The Cambridge Handbook of Cognition and Education

This handbook reviews a wealth of research in cognitive and educational psychology that investigates how to enhance learning and instruction to aid students struggling to learn and to advise teachers on how best to support student learning. The handbook includes features that inform readers about how to improve instruction and student achievement based on scientific evidence across different domains, including science, mathematics, reading, and writing. Each chapter supplies a description of the learning goal, a balanced presentation of the current evidence about the efficacy of various approaches to obtaining that learning goal, and a discussion of important future directions for research in this area. It is the ideal resource for researchers continuing their study of this field or for those only now beginning to explore how to improve student achievement.

JOHN DUNLOSKY is a professor of psychology in the Department of Psychological Sciences and Director of the Science of Learning and Education Center at Kent State University, USA. He received the Distinguished Scholar Award in 2010 from Kent State University and is a founder of the International Association for Metacognition.

KATHERINE A. RAWSON is a professor of psychology in the Department of Psychological Sciences at Kent State University, USA. She has received numerous awards for her research, including the US Presidential Early Career Award for Scientists and Engineers, the Outstanding Research and Scholarship Award from Kent State University, and the Outstanding Early Career Award from the Psychonomic Society.

The Cambridge Handbook of Cognition and Education

Edited by

John Dunlosky
Kent State University

Katherine A. Rawson
Kent State University

CAMBRIDGE
UNIVERSITY PRESS

CAMBRIDGE
UNIVERSITY PRESS

University Printing House, Cambridge CB2 8BS, United Kingdom

One Liberty Plaza, 20th Floor, New York, NY 10006, USA

477 Williamstown Road, Port Melbourne, VIC 3207, Australia

314–321, 3rd Floor, Plot 3, Splendor Forum, Jasola District Centre, New Delhi – 110025, India

79 Anson Road, #06–04/06, Singapore 079906

Cambridge University Press is part of the University of Cambridge.

It furthers the University's mission by disseminating knowledge in the pursuit of education, learning, and research at the highest international levels of excellence.

www.cambridge.org
Information on this title: www.cambridge.org/9781108416016
DOI: 10.1017/9781108235631

© Cambridge University Press 2019

First published 2019

A catalogue record for this publication is available from the British Library.

Library of Congress Cataloging-in-Publication Data
Names: Dunlosky, John, editor.
Title: The Cambridge handbook of cognition and education / edited by John Dunlosky, Kent State University, Katherine A. Rawson, Kent State University.
Description: New York : Cambridge University Press, 2019. | Includes bibliographical references and index.
Identifiers: LCCN 2018033895 | ISBN 9781108416016 (alk. paper)
Subjects: LCSH: Cognitive learning – Handbooks, manuals, etc. | Cognition – Handbooks, manuals, etc.
Classification: LCC LB1062 .C36 2019 | DDC 371.39–dc23
LC record available at https://lccn.loc.gov/2018033895

ISBN 978-1-108-41601-6 Hardback
ISBN 978-1-108-40130-2 Paperback

Contents

Figures

Tables

Contributors

ROGER AZEVEDO, Department of Learning Sciences and Educational Research, University of Central Florida, USA

LINDA BOL, Educational Foundations and Leadership, Old Dominion University, USA

JULIE L. BOOTH, College of Education, Temple University, USA

AMANDA E. BRADBURY, Department of Psychology, North Carolina State University, USA

JONATHAN L. BRENDEFUR, Department of Curriculum, Instruction and Foundational Studies, Boise State University, USA

M. ANNE BRITT, Department of Psychology, Northern Illinois University, USA

HEATHER A. BUTLER, Department of Psychology, California State University, Dominguez Hills, USA

MICHELE B. CARNEY, Department of Curriculum, Instruction and Foundational Studies, Boise State University, USA

PAULO F. CARVALHO, Human-Computer Interaction Institute, Carnegie Mellon University, USA

ANNE E. COOK, Educational Psychology Department, University of Utah, USA

EMMALINE DREW ELISEEV, Department of Psychology and Neuroscience, Duke University, USA

JOHN DUNLOSKY, Department of Psychological Sciences, Kent State University, USA

ALEXANDER EITEL, University of Freiburg, Germany

VANESSA FOOT-SEYMOUR, Department of Psychology, LaMarsh Centre for Child and Youth Research, York University, Canada

SONIYA GADGIL, The Eberly Center for Teaching Excellence and Educational Innovation, Carnegie Mellon University, USA

SUSAN GOLDIN-MEADOW, Department of Psychology and Department of Comparative Human Development, University of Chicago, USA

ROBERT L. GOLDSTONE, Department of Psychological and Brain Sciences and Program in Cognitive Science, Indiana University, USA

THOMAS D. GRIFFIN, Department of Psychology, University of Illinois at Chicago, USA

ELIZABETH A. GUNDERSON, Department of Psychology, Temple University, USA

DOUGLAS J. HACKER, Department of Educational Psychology, University of Utah, USA

DIANE F. HALPERN, Claremont McKenna College and Minerva Schools at KGI, USA

IRINA V. KAPLER, Department of Psychology, LaMarsh Centre for Child and Youth Research, York University, Canada

ALICE S. N. KIM, Department of Psychology, York University, Canada; Rotman Research Institute of Baycrest, Canada

DAVID KLAHR, Department of Psychology, Carnegie Mellon University, USA

PERRY D. KLEIN, The Faculty of Education, Western University, Canada

JUDITH F. KROLL, Department of Psychology, University of California, Riverside, USA

CAROLINA E. KÜPPER-TETZEL, School of Social Sciences, Psychology, University of Dundee, Scotland

JOEL R. LEVIN, University of Arizona, USA

JERI L. LITTLE, Department of Psychology, Hillsdale College, USA; now at Department of Psychology, California State University, East Bay, USA

GIGI LUK, Harvard Graduate School of Education, USA

ELIZABETH J. MARSH, Department of Psychology and Neuroscience, Duke University, USA

ZAHIA MARZOUK, Faculty of Education, Simon Fraser University, Canada

BRYAN J. MATLEN, Department of Psychology, Carnegie Mellon University, USA

RICHARD E. MAYER, Department of Psychological and Brain Sciences, University of California, Santa Barbara, USA

MARK A. MCDANIEL, Department of Psychological and Brain Sciences, Washington University in St. Louis, USA

MARTA K. MIELICKI, Department of Psychology, University of Illinois at Chicago, USA

NICHOLAS V. MUDRICK, Department of Psychology, North Carolina State University, USA

NORA S. NEWCOMBE, Department of Psychology, Temple University, USA

TIMOTHY J. NOKES-MALACH, Department of Psychology and Learning Research and Development Center, University of Pittsburgh, USA

EDWARD J. O'BRIEN, Psychology Department, University of New Hampshire, USA

JOHN E. OPFER, Department of Psychology, The Ohio State University, USA

RICHARD D. OSGUTHORPE, College of Education, Boise State University, USA

STEVEN OSWALT, College of Education, Boise State University, USA

STEPHEN T. PEVERLY, Teachers College, Columbia University, USA

ANNA POTOCKI, Department of Psychology, Université de Poitiers, France

KATHERINE A. RAWSON, Department of Psychological Sciences, Kent State University, USA

ALEXANDER RENKL, Department of Psychology, University of Freiburg, Germany

J. ELIZABETH RICHEY, Human-Computer Interaction Institute, Carnegie Mellon University, USA

BETHANY RITTLE-JOHNSON, Department of Psychology and Human Development, Peabody College, Vanderbilt University, USA

DANIEL H. ROBINSON, University of Texas at Arlington, USA

JEAN-FRANÇOIS ROUET, Centre national de la recherche scientifique (CNRS), Poitiers, France

NIKOL RUMMEL, Institute of Educational Research, Ruhr-Universität Bochum, Germany

KEITH SAWYER, School of Education, University of North Carolina at Chapel Hill, USA

POOJA G. SIDNEY, Department of Psychological Sciences, Kent State University, USA

ELIZABETH A. STEVENS, Department of Special Education and The Meadows Center for Preventing Educational Risk, The University of Texas at Austin, USA

MICHELLE TAUB, Department of Learning Sciences and Educational Research, University of Central Florida, USA

KEITH W. THIEDE, College of Education, Boise State University, USA

CLARISSA A. THOMPSON, Department of Psychological Sciences, Kent State University, USA

AARTJE VAN DIJK, Department of Teacher Training, Rotterdam University of Applied Sciences, the Netherlands

TAMARA VAN GOG, Department of Education, Utrecht University, the Netherlands

SHARON VAUGHN, Department of Special Education and The Meadows Center for Preventing Educational Risk, The University of Texas at Austin, USA

ELIZABETH M. WAKEFIELD, Department of Psychology, Loyola University Chicago, USA

TINA WESTON, Department of Psychology, LaMarsh Centre for Child and Youth Research, Centre for Aging Research and Education, York University, Canada

JENNIFER WILEY, Department of Psychology, University of Illinois at Chicago, USA

PHILIP H. WINNE, Faculty of Education, Simon Fraser University, Canada

MELODY WISEHEART, Department of Psychology, LaMarsh Centre for Child and Youth Research, Centre for Aging Research and Education, York University, Canada

AMIE D. WOLF, Teachers College, Columbia University, USA

CRISTINA D. ZEPEDA, Learning Research and Development Center, University of Pittsburgh, USA

CORINNE ZIMMERMAN, Department of Psychology, Illinois State University, USA

How Cognitive Psychology Can Inform Evidence-Based Education Reform

An Overview of *The Cambridge Handbook of Cognition and Education*

John Dunlosky and Katherine A. Rawson

Formal education has had a major and positive impact on society, but it is also true that not all students meet their learning aspirations. Many children and adults struggle to learn and many are left behind. The problems that undermine their efforts to succeed (and instructors' efforts to help them) arise from numerous sources; a short list includes poor nutrition, poor physical or mental health, a lack of motivation, boredom, social and interpersonal problems at school or at home, ineffective approaches to learning, learning disabilities, and poor access to educational resources. Successfully solving these problems will require many solutions and only a subset of them are targeted by cognitive psychologists. This subset of problems is nevertheless fundamental to education and, in general, includes the difficulties that many students have in effectively learning and understanding new ideas and concepts, correcting misconceptions, achieving proficiency in math and reading, and thinking critically. Even in the best of circumstances, many students will still struggle, and many of the efforts of cognitive and educational psychologists – and certainly those represented in this handbook – are aimed at helping students more effectively learn and teachers more effectively teach.

An Overview of *The Cambridge Handbook of Cognition and Education*

One implicit take-home message from the chapters of this handbook is that even with respect to the challenge of enhancing student learning, there are numerous problems and subsequently numerous solutions for them. One reason for such diversity pertains to the variety of content, concepts, and procedures that students are expected to learn. An effective tool for students who struggle with mathematics may not be as applicable for students trying to become proficient in a foreign language, and tools that are highly effective for learning a foreign language may not be as useful when students are learning to reason scientifically. For instance, effective reading may require techniques such as identifying main ideas, making predictive inferences, and summarizing (Stevens & Vaughn, Chapter 15, this volume). By contrast, learning how to solve math problems will involve a different set of tools, such as studying worked examples (van Gog, Rummel, & Renkl,

Chapter 8, this volume). As another example, using appropriate gestures during instruction promises to improve math instruction (Wakefield & Goldin-Meadow, Chapter 9, this volume), but gestures will likely not be as relevant to a student who is struggling to integrate ideas across multiple sources about a historical event (Rouet, Britt, & Potocki, Chapter 14, this volume).

Although domain-specific or content-specific tools may be required to improve student achievement for some domains and tasks, a variety of tools are more domain-general and promise to benefit learning across many domains. For example, retrieval practice can be used to improve student learning in the classroom (McDaniel & Little, Chapter 19, this volume), and spaced schedules of practice can support durable learning across many domains (Wiseheart, Küpper-Tetzel, Weston, Kim, Kapler, & Foot-Seymour, Chapter 22, this volume). Both techniques are domain-general, and for anyone who has used, heard, and believed the expression "practice makes perfect," these two techniques are fundamental for much of the practice that results in mastery and expertise.

Improving potentially general skills (such as critical thinking, scientific reasoning, and metacognition) also promises to benefit students in many domains. For example, accurately monitoring progress toward a learning goal – a form of personalized formative evaluation – presumably can enhance the effectiveness of subsequent learning. Even so, it is clear that this general skill (i.e., accurately monitoring) is rather challenging, both for students when preparing for exams (Hacker & Bol, Chapter 25, this volume) and for teachers who are evaluating the progress of their individual students (Thiede, Oswalt, Brendefur, Carney, & Osguthorpe, Chapter 26, this volume). Even more general, Winne and Marzouk (Chapter 27, this volume) describe how ideal self-regulated learning involves engaged learners who must cope with a learning task by identifying relevant conditions within the environment (external and internal) that can influence performance. Students would then apply the best strategies (or operations) for the task at hand and subsequently compare progress against learning standards to decide if further effort is needed to obtain a learning goal.

Given the diversity in approaches to improving student achievement, important aims of this handbook were to showcase this diversity by inviting experts to discuss (1) approaches to promoting education within specific domains; (2) general strategies for improving student learning and thinking; and (3) the promise of improving domain-general skills (e.g., metacognition) toward helping students learn more effectively.

Why this handbook and why now? As cognitive psychologists who are dedicated to helping students succeed, we (Dunlosky and Rawson) have been doing our best to keep informed about all the work relevant to our own areas of expertise and also trying to find out about advances being made by others who are exploring different issues. After all, we not only want to discover and evaluate strategies that may enhance student learning (one of our particular areas of interest) but also want to know about other discoveries and advances. Put simply, as educators, we want to know what works best and the strength of evidence for the effectiveness of different approaches. Given our assumption that many readers will share these interests, we encouraged authors to tell us what works best and, where possible, to offer prescriptions to students and instructors based on evidence demonstrating that the prescribed approach or technique is effective (e.g., by outperforming an often used but less effective approach in the area).

When making prescriptions, Robinson and Levin (Chapter 2, this volume) provocatively argue for caution, because even promising educational advances may "in fact [be] overpromises, in that the research from which the advances are derived is not based on replicable, scientifically 'credible' evidence" (p. 35). We agree, and apparently so do contributors to this volume who described the best evidence for an approach and evaluated its promise against well-established scientific criteria. In some cases, a great deal of evidence has experimentally established the efficacy of a particular approach. In other cases, however, evidence is promising but suggestive rather than definitive. For example, correlational research has revealed a meaningful relation between spatial skills, reasoning, and mathematics (Newcombe, Booth, & Gunderson, Chapter 5, this volume). These outcomes suggest that improving spatial skills may have broad benefits but they do not guarantee such benefits. In such cases, authors understandably did not offer strong prescriptions but instead highlighted viable future directions that could further establish the causal efficacy of an approach.

Reviewing the strength of evidence concerning the efficacy of any one approach can require considerable time. Despite some of our best attempts (e.g., Dunlosky et al., 2013), so much progress has been made recently that we have not been able to keep up. So, we selfishly discussed coediting a volume on cognition and education – why not have experts provide us with a bird's eye view on their areas? This selfishness is also reflected in our charge to the authors. We wanted each handbook chapter to satisfy both seasoned researchers who are interested in catching up on familiar areas of research and researchers who are looking for good entry points to begin new research within a less familiar area. For each chapter, we asked authors to start by defining their area of research and, if possible, by providing a brief history. We encouraged authors to then showcase some of their own favorite cutting-edge work, and the bulk of most chapters is aimed at helping readers develop a solid grasp of the current state of a particular area.

Finally, the origin of this particular handbook is significant. Keith Sawyer recently edited an outstanding volume, *The Cambridge handbook of the learning sciences*. The contribution of cognitive psychology is represented in that volume, but Dr. Sawyer also realized that much of the experimental work by cognitive psychologists was not included. As a consulting editor, he approached us to develop a companion handbook. We believe this handbook is a fitting companion, given that learning scientists and cognitive psychologists share the same primary goals of helping students succeed (for more on the learning sciences versus cognitive psychology, see Sawyer & Dunlosky, Chapter 1, this volume). We also hope that other companions to this handbook will be forthcoming; despite our desire to develop a handbook to survey all of the great work in cognitive psychology and education, much more excellent work is going on than could be covered in just a single volume. Even so, the current set of chapters does provide a representative and broad-ranging selection of topics from the intersection of cognition and education.

How the Handbook Is Organized

As suggested above, one way to categorize approaches to improving education is to separate them into those that focus on identifying strategies (or skills) that are effective for a specific domain and those that focus on identifying strategies that are more domain-general. An example of a relatively domain-specific strategy could involve developing an effective technique aimed at helping children to understand fractions, which is arguably an essential skill for developing math expertise (Sidney, Thompson, & Opfer, Chapter 7, this volume). An example of a domain-general approach is using multimedia presentations, which involve developing lessons that combine pictures and words. As Mayer's synthesis (Chapter 18, this volume) of multimedia research indicates, some approaches to using multimedia can undermine learning, whereas a properly designed multimedia presentation can have a meaningful impact on students' ability to gain knowledge and transfer it to solving problems in new contexts.

This domain-specific versus domain-general taxonomy is reflected in how we organized the chapters, grouping those about particular domains (*Science and Math; Reading and Writing*) and those about more domain-general strategies or skills (*General Strategies; Metacognition*). Of course, taxonomies can oversimplify, and we acknowledge the fuzzy boundaries between these groupings. For instance, although Luk and Kroll (Chapter 12, this volume) discuss some learning approaches that are specifically relevant to second-language acquisition (e.g., immersion, trans-languaging), they also note the relevance of domain-general strategies such as interleaving. As another example, we placed Peverly and Wolf's overview (Chapter 13, this volume) on note-taking under *Reading and Writing* (given that taking notes can involve a great deal of both). Even so, their opening statement discloses the domain-general importance of good note-taking skills: "Note-taking is a pervasive and important activity that includes notes taken on lectures in classrooms but also notes taken in other contexts such as trials (jurors' notes), physician and clinicians' offices, and boardrooms, among others" (p. 320). Likewise, we included Griffin, Mielicki, and Wiley's contribution (Chapter 24) under *Metacognition*, which includes people's monitoring of their task progress and hence can be relevant to any ongoing activity. Despite the fact that such metacognitive skills are often viewed as domain-general (e.g., in the COPES model; Winne & Marzouk, Chapter 27, this volume), students likely will need to use different tools to accurately monitor their progress for different learning tasks and domains. In the present case, Griffin, Mielicki, and Wiley (Chapter 24, this volume) discuss current theory and evidence for helping students monitor their learning and understanding of *text materials* (and hence that chapter could also have been grouped within the *Reading and Writing* section).

Further blurring the boundaries, even domain-general approaches may need domain-specific adjustments to maximize their promise as a learning tool for particular domains. For example, Renkl and Eitel (Chapter 21, this volume) discuss research on self-explanation, which occurs when a student explains why a particular idea is true, why a particular solution is correct, why a particular procedure is appropriate, and so on. As these cases illustrate, self-explanation can be instantiated in many different ways and thus can be applied to many domains, such as when a student is trying to understand abstract principles of science writing or learning math using worked examples. Despite self-explanation being a rather general learning tool, Renkl and Eitel (Chapter 21, this volume) acknowledge that "It is highly probable that different types of self-explanations have different functions, lead to better learning via different mechanisms, and should not be regarded as a unitary construct when providing practice recommendations" (p. 531). Thus, applying this general learning technique may require task-specific adjustments.

Likewise, given that students may be limited in their ability to monitor their progress in some domains, Azevedo and colleagues have been systematically evaluating how computer-assisted learning systems can be developed to help students better regulate their learning by providing appropriate feedback about guiding their learning, using strategies, and monitoring progress (Azevedo, Mudrick, Taub, & Bradbury, Chapter 23, this volume). This general approach to developing learning systems that scaffold effective self-regulated learning has been successfully applied to a variety of specific domains, such as learning about the human circulatory system and learning to foster scientific reasoning. Certainly, depending on the targeted content or skills, we suspect that the most successful approach to fostering self-regulation skills will not be identical across domains. For instance, computer-assisted learning systems that help students regulate unwanted emotions during a math lesson may not be as critical for systems that help students learn about ecology.

In sum, although we organized the volume in an attempt to reflect domain-general versus domain-specific approaches, other arrangements would have been viable. We invite readers to keep an open mind, given that many chapters have relevance to both general and specific approaches.

Common Themes and Next Steps

A variety of themes emerged across chapters, including (1) understanding the psychological mechanisms that are relevant to a given activity; (2) exploring the promise of a particular learning technique through well-controlled investigations and for multiple learning outcomes; (3) establishing that an approach showing promise in the laboratory works in a real-world setting; and (4) mapping out the most important next steps for research in their field. We briefly consider these themes (and a few others) in the next sections.

Theory and application. A major goal of cognitive research is to reveal the basic cognitive mechanisms involved in skilled performance (e.g., reading and math). In some areas, a great deal of the theoretically motivated research is being conducted with the applied aim of directly improving student achievement. In some areas, however, a gap still exists between theory and application. For example, as aptly noted by Cook and O'Brien (Chapter 10, this volume) in the context of reading research:

> Since the early 1970s, the psychological study of reading has focused primarily on the basic cognitive processes and mechanisms involved in every stage of reading – from decoding to parsing to comprehension. Research on reading in education, however, has focused more on reading outcomes. Although research in reading is becoming increasingly interdisciplinary, the divide between psychological theory and educational practices remains wide ... [T]he value of understanding basic comprehension processes is in the service of researchers whose aim is to develop improved methods of teaching reading and/or to develop effective interventions to assist struggling readers. (p. 237)

Cook and O'Brien argue for the importance of bridging the gap between theory and practice and offer examples of the positive impact of using theory to inform best practices in early literacy education.

The volume is packed with chapters that discuss current theories of how people perform various educationally relevant tasks, which have implications for improving student learning and task performance. For instance, the value of understanding basic processes is exemplified by Carvalho and Goldstone (Chapter 16, this volume), who consider the potential benefit of interleaving practice over blocked practice. Although interleaving has been shown to boost performance in learning concepts, their Sequential Attention Theory indicates that interleaving will not always be better than blocking practice and, more important, it describes those conditions in which each technique will benefit learning the most. Another example comes from Klahr, Zimmerman, and Matlen (Chapter 4, this volume). They describe the Scientific Discovery as Dual Search model that both defines and explains scientific thinking and has direct implications for improving people's scientific reasoning. They even highlight studies focusing on children's domain-specific and domain-general knowledge, which affirms our observation above that (despite how we organized chapters in this handbook) many chapters have relevance to more than one domain. Importantly, the theories offered in these and other chapters can be used to guide future theoretical and applied work, and we hope readers will be inspired by these theoretical advances and seek to test their implications in the laboratory and in authentic educational settings.

For a final example, Nokes-Malach, Zepeda, Richey, and Gadgil (Chapter 20, this volume) review the benefits and costs of collaborative learning. Importantly, they describe the mechanisms that result in these benefits and costs, and then subsequently appeal to these mechanisms for offering prescriptions to educators on how to maximize benefits and minimize costs when students collaborate while learning. Certainly, these prescriptions will require further evaluation in classroom settings, but as Nokes-Malach and colleagues emphasize, "There is also extensive evidence from the educational psychology approach for the benefits of learning in a group versus learning individually, especially outside of the laboratory in classroom contexts" (p. 508). The key point here is that revealing the underlying mechanisms can sharpen prescriptions and lead to systematic research aimed at (1) evaluating and improving an approach to learning (in this case, collaborative learning) and (2) potentially revising and updating the theory.

What techniques work and what counts as working? Although many of the approaches to learning or instruction offered in these chapters are partly (or entirely) informed by well-vetted theories, at least some approaches have been shown to work before researchers have fully understood why they work. Notable examples here include the use of retrieval practice (in which theory development has been relatively recent) and spaced practice (in which theoretical debates continue). Thus, even though theories often have implications for improving the efficacy of particular techniques or interventions, theory is not essential for establishing that a particular technique works.

Of course, this claim may lead one to ask, what counts as "working"? Part of the answer to this question is that a technique is working when students perform better on the targeted educational outcome. But this immediately begs a subsequent question: Better than what? Effectiveness studies often involve comparing a new technique or approach to business as usual. However, as argued by Hattie (2009), almost any intervention in the classroom is bound to produce some effect, partly because students and teachers get appropriately excited by any changes that occur and by new and enthusiastic faces (i.e., education researchers) visiting the classroom. Thus, appropriate comparison conditions or groups are needed to establish that the particular approach being evaluated (and not just social engagement or interest in trying something new) is responsible for any improvements.

The search for such evidence is analogous to the concern raised by Samuel Hopkins Adams (1905) in *Collier's Weekly* about the patent medicine business and subsequent calls for experimental evidence to establish that new medical treatments actually help people. In contrast to the Food and Drug Administration that oversees medical recommendations in the United States, there is no similar agency to ensure that educational interventions marketed to and adopted by schools and educators actually work.[1] Firmly establishing that an intervention works in authentic educational settings raises many challenges, and this handbook includes innovative examples of how this is done (for some specific recommendations on how to meet these challenges, see Dunlosky et al., in press). Moreover, in an address to the American Education Research Association, Dr. Whitehurst (2003) (Director of the Institute of Education Sciences [IES] at the time) emphasized that the position of IES is that "randomized trials are the only sure method for determining the effectiveness of education programs and practices." Importantly, this position does not mean that other approaches are invalid or uninformative, because randomized trials do not address all relevant educational issues and other approaches (e.g., case studies and

---

[1] However, see the What Works Clearing House, https://ies.ed.gov/ncee/wwc/

surveys) can mutually inform why a particular approach works and/or how to improve it. Readers will find a multiplicity of methodological approaches in the current handbook, all aimed at revealing how people learn and how to improve their learning.

Given the range of educational content areas represented in this volume, it is perhaps no surprise that the targeted educational outcomes vary greatly. A common theme pertains to the degree to which a particular intervention produces transfer to new contexts, tasks, and so forth (for a general framework of transfer, see Barnett & Ceci, 2002). Halpern and Butler's chapter (Chapter 3, this volume) captures the key question in their own domain: "Can students enhance their critical thinking skills in ways that endure over time and transfer across domains?" Spoiler alert: their emphatic answer to this question is "Yes", and they provide concrete recommendations on how to teach critical thinking to promote its widespread transfer. In this (and most other) cases, transfer is a good thing – it's often what we strive for when developing educational interventions. Thus, it may be surprising that some forms of transfer can be detrimental, causing problems instead of solving them. In the domain of math, Sidney, Thompson, and Opfer (Chapter 7, this volume) convincingly argue for the importance of children's fraction knowledge for subsequent achievement in mathematical cognition. Unfortunately, however, children's knowledge of whole numbers can negatively bias their conceptions of fractions! Thus, an important goal for all education research will be to understand how to maximize positive transfer and minimize negative transfer.

In our own work exploring interventions to boost learning (e.g., Rawson & Dunlosky, 2011), we have argued that researchers and practitioners should be concerned not only with the level and durability of learning achieved but also with the efficiency of using a given educational tool. Students are required to learn a vast amount of information and to master many tasks and procedures, but the amount of time and effort they have to expend is necessarily limited. Being a successful student can be overwhelming, so recommending an approach that takes a great deal of time to implement may not be feasible and, even if it is, students may simply not want to use that much time. Certainly, learning is difficult and takes time – thinking scientifically, understanding fractions, integrating information from multiple texts, and so forth is likely going to take a great deal of time and effort to do well. Nevertheless, all else equal, more efficient approaches to obtaining a learning goal are obviously preferable. In discussing best practices for correcting student misconceptions, Marsh and Eliseev (Chapter 17, this volume) note that providing feedback after a student responds correctly is rather inert and thus simply a waste of time. Likewise, as van Gog, Rummel, and Renkl (Chapter 8, this volume) emphasize, studying worked examples rather than attempting to solve problems may be the best way to begin for novice learners – not only do worked examples often yield higher levels of learning than problem-solving but they also typically have a significant advantage with respect to efficiency. In this case, novice learners can obtain the same or better level of performance and do so using less time.

Another important factor to consider when evaluating approaches to improving education is usability. Even a well-vetted technique that has been shown to boost student learning above business as usual can be inert if students or instructors cannot or do not use it with fidelity. Many educational tools discussed in the present handbook show promise partly because they are inexpensive and presumably easy-to-use, which means that the use of the tool can be widespread and inclusive. Along these lines, one exciting discovery is that using simple hand gestures can improve instruction and learning. Wakefield and Goldin-Meadow (Chapter 9, this volume) note that "A good teaching tool is one that can be implemented broadly," and they provide evidence that supplementing math instruction with the right kind of gestures can improve students' understanding of difficult math lessons (e.g., equivalence). Other approaches may be broad and cost-free, yet students may need instruction and practice using the tool to reap its benefits. For example, in the context of writing to learn, Klein and Van Dijk (Chapter 11, this volume) argue that elementary students will "need explicit instruction and examples of how to use strategies, as well as prompting to actually apply them . . . [The importance of strategy instruction] has also been independently demonstrated with respect to genres such as summary, discourse synthesis, and argumentation" (p. 284).

Another key theme that is prevalent in this handbook is that some strategies are effective for some students but not others. That is, individual differences on a variety of dimensions may moderate the impact of a given educational intervention (i.e., *Treatment X Aptitude* interactions). A non-exhaustive list of factors that can moderate the effectiveness of a given technique includes the grade level of students (Stevens & Vaughn, Chapter 15, this volume), the diversity of materials being used within an intervention (Halpern & Butler, Chapter 3, this volume), differences in the structure of to-be-learned concepts (Carvalho & Goldstone, Chapter 16, this volume), and the level of prior knowledge that students have about a targeted domain (van Gog, Rummel, & Renkl, Chapter 8, this volume). Prior knowledge is a particularly likely suspect, given its long history of moderating effects in many different literatures. For example, prior knowledge has long been known to moderate how well students learn from individual texts (e.g., McNamara et al., 1996), and Rouet, Britt, and Potocki (Chapter 14, this volume) conclude that prior knowledge also is relevant to integrating and comprehending content across multiple texts:

> Our brief review of the literature demonstrates that some specific task instructions are effective at enhancing students' multiple text comprehension. However, it is worth noting that several of these studies also showed that not all readers respond in the same way . . . Indeed, [prior knowledge] of the readers themselves [is] likely to influence multiple text processing and to mediate the effects of task instructions. (p. 370)

We invite readers to consider this and other factors that may moderate the benefits of each educational intervention or strategy, because discovering these moderators is an important goal for education researchers.

In summary, our major thesis in this section is simply that a particular technique or approach can work (or fail to do so) for many reasons. Of course, if it simply fails to promote better learning than business as usual, then adopting it likely makes no sense. Nevertheless, even approaches that have been shown to promote learning may not work because (1) they are prohibitively inefficient; (2) they are too difficult to use; or (3) students and/or teachers hold misconceptions about the effectiveness of the strategy or technique (for details, see Bjork, Dunlosky, & Kornell, 2013). In such cases, students and teachers may be unlikely to adopt an effective strategy. Thus, another avenue for research will be to understand how to sidestep these barriers, so as to better inform students and teachers about what works best and to modify effective strategies to make them more useable.

Exploring the impact of educational interventions in the wild. Many cognitive and education researchers conduct a great deal of research in their laboratories and some of us are a bit afraid to venture beyond them. Nevertheless, regardless of how well a particular intervention performs in the laboratory, it may not have the same impact when implemented in a classroom or in environments in which students are regulating their own learning. In reviewing the chapters in this handbook, we were gratified to find that the efficacy of many approaches is being evaluated outside of the laboratory. Conducting classroom-based research (or any research outside of the laboratory) poses challenges, especially if one aims to firmly establish efficacy using randomized trials; it can often take a great deal of time and resources to complete. Such investigations and demonstrations are critical, and we briefly consider two (perhaps obvious) reasons next.

First, realizing that experimental outcomes will not always transfer outside of the laboratory, researchers should use caution when making prescriptions to students and teachers in general until some questions are empirically addressed. Does the intervention work for the intended material and students when delivered in a classroom setting? Does the intervention produce educationally meaningful gains on the targeted knowledge or skills, whether that involves high-stakes exams, the quality of student projects, how well students write, and so forth? Does the intervention work only when the research team delivers it to a particular class or will it benefit students even when implemented by teachers or by students on their own? These are just a few of the important questions that can be addressed when one wishes to establish the efficacy of an approach outside the laboratory. Note, however, we are not arguing that all of these questions must be answered before making prescriptions to educators and students. Instead, we encourage researchers to address them when possible, and when they cannot, to consider qualifying their prescriptions by explaining the breadth and strength of the evidence supporting them.

Second, experimental evidence that a given intervention or strategy works outside the laboratory (e.g., boosts performance above an appropriate comparison group or control in an authentic educational context) may be helpful in convincing students and teachers to adopt the technique. We suspect that enthusiastic and charismatic champions of a particular approach can make a great deal of headway in promoting buy-in by administrators, teachers, and students. Like patent medicine in the early 1900s, however, stakeholders in education reform can be persuaded to adopt practices that can be costly (at minimum, adopting a new approach will require extra time) but do not work well. One high-profile example is how an emphasis on learning styles has had a negative impact on education – tailoring instruction to align with a student's learning style does not work, yet many schools are spending a great deal of time assessing students' styles and trying to teach to them (for evidence and rationale, see Pashler et al., 2009). As cogently put by Dan Willingham (2012), author of *When can you trust the experts? How to tell good science from bad science in education,*

> there is no support for the learning styles idea . . . Yet if you search for "learning styles" on the Internet, you will not find a brief, academic obituary for this interesting idea that turned out to be wrong. You'll find almost two million hits . . . And you'll find lots and lots of products that promise improved educational outcomes once you know students' learning styles . . . The main cost of learning styles seems to be wasted time and money. (p. 13)

As educators ourselves, we will admit that we want to believe in the techniques we are recommending, and we want to recommend them with enthusiasm. As cognitive researchers, we try to be as patient as possible, because we want our beliefs to be based on evidence that supports causal claims of efficacy. Just like when evaluating the potential pros and cons of a promising new treatment for a medical condition, vetting new approaches to enhancing education can take a great deal of time. Our hope is that eventually administrators, teachers, and educators will demand to see the evidence before buying or adopting a particular technique, regardless of how well polished, sexy, or intuitive it appears.

Importantly, many of the chapters in this handbook point to evidence relevant to the efficacy of a given technique or approach when used in an authentic educational context. We encourage cognitive psychologists who are exploring promising techniques to expand their research beyond their laboratories. Many cognitive psychologists teach, so why not put your promising technique where your teaching is and try it out for real? Many will not work at first, but even failures can lead to a deeper understanding of why a technique is limited and can cycle back into additional laboratory and classroom research to investigate how to improve it.

Important next steps. Another motivation for developing this handbook was to allow experts to identify the most important next steps or future directions for research in their area. The authors were charged with inciting excitement and direction within their areas, and they delivered. Just skimming the end of most chapters will provide guidance on what needs to be done next and, in some areas, this includes bridging the gap between laboratory research and exploring the efficacy of an intervention in the wild. Regardless of how much translational work has been carried out in any given area, we are pretty sure that more needs to be done to answer the vast number of questions that should be addressed to fully vet the efficacy of a particular intervention. Moreover, in many cases, even a negative answer to a question (e.g., Will it work in a classroom without supervision by researchers? No.) will lead to further research (e.g., How can we restructure the instructor manual to ensure the intervention is run with fidelity even when researchers are not running the show?).

To close this section, we want to highlight future directions from Rittle-Johnson (Chapter 6, this volume), who discusses how developing math competence requires acquiring both conceptual and procedural knowledge. Rittle-Johnson's next steps squarely focus on translational research and her recommendations would apply to many domains:

> First, instead of trying to *apply* our research to practice, we need to do research that is inherently relevant to and driven by the needs of practice. We need to incorporate research topics and methods that take into consideration current problems of practice (e.g., what mathematics educators identify as their most pressing concerns, such as optimal ordering of instruction). Second, our experimental evidence from studies done one-on-one with students on educationally relevant content is a first step. But it is only a first step, and few psychologists take the next steps. We must conduct research *within* educational settings in order to ensure the method is feasible outside of a controlled lab setting and that the findings generalize to those settings . . . Translation of psychological principles and findings into useable practices is not straightforward. (p. 140)

We could not agree more and our sincere hope is that this *Cambridge handbook of cognition and education* inspires both seasoned researchers and newcomers to address the most pressing questions relevant to translating psychological principles to authentic educational settings. Achieving this ambitious goal may require iterative research inside and outside the laboratory, so many productive efforts need not be rooted in authentic educational settings. Nevertheless, as cognitive researchers aimed at making an impact on education, taking steps toward implementation (which involves collaborating with instructors and understanding their practical challenges) within real-world settings will be necessary.

Closing Remarks

After reading the chapters in this volume, we hope you agree that our selfish plan to have experts bring us up to date in their areas was a success. We thoroughly enjoyed reading and reviewing all of the chapters and we learned a great deal. We would like to extend many thanks to all of the contributors to this volume, both for conducting excellent research aimed at improving student achievement and for the time-consuming effort it takes to develop hard-hitting chapters that overview the state of their research areas. Many thanks also go to Keith Sawyer for encouraging us to edit this volume and to David Repetto and the staff at Cambridge University Press for guidance and assistance throughout the process. If everyone learns as much and has as much fun reading this volume as we did in editing it, then we know it will be a major success.

References

Adams, S. H. (1905). The Great American Fraud. Collier's, October 7, 29, 14–15.

Barnett, S. M. & Ceci, S. J. (2002). When and where do we apply what we learn? A taxonomy for far transfer. *Psychological Bulletin, 128*, 612–637.

Bjork, R. A., Dunlosky, J., & Kornell, N. (2013). Self-regulated learning: Beliefs, techniques, and illusions. *Annual Review of Psychology, 64*, 417–444.

Dunlosky, J., Morehead, K., Zamary, A., & Rawson, K. A. (in press). From the laboratory to the classroom: Challenges and solutions for conducting memory research in educational contexts. In H. Otani & B. Schwartz (eds.), *Handbook of research methods in human memory*. New York: Routledge.

Dunlosky, J., Rawson, K. A., Marsh, E. J., Nathan, M. J., & Willingham, D. T. (2013). Improving students' learning with effective learning techniques: Promising directions from cognitive and educational psychology. *Psychological Science in the Public Interest, 14*, 4–58.

Hattie, J. (2009). *Visible learning: A synthesis of over 800 meta-analyses relating to achievement*. New York: Routledge.

McNamara, D. S., Kintsch, E., Songer, N. B., & Kintsch, W. (1996). Are good texts always better? Interactions of text coherence, background knowledge, and levels of understanding in learning from text. *Cognition and Instruction, 14*, 1–43.

Pashler, H., McDaniel, M., Rohrer, D., & Bjork, R. (2009). Learning styles: Concepts and evidence. *Psychological Science in the Public Interest, 9*, 105–119.

Rawson, K. A. & Dunlosky, J. (2011). Optimizing schedules of retrieval practice for durable and efficient learning: How much is enough? *Journal of Experimental Psychology: General, 140*, 283–302.

Whitehurst, G. (2003). *The Institute of Education Sciences: New wine, new bottles*. Paper presented at the annual meeting of the American Educational Research Association, Chicago, IL.

Willingham, D. T. (2012). *When can you trust the experts? How to tell good science from bad science in education*. San Francisco, CA: Jossey-Bass.

PART I

Foundations

1 How the Learning Sciences Can Inform Cognitive Psychology

Keith Sawyer and John Dunlosky

Introduction

In this chapter, we explore the similarities and differences between the learning sciences (LS) and cognitive psychology applied to education (CP) and the potential synergy created through further integrating them. We believe that their mutual strengths can result in a deeper understanding of how learning occurs and how to design learning environments that maximally foster learning. We argue that LS provides evidence-based, scientific, and methodologically rigorous empirical findings that complement CP, and yet LS adds to our understanding of learning in ways not possible with CP methods alone.

We argue that:

- Both LS and CP share the same goal: To better understand learning and to use that understanding to improve the design of learning environments.
- LS and CP both agree on the importance of scientific, evidence-based approaches to support policy and recommendations for improving instruction and student achievement.
- CP and LS each have unique strengths and take different approaches toward this goal.

And, based on these points, we further argue that LS and CP should come together because their strengths when combined would be synergistic.

The distinctions between CP and LS are difficult to discern, because both are fuzzy categories and not well defined. Speaking of LS, Nathan, Rummel, and Hay (2016) interviewed thirty LS researchers and it turns out that they do not agree about what LS is: "all of the groups wanted more information about how to define LS. In addition, many wanted input on delineating the canon, in terms of core courses, common readings, and research methods" (p. 195). As a result, it can be difficult to make firm statements about the contrasts between LS and CP. And yet, we believe there is a core disciplinary paradigm of LS and that the differences with CP are subtle and yet profound.

One of our goals (for the readers of this book who are likely to be focused on cognitive psychology applied to education, or CP) is to show what LS has to offer and to argue that CP can become stronger and more relevant by linking to and collaborating with LS. That is why we spend some time in this chapter struggling to pinpoint the definition and scope of each – otherwise, overly simplistic characterizations of one or the other may cause one to be dismissed by the other and opportunities for collaboration would be missed. You may disagree with some of our distinctions (and, admittedly, we do verge on advancing stereotypes that may not entirely apply to any given researcher), but even if you do, we are positive that you still will appreciate our take-home message – that a CP informed by LS will be better equipped to advance education.

The differences between CP and LS can be difficult to articulate, because each is grounded in different epistemologies and theoretical traditions, and each uses different methodologies. Our chapter is intended to articulate these contrasts and to use those descriptions to identify barriers to collaboration and potential opportunities for collaboration.

Cognitive Psychology: Definitions, Scope, and Origins

In general, cognitive psychology is the scientific investigation of how the mind works. Interest in mental processes as an object of scientific investigation arose in the mid to late 1800s (for a detailed history of cognitive psychology, see Lachman, Lachman, & Butterfield, 1979), when Gustav Fechner demonstrated that carefully controlled observations could be used to reveal a general law relating the intensity of physical stimuli to perception, and later with scientists and philosophers – notables including Wilhelm Wundt and William James – who put unraveling the mysteries of the mind and consciousness as a primary goal for psychological inquiry. Unfortunately, some of the methods used by these pioneers relied on trained introspection, which did not produce replicable outcomes across laboratories. In the early 1900s, John B. Watson mocked these unreliable methods and also strongly argued that psychologists should refrain from investigating consciousness and the mind (which presumably could be investigated only with introspection) and instead should focus exclusively on explaining observable outcomes (e.g., the relationship between stimuli and responses).

Accordingly, psychology lost its mind in the first decades of the 1900s, but soon recovered it, partly based on outcomes from animal research. Examples include goal gradient and latent learning. The former occurs when an animal speeds up as it approaches its goal, which can be explained by assuming the animal is expecting a reward. The latter occurs when animals are navigating a maze but do not receive a reward; after repeated trials, the animals show little reduction in errors to reach the (empty) goal box. This outcome is expected according to behaviorism – the animals are not being reinforced and hence should not develop stimulus–response associations relevant to efficiently navigating the maze. Nevertheless, when a reward is then introduced in later trials, the animals perform the maze as well as if they had always been rewarded. Thus, the animals were learning without reinforcement and Edward Tolman explained his discovery by proposing that the animals were developing a map of the environment even when they were not being reinforced. Both expectations and maps are mental constructs and research along these lines led many researchers to begin studying mental processes again. This cognitive renaissance was also marked by treatises from major leaders in the field, including Noam Chomsky's dismantling of behaviorist approaches to language, Broadbent's (1958) theoretical analysis of attention using information-processing models, and Miller, Galanter, and Pribram's (1960) classic volume *Plans and the Structure of Behavior.*

A major goal of CP is to develop models of how the mind operates and empirically evaluate predictions from these models. A driving assumption is that (normally developing) minds operate similarly, so in turn, cognitive psychologists have sought to reveal the general principles, processes, and structures of the mind. For instance, cognitive psychologists assume that memory operates similarly for all normally developing humans and they seek to reveal these generalities. This assumption does not mean individual differences will not occur or that particular effects will be domain general. In the case of memory, CP has demonstrated in many domains that individual differences in domain-specific knowledge will impact how well people will understand and learn about an event. Such differences in knowledge can produce different learning outcomes that may lead one to believe that memory operates differently for different individuals and in different contexts, when in fact general theories of memory can account for these individual differences.

Another example is particularly relevant to CP's contribution to improving student achievement. One principle based on a hundred years of evidence is that retrieval practice (as compared to restudying) of to-be-learned materials can improve long-term retention (for details, see McDaniel and Little, Chapter 19, this volume). Retrieval practice, however, need not be uniformly effective across all people and contexts; for instance, students with little knowledge may be better off studying materials first, because they do not yet know enough to accurately retrieve any of the to-be-learned materials. By contrast, students with moderate knowledge may gain a great deal by struggling to retrieve what they have learned. CP who are interested in education attempt to understand these moderators by appealing to general theories or hypotheses that can explain why differences in individuals, contexts, and materials impact the efficacy of a particular learning technique or approach. Put differently, although CP assumes that the basic structure and processes of minds are similar, depending on learners' prior experiences, motivations, the current context, and so on, the same underlying mechanisms will give rise to different outcomes. Thus, a main goal of CP is to discover these mechanisms so as to better understand individual variability and to inform best practices for improving people's learning and achievement.

The Learning Sciences: Definitions, Scope, and Origins

In the 1970s and 1980s, cognitive psychologists increasingly began to work with computer scientists studying artificial intelligence (AI) and it seemed inappropriate to call this new combination by either AI or cognitive psychology. The name *cognitive science* came to be used to describe this new interdisciplinary field. Cognitive science is the study of intelligence and intelligent behavior in man and machine. Like cybernetics before it, the 1950s precursor to cognitive science, cognitive science research and theory is agnostic about what systems manifest intelligence. For example, intelligent systems might include carbon-based life-forms, silicon-based machines, or even society as a collective entity. Cybernetics had its roots in mathematics and information theory; AI similarly has roots in the formalisms and models of logic theory and mathematics.

This new reframing of the study of intelligence soon drew in disciplines beyond cognitive psychology and AI, adding new perspectives that contributed to our understanding of intelligence. These disciplines include linguistics, anthropology, philosophy, and neuroscience (Gardner, 1985). The chapters in this handbook are by scholars who mostly affiliate with cognitive psychology. In contrast, LS aligns with the more interdisciplinary field of cognitive science. It draws on cognitive psychology, as one of many disciplinary influences, but also draws on AI and education, instructional technology, anthropology, and linguistics.

LS Today

LS argues that teaching and learning cannot be accurately and completely understood when considered to be a transmission of information to a learner – whether by a human teacher, a video, a book, or a computer program. Rather, LS considers learning to be a transformation of patterns of participation in sociotechnical systems and communities of practice. Some key concepts in this definition of LS:

- "Patterns of participation" refer to (1) symbolic interactions between group members; (2) roles and responsibilities of each member; (3) interactions with technological artifacts.
- "Community of practice" refers to a set of individuals who share a common culture, a knowledge of those practices characteristic of a culture, an understanding of the value of those practices to the culture, and a knowledge of how to participate appropriately in these practices.
- "Technological artifacts" refer to a wide range of modernity and sophistication. Such artifacts include paper and pencil, books and printing, video, continuing with today's technologies.
- "Sociotechnical system" refers to people and technological artifacts, closely intertwined. With contemporary technologies, it becomes increasingly difficult to consider human–computer interaction as a "human user" employing a "tool" to accomplish a task. This conceptualization implies a clear distinction between the user and the tool. But with augmented reality, for example, the line between user and tool blurs. The line between interacting with a tool and interacting with another person also blurs – for example, if those other people are avatars in a virtual reality world.

Contrasting Learning Sciences and Cognitive Psychology

The Role of Technology

LS has its roots in the 1980s in technology-heavy research organizations such as Xerox PARC, Vanderbilt's Learning Technology Center, and the education department of the IT and networking consulting firm Bolt Beranek and Newman (BBN), and also has roots in a few key universities, including primarily those with strong computer programs, such as MIT and CMU. LS emerged in opposition to behaviorist-based 1960s work in computer-assisted instruction (CAI). These new systems were based on cognitive models, proposed and studied by both AI and cognitive psychology. LS brought together anthropologists, educators, media developers, and developmental psychologists (e.g., Roy Pea's research group at Bank Street). Seymour Papert's MIT group, which developed the programming language Logo and Logo-based curricula, was also a strong influence on the founding of LS. Pea (2016) described the heart of LS as "cognition, technologies, pedagogies, and social relations" (p. 38).

LS received its name from computer scientist Roger Schank. In 1989, when Schank was hired away from Yale by Northwestern, he founded an "Institute for the Learning Sciences." In the 1991 editorial introduction to the inaugural issue of the *Journal of the Learning Sciences*, Janet Kolodner (1991) made a direct connection between cognitive psychology and the emerging LS:

> [this journal] provides a multidisciplinary forum ... to allow cognitive psychology to have an impact on the practices of education ... [Cognitive scientists] housed in psychology departments have added the study of knowledge structure and content and high-level cognitive processes to their more traditional endeavors. Some are refining old experimental paradigms and evolving new ones to allow them to better explore these issues [on how to improve learning in real-world environments]. (pp. 1, 2)

Several other journals at the time were aligned with cognitive science and these provided the context within which LS was founded in 1991. *Instructional Science: An International Journal of Learning and Cognition* was founded in 1972. (A few years ago, this journal changed its subtitle to *An International Journal of the Learning Sciences*.) *Cognition and Instruction* was founded in 1984 and has been edited primarily by scholars who affiliate with LS (Rich Lehrer, Andrea diSessa, Rogers Hall). In 1992, Richard Mayer (1992) referred to this journal when he said "the reemergence of cognitive approaches to instruction [is] now in full swing" (p. 409). Other early journals that influenced LS included *AI and Education*. The Cognitive Science Society brought together an interdisciplinary group of learning researchers (according to Pea, 2016).

This historical account makes it clear that LS research has been closely linked to information technologies since its origins in the 1980s. Through the decades, LS researchers have continued to expand their research to include new technologies as they emerge. Contemporary technologies that are currently being studied by LS include

- Open learner models (OLM)
- Learning analytics and knowledge (LAK)
- Automated assessment
- Computer supported collaborative learning (CSCL)
- Virtual and augmented reality (VR and AR)
- Mobile computing (smartphones and tablets)

In contrast to the way that technology is deeply embedded in LS research, CP is almost completely missing from most of the exciting new developments in educational technologies, including:

- Informal science education (enabled by smaller and more interactive technologies – tablets, desktop programmable robots such as Sphero, etc.)
- Educational data mining/learning analytics and knowledge (EDM/LAK) (enabled and advanced by developments in big data analytics)
- Embodied and augmented and virtual systems (enabled by greater processing power for 3D rendering, by lower cost VR goggles and even Google Cardboard's low price point)
- Computer support collaborative learning (CSCL) (enabled and advanced by rapid developments in Internet communication and networks)
- One-on-one learning environments (enabled by cheaper and more powerful tablets and smartphones)
- Human–computer interaction and user interface design (HCI and UIX)
- The maker movement and education (children programming, LEGO robotics, Scratch)

LS researchers are engaged, to varying degrees, in all of these developments. In contrast, few of these research and development efforts have CP involved. We need CP to contribute to these new systems and learning environments, but it cannot do so if it continues on the same course, of focusing on individuals and learning as entirely an internal mental state. Research on these new systems is more compatible with the LS epistemological and theoretical focus – on situated social practices, on socio-technical systems, on design-based thinking (which results in a combination of basic research and system development). Many LS researchers work closely in teams with software developers – contributing their research expertise to new system designs, while at the same time, conducting research on learning in these new innovative learning environments. So, how can we modify CP so that it can be a player and contribute to these new research projects and system developments?

Research Sites

LS is much more likely to study out-of-school learning environments. LS researchers have studied learning in science centers and workplace apprenticeships, but also how girls learn to play hopscotch; how children learn to weave from helping their parents; how kids learn taunting, rhyming insults from older kids. CP almost always focuses on formal schooling and learning for school-valued outcomes. Formal schooling designs are focused on individual learning – learners learn largely alone, are responsible for their own learning, and are assessed on their individual learning. For this reason, CP's epistemological focus on the individual learner may be an appropriate match with traditional instruction. But it can be hard to use these findings to improve the design of nonschool, informal learning environments (e.g., science center exhibits) and it can be hard to use these findings to analyze and explain sociotechnical systems, where individual learners are deeply embedded in a complex learning environment.

Domain-General vs. Domain-Specific

LS has more often collaborated with education researchers in the content areas, such as math educators and science educators. Much funded LS research involves collaborative teams with these education researchers, but rarely have CP researchers been involved with such collaborations.

Why?

(1) LS theory and research consider the unique representations and representational practices for each domain (e.g., Lehrer & Schauble, 2006, on "model based reasoning"), whereas CP often takes a domain-general approach to cognition. LS holds that learning always builds on existing knowledge, so that learning processes may/will differ, depending on the learner's prior cognitive state. Because the conceptual structures associated with each school subject are different, LS proceeds under the assumption that the nature of learning is likely to vary, so this is why so many LS researchers study *learning trajectories* – pathways of conceptual change from a beginning cognitive state to a desired end state (for a review, see diSessa, 2006).

(2) CP studies representations (of course) but does not study "representational practices." Students need to learn representational practices to both (1) learn the representations themselves that constitute knowledge; and (2) learn to apply the representations/knowledge they learn to real-world settings, to solve new and complex problems.

CP studies generalizable, context-independent structures and processes of individuals engaged in learning. Of course, CP researchers do realize the key role of prior knowledge in producing gains within a domain, but even here, a central goal is to reveal generalizable structures and processes relevant to a given domain.

The Unit of Analysis

Nathan and Sawyer (2014) make a contrast between "elemental" research approaches and "systemic" research approaches, and place CP as elemental and LS as systemic. They argue that CP and LS study different *levels of analysis*. The world can be considered to be organized into distinct levels of analysis and scientific disciplines are each focused on one level of analysis (a scientific division of labor).

The LS object of study is learners acting within learning environments, broadly defined to include sociotechnical systems within which learning occurs. In all social contexts, participants engage in situated social practices: collective activities that involve symbolic interaction between participants and that are appropriate for, and found in, that social context; and LS studies aspects of those systems that are causally relevant to learning. For LS, "learning environments" include school classrooms, but also include other sociotechnical systems, such as science centers, a child with parents, kids introducing a new kid to a playground game, and so forth. LS studies sociotechnical systems, which include multiple individuals as well as designed technological artifacts. The assumption is that these findings can be scientific and generalizable, even if they cannot lead to causal claims, and even when studying single systems, which may be idiosyncratic.

By contrast, the typical level of analysis of CP pertains to an individual learner, regardless of context, and is generalizable across contexts. CP's goal is to reveal mental processes that are associated with externally observed or operationalized measures of learning. One goal of CP applied to education is to develop research-based theoretical models that allow us to make predictions about which mental processes cause a particular learning outcome to occur. In some cases, however, the experimental demonstrations that a particular factor improves student learning have well preceded the theoretical work aimed at revealing how the factor impacts the mental processes responsible for those improvements. A case in point is the testing effect. Decades of research – including behaviorist experiments as early as the 1900s – had established its efficacy before cognitive psychologists began to explore why it works.

The contrasting conceptions of learning are directly related to the contrast in unit of analysis: individual or system. For cognitive psychologists interested in educational application, learning itself is conceptualized with respect to the learning goals relevant to a particular task. For instance, if a learning goal is to improve a student's memory for important class materials, then the measure of learning would be performance on a test of memory for those materials. If the goal is to write better, reason better, understand better, solve problems better, and so forth, then measures that objectively tap the quality (and sometimes efficiency) of these skills would be used to operationalize learning; in particular, a researcher would develop tests (or use those developed by a teacher collaborator) to objectively measure students' writing quality, reasoning, understanding, problem-solving, and so forth. In contrast to LS, however, CP researchers typically do not consider the sociocultural environment and how it jointly impacts learning outcomes. Even when they explore how individual differences impact learning outcomes (i.e., referred to as *treatment X aptitude* interactions), they do not consider the entire sociotechnical system that growth can take place in, and understanding the multifaceted interactions between individual aptitude and the sociotechnological environment is a key collaborative nexus for LS and CP.

On a humorous note, however, CP may be better equipped to make recommendations for how students can excel in one learning environment: students studying by themselves in their bedroom or dormitory. Quite a bit of learning occurs in these places and CP has many recommendations for college students who struggle to achieve. But, to have a broader impact on education, CP needs to get out of the proverbial dormitory and into more complex domains that also impact learning trajectories. A science center is an excellent example – a child can grow and even learn a great deal in a science center, but how visiting such a space along with family or friends on a field trip influences students' interest, engagement, and identity may, for a scientist, be as relevant to long-term learning outcomes as how an individual child represents the knowledge gained from that experience.

Conception of Learning

LS conceives of teaching and learning as a transformation of patterns of participation in communities of practice (e.g., Rogoff, 1990). In this conception, learning is defined as a change in an entire sociotechnical system – not as a change within one individual within that system (the learner). The goal of LS is to understand relations between learning, intended learning outcomes, and learning environment designs, and *to design learning environments that result in more effective learning*. They rarely say the goal is *to show teachers how to teach more effectively*. For LS, the role of the teacher is not to instruct; rather, the role of the teacher is to design the learning environment and then act as the "orchestrator" of the unfolding collective performance (Mercier et al., 2015).

Several decades of research, in both CP and LS, have demonstrated that instructionism is ineffective as compared to other approaches. Learning environments that are most effective are (Sawyer, 2014):

- Active, participatory
- Apprenticeship-based
- Project-oriented
- Collaborative (groups)
- Orchestrated so that the teacher participates in collaborative interactional processes

These learning environments cannot be fully explained by analyzing the participants as separate individuals. We have to analyze these learning systems as complex wholes. In educational studies of instructionist practices, it is thought that the teacher can be studied as an individual and the student can be studied as an individual. But when change in the sociotechnical system is the focus of study, as a complex set of elements that are continually interacting in complex ways, "learning" is a transformation in the complete system. A corollary is that the individual is inextricable from the learning context, and that individual learning can only be studied in its sociotechnical context. Of course, individual members of the system change, as part of this system transformation, and that change is what we think of as "individual learning." CP can contribute to our understanding of the individual as a component of the system, but CP does not study the complete system.

CP, as currently construed, is most appropriate for studying and influencing the design of instructionist learning environments. This is consistent with the CP focus on formal schooling, where instructionism is more likely to be found than in nonschool learning environments. And yet, we know that these are the least effective learning environments. As schools and other learning environments are redesigned, in ways grounded in the science of learning, LS may become more appropriate and CP may become less appropriate. CP researchers have been successful at developing models of how learning occurs within different domains for individual learners, and at developing models and theories that focus on representation of domain content and how individuals use it. And yet, a lot could be learned by exploring how these models are limited and need to be revised when tested within different (noninstructionist) environments. By combining approaches, CP and LS can practically meet in the middle in an attempt to model, understand, and promote learning of individuals and collaborative teams within different learning environments. Of course, a CP researcher still might be searching for generalizable conclusions that are relevant to all environments. Yet, even if this search is in vain, the collaborative effort should provide insight into promoting learning within environments that are rich and diverse.

The Relationship Between Basic and Applied Science (Methodology)

CP uses experimental methodologies that have the potential to result in generalizable, domain-general findings about how the mind operates. These findings can then be *applied to* or *used to contribute to the design of* educational interventions. This is a linear model of science, of the relationship between basic science and application: The scientist (the CP) does the research and identifies a finding, and then that basic finding can be used and applied. Sometimes the CP researcher is also involved in the application, but that's not required by the paradigm.

LS uses methods where basic research is embedded in application and intervention. LS (in general) rejects a linear model of science where the basic findings come first and then are general and applicable to a variety of settings. Instead, LS uses iterative, cyclical, nonlinear methodologies.

CP uses methodologies that study individuals (although see Nokes-Malach, Zepeda, Richey, Gadgil, Chapter 20, this volume): primarily, controlled experimental designs, random sampling from a single population, subjecting these randomly sampled individuals to two distinct designed experiences (independent variables modified in a "control" and an "experimental" "condition"), and then using some operationalization of a hypothesized mental state or process to measure dependent variables of each individual both before and after experiencing the condition. If there are differences in the dependent variable between the two groups, then one can make a causal claim that the difference was caused by the condition design.

Random sampling, combined with careful design of the two conditions so that everything is the same except for the independent variable, results in the ability to control for confounding variables: to be able to assert that differences in the dependent variable are indeed caused by differences in the independent variable. Even when such well-controlled designs cannot be used (e.g., when conducting classroom research where each student cannot be randomly assigned to an experimental group), CPs still strive to use the strongest quasi-experimental designs in an attempt to increase their confidence in causal conclusions (for discussion, see Dunlosky et al., in press). The reason for the focus on control is that almost any intervention in a classroom might be expected to result in short-term improvements (for detailed arguments, see Hattie, 2009), whether they be due to teacher (or researcher) enthusiasm, the novelty of doing something different, and so forth. Put differently, an important goal of conducting CP research is to establish sufficiently firm conclusions about what works by ruling out other plausible factors (e.g., the excitement of having a researcher visit class) as responsible.

LS uses methodologies that study learning in sociotechnical systems. Because these systems are complex, qualitative methods are often necessary. Many LS methodologies are designed to analyze data that is gathered through qualitative methodologies, such as ethnographies of naturally occurring learning environments or semi-structured interviews. Most learning scientists aspire to make the analysis of qualitative data as rigorous as possible – for example, by using grounded theory methodology, and the other methodologies named above.

A qualitative method that is widely used by learning scientists is *design based research* (DBR) (Barab, 2014). In DBR, researchers work with educators, students, and other participants in a real-world learning environment. DBR proceeds as an iterative process. First, the LS researcher designs a learning intervention, grounded in LS theory based on prior empirical research. Second, the learning intervention is implemented. Third, LS researcher conducts qualitative and quantitative analysis to determine whether the intervention was successful at enhancing the intended learning outcomes. Typically, an intervention is partially successful, but not completely. This is when an iteration takes place: The LS works to explain any complex outcomes, again by reference to theory and prior empirical studies. In a well-designed DBR study, the experience of the intervention and its analysis make a contribution to our scientific understanding of how to foster learning toward that learning outcome. A revision to the intervention is then developed, motivated by the observed results of the initial intervention. If that revision accomplished the theory-predicted change in learning outcomes, one can conclude that the theoretical contribution/development has empirically been supported and has generalizability beyond the specific research site. By using experimental methodologies, CP can make stronger causal claims; however, those claims are decontextualized. This is necessary to control for confounding variables, but as a result the findings may lack validity. For instance, a particular intervention that boosts student learning of biology concepts in the laboratory may be entirely inert when applied within a complex learning system, such as a biology classroom or when students are learning in social groups. In such cases, evaluating these findings in complex learning systems is essential. A case in point is provided by McDaniel and Little (Chapter 19, this volume) who discovered that a type of retrieval practice (using multiple-choice tests) that is relatively ineffective in the laboratory actually is rather beneficial when used in authentic education environments. The reason for this lack of generalizability is presumably that, although multiple-choice tests may not directly impact learning, they indirectly impact it by motivating students to subsequently learn material that they had not yet known. In laboratory studies, students often do not get the opportunity to self-regulate their learning and hence do not reap the indirect benefits of this kind of retrieval practice.

LS researchers study complex real-world learning environments so they can claim validity, but their causal claims must be hedged. DBR is designed to provide at least partial generalizability and, if effectively done, DBR can combine strong validity with partial claims to causality and generalizability.

Synergies

LS has much in common with cognitive psychology research applied to education. And yet there are also substantial differences, as we have discussed in this chapter. In this final section, we suggest some possible ways that LS approaches may contribute to CP research like that presented in this volume. We believe there are many potential synergies, because both fields share a common goals: To develop a scientific understanding of how learning happens. As with all scientific disciplines, both fields

- Design studies that gather empirical findings
- Extract meaningful patterns and themes from those findings
- Use those findings to develop theoretical frameworks that provide explanations for those findings
- Use these theoretical frameworks to suggest future empirical studies that have the potential to test, refine, and extend those theoretical frameworks

As with scientific research in most disciplines, both fields hold that theories are explanatory frameworks that provide enhanced understandings of learning.

In addition to this shared scientific approach, many LS and CP researchers alike then work to apply these findings to improve the development of real-world interventions to enhance learning, including curricular designs, teacher training, classroom materials, software and hardware designs, and social system designs such as collaborative and interactional tasks for learners.

LS, like the CP chapters in this volume, pursue research that is consistent with this scientific approach to the study of learning. As discussed, there are substantial differences between CP and LS scientific approaches and, in some cases, these differences are large enough that it can be hard to see how one might bridge the gap. And yet, as a result of this underlying, shared, scientific approach, quite a bit of LS research can be blended with CP approaches. In this concluding section, we identify potential synergies and make some tentative suggestions for how LS might contribute to CP.

Some connections are fairly easy to identify, but we also argue that one can identify an ever greater range of synergies if both CP and LS make the effort to "stretch" a bit, with slight modifications of what most people in their field do, but in ways that are still consistent with the core epistemology and methodology of both fields.

CP studies of how individuals learn could be considered to be a subset of LS research. CP studies how individuals learn, and individuals learn within the sociotechnical systems that LS studies. When individuals learn (in real-world learning environments, not necessarily in laboratory psychology experiments), they learn within systems that include other learners, within intentional learning environment designs, using designed artifacts (sometimes based on digital technologies, but not always), and from more experienced individuals for whom the learning environment is not explicitly designed to foster their learning, such as teachers in schools. LS researchers pursue scientific research that is designed to explain every element of the learning environment, including the individuals participating in that environment. To the extent that the study of the participating individuals can contribute to scientific explanation of how learning environments work, LS researchers either will be consumers of CP research or will sometimes pursue research that is quite similar to CP, in combination with other methodological approaches.

It has been difficult to write this chapter without portraying CP and LS differences to be more extreme than they actually are. The contrasts we've identified apply in many cases, but the risk is that we veer too close to stereotypes and misrepresentations. In our own experiences, Keith has often encountered LS researchers who disparage and stereotype CP, and John has likewise encountered CP researchers who are dismissive of LS. As with many stereotypes, there is some truth, as we've acknowledged here. We collaborated in writing this chapter because we believe that these differences can be productive and synergistic. If we focus only on contrasts between the two fields, our respective colleagues may perceive collaboration to be impossible, and we believe that this would be unfortunate, because some exciting collaborative research paths would be ignored or dismissed.

It may be overly simplistic, but we think of LS and CP as in a Venn diagram, with each circle having a large area of its own, but with the two intersecting for a significant portion of each field. Some great elemental work – studies of individual learning – is being done by researchers who affiliate with LS. Likewise, some CP researchers study individuals within context, not strictly as isolated laboratory subjects. We suspect that after reading our characterizations of LS and CP, some folks who identified with CP are now viewing themselves as more aligned with LS, and vice versa.

For those readers who are not in the overlapping area of the Venn diagram – those who align fairly closely with the characterization of CP that we've provided here – our intent has been to provide a concise overview of the LS approach and to describe situations in which the LS approach may have strengths vis-à-vis the prototypical CP approach of individual experimental laboratory research. As we've presented it here, LS has a greater capability to understand learning as it takes place within a sociotechnical context, when that individual learning is inextricably linked with the features of that context.

Some LS practitioners take a more extreme position that the individual learner can *never* be studied in isolation from context. In this view, even a student studying alone in a library must be analyzed as embedded in a sociocultural context. Libraries are historically and socially designed spaces, as is the very notion of studying there; the option of choosing to go there and the motivation to do so are socioculturally determined; the books used during study are technological artifacts, embedded in a specific culture and historical moment. And if so, the sociocultural context is just as important for a student sitting quietly in a lecture hall, taking notes, or a student completing a multiple-choice quiz. LS researchers who hold to this extreme position also fall outside of the center overlapping area in the Venn diagram.

By describing both LS and CP in some detail, we have to some extent emphasized the contrasts. We've done this for two reasons. First, to make explicit some of the unstated, taken-for-granted assumptions held by both LS and CP. Because both cognitive psychologists and learning scientists tend to work in environments where our collaborators and students share these same assumptions, we are likely to believe that these approaches are obviously true, and maximally scientific; and that other approaches are less scientific, almost by definition. This is what it means to have a disciplinary paradigm that is culturally shared. Second, we've done this because we believe that these contrasts represent the potential for strength when they are brought together.

In our view, these contrasts are not irreconcilable differences (as some of our colleagues think), but rather are equally valuable approaches toward our shared goal: To develop a scientifically grounded understanding of learning and to use that understanding to improve the design of learning environments and the learning of the participants in those environments.

Implications for Cognitive Psychology Applied to Education

Both CP and LS have lessons for the other approach. However, given the focus of this handbook on CP approaches to education, we suspect that the readership will largely be aligned with CP. Thus, in this section, we consider a few of the ways in which the LS approach might complement, or even strengthen, CP. We hope that this presentation may help bring LS and CP more closely together, given their joint goal is to have real-world impact on learning.

With the joint goal of improving education, we emphasize a handful of lessons for CP that were implied but not explicitly stated prior in the chapter:

1. *Studying technology-enhanced learning environments.* From the founding of LS, a central focus of research has been how new technologies impact learning environments. We've noted that CP has tended not to incorporate instructional technology into their studies (in part because CP focuses on individuals in isolation from learning environments, and in part because CP has tended to focus on traditional classroom instruction). CP research could be strengthened by expanding its contexts of study beyond traditional school classrooms.

2. *Using learning technologies to gather data on learning.* CP could strengthen its research by exploring ways to gather data using new technologies such as LAK and OLM. For example, when learners use smartphone apps or Internet apps, it is possible to gather second-by-second tracking data, resulting in substantial

volumes of quantitative data that could be integrated with existing CP methods to allow an analysis of individual learners in context.

3. *Increasing the range of learning environments studied.* For the most part, CP researchers have conducted studies in traditional school classrooms and have rarely studied other learning environments. We have mentioned only a few such learning environments in this chapter; they include, among many others, museums, after-school programs, web-based courses, and game-based learning. A limitation of CP's focus on school classrooms is simply that much learning happens outside of the classroom, even on topics that are primarily taught in schools – such as the increasing design of science centers to align with STEM learning in schools. Understanding how such informal learning works is a national priority, with substantial funding programs by the National Science Foundation, for example. In these contexts, a complete understanding of individual learning requires collaborative efforts that examine how these environments impact a learner's interest, identity, and efficacy, and how such impacts manifest differently for different social systems – for example, a family watching a program on space flight versus a group of children interacting with a display about space flight in a science center.

4. *Contributing to the improved design of learning environments.* CP generally follows a traditional model of "pure science," where research findings are gathered in controlled laboratory settings and only later are those findings used to modify learning environment designs. This linear path from research to application can work well, but it is not able to move through the rapid iterations made possible by design-based research – when research is conducted directly in those complex learning environments that we hope to improve.

5. *Studying multiple levels of analysis.* CP's focus on explanations of individual learning is a strength of the field. And yet, CP research could be strengthened by also incorporating analyses of the sociotechnical environments within which much learning occurs. By incorporating a complementary study of the features of learning environments that impact individual learning – from teamwork and collaboration, to the style of teacher–student interaction, to the role of technological artifacts from books to smartphones – CPs may gain more insight into why a particular intervention is (or is not) having an impact.

With the increasing use of research-based pedagogies in schools – those that move from instructionism toward project-based learning, collaborative work, and interaction through connected applications on personal devices – it is no longer possible to conceive of schooling as a row of students listening to a teacher deliver information. It has always been somewhat stereotypical to envision schools as a place where students learn quietly and in isolation. Students have worked in collaborative teams for decades. Students have been collaborating through computer networks for decades; computer-supported collaborative learning (CSCL) was first implemented and studied over local Intranets in schools in the 1980s, predating the Internet.

As learning technologies evolve in sophistication; as the price of these technologies rapidly decreases to a point where more schools can afford to purchase them;

and as school leaders and teachers become increasingly aware of the research showing the limitations of traditional school instruction, cognitive psychology will increasingly need to adapt, and in this chapter we have identified some ways that an awareness of LS research could contribute to the evolution of CP.

Conclusion: Collaboration Makes Us Stronger

As coauthors, we each represent the field we primarily affiliate with and our contributions to this jointly authored chapter are grounded in many years of participation in these fields. Keith has edited two editions of *The Cambridge handbook of the learning sciences* (2006, 2014) and John is the coeditor of this handbook, which appears in the same Cambridge University Press book series, Cambridge Handbooks in Psychology. We chose to work together on this chapter because we independently had come to the conclusion that each approach is equally valuable. We realized that researchers in both disciplines are committed to the same goals; that the two approaches were complementary; and that both could benefit by exploring links with the other. We also felt that this chapter was necessary because we have both frequently observed our colleagues being explicitly dismissive of the other approach, if not ignoring it entirely.

For many years prior to this collaboration, we both had a respect for research in the other's field. Then, the idea of coauthoring a chapter emerged naturally. Keith is the editor of this handbook series, and because of his respect for the field of cognitive psychology applied to education, he extended the invitation to John to create and edit this handbook. And then, because of John's respect for LS, and his belief that CP could benefit from understand LS and its approach to investigating education, he decided to include a chapter on LS and extended the invitation to Keith to coauthor this chapter. Our motivation was to benefit our colleagues in both of our fields and primarily the readers of this volume, who are likely to be cognitive psychologists. But, more than we expected, we also both benefited personally from our collaboration on this chapter. By exploring these issues together, we feel that each of us has gained insights into the merits of both approaches. In writing this chapter, we are more convinced than ever that our two approaches should come together. We should be active consumers of each other's research and readers of each other's journals. Our colleagues should collaborate more frequently in research grants and in the design of school interventions.

Early in our collaboration, we thought that our chapter might advocate that LS and CP should be considered to be part of one, subsuming, unified field – perhaps called "the science of learning." At one point, John generously suggested that CP was in fact a subfield of LS (because the individual learning studied by CP was a part of the larger system studied by LS). But after many months of working together, we no longer believe that LS and CP should merge together. Although we advocate for increased collaboration, we nonetheless believe that our shared goals would be better served by the two fields maintaining their differences. There are empirical phenomena that are best studied by CP and other phenomena that are best studied by LS (although with all learning, we believe that both fields have something to offer). For example, when the phenomenon being studied is a group learning together, LS would be the most appropriate scientific approach. As an example, envision two basketball teams playing against each other: To compete effectively, each team needs to learn collectively – from moment to moment – how to respond to the strengths and the changing strategies of the other team. To take a second example, a jazz ensemble playing together for the first time must learn how to work together quickly to create an effective performance for the audience. In a third example, in families, each child develops an identity and learns a set of culturally appropriate practices, including how to greet a stranger versus a family member; how to eat together; who it is appropriate to hug or to kiss; what is considered to be moral or immoral behavior. These forms of learning are deeply embedded in sociocultural systems.

We began the chapter by noting that our joint goal is to conduct scientific research to improve our understandings of learning and to use that scientific understanding to improve the design of learning environments – whether the goal is to improve the individual ability of each student, or to design more effective technological supports, or to improve the collective effectiveness of a social system. We conclude by restating our premise: Both LS and CP have unique strengths; there are valuable differences; and there are potentials for synergy that have not yet been fully explored. By working together, both of our research communities can better accomplish our goals of improving teaching and learning.

References

Barab, S. (2014). Design-based research: A methodological toolkit for engineering change. In R. K. Sawyer (ed.), *The Cambridge handbook of the learning sciences*, 2nd edn (pp. 151–170). New York: Cambridge University Press.

Broadbent, D. E. (1958). *Perception and communication*. London: Pergamon Press.

diSessa, A. A. (2006). A history of conceptual change research. In R. K. Sawyer (ed.), *The Cambridge handbook of the learning sciences* (pp. 265–281). New York: Cambridge University Press.

Dunlosky, J., Morehead, K., Zamary, A., & Rawson, K. A. (in press). From the laboratory to the classroom: Challenges and solutions for conducting memory research in educational contexts. In H. Otani & B. Schwartz (eds.), *Handbook of research methods in human memory*. New York: Routledge.

Gardner, H. (1985). *The mind's new science: A history of the cognitive revolution*. New York: Basic Books.

Hattie, J. (2009). *Visible learning: A synthesis of over 800 meta-analyses relating to achievement*. New York: Routledge.

Kolodner, J. L. (1991). *The Journal of the Learning Sciences*: Effecting changes in education. *The Journal of the Learning Sciences*, *1*(1), 1–6.

Lachman, R., Lachman, J. L., & Butterfield, E. C. (1979). *Cognitive psychology and information processing*. Hillsdale, NJ: Lawrence Erlbaum Associates.

Lehrer, R. & Schauble, L. (2006). Cultivating model-based reasoning in science education. In R. K. Sawyer (ed.), *The Cambridge handbook of the learning sciences* (pp. 371–387). New York: Cambridge.

Mayer, R. E. (1992). Cognition and instruction: Their historic meeting within educational psychology. *Journal of Educational Psychology, 84*(4), 405–412.

Mercier, E., Fong, C., Cober, R., Slotta, J. D., Forssell, K. S., Isreal, M., & Rummel, N. (2015). *Researching and designing for the orchestration of learning in the CSCL classroom.* Paper presented at the Exploring the Material Conditions of Learning: The Computer Supported Collaborative Learning (CSCL) Conference 2015, June 7–11, Gothenburg, Sweden.

Miller, G. A., Galanter, E., & Pribram, K. H. (1960). *Plans and the structure of behavior.* New York: Holt.

Nathan, M. J., Rummel, N., & Hay, K. E. (2016). Growing the learning sciences: Brand or big tent? In M. A. Evans, M. Packer, & R. K. Sawyer (eds.), *Reflections on the learning sciences* (pp. 191–209). New York: Cambridge University Press.

Nathan, M. J. & Sawyer, R. K. (2014). Foundations of the learning sciences. In R. K. Sawyer (ed.), *The Cambridge handbook of the learning sciences*, 2nd edn (pp. 21–43). New York: Cambridge University Press.

Pea, R. (2016). The prehistory of the learning sciences. In M. A. Evans, M. Packer, & R. K. Sawyer (eds.), *Reflections on the learning sciences* (pp. 32–58). New York: Cambridge University Press.

Rogoff, B. (1990). *Apprenticeship in thinking: Cognitive development in social context.* New York: Oxford University Press.

Sawyer, R. K. (2014). Introduction: The new science of learning. In R. K. Sawyer (ed.), *The Cambridge handbook of the learning sciences*, 2nd edn (pp. 1–18). New York: Cambridge University Press.

2 Quackery in Educational Research

Daniel H. Robinson and Joel R. Levin

> At the heart of science is an essential balance between two seemingly contradictory attitudes – an openness to new ideas, no matter how bizarre or counterintuitive they may be, and the most ruthless skeptical scrutiny of all ideas, old and new. This is how deep truths are winnowed from deep nonsense.
>
> Carl Sagan

Preliminary Remarks

Other chapters in this volume present promising instructional interventions and innovations that have been uncovered through thoughtfully crafted educational research. In this chapter, we take one big cautionary step backward and say "Whoa, not so fast!" Why? Because many similar "promising" educational advances are in fact overpromises, in that the research from which the advances are derived is not based on replicable, scientifically "credible" evidence (Levin, 1994). Most of our cautionary comments are directed at academic research within the field of education per se but other comments are directed at pseudoresearch prescriptions that emanate from the news media and popular magazine reports. At the same time, we do not mean to demean the vast amount of laudable, reputable research that can be found in the academic educational research literature, much of which has been produced by colleague contributors to this impressive *Handbook* volume. We are targeting only the not-so-laudable research that also can be found in that literature. In so doing, we frequently hyperbolize, with our primary intent being to emphasize a particular point or to highlight an example. To those readers who find the tone of our hyperbole too irreverent or light-hearted, we apologize in advance.

> There's a sucker born every minute. David Hannum, but commonly attributed to P. T. Barnum

Quackery Exposed

The term "quackery" has been used to describe the promotion of a method, technique, or procedure (generically, an intervention), which, by commonly accepted research standards, has not been proven to be effective. Following the American Civil War, charlatans from the North often tried to sell "snake oil" tonics that were in reality completely ineffective. This experience was captured in the movie *The Outlaw Josey Wales* (1976).[1] A similar quackery example appears at the beginning of the music video *Say, Say, Say* (1983).[2]

Quackery, as will be discussed here, is not exclusively a problem of concern for the dissemination of educational research findings. So, before we get to the specific educational-research focus of this chapter, let us broaden our scope to expose quackery in other research disciplines and contexts as well. We also note that quackery claims are not restricted to studies that purport to assess the effectiveness of some "new-fangled" innovative technique or intervention on the basis of researcher-manipulated intervention-versus-nonintervention comparisons. Even more "Aw!" inspiring instances are the quackery claims that stem from nonexperimental correlational studies in which no independent variables are manipulated and no controlled comparisons are conducted at all (Robinson et al., 2007; Shaw et al., 2010).

Scientific "advancements" that later turn out to be hoaxes are common. For example, in 1989, numerous physicists concluded that the "cold fusion energy" claims of Utah researchers could not be substantiated. Other questionable recent research "breakthroughs" include the health benefits of red wine (Wade, 2012), genetic bases of longevity (Schmid, 2011), and the development of a simple method for producing stem cells (Ritter, 2014), to name a few. It remains to be seen whether the recently hyped "Gaydar" Machine – a procedure to detect one's sexual orientation (Murphy, 2017) – has scientific validity but the initial research on which it is founded appears to be fraught with methodological problems.

Quackery in Medicine

Homeopathy is an alternative medicine widely characterized as pseudoscience. About a third of all Americans use some form of homeopathic medicine and spend almost $3 billion annually (Christensen, 2015). Recently, the UK's National Health Service banned prescriptions for homeopathy and other "low-value" treatments (McAfee, 2017). Homeopathy continues to thrive in the United States, where health insurance giant Blue Cross Blue Shield even devotes an entire website to alternative medicines such as homeopathy and herbalism.[3] Naturopathy is another alternative medicine that lacks scientific support. Nonetheless, recently, Massachusetts joined eighteen other states in passing a law that created a licensing board for naturopaths (Freyer, 2017). Such quackery nonsense reminds us of Steve Martin's (1978) outlandish Theodoric of York character in the early days of NBC's *Saturday Night Live* weekly TV show (www.nbc.com/saturday-night-live/video/theodoric-of-york/n8661?snl=1).

Does quackery in medicine still exist today? Wolf (2000) estimated that anywhere between 40,000 and 100,000 hospital patients die every year as a result of medical

---

[1] The clip from the movie *The Outlaw Josey Wales* may be viewed at www.youtube.com/watch?v=eUh5IShNwXo

[2] The music video for *Say, Say, Say* may be viewed at www.youtube.com/watch?v=aLEhh_XpJ-0

[3] See https://lifetimes.bcbstx.com/article/natural

errors. A chief cause of these errors is the failure of hospitals to base their daily practices on evidence (Berwick et al., 2006). In an article that startled many more than twenty-five years ago, the Evidence-Based Medicine Working Group (1992) suggested that current medical practice is not informed by science. Doctors rely too heavily on clinical experience alone when diagnosing and treating illnesses rather than also consulting the extant literature. The Evidence-Based Medicine Working Group called for "evidence-based" medicine. If medicine had only begun to rely on evidence in 1992, one must wonder what it relied on prior to 1992. Perhaps it followed a "faith-based" treatment procedure?

The popular TV personality Dr. Oz has been criticized by medical researchers for being more of an entertainer than a doctor in terms of some of his questionable recommendations. A group of ten doctors wrote a letter to a dean at Columbia University, where Dr. Oz is a faculty member in the School of Medicine, indicating that "Dr. Oz has repeatedly shown disdain for science and for evidence-based medicine [and that] he's pushing 'miracle' weight-loss supplements with no scientific proof that they work." Out of 479 recommendations from forty *Dr. Oz* episodes, researchers found that only 46 percent were evidence-based (McCoy, 2014).

> It ain't what you don't know that gets you into trouble. It's what you know for sure that just ain't so. Mark Twain

Quackery in Education

Since 1992, the term "evidence-based" has spread rapidly to several other fields, including corrections (Cullen & Gendreau, 2000; MacKenzie, 2001, 2006), crime prevention (Welsh & Farrington, 2006), education (Davies (1999), management (Pfeffer & Sutton, 2006), policing (Sherman, 1998), public health (Rychetnik et al., 2004), social work (Gilgun, 2005), and health and human services (Roberts & Yeager, 2004). Does quackery exist in education? When researchers make recommendations for practice, they are "selling" an intervention. Over the years, the fields of psychological and educational research have experienced their fair share of tempests in teapots with respect to interventions that have been "proven" to work.

Robinson and colleagues (2013) provided two examples of educational quackery where researchers clearly went beyond their correlational data to make recommendations warranted only by causally grounded data. In one study, teachers rated their current relationships with students and these ratings were correlated with parents' ratings of their child's behavior problems at home. The researchers concluded that high-quality teacher–child relationships buffered children from the risks of behavior problems. However, there was no causal link whatsoever between what the teachers did and children's behavior problems at home. In a second correlational study, the researchers concluded that their findings "suggest the importance of early and continued intervention by educators *all over the world*" (Robinson et al., 2013, p. 294, emphasis added) even though there were no data that warranted any causal link between the intervention and the student outcomes.

Reinhart and colleagues (2013) mentioned how the self-esteem movement of the 1970s through the 1990s provides another example of how recommendations based on observational data can lead to unjustified conclusions. The correlational link between high self-esteem and high academic achievement led some researchers to conclude that low self-esteem was the cause of many of society's problems. When further evidence was accumulated, however, it became clear that it was just as likely that self-esteem could be caused by achievement rather than vice versa. Moreover, efforts to increase achievement by boosting self-esteem not only did not work but actually could be counterproductive and lower achievement.

> *You can fool some of the people all of the time,*
> *and all of the people some of the time,*
> *but you can't fool all of the people all of the time.*
>
> Arguably attributed to Abraham Lincoln

Reminiscent of the capers of Clever Hans, the legendary horse that could perform many a wondrous "feet" of arithmetical dexterity (see Samhita & Gross, 2013), Lilienfeld and colleagues (2014) recently reported on the "facilitated communication" phenomenon. "Incredibly," orally noncommunicative children with autism were found to produce coherent messages via keyboards when their hand movements had been stabilized. Unfortunately for "true believers," however, subsequent carefully controlled research completely debunked the phenomenon. Similarly, despite widespread claims that children with behavioral and developmental disabilities benefit from sensory-based interventions (including a much heralded weighted-vest accoutrement), in a thorough review of the empirical literature, Barton and colleagues (2015) provided convincing evidence to refute those inflated claims.

Another recent quackery-in-education example is the widespread attention paid to a study linking fast food consumption to low academic performance (Purtell & Gershoff, 2014). Using a longitudinal data set, the authors studied more than 11,000 children who completed a food survey when they were in the 5th grade. The authors found that children who reported eating fast food made lower academic gains than those who did not. Although the authors stated that their study was observational rather than experimental, they were confident that fast food explained some of the difference in achievement gains: "Efforts to reduce parent stress around food preparation may be a promising way to reduce fast food consumption and thereby improve child achievement" (p. 5).

Even to a casual observer, this conclusion reeks of correlation-becoming-causation nonsensibility. It is well known that fast food consumption is more prevalent in lower-income families than in higher-income families (e.g., Kalenkoski & Hamrick, 2013). Similarly, the relationship between poverty and academic achievement is among the most well-established causal links that exist. But here, the media (and researchers to a lesser extent) have fanned the news-buzz flame so that these findings are interpreted as "If you want your children to succeed in school, cut out the French fries!" This is an example of educational quackery at its finest and what can happen when educational researchers are pressured/encouraged by the popular press (and even journal editors) to make eye-catching claims about their findings.

In 2008, the *New York Times* latched on to what they thought to be a whimsical study that appeared in the highly regarded scientific journal *Oikos* (Grim, 2008). In a sample of thirty-four surveyed Czech Republic avian evolutionary biology researchers, it was found that the greater the number of weekly beers the researchers reported having consumed, the lower their professional "success" with respect to the number of publications and citations of their work. Although beer drinking per se was not pinpointed as the proximate cause of academic sloth, Grim regarded this quaffing quackery as a useful proxy for how the researchers were spending their leisure time, which could well have "influenced" the quality and quantity of their academic work, which in turn led to the following Grim conclusion:

> The hypothesis of "social effects on publication success" and supporting correlative results between beer consumption rates and publication success presented herein have direct bearing not only on assessments of publication biases but also on understanding of human behavioural ecology. (p. 486)

A potentially intriguing hypothesis? We'll drink to that!

> All that glitters is not gold. Proverb

Quackery in Higher Education

An example of educational quackery in higher education comes from research on the first Synchronous Massive Online Course, or SMOC. According to Pennebaker, Gosling, and Ferrell (2013), and subsequently cited in a more widely read outlet (Clay, 2015), the SMOC "boosted performance half a letter grade, improved performance in other and subsequent classes and halved the socioeconomic achievement gap" (Clay, 2015, p. 54). However, a closer look at the data revealed that the tiny performance boosts could be attributed entirely to selection bias, whereas the achievement gap reduction could be explained by differential attrition (Robinson, 2017). Failure to adequately control for internal threats to validity led to false claims – claims based on observational, rather than on experimentally controlled, data. No worries, because surely nobody would take such claims seriously – or would they? Straumsheim (2013) interpreted them as follows:

> As more and more of the coursework continued to shift toward digital, the data showed a clear trend: Not only were students in the online section performing the equivalent of half a letter grade better than those physically in attendance, but taking the class online also slashed the achievement gap between upper, middle and lower-middle class students in half, from about one letter grade to less than half of a letter grade ... "We are changing the way students are approaching the class and the way they study," Pennebaker said ... "That's one thing that I'm actually most excited about ... This project could never have been built here at the university without heavy research behind it."
>
> And here's how the SMOC's potential has been discussed: Originally, the professors hoped the class would attract 10,000 non-university students willing to

> pay a few hundred dollars for the for-credit class. Indeed, the headline for a *Wall Street Journal* article about the pair's innovation trumpeted "Online class aims to earn millions." That hasn't happened. The class, offered each fall, still mostly consists of regular University of Texas undergrads. And while Gosling believes the model will eventually spread to other universities, as far as he knows it hasn't done so yet, perhaps because of the expertise and hefty investment required. Still, the model has been so successful the university has since developed SMOC versions of American government and U.S. foreign policy classes. (Clay, 2015, p. 54)

Let us hope that the "hefty investment" isn't too much. The last we looked, the University of Texas at Austin was committing a cool $16 million to Project 2021, which includes monies for increasing the number of SMOC production studios. The executive director of Project 2021 was recently quoted as saying, "experimentation is the beginning of progress in education" (Ritterbush, 2017). Too bad the "evidence" used to support the SMOC isn't based on carefully controlled comparisons between the SMOC and alternative course structures.

As a final example of unjustified recommendations based on "causation-squeezed-out-of-correlations" (Robinson & Levin, 2010), consider Colorado State University's Student Success Initiative. In 2008, Colorado State University began to examine student data with the goal of improving retention and graduation rates.

> Research also revealed that students who hadn't passed introductory composition and mathematics in the first year were much more likely to drop out. "After that, the goal was to get every freshman into those classes (or equivalent courses)," Hughes says. "The graduation rate is 40 percent higher for students who completed those courses their freshman year." (Phifer, 2017)

If the "cause" of poor retention and graduation rates is simply the failure of students to enroll in introductory courses, then there is an exceedingly simple solution: We should require *all* students to enroll in English and Mathematics courses during their first year. Then, magically, they will *all* pass, return after their first year, and graduate in four years! We know this because "research" revealed the truly amazing discovery that students who have trouble passing introductory English Composition and Math courses also have trouble graduating from college. Of course, one might wonder whether students who don't take or don't pass these introductory courses arrive at college lacking the prerequisite skills needed to pass the courses or to graduate from college.

What other new "fads" in education are likely to be quackery? Take the digital native/multitasker claim that young people who were born after 1984 have grown up with technology and naturally have the ability to multitask. Kirschner and de Bruyckere (2017) recently debunked this myth. They provided examples of other researchers who continue to perpetuate the myth and call for changes in how we teach these students. For example, Teras, Myllyla, and Teras (2011) claimed that "the natural skills of digital native learners … are not being supported in education" (p. 1). Blumenstyk (2017) reported that US colleges spend around $5 billion on educational technology products every year. However, virtually no efficacy research (i.e., research evaluating whether any of this educational technology "stuff" actually does any good) exists to inform these spending decisions. Do the public – and, more importantly, educators – believe in such quackery? In other words, are they buying it? A recent study by Macdonald and colleagues (2017) revealed that 93 percent of the general public and 76 percent of educators believed in students' preferred "learning styles," despite overwhelming evidence suggesting that such enduring learner traits are simply a myth (Pashler et al., 2008).

And what other educational "snake oil" is out there, waiting to be purchased? What educational reform efforts since 1965 have "worked"? Every day we hear about a new educational reform that will result in miraculous "turnaround" schools (i.e., changing schools from low performing to high performing within a few years). Perhaps even more wondrous (and, in terms of rareness, rivaling unicorns), there is talk of 90/90/90 schools, where a school has more than 90 percent of its students eligible for free or reduced lunch, more than 90 percent from ethnic minority populations, and more than 90 percent of students attaining high academic standards (Baeder, 2011). These initiatives and false claims that accompany them continue to give education a bad name. As Diane Ravitch (2011) suggested, "The news media and the public should respond with skepticism to any claims of miraculous transformation. The achievement gap between children from different income levels exists before children enter school" (p. 27).

Dramatic interlude. So, wherefore art thou, educational research? Is most of thee "credible" and the rest of thee "incredible" (Levin, 2004)? Are the conclusions produced by educational intervention research based on universally accepted scientific principles and methods, or merely on the hopes and dreams of would-be innovators? As a modest example of the latter – and we are not making this up! – perhaps educational research could even be "*couched in the sweet lilting strains of iambic pentameter, as one once opined*" (Cahnmann, 2003), though verily "*not without a response that was belatedly proffered in kind*" (Levin, 2011).

What to Do About Educational Prescriptions That Waddle?

So, what do we do? If we choose to do nothing, then educational quackery will continue to appear in the professional literature and in the popular press. We need fair-minded educational researchers to keep conducting scientifically valid tests of their claims. The goal is to not be cynical or pessimistic but simply skeptical. Medicine has taken steps to avoid quackery. The Food and Drug Administration was created to protect citizens from harmful quackery. In the field of education, the American Educational Research Association (AERA) could certainly step up to uphold the integrity of the field with the same ferocity and vigor that it employs to support social justice. Unfortunately, to provide a sense of AERA's current disposition toward research integrity – in addition to the just-cited article touting the potential of educational research as poetry (Cahnmann, 2003), which appeared in the *Educational Researcher*, the flagship journal of the organization – AERA has published articles touting autoethnography (Hughes, Pennington, & Makris, 2012) as a reputable educational research tool. Every year, the AERA annual meeting program is filled with sessions and titles that scream quackery to even a casual observer. As Ronald Reagan once famously said, "[G]overnment is not the solution to our problems. Government is the problem." Or to paraphrase somewhat more generously for the present context, "AERA may not be the solution to the problem of educational quackery because AERA contributes to the problem."

What, then, is the solution? The Department of Education has the What Works Clearinghouse (WWC) to rigorously evaluate the evidence published in intervention reports. The WWC to date has endorsed only a handful of educational interventions that actually "work." Perhaps that says something about the quality of the majority of educational research studies. In addition, the National Education Policy Center (NEPC) at the University of Colorado does yeoman service to the educational research community by screening research reports that purport to have "found X." In some cases, NEPC researchers agree that the study under scrutiny has plausibly, or even credibly, "found X"; and for those cases the NEPC reviews are appropriately complimentary. In other cases, however, upon a (typically painstaking) critique of the study's methodology and procedures, NEPC researchers argue that the evidence provided by the study's authors is not convincing enough to conclude that the study has "found X." As an example of the meticulous work that the NEPC is conducting, consider the following recent verbatim summary of a research critique that can be downloaded from the NEPC website:

> *Attempt to Refute Suspension's Harmful Academic Impact Falls Flat*
> Key Review Takeaway: Questionable methodological decisions cast doubt on validity of study's conclusions
> BOULDER, CO (June 1, 2017) – A new report from the Department of Education Reform at the University of Arkansas examines the association between out-of-school suspensions and student test scores. The findings and conclusions presented in the 'working paper,' however, lack validity on multiple grounds.
> "Understanding a Vicious Cycle: Do Out-of-School Suspensions Impact Student Test Scores?" was reviewed by Brea L. Perry of Indiana University and Daniel Losen of the University of California Los Angeles.
> Using dynamic and multilevel regression modeling of six years of student discipline records from all K-12 public schools in Arkansas, the paper purports to estimate a causal relationship between exclusionary discipline and academic performance. It concludes, in contrast to prior work, that the number of days of suspension a student receives has a very modest positive relationship to math and language arts test scores.
> The reviewers explain that the effects of out-of-school suspension are not measured in the academic year in which suspensions occurred, but instead are measured at least a full academic year later. In other words, the study design does not adequately capture lost instructional time, deterioration of student-teacher relationships, psychological distress, and other immediate consequences of suspension that would logically affect academic performance in the same academic year. Instead, the analyses only consider the delayed effect of suspension, without accounting for suspensions occurring more recently.
> The findings also have weak face validity in light of the weight of evidence suggesting that exclusionary discipline and school absences have adverse effects on key outcomes such as test scores, GPA, grade retention, and dropping out – including research conducted using the Arkansas dataset by a member of this same research team, examining grade retention.

For these and other reasons, the reviewers caution that this paper should not be used to guide disciplinary policy and practice. Find the review by Brea L. Perry and Daniel Losen at: http://nepc.colorado.edu/thinktank/review-discipline

In addition to the potential confounding and author-unconsidered factors enumerated in Perry and Losen's review, the Arkansas study affords a convenient illustration of "causal conclusions coming from correlational connections." As we have documented previously, causal conclusions have been flowing at an increased rate in professional education journals (Robinson et al., 2007; Shaw et al., 2010) and the unfortunately termed "causal" modeling statistical procedures themselves can be targeted as a plausible "causal" conclusions agent (Robinson & Levin, 2010).

In the extreme, and in dubious recognition of practice-and-policy–related educational research that truly "quacks," NEPC issues its annual "Bunkum Awards." Among the 2014 winners was a study that received a "Class Size *Reductio ad Absurdum*" award, based on the study's following di*stink*tion:

All that's needed is a pile of data and a mathematical model, and one can do creative things like rank countries' educational systems based on their 'efficiency.'
It apparently matters not how much sense it all makes, as long as it can be puffed up with something that sounds sufficiently intimidating, such as a stochastic frontier analysis, to lend an air of gravitas to an inherently silly idea.[4]

Beware of his false knowledge; it is more dangerous than ignorance. George Bernard Shaw

As we have argued throughout this chapter and elsewhere, recommendations for practice in education that are based on observational studies, rather than on experimentally grounded research, are at risk for being prescriptions of quackery ("prackery"?). Only when a sufficient number of independently conducted randomized intervention studies have been synthesized can one begin even to consider such prescriptions (Robinson et al., 2013). Fortunately, examples of truly evidence-based education policy recommendations, derived from scientifically credible research and comprehensive research syntheses, can be identified (e.g., Cooper & Valentine, 2001; Mosteller & Boruch, 2002). The Tennessee class size project was a large-scale randomized experiment that exemplifies the type of high-quality research that is needed in education (Finn et al., 2001; Mosteller, 1995). The study showed that reducing class size in elementary schools improves student achievement. It required organization that began with the governor and also was funded at $3 million per year for the first four years.

Unfortunately, such large-scale randomized controlled trial studies are the exception rather than the rule when it comes to informing educational policy. The best we can generally hope for are well-conceived and well-conducted small-scale experiments such as those by Whitehurst and colleagues (1994), where an emergent literacy intervention improved the literacy skills of children participating in Head Start. Ransford-Kaldon and colleagues (2010) subsequently implemented a similar

---

[4] The "Bunkum Award" 2014 list may be viewed at: http://nepc.colorado.edu/think-tank/bunkum-awards/2014

literacy intervention that improved the reading achievement for beginning readers. Without replication, however, recommendations based on such single-experiment (or "one-shot") studies are precarious and, as we have argued previously, should be avoided (Robinson et al., 2013).

Replications in educational research are extremely rare, representing only 0.13 percent of the articles in the top 100 education journals (Makel & Plucker, 2014). Although the WWC and NEPC have stepped up and helped to illuminate educational quackery, we would like to see the Department of Education go further and award small grants to fund replication research on promising educational interventions that are deemed worthy of replication. Sadly, even if the top 100 studies in education received replication attempts, the news would not likely be encouraging. If the replication success rate is similar to that experienced in psychology, where only about a third of replication studies successfully replicated the original effect (Open Science Collaboration, 2015), then the poor reputation of educational research is bound to continue.

In a recent article in *Nature*, Moher and colleagues (2017) discussed the destructive consequences of "predatory journals," defined essentially as low-level professional journals that publish quackery, pollute the target discipline, and erode the integrity of scientific scholarship. Those authors noted that currently more than 8,000 predatory journals exist. Omics International alone publishes more than 1,000 open-access journals. Almost every academic researcher receives daily emails laden with errors from unrecognized open-access journals. The *Directory of Open Access Journals* (*DOAJ*) was formed to discourage authors from submitting to open-access journals that do not appear on its list. This is helpful, but the previously summarized quackery examples (Pennebaker et al., 2013; Purtell & Gershoff, 2014) appeared in *PLoS One* and *Clinical Pediatrics*, both open-access journals that *do* appear on the *DOAJ* list, and that had 2016 impact factors of 2.81 and 1.37, respectively. Thus, even ensuring journal quality is not a panacea for eliminating all quackery.

Moher and colleagues (2017) suggested that "[w]hen seeking promotion or funding, researchers should include a declaration that their [vitas] are free of predatory publications" (p. 25). Perhaps researchers also ought to declare that their vitas are free of quackery. In the event that such declarations cannot be made in truth, the researchers could be advised to hawk their wise-quack wares either by hitching onto Barnum and Bailey's traveling circus or by joining the cast of the farcical Broadway musical *Something Rotten!* – a production that still succeeds in selling its Shakespearean snake oil nightly to sold-out audiences!

References

Baeder, J. (2011). The "90/90/90 Schools" myth. *Education Week*. May 30, 2017. http://blogs .edweek.org/edweek/on_performance/2011/05/909090_schools_revisited.html

Barton, E. E., Reichow, B., Schnitz, A., Smith, I. C., & Sherlock, D. (2015). A systematic review of sensory-based treatments for children with disabilities. *Research in Developmental Disabilities, 37*, 64–80.

Berwick, D. M., Calkins, D. R., McCannon, C. J., & Hackbarth, A. D. (2006). The 100,000 lives campaign: Setting a goal and a deadline for improving health care quality. *Journal of the American Medical Association, 295*, 324–327.

Blumenstyk, G. (2017). Quick hits. *Re:Learning*. July 25, 2017.

Cahnmann, M. (2003). The craft, practice, and possibility of poetry in educational research. *Educational Researcher, 32*(3), 29–36.

Christensen, J. (2015). Homeopathic medicine under FDA scrutiny. *CNN*. April 21, 2015. www.cnn.com/2015/04/20/health/homeopathic-medicine-fda/index.html

Clay, R. A. (2015). SMOCs: The next "great adventure." *Monitor on Psychology, 46*(7), 54. https://www.apa.org/monitor/2015/07-08/moocs-smocs.aspx

Cooper, H. & Valentine, J. C. (2001). Using research to answer practical questions about homework. *Educational Psychologist, 36*, 143–153.

Cullen, F. T. & Gendreau, P. (2000). Assessing correctional rehabilitation: Policy, practice, and prospects. In J. Horney (ed.), *Criminal justice 2000: Vol. 3. Policies, processes, and decisions of the criminal justice system* (pp. 109–175). Washington, DC: National Institute of Justice, US Department of Justice.

Davies, P. (1999). What is evidence-based education? *British Journal of Educational Studies, 47*, 108–121.

The Evidence-Based Medicine Working Group. (1992). Evidence-based medicine: A new approach to teaching the practice of medicine. *Journal of the American Medical Association, 268*, 2420–2425.

Finn, J. D., Gerber, S. B., Achilles, C. M., & Boyd-Zaharias, J. (2001). The enduring effects of small classes. *Teachers College Record, 103*, 45–83.

Freyer, F. J. (2017). Naturopaths get their own licensing board in Mass. *Boston Globe*. www.bostonglobe.com/metro/2017/01/11/naturopaths-get-their-own-licensingboard/Lk12PKB7jAYN1z8alxTw9K/story.html?et_rid=436855471&s_campaign=fast forward:newsletter.

Gilgun, J. F. (2005). The four consequences of evidence-based practice in social work. *Research on Social Work Practice, 15*, 52–61.

Grim, T. (2008). A possible role of social activity to explain differences in publication output among ecologists. *Oikos, 117*, 484–487.

Hughes, S., Pennington, J. L., & Makris, S. (2012). Translating autoethnography across the AERA standards: Toward understanding autoethnographic scholarship as empirical research. *Educational Researcher, 41*, 209–219.

Kalenkoski, C. M. & Hamrick, K. S. (2013). How does time poverty affect behavior? A look at eating and physical activity. *Applied Economic Perspectives and Policy, 35*, 89–105.

Kirschner, P. A., & de Bruyckere, P. (2017). The myths of the digital native and multitasker. *Teaching and Teacher Education, 67*, 135–142.

Levin, J. R. (1994). Crafting educational intervention research that's both credible and creditable. *Educational Psychology Review, 6*, 231–243.

Levin, J. R. (2004). Random thoughts on the (in)credibility of educational-psychological intervention research. *Educational Psychologist, 39*, 173–184.

Levin, J. R. (2011). Educational research, for better or verse. *Educational Psychology Review, 23*, 297.

Lilienfeld, S. O., Marshall, J., Todd, J. T., & Shane, H. C. (2014). The persistence of fad interventions in the face of negative scientific evidence: Facilitated communication for autism as a case example. *Evidence-Based Communication Assessment and Intervention, 8*, 62–101. http://dx.doi.org/10.1080/17489539.2014.976332.

Macdonald, K., Germine, L., Anderson, A., Christodoulou, J., & McGrath, L. M. (2017). Dispelling the myth: Training in education or neuroscience decreases but does not eliminate beliefs in neuromyths. *Frontiers in Psychology.* https://doi.org/10.3389/fpsyg.2017.01314

MacKenzie, D. L. (2001). Evidence-based corrections: Identifying what works. *Crime and Delinquency, 46*, 457–471.

MacKenzie, D. L. (2006). *What works in corrections: Reducing the criminal activities of offenders and delinquents.* New York: Cambridge University Press.

Makel, M. C. & Plucker, J. A. (2014). Facts are more important than novelty: Replication in the education sciences. *Educational Researcher, 43*, 304–316.

McAfee, D. G. (2017). England will ban prescriptions for homeopathy and other "low value" treatments. *Patheos.* July 23, 2017. www.patheos.com/blogs/friendlyatheist/2017/07/23/england-will-ban-prescriptions-for-homeopathy-and-other-low-value-treatments/?utm_medium=email&utm_source=BRSS&utm_campaign=Nonreligious&utm_content=361 on July 24, 2017.

McCoy, T. (2014). Half of Dr. Oz's medical advice is baseless or wrong, study says. *Washington Post*, December 19, 2014.

Moher, D., et al. (2017). Stop this waste of people, animals and money. *Nature, 549*, 23–25. https://doi.org/10.1038/549023a

Mosteller, F. (1995). The Tennessee study of class size in the early school grades. *The Future of Children, 5*(2), 114–127.

Mosteller, F. & Boruch, R. (eds.). (2002). *Evidence matters: Randomized trials in education research.* Washington, DC: Brookings Institution Press.

Murphy, H. (2017). The 'Gaydar' machine causes an uproar. *New York Times.* September 10, 2017.

Open Science Collaboration. (2015). Estimating the reproducibility of psychological science. *Science, 349*(6251), aac4716. https://doi.org/10.1126/science.aac4716

Pashler, H., McDaniel, M., Rohrer, D., & Bjork, R. (2008). Learning styles concepts and evidence. *Psychological Science in the Public Interest, 9*, 105–119. https://doi.org/10.1111/j.1539–6053.2009.01038.x

Pennebaker, J. W., Gosling, S. D., & Ferrell, J. D. (2013). Daily online testing in large classes: Boosting college performance while reducing achievement gaps. *PLoS One, 8*(11). https://doi.org/10.1371/journal.pone.0079774

Pfeffer, J. & Sutton, R. J. (2006). Evidence-based management. *Harvard Business Review, 84 (1)*, 62–74.

Phifer, T. (2017). Data shapes student success. *The Magazine.* http://magazine.colostate.edu/issues/spring-2017/data-shapes-student-success/ on June 19, 2017.

Purtell, K. M. & Gershoff, E. T. (2014). Fast food consumption and academic growth in late childhood. *Clinical Pediatrics, 54*, 871–877. https://doi.org/10.1177/0009922814561742.

Ransford-Kaldon, C., Flynt, E. S., Ross, C. L., Franceschini, L., Zoblotsky, T., Huang, Y., & Gallagher, B. (2010). *Implementation of effective intervention: An empirical study to evaluate the efficacy of Fountas & Pinnell's Leveled Literacy Intervention system (LLI).* Memphis, TN: Center for Research in Educational Policy, University of Memphis. https://eric.ed.gov/?&id=ED544374

Ravitch, D. (2011). Waiting for a school miracle. *New York Times*, May 31, 2011.

Reinhart, A. L., Haring, S. H., Levin, J. R., Patall, E. A., & Robinson, D. H. (2013). Models of not-so-good behavior: Yet another way to squeeze causality and recommendations for practice out of correlational data. *Journal of Educational Psychology, 105,* 241–247.

Ritter, M. (2014). Researchers withdraw papers about stem cells due to "extensive" errors. *Wisconsin State Journal*, July 3, 2014, A7.

Ritterbush, R. (2017). UT introduces Project 2021, new education innovation project. *Daily Texan.* March 31, 2017. www.dailytexanonline.com/2017/03/31/ut-introduces-project-2021-new-education-innovation-project

Roberts, A. R. & Yeager, K. R. (eds.). (2004). *Evidence-based practice manual: Research and outcome measures in health and human services.* New York: Oxford University Press.

Robinson, D. H. (2017). *An example of recommendations for practice gone bad.* Manuscript under review.

Robinson, D. H. & Levin, J. R. (2010). The not-so-quiet revolution: Cautionary comments on the rejection of hypothesis testing in favor of a "causal" modeling alternative. *Journal of Modern Applied Statistical Methods, 9,* 332–339.

Robinson, D. H., Levin, J. R., Schraw, G., Patall, E. R., & Hunt, E. (2013). On going (way) beyond one's data: A proposal to restrict recommendations for practice in primary educational research journals. *Educational Psychology Review, 25,* 291–302.

Robinson, D. H., Levin, J. R., Thomas, G. D., Pituch, K. A., & Vaughn, S. R. (2007). The incidence of "causal" statements in teaching and learning research journals. *American Educational Research Journal, 44,* 400–413.

Rychetnik, L., Hawe, P., Waters, E., Barratt, A., & Frommer, M. (2004). A glossary for evidence based public health. *Journal of Epidemiology and Community Health, 58,* 538–545.

Samhita, L. & Gross, H. J. (2013). The "Clever Hans Phenomenon" revisited. *Communicative & Integrative Biology, 6*(6), e27122. www.ncbi.nlm.nih.gov/pmc/articles/PMC3921203/

Schmid, R. E. (2011). Researchers retract paper on gene groups, longevity. *Seattle Times.* July 22, 2011.

Shaw, S. M., Walls, S. M., Dacy, B. S., Levin, J. R., & Robinson, D. H. (2010). A follow-up note on prescriptive statements in nonintervention research studies. *Journal of Educational Psychology, 102,* 982–988.

Sherman, L. J. (1998). *Evidence-based policing.* Washington, DC: Police Foundation.

Straumsheim, C. (2013). Don't call it a MOOC. *Inside Higher Ed.* August 27, 2013. www.insidehighered.com/news/2013/08/27/ut-austin-psychology-professors-prepare-worlds-first-synchronous-massive-online

Teras, H., Myllyla, M., & Teras, M. (2011). *Empowering teachers to meet their digital native learners.* Paper presented at the 2011 International E-Learning Conference, Bangkok, Thailand.

Wade, N. (2012). University suspects fraud by a researcher who studied red wine. *New York Times.* January 12, 2012.

Welsh, B. C., & Farrington, D. P. (eds.). (2006). *Preventing crime: What works with children, offenders, victims, and places.* New York: Springer.

Whitehurst, G. J., Epstein, J. N., Angell, A. L., Payne, A. C., Crone, D. A., & Fischel, J. E. (1994). Outcomes of an emergent literacy intervention in Head Start. *Journal of Educational Psychology, 86,* 542–555.

Wolf, F. M. (2000). Lessons to be learned from evidence-based medicine: Practice and promise of evidence-based medicine and evidence-based education. *Medical Teacher, 22,* 251–259.

PART II

Science and Math

3 Teaching Critical Thinking as if Our Future Depends on It, Because It Does

Diane F. Halpern and Heather A. Butler

Be very afraid. In the United States in 2014, almost 10 percent of adolescents were not immunized for measles (National Center for Health Statistics, 2015, table 67). It is not known what proportion of the unvaccinated teenagers is due to the belief that vaccines cause autism and other disorders, but if activity on the Internet and news reports can provide any indication, it is a substantial portion of those who refuse vaccines. By not immunizing their children, parents are putting others who cannot be vaccinated, for health-related reasons, at risk. In 2015, there was a large, multistate measles outbreak in the United States, so the risk of being unvaccinated is very real; yet some (unknown) proportion of parents, known as vaccine deniers, refuse to vaccinate their children despite the solid science behind its lifesaving benefits.

Are human activities responsible for global climate change? The Intergovernmental Panel on Climate Change and surveys of experts show a clear consensus among scientists that they are (van der Linden et al., 2015). Yet 37 percent of Americans believe that global warming is a hoax (van der Linden, 2013). Add to this list an assortment of beliefs that defy scientific knowledge, such as the growing number of Americans who endorse the belief that the earth is flat (Flat Earth Society, 2016), astrological claims about the ability to predict the future, and many similar beliefs.

The problem is not limited to vaccinations or global warming or the shape of the earth – there is a disregard for all aspects of science. In the US presidential election in 2016, one candidate wore a button that read "I Believe in Science," to show her support for what seems like a no-brainer to those of us who understand that science is the best method we have for reaching objective conclusions about what to believe and what to do. Otto (2016) warned readers of *American Scientist* that "Without objective truth, the nattering of warring pundits can go on forever, and can only be settled by those with the biggest stick or the loudest megaphone." We believe that deliberate, informed instruction that teaches critical thinking using what we know about best teaching/ learning practices so that these skills are durable (i.e., last long into the future) and transfer to novel situations is the best hope for creating informed citizens who can think about difficult issues, weigh evidence, determine credibility, and act rationally.

Historical Perspectives

During in-service training for teachers and in other venues, we have often heard people complain that "critical thinking is just another new-fangled idea thought up by bureaucrats with no teaching experience." It has been likened to the "new math" – ignore it and maybe it will go away. In fact, critical thinking has a long history in educational psychology. Dewey (1933) wrote about practical inquiry and reflective thinking. He even commented on the belief that the world is flat, probably never guessing that, over eight decades later, we would still be trying to convince people about the shape of the earth. His writings have a contemporary tone, as he addressed both "deep comprehension" and avoidance of biases, the two components of most definitions of critical thinking. There are also historical origins in the work of Jean Piaget, the famed developmental psychologist who posited different stages of cognitive development, culminating in abstract thinking. (As readers probably know, much of the specifics of Piaget's work, such as a strict sequence of stages that occur at specific ages, has been disproved, yet he remains a great pioneer for defining the field of cognitive development.)

There are several dual-process models of thinking, with the most widely known attributed to Daniel Kahneman (2013). He posits a fast, automatic, and intuitive thinking system that is error-prone but requires little effort or control, and an effortful thinking system that is deliberate, slow, and less error-prone. These are not independent systems. System 2, the slower and deliberate thinking system, can override and inform System 1. Critical thinking can be thought of as System 2 thinking. A commonly used example of these two systems can be found in the following short scenario (Frederick, 2005):

A bat and a ball cost $1.10. The bat costs $1.00 more than the ball. How much does the ball cost?

Most people, even well-educated adults at elite universities, answer $0.10, but the correct answer is $0.05. The ball is $0.05 and the bat is $1.05, $1.00 more than the ball. This does not mean that fast thinking is always wrong. The intuition of some experts can be surprisingly accurate, especially when their expertise is in a field in which they receive immediate feedback for their decisions, such as expert fire-fighters. We need fast thinking or else we would all be stymied when faced with tasks like selecting a brand of peanut butter from among a large array or deciding what to wear in the morning.

Teaching for Critical Thinking

Virtually every school district, university, and other formal learning site claims that they develop critical thinkers (e.g., for a list of exemplary schools and school districts, see P21, n.d.). Although it is difficult to find anyone who is actually opposed to critical thinking, there are a few blatant examples. In 2012, the Republican Party of Texas stated that they oppose the teaching of higher order thinking skills: "We oppose the teaching of Higher Order Thinking Skills (HOTS) (values clarification), critical thinking skills and similar programs that are simply a relabeling of Outcome-Based Education (OBE) (mastery learning) which focus on behavior modification and have the purpose of challenging the student's fixed beliefs and undermining parental authority" (Strauss, 2012). Later, the Republican Party of Texas stated that it was a mistake to oppose "critical thinking." Despite a few critics, the vast majority of people argue that critical thinking instruction is vital. Employers consistently list critical thinking among the top skills they want in new and continuing employees (Hart Research Associates, 2015). It is essential for a twenty-first-century military to exercise and use critical thinking skills, and we also need an educated citizenry to maintain a democracy; irrational voters are a threat to all of us.

Sometimes the term "critical" in "critical thinking" is assumed to mean disapproving comments or finding fault with something. In this context, the use of "critical" is meant as "critique" or a careful analysis of something. Although it is common to read that the term "critical thinking" is ill-defined or that there is little consensus about its meaning, in fact most of the definitions focus on the same few components. It is good or clear thinking that reflects a deep understanding and is relatively free of common biases. Critical thinkers consider the evidence that supports and fails to support a conclusion. They consider the relative strength of different types of evidence, the credibility of the information sources, relevant probabilities, the way language influences how we think, and much more. Halpern (2014) has used this definition for several decades:

> Critical thinking is the use of those cognitive skills and abilities that increase the probability of a desirable outcome. It is used to describe thinking that is purposeful, reasoned, and goal directed – the kind of thinking involved in solving problems, formulating inferences, calculating likelihoods, and making decisions, when the thinker is using skills that are thoughtful and effective for the particular context and type of thinking task. (p. 8)

Critical thinkers use these skills appropriately and without prompting in a variety of settings. There is also a dispositional aspect to critical thinking. Critical thinkers are willing to put in the hard work of persisting at a difficult thinking task, to be open-minded and willing to consider new information that does not fit well into their existing belief systems.

Not all thinking is critical thinking. It is different from but often relies upon simple recall (e.g., Is twenty an even number?), unsupported opinions (e.g., everyone should learn how to knit), and automated actions (e.g., tying shoelaces). Rote recall is often considered the antithesis of critical thinking but it is a necessary component of critical thinking. Everyone needs knowledge to think critically about a complex topic. For example, no one can think critically about vaccinations, global warming, or any other topic without the underlying knowledge that is relevant. No one can understand current conditions in Western Africa without knowledge of its colonial past, modern-day infrastructures, natural resources, and the threats posed by various diseases. By using this knowledge to make decisions and solve problems, a deeper understanding of the issues emerges. Thus, when we enhance critical thinking in ourselves or our students, we are promoting the development of deep comprehension (Franco, Butler, & Halpern, 2015).

Critical thinking is also a disposition. It is the willingness to engage in the challenging work of critical thinking and to persist when the task is difficult. Facione, Facione, and Giancarlo (2000) argue that it includes analyticity (e.g., being alert to problematic situations, anticipating consequences, valuing reason and evidence-based conclusions), systematicity (e.g., approaching problems in an organized, focused, diligent manner), inquisitiveness (e.g., values being well informed, wants to know things, values learning), open-mindedness (e.g., being tolerant of other viewpoints, sensitivity to one's own biases), critical thinking self-confidence (e.g., trusts their own good judgment and reasoning), truth-seeking (e.g., courageous pursuit of truth even if it contradicts your existing belief or opinion), and maturity (tolerance for uncertainty, understanding that there can be more than one correct answer). Critical thinkers need to be willing to change their beliefs when evidence and reasoning suggest a different one and to abandon nonproductive strategies. Someone with critical thinking skills but who does not care much about accuracy, or is unwilling to put in the cognitive effort to find the best solution to a problem, will be no better off than someone without these skills.

There is nothing about a thinking skills approach that would suggest that we cannot teach critical thinking. Schools teach writing, mathematics, communication, and more, with the implicit belief that these skills will be learned and will transfer to new contexts. There are individual differences in learning and some teaching/learning interchanges are more successful than others, but there is nothing inherent in critical thinking that would make it unteachable or unlearnable. Not *all* critical thinking interventions have been successful, but there is a large and growing body of literature demonstrating effective critical thinking interventions.

What Do We Mean by Critical Thinking Skills?

Critical thinking instruction is predicated on two assumptions: (1) that there are clearly identifiable and definable thinking skills, and (2) if recognized and used appropriately, students will be more effective thinkers. There are many lists of critical thinking skills, which apply across a wide variety of contexts. Table 3.1 is a short sampler of critical thinking skills. For a more comprehensive list, see Halpern (2014).

A thinking skills approach to critical thinking has face validity – even the most doubting skeptics would have a difficult time objecting to teaching and learning the skills on a list such as this. There may be disagreement over which of these skills is most important or easiest to teach but, taken as a whole, a list of skills similar to the ones in Table 3.1 is a good starting place for any intervention designed to help students think better.

Can Students Enhance Their Critical Thinking Skills in Ways That Endure Over Time and Transfer Across Domains?

"Yes!" There is a large research literature showing that it is possible to teach critical thinking skills in ways that endure over time and transfer across domains. The only reason why we have schools is the belief that whatever is learned in these formal learning settings will transfer across time and place. It would be meaningless if students only demonstrated critical thinking skills when their instructor was present and the topic was the same as the one used in class. Consider, for example, the critical

Table 3.1 *A sample of critical thinking skills*

- Reasoning: Drawing Deductively Valid Conclusions
  - Discriminating between deductive and inductive reasoning
  - Understanding the difference between truth and validity
  - Using quantifiers and negatives when reasoning
- The Relationship Between Thought and Language
  - Recognizing and defending against the inappropriate use of emotional language, labeling, name calling, ambiguity, vagueness, and arguments by etymology
  - Developing the ability to detect misuse of definitions, reification, euphemism, and bureaucratese
  - Understanding the use of framing with leading questions, and negation
  - Using analogies appropriately, which includes examining the nature of the similarity and its relationship to the conclusion
- Analyzing Arguments
  - Identifying arguments
  - Diagramming the structure of an argument
  - Evaluating premises for their acceptability
  - Examining the credibility of an information source
  - Determining the consistency, relevance to the conclusion, and adequacy in the way premises support a conclusion
- Thinking as Hypothesis Testing
  - Recognizing the need for and using operational definitions
  - Understanding the need to isolate and control variables in order to make strong causal claims
  - Checking for adequate sample size and unbiased sampling when a generalization is made
  - Understanding the limits of correlational reasoning
- Likelihood and Uncertainty (Understanding Probabilities)
  - Computing expected values in situations with known probabilities
  - Recognizing when regression to the mean is operating and adjust predictions to take this phenomenon into account
  - Utilizing base rates when making predictions
  - Using probability judgments to improve decision-making
  - Considering indicators such as historical data, risks associated with different parts of a decision, and analogies when dealing with unknown risks
- Decision-Making and Problem-Solving
  - Listing alternatives and considering the pros and cons of each
  - Reframing the decision so as to consider different types of alternatives
  - Recognizing the need to seek disconfirming evidence and deliberately seeking disconfirming evidence
  - Understanding the way emotional states such as reactance and anger can affect the way we evaluate alternatives and behaving in ways that minimize their effects
  - Using all of the following strategies: means–ends analysis; working backwards; simplification; generalization and specialization; random search and trial and error; rules; hints; split-half method; brainstorming; contradiction; analogies and metaphors; and consulting an expert

thinking skill of not confusing correlation and cause. Students need to recognize this skill in a research methods course, in a history course, and, more importantly, when reading the morning news and making everyday decisions. Most students can readily explain that correlation is not cause, but how often do they recognize this principle when reading that school grades tend to be low when marijuana sales are high or that children who attend preschool are better readers in 1st grade than those who do not attend preschool?

There is a huge research literature showing that it is possible to teach critical thinking skills so that they transfer to novel contexts. Although some believe that critical thinking instruction is best reserved for advanced classes, we believe that all students need to learn critical thinking skills to succeed in their future careers and college and to be effective citizens. In an earlier review, researchers found substantial gains in critical thinking (ds = 0.4 to 0.5; Bangert-Drowns & Bankert, 1990) from students who were guided through the use of thinking skills in programs that were intensive and continuously emphasized these skills. Of course, there are some examples in the research literature where the skills failed to transfer, but these failures do not mean that transfer is not possible. When all of the instruction relies on materials from one academic discipline, it should not be surprising that transfer to a different academic discipline is less likely to occur than other interventions that teach thinking skills in many different contexts. Let's consider an example where the researchers did not find evidence of transfer. The failure to get transfer was the main point in a recent study that was designed to improve critical thinking in freshman physics classes in Ethiopia (Tiruneh et al., 2016). The researchers found higher scores for critical thinking assessments within the domain of physics, but no effect on an assessment of "domain-general" critical thinking skills. They concluded that the lack of transfer was due to the way they designed their program, which used examples selected only from physics. Gains in critical thinking that cut across disciplines and contexts are not generally a by-product of "instruction as usual."

Sometimes, we think about transfer as something magical that either happens or does not happen, when in fact good instruction can make transfer much more likely. The learning sciences have provided educators with a number of deep learning principles that improve learning in general, and critical thinking skills in particular, such as spaced practice with multiple diverse examples. The first author of this chapter has also developed a model for teaching critical thinking (Halpern, 1998) that includes (1) explicitly teaching critical thinking skills; (2) encouraging a disposition toward thinking critically; (3) using practical activities connected to real life to make transfer more likely to occur; and (4) modeling overt metacognitive monitoring.

Critical thinking instruction is most effective when taught explicitly, using multiple examples from different disciplines, and in contexts where students have to recognize when a particular skill is relevant and, just as importantly, when it is not. In two experiments in a low-performing high school near Los Angeles, California, Marin and Halpern (2011) compared implicit and explicit instruction in critical thinking. In the first study, students were assigned at random to either mode of instruction. In the second study, entire classes were assigned at random to one of these two conditions. In the implicit instruction condition, students received standard instruction. In the explicit instruction condition, students were deliberately taught critical thinking skills. They were given many scenarios in diverse contexts and were asked to identify and label the appropriate skill to use (or not use). We focused on four broad categories of critical thinking skills, including analyzing arguments (recognizing reasons, conclusions, and persuasive appeals), correlations and causal claims, confirmation bias, and decision-making. Learning outcomes were assessed with a variety of measures of academic success and with the Halpern Critical Thinking Assessment (HCTA, described in the section "The Sequential Question" below). In accord with prior research, students who were in the explicit instruction group showed the greatest gains in critical thinking. Similar results were obtained by researchers at a Dutch university working with business and economics students (Heijltjes, Van Gog, & Paas, 2014). They found that explicit instruction with spaced practice was required to improve critical thinking. This conclusion was supported in a meta-analysis with 117 studies based on 20,698 participants; Abrami and colleagues (2008) concluded that "improvement in students' CT [critical thinking] skills and dispositions cannot be a matter of implicit expectation ... Educators must take steps to make CT objectives explicit in courses" (p. 1102).

Mosley, Miller, and Higgins (2003) worked with teams of educators from all sectors of education in the United Kingdom to determine if students actually benefited from explicit instruction in critical thinking. Based on their extensive review of the literature, they recommended that all students in post-16 schools (similar to community colleges in the United States) have explicit instruction in critical thinking. In a carefully worded document, they concluded that "strategic thinking and reflection should form part of all education and training" and "teacher training courses should include a more solid grounding in theories of thinking and learning than they do at present" (p. 4).

Positive results were also obtained in a series of studies using the computerized learning game Operation ARIES! (Acquiring Research Investigative Experimental Skills) whose name was later changed to Operation ARA (Acquiring Research Acumen; Forsyth et al., 2012; Forsyth et al., 2013). This serious learning game was written to teach students the critical thinking skills used in research methods (i.e., inductive reasoning). The game was designed to incorporate several key learning principles, including distributed/spaced practice that occurs in different domains and scenarios, explicit instruction, immediate feedback to the learner about performance, adaptive tutoring that adjusts to the skill level of the student, and other game features that enhanced engagement (e.g., a story line with aliens, an environmentally conscientious green theme, competition against other players, intrigue). We found that compared with control groups, students who played Operation ARA showed better learning both immediately after playing the game and after a delay (Halpern et al., 2012) and substantial gains were made by students in open-admissions community colleges, state universities, and at a private elite liberal arts college.

In their highly successful book *Academically Adrift: Limited Learning on College Campuses*, Arum and Roksa (2010) concluded that more than a third of students showed no improvement in critical thinking skills after four years at a university. In a radio interview, Arum (2011) said: "Our country today is part of a global economic system, where we no longer have the luxury to put large numbers of kids through college and university and not demand of them that they are developing these higher order skills that are necessary not just for them, but for our society as a whole."

Arum and Roksa's study has been criticized as being too pessimistic; one criticism concerned the measure and, more specifically, the lack of incentive used to measure critical thinking. It is difficult to get students to take seriously any assessment that has no impact on their grades, and many students may not have tried very hard to get correct answers on an assessment that had no meaning for them.

A new meta-analysis of critical thinking outcomes reached a different conclusion (Huber & Kuncel, 2016). It included seventy-one studies done on changes in critical thinking during college over the past forty years. The results suggest that both critical thinking skills and dispositions improve substantially over a normal college experience, but the researchers were unable to link critical thinking gains to specific programs or courses. This result is not surprising given the large number of classes and programs that purportedly teach critical thinking when, in fact, we have little or no idea about their pedagogy or outcome measures. Interestingly, Huber and Kuncel found that the critical thinking gains from recent studies were smaller (0.33 SD gained in 2011) than the gains found in older studies (1.22 SDs in 1963), indicating that gains in critical thinking is deteriorating over time. The authors suggest several reasons for this, including changes in curricula, student behavior, critical thinking being taught before they get to college and inflating their initial score, changes in research standards over time (a change of 1.22 SD is rather large), and other artifacts not accounted for in their research design. Still, it is a troubling finding that deserves more attention. Overall, critical thinking increased 0.59 SDs during college (cross-sectional and longitudinal combined). This number may appear small but the authors remind us that similar numbers were found when considering the contribution of a "general disposition towards learning" to predicting college success is only 0.61 SDs. The authors also explored gains in critical thinking disposition during college. Though the sample size was very small and the studies all used the same measure – the California Critical Thinking Disposition Inventory – the results are quite promising and consistent. Huber and Kuncel found increases in a disposition toward critical thinking, 0.55 SDs during college. We conclude from these reviews and other studies (see "Future Directions" below) that college students do improve their critical thinking skills and dispositions, but there is much room for improvement. We need more research on effective teaching strategies that will produce critical thinking gains and more research on assessing critical thinking.

Assessment as an Operational Definition for Critical Thinking

Central to the question of whether or not it is possible to teach critical thinking is the way we assess critical thinking and an essential part of any successful assessment is defining your construct. Recognizing the need for an operational definition is a critical thinking skill after all. If someone asked "Who is the greatest hip-hop artist of all time?," the answer will depend on how they operationalize the term "hip-hop artist." Similarly, if we apply this principle to the question of who is a good critical thinker, we would need to operationalize the term "critical thinking." In plain English, what will we include in our assessment of critical thinking? Assessments should be authentic (meaningful in real-world contexts), reliable, and valid. Based on the definition provided, an assessment would need to include real-life scenarios where the skills of verbal reasoning, argument analysis, hypothesis testing, using likelihood and uncertainty, and decision-making and problem solving would be recognized and used appropriately. When people are presented with a scenario (a synopsis of a story), they search their memory for relevant information. Cognitive psychologists distinguish between two types of remembering – free recall, where the person remembering has to generate the possible best answer, and forced choice, where the task is to recognize the best answer. As expected, people get more items correct when they have to recognize an answer from a list than when they have to generate an answer with few available cues. There are several commercially available critical thinking assessments but most rely entirely on recognition of a correct answer. It seems ironic to assess higher order thinking with a multiple-choice test. There are also several short essay critical thinking assessments available but they do not provide information as to whether a test taker could recognize a correct answer if it were presented in a list of several possible answers. Each of these two types of assessments has limitations, which is why the first author of this chapter developed the HCTA.

The Sequential Question

A critical thinking assessment that uses sequential questions offers measures of both free recall and recognition, and a combined score. The HCTA presents everyday scenarios with an open-ended response format, followed by the same scenario with forced choice responses. Table 3.2 presents an example similar to what is presented in the HCTA.

One reason why assessments avoid constructed response questions is the difficulty in grading them consistently. Despite this difficulty, most of the high-stakes examinations (College Board SAT for college admissions, admission to the judicial bar, medical licensing examinations, graduate school admissions tests, and many more) use constructed response formats because of the added validity. With HCTA, grading is done on the computer, with human graders responding to several prompts that then automatically score the questions. This method yields high levels of interrater reliability (Halpern, 2012).

The use of scenarios that embed the skill in a realistic context is similar to "situational judgment tests" which are commonly used in selection. There is a huge literature on their use (e.g., Jansen et al., 2013). As expected there are alternative forms to the HCTA to guard against exposure of test items and to prevent any recall of a specific scenario with pre- and postintervention testing. Most importantly, the HCTA has shown validity to real-world problems.

Table 3.2 *A sample item from the Halpern Critical Thinking Assessment (HCTA)*

The Welfare Department offered unemployed mothers the opportunity to take part in a new program called COMM-2-Work. The program involved taking a class that improved oral and written communication skills, because good communication skills are valued by employers. At the end of the year, the program was evaluated and the analysis indicated that the women who participated in the program were more likely to be employed than those who did not participate in the program. A policy analyst concluded that all unemployed mothers should be required to complete the program so they could find jobs.

In one or two sentences, explain your thinking about this program. Based solely on these data, would you require all unemployed mothers to participate in the program? (yes or no).

After responding to this constructed response question, the screen would go blank and the same scenario would appear a second time. The instructions would read:

Which of the following answers is the best argument *against* this proposal?

1. Because the program was voluntary, it is likely that the women who participated in the program were more motivated (or more intelligent or different in some other way) than those who did not participate in the program.
2. It might be a good idea but the cost could be prohibitive if we made every unemployed mother participate in the training.
3. There will always be some women who just don't want to work or for some reason cannot work, so it would be a waste of time and money. We just can't assume that because some women benefited from this program that all women would.
4. Training programs are not a good way to help unemployed women find jobs. There are plenty of jobs available if they would just go out and apply themselves.

As readers can probably guess, the constructed response should make the points that are listed in alternative 1.

Future Directions: Are There Real-Life Benefits for Critical Thinkers?

Several studies have indicated that critical thinking can predict some very important behaviors in our everyday lives. The HCTA was administered to college students and community adults in the United States (Butler, 2012), as well as in other countries (Butler et al., 2012), along with a behavioral inventory of life events. The inventory of life events produced a score that indicated the proportion of negative life events a person experienced in a given time frame. The severity of the life events ranged from relatively mild (e.g., paid a late fee for a movie rental) to severe (e.g., had an unplanned pregnancy) and encompassed a wide range of life domains, such as interpersonal outcomes (e.g., cheated on a romantic partner that you has been with for over a year), financial outcomes (e.g., had over $5,000 in credit card debt), health outcomes (e.g., contracted a sexually transmitted infection because you failed to use a condom), legal outcomes (e.g., were arrested for driving under the influence of drugs or alcohol), and educational outcomes (e.g., arrived to class to find there was an exam that day that you had not prepared for).[1] Critical thinkers experienced fewer negative life events, that is, those who scored higher on the HCTA reported experiencing fewer negative life events than those who scored lower. We are in the process of determining whether critical thinking just protects us from making poor choices or whether it also predicts the occurrence of positive life events (e.g., getting promoted). Our preliminary unpublished data indicates that the former may be true but another study suggests that wisdom (a very similar construct) may predict well-being (Grossmann et al., 2013). Clearly, further investigation is needed.

It is important to note that critical thinking was a stronger predictor of life events for community adults than for college students. This is probably due to the types of life events measured in the inventory. College students have different priorities and may be too young to have experienced the full range of life events that many community adults have experienced. For example, most college students do not own a home and many do not rent an apartment, so it is unlikely that they would have experienced a foreclosure or would have been asked to leave their apartment before the lease expired. Our colleagues argued this point for their sample of college students in the Netherlands. Despite finding evidence of good reliability for their Dutch translation of the HCTA, they did not find a relationship between scores on the HCTA and scores on the behavioral inventory (De Bie, Wilhelm, & Van der Meij, 2015). It is difficult to know how to interpret their results without further investigation into whether the lack of a relationship was caused by a measure that could not adequately capture the behavior of Dutch college students or whether it reflects a cultural difference in the impact that critical thinking has on decision-making and behavioral outcomes.

We argue that thinking critically results in better decision-making and can predict the life events we experience, perhaps even more so than other constructs that have received far more empirical attention, namely intelligence. The research literature on the real-world correlates of intelligence indicates that it has concurrent and predictive validity for many behaviors, experiences, and achievements. Intelligence predicts many academic outcomes, such as grades in school (Furnham & Monsen, 2009), academic achievement (Soars et al., 2015), learning outcomes in college (Kuncel, Hezlett, & Ones, 2004; Kuncel, Ones, & Sackett, 2010), and getting a doctorate degree and tenure in academic positions (Lubinski et al., 2006). Intelligence also predicts many nonacademic outcomes such as long-term job performance (Hunter & Schmidt, 1996), learning outcome in work settings (Kuncel et al., 2004; Kuncel, Ones, & Sackett, 2010), and criminal behaviors (negative relationship; Schwartz et al., 2015). Clearly, intelligence can predict a variety of everyday life outcomes and achievements, yet many people who score high on tests of intelligence do blatantly stupid things. There are so many possible examples, it is difficult to know which ones to choose to make this point. Consider Bill Clinton's highly publicized relationship with a White House intern. Some political pundits have suggested that this affair cost his wife the presidential election in 2016. Another

---

[1] The behavioral inventory was originally developed by De Bruin, Parker, and Fischhoff (2007) as a measure of decision-making competence. New items were added to make it more relevant to college students.

example from the political arena is President Reagan's reliance on astrology to schedule important events at the White House. The relationship between intelligence and good thinking is less clear, causing some to argue that the ability to think critically is what intelligence tests fail to adequately measure (Stanovich, 2010).

We argue that critical thinking may be a better predictor of behavior than intelligence, at least as intelligence is currently assessed with standardized assessments that yield IQ scores (e.g., vocabulary, visuospatial puzzles, digit recall, visual search for symbols), and we are not alone. Stanovich and his colleagues argue that intelligence tests are missing critical components of reasoning and rationality (Stanovich, 2010; (Stanovich, West, & Toplak, 2016). In their book *The Rationality Quotient*, they argue that intelligence (as currently defined and measured) and rationality are two different constructs (Stanovich et al., 2016). Rationality involves adaptive reasoning, good judgment, and good decision-making. They used the term "rational intelligence," which is consistent with most definitions of critical thinking. In fact, many definitions of critical thinking are more consistent with our intuitive beliefs about how an intelligent person thinks. When we think of the prototypical intelligent person we might imagine someone who is very knowledgeable and considers multiple perspectives on controversial issues, but our ideas about intelligent people may not be consistent with how intelligence is currently conceptualized. Stanovich and West (2008) assessed whether people who score high on intelligence tests were more likely to avoid certain cognitive biases, such as "my-side bias," which is the preference for evidence and conclusions consistent with one's own worldview. Intelligent people were not less likely to avoid my-side bias or prefer balanced perspectives on a controversial issue, indicating that intelligence may not be useful in predicting when someone will exercise good judgment or rational thinking.

We also mistakenly confuse intelligence with wisdom when wisdom is more closely associated with critical thinking and rationality. Grossmann and colleagues (2013) conceptualized wisdom as a set of reasoning strategies, including (1) considering the perspective of others; (2) recognizing the likelihood of change; (3) considering multiple possible outcomes; (4) searching for compromise; (5) recognizing uncertainty; and (6) predicting conflict resolution. The authors cite many studies that have failed to find a relationship between intelligence and positive life outcomes; they argue that intelligence tests fail to adequately measure real-world decision-making. They examined whether intelligence or wisdom (wise reasoning) would be associated with various positive life outcomes, such as greater life satisfaction, greater longevity, and better social relations. As expected, wise reasoning predicted well-being, whereas intelligence (cognitive ability) did not. Wise reasoning also marginally predicted longevity (through death records of older participants five years later) and better social relations.

We also tested whether intelligence or wisdom, in our case critical thinking, predicted real-world outcomes. Butler, Pentoney, and Bong (2017) compared the power of intelligence and critical thinking to predict the occurrence of negative life events using a behavioral inventory (the same inventory described previously). Community adults and college students took an intelligence test, a critical thinking assessment, and completed the life events inventory. Both those who scored high in intelligence and critical thinking ability experienced fewer negative life events but critical thinking was a slightly stronger predictor than intelligence in this study. Importantly, critical thinking accounted for unique variance in the model, indicating that critical thinking and intelligence measure different constructs and predict different behaviors in the real world. Future research could attempt to isolate what specific skills predict certain behaviors.

Conclusion

Critical thinking advocates argue that our future depends on our ability to think critically in a world that is growing more complex day by day. We know that critical thinking can be taught and, when it is taught explicitly, with multiple examples from different contexts, it will transfer across domains. Most importantly, we believe it should be a priority. Schools, colleges, and universities around the world acknowledge the importance of improving critical thinking and claim to be teaching critical thinking skills to the students they serve. Yet it does not appear that critical thinking skills are improving on a large enough scale for us to detect, and it is difficult to trace gains to specific pedagogies. Many universities have included critical thinking among their list of learning outcomes, and many have identified specific skills and even the classes in which their students will learn these skills, but we know very little about how this is actually being implemented in the classroom. Are students being taught these skills explicitly or implicitly? Is there spaced practice so that students get the opportunity to practice the skills throughout their education and in varying contexts? Do educators know best practices for teaching critical thinking skills effectively? How invested are educators in teaching critical thinking skills explicitly? Answers to these questions may well determine how effective we are at creating a better future for our children. They are worthy of a lifetime of research by many learning scientists. Teaching critical thinking successfully is probably the most difficult task any teacher/professor can take on but it is also the most important.

References

Abrami, P. C., Bernard, R. M., Borokhovski, E., Wade, A., Surkes, M. A., Tamim, R., & Zhang, D. (2008). Instructional interventions affecting critical thinking skills and dispositions: A Stage 1 meta-analysis. *Review of Educational Research, 78,* 1102–1134.

Arum, R. (2011). A Lack of Rigor Leaves Students "Adrift" in College. *NPR.* February 9, 2011. www.npr.org/2011/02/09/133310978/in-college-a-lack-of-rigor-leaves-students-adrift

Arum, R. & Roksa, J. (2010). *Academically adrift.* Chicago, IL: University of Chicago Press.

Bangert-Drowns, R. L. & Bankert, E. (1990). Meta-analysis of effects of explicit instruction for critical thinking. *ERIC, Collection of Educational Resources.* http://eric.ed.gov/?id=ED328614

Butler, H. A. (2012). Halpern Critical Thinking Assessment predicts real-world outcomes of critical thinking. *Applied Cognitive Psychology, 26*, 721–729. https://doi.org/10.1002/acp.2851

Butler, H. A., Dwyer, C. P., Hogan, M. J. et al. (2012). Halpern Critical Thinking Assessment and real-world outcomes: Cross-national applications. *Thinking Skills and Creativity, 7*, 112–121. https://doi.org/10.1016/j.tsc.2012.04.001

Butler, H. A., Pentoney, C., & Bong, M. (2017). Predicting real-world outcomes: Critical thinking ability is a better predictor of life decisions than intelligence. *Thinking Skills and Creativity, 25*, 38–46.

De Bie, H., Wilhelm, P., & Van der Meij, H. (2015). The Halpern Critical Thinking Assessment: Toward a Dutch appraisal of critical thinking. *Thinking Skills and Creativity, 17*, 33–44.

De Bruin, W. B., Parker, B., & Fischhoff, A. M. (2007). Individual differences in adult decision-making competence. *Journal of Personality and Social Psychology, 92* (5), 938–956.

Dewey, J. (1933). How we think. Boston: Heath.

Facione, P., Facione, N., & Giancarlo, C. (2000). The disposition toward critical thinking: Its character, measurement, and relationship to critical thinking skill. *Informal Logic, 20*(1), 61–84.

Flat Earth Society. (2016). The Flat Earth Society (website). www.theflatearthsociety.org/home/index.php

Forsyth, C .M., Graesser, A. C., Walker, B. et al. (2013). Didactic galactic: Acquiring knowledge learned in a serious game. In H. C. Lane, K. Yacef, J. Mostow, & P. Pavlik (eds.), *Proceedings of the International Conference on Artificial Intelligence in Education: 16th International Conference* (AIED 2013) (pp. 832–835). Berlin: Springer Verlag.

Forsyth, C. M., Pavlik, P., Graesser, A. C., Cai, Z., Germany, M., Millis, K., Butler, H., Halpern, D. F., & Dolan, R. (2012). Learning gains for core concepts in a serious game on scientific reasoning. In K. Yacef, O. Zaïane, H. Hershkovitz, M. Yudelson, & J. Stamper (eds.), *Proceedings of the 5th International Conference on Educational Data Mining* (pp. 172–175). Chania: International Educational Data Mining Society.

Franco, A. H. R., Butler, H. A., & Halpern, D. F. (2015). Teaching critical thinking to promote learning. In D. S. Dunn (ed.), *The Oxford handbook of psychology education* (pp. 65–74). New York: Oxford University Press. https://doi.org/0.1093/oxfordhb/9780199933815.013.007

Frederick S. (2005). Cognitive reflection and decision making. *Journal of Economic Perspectives, 19*, 25–42. https://doi.org/10.1257/089533005775196732

Furnham, A. & Monsen, J. (2009). Personality traits and intelligence predicts academic school grades. *Learning and Individual Differences, 19*, 28–33.

Grossmann, I., Varnum, M. E. W., Na, J., Kitayama, S., & Nisbett, R. E. (2013). A route to well-being: Intelligence versus wise reasoning. *Journal of Experimental Psychology: General, 142*, 944–953.

Halpern, D. F. (1998). Teaching critical thinking for transfer across domains: Dispositions, skills, structure training, and metacognitive monitoring. *American Psychologist*, 53, 449–455.

(2012). "Halpern Critical Thinking Assessment." SCHUHFRIED (Vienna Test System) (website). https://www.schuhfried.com/test/HCTA

(2014). *Thought and knowledge: An introduction to critical thinking*, 5th edn. New York: Routledge.

Halpern, D. F. & Hakel, M. D. (2003). Applying the science of learning to the university and beyond: Teaching for long-term retention and transfer. Change, July/August, 2–13.

Halpern, D. F., Millis, K., Graesser. A., Butler, H., Forsyth, C. & Cai, Z. (2012). Operation ARA: A computerized learning game that teaches critical thinking and scientific reasoning. *Thinking Skills and Creativity*, *7*, 93–100.

Hart Research Associates. (2015). *Falling short? College learning and career success* Washington, DC: Hart Research Associates. www.aacu.org/sites/default/files/files/LEAP/2015employerstudentsurvey.pdf

Heijltjes, A., Van Gog, T., & Paas, F. (2014). Improving students' critical thinking: Empirical support for explicit instructions combined with practice. *Applied Cognitive Psychology*, *28*, 518–530. https://doi.org/10.1002/acp.3025

Huber, C. R. & Kuncel, N. R. (2016). Does college teach critical thinking? A meta-analysis. *Review of Educational Research*, *86*, 431–468. https://doi.org/10.3102/0034654315605917

Hunter, J. E. & Schmidt, F. L. (1996). Intelligence and job performance: Economic and social implications. *Psychology, Public Policy, and Law*, *2*, 447–472.

Jansen, A., Melchers, K. G., Lievens, F., Kleinmann, M., Brändli, M., Fraefel, L., & König, C. J. (2013). Situation assessment as an ignored factor in the behavioral consistency paradigm underlying the validity of personnel selection procedures. *Journal of Applied Psychology*, *98*, 326–341. https://doi.org/10.1037/a0031257

Kahneman, D. (2013). *Thinking, fast and slow.* New York: Farrar, Straus and Giroux.

Kuncel, N. R., Hezlett, S. A., & Ones, D. S. (2004). Academic performance, career potential, creativity, and job performance: Can one construct predict them all? *Journal of Personality and Social Psychology*, *86*, 148–161.

Kuncel, N. R., Ones, D. S., & Sackett, P. R. (2010). Individual differences as predictors of work, educational, and broad life outcomes. *Personality and Individual Differences*, *49*, 331–336.

Lubinski, D., Benbow, C. P., Webb, R. M., & Bleske-Rechek, A. (2006). Tracking exceptional human capital over two decades. *Psychological Science*, *17*, 194–199. https://doi.org/10.1111/j.1467–9280.2006.01685.x

Marin, L. & Halpern, D. F. (2011). Pedagogy for developing critical thinking in adolescents: Explicit instruction produces greatest gains. *Thinking Skills and Creativity*, *6*, 1–13. https://doi.org/10.1016/j.tsc.2010.08

Mosley, D., Miller, J., & Higgins, S. (2003). *Thinking skills frameworks for use in education and training.* Paper prepared for the Knowledge and Skills for Learning to Learn Seminar. London, UK.

National Center for Health Statistics. (2015). *Health, United States, 2015, with special feature on racial and ethnic health disparities.* Washington, DC: US Government Printing Office.

Otto, S. (2016). A plan to defend against the war on science. *Scientific American*. October 9, 2016. www.scientificamerican.com/article/a-plan-to-defend-against-the-war-on-science/

P21 (Partnership for 21st Century Learning). (n.d.). "List of Exemplar Schools" (website). http://www.p21.org/exemplar-program-case-studies/about-the-program

Schwartz, J. A., Savolainen, J., Aaltonen, M., Merikukka, M., Paananen, R., & Gissler, M. (2015). Intelligence and criminal behavior in a total birth cohort: An examination of functional form, dimensions of intelligence, and the nature of offending. *Intelligence*, *51*, 109–118.

Soars, D. L., Lemos, G. C., Primi, R., & Almeida, L. S. (2015). *Learning and Individual Differences*, *41*, 73–78.

Stanovich, K. E. (2010). *What intelligence tests miss: The psychology of rational thought*. New Haven, CT: Yale University Press.

Stanovich, K. E. & West, R. F. (2008). On the failure of cognitive ability to predict myside and one-sided thinking biases. *Thinking & Reasoning*, *14*, 129–167. https://doi.org/10.1080/13546780701679764

Stanovich, K. E., West, R. F., & Toplak, M. E. (2016). *The rationality quotient: Toward a test of rational thinking*. Cambridge, MA: MIT Press.

Strauss, V. (2012). Texas GOP rejects "critical thinking" skills. Really. *The Washington Post*. July 9, 2012. www.washingtonpost.com/blogs/answer-sheet/post/texas-gop-rejects-critical-thinking-skills-really/2012/07/08/gJQAHNpFXW_blog.html

Tiruneh, D. T., Weldeslassie, A. G., Kassa, A., Tefera, Z., De Cock, M., & Elen, J. (2016). Systematic design of a learning environment for domain-specific and domain-general critical thinking skills. *Educational Technology Research and Development*, *64*(3), 481–505. https://doi.org/10.1007/s11423-015-9417-2

Van der Linden, S. (2013). New psychological research helps explain why some see intricate government conspiracies behind events like 9/11 or the Boston bombing. *Scientific American*. April 30, 2013. www.scientificamerican.com/article/moon-landing-faked-hy-people-believe-conspiracy-theories/

Van der Linden S. L., Leiserowitz, A. A., Feinberg, G. D., & Maibach, E. W. (2015). The scientific consensus on climate change as a gateway belief: Experimental evidence. *PLoS ONE*, *10*(2): e0118489. https://doi.org/10.1371/journal.pone.0118489

4 Improving Students' Scientific Thinking

David Klahr, Corinne Zimmerman, and Bryan J. Matlen

The production of a scientifically literate population is a fundamental goal of our educational system. The justifications for that goal, and descriptions of paths toward it, have been reiterated many times in recent decades, as exemplified by major policy statements and specific recommendations from prestigious organizations ranging from "Benchmarks of Scientific Literacy" (AAAS, 1993) to the recent "Framework for K-12 Science Education" (NRC, 2012). Consequently, substantial effort has been devoted to determining how to increase the likelihood that, as students progress through school, they will acquire at least a rudimentary understanding of fundamental domain-general scientific concepts and procedures, as well as a nontrivial amount of domain-specific concepts. However, given the vast number of those procedures and concepts, it is not surprising that the full science curriculum presented to students from pre-school through high school has often been characterized as "a mile wide and an inch deep" (Li, Klahr, & Siler, 2006; Santau et al., 2014).

Thus, the challenge facing researchers interested in improving science education is to enhance the quality and generality of the answers to two related questions: *What is scientific thinking?* and *How can it be taught?* In this chapter, we attempt to answer the first question by presenting a brief summary of a broad framework that characterizes the essential aspects of scientific thinking and reviewing the developmental origins of scientific thinking. We answer the second question by describing a few representative examples of research on teaching science in specific domains, such as physics, biology, and earth sciences – organized according to the framework – and selected from the extensive literature on different ways to improve children's basic ability to think scientifically.

What Is Scientific Thinking?

Scientific thinking is a particular form of human problem-solving that involves mental representations of (1) hypotheses about the structure and processes of the natural world and (2) various methods of inquiry used to determine the extent

Thanks to Audrey Russo for her painstaking proofreading and editing of the references. Preparation of this chapter was supported in part by grants from the Institute of Education Sciences to Carnegie Mellon University (R305A100404 and R305A170176), and from the National Science Foundation to the University of Chicago (1548292). Opinions expressed do not represent the views of the US Department of Education or the National Science Foundation.

to which those hypotheses are consistent with phenomena. Scientific discovery is a type of problem-solving that involves a high-level search through two complementary problem spaces (Newell & Simon, 1972). One such space is the *Hypothesis Space*, and the other is the *Experiment Space*. The two spaces are linked through the process of *Evaluating Evidence*. This dual-space framework, dubbed SDDS (for Scientific Discovery as Dual Search) by Klahr and Dunbar (1988), is used to frame the literature reviewed in this chapter.

The three cognitive processes from the SDDS model are listed in Table 4.1, along with corresponding science practices that have been elucidated in recent policy statements about science education (NRC, 2012). Hypothesis Space Search involves the formulation and refinement of hypotheses. The specific practices that support this search are (1) asking questions and (2) developing and using analogies and models. Experiment Space Search involves planning and carrying out investigations. Finally, Evaluating Evidence requires (1) analyzing and interpreting data and then (2) constructing explanations. Moreover, each of these science practices can vary along a dimension from being highly domain-specific to domain-general. In Table 4.1, we have listed some representative publications that focus on specific cells in the overall taxonomy of scientific thinking and we will describe some of them in more detail below.

The particular studies summarized in this chapter were chosen because they exemplify specific *psychological processes* subsumed in the aspects of scientific thinking that have been used to organize the rows in Table 4.1. We have further divided the studies into those focusing on children's domain-specific knowledge and those focusing on domain-general knowledge, even though many of those we have classified as domain-general are – of necessity – situated in specific domains. For example, we do not focus on children's developing knowledge about such *concepts* as the periodic table of the elements, or friction, or the definition of absolute zero. Nor do we focus on how children learn about particular domain-specific *processes* (e.g., alternating current, photosynthesis, Newton's Laws, or chemical equilibrium). Instead, we approach the topic of scientific thinking from the perspective of cognitive and developmental psychology. Using this perspective, we describe some highly general aspects of what it means to "think like a scientist" or to exhibit "scientific thinking" about some domain or problem, and we comment on how different instructional approaches and pedagogical strategies can facilitate children's acquisition and mastery of this kind of knowledge.

What Are the Developmental Origins of Scientific Thinking?

Beginning in infancy, children learn about the natural world in ways that will influence their later scientific thinking. A notable achievement in the early years of life is the ability to think representationally – that is, being able to think of an object both as an object in and of itself and as a representation of something else. Even three-year-old children are able to use scale models to guide their search for hidden objects in novel locations by applying the spatial relations in the model to the corresponding

Table 4.1 *A taxonomy for categorizing psychological investigations of aspects of science education, with representative examples of each type*

		Type of knowledge	
Cognitive processes	Science practices	Domain-specific	Domain-general
Forming and Refining Hypotheses (Hypothesis Space Search)	**Asking questions**	**A1** Samarapungavan, Mantzicopoulos, and Patrick (2008) King (1991)	**D1** Chouinard (2007) Jirout and Klahr (2012) Kuhn and Dean (2005)
	Developing and using analogies and models	**A2** Christie and Gentner (2010) Matlen et al. (2011) Clement (1993, 1982, 2000) Vendetti et al. (2015) Lehrer and Schauble (2004)	**D2** Raghavan and Glaser (1995)
Investigation Skills (Experiment Space Search)	**Planning and carrying out investigations**	**B** Metz (1997) Schwichow, Zimmerman et al. (2016)	**E** Chen and Klahr (1999) Sodian, Zaitchik, and Carey (1991) Siler and Klahr (2012) Zimmerman and Croker (2014)
Evaluating Evidence	**Analyzing and interpreting data/evidence**	**C1** Amsel and Brock (1996) Penner and Klahr (1996a, b) Kuhn (2011) Masnick, Klahr, and Knowles (2016)	**F1** Masnick and Morris (2008)
	Constructing explanations	**C2** Inagaki and Hatano (2008) Lehrer and Schauble (2004)	**F2** Mynatt, Doherty, and Tweney (1977, 1978) Kelemen et al. (2014)

Note: The structure of this table is taken from Zimmerman and Klahr (2018). The cognitive processes categories (row headings) and knowledge types (column headings) are adapted from Klahr and Dunbar (1988), Klahr (1994), and Klahr and Carver (1995). The science practice row subheadings are from the *Framework for K-12 Science Education* (NRC, 2012). Cell contents cite a few studies that exemplify the row and column headings for each cell. The corresponding text in the chapter cites additional examples.

relations in the real world (DeLoache, 1987), and four- to five-year-olds develop the ability to engage in pretend play, where one (usually mundane) object can represent another (often exotic) object (Hopkins, Dore, & Lillard, 2015; Sutherland & Friedman, 2013), such as when a stick becomes a magic wand or a sword. This fundamental ability lies at the heart of important scientific skills such as analogical reasoning and lays the groundwork for later scientific tasks such as interpreting and reasoning with models, maps, and diagrams (Uttal, Fisher, & Taylor, 2006).

The nature of knowledge acquisition in young children is a source of intense debate in developmental science. Some developmental theories espouse that children's acquisition of knowledge is similar, in many respects, to scientists' – that is, guided by top-down processes and theory-level explanations (e.g., Gelman & Coley, 1990; Gopnik & Sobel, 2000; Keil et al., 1998). Other theories espouse that knowledge is acquired through lower-level perceptual, attentional, and memory-based processes (e.g., Rakison, Lupyan, & Oakes, 2008; Sloutsky & Fisher, 2004; Smith, Jones, & Landau, 1996). Regardless of the way in which children acquire knowledge, it is clear that by the time they enter formal instruction they have strong ideas about the way in which the world works, that is, about what causes what. However, many of those ideas are partially or entirely incorrect (Vosniadou, 2013). In the science education literature, these mistaken, distorted, or partially correct notions, ideas, and beliefs about the world that children often bring to the science classroom are sometimes referred to as "preconceptions" and other times as "misconceptions." As Horton (2007) put it:

> "Misconceptions" seems excessively judgmental in view of the tentative nature of science and the fact that many of these conceptions have been useful to the students in the past. "Preconceptions" glosses over the fact that many of these conceptions arise *during* the course of instruction. (Horton, 2007, p. 4, emphasis added)

In this chapter we use both terms, roughly according to the context as described by Horton.

Children's preconceptions have been shown to influence learning in a variety of scientific domains including physics (Clement, 1982), thermodynamics (Lewis & Linn, 1994), astronomy (Vosniadou & Brewer, 1994), biology (Inagaki & Hatano, 2008; Opfer & Seigler, 2004), geoscience (Gobert & Clement, 1999), and chemistry (Wiser & Smith, 2008). Moreover, preconceptions can exist not only for domain-specific knowledge but also for domain-general science concepts, such as learning the principles of experimental design (Chen & Klahr, 1999; Lorch et al., 2010; Siler, Klahr, & Matlen, 2013) or understanding the purpose of scientific models (Grosslight, Unger, & Jay, 1991; Treagust, Chittleborough, & Mamiala, 2002).

One particularly interesting and widespread preconception was first reported in Vosniadou and Brewer's (1992, 1994) classic studies of children's mechanistic explanations regarding the day and night cycle. Prior to formal schooling, many children have ideas about how and why day turns to night, ideas that are deeply rooted in children's everyday concrete experiences (and which parallel the history of early prescientific notions). For instance, many children initially believe that the Earth is a flat plane and the sun travels from above to below the Earth to create day and night. Such preconceptions often continue to exist even after children receive formal instruction. For example, on being instructed that the Earth is in fact round, many children refine their conception of the Earth to being a flat disk-shaped object in order to account for what they are told (i.e., the Earth is round) and what they observe (i.e., the Earth is flat). Vosniadou and Brewer (1992) identified several similar morphed or synthetic understandings, such as the belief that the Earth is a hollow sphere with a flat bottom on which we live. One challenge to science education is the fact that such preconceptions are particularly resistant to formal instruction. Several studies have identified preconceptions that conflict with scientific conceptions even after semester-long or university-level courses (Clement, 1982; Lewis & Linn, 1994; Wiser & Smith, 2008; Zimmerman & Cuddington, 2007).

Chi (2013) has distinguished between two types of learning based on preconceptions. The first is knowledge acquisition, or *gap-filling*, where students' prior knowledge is incomplete and they need to acquire new knowledge. The second is where students have prior knowledge that is in conflict with to-be-learned knowledge (e.g., scientific concepts). For example, preschool-age children's tendency to believe that plants are inanimate objects conflicts with the scientific perspective that plants are living organisms. When children begin to conceive of plants as living organisms, it is said that they have undergone a recategorization of plants into a new ontological category – a *conceptual change*.

In sum, children come to school with the necessary prerequisites for scientific thinking, but they also bring with them strong beliefs about how the natural world works and these "theories" are often deeply flawed. As a result, science educators face three important challenges. First, although all educators are responsible for teaching that can be described as "gap-filling" (because of incomplete knowledge), they also have to deal with the many documented scientific misconceptions that are robust and continue into adulthood (Zimmerman & Cuddington, 2007). Second, children's understanding of the procedures used by scientists to investigate the world, such as the design of unconfounded experiments, is subject to conceptual difficulties and misconceptions (Chen & Klahr, 2008; Matlen & Klahr, 2013). Finally, learning to conduct scientific investigations involves the coordination of many science practices (see Table 4.1), which require extended instruction and refinement over the school years.

How Can Children's Scientific Thinking Be Taught?

Not only does scientific thinking require the development of several fundamental precursors, such as the ability to think representationally and to develop and revise causal theories about the world, but it is also highly culturally and educationally mediated (Zimmerman & Croker, 2014). Thus, the essential goal of science education can be characterized as having three primary aspects.

i. Fostering conceptual thinking in science: The aim here is to teach children something about scientific knowledge, that is, what has been learned from tens of thousands of years of human efforts to better understand the natural world.

This is the *product* of science and it includes a vast knowledge base. As noted at the beginning of the chapter, one of the challenges of science education is the fact that rather than coming to school with *no* knowledge of specific science concepts, children come with deep and often robust misconceptions (e.g., children – and many adults, alas! –often fail to distinguish between mass and weight, or they believe that the sun circles the Earth, or that energy and force are the same thing). These misconceptions must be detected and remediated based on an understanding of how misconceptions can be changed in the face of new information.

ii. Fostering procedural thinking in science: To teach children some of the ways that humans have devised to *acquire* that knowledge. That is, to teach them some of the fundamental *processes* of science. Here, too, children often have deep misconceptions. For example, with respect to experimental procedures, young children, even as late as their middle school years, do not know how to distinguish confounded experiments from unconfounded experiments (Chen & Klahr, 1999; Kuhn et al., 1995).

iii. Fostering the ability to apply "School Science Knowledge" to "Everyday Scientific Thinking": That is, to encourage and facilitate children's ability to use what they have learned about scientific products and scientific processes to extend and enrich both of them during their day-to-day engagement with the world around them – i.e., to teach children how to use what they know about science to do even more science. Of course this last goal has a wide range of objectives, from simply being able to approach everyday problems by proposing simple hypotheses and being able to identify causal factors ("Why is my basement wet?: Is the downspout at the front of the house clogged?"; "Why am I so jumpy this evening?: Is it because I ate a lot of candy at lunch?") to creating a research project for submission to the International Science and Engineering Fair.[1]

Fostering Conceptual Thinking

Science educators are responsible for ensuring that students understand both the *concepts* (i.e., the "Disciplinary Core Ideas"; NRC, 2012) and the *processes* of science. With respect to understanding the vast number of domain-specific science concepts, the literature is difficult to adequately summarize. As of 2009, Reinders Duit's bibliography of research studies on conceptual change in science had more than 8,400 entries.[2] To illustrate, consider a single chapter on children's understanding of physical science concepts. Hadzigeorgiou (2015) reviews studies of children's ideas about matter, heat, temperature, evaporation, condensation, the water cycle, forces, motion, floating, sinking, electricity, and light. Each of these topics can be further unpacked to constituent subcomponents (e.g., electricity concepts include current, voltage, charge, electrons, resistance, and circuits, to name a

[1] https://student.societyforscience.org/intel-isef-2017
[2] For the most recent update, see http://archiv.ipn.uni-kiel.de/stcse/

few). Given this daunting proliferation of specific topics, in this section, we briefly focus on key educational strategies that have been used *across* different conceptual domains to support scientific thinking.

As mentioned above, preconceptions significantly influence how children think about and learn scientific concepts. Therefore, facilitating scientific knowledge acquisition requires an understanding of both the preconceptions children bring and how likely that prior knowledge is to change in the face of new information. Work by Kelemen and colleagues (2014) has demonstrated that children's deep scientific misconceptions (in this case, about natural selection) can be remediated by relatively brief engagement in well-designed explicit instruction that directly targets the misconception. Other research has shown that sharpening children's observational skills is important because prior belief may influence what is "observed" (Chinn & Malhotra, 2002; Echevarria, 2003). For example, many children (and adults) assume that a heavy object falls faster than a light object; because it is difficult to observe both objects simultaneously, this ambiguous situation results in expectations of what will be observed, which in turn influences interpretation, generalization, and retention. Chinn and Malhotra (2002) concluded that belief change based on unexpected evidence is possible but making the correct observations is key. Instructional interventions with scaffolding were successful in promoting conceptual change such that children learned how to make observations unbiased by their initial conceptions.

One of the more effective strategies for effecting conceptual change is to (1) present information that conflicts with children's preconceptions and then (2) gradually support the adoption of scientifically accurate knowledge. For instance, a correct understanding of physical forces is a common source of difficulty for students. Many students believe that objects resting on top of a surface (e.g., books resting on a table) exhibit only a downward force (gravity) but not an upward force (the table). To confront this preconception, Minstrell (1992) developed an ingenious intervention to induce cognitive conflict. Specifically, Minstrell prompted students to hold a book in the outstretched palm of one hand, and then asked them to explain the forces that were acting on the object. Most students initially asserted that there was only a downward force (i.e., gravity). Then Minstrell started piling an increasing number of books onto the students' hands until they acknowledged that their hands were exerting an upward force in order to counteract the gravitational force. Using this revised conceptual model of compensating forces, students were able to generalize this new knowledge to new related instances (Minstrell, 1992). A similar strategy was used by Clement (1993), who attempted to anchor students' understanding of the same concept with a series of close analogies. Clement's first example consisted of a spring: Few students disagree that the spring exhibits an upward force if weight is placed on it. Before moving to the example of books on a table, Clement used an intermediate example – books resting on a foam base. The intermediate example acted as a bridge between the spring and the table examples, inducing students to recognize the similarity between the cases. Cognitive conflict has also been used to address procedural misconceptions that students have about how to conduct controlled experiments (Schwichow, Zimmerman, et al., 2016). This study will be described in more detail in the section below on "Early Experimentation Skills." These cases illustrate that students are most likely to undergo conceptual change when new information is progressively sequenced, starting from students' preconceptions and moving in well-designed instructional steps toward the resolution of the misconception. We return to related strategies in later sections.

Other strategies for fostering conceptual change include interventions designed to facilitate the process of making accurate observations and measurements, including the need to teach students that observations can be biased and measurements include error (Chinn & Malhotra, 2002). Koerber, Osterhaus, and Sodian (2017) demonstrated that scaffolds in the form of diagrams and explanations were effective in remediating misconceptions in kindergarteners and 2nd graders. Schuster and colleagues (2017) compared two different epistemic approaches to teaching Disciplinary Core Ideas. They found that both the "guided" and the "direct" instructional approaches, which both involved active student engagement, were effective at promoting conceptual learning gains.

Conceptual change is clearly essential for scientific thinking. Here, we focused on describing just a few educational strategies that may be used across scientific concepts. Shtulman (2017) argues that replacing the intuitive ideas that children have about the world is a key challenge of science education. Shtulman describes the conceptual challenges for a variety of physical and biological science topics (e.g., energy, motion, inheritance, illness). Intuitive theories, whether about growth or the cosmos, have many properties in common (e.g., they tend to be rooted in perceptual features). However, Shtulman (2017) argues that helping students develop more scientifically accurate theories requires educators to analyze individual concepts in depth to ascertain the most effective way to challenge intuitive theories: "Instruction that neglects the domain-specific nature of intuitive theories and their scientific counterparts has about as much chance of working as the chance of a nuclear physicist making an important discovery in immunology" (p. 249).

Fostering Procedural Thinking

As noted previously, the three key cognitive processes involved in scientific thinking that correspond with various science practices (see Table 4.1) can be applied to any domain of science. As children learn to engage in inquiry, these investigation skills can be fostered individually and in concert with other skills. For these scientific practices, we review some of what is known about children's developing abilities along with illustrative research on fostering these types of procedural thinking in science.

Forming and Refining Hypotheses

Of the three cognitive processes of SDDS, search in the hypothesis space has the most in common with conceptual thinking in science, as it typically involves a search of relevant domain-specific knowledge as represented in the hypothesis space. When one is engaged in inquiry or investigation activities, however, hypothesis-space search is instantiated in the service of the scientific practices of asking questions and developing or using models (NRC, 2012).

Asking questions and curiosity. Asking questions is one of the foundational process skills of scientific practice (NRC, 2012). However, rather than viewing science as a process of posing and then finding answers to questions, students often believe that the goal of science is to demonstrate what is already known (Kuhn, 2005), or to see if something "works" or to invent things (Carey et al., 1989). However, asking questions for which the answer is *not* yet known is a crucial element of inquiry that students must learn (Kuhn & Dean, 2005). Students must learn that *question-asking* is a defining feature of science. An essential precursor to asking good questions is *curiosity* (Klahr, Zimmerman, & Jirout, 2011). The fundamental importance of curiosity in science education is indicated by its nearly universal inclusion as a desired "habit of mind" across a variety of influential science curricula, educational standards, and assessment goals (AAAS, 1993; NEGP, 1993, 1995; NAEYC, 2012; NRC, 2000). For example, the National Science Teachers Association's official position statement on early childhood science education[3] recommends that teachers

> recognize the value and importance of nurturing young children's curiosity and provide experiences in the early years that focus on the content and practices of science with an understanding of how these experiences connect to the science content defined in the *Next Generation Science Standards*. (NSTA, 2014, p. 3)

Nevertheless, although "curiosity" is acknowledged to be an essential part of science at all ages and levels of sophistication, it remains a notoriously elusive psychological construct in both the adult (Lowenstein, 1994) and the child (Jirout & Klahr, 2012) literature.

Simple problem-solving tasks that require question-asking have been used to investigate children's ability to recognize specific instances of uncertainty and to evaluate information. Chouinard (2007) and others have demonstrated not only that young children can determine which questions to ask to address uncertainty but also that they can use information yielded by the answers to their questions to resolve it. Other research has examined children's abilities to ask questions in particular domains in order to investigate their understanding of various phenomena. For example, Greif and colleagues (2006) investigated young children's ability to ask domain-specific questions on a structured task. Children were instructed to ask questions about unfamiliar objects and animals, which they were able to do – averaging twenty-six questions asked across twelve pictures. Many questions were quite general, such as "What is it?" Other questions, however, showed that children recognized and understood that different questions should be asked of the different categories (i.e., objects and animals).

Several studies have gone beyond simply demonstrating young children's nascent ability to ask "good" questions about the natural world and have created procedures aimed at increasing the efficacy of such questions. For example, King (1991)

---

[3] www.nsta.org/about/positions/earlychildhood.aspx

demonstrated that 5th graders could be trained to use strategic questions to guide their cognitive and metacognitive activity during problem-solving with partners, and that when they did use such "good" questions, they learned more about the system they were investigating.

Analogical Thinking and Use of Scientific Models. Analogical reasoning is a very powerful way to form and refine hypotheses and to scaffold scientific understanding. It involves aligning representations based on their shared relations (Gentner, 1983, 2010). When one of the representations is better understood than the other, information from the familiar case (i.e., by convention, termed the "source") can be used to inform the scientist's understanding of the unfamiliar case (i.e., by convention, termed the "target"). For example, an important concept in molecular biology is how enzymes and substrates interact. This concept is easier to understand when it is compared to a lock and key – the key acts as an unlatching mechanism, fitting into the lock to open it, just as the enzyme fits into the substrate to break it apart. By putting these domains into correspondence based on their shared relations, further inferences might be drawn: for example, a specific key only fits a specific lock, therefore, enzymes may only react with specific substrates. This example illustrates the inferential power that can be derived from analogies, even where there is limited knowledge of the target domain.

Scientists frequently use analogies to generate hypotheses and explain scientific phenomena and to interpret and construct scientific models (Dunbar, 1997). Thus, it is not surprising that analogies have played a role in many scientific discoveries. A fitting example is that of Johannes Kepler (Gentner et al., 1997), who observed that the planets farther away from the sun moved in an elliptical path that was slower than that of the planets closer to the sun. To explain this phenomenon, Kepler drew an analogy to light – he reasoned that, just as light is weakened when viewed from a distance, the sun might dispense a moving power (*vis motrix* – an early predecessor to gravity) that becomes weakened when objects are farther away (Gentner et al., 1997). This analogy in turn contributed to his discovery of the laws of planetary motion.

In addition to the "classical" analogies underlying some of the great scientific discoveries, contemporary scientists use analogical reasoning in their everyday practice, such as the design and interpretation of experiments. Dunbar (1995), in his groundbreaking investigations of the thinking processes involved by scientists in several contemporary molecular biology laboratories, discovered that there are two general forms of analogies used by scientists in discussing and explaining their work. Within lab group discussions, the analogies tend to be fairly "local," as when one particularly well-known specific process in the lab is used as the base for analogically interpreting a recent empirical result. In contrast, when describing their work to outsiders (e.g., science reporters in the media), the scientists use "distant" analogies, in which the base domain is fairly familiar to the public and it is used to describe some important features of a new discovery in the lab.

Even early school-age children have at least rudimentary analogical reasoning abilities. However, owing in part to limited domain knowledge (Bulloch & Opfer, 2009; Goswami, 1991, 2001) and a less than fully developed prefrontal cortex

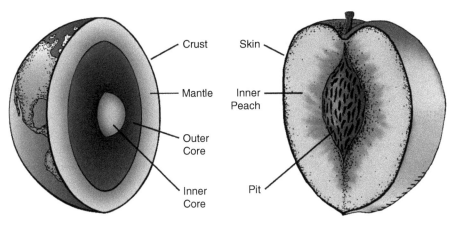

Figure 4.1 *Visual representation of the "Earth is like a peach" analogy (after Matlen et al., 2011)*

In this analogy, the peach, whose structure is known to the learner, serves as the source and the to-be-learned inner structure of the Earth serves as the target.

(Vendetti et al., 2015; Wright et al., 2008), young children are easily distracted by perceptual features of analogies at the expense of overlooking their relational structure, making them more prone to irrelevant encodings and conceptual misalignments. Despite young children's tendency to overlook relational information, researchers have identified strategies that children can be trained to use to support their scientific reasoning. One strategy is to prompt comparison-making between source and target domains (Christie & Gentner, 2010; Gick & Holyoak, 1983). Having been directly instructed to compare two domains, children are more likely to look beyond superficial features of problems and identify their common relational structure.

The process of comparison-making is facilitated when children's attention is directed toward relevant relationships (Vendetti et al., 2015). Visually representing both the source and the target of the analogy is one way in which comparison-making can be augmented (Gadgil, Chi, & Nokes, 2013; Richland & McDonough, 2010). As an illustration, Matlen and colleagues (2011) aimed to teach elementary-age students geological concepts, such as how mountains and volcanoes are formed. Matlen and colleagues (2011) presented children with analogy-enhanced text passages that were accompanied by either a visualization of both the source and the target (see Figure 4.1) of the analogy or a visualization of just the target (the latter of which is the most common form of presentation in elementary science texts). Matlen and colleagues (2011) found that children were more likely to learn and retain geoscience concepts when text passages were accompanied by visualizations of both the source and the target. Simultaneous visual presentation prompted students to compare the two domains and reduced the cognitive effort of having to recall each representation. Further, the impact of visual aids is enhanced when the to-be-aligned components are made perceptually similar (Jee et al., 2013) or when they are spatially aligned

(Matlen, Gentner, & Franconeri, 2014; Kurtz & Gentner, 2013), such that attention is directed to the corresponding components.

Scientific models also rely on the process of analogical reasoning and are frequently used in science. The source of the analogy constitutes a familiar case, which helps the scientist understand the phenomenon under study. Developing and using models constitute a "signature practice of the sciences" (Quellmalz et al., 2012, p. 366) that is related to the search for hypotheses or explanations. Models are commonly used in science and engineering to support theory-building, argumentation, and explanation (Nersessian, 2008). For example, Watson and Crick's physical model of the structure of DNA, drawings, and schematic representations (e.g., Faraday's sketches of electromagnetic tori or Darwin's tree of life) are cases of models that not only are used by practicing scientists but also provide powerful pedagogical value in teaching these concepts to students.

Because models are of central importance in scientific practice, they are now widely emphasized in science education and science assessment (Clement, 2000; Lehrer & Schauble, 2000, 2012; NRC, 2012). In both science and science education, the ability to develop and use models is becoming increasingly sophisticated due to the scaffolding provided by computers and computer simulations. Simulation models can be used to learn about and investigate phenomena that are "too large, too small, too fast, or too dangerous to study in classrooms" (Quellmalz et al., 2012, p. 367). Science education includes numerous domain-general and domain-specific examples of the instantiation of such model-based practices. Particular curricula are designed around the importance of models, such as the Model-Based Reasoning in Science (MARS) curriculum (Ragavan & Glaser, 1995; Zimmerman, Raghavan, & Sartoris, 2003). Domain-general examples include learning about variability (Lehrer & Schauble, 2004) and decomposition (Ero-Tolliver, Lucas, & Schauble, 2013) and domain-specific examples include evolution in elementary school (Keleman et al., 2014; Lehrer & Schauble, 2012), ecosystems in 6th grade (Lehrer, Schauble, & Lucas, 2008), and biomechanics of the human elbow (Penner et al., 1997; Penner, Lehrer, & Schauble, 1998).

It is important to recognize that although analogies and models have the potential to be powerful teaching tools, teachers must help students to differentiate between perceptual and conceptual similarities between the model and what is being modeled. In learning about multicomponent dynamic systems, young children tend to focus initially on perceptual features rather than on relations among components. However, with appropriate instruction, in which a model's relational structure rather than its perceptual features is reinforced, children can learn how to engage in relatively sophisticated reasoning. For example, Penner and colleagues (1997) asked 1st grade children to construct models of their elbow. Although children's models retained many superficial similarities to the arm (e.g., children insisted that their models include a hand with five fingers, represented by a foam ball and popsicle sticks), children were eventually able to construct models of their elbow that retained functional characteristics (e.g., incorporating the constraint that the elbow is unable to rotate 360 degrees), and were also more likely than a nonmodeling peer group to ignore superficial distractors when identifying functional models. With sustained practice and scaffolding, children can overcome the tendency to attend to superficial similarities and can begin to reason with more abstract models that retain mostly relational structure, such as graphing the relationship between plant growth and time (Lehrer & Schauble, 2004) or modeling variability in nature through a coin flip (Lehrer & Schauble, 2000). Early on, perceptual features serve as an invitation for children to compare the cases at a relational level (Gentner, 2010). Gradually weaning away these irrelevant perceptual features has proven to be an effective way to scaffold understanding with analogies and models (e.g., Clement 1993; Kotovsky & Gentner, 1996).

Investigation Skills: Searching the Experiment Space

Science and engineering practices, such as designing fair tests and interpreting evidence generated from controlled experiments, are included at every grade level from kindergarten through Grade 12 in the Next Generation Science Standards (NGSS Lead States, 2013). The design of an experiment to answer a question or to test a hypothesis can be construed as a problem to be solved, via search in a space of experiments (Klahr, 2000; Newell & Simon, 1972). Of course, experimentation is just one of several types of legitimate scientific inquiry processes that are involved in planning and carrying out investigations (see Lehrer, Schauble, & Petrosino, 2001), but here we focus on the substantial body of literature on ways to improve children's experimentation skills. In the following sections, we first describe research on the developmental precursors of experimentation skills, followed by studies in which participants are engaged in the full cycle of experimentation.

Early experimentation skills. Science education for young children tends to focus on investigation skills such as observing, describing, comparing, and exploring (NAEYC, 2012; NSTA, 2007). Until fairly recently, Piaget's stage theory (e.g., Inhelder & Piaget 1958; Piaget, 1970) was used to justify waiting until adolescence before attempting to teach science process skills (French & Woodring, 2013; Metz, 1995, 1997). However, an accumulation of evidence about human learning (e.g., NRC, 2000) has resulted in a more nuanced story about the developmental course of experimentation and investigation skills and the extent to which well-designed instruction can accelerate that development (NRC, 2007). Learning to conduct experiments involves the coordination of several component processes such as identifying and manipulating variables and observing and measuring outcomes. Not until the later school years, after extended instruction, scaffolding, and practice can children successfully coordinate all of these steps (e.g., Kuhn et al., 2000). Several studies have examined the precursors of the later ensemble of experimentation skills.

One of the fundamental skills in experimental design is the ability to construct a situation in which causal factors can be unambiguously identified. In her classic study, Tschirgi (1980) presented children and adults with a variety of everyday problem-solving situations (e.g., baking cakes, making paper airplanes) that involved a positive or negative outcome and several potential causal variables such as "John baked a cake using honey, white flour, and butter, and it turned out terrible" or "Susan made a paper airplane and it turned out great." The character would propose a hypothesis about a variable that may have caused the outcome (e.g., "John thinks that the honey made it taste bad" in the cake story). The participant in the study would then be asked to select one of three options in order to help the character (John) test the hypothesis. In the vary-one-thing-at-a-time (VOTAT) option, the proposed variable was changed, but the others were kept the same (e.g., bake another cake with everything the same except the sweetener: use sugar instead of honey). This strategy would produce an unconfounded experiment. In the hold-one-thing-at-a-time (HOTAT) option, the hypothesized variable was kept the same but the other variables were changed (e.g., bake another cake with the same sweetener but change the type of flour and shortening). The change-all (CA) option consisted of changing all of the variables (bake a cake with sugar, wholewheat flour, and margarine). All participants were more likely to select the HOTAT strategy when the outcome was *positive*. That is, the presumed causal variable was not changed, while all the other variables *were* changed (thus producing a confounded experiment) in the hope of maintaining the positive outcome. For a *negative* outcome, the logically correct VOTAT strategy (consistent with a controlled experiment) was chosen more frequently than HOTAT or CA, suggesting that participants were searching for the one variable to change in order to eliminate the negative outcome. Although 2nd and 4th graders were more likely to select the CA strategy for the negative outcomes (hoping to eliminate all possible offending variables at once), all participants were influenced by the desire to reproduce good effects and eliminate bad effects by choosing a strategy based on pragmatic outcomes (rather than logical grounds).

Croker and Buchanan (2011) used a task similar to Tschirgi's, but included contexts for which three-and-a-half–year-olds to eleven-year-olds held strong prior beliefs (e.g., the effect of cola vs. milk on dental health). For all age groups, there was an interaction of prior belief and outcome type. The logically correct VOTAT strategy was more likely to be selected under two conditions: (1) when the outcome was positive (i.e., healthy teeth) and consistent with prior belief or (2) when the outcome was negative (i.e., unhealthy teeth) and inconsistent with prior belief. Even the youngest children were influenced by the context and the plausibility of the domain-specific content of the situations that they were reasoning about.

In what has become a classic example of an ingenious study of young children's scientific reasoning, Sodian, Zaitchik, and Carey (1991) presented 1st and 2nd grade children with the challenge of designing a simple experiment to distinguish between two possible causal factors. Children were told that they had to figure out whether their home contained a large mouse or a small mouse. Children were shown "mouse houses" in which they could put some food that mice like. One house had a door through which either a large or a small mouse could pass. The other house had a door that only a small mouse could traverse. In the "find out" condition, the children were asked to decide which house should be used to determine the size of the mouse (i.e., to test a hypothesis). Of course, if the house with the small door is used, and the food is gone in the morning, then only a small mouse could have taken the food. If the food remains, they have a large (and now hungry!) mouse. Importantly, Sodian and colleagues had a second condition, the "feed" condition, in which children were asked what house to use if they wanted to make sure that the mouse would get fed no matter what his size. If a child can distinguish between the goals of testing a hypothesis with an experiment versus generating an effect (i.e., feeding the mouse), then he or she should select the small house in the *find out* condition and the large house in the *feed* condition. Sodian and colleagues found that children as young as six could distinguish between a conclusive and inconclusive experimental test of a simple hypothesis when provided with the two mutually exclusive and exhaustive hypotheses or experiments. Piekny and Maehler (2013) used the mouse house task with preschoolers (four- and five-year-olds) and school children (seven-, nine-, and eleven-year-olds). It was not until age nine that children scored significantly above chance, and not until age seven (a year later than in the Sodian et al. study) that children showed a recognition of, and justification for, conclusive or inconclusive tests of a hypothesis.

Klahr, Fay, and Dunbar (1993) investigated developmental differences in adults' and 3rd and 6th grade children's experimentation skills by presenting them with a programmable toy robot, in which participants first mastered most of the basic commands (see Figure 4.2). They were then challenged to find out how a "mystery key" worked by writing and then running programs that included the mystery key. In order to constrain the "hypothesis space" participants were provided with various hypotheses about the mystery key (only one of which was correct). Some examples of what the mystery key might do include (1) repeat the whole program *N* times, (2) repeat the last step *N* times, and (3) repeat the last *N* steps once. Some of these hypotheses were deemed highly plausible (i.e., likely to be correct) and others were deemed implausible. When presented with a hypothesis that was plausible, all participants set up experiments to *demonstrate the correctness* of the hypothesis (e.g., Experiment 1 in Figure 4.2).

When given an implausible hypothesis to test, adults and some 6th graders proposed a plausible *rival hypothesis* and set up an experiment that would discriminate between the two. The 3rd graders also proposed a plausible rival hypothesis but got sidetracked in the attempt to demonstrate that the rival plausible hypothesis was correct. Klahr, Fay, and Dunbar (1993) identified two useful heuristics that participants used: (1) design experiments that produce informative and interpretable results and (2) attend to one feature at a time. The 3rd and 6th grade children were far less likely than adult participants to restrict the search of possible experiments to those that were informative.

Bullock and Ziegler (1999) collected longitudinal data on participants, starting when they were age eight and following them through to age twelve. They examined the process skills required for experimentation, using separate assessments to tease apart an *understanding* of experimentation from the ability to *produce* controlled experiments. When the children were eight-year-olds they were able to *recognize* a controlled experimental test. The ability to *produce* a controlled experiment at levels comparable to adults did not occur until the children were in the 6th grade. This study

Hx: RPT N repeats the entire program N times.

Hy: RPT N runs program, then repeats the Nth step once.

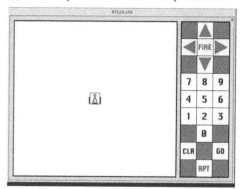

E1: ↑1   RPT 1

<u>Hx prediction</u>:   ↑ 2

<u>Hy prediction</u>:   ↑ 2

BT's behavior: ↑2

E2: ↑1   FIRE 2   ↓1   RPT 2

<u>Hx prediction</u>:	↑ 1 FIRE 2 ↓ 1	↑1 FIRE 2 ↓ 1
<u>Hy prediction</u>:	↑ 1 FIRE 2 ↓ 1	FIRE 2
<u>BT's behavior</u>:	↑ 1 FIRE 2 ↓ 1	FIRE 2 ↓ 1

Figure 4.2 *The control panel and two sample programs for discovering how the "mystery key" (labeled "RPT") works on a simulated robot (shown in its "home" position in the center of the screenshot) (after Klahr, Fay, & Dunbar, 1993)*

Hypothesis X (Hx) is that if a number N is appended to the RPT key, then the robot will repeat the entire preceding program N times. Hypothesis Y (Hy) is that the robot will repeat only the Nth step once.

For the first experiment (E1), the participant runs a very short program with only one step preceding the RPT key, that instructs the robot to go forward one unit, and then to do whatever RPT does, one time. Because the program is so short, both hypotheses make the same prediction about the robot's behavior and the robot's behavior is consistent with both.

For the second experiment (E2), a longer program with more steps is used: move forward one unit, fire laser cannon twice, backup 1 unit. Then the RPT 2 command is encountered. Hypothesis X predicts that the entire three-step program preceding RPT will be executed two times. Hypothesis Y predicts that the full program will be executed, followed by one repeat of the 2nd step (the FIRE2 command). The robot's behavior does not match either of these two predictions. Instead, it repeats the last two steps in the program once, thus refuting both hypotheses. In reality, RPT repeats the last N steps, preceding the RPT command, one time.

provides additional support for the idea that young children are able to understand the "logic" of experiments long before they are able to produce them.

When task demands are reduced – such as in simple story problems or when one can select (rather than produce) an experimental test from a set of a few alternatives – even young children show competence with rudimentary science process skills. Children, like adults, are sensitive to the context and the content of what is being reasoned about. Such precursors are important for understanding the challenges of teaching students how to conduct scientific investigations and the types of factors that can be used to facilitate or scaffold developing skills.

Planning and carrying out investigations. Much of the research on the development of investigation skills in older children and adults involves presenting participants with a multivariable causal system, such as physical apparatus or a computer simulation. The participants' goal is to investigate the system so as to identify the causal and noncausal variables in the system; they propose hypotheses, make predictions, plan and conduct experiments, collect and evaluate evidence, make inferences, and draw conclusions in the form of either new or updated knowledge (i.e., although the focus is on cells B or E in Table 4.1, other scientific practices come into play). For example, Schauble's (1996) participants conducted experiments in hydrodynamics, where the goal was to determine which variables have an effect on boat speed.

One foundational, and domain-general, science process skill is the control-of-variables strategy (CVS). The fundamental goal of an experiment is to unambiguously identify causal factors and their effects, and the essential procedure for doing this is to contrast conditions that differ only with the respect to the variable whose causal status is under investigation. *Procedurally*, CVS includes the ability to create experiments in which conditions differ with respect to only a single contrasting variable as well as the ability to recognize confounded and unconfounded experiments. *Conceptually*, CVS involves the ability to make appropriate inferences from the results of unconfounded experiments (e.g., that only inferences about the causal status of the variable being tested are warranted) as well as an awareness of "the inherent indeterminacy of confounded experiments" (Chen & Klahr, 1999, p. 1098). The conceptual aspects of CVS are relevant for argumentation and reasoning about causality in science and everyday life, as CVS includes an understanding of the invalidity of evidence from confounded experiments (or observations) and the importance of comparing controlled conditions (Kuhn, 2005). Thus, CVS is relevant to broader educational and societal goals, such as inquiry, reasoning skills, and critical thinking.

Mastery of CVS is required for successful inquiry learning as it enables students to conduct their own informative investigations. However, without instruction, students – and even adults – have poor inquiry skills (e.g., Kuhn, 2007; for review, see Zimmerman & Croker, 2014). Siler and Klahr (2012) identified the various "misconceptions" that students have about controlling variables. Typical mistakes include (1) designing experiments that vary the wrong (or "nontarget") variable, (2) varying more than one variable, and (3) not varying anything between the contrasted experimental conditions (i.e., overextending the "fairness" idea so both conditions are identical). Methods for determining children's mastery of CVS have varied from the kind of typical high-stakes test item shown in Figure 4.3 to computer-based interactive assessments of the kind shown in Figure 4.4.

A recent meta-analysis of CVS instructional interventions (Schwichow, Croker, et al., 2016) summarized the results of seventy-two studies. Possible moderators of the overall effect size included design features (e.g., quasi-experimental vs.

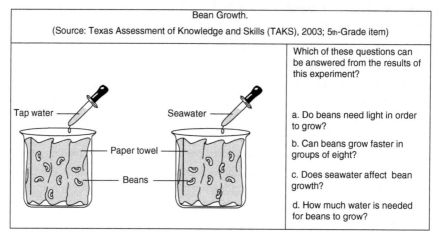

Figure 4.3 *A typical item from a "high-stakes" state assessment of domain-general experimentation skills and knowledge*

experimental studies), instructional features (e.g., use of demonstrations), training features (e.g., use of hands-on experiences), and assessment features (e.g., test format). Of the various instructional features coded for, only two were found to be effective: (1) interventions that induced a *cognitive conflict* and (2) teacher *demonstrations* of good experimental design. In this context, a teacher draws attention to a particular (confounded) comparison and asks what conclusions can be drawn about the effect of a particular variable. For example, to return to the cake baking example described earlier in the section, a teacher might note that although the cake made with butter, wholewheat flour, and sugar tasted much better than the cake made with margarine, white flour, and sugar, one could not tell for sure if the effect was due to the type of flour or the type of sweetener. Because the comparison was confounded, with two possible causal factors, either one of these potential causes might have determined the outcome.

Cognitive conflict is induced in students by drawing attention to a current experimental procedure or interpretation of data; the teacher attempts to get the student to notice that the comparison is confounded or that the conclusion is invalid or indeterminate (Adey & Shayer, 1990). Interestingly, the cognitive conflict technique is often presented *via* a demonstration by the teacher and so additional research is necessary to disentangle the unique effects of these two instructional techniques (Schwichow, Croker et al., 2016). Other instructional techniques that are often presumed to be important, such as the need for "hands-on" engagement with experimental materials, did not have an impact on student learning of CVS. And when hands-on procedures are used, at least one study demonstrated that it does not matter whether students' hands are on physical or virtual materials (Triona & Klahr, 2008). In a follow-up to the meta-analysis, Schwichow, Zimmerman, and colleagues (2016) determined that it is important for there to be a match between the way students learn CVS and the test format used to assess the extent to which they have learned it.

Q5. Suppose you want to find out what affects how much people can remember. You can do this by setting up two ways to memorize and then comparing how much people can remember.

There are three things that might make a difference in how much people can remember:

- The lighting of the room (Bright or Dim)
- A type of flashcard to memorize (10 Words or 10 Pictures)
- How much time they have to memorize (15 Seconds or 45 Seconds)

a. Figure out a way to find out whether the **lighting of the room** makes a difference in how much people can remember.

For each person, choose the lighting of the room (Bright or Dim), a type of flashcard to memorize (10 Words or 10 Pictures), and how much time they're given (15 seconds or 45 seconds).

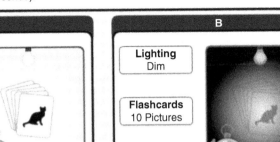

A

| Lighting |
| Bright |

| Flashcards |
| 10 Pictures |

| Time |
| 45 Seconds |

B

| Lighting |
| Dim |

| Flashcards |
| 10 Pictures |

| Time |
| 45 Seconds |

Figure 4.4 *Typical computer-interface item for assessing children's ability to design unconfounded experiments as part of their CVS training*

Evaluating Evidence

The goal of most experiments is to produce evidence that bears on a hypothesis, and once that evidence is generated it must be interpreted. (We say "most" here because, in some cases, scientists may perform experiments in the absence of any clearly articulated hypothesis, just to get a "feel" for the nature of the phenomenon.) The final cognitive process and scientific practices we will discuss are those that enable people to *evaluate, analyze,* and *explain* how evidence relates to the hypothesis that inspired it (i.e., cells C and F in Table 4.1). Evidence evaluation is the part of the cycle of inquiry aimed at determining whether the result of an experiment (or set of experiments) is sufficient to reject or accept a hypothesis under consideration (or whether the evidence is inconclusive), and to construct possible explanations for how the hypothesis and evidence are related.

Evaluating patterns of evidence. One method of examining the developmental precursors of skilled evidence evaluation with children involves presenting them with pictorial representations of potential causes and effects. These are often simple representations such as those between types of food and health (e.g., Kuhn, Amsel, & O'Loughlin, 1988) or plant treatment (e.g., sun, water) and plant health (Amsel & Brock, 1996). The pictures may represent perfect covariation between cause and effect, partial covariation, or no covariation. This cognitive skill is facilitated by the meta-cognitive ability to make a distinction between a hypothesis and the evidence to support a hypothesis (Kuhn, 2005, 2011).

In their classic study, Ruffman and colleagues (1993) presented four- to seven-year-old children with simple story problems involving one potential cause (e.g., type of food: red or green) and an outcome (tooth loss). A "faked evidence task" was used to determine whether children could form different hypotheses based on varying patterns of evidence. For example, children would be shown that green food perfectly covaries with tooth loss: this situation represents the "real evidence." Next, the evidence was tampered with; anyone who was unaware of the original pattern would be led to believe that red food causes tooth loss (i.e., the "faked evidence"). Children were asked to interpret which hypothesis the faked evidence supported. The key advantage of this type of task is that it is diagnostic with respect to whether a child can make a distinction between a hypothesis and a pattern of evidence to support a hypothesis. This task requires children to understand that their own hypothesis would be different from that of a story character who only saw the faked evidence. When considering the responses to *both* the initial veridical-evidence task and the faked-evidence task, only the five- to seven-year-olds performed above chance level. Partial covariation evidence was used to determine if five- to seven-year-olds could form hypotheses based on *patterns* of evidence. When considering both hypothesis-evidence and faked-evidence questions, only the performance of the six- and seven-year-olds was above chance level. Most children understood that veridical versus faked evidence would lead to different beliefs and that a newly formed hypothesis can be used to generalize to future cases.

Ruffman and colleagues showed that some of the very basic prerequisite evidence evaluation skills required for scientific thinking are present as early as six years of age. In follow-up research, Koerber and colleagues (2005) examined the performance of four- to six-year-olds on a variety of evidence evaluation tasks to examine whether *existing causal beliefs* influence evidence evaluation in the preschool years. In situations where there are no strong prior beliefs and the outcomes are equally plausible, preschoolers correctly interpreted perfect and partial covariation evidence. Preschoolers had difficulty, however, with evidence that contradicts prior plausible beliefs; this finding is consistent with the performance of both older children and adults on scientific thinking tasks (Zimmerman & Croker, 2014). Although young children demonstrate some of the precursors to more advanced evidence-evaluation skills, they too are susceptible to the influences of prior beliefs and considerations of the plausibility of what is being evaluated.

From the foundational work of Kuhn and colleagues (1988), we know that the process of revising and acquiring knowledge on the basis of evidence is highly influenced by the prior knowledge that a participant brings to the task. Evaluating evidence is guided by an assessment of the *plausibility* of a hypothesized cause; we make judgments about the world in ways that "make sense" or are consistent with what we already know about how things work. Plausibility is a known constraint in belief formation and revision (Holland et al., 1986) and is a domain-general heuristic that is used to guide the choice of which hypotheses to test and which experiments to run (Klahr et al., 1993). Because the strength of existing beliefs and assessments of plausibility are considered when evaluating evidence, children and adults often choose to maintain their prior beliefs rather than changing them to be in line with newly acquired evidence (e.g., Chinn & Brewer, 1998; Chinn & Malhotra, 2002). A common finding is that it is generally more difficult to integrate evidence that disconfirms a prior causal belief (which involves restructuring one's belief system) than it is to integrate evidence that disconfirms a prior noncausal belief (which involves incorporating a newly discovered causal relation, or "gap-filling"; Chi, 2013). For example, children and adults have robust physics misconceptions about weight, mass, and density, and these misconceptions influence the evaluation of evidence in tasks that involve the motion (e.g., falling, sinking, rolling) of objects. In the case of sinking objects, it is difficult to give up the belief that weight matters but it is easy to add the belief that shape (sphere vs. cube) speeds up or slows down an object based on first-hand evidence (Penner & Klahr, 1996b). Other research shows pervasive difficulties with revising knowledge on the basis of evidence, even when that evidence is generated and observed directly (rather than being provided by researchers; e.g., Chinn & Malhotra, 2002; Renken & Nunez, 2010).

Analyzing and interpreting data. The NRC (2012) science standards include the scientific practice of analyzing and interpreting *data*, noting that "scientific investigations produce data that must be analyzed in order to derive meaning . . . data do not speak for themselves" (p. 51). One important aspect of data interpretation is the capacity to distinguish data patterns that are sufficient to reach a conclusion from data patterns that are ambiguous with respect to a conclusion. Fay and Klahr (1996) described the skill of differentiating determinate and indeterminate situations in terms of children's ability to distinguish "knowing" from "guessing." They found that in a simple logical puzzle context, four- and five-year-old children tend to prematurely terminate search for a cause rather than continuing to search for more information that might render their judgment as incorrect.

The Fay and Klahr research was based on puzzles designed to preclude any empirical "noise." However, an inescapable aspect of real empirical research is that all measurements in the physical world include some degree of error, and children must learn how to deal with this. Masnick, Klahr, and Morris (2007) describe the challenge for the young scientist:

> A young child eagerly awaits the day when she will pass the 100 cm minimum height requirement for riding on the "thriller" roller coaster at her local amusement park. She regularly measures her height on the large-scale ruler tacked to her closet door. As summer approaches, she asks her parents to measure her every week. A few weeks ago she measured 98 cm, last week 99.5 cm, but today only 99.0 cm. Disappointed and confused, when she gets to school she asks the school nurse to measure her, and is delighted to discover that her height is 100.1 cm. Success at last! But as she anticipates the upcoming annual class excursion to the amusement park, she begins to wonder: what is her real height? And more importantly, what will the

measurement at the entrance to the roller coaster reveal? Why are all the measurements different, rather than the same? Because she is a really thoughtful child, she begins to speculate about whether the differences are in the thing being measured (i.e., maybe her height really doesn't increase monotonically from day to day) or the way it was measured (different people may use different techniques and measurement instruments when determining her height). (p. 3)

Although the processes associated with understanding and interpreting error and data variability draw heavily on mathematical reasoning, and therefore are beyond the scope of this chapter, there are a few studies that capture the intersection of analyzing quantitative data and identifying sources of error. Masnick and Morris (2008) examined how the characteristics of measurement data, such as sample size and variability within the data set (e.g., magnitude of differences, presence of outliers), influenced conclusions drawn by 3rd and 6th graders and adults. Participants were shown data sets with plausible cover stories (e.g., testing new sports equipment) and asked to indicate what conclusions could be drawn and their reasons. The 3rd and 6th graders had rudimentary skills in detecting trends, overlapping data points, and the magnitude of differences. The 6th graders had developing ideas about the importance of variability and the presence of outliers for drawing conclusions from data. At all ages, participants were more confident of conclusions based on larger samples of observations.

Masnick and colleagues (2016) explored how adults and children (aged 9–11) responded to (1) variability in the data collected from a series of simple experiments and (2) the extent to which the data were consistent with their prior hypotheses. Participants conducted experiments in which they generated, recorded, and interpreted data to identify factors that affect the period of a pendulum. In Study 1, several children and most adults used observed evidence to revise their initial understanding but participants were more likely to change incorrect noncausal beliefs to causal beliefs than the reverse. In Study 2, participants were oriented toward either an "engineering" goal (to produce an effect) or a "science" goal (to discover the causal structure of the domain) and presented with variable data about potential causal factors. Science goals produced more belief revision than engineering goals. Numerical data, when presented in context and with appropriate structure, can help children and adults reexamine their beliefs and initiate and support the process of conceptual change and robust scientific thinking.

Constructing explanations. The National Research Council's Framework for Science Education (NRC, 2012) emphasizes the importance of scientific theories and explanations: "The goal for students is to construct logically coherent explanations of phenomena that incorporate their current understanding of science, or a model that represents it, and are consistent with the available evidence" (p. 52). Scientific explanations are typically constructed after investigations that produce evidence that is to be evaluated and, ultimately, explained.

Much has been written in the scientific thinking literature about the ability to differentiate between evidence (i.e., data, observation, patterns) and the explanation or theory that purports to account for that evidence. In particular, Kuhn's

(1989, 2005, 2011) research has emphasized that mature scientific thinking requires the cognitive and metacognitive skills to differentiate between *evidence* and the theory or *explanation* for that evidence. Kuhn argues that effective coordination of evidence and theory depends on three metacognitive abilities: (1) the ability to encode and represent evidence and theory separately, so that relations between them can be recognized; (2) the ability to treat theories or explanations as independent objects of thought (i.e., rather than a representation of "the way things are"); and (3) the ability to recognize that theories can be false and explanations flawed and that, having recognized that possibility, to assess the evidence in order to determine whether the theory is true or false. These metacognitive abilities are necessary precursors to sophisticated scientific thinking and representative of the ways in which children, adults, and professional scientists differ.

As noted previously, children are inclined to notice and respond to causal events in the environment; even infants and young children have been shown to have a rudimentary understanding of cause and effect (Bullock & Gelman, 1979; Piaget 1929). Keil's (2006; Keil & Wilson, 2000) work on the nature of explanation in general indicates that children and adults alike have a propensity to generate explanations. We often privilege causal explanations, which are arguably quite important in scientific thinking. Koslowski's (1996, 2012, 2013) research shows that people are good at noticing evidence for the covariation between events in the world but there is a tendency to only make causal inferences when the link can be explained with a causal mechanism. Participants consider or generate plausible causal mechanisms to explain the relationship between potential causes and their effects. Similarly, if a plausible causal mechanism exists to explain why a cause and effect *should* be linked, it is difficult to let go of that belief. Therefore, we see across many types of scientific thinking tasks that both children and adults have a strong tendency to maintain beliefs rather than change them based on evidence (e.g., Chinn & Brewer, 1998; Chinn & Malhotra, 2002) because the strength of existing beliefs, assessments of plausibility, causal mechanisms, and alternative causal mechanisms are all potentially salient and brought to bear when reasoning (Koslowski et al., 2008).

Conclusions: How Can Research Inform Practice in Science Education?

The studies reviewed in this chapter reveal important insights into the ways in which science is learned. Although there is substantial evidence that children enter the period of school-based instruction with cognitive abilities that are foundational for engaging in scientific reasoning (e.g., Gopnik, Meltzoff, & Kuhl, 2000), these developmental precursors require careful guidance and sustained effort before this nascent knowledge can be transformed into robust scientific practices. Science is a highly educationally and culturally mediated activity that is supported by cultural tools (Morris et al., 2012; Zimmerman & Croker, 2014). Prior research has suggested several ways in which effective instructional strategies can scaffold scientific learning, and it suggests some ways in which these strategies can be applied to classroom teaching and produce meaningful improvements in students' understanding of science. However, even though this body of research has advanced our knowledge about the development of scientific thinking and about how to enable students to understand the body of knowledge about the natural world that has been accumulated, as well as to begin to advance that knowledge beyond their intuitive theories, many challenges remain before a clear-cut reformulation for science teaching can emerge. Scientists and STEM professionals are immersed in years of disciplinary training to overcome the cognitive heuristics and biases that may work well enough in everyday problem-solving but which can lead to incorrect responses or strategies in scientific contexts (Lilienfeld, Ammirati, & David, 2012). Science educators recognize that, insofar as possible, students should be exposed to learning experiences that correspond to the ways in which real science is conducted and communicated (NRC, 2007, 2012). The problem is how best to engage students in inquiry activities that are simultaneously (1) developmentally appropriate (i.e., that do not exceed their cognitive capacity) and (2) scientifically authentic (i.e., that do not distort or oversimplify the fundamental scientific ideas being taught).

There have been several attempts to summarize findings on science education research in such a way that they can be used by classroom teachers to refine their instructional practices based on solid scientific evidence. For example, in 2007, the National Research Council published the report of a blue-ribbon panel of science education experts, entitled *Taking Science to School* (NRC, 2007), that has since been cited thousands of times in the research literature. However, they also published a companion volume, *Ready, Set, SCIENCE!* (NRC, 2008) that was carefully crafted to be accessible to, and used by, practicing science teachers from K-8. Similar NRC reports summarize the current state of the art with respect to translating research on teaching science at the college level into actionable suggestions for college instructors (NRC, 2015; Singer, Nielsen, & Schweingruber, 2012). In addition, the US Office of Education, through its research arm, the National Institute of Education, has produced dozens of "Practice Guides" that distill the basic research in a wide variety of education topics – a few of which include math and science education – into practical, actionable suggestions for classroom teachers.[4] Nevertheless, there remain substantial gaps between findings from scholarly research on how children learn science and how curricula and instruction are typically enacted in real-world settings. We outline some possible reasons for these gaps and some ideas for how to bridge them.

Findings from research need to be more broadly accessible. Currently, researchers are incentivized to publish in peer-reviewed academic journals. However, the audiences for such journals are other highly trained researchers with deep content

---

[4] The Practice Guides are available at: https://ies.ed.gov/ncee/wwc/PracticeGuides

knowledge and methodological and statistical backgrounds in cognitive and developmental psychology. Researchers often speak a language that is not easily comprehended by the general public, including teachers. For research to make a broader impact on educational practice, findings from research should be accessible to curriculum developers, educators, and policy makers. The need for this type of communication between researchers and teachers has been acknowledged by initiatives such as that by the National Science Teachers Association to identify "Research Worth Reading." The Publications Advisory Committee for the National Association of Research in Science Teaching selects a set of published articles for a teacher audience that have the potential to inform the practice of science teaching.

One way to advance this goal would be for research to be conducted in collaboration with science educators as true partners, rather than as entrée points to students for research projects. Although researchers and teachers often share similar goals, those goals are not entirely overlapping and, in some cases, are at variance with one another. For example, researchers are often interested in advancing theory and in producing generalizable findings, whereas teachers are mainly interested in what is feasible for their classroom application (i.e., "what works"). Nevertheless, their common ground is that both are interested in finding strategies that enhance student learning. Incentives should be in place to support research collaborations between both educators and researchers, so that the goals of both are aligned. We believe these kinds of collaborations will be the most fruitful in fostering work that is conducted at the most appropriate grain size to be impactful for educational practice and over the most educationally meaningful time periods.

References

AAAS (American Association for the Advancement of Science). (1993). *Benchmarks for scientific literacy: A project 2061 report*. New York: Oxford University Press.

Adey, P. & Shayer, M. (1990). Accelerating the development of formal thinking in middle and high school students. *Journal of Research in Science Teaching, 27*, 267–285.

Amsel, E. & Brock, S. (1996). The development of evidence evaluation skills. *Cognitive Development, 11*, 523–550.

Bulloch, M. J. & Opfer, J. E. (2009). What makes relational reasoning smart? Revisiting the perceptual-to-relational shift in the development of generalization. *Developmental Science, 12*(1), 114–122.

Bullock, M. & Gelman, R. (1979). Preschool children's assumptions about cause and effect: Temporal ordering. *Child Development, 50*(1), 89–96.

Bullock, M. & Ziegler, A. (1999). Scientific reasoning: Developmental and individual differences. In F. E. Weinert & W. Schneider (eds.), *Individual development from 3 to 12: Findings from the Munich longitudinal study* (pp. 38–54). Cambridge: Cambridge University Press.

Carey, S., Evans, R., Honda, M., Jay, E., & Unger, C. (1989) "An experiment is when you try it and see if it works": A study of grade 7 students' understanding of the construction of scientific knowledge. *International Journal of Science Education, 11*, 514–529.

Chen, Z. & Klahr, D. (1999). All other things being equal: Children's acquisition of the control of variables strategy, *Child Development, 70*(5), 1098–1120.

Chen, Z. & Klahr, D. (2008). Remote transfer of scientific-reasoning and problem-solving strategies in children. *Advances in Child Development and Behavior, 36,* 420.

Chi, M. T. (2013). Two kinds and four sub-types of misconceived knowledge, ways to change it, and the learning outcomes. In S. Vosniadou (ed.), *International handbook of research on conceptual change* (pp. 49–70). New York: Routledge.

Chinn, C. A. & Brewer, W. F. (1998). An empirical test of a taxonomy of responses to anomalous data in science. *Journal of Research in Science Teaching, 35,* 623–654.

Chinn, C. A. & Malhotra, B. A. (2002). Children's responses to anomalous scientific data: How is conceptual change impeded? *Journal of Educational Psychology, 94,* 327–343.

Chouinard, M. M. (2007). Children's questions: A mechanism for cognitive development. *Monographs of the Society for Research in Child Development, 72,* 1–129.

Christie, S. & Gentner, D. (2010). Where hypotheses come from: Learning new relations by structural alignment. *Journal of Cognition and Development, 11*(3), 356–373.

Clement, J. (1982). Students' preconceptions in introductory mechanics. *The American Journal of Physics, 50*(1), 66–71.

   (1993). Using bridging analogies and anchoring intuitions to deal with students' preconceptions in physics. *Journal of Research in Science Teaching, 30*(10), 1241–1257.

   (2000). Model based learning as a key research area for science education. *International Journal of Science Education, 22,* 1041–1053.

Croker, S. & Buchanan, H. (2011). Scientific reasoning in a real world context: The effect of prior belief and outcome on children's hypothesis testing strategies. *British Journal of Developmental Psychology, 29,* 409–424.

DeLoache, J. S. (1987). Rapid change in the symbolic functioning of very young children. *Science, 238*(4833), 1556–1557.

Dunbar, K. (1995). How scientists really reason: Scientific reasoning in real-world laboratories. In R. J. Sternberg & J. E. Davidson (eds.), *The nature of insight* (pp. 365–395). Cambridge, MA: MIT Press.

   (1997). How scientists think: On-line creativity and conceptual change in science. In T. B. Ward, S. M. Smith, & J. Viad (eds.), *Creative thought: An investigation of conceptual structures and processes* (pp. 461–493). Washington, DC: American Psychological Association.

Echevarria, M. (2003). Anomalies as a catalyst for middle school students' knowledge construction and scientific reasoning during science inquiry. *Journal of Educational Psychology, 95,* 357–374.

Ero-Tolliver, I., Lucas, D., & Schauble, L. (2013). Young children's thinking about decomposition: Early modeling entrees to complex ideas in science. *Research in Science Education, 43,* 2137–2152.

Fay, A. & Klahr, D. (1996). Knowing about guessing and guessing about knowing: Preschoolers' understanding of indeterminacy. *Child Development, 67,* 689–716.

French, L. A. & Woodring, S. D. (2013). Science education in the early years. In O. N. Saracho & B. Spodek (eds.), *Handbook of research on the education of young children,* 3rd edn (pp. 179–196). New York: Routledge.

Gadgil, S. M., Nokes, T. J., & Chi, M. T. H. (2013). Effectiveness of holistic mental model confrontation in driving conceptual change. *Learning and Instruction, 22,* 47–61.

Gelman, S. A., & Coley, J. D. (1990). The importance of knowing a dodo is a bird: Categories and inferences in 2-year-old children. *Developmental Psychology, 26*(5), 796.

Gentner, D. (1983). Structure-mapping: A theoretical framework for analogy. *Cognitive Science, 7*, 155–170.

(2010). Bootstrapping the mind: Analogical processes and symbol systems. *Cognitive Science, 34*, 752–775.

Gentner, D., Brem, S., Ferguson, R. W., Markman, A. B., Levidow, B. B., Wolff, P., & Forbus, K. D. (1997). Analogical reasoning and conceptual change: A case study of Johannes Kepler. *Journal of the Learning Sciences, 6*, 3–40.

Gick, M. L. & Holyoak, K. J. (1983). Schema induction and analogical transfer. *Cognitive Psychology, 15*(1), 1–38.

Gobert, J. D. & Clement, J. J. (1999). Effects of student-generated diagrams versus student-generated summaries on conceptual understanding of causal and dynamic knowledge in plate tectonics. *Journal of Research in Science Teaching, 36*(1), 39–53.

Gopnik, A., Meltzoff, A. N., & Kuhl, P. K. (2000). *The scientist in the crib: What early learning tells us about the mind.* New York: Harper Collins.

Gopnik, A. & Sobel, D. M. (2000). Detecting blickets: How young children use information about novel causal powers in categorization and induction. *Child Development, 71*(5), 1205–1222.

Goswami, U. (1991). Analogical reasoning: What develops? A review of research and theory. *Child Development, 62*(1), 1–22.

Greif, M. L., Kemler Nelson, D. G., Keil, F. C., & Gutierrez, F. (2006). What do children want to know about animals and artifacts? Domain-specific requests for information. *Psychological Science, 17*, 455.

Grosslight, L., Unger, C., Jay, E., & Smith, C. L. (1991). Understanding models and their use in science: Conceptions of middle and high school students and experts. *Journal of Research in Science Teaching, 28*(9), 799–822.

Hadzigeorgiou, Y. (2015). Young children's ideas about physical science concepts. In K. C. Trundle & M. Sackes (eds.), *Research in early childhood science education* (pp. 67–97). Dordrecht: Springer.

Holland, J. H., Holyoak, K. J., Nisbett, R. E., & Thagard, P. R. (1986). *Induction.* Cambridge, MA: MIT Press.

Hopkins, E. J., Dore, R. A., & Lillard, A. S. (2015). Do children learn from pretense?, *Journal of Experimental Child Psychology, 130*, 1–18. http://doi.org/10.1016/j.jecp.2014.09.004

Horton, C. (2007) Student alternative conceptions in chemistry. *California Journal of Science Education, 7*(2), 23–38.

Inagaki, K. & Hatano, G. (2008). Conceptual change in naïve biology. In S. Vosniadou (ed.), *International handbook of research on conceptual change* (pp. 240–262). New York: Routledge

Inhelder, B. & Piaget, J. (1958). *The growth of logical thinking from childhood to adolescence.* New York: Basic Books.

Jee, B. D., Uttal, D. H., Gentner, D., Manduca, C., Shipley, T. F., & Sageman, B. (2013). Finding faults: Analogical comparison supports spatial concept learning in geoscience. *Cognitive Processing, 14*(2), 175–187.

Jirout, J. & Klahr, D. (2012). Children's scientific curiosity: In search of an operational definition of an elusive concept. *Developmental Review, 32*, 125–160.

Keil, F. C. (2006). Explanation and understanding. *Annual Review of Psychology, 57*, 227–254.

Keil, F. C., Smith, W. C., Simons, D. J., & Levin, D. T. (1998). Two dogmas of conceptual empiricism: Implications for hybrid models of the structure of knowledge. *Cognition*, *65*(2), 103–135.

Keil, F.C. & Wilson, R.A. (eds.) (2000). *Explanation and cognition*. Cambridge, MA: MIT Press.

Kelemen, D., Emmons, N., Seston, R., & Ganea, P. (2014). Young children can be taught basic natural selection using a picture storybook intervention. *Psychological Science*, *25*, 893–902.

King, A. (1991). Effects of training in strategic questioning on children's problem-solving performance. *Journal of Educational Psychology*, *83*, 307–317.

Klahr, D. (1994). Searching for the cognition in cognitive models of science. *Psycoloquy*, *5* (94), 7–13.

  (2000). *Exploring science: The cognition and development of discovery processes*. Cambridge, MA: MIT Press.

Klahr, D. & Carver, S. (1995). Scientific thinking about scientific thinking. *Monographs of the Society for Research in Child Development*, *60*(4), 137–151.

Klahr, D. & Dunbar, K. (1988). Dual search space during scientific reasoning. *Cognitive Science*, *12*, 1–48.

Klahr, D., Fay, A., & Dunbar, K. (1993). Heuristics for scientific experimentation: A developmental study. *Cognitive Psychology*, *25*, 111–146.

Klahr, D., Zimmerman, C., & Jirout, J. (2011). Educational interventions to advance children's scientific thinking. *Science*, *333*, 971–975.

Koerber, S., Sodian, B., Thoermer, C., & Nett, U. (2005). Scientific reasoning in young children: Preschoolers' ability to evaluate covariation evidence. *Swiss Journal of Psychology*, *64*, 141–152.

Koslowski, B. (1996). *Theory and evidence: The development of scientific reasoning*. Cambridge, MA: MIT Press.

  (2012) How explanation makes information evidentially relevant. In R. Proctor & J. Capaldi (eds.), *The psychology of science: Implicit and explicit processes* (pp. 112–136). New York: Oxford University Press.

  (2013). Scientific reasoning: Explanation, confirmation bias, and scientific practice. In G. Feist & M. Gorman (eds.), *Handbook of the psychology of science* (pp. 151–192). New York: Springer.

Koslowski, B., Marasia, J., Chelenza, M., & Dublin, R. (2008). Information becomes evidence when an explanation can incorporate it into a causal framework. *Cognitive Development*, *23*, 472–487.

Kotovsky, L. & Gentner, D. (1996). Comparison and categorization in the development of relational similarity. *Child Development*, *67*(6), 2797–2822. https://doi.org/10.2307/1131753

Kuhn, D. (1989). Children and adults as intuitive scientists. *Psychological Review*, *96*, 674–689.

  (2005). *Education for Thinking*. Cambridge, MA: Harvard University Press.

  (2007). Reasoning about multiple variables: Control of variables is not the only challenge. *Science Education*, *91*, 710–726.

  (2011). What is scientific thinking and how does it develop? In U. Goswami (ed.), *Handbook of childhood cognitive development*, 2nd edn (pp. 497–523). Oxford: Wiley-Blackwell.

Kuhn, D., Amsel, E., & O'Loughlin, M. (1988). *The development of scientific thinking skills*. Orlando, FL: Academic Press.

Kuhn, D., Black, J., Keselman, A., & Kaplan, D. (2000). The development of cognitive skills to support inquiry learning. *Cognition and Instruction, 18*, 495–523.

Kuhn, D. & Dean, D. (2005). Is developing scientific thinking all about learning to control variables?, *Psychological Science, 16*, 866–870.

Kuhn, D., Garcia-Mila, M., Zohar, A., & Andersen, C. (1995). Strategies of knowledge acquisition. *Monographs of the Society for Research in Child Development, 60*, v–128

Kurtz, K. J. & Gentner, D. (2013). Detecting anomalous features in complex stimuli: The role of structured comparison. *Journal of Experimental Psychology: Applied, 19*(3), 219.

Lehrer, R. & Schauble, L. (2000). Developing model-based reasoning in mathematics and science. *Journal of Applied Developmental Psychology, 21*, 39–48.

(2004). Modeling natural variation through distribution. *American Educational Research Journal, 41*, 635–679.

(2012). Seeding evolutionary thinking by engaging children in modeling its foundations. *Science Education, 96*, 701–724.

Lehrer, R., Schauble, L., & Lucas, D. (2008). Supporting development of the epistemology of inquiry. *Cognitive Development, 23*, 512–529.

Lehrer, R., Schauble, L., & Petrosino, A. J. (2001). Reconsidering the role of experiment in science education. In K. Crowley, C. Schunn, & T. Okada (eds.), *Designing for science: Implications from everyday, classroom, and professional settings* (pp. 251–277). Mahwah, NJ: Lawrence Erlbaum Associates.

Lewis, E. L. & Linn, M. C. (1994). Heat energy and temperature concepts of adolescents, adults, and experts: Implications for curricular improvements. *Journal of Research in Science Teaching, 31*(6), 657–677.

Li, J., Klahr, D., & Siler, S. (2006). What lies beneath the science achievement gap? The challenges of aligning science instruction with standards and tests. *Science Educator, 15*, 1–12.

Lilienfeld, S.O., Ammirati, R., & David, M. (2012). Distinguishing science from pseudoscience in school psychology: Science and scientific thinking as safeguards against human error. *Journal of School Psychology, 1*, 7–36.

Loewenstein, G. (1994). The psychology of curiosity: A review and reinterpretation. *Psychological Bulletin, 116*(1), 75–98.

Lorch, R.F., Jr., Lorch, E.P., Calderhead, W.J. et al. (2010). Learning the control of variables strategy in higher- and lower-achieving classrooms: Contributions of explicit instruction and experimentation. *Journal of Educational Psychology, 1*, 90–101.

Masnick, A. M., Klahr, D., & Morris, B. J. (2007). Separating signal from noise: Children's understanding of error and variability in experimental outcomes. In M. Lovett & P. Shaw (eds.), *Thinking with data* (pp. 3–26). Mahwah, NJ: Erlbaum.

Masnick, A. M., Klahr, D, & Knowles, E. R. (2016). Data-driven belief revision in children and adults. *Journal of Cognition and Development, 18*(1), 87–109.

Masnick, A. M. & Morris, B. J. (2008). Investigating the development of data evaluation: The role of data characteristics. *Child Development, 79*, 1032–1048.

Matlen, B.J., Vosniadou, S., Jee, B., & Ptouchkina, M. (2011). Enhancing the comprehension of science text through visual analogies. In L. Carlson, C. Holscher, and T. Shipley (eds.), *Proceedings of the 34th annual conference of the Cognitive Science Society* (pp. 2910–2915).

Matlen, B.J., Gentner, D., & Franconeri, S. (2014). Structure mapping in visual comparison: Embodied correspondence lines? Poster presented at the 37th Annual Conference of the Cognitive Science Society, Pasadena, California, July 22–25.

Matlen, B.J. & Klahr, D. (2013) Sequential effects of high and low instructional guidance on children's acquisition and transfer of experimentation skills. *Instructional Science, 41,* 621. https://doi.org/10.1007/s11251-012-9248-z

Metz, K. E. (1995). Reassessment of developmental constraints on children's science instruction. *Review of Educational Research, 65,* 93–127.

 (1997). On the complex relation between cognitive developmental research and children's science curricula. *Review of Educational Research, 67,* 151–163.

Minstrell, J. (1992). Facets of students' knowledge and relevant instruction. In R. Duit, F. Goldberg, & H. Niedderer (eds.), *Research in physics learning: Theoretical issues and empirical studies, proceedings of an international workshop* (pp. 110–128). Kiel: IPN.

Morris, B. J., Croker, S., Masnick, A. M., & Zimmerman, C. (2012). The emergence of scientific reasoning. In H. Kloos, B. J. Morris, and J. L. Amaral (eds.), *Current topics in children's learning and cognition* (pp. 61–82). Rijeka: InTech.

Mynatt, C. R., Doherty, M. E., & Tweney, R. D. (1977). Confirmation bias in a simulated research environment: An experimental study of scientific inference. *The Quarterly Journal of Experimental Psychology, 29,* 85–95.

 (1978). Consequences of confirmation and disconfirmation in a simulated research environment. *The Quarterly Journal of Experimental Psychology, 30,* 395–406.

NAEYC (National Association for the Education of Young Children). (2012). All criteria document. https://www.naeyc.org/our-work/families/10-naeyc-program-standards

NEGP (National Education Goals Panel). (1993). *Promises to keep: Creating high standards for American students.* Washington, DC: National Education Goals Panel.

 (1995). *The 1995 national education goals report: Building a nation of learners.* Washington, DC: National Education Goals Panel.

Nersessian, N. J. (2008). *Creating scientific concepts.* Cambridge MA: MIT Press.

Newell, A. & Simon, H. A. (1972). *Human problem solving.* New York: Prentice Hall.

NGSS Lead States. (2013). *Next Generation Science Standards: For states, by states.* Washington, DC: The National Academies Press.

NRC (National Research Council). (2000). *How people learn: Brain, mind, experience, and school.* Washington, DC: National Academies Press.

 (2007). *Taking science to school: Learning and teaching science in grades K-8.* Washington, DC: National Academies Press.

 (2008). *Ready, Set, SCIENCE! Putting Research to Work in K-8 Science Classrooms.* Washington, DC: National Academies Press.

 (2012). *A framework for K-12 science education: Practices, crosscutting concepts, and core ideas.* Washington, DC: National Academies Press.

 (2015) *Reaching students: What research says about effective instruction in undergraduate science and engineering.* Washington, DC: National Academies Press. https://doi.org/10.17226/18687

NSTA (National Science Teachers Association). (2007). NSTA position statement: The integral role of laboratory investigations in science instruction. www.nsta.org/about/positions/laboratory.aspx. Accessed March 18, 2013.

Opfer, J. E. & Siegler, R. S. (2004). Revisiting preschoolers' living things concept: A microgenetic analysis of conceptual change in basic biology. *Cognitive Psychology, 49*(4), 301–332.

Osterhaus, C., Koerber, S., & Sodian, B. (2017). Scientific thinking in elementary school: Children's social cognition and their epistemological understanding promote experimentation skills. *Developmental Psychology, 53*(3), 450–462.

Penner, D. E., Giles, N. D., Lehrer, R., & Schauble, L. (1997). Building functional models: Designing an elbow. *Journal of Research in Science Teaching, 34*(2), 125–143.

Penner, D. E. & Klahr, D. (1996a). The interaction of domain-specific knowledge and domain-general discovery strategies: A study with sinking objects. *Child Development, 67,* 2709–2727.

(1996b). When to trust the data: Further investigations of system error in a scientific reasoning task. *Memory and Cognition, 24,* 655–668.

Penner, D. E., Lehrer, R., & Schauble, L. (1998). From physical models to biomechanics: A design-based modeling approach. *Journal of the Learning Sciences, 7*(3–4), 429–449.

Piaget, J. (1929*). The child's conception of the world.* London: Kegan Paul.

(1970). *Genetic epistemology.* New York: Columbia University Press.

Piekny, J. & Maehler, C. (2013). Scientific reasoning in early and middle childhood: The development of domain-general evidence evaluation, experimentation, and hypothesis generation skills. *British Journal of Developmental Psychology, 31,* 153–179.

Quellmalz, E. S., Timms, M. J., Silberglitt, M. D., & Buckley, B. C. (2012). Science assessments for all: Integrating science simulations into balanced state science assessment systems. *Journal of Research in Science Teaching, 49,* 363–393.

Raghavan, K. & Glaser, R. (1995). Model–based analysis and reasoning in science: The MARS curriculum. *Science Education, 79*(1), 37–61.

Rakison, D. H., Lupyan, G., Oakes, L. M., & Walker-Andrews, A. S. (2008). Developing object concepts in infancy: An associative learning perspective [Monograph]. *Monographs of the Society for Research in Child Development, 73*(1), i–127.

Renken, M. D. & Nunez, N. (2010). Evidence for improved conclusion accuracy after reading about rather than conducting a belief-inconsistent simple physics experiment. *Applied Cognitive Psychology, 24,* 792–811.

Richland, L. E. & McDonough, I. M. (2010). Learning by analogy: Discriminating between potential analogs. *Contemporary Educational Psychology, 35*(1), 28–43.

Ruffman, T., Perner, J., Olson, D. R., & Doherty, M. (1993). Reflecting on scientific thinking: Children's understanding of the hypothesis-evidence relation. *Child Development, 64,* 1617–1636.

Samarapungavan, A., Mantzicopoulos, P., & Patrick, H. (2008). Learning science through inquiry in kindergarten. *Science Education, 92,* 868–908.

Santau, A. O., Maerten-Rivera, J. L., Bovis, S., & Orend, J. (2014). A mile wide or an inch deep? Improving elementary preservice teachers' science content knowledge within the context of a science methods course. *Journal of Science Teacher Education, 25,* 953. https://doi.org/10.1007/s10972-014-9402-3

Schauble, L. (1996). The development of scientific reasoning in knowledge-rich contexts. *Developmental Psychology, 32,* 102–119.

Schuster, D., Cobern, W. W., Adams, B. A., Undreiu, A., & Pleasants, B. (2017). Learning of core disciplinary ideas: Efficacy comparison of two contrasting modes of science instruction. *Research in Science Education, 43,* 1–47.

Schwichow, M., Croker, S., Zimmerman, C., Höffler, T., & Härtig, H. (2016). The control-of-variables strategy: A meta-analysis. *Developmental Review, 39*, 37–63.

Schwichow, M., Zimmerman, C., Croker, S., & Härtig, H. (2016). What students learn from hands-on activities. *Journal of Research in Science Teaching, 53*, 980–1002.

Shtulman, A. (2017). *Scienceblind: Why our intuitive theories about the world are so often wrong.* New York: Basic Books.

Siler, S. & Klahr, D. (2012). Detecting, classifying and remediating children's explicit and implicit misconceptions about experimental design. In R. W. Proctor & E. J. Capaldi (eds.), *Psychology of science: Implicit and explicit processes* (pp. 137–180). New York: Oxford University Press.

Siler, S., Klahr, D., & Matlen, B. (2013). Conceptual change in experimental design: From engineering goal to science goals. In S. Vosniadau (ed.), *Handbook of research on conceptual change*, 2nd edn. New York: Routledge.

Singer, S. R., Nielsen, N. R. & Schweingruber, H. A. (eds.) (2012). *Discipline-based education research: Understanding and improving learning in undergraduate science and engineering.* Washington, DC: National Academies Press.

Sloutsky, V. M. & Fisher, A. V. (2004). Induction and categorization in young children: A similarity-based model. *Journal of Experimental Psychology: General, 133*(2), 166–188.

Smith, L. B., Jones, S. S., & Landau, B. (1996). Naming in young children: A dumb attentional mechanism? *Cognition, 60*(2), 143–171.

Sodian, B., Zaitchik, D., & Carey, S. (1991). Young children's differentiation of hypothetical beliefs from evidence. *Child Development, 62*, 753–766.

Sutherland, S. L. & Friedman, O. (2013). Just pretending can be really learning: Children use pretend play as a source for acquiring generic knowledge. *Developmental Psychology, 49*(9), 1660–1668. http://doi.org/10.1037/a0030788

Treagust, D. F., Chittleborough, G., & Mamiala, T. L. (2002). Students' understanding of the role of scientific models in learning science. *International Journal of Science Education, 24*(4), 357–368.

Triona, L. & Klahr, D. (2008). Hands-on science: Does it matter what the students' hands are on? *The Science Education Review, 6*(4), 126–130.

Tschirgi, J. E. (1980). Sensible reasoning: A hypothesis about hypotheses. *Child Development, 51*, 1–10.

Uttal, D. H., Fisher, J. A., & Taylor, H. A. (2006). Words and maps: Children's mental models of spatial information acquired from maps and from descriptions. *Developmental Science, 9*(2), 221–235.

Vendetti, M. S., Matlen, B. J., Richland, L. E., & Bunge, S. A. (2015). Analogical reasoning in the classroom: Insights from cognitive science. *Mind, Brain, and Education, 9*(2), 100–106.

Vosniadou, S. (ed.) (2013). *International handbook of research on conceptual change.* 2nd edn. New York: Routledge.

Vosniadou, S. & Brewer, W. F. (1992). Mental models of the earth: A study of conceptual change in childhood. *Cognitive Psychology, 24*, 535–585.

(1994). Mental models of the day/night cycle. *Cognitive Science, 18*, 123–183.

Wiser, M. & Smith, C. L. (2008). Learning and teaching about matter in grades K-8: When should the atomic-molecular theory be introduced. In S. Vosiadou (ed.), *International handbook of research on conceptual change* (pp. 205–239). New York: Routledge.

Wright, S. B., Matlen, B. J., Baym, C. L., Ferrer, E., & Bunge, S. A. (2008). Neural correlates of fluid reasoning in children and adults. *Frontiers in Human Neuroscience*, *1*(8). http://dx.doi.org/10.3389/neuro.09.008.2007

Zimmerman, C. & Croker, S. (2014). A prospective cognition analysis of scientific thinking and the implications for teaching and learning science. *Journal of Cognitive Education and Psychology*, *13*, 245–257.

Zimmerman, C. & Cuddington, K. (2007). Ambiguous, circular and polysemous: Students' definitions of the "balance of nature" metaphor. *Public Understanding of Science*, *16*, 393–406.

Zimmerman, C. & Klahr, D. (2018). Development of scientific thinking. In S. Ghetti (ed.), *The Stevens' handbook of experimental psychology and cognitive neuroscience*, *Vol. 3: Developmental & Social Psychology* (pp. 223–248). New York: Wiley.

Zimmerman, C., Raghavan, K., & Sartoris, M. L. (2003). The impact of the MARS curriculum on students' ability to coordinate theory and evidence. *International Journal of Science Education*, *25*, 1247–1271.

5   Spatial Skills, Reasoning, and Mathematics

Nora S. Newcombe, Julie L. Booth, and Elizabeth A. Gunderson

Modern technological societies are built on a foundation of mathematics. We could not have extensive trade without book-keeping – we would be stuck with a barter system. We could not build our long bridges without calculation – we would still be relying on ferries to cross bodies of water. We have made impressive improvements in agricultural science in the past century based in part on experiments using the statistics of "split plots." The examples could be multiplied but the lesson is clear. Given the importance of numeracy, there is good reason for educational systems to strive to teach mathematics effectively. Even though many children in contemporary schools succeed in learning to calculate, many others struggle or progress slowly, and even more never achieve the levels required for full participation in our technological society. There are many reasons for this situation and many proposed remedies. One potential way to improve mathematics education involves harvesting our growing understanding of how human minds and brains process quantitative information and how these processes develop. The teaching of reading has already benefited from the insights of cognitive science (Rayner et al., 2001; Castles, Rastle, & Nation, 2018) and the teaching of mathematics is starting to keep pace (Ansari & Lyons, 2016).

The purpose of this chapter is to evaluate the potential of leveraging mathematics learning based on the links between spatial thinking and mathematical learning. A few sample findings give some sense of the variety of the evidence, which is derived from many levels of analysis. At the neural level, for example, Amalric and Dehaene (2016) found a great deal of overlap between the brain areas used for spatial and mathematical processing, even in expert mathematicians and across a wide range of mathematical fields. In terms of development, spatial–numerical associations are apparently basic, present at birth and even shared with other species, although also modified by culture (Rugani & de Hevia, 2017). Behaviorally, there is a longitudinal link between spatial skills and mathematical achievement, evident as young as preschool and continuing into high school and university (Casey et al., 1995; Kyttälä et al., 2003; Shea, Lubinski, & Benbow, 2001; Verdine et al., 2017; Wai, Lubinski, & Benbow, 2009).

Thus, one hope is that improving spatial skills will improve mathematics achievement.

This strategy would benefit, however, from delineating the pathways linking spatial skills to numeracy skills. We know that spatial skills and numeracy skills are both multidimensional constructs (Mix & Cheng, 2012; Uttal et al., 2012), so specific spatial skills may underlie specific mathematical achievements, in which case intervention should focus on the relevant spatial skills. Alternatively or in addition, mathematics learning may be facilitated overall by a general spatial way of thinking, what has been called a *spatial turn of mind*. For example, children and adults with the habit of visualizing problems, or perhaps even actually sketching them, may find mathematical reasoning easier. We discuss what we know about the nature of spatial–mathematical linkages in two major sections, concentrating first on elementary school mathematics and then on secondary school mathematics.

Spatial–Mathematical Linkages in Preschool and Elementary School

Understanding spatial–mathematical linkages requires some understanding of the nature of development of both domains. In this section, we begin with a short summary of early mathematical development and then turn to three kinds of spatial processes that may be relevant to mathematical development in this age range. One process is visuospatial working memory (VSWM), which is arguably a resource more than a skill. As we turn to skills, although there are a variety of spatial skills, only some have been extensively investigated. In this section, we concentrate on mental rotation and on proportional reasoning/spatial scaling. Proportional reasoning and spatial scaling have been studied separately but turn out to have a great deal in common. We close with a consideration of spatial strategies, the more general way in which spatial thinking may influence mathematical reasoning.

The Nature of Early Mathematical Learning

One important distinction for young children is between symbolic approximation skills (sometimes referred to as "number sense") and exact numeracy skills. Symbolic approximation skills involve rapidly estimating relations between symbolic quantities (e.g., approximate symbolic calculation and numerical comparison) and are thought to rely on a mapping between the evolutionarily old, nonsymbolic approximate number system (ANS) and a set of culturally created symbolic representations (number words and Arabic numerals) (Carey, 2009; Feigenson, Dehaene, & Spelke, 2004). Both symbolic and nonsymbolic approximate number representations become more fine-tuned with age and education (Halberda & Feigenson, 2008; Sekuler & Mierkiewicz, 1977), allowing adults to make faster and more precise judgments about numerical quantity than young children. Interestingly, approximation tasks involve activation in the intraparietal sulcus (IPS) in children and adults (Halberda & Feigenson, 2008; Kaufmann et al., 2011), a region also implicated in mental rotation skill (Zacks, 2007).

In contrast, exact numeracy skills involve concepts and procedures necessary to precisely represent and manipulate quantities (e.g., cardinality and exact arithmetic). These exact numeracy skills, which for young children involve whole-number concepts and procedures, are thought to rely on different processes and neural substrates than approximate numeracy skills. Children ages 3–5 who are just learning the cardinal meanings of the first few count words (i.e., "one," "two," and "three") appear to map them onto an object-based representation system that can hold up to three or four items in memory (Carey, 2009) and only later map them to approximate representations in the ANS (Le Corre, 2014; Le Corre & Carey, 2007). In adults, performing exact calculations through direct retrieval involves activation of the left angular gyrus (Grabner et al., 2007, 2009), which is close to language processing areas but distinct from the IPS, the area that is implicated in approximation tasks. Thus, the neural data suggest that exact calculation in adults is supported by verbal processes.

In addition to skills involving approximate calculation, number comparison, counting, and exact calculation, another important numerical representation that develops in childhood is the number line. Humans are predisposed to associate spatial magnitude (such as line length or area) with numerical magnitude, even in the absence of formal schooling (Dehaene, Bossini, & Giraux, 1993; Dehaene et al., 2008; de Hevia & Spelke, 2010; Lourenco & Longo, 2010; Pinel et al., 2004; Zorzi, Priftis, & Umiltà, 2002). Children in Western societies begin to map symbolic numbers (Arabic numerals) to space in a left-to-right orientation as early as preschool and kindergarten (Ebersbach, 2015; Sella et al., 2017). Theoretical accounts describe children's number line representations as initially logarithmic, in which they allocate more space to smaller numbers and less space to larger numbers (Opfer & Siegler, 2007; Opfer, Siegler, & Young, 2011; Siegler & Opfer, 2003). However, with age and experience, children's number line representations shift toward greater linearity, such that numbers that are equally distant in terms of numerical magnitude are represented in a spatially equidistant manner (Booth & Siegler, 2006; Siegler, 2009; Siegler & Booth, 2004, 2005; Siegler & Opfer, 2003). Developing a linear number line representation may involve narrowing the neural "tuning curves" associated with each Arabic numeral in the IPS (for a review, see Kaufmann et al., 2011), so that the amount of representational overlap between successive numbers is similar regardless of the size of the numbers.

Although it seems clear that mature performance on a typical number line task involves proportional judgments about a number in relation to the number line's endpoints (Slusser, Santiago, & Barth, 2013), there is controversy regarding how to best describe the earlier, logarithmic (or pseudo-logarithmic) stage (Barth & Paladino, 2011; Barth et al., 2011; Ebersbach et al., 2008; Kim & Opfer, 2017; Moeller et al., 2009; Opfer, Thompson, & Kim, 2016). Despite this controversy, there is strong evidence that the accuracy of children's number line estimations is a strong predictor of other numeracy skills, including numerical magnitude comparison, number recall, approximate calculation, and symbolic estimation (Booth & Siegler, 2008; Laski & Siegler, 2007; Siegler & Ramani, 2008, 2009). Further, lessons incorporating number lines are effective for teaching children concepts and procedures related to whole numbers and fractions (Fuchs et al., 2013; Hamdan & Gunderson, 2016; Saxe, Diakow, & Gearhart, 2013).

Visuospatial Working Memory

VSWM is one component of the three-part model of working memory (central executive, phonological loop, and VSWM) proposed by Baddeley and Hitch (1974). It is thought to store and process information in terms of its visual and spatial features. VSWM undergoes substantial development in early childhood (Gathercole et al., 2004) and is a robust predictor of numeracy skills in pre-k through 3rd grades. In prekindergarten, VSWM predicts counting skills (Kyttälä et al., 2003) and non-verbal addition (Rasmussen & Bisanz, 2005). In kindergarten, VSWM correlates with number line estimation (0–100), rapid identification of groups that add to 5 (Geary et al., 2007), and arithmetic performance (McKenzie, Bull, & Gray, 2003; Xenidou-Dervou, van der Schoot, & van Lieshout, 2015). In 1st grade, experimental disruption of VSWM using a dual task harms arithmetic performance (McKenzie et al., 2003). In 2nd and 3rd grades, VSWM relates to calculation skills (Nath & Szücs, 2014) and general math achievement (Gathercole & Pickering, 2000; Meyer et al., 2010). These relations are not only concurrent but also predictive. In one study, VSWM at age five predicts general math achievement in 3rd grade, mediated by quantity-number competencies at age six (Krajewski & Schneider, 2009). In another longitudinal study, four-year-olds' VSWM predicted growth in calculation skills over a fourteen-month period, even after accounting for vocabulary, processing speed, and nonsymbolic numerical discrimination skills (Soto-Calvo et al., 2015).

VSWM, as a versatile "mental visual sketchpad," may impact multiple aspects of numeracy that rely on this capacity, both approximate and exact. In a study of kindergarteners completing single-digit calculations, VSWM, but not verbal working memory, related to approximate symbolic calculation skills, and verbal working memory, but not VSWM, related to exact symbolic calculation skills (Xenidou-Dervou et al., 2015). Although exact calculations, particularly those involving rote memorization, rely heavily on verbal processes (e.g., Grabner et al., 2007; Spelke & Tsivkin, 2001), other strategies for exact calculation rely more heavily on VSWM. For example, VSWM may help children keep track of objects while counting and visualize nonsymbolic "mental models" of simple arithmetic problems (e.g., visualizing 2 objects and 3 objects to compute 2 + 3) (Alibali & DiRusso, 1999; Geary et al., 2004; Huttenlocher, Jordan, & Levine, 1994). Further, mentally computing a multistep symbolic calculation requires VSWM to remember intermediate steps involving carry operations and place value, especially when problems are presented vertically (Caviola et al., 2012; Trbovich & LeFevre, 2003). In addition, VSWM may help children to remember and later hold in mind the number line representation, which may, in turn, foster other numeracy skills (e.g., Booth & Siegler, 2008; Siegler & Ramani, 2008).

Mental Rotation

Mental rotation is the ability to hold in mind and mentally rotate representations of 2-D or 3-D visual stimuli (e.g., to decide whether a rotated puzzle piece would fit into a puzzle) (Shepard & Metzler, 1971). Mental rotation has been found to predict

(a)

"Which one of these (*point to four shapes on right*) makes a
square with this one (*point to shape on left*)?"

(b)

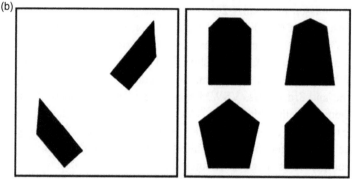

"Look at these pieces. Now look at these shapes. If you put the
pieces together, they will make one of these shapes. Point to
the shape the pieces make."

Figure 5.1 *(a) Illustration of the type of items used on the Thurstone mental rotation task; (b) A sample item from the Children's Mental Transformation Task (from Gunderson, et al., 2012, p. 1233. Reprinted with permission from the American Psychological Association)*

several measures of numeracy in young children (pre-k to 4th grade) using age-appropriate tasks (Figure 5.1). In pre-k, mental rotation skill correlates with a composite of numeracy skills (including counting, cardinality, number comparison, and ordering) (Kyttälä et al., 2003). Among 1st grade girls, mental rotation skill correlates with arithmetic proficiency (Casey et al., 2014). Further, mental rotation skills in 1st and 2nd grade predicted growth in number line knowledge over the course of the school year (Gunderson et al., 2012).

In a separate sample, mental rotation skills at age five predicted approximate symbolic arithmetic performance at age eight. The strongest correlational evidence to date shows that mental rotation skills uniquely relate to kindergarten and 3rd graders' (but not 6th graders') concurrent math skills (measured as a single factor), even after controlling for a variety of other spatial skills (Mix et al., 2016). Finally, one experimental study found that experimentally training mental rotation skill yielded improvements in arithmetic among six- to eight-year-olds, especially on missing-term problems (Cheng & Mix, 2012), although one attempt to replicate this effect of mental rotation training on numeracy was unsuccessful (Hawes et al., 2015). However, encouragingly, several recent randomized studies using more varied spatial training regimes, including mental rotation as well as other spatial skills (often in a playful context), have found positive effects of spatial training on

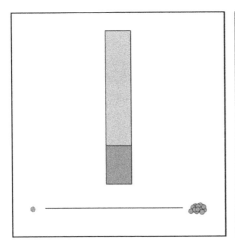 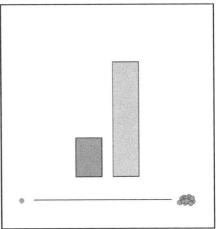

Figure 5.2 *Proportional reasoning measure*

numerical skills in young children (Grissmer et al., 2013; Hawes et al., 2017; Lowrie, Logan, & Ramful, 2017). Taken together, the research robustly supports a correlation between mental rotation skill and numeracy. The causal impact of spatial training (in general) on numeracy is increasingly well-supported, although evidence for transfer from mental rotation training (in particular) to numeracy is more mixed.

Despite the strong correlation between mental rotation skills and multiple aspects of numeracy, the mechanisms through which mental rotation skill would affect numeracy are not obvious. One mechanism, proposed by Cheng and Mix (2012), is that mental rotation skills help children to "rotate" missing-term arithmetic problems (e.g., 1 + __ = 5) into a more conventional format (e.g., __ = 5 − 1). Another possibility is that mental rotation skills are one component of a broader skill of spatial visualization – the ability to manipulate mental representations of objects in space – and that this spatial visualization skill can be brought to bear in a variety of numerical contexts that involve grounding new or complex concepts in a spatial mental model. Consistent with this hypothesis, block design (another measure of spatial visualization) was uniquely related to newly learned math concepts, but not familiar math concepts, among children in kindergarten, 3rd, and 6th grades; mental rotation was related to both new and familiar concepts among kindergarten and 3rd graders (Mix et al., 2016).

Proportional Reasoning and Spatial Scaling

Proportional reasoning and spatial scaling are two spatial skills that have only recently begun to be investigated in terms of individual differences (Frick & Newcombe, 2012; Möhring et al., 2014, 2016). Proportional reasoning involves understanding part–whole or part–part relations between spatial extents (see Figure 5.2); spatial scaling involves reasoning about a representation that differs in size from its referent (e.g., a map that differs in size from the city it represents).

These skills are deeply related: Proportional reasoning requires recognizing equivalent proportions at different scales (e.g., 2 cm of a 10 cm line is proportionally equivalent to 20 cm of a 100 cm line), and spatial scaling involves using proportional information to map locations between scales (e.g., a location on a map that is one-third of the way between two buildings will also be one-third of the way between those buildings at full scale). Indeed, recent work indicates that proportional reasoning (using nonsymbolic spatial extents) and spatial scaling are significantly correlated in childhood (Möhring, Newcombe, & Frick, 2015).

Although classic work by Piaget and Inhelder (1975) argued that proportional reasoning skill did not emerge until around eleven years of age, more recent work has shown sensitivity to proportions even in infancy (Duffy, Huttenlocher, & Levine, 2005; Huttenlocher, Duffy, & Levine, 2002). Starting at six months of age, infants and young children are quite sensitive to proportional relations between spatial extents (e.g., lengths), while the ability to discriminate exact spatial extents emerges much later, after age four (Duffy et al., 2005; Huttenlocher et al., 2002). Both children and adults spontaneously use proportional strategies, biased toward the center of salient spatial categories (such as quadrants of a circle or number line), to remember locations and make explicit proportion judgments related to 1-D and 2-D spaces (Huttenlocher, et al., 2004; Huttenlocher, Hedges, & Vevea, 2000; Huttenlocher, Newcombe, & Sandberg, 1994; Spence & Krizel, 1994). Spatial scaling ability also develops early: Children ages 3–6 show individual differences in the ability to use a 2-D map to find a location in another 2-D space that differs in size (Frick & Newcombe, 2012; Möhring et al., 2014; Vasilyeva & Huttenlocher, 2004).

Work on proportional reasoning and scaling is relatively new, and their links to numeracy are less well-tested than for mental rotation and VSWM. One recent study has shown that proportional reasoning skill is correlated with symbolic fraction concepts in children ages 8–10 (Möhring et al., 2016). Further, there are strong theoretical reasons to believe that proportional reasoning should relate to number line knowledge, since the number line also requires estimating quantities and relating parts to wholes. In fact, there is evidence that mature performance on a symbolic number line task involves proportion judgments that are biased toward the center of salient categories (such as halves or quarters of the number line), similar to proportion judgments in nonsymbolic, visual tasks (Barth & Paladino, 2011; Barth et al., 2011). Consistent with this, 5th graders' nonsymbolic proportional reasoning skills loaded onto the same factor as number line estimation (Ye et al., 2016). If proportional reasoning helps children's number line estimation, this may in turn benefit their numeracy skills more broadly.

The Linear Number Line

Despite decades of research showing a correlation between spatial skills and numeracy, relatively little work has probed the mechanisms that might explain this link. One potential mechanism is that the acquisition of a specific cultural tool that brings together spatial and numerical representations – *the linear number line* – may help to explain the relation between spatial skills and symbolic numeracy skills (Gunderson et al., 2012). Spatial skills may facilitate the development (i.e., learning, retention, and use) of the linear number line representation, which in turn enhances other numeracy skills, especially those related to symbolic approximation (Gunderson et al., 2012). Gunderson et al. (2012) reported on two longitudinal studies supporting this theory. In the first study, 1st and 2nd graders' beginning-of-year mental rotation skills predicted improvement in number line knowledge over the course of the school year, even after accounting for beginning-of-year math and reading achievement. In the second study, children's mental rotation skills at age five predicted approximate symbolic calculation ability at age eight, mediated by number line knowledge at age six. A separate study of 2nd through 4th graders replicated and extended these results, finding that the longitudinal relation between spatial skills and later calculation skill was partially mediated by number line knowledge (LeFevre et al., 2013).

Mental rotation may contribute to a visual transformation strategy (e.g., zooming) during number line estimation. Additional spatial skills may also be involved. As noted previously, proportional reasoning (Ye et al., 2016) and VSWM (Geary et al., 2007) have also been linked to number line estimation skill. Proportional reasoning may contribute to a proportion judgment strategy, and VSWM may help children to recall locations on number lines they have encountered in school. However, because the relations of mental rotation, proportional reasoning, and VSWM to number line knowledge have been investigated in separate studies, more work is needed to determine whether all three skills contribute uniquely to children's number line knowledge. Despite these limitations and open questions, research to date is consistent with the hypothesized causal chain linking spatial skills to number line knowledge to symbolic calculation skills, both exact (LeFevre et al., 2013) and approximate (Gunderson et al., 2012).

In terms of its relation to numeracy, one theoretical possibility is that the number line representation is particularly helpful for approximate symbolic numeracy skills, to the extent that improvement on the number line task indicates more finely tuned magnitude representations that are especially critical for approximation. Indeed, many studies showing the impact of number line estimation on numerical skill have used approximate measures (Booth & Siegler, 2008; Gunderson et al., 2012; Laski & Siegler, 2007; Siegler & Ramani, 2008, 2009). However, even if it is especially important for approximation, number line estimation skill may impact exact symbolic numeracy skills as well, perhaps by increasing children's ability to notice and correct errors in exact calculation procedures. Consistent with this, recent studies have also shown a strong relation between number line estimation and exact calculation skill (LeFevre et al., 2013; Xenidou-Dervou et al., 2015).

Spatial Strategy Use

Another potential mechanism linking spatial skills and numeracy is the use of spatial strategies (i.e., use of explicit visualization or external representations, such as schematic spatial images or sketches) to represent and solve a math problem. Use of spatial strategies is related to both spatial skills and math achievement (Blazhenkova, Becker, & Kozhevnikov, 2011; Hegarty & Kozhevnikov, 1999), which gives reason to believe that spatial strategy use may mediate the relation between spatial skills and numeracy skills. Children as young as age eight, as well as adults, can reliably self-report their preference for the use of spatial visualization strategies, object visualization strategies (i.e., detailed pictorial images of objects in the relevant problem), and verbal strategies (Blajenkova, Kozhevnikov, & Motes, 2006; Blazhenkova et al., 2011). Among older children (ages 8–18), spatial strategy preference is significantly related to children's mental rotation skill and relates to children's intention to pursue STEM fields (physics, chemistry, math, and computer science) (Blazhenkova et al., 2011). In addition, children's actual use of spatial strategies while completing math word problems predicts success on those problems (Hegarty & Kozhevnikov, 1999). Thus, children with higher levels of spatial skills may be more likely to use spatial strategies while completing numerical tasks (especially novel or difficult ones), leading to improved performance. However, given the paucity of research in this area, it may be fruitful for researchers to investigate the relations between specific spatial skills (such as mental rotation, VSWM, and proportional reasoning), spatial strategy preference and use, and math achievement among young children.

Spatial–Mathematical Linkages in Secondary School

Much like findings for primary mathematics content, there is evidence for the influence of spatial skills on higher-level mathematics skills, such as those learned in secondary school. Both VSWM and mental rotation (but not verbal working memory) are predictive of higher-level mathematics achievement scores (Reuhkala, 2001), and 3-D spatial visualization tasks such as mental rotation and paper folding have been found to predict students' SAT-M scores as they exit secondary school, as well as to mediate the observed relation between verbal working memory and SAT-M scores (Tolar, Lederberg, & Fletcher, 2009). Correlations between these types of 3-D spatial visualization measures and mathematics achievement tend to be greater for higher-level mathematics skills than for elementary mathematics skills (Casey, Nuttall, & Pezaris, 1997; Friedman, 1995; Reuhkala, 2001).

In the following sections, we first describe the types of mathematical content studied in secondary schools and then describe evidence for relations between spatial skills and these various areas of higher-level mathematics. We then discuss the mechanisms that may explain the connections between spatial reasoning and these higher-level mathematics skills.

The Nature of Secondary Mathematical Learning

In secondary schools, mathematics learning typically encompasses three types of content through which students progress at different speeds and to different degrees. Secondary mathematics often begins with the study of algebra in middle or early high school. Algebra focuses on the understanding of variables and their opera-tions (Usiskin, 1988) and generally contains component skills such as solving equa-tions and word problems and graphing linear, quadratic, and exponential functions. The next facet of secondary mathematics is typically geometry, which is typically studied in a stand-alone course in high school in the United States, but significant content on 2-D and 3-D figures is also addressed in middle school. Geometry has been defined as "branches of mathematics that exploit visual intuition ... to remember theorems, understand proof, inspire conjecture, perceive reality, and give global insight" (Royal Society and JMC, 2001). Finally, students who are successful in these earlier mathematics courses may begin the study of calculus, which is typically restricted to advanced high school and college students. Calculus can be thought of as the study of change in mathematical quantities, typically encompassing knowledge of derivatives, integrals, and limits (Zuccheri & Zudini, 2014).

Perhaps because they are studied by most secondary students, algebra and geo-metry topics dominate the literature on secondary mathematics learning. However, there are surprisingly few studies on connections between spatial skills and algebra (Kinach, 2012).

Compared with algebra, a greater amount of research has established the link between spatial ability and geometry (e.g., Battista, Wheatley, & Talsma, 1982, Delgado & Prieto, 2004). Unfortunately, there is a relative dearth of research on learning calculus at all, much less on the role of spatial abilities.

Here, we review the extant literature on two types of spatial skills: VSWM and mental rotation. Where available, we include findings on how spatial skills are related to all three of these types of secondary mathematics content; though geome-try may be considered the most obvious example of how spatial reasoning is relevant to secondary mathematics, mathematicians argue that "much of the thinking that is required in higher mathematics is spatial in nature" (Jones 2001, p. 55).

Visuospatial Working Memory

Since 2008, several studies have examined potential connections between various higher-level mathematics skills and VSWM. For instance, VSWM was shown to predict Australian high school students' ability to solve symbolic algebraic problems (Trezise & Reeve, 2014). Kyttälä and Lehto (2008) also found a direct relation between VSWM and performance on algebraic word problems for Finnish high school students; however, they did not find a comparable relation between VSWM and geometry problem-solving in that population.

Even in cases where such a relation is found, the link between VSWM and geometry achievement appears to be very weak and perhaps limited only to tasks involving mental manipulation (Giofrè et al., 2013). Using Dehaene and colleagues' (2006) distinction between types of geometric principles, Giofrè and colleagues (2013) also found that the relation between VSWM and geometry was limited to culturally mediated principles of geometry (i.e., symmetry, chirality, metric properties, and geometrical transformations) and not to core principles of geometry (i.e., topol-ogy, Euclidean geometry, and geometric figures; see Figure 5.3).

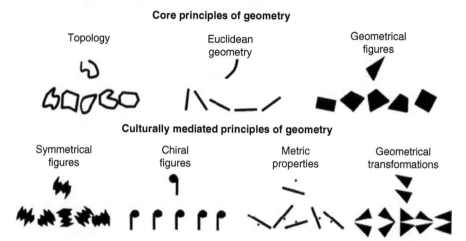

Figure 5.3 *Examples of core vs. culturally mediated principles of geometry (from Giofrè, et al., 2013, p. 117. Copyright 2013 by Elsevier. Reprinted with permission)*

In a recent meta-analysis, Peng and colleagues (2015) aimed to compare the impact of different facets of working memory on various aspects of secondary mathematics learning. They concluded that the role of working memory in geometry performance was generally small and that VSWM was no more influential than any other type of WM. They did not draw conclusions regarding VSWM and other facets of secondary mathematics, however, due to an insufficient number of studies on VSWM in algebra or any type of working memory at all in calculus.

Mental Rotation

Compared with those for VSWM, studies on the links between mental rotation (or other sorts of 3-D spatial visualization) and higher-level mathematics have yielded more conclusive findings. In general, much stronger evidence exists linking 3-D spatial visualization to geometry compared with algebra (Battista, 1990; Delgado & Prieto, 2004). For instance, Kyttälä and Lehto (2008) found a direct relation between mental rotation and solving geometry problems but only an indirect relation between mental rotation and solving algebraic word problems. High school students' performance on the Mental Rotation Test (MRT) has been found to relate to both geometry course grades and performance on a geometry achievement test, as well as to the students' perceptions of how well they do in geometry (Weckbacher & Okamoto, 2014); Mental rotation was also positively related to the students' perceptions of how well they do in algebra but not to their actual algebra course grades (Weckbacher & Okamoto, 2014). One recent study, however, found that scores on a paper folding task were predictive of both algebra pattern knowledge and geometry problem-solving for 6th grade students in Singapore (Logan, 2015).

Three-dimensional spatial visualization has also been linked to calculus performance. Cromley and colleagues (2017) demonstrated a relationship between mental rotation and high school and college calculus students' scores on items from the AP calculus test, though mental rotation was not related to performance on a conceptual calculus measure. Similarly, Samuels (2010) found a significant correlation between scores on the Purdue Spatial Visualization Tests (PSVT) Development (3-D paper folding) task and solution of problems involving finding the derivative in a college calculus class. There is also some causal evidence of the relation, as practice reasoning about the rotation of 3-D objects led to improved calculus grades for low-spatial undergraduate engineering students (Sorby et al., 2013).

Pittalis and Christou (2010) isolated the effects of a composite spatial abilities measure (which included both mental rotation and paper folding tasks but not VSWM) across the board for four separate types of geometry reasoning (see Figure 5.4) in Cyprian middle-grade students; strong relations were found between spatial abilities and students' representations of 3-D objects and measurement skills with 3-D objects (i.e., calculating surface area and volume), while slightly weaker relations were found with spatial structuring tasks (i.e., arranging and enumerating unit cubes) and conceptualizing properties of 3-D shapes. A different composite spatial ability measure (that still included both mental rotation and paper folding tasks) was related not only to Canadian 7th and 8th graders' initial knowledge about representation of 3-D geometric shapes but also to how much they were able to learn from geometry instruction (Kirby & Boulter, 1999). However, only a weak link between a 3-D spatial visualization composite (mental rotation and paper folding) and algebraic equation solving was found in undergraduate students (Tolar et al., 2009).

Mechanisms for Explaining Spatial–Achievement Relations in Secondary Mathematics

In algebra, VSWM seems to be more influential than 3-D spatial visualization, whereas the opposite may be true in geometry and calculus. The effect of 3-D spatial visualization seems to manifest across the board for geometry content but only certain facets of algebra and calculus may be influenced by spatial skills. Why might particular facets of spatial ability influence particular domains (or subcomponents of domains) of mathematics achievement?

Perhaps the most obvious mechanism is that many mathematical domains are inherently spatial. Geometry involves working with two and three dimensional figures, and both algebra and calculus involve working with lines or curves on Cartesian graphs. Perhaps the reason why mental rotation and other forms of 3-D spatial visualization are especially influential in the domains of geometry and calculus is that the spatial aspects of the requisite mathematics are not static. In geometry, students learn about their invariance, symmetry, and *transformations* of shapes (Jones, 2002). Calculus is similarly about transformations – to find an integral, one must consider the cumulative area of rectangles under a curve over a range of x values; finding a derivative requires considering how the slope of the

Ability	Description of Tasks	Example
Recognition and construction of nets	1. Identification of cuboids nets 2. Construction of a cylinder net 3. Construction of a triangular prism net 4. Identification of pyramid nets	Complete the following net in a proper manner to construct a triangular prism when folded.
Manipulation of 3D shapes representation modes	5. Translation of an orthogonal view to isometric 6. Translation of a side projection view to an orthogonal one 7&8. Recognition of parallel/perpendicular edges of a cube drawn in an isometric view 9&10. Enumeration of the triangular faces of a triangular pyramid/prism drawn in a transparent view	Draw the front, side and top view of the object. 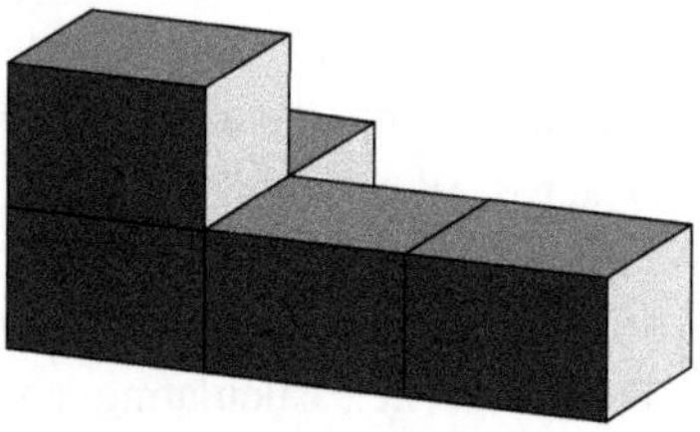
Structuring 3D arrays of cubes	11. Enumeration of the cubes needed to transform an object to a cuboid 12. Enumeration of the cubes and cuboids that fit in a box (the box is not empty) 13. Enumeration of the cubes that fit in an open/not empty box 14&15. Enumeration of the cubes that fit in an empty box	How many unit-sized cubes can fit in the box? 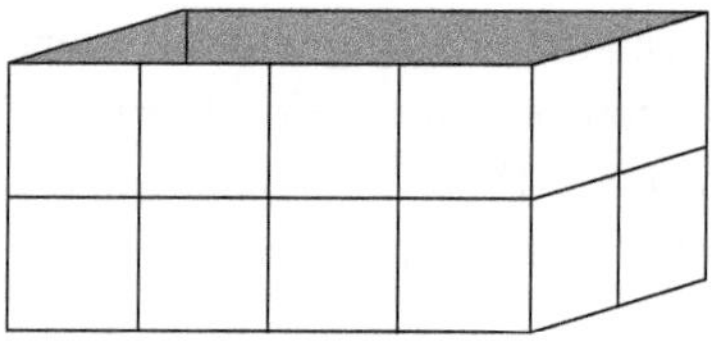
Recognition of 3D shapes' properties	16. Recognition of cuboids 17. Recognition of solids that have a specific number of vertices 18,19&20. Enumerating the vertices/faces/edges of pyramids	Circle the solids that have at least 8 vertices. 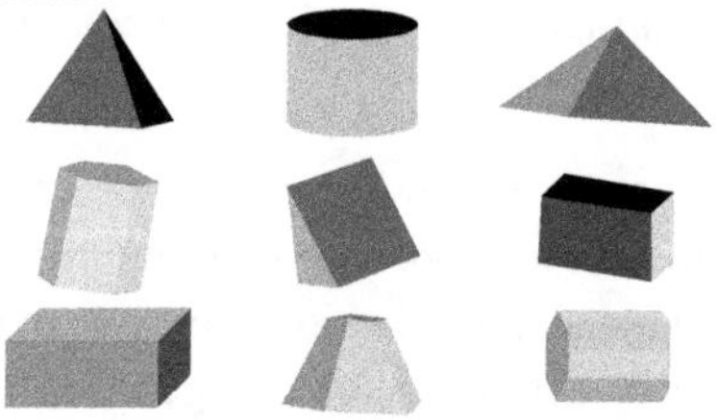
Calculation of the volume and the area of solids	21. Calculation of the area of a solid constructed by unit-sized cubes 22&23. Calculation of the area /volume of cuboids presented as open nets 24. Comparing the capacity of rectangular and cylinder reservoirs	How much paper is needed to wrap the box? 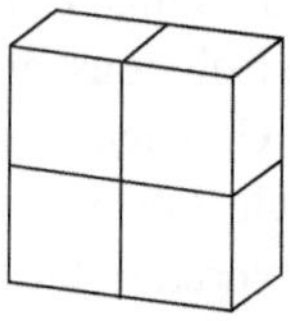
Comparison of 3D shapes properties	25. Right/wrong statements referring to the elements and properties of three solids 26&27. Exploration of the Euler's rule in pyramids/extension in prisms	Which of the following statements are wrong? (a) The faces of prisms and cuboids are rectangles, (b) the base of prisms and cuboids could be a rectangle and (c) the base of prisms and cuboids could be a triangle

Figure 5.4 *Classifications of spatial abilities (from Christou, 2010, p. 209. Copyright 2010 by Springer Science+Business Media B.V. Reprinted with permission)*

tangent to the curve changes as the x value changes (Bremigan, 2005; Sorby et al., 2013). Thus, effective mathematics instruction in these fields involves a lot of object manipulation and visualization (Kirby & Boulter, 1999), and mentally imagining these phenomena in class may draw on exactly the same components skills as imagining the rotation of block figures or flat paper being folded into 3-D shapes. Perhaps the observed lower impact of spatial skills such as mental rotation on algebra compared with geometry and calculus is due to the fact that algebra (especially solving equations) is not as dependent on visualization and rotation of objects or figures (Battista, 1981; Weckbacher & Okamoto, 2014). As previously mentioned, the graphing functions component of algebra may be more linked to 3-D spatial processing but this connection has not yet been tested.

The mechanism by which VSWM impacts mathematics performance is that VSWM capacity is thought to be a "mental blackboard" on which operations are carried out with the help of internal visual imagery (Heathcote, 1994). The connection between VSWM and mental arithmetic is well established (Trbovich & LeFevre, 2003) and, while not necessarily the focus, mental arithmetic certainly occurs in higher-level mathematics. Ashcraft (1996) argues that VSWM is necessary for success in math because one must accurately perceive the visuospatial location of digits and variables within mathematics problems in order to solve them. Perhaps this explains the potentially greater impact of VSWM in algebra compared with geometry – the symbolic nature of algebraic equations may require more processing of numerical and variable locations, operations, and mental arithmetic. The role of VSWM has not yet been tested in calculus, but it could be predicted that students with greater VSWM capacities should have greater success with the symbolic, algebraic components in calculus as well.

It could also be argued that VSWM is where mental rotation and other visuospatial processing takes place (Heathcote, 1994), so limited VSWM necessarily restricts the spatial processing that can occur, regardless of individuals' skill with particular types of processing. However, for geometry, calculus, and some component skills in algebra (and likely other facets of algebra that are yet untested), 3-D spatial visualization may mediate the relation between working memory and math achievement (Tolar et al., 2009). Further research is certainly necessary to tease apart the relations between these two key spatial variables.

Regardless of the specific spatial skills that are influential for mathematics success, there is one other important mechanism to consider. This stems from the fact that students who do not have strong spatial skills perceive themselves to be poorer in math – even if they don't actually earn lower math scores (Weckbacher & Okamoto, 2014). Countless studies have shown that believing you will not succeed in mathematics leads to failure in mathematics, while liking or feeling you are competent in math leads to success (e.g., Eccles et al., 1983; Elliot & Church, 1997). If deficits in spatial skills cause students to doubt their competence, they are unlikely to succeed in or to pursue further study of mathematics. To date, this has only been tested explicitly with mental rotation; however, it is conceivable that the same kind of effect would be found for deficits in other spatial skills, perhaps especially VSWM as math anxiety/worry has been shown to be particularly problematic for students with low working memory (Ashcraft & Kirk, 2001).

Future Directions

It is now well established that spatial skills predict numerical skills, cross-sectionally and longitudinally, across a wide variety of age spans and using appropriate statistical controls. However, although this accomplishment is a solid one, leveraging it in education requires further work. We need to move beyond correlational analyses to evaluation of causal effects. The most obvious experiments involve intervening to improve spatial skills, and we know we can do so effectively, although it would be nice to know more about best methods, necessary duration, and other parameters of training (Uttal et al., 2013). Showing transfer to numerical skills may be a challenge, however; existing studies have shown a mixed bag of positive and negative results. One fear is that changes may be only local or at best only moderately generalizable, as research attempting to increase performance on various cognitive tasks by training working memory has arguably shown (Shipstead, Redick, & Engle, 2012).

We may be able to improve training experiments by probing more deeply into the nature of spatial–numerical linkages. As discussed in this chapter, there are many different spatial skills as well as many different mathematical operations taught at widely different ages. So, for example, it is possible that effects may vary with children's age and whether they are learning a new mathematical concept or operation or practicing one already acquired. Novice learners might rely on spatial representations to aid them in acquiring new numerical concepts (Jordan et al., 2008; McKenzie et al., 2003; Uttal & Cohen, 2012) but spatial representations might become less critical as children acquire domain-specific knowledge (e.g., memorized arithmetic facts) and algorithms for solving problems. This phenomenon has been observed among adults, for whom spatial skills are strongly related to STEM performance among novices but less so among experts, who come to rely on more knowledge-based, verbal, and analytical strategies (Hambrick et al., 2012; Stieff, 2007; Uttal & Cohen, 2012).

However, there is some contrary evidence. For example, Mix and colleagues (2016) performed an analysis in which they divided mathematics tests into those covering familiar versus novel content at each grade level and found few clear patterns of spatial predictors (although block design did predict a better grasp of novel content at all three grade levels). Furthermore, recall that Amalric and Dehaene (2016) found a great deal of overlap between the brain areas used for spatial and mathematical processing, even in expert mathematicians. Along similar lines, one study found that VSWM predicts arithmetic performance among younger children (ages 6–7, the age at which arithmetic is first introduced in school) but not older children (ages 8–9) (McKenzie et al., 2003). But another study found that VSWM predicted mathematics performance at kindergarten, 3rd grade, and 6th grade, and indeed was the strongest spatial predictor at 6th grade (Mix et al.,

2016). Thus, caution is warranted about the idea that spatial thinking is most important for initial mathematics learning.

There are other versions of the general hypothesis that we need to get more specific about in terms of the nature of the linkage between spatial and mathematical cognition – for example, the work on spatial scaling and proportional reasoning discussed earlier in this chapter or the possibility that a spatial turn of mind is most important because it suggests strategies such as sketching during problem-solving that are known to be helpful (Miller-Cotto et al., under review). Evaluating these ideas will be the challenge for the next decade.

References

Alibali, M. W. & DiRusso, A. A. (1999). The function of gesture in learning to count: More than keeping track. *Cognitive Development, 14*(1), 37–56. https://doi.org/10.1016/s0885-2014(99)80017-3

Amalric, M. & Dehaene, S. (2016). Origins of the brain networks for advanced mathematics in expert mathematicians.*Proceedings of the National Academy of Sciences, 113*, 4909–4917. https://doi.org/10.1073/pnas.1603205113

Ansari, D. & Lyons, I.M. (2016). Cognitive neuroscience and mathematics learning: How far have we come? Where do we need to go? *ZDM Mathematics Education, 48*, 379–383. https://doi.org/10.1007/s11858-016–0782-z

Ashcraft, M. H. (1996). Cognitive psychology and simple arithmetic: A review and summary of new directions. In B. Butterworth (ed.), *Mathematical cognition. Vol. 1* (pp. 3–34). Hove, UK: Psychology Press. https://doi.org/10.1037/0096–3445.130.2.224

Ashcraft, M. H. & Kirk, E. P. (2001). The relationships among working memory, math anxiety, and performance. *Journal of Experimental Psychology: General, 130*(2), 243–248. https://doi.org/10.1037/0096–3445.130.2.224

Baddeley, A. D. & Hitch, G. (1974). Working memory. In G. Bower (ed.), *Recent advances in learning and motivation* Vol. *8* (pp. 47–89). New York: Academic Press.

Barth, H. & Paladino, A. M. (2011). The development of numerical estimation: Evidence against a representational shift. *Developmental Science, 14*(1), 125–135. https://doi.org/10.1111/j.1467–7687.2010.00962.x

Barth, H., Slusser, E., Cohen, D., & Paladino, A. (2011). A sense of proportion: Commentary on Opfer, Siegler and Young. *Developmental Science, 14*(5), 1205–1206. https://doi.org/10.1111/j.1467–7687.2011.01081.x

Battista, M. (1981). The interaction between two instructional treatments of algebraic structures and spatial-visualization ability. *The Journal of Educational Research, 74*(5), 337–341. https://doi.org/10.1080/00220671.1981.10885326

(1990). Spatial visualization and gender differences in high school geometry. *Journal for Research in Mathematics Education, 21*(1), 47–60. https://doi.org/10.2307/749456

Battista, M. T., Wheatley, G. H., & Talsma, G. (1982). The importance of spatial visualization and cognitive development for geometry learning in preservice elementary teachers. *Journal for Research in Mathematics Education, 13*(5), 332–340. https://doi.org/10.2307/749007

Blajenkova, O., Kozhevnikov, M., & Motes, M. A. (2006). Object-spatial imagery: A new self-report imagery questionnaire. *Applied Cognitive Psychology*, *20*(2), 239–263. https://doi.org/10.1002/acp.1182

Blazhenkova, O., Becker, M., & Kozhevnikov, M. (2011). Object–spatial imagery and verbal cognitive styles in children and adolescents: Developmental trajectories in relation to ability. *Learning and Individual Differences*, *21*(3), 281–287. https://doi.org/10.1016/j.lindif.2010.11.012

Booth, J. L. & Siegler, R. S. (2006). Developmental and individual differences in pure numerical estimation. *Developmental Psychology*, *41*(6), 189–201. https://doi.org/10.1037/0012–1649.41.6.189

   (2008). Numerical magnitude representations influence arithmetic learning. *Child Development*, *79*(4), 1016–1031. https://doi.org/10.1111/j.1467–8624.2008.01173.x

Bremigan, E. G. (2005). An analysis of diagram modification and construction in students' solutions to applied calculus problems. *Journal for Research in Mathematics Education*, *36*(3), 248–277.

Carey, S. (2009). *The origin of concepts*. Oxford: Oxford University Press.

Casey, B. M., Dearing, E., Dulaney, A., Heyman, M., & Springer, R. (2014). Young girls' spatial and arithmetic performance: The mediating role of maternal supportive interactions during joint spatial problem solving. *Early Childhood Research Quarterly*, *29*(4), 636–648. https://doi.org/10.1016/j.ecresq.2014.07.005

Casey, M. B., Nuttall, R. L., & Pezaris, E. (1997). Mediators of gender differences in mathematics college entrance test scores: A comparison of spatial skills with internalized beliefs and anxieties. *Developmental Psychology*, *33*(4), 669. http://dx.doi.org/10.1037/0012–1649.33.4.669

Casey, M. B., Nuttall, R., Pezaris, E., & Benbow, C. P. (1995). The influence of spatial ability on gender differences in mathematics college entrance test-scores across diverse samples. *Developmental Psychology*, *31*(4), 697–705. https://doi.org/10.1037/0012–1649.31.4.697

Castles, A., Rastle, K., & Nation, K. (2018). Ending the reading wars: Reading acquisition from novice to expert. *Psychological Science in the Public Interest*, *19*(1), 5–51.

Caviola, S., Mammarella, I. C., Cornoldi, C., & Lucangeli, D. (2012). The involvement of working memory in children's exact and approximate mental addition. *Journal of Experimental Child Psychology*, *112*(2), 141–160. https://doi.org/10.1016/j.jecp.2012.02.005

Cheng, Y. L. & Mix, K. S. (2012). Spatial training improves children's mathematics ability. *Journal of Cognition and Development*, *15*(1), 2–11. https://doi.org/10.1080/15248372.2012.725186

Cromley, J. G., Booth, J. L., Wills, T.W., Chang, B.L., Shipley, T.F., Zahner, W., Tran, N., & Madeja, M. (2017). Relation of spatial skills to high school calculus proficiency: A brief report. *Mathematical Thinking and Learning*, *19*(1), 55–68.

Dehaene, S., Bossini, S., & Giraux, P. (1993). The mental representation of parity and number magnitude. *Journal of Experimental Psychology: General*, *122*(3), 371–396. https://doi.org/10.1037/0096–3445.122.3.371

Dehaene, S., Izard, V., Pica, P., & Spelke, E. (2006). Core knowledge of geometry in an Amazonian indigene group. *Science*, *311*(5759), 381–384.

Dehaene, S., Izard, V., Spelke, E., & Pica, P. (2008). Log or linear? Distinct intuitions of the number scale in western and Amazonian indigene cultures. *Science*, *320*(5880), 1217–1220. https://doi.org/10.1126/science.1156540

de Hevia, M. D. & Spelke, E. S. (2010). Number-space mapping in human infants. *Psychological Science*, *21*(5), 653–660. https://doi.org/10.1177 /0956797610366091

Delgado, A. R. & Prieto, G. (2004). Cognitive mediators and sex-related differences in mathematics. *Intelligence*, *32*(1), 25–32. https://doi.org/10.1016/S0160-2896(03) 00061-8

Duffy, S., Huttenlocher, J., & Levine, S. (2005). It is all relative: How young children encode extent. *Journal of Cognition & Development*, *6*(1), 51–63. https://doi.org/10.1207 /s15327647jcd0601_4

Ebersbach, M. (2015). Evidence for a spatial–numerical association in kindergartners using a number line task. *Journal of Cognition and Development*, *16*(1), 118–128. https:// doi.org/10.1080/15248372.2013.805134

Ebersbach, M., Luwel, K., Frick, A., Onghena, P., & Verschaffel, L. (2008). The relationship between the shape of the mental number line and familiarity with numbers in 5- to 9-year old children: Evidence for a segmented linear model. *Journal of Experimental Child Psychology*, *99*(1), 1–17. https://doi.org/10.1016/j.jecp.2007 .08.006

Eccles, J., Adler, T. F., Futterman, R., Goff, S. B., Kaczala, C. M., Meece, J., & Midgley, C. (1983). Expectancies, values and academic behaviors. In J. T. Spence (ed.), *Achievement and achievement motives*. San Francisco: W. H. Freeman.

Elliot, A. J. & Church, M. A. (1997). A hierarchical model of approach and avoidance achievement motivation. *Journal of Personality and Social Psychology*, *72*(1), 218–232. https://doi.org/10.1037/0022–3514.72.1.218

Feigenson, L., Dehaene, S., & Spelke, E. (2004). Core systems of number. *Trends in Cognitive Sciences*, *8*(7), 307–314. https://doi.org/10.1016/j.tics.2004.05.002

Frick, A. & Newcombe, N. S. (2012). Getting the big picture: Development of spatial scaling abilities. *Cognitive Development*, *27*(3), 270–282. https://doi.org/10.1016/j.cogdev .2012.05.004

Friedman, L. (1995). The space factor in mathematics: Gender differences. *Review of Educational Research*, *65*(1), 22–50.

Fuchs, L. S., Schumacher, R. F., Long, J., Namkung, J., Hamlett, C. L., Cirino, P. T., Changas, P. (2013). Improving at-risk learners' understanding of fractions. *Journal of Educational Psychology*, *105*(3), 683–700. https://doi.org/10.1037 /a0032446

Gathercole, S. E. & Pickering, S. J. (2000). Working memory deficits in children with low achievements in the national curriculum at 7 years of age. *British Journal of Educational Psychology*, *70*(2), 177–194. https://doi.org/10.1348 /000709900158047

Gathercole, S. E., Pickering, S. J., Ambridge, B., & Wearing, H. (2004). The structure of working memory from 4 to 15 years of age. *Developmental Psychology*, *40*(2), 177–190. https://doi.org/10.1037/0012–1649.40.2.177

Geary, D. C., Hoard, M. K., Byrd-Craven, J., & Catherine DeSoto, M. (2004). Strategy choices in simple and complex addition: Contributions of working memory and counting knowledge for children with mathematical disability. *Journal of Experimental Child Psychology*, *88*(2), 121–151. https://doi.org/10.1016/j.jecp .2004.03.002

Geary, D. C., Hoard, M. K., Byrd-Craven, J., Nugent, L., & Numtee, C. (2007). Cognitive mechanisms underlying achievement deficits in children with mathematical learning disability. *Child Development, 78*(4), 1343–1359. https://doi.org/10.1111/j .1467–8624.2007.01069.x

Giofrè, D., Mammarella, I. C., Ronconi, L., & Cornoldi, C. (2013). Visuospatial working memory in intuitive geometry, and in academic achievement in geometry. *Learning and Individual Differences, 23*, 114–122. https://doi.org/10.1016/j.lindif.2012.09 .012

Grabner, R. H., Ansari, D., Koschutnig, K., Reishofer, G., Ebner, F., & Neuper, C. (2009). To retrieve or to calculate? Left angular gyrus mediates the retrieval of arithmetic facts during problem solving. *Neuropsychologia, 47*(2), 604–608. https://doi.org/10 .1016/j.neuropsychologia.2008.10.013

Grabner, R. H., Ansari, D., Reishofer, G., Stern, E., Ebner, F., & Neuper, C. (2007). Individual differences in mathematical competence predict parietal brain activation during mental calculation. *NeuroImage, 38*(2), 346–356. https://doi.org/10.1016/j .neuroimage.2007.07.041

Grissmer, D., Mashburn, A., Cottone, E., Brock, L., Murrah, W., Blodgett, J., Cameron, C. (2013). *The efficacy of minds in motion on children's development of executive function, visuo-spatial and math skills.* Paper presented at the Society for Research in Educational Effectiveness Conference, Washington, DC.

Gunderson, E. A., Ramirez, G., Beilock, S. L., & Levine, S. C. (2012). The relation between spatial skill and early number knowledge: The role of the linear number line. *Developmental Psychology, 48*(5), 1229–1241. https://doi.org/10.1037/a0027433

Halberda, J. & Feigenson, L. (2008). Developmental change in the acuity of the "number sense": The approximate number system in 3-, 4-, 5-, and 6-year-olds and adults. *Developmental Psychology, 44*(5), 1457–1465. https://doi.org/10.1037/a0012682

Hambrick, D. Z., Libarkin, J. C., Petcovic, H. L., Baker, K. M., Elkins, J., Callahan, C. N., . . . LaDue, N. D. (2012). A test of the circumvention-of-limits hypothesis in scientific problem solving: The case of geological bedrock mapping. *Journal of Experimental Psychology: General, 141*(3), 397–403. https://doi.org/10.1037/a0025927 and https://doi.org/10.1037/a0025927.supp (Supplemental)

Hamdan, N. & Gunderson, E. A. (2016). The number line is a critical spatial-numerical representation: Evidence from a fraction intervention. *Developmental Psychology,* https://doi.org/10.1037/dev0000252 and https://doi.org/10.1037/dev0000252.supp (Supplemental)

Hawes, Z., Moss, J., Caswell, B., Naqvi, S., & MacKinnon, S. (2017). Enhancing children's spatial and numerical skills through a dynamic spatial approach to early geometry instruction: Effects of a 32-week intervention. *Cognition and Instruction, 35*(3), 236–264. https://doi.org/10.1080/07370008.2017.1323902

Hawes, Z., Moss, J., Caswell, B., & Poliszczuk, D. (2015). Effects of mental rotation training on children's spatial and mathematics performance: A randomized controlled study. *Trends in Neuroscience and Education, 4*(3), 60–68. https://doi.org/10.1016/j.tine .2015.05.001

Heathcote, D. (1994). The role of visuo-spatial working memory in the mental addition of multi-digit addends. *Current Psychology of Cognition, 13*, 207–245.

Hegarty, M. & Kozhevnikov, M. (1999). Types of visual-spatial representations and mathe-matical problem solving. *Journal of Educational Psychology, 91*(4), 684–689. https://doi.org/10.1037/0022–0663.91.4.684

Huttenlocher, J., Duffy, S., & Levine, S. (2002). Infants and toddlers discriminate amount: Are they measuring? *Psychological Science, 13*(3), 244.

Huttenlocher, J., Hedges, L. V., Corrigan, B., & Crawford, L. E. (2004). Spatial categories and the estimation of location. *Cognition, 93*(2), 75–97. https://doi.org/10.1016/j.cognition.2003.10.006

Huttenlocher, J., Hedges, L. V., & Vevea, J. L. (2000). Why do categories affect stimulus judgment? *Journal of Experimental Psychology: General, 129*(2), 220–241. https://doi.org/10.1037/0096–3445.129.2.220

Huttenlocher, J., Jordan, N. C., & Levine, S. C. (1994). A mental model for early arithmetic. *Journal of Experimental Psychology: General, 123*(3), 284–296. https://doi.org/10.1037/0096–3445.123.3.284

Huttenlocher, J., Newcombe, N., & Sandberg, E. H. (1994). The coding of spatial location in young children. *Cognitive Psychology, 27*(2), 115–147. https://doi.org/10.1006/cogp.1994.1014

Jones, K. (2001). Spatial thinking and visualisation. In K. Jones, *Teaching and learning geometry.* (pp. 55–56). London: Royal Society.

(2002). Issues in the teaching and learning of geometry. In L. Haggarty (ed.), *Aspects of teaching secondary mathematics: Perspectives on practice* (pp. 121–139). London: Routledge. https://doi.org/10.4324/9780203165874

Jordan, N. C., Kaplan, D., Ramineni, C., & Locuniak, M. N. (2008). Development of number combination skill in the early school years: When do fingers help? *Developmental Science, 11*(5), 662–668. https://doi.org/10.1111/j.1467–7687.2008.00715.x

Kaufmann, L., Wood, G., Rubinsten, O., & Henik, A. (2011). Meta-analyses of developmental fMRI studies investigating typical and atypical trajectories of number processing and calculation. *Developmental Neuropsychology, 36*(6), 763–787. https://doi.org/10.1080/87565641.2010.549884

Kim, D. & Opfer, J. E. (2017). A unified framework for bounded and unbounded numerical estimation. *Developmental Psychology, 53*(6), 1088. http://dx.doi.org/10.1037/dev0000305

Kinach, B. M. (2012). Fostering spatial vs. metric understanding in geometry. *Mathematics Teacher, 105*(7), 534–540.

Kirby, J. R. & Boulter, D. R. (1999). Spatial ability and transformational geometry. *European Journal of Psychology of Education, 14*(2), 283–294. https://doi.org/10.1007/BF03172970

Krajewski, K. & Schneider, W. (2009). Exploring the impact of phonological awareness, visual–spatial working memory, and preschool quantity–number competencies on mathematics achievement in elementary school: Findings from a 3-year longitudinal study. *Journal of Experimental Child Psychology, 103*(4), 516–531. http://dx.doi.org/10.1016/j.jecp.2009.03.009

Kyttälä, M., Aunio, P., Lehto, J. E., Van Luit, J. E. H., & Hautamäki, J. (2003). Visuospatial working memory and early numeracy. *Educational and Child Psychology, 20*(3), 65–76.

Kyttälä, M. & Lehto, J. E. (2008). Some factors underlying mathematical performance: The role of visuospatial working memory and non-verbal intelligence. *European Journal of Psychology of Education, 23*(1), 77–94. https://doi.org/10.1007/BF03173141

Laski, E. V. & Siegler, R. S. (2007). Is 27 a big number? Correlational and causal connections among numerical categorization, number line estimation, and numerical magnitude comparison. *Child Development, 78*(6), 1723–1743. https://doi.org/10.1111/j.1467–8624.2007.01087.x

Le Corre, M. (2014). Children acquire the later-greater principle after the cardinal principle. *British Journal of Developmental Psychology*, *32*(2), 163–177. https://doi.org/10.1111/bjdp.12029

Le Corre, M. & Carey, S. (2007). One, two, three, four, nothing more: An investigation of the conceptual sources of the verbal counting principles. *Cognition*, *105*, 395–438. https://doi.org/10.1016/j.cognition.2006.10.005

LeFevre, J.-A., Jimenez Lira, C., Sowinski, C., Cankaya, O., Kamawar, D., & Skwarchuk, S.-L. (2013). Charting the role of the number line in mathematical development. *Frontiers in Psychology*, *4*, 1–9. https://doi.org/10.3389/fpsyg.2013.00641

Logan, T. (2015). The influence of test mode and visuospatial ability on mathematics assessment performance. *Mathematics Education Research Journal*, *27*(4), 423–441. https://doi.org/10.1007/s13394-015-0143-1

Lourenco, S. F. & Longo, M. R. (2010). General magnitude representation in human infants. *Psychological Science*, *21*(6), 878–881. https://doi.org/10.1177/0956797610370158

Lowrie, T., Logan, T., & Ramful, A. (2017). Visuospatial training improves elementary students' mathematics performance. *British Journal of Educational Psychology*, *87*(2), 170–186. https://doi.org/10.1111/bjep.12142

McKenzie, B., Bull, R., & Gray, C. (2003). The effects of phonological and visuospatial interference on children's arithmetical performance. *Educational and Child Psychology*, *20*(3), 93–108.

Meyer, M. L., Salimpoor, V. N., Wu, S. S., Geary, D. C., & Menon, V. (2010). Differential contribution of specific working memory components to mathematics achievement in 2nd and 3rd graders. *Learning and Individual Differences*, *20*(2), 101–109. https://doi.org/10.1016/j.lindif.2009.08.004

Miller-Cotto, D., Booth, J. L., Chang, B. L., Cromley, J. G., Newcombe, N. S., & Williams, T. A. (under review). Sketching and verbal self-explanation: Do they help middle school children solve math and science problems?

Mix, K. S. & Cheng, Y. L. (2012). The relation between space and math: developmental and educational implications. In J. B. Benson (ed.), *Advances in child development and behavior*, Vol. 42 (pp. 197–243). New York: Elsevier.

Mix, K. S., Levine, S. C., Cheng, Y.-L., Young, C., Hambrick, D. Z., Ping, R., & Konstantopoulos, S. (2016). Separate but correlated: The latent structure of space and mathematics across development. *Journal of Experimental Psychology: General*, *145*(9), 1206–1227.

Moeller, K., Pixner, S., Kaufmann, L., & Nuerk, H.-C. (2009). Children's early mental number line: Logarithmic or decomposed linear? *Journal of Experimental Child Psychology*, *103*(4), 503–515. https://doi.org/10.1016/j.jecp.2009.02.006

Möhring, W., Newcombe, N. S., & Frick, A. (2015). The relation between spatial thinking and proportional reasoning in preschoolers. *Journal of Experimental Child Psychology*, *132*, 213–220. https://doi.org/10.1016/j.jecp.2015.01.005

Möhring, W., Newcombe, N., Levine, S. C., & Frick, A. (2014). *A matter of proportions: Spatial scaling is related to proportional reasoning in 4- and 5-year-olds*. Paper presented at the Spatial Cognition Conference, Bremen, Germany.

  (2016). Spatial proportional reasoning is associated with formal knowledge about fractions. *Journal of Cognition and Development*, *17*(1), 67–84. https://doi.org/10.1080/15248372.2014.996289

Nath, S. & Szücs, D. (2014). Construction play and cognitive skills associated with the development of mathematical abilities in 7-year-old children. *Learning and Instruction*, *32*(0), 73–80. https://doi.org/10.1016/j.learninstruc.2014.01.006

Opfer, J. E. & Siegler, R. S. (2007). Representational change and children's numerical estimation. *Cognitive Psychology*, *55*(3), 169–195. https://doi.org/10.1016/j.cogpsych.2006.09.002

Opfer, J. E., Siegler, R. S., & Young, C. J. (2011). The powers of noise-fitting: Reply to Barth and Paladino. *Developmental Science*, *14*(5), 1194–1204. https://doi.org/10.1111/j.1467–7687.2011.01070.x

Opfer, J. E., Thompson, C. A., & Kim, D. (2016). Free versus anchored numerical estimation: A unified approach. *Cognition*, *149*, 11–17. https://doi.org/10.1016/j.cognition.2015.11.015

Peng, P., Namkung, J., Barnes, M., & Sun, C. (2016). A meta-analysis of mathematics and working memory: Moderating effects of working memory domain, type of mathematics skill, and sample characteristics. *Journal of Educational Psychology*, *108*(4), 455. https://doi.org/10.1037/edu0000079

Piaget, J. & Inhelder, B. (1975). *The origins of the idea of chance in children*. New York: Norton.

Pinel, P., Piazza, M., Le Bihan, D., & Dehaene, S. (2004). Distributed and overlapping cerebral representations of number, size, and luminance during comparative judgments. *Neuron*, *41*, 1–20. https://doi.org/10.1016/S0896-6273(04)00107–2

Pittalis, M. & Christou, C. (2010). Types of reasoning in 3D geometry thinking and their relation with spatial ability. *Educational Studies in Mathematics*, *75*(2), 191–212. https://doi.org/10.1007/s10649-010–9251-8

Rasmussen, C. & Bisanz, J. (2005). Representation and working memory in early arithmetic. *Journal of Experimental Child Psychology*, *91*(2), 137–157. https://doi.org/10.1016/j.jecp.2005.01.004

Rayner, K., Foorman, B., Perfetti, C., Pesetsky, D., & Seidenberg, M. (2001). How psychological science informs the teaching of reading. *Psychological Science in the Public Interest*, *2*(2), 31–74. https://doi.org/10.1111/1529–1006.00004

Reuhkala, M. (2001). Mathematical skills in ninth-graders: Relationship with visuo-spatial abilities and working memory. *Educational Psychology*, *21*(4), 387–399. https://doi.org/10.1080/01443410120090786

Royal Society and JMC (Joint Mathematical Council). (2001), *Teaching and Learning Geometry 11–19*. London: Royal Society and JMC.

Rugani, R & de Hevia, M.-D. (2017). Number-space associations without language: Evidence from 4 preverbal human infants and non-human animal species. *Psychonomic Bulletin & Review*, *24*, 352–369.

Samuels, J. (2010). The use of technology and visualization in calculus instruction (Unpublished doctoral dissertation). Teachers College, New York.

Saxe, G. B., Diakow, R., & Gearhart, M. (2013). Towards curricular coherence in integers and fractions: A study of the efficacy of a lesson sequence that uses the number line as the principal representational context. *ZDM Mathematics Journal*, *45*(3), 343–364. https://doi.org/10.1007/s11858-012–0466-2

Sekuler, R. & Mierkiewicz, D. (1977). Children's judgments of numerical inequality. *Child Development*, *48*(2), 630–633. https://doi.org/10.2307/1128664

Sella, F., Berteletti, I., Lucangeli, D., & Zorzi, M. (2017). Preschool children use space, rather than counting, to infer the numerical magnitude of digits: Evidence for a spatial mapping principle. *Cognition, 158,* 56–67. http://dx.doi.org/10.1016/j.cognition .2016.10.010

Shea, D. L., Lubinski, D., & Benbow, C. P. (2001). Importance of assessing spatial ability in intellectually talented young adolescents: A 20-year longitudinal study. *Journal of Educational Psychology, 93*(3), 604–614. https://doi.org/10.1037/0022–0663.93.3.604

Shepard, R. N. & Metzler, J. (1971). Mental rotation of three-dimensional objects. *Science, 171*(3972), 701–702.

Shipstead, Z., Redick, T. S., & Engle, R. W. (2012). Is working memory training effective?. *Psychological Bulletin, 138*(4), 628–154.

Siegler, R. S. (2009). Improving the numerical understanding of children from low-income families. *Child Development Perspectives, 3*(2), 118–124. https://doi.org/10.1111/j .1750–8606.2009.00090.x

Siegler, R. S. & Booth, J. L. (2004). Development of numerical estimation in young children. *Child Development, 75,* 428–444. https://doi.org/10.1111/j.1467–8624.2004.00684.x

(2005). Development of numerical estimation. In J. I. D. Campbell (ed.), *Handbook of mathematical cognition* (pp. 197–212). New York: Psychology Press.

Siegler, R. S. & Opfer, J. E. (2003). The development of numerical estimation: Evidence for multiple representations of numerical quantity. *Psychological Science, 14*(3), 237–243. https://doi.org/10.1111/1467–9280.02438

Siegler, R. S. & Ramani, G. B. (2008). Playing linear numerical board games promotes low-income children's numerical development. *Developmental Science, 11*(5), 655–661. https://doi.org/10.1111/j.1467–7687.2008.00714.x

(2009). Playing linear number board games – but not circular ones – improves low-income preschoolers' numerical understanding. *Journal of Educational Psychology, 101*(3), 545–560. https://doi.org/10.1037/a0014239

Slusser, E. B., Santiago, R. T., & Barth, H. C. (2013). Developmental change in numerical estimation. *Journal of Experimental Psychology: General, 142*(1), 193–208. https:// doi.org/10.1037/a0028560

Sorby, S., Casey, B., Veurink, N., & Dulaney, A. (2013). The role of spatial training in improving spatial and calculus performance in engineering students. *Learning and Individual Differences, 26,* 20–29. https://doi.org/10.1016/j.lindif.2013.03.010

Soto-Calvo, E., Simmons, F. R., Willis, C., & Adams, A.-M. (2015). Identifying the cognitive predictors of early counting and calculation skills: Evidence from a longitudinal study. *Journal of Experimental Child Psychology, 140,* 16–37. https://doi.org/10 .1016/j.jecp.2015.06.011

Spelke, E. S. & Tsivkin, S. (2001). Language and number: A bilingual training study. *Cognition, 78,* 45–88.

Spence, I. & Krizel, P. (1994). Children's perception of proportion in graphs. *Child Development, 65*(4), 1193–1213. https://doi.org/10.2307/1131314

Stieff, M. (2007). Mental rotation and diagrammatic reasoning in science. *Learning and Instruction, 17*(2), 219–234. https://doi.org/10.1016/j.learninstruc.2007.01.012

Tolar, T. D., Lederberg, A. R., & Fletcher, J. M. (2009) A structural model of algebra achievement: Computational fluency and spatial visualisation as mediators of the effect of working memory on algebra achievement. *Educational Psychology, 29*(2), 239–266. https://doi.org/10.1080/01443410802708903

Trbovich, P. & LeFevre, J. A. (2003). Phonological and visual working memory in mental addition. *Memory* and *Cognition, 31*(5), 738–745. https://doi.org/10.3758 /bf03196112

Trezise, K. & Reeve, R. A. (2014). Working memory, worry, and algebraic ability. *Journal of Experimental Child Psychology, 121*, 120–136.

Usiskin, Z. (1988). Conceptions of school algebra and uses of variables. In A. Coxford (ed.), *Ideas* of *algebra, K-12* (pp. 8–19). Reston, VA: NCTM.

Uttal, D. H. & Cohen, C. A. (2012). Spatial thinking and STEM education: When, why, and how? *Psychology of Learning and Motivation, 57*, 147–181. https://doi.org/10.1016/B978-0-12-394293-7.00004-2

Uttal, D. H., Meadow, N. G., Tipton, E., Hand, L. L. Alden, A. R., Warren, C., & Newcombe, N. S. (2013). The malleability of spatial skills: A meta-analysis of training studies. *Psychological Bulletin, 139*, 352–402.

Vasilyeva, M. & Huttenlocher, J. (2004). Early development of scaling ability. *Developmental Psychology, 40*(5), 682–690. https://doi.org/10.1037/0012-1649.40.5.682

Verdine, B. N., Golinkoff, R. M., Hirsh-Pasek, K., & Newcombe, N. S. (2017). Links between spatial and mathematical skills across the preschool years [Monograph]. Monographs of the Society for Research in Child Development, 82,(1), Serial Number 124.

Wai, J., Lubinski, D., & Benbow, C. P. (2009). Spatial ability for STEM domains: Aligning over 50 years of cumulative psychological knowledge solidifies its importance. *Journal of Educational Psychology, 101*, 817–835. https://doi.org/10.1037/a0016127

Weckbacher, L. M. & Okamoto, Y. (2014). Mental rotation ability in relation to self-perceptions of high school geometry. *Learning and Individual Differences, 30*, 58–63. https://doi.org/10.1016/j.lindif.2013.10.007

Xenidou-Dervou, I., van der Schoot, M., & van Lieshout, E. C. D. M. (2015). Working memory and number line representations in single-digit addition: Approximate versus exact, nonsymbolic versus symbolic. *The Quarterly Journal of Experimental Psychology, 68*(6), 1148–1167. https://doi.org/10.1080/17470218.2014.977303

Ye, A., Resnick, I., Hansen, N., Rodrigues, J., Rinne, L., & Jordan, N. C. (2016). Pathways to fraction learning: Numerical abilities mediate the relation between early cognitive competencies and later fraction knowledge. *Journal of Experimental Child Psychology, 152*, 242–263. http://dx.doi.org/10.1016/j.jecp.2016.08.001

Zacks, J. M. (2007). Neuroimaging studies of mental rotation: A meta-analysis and review. *Journal of Cognitive Neuroscience, 20*(1), 1–19. https://doi.org/10.1162/jocn.2008.20013

Zorzi, M., Priftis, K., & Umilta, C. (2002). Brain damage: Neglect disrupts the mental number line. *Nature, 417*, 138–139. https://doi.org/10.1038/417138a

Zuccheri, L. & Zudini, V. (2014). History of teaching calculus. In A. Karp & G. Schubring (eds.), *Handbook on the history of mathematics education* (pp. 493–513). New York: Springer .

6 Iterative Development of Conceptual and Procedural Knowledge in Mathematics Learning and Instruction

Bethany Rittle-Johnson

When children practice solving problems, does this also enhance their understanding of the underlying concepts? Under what circumstances do abstract concepts help children invent or implement correct procedures? These questions tap a central research topic in the fields of cognitive development and educational psychology: the relations between conceptual and procedural knowledge. Delineating how these two types of knowledge interact is fundamental to understanding how knowledge development occurs.

This topic is also central to improving mathematics teaching and learning. "The relationship between computational skill and conceptual understanding is one of the oldest concerns in the psychology of mathematics" (Resnick & Ford, 1981, p. 246) and continues to be a central challenge for understanding mathematical cognition (Alcock et al., 2016). This is because proficiency in mathematics requires multiple types of knowledge, and conceptual and procedural knowledge are the most fundamental types of mathematics knowledge (Kilpatrick, Swafford, & Findell, 2001). For example, the National Assessment of Educational Progress (NAEP) focuses on measuring students' conceptual and procedural knowledge of mathematics (National Assessment Governing Board, 2014).

The first section of this chapter provides a brief history of (1) how conceptual and procedural knowledge are defined, (2) perspectives on the developmental relations between the two types of knowledge, and (3) perspectives on the ordering of instruction on the two types of knowledge. The second section reviews recent research on each of these topics: (1) methods for assessing each type of mathematics knowledge, (2) evidence for the developmental relations between the two types of knowledge, and (3) evidence for how the two types of knowledge should be taught. The chapter concludes with a discussion of the promise of research in this area for improving education.

A Brief History

Although conceptual and procedural knowledge cannot always be separated, it is useful to distinguish between the two types of knowledge to better understand knowledge development. After briefly reviewing how conceptual and procedural knowledge have been defined, I review perspectives on the developmental relations between the two types of knowledge and on the ordering of instruction on the two types of knowledge.

Defining Conceptual and Procedural Knowledge

Conceptual Knowledge. A concept is "an abstract or generic idea generalized from particular instances."[1] Knowledge of concepts is often referred to as *conceptual knowledge* (e.g., Byrnes & Wasik, 1991; Canobi, 2009; Rittle-Johnson, Siegler, & Alibali, 2001). This knowledge includes both general principles and principles underlying procedures (e.g., the order in which objects are counted does not change the cardinality of a set) (Crooks & Alibali, 2014). It can be implicit or explicit, and thus does not have to be verbalizable (e.g., Goldin Meadow, Alibali, & Church, 1993). The National Research Council adopted a similar definition in their review of the mathematics education research literature, defining it as "comprehension of mathematical concepts, operations, and relations" (Kilpatrick et al., 2001, p. 5). This type of knowledge is sometimes also called conceptual understanding or principled knowledge.

At times, mathematics education researchers have used a more constrained definition. Star (2005a) noted that: "The term *conceptual knowledge* has come to encompass not only what is known (knowledge of concepts) but also one way that concepts can be known (e.g. deeply and with rich connections)" (p. 408). This definition is based on Hiebert and LeFevre's (1986) definition in the seminal book Conceptual and procedural knowledge: The case of mathematics edited by Hiebert:

> Conceptual knowledge is characterized most clearly as knowledge that is rich in relationships. It can be thought of as a connected web of knowledge, a network in which the linking relationships are as prominent as the discrete pieces of information. Relationships pervade the individual facts and propositions so that all pieces of information are linked to some network. (pp. 3–4)

After interviewing a number of mathematics education researchers, Baroody, Feil, and Johnson (2007) suggested that conceptual knowledge should be defined as "knowledge about facts, [generalizations,] and principles" (p. 107), without requiring that the knowledge be richly connected. Empirical support for this notion comes from research on conceptual change that shows that (1) novices' conceptual knowledge is often fragmented and needs to be integrated over the course of learning and (2) experts' conceptual knowledge continues to expand and become better organized (diSessa, Gillespie, & Esterly, 2004; Schneider & Stern, 2009). Thus, there is general consensus that conceptual knowledge should be defined as knowledge of concepts. A more constrained definition requiring that the knowledge be richly connected has sometimes been used in the past, but more recent thinking views the richness of connections as a feature of conceptual knowledge that increases with expertise rather than a defining feature.

---

[1] *Merriam-Webster's Collegiate Dictionary* (2012), s.v. "concept."

Procedural Knowledge. A procedure is a series of steps or actions taken to accomplish a goal. Knowledge of procedures is often termed *procedural knowledge* (e.g., Canobi, 2009; Rittle-Johnson et al., 2001). For example, "Procedural knowledge . . . is 'knowing how,' or the knowledge of the steps required to attain various goals. Procedures have been characterized using such constructs as skills, strategies, productions, and interiorized actions" (Byrnes & Wasik, 1991, p. 777). The procedures can be (1) algorithms – a predetermined sequence of actions that will lead to the correct answer when executed correctly or (2) possible actions that must be sequenced appropriately to solve a given problem (e.g., equation-solving steps). This knowledge develops through problem-solving practice and thus is tied to particular problem types. Further, "It is the clearly sequential nature of procedures that probably sets them most apart from other forms of knowledge" (Hiebert & LeFevre, 1986, p. 6).

As with conceptual knowledge, the definition of procedural knowledge has sometimes included additional constraints. Within mathematics education, Star (2005b) noted that sometimes "the term procedural knowledge indicates not only what is known (knowledge of procedures) but also one way that procedures (algorithms) can be known (e.g., superficially and without rich connections)" (p. 408). Baroody and colleagues (2007) acknowledged that:

> some mathematics educators, including the first author of this commentary, have indeed been guilty of oversimplifying their claims and loosely or inadvertently equating "knowledge memorized by rote . . . with computational skill or procedural knowledge" (Baroody, 2003, p. 4). Mathematics education researchers (MERs) usually define procedural knowledge, however, in terms of knowledge type—as sequential or "step-by-step [prescriptions for] how to complete tasks." (p. 116)

Thus, historically, procedural knowledge has sometimes been defined more narrowly within mathematics education but there appears to be agreement that it should not be.

Within psychology, particularly in computational models, there has sometimes been the additional constraint that procedural knowledge is implicit knowledge that cannot be verbalized directly (Anderson, 1993). For example, Sun, Merrill, and Peterson (2001) concluded that: "The inaccessibility of procedural knowledge is accepted by most researchers and embodied in most computational models that capture procedural skills" (p. 206). In part, this is because the models are often of procedural knowledge that has been automatized through extensive practice. However, at least in mathematical problem-solving, people often know and use procedures that are not automatized but rather require conscious selection, reflection, and sequencing of steps (e.g., solving complex algebraic equations) and this knowledge of procedures can be verbalized (e.g., Star & Newton, 2009).

Overall, there is a general consensus that procedural knowledge is the ability to execute action sequences (i.e., procedures) to solve problems. Additional constraints on the definition have been used in some past research but are typically not made in current research on mathematical cognition.

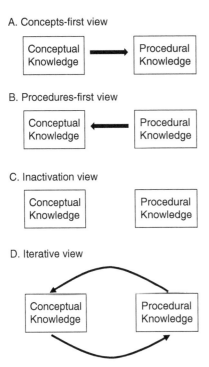

A. Concepts-first view

B. Procedures-first view

C. Inactivation view

D. Iterative view

Figure 6.1 *Schematic of four theoretical viewpoints on the causal relations between conceptual and procedural knowledge*

The majority of evidence supports an iterative view

Relations Between Conceptual and Procedural Knowledge

Historically, there have been four different theoretical viewpoints on the causal relations between conceptual and procedural knowledge (see Baroody, 2003; Haapasalo & Kadijevich, 2000; Rittle-Johnson & Siegler, 1998). See Figure 6.1 for a schematic of each view. *Concepts-first views* posit that children initially acquire conceptual knowledge, for example through parent explanations or guided by innate constraints, and then derive and build procedural knowledge from it through experience, such as repeated practice solving problems (e.g., Gelman & Williams, 1998; Gilmore, McCarthy, & Spelke, 2010; Halford, 1993). *Procedures-first views* posit that children first learn procedures, for example by means of explorative behavior, and then gradually derive conceptual knowledge from them by abstraction processes, such as representational redescription (e.g., Karmiloff-Smith, 1992; Siegler & Stern, 1998). A third possibility, sometimes labeled *inactivation view* (Haapasalo & Kadijevich, 2000), is that conceptual and procedural knowledge develop independently (Resnick, 1982; Resnick & Omanson, 1987). A fourth possibility is an *iterative view*. The causal relations are said to be bidirectional, with increases in conceptual knowledge leading to subsequent increases in procedural knowledge and vice versa (Baroody, 2003; Rittle-Johnson & Siegler, 1998; Rittle-Johnson et al., 2001).

An iterative view has several advantages over other perspectives. First, it accommodates gradual improvements in each type of knowledge over time. If knowledge is measured using continuous rather than categorical measures, it becomes clear that one type of knowledge is not well developed before the other emerges, arguing against a strict concepts- or procedures-first view. In addition, an iterative view accommodates evidence in support of concepts-first and procedures-first views, as initial knowledge can be conceptual or procedural, depending on environmental input and relevant prior knowledge of other topics. For example, even if children are born with a basic ability to track and discriminate between numerical magnitudes (Xu, Spelke, & Goddard, 2005), conceptual knowledge of numerical magnitude develops in concert with experience counting and learning the counting procedure (Muldoon et al., 2013). Third, an iterative view recognizes the role that each type of knowledge can play in the development of the other. Conceptual knowledge can help with the construction, selection and appropriate execution of problem-solving procedures (Hiebert & LeFevre, 1986). At the same time, practice implementing procedures may help students develop and deepen understanding of concepts, especially if the practice is designed to make underlying concepts more apparent (Canobi, 2009). An iterative view was not considered in early research on conceptual and procedural knowledge (for a review of this research in mathematics learning, see Rittle-Johnson & Siegler, 1998).

Ordering of Instruction on Concepts and Procedures

Mathematics educators are more concerned about the most effective way to teach content rather than how knowledge typically develops (i.e., under typical instructional conditions). Traditional mathematics instruction often focused on developing procedural knowledge, with limited attention to directly supporting conceptual knowledge. It is widely agreed that focusing instruction on procedural knowledge is not sufficient for supporting mathematics competency, in part because many students do not develop sufficient conceptual knowledge from this approach (for historical reviews, see Baroody, 2003; Kilpatrick et al., 2001; Resnick & Ford, 1981).

Currently, there is broad agreement that students need instruction that directly targets each type of knowledge. However, there is an ongoing debate between a unidirectional and a bidirectional perspective on how instruction should be sequenced (Rittle-Johnson, Schneider, & Star, 2015). The unidirectional perspective is a *conceptual-to-procedural-knowledge* perspective. The belief is that conceptual knowledge should be developed over an extended period of time prior to instruction and practice with procedures. This is based on the belief that procedural instruction interferes with gaining conceptual knowledge (Kamii & Dominick, 1997, 1998). Reform efforts in mathematics education in the United States have tended to focus on this conceptual-to-procedural-knowledge perspective (Grouws & Cebulla, 2000; NCTM, 1989, 2000, 2014). Most recently, the National Council of Teachers of Mathematics (NCTM, 2014) explicitly asserted a conceptual-to-procedural perspective in their principle that "procedural fluency follows and builds on a foundation of conceptual understanding" (p. 42). "Conceptual understanding (i.e., the comprehension and connection of concepts, operations, and relations) establishes the foundation, and is necessary, for developing procedural fluency (i.e., the meaningful and flexible use of procedures to solve problems)" (p. 7). This principle indicates that students should initially develop a foundation of conceptual understanding and that procedural knowledge should not be developed prior to the extended development of conceptual knowledge.

Alternatively, a *bidirectional* perspective is that conceptual and procedural knowledge develop iteratively, so instruction should focus on each type of knowledge from the beginning rather than waiting to teach procedural knowledge until conceptual knowledge is well established.

This perspective is implied, although not directly stated, in several consensus documents. For example, an influential report from the National Research Council identified conceptual understanding and procedural fluency as equally important and interdependent strands of mathematical proficiency (Kilpatrick, 2001). Procedural fluency was defined as "skill in carrying out procedures flexibly, accurately, efficiently and appropriately" (p. 116) and thus encompasses procedural knowledge. "Procedural fluency and conceptual understanding are often seen as competing for attention in school mathematics. But pitting skills against understanding creates a false dichotomy. As we noted earlier, the two are interwoven" (p. 122). The National Mathematics Advisory Panel (2008) came to a similar conclusion, noting the mutually reinforcing benefits of both types of knowledge. The terms "interwoven" and "mutually reinforcing" imply bidirectional relations between the two types of knowledge, although the reports do not explicitly address how instruction should support both types of knowledge.

Overall, there has been variability in how conceptual and procedural knowledge were defined and in the predicted developmental relations and the optimal ordering of instruction for conceptual and procedural knowledge. There is now general consensus for how to define each type of knowledge. In the next section, I consider evidence that addresses the second two topics.

Methods and Evidence

Ultimately, how each type of knowledge is *measured* is critical for interpreting evidence on the relations between conceptual and procedural knowledge. After reviewing different methods for measuring each type of knowledge, I consider the evidence for the developmental relations between the two types of knowledge and the impact of different instructional orderings.

Measuring Conceptual and Procedural Knowledge

The two types of knowledge must be assessed independently in order to study the relations between them, preferably using multiple measures for each type of knowledge (Schneider & Stern, 2010). Conceptual knowledge has been assessed in a large variety of ways, whereas there is much less variability in how procedural knowledge is measured.

Measures of conceptual knowledge vary in whether the tasks focus on general principles or on principles underlying procedures (Crooks & Alibali, 2014), and common tasks are outlined in Table 6.1. These tasks also vary in whether they require explicit, verbalizable knowledge or can be answered using more implicit knowledge that does not need to be explained. Measures of knowledge of general principles include translating between representational formats (e.g., matching a picture to the appropriate symbolic fraction) and comparing quantities, which are more implicit measures. Explicit measures include explaining an evaluation and generating or selecting definitions for concepts. Measures of knowledge of principles underlying procedures most often involve evaluation tasks on which children evaluate a procedure by making a categorical choice (e.g., judge the correctness of an example procedure) or by making a quality rating (e.g., rate an example procedure as very smart, kind of smart, or not so smart). In addition to these more implicit measures, children are sometimes asked to verbally justify why procedures work. All of these tasks may be completed as paper-and-pencil assessment items or answered verbally during standardized or clinical interviews (Ginsburg, 1997).

A critical feature of conceptual tasks is that they be relatively unfamiliar to participants, so that participants have to derive an answer from their conceptual knowledge rather than implement a known procedure for solving the task. For example, magnitude comparison problems are sometimes used to assess children's conceptual knowledge of number magnitude (e.g., Hecht, 1998; Schneider, Grabner, & Paetsch, 2009). However, children are sometimes taught procedures for comparing magnitudes or develop procedures with repeated practice; for these children, magnitude comparison problems are likely measuring their procedural knowledge, not their conceptual knowledge. Faulkenberry (2013) describes several other examples of conceptual tasks that could be solved using a taught procedure and suggests researchers classify the strategies children use to solve the task rather than classifying tasks themselves as conceptual or procedural. Although a fair critique, it is not feasible in most research to collect and reliably code strategy reports. Alternatively, researchers can gather information on participants' instructional histories and try to avoid using highly familiar tasks to assess conceptual knowledge.

In addition, conceptual knowledge measures are stronger if they use multiple tasks. First, use of multiple tasks intended to assess the same concept reduces the influence of task-specific characteristics (Schneider & Stern, 2010). Second, conceptual knowledge in a domain often requires knowledge of many concepts, leading to a multidimensional construct. For example, for counting, key concepts include cardinality and order-irrelevance and, for arithmetic, key concepts include place value and the commutativity and inversion principles. Although knowledge of each is related, there can be individual differences in these relationships, without

Table 6.1 *Range of tasks used to assess conceptual knowledge*

Type of task	Sample items
Knowledge of general principles	
A. Translate between representational formats	A1. Represent symbolic fractions with pictures (Hecht, 1998)
	A2. Place symbolic numbers on number lines (Siegler & Booth, 2004; Siegler, Thompson, & Schneider, 2011)
B. Compare quantities	B. Indicate which symbolic integer or fraction is larger (or smaller) (Hecht, 1998; Laski & Siegler, 2007)
C. Evaluate quality of answers given by others	C. Evaluate how much someone knows based on the quality of their errors, which are or are not consistent with principles of arithmetic (Prather & Alibali, 2008)
D. Encode key features	D. Success reconstructing examples from memory (e.g., equations), because greater conceptual knowledge helps people notice key features and chunk information, allowing for more accurate recall (McNeil & Alibali, 2004)
E. Sort examples into categories	E. Sort twelve statistics problems based on how they best go together (Lavigne, 2005)
F. Evaluate examples of concept	F1. Decide whether the number sentence 3 = 3 makes sense (Rittle-Johnson & Alibali, 1999) F2. 35 + 29 = 64. Does Alex need to count to figure out 29 + 35? (Canobi et al., 1998)
G. Explain evaluations	G. On evaluation task, provide correct explanation of choice (e.g., "29 + 35 has the same numbers as 35 + 29, so it equals 64, too.") (Canobi, 2009)
H. Generate or select definitions of concepts	H1. Define the equal sign (Knuth et al., 2006) H2. "The equal sign means two amounts are the same." Is this a good definition or not? (Matthews et al., 2012)
I. Draw concept maps	I. Construct a map that identifies main concepts in introductory statistics, showing how the concepts are related to one another (Lavigne, 2005)
Knowledge of principles underlying procedures	
J. Evaluate unfamiliar procedures	J. Decide whether it is okay for puppet to skip some items when counting (Gelman & Meck, 1983)
K. Invent principle-based shortcut procedures	K. On inversion problems such as 12 + 7 − 7, quickly stating the first number without computing (Rasmussen, Ho, & Bisanz, 2003)
L. Explain why procedures work	L. Explain why it is okay to borrow when subtract (Fuson & Kwon, 1992)

a standard hierarchy of difficulty (Dowker, 2008; Jordan, Mulhern, & Wylie, 2009; Robinson, Dube, & Beatch, 2016).

Measures of procedural knowledge are much less varied. The task is almost always to solve problems and the outcome measure is usually accuracy of the answers or procedures. On occasion, researchers also consider solution time (Canobi, Reeve, & Pattison, 1998; LeFevre et al., 2006; Schneider & Stern, 2010). Procedural tasks are familiar – they involve types of problems people have solved before and thus should know procedures for solving. Sometimes the tasks include near transfer problems – those with an unfamiliar problem feature that require either recognition that a known procedure is relevant or small adaptations of a known procedure to accommodate the unfamiliar problem feature (e.g., Renkl et al., 1998; Rittle-Johnson, 2006).

There are additional measures that have been used to tap particular ways in which procedural knowledge can be known. When interested in how flexible procedural knowledge is, researchers assess students' knowledge of multiple procedures and their ability to flexibly choose among them to solve problems efficiently (e.g., Blöte, Van der Burg, & Klein, 2001; Star & Rittle-Johnson, 2008; Verschaffel et al., 2009). However, this research is beyond the scope of this chapter.

Although it is important to separate measures of conceptual and procedural knowledge, it is also important to recognize that it is difficult for an item to measure one type of knowledge to the exclusion of the other. To respond to items designed to tap conceptual knowledge, people often follow a set of steps. To solve familiar problems, people may rely on their conceptual knowledge to interpret the problem and select a solution procedure. Thus, items are thought to predominantly measure one type of knowledge or the other rather than exclusively tapping a single type of knowledge.

One serious limitation within this literature is that no standardized approaches for assessing the different types of knowledge with proven validity, reliability, and objectivity have been developed (Rittle-Johnson & Schneider, 2015; Schneider & Stern, 2010). Rather, researchers develop their own study-specific measures, often without evidence of convergent or divergent validity. Consistency in findings using a variety of measures lends support to the accuracy of the findings but greater attention to measurement validation would clearly strengthen this literature.

Evidence for Developmental Relations

An iterative view was not considered in early research on the development of conceptual and procedural knowledge (for a review of this research in mathematics learning, see Rittle-Johnson & Siegler, 1998); however, since 2009, there has been an accumulation of evidence in support of it. An iterative view is now the most commonly endorsed perspective within psychology. Evidence in support of the iterative view comes from evidence from longitudinal research demonstrating bidirectional relations between the two types of knowledge over time and from experimental research demonstrating that manipulating one type of knowledge can lead to increases in the other type of knowledge. Additional research evaluates whether and when the bidirectional relations between conceptual and procedural knowledge are symmetrical.

First consider longitudinal studies on the predictive relations between the two types of knowledge over time. For example, in two samples differing in prior

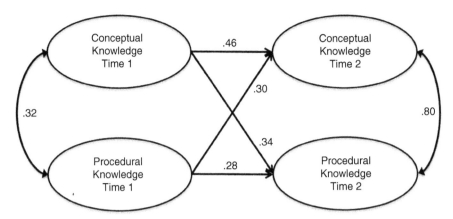

Figure 6.2 *Regression paths of the best-fitting structural equation model of the relations among conceptual and procedural knowledge in Study 1 (from Schneider, Rittle-Johnson and Star, 2011. Reprinted with permission from the American Psychological Association)*

knowledge, middle school students' conceptual and procedural knowledge for equation-solving was measured before and after a three-day classroom intervention in which students studied and explained worked examples with a partner (Schneider, Rittle-Johnson, & Star, 2011). Conceptual and procedural knowledge were modeled as latent variables and a cross-lagged panel design was used to directly test and compare the predictive relations from conceptual knowledge to procedural knowledge and vice versa. As shown in Figure 6.2, each type of knowledge predicted gains in the other type of knowledge. Further, the relations were symmetrical – procedural knowledge was as predictive of conceptual knowledge as vice versa. Similar bidirectional relations have been found for preschool children learning about counting (e.g., Baroody, 1992; Fuson, 1988; Muldoon, Lewis, & Berridge, 2007) and elementary school children learning addition and subtraction (Baroody & Ginsburg, 1986; Canobi, 2009) and about decimals (Rittle-Johnson et al., 2001; Rittle-Johnson & Koedinger, 2009).

An iterative view predicts that the bidirectional relations between conceptual and procedural knowledge persist over time, with increases in one supporting increasing in the other, *which in turn supports increases in the first type of knowledge.* Indeed, prior conceptual knowledge of decimals predicted gains in procedural knowledge after a brief problem-solving intervention, which in turn predicted gains in conceptual knowledge (Rittle-Johnson et al., 2001).

Bi-directional, predictive relations between conceptual and procedural knowledge are even present over several years (Cowan et al., 2011). For example, elementary school children's knowledge of fractions was assessed in the winter of Grade 4 and again in the spring of Grade 5 (Hecht & Vagi, 2010). Conceptual knowledge in Grade 4 predicted about 5 percent of the variance in procedural knowledge in Grade 5 after controlling for other factors, and procedural knowledge in Grade 4 predicted about 2 percent of the variance in conceptual knowledge in Grade 5.

Second, consider experimental studies that manipulated one type of knowledge and evaluate whether it led to increases in the other type of knowledge, providing evidence for causal relations. For example, direct instruction on one type of knowledge can lead to improvements in the other type of knowledge (Rittle-Johnson & Alibali, 1999). Elementary school children were given either a very brief lesson on a procedure for solving mathematical equivalence problems (e.g., $6 + 3 + 4 = 6 + \_\_$) or a lesson on the concept of mathematical equivalence, or were given no lesson. Children who received the procedure lesson gained a better understanding of the concept, and children who received the concept lesson generated correct procedures for solving the problems. The relations were bidirectional.

In addition, practice solving problems can support improvements in conceptual knowledge when constructed appropriately (Canobi, 2009; McNeil et al., 2012). For example, nontraditional arithmetic practice (e.g., problems with operations on the right side of the equal sign) can improve 2nd and 3rd grade students' procedural knowledge as well as their conceptual knowledge of the equal sign relative to traditional practice formats or no practice (McNeil, Fyfe, & Dunwiddie, 2014). Similarly, beginning a problem-solving session with a set of problems that facilitate noticing of a shortcut procedure promotes use of the procedure as well as conceptual knowledge of the concept that justifies the shortcut (DeCaro, 2016). Together, this evidence indicates that there are causal, bidirectional links between the two types of knowledge; improving procedural knowledge can lead to improved conceptual knowledge and vice versa, especially if potential links between the two are made salient.

Overall, there is extensive evidence from a variety of mathematical domains indicating that the development of conceptual and procedural knowledge of mathematics is often iterative, with one type of knowledge supporting gains in the other knowledge, which in turn supports gains in the former type of knowledge. Conceptual knowledge may help with the construction, selection, and appropriate execution of problem-solving procedures. At the same time, practice implementing procedures may help students develop and deepen understanding of concepts, especially if the practice is designed to make underlying concepts more apparent. Both kinds of knowledge are intertwined and can strengthen each other over time.

However, the relations between the two types of knowledge are not always symmetrical. In Schneider, Rittle-Johnson and Star (2011), the relations were symmetrical – the strength of the relationship from prior conceptual knowledge to later procedural knowledge was the same as from prior procedural knowledge to later conceptual knowledge. However, in other studies, conceptual knowledge or conceptual instruction has had a stronger influence on procedural knowledge than vice versa (Hecht & Vagi, 2010; Matthews & Rittle-Johnson, 2009; Rittle-Johnson & Alibali, 1999; Rittle-Johnson, Fyfe, & Loehr, 2016). Furthermore, brief procedural instruction or practice solving problems does not always support growth in conceptual knowledge (Canobi, 2009; Perry, 1991; Rittle-Johnson, 2006).

How much gains in procedural knowledge support gains in conceptual knowledge is influenced by the nature of the procedural instruction or practice. For example, in Canobi (2009) and McNeil and colleagues (2012), sequencing arithmetic practice problems so that conceptual relations were easier to notice supported conceptual knowledge, while random ordering of practice problems did not. In Peled and Segalis (2005), instruction that encouraged students to generalize procedural steps and connect subtraction procedures across whole numbers, decimals, and fractions led to greater conceptual knowledge than instruction on individual procedures. In general, it is best if procedural lessons are crafted to encourage noticing of underlying concepts.

The symmetry of the relations between conceptual and procedural knowledge also varies between individuals. Children in Grades 4 and 5 completed a measure of their conceptual and procedural knowledge of fractions (Hallett, Nunes, & Bryant, 2010). A cluster analysis on the two measures suggested five different clusters of students, with clusters varying in the strength of conceptual and procedural knowledge. For example, one cluster had above-average conceptual knowledge and below-average procedural knowledge, another cluster was the opposite, and a third cluster was high on both measures. These cluster differences suggest that, although related in all clusters, the strength of the relations varied. Similar findings were reported for primary school children's knowledge of addition and subtraction (Canobi, 2005), including a meta-analysis over fourteen studies (Gilmore & Papadatou-Pastou, 2009). At least in part, these individual differences may reflect different instructional histories between children.

In line with the importance of instructional histories, new research suggests that the potential asymmetry of the relations reported above may not generalize beyond Western countries, where all of the above research was conducted. In research contrasting the fraction knowledge of US and Chinese children, Chinese children had much greater procedural knowledge for fraction arithmetic and their procedural knowledge accounted for their greater conceptual knowledge for fraction magnitude (Bailey et al., 2015). The authors proposed that Chinese children's superior procedural knowledge was based on greater practice with procedures in their mathematics instruction, and that this greater procedural knowledge facilitated greater conceptual knowledge of fraction magnitude. Because this study was not longitudinal or experimental, this proposal is tentative. Nevertheless, it highlights the potential impact of instruction on the developmental relations between conceptual and procedural knowledge.

Overall, the relations between conceptual and procedural knowledge are bidirectional but sometimes they are not symmetrical. At times, conceptual knowledge more consistently and strongly supports procedural knowledge than the reverse. Crafting procedural lessons to encourage noticing of underlying concepts can promote a stronger link from improved procedural knowledge to gains in conceptual knowledge.

Table 6.2 *Limited empirical evidence relevant for identifying optimal ordering of instruction on concepts and procedures*

Study design	Condition that learned more	Context	Authors
Concepts-then-procedures vs. procedures-then-concepts			No studies identified
Procedures-and-concepts vs. concepts-only	No difference	Classroom	Pesek & Kirshner (2000)
	Concepts-only	Lab	Perry (1991)
	Concepts-only	Classroom	Rittle-Johnson, Fyfe, & Loehr (2016)
Concepts-only vs. procedures-only	Concepts-only	Lab	Perry (1991)
	Concepts-only	Lab	Matthews & Rittle-Johnson (2009)
	Concepts-only	Lab	Rittle-Johnson & Alibali (1999)
Concepts-then-procedures vs. iterative	Iterative	Classroom	Rittle-Johnson & Koedinger (2009)

Note: See text for additional details.

Evidence for Ordering of Instruction

Although the relations between the two types of knowledge are bidirectional, it still may be optimal for instruction to follow a particular ordering. Unfortunately, empirical evidence that directly evaluates claims for an optimal ordering of instruction is not available. For example, no published study has compared the effectiveness of instruction on concepts-then-procedures to instruction on procedures-then-concepts.

Rather, much of the evidence used to support the claim within mathematics education that instruction is best done in a concepts-then-procedures order comes from studies that document learning from reform-oriented instruction. Reform-oriented instruction often follows a concepts-then-procedures instructional order and is associated with greater student learning than traditional instruction that focuses on procedural knowledge (Blöte et al., 2001; Cobb et al., 1991; Fuson & Briars, 1990; Hiebert & Wearne, 1996; Hiebert & Grouws, 2007). These studies indicate that learning procedures in conjunction with concepts appears to be better than learning procedures with little or no attention to concepts. Multiple ways to support both types of knowledge were not considered. Furthermore, in all of these studies, the two instructional conditions differed on many dimensions (e.g., the amount and quality of student discussion).

Next consider studies that have manipulated the type(s) of instruction, which are outlined in Table 6.2. In one widely cited classroom study, 5th grade students were randomly selected to receive instruction on conventional procedures for finding area and perimeter prior to conceptually focused instruction (procedural-then-conceptual instruction) or to receive no relevant instruction prior to the conceptually focused instruction (only conceptual instruction) (Pesek & Kirshner, 2000). Students in the two conditions had similar performance on a posttest and retention test on finding the areas and perimeters of shapes. However, the only-conceptual-instruction condition had slightly (but not statistically significantly) better performance than the procedural-then-conceptual condition (e.g., 48 percent vs. 42 percent correct at posttest) that the authors argued may have been reliable with a substantially larger sample. In addition, qualitative descriptions of interviews with twelve students suggested subtle benefits for the only-conceptual-instruction condition on a few of the interview questions. Overall, differences between the conditions were small and not reliable, but the authors and others sometimes claim the study supports the use of extended conceptual instruction prior to procedural instruction.

Two other studies compared instruction on concepts and procedures to only instruction on concepts, although these studies are rarely cited in the mathematics education research literature. In Perry (1991), 4th and 5th grade students were randomly assigned to receive instruction on a concept and procedure, only on the concept, or only on the procedure. In this lab study, children received a few minutes of instruction in the context of two mathematical equivalence problems. For the concept-and-procedure condition, the instruction was provided one after the other on each problem and the order of the two types of instruction on each problem was counterbalanced across children and did not impact learning outcomes. Children who received only instruction on concepts showed the greatest procedural transfer, with children in the two other conditions performing similarly. Rittle-Johnson and colleagues (2016) found similar results in a classroom-based study, and the advantages of the concepts-only instruction held regardless of whether instruction was provided before or after a problem exploration phase. Thus, these studies provide some support for the claim that instruction on procedures should not be included concurrently with instruction on concepts, at least early in instruction on mathematical equivalence. Additional research is needed to evaluate whether this finding would generalize to other mathematics topics and to typical classroom contexts with much more extensive instruction and problem-solving experience.

Two additional laboratory-based experimental studies contrasted instruction on a concept versus a procedure. Children received brief one-on-one instruction on mathematical equivalence (less than ten minutes). As in Perry (1991), children who received brief instruction on a concept showed greater knowledge at posttest than children who received brief instruction on a procedure (Matthews & Rittle-Johnson, 2009; Rittle-Johnson & Alibali, 1999). These findings support the importance of including instruction on concepts and suggest that instruction on a procedure may not be necessary for some topics and for some learning goals. Yet note that neither of these studies provides direct evidence on the optimal sequencing of instruction on concepts and procedures.

Finally, one study suggests that a small dosage of instruction on concepts-first is preferable to a large dosage of instruction on concepts-first. In two classroom experiments, 6th grade students completed six lessons on decimals using an

Table 6.3 *Design of intervention conditions in Rittle-Johnson and Koedinger (2009)*

Condition	Lesson 1	Lesson 2	Lesson 3	Lesson 4	Lesson 5	Lesson 6
Concepts-first	Concept lesson (a)	Concept lesson (b)	Concept lesson (c)	Procedure lesson (a)	Procedure lesson (b)	Procedure lesson (c)
Iterative	Concept lesson (a)	Procedure lesson (a)	Concept lesson (b)	Procedure lesson (b)	Concept lesson (c)	Procedure lesson (c)

Note: Individual lessons were the same across conditions; only the ordering of the lessons differed. Lessons were implemented in an intelligent tutoring system.

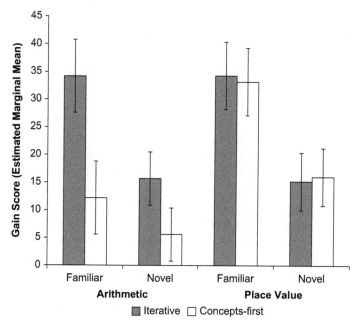

Figure 6.3 *Experiment 1 gain scores by condition for each item type (from Rittle-Johnson & Koedinger, 2009, p. 491. Copyright 2009 by the British Psychological Society. Reprinted with permission)*
Scores are estimated marginal means. Error bars represent standard errors.
Concepts-first condition received conceptual-then-procedural instruction.

intelligent-tutoring system in one of two randomly assigned conditions, as outlined in Table 6.3 (Rittle-Johnson & Koedinger, 2009). In the concepts-first condition, all conceptual knowledge lessons on place value were presented before the procedural knowledge lessons on adding and subtracting decimals. In an iterative condition, lessons iterated between a focus on concepts and a focus on procedures, beginning with a conceptual knowledge lesson. As shown in Figure 6.3, the iterative order supported equivalent conceptual knowledge and greater procedural knowledge (on both familiar and novel problem types) relative to the concepts-first sequence. This finding suggests that conceptual knowledge does not need to be well developed before beginning instruction on procedures. However, because there was no procedural-then-conceptual condition or iterative condition that began with a procedural lesson, this study does not directly inform the debate on a conceptual-then-procedural versus procedural-then-conceptual approach.

In summary, prior research has not directly evaluated whether a conceptual-then-procedural instructional sequence leads to greater learning than alternative orderings of instruction that also focus on developing both types of knowledge. A few laboratory-based studies suggest that it may be more effective to begin instruction with a brief conceptual lesson than a brief procedural lesson. An experimental, classroom-based study suggests that iterating between lessons on concepts and procedures is more effective than providing extensive instruction on concepts before introducing instruction on procedures. However, much more research is needed on the most effective dosage and timing of instruction on concepts and procedures. I suspect there are multiple routes to mathematical competence, such as instruction that iterates between a focus on concepts and procedures throughout instruction.

Conclusion and Future Directions

Mathematical competence rests on developing both conceptual and procedural knowledge, and there is clear evidence that conceptual and procedural knowledge often develop in an iterative, hand-over-hand fashion. However, evidence relevant to the optimal ordering of instruction is sparse.

Overall, existing research has general implications for mathematics education but its direct application to practice is limited. Current research confirms the importance of developing both types of knowledge and offers some possible ways to assess each type of knowledge (see Table 6.1 for examples). However, measures of conceptual and procedural knowledge of particular topics with evidence of strong reliability and validity are rare. Current research also suggests that there are likely multiple routes to strong mathematics competence given the potential for bidirectional and iterative relations between conceptual and procedural knowledge. However, past research has rarely evaluated alternative instructional sequences.

Educators care most about optimal instructional orderings and less about typical developmental relations. Thus, to be directly relevant to education, we must directly evaluate alternative instructional sequences for supporting both types of knowledge over time and in classroom contexts. Mathematics education research and advocates typically focus on only one of those routes: a conceptual-then-procedural ordering of instruction. However, there are alternative sequencings that also include a strong focus on conceptual as well as procedural knowledge. In particular, iterative sequencing of instruction appears promising based on evidence for developmental relations between the two types of knowledge as well as one short-term instructional experiment (Rittle-Johnson & Koedinger, 2009). Future research is needed to evaluate this sequencing, including whether beginning with one type of instruction or the other is preferable. At least for some topics, it might be optimal for an initial lesson to focus on concepts rather than procedures (Perry, 1991; Rittle-Johnson et al., 2016). In addition, current research provides little guidance on how often or at what grain size to iterate instruction (e.g., within a lesson, from lesson-to-lesson, from week-to-week). Further, some instructional activities may simultaneously support fluent use of procedures and understanding of underlying concepts, such as solving carefully sequenced practice problems (Canobi, 2009; McNeil et al., 2012) or prompting for self-explanation when studying worked examples (see Renkl and Eitel, Chapter 21, this volume). However, we need additional evidence and guidelines for the conditions under which carefully crafted practice problems effectively promote both conceptual and procedural knowledge.

Such needs-driven, classroom-based research is rare within psychology. First, instead of trying to *apply* our research to practice, we need to do research that is inherently relevant to and driven by the needs of practice. We need to incorporate research topics and methods that take into consideration current problems of practice (e.g., what mathematics educators identify as their most pressing concerns, such as optimal ordering of instruction). Second, our experimental evidence from studies carried out one-on-one with students on educationally relevant content is a first step. But it is only a first step and few psychologists take the next steps. We must conduct research *within* educational settings in order to ensure the method is feasible outside of a controlled lab setting and that the findings generalize to those settings. For example, I have capitalized on the common educational practice of partner work and randomly assigned pairs of students to different conditions within classrooms and had students work on our materials with a partner during their mathematics class on content relevant for that course (Rittle-Johnson & Star, 2011). But even this research covered only a few lessons and was researcher-led. A further step is to be directly involved in translating research-based findings into curricular materials and professional development that promotes their use by teachers. Translation of psychological principles and findings into usable practices is not straightforward. Psychological research often focuses on isolating particular processes and knowledge components, and how to combine and integrate different processes and components to address broad learning goals is rarely addressed by research but is necessary in practice. For example, the Institute of Education Sciences funded a National Research and Development Center on Cognition and Mathematics Instruction to redesign a widely used middle school mathematics curriculum using four principles derived from cognitive and learning sciences (Pashler et al., 2007). At times, implementing an evidence-based principle, such as removing potentially distracting or unnecessary visuals, was difficult because it was unclear how much a picture helped activate relevant background knowledge or served other social and motivational goals, such as illustrating that a wide variety of people do and use mathematics. Further, the impact of using the revised curriculum on student learning, compared to using the original curriculum, was modest, with a significant positive effect on only one of seven unit tests. There was some evidence that the revisions improved student learning for some subgroups on particular unit tests (Kao et al., 2017). We have faced similar difficulties in our own efforts to translate our research on the use of comparison and explanation of multiple strategies to a set of supplementary materials and professional development for Algebra I teachers (Star et al., 2015). In our case, teacher use of our materials was quite limited. We are currently working to better integrate our materials with existing curriculum and design better professional development. Nevertheless, this is the type of research that must be conducted if psychological research is going to have a direct impact on education.

Despite the obstacles of bridging between research and educational practice, it is essential research. Conducting research in educational contexts reveals new theoretical issues, such as how different sequencing of instruction might impact learning. Thus, it yields benefits for both research and practice and will help advance our understanding of how people learn and how we can better promote this learning.

References

Alcock, L., Ansari, D., Batchelor, S., Bisson, M.-J., De Smedt, B., Gilmore, C. K., . . . Weber, K. (2016). Challenges in mathematical cognition: A collaboratively-derived research agenda. *Journal of Numerical Cognition*, 2, 20–41. https://doi.org/10.5964/jnc.v2i1.10

Anderson, J. R. (1993). *Rules of the mind*. Hillsdale, NJ: Erlbaum.

Bailey, D. H., Zhou, X., Zhang, Y., Cui, J., Fuchs, L. S., Jordan, N. C., . . . Siegler, R. S. (2015). Development of fraction concepts and procedures in U.S. and Chinese children. *Journal of Experimental Child Psychology*, *129*, 68–83. https://doi.org/10.1016/j.jecp.2014.08.006

Baroody, A. J. (1992). The development of preschoolers' counting skills and principles. In J. Bideaud, C. Meljac, & J. P. Fischer (eds.), *Pathway to numbers: Children's developing numerical abilities* (pp. 99–126). Hillsdale, NJ: Erlbaum.

(2003). The development of adaptive expertise and flexibility: The integration of conceptual and procedural knowledge. In A. J. Baroody & A. Dowker (eds.), *The development of arithmetic concepts and skills: Constructing adaptive expertise* (pp. 1–34). Mahwah, NJ: Erlbaum.

Baroody, A. J., Feil, Y., & Johnson, A. R. (2007). An alternative reconceptualization of procedural and conceptual knowledge. *Journal for Research in Mathematics Education*, *38*, 115–131.

Baroody, A. J. & Ginsburg, H. (1986). The relationship between initial meaningful and mechanical knowledge of arithmetic. In J. Hiebert (ed.), *Conceptual and procedural knowledge: The case of mathematics*. Hillsdale, NJ: Lawrence Erlbaum.

Blöte, A. W., Van der Burg, E., & Klein, A. S. (2001). Students' flexibility in solving two-digit addition and subtraction problems: Instruction effects. *Journal of Educational Psychology*, *93*, 627–638. https://doi.org/10.1037//0022-0663.93.3.627

Byrnes, J. P., & Wasik, B. A. (1991). Role of conceptual knowledge in mathematical procedural learning. *Developmental Psychology*, *27*, 777–786. https://doi.org/10.1037//0012-1649.27.5.777

Canobi, K. H. (2005). Children's profiles of addition and subtraction understanding. *Journal of Experimental Child Psychology*, *92*, 220–246. https://doi.org/10.1016/j.jecp.2005.06.001

(2009). Concept-procedure interactions in children's addition and subtraction. *Journal of Experimental Child Psychology*, *102*, 131–149. https://doi.org/10.1016/j.jecp.2008.07.008

Canobi, K. H., Reeve, R. A., & Pattison, P. E. (1998). The role of conceptual understanding in children's addition problem solving. *Developmental Psychology*, *34*, 882–891. https://doi.org/10.1037//0012-1649.34.5.882

Cobb, P., Wood, T., Yackel, E., Nicholls, J., Wheatley, G., Trigatti, B., & Perlwitz, M. (1991). Assessment of a problem-centered second-grade mathematics project. *Journal for Research in Mathematics Education*, *22*, 3–29. https://doi.org/10.2307/749551

Cowan, R., Donlan, C., Shepherd, D.-L., Cole-Fletcher, R., Saxton, M., & Hurry, J. (2011). Basic calculation proficiency and mathematics achievement in elementary school children. *Journal of Educational Psychology*, *103*, 786–803. https://doi.org/10.1037/a0024556

Crooks, N. M. & Alibali, M. W. (2014). Defining and measuring conceptual knowledge in mathematics. *Developmental Review*, *34*, 344–377. https://doi.org/10.1016/j.dr.2014.10.001

DeCaro, M. S. (2016). Inducing mental set constrains procedural flexibility and conceptual understanding in mathematics. *Memory and Cognition*, *44*, 1138–1148. https://doi.org/10.3758/s13421-016-0614-y

diSessa, A. A., Gillespie, N. M., & Esterly, J. B. (2004). Coherence versus fragmentation in the development of the concept of force. *Cognitive Science*, *28*, 843–900.

Dowker, A. (2008). Individual differences in numerical abilities in preschoolers. *Developmental Science*, *11*, 650–654. https://doi.org/10.1111/j.1467-7687.2008.00713.x

Faulkenberry, T. J. (2013). The conceptual/procedural distinction belongs to strategies, not tasks: A comment on Gabriel et al. (2013). *Frontiers in Psychology*, *4*, 820. https://doi.org/10.3389/fpsyg.2013.00820

Fuson, K. C. (1988). *Children's counting and concept of number*. New York: Springer-Verlag.

Fuson, K. C. & Briars, D. J. (1990). Using a base-ten blocks learning/teaching approach for first- and second-grade place-value and multidigit addition and subtraction. *Journal for Research in Mathematics Education*, *21*, 180–206. https://doi.org/10.2307/749373

Fuson, K. C. & Kwon, Y. (1992). Korean children's understanding of multidigit addition and subtraction. *Child Development*, *63*, 491–506. https://doi.org/10.1111/j.1467-8624.1992.tb01642.x

Gelman, R. & Meck, E. (1983). Preschoolers' counting: Principles before skill. *Cognition*, *13*, 343–359. https://doi.org/10.1016/0010-0277(83)90014-8

Gelman, R. & Williams, E. M. (1998). Enabling constraints for cognitive development and learning: Domain specificity and epigenesis. In D. Kuhn & R. S. Siegler (eds.), *Handbook of child psychology: Cognition, perception, and language*, Vol. 2, 5th edn (pp. 575–630). New York: John Wiley & Sons.

Gilmore, C. K. & Papadatou-Pastou, M. (2009). Patterns of individual differences in conceptual understanding and arithmetical skill: A meta-analysis. *Mathematical Thinking and Learning*, *11*, 25–40.

Gilmore, C. K., McCarthy, S. E., & Spelke, E. S. (2010). Non-symbolic arithmetic abilities and mathematics achievement in the first year of formal schooling. *Cognition, 115*, 394–406. https://doi.org/10.1016/j.cognition.2010.02.002

Ginsburg, H. P. (1997). *Entering the child's mind: The clinical interview in psychological research and practice*. New York: Cambridge University Press.

Goldin Meadow, S., Alibali, M. W., & Church, R. B. (1993). Transitions in concept acquisition: Using the hand to read the mind. *Psychological Review, 100*, 279–297. https://doi.org/10.1037//0033-295X.100.2.279

Grouws, D. A. & Cebulla, K. J. (2000). *Improving student achievement in mathematics*. Geneva.

Haapasalo, L. & Kadijevich, D. (2000). Two types of mathematical knowledge and their relation. *JMD – Journal for Mathematic-Didaktik, 21*, 139–157.

Halford, G. S. (1993). *Children's understanding: The development of mental models*. Hillsdale, NJ: Erlbaum.

Hallett, D., Nunes, T., & Bryant, P. (2010). Individual differences in conceptual and procedural knowledge when learning fractions. *Journal of Educational Psychology, 102*, 395–406. https://doi.org/10.1037/a0017486

Hecht, S. A. (1998). Toward an information-processing account of individual differences in fraction skills. *Journal of Educational Psychology, 90*, 545–559. https://doi.org/10.1037/0022-0663.90.3.545

Hecht, S. A. & Vagi, K. J. (2010). Sources of group and individual differences in emerging fraction skills. *Journal of Educational Psychology, 102*, 843–859. https://doi.org/10.1037/a0019824

Hiebert, J. & Grouws, D. (2007). *Effective teaching for the development of skill and conceptual understanding of number: What is most effective?* Reston, VA: National Council of Teachers of Mathematics. www.nctm.org/Research-and-Advocacy/Research-Brief-and-Clips/Effective-Instruction/.

Hiebert, J. & LeFevre, P. (1986). Conceptual and procedural knowledge in mathematics: An introductory analysis. In J. Hiebert (ed.), *Conceptual and procedural knowledge: The case of mathematics* (pp. 1–27). Hillsdale, NJ: Lawrence Erlbaum.

Hiebert, J. & Wearne, D. (1996). Instruction, understanding, and skill in multidigit addition and subtraction. *Cognition and Instruction, 14*, 251–283. https://doi.org/10.1207/s1532690xci1403_1

Jordan, J.-A., Mulhern, G., & Wylie, J. (2009). Individual differences in trajectories of arithmetical development in typically achieving 5- to 7-year-olds. *Journal of Experimental Child Psychology, 103*, 455–468. https://doi.org/10.1016/j.jecp.2009.01.011

Kamii, C. & Dominick, A. (1997). To teach or not to teach algorithms. *Journal of Mathematical Behavior, 16*, 51–61. https://doi.org/10.1016/S0732-3123(97)90007-9

    (1998). The harmful effects of algorithms in grades 1–4. In L. J. Morrow & M. J. Kenney (eds.), *The teaching and learning of algorithms in school mathematics. 1998 yearbook* (pp. 130–140). Reston, VA: National Council of Teachers of Mathematics.

Kao, Y. S., Davenport, J., Matlen, B., Thomas, L., & Schneider, S. A. (2017). *The effectiveness of cognitive principles in authentic education settings: Research to practice*. Paper presented at the Society for Research in Educational Effectiveness, Washington, DC. www.iesmathcenter.org/research/2017_KaoSREESpring2017PaperAbstract.pdf

Karmiloff-Smith, A. (1992). *Beyond modularity: A developmental perspective on cognitive science*. Cambridge, MA: MIT Press.

Kilpatrick, J., Swafford, J. O., & Findell, B. (2001). *Adding it up: Helping children learn mathematics*. Washington, DC: National Academy Press.

Knuth, E. J., Stephens, A. C., McNeil, N. M., & Alibali, M. W. (2006). Does understanding the equal sign matter? Evidence from solving equations. *Journal for Research in Mathematics Education, 37*, 297–312.

Laski, E. V. & Siegler, R. S. (2007). Is 27 a big number? Correlational and causal connections among numerical categorization, number line estimation, and numerical magnitude comparison. *Child Development, 78*, 1723–1743.

Lavigne, N. C. (2005). Mutually informative measures of knowledge: Concept maps plus problem sorts in statistics. *Educational Assessment, 101*, 39–71. https://doi.org 10.1207/s15326977ea1001_3

LeFevre, J.-A., Smith-Chant, B. L., Fast, L., Skwarchuk, S.-L., Sargla, E., Arnup, J. S., ... Kamawar, D. (2006). What counts as knowing? The development of conceptual and procedural knowledge of counting from kindergarten through grade 2. *Journal of Experimental Child Psychology, 93*, 285–303. https://doi.org/10.1016/j .jecp.2005.11.002

Matthews, P. & Rittle-Johnson, B. (2009). In pursuit of knowledge: Comparing self-explanations, concepts, and procedures as pedagogical tools. *Journal of Experimental Child Psychology, 104*, 1–21. https://doi.org/10.1016/j .jecp.2008.08.004

Matthews, P., Rittle-Johnson, B., McEldoon, K., & Taylor, R. (2012). Measure for measure: What combining diverse measures reveals about children's understanding of the equal sign as an indicator of mathematical equality. *Journal for Research in Mathematics Education, 43*, 316–350.

McNeil, N. M. & Alibali, M. W. (2004). You'll see what you mean: Students encode equations based on their knowledge of arithmetic. *Cognitive Science, 28*, 451–466. https://doi .org/10.1016/j.cogsci.2003.11.002

McNeil, N. M., Chesney, D. L., Matthews, P. G., Fyfe, E. R., Petersen, L. A., Dunwiddie, A. E., & Wheeler, M. C. (2012). It pays to be organized: Organizing arithmetic practice around equivalent values facilitates understanding of math equivalence. *Journal of Educational Psychology*. https://doi.org/10.1037/a0028997

McNeil, N. M., Fyfe, E. R., & Dunwiddie, A. E. (2014). Arithmetic practice can be modified to promote understanding of mathematical equivalence. *Journal of Educational Psychology, 107*, 423–436. https://doi.org/10.1037/a0037687

Muldoon, K. P., Lewis, C., & Berridge, D. (2007). Predictors of early numeracy: Is there a place for mistakes when learning about number? *British Journal of Developmental Psychology, 25*, 543–558. https://doi.org/10.1348/026151007x174501

Muldoon, K. P., Towse, J., Simms, V., Perra, O., & Menzies, V. (2013). A longitudinal analysis of estimation, counting skills, and mathematical ability across the first school year. *Developmental Psychology, 49*, 250–257. https://doi.org/10.1037/a0028240

National Assessment Governing Board. (2014). *Mathematics framework for the 2015 National Assessment of Educational Progress*. Washington, DC: US Government Printing Office.

National Mathematics Advisory Panel. (2008). *Foundations of success: The final report of the National Mathematics Advisory Panel*. Washington, DC: US Department of Education.

NCTM (National Council of Teachers of Mathematics). (1989). *Curriculum and evaluation standards for school mathematics*. Reston, VA: NCTM.

(2000). *Principles and standards for school mathematics*. Reston, VA: NCTM.

(2014). *Principles to actions: Ensuring mathematical success for all*. Reston, VA: NCTM.

Pashler, H., Bain, P., Bottge, B., Graesser, A. C., Koedinger, K., McDaniel, M. A., & Metcalfe, J. (2007). *Organizing instruction and study to improve student learning* Washington, DC: National Center for Education Research, Institute of Education Sciences, and US Department of Education. https://ies.ed.gov/ncer/pubs/practice guides/20072004.asp

Peled, I. & Segalis, B. (2005). It's not too late to conceptualize: Constructing a generalized subtraction schema by abstracting and connecting procedures. *Mathematical Thinking and Learning, 7*, 207–230. https://doi.org/10.1207/s15327833mtl0703_2

Perry, M. (1991). Learning and transfer: Instructional conditions and conceptual change. *Cognitive Development, 6*, 449–468. https://doi.org/10.1016/0885-2014(91)90049-J

Pesek, D. D. & Kirshner, D. (2000). Interference of instrumental instruction in subsequent relation learning. *Journal for Research in Mathematics Education, 31*, 524–540. https://doi.org/10.2307/749885

Prather, R. W. & Alibali, M. W. (2008). Understanding and using principles of arithmetic: Operations involving negative numbers. *Cognitive Science, 32*, 445–457. https://doi.org/10.1080/03640210701864147

Rasmussen, C., Ho, E., & Bisanz, J. (2003). Use of the mathematical principle of inversion in young children. *Journal of Experimental Child Psychology, 85*, 89–102. https://doi.org/10.1016/s0022-0965(03)00031-6

Renkl, A., Stark, R., Gruber, H., & Mandl, H. (1998). Learning from worked-out examples: The effects of example variability and elicited self-explanations. *Contemporary Educational Psychology, 23*, 90–108. https://doi.org/10.1006/ceps.1997.0959

Resnick, L. B. (1982). Syntax and semantics in learning to subtract. In T. P. Carpenter, J. M. Moser, & T. A. Romberg (eds.), *Addition & subtraction: A cognitive perspective* (pp. 136–155). Hillsdale, NJ: Lawrence Erlbaum.

Resnick, L. B. & Ford, W. W. (1981). *The psychology of mathematics for instruction*. Hillsdale, NJ: Lawrence Erlbaum.

Resnick, L. B. & Omanson, S. F. (1987). Learning to understand arithmetic. In R. Glaser (ed.), *Advances in instructional psychology*, Vol. 3 (pp. 41–95). Hillsdale, NJ: Lawrence Erlbaum.

Rittle-Johnson, B. (2006). Promoting transfer: Effects of self-explanation and direct instruction. *Child Development, 77*, 1–15. https://doi.org/10.1111/j.1467-8624.2006.00852.x

Rittle-Johnson, B. & Alibali, M. W. (1999). Conceptual and procedural knowledge of mathematics: Does one lead to the other? *Journal of Educational Psychology, 91*, 175–189. https://doi.org/10.1037//0022-0663.91.1.175

Rittle-Johnson, B., Fyfe, E. R., & Loehr, A. M. (2016). Improving conceptual and procedural knowledge: The impact of instructional content within a mathematics lesson. *British Journal of Educational Psychology, 86*, 576–591. https://doi.org/10.1111/bjep.12124

Rittle-Johnson, B. & Koedinger, K. R. (2009). Iterating between lessons concepts and procedures can improve mathematics knowledge. *British Journal of Educational Psychology, 79*, 483–500. https://doi.org/10.1348/000709908X398106

Rittle-Johnson, B. & Schneider, M. (2015). Developing conceptual and procedural knowledge of mathematics. In R. C. Kadosh & A. Dowker (eds.), *Oxford handbook of numerical cognition* (pp. 1118–1134). Oxford: Oxford University Press.

Rittle-Johnson, B., Schneider, M., & Star, J. R. (2015). Not a one-way street: Bidirectional relations between procedural and conceptual knowledge of mathematics. *Educational Psychology Review*, *27*, 587–597. https://doi.org/10.1007/s10648-015-9302-x

Rittle-Johnson, B. & Siegler, R. S. (1998). The relation between conceptual and procedural knowledge in learning mathematics: A review. In C. Donlan (ed.), *The development of mathematical skills* (pp. 75–110). London: Psychology Press.

Rittle-Johnson, B., Siegler, R. S., & Alibali, M. W. (2001). Developing conceptual understanding and procedural skill in mathematics: An iterative process. *Journal of Educational Psychology*, *93*, 346–362. https://doi.org/10.1037//0022-0663.93.2.346

Rittle-Johnson, B. & Star, J. R. (2011). The power of comparison in learning and instruction: Learning outcomes supported by different types of comparisons. In J. P. Mestre & B. H. Ross (eds.), *Psychology of learning and motivation: Cognition in education*, Vol. 55 (pp. 199–222). Waltham, MA: Elsevier.

Robinson, K. M., Dube, A. K., & Beatch, J. A. (2016). Children's understanding of additive concepts. *Journal of Experimental Child Psychology*, *156*, 16–28. https://doi.org/10.1016/j.jecp.2016.11.009

Schneider, M., Grabner, R., & Paetsch, J. (2009). Mental number line, number line estimation, and mathematical achievement: Their interrelations in grades 5 and 6. *Journal of Educational Psychology*, *101*, 359–372. https://doi.org/10.1037/a0013840

Schneider, M., Rittle-Johnson, B., & Star, J. R. (2011). Relations between conceptual knowledge, procedural knowledge, and procedural flexibility in two samples differing in prior knowledge. *Developmental Psychology*. https://doi.org/10.1037/a0024997

Schneider, M. & Stern, E. (2009). The inverse relation of addition and subtraction: A knowledge integration perspective. *Mathematical Thinking and Learning*, *11*, 92–101. https://doi.org/10.1080/10986060802584012

(2010). The developmental relations between conceptual and procedural knowledge: A multimethod approach. *Developmental Psychology*, *46*, 178–192. https://doi.org/10.1037/a0016701

Siegler, R. S. & Booth, J. L. (2004). Development of numerical estimation in young children. *Child Development*, *75*, 428–444. https://doi.org/10.1111/j.1467-8624.2004.00684.x

Siegler, R. S. & Stern, E. (1998). Conscious and unconscious strategy discoveries: A microgenetic analysis. *Journal of Experimental Psychology: General*, *127*, 377–397. https://doi.org/10.1037/0096-3445.127.4.377

Siegler, R. S., Thompson, C. A., & Schneider, M. (2011). An integrated theory of whole number and fractions development. *Cognitive Psychology*, *62*, 273–296. https://doi.org/10.1016/j.cogpsych.2011.03.001

Star, J. R. (2005a). Reconceptualizing procedural knowledge. *Journal for Research in Mathematics Education*, *36*, 404–411. www.jstor.org/stable/30034943

Star, J. R. (2005b). Re-conceptualizing procedural knowledge: Innovation and flexibility in equation solving. *Journal for Research in Mathematics Education*, *36*, 404–411.

Star, J. R., & Newton, K. J. (2009). The nature and development of expert's strategy flexibility for solving equations. *ZDM Mathematics Education*, *41*, 557–567. https://doi.org/10.1007/s11858-009-0185-5

Star, J. R., Pollack, C., Durkin, K., Rittle-Johnson, B., Lynch, K., Newton, K., & Gogolen, C. (2015). Learning from comparison in algebra. *Contemporary Educational Psychology, 40*, 41–54. https://doi.org/10.1016/j.cedpsych.2014.05.005

Star, J. R., & Rittle-Johnson, B. (2008). Flexibility in problem solving: The case of equation solving. *Learning and Instruction, 18*, 565–579. https://doi.org/10.1016/j.learninstruc.2007.09.018

Sun, R., Merrill, E., & Peterson, T. (2001). From implicit skill to explicit knowledge: A bottom-up model of skill learning. *Cognitive Science, 25*, 203–244.

Verschaffel, L., Luwel, K., Torbeyns, J., & Van Dooren, W. (2009). Conceptualizing, investigating, and enhancing adaptive expertise in elementary mathematics education. *European Journal of Psychology of Education, 24*, 335–359. https://doi.org/10.1007/bf03174765

Xu, F., Spelke, E. S., & Goddard, S. (2005). Number sense in human infants. *Developmental Science, 8*, 88–101. https://doi.org/10.1111/j.1467-7687.2005.00395.x

7 Development of Fraction Understanding

Pooja G. Sidney, Clarissa A. Thompson, and
John E. Opfer

Consider Julie (described in Mack, 1990, p. 22), a 6th grader who knows little about fractions. Julie knows that when you have two pizzas of the same size and one is cut into six equal-sized pieces but the other cut into eight equal-sized pieces, she'll get more pizza if she chooses a slice from the first pizza rather than the second (see Figure 7.1). However, when asked which fraction is bigger, 1/6 or 1/8, she says, "One eighth is bigger. [Eight] is a bigger number I think. [Eight] is bigger than [six]."

Like Julie, many children have sound intuitions about the mathematical patterns in our world. These mathematical intuitions enable them to predict, for example, that dividing an amount into two groups will result in two, smaller groups that are approximately one-half of the original amount (McCrink et al., 2013) and that combining two quantities will result in a bigger quantity that is approximately equal to the sum of the parts (Knops, Viarouge & Dehaene, 2009; Mix, Levine, & Huttenlocher, 1999; Wynn, 1998). As children's mathematics knowledge develops in educational and informal settings, they link these intuitions about numbers and mathematical relationships to formal symbolic mathematics, extend their early formal knowledge to support more complex mathematical thinking, and develop new intuitions and concepts about the relations among symbolic quantities.

In this chapter, we review the empirical research on children's understanding of fraction concepts, symbols, and procedures. In the first two sections, we argue for the practical and theoretical importance of examining children's fraction understanding. In the third section, we describe children's and adults' fraction reasoning, while highlighting the common methodologies in this literature, and present the developmental picture painted by current research across the life span. In the fourth section, we explore the educational implications of developmental research on children's fraction reasoning. Finally, we conclude by considering the directions for future research.

Mathematical Cognition and Education

Mathematical thinking has long been an important and productive area of cognitive and developmental research, for both practical and theoretical reasons. Practically, understanding how children learn mathematics – particularly which

This chapter was supported in part by IES grant: R305A160295.

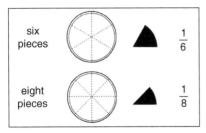

Figure 7.1 *An illustration of children's intuitions about mathematical patterns vs. difficulty reasoning about the formal symbolic fractional notation used to represent those magnitudes*

While children may have intuitions about the size of pieces, they often have difficulty reasoning about the formal symbolic fractional notation used to represent those magnitudes. In this example, a child who can reason about two pizzas cut into different numbers of slices may be unable to accurately reason about fraction symbols meant to represent the size of each slice. One goal of mathematics education is to support students' reasoning about the formal mathematical symbols.

experiences are most beneficial for robust learning – helps us to improve mathematics education in the United States and abroad. Development of mathematical thinking is an essential aspect of children's cognitive development. As adults, we reason about numbers and mathematics relationships every day. We reason with decimal numbers when calculating how much something costs or how much change we should receive. We measure, add, and transform fractions of ingredients while cooking. We consider and compare percentages when making decisions about interest rates at the bank and false positive rates at the doctor's office. In addition to using mathematics in everyday contexts such as these, many professions require advanced mathematical skills.

Given the critical role of mathematical thinking across a variety of contexts, the vast variability in children's mathematical knowledge across cultures – even among economically developed nations – is concerning. For example, children in the United States have been lagging behind those in many other developed countries on international assessments of mathematics achievement, despite sufficient access to public education. Among the 72 countries participating in the OECD's Programme for International Student Assessment (PISA), a survey of science, reading, and mathematics literacy among fifteen-year-olds, the United States scored below average in mathematics in the 2015 survey, with a significantly *lower* average score than the previous 2012 survey (OECD, 2016). The top-scoring countries included Singapore, China, and Japan. Furthermore, the survey showed that only about 1 percent of students in the United States reached the most advanced levels of mathematics reasoning, compared to about 10 percent in higher achieving countries. This raises a variety of questions about what facets of students' educational experience in higher-performing countries result in more mathematical proficiency, and which of these could be implemented in other, underperforming countries. Cross-cultural comparisons of American and East Asian classrooms have uncovered a variety of differences that may contribute to differential mathematics knowledge, including differences in teacher preparation (e.g., Ma, 1999), classroom practices (e.g., Richland, Zur, & Holyoak, 2007), and attitudes toward mathematics learning and practice (e.g., Stevenson, Chen, & Lee, 1993). One goal of research in mathematics cognition and development is to uncover the psychological mechanisms that propel development and shape children's emerging ideas and to identify experiences that enhance children's understanding in order to inform the best practices for mathematics education in the United States (e.g., Siegler et al., 2010, an IES Practice Guide) and abroad.

The development of children's fraction knowledge also appears to play an important role in the development of mathematical cognition. Children's understanding of fraction magnitudes is highly correlated with their current standardized mathematics achievement scores (Siegler, Thompson, & Schneider, 2011) and is a better predictor for students' readiness for learning algebra (i.e., knowledge of symbols and proficiency with solving equations and word problems) than their understanding of whole number magnitudes (Booth & Newton, 2012). More strikingly, 5th grade students' fraction knowledge predicts later high school mathematics achievement, even after controlling for children's other early mathematics knowledge, domain-general capacities (i.e., verbal IQ, nonverbal IQ, and working memory), and social factors (i.e., family education and family income; Siegler et al., 2012).

Despite its critical importance in mathematics education, and therefore educational success more broadly, American children continue to struggle to understand the magnitudes associated with fraction symbols (e.g., NCTM, 2007), procedures for solving fraction problems (e.g., Siegler et al., 2011; Siegler & Pyke, 2013), and the concepts underlying fraction operations (e.g., Richland & Hansen, 2013; Sidney & Alibali, 2015). For example, in a recent US National Assessment of Educational Progress (NAEP) survey, half of the tested 8th graders incorrectly ordered three fractions (2/7, 1/12, and 5/9) from smallest to largest (NCTM, 2007). This is particularly striking given that current standards for mathematics education recommend introducing symbolic fractions as early as 3rd grade (NGA & CCSSO, 2010). Indeed, in a survey of 1,000 US algebra teachers evaluating their students' preparation for Algebra 1, teachers reported that students' fraction understanding was the second "biggest problem," out of fifteen possible areas, in their algebra preparation (Hoffer et al., 2007). Even elementary school *teachers* often struggle with fraction concepts (e.g., Lo & Leu, 2012; Ma, 1999). For example, in one cross-cultural study of American and Chinese early mathematics teachers, nearly all of the twenty-three American teachers who were interviewed struggled to accurately solve and generate word problems about fraction division (Ma, 1999). In contrast, all of the Chinese teachers not only could accurately solve fraction division problems but were also able to describe multiple ways of conceptualizing fraction division and multiple strategies for approaching this topic with their students. Given the alarming gaps in students' knowledge, it is crucial to examine the ways in which children's fraction knowledge, and their educational success more generally, can be improved.

Mathematical Cognition and Developmental Theory

In addition to the practical applications of research to education, research on mathematical cognition often sheds light on a variety of fundamental questions about cognition generally. What is the nature of our *mental representations* of quantity? How do these mental representations *change over time*? What kinds of *environmental experiences* have formative and lasting effects? To what extent is mathematics cognition supported by *domain-specific* knowledge about mathematics or by *domain-general* competencies and processes? Which aspects of children's cognition are *innate* or very early emerging? Historically, many of these questions have been primarily addressed within children's mathematics cognition with respect to children's developing understanding of natural, whole numbers. As we will show, many findings from this research generalize to development of fraction knowledge.

Representing Whole Numbers

Researchers have long been interested in how children represent and estimate the numerosity of sets and the magnitudes of symbolic numbers. Using numerosity comparison tasks in which participants are asked to choose the more numerous of two sets of dots (see Figure 7.2, Panel A), a variety of studies have shown that infants to adults can rapidly choose which set has more, without the need for counting (e.g., Barth et al., 2003; Halberda, Mazzocco, & Feigenson, 2008; Xu & Spelke, 2000; Xu, 2003). Importantly, the *ratio* between two numerosities (or the difference in their *logarithms*) governs our ability to distinguish them, such that lower ratios between sets (i.e., 1:2) are more easily distinguished than higher ratios (i.e., 7:8), regardless of the number of items in each set. This ability to represent the numerosity of items has been attributed to an approximate number system (ANS) that supports estimating the numerosity of sets in an inexact way, with decreasing precision with increasing numerosity, and appears to be present in even very young children. Similar magnitude estimation abilities have also been documented in other primates (e.g., Brannon & Terrace, 1998) and rats (Meck & Church, 1983), suggesting that the ability to extract quantity information from nonsymbolic sets is an evolutionarily primary, and perhaps innately specified, ability.

This early emerging ability to represent the magnitude of nonsymbolic sets appears to support the more advanced ability to represent numeric magnitudes with numeric symbols, such as representing the numerosity of a set of two with the numeral 2. Using a number line task, in which participants are asked to locate a number on a given number line (see Figure 7.2, Panel B), Siegler and colleagues (e.g., Siegler & Opfer, 2003) have demonstrated that children's early magnitude judgments of symbolic whole numbers follow similar, ratio-governed patterns as their judgments of nonsymbolic magnitudes – unit differences between smaller numbers are overestimated while unit differences between larger numbers are underestimated. With experience, children's mental representations of numerical magnitude become increasingly linear (for a review, see Siegler & Opfer, 2003; Siegler, Thompson, & Opfer, 2009). Siegler and Opfer (2003) have argued that as children

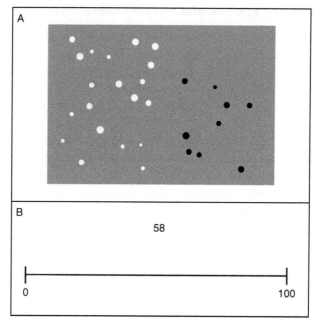

Figure 7.2 *Tasks for assessing knowledge of natural, whole number magnitudes*

Panel A shows an example of the dot comparison task, which is used to measure nonsymbolic whole number magnitude comparison (e.g., Halberda, Mazzocco, & Feigenson, 2008). In this task, people are asked to choose the larger number of dots without sufficient time to count them. Panel B shows an example of the number line task, which is used to measure symbolic whole number magnitude estimation (e.g., Siegler & Opfer, 2003). In this task, people are asked to mark the number line to show where 58 is located.

gain experience with whole number symbols and their relative magnitudes, they develop linear representations of number akin to a mental number line, on which small numbers are represented on the left and large numbers on the right, and unit differences (i.e., differences of one) are represented in the same way across the entire scale.

Development of nonsymbolic and symbolic number representations appear to occur concurrently and as a result of numerical experience. The ANS acuity, or highest ratio of sets that can be compared accurately, increases over developmental time (Halberda & Feigenson, 2008) and in response to practice (DeWind & Brannon, 2012). Children's number line representations also become linear across increasingly large scales as they gain practice with larger numbers (e.g., Siegler & Opfer, 2003; Siegler & Booth, 2004), with experiences that link symbolic numbers with linear, number line–like representations of numerical magnitude (e.g., Ramani & Siegler, 2008), with feedback about critical magnitudes (Opfer & Siegler, 2007), and via analogies between smaller number scales and larger number scales (Thompson & Opfer, 2010).

It remains somewhat controversial whether these mental representations are domain-specific representations of numerical magnitude or are based on domain-general representations of magnitude that also support the measurement of other nonsymbolic magnitudes, such as area and time. The ANS has been described as a domain-specific representation (e.g., Feigenson, Dehaene, & Spelke, 2004). Alternatively, the classic view is that the brain uses a general analog magnitude system to represent number (Dehaene, 2003; Meck & Church, 1983; Moyer & Landauer, 1967). Still a third view was recently proposed by Leibovich and colleagues (Leibovich et al., 2017; Leibovich, Kallai, & Itamar, 2016), who have suggested that numerical estimation of nonsymbolic sets is supported by a domain-general, approximate magnitude system (AMS), which becomes specialized to support numerical reasoning. Regardless of the specific nature of the magnitude representations, any truly domain general process, such as working memory (Namkung & Fuchs, 2016) and inhibitory control (e.g., Fuhs & McNeil, 2013), must also play a role in children's ability to map between symbolic numbers and magnitude representations.

Understanding Fractions

One challenge of research in children's mathematical thinking is to build a theory of mathematical development that incorporates children's thinking about numbers more broadly (Sidney et al., 2017; Siegler et al., 2011, 2013). Under this goal, the study of children's fraction reasoning has emerged as an important topic in children's mathematical thinking and development (Siegler, 2016; Siegler & Lortie-Forgues, 2014; Siegler et al., 2011, 2013). Natural, whole numbers comprise a very small subset of the kinds of numbers we use in complex mathematics and even in our everyday lives. As illustrated by the examples given at the beginning of the chapter, in addition to reasoning about whole number sets, we also reason about ratios and proportions represented with rational numbers, such as fractions, decimals, and percentages.

Examining children's developing understanding of fraction magnitudes, symbols, and operations allows us to broaden our characterization of mathematical development. Critically, fractions can serve as an illuminating test case for theories of mathematical development that have been based primarily on studies of children's whole number reasoning. Studies of fraction reasoning allow us to examine whether these theories generalize. For example, as we will discuss further in the next section, Siegler and colleagues (2011) examined whether the mental representations that support symbolic whole number reasoning (i.e., the mental number line) are similar to those that support symbolic fraction reasoning. Fractions also allow us to evaluate assumptions about the relationships between early emerging whole number competencies and later complex mathematics. For example, many researchers have argued that whole number reasoning is early emerging because the mind is innately equipped to reason about natural whole numbers, whereas fraction representations must be constructed from whole number representations. Recently, some researchers (Lewis, Matthews, & Hubbard, 2015; Matthews & Hubbard, 2017) have pointed to evidence for early competence in ratio reasoning, arguing for an intuitive ratio processing system (RPS) that should support early fraction reasoning as well. This work will also be further discussed in the next section. Furthermore, researchers who argue against the domain specificity of our understanding of numerical magnitude, such as Leibovich and colleagues (Leibovich et al., 2016, 2017) who argue for the AMS rather than ANS, leave room for whole number and fraction reasoning to develop in parallel rather than in sequence. As these examples illustrate, examining the development of fraction reasoning opens up several intriguing questions about the relationship between natural, whole number reasoning and more complex mathematics.

In addition to these questions about mathematical development, examining the development of fraction reasoning also allows us to test key theories of general cognitive development, in particular those concerning the development of *relational reasoning* and *transfer*. Fractions are fundamentally a relational concept. Their meaning is not derived from a single component, either the numerator or the denominator alone, but from the ratio relationship between these two components. The ability to represent relations among elements requires representing individual elements and thus develops later than the ability to represent the individual elements. For example, the ability to match sets based on relational patterns across elements within sets (e.g., small-medium-large or A-B-A patterns) rather than matching based on the perceptual details of the elements increases with age (e.g., Gentner, 1988). Furthermore, children's attention to relational structure can be supported by using relational language (e.g., referring to a small-medium-large pattern as "Baby, Mommy, Daddy"; Rattermann & Gentner, 1998), making an analogy to relationships in more familiar contexts (e.g., Goswami & Brown, 1990; Goswami, 1995), and by reducing the working memory demands of tasks relying on relational reasoning (e.g., Richland & McDonough, 2010; Thompson & Opfer, 2010). Although only a small subset of research on children's relational reasoning is situated in mathematical contexts, many mathematical concepts, such as fraction magnitudes, are inherently relational. Therefore, by examining whether these cognitive supports also enhance children's ability to reason about fractions, we can test the generalizability of these prior findings.

Similarly, by examining the relationship between children's emerging fraction understanding and their prior knowledge of whole number magnitudes and operations, we can test and further illuminate our theories of transfer. Children's whole number knowledge sometimes appears to negatively bias their fraction concepts (e.g., Ni & Zhou, 2005), suggesting that children's prior numerical knowledge transfers to new fraction concepts in ways that are unhelpful for new learning. Yet several aspects of children's whole number and fraction knowledge are strongly correlated (e.g., Bailey, Siegler, & Geary, 2014) and their knowledge of arithmetic operations with whole numbers can directly support learning about fraction arithmetic through analogical transfer (e.g., Richland & Hansen, 2013; Sidney & Alibali, 2015). Further investigation of when and how children spontaneously transfer from their prior knowledge of whole numbers when making sense of fractions may further illuminate the mechanisms of such transfer and contextual features of instruction that would further support appropriate transfer from students' prior knowledge. The relationship between children's knowledge of whole numbers and their developing understanding of fractions will be further discussed in the next section.

The Development of Fraction Skills

In this section, we review the current state of evidence of children's and adults' understanding of fractions, as well as some comparative evidence. First, we describe the nature of children's nonsymbolic proportion and ratio reasoning, as children typically show early competence with matching and comparing nonsymbolic fractions, similar to that of nonhuman animals. Next, we describe the nature of children's and adults' reasoning about the magnitudes of symbolic fractions, which are first introduced in early childhood and appear to cause difficulty for some students. Then, we will turn to more complex symbolic reasoning (e.g., arithmetic operations with fractions), which often depends on having adequate knowledge of fraction magnitudes. Along the way, we will discuss the methodology used to examine children's nonsymbolic and symbolic fraction understanding. Finally, we will consider the developmental pathways to fraction understanding, including the evidence for relationships between nonsymbolic and symbolic reasoning, the relationship between facets of children's fraction knowledge and other mathematics knowledge, and the role of domain-general processes in the development of children's fraction skills.

Nonsymbolic Proportions and Ratios

Children, adults, infants, and even nonhuman animals are able to reason about proportions and ratios in nonsymbolic contexts. Children as young as four years old can easily match visual stimuli representing the same proportions, despite different overall size (Duffy, Huttenlocher, & Levine, 2005; Sophian, 2000; Spinillo & Bryant, 2001) or even vastly different perceptual details (Singer-Freeman & Goswami, 2001). Furthermore, children as young as four years old can predict the outcome of simple addition and subtraction of nonsymbolic proportions, represented as parts of a circle, and this ability appears to develop from three to five years in parallel with the ability to add and subtract discrete, whole number, sets of objects (Mix et al., 1999). One limitation of these earlier studies is that they leave open the possibility that children may be completing the tasks via mechanisms other than attending to proportion, such as object-matching or attending to overall amount rather than proportion per se; similar criticisms have also been leveled at studies of nonsymbolic whole number reasoning (see Gebuis & Reynvoet, 2012; Leibovich et al., 2017; Mix, Huttenlocher, & Levine, 2002).

More recently, interest in children's fraction reasoning has led many researchers to examine children's and adults' abilities to compare one *ratio* of two numerosities to another *ratio* of two numerosities, in magnitude comparison tasks that are parallel to those used to investigate whole number reasoning (i.e., the dot comparison tasks used in studies of the ANS, see Figures 7.2 and 7.3) and tasks that better reflect

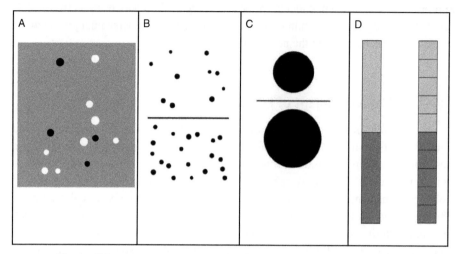

Figure 7.3 *Example stimuli for tasks assessing infants', children's, and adults' ability to represent and compare nonsymbolic ratios and proportions*

Panel A shows an example of a dot ratio stimulus in which the component numerosities are intermixed, as in Fazio et al. (2014) and McCrink & Wynn (2007). Panel B shows an example of a dot ratio stimulus in which the component numerosities are represented separately, in a fraction format. Panel C shows an example of an area ratio stimulus. Panels B and C reprinted from Matthews and Chesney (2015) with permission from Elsevier. Panel D shows two examples of area proportion stimuli, one continuous and one discretized, as in Boyer, Levine, and Huttenlocher (2008). Each panel shows an example of a 1:2 ratio.

symbolic fractional notation (e.g., two sets of dots separated by a fraction bar, with one taking the place of the numerator and the other taking the place of the denominator; see Figure 7.3, Panel B). These studies more closely target participants' sense of fractions as a ratio between two numbers or quantities.

In one such study, Fazio and colleagues (2014) administered a variety of fraction and whole number tasks to 5th grade children, including a nonsymbolic fraction magnitude comparison task. In this task, children viewed displays with two sets of yellow and blue dots, intermixed, of varying sizes (see Figure 7.3, Panel A for an example with black and white dots). Each set represented a specific ratio (e.g., 3:8 was represented with three blue dots and five yellow dots). Children were told that the dots represented candies and the blue dots taste the best, therefore, they should choose the side that would give them the best chance of picking a blue candy. Fazio and colleagues found that children were fairly successful at this task, choosing the larger ratio, on average, on 70 percent of trials. Similar to studies of whole number magnitude comparison, children were more accurate on the largest ratio differences (76 percent) than on the smallest ratio differences (65 percent).

Adults are also adept at perceiving and comparing nonsymbolic ratios and proportions (e.g., Matthews & Chesney, 2015; Meert et al., 2012). In their experiments with adult participants, Matthews and Chesney used symbolic fractional notation with sets of dots to represent component numerosities (i.e., one set of dots in the numerator position of the fraction and another set of dots in the denominator) or differently sized circular areas to represent component magnitudes (i.e., a smaller circle in the numerator position and a larger circle in the denominator; see Figure 7.3, Panels B and C). In their tasks, adults were able to accurately choose the greater ratio when comparing symbolic fractions to nonsymbolic dot fractions, symbolic fractions to nonsymbolic area fractions, and nonsymbolic dot fractions to nonsymbolic area fractions. In all cases, participants demonstrated *the distance effect*: they were faster and more accurate for more distant ratios and slower and less accurate for closer ratios, in parallel to earlier studies of adults' whole number comparisons. Furthermore, in a supplemental experiment, Matthews and Chesney found that adults were slower to make comparisons across two symbolic fractions than two nonsymbolic fractions in the same format, making it improbable that adults were converting nonsymbolic ratios to symbolic fractions in order to make the comparisons across ratios. Thus, adults can automatically represent ratio magnitudes in fractional formats, and the mental representations of these ratio magnitudes show an important similarity to adults' mental representations of whole number magnitudes – the comparison process itself is affected by the distance between ratios.

Furthermore, the ability to compare ratio magnitudes appears to be quite early emerging. McCrink and Wynn (2007) found that infants as young as six months old were sensitive to changes in ratios of items, as long as the ratios differed by at least a factor of 2. Their study used a habituation paradigm to test infants' ratio perception, in which infants were first habituated to stimuli with one ratio and then tested with stimuli that either matched or did not match the ratio of the habituated stimuli. Critically, habituation paradigms are used to test whether participants can perceive differences between habituated stimuli and test stimuli. If infants *dishabituate*, or begin to look longer at the new stimuli, during the test phase, researchers can infer that infants perceive the test stimuli as being different from habituated stimuli. In contrast, if infants do not look longer at the new stimuli during the test phase, then researchers can infer that infants *do not* perceive the new stimuli as being different from the habituated stimuli.

During the habituation phase, infants viewed a series of displays with yellow Pac-Men and blue pellets in different numbers, but constant ratio in each display (e.g., 8 blue pellets and 4 Pac-Men and 14 blue pellets and 7 Pac-Men are both a 2:1 ratio), until habituated. As in the adult work, the size of the dots varied within and across displays. To test whether infants can perceive ratio, McCrink and Wynn (2007) then tested whether infants would dishabituate to new ratios of items. The infants were assigned to one of two groups, a distant ratio group and a close ratio group (see Table 7.1). In the distant ratio group, the new ratio differed from the old ratio by a factor of 2. For example, some infants were habituated to displays with a 2:1 ratio and tested with displays with a 4:1 ratio. In the close ratio group, the new ratio differed from the old ratio by a factor of 1.5. For example, some infants were habituated to displays with a 2:1 ratio and tested with displays with a 3:1 ratio. Importantly, the numbers of items in the testing displays were different than in the habituation items seen by both groups.

Table 7.1 *Experimental design and findings from McCrink and Wynn (2007)*

Group	Habituated ratio	Test ratios	Difference factor[b]	Outcome
Distant Ratio[a]	Infants habituated to 2:1 (8:4, 38:19, 22:11, 14:7, 30:15)	2:1 (20:10, 32:16) 4:1 (40:10, 32:8)	1 2	Infants looked longer at new, 4:1 test stimuli
	Infants habituated to 4:1 (12:3, 48:12, 28:7, 24:6, 36:9)	2:1 (20:10, 32:16) 4:1 (40:10, 32:8)	2 1	Infants looked longer at new, 2:1 test stimuli
Close Ratio[c]	Infants habituated to 2:1 (8:4, 38:19, 22:11, 14:7, 34:17)	2:1 (20:10, 32:16) 3:1 (18:6, 30:10)	1 1.5	Infants *did not* look longer at new 3:1 test stimuli
	Infants habituated to 3:1 (9:3, 48:16, 27:9, 15:5, 36:12)	2:1 (20:10, 32:16) 3:1 (18:6, 30:10)	1.5 1	Infants *did not* look longer at new 2:1 test stimuli

[a] The distance, or difference factor, between the habituated ratio and the new test ratio is greater.
[b] The difference factor indicates the magnitude of the difference between the habituated and test ratios. A 2:1 ratio differs from a 4:1 ratio by a factor of 2 and differs from 3:1 by a factor of 1.5.
[c] The distance, or difference factor, between the habituated ratio and new test ratio is smaller.

McCrink and Wynn (2007) found that infants in the distant ratio group, on average, paid more attention to new ratios that differed by a factor of 2, whereas infants in the close ratio group did not pay attention to the new ratios that differed by a factor of 1.5. In other words, when the ratios of objects in the habituated and tested displays were very different, infants perceived them to be different. When the ratios of objects was less different, the infants did not appear to perceive the difference, even though the *number* of items was different in both conditions. Their findings suggest that infants can perceive differences in ratios, when they are sufficiently large, and thus must also be able to perceive the individual ratios between numbers of objects.

This work with infants has at least two implications for the development of nonsymbolic ratio reasoning. First, it demonstrates that the ability to represent and discriminate between ratios across numbers is early emerging, and thus likely supported by innate cognitive capacities. This idea is further supported by many similar studies with animals demonstrating sensitivity to differences or changes in proportions (Drucker, Rossa, & Brannon, 2016; Emmerton, 2001; Harper, 1982; McComb, Packer, & Pusey, 1994; Vallentin & Nieder, 2008). For example, recently, Drucker, Rossa, and Brannon (2016) demonstrated that rhesus macaques were able to choose a display with the larger ratio for a candy reward and, resembling the six-month-old infants, their accuracy was modulated by the differences in ratio. Second, the role of distance in infants', adults', and other animals' ability to discriminate proportions bears a striking similarity to the role of distance in infants' ability to discriminate numerosities of sets. As McCrink and Wynn (2007) discuss, six-month-old infants' approximate representations of numerosities appear parallel to their approximate representations of proportions, as, in both contexts, infants can discriminate sets that differ by a factor of 2 (20 dots vs. 40 dots, 2:1 dot ratio vs. 4:1 dot ratio), but not sets that differ by a factor of 1.5. Their work suggests a similar mechanism for numerical (whole number) discrimination and ratio (fraction) discrimination, although the exact mechanism remains unclear.

Despite these early competencies with nonsymbolic ratios and proportions, older children's and adults' nonsymbolic fraction reasoning sometimes appears to be sensitive to the nature of the proportional stimuli, specifically, whether the fraction is represented as a ratio of discrete, countable segments or a ratio of continuous amounts (Boyer & Levine, 2015; Boyer, Levine, & Huttenlocher, 2008; DeWolf, Bassok, & Holyoak, 2015). For example, Boyer and colleagues (2008) asked 1st, 2nd, 3rd, and 4th grade students to choose a mix of juice and water that matched a sample "recipe" (i.e., in the right proportions) to give to a very particular teddy bear. Children were shown a picture of a juice and water mixture in one of four conditions, which varied on how the "recipe" sample and the target proportion were displayed, either as continuous amounts of juice and water (e.g., as in an unmarked cylinder) or as discretized, countable sections of juice and water (e.g., as in a graduated cylinder; see Figure 7.3, Panel D). Then, they were asked to choose between a target which matched on juice:water ratio, but not the overall amount of fluid, or a foil which matched on the amount of juice or overall amount of fluid, but not the juice:water ratio. When both proportions were represented in a discretized way, children were less likely to choose the correct, proportion-match, and, instead, likely to choose a foil that matched the number of juice "sections." Thus, although children are able to reason about proportions and ratio when the components are continuous or not easily countable (e.g., in the dot ratio tasks), when ratio components are easily countable, children appear to rely on independent whole number components, rather than ratio, to match. Studies of children's symbolic fraction reasoning have uncovered parallel strategies during symbolic fraction comparison, and this reliance on only one ratio component has been attributed to a *whole number bias* (e.g., Ni & Zhou, 2005), which we will discuss further in the following section.

Symbolic Fractions

Given an early emerging ability to discriminate ratios, it might be expected that symbolic fractions would pose no special problems for young children. However, a wealth of research demonstrates that children, in particular those educated in the United States, have difficulty understanding the magnitudes and ratios expressed by symbolic fractions. For example, in interviews with elementary-aged children, Mack (1990, 1995) found that children learning about symbolic fractions in school displayed a range of misconceptions about the meanings of various fractions, many based on incorrect application of counting strategies to assess magnitude. For example, one young student reported 3/5 as meaning: "Oh, three fifths, that's three whole pumpkin pies with five pieces in each pie" (Mack, 1995, p. 431). As the example at the beginning of this chapter illustrates, even when children have an informal understanding of the magnitudes of fractional parts, this intuition is not always connected to their symbolic reasoning. Instead, often children, and sometimes adults, focus on the magnitudes of individual, whole number components of symbolic fractions in order to make sense of fraction symbols.

Children's systematic tendency to interpret fractions in a way that reflects robust transfer of children's early counting and whole number knowledge is often referred to as the *whole number bias* (e.g., Ni & Zhou, 2005). One common example of the whole number bias occurs when children are comparing fraction magnitudes and rely only on the denominator or the numerator component (i.e., the independent whole number component) to judge relative size. For example, children will often judge 1/3 as less than 1/4, because 3 is less than 4 (Behr et al., 1984) or judge 2/2 as less than 3/4, because 2 is less than 3 and 4 (Hartnett & Gelman, 1998). Even adults' fraction comparison is sometimes influenced by whole number components. Bonato and colleagues (2007) found that even adults rely on whole number magnitude representations while comparing unit fractions, fractions with 1 in the numerator (e.g., 1/5 vs. 1/4). When asked to decide which of the two symbolic fractions is bigger, Bonato and colleagues found that distances between *denominator components* significantly influenced the comparison speed (e.g., 5–4, for 1/5 vs. 1/4), such that participants were faster when the distances between denominator components was larger. The distances between the ratios (e.g., 0.20–0.25, for 1/5 vs. 1/4) did not significantly predict comparison speed, as it does in many nonsymbolic fraction comparison tasks, suggesting that adults were only attending to denominator components to make the comparison.

However, adults' reliance on independent whole number components during fraction comparison tasks is often constrained to pairs for which relying on either the numerator or the denominator to make comparisons is an efficient strategy. For example, when comparing two unit fractions, one can rely on their knowledge of the heuristic that larger denominators indicate smaller fractions, thus a comparison across denominator components will always result in a quick, accurate answer (see Table 7.2). Schneider and Siegler (2010) demonstrated a distance effect based on overall ratio, rather than components, when more complex, non-unit fractions (e.g., 7/9 vs. 3/5) were included in the task, preventing strategies based on independent components alone. This distance effect, based on the decimal distance between the two to-be-compared fractions, was taken as evidence that adults could reason about the holistic magnitude of fractions. Adults were more accurate when they compared more distant fractions.

Although relying on independent components to judge whether one fraction is larger than another can be advantageous in the magnitude comparison task, it should be noted that relying on only the denominator to estimate magnitude more precisely (e.g., when estimating the size of 1/60 relative to 1/1 and 1/1440) can decrease the accuracy of the estimate (Opfer & DeVries, 2008; Thompson & Opfer, 2008). Thus, by adulthood, people can accurately reason about the magnitude of symbolic

Table 7.2 *Common strategies for comparing fraction magnitudes among adults*

Strategy type	Strategy	Description	Example pairs[a]	
Strategies that rely on only the numerator or denominator magnitude	Equal denominators	When the denominators are equal, the fraction with the larger numerator is larger	2/5	3/5
	Equal numerators	When the numerators are equal, the fraction with the smaller denominator is larger	2/7	2/5
	Multiply for a common denominator	Multiply the numerator and denominator of one fraction by a whole number so that the denominators become equal, deploy *Equal Denominators* strategy	2/5	7/10
	Multiply for a common numerator	Multiply the numerator and denominator of one fraction by a whole number so that the numerators become equal, deploy *Equal Numerators* strategy	2/5	4/7
Strategies that rely on considering the numerator and denominator magnitudes	Larger numerator and smaller denominator	Fractions with larger numerators AND smaller denominators are larger in magnitude	2/5	3/4
	Difference between numerator and denominators	Fractions with smaller differences between denominators and numerators are larger	2/5	8/9
Strategies that rely on considering the ratio between numerator and denominator	Halves reference	When one fraction is less than 1/2, the fraction that is greater than 1/2 is larger	2/5	6/11
	Numerator goes into the denominator fewer times	Divide the denominator by the numerator; the smaller quotient is the larger fraction	2/5	7/17

Note. This strategy table is adapted from Fazio, DeWolf, and Siegler (2016). They found that adults rely on a range of strategies for magnitude comparison. These strategies can lead to accurate comparisons when used effectively.
[a] Larger fractions appear on the right.

fractions, using a variety of strategies, although they still have difficulty representing their magnitudes precisely. Given that fraction magnitude estimation is often a strategic, rather than automatic process, adults are slower to process fraction magnitudes than other kinds of numbers (e.g., decimals; DeWolf et al., 2014).

Siegler and colleagues (2011) demonstrated that, like adults, children also rely on a variety of strategies for estimating the magnitude of symbolic fractions. Siegler and colleagues examined 6th and 8th grade students' fraction understanding in a variety of tasks, including a fraction number line task. The fraction number line task is adapted from the original number line task (see Figure 7.2, Panel B) used to assess the nature of people's whole number magnitude representations (e.g., Siegler & Opfer, 2003). This task assesses symbolic fraction magnitude estimation by requiring participants to place fractions (e.g., 3/5) on a number line with given endpoints, often 0 and 1 or 0 and 5. Accuracy is measured with percentage absolute error (PAE), an index of the measured difference between the participant's placement of the fraction and the correct location of the fraction relative to the total length of the number line, such that higher PAE indicates lower accuracy.

Children use a wide variety of strategies in order to estimate fraction magnitudes on the fraction number line task (Siegler, et al., 2011; Siegler & Thompson, 2014), including highly advantageous strategies, such as transforming less familiar fractions into more familiar fractions and comparing fractions to subjective landmarks on the number line (e.g., using their knowledge of 1/2, the midpoint of the 0–1 line, as a landmark for estimating other fraction magnitudes), and less advantageous strategies, such as using the numerator or denominator magnitude to guide magnitude estimation (e.g., placing 3/7 near 0, since 3 is a small number). The highly advantageous transformation and landmarks strategies are common and often significantly related to lower PAE. As a further indicator of children's reliance on their strategic knowledge to estimate fraction magnitudes, children's estimations are often time-consuming compared to the time it typically takes younger children to estimate whole number magnitudes, and their estimates of fraction magnitudes are less accurate overall than whole number magnitudes (Fazio et al., 2014).

Taken together, this research (Bonato et al., 2007; DeWolf et al., 2014; Schneider & Siegler, 2010; Siegler et al., 2011; Siegler & Thompson, 2014) demonstrates that children's and adults' estimation of the magnitude of symbolic fractions requires them to process the ratio across component numbers, rather than automatically perceive that ratio, and both children and adults often rely on strategic knowledge to make estimations and comparisons. Importantly, this contrasts with the research on nonsymbolic fraction understanding, which likely relies on automatic processes.

The variability in children's and adults' strategy use across tasks and stimuli can account for the variability in evidence for the whole number bias. On the basis of this research, Alibali and Sidney (2015) have argued for a *dynamic strategy choice* account of the whole number bias, suggesting that people's strategy choices are guided by the strength of their magnitude representations for the numbers in the problems (e.g., how easily a person can directly estimate the magnitude of a number), their repertoire of available strategies, and the context or affordances of the task at hand. For example, among children who are still learning about fraction symbols, fraction magnitude representations and strategic knowledge are not well developed. In contrast, their knowledge of whole number magnitude representations and strategies may be quite well developed, and automatically activated, causing children to rely on their whole number knowledge and often resulting in the whole number bias. Similarly, adults may rely on whole number magnitude knowledge when the task stimuli afford whole number–based reasoning (e.g., as in Bonato et al.,

2007) or when their fraction magnitude representations are not precise enough to support a direct comparison (e.g., when comparing fractions that are close in magnitude, e.g., 4/5 and 7/9). Among older children and adults, having rich strategic knowledge helps them to leverage their whole number knowledge and avoid the pitfalls of the whole number bias.

Advanced Fraction Concepts

Children's knowledge of fractions extends beyond understanding the magnitudes of fraction symbols. For example, children also learn about other fraction properties, such as the idea that unlike natural, whole numbers, fractions cannot be counted in a sequence and that there are an infinite number of fractions between any two fractions. This latter idea is referred to as *numerical density*, and children's understanding of numerical density lags behind their understanding of fraction magnitudes (e.g., McMullen et al., 2015). Even when children understand the idea of numerical density in the context of whole numbers (i.e., there are an infinite number of numbers between any two whole numbers), they are less likely to understand this same idea in the context of fractions (i.e., there are an infinite number of numbers between any two fractions; e.g., Vamvakoussi & Vosniadou, 2010). Instead, 7th, 9th, and even 11th graders may claim, for example, that there are no fractions between 3/5 and 4/5 because there are no whole numbers between 3 and 4. Children may have difficulty reasoning about numerical density between fractions in part because of poorly developed or imprecise mental representations of fraction magnitudes or strategies for thinking about fraction magnitudes, thus relying on their knowledge of countable, whole number sequences to reason about density (for a discussion, see Alibali & Sidney, 2015). Even adults show evidence of a whole number bias, for example responding that there is only one number between 1/2 and 1/4 (e.g., 1/3), particularly when the experimenter highlights this possibility by gesturing once between 1/2 and 1/4 printed on paper (Brown, Donovan, & Alibali, 2016).

Furthermore, a great deal of research has examined children's ability to calculate and understand addition, subtraction, multiplication, and division with fractions. Children, and even adults, show deficits in their ability to apply fraction arithmetic procedures to symbolic problems. For example, Siegler and colleagues (Siegler et al., 2011; Siegler & Pyke, 2013) found that 6th and 8th grade children showed poor accuracy on fraction arithmetic problems across all four operations. Children often implemented incorrect strategies, such as operating on the numerators and denominators independently (e.g., 3/5 + 1/2 = 4/7) or inappropriately applying a problem-solving strategy meant for one operation on another, such as only operating on the numerators when the denominators are the same (e.g., 3/5 × 2/5 = 6/5), a correct procedure for fraction addition but not fraction multiplication. Both types of errors suggest spontaneous transfer for children's prior knowledge to these difficult problems. Furthermore, children's knowledge of fraction division appears to be especially poor. Even at 8th grade, long after fraction arithmetic instruction typically occurs in 5th and 6th grade (NGA & CCSSO, 2010), children's proficiency with fraction division calculation is quite low (46 percent correct; Siegler et al., 2011).

In addition, children often have a poor conceptual understanding of fraction operations and, most notably, fraction division (e.g., Sidney & Alibali, 2015; Richland & Hansen, 2013). As described in the "Mathematical Cognition and Education" section, even American elementary teachers are unsure of how fraction division might be represented in a "real-world" context (e.g., Ma, 1999). Studies assessing conceptual knowledge of fraction division often employ tasks in which people are asked to generate a story (e.g., Ball, 1990; Ma, 1999; Sidney & Alibali, 2015; Sidney, Hattikudur, & Alibali, 2015) or a diagram (e.g., Richland & Hansen, 2013; Sidney, 2016; Sidney et al., 2015) to represent a fraction division problem (see Figure 7.4). Similar to children's errors on solving symbolic fraction problems (e.g., Siegler & Pyke, 2013), children's errors on conceptual items often also reflect inappropriate transfer from their prior knowledge of other fraction operations. For example, children may write stories that represent multiplication and subtraction rather than division (e.g., for 5 ÷ ¼, representing ¼ of five units taken away from five whole units or 5 × (5 – ¼); see Figure 7.4, Panel B). Such errors are common (e.g., Sidney & Alibali, 2017) and are consistent with the misconception that "*division makes smaller*" (Fischbein et al., 1985). However, children's conceptual understanding of fraction division is improved by instruction that draws on children's more familiar, whole number division concepts (e.g., Richland & Hansen, 2013; Sidney, 2016; Sidney & Alibali, 2015). Such educational interventions will be further discussed in the "Implications for Instruction" section.

Developmental Pathways

Which aspects of children's early fraction understanding support children's later fraction understanding as well as their later mathematics achievement? Although the complete developmental picture is still emerging, we examine several correlational and longitudinal studies that shed light on what these pathways may be. First, we discuss the role of symbolic fraction magnitude understanding in fraction arithmetic and mathematics achievement. Second, we discuss the role of nonsymbolic fraction understanding in fraction development, and mathematics development more broadly. Finally, we consider the role of whole number knowledge and general cognitive predictors in children's fraction development.

As discussed in the "Mathematical Cognition and Education" section, much of the research on children's numerical development has occurred in the context of their whole number reasoning. Children's estimation and comparison of whole number magnitudes in nonsymbolic (e.g., Halberda et al., 2008; Schneider et al., 2017) and symbolic tasks (e.g., Booth & Siegler, 2008; Schneider et al., 2016) are correlated to mathematics achievement more broadly. In particular, children's whole number magnitude estimation on the number line task appears to be important for later success in mathematics. Children who are better able to estimate the magnitude of symbolic whole numbers on a number line are more proficient with whole number arithmetic (e.g., Geary et al., 2007; Geary et al., 2008) and have better memory for numbers (e.g., Thompson & Siegler, 2010). Furthermore, providing training that increases children's accuracy on a number line estimation task (e.g., by playing

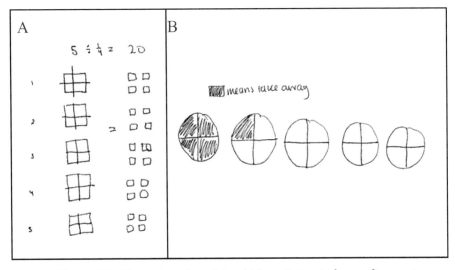

Figure 7.4 *Illustration of a task in which participants draw a diagram to represent a fraction division problem*

In some studies, children's and adults' understanding of the conceptual structure of fraction division is assessed by asking participants to draw a diagram to represent a fraction division problem. Panels A and B are examples of participants' drawings to represent 5 ÷ 1/4 from Sidney and Alibali (2012). Panel A shows accurate reasoning; 5 is divided in 20 subsections of 1/4. Panel B reflects the "division makes smaller" misconception, and represents a combination of multiplication and subtraction instead of division. Sidney and Alibali (2017) also documented this error using an object modeling task assessing fraction division concepts.

a board game in a left-to-right orientation, in parallel with the hypothesized mental number line) results in improvements in counting ability (Ramani & Siegler, 2008; Whyte & Bull, 2008) and arithmetic proficiency (e.g., Booth & Siegler, 2008; Siegler & Ramani, 2009). These findings suggest that the ability to precisely estimate the magnitude of numbers, as measured by the number line task, is a fundamental mathematics development.

Siegler and colleagues (2011) proposed that estimating the magnitude of symbolic fractions on a number line is similarly central to later mathematics understanding. Their *integrated theory of numerical development* posits an important role for the number line representation, in general. Thinking about numbers as represented on a continuous number line can support children's thinking about magnitudes of both whole numbers and fractions relative to 0, 1, and other numbers as well as children's thinking about other important numerical concepts such as numerical density between whole numbers and fractions.

In support of their hypothesis, and in parallel with the research of children's whole number development, both correlational and longitudinal studies have demonstrated that children's fraction magnitude understanding indeed supports more complex mathematics skills. Children's fraction magnitude understanding is correlated with their fraction arithmetic skills (Hecht & Vagi, 2010; Siegler et al., 2011), and both fraction magnitude understanding and fraction arithmetic skills are independently correlated with children's concurrent mathematics achievement (Fazio et al., 2014; Siegler 2011; Torbeyns et al., 2015). Knowledge of fraction magnitudes is necessary, although not sufficient, for understanding the density of rational numbers (McMullen et al., 2015). Furthermore, children's fraction knowledge predicts later, high school mathematics achievement over and above their knowledge of whole number arithmetic, IQ, working memory, and family education and income (Siegler et al., 2012). These findings clearly point to a central role of children's understanding of the magnitude of fraction symbols in numerical development more generally. However, the role of children's understanding of nonsymbolic ratios and proportions in their understanding of symbolic fractions, advanced fraction concepts, and mathematics achievement is less clear.

Children's and adults' nonsymbolic ratio understanding is correlated with symbolic fraction understanding (Fazio et al., 2014; Matthews, Lewis, & Hubbard; 2016; Möhring et al., 2016), algebra proficiency (Matthews, Lewis, & Hubbard, 2016), and general mathematics achievement (Fazio et al., 2014), although the relationships between symbolic fraction knowledge and achievement appear to be stronger than the correlations between nonsymbolic ratio understanding and achievement (Fazio et al., 2014). Furthermore, in a mediation model that included both whole number and fraction nonsymbolic and symbolic tasks, Fazio and colleagues examined the hypothesis that symbolic understanding of magnitudes mediates the relationship between nonsymbolic understanding and mathematics achievement – in other words, that nonsymbolic understanding is a precursor to symbolic magnitude understanding, which in turn affects children's general mathematics knowledge. They did not find support for this hypothesis. Instead, they found that nonsymbolic and symbolic magnitude understanding independently correlated with mathematics achievement, with a stronger correlation between symbolic knowledge and achievement, consistent with a recent meta-analysis (Schneider et al., 2017). However, their conclusions may be in part due to a reliance on measures of nonsymbolic and symbolic magnitude knowledge that include both whole number and fraction measures. Matthews and colleagues (2016) found that nonsymbolic ratio understanding, but *not* nonsymbolic whole number magnitude knowledge, was associated with algebra proficiency. Likewise, recent longitudinal work suggests that the relationships between nonsymbolic whole number magnitude comparison and later mathematics proficiency may be quite small when controlling for other general cognitive competencies (e.g., Sullivan, Frank, & Barner, 2016). Therefore, it remains unclear whether nonsymbolic ratio understanding directly affects the development of nonfraction mathematical knowledge or whether students' understanding of symbolic fractions, specifically, mediates this relationship.

In addition to nonsymbolic ratio reasoning, facets of children's early mathematics knowledge of whole numbers as well as several domain general processes support the development of children's fraction concepts and skills. For example, knowledge of whole number magnitudes is correlated with knowledge of fraction magnitudes in

5th grade (e.g., Fazio et al., 2014) and children's whole number division knowledge predicts concurrent fraction arithmetic proficiency in 6th and 8th grade (Siegler & Pyke, 2013). Furthermore, children's analogical reasoning ability supports their estimation of whole number magnitudes (Alvarez et al., 2017; Sullivan & Barner, 2014; Thompson & Opfer, 2010) and is related to their ability to complete number analogies (i.e., 30:60 is like 50:__) akin to symbolic fraction matching (Alvarez et al., 2017).

A handful of longitudinal studies have begun to reveal some of the developmental precursors of children's early symbolic fraction reasoning in 4th grade (Jordan et al., 2013; Vukovic et al., 2014). Children's early symbolic fraction knowledge in 4th grade is related to a variety of domain-general processes in 3rd grade, including their attentive behaviors in the classroom, language ability, nonverbal reasoning, and working memory (Jordan et al., 2013), and in 1st grade, including their language ability, attentive behaviors, and visuospatial memory (Vukovic et al., 2014). However, among the strongest predictors of children's 4th grade fraction understanding is children's 2nd (Vukovic et al., 2014) and 3rd grade (Jordan et al., 2013) whole number magnitude knowledge, as measured by the number line task. Moreover, Vukovic and colleagues (2014) found that children's number line estimation and whole number arithmetic fluency in 2nd grade fully mediated the relationships between 4th grade fraction knowledge and 1st grade domain-general skills.

Taken together, this research suggests that children's language ability, their ability to attend to instruction in the classroom, their working memory, and their analogical skills support mathematics learning more generally, and that children's whole number magnitude understanding is positively related to their fraction knowledge. This latter point is especially important in the context of research on the whole number bias. Although some aspects of children's whole number knowledge appear to interfere with fraction reasoning, understanding how to map whole numbers symbols to magnitudes on a number line provides an advantage for understanding fraction magnitudes as well.

Implications for Instruction

As we discussed at the beginning of the chapter, students' understanding of fraction concepts, such as the magnitudes associated with fraction symbols, and their understanding of fraction procedures, such as those for adding, subtracting, multiplying, and dividing fractions, is highly, and often uniquely, predictive of more complex mathematics and later mathematics achievement. Yet many students struggle with fractions, more so than other areas of mathematics (e.g., Hoffer et al., 2007). In this section, we consider the implications of the research on children's and adults' fraction reasoning for improving classroom instruction of this important area of early mathematics. First, we consider the aspects of children's fraction understanding on which educational interventions may have the broadest impact.

Areas for Intervention

The psychological research on children's ratio and fraction reasoning, as well as the developmental theory, points to children's mental representations of symbolic fractions as particularly important in mathematics education. As we have described in earlier sections, the accuracy of children's magnitude representations for symbolic fractions and, more generally, their ability to understand the magnitudes, ratios, and proportions to which symbolic fractions refer, critically support both later fraction reasoning as well as later mathematics skills, such as algebra reasoning. Although children's nonsymbolic reasoning and fraction arithmetic proficiency are correlated with later mathematics achievement, these correlations tend to be considerably weaker. One implication of these weaker correlations, coupled with the evidence that children appear to have competency representing and comparing nonsymbolic ratios quite early on, is that intervening on children's nonsymbolic reasoning may not be optimally productive. In contrast, although fraction arithmetic is not always correlated with later mathematics achievement, competency with fraction arithmetic is a practical skill and an important component of school mathematics (NGA & CCSSO, 2010) as well as the standardized tests used to measure mathematics proficiency (e.g., the NAEP and PISA; see the "Mathematical Cognition and Education" section). Thus, the research we have discussed in this chapter points to two areas in which educational interventions may be most impactful: children's understanding of symbolic fraction magnitudes and children's understanding of fraction arithmetic concepts and procedures.

Improving Magnitude Representations

Children's mental representations of symbolic fractions might be improved through several avenues. One possibility is to improve the accuracy and precision of children's nonsymbolic ratio representations in order to provide a better basis for understanding the magnitudes of symbolic fractions. This logic has also been applied to children's whole number reasoning, and some researchers have suggested that improving children's ANS acuity through training improves their ability to estimate the magnitudes of symbolic whole numbers (e.g., Park & Brannon, 2013). However, although nonsymbolic ratio reasoning is correlated with symbolic fraction reasoning, it remains unclear whether or how nonsymbolic ratio reasoning may be improved and whether greater accuracy at matching or estimating nonsymbolic ratios would necessarily, and spontaneously, result in substantive improvements in symbolic fraction magnitude estimation.

There may be more promise in interventions that target the links between children's nonsymbolic magnitude estimations and their symbolic reasoning. Tasks such as the number line estimation task directly address the link between the symbolic fraction that is placed on the number line and a nonsymbolic ratio (e.g., the ratio between the line length between 0 and the fraction and the total line length between 0 and 1; for discussion, see Sidney et al., 2017). Indeed, as discussed in the section "Developmental Pathways," Siegler and colleagues' (2011) integrated theory of numerical development suggests that the number line is a powerful tool for representing magnitudes of all rational numbers, including both whole numbers and fractions, and children's ability to represent numbers on a number line is highly predictive of later mathematics success. Furthermore, similar work on children's whole number understanding has shown that experience with linear, continuous representations of whole number magnitudes is causally related to improvements in children's understanding of the magnitudes that underlie symbolic numbers (e.g., Ramani & Siegler, 2008) as well as improvements in arithmetic (e.g., Siegler & Ramani, 2009).

One critical characteristic of the number line as a visual representation for understanding the magnitudes of symbolic fractions may be its continuous nature. Often, early fraction education in the United States includes area models of fractions that are discrete in nature (NGA & CCSSO, 2010). For example, in an area model, the fraction 3/5 might be represented as a circle with five sections, three of which are shaded. In contrast, on a number line, the fraction 3/5 might be represented as a continuous length that is 3/5 of the line length from 0 to 1 (see Figure 7.5). Boyer and colleagues' (Boyer & Levine, 2015; Boyer et al., 2008) studies of children's nonsymbolic ratio comparison suggest that children are better able to compare ratios across continuous representations than discretized, countable representations. Discrete representations afford counting, which in turn can cause whole number bias–type errors.

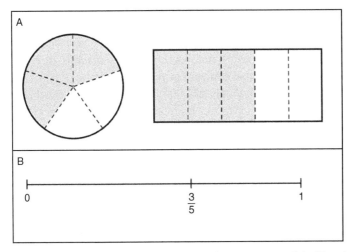

Figure 7.5 *Fractions can be represented using area models (Panel A) and number lines (Panel B)*

Research suggests that number lines are powerful tools for reasoning about the magnitudes of number symbols (e.g., Hamdan & Gunderson, 2017; Siegler, Thompson, & Schneider, 2011). Panel A shows a circular area model and rectangular area model, also known as a tape diagram, for the fraction 3/5. Panel B shows 3/5 represented on a continuous 0 to 1 number line.

Indeed, some educational interventions have demonstrated that including number line representations in instruction improves children's understanding of fraction magnitudes (e.g., Cramer, Post, & delMas, 2002). In their Rational Number Project (RNP), Cramer and colleagues designed fraction instruction that represented fractions with both area models and number line models to introduce fraction symbols and their magnitudes. The intervention also included opportunities to compare and contrast across different fraction representations. Cramer and colleagues found that RNP instruction was more effective in helping students learn about the magnitudes of fraction symbols, which in turn supported their understanding of fraction arithmetic, in comparison to fraction instruction that only included area models. This work provides some evidence that more continuous, number line representations are beneficial for children's fraction learning. However, there were many differences between the activities in the intervention and those in the control instruction, rendering it difficult to make a strong conclusion about the number line per se.

In one recent experimental study, Hamdan and Gunderson (2017) directly, and rigorously, compared children's learning about fraction magnitudes from number line and area models of fractions. In this study, 2nd and 3rd grade children were introduced to fraction symbols for the first time using continuous, number line representations or discrete, area representations of their magnitudes. After the lesson, children who learned about fraction magnitudes using number line representations were not only better able to represent fractions on a number line than children who learned about fractions using area representations but also more accurate at comparing symbolic fractions, a task that had not been introduced in the lesson. Furthermore, children in the number line condition displayed less evidence of errors stemming from a whole number bias. Thus, learning about the magnitudes represented by fraction symbols using number line representations directly supports children's ability to estimate and compare symbolic fractions.

Number line representations may also be advantageous to children's fraction learning because they are *abstract* representations of numerical magnitude. Mathematics textbooks often represent number concepts with real objects and sometimes visually detailed illustrations. Researchers across psychology, educational psychology, and mathematics education have questioned whether concrete representations of mathematical concepts benefit or limit students' learning about those mathematical concepts, in comparison to more abstract representations. Although concrete representations can sometimes constrain children's errors during problem-solving and learning, by providing familiar contexts for thinking about abstract concepts (e.g., Koedinger, Alibali, & Nathan, 2008; McNeil et al., 2009), learners are better able to generalize their knowledge to new problems when they learn with abstract representations (e.g., Kaminski, Sloutsky, & Heckler, 2008). The abstract nature of the number line representation, compared to representing fractions as pies or pizzas for example, may be yet another reason why learning about fractions on number lines results in generalizable knowledge.

In addition to including number line representations in instruction, children's understanding of fraction magnitudes may also be supported by drawing on their knowledge of whole number magnitudes. Despite evidence of the whole number bias in children's fraction reasoning, the developmental research makes clear that children's whole number magnitude estimation is correlated with their fraction magnitude estimation. Thus, interventions that focus on integration of children's fraction understanding with their prior knowledge of whole number magnitudes may also prove successful.

In one such intervention, Moss and Case (1999) developed a rational number curriculum in which children's experiences with fractions drew on earlier lessons including decimal and whole number magnitudes. In their instruction, children were first shown how to connect their understanding of whole numbers between 0 and 100 to representations of percentage (i.e., 0 percent to 100 percent). Then, the instructor linked between percentages and decimals (i.e., 0.00 to 1.00). Finally, the instructors built on children's understanding of decimals between 0 and 1 to make sense of fractions between 0 and 1. Along the way, the instructor used continuous linear representations, akin to the number line, to ground students' understanding of numerical magnitude. Children who received the experimental instruction, in which their whole number knowledge was leveraged to make sense of rational number magnitudes, showed a better understanding of fraction magnitudes and fewer whole number bias errors than children who learned via typical instruction. Although, as in the RNP curriculum (Cramer et al., 2002), any of the components of the instruction may have contributed to student learning, this study provides converging evidence with that of the longitudinal studies that children's whole number magnitude knowledge underlies their understanding of numerical magnitude, more generally.

Improving Fraction Arithmetic

Few experimental interventions are specifically aimed at improving children's fraction arithmetic skills, rather than at improving children's arithmetic skill through their understanding of symbolic fraction magnitudes. Indeed, competence at estimating the magnitude of symbolic fractions is correlated with fraction arithmetic skill, and improvements in magnitude estimation are likely causally related to improvements in addition and subtraction of fractions. In children's whole number reasoning, providing support for children's visualization of whole number magnitudes improves their ability to add whole numbers (Booth & Siegler, 2008). Similarly, being able to visualize or estimate the magnitude of a fraction may also support children's ability to estimate or predict the answer to fraction addition and subtraction problems.

Although children's fraction magnitude knowledge may help them better estimate or predict the answer to fraction addition or subtraction problems, children's knowledge of the multiplicative operations, and of division specifically, tends to be much less robust than their knowledge of addition and subtraction (Dixon, Deets, & Bangert, 2001). Thus, improving children's knowledge of fraction magnitudes may not be sufficient to improve children's understanding of fraction division, without also supporting children's understanding of the division concepts.

A handful of studies suggest that drawing on students' prior knowledge of whole number division concepts during fraction division instruction can improve students' fraction division learning (Richland & Hansen, 2013; Sidney, 2016; Sidney & Alibali, 2015). In these studies, the instructor first reminds 5th and 6th grade children about what it means to divide by a whole number (e.g., division can be construed as dividing into groups as big as the divisor) and then introduces the analogous concept in the context of fraction division. Reminding children about their relevant prior knowledge of whole number division before the lesson improves children's mental models for fraction division (Richland & Hansen, 2013; Sidney, 2016; Sidney & Alibali, 2015) and their problem-solving accuracy (Sidney & Alibali, 2015).

However, these studies have mixed recommendations on the extent to which this link should be made explicitly for students. Richland and Hansen (2013) found that making the analogy between whole number division and fraction division with a high degree of instructional support (e.g., using similar visual representations, using gesture to indicate corresponding features across whole number and fraction division) was beneficial for student learning. In contrast, Sidney and Alibali (Sidney, 2016; Sidney & Alibali, 2015) have found that reminding students about whole number division prior to fraction division instruction, but not explicitly making analogies between division problems, results in fewer misconceptions and better transfer to novel problems than making explicit analogies either with or without a high degree of instructional support. Although these studies highlight the benefits of drawing on children's prior knowledge of whole numbers during fraction learning, the specific aspects of instruction that might best support this link remain unclear. In the next section, we outline future directions, both for applied research on fraction instruction and basic research on the development of children's mathematical reasoning.

Future Directions

Recently, several experts across the fields of mathematics education, educational psychology, psychology, and neuroscience engaged in a collaborative exercise to outline the most important questions about children's mathematical cognition, given the current state of research and theory (Alcock et al., 2016). Their agenda included questions pertaining to the developmental pathways of mathematical cognition (e.g., "What are reliable early and later longitudinal predictors of the development of number skills, arithmetic, and other aspects of mathematics?," p. 26) as well as to the interactions between developmental trajectories (e.g., "How are different mathematical skills (including representing number, counting, performing arithmetic, using fractions) and their developmental trajectories related to each other?," p. 27). They also challenged mathematics cognition researchers to shed light on educational interventions (e.g., "Which domain-specific foundational competencies are most malleable and when in developmental time? And does their malleability impact on other aspects of mathematical performance?") and develop measures that would allow for better comparison across studies. As we have discussed in this chapter, many researchers have addressed these questions in the context of children's fraction development. Still, we see several avenues for future research that would contribute to our understanding of both children's fraction development and children's mathematics development more generally.

First, although longitudinal and other correlational studies are beginning to uncover the precursory whole number competencies for later fraction reasoning, further research is needed to provide a more comprehensive account of the relationship between the development of children's whole number reasoning and the development of children's fraction reasoning. Young children demonstrate early competence in reasoning about both nonsymbolic sets and ratios, and symbolic whole number magnitude estimation is correlated with symbolic fraction magnitude estimation. However, the specific relationships between nonsymbolic and symbolic whole number and fraction competencies, and the interactions between their developmental trajectories, remain unclear. For example, what is the relationship between children's ability to estimate numerosity of sets and their ability to estimate ratios? Do these competencies develop independently or in parallel? Is it advantageous for children to develop symbolic knowledge of whole numbers prior to understanding symbolic fractions, or would it be more advantageous to introduce fractions earlier, to prevent a strong whole number bias?

Second, although several researchers have found positive correlations across fraction tasks and between fraction tasks and general mathematics achievement, some of the evidence shows mixed results – for example, the evidence for relationships between nonsymbolic ratio reasoning and mathematics achievement. Furthermore, much of this research is correlational, therefore, it remains unclear which pathways are causal and open to intervention.

One barrier to both of these goals is that mixed findings across studies may be due in part to differences across tasks used to measure ostensibly the same underlying competency. For example, some nonsymbolic tasks represent fractions as ratios across dots whereas others represent ratios across line lengths (see Matthews & Chesney, 2015). In some studies, the components are separated and in others they are joined (see Möhring et al., 2016). Future research is needed to further explore the consequences of differences across tasks and create standardized measures to facilitate comparison across studies and research labs.

In addition to these questions about the developmental pathways toward fraction understanding, current research on children's fraction development has opened up several new questions about children's analogical and relational reasoning. For example, given the relationships between children's whole number and fraction reasoning, more research is needed to understand the roles of analogical mapping and transfer in integrating children's knowledge about whole numbers, fractions, and other kinds of numbers. Do the same types of instructional features (i.e., visual representations, familiar source domain, shared labels) that support children's analogical and relational reasoning also support learning about fraction concepts? What is the relationship between the development of children's relational reasoning, the general cognitive competencies that support relational reasoning (e.g., executive functioning), and their understanding of fractions as a relational concept?

Finally, there are many more applied questions to pursue. Here, we have argued for the number line as critically important for grounding children's mental representations of fraction magnitudes. Although Hamdan and Gunderson (2017) have empirically demonstrated the promise of number line representations for children's learning, more research is needed to examine the instructional activities that would support further learning, such as learning about arithmetic operations with fractions. Furthermore, several of the theoretical questions we have posed here may also further efforts to design fraction instruction that fully supports children's early fraction concepts, as well as the specific aspects of fraction competencies that underlie students' success with algebra and more advanced mathematics concepts.

Conclusions

Children's understanding of fractions, including their symbols, concepts, and arithmetic procedures, is an important facet of both developmental research on mathematics cognition and mathematics education. Research on infants', children's, and adults' fraction and ratio reasoning allows us to test a range of proposals about the development of numerical cognition that have largely been developed with natural, whole numbers in mind. As with whole numbers, even young infants can reason about nonsymbolic ratios, people's ability to compare nonsymbolic ratios is governed by the ratio between ratios, and children's ability to accurately place fractions on a number line predicts later competencies and mathematics achievement on standardized measures. However, as with whole numbers, the causal relationships between early emerging nonsymbolic competencies and later symbolic competencies remain underspecified. The developmental research opens several avenues for improving mathematics education. Here, we have focused on the inclusion of the number line representation and analogies between children's prior knowledge of whole numbers and related fraction concepts as two beneficial facets of fraction instruction. Although children's fraction understanding has recently received a great deal of attention, this work has opened up many additional questions, and more empirical research on the relationships between nonsymbolic and symbolic whole number and fraction tasks is necessary to paint a clearer picture of the development of children's understanding of fractions.

References

Alcock, L., Ansari, D., Batchelor, S., Bisson, M.-J., De Smedt, B., Gilmore, C., . . . Weber, K. (2016). Challenges in mathematical cognition: A collaboratively-derived research agenda. *Journal of Numerical Cognition, 2*(1), 20–41. https://doi.org/10.5964/jnc .v2i1.10

Alibali, M. W. & Sidney, P. G. (2015). Variability in the natural number bias: Who, when, how, and why?. *Learning and Instruction, 37*, 56–61. https://doi.org/10.1016/j .learninstruc.2015.01.003

Alvarez, J., Abdul-Chani, M., Deutchman, P., DiBiasie, K., Iannucci, J., Lipstein, R., ..., Sullivan, J. (2017). Estimation as analogy-making: Evidence that preschoolers' analogical reasoning ability predicts their numerical estimation. *Cognitive Development*, 41, 73–84. http://dx.doi.org/10.1016/j.cogdev.2016.12.004

Bailey, D. H., Siegler, R. S., & Geary, D. C. (2014). Early predictors of middle school fraction knowledge. *Developmental Science*, *17*(5), 775–785. https://doi.org/10.1111/desc.12155

Ball, D. L. (1990). Prospective elementary and secondary teachers' understandings of division. *Journal for Research in Mathematics Education*, *21*(2), 132–144. https://doi.org/10.2307/749140

Barth, H., Kanwisher, N., & Spelke, E. (2003). The construction of large number representations in adults. *Cognition*, *86*(3), 201–221. https://doi.org/10.1016/S0010-0277(02)00178-6

Behr, M., Wachsmuth, I., Post T., & Lesh R. (1984). Order and equivalence of rational numbers: A clinical teaching experiment. *Journal for Research in Mathematics Education*, *15*(5), 323–341. https://doi.org/10.2307/748423

Bonato, M., Fabbri, S., Umilta, C., & Zorzi, M. (2007). The mental representation of numerical fractions: Real or integer?. *Journal of Experimental Psychology: Human Perception and Performance*, *33*(6), 1410–1419. https://doi.org/10.1037/0096-1523.33.6.1410

Booth, J. L. & Newton, K. J. (2012). Fractions: Could they really be the gatekeeper's doorman? *Contemporary Educational Psychology*, *37* (4), 247–253. http://dx.doi.org/10.1016/j.cedpsych.2012.07.001.

Booth, J. L. & Siegler, R. S. (2008). Numerical magnitude representations influence arithmetic learning. *Child Development*, *79*(4), 1016–1031. https://doi.org/10.1111/j.1467-8624.2008.01173.x

Boyer, T. W. & Levine, S. C. (2015). Prompting children to reason proportionally: Processing discrete units as continuous amounts. *Developmental Psychology*, *51*(5), 615–620. http://dx.doi.org/10.1037/a0039010

Boyer, T. W., Levine, S. C., & Huttenlocher, J. (2008). Development of proportional reasoning: Where young children go wrong. *Developmental Psychology*, *44*(5), 1478–1490. https://doi.org/10.1037/a0013110

Brannon, E. M. & Terrace, H. S. (1998). Ordering of numerosities 1 to 9 by monkeys. *Science*, *282*(5389), 746–749. https://doi.org/10.1126/science.282.5389.746

Brown, S. A., Donovan, A. M., & Alibali, M. W. (2016). *Gestural schematization influences understanding of infinite divisibility*. Paper presented at the Fourth Annual Midwest Meeting on Mathematical Thinking, Madison, WI.

Cramer, K. A., Post, T. R., & delMas, R. C. (2002). Initial fraction learning by fourth- and fifth-grade students: A comparison of the effects of using commercial curricula with the effects of using the rational number project curriculum. *Journal for Research in Mathematics Education*, *33*(2), 111–144. https://doi.org/10.2307/749646

Dehaene, S. (2003). The neural basis of Weber-Fechner's law: Neuronal recordings reveal a logarithmic scale for number. *Trends in Cognitive Science*, *7*(4), 145–147.

DeWind, N. K., & Brannon, E. M. (2012). Malleability of the approximate number system: Effects of feedback and training. *Frontiers in Human Neuroscience*, *6* (68). https://doi.org/10.3389/fnhum.2012.00068

DeWolf, M., Bassok, M., & Holyoak, K. J. (2015). From rational numbers to algebra: Separable contributions of decimal magnitude and relational understanding of

fractions. *Journal of Experimental Child Psychology, 133*(1), 72–84. http://dx.doi
.org/10.1016/j.jecp.2015.01.013

DeWolf, M., Grounds, M. A., Bassok, M., & Holyoak, K. J. (2014). Magnitude comparison
with different types of rational numbers. *Journal of Experimental Psychology:
Human Perception and Performance, 40*(1), 71–82. https://doi.org/10.1037/
a0032916

Dixon, J. A., Deets, J. K., & Bangert, A. (2001). The representation of the arithmetic
operations include functional relationships. *Memory and Cognition, 29*(3),
462–477.

Drucker,C. B., Rossau, M. A., & Brannon, E. M. (2016). Comparison of discrete ratios by
rhesus macaques (*Macaca mulatta*). *Animal Cognition, 19*(1), 75–89. https://doi
.org/10.1007/s10071-015-0914-9

Duffy, S., Huttenlocher, J., & Levine, S. C. (2005). How infants encode spatial extent. *Infancy,
8*(1), 81–90. https://doi.org/10.1207/s15327078in0801_5

Emmerton, J. (2001). Pigeons' discrimination of color proportion in computer-generated
visual displays. *Animal Learning and Behavior, 29*(1), 21–35. https://doi.org/
10.3758/BF03192813

Fazio, L. K., Bailey, D. H., Thompson, C. A., & Siegler, R. S. (2014). Relations of different
types of numerical magnitude representations to each other and to mathematics
achievement. *Journal of Experimental Child Psychology, 123*(1), 53–72, http://dx
.doi.org/10.1016/j.jecp.2014.01.013.

Feigenson, L., Dehaene, S., & Spelke, E. (2004). Core systems of number. *Trends in Cognitive
Science, 8*(7), 308–314. https://doi.org/10.1016/j.tics.2004.05.002

Fischbein, E., Deri, M., Nello, M. S., & Marino, M. S. (1985). The role of implicit models in
solving verbal problems in multiplication and division. *Journal for Research in
Mathematics Education, 16*(1), 3–17. https://doi.org/10.2307/748969

Fuhs, M. W. & McNeil, N. M. (2013). ANS acuity and mathematics ability in preschoolers
from low-income homes: Contributions of inhibitory control. *Developmental
Science, 16*(1), 136–148. https://doi.org/10.1111/desc.12013

Geary, D. C., Hoard, M. K., Nugent, L., & Byrd-Craven, J. (2008). Development of number
line representations in children with mathematics learning disability.
Developmental Neuropsychology, 33(3), 277–299. https://doi.org/10.1080/
87565640801982361

Geary, D. C., Hoard, M. K., Byrd-Craven, J., Nugent, L., & Numtee, C. (2007). Cognitive
mechanisms underlying achievement deficits in children with mathematics learning
disability. *Child Development, 78*(4), 1343–1359. https://doi.org/10.1111/j.1467-
8624.2007.01069.x

Gebuis, T. & Reynvoet, B. (2012). The interplay between nonsymbolic number and its
continuous visual properties. *Journal of Experimental Psychology: General, 141*
(4), 642–648. https://doi.org/10.1037/a0026218

Gentner, D. (1988). Metaphor as structure mapping: The relational shift. *Child Development,
59*(1), 47–59. https://doi.org/10.2307/1130388

Goswami, U. (1995). Phonological development and reading by analogy: What is analogy and
what is it not?. *Journal of Research in Reading, 18*(2), 139–145. https://doi.org/
0.1111/j.1467-9817.1995.tb00080.x

Goswami, U. & Brown, A. L. (1990). Melting chocolate and melting snowman: Analogical
reasoning and causal relations. *Cognition, 35*(1), 69–95. http://dx.doi.org/10.1016/
0010-0277(90)90037-K

Halberda, J. & Feigenson, L. (2008). Developmental change in the acuity of the "Number Sense": The approximate number system in 3-, 4-, 5-, 6-year-olds and adults. *Developmental Psychology, 44*(5), 1457–1465. https://doi.org/10.1037/a0012682

Halberda, J., Mazzocco, M. M. M., & Feigenson, L. (2008). Individual differences in non-verbal number acuity correlate with maths achievement. *Nature, 455*, 665–668. https://doi.org/10.1038/nature07246

Hamdan, N. & Gunderson, E. A. (2017). The number line is a critical spatial-numerical representation: Evidence from a fraction intervention. *Developmental Psychology.* 53(3), 587–596. http://dx.doi.org/10.1037/dev0000252

Harper, D. (1982). Competitive foraging in mallards: "ideal free" ducks. *Animal Behavior, 30*, 575–584.

Hartnett, P., & Gelman, R. (1998). Early understandings of numbers: Paths or barriers to the construction of new understandings? Learning and Instruction, 8(4), 341–374.

Hecht, S. A. & Vagi, K. J. (2010). Sources of group and individual differences in emerging fraction skills. *Journal of Educational Psychology, 102*, 843–858. http://dx.doi.org/10.1037/a0019824

Hoffer, T. B., Venkataraman L., Hedberg, E. C., & Shagle, S. (2007). *Final report on the National Survey of Algebra Teachers (for the National Mathematics Advisory Panel Subcommittee).* Washington, DC: US Department of Education (Conducted by the National Opinion Research Center at the University of Chicago). http://www2.ed .gov/about/bdscomm/list/mathpanel/report/nsat.pdf

Jordan, N. C., Hansen, N., Fuchs, L. S., Siegler, R. S., Gersten, R., & Micklos, D. (2013). Developmental predictors of fraction concepts and procedures. *Journal of Experimental Child Psychology, 116*(1), 45–58. http://dx.doi.org/10.1016/j .jecp.2013.02.001

Kaminski, J. A., Sloutsky, V. M., & Heckler, A. F. (2008). The advantage of abstract examples in learning math. *Science, 320*(5875), 454–455. https://doi.org/10.1126/ science.1154659

Knops, A., Viarouge, A., & Dehaene, S. (2009). Dynamic representations underlying symbolic and nonsymbolic calculation: Evidence from the operational momentum effect. *Attention Perception and Psychophysics, 71*(4), 803–821. https://doi.org/ 10.3758/APP.71.4.803

Koedinger, K. R., Alibali, M. W., & Nathan, M. J. (2008). Trade-offs between grounded and abstract representations: Evidence from algebra problem solving. *Cognitive Science, 32*(2),366–397. https://doi.org/10.1080/03640210701863933

Leibovich, T., Kallai, A. Y., & Itamar, S. (2016). What do we measure when we measure magnitudes? In A. Henik (ed.), *Continuous issues in numerical cognition* (pp. 355–373). Cambridge, MA: Academic Press.

Leibovich, T., Katzin, N., Harel, M., & Henik, A. (2017). From "sense of number" to "sense of magnitude": The role of continuous magnitudes in numerical cognition. *Behavior and Brain Sciences*, 40, e164. https://doi.org/10.1017/S0140525X16000960

Lewis M. R., Matthews P. G., & Hubbard E. M. (2015). Neurocognitive architectures and the nonsymbolic foundations of fractions understanding. In D. B. Berch, D. C. Geary, & K. M. Koepke (eds.), *Development of mathematical cognition: Neural substrates and genetic influences* (pp. 141–160). San Diego, CA: Academic Press.

Lo, J.-J. & Leu, F. (2012). Prospective elementary teachers' knowledge of fraction division. *Journal of Mathematics Teacher Education, 15*(6), 481–500. https://doi.org/ 10.1007/s10857-012-9221-4

Ma, L. (1999).*Knowing and teaching elementary mathematics: Teachers' understanding of fundamental mathematics in China and the United States*. Mahwah, NJ: Lawrence Erlbaum.

Mack, N. K. (1990). Learning fractions with understanding: Building on informal knowledge. *Journal for Research in Mathematics Education, 21*(1), 16–32. https://doi.org/ 10.2307/749454

(1995). Confounding whole-number and fraction concepts when building on informal knowledge. *Journal for Research in Mathematics Education, 26*(5), 422–441. https://doi.org/10.2307/749431

Matthews, P. G. & Chesney, D. L. (2015). Fractions as percepts? Exploring cross-format distance effects for fractional magnitudes. *Cognitive Psychology, 78*, 28–56. http:// dx.doi.org/10.1016/j.cogpsych.2015.01.006

Matthews, P. G. & Hubbard, E. M. (2017). Making space for spatial proportions. *Journal of Learning Disabilities. 50*(6), 644–647. https://doi.org/10.1177/0022219416679133

Matthews, P. G., Lewis, M. R., & Hubbard, E. M. (2016). Individual differences in nonsymbolic ratio processing predict symbolic math performance. *Psychological Science, 27*(2), 191–202. https://doi.org/10.1177/0956797615617799

McComb, K., Packer, C., & Pusey, A. (1994). Roaring and numerical assessment in contests between groups of female lions, Panthera leo. *Animal Behavior, 47*(2), 379–387. http://dx.doi.org/10.1006/anbe.1994.1052

McCrink, K., Spelke, E. S., Dehaene, S., & Pica, P. (2013). Non-symbolic halving in an Amazonian indigene group. *Developmental Science, 16*(3), 451–462. https://doi .org/10.1111/desc.12037

McCrink, K. & Wynn, K. (2007). Ratio abstraction by 6-month-old infants. *Psychological Science, 18*(8), 740–175. https://doi.org/10.1111/j.1467-9280.2007.01969.x

McMullen, J., Laakkonen, E., Hannula-Sormunen, M., & Lehtinen, E. (2015). Modeling the developmental trajectories of rational number concept(s). *Learning and Instruction, 37*, 14–20. http://dx.doi.org/10.1016/j.learninstruc.2013.12.004

McNeil, N. M., Uttal, D. H., Jarvin, L., & Sternberg, R. J. (2009). Should you show me the money? Concrete objects both hurt and help performance on mathematics problems. *Learning and Instruction, 19*, 171–184. https://doi.org/10.1016/j.learninstruc .2008.03.005

Meck, W. H. & Church, R. M. (1983). A mode control model of counting and timing processes. *Journal of Experimental Psychology: Animal Behavior Processes, 9*(3), 320–334. http://dx.doi.org/10.1037/0097-7403.9.3.320

Meert, G., Grégoire, J., Seron, X., & Noël, M. P. (2012). The mental representation of the magnitude of symbolic and nonsymbolic ratio in adults. *Quarterly Journal of Experimental Psychology, 65*(4), 702–724. https://doi.org/10.1080/17470218.2011 .632485

Mix, K. S., Huttenlocher, J., & Levine, S. C. (2002). Multiple cues for quantification in infancy: Is number one of them? *Psychological Bulletin, 128*(2), 278–294. http://dx .doi.org/10.1037/0033-2909.128.2.278

Mix, K. S., Levine, S. C., & Huttenlocher, J. (1999). Early fraction calculation ability. *Developmental Psychology, 35*(1), 164–174.

Möhring, W., Newcombe, N. S., Levine, S. C., & Frick, A. (2016). Spatial proportional reasoning is associated with formal knowledge about fractions. *Journal of Cognition and Development, 17*(1), 67–84. https://doi.org/10.1080/15248372.2014 .996289

Moss, J. & Case, R. (1999). Developing children's understanding of the rational numbers: A new model and an experimental curriculum. *Journal for Research in Mathematics Education, 30*(2), 127–147. https://doi.org/10.2307/749607

Moyer, R. S. & Landauer, T. K. (1967). Time required for judgements of numerical inequality. *Nature, 215*, 1519–1520. https://doi.org/10.1038/2151519a0

Namkung, J. M. & Fuchs, L. S. (2016). Cognitive predictors of calculations and number line estimation with whole numbers and fractions among at-risk students. *Journal of Educational Psychology, 108*(2), 214–228. https://doi.org/10.1037/edu0000055

NCTM (National Council of Teachers of Mathematics). (2007). *Second handbook of research on mathematics teaching and learning.* Washington, DC: NCTM.

NGA & CCSSO (National Governors Association & Council of Chief State School Officers). (2010). *Common core state standards for mathematics.* www.corestandards.org/assets/CCSSI_Math%20Standards.pdf

Ni, Y. & Zhou, Y. (2005). Teaching and learning fraction and rational numbers: The origins and implications of whole number bias. *Educational Psychology, 40*(1), 27–52. http://dx.doi.org/10.1207/s15326985ep4001_3

OECD (Organisation for Economic Co-operation and Development). (2016). *PISA 2015: PISA results in focus.* www.oecd.org/pisa/pisa-2015-results-in-focus.pdf

Opfer, J. E. & DeVries, J. M. (2008). Representational change and magnitude estimation: Why young children can make more accurate salary comparisons than adults. *Cognition, 108*(3), 843–849. http://dx.doi.org/10.1016/j.cognition.2008.05.003

Opfer, J. E. & Siegler, R. S. (2007). Representational change and children's numerical estimation. *Cognitive Psychology, 55*(3), 169–195. https://doi.org/10.1016/j.cogpsych.2006.09.002

Park, J. & Brannon, E. M. (2013). Training the approximate number system improves math proficiency. *Psychological Science, 24*(10), 2013–2019. https://doi.org/10.1177/0956797613482944

Ramani, G. B. & Siegler, R. S. (2008). Promoting broad and stable improvements in low-income children's numerical knowledge through playing number board games. *Child Development, 79*(2), 375–394.

Rattermann, M. J. & Gentner, D. (1998). More evidence for a relational shift in the development of analogy: Children's performance on a causal-mapping task. *Cognitive Development, 13*(4), 453–478. http://dx.doi.org/10.1016/S0885-2014(98)90003-X

Richland, L. E. & Hansen, J. H. (2013). Reducing cognitive load in learning by analogy. *International Journal of Psychological* Studies, 5(4), 69–80. https://doi.org/10.5539/ijps.v5n4p

Richland, L. E. & McDonough, I. M. (2010). Learning by analogy: Discriminating between two potential analogs. *Contemporary Educational Psychology, 23*(1), 28–43. https://doi.org/10.1016/j.cedpsych.2009.09.001

Richland, L. E., Zur, O., & Holyoak, K. J. (2007). Cognitive supports for analogies in the mathematics classroom. *Science, 316*(5828), 1128–1129. https://doi.org/10.1126/science.1142103

Schneider, M., Beeres, K., Coban, L., Merz, S., Schmidt, S. S., Stricker, J., & De Smedt, B. (2017). Associations of non-symbolic and symbolic numerical magnitude processing with mathematical competence: A meta-analysis. *Developmental Science. 20*(3), 1–16. https://doi.org/10.1111/desc.12372

Schneider, M. & Siegler, R. S. (2010). Representations of the magnitudes of fractions. *Journal of Experimental Psychology: Human Perception and Performance, 36*(5), 1227–1238. https://doi.org/10.1037/a0018170

Sidney, P. G. (2016). Does new learning provide new perspectives on familiar concepts? Exploring the role of analogical instruction in conceptual change in arithmetic. (Unpublished doctoral dissertation). University of Wisconsin-Madison.

Sidney, P. G. & Alibali, M. W. (2012). Supporting conceptual representations of fraction division by activating prior knowledge domains. In L. R. Van Zoest, J.-J. Lo, & J. L. Kratky (eds.) *Proceedings of the 34th annual meeting of the North American Chapter of the International Group for the Psychology of Mathematics Education* (1012). Kalamazoo: Western Michigan University.

Sidney, P. G. & Alibali, M. W. (2015). Making connections in math: Activating a prior knowledge analogue matters for learning. *Journal of Cognition and Development*, *16*(1), 160–185. https://doi.org/10.1080/15248372.2013.792091

(2017). Creating a context for learning: Activating children's whole number knowledge prepares them to understand fraction division. *Journal of Numerical Cognition, 3* (1), 31–57. https://doi.org/10.5964/jnc.v3i1.71

Sidney, P. G., Hattikudur, S., & Alibali, M. W. (2015). How do contrasting cases and self-explanation promote learning? Evidence from fraction division. *Learning and Instruction*, *40*, 29–38. https://doi.org/10.1016/j.learninstruc.2015.07.006

Sidney, P. G., Thompson, C. A., Matthews, P. G., & Hubbard, E. M. (2017). From continuous magnitudes to symbolic numbers: The centrality of ratio. Behavioral and Brain Sciences, 40, e190. https://doi.org/10.1017/S0140525X16002284

Siegler, R. S. (2016). Magnitude knowledge: The common core of numerical development. *Developmental Science*, *19*(3), 341–361. https://doi.org/10.1111/desc.12395

Siegler, R. S. & Booth, J. L. (2004). Development of numerical estimation in young children. *Child Development*, *75*(2), 428–444. https://doi.org/10.1111/j.1467-8624.2004.00684.x

Siegler, R., Carpenter, T., Fennell, F., Geary, D., Lewis, J., Okamoto, Y., Thompson, L., & Wray, J. (2010). *Developing effective fractions instruction for kindergarten through 8th grade: A practice guide* (NCEE #2010-4039). Washington, DC: National Center for Education Evaluation and Regional Assistance, Institute of Education Sciences, US Department of Education. whatworks.ed.gov/ publications/practiceguides.

Siegler, R. S., Duncan, G. J., Davis-Kean, P. E. et al. (2012). Early predictors of high school mathematics achievement. *Psychological Science*, *23*(7), 691–697. https://doi.org/10.1177/0956797612440101

Siegler, R. S., Fazio, L. K., Bailey, D. H., & Zhou, X. (2013). Fractions: The new frontier for theories of numerical development. *Trends in Cognitive Science*, *17*(1), 13–19.

Siegler, R. S. & Lortie-Forgues, H. (2014). An integrative theory of numerical development. *Child Development Perspectives*, *8*(3), 144–150, https://doi.org/10.1111/cdep.12077

Siegler, R. S., & Opfer, J. E. (2003). The development of numerical estimation: Evidence for multiple representations of numerical quantity. *Psychological Science*, 14(3), 237–243.

Siegler, R. S. & Pyke, A. A. (2013). Developmental and individual differences in understanding of fractions. *Developmental Psychology*, *49*(10), 1994–2004, https://doi.org/10.1037/a0031200

Siegler, R. S. & Ramani, G. B. (2009). Playing linear numerical board games promotes low-income children's numerical development. *Developmental Science*, *11*(6), 655–661. https://doi.org/10.1111/j.1467-7687.2008.00714.x

Siegler, R. S. & Thompson, C. A. (2014). Numerical landmarks are useful – Except when they're not. *Journal of Experimental Child Psychology, 120*(1), 39–58, http://dx.doi.org/10.1016/j.jecp.2013.11.014

Siegler, R. S., Thompson, C. A., & Opfer, J. E. (2009). The logarithmic-to-linear shift: One learning sequence, many tasks, many time scales. *Mind, Brain, and Education, 3*(3), 143–150. https://doi.org/10.1111/j.1751-228X.2009.01064.x

Siegler, R. S., Thompson, C. A., & Schneider, M. (2011). An integrated theory of whole number and fractions development. *Cognitive Psychology, 62*(4), 273–296. https://doi.org/10.1016/j.cogpsych.2011.03.001

Singer-Freeman, K. & Goswami, U. (2001). Does half a pizza equal half a box of chocolates? Proportional matching in an analogy task. *Cognitive Development, 16*(3), 811–829. http://dx.doi.org/10.1016/S0885-2014(01)00066-1

Sophian, C. (2000). Perceptions of proportionality in young children: Matching spatial ratios. *Cognition, 75*(2), 145–170. http://dx.doi.org/10.1016/S0010-0277(00)00062-7

Spinillo, A. G., & Bryant, P. (2001). Children's proportional judgements: The importance of "half." *Child Development, 62*(3), 427–440. https://doi.org/10.2307/1131121

Stevenson, H. W., Chen, C., & Lee, S. Y. (1993). Mathematics achievement of Chinese, Japanese, and American children: Ten years later. *Science, 259*(5091), 53–58. https://doi.org/10.1126/science.8418494

Sullivan, J. & Barner, D. (2014). The development of structural analogy in number-line estimation. *Journal of Experimental Child Psychology, 128*(1), 171–189. https://doi.org/10.1016/j.jecp.2014.07.004

Sullivan, J., Frank, M. C., & Barner, D. (2016). Intensive math training does not affect approximate number acuity: Evidence from a three-year longitudinal curriculum intervention. *Journal of Numerical Cognition, 2*(2), 57–76. https://doi.org/10.5964/jnc.v2i2.19

Thompson, C. A. & Opfer, J. E. (2008). Costs and benefits of representational change: Effects of context on age and sex differences in magnitude estimation. *Journal of Experimental Child Psychology, 101*(1), 20–51.

(2010). How 15 hundred is like 15 cherries: Effect of progressive alignment on representational changes in numerical cognition. *Child Development, 81*(6), 1768–1786. https://doi.org/10.1111/j.1467-8624.2010.01509.x

Thompson, C. A. & Siegler, R. S. (2010). Linear numerical magnitude representations aid children's memory for numbers. *Psychological Science, 21*(9), 1274–1281.

Torbeyns, J., Schneider, M., Xin, Z., & Siegler, R. S. (2015). Bridging the gap: Fraction understanding is central to mathematics achievement in students from three different continents. *Learning and Instruction, 37*, 5–13. http://dx.doi.org/10.1016/j.learninstruc.

Vallentin, D. & Nieder, A. (2008). Behavioral and prefrontal representations of spatial proportions in the monkey. *Current Biology, 18*(8), 1420–1425. http://dx.doi.org/10.1016/j.cub.2008.08.042

Vamvakoussi, X. & Vosniadou, S. (2010). How many decimals are there between two fractions? Aspects of secondary school students' understanding of rational numbers and their notation. *Cognition and Instruction, 28*(2), 181–209. https://doi.org/10.1080/07370001003676603

Vukovic, R. K., Fuchs, L. S., Geary, D. C., Jordan, N. C., Gersten, R., & Siegler, R. S. (2014). Sources of individual differences in children's understanding of fractions. *Child Development, 85*(4), 1461–1476. https://doi.org/10.1111/cdev.12218

Whyte, J. C. & Bull, R. (2008). Number games, magnitude representation, and basic number skills in preschoolers. *Developmental Psychology, 44*(2), 588–596. https://doi.org/10.1037/0012-1649.44.2.588

Wynn, K. (1998). Psychological foundations of number: Numerical competence in human infants. *Trends in Cognitive Science, 2*(8), 296–303. http://dx.doi.org/10.1016/S1364-6613(98)01203-0

Xu, F. (2003). Numerosity discrimination in infants: Evidence for two systems of representations. *Cognition, 89*(1), B15–B25. http://dx.doi.org/10.1016/S0010-0277(03)00050-7

Xu, F. & Spelke, E. (2000). Large number discrimination in 6-month-old infants. *Cognition, 74*(1), B1–B11. https://doi.org/10.1016/S0010-0277(99)00066–9

8 Learning How to Solve Problems by Studying Examples

Tamara van Gog, Nikol Rummel, and Alexander Renkl

Problem-solving tasks make up an important part of the learning activities in many school subjects and particularly in STEM domains (science, technology, engineering, and mathematics). We speak of problem-solving tasks when students have to get from A (given information on an initial state) to B (a described goal state) without knowing what series of actions they should perform to get there (although they may have received rules regarding what actions are or are not allowed; Newell & Simon, 1972). Learning to solve problems requires the acquisition of both the procedural knowledge of *what* actions to perform and *how* to perform them and the conceptual knowledge of *why* to perform those actions. Conceptual knowledge is particularly relevant when solving transfer problems in which a solution procedure has to be adapted. This chapter is concerned with an effective and efficient way of acquiring such knowledge: example-based learning.

What Is Example-Based Learning?

In example-based learning, rather than engaging in finding a way to get from the initial state to the goal state by themselves (i.e., learning by doing), students are provided with examples in which the solution procedure is demonstrated. As example-based learning involves learning by observing the solution procedure of someone else who has solved or is solving a (similar) problem, it is a form of observational learning (Bandura, 1986; Sweller & Sweller, 2006). Note, though, that observational learning can apply to the acquisition of all kinds of skills, attitudes, or behaviors (including negative ones) from observing others (Bandura, 1986). Our use of the term example-based learning is more specific, being limited to to-be-learned tasks or skills. As the to-be-learned tasks or skills in academic contexts are mostly cognitive, the focus is mainly on *abstract modeling*: the acquisition of cognitive skills based on underlying (abstract) rules or principles that are exemplified or verbalized by the models (i.e., in contrast to models whose behavior can simply be "copied" one-on-one). Finally, we should note that example-based learning is different from another type of observational learning, namely vicarious learning. Vicarious learning refers to learning by *observing someone else being taught* (e.g., observing a fellow student while s/he is interacting with a teacher or tutor in the classroom or on a video; cf. Chi, Roy, & Hausmann, 2008).

Tamara van Gog was supported by a Vidi grant (# 452-11-006) from the Netherlands Organization for Scientific Research.

Historically, research on example-based learning originated from different theoretical perspectives, which differed in the kinds of examples presented to learners and in the reasoning behind implementing examples (Renkl, 2014; Van Gog & Rummel, 2010). In cognitive research conducted on analogical reasoning (Gick & Holyoak, 1983; Holyoak, 2005), on adaptive control of thought–rational (ACT-R) theory (Anderson, 1993; Anderson, Fincham, & Douglass, 1997), or on cognitive load theory (Sweller, 1988; Sweller, Ayres, & Kalyuga, 2011), *worked examples* have been used. Worked examples typically show students the full (and correct) solution procedure in writing (see Figure 8.1 for an illustration). They are usually didactical examples, showing the procedure as novice students first need to acquire it, which is not necessarily as an expert would perform it. Students can use these worked examples either directly, while the example is still present (e.g., Reed, Willis, & Guarino, 1994; Van Loon-Hillen, Van Gog, & Brand-Gruwel, 2012), or later on, when the example is no longer present, based on a schema they formed of the example in memory, as an analogue for solving similar or slightly different problems. The focus in cognitive research on example-based learning has mainly been on investigating the effectiveness and efficiency of examples (as compared to practice problems) for acquiring problem-solving skills.

In research on social learning, tracing back to Bandura's social cognitive theory (e.g. Bandura, 1986), the focus has been on *modeling examples*. In modeling examples, students observe a live or video demonstration of the problem being solved by another person (i.e., an expert, teacher, tutor, or peer student; see Figure 8.2 for an illustration). Like worked examples, modeling examples may be didactical in nature; however, they may also show natural behavior – for instance, a peer student struggling with a task (e.g., Schunk, Hanson, & Cox, 1987). In research on social learning, the focus has frequently been on investigating how examples affect problem-solving skill acquisition via effects on students' *self-efficacy.*

Nowadays, with the advent of modern technology, "hybrid" types of examples have started to appear. Take, for instance, a video modeling example in mathematics. In a "classic" modeling example, one would see a video of the model as s/he is working out the solution procedure on a blackboard or whiteboard. It is also possible nowadays, however, to record the model's computer screen, while s/he is writing out the solution procedure on a track pad.[1] This is 'hybrid' in the sense that there are characteristics of both modeling examples and worked examples: the written steps of the example appear step-by-step, but the student no longer sees the model (though the model may be heard in a voice-over). In the end, when all steps have been written out, what is visible is essentially a worked example.

Why Is Example-Based Learning Effective?

A large body of experimental research in lab, school, or professional training contexts has established the efficacy of example-based learning in comparison to problem-solving practice (for reviews, see Atkinson et al., 2000; Renkl, 2014,

---

[1] Cf. the examples on the popular Khan Academy: www.khanacademy.org.

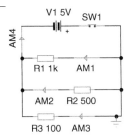

1. Determine how this circuit <u>should</u> function using Ohm's law, that is, determine what the current is that you should measure at AM1 to AM4

In parallel circuits, the total current (I_t) equals the sum of the currents in the parallel branches (I_1, I_2, etc.).

The total current should be: $I_t = I_1 + I_2 + I_3$

or: $\quad I_t = \dfrac{U}{R_1} + \dfrac{U}{R_2} + \dfrac{U}{R_3} = \dfrac{5V}{1k\Omega} + \dfrac{5V}{500\Omega} + \dfrac{5V}{100\Omega} = 5mA + 10mA + 50mA = 65mA$

This means you should measure:

AM1 = 5mA AM2 = 10mA AM3 = 50mA Am4 = 65mA

2. Suppose the ammeters indicate the following measurements:

AM1 = 5mA AM2 = 7,14mA AM3 = 50mA AM4 = 62,14mA

The calculation of what you should measure does not correspond to the actual measures, so something is wrong in this circuit.

3. What is the fault and in which component is it located? Also compute the actual value of the component

If the current in a branch is <u>lower</u> than it should be, the resistance in that branch is <u>higher than it should be</u> (equal U divided by higher R results in lower I).

The current in the second branch is lower than it should be if the circuit were functioning correctly: $I_2 = 7,14mA$ instead of 10mA. Thus, R_2 has a higher resistance than the indicated 500Ω. The actual resistance of R_2 can be calculated using the <u>measured</u> current:

$$R_2 = \dfrac{U}{I_2} = \dfrac{5V}{7,14mA} = 7,0k\Omega = 700\Omega$$

Figure 8.1 *Worked example of an electrical circuits troubleshooting task (after Van Gog, Kester, & Paas, 2011; Van Gog et al., 2015)*

In a practice problem format of this task, students had to answer questions 1 and 3 themselves; they could use a calculator and a "formula sheet" on which Ohm's law was explained and the different forms of the formula were given while doing so (i.e., R = U/I; U = R*I; I = U/R).

2017; Sweller, Ayres, & Kalyuga, 2011; Paas, Sweller, & Van Merriënboer, 1998; Van Gog & Rummel, 2010). This research has shown that for novice learners (i.e., in the early stages of skill acquisition on a task), replacing a substantial part of conventional practice problems with worked examples is more effective – as evidenced by higher posttest performance – and/or efficient – as evidenced by higher or

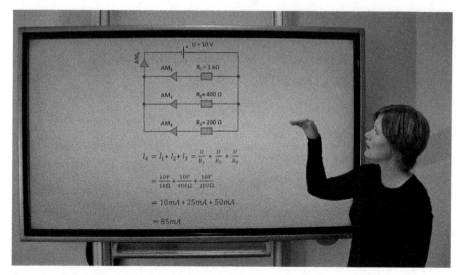

Figure 8.2 *Screenshot of a video modeling example (used in Hoogerheide, Van Wermeskerken et al., 2016) in which it is demonstrated and explained how to solve an electrical circuits troubleshooting task (the steps of the procedure are presented on the slides)*

equal posttest performance being reached with less investment of study time or mental effort. This has become known as "the worked example effect" (Sweller, Ayres, & Kalyuga, 2011).

Cognitive load theorists attribute the greater effectiveness and efficiency of example-based learning compared with solving practice problems to the cognitive processes involved. When beginning to acquire a cognitive skill, novices have to rely on general, weak strategies (e.g., trial-and-error, means-ends analysis) when solving problems, as they have not yet learned effective specific procedures for doing so. These general, weak problem-solving strategies are not very efficient for learning, in that they lead to learning only slowly; learners may succeed in solving the problem eventually, but as a consequence of the high working memory load they often fail to remember what steps were actually effective. Therefore, they fail to construct schemas connecting problem types and effective solution procedures and remain unable to subsequently solve similar problems (see Sweller & Levine, 1982). As they impose a high load on working memory and are very time-consuming, these weak strategies are not only ineffective but also inefficient for learning (Sweller, 1988). By showing learners how to solve a problem, worked examples obviate the need for applying general, weak problem-solving strategies. Moreover, they allow learners to devote all available working memory capacity to learning, that is, to constructing a cognitive schema of the solution procedure that can guide future problem-solving (Sweller, Ayres, & Kalyuga, 2011).

Research on analogical reasoning, which, like cognitive load research, commenced intensively in the 1980s (e.g., Gick & Holyoak, 1983), has provided insights into how schemas guide problem-solving (and become more refined in this process). Usually, four phases are distinguished in analogical reasoning (Holyoak, 2005; Reeves & Weisberg, 1993): (1) encoding of examples (initial schema construction); (2) activating relevant analogs from memory when a new (transfer) problem is to be solved; (3) mapping the problem to be solved onto the analog, that is, learners determine commonalities and differences between a known problem (analog) and the new problem at hand; and (4) inducing an *abstract* schema out of this mapping process or modifying a schema constructed in phase 1; for instance, learners may notice that some superficial features (e.g., concrete numbers and objects in a mathematics word problem) are not relevant to the appropriate solution method and instead encode the relevant *structural* features (i.e., what actions to perform in the solution procedure for a particular problem type) as a schema (e.g., Ross, 1989; Ross & Kennedy, 1990).

The assumption that examples are effective because of the particular combination of reducing cognitive load imposed by ineffective search processes *and* providing strong guidance for schema construction has recently received support from research in which example-based learning was compared with other types of tasks that also provide instructional guidance. Conventional practice problem-solving has been criticized as a "lousy control condition" for example-based learning, because a high instructional guidance condition (examples) is compared to a control condition (practice problems) in which learners do not receive any assistance (Koedinger & Aleven, 2007; see also Schwonke et al., 2009). In response to this criticism, recent research has compared example-based learning with tutored problem-solving practice conditions, in which learners can request hints when they do not know how to proceed on a problem-solving step and get feedback when they make errors (Koedinger & Aleven, 2007). In this work (for a review, see Salden et al., 2010), combining worked example study with tutored problem-solving was not consistently found to improve learning outcomes compared to tutored problem solving only. Yet it does have substantial efficiency benefits (i.e., same learning outcomes reached with less study time). A recent study comparing studying worked examples with tutored practice problem-solving and conventional practice problem-solving showed a large time efficiency benefit: worked example study took up to 60 percent less time (McLaren et al., 2016). These findings suggest that the benefit of example study indeed lies in reducing search processes and simultaneously enabling relatively rapid schema construction.

Research inspired by Bandura's social cognitive learning theory (Bandura 1977, 1986) has mainly focused on explaining the effectiveness of *modeling examples* in terms of the general cognitive processes that need to take place for observational learning to be effective, rather than on comparing example-based learning with other types of learning. Bandura postulated that observers acquire a cognitive (symbolic) representation (cf. cognitive schema) of the model's behavior that outlasts the modeling situation and thus enables learners to exhibit the observed and novel behavior at later occasions. To acquire this representation, learners must pay attention to the relevant aspects of the modeled behavior (Bandura, 1986). The learner's attention is influenced both by the salience of those aspects and by the characteristics of the model. The information that the learner attended to then needs to be retained in memory, which requires encoding this information. Rehearsal (i.e., imitation), either mentally or physically, is considered to play an important role in retention, as well as in improvement of performance. However, learners may not always be able to produce the observed behaviors themselves. Whether or not they are able to do so depends on the quality of the cognitive representation they have acquired and on the extent to which they master the component skills. Finally, motivational processes determine whether or not the learner will actually exhibit the behavior that was learned through observation.

It is relevant to note that both Sweller and colleagues (e.g., Sweller & Sweller 2006) and Bandura (1977, 1986) stress that example-based learning does not entail a one-on-one mapping of the observed information to the memory of the learner. Instead, learning is considered to be a constructive process during which information is actively abstracted, (re)organized, and integrated with the learner's existing knowledge. Similarly, both cognitive load theory and social learning theory perspectives on example-based learning emphasize the need for focused processing of the demonstrated task or skill.

How Can Example-Based Learning Best Be Implemented?

Sequencing Example Study and Practice Problem-Solving

What should educators who wish to implement example-based learning in their lessons, make of the worked example effect? The recommendation to "replace a substantial part of conventional practice problems with worked examples" is rather vague. One could simply replace all practice problems by examples (which has been shown to be more effective than practice problem-solving only: Van Gerven, Paas, Van Merriënboer, & Schmidt, 2002; Van Gog, Paas, & Van Merriënboer, 2006). One could also alternate example study and practice problem-solving in different manners. For instance, many studies have shown example–problem pairs to be more effective than practice problem-solving only (Carroll, 1994; Cooper & Sweller, 1987; Kalyuga et al., 2001; Mwangi & Sweller, 1998; Rourke & Sweller, 2009; Sweller & Cooper, 1985; see also studies with example–example–problem triplets: Paas, 1992; Paas & Van Merriënboer, 1994). And one could also argue that problem–example pairs would be effective by allowing learners to first experience what they do and do not yet know before providing them with examples (e.g., Reisslein et al., 2006; Stark et al., 2000).

Because direct comparisons of those different strategies had not yet been made, it was unclear which would be most effective. Therefore, Van Gog, Kester, and Paas (2011) set out to compare the effectiveness of example study only, practice problem-solving only, or alternating example study and practice problem-solving by providing students with example–problem pairs or problem–example pairs, within one experiment in the domain of physics (problems on troubleshooting electrical circuits; see Figure 8.1). They found that example study only and example–problem pairs required less effort during the learning phase and led to significantly higher test performance than problem-solving only and problem–example pairs. This pattern of results has meanwhile been replicated with different tasks (video modeling examples in science: Kant, Scheiter, & Oschatz, 2017; worked examples in statistics: Leppink et al., 2014).

The findings by Van Gog, Kester, and Paas (2011) replicated prior research on the worked example effect by showing that both examples only and example–problem pairs were more effective than solving practice problems only. Two other findings were more interesting, however. First, the study by Van Gog, Kester, and Paas (2011) was the first to compare effects of examples only and example–problem pairs. It was interesting that no differences between those conditions in effort investment or test performance were revealed, because one might expect practice problem-solving after example study to be more motivating than example study only (as suggested – but not tested – by Sweller & Cooper, 1985) and to be more effective for retention as it allows for retrieval practice (the benefits of which should primarily show at a one-week delayed test; see Roediger & Karpicke, 2006). Nevertheless, the finding that examples only and example–problem pairs did not differ significantly in their effects on learning has meanwhile been replicated several times and even with one-week delayed tests (Leahy, Hanham, & Sweller, 2015; Van Gog & Kester, 2012; Van Gog et al., 2015). Note, though, that in the absence of significant differences among these conditions, example–problem pairs may be preferable from a metacognitive perspective: Solving a practice problem after example study seems to give students better insight into their current level of understanding than example study only (Baars et al., 2014, 2017).

The second intriguing finding is that the problem–example pairs condition did not outperform the practice problems only condition. In other words, receiving examples to study after problem-solving did not benefit learning compared to receiving no examples at all. How can that be, when examples are so effective? This should also be considered in light of the finding that the sequencing of examples mattered: The problem–example pairs condition did worse than the example–problem pairs condition. Whereas this replicated prior findings for novice learners from another study in physics (Reisslein et al., 2006), a study using a puzzle problem did not find differences between example–problem and problem–example pairs on learning outcomes (Van Gog, 2011). These findings may point to self-efficacy as a potential explanation. When starting with a physics practice problem that they cannot yet solve, students might get frustrated, might feel that this is a task they will not be able to master anyway, and might therefore pay little attention to the example that follows (an effect that is much less likely to occur when they are working on puzzle tasks, as those are often more intrinsically motivating). Of course, this explanation remains to be tested in future research. However, it also nicely illustrates the potential added value of connecting aspects of the cognitive and social learning perspectives on example-based learning in future research.

In determining how to sequence example study and problem-solving, it is important to take students' (developing) prior knowledge into account. As mentioned earlier (see the section "Why Is Example-Based Learning Effective?"), example study is particularly effective for novices, that is, for students who have little if any prior knowledge of the demonstrated problem-solving task (Kalyuga et al., 2001). The high level of instructional guidance provided by examples, which fosters learning when no cognitive schemata are available yet, has been shown to be ineffective or even detrimental for advanced learners. They have already developed cognitive schemata that can guide their problem-solving and are in a stage where automating the acquired skill becomes important and, as such, advanced learners benefit more from solving practice problems (Kalyuga et al., 2001; this is an example of an "expertise reversal effect": Kalyuga, 2007). Thus, prior knowledge, or knowledge gained during example-based learning, will moderate the effectiveness of different sequences of examples and problems. For instance, whereas Reisslein and colleagues (2006) found example–problem pairs to be more effective than problem–example pairs for novices, the reverse was true for learners with more prior knowledge.

An alternative approach to alternating examples and practice problems that also takes into account students' developing knowledge would be to gradually transition from example study to problem-solving. This can be done by means of *completion problems* (Paas, 1992; Van Merriënboer et al., 2002) in a *fading strategy* (Renkl & Atkinson, 2003). In a fading strategy, students are initially presented with fully worked-out examples to study and are then asked to complete increasingly more steps in partially worked-out examples (i.e., completion problems) until they solve entire practice problems themselves. Studies have shown that a fading strategy, in which, for example, the last solution steps were omitted first in the completion problems, was more effective than the use of example–problem pairs (Renkl et al., 2002; Atkinson, Renkl, & Merrill, 2003).

Techniques to Foster Understanding and Transfer

Educators typically aim to teach for *transfer*, that is, the ability to use the acquired knowledge to solve novel problems that have not previously been encountered (Mayer & Wittrock, 1996). In most of the studies reviewed above, part of the posttest problems were isomorphic, meaning that they had the same structural features (i.e., the same solution procedure) as the problems that were demonstrated in the examples, but different surface features (e.g., a different cover story, different numbers). Thus, these findings suggest that students are capable of *near transfer* after example study by using the examples as an analog: Even if the surface features of the problem differ, learners are able to recognize the structural features of the problem and can map the solution procedure for solving problems of that category that they have abstracted from the examples.

In order to solve a novel problem from an as yet *unknown* problem category (*far transfer*), however, a learner needs to be able to recognize and flexibly apply the relevant parts of a previously learned procedure. To do so, it is imperative that a learner "not only knows the procedural steps for problem-solving tasks, but also *understands* when to deploy them and why they work" (Gott et al., 1993, p. 260; emphasis added). Thus, for "far" transfer to occur, understanding is critical (Mayer

& Wittrock, 1996; Ohlsson & Rees, 1991). As Ohlsson and Rees (1991) state, "procedures learned without conceptual understanding tend to be error prone, are easily forgotten, and do not transfer easily to novel problem types" (p. 104). According to their definition, "understanding of a procedure must involve both knowledge of its domain and of its teleology" (p. 118). Knowledge of a domain consists of principled knowledge about objects and events in that domain, and knowledge of the teleology of a procedure is knowledge of the rationale behind or purpose of the steps in a procedure (Ohlsson & Rees, 1991). This is why researchers have aimed to identify effective instructional principles for enhancing transfer by fostering students' understanding in example-based learning (Van Gog, Paas, & Van Merriënboer, 2004).

Providing (self-)explanations. Most worked examples research has used "product-oriented" examples that show a given state (i.e., the problem formulation), a sequence of operators (i.e., solution procedure), and the goal state (i.e., the final solution), but not the principles or rationale underlying the solution procedure (i.e., the explanation for the selection and application of operators), understanding of which is necessary for attaining transfer, especially far transfer (Van Gog, Paas, & Van Merriënboer, 2004). Because this information is not usually included in the examples, it does not become part of the learner's schema unless learners are able to generate adequate explanations for the selection and application themselves (i.e., self-explaining; Chi et al., 1989). However, learners do not always spontaneously engage in self-explaining and are not always capable of providing high-quality self-explanations (see Chi et al., 1989; Lovett, 1992; Renkl, 1997), so they need to be trained or prompted to do so (for reviews, see Renkl, 2017; and Renkl & Eitel, Chapter 21, this volume). An example of a prompt can be seen in Figure 8.3.

If this precondition of being able to provide high-quality self-explanations is not met, then providing high-quality instructional explanations may enhance learning from examples (Lovett, 1992). In providing instructional explanations, however, one should take into account that these may become redundant relatively quickly, at which point they need to be faded out or may start to hamper learning (Van Gog, Paas, & Van Merriënboer, 2008). Wittwer and Renkl (2010) reviewed the literature on instructional explanations in example-based learning and found positive effects when: (1) conceptual understanding is emphasized as the learning outcome (instead of procedural knowledge), (2) there are no simultaneous self-explanation prompts, and (3) they are provided automatically (instead of on learner demand).

Next to providing self-explanations, students may also benefit from explaining example content to (fictitious) other students. Like self-explaining and explaining to others in interactive situations (e.g., during tutoring, collaborative learning; e.g., Roscoe & Chi, 2007), explaining learned content to a nonpresent, fictitious other student on video has been found to be beneficial for fostering understanding and transfer (Fiorella & Mayer, 2013, 2014; Hoogerheide, Loyens, & Van Gog, 2014a; Hoogerheide et al., 2016). A recent study showed that the same applies when

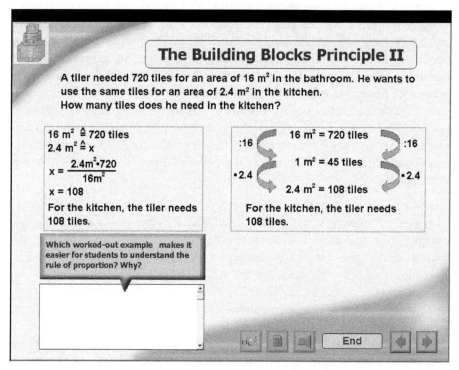

Figure 8.3 *Example of a self-explanation prompt (see bottom-left) and illustration of the difference between a molar (left) and modular (right) example (from Hilbert et al., 2008, reprinted with permission)*

studying worked examples and then explaining how to solve that type of problem to a (fictitious) other student on video (Hoogerheide et al., 2018).

Comparing (representations of) problem solutions within a problem category. Another way to enhance students' understanding of the principles behind (or function of) solution steps is to have them engage in comparing worked examples (Rittle-Johnson & Star, 2009; Rittle-Johnson, Star, & Durkin, 2009) or different representations of the same solution procedure (e.g., diagrams and equations; Berthold & Renkl, 2009) within a problem category. For example, being prompted to compare two worked examples of probability problems of the category "order relevant, without replacement," they can see that the surface features such as numbers or objects used may vary between the examples but are irrelevant for the solution procedure. It is important to guide the learner's attention to the structural features that remain constant across the examples; for instance, by prompting them to compare (and explain) the examples' or representations' commonalities and differences (Berthold & Renkl, 2009; Rittle-Johnson et al., 2009). We should note that some findings suggested that students may need to have some prior knowledge in order to benefit from comparing examples (Rittle-Johnson et al., 2009).

Comparing problem solutions between problem categories. Comparison among solution procedures for different problem categories demonstrated in worked examples (Paas & Van Merriënboer, 1994), completion problems (Van Merriënboer et al., 2002), and modeling examples (Wright, Li, & Coady, 1997) can be fostered by not presenting them in a typical blocked sequence by problem type or category (e.g., AAA-BBB-CCC-DDD) but in a random sequence (e.g., AC-D-B-B-C-A-D-A-B-D-C). Although random sequencing tends to increase cognitive load and decrease performance during training, it does usually lead to better learning and transfer outcomes (see also Carvalho & Goldstone, Chapter 16, this volume), so this increase in cognitive load is due to processes that are effective for learning (i.e., germane load). Whereas, in a blocked schedule, only one procedure has to be kept in mind during a block of tasks, a random sequence presumably challenges learners to compare the different procedures for solving the different types of problems. These comparisons may foster their understanding of which problem features are relevant for a certain solution procedure and which are not (Paas & Van Merriënboer, 1994).

Comparing correct and erroneous examples. Students may also come to understand the principles behind (or function of) solution steps better when they are asked to find and fix or explain errors in examples. The effects of studying erroneous examples or a mix of correct and erroneous examples have been investigated using a variety of tasks (e.g., communication skills: Baldwin, 1992; motor learning: Blandin & Proteau, 2000; mathematics: Adams et al., 2014; Durkin & Rittle-Johnson, 2012; Große & Renkl, 2007; medical diagnosis: Kopp, Stark, & Fischer, 2008; Kopp et al., 2009). Research in mathematics suggested that such a mix, with the instruction to find and fix the errors, was less effective for students with low prior knowledge than studying correct examples only, in particular when the errors were not labeled (Große & Renkl, 2007). Later research showed, however, that even novices could benefit from comparing correct and erroneous examples (as compared to studying correct examples only) when these were presented side by side (Durkin & Rittle-Johnson, 2012). Studies in medical education have also shown that studying only erroneous examples may also foster the acquisition of diagnostic knowledge compared to only correct examples, provided that the erroneous examples are accompanied by elaborate feedback that explains *why* a step was wrong, instead of indicating only *that* a step was wrong (Kopp et al., 2008, 2009).

Presumably, the reason why novices only benefit from erroneous examples when they can contrast them with correct examples or receive elaborate feedback explaining why a step was wrong is that "people cannot learn much by observation unless they attend to, and perceive accurately, the *significant features* of the modeled behavior" (Bandura, 1977, p. 24, emphasis added). Because novices have little, if any, prior knowledge of how a task should be performed, they also lack knowledge of the criteria and standards for what constitutes good performance (a phenomenon that has been dubbed "the double curse of incompetence"; Dunning et al., 2003). When contrasting correct and erroneous examples, or receiving elaborate feedback about what constitutes correct and incorrect performance, the correct example or the feedback can act as a reference for performance standards that can then be applied to evaluate or learn from the flawed performance (see also Van Gog, 2015), which also explains why comparing and explaining the differences between correct and incorrect examples is mostly effective when they are presented side by side (Renkl & Eitel, Chapter 21, this volume).

Labeling subgoals. As mentioned, it is critical that learners do not just memorize the single-solution steps but also know "when to deploy them and why they work" (Gott et al., 1993, p. 260) for them to be able to recognize and flexibly reassemble the relevant parts of a previously learned procedure for solving a novel problem in which, for example, the sequence of the steps has to be changed or steps have to be added or left out. In other words, learners need to encode the individual steps in a chain not as individual steps but as meaningful building blocks. One way to help them do so is by making subgoals in the solution procedure salient, for instance by visually isolating or labeling them (Catrambone, 1996, 1998). In video modeling examples, or animated modeling examples in which an animated agent functions as a model, this can be achieved through segmenting, that is, pausing after meaningful event units, which has been shown to foster novices' learning (Spanjers et al., 2012; Spanjers et al., 2011; see also Ertelt, Renkl, & Spada, 2006). Another option would be to not present novices with *molar* solution procedures connected to problem categories but present the finer-grained *modular* components of which the procedure is built up (Atkinson, Catrambone, & Merrill, 2003; Gerjets, Scheiter, & Catrambone, 2004, 2006; see also Figure 8.3).

Imagining/cognitively rehearsing the procedure. After initial example study, imagining (Cooper et al., 2001) or cognitively rehearsing (Bandura, 1986) the procedure presented in examples, has been shown to enhance learning outcomes compared with studying only. The "imagination effect" has been found to apply mainly when students have at least some prior knowledge (for students with little or no prior knowledge, further example study is more effective; Cooper et al., 2001; Ginns, Chandler, & Sweller, 2003)[2] and for complex materials (i.e., materials that are high in intrinsic load, containing many interacting information elements; Leahy & Sweller, 2005, 2008). This is in line with findings reviewed by Bandura, showing that cognitive rehearsal of observed behavior may enhance learning, provided it is accurate, and that the effect is more likely to occur on tasks that require more extensive cognitive processing (see also Driskell, Copper, & Moran, 1994; Feltz & Landers, 1983).

What Should Be Considered When Designing (Video) Examples?

After some early studies demonstrating the worked example effect (e.g., Cooper & Sweller, 1987; Sweller & Cooper, 1985), Tarmizi and Sweller (1988) initially failed to replicate this effect. They discovered that the design of the examples was crucial (Tarmizi & Sweller, 1988). Research on this issue led to the establishment of design

---

[2] Note that this is another instance of the expertise reversal effect (Kalyuga, 2007).

guidelines. For instance, one well-known guideline states that *split-attention* should be avoided by integrating mutually referring information sources such as text and picture/diagram (this can also be accomplished by using spoken instead of written text with pictorial information; e.g., Mousavi, Low, & Sweller, 1995). Another design guideline indicates that *redundancy* should be avoided, that is, multiple sources of information (e.g., text and a diagram) should only be presented when they are *both* necessary for comprehension; when they are understandable in isolation, one of the sources is redundant and should be left out (Chandler & Sweller, 1991).

Split-attention and redundancy are also important considerations in the design of video modeling examples but other issues come into play there as well. With modern technology, we now have a myriad of possibilities for designing video modeling examples. For instance, in "lecture-style" video examples, the learner may see the model standing next to a board on which s/he is writing out the steps or projecting slides that visualize each step in the task completion process (see Figure 8.2), or the learner may only see the writing or the slides accompanied by the model's verbal explanation in a voiceover. In examples in which the model is manipulating (virtual) objects, the model can be visible in the video entirely, partly (e.g., only the hands), or not at all (e.g., in examples that consist of a screen-recording, showing the model engaging in clicking, typing, drawing, or dragging objects on a computer screen). This myriad of design possibilities raises questions that are specific to video modeling examples.

Model visibility. A first question is, does it matter for attention and learning whether the model (and in particular the model's face) is visible in the video modeling examples? To learn from video modeling examples, it is imperative that learners attend to relevant information while the model is verbally referring to it or they will not be able to make sense of the model's explanation and task demonstration. Because our attention is automatically drawn to other people's faces (and especially their eyes; Langton, Watt, & Bruce, 2000), seeing the model's face in a video example is likely to attract students' attention. If this attention to the face would go at the expense of attending timely (i.e., in synchrony with the verbal explanation) to the relevant information on the slides or in the object demonstration, learning might be hampered. Although the model's face seems to attract a substantial amount of the learner's (visual) attention, this does not seem to significantly hamper learning (*object demonstration examples*: Van Gog, Verveer, & Verveer, 2014; Van Wermeskerken & Van Gog, 2017; Van Wermeskerken, Grimmius, & Van Gog, 2018; *lecture style examples*: Van Wermeskerken, Ravensbergen, & Van Gog, 2018; see also findings on learning outcomes only by Hoogerheide, Loyens, & Van Gog, 2014b). One study even reported a beneficial effect on learning (Van Gog, Verveer, & Verveer, 2014). A (tentative) explanation for this positive effect might lie in the fact that the students who saw the model's face in this study could see her switching her gaze toward an object prior to manipulating it. Such "gaze cues" might help align the learner's attention to the model's attention (a kind of "joint attention"), which should help them make sense of the model's explanation.

Establishing joint attention. Joint attention (i.e., two people looking at the same thing at the same time) has been shown to improve communication and sense-making in social (learning) situations (Langton et al., 2000; Meltzoff & Brooks, 2013). When the model is visible in the video, we may be able to exploit the tendency of human beings to automatically follow another person's eye gaze (Langton et al., 2000) and deictic gestures (Goldin-Meadow & Alibali, 2012) to establish a kind of joint attention ("a kind of," as the model has been prerecorded). A recent, small-scale eye-tracking study on lecture-style examples established that students spent more time looking at the model than at the parts of the task that the model was referring to when she looked straight into the camera. Gaze cues (looking at the task) or gaze + gesture cues (looking + pointing at the task) seemed successful at shifting learners' attention away from the model and toward the referred parts of the task (Ouwehand, Van Gog, & Paas, 2015). However, it remains to be determined whether gaze and gaze + gesture cues can not only establish joint attention but also foster learning. Studies with animated pedagogical agents (at which learners look much as they do at human models; Louwerse et al., 2009) do suggest that such social cues can indeed guide attention and foster understanding (Wang et al., 2017; see also Atkinson, 2002; Mayer & DaPra, 2012).

When the model is not visible, gaze cues can be provided "indirectly" by means of eye-tracking technology. Screen-recording video examples show learners what the model is seeing (i.e., the screen content) and doing on his/her computer screen (e.g., drawing, typing, clicking), usually with the model's explanations as a voiceover. Eye-tracking technology allows for recording the model's eye movements while s/he is giving the example and for displaying the recorded eye movements to the learner overlaid on the video example (e.g., as a colored circle or dot). Such eye movement modeling examples (EMME) allow the learner to see what the model is looking at and, again, this alignment of the learner's attention with the model's attention can be expected to help learners make sense of the demonstration and (when present) explanation by the model. EMME have been shown to improve "joint attention" (i.e., during example study, students attend faster or more to the information the model was looking at and referring to; Jarodzka et al., 2013; Van Marlen et al., 2016, 2018). EMME have been shown to improve learning of classification (Jarodzka et al., 2013) and diagnosis tasks (Jarodzka et al., 2012), and of learning strategies (i.e., text–picture integration; Mason, Pluchino, & Tornatora, 2015; Mason, Scheiter, & Tornatora, 2017) compared with regular screen-recording video modeling examples. Although several studies with university students failed to establish beneficial effects of EMME on problem-solving tasks (Van Gog et al., 2009; Van Marlen et al., 2016), a recent study showed that EMME were more beneficial than regular modeling examples for secondary education students' acquisition of geometry problem-solving skills (Van Marlen et al., 2018), which suggests that similar to effects of other types of cues (Richter, Scheiter, & Eitel, 2016), the attention guidance provided by gaze cues will only affect learning outcomes when learners have low prior knowledge.

Model characteristics. A question that received a lot of attention in early research on modeling (see Schunk, 1987) is also highly relevant for the design of video modeling examples: Do model characteristics such as gender, age, or (perceived) competence affect students' self-efficacy and learning outcomes? According to the model–observer similarity hypothesis, the perceived similarity to the model in terms of such characteristics will affect students' self-efficacy and (thereby) their learning outcomes (Bandura, 1994). However, research on the model–observer similarity hypothesis has produced inconsistent findings.

For example, studies on model competence that compared effectiveness of mastery models (displaying faultless performance from the start) with coping models (whose performance includes errors that are corrected and expressions of uncertainty that are gradually reduced) showed mixed results. In mathematics, no differences in the effectiveness of a peer coping model or a peer mastery model were found for low-ability students who had had prior successful experiences with the task (both were better than an adult model, which was better than no model; Schunk & Hanson, 1985) or for average-ability students (Schunk & Hanson, 1989). However, for low-ability students without prior success with the task, coping peer models were more effective for learning than mastery peer models, and children who observed coping peer models judged themselves to be more similar in competence to the models (Schunk et al., 1987). Later research found that students who had weak writing skills benefited more from being instructed to focus on video examples by weak models who explained and demonstrated how to write an argumentative text than from focusing on competent models, whereas students with better writing skills profited more from focusing on competent models (Braaksma, Rijlaarsdam, & Van den Bergh, 2002; note, though, that this finding was not replicated with video modeling examples on creative tasks such as poetry writing or collage making: Groenendijk et al., 2013).

Findings regarding model observer similarity in terms of gender or age were also inconsistent (Schunk, 1987). However, one issue in many model–observer similarity studies is that not only the model characteristics but also the content of the examples (i.e., what was demonstrated or explained) differed across conditions, which may be a partial explanation for the mixed findings. Recent studies that kept the content of video modeling examples equal across conditions found no evidence that the model's gender affected learning (Hoogerheide, Loyens, & Van Gog, 2016; Hoogerheide et al., 2018), but the model's age did (Hoogerheide et al., 2016): secondary education students who had observed an adult model (see Figure 8.2) rated the quality of the model's explanation as being higher and showed better posttest performance than students who had observed a peer model, even though the examples had the exact same content. The alleged expertise of the model, which was manipulated prior to example study, also affected students' ratings of the quality of the explanations but this did not affect their learning outcomes (Hoogerheide, Van Wermeskerken, et al., 2016).

Viewing perspective. Finally, in modeling examples in which the model is manipulating objects as part of the task performance, the perspective from which the example is filmed may affect learning. A recent study showed that learning outcomes (as measured by students' subsequent performance of the task) were higher when a video modeling example demonstrating how to build an electrical circuit was filmed from a first-person perspective than when it was filmed from a third-person perspective (Fiorella et al., 2017).

Future Research

One important direction for future research on example-based learning is to address the effects over time in real classroom contexts. Most studies on the effectiveness of example-based learning have been of the highly controlled single-session variety in a lab or school. There are some classroom studies spanning multiple sessions over different days, with promising results in terms of time efficiency: students achieving the same level of learning outcomes in up to 60 percent less study time (McLaren et al., 2016; Salden et al., 2010; Van Loon-Hillen, Van Gog, & Brand-Gruwel, 2012; Zhu & Simon, 1987). Thus, undertaking large-scale classroom studies would seem a promising and potentially very worthwhile endeavor for educational practice.

When taking example-based learning to school, other important questions concern how students self-regulate their learning from examples and practice problems, and motivational variables (e.g., interest and engagement; feelings of self-efficacy and perceived competence) may play an important role in this. Some studies suggest, for instance, that completing steps in examples (Baars et al., 2013) or solving a practice problem after example study (Baars et al., 2014; Baars et al., 2017) may help students to make more accurate judgments of learning compared to (fully worked-out) example study only. Having better insight into what they do and do not yet understand is important for learners, as it will affect their subsequent study behavior. We also know very little about students' study behavior when they engage in self-regulated learning (i.e., have a choice over what tasks to select) with fully or partially worked-out examples and practice problems. A recent study with university students found that when students were given a choice over what tasks to work on, the ratio of students' selection of worked examples versus practice problems was on average about 40 percent versus 60 percent. The percentage of examples selected decreased and the percentage of practice problems increased over time and there was a higher probability of an example being selected after a failed than after a correct problem-solving attempt (Foster, Rawson, & Dunlosky, 2018). Coming full circle, there are also some studies that have shown that video modeling examples may be a suitable method for teaching students how to effectively select tasks during self-regulated learning (Kostons, Van Gog, & Paas, 2012; Raaijmakers et al., 2018).

Another interesting future direction would be to connect the research on example-based learning with that on productive failure. Productive failure is defined as an instructional method designed to let students attempt (and fail) to generate the "canonical," correct solution to a given problem before instruction on this solution is provided (Kapur, 2008; Kapur & Rummel, 2012). Several studies, using math problems, have shown this to be more effective for conceptual knowledge acquisition than providing instruction first and then having students engage in problem-solving, without hampering procedural knowledge acquisition (i.e., ability to apply the canonical solution; for a review, see Loibl, Roll, & Rummel, 2017). Although this seems at odds with findings (discussed in the section "How Can Example-Based Learning Best Be Implemented?") regarding the sequencing of example study and practice problem-solving, it is important to note that the problem-solving activity in productive failure has a different nature and aim. An interesting question for future research would be to address whether failure should be experienced first-hand or whether observing (video) modeling examples of others engaging in problem-solving activities in the context of productive failure could also be effective for conceptual knowledge acquisition (Hartmann, Rummel, & Van Gog, 2017).

Finally, an open question that is both scientifically and practically relevant is whether individual differences would affect the effectiveness of example-based learning. Example-based learning has been studied at all levels of education (including for learners with special needs), in workplace learning contexts, and for aging adults, so it seems to be effective for a wide variety of learners. However, with the exception of prior knowledge (as discussed in the section "How Can Example-Based Learning Best Be Implemented?"), there has been little research on the influence of individual differences (e.g., intelligence, working memory capacity; for an exception, see, e.g., Schwaighofer, Bühner, & Fischer, 2016) on the effectiveness of example-based learning.

References

Adams, D. M., McLaren, B. M., Durkin, K., Mayer, R. E., Rittle-Johnson, B., Isotani, S., & Van Velsen, M. (2014). Using erroneous examples to improve mathematics learning with a web-based tutoring system. *Computers in Human Behavior*, *36*, 401–411. https://doi.org/10.1016/j.chb.2014.03.053

Anderson, J. R. (1993). *Rules of the mind*. Hillsdale, NJ: Lawrence Erlbaum.

Anderson, J. R., Fincham, J. M., & Douglass, S. (1997). The role of examples and rules in the acquisition of a cognitive skill. *Journal of Experimental Psychology: Learning, Memory, and Cognition*, *23*, 932–945. https://doi.org/10.1037/0278-7393.23.4.932

Atkinson, R. K. (2002). Optimizing learning from examples using animated pedagogical agents. *Journal of Educational Psychology*, *94*, 416–427. https://doi.org/10.1037/0022-0663.94.2.416

Atkinson, R. K., Catrambone, R., & Merrill, M. M. (2003). Aiding transfer in statistical learning: Examining the use of conceptually-oriented equations and elaborations. *Journal of Educational Psychology*, *95*, 762–773. https://doi.org/10.1037/0022-0663.95.4.762

Atkinson, R. K., Derry, S. J., Renkl, A., & Wortham, D. (2000). Learning from examples: Instructional principles from the worked examples research. *Review of Educational Research*, *70*, 181–214. https://doi.org/10.3102/00346543070002181

Atkinson, R. K., Renkl, A., & Merrill, M. M. (2003). Transitioning from studying examples to solving problems: Effects of self-explanation prompts and fading worked-out steps.

Journal of Educational Psychology, 95, 774–783. https://doi.org/10.1037/ 0022-0663.95.4.774

Baars, M., Van Gog, T., De Bruin, A., & Paas, F. (2014). Effects of problem solving after worked example study on primary school children's monitoring accuracy. *Applied Cognitive Psychology, 28,* 382–391. https://doi.org/10.1002/acp.3008

(2017). Effects of problem solving after worked example study on secondary school children's monitoring accuracy. *Educational Psychology, 37,* 810–834. https://doi .org/10.1080/01443410.2016.1150419

Baars, M., Visser, S., Van Gog, T., De Bruin, A., & Paas, F. (2013). Completion of partially worked-out examples as a generation strategy for improving monitoring accuracy. *Contemporary Educational Psychology, 38,* 395–406. https://doi.org/10.1016/j .cedpsych.2013.09.001

Baldwin, T. T. (1992). Effects of alternative modelling strategies on outcomes of interpersonal-skills training. *Journal of Applied Psychology, 77,* 147–154. https:// doi.org/10.1037/0021-9010.77.2.147

Bandura, A. (1977). *Social learning theory.* Englewood Cliffs, NJ: Prentice Hall.

(1986). *Social foundations of thought and action: A social cognitive theory.* Englewood Cliffs, NJ: Prentice-Hall.

(1994). Self-efficacy. In V. S. Ramachaudran (ed.), *Encyclopedia of human behavior,* Vol. 4 (pp. 71–81). New York: Academic Press.

Berthold, K. & Renkl, A. (2009). Instructional aids to support a conceptual understanding of multiple representations. *Journal of Educational Psychology, 101,* 70–87. https:// doi.org/10.1037/a0013247

Blandin, Y. & Proteau, L. (2000). On the cognitive basis of observational learning: Development of mechanisms for the detection and correction of errors. *The Quarterly Journal of Experimental Psychology, 53A,* 846–867. https://doi .org/10.1080/713755917

Braaksma, M. A. H., Rijlaarsdam, G., & Van den Bergh, H. (2002). Observational learning and the effects of model-observer similarity. *Journal of Educational Psychology, 94,* 405–415. https://doi.org/10.1037/0022-0663.94.2.405

Carroll, W. M. (1994). Using worked examples as an instructional support in the algebra classroom. *Journal of Educational Psychology, 86,* 360–367. https://doi.org/ 10.1037/0022-0663.86.3.360

Catrambone, R. (1996). Generalizing solution procedures learned from examples. *Journal of Experimental Psychology: Learning, Memory, and Cognition, 22,* 1020–1031. https://doi.org/10.1037/0278-7393.22.4.1020

(1998). The subgoal learning model: Creating better examples so that students can solve novel problems. *Journal of Experimental Psychology: General, 127,* 355–376. https://doi.org/10.1037/0096-3445.127.4.355

Chandler, P. & Sweller, J. (1991). Cognitive load theory and the format of instruction. *Cognition and Instruction, 8,* 293–332. https://doi.org/10.1207/s1532690xci0804_2

Chi, M. T. H., Bassok, M., Lewis, M. W., Reimann, P., & Glaser, R. (1989). Self-explanations: How students study and use examples in learning to solve problems. *Cognitive Science, 13,* 145–182. https://doi.org/10.1207/s15516709cog1302_1

Chi, M. T. H., Roy, M., & Hausmann, R. G. M. (2008). Observing tutorial dialogues collaboratively: Insights about human tutoring effectiveness from vicarious learning. *Cognitive Science, 32,* 301–341. https://doi.org/10.1080/ 03640210701863396

Cooper, G. & Sweller, J. (1987). Effects of schema acquisition and rule automation on mathematical problem-solving transfer. *Journal of Educational Psychology, 79,* 347–362. https://doi.org/10.1037/0022-0663.79.4.347

Cooper, G., Tindall-Ford, S., Chandler, P., & Sweller, J. (2001). Learning by imagining. *Journal of Experimental Psychology: Applied, 7,* 68–82. https://doi.org/10.1037/1076-898X.7.1.68

Driskell, J. E., Copper, C., & Moran, A. (1994). Does mental practice enhance performance? *The Journal of Applied Psychology, 79,* 481–492. https://doi.org/10.1037/0021-9010.79.4.481

Dunning, D., Johnson, K., Erlinger, J., & Kruger, J. (2003). Why people fail to recognize their own incompetence. *Current Directions in Psychological Science, 12,* 83–87. https://doi.org/10.1111/1467-8721.01235

Durkin, K. & Rittle-Johnson, B. (2012). The effectiveness of using incorrect examples to support learning about decimal magnitude. *Learning and Instruction, 22,* 206–214. https://doi.org/10.1016/j.learninstruc.2011.11.001

Ertelt, A., Renkl, A., & Spada, H. (2006). Making a difference: Exploiting the full potential of instructionally designed on-screen videos. In S. A. Barab, K. E. Hay, & D. T. Hickey (eds.), *Proceedings of the 7th International Conference of the Learning Sciences* (pp. 154–169). Mahwah, NJ: Lawrence Erlbaum.

Feltz, D. L. & Landers, D. M. (1983). The effects of mental practice on motor skill learning and performance: A meta-analysis. *Journal of Sport Psychology, 5,* 25–57. https://doi.org/10.1123/jsp.5.1.25

Fiorella, L. & Mayer, R. E. (2013). The relative benefits of learning by teaching and teaching expectancy. *Contemporary Educational Psychology, 38,* 281–288. https://doi.org/10.1016/j.cedpsych.2013.06.001

(2014). Role of expectations and explanations in learning by teaching. *Contemporary Educational Psychology, 39,* 75–85. https://doi.org/10.1016/j.cedpsych.2014.01.001

Fiorella, L., Van Gog, T., Hoogerheide, V., & Mayer, R. E. (2017). It's all a matter of perspective: Viewing first-person video modeling examples promotes learning of an assembly task. *Journal of Educational Psychology, 109,* 653–665. https://doi.org/10.1037/edu0000161Issn

Foster, N. L., Rawson, K. A., & Dunslosky, J. (2018). Self-regulated learning of principle-based concepts: Do students prefer worked examples, faded examples, or problem solving? *Learning and Instruction. 55,* 124–138. https://doi.org/10.1016/j.learninstruc.2017.10.002

Gerjets, P., Scheiter, K., & Catrambone, R. (2004). Designing instructional examples to reduce intrinsic cognitive load: Molar versus modular presentation of solution procedures. *Instructional Science, 32,* 33–58. https://doi.org/10.1023/B:TRUC.0000021809.10236.71

(2006). Can learning from molar and modular worked-out examples be enhanced by providing instructional explanations and prompting self-explanations? *Learning and Instruction, 16,* 104–121. https://doi.org/10.1016/j.learninstruc.2006.02.007

Gick, M. L. & Holyoak, K. J. (1983). Schema induction and analogical transfer. *Cognitive Psychology, 15,* 1–38. https://doi.org/10.1016/0010-0285(83)90002-6

Ginns, P., Chandler, P., & Sweller, J. (2003). When imagining information is effective. *Contemporary Educational Psychology, 28,* 229–251. https://doi.org/10.1016/S0361-476X(02)00016-4

Goldin-Meadow, S. & Alibali, M. W. (2012). Gesture's role in learning and development. In P. Zelazo (ed.), *Oxford handbook of developmental psychology* (pp. 953–973). Oxford: Oxford University Press.

Gott, S. P., Parker Hall, E., Pokorny, R. A., Dibble, E., & Glaser, R. (1993). A naturalistic study of transfer: Adaptive expertise in technical domains. In D. K. Detterman & R. J. Sternberg (eds.), *Transfer on trial: Intelligence, cognition, and instruction* (pp. 258–288). Norwood, NJ: Ablex.

Groenendijk, T., Janssen, T., Rijlaarsdam, G., & Van den Bergh, H. (2013). Learning to be creative: The effects of observational learning on students' design products and processes. *Learning and Instruction, 28,* 35–47. https://doi.org/10.1016/j.learninstruc.2013.05.001

Große, C. S., & Renkl, A. (2007). Finding and fixing errors in worked examples: Can this foster learning outcomes? *Learning and Instruction, 17,* 612–634. https://doi.org/10.1016/j.learninstruc.2007.09.008

Hartmann, C., Rummel, N., & Van Gog, T. (2017). *Productive or vicarious failure: Do students need to make every mistake by themselves?* Paper presented at the 17th International Conference of the European Association for Research on Learning and Instruction (EARLI), Tampere, Finland.

Hilbert, T. S., Renkl, A., Schworm, S., Kessler, S., & Reiss, K. (2008). Learning to teach with worked-out examples: A computer-based learning environment for teachers. *Journal of Computer-Assisted Learning, 24,* 316–332. https://doi.org/10.1111/j.1365-2729.2007.00266.x

Holyoak, K. J. (2005). Analogy. In K. J. Holyoak & R. G. Morrison (eds.), *The Cambridge handbook of thinking and reasoning* (pp. 117–142). New York: Cambridge University Press.

Hoogerheide, V., Deijkers, L., Loyens, S. M. M., Heijltjes, A. E. G., & Van Gog, T. (2016). Gaining from explaining: Learning improves from explaining to fictitious others on video, not from writing to them. *Contemporary Educational Psychology, 44–45,* 95–106. https://doi.org/10.1016/j.cedpsych.2016.02.005

Hoogerheide, V., Loyens, S. M. M., & Van Gog, T. (2014a). Effects of creating video-based modeling examples on learning and transfer. *Learning and Instruction, 33,* 108–119. https://doi.org/10.1016/j.learninstruc.2014.04.005

(2014b). Comparing the effects of worked examples and modeling examples on learning. *Computers in Human Behavior, 41,* 80–91. https://doi.org/10.1016/j.chb.2014.09.013

(2016). Learning from video modeling examples: Does gender matter? *Instructional Science, 44,* 69–86. https://doi.org/10.1007/s11251-015-9360-y

Hoogerheide, V., Renkl, A., Fiorella, L., Paas, F., & Van Gog, T. (2018). Enhancing example-based learning: Teaching on video increases arousal and improves problem-solving performance. *Journal of Educational Psychology.* http://dx.doi.org/10.1037/edu0000272

Hoogerheide, V., Van Wermeskerken, M., Loyens, S. M. M., & Van Gog, T. (2016). Learning from video modeling examples: Content kept equal, adults are more effective models than peers. *Learning and Instruction, 44,* 22–30. https://doi.org/10.1016/j.learninstruc.2016.02.004

Hoogerheide, V., Van Wermeskerken, M. M., Van Nassau, H., & Van Gog, T. (2018). Model-observer similarity and task-appropriateness in learning from video-modeling examples: Do model and student gender affect test performance, self-efficacy, and perceived competence? *Computers in Human Behavior, 89,* 457–464. https://doi.org/10.1016/j.chb.2017.11.012

Jarodzka, H., Balslev, T., Holmqvist, K. et al. (2012). Conveying clinical reasoning based on visual observation via eye-movement modelling examples. *Instructional Science, 40,* 813–827. https://doi.org/10.1007/s11251-012-9218-5

Jarodzka, H., Van Gog, T., Dorr, M., Scheiter, K., & Gerjets, P. (2013). Learning to see: Guiding students' attention via a model's eye movements fosters learning. *Learning and Instruction, 25,* 62–70. https://doi.org/10.1016/j.learninstruc.2012.11.004

Kalyuga, S. (2007). Expertise reversal effect and its implications for learner-tailored instruction. *Educational Psychology Review, 19,* 509–539. https://doi.org/10.1007/s10648-007-9054-3

Kalyuga, S., Chandler, P., Tuovinen, J., & Sweller, J. (2001). When problem solving is superior to studying worked examples. *Journal of Educational Psychology, 93,* 579–588. https://doi.org/10.1037/0022-0663.93.3.579

Kant, J. M., Scheiter, K., & Oschatz, K. (2017). How to sequence video modeling examples and inquiry tasks to foster scientific reasoning. *Learning and Instruction, 52,* 46–58. https://doi.org/10.1016/j.learninstruc.2017.04.005

Kapur, M. (2008). Productive failure. *Cognition and Instruction, 26,* 379–424. https://doi.org/10.1080/07370000802212669

Kapur, M. & Rummel, N. (2012). Productive failure in learning from generation and invention activities. *Instructional Science, 40*(4), 645–650. https://doi.org/10.1007/s11251-012-9235-4

Koedinger, K. R. & Aleven, V. (2007). Exploring the assistance dilemma in experiments with cognitive tutors. *Educational Psychology Review, 19,* 239–264. https://doi.org/10.1007/s10648-007-9049-0

Kopp, V., Stark, R., & Fischer, M. R. (2008). Fostering diagnostic knowledge through computer-supported, casebased worked examples: Effects of erroneous examples and feedback. *Medical Education, 42,* 823–829. https://doi.org/10.1111/j.1365-2923.2008.03122.x

Kopp, V., Stark, R., Kühne-Eversmann, L., & Fischer, M. R. (2009). Do worked examples foster medical students' diagnostic knowledge of hyperthyroidism? *Medical Education, 43,* 1210–1217. https://doi.org/10.1111/j.1365-2923.2009.03531.x

Kostons, D., Van Gog, T., & Paas, F. (2012). Training self-assessment and task-selection skills: A cognitive approach to improving self-regulated learning. *Learning and Instruction, 22,* 121–132. https://doi.org/10.1016/j.learninstruc.2011.08.004

Langton, S. R. H., Watt, R. J., & Bruce, V. (2000). Do the eyes have it? Cues to the direction of social attention. *Trends in Cognitive Sciences, 4,* 50–59. https://doi.org/10.1016/S1364-6613(99)01436-9

Leahy, W., Hanham, J., & Sweller, J. (2015). High element interactivity information during problem solving may lead to failure to obtain the testing effect. *Educational Psychology Review, 27,* 291–304. https://doi.org/10.1007/s10648-015-9296-4

Leahy, W. & Sweller, J. (2005). Interactions among the imagination, expertise reversal and element interactivity effects. *Journal of Experimental Psychology: Applied, 11,* 266–276. https://doi.org/10.1037/1076-898X.11.4.266

(2008). The imagination effect increases with an increased intrinsic cognitive load. *Applied Cognitive Psychology, 22,* 273–283. https://doi.org/10.1002/acp.1373

Leppink, J., Paas, F., Van Gog, T., Van der Vleuten, C. P. M., & Van Merriënboer, J. J. G. (2014). Effects of pairs of problems and examples on task performance and different types of cognitive load. *Learning and Instruction*, *30*, 32–42. https://doi.org/10.1016/j.learninstruc.2013.12.001

Loibl, K., Roll, I., & Rummel, N. (2017). Towards a theory of when and how problem solving followed by instruction supports learning. *Educational Psychology Review*, *29*, 693–715. https://doi.org/10.1007/s10648-016-9379-x

Louwerse, M. M., Graesser, A. C., McNamara, D. S., & Lu, S. (2009). Embodied conversational agents as conversational partners. *Applied Cognitive Psychology*, *23*, 1244–1255. https://doi.org/10.1002/acp.1527

Lovett, M. C. (1992). Learning by problem solving versus by examples: The benefits of generating and receiving information. *Proceedings of the 14th annual conference of the Cognitive Science Society* (pp. 956–961). Hillsdale: Erlaum.

Mason, L., Pluchino, P., & Tornatora, M. C. (2015). Eye-movement modeling of integrative reading of an illustrated text: Effects on processing and learning. *Contemporary Educational Psychology*, *41*, 172–187 https://doi.org/10.1016/j.cedpsych.2015.01.004

Mason, L., Scheiter, K., & Tornatora, C. (2017). Using eye movements to model the sequence of text-picture processing for multimedia comprehension. *Journal of Computer Assisted Learning*, *33*, 443–460. https://doi.org/10.1111/jcal.12191

Mayer, R. E. & DaPra, C. S. (2012). An embodiment effect in computer-based learning with animated pedagogical agents. *Journal of Experimental Psychology: Applied*, *18*, 239–252. https://doi.org/10.1037/a0028616

Mayer, R. E. & Wittrock, M. C. (1996). Problem-solving transfer. In D. C. Berliner & R. C. Calfee (eds.), *Handbook of educational psychology* (pp. 47–62). New York: Macmillan.

McLaren, B. M., Van Gog, T., Ganoe, C., Karabinos, M., & Yaron, D. (2016). The efficiency of worked examples compared to erroneous examples, tutored problem solving, and problem solving in computer-based learning environments. *Computers in Human Behavior*, *55*, 87–99. https://doi.org/10.1016/j.chb.2015.08.038

Meltzoff, A. N. & Brooks, R. (2013). Gaze following and agency in human infancy. In J. Metcalfe & H. S. Terrace (eds.), *Agency and joint attention* (pp. 125–138). New York: Oxford University Press.

Mousavi, S. Y., Low, R., & Sweller, J. (1995). Reducing cognitive load by mixing auditory and visual presentation modes. *Journal of Educational Psychology*, *87*, 319–334.

Mwangi, W. & Sweller, J. (1998). Learning to solve compare word problems: The effect of example format and generating self-explanations. *Cognition and Instruction*, *16*, 173–199.

Newell, A. & Simon, H. A. (1972). *Human problem solving*. Englewood Cliffs, NJ: Prentice-Hall.

Ohlsson, S. & Rees, E. (1991). The function of conceptual understanding in the learning of arithmetic procedures. *Cognition and Instruction*, *8*, 103–179. https://doi.org/10.1207/s1532690xci0802_1

Ouwehand, K., Van Gog, T., & Paas, F. (2015). Designing effective video-based modeling examples using gaze and gesture cues. *Educational Technology and Society*, *18*, 78–88.

Paas, F. (1992). Training strategies for attaining transfer of problem-solving skill in statistics: A cognitive load approach. *Journal of Educational Psychology*, *84*, 429–434. https://doi.org/10.1037/0022-0663.84.4.429

Paas, F. & Van Merriënboer, J. J. G. (1994). Variability of worked examples and transfer of geometrical problem solving skills: A cognitive load approach. *Journal of Educational Psychology*, *86*, 122–133. https://doi.org/10.1037/0022-0663.86.1.122

Raaijmakers, S. F., Baars, M., Schaap, L., Paas, F., Van Merriënboer, J. J. G., & Van Gog, T. (2018). Training self-regulated learning skills with video modeling examples: Do task-selection skills transfer? Instructional Science, *64*, 273–290. https://doi.org/10.1007/s11251-017-9434-0

Reed, S. K., Willis, D., & Guarino, J. (1994). Selecting examples for solving word problems. *Journal of Educational Psychology*, *86*, 380–388. https://doi.org/10.1037/0022-0663.86.3.380

Reeves, L. M. & Weisberg, R. W. (1993). On the concrete nature of human thinking: Content and context in analogical transfer. *Educational Psychology*, *13*, 245–258. https://doi.org/10.1080/0144341930130303

Reisslein, J., Atkinson, R., Seeling, P., & Reisslein, M. (2006). Encountering the expertise reversal effect with a computer-based environment on electrical circuit analysis. *Learning and Instruction*, *16*, 92–103. https://doi.org/10.1016/j.learninstruc.2006.02.008

Renkl, A. (1997). Learning from worked-out examples: A study on individual differences. *Cognitive Science*, *21*, https://doi.org/1-29. 10.1207/s15516709cog2101_1

  (2014). Towards an instructionally-oriented theory of example-based learning. *Cognitive Science*, *38*, 1–37. https://doi.org/10.1111/cogs.12086

  (2017). Instruction based on examples. In R. E. Mayer & P. A. Alexander (eds.), *Handbook of research on learning and instruction*, 2nd edn (pp. 325–348). New York: Routledge.

Renkl, A. & Atkinson, R. K. (2003). Structuring the transition from example study to problem solving in cognitive skills acquisition: A cognitive load perspective. *Educational Psychologist*, *38*, 15–22. https://doi.org/10.1207/S15326985EP3801_3

Renkl, A., Atkinson, R. K., Maier, U. H., & Staley, R. (2002). From example study to problem solving: Smooth transitions help learning. *Journal of Experimental Education*, *70*, 293–315. https://doi.org/10.1080/00220970209599510

Richter, J., Scheiter, K., & Eitel, A. (2016). Signaling text-picture relations in multimedia learning: A comprehensive meta-analysis. *Educational Research Review*, *17*, 19–36. https://dx.doi.org/10.1016/j.edurev.2015.12.003

Rittle-Johnson, B. & Star, J. R. (2009). Compared with what? The effects of different comparisons on conceptual knowledge and procedural flexibility for equation solving. *Journal of Educational Psychology*, *101*, 529–544. https://doi.org/10.1037/a0014224

Rittle-Johnson, B., Star, J. R., & Durkin, K. (2009). The importance of prior knowledge when comparing examples: Influences on conceptual and procedural knowledge of equation solving. *Journal of Educational Psychology*, *101*, 836–852. https://doi.org/10.1037/a0016026

Roediger, H. L. & Karpicke, J. D. (2006). The power of testing memory: Basic research and implications for educational practice. *Perspectives on Psychological Science*, *1*, 181–210. https://doi.org/10.1111/j.1745-6916.2006.00012.x

Roscoe, R. & Chi, M. (2007). Understanding tutor learning: Knowledge-building and knowledge-telling in peer tutors' explanations and questions. *Review of Educational Research*, *77*, 534–574. http://dx.doi.org/10.3102/0034654307309920

Ross, B. H. (1989). Distinguishing types of superficial similarities: Different effects on the access and use of earlier problems. *Journal of Experimental Psychology: Learning, Memory, and Cognition, 15*, 456–468.

Ross, B. H. & Kennedy, P. T. (1990). Generalizing from the use of earlier examples in problem solving. *Journal of Experimental Psychology: Learning, Memory, and Cognition, 16*, 42–45. https://doi.org/10.1037/0278-7393.16.1.42

Rourke, A. J. & Sweller, J. (2009). The worked-example effect using ill-defined problems: Learning to recognise designers' styles. *Learning and Instruction, 19*, 185–199. https://doi.org/10.1016/j.learninstruc.2008.03.006

Salden, R. J. C. M., Koedinger, K. R., Renkl, A., Aleven, V., & McLaren, B. M. (2010). Accounting for beneficial effects of worked examples in tutored problem solving. *Educational Psychology Review, 22*, 379–392. https://doi.org/10.1007/s10648-010-9143-6

Schunk, D. H. (1987). Peer models and children's behavioral change. *Review of Educational Research, 57*, 149–174. https://doi.org/10.3102/00346543057002149

Schunk, D. H. & Hanson, A. R. (1985). Peer models: Influence on children's self-efficacy and achievement. *Journal of Educational Psychology, 77*, 313–322. https://doi.org/10.1037/0022-0663.77.3.313

(1989). Influence of peer-model attributes on children's beliefs and learning. *Journal of Educational Psychology, 81*, 431–434. https://doi.org/10.1037/0022-0663.81.3.431

Schunk, D. H., Hanson, A. R., & Cox, P. D. (1987). Peer-model attributes and children's achievement behaviors. *Journal of Educational Psychology, 79*, 54–61. https://doi.org/10.1037/0022-0663.79.1.54

Schwaighofer, M., Bühner, M., & Fischer, F. (2016). Executive functions as moderators of the worked example effect: When shifting is more important than working memory capacity. *Journal of Educational Psychology, 108*, 982–1000. https://doi.org/10.1037/edu0000115

Schwonke, R., Renkl, A., Krieg, C. et al. (2009). The worked example effect: Not an artefact of lousy control conditions. *Computers in Human Behavior, 25*, 258–266. https://doi.org/10.1016/j.chb.2008.12.011

Spanjers, I. A. E., Van Gog, T., Wouters, P., & Van Merriënboer, J. J. G. (2012). Explaining the segmentation effect in learning from animations: The role of pausing and temporal cueing. *Computers & Education, 59*, 274–280. https://doi.org/10.1016/j.compedu.2011.12.024

Spanjers, I. A. E., Wouters, P., Van Gog, T., & Van Merriënboer, J. J. G. (2011). An expertise reversal effect of segmentation in learning from animated worked-out examples. *Computers in Human Behavior, 27*, 46–52. https://doi.org/10.1016/j.chb.2010.05.011

Stark, R., Gruber, H., Renkl, A., & Mandl, H. (2000). Instruktionale effekte einer kombinierten lernmethode: Zahlt sich die kombination von lösungsbeispielen und problemlöseaufgaben aus? [Instructional effects of a combined learning method: Does the combination of worked-out examples and problem-solving tasks pay off?]. *Zeitschrift für Pädagogische Psychologie, 14*, 205–217. https://doi.org/10.1024//1010-0652.14.4.206

Sweller, J. (1988). Cognitive load during problem-solving: Effects on learning. *Cognitive Science, 12*, 257–285. https://doi.org/10.1207/s15516709cog1202_4

Sweller J., Ayres P. L., & Kalyuga S. (2011). *Cognitive load theory*. New York: Springer. https://doi.org/10.1007/978-1-4419-8126-4

Sweller, J. & Cooper, G. A. (1985). The use of worked examples as a substitute for problem solving in learning algebra. *Cognition and Instruction, 2*, 59–89. https://doi.org/10.1207/s1532690xci0201_3

Sweller, J. & Levine, M. (1982). Effects of goal specificity on means-ends analysis and learning. *Journal of Experimental Psychology: Learning, Memory, and Cognition, 8*, 463–474. https://doi.org/10.1037/0278-7393.8.5.463

Sweller, J. & Sweller, S. (2006). Natural information processing systems. *Evolutionary Psychology, 4*, 434–458. https://doi.org/10.1177/147470490600400135

Sweller, J., Van Merriënboer, J. J. G., & Paas, F. G. (1998). Cognitive architecture and instructional design. *Educational Psychology Review, 10*, 251–296. https://doi.org/10.1023/A:1022193728205

Tarmizi, R. & Sweller, J. (1988). Guidance during mathematical problem solving. *Journal of Educational Psychology, 80*, 424–436. https://doi.org/10.1037/0022-0663.80.4.424

Van Gerven, P. W. M., Paas, F., Van Merriënboer, J. J. G., & Schmidt, H. G. (2002). Cognitive load theory and aging: Effects of worked examples on training efficiency. *Learning and Instruction, 12*, 87–105. https://doi.org/10.1016/S0959-4752(01)00017-2

Van Gog, T. (2011). Effects of identical example-problem and problem-example pairs on learning. *Computers & Education, 57*, 1775–1779. https://doi.org/10.1016/j.compedu.2011.03.019

   (2015). Commentary: Learning from erroneous examples in medical education. *Medical Education, 49*, 142–144. https://doi.org/10.1111/medu.12655

Van Gog, T., Jarodzka, H., Scheiter, K., Gerjets, P., & Paas, F. (2009). Attention guidance during example study via the model's eye movements. *Computers in Human Behavior, 25*, 785–791. https://doi.org/10.1016/j.chb.2009.02.007

Van Gog, T. & Kester, L. (2012). A test of the testing effect: Acquiring problem-solving skills from worked examples. *Cognitive Science, 36*, 1532–1541. https://doi.org/10.1111/cogs.12002

Van Gog, T., Kester, L., Dirkx, K. et al. (2015). Testing after worked example study does not enhance delayed problem-solving performance compared to restudy. *Educational Psychology Review, 27*, 265–289. https://doi.org/10.1007/s10648-015-9297-3

Van Gog, T., Kester, L., & Paas, F. (2011). Effects of worked examples, example-problem, and problem-example pairs on novices' learning. *Contemporary Educational Psychology, 36*, 212–218. https://doi.org/10.1016/j.cedpsych.2010.10.004

Van Gog, T., Paas, F., & Van Merriënboer, J. J. G. (2004). Process-oriented worked examples: Improving transfer performance through enhanced understanding. *Instructional Science, 32*, 83–98. https://doi.org/10.1023/B:TRUC.0000021810.70784.b0

   (2006). Effects of process-oriented worked examples on troubleshooting transfer performance. *Learning and Instruction, 16*, 154–164. https://doi.org/10.1016/j.learninstruc.2006.02.003

   (2008). Effects of studying sequences of process-oriented and product-oriented worked examples on troubleshooting transfer efficiency. *Learning and Instruction, 18*, 211–222. https://doi.org/10.1016/j.learninstruc.2007.03.003

Van Gog, T. & Rummel, N. (2010). Example-based learning: Integrating cognitive and social-cognitive research perspectives. *Educational Psychology Review, 22*, 155–174. https://doi.org/10.1007/s10648-010-9134-7

Van Gog, T., Verveer, I., & Verveer, L. (2014). Learning from video modeling examples: Effects of seeing the human model's face. *Computers & Education, 72*, 323–327. https://doi.org/10.1016/j.compedu.2013.12.004

Van Loon-Hillen, N. H., Van Gog, T., & Brand-Gruwel, S. (2012). Effects of worked examples in a primary school mathematics curriculum. *Interactive Learning Environments, 20*, 89–99. https://doi.org/10.1080/10494821003755510

Van Marlen, T., Van Wermeskerken, M. M., Jarodzka, H., & Van Gog, T. (2016). Showing a model's eye movements in examples does not improve learning of problem-solving tasks. *Computers in Human Behavior, 65*, 448–459. https://doi.org/10.1016/j.chb.2016.08.041

(2018). Effectiveness of Eye Movement Modeling Examples in problem solving: The role of verbal ambiguity and prior knowledge. *Learning and Instruction, 58*, 274–283. https://doi.org/10.1016/j.learninstruc.2018.07.005

Van Merriënboer, J. J. G., Schuurman, J. G., De Croock, M. B. M., & Paas, F. (2002). Redirecting learners' attention during training: Effects on cognitive load, transfer test performance and training. *Learning and Instruction, 38*, 11–39. https://doi.org/10.1016/S0959-4752(01)00020-2

Van Wermeskerken, M., Grimmius, B., & Van Gog, T. (2018). Attention to the model's face when learning from video modeling examples in adolescents with and without autism spectrum disorder. *Journal of Computer Assisted Learning, 34*, 32–41. https://doi.org/10.1111/jcal.12211

Van Wermeskerken, M., Ravensbergen, S. J., & Van Gog, T. (2018). Effects of instructor presence in video modeling examples on attention and learning. *Computers in Human Behavior, 89*, 430–438. https://doi.org/10.1016/j.chb.2017.11.038

Van Wermeskerken, M. & Van Gog, T. (2017). Seeing the instructor's face and gaze in demonstration video examples affects attention allocation but not learning. *Computers and Education, 113*, 98–107. https://doi.org/10.1016/j.compedu.2017.05.013

Wang, F., Li, W., Mayer, R. E., & Liu, H. (2017). Animated pedagogical agents as aids in multimedia learning: Effects on eye-fixations during learning and learning outcomes. *Journal of Educational Psychology, 110*(2), 250–268. http://dx.doi.org/10.1037/edu0000221

Wittwer, J. & Renkl, A. (2010). How effective are instructional explanations in example-based learning? A meta-analytic review. *Educational Psychology Review, 22*, 393–409. https://doi.org/10.1007/s10648-010-9136-5

Wright, D. L., Li, Y., & Coady, W. (1997). Cognitive processes related to contextual interference and observational learning: A replication of Blandin, Proteau and Alain (1994). *Research Quarterly for Exercise and Sport, 68*, 106–109. https://doi.org/10.1080/02701367.1997.10608872

Zhu, X. & Simon, H. A. (1987). Learning mathematics from examples and by doing. *Cognition and Instruction, 4*, 137–166. https://doi.org/10.1207/s1532690xci0403_1

9 Harnessing Our Hands to Teach Mathematics

How Gesture Can Be Used as a Teaching Tool in the Classroom

Elizabeth M. Wakefield and Susan Goldin-Meadow

The Body Plays a Role in Learning

The notion that the actions we perform with our bodies affect how we think and learn is not new. In the early twentieth century, Maria Montessori developed an educational philosophy based on the idea that children could better acquire knowledge by *actively* exploring the world around them rather than through traditional, verbal instruction (Lillard & Else-Quest, 2006; Montessori, 1995). Today, the Montessori approach is used in roughly 5,000 schools in the United States (Lillard & Else-Quest, 2006), as well as in many other countries around the world. In the mid-twentieth century, Jean Piaget (1952), famous for his work as a developmental psychologist, also focused on the importance of a child's motor exploration of the world for shaping cognition. He viewed cognitive development in terms of a stage theory in which children's actions – first, simple repetitive movements and, later, more complex explorative actions – play a role in the development of intelligence.

Both Montessori's and Piaget's frameworks highlight the importance of acting on objects to learn, especially in childhood. Building on these theories, a large body of research has shown that learning through producing one's own actions versus learning through observing others' actions *does* differentially impact how children think. For instance, physically manipulating a novel object (e.g., picking it up, turning it over, shaking it) will lead to better recall and recognition of the object than viewing these same actions produced by another person (e.g., Butler & James, 2013; Butler, James, & James, 2011; Harman, Humphrey, & Goodale, 1999). Many current educational techniques reflect these findings. For example, in mathematics classrooms, especially in early elementary school, teachers encourage children to interact with *manipulatives* when they are acquiring ideas such as quantity, addition, and subtraction (Mix, 2010).

Acting on objects is an important educational tool. However, focusing exclusively on actions that *manipulate* objects ignores another type of movement that teachers and students use in the classroom – gestures. Gestures are movements of the hands that can express ideas through their form and trajectory. In this chapter, we focus on the utility of gesture in educational practice, as gesture has been shown not only to reflect children's thought but also to *change* those thoughts (Goldin-Meadow, 2003).

Broadly speaking, gestures and actions on objects share a number of properties. Physically, gestures are movements of the hand that accompany speech and are, in this sense, actions. Functionally, gesture and action both shape cognition (e.g., Calvo-Merino et al., 2005; Casile & Giese, 2006; Chao & Martin, 2000; Cook, Mitchell, & Goldin-Meadow, 2008; Goldin-Meadow, Cook, & Mitchell, 2009; James, 2010; James & Atwood, 2009; James & Gauthier, 2006; James & Maouene, 2009; James & Swain, 2011; Longcamp et al., 2003; Longcamp, Tanskanen, & Hari, 2006; Novack et al., 2014; Pulvermüller, 2001; Singer & Goldin-Meadow, 2005; Wakefield & James, 2015) – hence their inclusion in a handbook on educational practice – and they may affect cognition in some of the same ways.

However, gesture also has some unique properties. Actions that are performed on objects have a direct effect on the world. In contrast, gestures that are performed off objects in the air do not bring about direct change. For example, twisting the cap of a bottle can directly open the bottle; gesturing a twisting motion over the bottle cannot. Actions complete a goal; gestures represent ideas. Because gestures are free from the constraints imposed on actions on objects, they are more flexible in their form. In gesture, we find a naturally used tool through which instructors and students can represent and manipulate ideas (e.g., Flevares & Perry, 2001) and, as will be reviewed later, a tool that shapes cognition when it is both produced and observed. Given these properties, gesture has the potential to be exploited in the classroom.

We begin by defining what gestures are and asking why they occur. We then review research showing that gesture can promote learning in classrooms, particularly in math classrooms. Studies of gesture use in naturalistic circumstances establish gesture's relevance to classroom teaching but they rarely provide enough leverage to argue that gesture has a causal effect on learning. We turn to laboratory studies to make the case that gesture promotes learning, both the gestures that students produce and the gestures that their teachers produce. We end with recommendations for educational practice and future directions for research.

How Do We Define Gesture and Where Does It Come From?

Gesture can be defined in many ways. At the most general level, gestures are movements expressed with the hands, arms, fingers, facial features, or even the entire body that communicate something to another individual (Crais, Watson, & Baranek, 2009). But it is often more useful to consider gestures within more specific categories. In a well-known categorization scheme, Kendon (2004) arranges gesture types on a continuum from movements completely independent of speech to those that are rarely produced in the absence of speech. Here, we focus our attention on one end of the spectrum: gesticulations that co-occur with speech. Gesticulations are either *imagistic* (iconic or metaphoric gestures) or *nonimagistic* (deictic or beat gestures). Imagistic gestures depict a shape, an action of some kind, or a movement pattern related to a referent (Kendon, 2004; McNeill, 1992). In other words, the form and/or movement trajectory of the gesture is meaningful in the context of the speech it accompanies. *Iconic gestures* represent concrete objects and actions through visuospatial representations. For example, an elementary school teacher, explaining the concept of a balance, might show children weights on opposite sides of the scale and then use her gesture to visually depict different ways the scale would shift, based on which side held heavier weights. The same gesture could be used when describing how to balance a complex equation in a high school algebra class. This second gesture would be an example of a *metaphoric* gesture because it expresses aspects of an abstract concept in a concrete, visuospatial manner (for discussion, see Cooperrider & Goldin-Meadow, 2017).

Unlike imagistic gestures, nonimagistic gestures single out referents or segment speech rather than iconically or metaphorically representing a referent (Kendon, 2004; McNeill, 1992). *Deictics* are pointing movements, with either the fingers or palm, that are used to indicate objects, locations, or other parts of conversation. *Beats* are rhythmic movements that are used to emphasize parts of a spoken sentence (McNeill, 1992). Essentially, these are the small movements that speakers will make that do not appear to represent the ideas they are communicating but often emphasize parts of the message. For the remainder of this chapter, we use the term "gesture" to refer to gestures that represent information through their form or indicate referents – iconics, metaphorics, and deictics.

There are different theories of how gestures arise but, in conceptualizing gesture as a special kind of action, the most useful framework through which to understand gesture production is the Gesture-as-Simulated-Action (GSA) framework (Hostetter & Alibali, 2008). The GSA framework is based on the theory that cognition is embodied (e.g., Barsalou, 1999): The way we understand the world and process information is grounded in our interactions with the environment. Cognition is thus based in reactivation of sensory-motor representations that have been built through previous sensory experiences. Hostetter and Alibali (2008) suggest that when these reactivations reach a certain threshold, activation "spreads" to primary motor regions and we produce overt gestures. Gesture, then, is the result of simulated actions (neural activation in premotor, motor, and sensory regions involved in motor planning or motor representations) that become realized as overt motor movements. According to the GSA framework, whether a simulated action gives rise to gesture is influenced by a number of factors. Gesture is more likely to occur if an individual is already engaging the motor system for speech production, which is one reason that we do not see spontaneous gestures occurring without speech. Gesture is also more likely to occur if the topic of our conversation is tightly coupled to a motor representation, either because we have motor experiences linked to this topic or because our language is tightly coupled to a motor representation. This prediction has been tested: Hostetter and Alibali (2010) demonstrated that participants were more likely to gesture if they were describing a pattern that they had physically created, as compared to a pattern that they did not create, supporting the tenants of the framework. Thus, gesture is an outward realization of our mental processes, expressing our thoughts through our hands. Given this framework, gesture lies at the intersection of action and thought, which makes it a powerful tool for education.

Gesture in Naturalistic Classrooms: Gesture Is There and Is Used

Why might gesture be useful in an educational setting and, in particular, when we teach mathematics? We focus our attention on math education for two reasons. First, students tend to struggle in math classes. Because mathematical concepts build on each other, once students fall behind, they have difficulty catching up in subsequent courses. Not only do delays of this sort decrease students' likelihood of succeeding in other STEM courses, but they also affect students' academic success more broadly (Adelman, 2006; Department of Education, 1997, 1999; Hansen, 2014). For instance, failure in algebra is predictive of failure to complete high school (Allensworth & Easton, 2005). Because success in mathematics is integrally tied to academic achievement, developing tools that will help children master mathematical concepts is important. A second reason for focusing on the utility of gesture in mathematics classrooms is that mathematics is the domain where the effects of gesture use have been most widely studied. We can therefore be confident in making recommendations for educational practice within the realm of mathematics. This focus on the benefits of incorporating gesture into the teaching and learning of mathematics may be historical – much of the gesture work in laboratory settings stems from two studies using mathematical concepts: Piagetian conservation (Church & Goldin-Meadow, 1986) and mathematical equivalence (Perry, Church, & Goldin-Meadow, 1988). However, these concepts became the focus of laboratory studies *because* researchers had observed natural use of gesture during instruction of these concepts. We argue that gesture is a useful tool in mathematics education because (1) practically speaking, educational practices based on student and teacher gesture can be implemented broadly, as gesture is naturally produced and universally accessible, regardless of the monetary resources available at a particular school; and (2) gesture is uniquely situated for expressing ideas that are integral to a mathematics classroom.

Implementing Gesture Instruction Is Feasible

A good teaching tool is one that can be implemented broadly. If a tool is difficult for educators and students to use, it is unlikely to be adopted. Likewise, if a tool is costly, it may not be accessible to schools in underprivileged communities – schools that are arguably in most need of good teaching techniques and student support. An important place to begin, then, in advocating for gesture as a teaching tool is to show that gestures are already in use in classrooms and that they can be easily encouraged without a major time commitment from instructors. Support for both of these ideas is found in classroom studies.

Although most research on gesture's effects on learning have been conducted in a laboratory setting, there is a small but growing body of literature documenting gesture's use in the classroom. Focusing on natural instruction in elementary and middle school, Flevares and Perry (2001) studied the use of nonverbal representations (e.g., pictures, objects, gestures) during instruction about place value. They found that, on average, teachers used five to seven nonverbal representations per minute and that the predominant type of nonverbal representation used in the classroom was gesture. This work has been corroborated by other classroom-based studies (e.g., Alibali & Nathan, 2012; Alibali et al., 2014; Richland, Zur, & Holyoak, 2007). Moreover, teachers spontaneously increase the amount of gesture during instruction when it becomes clear that students do not understand a particular concept in a lesson (Alibali, Nathan et al., 2013). In turn, students gesture spontaneously when asking questions or describing their solutions to problems, which can provide insight into their understanding of mathematical concepts (Alibali & Nathan, 2012). Together, these studies suggest that gesture is already used in classrooms by teachers and students, and that teachers are even more prone to use it when students are struggling with concepts.

Not only is gesture naturally used by teachers, but its use can easily be encouraged. Recent work has shown that teachers, when told about the importance of gestures for student learning, can intentionally increase the amount of gesture they use during instruction (Alibali, Young et al., 2013b). This study illustrates that a very simple intervention – telling teachers that gesture can help students learn – is enough to shape their behavior. Such an intervention would be quick and inexpensive, suggesting it could be implemented broadly, regardless of the financial resources of a school.

Gesture Can Make Complex Ideas Accessible

Part of understanding how gesture functions in an instructional setting comes from determining what gesture adds to instruction. Evidence for gesture's effects on learning in laboratory studies will be discussed in the next section, but observations in naturalistic classrooms can highlight ways that gesture is uniquely situated for expressing ideas that are important in a mathematics classroom. In general, an educator's goal is to communicate new ideas to students in a way that is accessible and will create long-lasting change in students' understanding of various concepts. In a mathematics classroom, students must learn overarching algebraic and geometric concepts, as well as strategies for solving problems that instantiate these concepts. Students must also learn how symbolic representations map onto abstract quantities and operational procedures, and how to move between different representational systems. In other words, they must be able to link abstract ideas to concrete symbols and apply arithmetic procedures to manipulate these ideas. In a review, Alibali and Nathan (2012) characterized the types of gestures used by instructors and suggest that gesture fulfills these functions when naturally used in mathematics instruction.

Pointing (deictic) gestures are the predominant form of gesture used during math instruction (Alibali, Nathan, & Fujimori, 2011). Teachers use points to link spoken instruction to concrete representations in the classroom or to link analogous elements within two or more representations. Classroom observations have revealed that linking ideas through pointing in conjunction with spoken instruction is more common than linking ideas through spoken instruction by itself. In fact, gestures are more often used when teachers link concepts or representations to each other than when they use other forms of narrative – in a sample of six teachers, Alibali, Nathan, and colleagues (2013) found that linking gestures were used 16.9 times per 100 words when teachers linked ideas together in speech, which is more than 1.5 times the frequency of gesture during storytelling (Alibali, Heath, & Myers, 2011).

This prevalent use of gesture suggests that teachers naturally find gesture to be a useful teaching tool and, indeed, linking gestures have been found to play important functions in classrooms. Linking spoken language to concrete representations in the classroom using points can elucidate or disambiguate spoken instruction that students find confusing or ambiguous on its own. For example, a teacher may point to the two sides of an equation, written on the board, when explaining the concept of mathematical equivalence with language such as, "We need to make the two sides of the equation equal to each other." Many students misinterpret an equal sign as an indication to add numbers together rather than as a symbol that separates sides of an equation. Thus, highlighting the sides of the equation with gesture may disambiguate the teacher's spoken instruction (Figure 9.1). When pointing is used to link analogous elements within two or more representations, it can help students move between different representational systems and integrate ideas into common mental representations. Alibali and Nathan (2012) provide an example of a teacher pointing to the short side of two different rectangles to show that these sides correspond to one another. Providing these gestures highlights a relation between the rectangles that may not have been apparent to students in the class, a connection that may need to be made before introducing an equation relating the two shapes.

In addition to points, teachers use iconic and metaphoric gestures in the classroom (Alibali & Nathan, 2012). Pointing gestures can create clear links between pieces of information but representational gestures can provide a visual depiction of abstract concepts being described in spoken instruction. Representational gestures therefore offer a second window onto these concepts. For example, in a naturalistic observation, a teacher illustrated how altering the slope of a line within an equation was represented in graphical form. First, the teacher pointed to the graphical representation of the two different slopes and the equations with the two different slopes – a linking gesture clarifying a relation. But then, the teacher went a step further, varying the angle of his outstretched arm to demonstrate slope changes using an iconic gesture (Figure 9.2). This physical embodiment grounds the abstract idea of slope in something more tangible for students. In a second example, a teacher explained balancing an equation and used metaphoric gesture to make an abstract concept concrete. The teacher talked about the elements on either side of the equation as spheres on two sides of a scale. She used gesture to "move" the spheres and showed how this affected the balance of the equation, making the concept more accessible to students by grounding instruction in the physical world and concrete experiences.

Gesture is thus used in the classroom during mathematics instruction by teachers and their students. But is there evidence that these gestures actually facilitate learning rather than their being a natural, but not relevant, part of instruction? Most evidence about the benefits of gesture comes from laboratory studies, but there is one naturalistic study that provides compelling evidence of gesture's power in the classroom. Richland (2015) analyzed ten videotaped fifty-minute

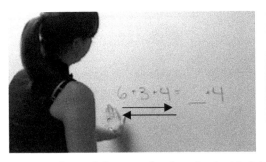

Figure 9.1 *Example of teacher highlighting two sides of an equation through gesture*

Figure 9.2 *Example of teacher demonstrating slope changes using iconic gesture (from Alibali & Nathan, 2012, with permission from Taylor & Francis)*

long classroom sessions from teachers instructing 8th grade children in the United States, Hong Kong, and Japan (thirty total), randomly selected from the Trends in International Mathematics and Science Study-Repeat (TIMSS-R). Both Hong Kong and Japan have significantly higher test scores in mathematics than the United States; the purpose of the study was to ask whether this difference corresponded to variations in how linking gestures were used during instruction. Richland found that, even though teachers from all countries used gesture in instruction, teachers from Hong Kong and Japan used significantly more linking gestures that physically displayed connections between two or more representations than teachers from the United States. Teachers from these Asian countries also displayed an increased tendency to adapt gesture to prior student knowledge, compared to teachers from the United States. For example, teachers in the Asian countries were more likely to use linking gestures for new concepts than for previously introduced concepts. These findings are consistent with the hypothesis that tailoring gesture to support mathematics understanding in classrooms can improve learning outcomes. We now turn to experimental evidence that gesture does indeed play a causal role in learning.

Gesture in Laboratory Studies: Gesture Promotes Learning

Laboratory studies targeting gesture's role in learning can be traced back to the mid-1980s. Before reviewing studies that explore whether gesture plays a causal role in learning, we turn to the original studies establishing gesture as a window onto cognition.

Student Gesture Is Relevant to Cognition

Much of the research on gesture and learning has involved manipulating teacher or student gesture and asking how these manipulations affect learning outcomes. However, initial work in this area focused on gestures that children *naturally* produce; gestures that were hypothesized to reflect a child's thought processes. Researchers asked whether teachers could use a child's gesture to identify when she was most likely to benefit from instruction on a particular concept, or, in more formal terms, when the child was in a *transitional knowledge state* (Church & Goldin-Meadow, 1986; Perry, et al., 1988).

From a Piagetian prospective, a transitional knowledge state occurs when a child holds inconsistent ideas about a concept, some incorrect and some correct, for which she previously held only incorrect ideas. A child is therefore at a point developmentally when instruction about the concept will be particularly beneficial because she is no longer committed to an incorrect understanding of a concept but has not yet embraced a new, more adult-like understanding (Perry et al., 1988). Consider a child who expresses an incorrect understanding of a concept in speech. Because gesture does not always convey the same information as the speech it accompanies (Goldin-Meadow, 2003), the gestures that the child produces have the potential to reveal a different understanding of that concept than is found in her speech. This general phenomenon (illustrated in Figure 19.3) – when gesture conveys different information from the speech with which it occurs – has been called "gesture–speech mismatch" (Church & Goldin-Meadow, 1986). In contrast, when gesture and speech express the same information, the response is called "gesture–speech match." A child who produces many gesture–speech mismatches when explaining how she solved problems probing a particular concept may be in a transitional knowledge state and thus ready to learn this particular concept.

To put the hypothesis that a child's gesture indexes whether she is in a transitional knowledge state to empirical test, Church and Goldin-Meadow (1986) and Perry and colleagues (1988) observed how many gesture–speech mismatches were produced by children explaining their solutions to problems with underlying concepts they had yet to master. They then asked whether producing many mismatches predicted a child's likelihood of learning from subsequent instruction in the concept. Finding that children who produced many gesture–speech mismatches before instruction have better learning outcomes than their peers who predominately produced gesture–speech matches would support the hypothesis that gesture reflects children's cutting-edge knowledge of a concept. If so, gesture can be used to identify children who are particularly ready to learn a new concept.

In both seminal studies (Church & Goldin-Meadow, 1986; Perry et al., 1988), children completed a pretest, instruction session, and posttest, while being video-recorded. During the pretest, children solved six problems and explained their solutions to an experimenter. Children between the ages of five and eight years were asked to complete Piagetian conservation questions related to number, liquid quantity, and length (Church & Goldin-Meadow, 1986), and children between the ages of ten and eleven years were asked to solve mathematical equivalence questions of the form $5 + 7 + 3 = \_\_\_ + 3$ (Perry et al., 1988). These age groups were chosen because these are the time periods during which children typically acquire an understanding of the respective concepts.

Children who answered all questions incorrectly on the math pretest and some questions incorrectly on the conservation pretest remained in the study and were given a standardized instruction session in which the researcher taught them how to solve problems similar to those they had just been tested on during the pretest. Children took an active role in the instruction session by working through problems with the instructor. Finally, children completed a posttest containing six problems in the same format but with new numbers for math, or the original six problems for conservation. Again, children were asked to explain their solutions to an experimenter. This protocol provided the template for experimental designs in subsequent studies.

In order to determine whether gesture–speech mismatch production before instruction predicted a child's learning outcome after instruction, children's explanations of their pretest problem solutions had to be coded. Researchers considered spoken and gestured explanations separately, so that coding a child's spoken explanation would not be influenced by the child's gestures, and vice versa. Each explanation was assigned a code based on the meaning it expressed. For example, when solving a mathematical equivalence problem such as $3 + 4 + 5 = \_\_\_ + 5$, a common mistake made by children at pretest was to answer "12." When explaining this solution, a child might say "I added up the 3, 4, and 5, and got 12." This explanation would be assigned an "Add-to-Equal Sign" code because the child's strategy was to add the numbers to the left of the equal sign to arrive at a solution. The gestures produced during this solution would then be considered separately, without the context of the child's speech. If a child pointed to the 3, 4, and 5 on the left side of the equal sign, and then the blank, this response would be assigned the same "Add-to-Equal Sign" code, as the gestures reflected this same strategy (Figure 9.3, Panel A). After spoken and gestured explanations were coded separately, the researchers considered the relation between the codes. In the example just given, the child's explanation would have been coded as a gesture–speech match, as the same strategy was reflected in both modalities. However, the researchers found that many children's gestures did *not* express the same strategy as their speech. Take, for example, a child who gave the same speech strategy "I added up the 3, 4, and 5, and got 12" but pointed at the 3, 4, 5, and the 5 on the right side of the equation. This gesture strategy would be assigned an "Add-All-Numbers" code, as the child's gestures indicate all of the numbers in the problem (Figure 9.3, Panel B). This explanation would have been coded as a gesture–speech mismatch because the information expressed in gesture was different from the information expressed in speech. An analogous system was designed for coding explanations given by children solving Piagetian conservation problems (Church & Goldin-Meadow, 1986). These coding systems have continued to be used in subsequent studies in which children were taught either conservation or mathematical equivalence.

Church and Goldin-Meadow (1986) and Perry and colleagues (1988) hypothesized that children who produced gesture–speech mismatches on at least half of their explanations of the pretest solutions (three or more out of six problems) – mismatchers – were in a transitional knowledge state. The next question was whether mismatchers respond differently to instruction than matchers, that is, than children who primarily produced gesture–speech matches (e.g., producing an incorrect "Add-to-Equal Sign" explanation in both gesture and speech when explaining a mathematical equivalence problem). Results from both studies indicated that children who were mismatchers before instruction showed significantly more improvement between pretest and posttest than children who were matchers before instruction. In addition, children who were mismatchers prior to instruction were more likely to successfully transfer the knowledge they had gained to similar, but not identical, problem types after instruction than children who were matchers.

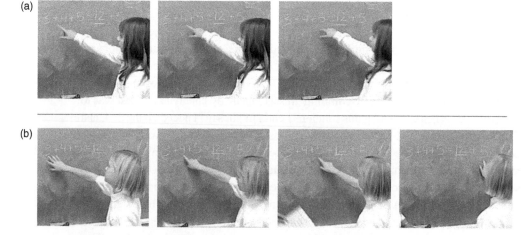

Figure 9.3 *Examples of gesture strategies produced by children*

(a) Add-to-Equal Sign. Child points to each addend on the left side of the problem.
(b) Add-All-Numbers. Child points to all four addends. In these examples, both children produced an Add-to-Equal Sign strategy in speech ("I added up the 3, 4, and 5, and got 12"). Thus, the child in panel (a) produced a gesture–speech match, and the child in panel (b) produced a gesture–speech mismatch.

These results suggest that producing gesture–speech mismatches on a particular problem can index whether a child is in a transitional state with respect to that problem.

The findings by Church and Goldin-Meadow (1986) and Perry and colleagues (1988) are of theoretical interest. However, it is not practical for teachers to video-record their students and code speech and gesture strategies in order to determine which children will benefit most from instruction before providing instruction. But, happily, it turns out that teachers and other adults *naturally* glean information from children's gestures (Alibali, Flevares, & Goldin-Meadow, 1997; Goldin-Meadow, Wein, & Chang, 1992). Alibali and colleagues (1997) asked adults to watch videotapes of children explaining their responses to mathematical equivalence problems; half of the children produced gesture–speech mismatches in their explanations, half produced matches. They then asked the adults to assess each child's knowledge about mathematical equivalence. Adults were more likely to mention strategies that the child had not produced in speech when observing mismatches than when observing matches. Moreover, many of these additional strategies could be traced to the mismatching gesture that the child produced. Interestingly, most of the adults said they were unaware that children were gesturing during the study.

But do teachers make use of the information that they glean from a child's gestures when deciding how to teach the child? The short answer is "yes." Teachers have been found to naturally modify their instruction in response to children who produce gesture–speech mismatches (Goldin-Meadow & Singer, 2003). Teachers were asked to teach six children how to solve mathematical equivalence problems. The teachers watched the children they were to teach as they explained their solutions to the pretest questions to the experimenter and then taught each child how to solve the problem. The teachers produced significantly more different strategies for solving the problem when teaching children who produced mismatches during the pretest or during the instruction period compared with children who never produced mismatches. This finding suggests that teachers are sensitive to the implicit knowledge a child expresses in gesture and that they adjust their instruction accordingly. If a child is producing mismatches on the math task, he or she is ready to learn that task and therefore should be able to take advantage of the additional strategies that the teacher produces. In contrast, a child who produces matches is not particularly close to a conceptual breakthrough on the problem and therefore may not have the capacity to benefit from relatively rich instruction. Thus, in a free-form, seminaturalistic instruction session, teachers are not only sensitive to whether a child produces gesture–speech mismatches but also change their teaching style in response to those mismatches.

These studies tell us that gesture can index a child's conceptual understanding and that teachers are sensitive to those gestures and alter their instruction accordingly. But they do not tell us whether gesture plays a *causal* role in changing thought. In other words, we know from these studies only that gesture is useful as a diagnostic tool to determine readiness to learn. The crucial question is whether incorporating gesture into a lesson, either by producing gestures that children can see or by asking children to produce gestures of their own, has an impact on learning. To address these questions, researchers use the same general experimental design (pretest–training–posttest) but add various manipulations. In some studies, the effect of teacher gesture on learning has been explored by designing teaching strategies that do, or do not, include various types of gesture and asking whether children's posttest performance varies accordingly. In other studies, child gesture is manipulated. Sometimes this manipulation is as simple as encouraging children to use their hands when they explain how to solve problems. In other cases, children are taught to perform specific gestures during training. In all cases, the dependent measure is the child's posttest performance. In the following sections, we consider (1) how a teacher's gesturing affects a student's comprehension of lesson material, and (2) how a student's gesturing affects how he or she processes the lesson material.

Teacher Gesture Has an Impact on What Students Learn

Teachers may change their style of instruction depending on a child's production of mismatches, but does this change affect learning? To address this question, it is essential to systematically manipulate whether gesture is included in a lesson. Overall, findings suggest that the gestures teachers produce facilitate student learning in preschool when children learn the concept of bilateral symmetry (Valenzeno, Alibali, & Klatzky, 2003), as well as in elementary school when children learn pre-algebraic concepts such as mathematical equivalence (Cook et al., 2008; Wakefield et al., 2018a; Singer & Goldin-Meadow, 2005). Students show more improvement from pretest to posttest when an instructor uses both gesture and speech strategies to explain a concept than when the instructor uses only speech strategies.

Research has also moved beyond showing that teacher gesture can help children learn to showing that the meaning expressed through teacher gesture affects what is learned. For example, teacher gesture has been found to be more powerful when it provides information not found in the teacher's speech, that is, when teachers use gesture–speech mismatches during instruction. In this case, the mismatches produced by a teacher provide two *correct* strategies, one in gesture and one in speech. These mismatches differ from the mismatches that signal a child's transitional knowledge state in that teacher mismatches contain two correct strategies whereas child mismatches contain at least one incorrect strategy, typically in speech. Singer and Goldin-Meadow (2005) conducted a study using a pretest–training–posttest design in which they manipulated the number of spoken strategies used by a teacher (one, two) and whether the spoken strategy was accompanied by gesture and, if so, the type of gesture (speech alone; speech and matching gesture; speech and mismatching gesture). Children taught with one spoken strategy performed significantly better at posttest than children taught with two spoken strategies. However, giving children two strategies in instruction could be effective, but only if one of the strategies was produced in gesture and the other in speech – that is, only if the instruction contained a gesture–speech mismatch. Children performed significantly better at posttest when taught with gesture–speech mismatches (where gesture and speech expressed different, correct strategies for solving the problems) than when taught with gesture–speech matches (where gesture and speech expressed the same correct strategy) or speech alone (see also, Congdon et al., 2017; Wakefield et al., 2018a). In fact, there was no significant difference between a child's performance after being taught with matching speech and gesture than with speech alone. Taken together, these studies suggest that gesture produced by a teacher may be particularly beneficial to students when it provides correct (and relevant) information *not* found in the teacher's speech.

It is important to point out that teacher gesture can be a powerful teaching tool even when it expresses the same information as the teacher's speech in both conservation (Church, Ayman-Nolley, & Mahootian, 2004) and mathematical equivalence (Cook, Duffy, & Fenn, 2013). For example, Cook and her colleagues (2013) created videotaped mathematical equivalence instruction in which the teacher stressed that two sides of the problem were equal to each other in speech. The teacher either produced this spoken strategy with no gesture (Speech Alone) or she produced the strategy while simultaneously underlining first one side and then the other side of the problem in gesture, a gesture–speech match (Speech + Gesture). Videotapes were shown to classrooms of students who completed pre- and posttests before and after instruction. Children who learned through instruction containing speech and gesture performed better than those who learned through instruction containing speech alone immediately after instruction and also after a twenty-four-hour delay. The children who saw the speech + gesture instruction also outperformed their peers on a more difficult test, one in which they had to solve multiplication problems of the same structure instead of addition problems. These studies bridge laboratory and school studies by showing that controlled instruction can be used at a classroom level to facilitate learning. Although this work supports using gesture that expresses the same information as speech in instruction, there is one caveat – the instruction in these studies was videotaped, and recent work suggests that videotaped gesture instruction is more powerful than live instruction (Koumoutsakis et al., 2016). Further work is needed to establish whether gesture expressing the same information as spoken instruction is useful when produced live by classroom teachers.

Student Gesture Also Has an Impact on What Students Learn

If gesture is powerful in the hands of the instructor, it stands to reason that it may also be powerful in the hands of a learner. Both naturalistic observation (Alibali & Nathan, 2012) and early laboratory work (Church & Goldin-Meadow, 1986; Perry et al., 1988) demonstrate that children use gesture when explaining their solutions to problems. Subsequent laboratory studies have shown that encouraging children to move their hands while explaining their solutions to a problem, or telling them precisely which hand movements to make, facilitates learning.

Interestingly, teachers may be able to encourage children to gesture simply by using their own gestures. Cook and Goldin-Meadow (2006) found that when the teacher used gesture, students were more likely to gesture as they explained solutions to problems than when the teacher did not use gesture. These students who spontaneously increased their gesture use, presumably in response to their teacher's gesture use, performed better after instruction than their peers. But the students who spontaneously increased their gesture use in response to the teacher might have been ready to learn in the first place. Thus, although the findings show that teacher gesture can lead to an increase in child gesture, the findings do not definitely show that child gesture has an impact on child learning.

To circumvent this problem, Broaders and colleagues (2007) gave some children explicit instructions to gesture. Children were given six math problems and asked to explain their answers. They were then asked to solve and explain six more problems, and were divided into three groups: one group was told to move their hands while explaining their answers to this second set of problems; one group was told not to move their hands; and a third group was given no instructions about their hands. After explaining their answers, children were given instruction about the problems and then asked to complete a posttest. Children who had been told to gesture on the second set of problems prior to instruction solved significantly more problems correctly than children who had been told not to gesture or had received no instructions about their hands. Interestingly, many of the gestures that the children produced when told to gesture on the second set of six problems conveyed strategies that could not be found in either speech or gesture on the first set of six problems. Being told to gesture thus brought out implicit knowledge (knowledge not evident in speech) that seemed to help the children benefit from instruction. Asking children to gesture can thus have positive effects on learning outcomes.

Children also benefit from being taught specific gesture strategies. When children are taught to produce a gesture strategy, with or without an accompanying speech strategy, they show better learning outcomes than when they are taught to produce a speech strategy alone (Cook et al., 2008; Goldin-Meadow et al., 2009). For example, Cook and colleagues (2008) taught children to produce an equalizer strategy for solving mathematical equivalence problems through speech ("make the two sides of the equation equal"), gesture (a sweeping gesture under one side of the equation and then the other side of the equation), or speech + gesture. All groups improved in solving posttest problems immediately after repeating the strategy during training. However, on a follow-up test given three weeks later, only children who had produced gesture (with or without speech) during training retained their newfound knowledge. Gesturing can make learning last.

Children can thus benefit from being taught to produce correct strategies for solving problems either through gesture–speech matches (Cook et al., 2008) or through gesture–speech mismatches (Goldin-Meadow et al., 2009). No study has directly compared learning outcomes after children are taught to use a gesture–speech match versus a gesture–speech mismatch in mathematical equivalence. However, the impact of producing matches versus mismatches has been assessed in a different domain – learning palindromes. A palindrome is a word or phrase that is read the same, whether read from left-to-right or right-to-left. For example, the words "mom" and "dad" are palindromes. Children were taught to produce a speech strategy ("A palindrome reads the same forwards and backwards") with either a matching gesture (sweeping the hand from left-to-right under a palindrome written on the board and then right-to-left) or mismatching gesture (pointing simultaneously to the first and last letter of the palindrome and then to the second and second-to-last letter, showing the symmetry of the spelling). Children benefited equally from these gesture strategies. Moreover, producing speech with either gesture strategy was more effective than producing speech without gesture (Wakefield & James, 2015). Future work is needed to determine how general this effect is and, in particular, whether it extends to concepts like mathematical equivalence (recall that, on the math task, mismatching gesture was more effective than matching gesture when it was produced by the *teacher*, Singer & Goldin-Meadow, 2005).

What We Know About Mechanism

To understand why gesture helps learners, we need to ask questions about mechanism. Gesture could facilitate learning by directing a child's visual attention toward relevant information. We know that even young infants will follow a pointing gesture and look at the indicated referent (Rohlfing, Longo, & Bertenthal, 2012), and that visually attending to a referent while it is being labeled positively predicts a young child's ability to remember that label (Yu & Smith, 2012). To determine whether guiding visual attention is the sole way that gesture affects learning, Goldin-Meadow and colleagues (2009) taught some children to point at the wrong numbers. One group of children were taught to place a V-shaped hand under the first two addends on the left side of a mathematical equivalence problem (the 3 and the 4 in the problem $3 + 4 + 5 = \underline{} + 5$) and then to point at the blank, a correct "grouping" strategy in gesture, while expressing an equalizer strategy in speech ("I want to make one side, equal to the other side"; Figure 9.4, Panel A). Another group was taught to point to the *second* and *third* addends (the 4 and the 5 in the problem $3 + 4 + 5 = \underline{} + 5$) and then to the blank, a partially correct "grouping" strategy in gesture, while expressing the equalizer strategy in speech (Figure 9.4, Panel B). This gesture strategy is partially correct because it conveys the notion of grouping in the V-shaped hand, and it also highlights the fact that there are two sides to the equation with the point at the blank; the strategy is incorrect in that it encourages grouping and adding the wrong two numbers. A third group was taught only the equalizer strategy without any gesture at all. If gesture serves *only* as an attentional cue, children taught the partially correct grouping strategy should perform significantly worse than the other two groups. However, this group outperformed children who learned through speech alone, although they did perform worse than children taught to use the correct grouping strategy. Children thus seem to be gleaning information not only from the V-point that directs attention to the numbers but also from the shape of the V (which encourages grouping) and the sequence of the gestures (which highlights the two sides of the problem).

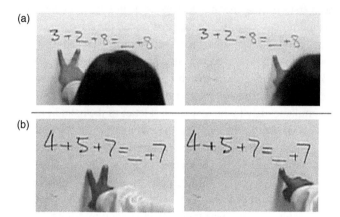

Figure 9.4 *Examples of the gesture strategies children were taught to produce in Goldin-Meadow, Cook, & Mitchell (2009)*

(a) Correct grouping strategy (b) Partially correct grouping strategy. In both cases, children were taught to produce the equalizer strategy in speech, "I want to make one side equal to the other side."

In a recent study using eye tracking technology, Wakefield and colleagues (2018a) asked about the effects of teacher gesture on children's visual attention during mathematical equivalence instruction. Two of the conditions in Goldin-Meadow, Cook, and Mitchell (2009) were adapted for this study – either children saw videotaped instruction in which the teacher expressed the equalizer strategy in speech alone or the teacher expressed the equalizer strategy in speech accompanied by a correct grouping strategy in gesture. As expected, children who received instruction that included gesture had significantly better learning outcomes than children who received speech-alone instruction. Using the eye tracker, the researchers also examined where the children allocated attention during the lesson and found that children who watched instruction with gesture allocated their visual attention differently than children who watched instruction without gesture – they looked more to the problem being explained, less to the instructor, and were more likely to synchronize their visual attention with information presented in the instructor's speech (i.e., they *followed along with speech*) than children who watched the instruction without gesture. But, as in Goldin-Meadow and colleagues (2009), Wakefield et al. (2018a) found that these differences in visual attention between groups could not fully explain gesture's beneficial effects. Even though the looking patterns characteristic of children in the gesture-instruction group predicted learning outcomes, the patterns did not *mediate* the effects of condition on posttest success. There was instead a complex relation between gesture and visual attention in which gesture *moderated* the impact of visual looking patterns on learning – *following along with speech* predicted learning for children who watched gesture instruction but not for children who watched speech-alone instruction. This study provides further evidence that visual attention plays some role in the effects gesture has on learning but suggests that another mechanism may also be at play – gesture's ability to synchronize with, and supplement, information found in speech.

Throughout this chapter, we have considered how meaning expressed through gesture relates to meaning simultaneously expressed through speech. It may, in fact, be gesture's tight relation to speech that underlies its power in learning. We know that gesture has a privileged relation to speech in that it is synchronized, both temporally and semantically, with speech (Kelly et al., 2014; Kendon, 1980; McNeill, 1992). Because the two modalities can be produced at the same time, gesture has the potential to promote the integration of information conveyed in speech and gesture. In a recent study, Congdon and colleagues (2017) tested whether gesture is more powerful when the strategy it conveys is produced simultaneously with a different strategy conveyed in speech (S + G) than when the strategy conveyed in gesture is produced sequentially with a different strategy conveyed in speech (S→G) or when the two strategies are produced sequentially both conveyed in speech (S→S). Children in all three instruction groups showed the same improvement on the posttest problems that were identical in form to those taught during instruction. However, when children were asked to generalize what they had learned to problems with new forms, children who received instruction containing simultaneous speech and gesture (S + G) outperformed the other two groups (S→S and S→G). These children were also significantly more likely to retain what they had learned one day and four weeks after training than were the children in the other two groups. Although future work is needed to determine whether this finding holds when children are asked to produce the strategies themselves, the current work does suggest that part of gesture's power to promote flexible learning that can be retained lies in its inherent synchrony with speech.

A final property of gesture that may contribute to its ability to help children learn is that gesture brings the motor system into the learning process. At the beginning of this chapter, we reviewed evidence that cognition is embodied and that action affects thought. Part of the reason teachers use manipulatives in the classroom may be to give children active motor experience through which they can learn new concepts. Given that there are both similarities and differences between the motoric experience provided by actions on objects versus gesture, we can ask whether these motor movements have the same or different effects on how children learn.

In a neuroimaging study, Wakefield and colleagues (2014) found that children who produced both speech and gesture while learning mathematical equivalence showed significantly greater activation in sensorimotor areas when subsequently solving problems in the scanner (where no movement was taking place) than children who produced only speech during learning. The network of activation found in children in the gesture condition is similar to the network in children tested after they learned a concept through actions on objects (e.g., James & Swain, 2011). Learning through gesture has also been found to build sensorimotor representations in adults in a word learning paradigm (Macedonia, Muller, & Friederici, 2011). However, a study conducted by Novack and colleagues (2014) suggests that gesture can have different effects on learning than action on objects. Plastic numbers were placed on top of the numbers in a mathematical equivalence problem, which was written on a whiteboard.

In the gesture condition, children were taught to produce a V-point with their index and middle fingers under the 5 and 7 on the left side of the problem, and then point to the blank on the right side, instantiating the *grouping* procedure. In the action condition, children were taught to remove the 5 and the 7 number tiles and hold the two numbers under the blank, a concrete instantiation of the *grouping* procedure. Children in both groups produced these strategies while saying the equalizer strategy in speech as they attempted to solve each problem during the lesson. Gesture and action were equally effective in promoting success on posttest problems of the same form as the problems on which the children had been trained ($3 + 8 + 7 = \_\_ + 7$), providing further evidence that motor experience in general can benefit learning. However, gesture also promoted success on posttest problems that required generalization ($3 + 8 + 7 = 3 + \_\_$ and $3 + 8 + 7 = \_\_ + 5$) – action did not. The findings suggest that although recruiting the motor system overall promotes the learning process, producing movement that represents information (as opposed to manipulating objects) – that is, producing gesture – facilitates flexible learning that can be transferred to new problems. This finding has been conceptually replicated in a second domain, word learning, with younger children (Wakefield et al., 2018b), demonstrating that gesture can play an important role in generalizing new knowledge in a variety of domains. Future work using neuroimaging will explore whether learning through gesture versus action on objects leads to activation in different parts of the motor network (e.g., areas in the brain that are associated with abstraction for learning through gesture).

The studies that have been conducted to unpack how gesture shapes thought have begun to tell a narrative. It is likely that gesture is not powerful because of one property. Rather, gesture may be a powerful learning tool because it brings together in a single behavior a variety of skills that support learning.

Recommendations for Educational Practice

The reviewed literature suggests that gesture is a powerful educational tool that can facilitate children's understanding of mathematical ideas – both when it is performed by teachers and when it is performed by students. Iconic and metaphoric gestures can express difficult mathematical concepts in an accessible visuospatial format, and deictic gestures can link together concepts and representations as well as direct visual attention to relevant parts of an equation or diagram. Although most of the research on gesture's effects has been conducted one-on-one in controlled settings, gesture is spontaneously used in classrooms by both teachers and students and, in the few classroom studies that have been done, has been found to be effective. We can feel confident that teachers will be able to implement gesture-based educational tools in the classroom because they *already* use this tool, as do their students. We also know that gesture remains effective when we "scale up" from a single child to a classroom of children – Richland (2015) found evidence that, around the globe, teachers' use of linking gestures is associated with good student mathematics performance. And importantly, gesture is *free*, which means that teachers can take advantage of it as a tool regardless of the monetary resources available to them.

Before providing basic recommendations to educators about gesture use, we feel it important to mention a caveat: Gesture is a powerful tool, but as we learn more about its underlying mechanisms and the nuances of its effects, we also discover the boundaries of its benefits and places where other tools might be more effective. To illustrate this point, we consider two examples: (1) evidence that *doing* gesture may have a more powerful effect on learning than *seeing* a teacher gesture, and (2) evidence that there are times when actions on objects may be more useful to children than gesture.

If gesture is helpful because it involves the motor system in learning, children's own gesture might be expected to have a more powerful effect on their understanding of a concept than teacher gesture. Research in the action-learning literature has, in fact, shown that *doing* action has a more powerful effect on learning than *seeing* action (e.g., Butler et al., 2011; Harman et al., 1999; Kontra et al., 2015). Although the differences in doing versus seeing gesture have been relatively unexplored, one study of mental rotation has found that children *doing* gesture had better learning outcomes than children *seeing* gesture (Goldin-Meadow et al., 2012). Further research is needed, but the findings to date suggest that although teacher gesture is powerful, to get optimal effects, children should be encouraged to gesture as well.

There also may be instances when gesture is not the optimal tool to use. Although we have reviewed literature suggesting that gesture leads to more flexible learning than actions on objects, there may be times when children would benefit more from action experience than gesture. *Action* on objects may be more useful when children are first learning a concept because it is more concrete than gesture. Through manipulatives, students gain physical representations of concepts that allow them to offload some of the mental effort involved in learning (Lillard, 2005), and research has shown that this experience can be helpful to students (Kennedy & Tipps, 1994; Tooke et al., 1992). For children who are struggling with a new concept, manipulatives may provide a necessary foothold into the concept, allowing them to build a rudimentary understanding of the concept. This understanding could then be expanded through gesture. Indeed, there is evidence that being exposed to concrete instantiations of a concept before being exposed to a relatively abstract instantiation of the concept can, in some circumstances, promote learning. For example, Goldstone and Son (2005) found that having students manipulate displays that began as concrete and became abstract was a more effective teaching protocol than having them manipulate either concrete or abstract displays on their own. Thus, using action and gesture to complement each other may create an ideal learning situation for students. As the previous section makes clear, we are just beginning to understand the mechanisms that underlie the effects of gesture. By continuing this line of work, researchers will be able to make more specific recommendations about when and how gesture can be most effectively used for teaching and learning, transforming it from a relatively blunt hammer into a finely tuned instrument.

Even with the caveat that gesture may not always be the silver bullet in the classroom, ample evidence supports implementing gesture as an educational tool. Given that we know gesture can be used to facilitate student learning and is relatively easy to implement in the classroom, what are the next steps that will move gesture out of the lab and into the hands of teachers and their students? We share two basic recommendations that can be made on the basis of the current literature below.

Putting Gesture in the Hands of Teachers

It may seem obvious, but a first step in implementing gesture-based teaching strategies should be to teach educators the power of gesture for learning. We know that teachers adjust their instruction unknowingly, based on whether or not students express implicit knowledge about a new concept (e.g., Goldin-Meadow & Singer, 2003). We also know that if told to increase their gesture, teachers will do so (Alibali, Young et al., 2013) and will also alter their gesture use after instruction on how gesture promotes learning (Kelly et al., 2002). Thus, teachers who are aware of the role that gesture can play in changing the minds of their students are likely to move their hands during instruction. Teachers can be made aware of the utility of linking gestures for helping students integrate mathematical concepts and representations. Teachers can also be encouraged to think of ways to ground the concepts they teach in iconic and metaphoric gestures. A mathematics teacher knows more about the concepts she is teaching than gesture researchers do. If taught about how iconic and metaphoric gestures express information, teachers may realize they already have intuitions about gestures that could represent difficult concepts. These gestures could then be deliberately used in the classroom.

Putting Gesture in the Hands of Students

The gestures teachers make matter for student learning, but so do students' own gestures. Although designing specific gestures to teach to children (like the grouping or equivalence gestures used in math lessons discussed earlier) may be useful, an easy initial step would be to encourage children to reason out loud about problems and concepts they are learning and move their hands while doing so. Work from other areas shows that self-explanation can be a powerful tool in its own right (DeCaro & Rittle-Johnson, 2012; McEldoon, Durkin, & Rittle-Johnson, 2013). Combining it with gesture may be even better for a learner. Implementing this practice may not always be trivial. Often teachers must discipline students, so inviting them to talk and move around may seem counterintuitive. Yet what children do with their hands has the power to change how they think and, as long as gesturing is implemented in a way that does not disrupt the classroom, having students move may be a *good* thing.

Conclusions

In this chapter, we have provided evidence that gesture is a tool that can promote learning mathematical concepts. Because teachers and students naturally use gesture, it is an obvious tool to target and harness in the classroom. Based on current work, we suggest that teachers should be informed of the effects that different forms of gesture can have on students' learning outcomes so that they can be mindful of using gesture in the classroom, and can encourage their students to use gestures of their own. Future work will help us understand *when* and *how* gesture promotes learning so that this continuously accessible tool can be put to optimal use.

References

Adelman, C. (2006). *The toolbox revisited: Paths to degree completion from high school through college*. Washington, DC: US Department of Education.

Alibali, M. W., Flevares, L. M., & Goldin-Meadow, S. (1997). Assessing knowledge conveyed in gesture: Do teachers have the upper hand? *Journal of Educational Psychology, 89*, 183–193. https://doi.org/10.1037/0022–0663.89.1.183

Alibali, M. W., Heath, D. C., & Myers, H. J. (2011). Effects of visibility between speaker and listener on gesture production: Some gestures are meant to be seen. *Journal of Memory and Language, 44*, 169–188. https://doi.org/10.1006/jmla.2000.2752

Alibali, M. W., & Nathan, M. J. (2012). Embodiment in mathematics teaching and learning: Evidence from learners' and teachers' gestures. *Journal of the Learning Sciences, 21*, 247–286. https://doi.org/10.1080/10508406.2011.611446

Alibali, M. W., Nathan, M. J., Church, R. B., Wolfgram, M. S., Kim, S., & Knuth, E. J. (2013). Teachers' gestures and speech in mathematics lessons: Forging common ground by resolving trouble spots. *Mathematics Education, 45*, 425–440. https://doi.org/10.1007/s11858-012-0476-0

Alibali, M. W., Nathan, M. J., & Fujimori, Y. (2011). Gesture in the mathematics classroom: What's the point? In N. Stein & S. Raudenbush (eds.), *Developmental cognitive science goes to school* (pp. 219–234). New York: Routledge.

Alibali, M. W., Nathan, M. J., Wolfgram, M. S., Church, R. B., Jacobs, S. A., Maritinex, C. J., & Knuth, E. J. (2014). How teachers link ideas in mathematics instruction using speech and gesture: A corpus analysis. *Cognition and Instruction, 32*, 65–100. https://doi.org/10.1080/07370008.2013.858161

Alibali, M. W., Young, A. G., Crooks, N. M., Yeo, A., Wolfgram, M. S., Ledesma, I. M., … Knuth, E. J. (2013). Students learn more when their teacher has learned to gesture effectively. *Gesture, 13*, 210–233. https://doi.org/10.1075/gest.13.2.05ali

Allensworth, E. M., & Easton, J. Q. (2005). *The on-track indicator as a predictor of high school graduation*. Chicago: Consortium on Chicago school research. https://consortium.uchicago.edu/sites/default/files/publications/p78.pdf

Barsalou, L. (1999). Perceptual symbol systems. *Behavioral and Brain Sciences, 22*, 577–660. https://doi.org/10.1017/S0140525X99002149

Broaders, S. C., Cook, S. W., Mitchell, Z., & Goldin-Meadow, S. (2007). Making children gesture brings out implicit knowledge and leads to learning. *Journal of Experimental Psychology, 136*, 539–550. https://doi.org/10.1037/0096–3445.136.4.539

Butler, A. J., & James, K. H. (2013). Active learning of novel sound-producing objects: Motor reactivation and enhancement of visuo-motor connectivity. *Journal of Cognitive Neuroscience, 25*, 203–218. https://doi.org/10.1162/jocn_a_00284

Butler, A. J., James, T. W., & James, K. H. (2011). Enhanced multisensory integration and motor reactivation after active motor learning of audiovisual associations. *Journal of Cognitive Neuroscience, 23*, 3515–3528. https://doi.org/10.1162/jocn_a_00015

Calvo-Merino, B., Glaser, D. E., Grezes, J., Passingham, R. E., & Haggard, P. (2005). Action observation and acquired motor skills: An fMRI study with expert dancers. *Cerebral Cortex*, *15*, 1243–1249. https://doi.org/10.1093/cercor/bhi007

Casile, A., & Giese, M. A. (2006). Nonvisual motor training influences biological motion perception. *Current Biology*, *16*, 69–74. https://doi.org/10.1016/j.cub.2005.10.071

Chao, L. L., & Martin, A. (2000). Representation of manipulable man-made objects in the dorsal stream. *Neuroimage*, *12*, 478–484. https://doi.org/10.1006/nimg.2000.0635

Church, R. B., Ayman-Nolley, S., & Mahootian, S. (2004). The role of gesture in bilingual education: Does gesture enhance learning? *International Journal of Bilingual Education and Bilingualism*, *7*, 303–319. https://doi.org/10.1080/13670050408667815

Church, R. B., & Goldin-Meadow, S. (1986). The mismatch between gesture and speech as an index on transitional knowledge. *Cognition*, *23*, 43–71. https://doi.org/10.1016/0010–0277(86)90053–3

Congdon, E. L., Novack, M. A., Brooks, N., Hemani-Lopez, N., O'Keefe, L., & Goldin-Meadow, S. (2017). Better together: Simultaneous presentation of speech and gesture in math instruction supports generalization and retention. *Learning and Instruction*, *50*, 65–74. https://doi.org/10.1016/j.learninstruc.2017.03.005

Cook, S. W., Duffy, R. G., & Fenn, K. M. (2013). Consolidation and transfer of learning after observing hand gesture. *Child Development*, *84*, 1863–1871. https://doi.org/10.1111/cdev.12097

Cook, S. W., & Goldin-Meadow, S. (2006). The role of gesture in learning: Do children use their hands to change their minds? *Journal of Cognition and Development*, *7*, 211–232. https://doi.org/10.1207/s15327647jcd0702_4

Cook, S. W., Mitchell, Z., & Goldin-Meadow, S. (2008). Gesturing makes learning last. *Cognition*, *106*, 1047–1058. https://doi.org/10.1016/j.cognition.2007.04.010

Cooperrider, K., & Goldin-Meadow, S. (2017). When gesture becomes analogy. Topics in Cognitive Science, *9*, 719–737. https://doi.org/10.1111/tops.12276

Crais, E. R., Watson, L. R., & Baranek, G. T. (2009). Use of gesture development in profiling children's prelinguistic communication skills. *American Journal of Speech-Language Pathology*, *18*, 95–108. https://doi.org/10.1044/1058–0360(2008/07–0041

DeCaro, M. S., & Rittle-Johnson, B. (2012). Exploring mathematics problems prepares children to learn from instruction. *Journal of Experimental Child Psychology*, *113*, 552–568. https://doi.org/10.1016/j.jecp.2012.06.009

Department of Education. (1997). *Mathematics equals opportunity*. White Paper prepared for US Secretary of Education R. W. Riley.

  (1999). *Do gatekeeper courses expand education options?*. National Center for Education Statistics.

Flevares, L. M., & Perry, M. (2001). How many do you see? The use of nonspoken representations in first-grade mathematics lessons. *Journal of Educational Psychology*, *93*, 330–345. https://doi.org/10.1037//0022–0663.93.2.330

Goldin-Meadow, S. (2003). *Hearing gesture: How our hands help us think*. Cambridge, MA: Belknap Press of Harvard University Press.

Goldin-Meadow, S., Cook, S. W., & Mitchell, Z. (2009). Gestures gives children new ideas about math. *Psychological Science*, *20*, 267–271. https://doi.org/10.1111/j.1467–9280.2009.02297.x

Goldin-Meadow, S., Levine, S. C., Zinchenko, E., Yip, T. K., Hemani, N., & Factor, L. (2012). Doing gesture promotes learning a mental transformation task better than seeing gesture. *Developmental Science, 15*, 876–884. https://doi.org/10.1111/j.1467–7687 .2012.01185.x

Goldin-Meadow, S., & Singer, M. A. (2003). From children's hands to adults' ears: Gesture's role in the learning process. *Developmental Psychology, 39*, 509–520. https://doi .org/10.1037/0012–1649.39.3.509

Goldin-Meadow, S., Wein, D., & Chang, C. (1992). Assessing knowledge through gesture: Using children's hands to read their minds. *Cognition and Instruction, 9*, 201–219. https://doi.org/10.1207/s1532690xci0903_2

Goldstone, R. L., & Son, J. Y. (2005). The transfer of scientific principles using concrete and idealized simulations. *The Journal of Learning Sciences, 14*, 69–110. https://doi.org /10.1207/s15327809jls1401_4

Hansen, M. (2014). Characteristics of schools successful in STEM: Evidence from two states' longitudinal data. *The Journal of Educational Research, 107*, 374–391. https://doi .org/10.1090/00220671.2013.823364

Harman, K. L., Humphrey, G. K., & Goodale, M. A. (1999). Active manual control of object views facilitates visual recognition. *Current Biology, 9*, 1315–1318. https://doi.org /10.1016/S0960-9822(00)80053-6

Hostetter, A. B., & Alibali, M. W. (2008). Visible embodiment: Gestures as simulated action. *Psychonomic Bulletin & Review, 15*, 495–514. https://doi.org/10.3758/pbr.15.3.495

(2010). Language, gesture, action! A test of the Gesture as Simulated Action framework. *Journal of Memory and Language, 63*, 245–257. https://doi.org/10.1016/j.jml.2010 .04.003

James, K. H. (2010). Sensori-motor experience leads to changes in visual processing in the developing brain. *Developmental Science, 13*, 279–288. https://doi.org/10.1111/j .1467–7687.2009.00883.x

James, K. H., & Atwood, T. P. (2009). The role of sensorimotor learning in the perception of letter-like forms: Tracking the causes of neural specialization for letters. *Cognitive Neuropsychology, 26*, 91–110. https://doi.org/10.1080/02643290802425914

James, K. H., & Gauthier, I. (2006). Letter processing automatically recruits a sensory-motor brain network. *Neuropsychologia, 44*, 2937–2949. https://doi.org/10.1016/j .neuropsychologia.2006.06.026

James, K. H., & Maouene, J. (2009). Auditory verb perception recruits motor developing brain: An fMRI investigation. *Developmental Psychology, 12*, F26–34. https://doi .org/10.1111/j.1467–7687.2009.00919.x

James, K. H., & Swain, S. N. (2011). Only self-generated actions create sensori-motor systems in the developing brain. *Developmental Psychology, 14*, 1–6. https://doi .org/10.1111/j.1467–7687.2010.01011.x

Kelly, S. D., Healy, M., Ozyurek, A., & Holler, J. (2014). The processing of speech, gesture, and action during language comprehension. *Psychonomic Bulletin and Review*. https://doi.org/10.3758/s13423-014–0681-7

Kelly, S. D., Singer, M., Hicks, J., & Goldin-Meadow, S. (2002). A helping hand in assessing children's knowledge: Instructing adults to attend to gesture. *Cognition and Instruction, 20*, 1–26. https://doi.org/10.1207/S1532690XCI2001_1

Kendon, A. (1980). Gesticulation and speech: Two aspects of the process of utterance. In M. R. Key (ed.), *The Relationship of Verbal and Nonverbal Communication* (pp. 207–227). The Hague: Mouton and Co.

(2004). *Gesture: Visible Action as Utterance*. Chicago, IL: University of Chicago Press.

Kennedy, L. M., & Tipps, S. (1994). *Guiding children's learning of mathematics, 7th edition*. Belmont, CA: Wadsworth.

Kontra, C., Lyons, D. J., Fischer, C., & Beilock, S. L. (2015). Physical experience enhances science learning. *Psychological Science, 26*, 737–749. https://doi.org/10.1177/0956797615569355

Koumoutsakis, T., Church, R. B., Alibali, M. W., Singer, M., & Ayman-Nolley, S. (2016). Gesture in instruction: Evidence from live and video lessons. *Journal of Nonverbal Behavior, 40*, 301–315. https://doi.org/10.1007/s10919-016-0234-z

Lillard, A. (2005). *Montessori: The science behind the genius*. New York: Oxford University Press.

Lillard, A., & Else-Quest, N. (2006). Evaluating Montessori method. *Science, 313*, 1893–1894. https://doi.org/10.1126/science.1132362

Longcamp, M., Anton, J.-L., Roth, M., & Velay, J.-L. (2003). Visual presentation of single letters activates a premotor area involved in writing. *Neuroimage, 19*, 1492–1500. https://doi.org/10.1016/s1053-8119(03)00088-0

Longcamp, M., Tanskanen, T., & Hari, R. (2006). The imprint of action: Motor cortex involvement in visual perception of handwritten letters. *Neuroimage, 33*, 681–688. https://doi.org/10.1016/j.neuroimage.2006.06.042

Macedonia, M., Muller, K., & Friederici, A. D. (2011). The impact of iconic gestures on foreign language word learning and its neural substrate. *Human Brain Mapping, 32*, 982–998. https://doi.org/10.1002/hbm.21084

McEldoon, K. L., Durkin, K. L., & Rittle-Johnson, B. (2013). Is self-explanation worth the time? A comparison to additional practice. *British Journal of Educational Psychology, 83*, 615–632. https://doi.org/10.1111/j.2044-8279.2012.02083.x

McNeill, D. (1992). *Hand and Mind: What Gestures Reveal about Thought*. Chicago, IL: University of Chicago Press.

Mix, K. S. (2010). Spatial tools for mathematical thought. In K. S. Mix, L. B. Smith, & M. Gasser (eds.), *Space and Language* (pp. 41–66). New York: Oxford University Press.

Montessori, M. (1995). *The Absorbent Mind*. New York: Henry Holt and Company.

Novack, M., Congdon, E., Hemani-Lopez, N., & Goldin-Meadow, S. (2014). From action to abstraction: Using the hands to learn math. *Psychological Science, 25*, 903–910. https://doi.org/10.1177/0956797613518351

Perry, M., Church, R. B., & Goldin-Meadow, S. (1988). Transitional knowledge in the acquisition of concepts. *Cognitive Development, 3*, 359–400. https://doi.org/10.1016/0885-2014(88)90021-4

Piaget, J. (1952). *The Origins of Intelligence in Children*. New York: International University Press.

Pulvermüller, F. (2001). Brain reflections of words and their meaning. *Trends in Cognitive Sciences, 5*, 517–524. https://doi.org/10.1016/S1364-6613(00)01803-9

Richland, L. E. (2015). Linking gestures: Cross-cultural variation during instructional analogies. *Cognition and Instruction, 33*, 295–321. https://doi.org/10.1080/07370008.2015.1091459

Richland, L. E., Zur, O., & Holyoak, K. J. (2007). Cognitive supports for analogies in the mathematics classroom. *Science, 316*, 1128–1129. https://doi.org/10.1126/science.1142103

Rohlfing, K. J., Longo, M. R., & Bertenthal, B. I. (2012). Dynamic pointing triggers shifts of visual attention in young infants. *Developmental Science, 15*, 426–435. https://doi.org/10.1111/j.1467–7687.2012.01139.x

Singer, M. A., & Goldin-Meadow, S. (2005). Children learn when their teacher's gestures and speech differ. *Psychological Science, 16*, 85–89. https://doi.org/10.1111/j.0956–7976.2005.00786.x

Tooke, D. J., Hyatt, B., Leigh, M., Snyder, B., & Borda, T. (1992). Why aren't manipulatives used in every middle school mathematics classroom? *Middle School Journal, 24*, 61–62.

Valenzeno, L., Alibali, M. W., & Klatzky, R. (2003). Teachers' gestures facilitate students' learning: A lesson in symmetry. *Contemporary Educational Psychology, 28*, 187–204. https://doi.org/10.1016/s0361-476x(02)00007-3

Wakefield, E. M., Hall, C., James, K. H., & Goldin-Meadow, S. (2018b). Gesture for generalization: Gesture facilitates flexible learning of words for actions on objects. *Developmental Science*. Doi: 10.1111/desc.12656

Wakefield, E. M., & James, K. H. (2015). Effects of learning with gesture on children's understanding of a new language concept. *Developmental Psychology, 5*, 1105–1114. https://doi.org/10.1037/a0039471

Wakefield, E. M., Novack, M., Congdon, E., Franconeri, S., & Goldin-Meadow, S. (2018a). Gesture helps learners learn, but not merely by guiding their visual attention. *Developmental Science*, https://doi.org/10.1111/desc.12664

Wakefield, E. M., Novack, M., Congdon, E., Goldin-Meadow, S., & James, K. H. (2014). Understanding the neural effects of learning with gesture: Does gesture help learners because it is grounded in action? Talk presented at the International Society of Gesture Studies meeting, July, San Diego, California.

Yu, C., & Smith, L. B. (2012). Embodied attention and word learning by toddlers. *Cognition, 125*, 244–262. https://doi.org/10.1016/j.cognition.2012.06.016

PART III

Reading and Writing

10 Fundamental Components of Reading Comprehension

Anne E. Cook and Edward J. O'Brien

Studying Reading Comprehension

Since the early 1970s, the psychological study of reading has focused primarily on the basic cognitive processes and mechanisms involved in every stage of reading – from decoding to parsing to comprehension. Research on reading in education, however, has focused more on reading outcomes. Although research in reading is becoming increasingly interdisciplinary, the divide between psychological theory and educational practices remains wide. Development of theories of reading comprehension are valuable in their own right simply because they increase our understanding of this complex process. However, and likely more important, the value of understanding basic comprehension processes is in the service of researchers whose aim is to develop improved methods of teaching reading and/or to develop effective interventions to assist struggling readers. The goal of this chapter is to describe fundamental passive processes (i.e., those not under the control of the reader) that underpin and underlie successful comprehension. Our hope is to convince researchers developing improved strategies for teaching reading or developing interventions to consider how new strategies and interventions are likely to interact and therefore be impacted by the basic processes reviewed in this chapter.

Crossover between the two fields (i.e., theory and application) has been strongest at lower levels of processing. Psychological theories have had considerable influence on educational interventions and practices in early literacy education. For example, as psychological models have moved from emphasizing importance of encoding meaning and whole word recognition (Goodman, 1967; Routman, 1991; Smith, 1971, 1973, 2004; Smith & Goodman, 1971) to phonics-based decoding (e.g., Beck, 2006; Gough & Hillinger, 1980; National Reading Panel, 2000; Rayner et al., 2001) and, more recently, to a balanced perspective (Fountas & Pinnell, 2006, 2008), educational practices have shifted accordingly.

The disciplinary divide between psychology and education becomes much wider, though, when higher level comprehension is considered. This is because while psychological research on comprehension focuses, for the most part, on the passive processes involved, educational research on comprehension tends to focus on strategies and interventions. In most US schools, the instructional emphasis shifts from decoding and fluency to comprehension around 3rd grade, and the educational research on comprehension focuses primarily on teaching methods, strategies, and interventions. Cognitive psychology research on reading, however, has largely described comprehension as driven by passive processes (e.g., Cook & O'Brien, 2014; Kintsch, 1988; Myers & O'Brien, 1998; O'Brien & Cook, 2016a, 2016b; O'Brien & Myers, 1999; Sanford & Garrod, 1998, 2005). We contend that it is essential for anyone studying these interventions to take into account the underlying passive processes involved in comprehension, and how interventions might interact with these processes. Although this is true for all levels of comprehension (e.g., decoding, parsing, higher level comprehension), it is particularly relevant for comprehension of connected texts, or discourse. In this chapter, we focus on describing fundamental assumptions and processes from psychological models of discourse comprehension that may have particular relevance for educational interventions.

Psychological Assumptions About Reading Comprehension

Psychological models may differ in the extent to which they assume an active role on the part of the reader (for a review, see O'Brien & Cook, 2015) but there are some common assumptions that apply to nearly every model. This section will review those assumptions while presenting empirical evidence and typical methodologies for testing these assumptions in the psychology of reading.

Levels of Representation

First, almost all models adopt Kintsch and van Dijk's (1978) assertion that readers generate multiple levels of representation of a text during reading. The first level, the surface structure, is a verbatim representation of the text. This representation quickly decays from memory, though, and the reader is left with a more gist-based representation, the text-base. The text-base is a representation of the information explicitly stated within the text, but it is assumed to be based on propositional idea units that represent and replace the original surface structure (e.g., "The dog bit the boy" and "The male child was bitten by the canine" have different surface features but convey the same idea unit). Propositions within the text structure are connected to one another as a function of argument overlap, in which propositions that contain the same concepts are connected to one another (Kintsch, 1988; Kintsch & van Dijk, 1978; Kintsch & Vipond, 1979), and causal relations (Keenan, Baillet, & Brown, 1984; O'Brien & Myers, 1987; Trabasso, Secco, & van den Broek, 1984). Although the text-base is not a veridical representation of the text, it is limited to the information and relations explicitly stated in the text along with inferences necessary to repair coherence breaks. In contrast, the third and highest level of representation – the situation model – includes both the information represented in the text-base and the more implicit relations that are intended by the author; it is a representation of what the text is about. Thus, the situation model represents the information explicitly stated in the text as well as information from the reader's general world knowledge that is unstated, but undeniably related to the message conveyed by the text. From the standpoint of almost all psychological models of comprehension, the development of a coherent situation model is a minimum requirement for successful comprehension.

Maintenance of Coherence via Passive Activation

When discussing representation, it is essential to consider the underlying processes and the constraints placed on those processes. One such constraint is the assumption that all of cognition operates within a limited capacity system. In reading, this means that individuals can only hold active in memory and process a small amount of information at a time (Kintsch & van Dijk, 1978; van Dijk & Kintsch, 1983). Within Kintsch's view, reading is a cyclical process; within each cycle, a small number of propositions are encoded and connected to propositions in working memory. Some of these propositions are held active in memory for integration with future input and the remaining propositions become part of the evolving discourse representation in long-term memory. When new propositions are encoded and can be easily integrated with the contents of active memory, local coherence is maintained. That is, the text "flows" smoothly from one sentence to another.

More interesting, however, are the situations in which coherence is not maintained. This can occur because there is no connection between encoded concepts and the currently active information in memory (local coherence break). In such an event, readers must access information from long-term memory in order to reestablish coherence; this may result in activation of relevant information from earlier in the text, or information from general world knowledge that serves as a connection that allows the reader to regain coherence. Coherence breaks can also occur, though, when newly encoded concepts are locally coherent with information in active memory but cannot be readily integrated with previously encoded information that is no longer active in memory (global coherence break; e.g., Albrecht & O'Brien, 1993). That is, although local coherence is maintained, readers experience processing difficulty because newly encoded information is incompatible with previously encoded (and no longer active) content. In both cases (i.e., local or global coherence breaks), readers experience difficulty establishing a connection between incoming information and previously encountered content. We have described elsewhere (e.g., Cook & O'Brien, 2015; O'Brien & Cook, 2015) that maintenance of both local and global coherence rely on passive activation of information from long-term memory. This is a fundamental assumption of memory-based models of text processing (Kintsch, 1988, 1998; Myers & O'Brien, 1998; O'Brien & Myers, 1999; Sanford & Garrod, 1998, 2005; van den Broek et al., 1996).

The passive activation mechanism adopted by memory-based models of comprehension resembles a resonance process (Myers & O'Brien, 1998; O'Brien & Myers, 1999), which was derived from research and theory in memory retrieval (Gillund & Shiffrin, 1984; Hintzman, 1988; Ratcliff, 1978). Within the resonance model, as it applies to comprehension (e.g., Myers & O'Brien, 1998; O'Brien & Myers, 1999), newly encoded information, along with information already active in memory, serve as signals to all of long-term memory; the signal is unrestricted in that it goes out to both previously encoded information from the current text and general world knowledge. The signal's intensity varies as a function of attention but the signal itself proceeds autonomously. Concepts in memory resonate as a function of the degree of conceptual match or overlap with the input. Concepts that resonate in response to this signal may in turn signal to other concepts in memory. The resonance process builds in this manner until it stabilizes and the most active elements (i.e., those that resonate the most) enter working memory. In addition to being autonomous and unrestricted, the resonance process is also assumed to be dumb; information that resonates sufficiently will be reactivated regardless of whether it is relevant to the current discourse model and independent of whether it facilitates or hinders comprehension.

In the next section, we will provide an overview of evidence supporting passive activation of inferences needed to maintain coherence (i.e., necessary inferences); evidence supporting the activation of elaborative inferences – those that are not needed for coherence; and, finally, we will review evidence for the activation of information necessary for maintenance of global coherence.

Necessary Inferences. Inferences fall into two very broad classes of inference type: necessary and elaborative. Necessary inferences are those inferences that are necessary for comprehension because the reader has encountered a coherence break that needs to be repaired, whereas elaborative inferences are not necessary for coherence; instead, they expand on explicitly stated information in a manner that helps "flesh in" the situation model (for a more thorough review of both necessary and elaborative inferences, see Cook and O'Brien, 2015).

Consider first necessary inferences. Probably the most studied type of necessary inference is the anaphoric reference, in which the reader must connect a pronoun, noun, or referential phrase to information presented earlier in a text. Evidence for the activation of anaphoric inferences was first established by McKoon and Ratcliff (1980). They showed that when a sentence presented late in a passage mentioned an anaphor (e.g., "criminal"), it reactivated its antecedent from earlier in the passage (e.g., "burglar"). McKoon and Ratcliff (1980; Dell, McKoon, & Ratcliff, 1983) and O'Brien (1987; O'Brien, Duffy, & Myers, 1986) argued that in these cases, the "search" for an antecedent actually occurs via a passive reactivation process. Most studies on anaphoric inferences set up contexts in which one or more antecedents are presented in the text, followed by a sentence that contains an anaphor designed to reactivate (i.e., reinstate) that antecedent. Researchers measure the time to read the reinstatement sentence, as well as time to respond to a probe that reflects the antecedent concept. Using paradigms like this, researchers have found that ante-cedents are passively reactivated on encountering an anaphoric phrase, and that the speed with which they are reactivated can depend on factors such as distance between the anaphor and the antecedent in the text (O'Brien, 1987), causal related-ness between the anaphor and the antecedent (O'Brien & Myers, 1987), elaboration of the antecedent (O'Brien, Plewes, & Albrecht, 1990), presence of alternate ante-cedent concepts (O'Brien et al., 1995), and conceptual overlap between the anaphor and antecedent (Cook, 2014; Garrod & Sanford, 1977; O'Brien & Albrecht, 1991; O'Brien et al., 1997). Because the reactivation process is passive, it is also unrestricted. This means it is quite possible that an anaphor will end up reactivating a potential antecedent from general world knowledge that is related to the context of the passage, even though that particular concept was never mentioned in the passage and is actually "the wrong" antecedent (e.g., O'Brien & Albrecht, 1991). A further consequence of the reactivation process being dumb is that concepts in the text specifically designated as not the antecedent can be reactivated (Cook, Myers, & O'Brien, 2005), as well as those that are related to the anaphor but are inappropriate antecedent candidates (Klin et al., 2004; Klin et al., 2006; Levine, Guzman, & Klin, 2000).

Another type of necessary inference that is passively activated during reading is one in which readers must infer a link between an event in the text and its causal antecedent. This type of inference is commonly called a backward causal bridging inference. Keenan et al. (1984; see also Albrecht & O'Brien, 1995; Myers, Shinjo, & Duffy, 1987) demonstrated that ease of generating these inferences was predicted by the degree of causal relatedness between a consequence and its causal antecedent. For example, reading times on the sentence "The next day his body was covered with bruises" were much faster following, "Joey's big brother punched him again and again" than "Joey's crazy mother became furiously angry with him," suggesting that readers were able to make the causal bridge between bruises and the antecedent event much more easily in the former case than in the latter case. In the example just presented, reading times for the target sentence increased as its causal relatedness to the preceding sentence decreased. This research was extended by Singer and colleagues (Singer, 1993; Singer & Ferreira, 1983; Singer & Halldorson, 1996; Singer et al., 1992), who provided evidence that causal bridging inferences are activated, even when the events are separated by several sentences of text. Moreover, Rizzella and O'Brien (1996) found that the activation of distant causal antecedents occurs even when there is a sufficient causal antecedent available in active memory. Consistent with the assumptions of a passive inference activation process, Rizzella and O'Brien argued that activation of causal information was driven by the same memory-based factors that drive the activation of nominal antecedents (e.g., distance and elaboration), rather than sufficiency (see also Albrecht & Myers, 1995, 1998; Myers et al., 2000).

Elaborative inferences. As noted earlier, elaborative inferences are inferences that are not necessary for coherence but instead expand on explicitly stated information. Early evidence for passive activation of elaborative inferences was obtained by researchers who demonstrated that readers activate an unnamed instrument (e.g., broom) when reading related contextual information (e.g., The boy cleared the snow from the stairs) (Singer, 1979). Subsequent research on instrumental inferences, however, revealed that instrument activation is highly dependent on the amount of contextual support in the text (Harmon-Vukic et al., 2009; Lassonde & O'Brien, 2009; Lucas, Tanenhaus, & Carlson, 1990; McKoon & Ratcliff, 1981). O'Brien et al. (1988; Garrod et al., 1990) also found that in the presence of a highly supportive context (e.g., picnic setting), readers would infer/activate specific exemplars (e.g., ants) when only category names (e.g., bugs) were explicitly mentioned in the text.

Reading times on a subsequent encounter of the exemplar were just as fast when it had been inferred as in conditions in which it had been explicitly stated in the text. And, finally, Lea and colleagues (Lea, 1995; Lea & Mulligan, 2002; Lea, Mulligan, & Walton, 2005) have demonstrated that readers will activate implicit conclusions for logical arguments (e.g., if p then q, p/therefore q), but only when the premises supporting the conclusion are accessible in memory. In all three cases just outlined (i.e., instrument inferences, exemplar inferences, and logical inferences), there is no local coherence break that requires an anaphoric or causal bridging connection to preceding content. Instead, contextual information autonomously signals long-term memory (including general world knowledge; see Cook & Guéraud, 2005), and if contacted information resonates sufficiently, it is automatically reactivated. Thus, a passive activation process allows readers to fill in "gaps" in the text-base, even when those gaps do not negatively impact comprehension.

Another case in which readers have been shown to passively activate inferences without coherence breaks or "gaps" in the text is when they make predictions about future events. Predictive inferences are not only not required for comprehension but they could actually result in processing difficulty if the predictions made are inconsistent with subsequently presented information (e.g., Peracchi & O'Brien, 2004). In a particularly influential study, the first evidence for predictive inferences was obtained by McKoon and Ratcliff (1986). Their participants read statements like, "The director and cameraman were ready to shoot close-ups when suddenly the actress fell from the 14th story," and then were asked to respond to a probe word reflecting the inference "dead." Response times to this probe were faster than in a control condition, suggesting that "dead" was activated in memory. McKoon and Ratcliff's study launched multitudes of studies on the circumstances under which predictive inferences are activated during reading. From this research, it is clear that predictive inferences are initially activated but that this activation is not long-lasting, particularly if the text continues with unrelated information (Keefe & McDaniel, 1993; Murray, Klin, & Myers, 1993; Potts, Keenan, & Golding, 1988). As with other elaborative inferences, predictive inferences are highly dependent on contextual support (Cook, Limber, & O'Brien, 2001; Klin, Guzman, & Levine, 1999; Peracchi & O'Brien, 2004) and are the product of activation that emanates from both the context and the inference-evoking information (Guéraud, Tapiero, & O'Brien, 2008). The specificity of this activation depends on the constraints placed by the context (Lassonde & O'Brien, 2009). Consistent with a dumb resonance process, we have shown that readers will activate predictive inferences that are related to preceding context, even if that context is no longer relevant (i.e., it is outdated or untrue) to the current discourse model (Cook et al., 2014).

Based on the assumption of resonance continuously activating related information, Gerrig and O'Brien (2005) argued that there really is no need for a taxonomy of inferences (some necessary, some elaborative) that a reader would activate. Instead, all types of inferences are viewed just like any other type of information that has the potential to be passively reactivated from memory. The likelihood of activating any inference is a function of the degree to which the potential inference shares featural overlap with information currently in working memory. This is regardless of whether the inference in question is necessary for local coherence or just elaborates on information explicitly stated in the text (Garrod et al., 1990; McKoon & Ratcliff, 1986, 1992; O'Brien et al., 1988). That is, within the memory-based view, both the "necessity" of the inference for coherence and the goal-meeting properties of the inference are irrelevant (at least with respect to initial activation); if the inference in question is strongly related to information in working memory, it has the potential to be activated. As we will discuss in a subsequent section, the consequences for comprehension resulting from activation of (or failure to activate) inferences require additional cognitive mechanisms beyond the resonance mechanism discussed. In addition, the inferences reviewed in this section are just selected examples of the types of inferences that may be passively activated during reading (for a more thorough review, see Cook and O'Brien, 2015).

Maintaining Global Coherence. While maintaining local coherence requires mapping newly encoded information onto the information in active memory, or activating an inference that helps to establish broken connections, readers must also maintain global coherence. This requires mapping newly encoded content onto information that is no longer active in memory but resides in the reader's long-term memory representation of the text.

Much of the evidence for the role of a passive activation mechanism in the maintenance of global coherence comes from studies employing the inconsistency paradigm. This paradigm was first developed by O'Brien and Albrecht (1992). They presented readers with passages in which information stated early on in the passage was either consistent (e.g., Kim stood inside the health club) or inconsistent (e.g., Kim stood outside the health club) with a target sentence presented later in the passage (e.g., She decided to go outside and stretch her legs a little). Importantly, these two pieces of information were separated by several sentences of text so that the initial information about Kim's location was no longer active in memory when the target sentence was presented; that is, the only coherence break was global in nature. O'Brien and Albrecht found that reading times were slowed in the inconsistent condition, suggesting that readers did in fact maintain global coherence in the absence of a local coherence break.

An even better known utilization of the inconsistency paradigm and demonstration of the role of a passive reactivation mechanism in global coherence maintenance comes from another series of experiments conducted by O'Brien and colleagues (Albrecht & O'Brien, 1993; Cook, Halleran, & O'Brien, 1998; Cook & O'Brien, 2014; Guéraud, Harmon, & Peracchi, 2005; Guéraud et al., in press; Hakala & O'Brien, 1995; Kendeou, Smith, & O'Brien, 2013; O'Brien, Cook, & Guéraud, 2010; O'Brien, Cook, & Peracchi, 2004; O'Brien et al., 1998). Albrecht and O'Brien (1993) presented readers with passages that described characteristics of a protagonist (e.g., Mary loved junk food, or Mary was a vegetarian) that were either consistent or inconsistent with a subsequent target sentence (e.g., Mary ordered a cheeseburger and fries). As in the previously described study, the protagonist information and the target sentence were separated by several sentences of text so that the protagonist information was no longer active in memory when the target sentence was presented

(Myers et al., 1994) and there was no break in local coherence. Albrecht and O'Brien found that reading times were longer on the target sentence in the inconsistent condition than in the consistent condition and argued that the simplest explanation for this was a passive reactivation mechanism. When the target sentence was encoded, a signal was sent to long-term memory and related information resonated in response and was reactivated. This included activation of Mary's eating habits in the inconsistent condition, which could not be easily reconciled with the information about her food choice in the target sentence. This created a global coherence break and processing was disrupted as a result.

Subsequent studies in this series served to clarify critical characteristics of the resonance process. As mentioned earlier, the resonance mechanism is dumb; information is reactivated on the basis of its relation to current input regardless of its relevance. The best demonstration of this came from O'Brien and colleagues (1998), who created a qualified protagonist characteristic condition, in which the inconsistent characteristic (e.g., Mary was a vegetarian) was clearly indicated as outdated or no longer true (e.g., " ... but she wasn't anymore. She now ate meat"). If the resonance process is dumb, it should reactivate information about Mary's vegetarianism even though it is no longer relevant to the current state of affairs in the text; this should lead to difficulty processing the target sentence relative to the consistent condition. Across five experiments, O'Brien and colleagues found slower reading times in the qualified condition than in the consistent condition. These findings were later replicated in other related studies, in which the order of information in the qualified condition was manipulated (Guéraud et al., 2005, in press) or included irreversible changes in state (e.g., someone died or a tree was cut down; O'Brien et al., 2010).

The resonance process is also sensitive to the quantity and quality of the representation of concepts it contacts. Kendeou and colleagues (2013) added a causal justification to the qualified condition (e.g., Mary began eating meat to overcome anemia), arguing that adding a causal component would result in a more richly elaborated and interconnected representation of the qualified information; more interconnected concepts (e.g., not a vegetarian) should be more likely to become reactivated during reading and thus more likely to compete with the inconsistent information (e.g., vegetarian) for activation. Kendeou and colleagues found that when the causal justification was just a single sentence, the impact of the inconsistent information was reduced such that it was activated in memory on presentation of the target sentence but it no longer impacted processing (i.e., did not slow reading times). When the causal justification was extended to three sentences, not only was processing difficulty eliminated but the inconsistent information was no longer measurably active in memory after the target sentence was presented. That is, as the interconnectivity of the qualified representation increased, so did the likelihood that it would draw activation while also reducing any activation reaching the inconsistent information. Given the constraints of a limited capacity system, highly interconnected information will compete with, and can override, other information for activation and influence on subsequent processing.

Finally, as previously noted, the resonance signal to long-term memory is unrestricted; it goes out to the episodic text representation as well as general world knowledge. Given this, Cook and O'Brien (2014) argued that any reactivation of previously stated information from the text (e.g., Mary is a vegetarian) in response to the contents of the target sentence must be mediated by its underlying relation in general world knowledge. In the case of Mary, the tie that binds vegetarian to cheeseburger is the underlying concept "meat," which was never explicitly stated in the passage but resides in general world knowledge. Consistent with the unrestricted nature of resonance, and the corresponding influence of general world knowledge, Cook and O'Brien found that reactivation of "vegetarian" was faster and it had a stronger influence on comprehension when it was more highly related to the contents of the target sentence (e.g., she ordered a cheeseburger) than when it was less related (e.g., she ordered a tuna salad).

The studies described in this section provide evidence for the role of a passive, dumb, and unrestricted activation mechanism in reading comprehension. It is important to note that the resonance model only describes the activation process and not what happens thereafter. The next section will focus on models of comprehension that provide a wider view of how readers activate and ultimately utilize that activated information during reading.

Beyond Passive Activation

Nearly every psychological model of reading comprehension carries the general assumption that successful comprehension is a two-stage process that involves (1) reactivation of information from long-term memory, as described in the previous section, and (2) integration of reactivated content with incoming information. Although the reactivation process has been relatively well defined, less is known about the processes that follow and the specific constraints that pertain to them.

The most complete and most commonly adopted two-stage activation + integration model is Kintsch's (1988, 1998) construction–integration model. During the construction stage, readers develop a text-base–level representation (Kintsch & van Dijk, 1978) for the text information currently being processed in that cycle, which is elaborated with related information reactivated from long-term memory. Similar to the resonance model, it is assumed that related information will be added to this initial network regardless of whether it is coherent or whether it will ultimately facilitate or hinder comprehension. Then, during integration, activation is assumed to spread throughout the network until it stabilizes; in most cases, this means that irrelevant or incoherent nodes activated during the initial stage will be eliminated. Through this continuous two-stage process, the reader is assumed to develop a coherent representation without employing any strategic processes. If this does not occur, Kintsch argued that failure, or comprehension difficulty, may result in a reinitiation of the construction–integration cycle.

What has become increasingly clear, however, is that a simple activation-then-linkage approach to describing comprehension is elegant but incomplete. Long and Lea (2005) argued that the linkage (i.e., integration) process must also contain an evaluative component that allows for the system to determine what does and does not make sense (see also Isberner & Richter, 2014; Richter, 2015; Singer, 2006, 2013; Singer & Doering, 2014). More recently, we, along with other researchers, have argued for a third comprehension stage through which linkages are verified or validated against information in active memory (e.g., Cook & O'Brien, 2014; O'Brien & Cook 2016a, 2016b). Before describing the theoretical model into which this third processing stage is incorporated, we will first provide evidence that validation occurs during reading.

As we indicated in the section "Maintenance of Coherence via Passive Activation," in most situations, inferences are passively activated during reading. What we left out, however, is what happens after activation. In some cases, as with unsubstantiated predictive inferences, activation may quickly dissipate (Keefe & McDaniel, 1993; Murray et al., 1993; Potts et al., 1988). In other cases, activated inferences may be instantiated into the reader's long-term memory representation of the text. Although the specificity of what is encoded may depend on the degree of contextual support (Cook et al., 2001; Lassonde & O'Brien, 2009), the factors that influence which inferences are instantiated and which are not have not been clear in the literature. Cook and colleagues (2014) found that predictive inferences are activated regardless of whether they are based on contextual information that is currently relevant to the evolving discourse model, suggesting that they are activated via a dumb and passive process. More pertinent to the issue of validation, however, is their finding that only relevant inferences were subsequently instantiated into the reader's long-term memory representation. That is, after activation, the activated content must have been submitted to some evaluative process through which irrelevant information was "pruned" from the evolving discourse representation.

It is important to clarify that this evaluative process involved in inference instantiation is not assumed to be a "smart" process. In fact, in some cases, it is possible for it to lead to the instantiation of content that is incorrect but highly related to the text. For example, O'Brien and Albrecht (1991) found that when contextual support in a passage (e.g., a small black cat with a white stripe down its back) strongly supported a concept from general world knowledge (e.g., skunk), readers would activate "skunk" even when the actual antecedent was explicitly stated in the text (e.g., cat). Not only did readers activate "skunk" in place of the appropriate antecedent but they also instantiated it into their long-term memory representation of the text. A recall experiment demonstrated that readers incorrectly instantiated and subsequently retrieved "skunk" from memory when they had actually read about a black and white cat.

Cook and O'Brien (2014) argued that it is also necessary to assume a validation-like process in order to fully explain results like those found with the inconsistency paradigm. As previously discussed, information is reactivated via a passive resonance-like mechanism and then it must be linked to incoming information. The processing difficulty that results from "Mary ordered a cheeseburger and fries" does not occur during activation or the linkage of activated to incoming information. Several findings have confirmed that information can be activated but fail to lead to processing difficulty (e.g., Cook et al., 1998; Kendeou et al., 2013). Instead, processing difficulty results when the linkage between the reactivated node that "Mary is a vegetarian" and the incoming information that "Mary ordered a cheeseburger" is validated, or checked, against the underlying information from general world knowledge that cheeseburgers contain meat, which vegetarians do not eat. Since speed and strength of activation is a function of the relation between the to-be-reactivated information and the cue, validation of the linkage is also mediated by that underlying relation in general world knowledge.

RI-Val Model of Comprehension

Given the need for a validation component in reading, Cook and O'Brien (2014; O'Brien & Cook, 2016a, 2016b) proposed the RI-Val model of comprehension. This model builds on previous two-stage activation + integration models of comprehension (Kintsch, 1988, 1998; Sanford & Garrod, 1989, 2005; van den Broek et al., 1996) and includes three distinct yet interdependent stages: *resonance, integration*, and *validation*. These three stages are depicted in Figure 10.1. Resonance operates as originally assumed by Myers and O'Brien (1998; O'Brien & Myers, 1999); incoming information autonomously signals all of long-term memory, contacted elements may in turn signal other elements, and this process continues until it stabilizes. Contacted elements resonate as a function of their overlap with information in active memory, and those elements that resonate the most will be reactivated.

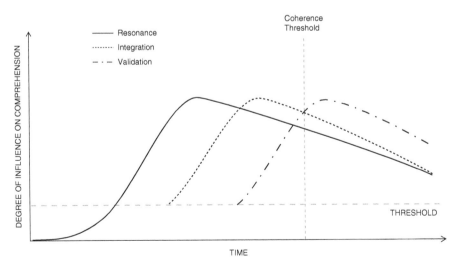

Figure 10.1 *The RI-Val model of comprehension. This figure represents the parallel asynchronous nature of the Resonance, Integration and Validation stages assumed by the model (from O'Brien & Cook, 2016a)*

Activation is not all-or-none but occurs along a continuum; some elements will be activated but will not meet a minimum threshold for impacting subsequent stages of comprehension, whereas others will exceed the threshold and will serve as input for subsequent stages. In the Integration phase, reactivated elements that exceed the minimum threshold are linked to information already active in memory on the basis of conceptual overlap, or goodness of fit, presumably in a proposition-like manner (Kintsch, 1988, 1998; Kintsch & van Dijk, 1978; van Dijk & Kintsch, 1983). These linkages then, are Validated, or evaluated, in a third stage.

The Resonance and Integration stages of the RI-Val model are largely adapted from previous theoretical models (Kintsch, 1988, 1998; Sanford & Garrod, 1989, 2005; van den Broek et al., 1996), but there has been less research on the mechanisms that underlie Validation. Consistent with a passive, memory-based view of comprehension, we have adopted a passive approach to validation that is based on a pattern matching process similar to that described by Reder and colleagues (partial matching hypothesis; Kamas & Reder, 1995; Kamas, Reder & Ayers, 1996; Reder & Cleeremans, 1990). Linkages from the integration stage are evaluated on the basis of how the elements within those linkages match at a featural level; this is important because clusters of features can "match" even if they are not identical. Ease of validation processing (e.g., reading time) is a function of the degree of match among elements within these linkages in active memory. The use of this type of pattern matching mechanism to explain validation allows for an evaluative sense-making component of comprehension to operate without employing rigid algorithms or any strategic component on the part of the reader.

Figure 10.1, originally presented in O'Brien and Cook (2016a; see also O'Brien & Cook, 2016b), can be used to illustrate some of the fundamental assumptions of the RI-Val model. First, all three processes, resonance, integration, and validation, represented by the three curves in the figure, are passive; this implies that once each process starts, it runs to completion. The resonance process (R) (solid curve) begins as soon as new information is encoded. Information that is activated above a minimum threshold (horizontal dotted line) has the potential to influence comprehension, with information at higher levels of activation having a greater potential for influence. Activation operates along a continuum; it builds over time, peaks, and then eventually decays below threshold. The information that is activated above threshold in the R stage will be linked to incoming information in the Integration stage (I), represented by the dotted curve. Finally, linkages from the I stage are validated (Val) (dashed curve).

The abscissa in the figure represents time, capturing the idea that the RI-Val processes are assumed to play out over time. Because processing is assumed to be continuous and cyclical (see also Kintsch, 1988, 1998), once each process starts, all three run in parallel. They are also asynchronous; each process depends and operates on the output of the previous stage. Because all stages are ultimately dependent on the output of the resonance process, all stages are mediated by factors that influence activation. This means that information that is highly related to current input is likely to be reactivated, integrated, and validated before information that is less related to current input.

R, I, and Val are assumed to play out over time, and this is somewhat independent of the internal "gauge" that guides when the reader will move on in the text. We have argued that the coherence threshold (vertical dashed line in Figure 10.1) represents the point in time marking when the reader moves from one unit of text to another. That is, the coherence threshold marks the extent to which the R, I, and Val processes run before attention shifts to subsequent information. We have clarified elsewhere (O'Brien & Cook, 2016a, 2016b) that the coherence threshold marks the point in time at which the match accrued by the validation process results in sufficient coherence for the reader to shift their attention to new information in the text. This term is adapted from van den Broek and colleagues' more general concept of "standards of coherence" (e.g., van den Broek et al., 2002, 2011; van den Broek, Risden, & Husbye-Hartman, 1995). Because the coherence threshold is just a point on a temporal continuum, it means that effects from the three processes can potentially occur on either side of the continuum; processing effects could be immediate (to the left of the threshold), delayed (to the right of the threshold), or both.

The last point – that processing is continuous and can be observed immediately and/or after a delay – has led to a renewed interest in understanding how effects of different types of information may play out over the time course of comprehension. This requires the use of measures that allow researchers to observe effects at more than one window in time. For example, in self-paced reading experiments, we have argued for the measurement of processing times on a target sentence as well as on a spillover sentence (e.g., Albrecht & O'Brien, 1993; Cook et al., 1998; Cook & O'Brien, 2014; O'Brien et al., 1998, 2004, 2010). We stated earlier that Cook and O'Brien (2014) found that inconsistency effects were stronger and appeared earlier when the underlying relation in general world knowledge between the target sentence was strong than when it was weak. That is, in the context of the current discussion, the processing difficulty due to the inconsistency appeared on the target sentence itself in the high-related condition but did not appear until a subsequent, spillover, sentence in the low-related version. Similarly, Cook (2014) found that processing difficulties due to low-related, anomalous anaphors appeared immediately (i.e., on the target sentence) but difficulties due to high-related anomalous anaphors were not fully validated until a sentence later (i.e., the spillover sentence) (see also Williams, Cook, & O'Brien, 2018).

The time course of processing effects can also be mapped out with more precise reading-based measures, such as those provided by eye tracking data (e.g., Cook & Wei, 2017; Wei & Cook, 2016). Cook and Myers (2004) tracked readers' eye movements as they processed narratives about scripted events (e.g., rock concert). Within these narratives, scripted role fillers (e.g., band manager, guitarist) performed either script appropriate (e.g., song was played by a guitarist) or script-inappropriate (e.g., song was played by the manager) actions across two encounters. On the first encounter, the appropriateness of the role filler's actions impacted processing time. On the second encounter, early processing effects were impacted by whether or not the information matched the first encounter, but delayed processing effects were influenced by the appropriateness of the action. Thus, Cook and Myers were able to map the time course of how different kinds of information (i.e., previously encountered text and script-based knowledge) influenced comprehension.

The combination of the unrestricted nature of the resonance process and the continuous nature of RI-Val processing provides the perfect theoretical context in which to study the interplay of information from different sources during reading, such as that examined by Cook and Myers (2004; see also Albrecht & O'Brien, 1991; Rizzella & O'Brien, 2002). More recently, we have shifted from examining inconsistencies in narratives (e.g., vegetarians who order cheeseburgers) to examining contexts in which ordinary validation processes seem to fail. These include scenarios in which readers do not experience difficulty (at least not right away) when processing information that is clearly incorrect or inconsistent with general world knowledge. Thus, the shift in our research on comprehension has moved from examining the reactivation and integration processes to examining the validation process. The next section will describe examples of different lines of research designed to elucidate factors influencing validation.

Studying Validation Processes

Semantic Anomalies. As just noted, one way to study validation is by examining situations in which it breaks down. The first example of validation "failure" that we will discuss comes from studies of semantic anomalies. Semantic anomalies, or illusions, contain purposefully incorrect information that often goes undetected by readers. For example, Erickson and Mattson (1981) found that readers frequently miss the error in "How many animals of each kind did Moses take on the Ark?" and incorrectly respond "two" (see also Kamas et al., 1996; Reder & Cleeremans, 1990; Reder & Kusbit, 1991), presumably because the erroneous "Moses" still shares many features in common with the correct term, "Noah." These kinds of detection failures have typically been attributed to shallow, incomplete, or "good enough" processing (Ferreira, Bailey, & Ferraro, 2002; Ferreira & Patson, 2007; Sanford, 2002; Sanford & Emmott, 2012; Sanford & Graesser, 2006; Sanford & Sturt, 2002) that is not based on a fully validated match between recent linkages and activated information from memory.

Williams and colleagues (2018) recently embedded anomalies like the Moses Illusion in narrative contexts; the anomaly appeared in a target sentence, followed by a spillover sentence. This allowed Williams and colleagues to manipulate the amount of preceding passage context that supported the Illusion, as well as to study processing over a broader window of time than typically afforded in anomaly detection tasks. They found that when passage context was elaborated and highlighted the *shared* features between the anomalous (e.g., Moses) and correct (e.g., Noah) information, any processing difficulty due to the anomaly was delayed until a spillover sentence (see the shared features conditions in Figure 10.2); initial validation of the information in the target sentence was dominated by the strong contextual information that supported both terms, and additional time was needed for information from general world knowledge that distinguished between the anomalous and correct terms to be reactivated, integrated, and validated.

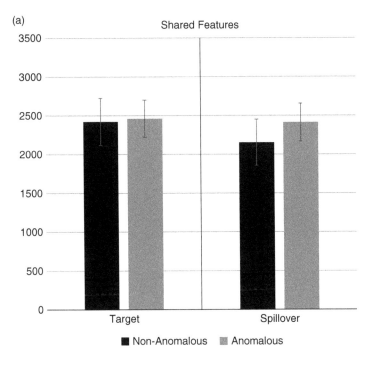

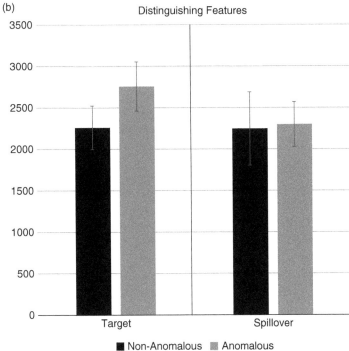

Figure 10.2 *Reading times in milliseconds for nonanomalous and anomalous target and spillover sentences as a function of context conditions – (a) shared vs. (b) distinguishing features (from Williams, Cook, & O'Brien, 2018)*

(a) shows no effect of anomaly until the spillover sentence, when the context focused on shared features, whereas (b) shows an immediate effect of the anomaly on the target sentence when the context focused on distinguishing features.

In contrast, when there was minimal contextual information about shared features between the anomalous and correct terms present in the narrative, or the context elaborated on features that *distinguished* between anomalous and correct information, processing difficulty appeared immediately (i.e., on the target sentence) (see the distinguishing features conditions in Figure 10.2). In this case, the overwhelming majority of concepts reactivated from memory served to distinguish between the two terms and this information was used to quickly integrate and validate the information in the target sentence. These findings highlighted the strong interplay between contextual information and information from general world knowledge during validation, and how the timing of these effects is dependent on strength and speed of information activation.

Similarly, Cook and colleagues (2018) used eye tracking to study the time course of how readers processed Moses Illusion items and found that low-related anomalies (e.g., Nixon took two animals of each kind on the Ark) resulted in immediate processing difficulty on the anomalous term. High-related anomalies (e.g., Moses) led to processing difficulty but only after a delay. Interestingly, this occurred regardless of whether anomalies were detected (i.e., a correct "false" answer was provided in response to the statement) or undetected by the reader. Consistent with other work supporting the RI-Val model (e.g., Cook & O'Brien, 2014), Cook and colleagues argued that validation of the information in the statements was mediated by its underlying relation with the correct information in general world knowledge. And importantly, detection of the anomaly appeared to be independent of this validation process.

These studies highlight the importance of understanding how contextual cues in a narrative may reactivate information from general world knowledge and how these two sources ultimately compete for influence on validation processes. A common comprehension instructional approach is to encourage readers to relate a text to their own prior knowledge (e.g., Dole et al., 1991; National Reading Panel, 2000). The studies just described indicate that this activation of knowledge occurs autonomously and continuously and can be influenced by the strength of quite subtle cues in a text.

Fantasy Text Comprehension. Another instance in which validation seems to "fail" is in comprehension of fantasy texts, where events routinely violate norms established in the reader's general world knowledge. Creer, Cook, and O'Brien (2018) expanded on previous work in fantasy comprehension (e.g., Ferguson & Sanford, 2008; Foy & Gerrig, 2014; Nieuwland & van Berkum, 2006) to test how fantasy story contexts interact with general world knowledge to influence validation. They manipulated whether the opening lines of a story supported a narrative in a commonplace world, or a fantasy environment. Passages went on to describe either a well-known fictional character (e.g., Superman) or an unknown individual. Later in the passage, a target sentence referenced the protagonist and an event that violated general world knowledge (e.g., bullets bounced off his chest). Creer and colleagues argued that readers should be able to easily validate the target sentence event when reading about familiar fantasy characters, because they can rely on information from general world knowledge about the character and all their fantasy-relevant characteristics. But when unknown characters are featured in a narrative, more elaborated fantasy contexts may be necessary to override violations of general world knowledge during reading. This is exactly what they found. Just as important, this was not true when fantasy contexts were reduced to a single sentence.

The idea that readers build fantasy representations of a narrative over time was investigated in depth by Walsh, Cook, and O'Brien (2018). They had participants read an extended fantasy narrative, in which embedded target sentences conflicted either with general world knowledge or with aspects of the fantasy narrative. When the inconsistencies in the text were unrelated to the evolving fantasy narrative but depended on the activation, integration, and validation of information from general world knowledge, readers experienced immediate disruption (see Target Sentence conditions in Figure 10.3a). When inconsistencies in the text pertained to information that was an integral part of the broad fantasy narrative, readers also experienced immediate processing difficulty, but only when the inconsistencies appeared early on in the narrative. Later on in the same extended narrative, the reader had developed a richly elaborated fantasy-based representation from which fantasy-relevant information could be reactivated, integrated, and validated prior to any influence of information from general world knowledge on validation; readers still experienced processing due to the inconsistency, but it was now delayed until a spillover sentence (see spillover sentence conditions in Figure 10.3b).

Taken together, the findings of Creer and colleagues (2018) and Walsh and colleagues (2018) provide clear evidence that the reader's "immersion" in a fantasy world is not a result of compartmentalization of information about the text (e.g., Rapp et al., 2014), the reader suspending disbelief of general world violations (e.g., Gerrig, 1989, 1993), or a qualitative shift in processing or attention. Instead, literary immersion is a function of the cumulative representation of contextual information in a narrative. As the amount of contextual information increases, so does the likelihood that it will have a strong and earlier impact on validation processes. Thus, even though different types of text manipulations can impact the strength and timing of informational influence on comprehension, the processes that underlie comprehension are the same regardless of text genre, length, or contents.

Manipulating the Coherence Threshold. So far, our discussion of the coherence threshold has focused on it as a temporal mark for measuring immediate and delayed processing. Originally, though, this concept grew out of van den Broek and colleagues' "standards of coherence" which is a general and somewhat abstract gauge by which readers judge whether current text is coherent and how and when to engage in more strategic processing (for a discussion of this concept, see O'Brien & Cook, 2016a). Manipulations of readers' standards of coherence have typically demonstrated that readers may engage in different levels or "depths" of processing as a function of reader, text, or task variables (Linderholm & van den Broek, 2002; Linderholm & Zhao, 2008; van den Broek et al., 2001). Although these studies have demonstrated that processing may shift as a function of individual differences or

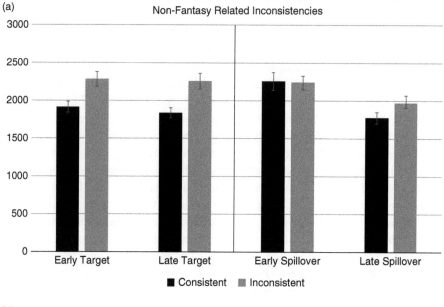

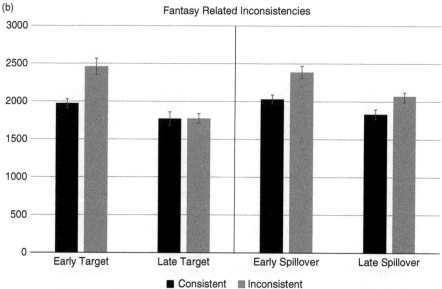

Figure 10.3 *Reading times in milliseconds for target and spillover sentences as a function of consistency and passage position (early vs. late) – (a) nonfantasy-related inconsistencies, (b) fantasy-related inconsistencies (from Walsh, Cook, & O'Brien, 2018)*

In (a), passage inconsistencies were not fantasy-related and pertained to readers' general world knowledge; differences between the consistent and inconsistent conditions appeared on the target sentence regardless of passage position. In (b), passage inconsistences depended on fantasy-based
information; differences between the consistent and inconsistent condition appeared on the target sentence when positioned early in the narrative but were delayed to the spillover sentence when positioned late in the narrative.

external influences, they have not been linked to understanding how these variables impact processing over time.

For example, the work of van den Broek and colleagues has made clear that processing may shift as a function of tasks. Van den Broek and colleagues (2001) found that when individuals read a text for entertainment versus for study, readers' processing (as measured by talk aloud protocols recorded during reading) changed from comprehension monitoring and associations to generation of more in-depth elaborative and predictive inferences. This study imposed a change in task expectations on readers, but often the standards by which readers gauge whether sufficient coherence goals have been met are more subtle. Williams and colleagues (2018) manipulated readers' coherence thresholds without making any changes to the instructions given to participants but by simply changing the number of comprehension questions asked throughout the experimental session. That is, they were able to shift the level of featural match required for the reader to move on to an either higher (i.e., later in time) or lower (i.e., earlier in time) threshold without ever adjusting the task itself. And the adjustment of the coherence threshold affected the timing of anomaly processing effects. When they increased the number of comprehension questions asked per passage, the threshold was raised and a higher degree of match was required for comprehension before readers' attention shifted to subsequent information. In this case, readers waited for more information to accrue activation, be integrated, and validated before moving on to subsequent text; processing difficulty due to the anomalous term in the target sentence appeared immediately. When they decreased comprehension questions to only one every four passages, however, the coherence threshold was lowered and only a minimal match was required for readers to move on in the text. In this case, any processing difficulty due to the anomaly was delayed until the spillover sentence, if present at all. Williams and colleagues' study demonstrates that very subtle changes in task expectations can lead to measurable changes in processing.

Although further refinement of the coherence threshold and the variables that impact it are necessary, our preliminary work points to the importance of considering how it affects timing of comprehension processing effects. The next section will focus on another variable that may interact with RI-Val processes and have important consequences for comprehension – individual differences in reader ability.

Understanding Reader Differences. The processes discussed above are passive and therefore assumed to be universal to all readers. They may not "look" the same in all readers, because readers may differ on variables such as working memory capacity (Baddeley, Gathercole, & Papagno, 1998; Engle, 2002), lack of accessible domain knowledge (McNamara, 1997; McNamara & McDaniel, 2004), and ability to suppress irrelevant information (Gernsbacher, 1993; Henderson, Snowling, & Clark, 2013). Presumably, these variables influence the amount and type of information that could be made available via passive reactivation for influence on later processing.

While there have been some investigations into differences in reading style, or the general processing approach readers adopt when reading a text, there has not been as much research on how these reading styles impact or interact with the processes underlying comprehension, such as those outlined in the RI-Val model. For example, Hyona, Lorch, & Kaakinen (2002; see also Hyona & Nurminen, 2006) examined readers' eye movements as they processed expository texts and reported that their participants could be divided into four general groups based on general reading style: fast linear readers, slow linear readers, topic structure processors, and nonselective reviewers. These groups differed with respect to their overall reading speed, number of regressions made, and amount of processing time devoted to reading headings and topic sentences versus other text content. Although Hyona and Nurminen (2006) found amount of rereading was correlated with general comprehension of the text, it is not clear how or whether reading speed or likelihood of rereading corresponded to individual comprehension processes. Similarly, Rayner, Slattery, and Belanger (2010) found that fast readers had larger perceptual spans and spent less time rereading than slow readers, but they did not investigate how these differences might relate to more fundamental processes involved in comprehension. Rayner (2016) did, however, provide convincing evidence that, contrary to claims made by popular speed reading programs, reading speed cannot be dramatically increased without having a serious and detrimental impact on comprehension.

With respect to understanding reader differences in comprehension, the most relevant studies on how individual differences affect processing have come from work on differences in reading skill. Traditionally, reading skill is measured independently via standardized tests, such as the Nelson–Denny (Nelson, Brown, and Denny, 1960) or the Gates–MacGinitie (MacGinitie et al., 2000), and readers are divided based on a median split into "high skill" and "low skill" groups. Processing differences on reading comprehension tasks such as those presented in earlier sections of this chapter are then compared as a function of reading skill. Studies of this nature have demonstrated that although low skill readers may reactivate previously encountered information, they may not always fully integrate and validate that reactivated content against incoming information (Long & Chong, 2001; Steigler & O'Brien, 2009). This difficulty in mapping reactivated content, including information from previously encountered text and general world knowledge, onto incoming content could, over time, result in weak or impoverished mental representations of a text (Ericcson & Kintsch, 1995). A weak representation would not contain the interconnections and associations that are needed to facilitate subsequent processing (e.g., Smith & O'Brien, 2016; Steigler & O'Brien, 2009). Smith and O'Brien (2016), however, found that this is not irreversible; with subtle interventions such as the use of elaborated contexts and/or stronger retrieval cues that would serve to increase activation levels, it was possible to increase the accessibility of previously encountered information such that it was more likely to be reactivated and have an influence on comprehension.

Findings like those of Smith and O'Brien (2016) make clear that successful interventions for readers can be developed by appealing to the fundamental processes that make up comprehension. The RI-Val model's view of parallel, asynchronous processing requires researchers to attend to the interdependent nature of reactivation, integration, and validation mechanisms, and that manipulations designed to influence one stage can have consequences for other stages downstream. Depending on the underlying processes targeted, it might be possible to design effective interventions that are quite subtle in appearance. These may involve providing more time for processing to unfold, stronger elaborations of critical information in texts, or stronger cues for retrieval of critical contents. Future research in this area might focus on specific manipulations that support validation processes and/or that that impact the reader's coherence threshold.

Beyond Fundamental Components of Reading Comprehension

The primary goal of the RI-Val model and its predecessors has been to outline the fundamental processes that have to be core components of any full model of comprehension. Understanding these fundamental components of comprehension is critical to anyone interested in studying reading – whether they are interested in basic processes, designing interventions, or teaching reading (see also Rayner et al., 2001).

As we noted in O'Brien and Cook (2015), however, no complete theoretical model of comprehension exists. The RI-Val model and other memory-based accounts (Kintsch, 1988, 1998; Sanford & Garrod, 1989, 2005; van den Broek et al., 1996) have focused on the extent to which passive processes can explain critical issues in comprehension, such as the activation of inferences or maintenance of coherence. These processes, however, cannot fully explain what researchers have referred to as deeper comprehension (Graesser, 2015) – comprehension that goes far beyond the simple development of a situation model; that is, they do not include higher-order thinking such as analysis, synthesis, and evaluation (McNamara, Jacovina, & Allen, 2016). An excellent example of comprehension that goes beyond the situation model is demonstrated in Goldman's recent work on the comprehension of literary texts (e.g., narratives, folk tales, poems, science fiction), as exemplified by the differences between a "literal stance" and an "interpretive stance" (Goldman, McCarthy, & Burkett, 2015). Literal stance involves an orientation toward developing an understanding of what the text is about akin to Kintsch's (1988, 1998) situation model level of representation. In contrast, deeper comprehension, such as taking an interpretive stance, involves an orientation toward what the text "means" (e.g., comprehending the intended meaning of a fable or parable). For example, an interpretive understanding of the fable about "the tortoise and the hare" requires far more than the development of a situation model of a race between a tortoise and a hare; it requires a much deeper interpretive understanding (i.e., slow and steady wins the race).

The work being done on "deeper comprehension" clearly points out the limitations of memory-based models such as RI-Val. However, as we argued at the beginning of this chapter, one of the primary goals of memory-based models is to capture the fundamental processes involved in comprehension in order to serve more complex models of comprehension that tackle markedly more complex processes such as those involved in deeper comprehension, as well as to assist researchers working on developing effective reading interventions. We contend that memory-based models of comprehension and models of comprehension that focus more on the strategies that readers bring to bear (e.g., Gernsbacher, 1990; Graesser, Singer, & Trabasso, 1994; Singer, Graesser, & Trabasso, 1994; Zwaan, 1999) are not in competition with each other (except on issues of parsimony); instead, we believe that memory-based models are designed to facilitate the development of more complete models of comprehension that undoubtedly require strategic processing (see O'Brien & Cook, 2015). To the extent that memory-based models have accurately captured some fundamental processes, these findings could well serve researchers as they develop improved strategies for teaching reading as well as interventions to assisted less-skilled readers.

References

Albrecht, J. E. & Myers, J. L. (1995). Role of context in accessing distant information during reading. *Journal of Experimental Psychology: Learning, Memory, and Cognition*, *21*, 1459–1468.

(1998). Accessing distant text information during reading: Effects of contextual cues. *Discourse Processes*, *26*, 87–107.

Albrecht, J. E. & O'Brien, E. J. (1991). Effects of centrality on retrieval of text-based concepts. *Journal of Experimental Psychology: Learning, Memory, and Cognition*, *17*, 932–939.

(1993). Updating a mental model. *Journal of Experimental Psychology: Learning, Memory, and Cognition*, *19*, 1061–1070.

(1995). Goal processing and the maintenance of coherence. In R. F. Lorch & E. J. O'Brien (eds.), *Sources of coherence in reading* (pp. 263–278). Hillsdale, NJ: Erlbaum.

Baddeley, A., Gathercole, S., & Papagno, C. (1998). The phonological loop as a language learning device. *Psychological Review*, *105*(1), 158.

Beck, I. L. (2006). *Making sense of phonics*. New York: Guilford Press.

Cook, A. E. (2014). Processing anomalous anaphors. *Memory & Cognition*, *42*, 1171–1185.

Cook, A. E. & Guéraud, S. (2005). What have we been missing? The role of general world knowledge in discourse processing. *Discourse Processes*, *39*, 365–378.

Cook, A. E., Halleran, J. G., & O'Brien, E. J. (1998). What is readily available during reading? A memory-based text processing view. *Discourse Processes*, *26*, 109–129.

Cook, A. E., Lassonde, K. A., Splinter, A. et al. (2014). The role of relevance in the activation and instantiation of predictive inferences. *Language and Cognitive Processes*, *29*, 244–257.

Cook, A. E., Limber, J. E., & O'Brien, E. J. (2001). Situation-based context and the availability of predictive inferences. *Journal of Memory and Language*, *44*, 220–234.

Cook, A. E. & Myers, J. L. (2004). Processing discourse roles in scripted narratives: The influences of context and world knowledge. *Journal of Memory and Language*, *50*, 268–288.

Cook, A. E., Myers, J. L., & O'Brien, E. J. (2005). Processing an anaphor when there is no antecedent. *Discourse Processes*, *39*, 101–120.

Cook, A. E. & O'Brien, E. J. (2014). Knowledge activation, integration, and validation during narrative text comprehension. *Discourse Processes*, *51*, 26–49.

(2015). Passive activation and instantiation of inferences during reading. In E. J. O'Brien, A. E. Cook, & R. F. Lorch, Jr. (eds.), *Inferences during reading* (pp. 19–41). New York: Cambridge University Press.

Cook, A. E., Walsh, E., Bills, M. A. A., Kircher, J. C., & O'Brien, E. J. (2018). Validation of semantic illusions independent of anomaly detection: Evidence from eye movements. *Quarterly Journal of Experimental Psychology*, 7, 113–121.

Cook, A. E. & Wei, W. (2017). Using eye movements to study reading processes: Methodological considerations. In C. A. Was, F. J. Sansoti, & B. J. Morris (eds.), *Eye tracking technology applications in educational research* (pp. 27–47). Hershey, PA: IGI Global.

Creer, S. D., Cook, A. E., & O'Brien, E. J. (2018). Competing activation during fantasy text comprehension. *Scientific Studies of Reading*, *22*, 308–320.

Dell, G. S., McKoon, G., & Ratcliff, R. (1983). The activation of antecedent information during the processing of anaphoric reference in reading. *Journal of Verbal Learning and Verbal Behavior*, *22*(1), 121–132.

Dole, J. A., Valencia, S. W., Greer, E. A., & Wardrop, J. L. (1991). Effects of two types of prereading instruction on the comprehension of narrative and expository text. *Reading Research Quarterly*, *26(2)*, 142–159.

Engle, R. W. (2002). Working memory capacity as executive attention. *Current Directions in Psychological Science*, *11*(1), 19–23.

Ericsson, K. A. & Kintsch, W. (1995). Long-term working memory. *Psychological Review*, *102*(2), 211–245.

Erickson, T. D. & Mattson, M. E. (1981). From words to meaning: A semantic illusion. *Journal of Verbal Learning and Verbal Behavior*, *20*, 540–551.

Ferguson, H. J. & Sanford, A. J. (2008). Anomalies in real and counterfactual worlds: An eye-movement investigation. *Journal of Memory and Language*, *58*, 609–626.

Ferreira, F., Bailey, K. G.,& Ferraro, V. (2002). Good-enough representations in language comprehension. *Current Directions in Psychological Science*, *11*, 11–15.

Ferreira, F. & Patson, N. D. (2007). The "good enough" approach to language comprehension. *Language and Linguistics Compass*, *1*(1-2), 71–83.

Fountas, I. C. & Pinnell, G. S. (2006). *Teaching for comprehending and fluency: Thinking, talking, and writing about reading, K-8*. Portsmouth, NH: Heinemann.

(2008). *When readers struggle: Teaching that works*. Portsmouth, NH: Heinemann.

Foy, J. E. & Gerrig, R. J. (2014). Flying to Neverland: How readers tacitly judge norms during comprehension. *Memory and Cognition*, *42*(8), 1250–1259.

Garrod, S., O'Brien, E. J., Morris, R. K., & Rayner, K. (1990). Elaborative inferencing as an active or passive process. *Journal of Experimental Psychology: Learning, Memory, and Cognition*, *16*(2), 250–257.

Garrod, S. & Sanford, A. (1977). Interpreting anaphoric relations: The integration of semantic information while reading. *Journal of Verbal Learning and Verbal Behavior*, *16*(1), 77–90.

Gernsbacher, M. (1990). *Language comprehension as structure building*. Hillsdale, NJ: Lawrence Erlbaum.

(1993). Less-skilled readers have less efficient suppression mechanisms. *Psychological Science*, *4*, 294–298.

Gerrig, R. J. (1989). Suspense in the absence of uncertainty. *Journal of Memory and Language*, *28*(6), 633–648.

(1993). *Experiencing narrative worlds: On the psychological activities of reading.* New Haven, CT: Yale University Press.

Gerrig, R. J. & O'Brien, E. J. (2005). The scope of memory-based processing. *Discourse Processes, 39*(2–3), 225–242.

Gillund, G. & Shiffrin, R. M. (1984). A retrieval model for both recognition and recall. *Psychological Review, 91,* 1–67.

Goldman, S. R., McCarthy, K. S., & Burkett, C. (2015). Interpretive inferences in literature. In E. J. O'Brien, A. E. Cook, & R. F. Lorch, Jr. (eds.), *Inferences during reading* (pp. 386–415). New York: Cambridge University Press.

Goodman, K. S. (1967). Reading: A psycholinguistic guessing game. *Journal of the Reading Specialist, 6,* 125–135.

Gough, P. B. & Hillinger, M. L. (1980). Learning to read: An unnatural act. *Bulletin of the Orton Society, 20,* 179–196.

Graesser, A. C. (2015). Deeper learning with advances in discourse science and technology. *Policy Insights from the Behavioral and Brain Sciences, 2*(1), 42–50.

Graesser, A. C., Singer, M., & Trabasso, T. (1994). Constructing inferences during narrative text comprehension. *Psychological Review, 101,* 371–395.

Guéraud, S., Harmon, M. E., & Peracchi, K. A. (2005). Updating situation models: The memory-based contribution. *Discourse Processes, 39,* 243–263.

Guéraud, S., Tapiero, I., & O'Brien, E. J. (2008). Context and the activation of predictive inferences. *Psychonomic Bulletin & Review, 15*(2), 351–356.

Guéraud, S., Walsh, E., Cook, A. E., & O'Brien, E. J. (in press). Validating character profiles during reading: The effect of recency. *Journal of Research in Reading.*

Hakala, C. M. & O'Brien, E. J. (1995). Strategies for resolving coherence breaks in reading. *Discourse Processes, 20*(2), 167–185.

Harmon-Vukić, M., Guéraud, S., Lassonde, K. A., & O'Brien, E. J. (2009). The activation and instantiation of instrumental inferences. *Discourse Processes, 46*(5), 467–490.

Henderson, I., Snowling, M., & Clark, P. (2013). Accessing, integrating, and inhibiting word meaning in poor comprehenders. *Scientific Studies of Reading, 17,* 177–198.

Hintzman, D. L. (1988). Judgments of frequency and recognition memory in a multiple-trace memory model. *Psychological Review, 95,* 528–551.

Hyönä, J., Lorch Jr, R. F., & Kaakinen, J. K. (2002). Individual differences in reading to summarize expository text: Evidence from eye fixation patterns. *Journal of Educational Psychology, 94*(1), 44–55.

Hyönä, J. & Nurminen, A. M. (2006). Do adult readers know how they read? Evidence from eye movement patterns and verbal reports. *British Journal of Psychology, 97*(1), 31–50.

Isberner, M. B. & Richter, T. (2014). Does validation during language comprehension depend on an evaluative mindset?. *Discourse Processes, 51,* 7–25.

Kamas, E. N. & Reder, L. M. (1995). The role of familiarity in cognitive processing. In R. F. Lorch, & E. J. O'Brien (eds.), *Sources of coherence in reading* (pp. 177–202). Hillsdale, NJ: Lawrence Erlbaum.

Kamas, E. N., Reder, I. M., & Ayers, M. S. (1996). Partial matching in the Moses Illusion: Response bias not sensitivity. *Memory and Cognition, 24,* 687–699.

Keefe, D. E. & McDaniel, M. A. (1993). The time course and durability of predictive inferences. *Journal of Memory and Language, 32*(4), 446–463.

Keenan, J. M., Baillet, S. D., & Brown, P. (1984). The effects of causal cohesion on comprehension and memory. *Journal of Verbal Learning and Verbal Behavior, 23* (2), 115–126.

Kendeou, P., Smith, E. R., & O'Brien, E. J. (2013). Updating during reading comprehension: Why causality matters. *Journal of Experimental Psychology: Learning, Memory, and Cognition, 39*, 854–865.

Kintsch, W. (1988). The role of knowledge in discourse comprehension: A construction-integration model. *Psychological Review, 95*, 163–182.

(1998). *Comprehension: A paradigm for cognition.* New York: Cambridge University Press.

Kintsch, W. & Van Dijk, T. A. (1978). Toward a model of text comprehension and production. *Psychological Review, 85*, 363–394.

Kintsch, W. & Vipond, D. (1979). Reading comprehension and readability in educational practice and psychological theory. In L. G. Nilsson (ed.), *Perspectives on memory research* (pp. 329–365). Hillsdale, NJ: Lawrence Erlbaum.

Klin, C. M., Guzmán, A. E., & Levine, W. H. (1999). Prevalence and persistence of predictive inferences. *Journal of Memory and Language, 40*(4), 593–604.

Klin, C. M., Guzmán, A. E., Weingartner, K. M., & Ralano, A. S. (2006). When anaphor resolution fails: Partial encoding of anaphoric inferences. *Journal of Memory and Language, 54*(1), 131–143.

Klin, C. M., Weingartner, K. M., Guzmán, A. E., & Levine, W. H. (2004). Readers' sensitivity to linguistic cues in narratives: How salience influences anaphor resolution. *Memory and Cognition, 32*(3), 511–522.

Lassonde, K. A. & O'Brien, E. J. (2009). Contextual specificity in the activation of predictive inferences. *Discourse Processes, 46*(5), 426–438.

Lea, R. B. (1995). On-line evidence for elaborative logical inferences in text. *Journal of Experimental Psychology: Learning, Memory, and Cognition, 21*(6), 1469–1482.

Lea, R. B. & Mulligan, E. J. (2002). The effect of negation on deductive inferences. *Journal of Experimental Psychology: Learning, Memory, and Cognition, 28*(2), 303–317.

Lea, R. B., Mulligan, E. J., & Walton, J. L. (2005). Accessing distant premise information: How memory feeds reasoning. *Journal of Experimental Psychology: Learning, Memory, and Cognition, 31*(3), 387–395.

Levine, W. H., Guzmán, A. E., & Klin, C. M. (2000). When anaphor resolution fails. *Journal of Memory and Language, 43*(4), 594–617.

Linderholm, T. & van den Broek, P. (2002). The effects of reading purpose and working memory capacity on the processing of expository text. *Journal of Educational Psychology, 94*(4), 778–784.

Linderholm, T. & Zhao, Q. (2008). The impact of strategy instruction and timing of estimates on low and high working-memory capacity readers' absolute monitoring accuracy. *Learning and Individual Differences, 18*, 135–143.

Long, D. L. & Chong, J. L. (2001). Comprehension skill and global coherence: A paradoxical picture of poor comprehenders' abilities. *Journal of Experimental Psychology: Learning, Memory, and Cognition, 27*(6), 1424–1429.

Long, D. L. & Lea, R. B. (2005). Have we been searching for meaning in all the wrong places? Defining the "search after meaning" principle in comprehension. *Discourse Processes, 39*, 279–298.

Lucas, M. M., Tanenhaus, M. K., & Carlson, G. N. (1990). Levels of representation in the interpretation of anaphoric reference and instrument inference. *Memory and Cognition, 18*(6), 611–631.

MacGinitie, W. H., MacGinitie, R. K., Maria, K., & Dreyer, L. G. (2000). *Gates-MacGinitie reading test,* 4th edn. Itasca, IL: Riverside.

McKoon, G. & Ratcliff, R. (1980). The comprehension processes and memory structures involved in anaphoric reference. *Journal of Verbal Learning and Verbal Behavior, 19*(6), 668–682.

(1981). The comprehension processes and memory structures involved in instrumental inference. *Journal of Verbal Learning and Verbal Behavior, 20*(6), 671–682.

(1986). Inferences about predictable events. *Journal of Experimental Psychology: Learning, Memory, and Cognition, 12*(1), 82–91.

(1992). Inference during reading. *Psychological Review, 99,* 440–466.

McNamara, D. (1997). Comprehension skill: A knowledge-based account. In S. Langley (eds.), *Proceedings of the nineteenth annual conference of the cognitive science society* (pp. 508–513). Hillsdale, NJ: Lawrence Erlbaum.

McNamara, D. S., Jacovina, M. E., & Allen, L. K. (2016). Higher order thinking in comprehension. In P. Afflerbach (ed.), *Handbook of individual differences in reading: Text and context* (pp. 164–176). New York: Routledge.

McNamara, D. & McDaniel, M. (2004). Suppressing irrelevant information: Knowledge activation or inhibition. *Journal of Experimental Psychology: Learning, Memory, and Cognition, 30,* 465–482.

Murray, J. D., Klin, C. M., & Myers, J. L. (1993). Forward inferences in narrative text. *Journal of Memory and Language, 32*(4), 464–473.

Myers, J. L., Cook, A. E., Kambe, G., Mason, R. A., & O'Brien, E. J. (2000). Semantic and episodic effects on bridging inferences. *Discourse Processes, 29,* 179–199.

Myers, J. L. & O'Brien, E. J. (1998). Accessing the discourse representation during reading. *Discourse Processes, 26,* 131–157.

Myers, J. L., O'Brien, E. J., Albrecht, J. E., & Mason, R. A. (1994). Maintaining global coherence during reading. *Journal of Experimental Psychology: Learning, Memory, and Cognition, 20*(4), 876–886.

Myers, J. L., Shinjo, M., & Duffy, S. A. (1987). Degree of causal relatedness and memory. *Journal of Memory and Language, 26*(4), 453–465.

National Reading Panel. (2000). *Teaching children to read: An evidence-based assessment of the scientific research literature on reading and its implications for reading instruction (NIH Publication No. 00–4769).* Washington, DC: National Institute of Child Health and Human Development.

Nelson, M. J., Brown, J. I., & Denny, M. J. (1960). *The Nelson-Denny Reading Test: Vocabulary, Comprehension, Rate.* Boston, MA: Houghton Mifflin.

Nieuwland, M. S. & Van Berkum, J. J. (2006). When peanuts fall in love: N400 evidence for the power of discourse. *Journal of Cognitive Neuroscience, 18*(7), 1098–1111.

O'Brien, E. J. (1987). Antecedent search processes and the structure of text. *Journal of Experimental Psychology: Learning, Memory, and Cognition, 13*(2), 278–290.

O'Brien, E. J. & Albrecht, J. E. (1991). The role of context in accessing antecedents in text. *Journal of Experimental Psychology: Learning, Memory, and Cognition, 17*(1), 94–102.

(1992). Comprehension strategies in the development of a mental model. *Journal of Experimental Psychology: Learning, Memory, and Cognition, 18,* 777–784.

O'Brien, E. J., Albrecht, J. E., Hakala, C. M., & Rizzella, M. L. (1995). Activation and suppression of antecedents during reinstatement. *Journal of Experimental Psychology: Learning, Memory, and Cognition*, *21*(3), 626–634.

O'Brien, E. J. & Cook, A. E. (2015). Models of discourse comprehension. In A. Pollatsek, & R. Treiman (eds.), *Handbook on reading* (pp. 217–231). New York: Oxford University Press.

(2016a). Coherence threshold and the continuity of processing: The RI-Val model of comprehension. *Discourse Processes*, 53, 326–338.

(2016b). Separating the activation, integration, and validation components of reading. *Psychology of Learning and Motivation*, 65, 249–276.

O'Brien, E. J., Cook, A. E., & Guéraud, S. (2010). Accessibility of outdated information. *Journal of Experimental Psychology: Learning, Memory, & Cognition*, *36*, 979–991.

O'Brien, E. J., Cook, A. E., & Peracchi, K. A. (2004). Updating situation models: A reply to Zwaan and Madden. *Journal of Experimental Psychology: Learning, Memory, and Cognition*, *30*, 289–291.

O'Brien, E. J., Duffy, S. A., & Myers, J. L. (1986). Anaphoric inference during reading. *Journal of Experimental Psychology: Learning, Memory, and Cognition*, *12*(3), 346–352.

O'Brien, E. J. & Myers, J. L. (1987). The role of causal connections in the retrieval of text. *Memory and Cognition*, *15*(5), 419–427.

(1999). Text comprehension: A view from the bottom up. In S. R. Goldman, A. C. Graesser, & P. van den Broek (eds.), *Narrative comprehension, causality, and coherence: Essays in honor of Tom Trabasso* (pp. 35–53). Mahwah, NJ: Lawrence Erlbaum.

O'Brien, E. J., Plewes, P. S., & Albrecht, J. E. (1990). Antecedent retrieval processes. *Journal of Experimental Psychology: Learning, Memory, and Cognition*, *16*(2), 241–249.

O'Brien, E. J., Raney, G. E., Albrecht, J. E., & Rayner, K. (1997). Processes involved in the resolution of explicit anaphors. *Discourse Processes*, *23*(1), 1–24.

O'Brien, E. J., Rizzella, M. L., Albrecht, J. E., & Halleran, J. G. (1998). Updating a situation model: A memory-based text processing view. *Journal of Experimental Psychology: Learning, Memory, & Cognition*, *24*, 1200–1210.

O'Brien, E. J., Shank, D. M., Myers, J. L., & Rayner, K. (1988). Elaborative inferences during reading: Do they occur on-line?. *Journal of Experimental Psychology: Learning, Memory, and Cognition*, *14*(3), 410–420.

Peracchi, K. A. & O'Brien, E. J. (2004). Character profiles and the activation of predictive inferences. *Memory and Cognition*, *32*(7), 1044–1052.

Potts, G. R., Keenan, J. M., & Golding, J. M. (1988). Assessing the occurrence of elaborative inferences: Lexical decision versus naming. *Journal of Memory and Language*, *27* (4), 399–415.

Rapp, D. N., Hinze, S. R., Slaten, D. G., & Horton, W. S. (2014). Amazing stories: Acquiring and avoiding inaccurate information from fiction. *Discourse Processes*, *51*, 50–74.

Ratcliff, R. (1978). A theory of memory retrieval. *Psychological Review*, *85*, 59–108.

Rayner, K., Foorman, B. R., Perfetti, C. A., Pesetsky, D., & Seidenberg, M. S. (2001). How psychological science informs the teaching of reading. *Psychological Science in the Public Interest*, *2*, 31–74.

Rayner, K., Schotter, E. R., Masson, M. E., Potter, M. C., & Treiman, R. (2016). So much to read, so little time: How do we read, and can speed reading help?. *Psychological Science in the Public Interest*, *17*(1), 4–34.

Rayner, K., Slattery, T. J., & Bélanger, N. N. (2010). Eye movements, the perceptual span, and reading speed. *Psychonomic Bulletin & Review, 17*(6), 834–839.

Reder, L. M. & Cleeremans, A. (1990). The role of partial matches in comprehension: The Moses Illusion revisited. In A. C. Graesser & G. H. Bower (eds.), *The psychology of learning and motivation* (Vol. 25, pp. 233–258). San Diego, CA: Academic Press.

Reder, L. M. & Kusbit, G. W. (1991). Locus of the Moses Illusion: Imperfect encoding, retrieval, or match?. *Journal of Memory and Language, 30*, 385–406.

Richter, T. (2015). Validation and comprehension of text information: Two Sides of the Same Coin. *Discourse Processes, 52*, 337–354.

Rizzella, M. L., & O'Brien, E. J. (1996). Accessing global causes during reading. *Journal of Experimental Psychology: Learning, Memory, and Cognition, 22*, 1208–1218.

   (2002). Retrieval of concepts in script-based texts and narratives: The influence of general world knowledge. *Journal of Experimental Psychology: Learning, Memory, and Cognition, 28*, 780–790.

Routman, R. (1991). *Invitations: Changing as teachers and learners K-12*. Portsmouth, NH: Heinemann.

Sanford, A. J. (2002). Context, attention and depth of processing during interpretation. *Mind and Language, 17*(1-2), 188–206.

Sanford, A. J. & Emmott, C. (2012). *Mind, brain and narrative*. Cambridge: Cambridge University Press.

Sanford, A. J. & Garrod, S. C. (1989). What, when, and how? Questions of immediacy in anaphoric reference resolution. *Language and Cognitive Processes, 4*, 235–262.

   (1998). The role of scenario mapping in text comprehension. *Discourse Processes, 26*, 159–190.

   (2005). Memory-based approaches and beyond. *Discourse Processes, 39*(2–3), 205–224.

Sanford, A. J. & Graesser, A. C. (2006). Shallow processing and underspecification. *Discourse Processes, 42*(2), 99–108.

Sanford, A. J. & Sturt, P. (2002). Depth of processing in language comprehension: Not noticing the evidence. *Trends in Cognitive Sciences, 6*(9), 382–386.

Singer, M. (1979). Processes of inference during sentence encoding. *Memory and Cognition, 7*, 192–200.

   (1993). Causal bridging inferences: Validating consistent and inconsistent sequences. *Canadian Journal of Experimental Psychology, 47*(2), 340–359.

   (2006). Verification of text ideas during reading. *Journal of Memory and Language, 54*, 574–591.

   (2013). Validation in reading comprehension. *Current Directions in Psychological Science, 22*, 361–366.

Singer, M. & Doering, J. C. (2014). Exploring individual differences in language validation. *Discourse Processes, 51*, 167–188.

Singer, M. & Ferreira, F. (1983). Inferring consequences in story comprehension. *Journal of Verbal Learning and Verbal Behavior, 22*, 437–448.

Singer, M., Graesser, A. C., & Trabasso, T. (1994). Minimal or global inference during reading. *Journal of Memory and Language, 33*(4), 421–441.

Singer, M. & Halldorson, M. (1996). Constructing and validating motive bridging inferences. *Cognitive Psychology, 30*, 1–38.

Singer, M., Halldorson, M., Lear, J. C., & Andrusiak, P. (1992). Validation of causal bridging inferences. *Journal of Memory and Language, 31*, 507–524.

Smith, E. R. & O'Brien, E. J. (2016). Enhancing memory access for less-skilled readers. *Scientific Studies of Reading*, *20*, 421–435.

Smith, F. (1971). *Understanding reading: A psycholinguistic analysis of reading and learning to read*. New York: Holt, Rinehart & Winston.

(1973). *Psycholinguistics and reading*. New York: Holt, Rinehart & Winston.

(2004). *Understanding reading*, 6th edn. Mahwah, NJ: Lawrence Erlbaum.

Smith, F. & Goodman, K. S. (1971). On the psycholinguistic method of teaching reading. *Elementary School Journal*, *71*, 177–181.

Trabasso, T., Secco, T., & van den Broek, P. W. (1984). Causal cohesion and story coherence. In H. Mandl, N. L. Stein, & T. Trabasso (eds.), *Learning and comprehension of text* (pp. 83–111). Hillsdale, NJ: Lawrence Erlbaum.

van den Broek, P., Bohn-Gettler, C. M., Kendeou, P., Carlson, S., & White, M. J. (2011). When a reader meets a text: The role of standards of coherence in reading comprehension. In M. T. McCrudden, J. Magliano, & G. Schraw (eds.), *Text relevance and learning from text* (pp. 123–139). Greenwich, CT: Information Age Publishing.

van den Broek, P., Lorch, R. F., Linderholm, T., & Gustafson, M. (2001). The effects of readers' goals on inference generation and memory for texts. *Memory and Cognition*, *29*(8), 1081–1087.

van den Broek, P., Risden, K., Fletcher, C. R., & Thurlow, R. (1996). A "landscape" view of reading: Fluctuating patterns of activation and the construction of a stable memory representation. In B. K. Britton & A. C. Graesser (eds.), *Models of understanding text* (pp.165–187). Mahwah, NJ: Lawrence Erlbaum.

van den Broek, P., Risden, K., & Husebye-Hartmann, E. (1995). The role of readers' standards for coherence in the generation of inferences during reading. In R. F. Lorch & E. J. O'Brien (eds.), *Sources of coherence in reading* (pp. 353–373). Mahwah, NJ: Lawrence Erlbaum.

van den Broek, P., Virtue, S., Everson, M. G., Tzeng, Y., & Sung, Y. C. (2002). Comprehension and memory of science texts: Inferential processes and the construction of a mental representation. In J. Otero, J. Leon, & A. C. Graesser (eds.), *The psychology of science text comprehension* (pp. 131–154). Mahwah, NJ: Lawrence Erlbaum.

van Dijk, T. A., & Kintsch, W. (1983). *Strategies of discourse comprehension*. New York: Academic Press.

Walsh, E. K., Cook, A. E., & O'Brien, E. J. (2018). Processing real-world violations embedded within a fantasy-world narrative. *Quarterly Journal of Experimental Psychology*, *17*, 2282–2294.

Wei, W., & Cook, A. E. (2016). Semantic size and contextual congruency effects during reading: Evidence from eye movements. *Discourse Processes*, *53*, 415–429.

Williams, C. R., Cook, A. E., & O'Brien, E. J. (2018). Validating semantic illusions: Competition between context and general world knowledge. *Journal of Experimental Psychology: Learning, Memory, and Cognition*, 44, 1414–1429.

Zwaan, R. A. (1999). Five dimensions of narrative comprehension: The event-indexing model. In S. R. Goldman, A. C. Graesser, & P. van den Broek (eds.), *Narrative comprehension, causality, and coherence: Essays in honor of Tom Trabasso* (pp. 93–110). Hillsdale, NJ: Lawrence Erlbaum.

11 Writing as a Learning Activity

Perry D. Klein and Aartje van Dijk

Introduction

Writing to learn is a set of practices, used in a variety of disciplines, in which students compose in order to think and learn about subject matter. Since 2000, research has confirmed that the effects of writing on learning are significant but variable; several writing activities and moderators have been identified that produce medium or large effects on learning (for a review, see Klein & Boscolo, 2016). At the same time, a recent survey indicated that teachers only sometimes use writing practices that have been found to support learning (Gillespie et al., 2014). Thus, it is important to understand how writing contributes to learning and how educators and students can make writing most effective.

History of Research on Writing to Learn

During the language experience movement of the 1970s, several authors advocated the importance of writing as a means of learning. Britton and colleagues argued that schools should make greater use of "expressive" writing, that is, informal spontaneous writing, which was thought to allow unconscious ideas to coalesce as they were translated into language (Britton, 1982; Britton et al., 1975). This conception of writing to learn was taken up by educators in a variety of disciplines as part of the "writing across the curriculum" movement (e.g., Gere, 1985). The notion that brief, informal writing activities contribute to learning continued to be influential during the subsequent four decades (e.g., Galbraith, 2009). On the one hand, eventually, the practice of asking students to reflect on their learning would garner strong empirical support (Bangert-Drowns, Hurley, & Wilkinson, 2004; Berthold, Nückles, & Renkl, 2007). On the other hand, the idea that writing contributes to learning by rendering unconscious ideas explicit, and that writing should be spontaneous, would generate more limited empirical research and support (Galbraith, 2009; Ong, 2013).

In the meantime, during the 1970s and early 1980s, several experimental studies on writing to learn took place, conducted by researchers other than Britton and colleagues. At this time, several authors theorized that analytical writing, that is, essay writing, would encourage critical thinking and learning (e.g., Applebee, 1984; Langer & Applebee, 1987). Consequently, this research focused on comparing the effects of either analytical writing or journal writing with other kinds of activities. During this time frame, cognitive theories of writing were also being developed, which identified circumstances under which writing could lead to learning (Hayes & Flower, 1980). The early experimental literature on writing to learn was subject to repeated reviews, each of which reported mixed and modest results for the effect of writing on learning (Ackerman, 1993; Applebee, 1984). These mixed results led psychological researchers to treat writing to learn as an intriguing but unproven, practice (e.g., Klein, 1999).

During the late 1980s and 1990s, social theories and practices of writing emerged and grew in influence (e.g., Childers, Gere, & Young, 1994; Hewitt & Scardamalia, 1998). These theories included distributed cognition, sociocultural theory, and activity theory (Bazerman, 2009; Hewitt & Scardamalia, 1998; Newell, 2006). Key ideas were that learners need to be apprenticed into writing; that writing takes place in collaborative networks of individuals; and that external resources, such as technology, affect the writing process. The distributed cognitive approach was influential in computer supported collaborative learning (CSCL), and although CSCL and writing in wikis and weblogs include writing as a learning activity, research in CSCL mostly diverged into a separate literature (e.g., Hewitt & Scardamalia, 1998), with a few exceptions (Petko, Egger, & Graber, 2014).

The period since 2000 has been the most productive in the history of research on writing to learn. Several important developments have occurred: an increase in the number of experimental studies of writing to learn; investigation of new theoretical concepts such as self-regulatory theory of writing and cognitive load theory (Berthold, Nückles, & Renkl, 2007; Klein, Haug, & Arcon, 2017); testing of cognitive hypotheses about writing to learn using mediational analysis (Leopold, Sumfleth, & Leutner, 2013); greater use of meta-analysis, including examination of moderator variables (e.g., Graham & Hebert, 2011); integration of proven methods of writing instruction, such as Self-Regulated Strategy Development, into writing to learn (De La Paz & Felton, 2010; Reynolds & Perin, 2009); and the launch of large systematic research programs, such as the Science Writing Heuristic (Keys et al., 1999; Nückles et al., 2004; for a review, see Klein & Boscolo, 2016). We will explore these changes in later sections.

Chapter Overview

This chapter will focus largely on the core of recent writing to learn literature. This core is largely cognitive in theoretical orientation, with a growing attention to motivation, and it is largely experimental or quasi-experimental (Klein & Boscolo, 2016). Much of the chapter will address two main questions: First, what kind of classroom writing activities and programs contribute significantly to learning during writing? Second, what are the cognitive processes that contribute to learning during writing? A limitation of this chapter is that we will reference many of the experimental and quasi-experimental studies since 2000, but not all of them. We have selected mainly studies that test cognitive theories and studies that are relatively recent. A second issue is that the roles of writing in the construction of knowledge and individual learning have been discussed extensively in the social sciences and humanities; for example, there is a large literature on writing across the curriculum in postsecondary education, which is largely based on theory and case studies. However, given our focus on experimental studies, we do not address these.

Theory

There have been numerous theories, as well as less fully developed ideas, about how writing contributes to learning (for reviews, see Klein, 1999; Newell, 2006). In this section, we will focus on three theories that have been particularly influential.

The Knowledge Transforming Model

Bereiter and Scardamalia's (1987) knowledge transforming model has perhaps been the most discussed theory of how writing contributes to learning. It is based on a model of writing as a dialectical search through two problem spaces. In the rhetorical space, the writer adopts a communicative goal concerning what he or she wishes to say. For example, the writer may wish to persuade the reader of a particular claim. If the writer has a knowledge transforming strategy, she or he may then translate this rhetorical goal into a content subgoal, such as examining data relevant to the claim. The writer then pursues this content subgoal in the content problem space, using content operators such as making inferences; for example, the writer may compare the claim to the evidence on the issue. This problem-solving in the content space transforms the knowledge; for example, an examination of the evidence may lead the writer to change her or his mind about the claim. The writer may then pursue the other side of the dialectic, setting the rhetorical goal of persuading the reader of this new claim; for example, the writer might adapt the choice of language to the audience. Notice that this is a very "writerly" conception of writing to learn, in that it treats rhetorical intention as the driving force in the learning process and it implies that writing that is meant to communicate effectively with a reader is also likely to lead to learning for the writer.

The knowledge transforming model has good empirical support as a conception of the difference between expert and novice writers (Bereiter & Scardamalia, 1987). As a model of how writing transforms content knowledge it has some limited support (for a review, see Klein, 1999). For example, there is evidence that assigning rhetorical goals, such as the goal to write an argument, contributes to learning (Wiley & Voss, 1999); prompting writers with rhetorical subgoals increases learning (Klein et al., 2017); rhetorical knowledge, e.g., knowledge about characteristics of good arguments, mediates learning during argumentation writing tasks (Klein & Kirkpatrick, 2010); and generating content to satisfy rhetorical goals contributes to learning and text quality (Galbraith, Walker, & Ford, 2005). However, the theory is also somewhat difficult to falsify empirically. For example, either content goals or rhetorical goals can occur at various levels of generality, from the clause (or proposition) to the gist of the entire text, so the model is very general in that respect. We are aware of very few empirical studies of writing to learn that were designed as empirical tests of a knowledge transforming model of writing to learn (for an exception, see Klein et al., 2017). Consequently, possibly the main importance of the knowledge transforming model for writing to learn has been to inspire interest in the idea that writing contributes to learning.

The Self-Regulation View of Writing to Learn

The theory of writing to learn that has been most strongly supported empirically is what has been called the "self-regulation view of writing to learn," developed by researchers at the University of Freiburg (e.g., Berthold, Nückles, & Renkl, 2003; Schwonke et al., 2006). It claims that "writing enhances learning if beneficial cognitive and metacognitive strategies are triggered by the writing task" (Hübner, Nückles, & Renkl, 2010, p. 19). Cognitive strategies include two types: Organizational strategies build connections internal to new material to be learned, e.g., organizing the information and identifying main ideas. Elaboration strategies build external connections between the new information and the learner's prior knowledge, e.g., creating examples or analogies. Additionally, writing depends on metacognitive strategies through which writers monitor their learning.

   For educational purposes, the researchers have connected this theory to previous research on the development of strategy learning, noting that students may have performance deficits, mediational deficits, or utilization deficits and so they need some level of prompting or instruction to apply these strategies to the writing task. In a performance deficit (or "deficiency"), the student is capable of using the strategy but does not do so spontaneously. In a mediational deficiency, the student lacks some cognitive skills required to implement the strategy. In a utilization deficit, the student is able to apply the strategy but it initially does not contribute to learning because of the working memory load associated with implementing the strategy itself (Hübner et al., 2010). Since 2003, researchers have tested the self-regulation theory of writing to learn multiple times. They have found that prompting cognitive and metacognitive strategies during writing significantly enhances learning; additionally, statistical analysis of the students' writing has shown that the effect of instruction on learning is mediated by the student's use of these strategies (Glogger et al., 2009; Glogger et al. 2012; Hübner et al., 2010).

Multimodality and Composing to Learn

"Multimodality" will be defined here as the theory that literacy is comprised of interpreting and composing in a variety of media and types of representations, including the graphic or auditory representations. Multimodality has grown in importance in recent years, because digital technology has allowed students to more readily acquire, create, and disseminate a variety of kinds of media (Bezemer & Kress, 2015). It is discussed here because it can be considered either an extension or a threat to writing to learn and because, to date, experiments have shown that graphical, or mixed textual and graphical representations, have a significantly greater effect on learning than writing alone. For example, Hand and colleagues have carried out a program of research that has shown that embedding representations such as diagrams and equations in text enhances learning, relative to writing text alone (Gunel, Hand, & Gunduz, 2006; McDermott & Hand, 2013). We will explore these studies in greater depth in the section on research on learning.

The literature on multimodality in writing to learn has been inspired by several possible explanations. One idea is that each discipline uses representations that are appropriate to its domain of knowledge, so that learners need to learn to create and interpret these representations, in order to engage meaningfully with the discipline (McDermott & Hand, 2013; Prain & Hand, 2016). A second idea is that cognitive structure is such that dual coding of information, using both visual and linguistic forms, enhances learning (Mayer, 2009; Paivio, 2007). A third idea is that translating knowledge from one modality of representation to another contributes to learning (Mayer, 2009; Pineda & Garza, 2000). A fourth idea is that whereas writing may focus students on creating a propositional model that represents connections among words, drawing may create a situational model that focuses students on spatial relations (Leopold & Leutner, 2012). These ideas are not mutually exclusive and each is consistent with the empirical results summarized above.

Research on Writing to Learn

In this section, we will discuss the empirical research on writing to learn. We will begin by outlining the five types of research methods commonly used in experimental research on writing to learn. The remainder of the review will examine empirical research on writing to learn, with an emphasis on more recent work. Each section will focus on one educational level: elementary, secondary, and postsecondary. Within each educational level, we will discuss some recent experimental studies in four broad categories, to the extent that they have been conducted at that level: journal/reflective writing; argumentation and other informational genres; the Science Writing Heuristic; and multimodal composing. Finally, we will present some conclusions about cognitive processes in writing to learn and implications for educational practice.

Writing to learn research has included a variety of genres of writing. In Table 11.1, we have listed the genres that are discussed in the chapter. The meaning of genre, and the classification of texts, is itself a complex and controversial topic. However, this table provides a quick reference for genres that appear in the writing to learn literature.

Methods

As noted above, since 2000, most studies that are explicitly identified as writing to learn have been experiments or quasi-experiments. Because these studies have been important in testing the effect of writing on learning, as well as the effects of

Table 11.1 *Text genres in the writing to learn literature*

Genre	Related terms and similar genres	Description	Example from the writing to learn literature
Journal entry	Learning protocol	Reflects on writer's own learning	Berthold, Nückles, and Renkl (2007)
Argumentation	Persuasive, analytic, discussion, deliberation	Persuades a reader or critically explores an issue	Klein, Haug, and Arcon (2017)
Analogy		A comparison, often focused on relations between elements	Mason and Tornatora (2016)
Summary		Presents the gist of a longer source text	Gelati, Galvan, and Boscolo (2014)
Discourse synthesis	Research report	Provides an integrated summary, discussion or argument based on multiple source texts	Martínez, Mateos, Martín, and Rijlaarsdam (2015)
Multimodal		A text that combines modalities, e.g., text as well as graphics, equations, or graphs	McDermott and Hand (2013)
Pictorial summary		A series of diagrams representing key ideas in a text	Leopold, Sumfelth, and Leutner (2013)

moderator variables and mediating cognitive processes, they will be the focus of this chapter. Most of these studies have happened in elementary, secondary, or university classrooms.

Typically, studies of writing to learn include a posttest and, frequently, a pretest of knowledge. Many posttests include a mixture of recall, conceptual understanding, and transfer items (Klein et al., 2017; Wiley & Voss, 1999). Conversely, a limitation of several studies of writing to learn, documented in a recent meta-analysis, has been the use of "treatment inherent measures," in which the posttest measure is based on content taught in one of the experimental conditions (for a review, see Hebert, Gillespie, & Graham, 2013).

In several recent studies, researchers have tested hypotheses about mediating variables (Glogger et al., 2012; Leopold et al., 2013; Wäschle et al., 2015). In writing to learn research, the independent variable typically represents manipulation of participation in some writing activity; the hypothetical mediating variable is a theoretically motivated measure of some cognitive processes or linguistic act that is thought to be the "active ingredient" in writing to learn; and the dependent variable is a posttest measure of learning. Empirically, in a structural equation model, the mediating variable appears "between" the independent variable and the learning measure, that is, when entered into the model, it reduces the amount of variance in the dependent variable accounted for the independent variable. For example, in a comparison of the effects of drawing versus summary writing on learning about molecules, researchers used a path analysis to show that modality condition affected students' knowledge about spatial relations, which in turn affected learning about molecules (Leopold et al., 2013).

Below, we discuss five types of research designs commonly used in experimental and quasi-experimental studies of writing to learn. These designs are differentiated mainly by the level of scaffolding provided to the learners, ranging from no scaffolding, to sustained instruction in the writing strategy that students use for learning. A second dimension that differentiates experimental studies of writing to learn is the complexity of the writing activity; some studies involve individual writing of a single draft text; other studies involve additional elements such as multiple writing activities, hands-on inquiry, and collaboration among students. The five types of experimental studies each test a different kind of hypothesis:

(1a) **Effect of an independent writing activity on learning**. In this type of experiment, the participants are assigned a writing task and its effect on learning is measured. The learner is not provided with assistance or instruction. Typically, learners have access to some source of information, such as a set of readings or a lecture, and they use the writing activity to interpret this information. The type of control or comparison condition varies across studies; examples include talk, i.e., either monologue or discussion (Klein, Piacente-Cimini, & Williams, 2007; Rivard, 2004); nonwriting learning activities (Rouse, Graham, & Compton, 2017); a writing activity in a genre different from the treatment condition (e.g., Wiley & Voss, 1999); a writing activity about a different topic (Rouse et al., 2016); or writing a text that requires minimal composition, such as taking notes (Hebert et al., 2014).

(1b) **Effect of a unit of study with multiple writing activities on learning**. A second type of study, frequently quasi-experimental, similarly requires learners to write independently but here the treatment includes several writing activities (for a review, see Bangert-Drowns et al., 2004). This type of study is often conducted, e.g., in university courses that include frequent, brief, informal writing activities (Drabick et al., 2007; Gingerich et al. 2014). The control condition may be comprised of an alternative activity in which students think about or discuss the same questions that treatment students write about (Drabick et al., 2007; Linton et al., 2014). The control condition may be a different section of the same course; or a within-subjects design may be used in which students in a given section are switched between treatment and control conditions (Gingerich et al., 2014; Linton et al., 2014). Learning is typically measured by a test at the end of the unit of study.

(2a) **Effect of writing with scaffolding on learning**. In the treatment condition, the participants complete a writing activity with scaffolding provided by a researcher or teacher, often in the form of a series of writing prompts or a more extended set of instructions for the writing activity, which guides them through composing the text. In the control condition, participants complete the same writing activity without prompts or with a different type of writing prompt (e.g., Felton, Garcia-Mila, & Gilabert, 2009; Klein et al., 2017).

(2b) **Writing to learn in a complex environment.**The defining feature of this type of study is that writing is embedded in a complex intervention comprised of several elements, such as inquiry, group discussion, and reader feedback. An example is the Science Writing Heuristic, a writing-intensive method of science education, which is modeled on a community of scientists (Keys et al., 1999). In some studies, the entire complex treatment is compared to a control group comprised of business as usual (Akkus, Gunel, & Hand, 2007); in other studies, the entire treatment is provided to both the treatment and the control group, but a specific component, such as type of audience, is varied to comprise the independent variable (Gunel et al., 2009; Hand, Hohenshell, & Prain, 2004).

(3a) **Effect of writing strategy instruction on writing to learn**. The defining feature of this type of study is that the participants receive training in the writing strategy that they are to apply in a subsequent writing to learn activity. An early study of this type was Reynolds and Perin (2009), in which students were trained in a strategy for writing summaries using the Self-Regulated Strategy Development method (cf., Harris, Graham, & Mason, 2006; Martinez et al., 2015). The control group completes the same writing to learn activity but without training in the writing strategy, or with a different kind of training in writing.

Research on Writing to Learn in the Elementary Grades

Elementary education is defined here as preschool through 6th grade.

Journal/reflective writing. The same Bangert-Drowns and colleagues (2004) meta-analysis cited above analyzed the effect of the type of questions used as writing prompts and showed that metacognitive questions significantly increased the effect of writing activities. These were prompts in which "students were asked to reflect on their ongoing learning processes: their current level of comprehension in a content area, comprehension failures and successes, or affective or motivational responses to content that might facilitate or debilitate learning" (p. 38). Compared with writing tasks that did not require metacognitive writing, these had a significant positive effect on learning. The role of metacognition in writing to learn was subsequently taken up in the self-regulation theory of writing to learn, described at the beginning of the chapter (Hübner et al., 2010; Nückles et al. 2004).

To date, most studies of the self-regulatory model have been conducted with secondary and postsecondary students. However, a study with Grade 5 students (Roelle et al., 2012), addressed the point that elementary students often not only have production deficits but also have mediational deficits, that is, they lack the knowledge or skills required to apply strategies. To address these mediational deficits, in this study, all students received a lesson about cognitive and metacognitive strategies that they could use in the learning protocol. Additionally, the treatment group was presented with a worked example of a completed protocol. Next, they completed a writing activity, with continuing access to this protocol as a model. The worked examples group showed significantly greater use of cognitive and metacognitive strategies; on a posttest, they showed greater conceptual understanding of fractional arithmetic, relative to the control group. In the next phase of the study, the conditions were reversed, so that the experimental group used the strategy with the support phased out, while the former control group had the worked example phased in. The delayed provision produced an increase in metacognitive strategies relative to their previous performance, but a reduction in cognitive strategies, and no significant effect on learning.

There have also been studies of reflective writing outside of the program of research on self-regulatory theory. For example, in one recent study, in one condition students completed an extended writing activity in which they compared and contrasted their own experiences with a text that they read; in the other condition, students took notes. Extended writing resulted in superior performance on a multiple-choice inference measure but not on two other measures (Hebert et al., 2014).

Several older studies on reflective writing showed positive effects on learning (Jennings 1990; Konopak, Martin, & Martin, 1990) but others produced nonsignificant results (Saunders & Goldenberg, 1999). In understanding the evolution of research on reflective writing, it should be noted that earlier research defined reflective writing in terms of somewhat disparate features: personal writing (versus nonpersonal); spontaneous versus planned or rhetorically focused writing; and receiving metacognitive prompts versus other prompts or no prompts (Bangert-Drowns et al., 2004; Britton et al., 1975). Self-regulatory theory implies that writing that includes cognitive processes plus metacognitive processes plus training that addresses elementary mediational deficits will contribute to learning for elementary students. The evolution from an earlier literature with conflicting results to the self-regulatory approach, which has produced more consistently positive results, is consistent with this theory.

Argumentation and other informational writing. We define informational writing as a broad category, which includes various nonfiction genres; those used in the writing to learn literature include arguments, summary, discourse synthesis, and occasionally compare-and-contrast, explanation, and analogy (see Table 11.1). In a recent study on argumentation, students learned about classification by writing about animals that were difficult to classify, such as dolphins (Klein et al., 2017). In all conditions, students were provided with background information about the animals and asked to classify them and to write an argument for their classification decision. Students in the control condition received the main argument question only; students in a rhetorical subgoal prompt condition received the argument question plus a series of prompts to address six types of argument subgoals (evidence, other opinion, reasons for other opinion, etc.); students in a content subgoal condition received the argument question plus six prompts to address content subtopics related to classification in their argument (respiration, body covering, reproduction). On a unit posttest comprised of recall of information, and inference items that assessed multiple dimensions of understanding animal classification, the rhetorical subgoal condition resulted in significantly greater learning than the argument goal-only condition; the content subgoal condition scored between these two other groups and did not differ significantly from them.

Summary writing appears to be the informational genre that has most frequently been investigated with respect to its effects on learning for elementary students. In a recent meta-analysis of research on the effects of writing on reading comprehension, Graham and Hebert (2011) found that summary writing, compared with non-writing activities, had significant positive effects on reading comprehension. However, in a second meta-analysis, Hebert, Gillespie, and Graham (2013) found that summarization was not more effective than note-taking, and was more effective than question-answering only on free recall measures. Gelati, Galvan, and Boscolo (2014) found that training 5th grade students in a strategy for writing summaries had positive effects on expository text comprehension. This finding is consistent with several earlier studies showing that summarization had positive effects on text comprehension for elementary students (cf., Jennings, 1990; Rinchart, Stahl, & Erickson, 1986). More recently, Martinez and colleagues (2015) compared a group that participated in strategy instruction in discourse synthesis with an untrained group. The strategy instruction group showed greater learning, as measured by a posttest comprised of recall and inferences concerning source texts.

Analogy is a form of reasoning that is thought to be central to thinking and learning (Gentner, 2003). Mason and Tornatora (2016) asked students to write analogies to understand two science demonstrations, which were perceptually dissimilar but based on the same underlying structure. In the treatment condition, students were instructed to "compare the two scenarios, think of what they have in common, and explain what is happening in the scenarios." In two control conditions, students completed the same analogy but without instructions to explain each of the scenarios. At posttest, the students were required to list the differences between the scenarios, explain each scenario, and rate how similar they were to one another and justify their rating. The condition that combined joint presentation with instructions to compare resulted in significantly greater analogical encoding on most measures.

Conversely, a recent study on explanation writing produced null results. Rouse, Graham, and Compton (2017) asked students to complete a balance scale experiment for learning about levers. Four times during the experiment the students wrote brief observations and explanations; the control group of students completed the experiment without writing. Writing did not produce significantly different effects on a posttest of understanding of the balance scale, as measured by a posttest that required students to view diagrams and predict if the balance scale would tilt left, tilt right, or balance. The authors noted several difficulties with the students' writing, including the fact that many wrote minimal responses to the prompts, sometimes only a few words in length.

What we have learned about elementary writing to learn? In considering the literature on writing to learn with elementary students, it appears that the task that has been most frequently investigated has been summarization, which has produced positive effects on learning. In a second pattern that appears to emerge across various genres, elementary writers require guidance in the form of writing prompts (e.g., Klein et al., 2016; Mason & Tornatora, 2014; Ritchie, Tomas, & Tones, 2011). Moreover, in keeping with analysis by self-regulatory theorists, elementary students may have not only production deficits but also mediational deficits in strategy use (Glogger et al., 2012; Hübner et al., 2010). Therefore, instruction in the genre that they are expected to write contributes to their learning. This systematic instruction includes practices such as explicitly teaching the strategy, modeling, scaffolded writing, and the study of worked examples (Roelle et al., 2012; cf., Martinez et al., 2015; Rinehart et al., 1986). In conclusion, more research is needed concerning writing to learn in elementary school; in earlier decades, summary writing was extensively studied but there have been very few experimental studies on writing to learn in genres such as persuasive writing (Klein et al., 2017), learning protocols (i.e., metacognitive journals; Roelle et al., 2012), and narrative (Ritchie, Tomas, & Tones, 2011). Additionally, given that drawing is a popular activity with elementary students, further experimental research should be conducted on the effects of multimodal activities at this grade level.

Research on Writing to Learn in Secondary Education

The literature on writing to learn in secondary classes appears to be more extensive than that in elementary classes: Studies in this section explore various genres of writing activities, including reflective writing, the Science Writing Heuristic, multimodal writing, and argument writing. These can be discipline-specific, such as a science laboratory report, but may also be types of writing that students encounter daily, for instance a letter or a newspaper article.

Journal/reflective writing. The studies on reflective writing activities support the outcomes of the meta-analysis of Bangert-Drowns and colleagues (2004) by confirming that applying metacognitive prompts to journal-style writing results in positive effects on learning. These effects have been shown in the context of various types of control conditions; for instance, the use of the metacognitive prompts has been compared to summary journal writing (Cantrell, Fusaro, & Dougherty, 2000) as well as to a business-as-usual condition (Wäschle et al., 2015) and a no-writing condition (Wong et al., 2002).

Wäschle and colleagues (2015) conducted two experiments. First, they compared the application of cognitive and metacognitive prompts on the writing of learning journals to a business-as-usual condition in Grade 7 biology classes. The researchers measured comprehension and interest after the treatment respectively by means of open-ended questions and a questionnaire. The experimental students showed larger effects than the control students on comprehension ($\eta^2 = 0.18$) and interest increased in both conditions. On a delayed posttest after eight weeks, experimental students scored significantly higher than the control students on the same comprehension test ($\eta^2 = 0.31$) and on a writing task on critical reflection ($\eta^2 = 0.24$). Compared with the results on the first posttest, experimental students' interest increased ($\eta^2 = 0.15$), whereas interest of control students decreased. Mediation analyses showed that the prompted condition enhanced comprehension and that enhanced comprehension increased interest into subject matter. Furthermore, increased interest enhanced critical reflection. The researchers concluded that the effects of journal writing on experimental students' interest did not happen immediately after the treatment. They theorized that effects of journal writing could even be larger, when students received a motivational prompt aimed at stimulating their interest at the start of the experiment.

Therefore, in the second experiment in Grade 10 philosophy classes, they compared two conditions. In the first condition, cognitive and metacognitive prompts were used again. In the second condition, a motivational prompt ("Why is the learning material personally relevant for you at present or in future out of school?") was added to cognitive and metacognitive prompts. When comparing the effect of the conditions on comprehension, no significant differences were found on the measure consisting of open-ended questions ($\eta^2 = 0.05$). However, interest increased in the added motivational prompt condition (($\eta^2 = 0.24$) but not in the other condition. The effects on critical reflection of the added motivational prompt condition were larger than the effects of the cognitive/metacognitive prompts condition ($\eta^2 = 0.41$). Furthermore, a mediation analysis has been conducted, in which critical reflection was the dependent variable, the added motivational prompt condition was the independent variable, and interest was the mediator variable. Researchers found significant effects of the added motivational prompt condition on critical reflection and on interest. After regressing critical reflection on both the experimental condition (predictor) and the interest (mediator), the effect of interest on critical reflection was significant, $t(21) = 2.27, \beta = 0.37, p < 0.05$ (cf., Hübner et al., 2010).

Argument writing. Argument writing has been used in research on writing to learn since the 1980s. It always has been considered an important skill in education. For instance, Langer and Applebee (1987) concluded in their study on the relation between writing and learning, titled *How writing shapes thinking*, that argument-writing activities could elicit critical thinking, in contrast to restricted writing activities.

Argument writing is often used as a means for learning about history (De La Paz & Felton, 2010), literature (Boscolo & Carotti, 2003), and philosophy (Corcelles Seuba & Castelló, 2015) because learning tasks in these disciplines often require reading multiple sources and reasoning critically about them. De La Paz and Felton (2010) hypothesized that instruction in historical reasoning would enhance the quality of arguments in students' texts, and also their reasoning abilities. Their task required reading of historical source texts, including primary historical sources. They compared strategy instruction with a control condition comprised of applying key concepts in writing historical essays, which was consistent with the usual approach of the teacher. For posttesting, students wrote an essay. Effects of strategy instruction on text quality and historical reasoning were found.

Van Drie, Braaksma, and Van Boxtel (2015) investigated the effects of discipline-based writing instruction on Grade 11 students' knowledge and compared this instruction with general writing instruction, using open-ended questions and a writing task for measuring. They expected to find larger effects of discipline-based instruction on historical knowledge. Instead, they found growth of students' knowledge in both experimental conditions, and no significant differences between them. However, they found effects of discipline-based instruction on the quality of historical reasoning (cf. De La Paz & Felton, 2010). The researchers concluded that discipline-based writing instruction needs more research.

In the field of literature, other types of instruction on argument writing have been explored. For instance, researchers have refined argument instruction by adapting it to students' preferred writing strategy, either planning or revising (Kieft, Rijlaarsdam, & Van den Bergh, 2006; Kieft, Rijlaarsdam, & Van den Bergh, 2008). Kieft and colleagues (2006) measured students' preferred strategy with a questionnaire, and understanding by means of open-ended questions. They did not report an interaction effect between writing strategy and learning. However, Kieft and colleagues (2008) showed an interaction effect on literary interpretation for matching instruction to students' preferred writing style, by using the same types of posttests.

In a second type of approach to writing to learn about literature, Boscolo and Carotti (2003) taught students to write a variety of texts about literary topics during a period of twenty-eight weeks; examples included a synthesis of a literary text and the minutes of an interesting lesson. These lessons were meant to prepare students for learning to write an argument and for attaining literary understanding by writing an argument. Boscolo and Carotti (2003) found that this intervention had significantly larger effects on literary understanding, measured by means of a writing task, than business-as-usual in the control condition.

Argument writing has been used to support learning for several decades. However, in the past decade, researchers in secondary education have increasingly gone beyond simple comparisons of argument to nonargument conditions. Instead, they have investigated various approaches to teaching argumentation, and different types of argument writing, with respect to their effects on learning.

The Science Writing Heuristic. The Science Writing Heuristic (SWH) is an inquiry-based approach, in which writing occupies a role analogous to its role in a community of scientists. The SWH guides students through the process of laboratory research, including three types of activities that they perform partly individually and partly collaboratively: (1) execution of observations and other elements of laboratory research; (2) writing of short texts such as notes or conclusions; and (3) reading and understanding theory. After finishing these activities, students write a laboratory report to describe and discuss the results of their research. For writing, students are provided with a template that includes aspects of both a laboratory report and an argument. In this way, the traditional laboratory report has been reimagined to support evidence-based reasoning and critical thinking. The writing of a laboratory report is meant to be a writing-to-learn activity that brings new insights into subject matter (for more detailed information, see Wallace, Hand, & Prain, 2004).

Researchers have conducted many studies on the SWH, with positive effects on learning, usually assessed by means of unit tests (e.g., Nam, Choi, & Hand, 2011; Kingir, Geban, & Gunel, 2013). After initial studies that showed the positive effects of the SWH on learning, researchers subsequently conducted studies on specific elements of writing, for instance writing for a specific audience (Gunel, Hand, & McDermott, 2009; Hand, Yang, & Bruxvoort, 2006; Hohenshell & Hand, 2006) or writing types of genres that are not common in science, such as a letter (Hand, Yang, & Bruxvoort, 2006). The latter choice of an everyday genre is based on the view that explaining subject matter to a less knowledgeable audience invites students into a process of translation of ideas into everyday language and connection to familiar concepts (Prain, 2006).

Some studies have investigated the effects of other combinations of variables, such as the timing of planning and multiple writing assignments (Hand, Hohenshell, & Prain, 2004). The researchers used three posttests, one consisting of a writing task and open-ended questions and two only consisting of open-ended questions. These were administered after writing one text, after writing two texts, and one was a delayed posttest. The researchers found larger effects for planning before writing than for planning after writing; additionally, they found that multiple writing assignments led to larger effects than single assignments (see also Hand, Hohenshell, & Prain, 2007).

The group of SWH researchers has given considerable attention to the training of teachers in using the SWH because, in their view, research has to be conducted in "real" educational settings. The SWH is designed for science and thus is discipline-bound. A new step in this research has been to explore the possibilities for other disciplines. Akkus and Hand (2005) started to design and examine a mathematics reasoning heuristic. Subsequently, Akkus (2006) investigated effects of the mathematics reasoning heuristic and found positive effects on learning.

Recently SWH researchers have been exploring the integration of graphical and mathematical representations into written texts. McDermott and Hand (2013) conducted two experiments in grades 10, 11, and 12 chemistry classes, in two different samples. The intervention was complex, containing strategy instruction on embedding graphs and formulas, and on writing. In the first experiment ($N = 70$), students were instructed to embed graphs and formulas in their texts, in two units of study. Students' learning was tested by means of two posttests (each a combination of multiple choice and open ended questions), after the first unit and after the second unit respectively. After the first unit, no significant effects were found. However, after the second unit embedding graphs led to positive effects on learning ($d = 0.53$). The research design of the second experiment was the same, but the sample was larger (95) and the intervention took place only once. Significant effects of the intervention on learning were found ($d = 0.62$) (cf., Gunel, Hand, and Gunduz, 2006). In Hand, Gunel, and Ulu (2009), the order in which students integrated graphic and mathematic modalities into text is topic of the study. They found that the sequence determined the effect on learning.

A promising approach in multimodality research is the use of drawing to represent the main ideas of a text. Leopold and Leutner (2012) compared four conditions: In the first, students studied a text with the aim of comprehending it; in the second, students were told to select main ideas in the text and to write them down; in the third, students were asked to read the text for comprehension and subsequently draw the main ideas; in the fourth, students drew main ideas and also wrote them down. The researchers reported significantly larger effects on deep learning of the drawing-only condition, as compared with the three other conditions. The same paper reported a second experiment, in which students in the conditions summarized the text instead of writing the main ideas. This experiment also resulted in effects of the drawing-only condition on deep learning, when compared with verbal conditions and a combined verbal and drawing condition.

In a second study on drawing to learn (Leopold, Sumfleth, & Leutner, 2013), four conditions for summarizing were compared: The first was on summarizing by means of drawing, scaffolded by predefined (model) pictorial summaries; the second was on verbal summarizing scaffolded by predefined verbal summaries; the third was on summarizing by drawing; the fourth was on verbal summarizing. The pictorial conditions resulted in significantly larger effects on comprehension, on transfer of knowledge and on visualization, than the verbal conditions. The conditions comprising the predefined summaries resulted in higher scores than the conditions demanding self-generated summaries. Furthermore, scores on a measure of participants' spatial representation mediated between the representation mode (verbal or pictorial) and the scores on the transfer test (application of knowledge). These initial results suggest that drawing is a more effective method of learning than textual summarizing, if subject matter can be visualized.

Writing to Learn in Postsecondary Education

In postsecondary education, the majority of studies have been conducted on reflective writing activities and informational writing activities. These are often used after lectures to elaborate on the subject matter.

Reflective writing activities. It was noted above that during the past decade researchers from the University of Freiburg have been conducting studies according to their view called "self-regulation of writing to learn" by using learning protocols. They define a learning protocol as "a writing assignment to be performed as a follow up course work activity." In a study that combined cognitive and metacognitive strategies, with additional strategies for revision (Nückles, Hübner, & Renkl, 2009), students received the text of an audio taped lecture they had attended, which they could use to revise their learning protocols. Providing students with this opportunity to revise their draft and to review subject matter stimulated the use of metacognitive strategies and increased learning. Schwonke and colleagues (2006) demonstrated that receiving adaptive revising prompts in a blended learning context also results in positive effects on learning. In this context, the term "adaptive" means that the content of the online prompts depended on students' answers on preceding prompts.

They used two posttests: a knowledge test and a test of understanding. Blended learning is a combination of online learning and class work.

The above-mentioned studies focused on writing one or two prompted learning journals in laboratory settings, thus they were short-term studies. Nückles and colleagues (2010) were interested in long-term effects of journal writing. They investigated the effects of strategy prompts on the writing of twelve journal entries during an instructional period of sixteen weeks. They compared an experimental group whose writing was supported by cognitive and metacognitive prompts with a control group that wrote without prompts. Students performed a posttest (open-ended questions) after eight weeks and a posttest (open-ended questions) after sixteen weeks. The researchers reported positive effects of cognitive and metacognitive prompts on learning after eight weeks but there were no significant differences between groups after sixteen weeks.

In a second experiment, the researchers compared two experimental conditions with a control group without prompts. In the first condition, students were presented cognitive and metacognitive prompts throughout the treatment; however, in the second condition, the cognitive and metacognitive prompts were gradually faded out. After eight weeks, both experimental conditions showed similar positive effects on learning when compared with a controlled control group; however, after sixteen weeks, the effects of the condition without fading treatment were significantly decreased compared with the results of the posttest performed eight weeks before, while the fading condition did not show significantly larger effects than the controlled control group. The researchers inferred that the prompts became superfluous, and interfered with students' own way to apply the strategies (see Nevid, Pastva, & McClelland, 2012).

Informational writing tasks. In this category first we will discuss brief tasks. These include the minute paper and the micro theme. They require only a minute or a few minutes to complete and may ask the student to create a statement, a question, a definition, and so on. Because they are brief, these tasks can be added regularly to an ongoing series of lectures or readings. Several studies have shown positive effects of these brief writing activities (Drabick et al. 2007; Gingerich et al., 2014; Stewart, Myers, & Culley, 2010).

Other forms of informational writing are more extended and require greater elaboration; these include explanation (Atasoy, 2013), summary (Yildiz, 2012), and analogy (Klein, Piacente-Cimini, & Williams, 2007). The latter (school) genre, analogy writing, has hardly been researched, though it offers opportunities for reasoning and thinking, as Klein and colleagues (2007) showed. After observing two comparable demonstrations on one physics topic, students composed analogies in one of three different modalities: by speaking, by writing, and by writing while thinking aloud. Students in both writing conditions scored significantly higher than in the speaking condition on a posttest that required transferring the scientific principle to a novel scenario. In an interaction effect, students with low spatial working memory scored higher on the posttest in the writing condition than in the speaking condition. The scores of students with high spatial working memory were similar in both conditions.

Conclusion

What Have We Learned About Writing Activities That Lead to Learning?

In Table 11.2, we briefly summarize our review of this literature. Note that we have not conducted a meta-analysis, partly because, in several instances, there are not enough papers with similar methods and this review has not been comprehensive; we have focused mostly on recent research.

Having noted this, there are three programs of research on the effects of writing on learning that stand out for the quantity of research and consistency of outcomes. First, the self-regulatory approach, in which students write learning protocols in response to prompts for cognitive and metacognitive strategies, has resulted in consistently positive results, from elementary school through university and for content in both mathematics and psychology (Glogger et al., 2009; Glogger et al., 2012; Nückles et al., 2010; Roelle et al., 2012). Second, there is an older literature that shows that writing summaries, particularly following summarization training, significantly improves text comprehension (for a review, see Graham & Hebert, 2011). More recently, this literature has been extended to the more complex genre of discourse synthesis, in which students produce an integrated summary of multiple texts, with similarly positive results (Martinez et al., 2015; Reynolds & Perin, 2009). The third extensive and successful program of research concerns the SWH. Both the SWH as a practice and specific elements of the practice, such as multiple writing activities and writing for specific audiences, have generally produced significant and positive results.

Table 11.2 *Summary of review of empirical research*

	Elementary	Secondary	Postsecondary
Journal writing/ learning protocols	Positive results with cognitive prompting and instruction†	Positive results with cognitive prompting	Positive results with cognitive prompting
Argumentation	Positive results with prompting†	Positive results with prompting/instruction	Mixed findings; research needed on prompting or instruction†
Informational genre (summary, discourse synthesis, analogy, literary review, one-minute response paper)	Positive results for summary, analogy, discourse synthesis with prompting / instruction†	Mixed results†	Positive results for brief in-class writing; research needed on other genres
Science Writing Heuristic	Positive initial results†	Positive results	Positive initial results†
Multimodal composing/pictorial summary	Research needed†	Positive results with prompting/instruction	Research needed†

† Few studies to date; research needed.

Conversely, Table 11.2 suggests that there are several gaps in the empirical literature on writing to learn. The elementary educational level has been under-researched relative to other educational levels in most genres. Secondly, some genres of activity, such as the learning protocol and the SWH, have been well explored; however, others, such as analogy writing and pictorial summaries, have not. Thirdly, when we consider the intersection of educational level with genre, there are some areas that are well covered and some that are sparsely covered. Moreover, some of these underresearched genres seem like "natural" choices for further investigation, such as elementary students creating pictorial summaries. Fourthly, while the past decade has seen a surge in research on prompting or teaching cognitive strategies for writing, there are some educational levels or genres to which this has not been applied extensively, such as prompting postsecondary argumentation for writing to learn.

It is equally informative to consider what widely held beliefs about the theory or practice of writing to learn have been disproven or have not yet been investigated experimentally. The idea that writing inherently leads to learning is no longer plausible – the effects of writing on learning have consistently proven inconsistent (e.g., Bangert-Drowns et al., 2004; Graham & Hebert, 2011; Klein, 1999). Additionally, the two genres that were the focus of greatest attention for several decades – argumentation and journal writing – do not consistently lead to learning. Recent meta-analyses have shown that while writing about material that has been read contributes to learning, it is not reliably the case that extended writing is more effective than brief writing (Bangert-Drowns et al., 2004; Hebert et al., 2013). These findings point to the importance of identifying the moderator variables that make writing to learn effective or ineffective.

In the same vein, it is noteworthy that the writing activities that have been most consistently shown to affect learning are not those that are most commonly required in school curricula or most authentic. In an influential paper, Duke and colleagues (2006) defined authentic writing as "writing to provide information for someone who needs or wants it – in addition to teaching or learning particular skills or content. To be authentic, a text (written or read) must be like texts that are used by readers or writers outside of a learning-to-read-or-write context (i.e. to serve communicative purposes or functions)" (p. 346). However authenticity is not a characteristic of two of the genres of writing (self-regulatory learning protocol, summary/discourse synthesis) that have been found to contribute to learning during writing. Rather, in the case of learning protocols, successful writing to learn represents a new genre, which looks more like "cognitive strategies on paper" (e.g., Roelle et al., 2012) than authentic communication with an actual reader. Similarly, summary writing and discourse synthesis are genres that are written in school, with the teacher as audience, rather than for an authentic readership. As a partial qualification to this critique, the interactive community of the SWH provides an authentic context for writing, and a readership has been found to contribute to its effectiveness. However, generally, the discrepancy between writing that is authentic and writing that stimulates learning shows that the quality of writing is not a one-dimensional construct – a text that is good for engaging a readership may be different from a text that allows students to deeply understand new material.

What Have We Learned About the Cognitive Basis of Writing to Learn?

Many theories and ideas about the cognitive basis of writing to learn have been put forward. The theory that has been most extensively researched and best supported to date is the self-regulatory theory (Nückles et al., 2004; Roelle et al., 2012). It has been supported by experimental research as well as mediational analysis. Both components – cognitive strategies and metacognitive strategies – have been shown to contribute to learning. Although this theory was tested with the use of learning protocols, it may also be used to explain the effects of writing on learning in some other genre, such as discourse synthesis, analogy, and argumentation, because these writing activities also involve elaborative or organizational processes (e.g., Klein et al., 2007; Martinez et al., 2015). For example, the process of learning science through analogy writing is dependent on the extent to which students compare elements and relations between the source and the target situations.

The other group of theories that should be mentioned are those that are socially oriented, such as distributed cognition and activity theory (e.g., Bazerman, 2009; Klein & Leacock, 2012, Newell, 2006). It is generally recognized that writing is a complex activity, which involves internal psychological processes, external sources of information, collaborators, external supports for writing such as writing prompts, and sometimes feedback from audiences. These social processes are particularly apparent in complex approaches to writing to learn, such as the SWH. In some instances, the effects of specific external supports have been tested empirically, with positive results (e.g., Gunel et al., 2009; Klein et al., 2017). Activity theory and distributed cognition have not been discussed in this chapter because they have seldom been tested experimentally in writing research and they have not been highly influential in the writing to learn literature. However, they are influential in the broader research literature on writing and they provide an important conceptual frame for understanding the broader context of writing activities.

Teaching Practice

For educators, we would point to the practical value of the three approaches to writing to learn as mentioned above: summarizing and discourse synthesis; the self-regulatory approach to writing learning protocols; and the SWH. Two of these practices, summary writing/discourse synthesis and self-regulatory learning protocols, can be implemented in a traditional classroom context. They comprise brief, easily prepared and managed activities, which provide a high level of student accountability. Learning protocols can be readily appended to traditional lessons or audiovisual presentations; and instruction in strategies for discourse synthesis are an extension of traditional classroom, report writing activities. In contrast, the SWH is a bolder reimagining of the classroom as a community of collaborative inquiry.

A second important consideration for educators is to be aware of developmental differences in strategy use and appropriate instructional responses to them. This has been most extensively discussed in the literature on self-regulatory theory of writing to learn (e.g., Roelle et al., 2012). As noted above, secondary students frequently show production deficits, but when scaffolded with a series of strategy prompts, many are able to use them successfully (Glogger et al., 2012; but cf. Glogger et al., 2009). Elementary students frequently show mediational as well as production deficits, so that they need explicit instruction and examples of how to use strategies, as well as prompting to actually apply them (Roelle et al., 2012). The importance of scaffolding and strategy instruction for elementary and secondary students has also been independently demonstrated with respect to genres such as summary, discourse synthesis, and argumentation (e.g., Klein et al., 2017; Martinez et al., 2015, Reynolds & Perin, 2009; Wäschle et al., 2015). Conversely, university students, after several activities in which they are prompted to use strategies, are frequently competent to apply strategies without prompting, and continued prompting may become counter-productive (Nückles et al., 2010).

A third consideration for educators is growing evidence for the effectiveness of multimodal composition, which integrates representations such as graphics or mathematics into text, or replaces text altogether with drawing (e.g., Hand et al., 2009; Leopold & Leutner, 2012). To date, this research has been focused in science, where spatial representations appear particularly important. This suggests that for tasks that require understanding spatial relations, it may be useful to supplement textual writing with creating mixed, embedded representations or even to replace writing with drawing.

Critique and Further Research Questions

As we noted above, to date, there have been several promising kinds of writing activities that have been the subject of relatively few experimental studies; there is a need to investigate further the effects of these genres on learning and to conduct studies at all educational levels (elementary, secondary, postsecondary). Similarly, with respect to cognitive processes, there has been a long-standing interest in the role of spontaneous processes in writing to learn but there have been only a few experimental studies on such processes, so they bear further investigation (for a review, see Galbraith, 2009; Ong, 2013). Additionally, cognitive load research has been a powerful influence in instructional psychology since the early 2000s; however, researchers have only recently begun to investigate the role of cognitive load in writing and writing to learn (Klein et al., 2017; Nückles et al., 2010).

Perhaps the most important issues for further research arise from the changing nature of writing: Already in schools, writing is becoming largely digital, both with respect to sources of information and the medium of composition; the continuing growth of wikis and CSCL both make writing more cooperative; and digital media is making writing more multimodal. To date, only a few experimental studies of writing to learn have focused on digital media (e.g., Petko, Egger, & Graber, 2014). So far, the results of research on multimodal writing have been positive – so positive that they challenge the normal practice of text-only as a medium for writing to learn. It would be desirable to continue research on writing with embedded representations. This is particularly important at the elementary level, where drawing appears to be a natural fit for children. The gradual coalescence of solid findings on writing to learn, combined with the emergence of new forms of writing, makes composition a promising educational practice both for the present and for the future.

References

Ackerman, J. (1993). The promise of writing to learn. *Written Communication, 10*, 334–370.

Akkus, R. (2006). The impact of writing on students' performances on the post test. In S. Alatorre, J. L. Cortina, M. Sáiz, & A. Méndez (eds.), *Proceedings of the 28th annual meeting of the North American chapter of the International Group for the Psychology of Mathematics Education* (p. 326). Mérida: Universidad Pedagógica Nacional.

Akkus, R., Gunel, M., & Hand, B. (2007). Comparing an inquiry-based approach known as the science writing heuristic to traditional science teaching practices: Are there differences? *International Journal of Science Education, 29*, 1745–1765.

Akkus R. & Hand, B. (2005). Mathematics reasoning heuristic: Writing-to-learn. In G. M. Lloyd, M. Wilson, J. L. M. Wilkins, & S. L. Behm (eds.), *Proceedings of the 27th annual meeting of the North American chapter of the International Group for the Psychology of Mathematics Education*, (pp. 1–3). Roanoke, VA: Virginia Polytechnic and State University.

Applebee, A. (1984). Writing and reasoning. *Review of Educational Research, 54*, 577–596.

Atasoy, Ş. (2013). Effect of writing-to-learn strategy on undergraduates' conceptual understanding of electrostatics. *The Asia-Pacific Education Researcher, 22*, 593–602.

Bangert-Drowns, R. L., Hurley, M. M., & Wilkinson, B. (2004). The effects of school-based writing-to-learn interventions on academic achievement: A meta-analysis. *Review of Educational Research, 74*, 29–58.

Bazerman, C. (2009). Genre and cognitive development: Beyond writing to learn. *Pratiques. Linguistique, littérature, didactique,* 143–144, 127–138.

Bereiter, C. & Scardamalia, M. (1987). *The psychology of written composition.* Hillsdale, NJ: Lawrence Erlbaum.

Berthold, K., Nückles, M., & Renkl, A. (2003.) Fostering the application of learning strategies in writing learning protocols. In F. Schmalhofer & R. Young (eds.), *Proceedings of the European cognitive science conference 2003.* Mahwah, NJ: Lawrence Erlbaum.

   (2007). Do learning protocols support learning strategies and outcomes? The role of cognitive and metacognitive prompts. *Learning and Instruction, 17*, 564–577.

Bezemer, J. & Kress, G. (2015). *Multimodality, learning and communication: A social semiotic frame.* New York: Routledge.

Boscolo, P. & Carotti, L. (2003). Does writing contribute to improving high school students' approach to literature? *L1-Educational Studies in Language and Literature, 3,* 197–224.

Boscolo, P. & Mason, L. (2001). Writing to learn, writing to transfer. In P. Tynjälä, L. Mason, & K. Lonka (eds.), *Studies in Writing: Vol. 7. Writing as a learning tool: Integrating theory and practice* (pp. 83–104). Dordrecht: Kluwer Academic Publishers.

Britton, J. (1982). Writing-to-learn and learning to write. In G. M. Pradl (ed.), *Prospect and retrospect: Selected essays of James Britton* (pp. 94–111.). Montclair, NJ: Boynton and Cook Publishers. (Reprinted from The Humanity of English: NCTE Distinguished Lectures 1972.)

Britton, J., Burgess, T., Martin, N., McLeod, A., & Rosen, H. (1975). *School councils research studies: The development of writing abilities* (pp. 11–18). London: Macmillan Education.

Cantrell, R. J., Fusaro, J. A., & Dougherty, E. A. (2000): Exploring the effectiveness of journal writing on learning social studies: A comparative study. *Reading Psychology, 21*, 1–11.

Childers, P. B., Gere, A. R., & Young, A. (eds.), (1994). *Programs and practices: Writing across the secondary school curriculum*. Montclair, NJ: Boynton and Cook Publishers.

Corcelles Seuba, M. & Castelló, M. (2015). Learning philosophical thinking through collaborative writing in secondary education. *Journal of Writing Research, 7*, 157–200. https://doi.org/10.17239 jowr-2015.07.01.07

De La Paz, S. & Felton, M. K. (2010). Reading and writing from multiple source documents in history: Effects of strategy instruction with low to average high school writers. *Contemporary Educational Psychology, 35*, 174–192.

Drabick, D. A., Weisberg, R., Paul, L., & Bubier, J. L. (2007). Keeping it short and sweet: Brief, ungraded writing assignments facilitate learning. *Teaching of Psychology, 34*, 172–176.

Duke, N. K., Purcell-Gates, V., Hall, L. A., & Tower, C. (2006). Authentic literacy activities for developing comprehension and writing. *The Reading Teacher, 60*(4), 344–355.

Felton, M., Garcia-Mila, M., & Gilabert, S. (2009). Deliberation versus dispute: The impact of argumentative discourse goals on learning and reasoning in the science classroom. *Informal Logic, 29*, 417–446.

Galbraith, D. (2009). Writing about what we know: Generating ideas in writing. In R. Beard, D. Myhill, J. Riley, & M. Nystrand (eds.), *The Sage handbook of writing development* (pp. 48–64). Los Angeles: SAGE Publications.

Galbraith, D., Ford, S., Walker, G., & Ford, J. (2005). The contribution of different components of working memory to knowledge transformation during writing. *L1-Educational Studies in Language and Literature, 5*, 113–145.

Gelati, C., Galvan, N., & Boscolo, P. (2014). Summary writing as a tool for improving the comprehension of expository texts: An intervention study in primary school. In P. D. Klein, P. Boscolo, L. C. Kirkpatrick, & C. Gelati (eds.), *Studies in writing. Vol. 28: Writing as a learning activity* (pp. 191–216). Leiden: Brill.

Gentner, D. (2003). Why we're so smart. In D. Gentner & S. Goldin-Meadow (eds.), *Language in mind: Advances in the study of language and thought* (pp. 195–235). Cambridge, MA: MIT Press.

Gere, A. R. (ed.). (1985). *Roots in the sawdust: Writing to learn across the disciplines*. Urbana: IL: National Council of Teachers of English.

Gillespie, A., Graham, S., Kiuhara, S., & Hebert, M. (2014). High school teachers' use of writing to support students' learning: a national survey. *Reading and Writing, 27*, 1043–1072.

Gingerich, K. J., Bugg, J. M., Doe, S. R., Rowland, C. A., Richards, T. L., Tompkins, S. A., & McDaniel, M. A. (2014). Active processing via write-to-learn assignments learning and retention benefits in introductory psychology. *Teaching of Psychology, 41*, 303–308.

Glogger, I., Holzäpfel, L., Schwonke, R., Nückles, M., & Renkl, A. (2009). Activation of learning strategies in writing learning journals. *Zeitschrift für pädagogische Psychologie, 23*, 95–104.

Glogger, I., Schwonke, R., Holzäpfel, L., Nückles, M., & Renkl, A. (2012). Learning strategies assessed by journal writing: Prediction of learning outcomes by quantity, quality, and combinations of learning strategies. *Journal of Educational Psychology, 104*, 452–468.

Graham, S. & Hebert, M. (2011). Writing to read: A meta-analysis of the impact of writing and writing instruction on reading. *Harvard Educational Review, 81*, 710–744.

Gunel, M., Hand, B., & Gunduz, S. (2006). Comparing student understanding of quantum physics when embedding multimodal representations into two different writing formats: Presentation format versus summary report format. *Science Education, 90*, 1092–1112.

Gunel, M., Hand, B., & McDermott, M. A. (2009). Writing for different audiences: Effects on high-school students' conceptual understanding of biology. *Learning and Instruction, 19*, 354–367.

Hand, B., Gunel, M., & Ulu, C. (2009). Sequencing embedded multimodal representations in a writing to learn approach to the teaching of electricity. *Journal of Research in Science Teaching, 46*, 225–247.

Hand, B., Hohenshell, L., & Prain, V. (2004). Exploring students' responses to conceptual questions when engaged with planned writing experiences: A study with year 10 science students. *Journal of Research in Science Teaching, 41*, 186–210.

(2007). Examining the effect of multiple writing tasks on year 10 biology students' understanding of cell and molecular biology concepts. *Instructional Science, 35*, 343–373. https://doi.org/10.1007/s11251-006–9012-3Hand, B., Wallace, C.W., & Yang, E. (2004). Using a Science Writing Heuristic to enhance learning outcomes from laboratory activities in seventh-grade science: Quantitative and qualitative aspects. *International Journal of Science Education*, 26, 131–149. https://doi.org/10.1080/0950069032000070252

Hand, B., Yang, O. E. M., & Bruxvoort, C. (2007). Using writing-to-learn science strategies to improve year 11 students' understandings of stoichiometry. *International Journal of Science and Mathematics Education*, 5, 125–143.

Harris, K. R., Graham, S., & Mason, L. H. (2006). Improving the writing, knowledge and motivation of struggling young writers: Effects of self-regulated strategy development with and without peer support. *American Educational Research Journal, 43*, 295–340.

Hayes, J. R. & Flower, L. (1980). Identifying the organization of the writing processes. In L. W. Gregg & E. R. Steinberg (eds.), *Cognitive processes in writing* (pp. 3–30). Hillsdale, NJ: Lawrence Erlbaum.

Hebert, M., Gillespie, A., & Graham, S. (2013). Comparing effects of different writing activities on reading comprehension: A meta-analysis. *Reading and Writing, 26*, 111–138.

Hebert, M., Graham, S., Rigby-Wills, H., & Ganson, K. (2014). Effects of note-taking and extended writing on expository text comprehension: Who benefits? *Learning Disabilities – A Contemporary Journal, 12*(1), 43–68.

Hewitt, J. & Scardamalia, M. (1998). Design principles for distributed knowledge building processes. *Educational Psychology Review, 10*, 75–96.

Hohenshell, L.M. & Hand, B. (2006). Writing-to-learn strategies in secondary school cell biology: A mixed method study. *International Journal of Science Education, 28*, 261–289. https://doi.org/10.1080/09500690500336965

Hübner, S., Nückles, M., & Renkl, A. (2010). Writing learning journals: Instructional support to overcome learning-strategy deficits. *Learning and Instruction, 20*, 18–29.

Jennings, J. H. (1990). A comparison of summary and journal writing as components of an interactive comprehension model. In J. Zuttell & S. McCormick (eds.), *Learner factors/teacher factors: Issues in literacy research and instruction: Fortieth year-book of the National Reading Conference* (pp. 67–82). Chicago: National Reading Conference.

Keys, C. W., Hand, B., Prain, V., & Collins, S. (1999). Using the Science Writing Heuristic as a tool for learning from laboratory investigations in secondary science. *Journal of Research in Science Teaching, 36*, 1065–1084.

Kieft, M., Rijlaarsdam, G., & van den Bergh, H. (2006). Writing as a learning tool: Testing the role of students' writing strategies. *European Journal of Psychology of Education, 21*, 17–34.

  (2008). An aptitude-treatment interaction approach to writing-to-learn. *Learning and Instruction, 18*, 379–390.

Kingir, S., Geban, O., & Gunel, M. (2013). Using the Science Writing Heuristic approach to enhance student understanding in chemical change and mixture. *Research in Science Education, 43*, 1645–1663. https://doi.org/10.1007/s11165-012–9326-x

Klein, P. D. (1999). Reopening inquiry into cognitive processes in writing-to-learn. *Educational Psychology Review, 11*, 203–270.

Klein, P. D. & Boscolo, P. (2016). Trends in research on writing as a learning activity. *Journal of Writing Research, 7*, 311–350.

Klein, P. D., Haug, K. N., & Arcon, N. (2017). The effects of rhetorical and content subgoals on writing and learning. *Journal of Experimental Education, 85*, 291–308.

Klein, P. D. & Kirkpatrick, L. C. (2010). A framework for content area writing: Mediators and moderators. *Journal of Writing Research, 2*(1), 1–46.

Klein, P. D. & Leacock, T. L. (2012). Distributed cognition as a framework for understanding writing. In V. W. Berninger (ed.), *Past, present, and future contributions of cognitive writing research to cognitive psychology* (pp. 133–152). New York: Psychology Press and Taylor & Francis Group.

Klein, P. D., Piacente-Cimini, S., & Williams, L. A. (2007). The role of writing in learning from analogies. *Learning and Instruction, 17*, 595–611.

Konopak, B. C., Martin, S. H., & Martin, M. A. (1990). Using a writing strategy to enhance sixth-grade students' comprehension of content material. *Journal of Reading Behavior, 22*, 19–37.

Langer, J. A., & Applebee, A. N. (1987). *How writing shapes thinking: A study of teaching and learning*. Urbana, IL: National Council of the Teachers of English.

Leopold, C. & Leutner, D. (2012). Science text comprehension: Drawing, main idea selection, and summarizing as learning strategies. *Learning and Instruction, 22*, 16–26.

Leopold, C., Sumfleth, E., & Leutner, D. (2013). Learning with summaries: Effects of representation mode and type of learning activity on comprehension and transfer. *Learning and Instruction, 27*, 40–49.

Linton, D. L., Pangle, W. M., Wyatt, K. H., Powell, K. N., & Sherwood, R. E. (2014). Identifying key features of effective active learning: The effects of writing and peer discussion. *CBE—Life Sciences Education*, 13, 469–477.

Martínez, I., Mateos, M., Martín, E., & Rijlaarsdam, G. (2015). Learning history by composing synthesis texts: Effects of an instructional program on learning, reading, and writing processes, and text quality. *Journal of Writing Research*, 7(2), 275–302.

Mason, L. & Tornatora, M. C. (2016). Analogical encoding with and without instructions for case comparison of scientific phenomena. *Educational Psychology*, 36, 391–412.

Mayer, R. E. (2009). *Multimedia learning*, 2nd edn. Cambridge: Cambridge University Press.

McDermott, M. A. & Hand, B. (2013). The impact of embedding multiple modes of representation within writing tasks on high school students' chemistry understanding. *Instructional Science*, 41, 217–246.

Nam, J., Choi, A., & Hand, B. (2011). Implementation of the science writing heuristic (SWH) approach in 8th grade science classrooms. *International Journal of Science and Mathematics Education*, 9, 1111–1133.

Nevid, J.S., Pastva, A., & McClelland, N. (2012). Writing-to-learn assignments in introductory psychology: Is there a learning benefit? *Teaching of Psychology*, 39, 272–275. https://doi.org/10.1177/0098628312456622

Newell, G. E. (2006). Writing to learn. In C. A. MacArthur, S. Graham, & J. Fitzgerald (eds.), *Handbook of writing research* (pp. 235–247). New York: The Guilford Press.

Nückles, M., Hübner, S., Dümer, S., & Renkl, A. (2010). Expertise reversal effects in writing-to-learn. *Instructional Science*, 38, 237–258.

Nückles, M., Hübner, S., & Renkl, A. (2009). Enhancing self-regulated learning by writing learning protocols. *Learning and Instruction*, 19, 259–271.

Nückles, M., Schwonke, R., Berthold, K., & Renkl, A. (2004). The use of public learning diaries in blended learning. *Journal of Educational Media*, 29, 49–66.

Ong, J. (2013). Discovery of ideas in second language writing task environment. *System*, 41, 529–542.

Paivio, A. (2007). *Mind and its evolution: A dual coding theoretical approach*. Mahwah, NJ: Lawrence Erlbaum.

Petko, D., Egger, N., & Graber, M. (2014). Supporting learning with weblogs in science education: A comparison of blogging and hand-written reflective writing with and without prompts. *Themes in Science and Technology Education*, 7(1), 3–17.

Pineda, L., & Garza, G. (2000). A model for multimodal reference resolution. *Computational Linguistics*, 26, 139–193.

Prain, V. (2006). Learning from writing in secondary science: Some theoretical and practical implications. *International Journal of Science Education*, 28, 179–201. https://doi.org/10.1080/09500690500336643

Prain, V. & Hand, B. (2016). Coming to know more through and from writing. *Educational Researcher*, 45, 430–434.

Reynolds, G. A. & Perin, D. (2009). A comparison of text structure and self-regulated writing strategies for composing from sources by middle school students. *Reading Psychology*, 30, 265–300.

Rinehart, S. D., Stahl, S. A., & Erickson, L. G. (1986). Some effects of summarization training on reading and studying. *Reading Research Quarterly*, 21, 422–438.

Ritchie, S. M., Tomas, L., & Tones, M. (2011). Writing stories to enhance scientific literacy. *International Journal of Science Education*, 33, 685–707.

Rivard, L. P. (2004). Are language-based activities in science effective for all students, including low achievers? *Science Education, 88*, 420–442.

Rivard, L.P. & Straw, S.B. (2000). The effect of talk and writing on learning science: An exploratory study. *Science Education, 84*, 566–593.

Roelle, J., Krüger, S., Jansen, C., & Berthold, K. (2012). The use of solved example problems for fostering strategies of self-regulated learning in journal writing. *Education Research International, 12*. https://doi.org/10.1155/2012/751625

Rouse, A., Graham, S., & Compton, D. (2017). Writing to learn in science: Effects on Grade 4 students' understanding of balance. *The Journal of Educational Research, 110*(4), 366–379.

Saunders, W. M. & Goldenberg, C. (1999). Effects of instructional conversations and literature logs on limited and fluent English proficient students' story comprehension and thematic understanding. *Elementary School Journal, 99*(4), 277–301.

Schwonke, R., Hauser, S., Nückles, M., & Renkl, R. (2006). Enhancing computer-supported writing of learning protocols by adaptive prompts. *Computers in Human Behavior, 22*, 77–92. https://doi.org/10.1016/j.chb.2005.01.002

Stewart, T. L., Myers, A. C., & Culley, M. R. (2010). Enhanced learning and retention through "writing to learn" in the psychology classroom. *Teaching of Psychology, 37*, 46–49. https://doi.org/10.1080/00986280903425813

Van Drie, J., Braaksma, M., & Van Boxtel, C. (2015). Writing in history: Effects of writing instruction on historical reasoning and text quality. *Journal of Writing Research, 7*, 123–156. https://doi.org/10.17239/jowr-2015.07.01.06

Wallace, C.S., Hand, B., & Prain, V. (2004). *Writing and learning in the science classroom.* Dordrecht: Kluwer Academic Publishers.

Wäschle, K., Gebhardt, A., Oberbusch, E. M., & Nückles, M. (2015). Journal writing in science: Effects on comprehension, interest, and critical reflection. *Journal of Writing Research, 7*(1), 41–64.

Wiley, J. & Voss, J. F. (1999). Constructing arguments from multiple sources: Tasks that promote understanding and not just memory for text. *Journal of Educational Psychology, 91*, 301–311.

Wong, B. Y. L., Kuperis, S., Jamieson, D., Keller, L., & Cull-Hewitt, R. (2002). Effects of guided journal writing on students' story understanding. *The Journal of Educational Research, 95*, 179–191. https://doi.org/10.1080/0022067020959658

Yildiz, A. (2012). Prospective teachers' comprehension levels of special relativity theory and the effect of writing for learning on achievement. *Australian Journal of Teacher Education, 37*, 15–28. https://doi.org/10.14221/ajte.2012v37n12.

12 Bilingualism and Education

Bridging Cognitive Science Research to Language Learning

Gigi Luk and Judith F. Kroll

Since 2000, there has been a dramatic increase in research on bilingualism (e.g., Kroll & Bialystok, 2013). In the United States, bilinguals have traditionally been considered an exception, with the presence of a second language (L2) or the absence of English as the first language (L1) seen as a complication for understanding language use and cognition and an obstacle for academic success. The language and learning sciences have now come to see that far from being a complication, bilingualism is a model for examining the cognitive and neural mechanisms that enable flexible language use. At the same time, the translation of this new research to language learning environments and the connections between research on language and education still remain distant. In 2017, the American Academy of Arts and Sciences issued a report on the status of language learning in the United States (Commission on Language Learning, 2017). The conclusion of that report was that it is critical that we change our understanding of the importance of language learning in the United States. The growing diversity of the population within the country has created an urgent need to understand the educational implications of research on bilingualism. In this chapter, we argue that researchers can benefit from understanding the current educational practices and policy involving diverse language learners to design impactful research programs. Simultaneously, recent research findings offer insights to breaking down stereotypes about diverse language learners concerning academic achievement in the US education system. Collaboration between researchers, practitioners, and policy makers is essential to advance intellectual and translational knowledge of language development and learning.

The goal of this chapter is to take a first step toward creating a bridge between research findings on language learning and bilingualism and the contexts in which learning occurs across the life span, in classrooms and beyond. We begin by providing an overview of the history of research concerning bilingualism. We then review the major findings on bilingual cognition and language processing that we believe hold critical implications for education and for learning more generally. Other recent chapters and papers provide comprehensive reviews of this work (e.g., Bialystok, 2017; Kroll & Dussias, 2017; Kroll et al., 2015; Kroll & Navarro-Torres, 2018). Our focus here is on those findings that have immediate consequences for learning and education, as well as potential topics where there are gaps between research and

The writing of this chapter was supported in part by NIH Grant HD082796 and NSF Grants BCS-1535124 and OISE-1545900 to J. F. Kroll and Spencer Foundation Grant #201700115 to G. Luk. The authors thank Audra Irvine and Hannah Pereira for their help in preparing the manuscript.

practice. We consider the context that young English learners (ELs) in the United States face when they enter school without strong skills in English as well as in contrast to English-proficient students. In many respects, ELs are the focal group in discussions of bilingual education, although this approach has potential to benefit all learners, regardless of their language backgrounds (Goldenberg & Romeo, 2015). In this context, we discuss the benefits of bilingualism and the wisdom of maintaining a child's home language when it is not the majority language, as well as the value of monolingual families actively investing in bilingualism in their children. While EL is a categorical label most widely recognized by educators, we recognize that all children, regardless whether English is their native language or not, are in the process of acquiring English. Therefore, we opt to use a more inclusive label, namely *emerging bilinguals* (EBs; García, Kleifgen, & Falchi, 2008), that signals these children's potential to acquire multiple languages. We also illustrate the importance of recognizing students' language background beyond whether they are categorically proficient in English or not. In addition to the children's perspective, we consider how learning a second language may change the minds and the brains of all learners over the course of the life span, particularly in adulthood, regardless of their native language. As part of that discussion, we consider the role of immersion learning, focusing on the environment and setting in which learning occurs. Finally, we describe, in broad strokes, an agenda for future research on bilingualism and education that promotes research–practice partnerships to design research programs relevant to contemporary educational contexts. We consider this chapter a starting point in facilitating cross-disciplinary discussion on improving learning support for children and adults of all language backgrounds.

Historical Overview of Research on Bilingualism

Early studies on bilingualism reported inferior performances in bilingual children and adults on general intelligence, verbal mental tests, and school achievement (Barke & Williams, 1938; Darcy, 1953; Jones & Stewart, 1951; Macnamara, 1966; Mitchell, 1937; Saer, 1923; F. Smith, 1923; M. E. Smith 1931). Although there were a few exceptions, researchers generally claimed that bilingualism had a detrimental effect on child development, particularly in intelligence and language. Terminologies such as "mental confusion" (Saer, 1923) or "language handicap" (Jones, 1952) were used to describe children growing up speaking multiple languages. The early findings on bilinguals that revealed a deficit in intelligence and language tests were largely because the bilingual children were from immigrant families who often had lower social economic status (SES). Furthermore, many bilingual children were not accustomed to completing standardized tests, such as the *Stanford–Binet Intelligence Scales*, which were constructed and normed in samples from middle-class children who had consistent schooling experience. Barke (1933) compared Welsh–English speaking bilinguals to Welsh monolinguals (SES favored bilinguals in this study) and found that bilinguals performed better than the monolinguals in nonverbal intelligence tests. However, when he conducted a follow-up study attempting to control for SES by recruiting children in "comparable" neighborhoods (comparability was not explicitly defined), there was no difference between monolingual and bilingual children in nonverbal intelligence performance, but the bilingual children had smaller vocabulary in the language of testing. Therefore, early comparisons between monolingual and bilingual children were confounded with social factors that interacted with bilingualism, which caused biased interpretations that bilingualism has a detrimental effect on development and learning. These social confounds, in some communities, continue to be associated with bilingualism to date.

The notion that bilingualism is associated with lower cognitive and language skills has persisted in academia and in the general public since these early reports. In 1962, Peal and Lambert published a seminal study demonstrating that bilingual children outperformed their monolingual peers in school grades, and in verbal and nonverbal intelligence measures. This study was critical to inform contemporary research on bilingualism. First, the study was conducted in Montreal, Canada, where English and French were prevalent in the community (English and French became the official languages of Canada following the enactment of Canada's first Official Languages Act in 1969; Fortier, 2009), cultivating the community to consider bilingualism as a social asset. Second, Peal and Lambert (1962) had ensured the monolingual and bilingual children in the study were comparable in SES, sex, and age. This careful matching overcame previous methodological issues and provided a fair and valid basis for investigating the cognitive and linguistic consequences of bilingualism. Since Peal and Lambert's (1962) study, subsequent studies that compared monolinguals and bilinguals matched on SES and other sociodemographic variables showed three major findings: (1) bilinguals showed better performances than monolinguals in cognitive tasks that do not heavily rely on lexical retrieval (e.g., Bain, 1974); (2) bilinguals had weaker language processing than monolinguals on measures such as vocabulary knowledge and comprehension (e.g., Carrow, 1972); and (3) bilinguals demonstrated stronger metalinguistic awareness than monolinguals (e.g., Ben-Zeev, 1977). The empirical evidence suggested that bilingualism has cognitive and linguistic consequences beyond the ability to converse in multiple languages.

Cognitive and Language Consequences Associated with Bilingualism in Children and Adults

The three major findings from the historical work gave rise to major research interests in understanding the mechanisms behind bilinguals' advanced cognitive performance, their weaker lexical retrieval and vocabulary, and their insightful metalinguistic awareness. The process of constantly managing two languages requires a bilingual individual to engage mental activities that are not specifically related to language. These include paying attention to one of the two language networks, ignoring irrelevant linguistic information activated in the other network, and suppressing the habitual tendency to converse in a dominant language when the second language is needed (Kroll et al., 2012). The processes involved in juggling the two languages are common to all bilinguals. With increasing empirical evidence concerning the ways that bilinguals manage the two languages, psycho-linguistic models have been proposed to capture these common processes, e.g., revised hierarchical model (RHM) (Kroll & Stewart, 1994), inhibitory control (IC) model (Green, 1998), and bilingual interactive activation model + (BIA+) (Van Heuven, Dijkstra, & Grainger, 1998). Interested readers can refer to Basnight-Brown (2014) for a comprehensive review of these models. In the next section, we will focus on the language, cognitive, and neural consequences associated with bilingualism in children and adults.

Language Processes Associated with Bilingualism

One of the most important developmental skills that children acquire is to connect sound to meaning, which forms a lexical-semantic relationship supporting subsequent language acquisition. For children growing up with multiple languages, this task may be more challenging as they must navigate the situation that one meaning may be represented by different sounds. To achieve a lexical-semantic mapping, children need to rely on their prior word knowledge and disambiguate irrelevant sounds from relevant ones associated with a specific meaning. This process takes place gradually during toddlerhood (Bion, Borovsky, & Fernald, 2013). Notably, disambiguation leading to successful vocabulary retention may seem more immense for children growing up in bilingual families as there are naturally more sounds associated with each meaning that they encounter in their linguistic environment. For example, a child growing up in a single-language environment may associate a cup with the sound "cup." This relationship is relatively consistent compared to that of a child growing up in a bilingual home where a cup can be "cup" in English and "la taza" in Spanish. To adapt to this linguistic complex-ity, researchers have observed that bilingual toddlers are less willing to assign a definitive meaning to a word compared to monolingual toddlers. In other words, bilingual toddlers adapt to the complex linguistic environment by tolerating a larger margin of error when mapping meaning to word. Indeed, toddlers show increased looking time at a target noun to the language that she or he hears more in the environment (Marchman et al., 2017), demonstrating their sensitivity to the preva-lence of linguistic information in the environment. Trilingual toddlers, who interact with even more immense linguistic complexities, showed no disambiguation of the lexical-semantic association (Byers-Heinlein & Werker, 2009). This finding is intri-guing because it demonstrated that infants are *active learners*, not just passive recipients of linguistic information in the environment. It turns out that infants growing up in a bilingual environment adapt to linguistic complexity by maintaining a malleable sound-to-meaning mapping system for longer than their monolingual peers.

One consequence of this adaptation is that bilingual infants will achieve the same developmental milestones in language acquisition on a different developmental trajectory relative to their monolingual peers. This adaptation reflects the increased cognitive demand associated with statistically tracking meaning to sound in bilinguals' complex linguistic environment (Werker, Yeung, & Yoshida, 2012). Infants' sensitivity to speech perception gradually narrows during the course of the first year of life. Perceptual narrowing reflects infants' responsiveness to the language(s) present in the environment such that sensitivity to more available language (i.e., native language) increases, while sensitivity to less present language decreases. Interestingly, fourteen-month-old infants growing up in monolingual and bilingual homes performed equally well when they had to differentiate two words with different syllables (e.g., /bev/ vs. /lon/; Fennell, Byers-Heinlein, & Werker, 2007). However, at seventeen months, monolingual infants were able to differentiate syllables with different phonemes (/bev/ vs. /dev/) (Werker et al., 2002), while bilingual infants demonstrated comparable performances at around twenty months (Fennell et al., 2007). These findings demonstrate that perceptual narrowing is most apparent at the phonemic level of speech processing. Phoneme is the smallest sound unit within a word. Recent research reports that infants were less responsive to native sounds between six and twelve months, with the initial observation of localization in the frontal region at six months to the disappearance of the frontal localization at twelve months (Ortiz-Mantilla et al., 2016). This neural adaptation parallels behavioral observation of perceptual narrowing, suggesting that language acquisition is an active learning process.

Another consequence that is associated with adapting to the linguistic complexity is that bilingual children are reported to know fewer words in each language compared with a monolingual child. Research showing this observation often compares children's performance on standardized tests that measure receptive vocabulary, e.g., the *Peabody Picture Vocabulary Test* (PPVT-4; Dunn & Dunn, 2007). The PPVT requires children or adults to respond to a word spoken by the experimenter by pointing to one of four pictures. The items are in increasing level of difficulty. A basal and a ceiling mark the beginning and termination of testing. A basal is established when a child has one or no error in a set of twelve items. After establishing the basal, testing proceeds to the next set of twelve items. A ceiling is established when a child has six or more errors in a set of twelve items. Raw scores are calculated by subtracting the number of errors from the total number of items responded. Raw scores are then transformed to standard scores, adjusting for a child's chronological age. The standard score reflects a child's performance relative to his or her age-matched peers. The interpretation of the standard score is similar to that of IQ scores with a population mean of 100 and a standard deviation of 15.

Using this task, Bialystok and colleagues (2010) reported bilingual children between ages 3 and 10 who speak a heritage language at home while being educated in English know fewer words in the language of testing (English, in this case) than their age-matched monolingual peers. Given that bilingual children are in the process of acquiring vocabulary in two languages, it is not surprising that bilingual children know fewer words in each of the languages they speak, particularly when compared with their monolingual peers. Therefore, researchers have also shown that scoring conceptual vocabulary by assessing children's vocabulary in *either* language is a more linguistically responsive way to tap into the lexical-semantic capacity of bilingual children (e.g., Gross, Buac, & Kaushanskaya, 2014). Vocabulary assessment is a common measure of word knowledge in school settings. Standardized, norm-criterion tests are often employed to provide an age-corrected standard score for a child. These scores are aligned to a normal distribution, similar to that involved in the psychometrics of measuring IQ, with a population mean at 100 and a standard deviation at 15. Given the stake is high when comparing an individual child's performance with his or her age-matched peers, it is essential to know whether the norming sample is adequate for a bilingual child. Surprisingly, many of the commercially available norming tests on language do not specify language background information of their norming samples (Luk & Christodoulou, 2016). Indeed, the lack of sensitivity in interpreting age-corrected standard scores obtained from bilingual children has significant ramifications in determining special education eligibility for emerging bilingual children, particularly in categories relating to language and literacy. These ramifications will be discussed in subsequent parts of this chapter. We now turn to the cognitive processes that are thought to be engaged by dual language use and then we consider how language and cognitive processes are recruited during adult second-language learning.

Cognitive Processes Associated with Bilingualism

Adapting to the increased cognitive demand of managing multiple languages, bilingual children and adults have demonstrated superior cognitive skills when the task at hand requires minimal language processing (Bialystok, 2017). Across the life span, the cognitive advantages associated with bilingualism are most apparent in children and older adults, with some mixed results in young adults. Given that there are multiple reviews addressing and reporting the cognitive consequences of bilingualism (e.g., Bialystok, 2017), we take a different approach in this section to outline the theoretical foundations describing bilingualism and cognition, followed by supplementing empirical findings in the literature.

Theoretical Frameworks for Bilingualism and Cognition

Much of the work on bilingualism and cognition has centered around executive functions (EFs), a set of domain-general processes that facilitate goal-directed behavior. EFs have conceptually been represented as a multidimensional construct (Miller & Cohen, 2001) and that the employment of this set of processes is effortful (Diamond, 2013). The general components include updating, shifting, and inhibition (Miyake et al., 2000), which are correlated but separable at the behavioral level. This feature of EFs is represented in the unity/diversity framework (Miyake & Friedman, 2012). While the general components of EFs include updating, shifting, and inhibition, other processes such as working memory and cognitive flexibility have also been considered components of the EFs (Friedman & Miyake, 2017).

Many researchers investigating bilingualism and EFs followed the unity/diversity framework of EFs to examine behavioral differences in monolingual and bilingual individuals across the life span. However, mapping the unity/diversity framework of EFs on bilingualism and cognition may be oversimplistic. First, adopting a group comparison approach using latent constructs implies the assumption of a linear relationship between bilingual experience and EFs. This assumption may be over-simplistic given bilingualism is neither readily quantifiable (Grosjean, 2013) nor unidimensional (Luk & Bialystok, 2013). Indeed, Guerrero, Smith, and Luk (2016) have reported that bilingual experience, as operationally defined as home language usage given all children were educated in English, has a nonlinear relationship with EFs, measured as accuracy rates in a flanker task for children (Rueda et al., 2004). Parents of the children were asked to indicate the proportion of English and non-English language usage on a balance scale ranging from 0 (all English) to 100 (all non-English language). Results showed that preschoolers whose parents reported that they use around 80 percent of the non-English language at home achieved the highest level of accuracy on the flanker task. This finding challenges the assumption of a linear relationship between bilingual experience and EFs. Second, like EFs, bilingualism is dynamic and multidimensional (Luk & Bialystok, 2013). There has not been sufficient empirical evidence to identify how these two multidimensional constructs correlate with each other. The components included in the unity/diversity framework of EF may not be comprehensive (Friedman & Miyake, 2017), which leads to a restricted view of cognitive consequences of bilingualism.

To this end, it is apparent that the prevalent view of EFs does not accurately depict the cognitive processes involved in bilinguals. Indeed, identifying a theoretical framework on EFs for bilingualism is challenging. Another representative model that describes the cognitive processes in bilinguals is Green's (1988) inhibitory control (IC) model. This model focuses on the *processes* of managing multiple languages and has been seen as the most representative model of cognitive control in bilinguals. In the IC model, a control mechanism is responsible for handling the two languages. This control mechanism does not operate on the amount of knowledge in either L1 or L2; instead, it operates to achieve a goal and allocates different amounts of attentional resources to either language network.

Based on the attention model of controlling motor actions devised by Norman and Shallice (1986), Green (1998) proposed that the control process for handling two languages is much like the control process for motor action. In general, language input is received by the bilingual lexico-semantic system. However, language output is not instant. The bilingual lexico-semantic system interacts with a conceptualizer, which is responsible for constructing concepts by recruiting information from long-term memory. The task of using either language as an output is framed as language task schemas. Schemas were defined as "mental devices or networks that individuals may construct or adapt on the spot in order to achieve a specific task and not simply ... structures in long-term memory" (Green, 1998, p. 69). Both concepts (conceptual) and language task schemas (intentional) are mediated by the Supervisory Attention System (SAS), which is constantly regulated by the active task goal. These processes focus primarily on management of attention and cognitive resources to solve the task at hand. After selecting a language as output, the bilingual lexico-semantic system represents concepts or ideas in their respective language and produces verbal output. In the IC model, the conceptualizer, SAS, language task schemas, and task goal are all represented at the cognitive level independent of languages. Languages are represented in the bilingual lexico-semantic system, which receives (decodes) and produces (encodes) verbal information into respective languages.

The IC model has combined the cognitive and linguistic processes involved in managing multiple languages. One element that was in Norman and Shallice's (1986) model but not in the IC model is the differentiation between *controlled* and *automatic* processes in cognition. The differentiation between controlled and automatic processes in Norman and Shallice's model has distinctive resemblance to bilingual processes. One interpretation of automatic processes refers to the ability to complete a task with minimal interference from other tasks whereas controlled processes involve planning, organizing, and/or overcoming a prepotent motor response or resisting a habitual behavioral outcome. The difference is important for understanding bilingual cognition because the demand on cognitive resources is likely different for bilinguals with different levels of L2 proficiency or bilinguals who speak their languages in different contexts.

Recent studies going beyond the monolingual versus bilingual comparison have shown that balanced bilinguals demonstrate advanced performance in tasks that require EFs (Heidlmayr et al., 2014; Prior et al., 2016). However, there are different ways to determine balance in bilinguals. In terms of proficiency, balance may refer to comparable level of word knowledge. Similarly, in terms of usage, balance refers to the amount of language use in a sustained and prolonged period of time. Following Norman and Shallice's differentiation of automatic and controlled processes, balanced bilinguals, in terms of both proficiency and usage, may engage in tasks through a rather automatic process while unbalanced bilinguals engage in EF task with controlled processes. For balanced bilinguals, who may have longer experience of managing two languages as well as more balanced proficiency in both languages, tackling EF tasks may be less cognitively demanding for them as they engage in solving the task with automatic processes. Similarly, for unbalanced bilinguals, who may have asymmetrical proficiency in both languages and shorter experience in managing two languages, engaging in EF tasks may reflect more effortful and controlled processes. Under Norman and Shallice's model, bilinguals with different levels of experience and proficiency will perform differently relative to each other, and relative to monolinguals. Depending on the tasks employed to measure EFs that are sensitive to the ages of the participants, bilinguals' performances may be observed in faster response times or achieving higher accuracy. If balanced bilinguals achieve tasks in a more automatic fashion, then it is reasonable to predict that they would have better performances when compared with their monolingual peers. For unbalanced bilinguals, the prediction is less clear since there is an uncertainty around the level of bilingual experience and whether the magnitude and intensity of the experience is significantly different from and sufficient for the observation of differential behavioral experience.

The theoretical model of automatic and controlled processes in cognition provides a platform to investigate how bilingual experience shapes the mind. Across different developmental stages, early childhood offers the opportunity to see correlating growth in language and cognition. To demonstrate how bilingual experience contributes to changes in EFs, a longitudinal design showing correlating growth in language and EFs is crucial. However, this correlation is not as simplistic. We know that bilingual children develop language at a different rate compared to their monolingual peers (Hoff, 2018). Since there is a demand to attend to multiple languages in the environment, to achieve comparable level of language proficiency may take more time. Nevertheless, there is no reason to predict bilingual children would be less capable of acquiring concepts even though the same concept may be represented in multiple languages. Using conceptual scores, comparable receptive vocabulary was observed in bilingual and monolingual children (Gross et al., 2014) and toddlers (Core et al., 2013). One measure of conceptual vocabulary in bilingual children is translation equivalents, which is related to children's bilingual exposure (Genesee & Nicoladis, 2007). While monolingual children had more productive conceptual vocabulary, Crivello and colleagues (2016) found that bilingual toddlers had better performance in the conflict tasks (shape Stroop task and reverse categorization task) even though these tasks may require a high level of understanding abstract language. Critically, within the bilinguals, there is a positive correlation between knowledge of translation equivalents growth in seven months and performance in the conflict tasks, indicating the growth in bilingual lexical knowledge is associated with growth in EFs. The role of second language proficiency and usage is important for considering the cognitive consequences of bilingualism since these characteristics of bilingualism are important indicators of the quality and quantity of bilingual experiences.

Adult Second-Language Learning and Bilingualism

While bilingualism may shape the minds of children who have been exposed to a second language in early childhood, investigating adults with bilingual experience offers insights into cognitive and neural flexibility associated with (second-)language learning. Traditional accounts of language learning assume that the process for adults who only begin to learn the L2 after the L1 is firmly established is quite different, relying primarily on transfer from the L1 to the L2 and mediated by cognitive rather than linguistic mechanisms (e.g., Pienemann et al., 2005). Bolstered by claims of a critical period for language learning (Lenneberg, 1967) and by evidence suggesting dramatic effects of age of acquisition for both speech (e.g., Piske, MacKay, & Flege, 2001) and grammar (e.g., Johnson & Newport, 1989), the assumption until recently has been that constraints on learning prevent adults from fully acquiring native-like language abilities in the L2 (e.g., Clahsen & Felser, 2006).

Recent research has challenged the traditional account on two important grounds. First, the claims for hard constraints on late acquisition have failed to find support in studies that use electrophysiology to examine brain activity in late L2 speakers (e.g., Steinhauer, 2014). A series of studies has asked whether late L2 learners who have achieved reasonably high proficiency in the L2 are able to process the syntax and morphosyntax of the L2 in a way that resembles that of native speakers. Although late L2 learners may differ from native speakers in some respects, the overwhelming conclusion of this new work is that it is possible to acquire the nuances of the L2 even when they are acquired after early childhood (e.g., Morgan-Short et al., 2012). The neural signatures of language processing in response to violations of the grammar appear to be similar to those generated by native speakers processing their L1. While there is evidence that the age of L2 acquisition has consequences that can be observed in both structural and functional imaging (e.g., Klein et al., 2014), those consequences do not prevent late acquirers from having access to the L2 grammar. The observation of a high level of plasticity among adult L2 learners better characterizes the grammar than the phonology. The tuning of speech to the language of exposure early in life appears to maintain its grip on speech, even for adult learners who are capable of acquiring the L2 grammar. While there are documented phonetic changes that occur in response to language contact (e.g., Chang, 2012), it is common for adult learners to persist in having a foreign accent in using the L2.

The second observation that has changed our understanding of adult bilingualism is that learning and using a L2 changes the native language (e.g., Kroll, Bobb, & Hoshino, 2014; Dussias & Sagarra, 2007). It might seem that consequences of having the two languages in contact would require a high level of proficiency and perhaps even attrition of the L1, but these findings have been reported from even early stages of L2 learning (e.g., Bice & Kroll, 2015). In traditional accounts of language learning, the native language was assumed to be stable, with cross-language interactions reflecting unidirectional transfer from the L1 to the L2. The robust parallel activation of the two languages when bilinguals read, speak, and listen to one language alone (e.g., Van Heuven et al., 1998; Kroll, Bobb & Wodniecka, 2006; Marian & Spivey, 2003), together with the evidence from neuroimaging studies showing that the two languages engage the same neural architecture (e.g. Perani & Abutalebi, 2005), creates a context in which the use of each language spills over to the other language. What is notable is that these cross-language interactions are not restricted to languages that are structurally similar to one another but extend to languages represented by different scripts (e.g., Hoshino & Kroll, 2008) and to bimodal bilingualism in which one language is spoken or read and the other signed (e.g., Emmorey, Giezen, & Gollan 2016; Morford et al., 2011).

If the two languages come to shape each other as they are used, then not only would we expect to see changes that reflect those interactions but we might also expect to see interference because the different properties of each language will come into conflict. What we have learned is that once individuals become skilled speakers of the two languages, they rarely experience conflict at a level that disrupts their fluency. To the contrary, they are able to stay with the language they intend to speak and, at the same time, switch languages, even in the middle of a spoken utterance. The transition of this ability mirrors the controlled and automatic processes in Norman and Shallice's (1986) model. The ability to keep the two languages separate and also to use them together suggests that bilinguals develop the ability to allocate cognitive resources effectively and in a way that enables efficient regulation of action involving multiple languages. The models described earlier of how language processes come to engage cognitive resources provided a first step in conceptualizing how bilinguals and second-language learners control the use of each language in a way that is skillful and amateur respectively. A more recent account of the actions that support language regulation has been proposed by Green and Abutalebi (2013) in the adaptive control hypothesis. The idea is that even bilinguals at a similar level of proficiency in each language will face cognitive demands that differ, depending on the context of language use. Some bilinguals live in their native language, L1, environment and have learned to use an L2 at a high level of proficiency. These bilinguals will have to prevent the L1 from intruding when L2 is used. Studies of control during language production suggest that there is differential inhibition of the more dominant L1 when speech is planned in the L2 (e.g., Misra et al., 2012; Van Assche, Duyck, & Gollan, 2013). Other bilinguals may be immersed in the L2 and may experience reduced access to the L1 (e.g., Linck, Kroll, & Sunderman, 2009). Likewise, some bilinguals may live in a context in which speakers frequently code switch with one another, moving in and out of the two languages with ease. Others may speak the same two languages but may never switch languages within a single utterance. And those who do switch may live in an environment in which everyone speaks the same languages or where only some speakers speak the same languages. The decision-making induced by the discourse environment may have critically important implications for understanding the cognitive consequences of bilingualism. The Adaptive Control Hypothesis provides an account of how the demands that dual language use make on cognitive resources may tune the control mechanisms that enable effective language regulation. The consequence is that bilinguals will differ among themselves (e.g., Luk & Bialystok, 2013) and those differences will determine the precise consequences of dual language use for the networks that underlie cognitive control (Hartanto & Yang, 2016).

In this brief overview, we have emphasized three aspects of adult second-language learning and bilingualism that have changed the way that we understand bilingualism and that potentially hold important implications for educational practice. One is that there are not hard constraints on L2 learning that make it impossible for adults to acquire the L2. The trajectory of learning for adults may differ from that for children but individuals past early childhood are able to acquire L2 to a level of high proficiency. Not only is late learning possible, but the positive consequences of bilingualism can be seen in late as well as early bilinguals (e.g., Vega-Mendoza et al., 2015). A second observation is that the two languages are continually active and interacting with one another, creating bidirectional transfer. A consequence is that each language of the proficient bilingual is potentially a bit different than the native language of monolingual speakers of those languages. The resulting changes have sometimes been misinterpreted as signs of reduced proficiency or even language disorders (e.g., Fabiano-Smith & Goldstein, 2010; Grosjean, 1989). We now know that these changes are typical of the most proficient L2 speakers and characterize the dynamics of dual language experience, not attrition or pathology. A third point is that the context of language learning and language use modulates the way in which the two languages interact, determining how cognitive resources are recruited to use each language and the way in which the neural networks that support language are tuned to enable control.

The Implications of a New Model of Adult Bilingualism for Learning and Educational Practice

We now consider the implications of each of these observations for considering the educational contexts that support adult L2 learning. Perhaps the most provocative implication of the new research on bilingualism is that the goal of L2 learning may not be to acquire native-like monolingual proficiency in the L2 but to acquire proficiency that has accommodated to the relation between the L2 and the L1. Indeed, Grosjean (1989) warned against expecting a bilingual to be a sum of two monolinguals in each of their languages. From this view, we might take a cue from proficient bilingualism to develop appropriate expectations for what successful L2 learning looks like. Proficient bilinguals have acquired the ability to regulate the competition that results when the two languages are in play. Learners need to acquire the representations to access the phonology, lexicon, and grammar of the L2. But they also need to learn to control the two languages. That ability may include being able to tolerate the costs to the native language under conditions in which its dominance may otherwise prevent the fluent use of the L2. Studies of language immersion (e.g., Baus, Costa, & Carreiras, 2013; Linck et al., 2009) make this issue salient by showing that there is at least momentary suppression of the more dominant L1 when individuals are immersed in the L2. During short-term experiences of traveling or studying abroad, the costs associated with L1 may appear to be an ordinary, frustrating experience. For long-term language learning, these costs may represent a first step toward the reorganization of the language system to accommodate the L2.

Under conditions of language immersion, the modulation of the native language may come for free, in the sense that the experience of increased exposure to the L2 may, in and of itself, be sufficient to enable regulation. What we do not know at this stage is whether conditions of immersion do more than reduce access to the L1. Linck and colleagues (2009) showed that native English-speaking learners immersed in Spain produced fewer exemplars in English than classroom learners in a speeded category fluency task. Because English was the L1 and dominant language for both groups, the results suggested that the L1 was suppressed for the learners in Spain. One might speculate that only conditions of active suppression might produce an enhancement of language regulation abilities. It will remain to be seen whether increasing the frequency of exposure to the L2 is sufficient to enhance regulation abilities among L2 learners.

The studies of L1 change during L2 learning suggests that there may be costs to the L1 that are part of the normal dynamic of learning. A notable gap in the literature on adult learning is the connection between L2 learning and research on learning and memory more generally. A prominent claim about domain-general learning and memory is that conditions that give rise to more active memory retrieval, semantic elaboration, and errors from which learners derive meaning are more likely to enhance long-term memory, although they may come at an initial cost during early stages of encoding (e.g., Bjork, Dunlosky, & Kornell, 2013; Bjork & Kroll, 2015; Healy & Bourne, 2013; Kornell, Hays, & Bjork, 2009). An intriguing suggestion about new language learning is that the need to acquire regulation of the dominant language engages cognitive mechanisms that may initially tax the learner but, when successful, produce enduring learning. Bogulski, Bice, and Kroll (2018) tested this hypothesis in a vocabulary learning study in which three bilingual groups and one group of monolingual English speakers learned words in Dutch, a language equally unfamiliar to all of them. At study, participants viewed a novel Dutch word that was paired with its English translation. The task was only to speak the English translation when it was understood as the meaning of the Dutch word. At test, all groups performed a Dutch lexical decision task. The three bilingual groups differed with respect to their native languages. One group had English as the L1 and Spanish as the L2, another had Spanish as the L1 and English as the L2, and a third group had Chinese as the L1 and English as the L2. Critically, both the monolinguals and English–Spanish bilinguals learned the new Dutch vocabulary via their dominant language, English. The other two bilingual groups learned the words via their L2. Bogulski and colleagues replicated the finding that bilinguals are better word learners than monolinguals but only for the bilinguals learning via their L1. The other two bilingual groups were no better than monolinguals. Of great interest was that the English–Spanish bilinguals who revealed the word learning advantage were also markedly slow to perform the encoding task relative to the other groups. Bogulski and colleagues hypothesized that the slow encoding time and superior memory for the bilinguals learning via the L1 reflected past experience in learning to regulate their dominant language. Monolinguals have no need to do so and the other bilingual groups likewise would have had experience with their respective L1s but not with English, the L2. When presented with a new learning task, only the one group of bilinguals were considered to have had experience using their L1 in this way.

A phenomenon that has been widely studied from this perspective about learning and memory is interleaving (e.g., Birnbaum et al., 2013). Interleaving is the idea that learning new information in categories that are neatly organized may appeal to learners but over time does not produce better learning outcomes. Having mixed or interleaved information during initial encoding makes learning more challenging but in a way that creates a desirable difficulty, with better memory for new information when initial learning occurred under mixed conditions. The potential implications for new language learning are broad and beyond the scope of this chapter to consider them in full. For present purposes, we focus on how the findings on interleaving in learning may relate to what is one of the most salient myths about bilingualism, namely that mixing the two languages is a sign of deficit. Not only is that belief misguided (e.g., Kroll & Dussias, 2017), but it also fails to recognize, along the lines of the Adaptive Control Hypothesis discussed in the previous section, that code switching may be at the heart of many of the cognitive consequences that have been observed in bilinguals (e.g., Green & Wei, 2014).

Not all bilinguals code switch within the same sentence, but those who do are typically highly proficient in each language and obey the syntactic constraints that determine which mixed utterances would be grammatically acceptable across the two languages (e.g., Myers-Scotton, 2002). For present purposes, perhaps the most critical feature of code switching is that it comes to modulate language processing in a way that creates tuning between production and comprehension (e.g., Beatty-Martínez & Dussias, 2017; Guzzardo Tamargo, Valdés Kroff, & Dussias, 2016). Not only is code switching not a deficit but it is potentially one of the most skilled acts of language processing. Code switching bilinguals learn to tune to their interlocutors to be able to predict when upcoming utterances are likely to include a switch of language (Fricke, Kroll, & Dussias, 2016). While we are only at an early stage of research in identifying the cognitive and neural consequences of code switching, the possible implications for new learning seem promising. Here we suggest a connection to one conversation in the literature on dual language education that may offer a direction to link research more closely to educational practice.

Recent approaches to dual language programs talk about an approach called translanguaging (e.g., García & Lin, 2017; García & Wei, 2014). The idea is to allow a more flexible use of both of a bilingual's two languages in new learning contexts. Translanguaging and code switching are not the same; one involves a more liberal flow of information from one task or context to another and not necessarily a strict rule-governed switch from one language to the other. Critically, they both exploit the simultaneous use of the two languages in a natural way. To our knowledge, there is very little, if any, research that examines the relationships between language processing, its cognitive and neural consequences, and the role of mixed language in new learning. If the claims about the benefits of interleaving are correct (e.g., Birnbaum et al., 2013), then we might hypothesize that mixed language learning environments may promote better learning. Exploring the optimal conditions of language mixing for enhancing new learning will be an important topic for planned research.

The Implications of Research on Emerging Bilingualism for US Education

Knowing that bilingualism changes language and cognitive processes in adults and children, it is expected that diverse language experiences influence learning or knowledge acquisition in general. While the implications for adult second-language learning highlights the potential and flexibility of adult second-language learning, in the US education system, emergent bilinguals remain a marginalized group of learners that have shown weaker academic achievement compared with those who are proficient in English (Murphey, 2014). We argue that the relative performance between emergent bilinguals and students who are proficient in English is too simplistic. This dichotomous comparison has placed the emphasis on a deficit view and does not offer sufficient information to empower emergent bilinguals in educational settings. Instead, drawing from research on bilingualism, we propose a shift from dichotomizing learners as having either limited English proficiency or being proficient in English to a gradient spectrum of language experiences through information in existing education data. This shift has the potential to dissolve the stereotypical notion that emerging bilingualism is an explanation for lower academic achievement. In this section, we outline the educational context relevant to emerging bilingualism and demonstrate with an analytic example.

For educators, understanding how research findings on bilingual children are relevant to education can be challenging. First, the context of research is very different from the context in a classroom. In particular, research requires samples that are rather homogeneous, such that the bilingual children may share similar language backgrounds. Indeed, inconsistent labels and descriptions for children's language background have been reported even among researchers (Surrain & Luk, 2017). Therefore, ecological validity in research should be considered when understanding how findings inform classroom teaching and learning. Second, psychology experiments often utilize elegantly designed tasks and children are tested in well-controlled laboratory contexts. The classroom environment is entirely different: children are often from diverse language backgrounds, with different levels of proficiency in the language that is crucial to acquire academic knowledge. We consider these two potential disconnections between research and practice and the opportunities to bridge the connections.

In the context of public education, particularly in the United States, bilingualism is a term typically associated with limited proficiency in English. Approximately 9.4 percent students (~4.6 million) in the United States are designated as English Language Learners (ELLs; National Center for Education Statistics, 2018a), which refers to "a child who does not speak English or who is not currently able to perform ordinary classroom work in English" (MA-DESE, 2016, p. 7). Although there is a lack of common definition of ELLs across the nation, both at the state and at the district level (Linquanti et al., 2016) and ELL classification criteria vary by state or district, it is common that ELL children (or emerging bilinguals) are tasked with the challenge of acquiring novel academic knowledge through their weaker but developing language. One consequence of this challenge is that a persistent and substantial achievement gap exists between ELLs and their English-proficient peers (Murphey, 2014). With research showing a clear cognitive advantage for bilingual children when compared with monolingual children, it seems that the cognitive advantages do not transfer to academic domains. However, there are a few notable details that need to be considered in order to unpack the stereotype of ELLs and academic achievement: first, the well-documented academic achievement gap is between ELLs and their English-proficient peers. A group of understudied students in the US education system is those who are bilingual *and* proficient in English. This group also includes students who were ELLs but have been reclassified as being English-proficient. Second, the academic achievement gap may be strongly confounded with the association between students' socioeconomic status and academic achievement. Third, the academic achievement gap is often discussed in the context of standardized assessments (Menken, 2008), which typically require a high level of language proficiency in English to achieve in English language arts (ELA) and mathematics. These three considerations can serve as potential anchors for bridging psychology research on bilingualism to the context of education.

The bridge between research and practice requires researchers to walk outside of one's comfort zone and employ innovative research methods. While developmental psychology research typically involves sample-based research using experimental tasks in a laboratory setting, adopting existing education data to test hypotheses derived from psychology research can increase the relevance to education. Here, we demonstrate an example of using the three anchoring issues, namely gradient bilingualism, socioeconomic status and bilingualism, and standardized assessments, to examine the relationship between bilingualism and learning in children who are part of the US education system. Specifically, we ask whether existing education data allow the examination of students' language experience beyond the binary category of English-proficient students and ELLs. Then, we ask whether children's language experience modulates their performance in standardized tests.

Using public data available from the Massachusetts Department of Elementary and Secondary Education (MA-DESE), we extracted the student demographic data for the academic year 2012/13. The data set includes de-identified demographic information, such as gender, race, years in schools, ELL status, lunch status, special education eligibility, and scaled scores on ELA and mathematics. Grade 3 and older students attending public schools in Massachusetts are required to participate in the Massachusetts Comprehensive Assessment System (MCAS), an annual standardized test that involves both multiple choices and short answer questions. Both ELA and mathematics tests are based on the state curriculum frameworks.

The data set included a total of 71,461 Grade 3 students attending public schools in Massachusetts in 2012/13. Excluding 12,420 children who were eligible for special education, a total of 59,041 students were included in this analysis. We further excluded students with incomplete data and those who did not participate in the standardized tests, resulting in a total sample size of 58,075 Grade 3 students. Prior to examining whether students' diverse language experience modulates performances on standardized academic tests, we need to ascertain that the data set includes pertinent information about students' diverse language background. Guided by the first anchoring point, a variable was needed to classify bilingual students beyond ELL and non-ELL statuses. Using the variable FIRSTLANGUAGE and LEP_OFF (Official status of Limited English Proficiency), we derived four groups:

(1) L1Eng: students whose parents reported that their first language was English
(2) English-Proficient Bilinguals (EPBs): students whose parents reported that a non-English language was a first language and have never received English-language services in schools
(3) Former ELLs (F-ELLs): students whose parents reported that a non-English language was a first language and were ELLs but have been reclassified as English-proficient
(4) Current ELLs (C-ELLs): students whose parents reported that a non-English language was a first language and were receiving ELL service during 2012/13

It should be noted that information about children's first language was collected on the Home Language Survey (MA-DESE, 2018). This survey was required as part of the school registration process. No information about home language was collected after school registration. Therefore, the information on home language was collected during school registration, which typically occurs during kindergarten or 1st grade. Furthermore, it is acknowledged that, in the United States, children with diverse language backgrounds were also likely to come from low-income homes (Murphey, 2014). This trend and other sociodemographic information is presented in Table 12.1. As expected, L1Eng formed the largest group in 3rd grade, followed by EPBs and C-ELLs. F-ELLs were the smallest group as reclassification typically occurred later in elementary school. There were comparable proportion of females within each language group and that the students spent a similar number of years in MA. It is noteworthy to state that many of the C-ELLs were not first-generation immigrants but second-generation immigrants born in the United States. Finally, a disproportionate number of F-ELLs and C-ELLs were eligible for free- or reduced-lunch at schools, a proxy measure for socio economic status. As for language diversity within groups, Spanish was the most representative first language in EPB (48.6 percent), F-ELLs (52.7 percent), and C-ELLs (47.4 percent), followed by Brazilian Portuguese, Chinese, and Vietnamese. The representativeness of these languages was the same across the bilingual groups.

Given that socioeconomic status was completely confounded with students' language background (second anchoring point), we conducted general linear models separately for students eligible for free/reduced lunch and those who were not eligible. ELA and mathematics scaled scores were dependent variables where language group (4) and gender (2) were between group factors. For children who were not eligible for free/reduced lunch, both gender and language group significantly predicted ELA scaled score, $F(7, 36673) = 105$, $p < 0.0001$. Female students had higher performance in ELA ($M = 247.5$, $SE = 0.52$) than male students ($M = 243.9$, $SE = 0.50$). The main effect of language group was driven by the lower performance of the C-ELLs ($M = 237.6$, $SE = 0.94$)

Table 12.1 *Sociodemographic information of Grade 3 general education children attending public schools in Massachusetts during the 2012/13 academic year*

	L1Eng[a]	EPB[a]	F-ELLs[a]	C-ELLs[a]
Sample size	47,402	9,252	433	988
% female within group	51.7%	52.5%	55.0%	48.5%
Mean number of years in MA schools (*SD*)	3.8 (0.6)	3.7 (0.7)	3.8 (0.5)	3.4 (0.9)
% free lunch within group	36.8%	30.4%	70.7%	82.7%

[a] L1Eng = Students with English as first language; EPB = English-Proficient Bilinguals; F-ELLs = Former English Language Learners; and C-ELLs = Current English Language Learners.

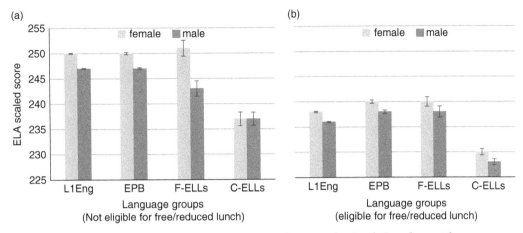

Figure 12.1 *English language arts (ELA) performance for Grade 3 students with diverse language backgrounds*

(a) language group by gender for children not eligible for free/reduced lunch; (b) language group by gender for children eligible for free/reduced lunch

compared with the other groups, which were not different from each other. For children who were eligible for free/reduced lunch, the model also significantly predicted ELA scores, $F(7, 21386) = 80.9, p < 0.0001$. Again, female students had higher performance in ELA ($M = 237.3$, $SE = 0.39$) than male students ($M = 235.3$, $SE = 0.32$), although the difference between gender was smaller. For the language groups, EPBs and F-CELLs had higher performances than L1Eng, followed by C-ELLs. The least squared means are shown in Figure 12.1. Similar analysis was conducted for the mathematics scaled scores. For children not eligible for free/reduced lunch, only language group significantly predicted mathematics scaled scores, $F(7, 36673) = 10.6, p < 0.0001$. Similar to findings for ELA, Tukey's multiple comparisons showed that L1Eng, EPBs, and F-CELLs had comparable performance than C-ELLs. For children eligible for free/reduced lunch, all groups were significantly different from each other, with the F-ELLs achieving the highest performance, followed by EPBs, L1Eng, and C-ELLs (Tukey, 1949). Again, gender was not a significant predictor for the mathematics scaled score. The least squared means are shown in Figure 12.2.

Anchored by three guidelines, the analysis demonstrated the value of combining knowledge from research on bilingualism with contemporary educational issues. By reexamining current education data recognizing the multifaceted nature of bilingualism, new knowledge relevant to education is identified. Results from this analysis confirmed previous findings showing the achievement gap between ELLs and their English-proficient peers as well as between students who were eligible for free/reduced lunch and those who were not eligible. Two significant findings were identified: First, language experience was significantly confounded with lunch status, a proxy for socioeconomic status, indicating that the achievement gap between ELLs and their English-proficient peers may reflect the combined influence of low socioeconomic status and learning academic knowledge in a developing

(a)   (b)

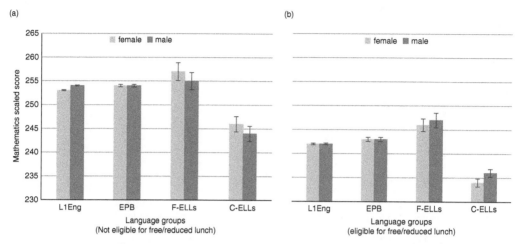

Figure 12.2 *Mathematics performance for Grade 3 students with diverse language backgrounds*

(a) language group by gender for children not eligible for free/reduced lunch; (b) language group by gender for children eligible for free/reduced lunch

language. Second, language experience modulated children's academic performances in ELA and mathematics. While it was clear that ELLs had more challenges in ELA and mathematics tests relative to their English-proficient peers, it is also important to acknowledge that EPBs and F-ELLs had comparable academic performance as their L1Eng peers. In the case of children eligible for free/reduced lunch, F-ELLs attained the highest scores among the groups. This finding is intriguing because F-ELLs shared similar sociodemographic backgrounds as C-ELLs, yet they outperformed other students in ELA and mathematics. It is possible that ELLs receiving English-language services at school acquired additional structured language support to facilitate their development of English.

Cummins (1991) has differentiated language proficiency into contextualized and decontextualized language skills. Contextualized language skills refer to skills that involve paralinguistic cues and other contextual information that facilitate communicative purposes, whereas decontextualized language skills refer to skills that are indirect and are often associated with academic learning. One possible research direction is to identify features of classroom language environment that are beneficial to emergent bilinguals and support their acquisition of adequate English proficiency for classroom learning. A second research direction is to consider supporting these students to maintain and continue to develop their heritage language.

Similar to how the strategy categorizing participants into monolingual and bilingual groups may be oversimplified, evaluating academic performance in ELLs and their English-proficient peers subsides the heterogeneity embedded in bilingualism. The many faces of bilingualism should be recognized and implications of the cognitive and linguistic consequences should be considered. In the following section, we address the potential to develop research–practice partnerships in eligibility for special education and second-language learning.

The Case for Special Education

When considering emerging bilingual learners' eligibility for special education, this task is particularly challenging for categories involving language and literacy skills, such as Specific Learning Disability (SLD). Students with SLD form the largest group receiving special education services in the United States. According to the National Center for Education Statistics (2018b), approximately 6.6 million children (13 percent) received special education services in public schools during the academic year 2014/15. Thirty-five percent of these students were classified as having SLD, which refers to those with "a disorder in one or more of the basic psychological processes involved in understanding or in using language, spoken or written, that may manifest itself in an imperfect ability to listen, think, speak, read, write, spell, or to do mathematical calculations" (Individuals with Disabilities Education Act (IDEA), 34 CFR 300.8(c)(10) (2004)). SLD includes students with a range of learning challenges, including those with dyslexia, dyscalculia, or dysgraphia. The imminent challenge is to identify ELLs who are at risk for SLD in order to provide adequate support and services.

Previous research has reported that ELLs have been disproportionately represented in special education, including those with SLD (Linn & Hemmer, 2011; Samson & Lesaux, 2009; Sullivan, 2011). Partially contributing to this situation is that there is little consensus on the process of identifying SLD in ELLs. Language assessments that are commonly used in school settings do not report the proportion of children from diverse language backgrounds in their norming samples (Luk & Christodoulou, 2016). Importantly, ELLs' non-English language proficiency should be included as part of the identification process in order to take into account the child's overall language competence (de Villiers, 2015); however, schools often lack assessments normed in non-English languages and personnel with the language proficiency necessary to assess students in their native language. These challenges have been scarcely investigated, and it is generally reported that special education assessments for ELs are not linguistically or culturally responsive (Harris et al., 2015). We know that emerging bilingual children reach language acquisition milestones at different developmental stages relative to their monolingual age-matched peers (for a review, see Kovács, 2015). Owing to this developmental timing difference, comparing ELLs against age-based standardized language measures in English may exaggerate discrepancies in performance. One potential consequence is an increased likelihood for ELLs to be considered eligible for special education services. Preliminary analysis suggests that the disproportionate eligibility in ELLs shifted from underidentification in 3rd grade to overidentification in 5th grade (Yamasaki & Luk, 2018). This finding may be related to inconsistencies between identification procedures and educators' reluctance to identify ELLs with SLD as it was unclear whether the child struggles with learning due to developing English proficiency. While there has been some research on the procedures of SLD identification (e.g., Cottrell & Barrett, 2016; Unruh & McKellar, 2013), there is little scholarly knowledge and practical guidance on the assessments that are applicable for ELLs (and bilingual children in general). Establishing research–practice partnerships will enrich our current understanding of how bilingualism interacts with learning difficulty and provide translatable knowledge to practice.

Conclusion

Bilingualism is a common life experience for many people around the world. The science of bilingualism has advanced our understanding of how diverse language experience can shape the development of our mind and brain across the life span. In children and adults, acquiring a second language entails cognitive and linguistic consequences. Understanding these consequences enables research diversity and promotes theoretical knowledge that is applicable and responsive to the increasingly linguistically diverse population around the world. Connecting scientific knowledge to educational practices and learning requires multidisciplinary collaboration. This reciprocal relationship is also necessary to facilitate and inspire researchers to engage in scientific inquiry that is relevant to the general public. Research on bilingualism offers a window for researchers and practitioners to engage in partnerships to promote respect for language diversity in schools and in the community.

References

Bain, B. (1974). Bilingualism and cognition: Toward a general theory. In S. T. Carey (ed.), *Bilingualism, biculturalism and education: Proceedings from the Conference at College Universitaire Saint Jean* (pp. 119–128). Edmonton: The University of Alberta.

Barke, E. (1933). A study of the comparative intelligence of children in certain bilingual and monoglot schools in South Wales. *British Journal of Educational Psychology, 3*, 237.

Barke, E. & Williams, D. E. P. (1938). A further study of the comparative intelligence of children in certain bilingual and monoglot schools in South Wales. *British Journal of Educational Psychology*, 8, 63–77. https://doi.org/10.1111/j.2044-8279.1938 .tb03183.x

Basnight-Brown, D. M. (2014). Models of lexical access and bilingualism. In R. Heredia & J. Altarriba (eds.) *Foundations of bilingual memory* (pp. 85–107). New York: Springer.

Baus, C., Costa, A., & Carreiras, M. (2013). On the effects of second language immersion on first language production. *Acta Psychologica, 142*, 402–409.

Beatty-Martínez, A. L. & Dussias, P. E. (2017). Bilingual experience shapes language processing: Evidence from codeswitching. *Journal of Memory and Language, 95*, 173–189.

Ben-Zeev, S. (1977). The influence of bilingualism on cognitive strategy and cognitive development. *Child Development, 48*(3),1009–1018.

Bialystok, E. (2017). The bilingual adaptation: How minds accommodate experience. *Psychological Bulletin, 143*, 233–262.

Bialystok, E., Luk, G., Peets, K. F., & Yang, S. (2010). Receptive vocabulary differences in monolingual and bilingual children. *Bilingualism: Language and Cognition, 13*(4), 525–531.

Bice, K. & Kroll, J. F. (2015). Native language change during early stages of second language learning. *Neuroreport, 26*(16), 966–971.

Bion, R. A. H., Borovsky, A., & Fernald, A. (2013). Fast mapping, slow learning: Disambiguation of novel word–object mappings in relation to vocabulary learning at 18, 24, and 30 months. *Cognition, 126*(1), 39–53.

Birnbaum, M. S., Kornell, N., Bjork, E. L., & Bjork, R. A. (2013). Why interleaving enhances inductive learning: The roles of discrimination and retrieval. *Memory and Cognition, 41*(3), 392–402.

Bjork, R. A., Dunlosky, J., & Kornell, N. (2013). Self-regulated learning: Beliefs, techniques, and illusions. *Annual Review of Psychology, 64*, 417–444.

Bjork, R. A. & Kroll, J. F. (2015). Desirable difficulties in vocabulary learning. *American Journal of Psychology, 128*, 241–252.

Bogulski, C. A., Bice, K., & Kroll, J. F. (2018). Bilingualism as a desirable difficulty: Advantages in word learning depend on regulation of the dominant language. *Bilingualism: Language* and Cognition. https://doi.org/10.1017/S1366728918000858

Byers-Heinlein, K. & Werker, J. F. (2009). Monolingual, bilingual, trilingual: Infants' language experience influences the development of a word-learning heuristic. *Developmental Science, 12*(5), 815–823.

Carrow, E. (1972). Auditory comprehension of English by monolingual and bilingual preschool children. *Journal of Speech, Language, and Hearing Research, 15*(2), 407–412.

Chang, C. B. (2012). Rapid and multifaceted effects of second-language learning on first-language speech production. *Journal of Phonetics, 40*(2), 249–268.

Clahsen, H. & Felser, C. (2006). Grammatical processing in language learners. *Applied Psycholinguistics, 27*, 3–42.

Commission on Language Learning. (2017). *America's languages: Investing in language education for the 21st century.* Cambridge, MA: American Academy of Arts and Sciences.

Core, C., Hoff, E., Rumiche, R., & Señor, M. (2013). Total and conceptual vocabulary in Spanish–English bilinguals from 22 to 30 months: Implications for assessment. *Journal of Speech, Language, and Hearing Research, 56*(5), 1637–1649.

Cottrell, J. M. & Barrett, C. A. (2016). Defining the undefinable: Operationalization of methods to identify specific learning disabilities among practicing school psychologists. *Psychology in the Schools*, 53, 143–157.

Crivello, C., Kuzyk, O., Rodrigues, M., Friend, M., Zesiger, P., & Poulin-Dubois, D. (2016). The effects of bilingual growth on toddlers' executive function. *Journal of Experimental Child Psychology*, *141*, 121–132.

Cummins, J. (1991). Interdependence of first- and second-language proficiency in bilingual children. In E. Bialystok (ed.), *Language processing in bilingual children* (pp. 70–89). New York: Cambridge University Press. http://dx.doi.org/10.1017/CBO9780511620652.006

Darcy, N. T. (1953). A review of the literature on the effects of bilingualism upon the measurement of intelligence. *The Pedagogical Seminary and Journal of Genetic Psychology*, *82*(1), 21–57.

De Villiers, J. (2015). Taking account of both languages in the assessment of dual language learners. *Seminars in Speech and Language*, 36, 120–132.

Diamond, A. (2013). Executive functions. *Annual Review of Psychology*, *64*(1), 135–168.

Dunn, L. M. & Dunn, D. M. (2007). *Peabody picture vocabulary test: PPVT-4*. Minneapolis, MN: Pearson Assessments.

Dussias, P. E. & Sagarra, N. (2007). The effect of exposure on syntactic parsing in Spanish–English bilinguals. *Bilingualism: Language and Cognition*, *10*, 101–116.

Emmorey, K., Giezen, M. R., & Gollan, T. H. (2016). Psycholinguistic, cognitive, and neural implications of bimodal bilingualism. *Bilingualism: Language and Cognition*, *19*(2), 223–242.

Fabiano-Smith, L., & Goldstein, B. A. (2010). Phonological acquisition in bilingual Spanish–English speaking children. *Journal of Speech, Language, and Hearing Research*, *53* (1), 160–178.

Fennell, C. T., Byers-Heinlein, K., & Werker, J. F. (2007). Using speech sounds to guide word learning: The case of bilingual infants. *Child Development*, *78*(5), 1510–1525.

Fortier, D. (2009). Official languages policies in Canada: A quiet revolution. *International Journal of the Sociology of Language*, *105–106*(1), 69–98.

Fricke, M., Kroll, J. F., and Dussias, P. E. (2016). Phonetic variation in bilingual speech: A lens for studying the production–comprehension link. *Journal of Memory and Language*, *89*, 110–137.

Friedman, N. P. & Miyake, A. (2017). Unity and diversity of executive functions: Individual differences as a window on cognitive structure. *Cortex*, *86*, 186–204.

Garcia, O., Kleifgen, J. A., & Falchi, L. (2008). *From English Language Learners to Emergent Bilinguals. Equity Matters*. Research Review No. 1. Campaign for Educational Equity, Teachers College, Columbia University.

García, O. & Lin, A. M. Y. (2017). Translanguaging in bilingual education. In O. García, A. M. Y. Lin., & S. May (eds.), *Bilingual and multilingual education* (pp. 117–130). Cham: Springer.

García, O. & Wei, L. (2014). Translanguaging and education. In W. E. Wright, S. Boun, & O. García(eds.), *Translanguaging: Language, bilingualism and education* (pp. 63–77). London: Palgrave Macmillan.

Genesee, F. & Nicoladis, E. (2007). Bilingual acquisition. In E. Hoff & M. Shatz (eds.), *Handbook of language development*, pp. 324–342. Oxford: Blackwell.

Goldenberg, C. & Romeo, K. (2015). ESL vs. EFL learners: The benefits of combining language acquisition and explicit instruction approaches. In L. Wong & A. Dubey-Jhaveri (eds.), *English language education in a global world: Practices, issues, and challenges*. Hauppauge, NY: Nova Science Publishers.

Green, D. W. (1998). Mental control of the bilingual lexico-semantic system. *Bilingualism: Language and Cognition*, *1*(2), 67–81.

Green, D. W. & Abutalebi, J. (2013). Language control in bilinguals: The adaptive control hypothesis. *Journal of Cognitive Psychology*, *25*, 515–530.

Green, D. W. & Wei, L. (2014). A control process model of code-switching. *Language, Cognition and Neuroscience*, *29*, 499–511.

Grosjean, F. (1989). Neurolinguists, beware! The bilingual is not two monolinguals in one person. *Brain and Language*, *36*, 3–15.

(2013). *From second language learning to bilingualism in schools*. ACI Information Group. http://scholar.aci.info/view/1427c2d263f114a0104/14ea95abe0600010008

Gross, M., Buac, M., & Kaushanskaya, M. (2014). Conceptual scoring of receptive and expressive vocabulary measures in simultaneous and sequential bilingual children. *American Journal of Speech and Language Pathology*, *23*, 574–586.

Guerrero, S. L., Smith, S., & Luk, G. (2016). Home language usage and executive function in bilingual preschoolers. In J. W. Schwieter (ed.) *Cognitive control and consequences of multilingualism* (pp. 351–374). Amsterdam: John Benjamins Publishing Company. https://doi.org/10.1075/bpa.2.15leo

Guzzardo Tamargo, R. E., Valdés Kroff, J. R., & Dussias, P. E. (2016). Examining the relationship between comprehension and production processes in code-switched language. *Journal of Memory and Language*, *89*, 138–161.

Harris, B., Sullivan, A. L., Oades-Sese, G. V., & Sotelo-Dynega, M. (2015). Culturally and linguistically responsive practices in psychoeducational reports for English language learners. *Journal of Applied School Psychology*, *31*, 141–166.

Hartanto, A., & Yang, H. (2016). Disparate bilingual experiences modulate task-switching advantages: A diffusion-model analysis of the effects of interactional context on switch costs. *Cognition*, *150*, 10–19.

Healy, A. F., & Bourne, L. E., Jr., (2013). Empirically valid principles for training in the real world. *The American Journal of Psychology*, *126*, 389–399.

Heidlmayr, K., Moutier, S., Hemforth, B., Heidlmayr, K., Moutier, S., Hemforth, B., Courtin, C., Tanzmeister, R., & Isel, F. (2014). Successive bilingualism and executive functions: The effect of second language use on inhibitory control in a behavioural Stroop colour word task. *Bilingualism: Language and Cognition*, *17*(3), 630–645.

Hoff, E. (2018). Bilingual development in children of immigrant families. *Child Development Perspectives*, 12, 80–86. https://doi.org/10.1111/cdep.12262

Hoshino, N. & Kroll, J. F. (2008). Cognate effects in picture naming: Does cross-language activation survive a change of script? *Cognition*, *106*(1), 501–511.

Johnson, J. S. & Newport, E. L. (1989). Critical period effects in second language learning: The influence of maturational state on the acquisition of English as a second language. *Cognitive Psychology, 21,* 60–99.

Jones, W. R. (1952). The language handicap of Welsh-speaking children. *British Journal of Educational Psychology, 22*(2),114–123.

Jones, W. R. & Stewart, W. A. C. (1951). Bilingualism and verbal intelligence. *British Journal of Statistical Psychology, 4*(1),3–8.

Klein, D., Mok, K., Chen, J.-K., & Watkins, K. E. (2014). Age of language learning shapes brain structure: A cortical thickness study of bilingual and monolingual individuals. *Brain and Language, 131,* 20–24.

Kornell, N., Hays, M. J., & Bjork, R. A. (2009). Unsuccessful retrieval attempts enhance subsequent learning. *Journal of Experimental Psychology: Learning, Memory, & Cognition, 35,* 989–998.

Kovács, Á. M. (2015). Cognitive adaptations induced by a multi-language input in early development. *Current Opinion in Neurobiology,* 35, 80–86.

Kroll, J. F. & Bialystok, E. (2013). Understanding the consequences of bilingualism for language processing and cognition. Journal of *Cognitive Psychology, 25*(5), 497–514.

Kroll, J. F., Bobb, S. C., & Hoshino, N. (2014). Two languages in mind: Bilingualism as a tool to investigate language, cognition, and the brain. *Current Directions in Psychological Science, 23*(3), 159–163.

Kroll, J. F., Bobb, S. C., & Wodniecka, Z. (2006). Language selectivity is the exception, not the rule: Arguments against a fixed locus of language selection in bilingual speech. *Bilingualism: Language and Cognition, 9*(2), 119–135.

Kroll, J. F. & Dussias, P. E. (2017). The benefits of multilingualism to the personal and professional development of residents of the US. *Foreign Language Annals, 50,* 248–259.

Kroll, J. F., Dussias, P. E., Bice, K., & Perrotti, L. (2015). Bilingualism, mind, and brain. *Annual Review of Linguistics, 1,* 377–394.

Kroll, J. F., Dussias, P. E., Bogulski, C. A., & Valdes Kroff, J. R. (2012). Juggling two languages in one mind: What bilinguals tell us about language processing and its consequences for cognition. *Psychology of Learning and Motivation, 56,* 229–262.

Kroll, J. F. & Navarro-Torres, C. (2018). Bilingualism. In J. Wixted (ed.), *The Stevens' Handbook of Experimental Psychology and Cognitive Neuroscience* (pp. 245–274), Hoboken, NJ: Wiley-Blackwell.

Kroll, J. F. & Stewart, E. (1994). Category interference in translation and picture naming: Evidence for asymmetric connections between bilingual memory representations. *Journal of Memory and Language, 33*(2), 149–174.

Lenneberg, E. H. (1967). The biological foundations of language. *Hospital Practice, 2*(12), 59–67.

Linck, J. A., Kroll, J. F., & Sunderman, G. (2009). Losing access to the native language while immersed in a second language: Evidence for the role of inhibition in second-language learning. *Psychological Science, 20,* 1507–1515.

Linquanti, R., Cook, H. G., Bailey, A. L., & MacDonald, R. (2016). *Moving toward a more common definition of English learner: Collected guidance for states and multi-state assessment consortia.* Washington, DC: Council of Chief State School Officers.

Luk, G. & Bialystok, E. (2013). Bilingualism is not a categorical variable: Interaction between language proficiency and usage. *Journal of Cognitive Psychology, 25,* 605–621.

Luk, G. & Christodoulou, J. A. (2016). Assessing and understanding the needs of dual-language learners. *Leading edge of early childhood education: linking science to policy for a new generation*, 67–90.

Macnamara, J. T. (1966). *Bilingualism and primary education: A study of Irish experience*. Edinburgh: Edinburgh University Press.

MA-DESE (Massachusetts Department of Elementary and Secondary Education). (2016). *School and district profiles [data file]*. www.doe.mass.edu/infoservices/research/

(2018). *Home Language Survey*. www.doe.mass.edu/ell/resources.html

Marchman, V. A., Martínez, L. Z., Hurtado, N., Grüter, T., & Fernald, A. (2017). Caregiver talk to young Spanish-English bilinguals: Comparing direct observation and parent-report measures of dual-language exposure. *Developmental Science, 20*(1). https://doi.org/10.1111/desc.12425

Marian, V. & Spivey, M. (2003). Competing activation in bilingual language processing: Within- and between-language competition. *Bilingualism: Language and Cognition*, 6(2),97–115.

Menken, K. (2008). *English learners left behind: Standardized testing as language policy*. Bristol: Multilingual Matters.

Miller, E. K. & Cohen, J. D. (2001). An integrative theory of prefrontal cortex function. *Annual Review of Neuroscience, 24*(1), 167–202.

Misra, M., Guo, T., Bobb, S. C., & Kroll, J. F. (2012). When bilinguals choose a single word to speak: Electrophysiological evidence for inhibition of the native language. *Journal of Memory and Language, 67*, 224–237.

Mitchell, A. J. (1937). The effect of bilingualism in the measurement of intelligence. *The Elementary School Journal, 38*(1), 29–37.

Miyake, A. & Friedman, N. P. (2012). The nature and organization of individual differences in executive functions: Four general conclusions. *Current Directions in Psychological Science, 21*(1), 8–14.

Miyake, A., Friedman, N. P., Emerson, M. J., Witzki, A. H., Howerter, A., & Wager, T. D. (2000). The unity and diversity of executive functions and their contributions to complex "Frontal Lobe" tasks: A latent variable analysis. *Cognitive Psychology, 41*(1), 49–100.

Morford, J. P., Wilkinson, E., Villwock, A., Piñar, P., & Kroll, J. F. (2011). When deaf signers read English: Do written words activate their sign translations? *Cognition, 118*, 286–292.

Morgan-Short, K., Steinhauer, K., Sanz, C., & Ullman, M. T. (2012). Explicit and implicit second language training differentially affect the achievement of native-like brain activation patterns. *Journal of Cognitive Neuroscience, 24*(4), 933–947.

Murphey, D. (2014). *The Academic Achievement of English Language Learners: Data for the U.S. and each of the States*. Research Brief, Child Trends, Publication No. 2014–62.

Myers-Scotton, C. (2002). *Contact linguistics: Bilingual encounters and grammatical outcomes*. Oxford: Oxford University Press.

National Center for Education Statistics (2018a). English language learners in public schools. *The Condition of Education*. Updated April 2018. https://nces.ed.gov/programs/coe/indicator_cgf.asp

(2018b). Children and youth with disabilities. *The Condition of Education*. Updated April 2018. https://nces.ed.gov/programs/coe/indicator_cgg.asp

Norman D. A. & Shallice T. (1986). Attention to action. In: R. J. Davidson, G. E. Schwartz, & D. Shapiro (eds.) *Consciousness and self-regulation*. Boston, MA: Springer.

Ortiz-Mantilla, S., Hämäläinen, J. A., Realpe-Bonilla, T., & Benasich, A. A. (2016). Oscillatory dynamics underlying perceptual narrowing of native phoneme mapping from 6 to 12 months of age. *Journal of Neuroscience*, *36*(48), 12095–12105.

Peal, E. & Lambert, W. E. (1962). *The Relation of Bilingualism to Intelligence*, *76*(27), 1–23.

Perani, D. & Abutalebi, J. (2005). The neural basis of first and second language processing. *Current Opinion in Neurobiology*, *15*, 202–206.

Pienemann, M., Di Base, B. Kawaguchi, S., & Håkansson, G. (2005). Processing constraints on L1 transfer. In J. F. Kroll & A. M. B. De Groot (eds.), *Handbook of bilingualism: Psycholinguistic approaches* (pp. 128–153). New York: Oxford University Press.

Piske, T., MacKay, I. R. A., & Flege, J. E. (2001). Factors affecting the degree of foreign accent in an L2: A review. *Journal of Phonetics*, *29*, 191–215.

Prior, A., Goldwasser, N., Ravet-Hirsh, R., & Schwartz, M. (2016). Executive functions in bilingual children: Is there a role for language balance?. In J. W. Schwieter (ed.), *Cognitive control and consequences in the multilingual mind* (pp. 323–350). Amsterdam: John Benjamins Publishing Company. https://doi.org/10.1075/bpa.2.14pri

Rueda, M. R., Fan, J., McCandliss, B. D., Halparin, J. D., Gruber, D. B., Lercari, L. P., & Posner, M. I. (2004). Development of attentional networks in childhood. *Neuropsychologia*, *42*(8), 1029–1040.

Saer, D. J. (1923). The effect of bilingualism on intelligence. *British Journal of Psychology. General Section*, *14*(1), 25–38.

Smith, F. (1923). Bilingualism and mental development. *British Journal of Psychology. General Section*, *13*(3), 271–282.

Smith, M. E. (1931). A study of five bilingual children from the same family. *Child Development*, *2*, 184–187.

Steinhauer, K. (2014). Event-related potentials (ERPs) in second language research: A brief introduction to the technique, a selected review, and an invitation to reconsider critical periods in L2. *Applied Linguistics*, *35*(4), 393–417.

Surrain, S. & Luk, G. (2017). Describing bilinguals: A systematic review of labels and descriptions used in the literature between 2005–2015. *Bilingualism: Language and Cognition*, 1–15. https://doi.org/10.1017/S1366728917000682

Tukey, J. (1949). Comparing individual means in the analysis of variance. Biometrics, 5, 99–114.

Unruh, S. & Mckellar, N. A. (2013). Evolution, not revolution: School psychologists' changing practices in determining specific learning disabilities. *Psychology in the Schools*, 50, 353–365.

Van Assche, E., Duyck, W., & Gollan, T. H. (2013). Whole-language and item-specific control in bilingual language production. *Journal of Experimental Psychology: Learning, Memory, and Cognition*, *39*, 1781.

Van Heuven, W. J. B., Dijkstra, T., & Grainger, J. (1998). Orthographic neighborhood effects in bilingual word recognition. *Journal of Memory and Language*, *39*(3), 458–483.

Vega-Mendoza, M., West, H., Sorace, A., & Bak, T. H. (2015). The impact of late, non-balanced bilingualism on cognitive performance. *Cognition*, *137*, 40–46.

Werker, J. F., Fennell, C. T., Corcoran, K. M., & Stager, C. L. (2002). Infants' ability to learn phonetically similar words: Effects of age and vocabulary size. *Infancy*, *3*(1), 1–30.

Werker, J. F., Yeung, H. H., & Yoshida, K. A. (2012). How do infants become experts at native-speech perception? *Current Directions in Psychological Science*, *21*(4), 221–226.

Yamasaki, B. & Luk, G. (2018). Eligibility for special education in elementary school: The role of diverse language experiences. *Language, Speech, and Hearing Services in Schools*, *49(4)*, 889–901.

13 Note-Taking

Stephen T. Peverly and Amie D. Wolf

Note-taking is a pervasive and important activity that includes notes taken on lectures in classrooms but also notes taken in other contexts such as trials (jurors' notes), physician and clinicians' offices, and boardrooms, among others. In this chapter, we present a definition of note-taking, and since almost all of the research is on lecture note-taking, we spend a majority of our time discussing the research that addresses lecture note-taking. Topics include the efficacy of and individual differences in lecture note-taking, research on ways to improve lecture note-taking and other topics on which we wish there was more research such as modes of note-taking (handwritten vs. computer), and the development of note-taking.

Characteristics of Note-Taking

Note-taking is the act of selecting and cryptically and idiosyncratically transcribing important information that can be used as a personal memory aid for later reference, review, and/or memorization by the note-taker. Notes can contain information abstracted from the environment (e.g., from teachers, judges, lawyers, textbooks, or other documents, or otherwise present in the environment such as diagrams and other visuospatial information) and personal reflections (Blair, 2004, e.g., ideas impressions, opinions, hypotheses). Further, note-taking can be a very time-constrained and cognitively challenging activity, especially in the case of lecture note-taking. Lectures are typically fast-paced and the information presented is often new, frequently very dense, and disappears quickly. Finally, notes are related to different goals. In the courtroom, the goal of taking notes is to facilitate memory in the service of effective decision-making. In school, note-taking is a critical part of "studying,"[1] an isolated, self-directed activity initiated by the student that involves setting goals, planning, searching for and integrating relevant information, enacting strategies for understanding, remembering and time management, and monitoring progress often for the purpose of performing well academically (Winne & Hadwin, 2009). Given the developmental and cultural importance of schooling and the importance of lectures in schools for defining course goals, content, and outcomes,

---

[1] While this point seems obvious, it has not been recognized by everyone. Anderson and Armbruster (1984), for example, defined studying as "a special form of reading" (p. 697) which focused on the techniques (e.g., underlining) and criteria (e.g., preparation for a test) students use to understand and remember information in texts, which by their definition excludes lecture note-taking.

almost all of the research on note-taking is on the critical activity of recording (and studying) notes from lecture. Thus, this chapter focuses on lecture note-taking primarily. After we review the literature on lecture note-taking, we will briefly review the research on note-taking in one other context – courtrooms.

Research on Lecture Note-Taking

In this section, we cover several topics on note-taking: its prevalence and perceived importance, functions and efficacy, individual differences, and research on ways to improve note-taking, among others.

The Perceived Importance and Ubiquity of Lecture Note-Taking

As students progress through elementary, secondary, and postsecondary education, the amount and difficulty of information students must understand, remember, and apply in myriad ways increases noticeably (Thomas, Iventosch, & Rohwer, 1987). Also, after elementary school, lecture is the primary mode of conveying that information (Mulcahy-Ernt & Caverly, 2009; Snow, 2002; Thomas et al., 1987), which students find somewhat difficult to process (Piolat, Olive, & Kellogg, 2005; Shernoff et al., 2003; Vogler, 2006). Therefore, students take notes to help them focus on and process lectures (DiVesta & Gray, 1972) because (1) the content presented is fleeting; (2) lectures present course-related goals and content critical to understanding the knowledge domain(s) addressed in the course, which in turn are strongly related to personal academic goals – learning, remembering, understanding, good test performance, and high class grades; and (3) the information may not be available elsewhere (e.g., in readings or other class-related materials). Not surprisingly, research on lecture note-taking has found that instructors expect students to take notes (Landrum, 2010), students think note-taking is important (Dunkel & Davy, 1989), and almost all students take notes (Armbruster, 2009). Decades ago, Palmatier and Bennett (1974), estimated that 99 percent of undergraduates take lecture notes. Results from a recent survey of undergraduates at different universities (2012–2013) from our laboratory indicated that 99.8 percent of respondents take lecture notes at least some of the time ($N = 421$; 94.5 percent take notes "often" or "always") (see Table 13.1, Question 1).

The Functions and Efficacy of Note-Taking

DiVesta and Gray (1972) argued that note-taking has two functions: encoding and storage (sometimes referred to as the process and product functions of note-taking, respectively). Encoding is the act of recording information from a lecture, which provides students with the opportunity to record and to elaborate on or to generate inferences in their notes based on prior knowledge or previous statements made during the lecture (Peper & Mayer, 1978, 1986). The storage function presents students with the opportunity, at some later point in time, to review, process, conceptualize, and commit the information to memory.

DiVesta and Gray (1972) were a catalyst for dozens of studies on the efficacy of each note-taking function on test performance. To evaluate the effectiveness of students' note-taking (encoding) on test performance, researchers have generally compared the test performance of a note-taking group who are not afforded the opportunity to review their notes with a listening-only group that did not take notes. To evaluate the efficacy of review (storage) in addition to encoding, researchers have typically compared the test performance of a listening- or reading-only group to a group that was allowed to take and review their notes. There is also a third group of investigations on the efficacy of providing notes to students, either the instructor's notes or other students' notes (e.g., for students who miss class). The usefulness of review alone has typically been investigated by comparing the test performance of three groups: (1) those who took notes but did not review them, (2) those who took and reviewed their notes, and (3) those who attended the lecture and did not take notes or did not attend the lecture and reviewed notes from another student or the instructor.

There have been a number of reviews of the note-taking literature over the years (e.g., Armbruster, 2009; Hartley & Davies, 1978; Kiewra, 1985, 1989; Kobayashi, 2005; 2006). For example, Kiewra (1985) qualitatively analyzed fifty-six studies on the efficacy of encoding (note-taking alone). Listening was better than note-taking in two, there were no significant differences between conditions in twenty-one studies, and thirty-three studies found effects in favor of note-taking. A meta-analysis by Kobayashi (2005) on the efficacy of encoding found a small effect in favor of encoding without review compared to listening only on test performance ($d = 0.22$).

Research on the efficacy of review presents a more optimistic picture. Kiewra (1985) found twenty-two studies that compared the test performance of students who were allowed to review their notes with those who were not allowed to review. Seventeen studies showed significantly positive effects for reviewing notes and five did not find a difference between those who reviewed their notes and those who did not. A meta-analysis by Kobayashi (2006) that compared no note-taking to note-taking and review found a relatively large effect for review ($d = 0.75$).

In conclusion, scores of studies have investigated the relative efficacy of taking and/or reviewing notes. The results are clear; review is the most important function of note-taking. Although some have postulated that taking notes encourages generative processing such as making connections between note-takers' knowledge and the information contained in lecture (e.g., Peper & Mayer, 1978, 1986), the low efficacy of note-taking alone suggests that most of the generative processing takes place at review (Kiewra, 1991; Kiewra & Fletcher, 1984).

Why Is Review Superior to Encoding?

There are several possible reasons why reviewing notes is much more strongly related to test performance than taking notes: differences between rates of speaking in lecture and handwriting, lack of supports to facilitate note-taking, and the lectures themselves (high density of information; low familiarity).

First, speaking rates in lectures and students' transcription rates are often not compatible. Although the speaking rate of lectures used in research can vary tremendously (Kiewra, 1987) they typically range from 100 to 140 words per minute (WPM). Students' handwriting rate is approximately 20 WPM during a lecture (Greene, 1928; see also the discussion about taking notes by paper/pencil vs. computer later in this chapter) and approximately 38 WPM on a three-minute handwriting speed test (Summers & Catarro, 2003). Thus, note-takers do not have time to record a great deal of information or process the information meaningfully. Second, researchers are interested in students' note-taking under typical classroom conditions. Thus, researchers do not typically provide supports for note-taking such as outlines or breaks, which can provide time for recording more elaborated notes (we discuss interventions in the section "Research on Ways to Improve Note-Taking, Review, and Test Performance").

In addition, lack of familiarity with the content (e.g., due to background knowledge) and/or the propositional density of the lecture may make it difficult to comprehend the lecture and to take notes. There are very little data on the effects of familiarity on note-taking. Hypothetically, since note-taking focuses strongly on main ideas (Armbruster, 2009) and domain knowledge is positively related to the identification/construction of main ideas (Kintsch, 1998), high-knowledge students *should* be able to take better notes from domain-related lectures than low-knowledge students. However, the opposite can be true as well; high-knowledge students may take fewer notes because they are already familiar with the material and do not need to record it. The evidence on this point is mixed. In an ethnographic study of college students' perceptions of lecture note-taking, students reported taking fewer notes when they were familiar with the content of the course, which suggests a negative relationship between notes and background knowledge for high-knowledge students (Van Meter, Yokoi, & Pressley, 1994). This was confirmed in a note-taking study in a hypermedia learning environment (HLE). Trevors, Duffy, and Azevedo (2014) found that high-knowledge students took fewer notes than low-knowledge students but only in the control condition when the HLE did not provide feedback or prompts. Also, low-knowledge students took more verbatim notes, which is less strongly correlated with test performance than generative notes (Mueller & Oppenheimer, 2014; see also Moos & Azevedo, 2008). However, two studies on text note-taking by Peverly and colleagues (Peverly et al., 2003; Peverly & Sumowski, 2012), which controlled for the effects of other cognitive variables on notes, did not find a significant relationship between background knowledge and notes.

Finally, propositional density is fairly strongly and positively correlated with text readability and comprehension (Kintsch, 1998; Kintsch & Vipond, 1979), which suggests that lecture density also may be related to the ease or difficulty of taking notes. Aiken, Thomas, and Shennum (1975) investigated whether the density of information in a lecture would have an impact on recall. They created two versions of the same lecture. Both had approximately the same number of words but the high-density lecture had twice as many information units as the low-density lecture. Results indicated that students in the high-density condition recalled a lower proportion of information units than those in the low-density condition.

Because handwriting rates are slow and lecture rates are rapid, lectures often do not include supports that facilitate note-taking and the lectures themselves may be problematic (high density of information; low familiarity), students do not typically record most of the information in lecture. According to Kiewra (2016), he and his colleagues conducted sixteen experiments in which they compared information contained in a lecture and recorded in notes. Although the information captured in notes from the lecture ranged from 20 percent to 70 percent, the average was 35 percent of presented information. In the half-dozen studies completed in our research group since 2011, the range has been 16 percent to 63 percent, with a mean that approximates Kiewra's. The results from Kiewra and our research group on the percentage of information included in notes from lecture confirms research spanning approximately ninety years (Crawford, 1925).

The question then is this: If there is so little information in notes, how are students able to profit so substantially from review? The good news is that information in notes is much more likely to be recalled than information stated in the lecture that is not included in notes (Aiken et al. 1975; Bretzing, Kulhavy, & Caterino, 1987; Rickards & Friedman, 1978; also Locke, 1977, found that better students include more information in notes than more average students) and college students effectively adapt to the constraints of note-taking; notes are typically strongly biased toward important information (Kiewra & Benton, 1988; Kiewra, Benton, & Lewis, 1987). For example, Kiewra and colleagues (1987) divided information in a lecture into propositions and rated them on importance from 1 (most important) to 4 (least important). While students recorded only 37 percent of the propositions contained in lecture, they recorded 91 percent, 60 percent, 35 percent, and 11 percent of levels 1 through 4, respectively. On the downside, however, note-takers have also been known to (1) omit many details which can provide critical support for important information (Kiewra et al., 1987), (2) omit context or qualifying information that can provide critical information on the conditions under which a particular important idea may or may not apply (Titsworth & Kiewra, 2004), (3) include vague or inaccurate statements (Hartley & Cameron, 1967; Howe, 1974, 1975; Maddox & Hoole, 1975), although the proportion of "c" is relatively small compared with correct information in notes (Maddox & Hoole, 1975), and (4) include too many verbatim statements that do not reflect a deeper understanding of the material (Kiewra, 1989, 2016). Thus, the most obvious answer to why review is so important is that the processes associated with review provide students with the time and the opportunity to correct errors, provide context, and add omitted information to notes as well as to engage in depth of processing (Kiewra, 1985a), that is, to engage in the processes needed to conceptualize, organize, consolidate, and remember the information in their notes.

Individual Differences in Note-Taking and Test-Taking

In this section, we review research on variables that may be related to individual differences in note-taking and on the variables that account for variance in test performance other than the variance accounted for by notes.

Note-taking. Since Crawford (1925), we have known that the quantity and quality of notes are related positively and significantly to test and class grades (for reviews, see Armbruster, 2009; Kiewra, 2016). Differences among students in the quality and quantity of notes have typically been attributed to environmental variables discussed in the previous section: speed of the lecture (Aiken et al., 1975) and informational density (Aiken et al., 1975) of the content of the lecture, among many other possibilities.

Historically, there has been very little research on the relationship between the quantity and the quality of notes and individual differences in the cognitive skills that may be related to note-taking, despite recognition that note-taking is a cognitively demanding task (Kiewra & Benton, 1988; Kiewra et al., 1987; Kobayashi, 2005; Peverly, 2006; Poliat et al., 2005). Students must hold lecture information in verbal working memory, use cognitive resources such as verbal ability and/or background knowledge to select, construct, and/or transform the information, transcribe it (via writing or typing) before the information in working memory is forgotten, and attend to the lecture over long periods of time. Research has found that note-taking is comparable in difficulty to the process of translating, planning, and revising during writing and more effortful than reading or engaging in intentional or incidental learning tasks (Piolat et al., 2005). Thus, note-taking skill may be related to several variables: handwriting speed, working memory, verbal ability, background knowledge, and the ability to attend, among others. Inadequate lecture notes could result from a breakdown in any one of these variables.

Research on the cognitive and demographic characteristics of good lecture note-takers has found skills that are positively, significantly, and relatively consistently related to the quantity and quality of lecture notes: (1) handwriting speed (Gleason, 2012; Peverly et al., 2007, 2013; Peverly, Garner, & Vekaria, 2014); (2) verbal ability (Gleason, 2012; Peverly et al., 2013; Reddington, Peverly, & Block, 2015; Vekaria & Peverly, 2018); (3) sustained attention (Gleason, 2012; Peverly et al., 2014; Schacter & Szpunar, 2015; Vekaria & Peverly, 2018); (4) field-independence/field-dependence (Frank [1984] but not Kiewra and Frank [1988] found that field-independent students took more notes and more efficient notes – they needed fewer words to adequately express ideas – than field-dependent students [Frank, 1984]);[2] and (5) gender, where females have been found to be better note-takers than males (Cohn, Cohn, & Bradley, 1995; Fisher & Harris, 1973; Nye, 1978; Reddington, et al., 2015). Some of these variables also seem to be related to *text* note-taking. Peverly and Sumowski (2012) found that handwriting speed and verbal ability were significantly associated with the quantity and quality of text notes. Collectively, these data suggest that students who write faster, have higher levels

---

[2] The continuum of field-dependence/field-independence, which originated in the perception literature (Witkin, 1959), refers to the ability to detect a visual element within a visual field. For example, those on the field-independence end of the continuum find it much easier to "find Waldo" in a cluttered visual array than those on the field-dependent end of the continuum. In note-taking, more field-independent individuals would find it easier to locate key information related to the topic than more field-dependent individuals.

of verbal skill and sustained attention, are female, and (possibly) have higher levels of field-independence take better notes.

Several studies have evaluated the relationship of working memory to notes. Some studies found a significant positive relationship between working memory and the quantity or quality of notes (Bui, Myerson, & Hale, 2013; Kiewra et al., 1987; Kiewra & Benton, 1988; McIntyre, 1992) and others have not (Cohn et al., 1995; Gleason, 2012; Hadwin et al., 1999; Peverly et al., 2007, 2013, 2014; Peverly & Sumowski, 2012; Vekaria & Peverly, 2018). We did not include working memory in our list of variables related to note-taking because (1) investigations that explicitly measured components of working memory, processing, and storage did not find a significant relationship with quality of notes (Cohn et al., 1995; Gleason, 2012; Hadwin et al., 1999; Peverly et al., 2007, 2013, 2014; Peverly & Sumowski, 2012; Vekaria & Peverly, 2018), with one exception (Bui et al., 2013). However, Bui and colleagues did not concurrently assess the contributions of other cognitive variables hypothesized to be related to note-taking (e.g., handwriting speed, language comprehension) to determine the amount of orthogonal variance contributed by working memory to note-taking (but, see Bui & Myerson, 2014).

Test-taking. While decades of research on note-taking indicate that taking and reviewing notes are significantly related to students' performance on tests (Kobayashi, 2005, 2006), individual differences in cognitive skills may influence test performance, either alone or in addition to notes. Also, their influence may vary by test type (e.g., essay, multiple choice) or what the test is measuring (memory, understanding). Although a variety of different test types have been used in note-taking research (recall, multiple choice, fact recognition, transfer, synthesis, etc.), they typically measure either (1) memory for information stated directly in lecture or (2) the ability to generate inferences.

According to Kintsch (1998), tests such as written recall and multiple-choice items that assess information stated directly in a lecture measure the *text-base*, a mental representation of the propositions derived from lecture and their interrelationships, which have not been elaborated on by students' knowledge and experiences. In his view, measures of the text-base are measures of memory but not necessarily understanding, since they do not explicitly assess understanding. Tests that measure inferences, however, are measures of the *situation model*, a text-base that has been more deeply processed and enriched by readers' or listeners' general and domain-specific knowledge, experiences, and so on. In Kintsch's view, tests that measure students' situation models of lectures and text (e.g., inference questions) measure understanding.

In what follows, we consider research that allows us to estimate the extent to which notes are related to test outcomes once the cognitive characteristics of the learner are taken into account. Prediction patterns in the studies by Peverly and colleagues suggest that notes are consistently related to tests of memory (text-base) but not understanding (situation model). Several studies found a significant relationship between notes and written recall (Peverly et al., 2007: Experiments 1 & 2;

Peverly et al., 2013, 2014; Peverly & Sumowski, 2012; Vekaria & Peverly, 2018) and memory multiple-choice items that measured information stated directly in the lecture or text (Gleason, 2012; Peverly & Sumowski, 2012; however, see Oefinger, 2014).[3]

Multiple-choice questions that measured understanding (via inferences) were not significantly related to notes. Only background knowledge was related to inference items in a text note-taking investigation by Peverly and Sumowski (2012) and verbal ability was the only variable related to inference items in Gleason (2012; a measure of background knowledge was not included in Gleason's investigation) and Oefinger (2014). Findings from other studies that evaluated the relationship of notes to test performance but did not measure the cognitive characteristics of learners largely agree with our conclusions with the caveat that note-taking interventions that produced more elaborated notes, such as outlines or matrices, are sometimes related to performance on tests based in inferences (Kiewra et al., 1989, 1991, 1995). Intuitively, these findings make sense. The rapidity of most lectures and the demands of note-taking (lecture or text; Piolat et al., 2005) may inhibit the deeper levels of cognitive processing required to generate inferences during note-taking unless students are given notes or required to generate notes with more elaborated relationships (e.g., through the use of matrices).

Taking and reviewing notes, cognitive processes, and test performance. Research reviewed in the previous sections on the relationship of cognitive and demographic variables related to taking notes and tests seems to suggest that notes mediate the relationship between the cognitive characteristics of the learner and performance on measures of memory but not measures of understanding (unless students are given the opportunity to more deeply process lectures through the use of matrices or other structural supports). However, the research we reviewed did not measure review and it may be that both notes and review mediate the relationship between individual differences in cognitive processing and test outcomes. One possible way of testing this is to code the quality of notes and a review product (e.g., a summary of notes) and relate these to each other and to test performance. Hadwin, Kirby, and Woodhouse (1999) evaluated the influence of working memory, prior knowledge, verbal ability, and review (researchers coded a summary that students wrote from their notes during a review period) on written (cued) recall. Hadwin and colleagues did not code notes since only one of their three experimental groups took and reviewed their own notes. Review was a significant predictor of cued recall, which suggests that review may mediate the relationship between notes and test performance.

In addition, in our laboratory, we are now analyzing data from an experiment on the relationships among notes, notes-review (students rewrote their notes), and test performance as well as some of the cognitive variables measured by

---

[3] Many studies have found note-taking to be related to students' performance on inference questions. Our point is that other variables may be more related to answering inference questions than notes and, if those other variables were not measured, we cannot evaluate whether it is notes and or those other variables that most consistently account for students' performance on inference questions.

Hadwin and colleagues (1999) and Peverly and colleagues. Only some of the results are presented here. Writing fluency and language comprehension were significant predictors of notes, and notes and language comprehension were significant predictors of notes-review. However, language comprehension was a significant predictor of performance on memory multiple-choice items (not notes) and notes-review was a significant predictor of inferences items. Thus, we need a great deal more research on the interrelationships among individual differences in cognitive processing, note-taking, notes-review, and different kinds of tests (memory and understanding) to begin to understand how all of these variables are related to good test outcomes.

Individual Differences in Note-Taking and Test-Taking: Students with Disabilities. There is relatively little note-taking research on students with disabilities. What exists has focused on students diagnosed with a learning disability (LD) or attention deficit hyperactivity disorder (ADHD). As one might expect, students with disabilities have more difficulty with note-taking and testing-taking than their peers (on LD, see Boyle, 2010a; Hughes & Suritsky, 1994; Oefinger, 2014; and on ADHD, see Gleason, 2012; Vekaria & Peverly, 2018). Also, the cognitive processes that underlie their difficulties in taking notes and doing well on tests are generally the same as those for their nonhandicapped peers (on LD, see Oefinger, 2014; and on ADHD, see Gleason, 2012; Vekaria & Peverly 2018). Finally, students with disabilities respond well to note-taking interventions (Boyle, 2010b, 2013; Boyle & Rivera, 2012; Boyle & Weishaar, 2001; Hamilton et al., 2000; Lazarus, 1993; Ruhl, 1996; Ruhl, Hughes, & Schloss, 1987; Ruhl & Suritsky, 1995), which we discuss more in the section "Research on Ways to Improve Note-Taking, Review, and Test Performance." Thus, data indicate that the cognitive processes that underlie effective note-taking and test-taking seem to be the same for students with (LD and ADHD only) and without disabilities. Differences between groups seem to be related to the level of development of those skills. Figure 13.1 offers a tentative summary of the relationship between cognitive processes and notes and test performance.

The Cognitive Similarities of Note-Taking to Other Academic Skills

From a general cognitive perspective, the ability to take notes does not seem to be different than the ability to execute other academic skills. For example, theories of performance in academic skills such as reading (Hulme & Snowling, 2011; Rayner et al., 2001; Vellutino et al., 2004), writing (Berninger, 2012; Berninger et al., 2006; McCutchen, 2012), and mathematics (Geary, 2011) all recognize that (1) competence in academic skills requires the parallel execution of domain-specific basic and higher level processes within a limited capacity working memory; (2) domain-specific basic skills must be executed automatically/fluently (e.g., word recognition) so that limited working memory resources can be more efficiently used for the application of higher level cognitive skills (e.g. language ability); and (3) once basic skills are sufficiently automatic or fluent, competence in a skill is largely

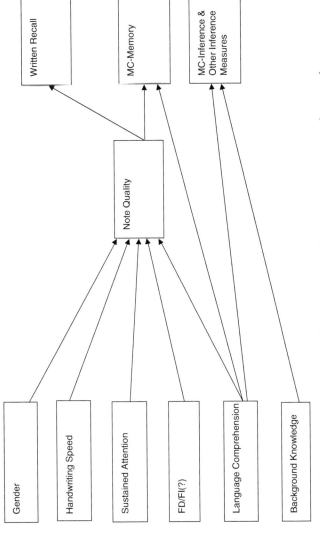

Figure 13.1 *Hypothesized relationships among cognitive processes, notes, and test performance* (reprinted from Peverly et al., 2012, with permission from John Wiley and Sons)

Table 13.1 *Selected questions from an unpublished note-taking questionnaire administered to college students* (N = 435)

Question 1. I take notes in class
  Never (0.46%); Sometimes (5.75%); Often (26.21%); Always (67.59%)

Question 2. I am good at taking notes
  Strongly Disagree (0%); Disagree (5.98%); Agree (67.13%); Strongly Agree (26.90%)

Question 3. The following items refer to taking notes during class, lectures, or discussions. Please select one answer for each item. (Only items pertaining to review are presented here.)
  a. I rewrite or reorganize my notes after class
    Never (42.52%); Sometimes (36.92%); Often (12.38%); Always (8.18%)
  b. I use my notes to study for tests or quizzes
    Never (2.10%); Sometimes (6.31%); Often (17.52%); Always (74.07%)
  c. I go over my notes before class even when there is not a test or a quiz
    Never (43.46%); Sometimes (42.76%); Often (8.88%); Always (4.19%)

Question 6. How do you take notes during class?
  a. I write notes on paper
    Never (3.55%); Sometimes (16.31%); Often (26.95%); Always (53.19%); Don't Know (0.00%)
  b. I type notes on a laptop
    Never (46.75%); Sometimes (26.00%); Often (17.49%); Always (9.93%); Don't Know (0.00%)
  c. I write notes using a digital note-taking pen
    Never (93.38%); Sometimes (1.18%); Often (1.42%); Always (2.84%); Don't Know (2.84%)
  d. I write notes with a stylus on a tablet computer
    Never (95.27%); Sometimes (0.95%); Often (1.42%); Always (0.71%); Don't Know (1.65%)
  e. I write notes with an iPad
    Never (94.33%); Sometimes (2.84%); Often (1.42%); Always (1.42%); Don't Know (0.00%)

Question 8. Below is a list of reasons why people review notes. Please check the two most important reasons you review notes.
  a. I review notes because it helps me learn the information presented during class – 83.69%
  b. I review notes because the instructor requires it – 2.36%
  c. I review note because it helps me earn better grades – 67.61%
  d. I review notes from class so I do not have to read the textbook or course readings – 9.69%
  e. I review notes from class to help me understand the textbook or course readings – 36.64%

Question 11. I would take better notes if ... (participants were given 10 options and asked to choose three):
  a. I wrote faster – 42.32%
  b. I was less anxious – 12.53%
  c. I paid more attention in class – 22.70%
  d. The instructor talked more slowly – 49.17%
  e. Someone taught me how to take notes – 18.68%
  f. I was better at figuring out what is important – 58.87%
  g. I could understand the lecture better – 18.20%
  h. I knew how to organize my notes better – 29.95%
  i. The instructor was better organized – 33.33%

determined by the quality of higher level skills (e.g. language ability). Similarly, in note-taking, research suggests that transcription must be sufficiently fluent so working memory can be used for the application of language skills and background knowledge to comprehend lectures. Interestingly, in the survey from our laboratory on undergraduates' views of note-taking mentioned previously, the most frequent responses to the question "I would take better notes if ... " (ten choices were presented and they were limited to three) were "the instructor talked more slowly" (49.17 percent), "I wrote faster" (42.32 percent), and "I was better at figuring out what is important," which correspond closely to the variables we have found to be related to note-taking (see Table 13.1, Question 11; for survey results from undergraduates that are very similar to ours, see also Reimer et al., 2009).

Mode of Note-Taking: Pen vs. Computer

Data discussed in the previous three sections suggest that one of the variables related to quality of notes is handwriting speed. If speed is important, then laptop computers should confer an advantage to taking lecture notes since students can write faster with computers than pen and paper. Even though computers are ubiquitous on college campuses (Dahlstrom, Walker, & Dziuban, 2013), surveys of undergraduates' preferences for note-taking by longhand or computer vary significantly from one study to another. As mentioned previously, in the survey from our lab, 99.54 percent indicated that they took notes at least "sometimes" (choices were "never," "sometimes," "often," and "always"), 53.19 percent indicated that they "always" take notes on paper (only 9.93 percent said they "always" take notes on computer), and 96.45 percent indicated that they took notes on paper at least "sometimes" (53.43 percent indicated that they take notes by computer at least "sometimes") (see Table 13.1, Question 6). More recent data gathered in our lab in 2015, on a much smaller sample of undergraduates ($N = 80$), found that 96.3 percent of undergraduates always take notes but only 18.8 percent "always used pen and paper" and only 2.5 percent "always used a computer." In Aguilar-Roca, Williams, and Dowd (2012), approximately 50 percent of their sample indicated a consistent preference for paper-based notes and approximately 22 percent indicated a consistent preference for taking notes with a computer. Fried (2008) found that the undergraduates they surveyed ($N = 128$) used laptops in approximately 49 percent of their class sessions for note-taking and other activities.

Despite the ubiquity of computers on campus and the potential benefits of using computers in college classrooms (e.g., Kay & Lauricella, 2011, 2014), the use of computers in classrooms is controversial (Fried, 2008). For example, laptop users have been found to be off-task more and participate less in class (Aguilar-Roca et al., 2012; Fried, 2008; Kay & Lauricella, 2014; Yamamoto, 2007), to have poorer comprehension of the lecture and poorer test performance (Hembrooke & Gay, 2003; Kraushaar & Novak, 2010; Sana, Weston, & Cepeda, 2013), to distract those sitting near them (Sana et al., 2013), and to report significantly less satisfaction with their education (Wurst, Smarkola, & Gaffney, 2008).

Despite the amount of research on the use of laptops in classrooms, there is very little research on the effects of laptops on note-taking and what exists is contradictory. Bui and colleagues (2013) found (1) notes taken by computer contained more idea units than notes taken by longhand ($\eta^2 = 0.19$) and (2) students who took notes by computer performed better on tests (free recall; short answer) than those who took notes by longhand ($\eta^2 = 0.08$ for free recall; an effect size for short answer was not provided). Mueller and Oppenheimer (2014), in Studies 1 and 2, tested the effects of taking longhand or typed notes, without review, on test performance. Study 3 investigated both functions of note-taking: taking and reviewing notes. Across studies, Mueller and Oppenheimer (2014) found that those who took longhand notes wrote significantly fewer words (Study 1, $d = 1.4$; Study 2, $d = 1.11$) than those in the laptop group but wrote a greater percentage of their notes in their own words (Study 1, $d = 0.94$; Study 2, $d = 1.12$),[4] which is typically related to better understanding. There were no differences between groups on factual test questions but those who took longhand notes performed significantly better on conceptual application questions.

The ambiguity of these results seems to be mirrored by undergraduates' nuanced understanding of the pros and cons of using computers to take notes. In a study that consisted of interviews and questionnaires, Reimer and colleagues (2009) found that students associated handwritten notes with better learning and greater flexibility in the organization of notes and greater ease in creating visual representations such as diagrams, figures, and the like. However, laptops enabled them to record more notes and more legible notes, which were easier to rewrite and reorganize than handwritten notes. Thus, a great deal more research is needed on the benefits, drawbacks, challenges, and personal preferences of taking and reviewing notes via pen/paper versus computer.

Definition of Note-Taking Revisited

As discussed above, we believe that the ability to take notes, from a cognitive, limited processing capacity perspective, is not different than the ability to read, write, or do math, that is, basic-level skills (e.g., handwriting speed) must be automatized or as fluent as possible to enable the application of higher order skills (e.g., language) to achieve a goal (e.g., comprehension).

It is also our belief that note-taking is a form of writing. Writing, as it is typically studied in the literature, is reader-based prose (e.g., narrative and expository essays written for others to read). Notes are best described as writer-based prose given their self-serving, idiosyncratic nature. Regardless, the cognitive processes that underlie the ability to take notes, outlined above, are to a significant extent the same as those that underlie the development of the ability to write. To create reader-based prose, theory and research suggest that writers must, within a limited capacity processing system, be fluent in (1) generating ideas, (2) transcribing them quickly before they

---

[4] For Study 2, only the effects sizes for the non-intervention group are reported, since Study 1 did not have an intervention group.

are forgotten, and (3) reading (understanding) what has been written so far to help formulate subsequent reader-based prose (Berninger & Richards, 2012; Berninger & Swanson, 1994; McCutchen, 2000; McCutchen et al., 1994; Olive & Kellogg, 2002; Olive, Alves, & Castro, 2009; Peverly, 2006). Efficiency in executing "a" and "b" significantly lessens the strain on working memory, which in turn enables writers to more efficiently access and use the metacognitive (Bereiter & Scardamalia, 1982, 1987; Hayes, 1996) and other cognitive resources (e.g., language comprehension, content knowledge; McCutchen, 2000) needed to recursively generate and edit written language to create high-quality reader-based prose.

Similarly, to take good notes students must have strong interpretation and transcription skills to record the conceptual essence of the lecture. To review notes, notetakers must have the background knowledge and the linguistic and metacognitive skills needed to add additional information to what has already been written and to organize and more thoroughly conceptualize the overall thematic content of the lecture. Although the end product will most likely be more writer-focused than reader-focused, the domain-general (limited capacity processing) and content-specific skills that underlie both are very similar. Thus, any definition of note-taking should include note-taking as a part of the continuum of writer-based to reader-based prose.

Research on Ways to Improve Note-Taking, Review, and Test Performance

To help students adapt to the cognitively demanding process of taking lecture notes and classroom learning, researchers have focused on several strategies. Predominant among these are methods that change (1) the lecture (e.g., lecture rate), (2) how students take and review their notes (for other reviews, see Kiewra, 1985a, 1991), and (3) teaching.

Changes in lecture. In our survey, the second most frequent response to the question on the conditions under which undergraduates felt they could take better notes was "if the instructor talked more slowly" (48.5 percent). Research on lecture modifications has focused on helping students compensate for the rate of lectures by repeating the lecture, inserting pauses in the lecture, or providing cues to help students process the lecture content more easily.

Lecture repetition. Kiewra and Mayer (1997) and Kiewra and colleagues (1991) had college students view a lecture one, two, or three times and take notes. The number of presentations (1) was directly related to the total number of idea units recorded in notes, with significant increases from one to two and from two to three presentations, and (2) did not have a strong differential effect on the proportion of idea units recorded by level. In general, students' notes were strongly biased toward Level 1 information, though students did record more Level 2 and 3 information from the second and third presentations (Kiewra, et al. 1991; Experiment 2 only). Regarding test performance, Kiewra and Mayer (1997) found that the number of presentations did not affect recall but did affect performance on a fact recognition test. Students who saw the presentation more than once performed better than those who saw it only once. In Kiewra and colleagues (1991), the number of presentations was related to significant increases in total recall and in recall at each level of idea unit importance in Study 1 but not Study 2. Students' recall (like notes) was strongly biased toward important information.

Pauses. Ruhl and colleagues measured the effect on test outcomes (Ruhl, 1996; Ruhl, Hughes, & Gajar, 1990; Ruhl et al., 1987; Ruhl & Suritsky, 1995) and on note-taking (Ruhl et al., 1987; Ruhl & Suritsky, 1995) of inserting pauses during a lecture. The procedure involved stopping a lecture three times for a period of 2 minutes each time. Lectures ranged in length from 22 to 45 minutes. During pauses, students discussed the lecture content with peers for corrections, elaborations, clarifications, and so on.

Although there are a number of differences in design across studies, we mention only two. While undergraduates were participants in all of the studies, two used participants who were diagnosed with an LD (Ruhl, 1996; Ruhl & Suritsky, 1995), one used typically functioning students only (Ruhl et al. 1987), and one used both (Ruhl et al. 1990). Also, two studies required note-taking (Ruhl & Suritsky, 1995; Ruhl, 1996). Across studies, results indicated that the pause procedure facilitated test performance for both disabled and nondisabled students (there were no differences between groups). Also, there were no differences between groups on the total number of complete idea units included in notes. Thus, the research by Ruhl and colleagues suggests that an effective way of compensating for rate is to use short pauses during lecture to allow students time to consult with their peers or instructors to update their notes, check understanding, and so on.

Verbal lecture cues. In a series of three studies, Titsworth (2001, 2004) and Titsworth and Kiewra (2004) evaluated the effects of organizational cues on note-taking (notes vs. no notes) and/or test performance provided in a lecture. All three studies used the same lecture, which covered four theories of communication and, within each theory, four subthemes. Lectures with organizational cues provided explicit statements that a theory or subtheme of the theory was about to be discussed ("First, we are going to discuss [name of theory or sub-theme].") The comparison group heard the same lecture but without cues as explicit as those in the organizational group ("Another [name of theory or subtheme] we are going to discuss ...") Results indicated that organizational cues and note-taking were significantly related to better test performance (Titsworth, 2001; Titsworth & Kiewra, 2004) and organizational cues were significantly related to better note-taking (Titsworth, 2004; Titsworth & Kiewra, 2004).

Summary. Research suggests that viewing lectures more than once (if they have been recorded, e.g., online courses) and inserting pauses and organizational cues in a lecture can lead to increases in the quality and quantity of information in notes as well as better test performance.

Changes in note-taking. Again, referring to our survey, students' most frequent response to the question "under what conditions they would take better notes" was "if I was better at figuring out what was important" (62.9 percent). Some of the techniques used to help students figure out what is important are structural supports, instructors' notes, and other students' notes.

Structural supports. The primary technique used by researchers to improve note-taking is to provide students with structural supports or handouts to help them focus on main ideas and their interrelationships. The most typical are (1) skeletal (linear) notes, which contain headings and subheadings related to main ideas, with spaces for students to record related information; (2) guided notes, which are similar to skeletal notes but also provide students with numbers or other cues to indicate how many ideas should be recorded; (3) matrices, which require students to record notes in cells created by the intersection of headings and subheadings; and (4) instructions on which categories to use to organize notes. Typically, groups given handouts or special instructions are compared with listening-only and/or conventional note-taking groups who are not provided with supports.

Overall, handouts facilitate note-taking and test-taking compared with listening-only or conventional notes. While students of all ability levels seem to benefit, lower ability students benefit more than higher ability students (Austin, Lee, & Carr, 2004; Benton et al., 1993; Boyle & Rivera, 2012; Cohn, et al., 1995; Grabe, Christopherson, & Douglas, 2005; Kaufman, Zhao, & Yang, 2011; Kiewra et al., 1989, 1991, 1995; Morgan, Lilly, & Boreham, 1988; Peverly et al., 2013; Neef, McCord, & Ferreri, 2006; Ruhl & Suritsky, 1995; Shimmerlick & Nolan, 1976; but see Frank, Garlinger, & Kiewra, 1989).

The reader should note that it is difficult to determine whether one type of handout is better than another given the diversity in handouts, materials, students, length of lecture, outcome measures, and time between lecture and test, among other variables across studies.

Providing instructors' notes. Another way of helping students to "figure out what is important" is to provide students with instructors' notes. The results are very mixed. Some have found (1) reviewing one's own notes is better than reviewing instructors' notes, especially when students are given very little time for review (Fisher & Harris, 1973; Kiewra, 1984, 1985); (2) reviewing instructors' notes is better than reviewing one's own notes when the former are very accurate and detailed and students have sufficient time to review them (Kiewra, 1985c; Kiewra, 1985d; Knight & McKelvie, 1986); (3) it depends on the timing of the examination during the semester (Grabe et al., 2005); and (4) it does not seem to make a difference if students took and studied their own notes or took notes but studied instructors' notes (Annis & Davis, 1975; Maqsud, 1980; Thomas, 1978).

Research discussed in the previous paragraph evaluated the relative effectiveness of the review of students' and instructors' notes on test performance. Kiewra and colleagues (1988) evaluated the effects of different types of instructors' notes provided for review on college students' test performance (students did not take notes). Specifically, students watched a lecture on creativity without taking notes and were randomly assigned a week later to one of four groups, all of which were provided with different types of notes to review: matrix notes (types of creativity on one axis and attributes of creativity on the other); linear outline notes (a list of all the important points raised in the lecture); a complete text of the lecture; and a control group (no notes; mental review only). After review, students took three tests: factual recognition, cued recall, and transfer. Given the importance of review, Kiewra and colleagues (1988) hypothesized that all three of the review groups would perform better than the control group on all of the tests. They also hypothesized that the outline and matrix groups would perform better than the complete text group on the cued recall and transfer tests, because performance on those tests was more dependent on the interrelationships among ideas in memory made clear in the outlines and matrices. Given the greater clarity among ideas in the matrix group, as compared with the outline group, and the greater clarity of understanding demanded by transfer tests, they hypothesized that students in the matrix group would perform best on the transfer test. Finally, they predicted that there would be no differences between groups on the factual recognition test because memory for isolated facts is not dependent on interrelationships. All hypotheses were confirmed. These data suggest that higher quality notes, that is, those that promote deeper more integrative processing, and a sufficient amount of time to review them, generally leads to better test performance. Indeed, research has demonstrated that students do not have to attend the lecture to perform well on the test so long as the notes they are given are sufficiently thorough and detailed (Kiewra, 1985d; Knight & McKelvie, 1986).

Providing students' notes. Instructors' notes are often not available. If students miss class, their only option may be to borrow another student's notes. Kiewra and colleagues (1991) assigned students to one of three groups, notes only ($N = 24$), notes and review ($N = 24$), and review only ($N = 48$; each student in the review-only group was assigned notes from another student in one of the other two groups), all of whom listened to a lecture on creativity. There were two tests: cued recall and synthesis (students had to identify two types of creativity that shared a characteristic). The notes and review group was superior to the others on cued recall; and the notes and review and review-only groups were superior to the notes-alone group on synthesis. Kiewra and colleagues (1989) more or less replicated the design of Kiewra and colleagues (1991), with the exception that they equated processing time among the groups because the notes and review group in Kiewra and colleagues (1991) had twice as much processing time as the other two groups. Thus, the notes-only group viewed the lecture and took notes twice and the review-only group reviewed the notes they were given twice. Results indicated that those who took and reviewed notes performed significantly better on recall than the other groups. There were no significant differences among groups on the other test types.

Summary. Findings presented in this section are a little hard to summarize. Nonetheless, they seem to indicate that providing a handout of some sort (e.g., skeletal), giving instructions on how to take notes, and/or providing instructors' notes, if they are accurate and detailed and students have enough time to process them, can facilitate test performance. The data are less clear on the benefits of students borrowing other students' notes when they miss class (although they may not have a choice).

Changes in review. Reviewing notes is important. The effect size for review of notes is three times larger than the act of taking notes on test performance (Kobayashi, 2006) and students understand the importance of reviewing notes. Approximately 98 percent (97.9 percent) of the respondents to our survey said they studied their notes at least "sometimes" (see Table 13.1, Question 3). The reasons why students study their notes are relatively straightforward. Because of the pressures and complexities of note-taking, students do not always have time to take notes that completely and thoroughly express all of the interrelations among ideas, like the notes given to students in Kiewra and colleagues (1988), nor can they effectively remember them. Most of the integration, reconceptualization, and memorization needed for examinations must be done by the learner by rewriting and reviewing their notes after class and/or while preparing for an examination. Unfortunately, however, students do not always engage in the most appropriate review activities. In our survey, approximately 43 percent said they "never" rewrite their notes after class and approximately 37 percent said they do it "sometimes," which suggests that reorganization and reconceptualization are not a priority (see Table 13.1, Question 3). Also, research indicates that students often prefer less effortful strategies such as repeated reading or passive review, which are minimally effective (Dunlosky et al., 2013; Karpicke, Butler, & Roediger, 2009; Tomes, Wasylkiw, & Mockler, 2011; Van Etten, Freeborn, & Pressley, 1997).

Surprisingly, given the importance of review, there is very little research on promoting review of personal notes. We summarize what exists but, given the importance of review, we turn to research on two other strategies – repeated retrieval and semantic maps – for strategies that might assist students with the processes of studying and review. Although the research on both has focused on studying and review, the strategy of repeated retrieval has not been applied to the review of notes. Semantic maps have been applied to the review of notes, albeit rarely.

Instructions or training on how to review. Kiewra (1983) gave college students notes and divided them into one of two review conditions: normal review or reorganization of notes using a matrix provided by the experimenter. There were no significant differences between groups on a cued recall test, but those in the organizational group performed best on a free recall test. Barnett, DiVesta, and Rogozinski (1981) conducted two experiments that investigated the effects of notes (no notes – listen only; take notes; given instructor's notes) and review (no review; review; elaboration review – integrating lecture information with prior knowledge) on college students' performance on a cued recall test (immediate or delayed). Results for both experiments were essentially the same. Students who took notes or had the instructor's notes did better than those who did not have notes regardless of the timing of the exam. There was no effect for review other than the finding that the no-review group performed better than the elaboration group. Thus, the review of notes, as it was operationalized in these studies, did not produce strong results.

King (1992) investigated the efficacy of training "underprepared" undergraduates enrolled in a remedial reading and study skills course on how to review their notes.

Students were assigned to one of two treatment groups – self-questioning or summarizing – or a control group. Training lasted for eight sessions. The self-questioning group was trained to use a rubric of thirteen generic questions (e.g., "explain why") to generate questions about the content of lectures. The summarization group was trained to generate summaries by linking main themes and subordinate supporting information into a coherent paragraph using their own words. Both groups were taught through teacher modeling, practice, and teacher feedback. The control group (note-taking review) discussed their notes in groups.

All students were pretested in the first session by viewing a lecture, taking notes, and answering fifteen multiple-choice questions on the content of the lecture (there were no significant differences between groups on note-taking and comprehension). The treatment groups received training on their strategies in Session 2, and, in Sessions 3 through 6, they viewed a lecture, took notes, practiced their strategies, and received modeling and feedback from the teacher. In Session 7, students took notes on another lecture, reviewed their notes by applying the strategies they had been taught in previous sessions, and then took a comprehension test. Session 8 was a retention test. Both tests consisted of ten multiple-choice questions. On the immediate comprehension test (Session 7) and note-taking, results indicated that the self-questioning and summarization groups were not significantly different from each other and both outperformed the review group. On the retention test, the self-questioning group performed significantly better than the review group. The summarization group was not significantly different from either group.

Improving recall of notes via repeated retrieval. Approximately 98 percent (97.3 percent) of the respondents to our survey said they studied their notes at least "sometimes" before exams. However, as mentioned, students prefer less effortful and less effective strategies such as repeated reading or passive review to more effortful and successful strategies such as self-testing (Dunlosky et al., 2013). In a direct test of the efficacy of review, research has shown consistently that repeated retrieval (called *the testing effect*) facilitates long-term memory more than repeated review (Roediger & Karpicke, 2006a). Roediger and Karpike (2006b: Experiment 2), for example, evaluated the relative efficacy of studying a passage (with full access to the passage) versus testing one's memory for the passage via written recall (without access to the passage). In the first session, participants learned a prose passage in one of the following conditions: (1) four study periods (SSSS), (2) three study periods and one testing period (SSST), or (3) one study period and three testing periods (STTT). After study/retrieval, participants predicted how well they would remember the passage in a week (1 = *not very well*; 7 = *very well*). In the second session, which took place either five minutes or one week after the first session, participants were asked to write down as much of the passage they could recall, without reference to the passage.

Results from the questionnaire indicated that participants in the SSSS condition were significantly more confident about recalling the passage in a week than participants in the other conditions. However, results of the experiment reflected the typical findings from comparisons of repeated review to repeated recall. On the immediate test, all conditions were significantly different from each other, in the following order: SSSS (83 percent), SSST (78 percent), and STTT (71 percent). On the delayed test, the pattern was the opposite, despite participants' prediction on the questionnaire: STTT (61 percent), SSST (56 percent), SSSS (40 percent). While the difference between the first two conditions was not significant, despite the fact that the SSST group reviewed the passage three times longer than the STTT group, both groups recalled significantly more than the SSSS condition. Thus, the testing effect (repeated retrieval) can have a substantially positive effect on long-term retention.

The testing effect has been replicated many times with different study materials, settings, levels of schooling, and so on. In the laboratory, findings have been replicated with paired associates, short prose and fiction passages (Butler et al., 2006), fact lists (Bouwmeester & Verkoeijen, 2011; Kang, McDermott, & Roediger, 2007), journal articles (Kang et al., 2007), different types of intermittent and final tests, including multiple choice (McDaniel et al., 2007), cued, and free recall (Pyc & Rawson, 2010), and tests of the ability to infer relationships (Butler, 2010; Karpicke & Blunt, 2011). In actual classrooms, the testing effect has been shown to be more efficacious than other study methods in elementary school (Gates, 1917; Spitzer, 1939), middle school (Glover, 1989; McDaniel et al., 2011; Roediger et al., 2011), and college (McDaniel et al., 2007).

Semantic maps. Semantic or concept maps are visuospatial and verbal representations of the conceptual organization of written (in this case notes) or spoken information (e.g., lecture), which typically include markers (e.g. arrows) and/or verbal phrases that can represent story grammars, causation, similarities and differences, and sequences in time, among other structures. They are often used as supports for learning from a lecture, text, studying, and other classroom-based activities. Research indicates that semantic maps promote understanding, memory, and transfer (e.g., Bahr & Dansereau, 2001, 2005; Chmielewski & Dansereau, 1998; O'Donnell et al., 2002; Robinson, 1998; Patterson, Dansereau, & Newbern, 1992; Stull & Mayer, 2007). In comparison to other methods, meta-analyses have typically found medium to large effect sizes in favor of maps (Moore & Readance, 1984; Nesbit & Odesope, 2006).

Research on semantic maps also indicates that they are especially helpful to struggling learners of different ages and difficulties (Amer, 1994; Chmielewski & Dansereau, 1998; DiCecco & Gleason, 2002; Horton, Lovitt, & Bergerud, 1990; O'Donnell, Dansereau, & Hall, 2002; O'Donnell & Adenwalla, 1991; Wiegmann et al., 1992). Finally, semantic maps adapt equally well to different content areas (e.g., science and social studies; Horton et al., 1990) and teaching students how to use maps, especially struggling learners, is essential (e.g., Chmielewski & Dansereau, 1998; Dicecco & Gleason, 2002; Stull & Mayer, 2007).

Summary. Data reviewed previously suggest that review is the most important function of note-taking. In this section, we reviewed research on the testing effect and semantic maps for the purpose of arguing that these methods, instead of rereading or passive review, should be used to study notes. The implications of both are straightforward. After students have determined that their notes thoroughly reflect the content of the lecture, they should engage in the reconstruction and reconceptualization of notes (semantic maps) and intermittent recall (without access to notes) until they have mastered the material. In addition, students should be taught to use other research-supported activities: (1) distributed rather than massed studying (e.g., Dempster, 1988); (2) try to anticipate (and answer) instructors' questions (Rosenshine, Meister, & Chapman, 1996; Weinstein, McDermott, & Roediger, 2010); and (3) answer questions in texts or readings that support the lecture (Hamaker, 1986; Peverly & Wood, 2001; Rothkopf, 1996; Weinstein, et al., 2010).

Note-Taking in Contexts Other Than a Lecture

Notes are taken in many contexts other than a lecture, and although there is comparatively little research on note-taking in any of them, most of what exists is on the influence of notes taken by jurors' on their memory for the contents of trials and on their deliberations and decision-making about verdicts and compensation. This research is not solely due to academics' interest in the value of notes in noneducational contexts. At least in part it is the result of a history of litigation on the use of notes by jurors because of the belief by some in the legal profession that note-taking during trials is inappropriate and may constitute misconduct (e.g., Heuer & Penrod, 1994 provide a brief review of the litigation). Thus, research on jurors' note-taking is evaluating whether note-taking inhibits, has no effect on, or improves jurors' participation in trials.

Research on jurors and note-taking has been conducted in two ways, primarily. Most are controlled experiments using mock jurors, audio- or videotapes or transcripts of actual trials, or reenactments of actual trials using lawyers or actors – in some experiments, the trials were shortened and/or evidence calibrated slightly to make clearer distinctions in the evidence presented (e.g., ForsterLee, Horowitz, & Bourgeois, 1994). In these experiments, jurors are randomly assigned to a group (e.g., notes; no notes) and data are gathered from jurors individually or jurors are formed into groups for deliberation on verdicts, compensation, and other tasks, as they would be in actual trials. A second way of studying the effects of note-taking on jurors is to ask actual judges (and the trials they are conducting) to participate in an experiment and, if they agree, to randomly assign them (and their trials) to condition. Since few researchers have attempted this type of investigation, our review focuses on the first approach – controlled experiments. For examples of the other approach, see Heuer and Penrod (1988; and, especially, 1994).

Juror note-taking research addresses two questions: Does note-taking improve jurors' memory for trial information? Does note-taking improve decision-making? The assumption, although rarely tested, is that note-taking improves memory, which mediates the relationship between notes and decision-making. Regardless of whether jurors worked individually or in groups, results typically indicated that note-takers had better free and cued recall and recognition memory for trial information and/or engaged in qualitatively better decision-making than those who do not take notes

(Fitzgerald, 2000; ForsterLee & Horowitz, 1997; ForsterLee, Kent, & Horowitz, 2005; Hope, Eales, & Mirashi, 2014; Horowitz & Bordens, 2002; Horowitz & ForsterLee, 2001; Rosenhan et al., 1994; Thorley, Baxter, & Lorek, 2016). However, in almost all of the aforementioned studies, note-takers had their notes available to them during the test. In other words, few have addressed a key question evaluated in the lecture note-taking literature – the impact of taking notes versus taking and reviewing notes on recall in the absence of notes. ForsterLee and colleagues (ForsterLee & Horowitz, 1997; ForsterLee et al., 1994) are among the few to address the question. Using methods similar to those discussed previously, they found that note-takers (some had access to notes during deliberations and some did not) (1) were better at distinguishing differences in the severity of plaintiffs' injuries than the no-notes group and (2) recalled more trial information (for similar results, see Thorley et al., 2016). There were no significant differences between the access and no access to notes groups. Also, ForsterLee and Horowitz (1997) found that recall mediated the relationship between notes and decision-making. The authors concluded that encoding rather than review is the most important function of note-taking.

In conclusion, these investigations provide support for the notion that taking notes in court is not harmful but can facilitate memory for information presented during trial and promote effective decision-making. However, unlike the research in class-rooms, the most important function of note-taking is encoding and the presence of notes during deliberations and decision-making, not the effects of notes on tests (e.g., recall) in the absence of notes.

There is research on note-taking in other contexts such as clinical settings and business meetings, among others (for reviews, see Hartley, 2002; Kiewra, 2016). Research should be conducted in these domains to determine the role notes play in clinical and business outcomes for clients and the role notes play in conducting therapy or making decisions, among other outcomes.

Future Research on Note-Taking

Since DiVesta and Gray (1972), research has focused predominately on the efficacy of the components of note-taking (encoding, review, or the combination of encoding and review) on test performance, as well as research on how to improve the efficacy of those components. Researchers, however, have not focused or have focused very little on two issues that we consider to be of seminal value to under-standing note-taking in particular and studying more broadly: the development of the strategies of studying and the efficacy of note-taking compared with other methods of learning from lecture. We first consider the research we feel is needed on the functions of note-taking. We then turn to the other issues.

Further Research on the Efficacy of the Functions of Note-Taking

In addition to the questions addressed in the work we have already reviewed, more research is needed on (1) how students review their notes in preparation for exams;

(2) note-taking among elementary, middle school, and high school students; (3) students who may struggle taking notes, such as students with disabilities or students who receive instruction in English when English is not their first language; (4) how students integrate the information in notes with other related information presented in class or found online; (5) the cognitive characteristics associated with individual differences in note-taking and review and their implications for instruction; (6) the efficacy of programs for teaching note-taking in elementary, middle, and high school; (7) the efficacy of taking notes by pen and paper or computer (or other devices); (8) the effect of technology other than computers on note-taking (e.g., PowerPoint); (9) taking notes on nonverbal information (e.g., graphs; equations); and (10) note-taking in contexts other than lectures, among many others. Research on any or all of these areas could advance our understanding of note-taking in particular and studying in general.

Future Research on the Development of Studying and Note-Taking

There is an extraordinary amount of research on the development of academic skills taught in elementary school that has had a strong impact on our understanding and teaching of those skills, especially in the areas of reading (Samuels & Farstrup, 2011) and writing (Berninger, 2012). We do not have a similar body of research on the development of the skills and strategies that might reasonably be included under the rubric of studying, such as note-taking (Rohwer, 1984), which could have a similar impact on instruction. In fact, there are very few studies on note-taking that include students other than college undergraduates. Regardless of the reasons for this, in what follows, we review briefly a series of studies published in the late 1970s and early 1980s by Ann Brown and her colleagues (Brown & Day, 1983; Brown, Day, & Jones, 1983; Brown & Smiley, 1977; Brown, Smiley, & Lawton, 1978), which began to lay the basis for a developmental psychology of studying. We review her work for three reasons: (1) note-taking is part of studying and her work is the only research that we know of on the development of studying; (2) two of her studies have a small amount of data on the developmental usefulness of (text) notes; and (3) we hope to encourage the rebirth of a developmental program of research on studying and note-taking.

Brown and colleagues carried out a series of cross-sectional developmental investigations on studying, which typically included subjects from the 3rd or 5th grades through college (e.g., 5th, 7th, 11th, and college), who had to read and process short 5th grade–level narratives that were approximately 500 words in length. Across studies, Brown and colleagues found lengthy developmental progressions in the ability to (1) consciously rate (differentiate) levels of importance of idea units in text (Brown & Day, 1983); (2) benefit from extra study time, that is, to consciously use strategies (e.g., underlining and note-taking) to focus on information that they did not recall earlier (Brown & Smiley, 1977; see also Kiewra et al., 1991: Experiment 2, discussed earlier); (3) choose appropriate retrieval cues for studying and to revise those cues based on the success of previous attempts at recall (Brown et al., 1978); (4) write coherent summaries (Brown et al., 1983); (5) write summaries in their own words (Brown et al., 1983); (6) use notes to plan their summaries (see also Richards et al., 2016); and (7) effectively use Kintsch and van Dyke's (Kintsch, 1998) summarization rules (Brown & Day, 1983). Research on note-taking needs to focus on these and other skills (e.g., the processes that underlie review) in developmental research on lecture note-taking and other components of studying that Rohwer (1984) called for decades ago.

Future Research on Whether Note-Taking Is the Best Way to Learn from Lecture?

Previously, we argued that after students have determined that their notes thoroughly reflect the content of the lecture, they should engage in the reconstruction and reconceptualization of notes via the use of semantic maps and intermittent recall (the testing effect) until they have mastered the material in preparation for an exam. In other words, one way of improving the review function of notes is to use repeated recall as part of the review process.

Szpunar and colleagues have taken a somewhat different approach. Rather than incorporating the testing effect into the review of notes, they compared note-taking to the testing effect directly, to determine which promoted more learning during a lecture (Jing, Szpunar, & Schacter, 2016; Schacter & Szpunar, 2015; Szpunar, Khan, & Schacter, 2013). Although the methods differ from study to study, all of the participants in these experiments watched a videotaped lecture that was divided into segments (e.g., four segments), with time for another activity between segments. In each experiment, participants were divided into groups and the groups differed on the activities they engaged in during the intervals. In Szpunar and colleagues (2013: Experiment 1) and Jing and colleagues (2016: Experiment 2), all participants in both experiments watched a lecture and were given lecture slides on which they could take notes, although they were not told to take notes. After each segment, the activities in which the participants engaged differed. In Szpunar and colleagues (2013: Experiment 1), the testing effect group spent a relatively short time doing math problems and then answered questions about the previous lecture segment. The participants in the other group did math problems for the entire interval. In Jing and colleagues (2016), both groups worked on math problems briefly during the intervals for the same amount of time. After the math problems, one group wrote down as much of the lecture as they could recall (the testing effect group) and the other group studied the slides they were given as well as any notes they might have taken. In the first experiment of both Szpunar and colleagues and Jing and colleagues, the testing effect groups performed significantly better on the final tests than the slides/notes groups. Also, the testing effect groups in both studies took more notes (for a replication of this finding, see also Szpunar et al., 2014); and, in another finding of note, participants in the testing effect groups reported fewer instances of mind wandering (i.e., attending to something else other than the content of the lecture) than those in the restudy group. The latter finding supports Peverly and colleagues (2014), Vekaria and Peverly, (2018), and Gleason (2012) on the significant and positive relationship between sustained attention and the quantity and quality of notes (for similar results, see also Kane et al. 2017).

The aforementioned results do not unequivocally support the efficacy of the testing effect compared with notes because the designs of the studies did not include more controlled comparisons between the testing effect and notes (e.g., all participants were given lecture slides, participants were not told to take notes, it is unknown how many took notes, and there was no direct comparison between the efficacy of the testing effect with and without notes). There is, however, more direct evidence on the relative efficacy of the testing effect and notes. In a text note-taking study, Rummer and colleagues (2017) asked participants to read a text repeatedly for 10 minutes in the first phase of the experiment. Subsequently, participants were divided into three groups: rereading, note-taking, or testing. In the next two, 10-minute phases of the experiment, participants either reread the text as many times as they could, took notes in their own words and in complete sentences, or wrote down as many facts as they could remember in their own words and in complete sentences without the text present. Testing (free recall) occurred 5 minutes, 1 week, or 2 weeks after the last session. Results indicated a main effect of time and a group × time interaction. There were significant decreases in the amount recalled over the three testing sessions. The interaction indicated that note-taking was superior to the other two groups at 5 minutes, which were not significantly different from each other. At 1 week, the note-taking and testing groups were superior to rereading but they were not significantly different from each other. At 2 weeks, the testing group was superior to the note-taking group, which was superior to the rereading group. Thus, although these data seem to indicate that the relative efficacy of note-taking to testing may be time-dependent, with testing showing better results over the long term, it appears that the note-taking group was not allowed to review their notes, which is the most important function of note-taking. Thus, the note-taking group may have been handicapped relative to the other two groups. Finally, Arnold and colleagues (2017) had undergraduates read scientific passages and complete one of four activities: writing an essay about what they read (activity 1), recalling what they read (activity 2, both without access to the text), underlining the text (activity 3), or taking notes (activity 4). Those participants who engaged in retrieval (writing an essay or recalling the text) performed better on the test than those who did not have to recall the text (underlining and note-taking). Again, however, the note-taking group was not allowed to review their notes.

In summary, although the testing effect appears to be superior to note-taking in producing better test outcomes, the design of the studies reviewed here precludes any strong conclusion in this regard. That said, the testing effect has proved to be a powerful and robust learning tool (Brown, Roediger, & McDaniel, 2014). Future research should explore more thoroughly the relative efficacy (the testing effect vs. note-taking) and complementarity (the testing effect as part of the review portion of note-taking) of these two approaches to learning and studying.

References

Aguilar-Roca, N. M., Williams, A. E., & O'Dowd, D. K. (2012). The impact of laptop-free zones on student performance and attitudes in large lectures. *Computers and Education, 59*, 1300–1308.

Aiken, G. A., Thomas, G. S., & Shennum, W. A. (1975). Memory for lecture: Effects of notes, lecture rate, and informational density. *Journal of Educational Psychology, 67*, 439–444.

Amer, A. A. (1994). The effect of knowledge-map and underlining training on the reading comprehension of scientific texts. *English for Specific Purposes, 13*, 35–45.

Anderson, T. H. & Anderson, B. B. (1984). Studying. In P. D. Pearson (ed.), *Handbook of reading research* (pp. 657–679). New York: Longman.

Annis, L. & Davis, J. K. (1975). The effect of encoding and an external memory device on note taking. *Journal of Experimental Education, 44*, 44–46.

Armbruster, B. (2009). Notetaking from lectures. In R. F. Flippo, & D. C. Caverly (eds.), *Handbook of college reading and study strategy research*, 2nd edn. (pp. 220–248). New York: Routledge.

Arnold, K. M. Umanath, S., Thio, K. et al. (2017). Understanding the cognitive processes involved in writing to learn. *Journal of Experimental Psychology: Applied, 23*, 115–127.

Austin, J., Lee, M., & Carr, J. (2004). The effects of guided notes on undergraduate students' recording of lecture content. *Journal of Instructional Psychology, 31*, 314–320.

Bahr, G. S. & Dansereau, D. F. (2001). Bilingual knowledge maps (BiK-Maps) in second-language vocabulary learning. *The Journal of Experimental Education, 70*, 5–24.

(2005). Bilingual knowledge maps (BiK-Maps) as a presentation format: Delayed recall and training effects. *The Journal of Experimental Education, 73*, 101–118.

Barnett, J. E., DiVesta, F. J., & Rogozinski, J. T. (1981). What is learned in note taking? *Journal of Educational Psychology, 73*, 181–192.

Benton, S. L., Kiewra, K. A., Whitfill, J. M., & Dennison, R. (1993). Encoding and external-storage effects on writing processes. *Journal of Educational Psychology, 85*, 267–280.

Bereiter, C. & Scardamalia, M. (1982). From conversation to composition: The role of instruction in a developmental process. In R. Glaser (ed.), *Advances in instruction*, Vol. 2 (pp. 1–64). Hillsdale, NJ: Lawrence Erlbaum.

(1987). *The psychology of written composition*. Hillsdale, NJ: Lawrence Erlbaum.

Berninger, V. (2012). *Past, present, and future contributions of cognitive writing research to cognitive psychology*. New York: Psychology Press.

Berninger, V. W., Abbott, R. D., Jones J., Wolf, B. J., Gould, L., Anderson-Youngstrom, M., Shimada, S., & Apel, K. (2006). Early development of language by hand: Composing-, reading-, listening-, and speaking- connections, three letter writing modes, and fast mapping in spelling. *Developmental Neuropsychology, 29*, 61–92.

Berninger, V. W. & Richards, T. L. (2012). The writing brain: Coordinating sensory/motor, language, and cognitive systems in working memory. In V. W. Berninger (ed.), *Past, present, and future contributions of cognitive writing research to cognitive psychology*. London: Psychology Press.

Berninger, V. W. & Swanson, H. L. (1994). Modifying Hayes and Flower's model of skilled writing to explain beginning and developing writing. In E. Butterfield (ed.),

Children's writing: Toward a process theory of the development of skilled writing (pp. 57–81). Greenwich, CT: JAI Press.

Blair, A. (2004). Note taking as an art of transmission. *Critical Inquiry, 31*, 85–107.

Bouwmeester, S. & Verkoeijen, P. P. J. L. (2011). Why do some children benefit more from testing than others? Gist trace processing to explain the testing effect. *Journal of Memory and Language, 65*(1), 32–41. https://doi.org/10.1016/j.jml.2011.02.005

Boyle, J. R. (2010a). Note-taking skills of middle school students with and without learning disabilities. *Journal of Learning Disabilities, 43(6)*, 530–540.

    (2010b). Strategic note-taking for middle-school students with learning disabilities in science classes. *Learning Disability Quarterly*, 33, 93–109.

    (2012). Note-taking and students with learning disabilities: Challenges and solutions. *Learning Disabilities Research and Practice*, 27, 90–101. https://doi.org/10.1111/j.1540-5826.2012.00354.x.

    (2013). Strategic note-taking for inclusive middle school science classrooms. *Remedial and Special Education, 34*(2), 78–90.

Boyle, J. R. & Rivera, T. Z. (2012). Note-taking techniques for students with disabilities: A systematic review of the research. *Learning Disability Quarterly, 35*, 131–143. https://doi.org/10.1177/0731948711435794

Boyle, J. R. & Weishaar, M. (2001). The effects of a strategic note-taking technique on the comprehension and long term recall of lecture information for high school students with LD. *LD Research and Practice, 16*, 125–133.

Bretzing, B. H., Kulhavy, R. W., & Caterino, L. C. (1987). Notetaking by junior high students. *Journal of Educational Research, 80*, 359–362.

Brown, A. L. & Day, J. D. (1983). Macrorules for summarizing text: The development of expertise. *Journal of Verbal Learning and Verbal Behavior, 22*, 1–14.

Brown, A. L., Day, J. D., & Jones, R. S. (1983). The development of plans for summarizing text. *Child Development, 54*, 968–979.

Brown, P. C., Roediger, H. L., & McDaniel, M. A., (2014). *Make it stick: The science of successful learning*. New York: Belknap Press.

Brown, A. L. & Smiley, S. S. (1977). Rating the importance of structural units of prose passages: A problem of metacognitive development. *Child Development, 48*, 1–8.

    (1978). The development of strategies for studying. *Child Development, 49*, 1076–1088.

Brown, A. L., Smiley, S. S., & Lawton, S. Q. C. (1978). The effects of experience on the selection of suitable retrieval cues for studying texts. *Child Development, 49*, 829–835.

Bui, D. C. & Myerson, J. (2014). The role of working memory abilities in lecture note-taking. *Learning and Individual Differences, 33*, 12–22.

Bui, D. C., Myerson, J., & Hale, S. (2013). Note-taking with computers: Exploring alternative strategies for improved recall. *Journal of Educational Psychology, 105*, 299–309. http://dx.doi.org/10.1037/a0030367

Butler, A. C. (2010). Repeated testing produces superior transfer of learning relative to repeated studying. *Journal of experimental psychology. Learning, memory, and cognition, 36*, 1118–33. https://doi.org/10.1037/a0019902

Butler, A. C., Marsh, E. J., Goode, M. K., & Roediger, H. L. (2006). When additional multiple-choice lures aid versus hinder later memory. *Applied Cognitive Psychology, 20*, 941–956. https://doi.org/10.1002/acp.1239

Chmielewski, T. L. & Dansereau, D. F. (1998). Enhancing the recall of text: Knowledge mapping training promotes implicit transfer. *Journal of Educational Psychology*, *90*, 407–413.

Cohn, E., Cohn, S., & Bradley, J. (1995). Notetaking, working memory, and learning in principles of economics. *Research in Economic Education*, *26*, 291–307.

Crawford, C. C. (1925). The correlation between lecture notes and quiz papers. *Journal of Educational Research*, *12*, 282–291.

Dahlstrom, E., Walker, J. D., & Dziuban, C. (2013). *ECAR study of undergraduate students and information technology, 2012*. Boulder, CO: Educause Center for Applied Research.

Dansereau, D. F. & Simpson, D. D. (2009). A picture is worth a thousand words: The case for graphic representations. *Professional Psychology: Research and Practice*, *40*, 104–110.

Dempster, F. N. (1988). The spacing effect: A case study in the failure to apply the results of psychological research. *American Psychologist*, *43*, 627–634.

DiCecco, V. M. & Gleason, M. M. *(*2002*)*. Using graphic organizers to attain relational knowledge from expository text. *Journal of Learning Disabilities*, *35*, 306–320.

DiVesta, F. J. & Gray, G. S. (1972). Listening and note taking. *Journal of Educational Psychology*, *64*, 321–325.

Dunkel, P. & Davy, S. (1989). The heuristic of lecture notetaking: Perceptions of American and international students regarding the value and practice of notetaking. *English for Specific Purposes*, 8, 33–50.

Dunlosky, J., Rawson, K. A., Marsh, E. J., Nathan, M. J., & Willingham, D. T. (2013). Improving students' learning with effective learning techniques: Promising directions from cognitive and educational psychology, *Psychological Science in the Public Interest*, *14*, 4–58.

Fisher, J. L. & Harris, M. B. (1973). Effect of note-taking and review on recall. *Journal of Educational Psychology*, *65*, 321–325.

Fitzgerald, J. M. (2000). Younger and older jurors: The influence of environmental supports on memory performance and decision making in complex trials. *The Journals of Gerontology Series B: Psychological Sciences and Social Sciences*, 55, 323–331. https://doi.org/10.1093/ geronb/55.6.P323

ForsterLee, L. & Horowitz, I. A. (1997). Enhancing juror competence in a complex trial. *Applied Cognitive Psychology*, *11*, 305–319. https://doi.org/10.1002/(SICI)1099-0720(199708)11:4%3C305::AID-ACP457%3E3.0.CO;2-J

ForsterLee, L., Horowitz, I. A., & Bourgeois, M. (1994). Effects of notetaking on verdicts and evidence processing in a civil trial. *Law and Human Behavior*, *18*, 567–578.

ForsterLee, L., Kent, L., & Horowitz, I. A. (2005). The cognitive effects of jury aids on decision-making in complex civil litigation. *Applied Cognitive Psychology*, *19*, 867–884. https://doi.org/10.1002/acp.1124

Frank, B. M. (1984). Effect of field independence-dependence and study technique on learning from lecture. *American Educational Research Journal*, *21*, 669–678.

Frank, B. M., Garlinger, D. K., & Kiewra, K. A. (1989). Use of embedded heading and intact online with videotaped instruction. *Journal of Educational Research*, *82*, 277–281.

Fried, C. B. (2008). In-class laptop use and its effects on student learning. *Computers and Education*, 50(3),906–914.

Gates, A. I. (1917). *Recitation as a factor in memorizing*. Archives of Psychology, 40th edn. (pp. 1–104). New York: The Science Press. Retrieved from http://books.google.com/

books/download/Recitation_as_a_factor_in_memorizing.pdf?id=Yin QHb3ZS8YC&output=pdf&sig=ACfU3U0dCJ-oJYvoQ6ESH62kUpQQVGL2vQ

Geary, D. C. (2011). Cognitive predictors of achievement growth in mathematics: A 5-year longitudinal study. *Developmental Psychology*, *47*, 1539–1552. http://dx.doi.org/10.1037/a0025510

Gleason, J. (2012). *An investigation of the lecture note-taking skills of adolescents with and without attention deficit/hyperactivity disorder: An extension of previous research.* Teachers College, Columbia University, New York City.

Glover, J. A. (1989). The "testing" phenomenon: Not gone but nearly forgotten. *Journal of Educational Psychology*, *81*, 392–399. https://doi.org/10.1037//0022–0663.81.3.392

Grabe, M., Christopherson, K., & Douglas, J. (2005). Providing introductory psychology students access to on-line notes: The relationship of note use to performance and class attendance. *Journal of Educational Technology Systems*, *33*, 295–308.

Greene, E. B. (1928). The relative effectiveness of lecture and individual reading as methods of college teaching, *Genetic Psychology Monographs*, *4*, 459–563.

Hadwin, A. F., Kirby, J. R., & Woodhouse, R. A. (1999). Individual differences in notetaking, summarization, and learning from lectures. *The Alberta Journal of Educational Research*, *45*, 1–17.

Hamaker, C. (1986). The effects of adjunct questions on prose learning. *Review of Educational Research*, *56*, 212–242.

Hamilton, S. L., Seibert, M. A., Gardner, R., & Talbert-Johnson, C. (2000). Using guided notes to improve the academic achievement of incarcerated adolescents with learning and behavior problems. *Remedial and Special Education*, *21*, 133–140.

Hartley, J. (2002). Notetaking in non-academic settings: a review. *Applied Cognitive Psychology*, *16*, 559–574.

Hartley, J. & Cameron, A. (1967). Some observations on the efficiency of lecturing. *Educational Review*, 20, 30–37.

Hartley, J. & Davies, I. K. (1978). Note-taking: A critical review. *Programmed Learning and Educational Technology*, *15*, 207–224.

Hayes, J. R. (1996). A new framework for understanding cognition and affect in writing. In C. M. Levy, & S. Ransdell (eds.), *The science of writing* (pp. 1–27). Mahwah, NJ: Lawrence Erlbaum.

Hembrooke, H. & Gay, G. (2003). The laptop and the lecture: The effects of multitasking in learning. *Journal of Computing in Higher Education*, *15*, 46–64.

Heuer L. & Penrod S. (1988). Increasing jurors' participation in trials: A field experiment with jury notetaking and question asking. *Law and Human Behavior*, *12*, 231–262.

(1994). Juror notetaking and question asking during trials. *Law and Human Behavior 18*, 121–150.

Hope, L., Eales, N., & Mirashi, A. (2014). Assisting jurors: Promoting recall of trial information through the use of a trial-ordered notebook. *Legal and Criminological Psychology*, *99*, 316–331. https://doi.org/10.1111/lcrp.12003

Horowitz, I. A. & Bordens, K. S. (2002). The effects of jury size, evidence complexity, and note taking on jury process and performance in a civil trial. *Journal of Applied Psychology*, *87*, 121–130. https://doi.org/10.1037/0021–9010.87.1.121

Horowitz, I. A. & ForsterLee, L. (2001). The effects of note-taking and trial transcript access on mock jury decisions in a complex civil trial. *Law and Human Behavior*, *25*, 373–391.

Horton, S. V., Lovitt, T. C., & Bergerud, D. (1990). The effectiveness of graphic organizers for three classifications of secondary students in content area classes. *Journal of Learning Disabilities, 23*, 12–22.Howe, M., J., A. (1974). The utility of taking notes as an aid to learning. *Educational Research, 16*, 222–227.

(1975). Taking notes and human learning. *Bulletin of the British Psychological Society, 28*, 158–161.

Hughes, C. A. & Suritsky, S. K. (1994). Note-taking skills of university students with and without learning disabilities. *Journal of Learning Disabilities, 27*, 20–24.

Hulme, C. & Snowling, M. J. (2011). Children's reading comprehension difficulties: Nature, causes, and treatments. *Current Directions in Psychological Science, 20*, 139–142.

Jing, H. G., Szpunar, K. K., & Schacter, D. L. (2016). Interpolated testing influences focused attention and improves integration of information during a video-recorded lecture. *Journal of Experimental Psychology: Applied, 22*, 305–318.

Kane, M. J., Smeekens, B. A., von Bastian, C. C. et al. (2017). A combined experimental and individual-differences investigation into mind wandering during a video lecture. *Journal of Experimental Psychology: General, 146*, 1649–1647.

Kang, S. H. K., McDermott, K. B., & Roediger, H. L. (2007). Test format and corrective feedback modify the effect of testing on long-term retention. *European Journal of Cognitive Psychology, 19*, 528–558. https://doi.org/10.1080/09541440601056620

Karpicke, J. D. & Blunt, J. R. (2011). Retrieval practice produces more learning than elaborative studying with concept mapping. *Science, 331*(6018), 772–775. https://doi.org/10.1126/science.1199327

Karpicke, J. D., Butler, A. C., & Roediger, H. L. (2009). Metacognitive strategies in student learning: Do students practice retrieval when they study on their own? *Memory, 17*, 471–9. https://doi.org/10.1080/09658210802647009

Kaufman, D. F., Zhao, R., & Yang, Y-S. (2011). Effects of online note taking formats and self-monitoring prompts on learning from online text: Using technology to enhance self-regulated learning. *Contemporary Educational Psychology, 36*, 313–322.

Kay, R. H. & Lauricella, S. (2011). Unstructured vs. structured use of laptops in higher education. *Journal of Information Technology Education, 10*, 33–42.

(2014). Investigating the Benefits and Challenges of Using Laptop Computers in Higher Education Classrooms. *Canadian Journal of Learning and Technology, 40*, 1–25.

Kiewra, K. A (1983). The process of review: A levels of processing approach. *Contemporary Educational Psychology, 8*, 366–374.

(1985a). Investigating note-taking and review: A depth of processing alternative. *Educational Psychologist, 20*, 23–32.

(1985b). A review of note-taking: The encoding-storage paradigm and beyond. *Educational Psychology Review, 1*, 147–172.

(1985c). Students' notetaking behaviors and the efficacy of providing the instructor's notes for review. *Contemporary Educational Psychology, 10*, 378–386.

(1985d). Learning from a lecture: An investigation of notetaking, review, and attendance at a lecture. *Human Learning, 4*, 73–77.

(1987). Notetaking and review: The research and its implications. *Instructional Science, 16*, 233–249.

(1989). A review of note-taking: The encoding-storage paradigm and beyond. *Educational Psychology Review, 1*, 147–172.

(1991). Aids to lecture learning. *Educational Psychologist, 26*, 37–53.

(2016). Note taking on trial: A legal application of note-taking research. *Educational Psychology Review, 28,* 377–384. https://doi.org/10.1007/s10648-015-9353-z

Kiewra, K. A. & Benton, S. L. (1988). The relationship between information processing ability and notetaking. *Contemporary Educational Psychology, 13,* 33–44.

Kiewra, K. A., Benton, S. L., Kim, S.-I., Risch, N., & Christensen, M. (1995). Effects of note-taking format and study technique on recall and relational performance. *Contemporary Educational Psychology, 13,* 33–44.

Kiewra, K. A., Benton, S. L., & Lewis, L. B. (1987). Qualitative aspects of notetaking and their relationship with information-processing ability and academic achievement. *Journal of Instructional Psychology, 14,* 110–117.

Kiewra, K. A., DuBois, N. F., Christensen, M., Kim, S.-I., & Lindberg, N. (1989). A more equitable account of the note-taking functions in learning from lecture and from text. *Instructional Sciences, 18,* 217–232.

Kiewra, K. A., DuBois, N. F., Christian, D., & McShane, A. (1988). Providing study notes: Comparison of three types of notes for review. *Journal of Educational Psychology, 80,* 595–597.

Kiewra, K. A., DuBois, N. F., Christian, D. et al. (1991). Note-taking functions and techniques. *Journal of Educational Psychology, 83,* 240–245.

Kiewra, K. A. & Fletcher, H. J. (1984). The relationship between levels of note-taking and achievement. *Human Learning, 3,* 273–280.

Kiewra, K. A. & Frank, B. M. (1988). Encoding and external-storage effects of personal lecture notes, skeletal notes, and detailed notes for field-independent and field-dependent learners. *Journal of Educational Research, 81,* 143–148.

Kiewra, K. A. & Mayer, R. E. (1997). Effects of advanced organizers and repeated presentations on students learning. *Journal of Experimental Education, 65,* 147–159.

Kiewra, K. A., Mayer, R. E., Christensen, M., Kim, S., & Risch, N. (1991). Effects of repetition on recall and note-taking: Strategies for learning from lectures. *Journal of Educational Psychology, 83,* 120–123.

King, A. (1992). Comparison of self-questioning, summarizing, and notetaking-review as strategies for learning from lectures. *American Educational Research Journal, 29,* 303–323.

Kintsch, W. (1998). *Comprehension: A paradigm for cognition.* Cambridge: Cambridge University Press.

Kintsch, W. J. & Vipond, D. (1979). Reading comprehension and readability in educational practice and psychological theory. In L. Nilsson (Ed.), *Perspectives on memory search* (pp. 325–366). Hillsdale, NJ: Lawrence Erlbaum.

Knight, L. J. & McKelvie, S. J. (1986). Effects of attendance, note taking and review on memory for a lecture: Encoding vs. external storage function of notes. *Canadian Journal of Behavioral Science, 18,* 52–61.

Kobayashi, K. (2005). What limit the encoding effect of note-taking? A meta-analytic examination. *Contemporary Educational Psychology, 30,* 242–262.

(2006). Combined effects of notetaking/-reviewing on learning and the enhancement through interventions: A meta-analytic review. *Contemporary Educational Psychology, 26,* 459–477.

Kraushaar, J. M. & Novak, D. C. (2010). Examining the effects of student multitasking with laptops during the lecture. *Journal of Information Systems Education, 21,* 241–251.

Landrum, R. E. (2010). Faculty and student perceptions of providing instructor lecture notes to students: Match or mismatch? *Journal of Instructional Psychology, 37,* 216–221.

Lazarus, B. D. (1993). Guided notes: Effects with secondary and post secondary students with mild disabilities. *Education and Treatment of Children, 16*, 272–289.

Locke, E. A. (1977). An empirical study of lecture notetaking among college students. *Journal of Educational Research, 77*, 93–99.

Maddox, H. & Hoole, E. (1975). Performance decrement in the lecture. *Educational Review, 28*, 17–30.

Maqsud, M. (1980). Effects of personal lecture notes and teacher-notes on recall of university students. *British Journal of Educational Psychology, 50*, 289–294.

McCutchen, D. (2000). Knowledge, processing, and working memory: Implications for a theory of writing. *Educational Psychologist, 35*, 13–23.

  (2012). Phonological, orthographic, and morphological word-level skills supporting multiple levels of the writing process. In V. Berninger (ed.), *Past, present, and future contributions of cognitive writing research to cognitive psychology*. New York: Psychology Press.

McCutchen, D., Covill, A., Hoyne, S. H., & Mildes, K. (1994). Individual differences in writing: Implications of translating fluency. *Journal of Educational Psychology, 86*, 256–266.

McDaniel, M. A., Agarwal, P. K., Huelser, B. J., McDermott, K. B., & Roediger, H. L. III (2011). Test-enhanced learning in a middle school science classroom: The effects of quiz frequency and placement. *Journal of Educational Psychology, 103*, 399–414. http://dx.doi.org/10.1037/a0021782

McDaniel, M. A., Anderson, J. L., Derbish, M. H., & Morrisette, N. (2007). Testing the testing effect in the classroom. *European Journal of Cognitive Psychology, 19*, 494–513.

McIntyre, S. (1992). Lecture notetaking, information processing, and academic achievement. *Journal of College Reading and Learning, 25*, 7–17.

Moore, D. W. & Readence, J. E. (1984). A quantitative and qualitative review of graphic organizer research. *Journal of Educational Research, 78*, 11–17.

Moos, D. C. & Azevedo, R. (2008). Self-regulated learning with hypermedia: The role of prior domain knowledge. *Contemporary Educational Psychology, 33*, 270–298.

Morgan, C. H., Lilly, J. D., & Boreham, N. C. (1988). Learning from lectures: The effect of varying detail in lecture handouts to note-taking and recall. *Applied Cognitive Psychology, 2*, 115–122.

Mueller, P. A. & Oppenheimer, D. M. (2014). The pen is mightier than the keyboard: Advantages of longhand over laptop note taking. *Psychological Science, 25*, 1159–1168.

Mulcahy-Ernt, P. I. & Caverly, D. C. (2009). Strategic study-reading. In R. F. Flippo, & D. C. Caverly (eds.), *Handbook of college reading and study strategy research*, 2nd edn (pp. 177–198). New York: Routledge.

Neef, N. A., McCord, B. E., & Ferreri, S. J. (2006). Effects of guided notes versus completed notes during lectures on college students' quiz performance. *Journal of Applied Behavior Analysis, 39*, 123–130.

Nesbit, J. C. & Adesope, O. O. (2006). Learning with concept and knowledge maps: A meta-analysis. *Review of Educational Research, 76*, 413–448.

Nye, P. (1978). Student variables in relations to note-taking during a lecture. *Programmed Learning and Educational Technology, 15*, 196–200.

Oefinger, L. M. (2014). *The lecture note-taking skills of adolescents with and without a learning disabilities. Teachers College*, Columbia University, New York City.

O'Donnell, A. M. & Adenwalla, D. (1991). Using cooperative learning and concept maps with deaf college students. In D. S. Martin (ed.), *Advances in cognition, learning, and deafness* (pp. 348–355). Washington, DC: Gallaudet University Press.

O'Donnell, A. M., Dansereau, D. F., & Hall, R. H. (2002). Knowledge maps as scaffolds for cognitive processing. *Educational Psychology Review, 14*, 71–86.

Olive, T., Alves, R. A., & Castro, S. L. (2009). Cognitive processes in writing during pauses and execution periods. *European Journal of Cognitive Psychology, 21*, 758–785.

Olive, T. & Kellogg, R. T. (2002). Concurrent activation of high- and low-level production processes in written composition. *Memory and Cognition, 30*, 594–600.

Palmatier, R. A. & Bennett, J. M. (1974). Notetaking habits of college students. *Journal of Reading, 18*, 215–218.

Patterson, M. E., Dansereau, D. F., & Newbern, D. (1992). Effects of communication aids and strategies on cooperative teaching. *Journal of Educational Psychology, 84*, 453–461.

Peper, R. J. & Mayer, R. E. (1978). Note taking as a generative activity. *Journal of Educational Psychology, 70*, 514–522. https://doi.org/10.1037/0022–0663.70.4.514

(1986). Generative effects of note-taking during science lectures. *Journal of Educational Psychology, 78*, 34–38. https://doi.org/10.1037/0022–0663.78.1.34

Peverly, S. T. (2006). The Importance of handwriting speed in adult writing. *Developmental Neuropsychology, 29*, 197–216.

Peverly, S. T., Brobst, K., Graham, M., & Shaw, R. (2003). College adults are not good at self-regulation: A study on the relationship of self-regulation, note-taking, and test-taking. *Journal of Educational Psychology, 95*, 335–346.

Peverly, S. T., Garner, J. K., & Vekaria, P. C. (2014). Both handwriting speed and selective attention are important to lecture note-taking. *Reading and Writing: An Interdisciplinary Journal, 27*, 1–30. https://doi.org/10.1007/s11145-013–9431-x

Peverly, S. T., Ramaswamy, V., Brown, C. et al. (2007). What predicts skill in lecture note taking? *Journal of Educational Psychology, 99*, 167–180.

Peverly, S. T. & Sumowski, J. F. (2012).What variables predict quality of text notes and are text notes related to performance on different types of tests? *Applied Cognitive Psychology*, 26: 104–117. https://doi.org/10.1002/acp.1802.

Peverly, S. T., Vekaria, P. C., Reddington, L. A. Sumowski, J. F. Johnson, K. R., & Ramsay, C. M. (2013). The relationship of handwriting speed, working memory, language comprehension and outlines to lecture Note-taking and Test-taking among college students. *Applied Cognitive Psychology, 27*, 115–126. https://doi.org/10.1002/acp.2881

Peverly, S. T. & Wood R. (2001). The effects of adjunct questions and feedback on improving the reading comprehension skills of learning-disabled adolescents. *Contemporary Educational Psychology, 26*, 25–43.

Piolat, A., Olive, T., & Kellogg, R. T. (2005). Cognitive effort during note taking. *Applied Cognitive Psychology, 19*, 291–312.

Pyc, M. A. & Rawson, K. A. (2010). Why testing improves memory: Mediator effectiveness hypothesis. *Science, 330*(6002), 335. https://doi.org/10.1126/science.1191465

Rayner, K., Foorman, B. R., Perfetti, C. A., Pesetsky, D., & Seidenberg, M. S. (2001). How psychological science informs the teaching of reading. *Psychological Science in the Public Interest, 2*, 31–74.

Reddington, L. A., Peverly, S. T., & Block, C. J. (2015). An examination of some of the cognitive and motivation variables related to gender differences in lecture note-taking. *Reading and Writing: An Interdisciplinary Journal*, 28, 1155–1185. https://doi.org/10.1007/s11145-015-9566-z

Reimer, J. R., Brimhall, E., Cao, C., & O'Reilly, K. (2009). Empirical user studies inform the design of an e-notetaking and information assimilation system for students in higher education. *Computers and Education*, 52, 893–913.

Rickards, J. P. & Friedman, F. (1978). The encoding versus the external storage hypothesis in note taking. *Contemporary Educational Psychology*, 3, 136–143.

Richards, T., Peverly, S., Wolf, A., Abbott, R., Tanimoto, S., Thompson, R., Nagy, W., & Berninger, V. (2016). Idea units in notes and summaries for read texts by keyboard and pencil in middle childhood students with specific learning disabilities: Cognitive and brain findings. *Trends in Neuroscience and Education*, 5, 146–155. http://dx.doi.org/10.1016/j.tine.2016.07.005

Robinson, D. H. (1998). Graphic organizers as aids to text learning. *Reading Research and Instruction*, 37, 85–105.

Roediger, H. L., Agarwal, P. K., McDaniel, M. A., & McDermott, K. B. (2011). Test-enhanced learning in the classroom: long-term improvements from quizzing. *Journal of Experimental Psychology. Applied*, 17, 382–95. https://doi.org/10.1037/a0026252

Roediger, H. L. & Karpicke, J. D. (2006a). The power of testing memory. *Perspectives on Psychological Science*, 17, 181–210. https://doi.org/10.1111/j.1745–6916.2006.00012.x (2006b). Test-enhanced learning: taking memory tests improves long-term retention. *Psychological Science*, 17, 249–55. https://doi.org/10.1111/j.1467–9280.2006.01693.x

Rohwer, W. D. (1984). An invitation to a developmental psychology of studying. In F. J. Morrison, C. A. Lord, & D. P. Keating (eds.), *Advances in applied developmental psychology*, Vol. 1 (pp. 1–57). New York: Academic Press.

Rosenhan, D. L., Eisner, S. L., & Robinson, R. J. (1994). Notetaking can aid juror recall. *Law and Human Behavior*, 18, 53–61.

Rosenshine, B., Meister, C., & Chapman, S. (1996). Teaching students to generate questions: A review of the intervention studies. *Review of Educational Research*, 66, 181–221.

Rothkopf, E. Z. (1996). Control of mathemagenic activities. In D. H. Jonassen (ed.), *Handbook of research for educational communications and technology* (pp. 879–896). New York: Simon & Schuster and Macmillan.

Ruhl, K. L. (1996). Does nature of student activity during lecture pauses affect notes and immediate recall of college students with learning disabilities? *Journal of Postsecondary education and Disability*, 12, 16–27.

Ruhl, K. L., Hughes, C. A., & Gajar, A. H. (1990). Efficacy of the pause procedure for enhancing learning disabled and nondisabled college students' long- and short-term recall of facts presented through lecture. *Learning Disability Quarterly*, 13, 55–64.

Ruhl, K. L., Hughes, C. A., & Schloss, P. J. (1987). Using the pause procedure to enhance lecture recall, *Teacher Education and Special Education*, 10, 14–18.

Ruhl, K. L. & Suritsky, S. (1995). The pause procedure and/or an outline: Effect on Immediate free recall and lecture notes taken by college students with disabilities. *Learning Disability Quarterly*, 18, 2–11.

Rummer, R, Schweppe, J., Gerst, K., & Wagner, S. (2017). Is testing a more effective strategy than note-taking? *Journal of Experimental Psychology*, 23, 293–300.

Samuels, S. J. & Farstrup, A. E. (eds.) (2011). *What research has to say about reading instruction*. Newark, DE: International Reading Association.

Sana, F., Weston, T., & Cepeda, N. J. (2013). Laptop multitasking hinders classroom learning for both users and nearby peers. *Computers and Education, 62*, 24–31.

Schacter, D. L. & Szpunar, K. K. (2015). Enhancing attention and memory during video-recorded lectures. *Scholarship of Teaching and Learning in Psychology, 1*, 60–71.

Shernoff, D. J., Csikszentmihalyi, M., Schneider, B., & Shernoff, E. S. (2003). Student engagement in high school classrooms from the perspective of flow theory. *School Psychology Quarterly, 18*, 158–176. http://dx.doi.org/10.1521/scpq.18.2.158.21860

Shimmerlick, S. M. & Nolan, J. D. (1976). Organization and the recall of prose. *Journal of Educational Psychology, 68*, 779–786.

Snow, C. (2002). (ed.) *Reading for understanding: Toward an R & D program in reading comprehension.* Santa Monica, CA: Rand.

Spitzer, H. F. (1939). Studies in retention. *Journal of Educational Psychology, 30*, 641–656.

Stanovich, K. E. (1986). Matthew effects in reading: Some consequences of individual differences in the acquisition of literacy. *Reading Research Quarterly, 21*, 360–407.

Stull, A. T. & Mayer, R. E. (2007). Learning by doing versus learning by viewing: Three experimental comparisons of learner-generated versus author-provided graphic organizers. *Journal of Educational Psychology, 99*, 808–820.

Summers, J. & Catarro, F. (2003). Assessment of handwriting speed and factors influencing written output of university students in examinations. *Australian Occupational Therapy Journal, 50*, 148–157.

Szpunar, K. K., Jing, H. G., & Schacter, D. L. (2014). Overcoming overconfidence in learning from video-recorded lectures: Implications for online education. *Journal of Applied Research in Memory & Cognition, 3*, 161–164. http://dx.doi.org/10.1016/j.jarmac.2014.02.001

Szpunar, K. K., Khan, N. Y., & Schacter, D. L. (2013). Interpolated memory tests reduce mind wandering and improve learning of online lectures. *Proceedings of the National Academy of Sciences of the United States of America, 110*, 6313–6317. http://dx.doi.org/10.1073/pnas.1221764110

Thomas, G. S. (1978). Use of students notes and lecture summaries as study guides for recall. *Journal of Educational Research, 71*, 316–319.

Thomas, J. W., Iventosch, L., Rohwer, W. D. (1987). Relationships among student characteristics, study activities, and achievement as a function of course characteristics. *Contemporary Educational Psychology, 12*, 344–364.

Thorley, C., Baxter, R.E., & Lorek, J. (2016). The impact of note taking style and note availability at retrieval on mock jurors' recall and recognition of trial information. *Memory, 24*, 560–574.

Titsworth, B. (2004). Students' notetaking: The effects of teacher immediacy and clarity. *Communication Education, 53*, 305–320.

Titsworth, B. S. & Kiewra, K. A. (2004). Spoken organizational lecture cures and student notetaking as facilitators of student learning. *Contemporary Educational Psychology, 29*, 447–461.

Titsworth, S. (2001). The effects of teacher immediacy, use of organizational lecture cues, and students' notetaking on cognitive learning. *Communication Education, 50*, 283–297.

Tomes, J. L., Wasylkiw, L., & Mockler, B. (2011). Studying for success: Diaries of students' study behaviours. *Educational Research and Evaluation, 17*, 1–12. https://doi.org/10.1080/13803611.2011.563087

Trevors, G., Duffy, M., & Azevedo, R. (2014). Note-taking within MetaTutor: Interaction between an intelligent tutoring system and prior knowledge on note-taking and learning. *Educational Technology Research and Development*, *62*, 507–528.

Van Etten, S., Freebern, G., & Pressley, M. (1997). College students' beliefs about exam preparation. *Contemporary Educational Psychology*, *22*, 192–212.

Van Meter, P., Yokoi, L., & Pressley, M. (1994). College students' theory of note taking derived from their perceptions of note taking. *Journal of Educational Psychology*, *86*, 323–338.

Vekaria, P. C. & Peverly, S. T. (2018). Lecture note-taking in postsecondary students with self-reported attention-deficit/hyperactivity disorder. *Reading and Writing: An Interdisciplinary Journal*. 31, 1551–1573, https://doi.org/10.1007/s11145-018-9849-2

Vellutino, F. R., Fletcher, J. M., Snowling, M. J., & Scanlon, D. M. (2004). Specific reading disability (dyslexia): What have we learned in the past four decades? *Journal of Child Psychology and Psychiatry*, *45*, 2–40.

Vogler, K. (2006). Impact of a high school graduation examination on Tennessee science teachers' instructional practices. *American Secondary Education*, *35*, 35–57.

Weinstein, Y., McDermott, K. B., & Roediger, H. L. (2010). A comparison of study strategies for passages: rereading, answering questions, and generating questions. *Journal of Experimental Psychology. Applied*, *16*, 308–16. https://doi.org/10.1037/a0020992

Wiegmann, D. A., Dansereau, D. F., & McCagg, E. C., Rewey, K. L., & Pitre, U. (1992). Effects of knowledge map characteristics on information processing. *Contemporary Educational Psychology*, *17*, 136–155.

Winne, P. H. & Hadwin, A. F. (2009). Studying as self-regulation. In D. J. Hacker, J. Dunlosky, & A. C. Graesser (eds.), *Metacognition in educational theory and practice* (pp. 277–304). New York: Routledge.

Witkin, H. A. (1959). The perception of the upright. *Scientific American*, *200*, 50–56

Wurst, C., Smarkola, C., & Gaffney, M. A. (2008). Ubiquitous laptop usage in higher education: Effects on student achievement, student satisfaction, and constructivist measures in honors and traditional class-rooms. *Computers & Education*, *51*(4), 1766–1783. https://doi.org/10.1016/j.compedu.2008.05.006

Yamamoto, K. (2007). Banning laptops in the classroom: Is it worth the hassle? *Journal of Legal Education*, *57*, 477–520.

14 Multiple-Text Comprehension

Jean-François Rouet, M. Anne Britt, and Anna Potocki

Multiple-text comprehension refers to the psychological resources and processes involved in readers' use of two or more texts in order to achieve their purposes. Multiple-text comprehension has emerged as a new and important avenue for discourse comprehension research and its educational applications. There are both practical and theoretical reasons for investigating multiple-text comprehension as a complex cognitive skill. At a practical level, the increased dissemination of information through print and electronic media has made it more common for readers to make use of several texts in order to achieve their goals, whether in school, work, or personal contexts. The advent of the Web and search engines has further established multiple-text comprehension as a common, if not dominant paradigm for reading.

At a theoretical level, a simple glance at multiple texts and how people read them is enough to raise a number of new and intriguing questions. One question concerns the texts themselves and how they make sense as a set. In this chapter, we refer to "multiple texts" as sets of texts that refer to a common topic (for instance, "the Battle of Lexington," "the growth of large cities throughout the world," or "the organization of a birthday party"). An important dimension of multiple texts is that each item in the set corresponds to a distinct source (i.e., where the text comes from). The construct of a source is complex and multifaceted. It involves information about the author, the context of production, and the dissemination medium. In addition, texts within a set may pertain to different genres, use different styles, address different readerships, and contain information at various levels of quality and accuracy. Finally, multiple texts are related through a number of relationships such as reference (one text refers to another), redundancy (the same piece of information can be found in several texts), and discrepancy (information in one text contradicts information in another text). A full grammar of sources, genres, and the relationships between items in a set of text is yet to be formulated. These relationships, however, extend beyond the coherence and cohesion principles that are employed in analyzing single texts (for discussions, see Perfetti, Rouet, & Britt, 1999; Rouet & Britt, 2014; Wineburg, 1994).

Another question concerns readers' goals and strategies when they read multiple texts as opposed to a single text. When reading multiple texts, people do not typically

Preparation of this chapter was supported in part through grant ANR – 17-CE28 SELEN from the French National Research Agency to the first and third authors.

pursue the goal of just accumulating information from one text to another, like they would do for instance when reading the chapters of a novel. Instead, readers of multiple texts may decide on a particular reading order; they may selectively scan the texts they choose to read, ignoring some passages and focusing on others; they may draw inferences not just within but also across the texts; and they may have to draw specific connections that are seldom found within single texts. For instance, readers may note that information in Text A opposes or contradicts information in Text B. Unlike within-text contradictions (which usually reflect some kind of mistake or anomaly), contradictions across texts are part of a normal state of affairs, whereby different authors may provide different and sometimes conflicting accounts of a situation as a function of their access to information, expertise in the domain, communicative intent, conflict of interest, and so forth. How readers manage to make sense of sets of texts that lack cohesiveness and perhaps include straight contradictions is an issue of great theoretical interest.

These issues have triggered attempts to expand comprehension theory in order to provide a full description of the information conveyed in multiple text sets and to account for the cognitive processes of selecting, evaluating, and integrating information from multiple texts, including readers' detection and handling of intertextual inconsistencies. This chapter seeks to provide an overview of how the domain has developed, the main conceptual underpinning of current theories, and what is known regarding the role of text, task, and reader dimensions on the comprehension of multiple texts. We start with a simple example, then we review the development of the field, and, finally, we examine some empirical evidence regarding factors that affect multiple-text comprehension.

A Simple Case of Multiple-Text Comprehension

As an example of the pervasiveness of multiple texts in current reading practice, consider this anecdote, which is based on actual facts. Ulysses is a French eleven-year-old boy who lives in a midsize town and attends 6th grade at a local public middle school. His geography teacher has started a series of classes on urban expansion in developed vs. less developed countries, in compliance with the national curriculum. During the first week, the class worked on the case of New York City, discussing constructs such as inner city vs. suburbs, daily migration, poverty vs. gentrification, as well as challenges such as traffic jams and waste management. On the second week, the class worked on the case of the Indian megalopolis of Mumbai. One evening, Ulysses came back from school with a homework assignment made of a worksheet containing a list of questions with references to pages of a Web-based electronic geography textbook (lelivrescolaire, 2017), which features several documents about Mumbai. One of Ulysses' parents (who also happens to be a coauthor of this chapter) helped him with the assignment.

Table 14.1 shows excerpts from two pages of the electronic textbook. Other pages not reprinted here show photographs of a very poor neighborhood and a gentrified historical district as well as definitions of words like "slum."

Table 14.1 *Two texts that form part of a 6th grade geography reading assignment. The texts are featured on two pages of an electronic textbook. The title* Getting housing in Mumbai *is displayed at the top of each page (our adaptation from French)*

Getting housing in Mumbai
Asma lives in a slum in Mumbai.
Shabbir (27), Asma and their two daughters live in a sort of solidified slum, in which each family has a single room without running water [. . .]. "When I go visit my relatives in the village, after some time I get bored, and I miss the city. At least here we have electricity and basic services. In my village there is nothing, my children get sick easily [. . .]" "In Mumbai, you will find a doctor or a grocery store at any corner [. . .]. That is also a difference between Mumbai and the other places."
(the passage below appears on a separate page)
Getting housing in Mumbai
Jyotsna Kunwar, 47, is a housewife in the Tardeo neighborhood.
Last December, Jyotsna Kunwar moved in a sumptuous 4-room apartment of 2,300 sq. ft. at the 22nd floor of the Imperial Building. She loves living in this 60-floor tower, the highest in India, inaugurated in 2010. "It could not be better. All our needs are taken care of [. . .]." From high-end security services to separate housing for the servants, the residents are entitled to first-class services.

The following are among the questions Ulysses had to answer in reference to the two texts presented in Table 14.1:

> "'Asma lives in a slum in Mumbai' What kind of population lives in this slum? Why don't the residents want to leave?"
> "By comparing Asma's testimony with that of Jyotsna Kunwar, what parallel can you draw with the organization of New York City?"

The first two questions are similar to simple literal and inference questions a reader may answer after reading a single text (Kintsch, 1988). The kind of population that lives in the slum is not specified but can be easily deducted from the fact that Asma's house has only one room and no running water, the pictures, and the definition of a slum: Like the other residents of the slum, Asma and her family are very poor. The reasons why Asma and her family do not want to leave the slum are also partly stated in the text: In comparison to the village where the family probably comes from, in the slum, they have access to basic services such as electric power, a doctor, and a grocery store nearby. What the text does not say explicitly is why Asma would not consider living in a better neighborhood in Mumbai but that can be explained in reference to the first question.

The third question, however, requires more than extracting and interpreting information from a single passage. In fact, the student is explicitly asked to compare information across two different texts and then to relate this comparison to the lesson learned a week before. So, what sort of challenge does a 6th grader face when comparing Asma's and Jyotsna's testimonies and drawing a comparison with what they have learned about New York City? First, they have to understand that each text conveys the perspective of a different person and that these perspectives reflect very different life experiences. Although, in this case, the persons and the perspectives seem quite explicit and easy to represent, some of their characteristics are left partly implicit. For instance, the respective incomes of Asma and Jyotsna have to be inferred from the description of where they live.

Another important challenge in comprehending multiple texts is the need for the reader to draw connections between two paragraphs that do not share any common explicit reference. The fact that Tardeo is located in the giant city of Mumbai may be inferred based on pragmatic cues: All the documents are presented as part of a textbook section about the city of Mumbai, therefore it is unlikely that the author would bring a document about another city without explicitly telling the reader. However, not all developing readers will readily draw this type of inference. For instance, Ulysses initially thought that Jyotsna and Asma lived in two different cities of India. He somehow related "Tardeo" to the village that Asma mentions in her testimony. The parent-generated cue that Tardeo is a district of Mumbai did help him reinterpret (and solve) the whole task.

Comparing information across texts requires the reader to identify comparable dimensions. The page headers indicate that the topic is housing in Mumbai and, indeed, the two texts clearly indicate that they are describing places where people live ("live," "moved to"). Terms such as "slum," "single room," "without running water," on the one hand, and "sumptuous," "4-room," "first-class services," on the other hand, may help establish a contrast on a dimension of "wealth." However, the dimension has to be inferred since the texts contain no explicit statement regarding the respective level of wealth associated with the two descriptions of living conditions.

In the above example, the final task consists of relating the contrast between Asma and Jyotsna to a similar contrast that the students have previously learned about New York City. This will require either that the student has a very good memory about the previous week's lessons and assignments or a look back at the lecture notes, documents, and assignments received a week before. These requirements may bring additional challenges to most 6th grade students.

Even disregarding these additional challenges, this simple case (arguably among the simplest ones we could come up with) is enough to illustrate some of the specific reading processes involved in multiple-text comprehension: the need to identify sources and relate them to specific contents and the need to draw connections across texts in the absence of explicit cues. Note that other significant challenges, such as finding out whether the text is relevant to a particular question (in this case, both are), or whether the texts contain accurate and reliable information (in this case, both are assumed to), are not represented in this example. Put together, this simple case suggests that there is considerable interest at theoretical and practical levels in eliciting the specific types of knowledge and skills involved in comprehending multiple texts.

Research conducted over the past decades has contributed to developing theoretical accounts of these and other important aspects of multiple-text comprehension.

Cognitive Theories of Multiple-Text Comprehension

A New Field in Text Comprehension Research

Quite logically, research on text comprehension conducted within cognitive psychology during the 1970s and 1980s focused on single texts and simple memory tasks. As of February 2017, Google Scholar retrieved a mere fifty-eight references to articles published until 1990 and matching the phrases "multiple text" and "comprehension." Most of them had to do with order effects in multitext assessments, with mismatches such as "multiple-text sentences" or – more interestingly – with pedagogical discussions of multiple-text use in the classroom (in general few with data). Wineburg (1991) contributed one of the earliest empirical studies of readers' strategies when making sense of multiple texts. The participants were a small group of high school students attending Advanced Placement history classes and another small group of experienced history students and scholars. In comparison with the simple example outlined above, Wineburg gave his participants a rather challenging task that comprised reading seven documents about the Battle of Lexington with the purpose of (trying) "to understand what happened at Lexington Green on the morning of April 19, 1775." Participants also rated each document for its usefulness and trustworthiness. The participants then received another task involving a set of pictures about the same event. Among a host of critical observations, Wineburg elicited three heuristics used by historians as they read the documents: sourcing (i.e., actively seeking and using information about who wrote the text), corroboration (relating information from various texts for confirmation), and contextualization (relating text information to one's prior knowledge of the situation). The high school participants seldom made use of these heuristics. Instead, they tended to read the texts linearly and in isolation, and showed a strong reliance on the textbook (even though in this case the textbook contained a factual mistake, as noted by several of the historians). Wineburg's (1991) seminal study was an early sign of a then-burgeoning interest for reading situations involving more than one text, an interest partly stimulated by the development of computer-based text presentation and the advent of hypertext and multimedia technologies (Rouet et al., 1996).

In recent decades, multiple-text comprehension has received growing interest, to become an acknowledged new area of research in scientific conferences and journals. As of February 2017, Google Scholar retrieved close to 1,500 publications matching the phrases "multiple text" and "comprehension" and published after 1990, a 2,500 percent increase compared with the period before 1991. Although the figure partly reflects a general increase in scholarly publications, it is impressive compared with other topics in discourse research. For instance, in the same period of time, publications matching the phrase "sentence comprehension" grew by only 20 percent.

Thus, a new line of research has emerged in an attempt to elicit the specific cognitive processes at work in the comprehension of multiple texts. Researchers have addressed two aspects of the issue. The first aspect concerns the mental representations a reader has to build when reading information from multiple texts, how these representations differ from single-text comprehension, and what type of reader resources they draw on. The second type focuses on the processes at work during the reading of multiple texts: which stages and processes do readers go through and, again, how these stages and processes differ compared with the sustained reading of a single passage. In the next sections, we review the main theoretical proposals that have emerged from research thus far.

The Importance of Source Information in Text Comprehension

Early research into multiple-text comprehension focused on what readers represent when they acquire information from a set of texts (Rouet et al., 1996; Wineburg, 1991). Perhaps one of the earliest and most significant outcomes of those early studies was a broader definition of what makes up the "meaning" of a text. Since the seminal works by psycholinguist Walter Kintsch and his colleagues in the 1970s and the creation of a technique to analyze the semantic contents of a text (Turner & Greene, 1977), researchers interested in text comprehension had tended to equate the meaning of a text with its propositional contents. This approach was perhaps reinforced by the frequent use of short narrative passages as stimuli in text comprehension experiments. As noted by Wineburg (1994), however, texts are rhetorical artifacts that emanate from a source and get communicated using some medium in the service of some communication intent. The source, the medium, the intent, and the propositional contents all contribute to the meaning of the text, considered as the outcome of a reader's active processing and inference production. In a meta-analysis of persuasion experiments, manipulations of source parameters such as expertise, trustworthiness, and attractiveness accounted for 9 percent of explained variance on a range of dependent measures (Wilson & Sherrell, 1993). Some of the studies included in the meta-analysis did use written texts as stimuli, suggesting that source effects are not limited to face-to-face interaction and extend to reading comprehension.

Wineburg's (1991) study found evidence that readers with expertise in the domain not only notice but actively seek source information as a means of enabling interpretive processes (i.e., the "sourcing heuristic"). Although younger and less knowledgeable readers do not exhibit such a heuristic, they do possess some source knowledge, as shown by their (over)reliance on information issued in a textbook as opposed to other types of sources (see also Bråten, Strømsø, & Salmerón, 2010). Rouet and colleagues (1996) asked college-level students with no specific experience in history to read sets of seven documents related to a specific aspect of the history of the Panama Canal, with the purpose of writing a short essay addressing a controversial question (e.g., "To what extent was the 1903 US military intervention in Panama justified?"). They found that students were able to tie some of the contents read to their respective sources (e.g., authors) in their postreading essay, as evidenced by their citation of the sources. Rouet and colleagues also observed that primary sources, i.e., texts whose authors were either participants or witnesses of the events, were more likely to be cited than second-hand accounts (Figure 14.1). Interestingly, there was never any explicit mention of the textbook as a source in students' essays.

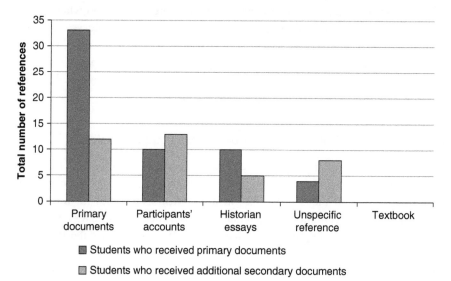

Figure 14.1 *References to documents in undergraduate students' short essays about historical controversies as observed in the study by Rouet et al. (1996, adapted with permission from the American Psychological Association)*

Note that the students who received additional secondary documents instead of primary documents could learn about the primary documents indirectly through their citation by secondary authors.

Thus, when faced with a demanding task involving a set of documents, university-level readers tend to hierarchize text information as a function of source features. Using a similar procedure, Rouet and colleagues (1997) observed that advanced history students were more prone to citing sources in their essays in comparison with psychology students matched for educational level. They concluded that as students gain expertise in a discipline (in this case, history), they acquire specific strategies to read, evaluate, and cite sources of information typical of that discipline. Discipline specialists can make use of discipline-relevant reading heuristics even though they may not have a lot of prior knowledge of the topic they are studying.

These studies suggest that source information plays a critical role when comprehending multiple texts because readers need to comprehend not just what is written but also who wrote it, when, and for what purpose, as well as a potentially long list of source features. Comprehending source information enables readers to index contents (i.e., Where did I read this?) and to integrate various pieces of discourse into coherent sets (i.e., Who says what on this issue?).

Integrating Information from Multiple Texts

In their seminal theory of (single-)text comprehension, Kintsch and van Dijk (1978) emphasized the importance of referential continuity for readers' integration of information across propositions, sentences, and paragraphs. The repetition of discourse objects (such as the name of a character, a place, an artifact) enables readers to connect semantic propositions into hierarchically organized networks. Subsequent research also found that narrative comprehension relies on readers' identification of causal links among events depicted in a text (Trabasso & van den Broek, 1985). Gaps in causal coherence tend to slow down and disrupt comprehension processes (Albrecht & O'Brien, 1993).

The crucial importance of cohesion (i.e., relations between linguistic textual elements such as sentences or paragraphs) and coherence (semantic relationships among agents, objects, and events in the situation described in the text) poses a problem for any theory of multiple-text comprehension. When shifting their attention from one text to another, readers almost always experience a gap in cohesion (see the example in Table 14.1). Moreover, multiple texts dealing with a given situation do not always provide coherent accounts. Readers have to handle issues ranging from minor discrepancies to blatant contradictions (Table 14.1 again offers a clear example of that phenomenon). And yet, even middle school students can achieve at least simple forms of multiple-text comprehension. Clearly, additional processes are at work to support the construction of a coherent mental representation despite the lack of cohesion and sometimes coherence across texts.

One of the earliest theories that attempted to account for readers' comprehension of multiple texts is the documents model framework by Perfetti and colleagues (1999). The documents model framework posits that under some circumstances readers encode information about where the text comes from (i.e., the source) in addition to the text contents per se. Source information may include a wide array of features, ranging from the name of the author to whether it is a book or a journal article, to its publication date, and to the intended audience and purpose (Britt et al., 1999). For instance, a reader may remember that "I have read a book chapter published in 2017 whose author is Anne Britt and whose purpose is to inform university students and scholarly audiences." This type of mental representation is called a "source node" in the documents model framework. Source nodes can be tied to the contents found in the text. For instance, the reader may remember that the chapter by Anne Britt discusses an anecdote about a 6th grader. Finally, source nodes can be connected to other source nodes, with "rhetorical predicates" such as corroborate, support, oppose, add to, and so forth. The representation of a set of sources (source nodes), together with their rhetorical predicates, is called an intertext model.

Among other benefits, building a documents model allows multiple-text readers to represent conflicting information without developing an inconsistent mental model, by "tagging" discrepant statements to their respective sources. However, the documents model is clearly less parsimonious that a mere situation model (i.e., representing the situation as described in the text(s) without retaining where the information comes from; van Dijk & Kintsch, 1983). Consequently, readers cannot be expected to routinely construct such elaborate models. Indeed, the evidence suggests that readers do not systematically encode source details or tie source nodes to specific contents. Instead, readers seem to operate on a selection of contents they need to tag (Britt et al., 1999) as a function of their perception of the task demands and most likely a range of other factors.

The precise circumstances under which readers will form a documents model as opposed to a simpler situation model remain in large part to be identified. However, over the past decades, empirical studies have come to identify a series of variables related to texts, tasks, and individuals that play a significant role in multiple-text comprehension. The next section highlights some of the main findings from that line of research.

Conditions That Affect Multiple-Text Comprehension

This section examines the conditions that influence readers' comprehension of multiple texts, considered as an integrated representation of the texts' sources and contents, with at least some selective tagging of content information onto the respective source and some linking across sources through rhetorical relationships such as "confirms," "supports," or "contradicts." We first review a range of text factors that promote readers' encoding and integration of source information; then we consider variations in multiple-text comprehension as a function of the task contexts; finally, we briefly review some key dimensions of individual differences. In the next section, we examine some instructional conditions that promote students' ability to comprehension multiple texts.

Text Factors

Let us consider a teenage history student who is given two text passages describing the same event, for instance "the construction of the Panama canal." Each text comes with some information about its source, such as the name of the author, the book or article the passage was excerpted from, when it was published and so forth. The student is asked to write a summary of the information acquired from the two texts. Let's assume that both texts convey in part the same information, for instance the year the construction started, how much time it took, the dimensions of the canal, and so forth. Let's further assume that one text focuses on the political circumstances surrounding the construction, whereas the other text focuses on the technical means needed to achieve the construction. How likely would it be for the student to remember precisely which information was present in both texts, which came uniquely from text A and which came from text B? In other words, how likely is the student to build a documents model in which the sources and the contents would be represented, with some links between sources and contents, so that the student could remember both the information and where it came from?

Both daily experience and research evidence suggest that under most circumstances the probability would be rather low. Just like Wineburg's (1991) high school students, nonexpert readers often treat source information as "peripheral" and tend to quickly forget it when they do not simple skip it on reading (or listening to) the materials. As a consequence, any link between the contents read and the source details is either not encoded or quickly forgotten. Memory for "who said what" might even decrease as readers or listeners process content information more deeply (see e.g., Braasch, McCabe, & Daniel, 2016; Jurica & Shinamura, 1999). In our example above, the average student might construct an integrated situation model of the canal construction and quickly forget which source they got the details from. Britt and colleagues (1999) called this type of memory representation a "mush" model.

The research to date suggests, however, that when reading for study purposes university-level readers spontaneously tag at least some information pieces to their respective source(s). This is the case, for instance, in history, when the source is a character involved in the events (i.e., an eyewitness account or a "primary source" as historians call it). As reviewed in the previous section, after reading multiple texts students are much more likely to cite a primary source in a postreading essay than any other type of document (for instance, a historian's essay or a textbook passage; Rouet et al., 1996). Students' preference for primary sources over other types of documents may come from the fact that the authors of primary sources are agents in the situation in addition to issuers of information about the situation. De Pereyra and colleagues (2014, Experiment 1) directly examined the effect of a source's "closeness" to the situation on readers' memory for the link between the source and what the source said in a short news story. Undergraduate students were given a set of short pieces of news with the task of rating the plausibility of the story as if they were screening it for the editor of a Web news agency. In half of the stories, the source was a participant close to the events; in the other half, the source was remote from the events (for instance, a commentator describing the events from a remote location). The participants were later asked to recall the source and a specific content detail in a fill-in-the-blank task, with the rest of the story as a recall cue. De Pereyra and colleagues found that close sources were more likely to be recalled than distant sources. Regardless of distance, however, sources were less likely to be retrieved than the specific details, confirming readers' tendency to overlook source information. To explain the better recall of close sources, De Pereyra and colleagues conjectured that a source's inclusion in the situation resulted in the creation of analogous types of links (Glenberg, Meyer, & Lindem, 1987) whereby the source was part of the mental model of the situation. At retrieval, these additional links between the source and the situation facilitated the recall of the source, compared with a source with no concrete links to the situation.

Based on a theoretical assumption by Britt and colleagues (1999), Braasch and colleagues (2012) tested whether two information sources that were featured within the same short text were more likely to be encoded when the sources disagreed with each other than when they agreed. The rationale was that source encoding would permit readers to restore coherence at a discourse level when the situation was conflicting or ambiguous, a core assumption of the documents model framework. Braasch and colleagues (2012) coined the phrase "Discrepancy-induced Source Comprehension," or DISC, to designate this process. Undergraduate students were asked to read short news stories presented on the screen of an eye tracker, with the goal of uttering a one-sentence summary of the story. In each critical story, two characters issued statements about a situation. For instance, a stage technician and an art critic each gave an account of the audience's response to an opera premiere. In half of the stories, the two sources provided consistent statements, whereas, in the other stories, their statements were discrepant (e.g., one claimed that the audience loved the show, whereas the other said that the audience hated it). Braasch and colleagues found that readers tended to look back to source phrases more often and for longer periods of time when the sources disagreed. Importantly, the increase in rereading was larger for source phrases compared with, for instance, the contents issued by the sources. The participants were also more likely to cite the sources in their summary of the story. Finally, the participants remembered the sources of discrepant stories better than the sources of consistent stories. Thus, contradiction seems to promote college-level readers' encoding and integration of source information. In terms of the document model framework, this finding can be interpreted as reflecting the organizing role of source information when information cannot be integrated in the form of a single, coherent situation model. In the example above, without encoding the sources the story would simply be incoherent, e.g., "the audience loved and hated the show." When tying the statements to their respective sources, readers manage to organize inconsistent information within a coherent discourse framework: "according to the art critic the audience loved the show, whereas, according to the stage technician, the audience hated it." Further evidence for the use of source information as a means to integrate discrepant information was reported by Rouet and colleagues (2016).

At this point, the reader may wonder if we are still talking about the comprehension of multiple texts or about multiple sources within single texts and whether that makes any difference. For instance, one may wonder whether presenting two conflicting views side by side in a short story artificially draws readers' attention to the conflict, magnifying the role of source information. In fact, there is some evidence that readers are even more prone to detecting conflict when information is presented in multiple as opposed to single texts. Britt and Aglinskas (2002, Experiment 3) asked high school students to study a historical topic through either a set of documents or a single integrated text in order to write a short integrative essay. The contents were equated in the two conditions. Nevertheless, readers of multiple texts wrote more integrated essays, whereas readers of the single text tended to reuse the single text's introductory section. The authors concluded that information presented as multiple texts prompts readers to read systematically and to actively integrate the sources and contents (see also Wiley & Voss, 1999). In a similar vein, Stadtler and colleagues (2013) found that university students displayed better memory for conflicting information when the information was presented as four separate documents rather than a single, integrated text within which the sources were mentioned. And Salmeron, Macedo-Rouet, and Rouet (2016) found that students at various grade levels tended to pay more attention to source features when they were faced with several messages about a topic than when they were faced with a single perspective. Thus, although some experiments used short, single texts to examine the comprehension of multiple sources, it is likely that the results would generalize to situations involving multiple texts.

Put together, the research so far suggests that readers are more likely to integrate source and content information into a documents model when the sources are close to the situation, when they provide conflicting as opposed to consistent statements, and when the information is presented as multiple texts rather than a single text.

Task Factors

As stated earlier, a documents model is a sophisticated mental representation whose construction presumably costs significant resources and effort on the part of a reader, compared with more basic (though possibly incomplete or inaccurate) representations of text contents. It is likely that readers will invest the extra effort only to the extent that they need to do so in order to achieve their goals.

Indeed, research has determined that some specific task instructions promote readers' integration of ideas across multiple texts. Studies of single-text comprehension had already shown that conditions that make reading more effortful can be beneficial for comprehension (e.g., Kintsch & Young, 1984; McNamara et al., 1996; Walczyk et al., 1999). Similarly, research into multiple-text comprehension has found that more demanding tasks promote more integrated and causal multiple-text comprehension than less demanding ones. For instance, studies have determined that undergraduate university students reading multiple texts in order to write an argument produced essays that reflect students' deeper comprehension. For instance, Wiley and Voss (1999) investigated the effects of a variety of writing tasks (writing an argument, a narrative, a summary, or an explanation) on undergraduate students' comprehension of a set of documents texts about the nineteenth-century Irish potato famine. Essays written under the "argument" instructions contained more sentences based on the source materials (i.e. "transformed" sentences), compared with sentences directly borrowed from the source texts or sentences added from scratch. Argumentative essays also included more connections between ideas or with background knowledge, and more connectives, compared with those by students reading the same texts in order to write a narrative, a summary, or an explanation. Argument writers also outperformed participants in the other conditions on two comprehension tasks (i.e., inference and analogy tasks), further suggesting that they gained a better understanding of the subject matter than the other students. Interestingly, no differences were found between the different task instructions in terms of just repeating text information.

Le Bigot and Rouet (2007) reported similar findings from a study conducted with undergraduate students. The participants read short texts on the topic of social influence. Summary and argument writing tasks did not result in significant differences in reading time or comprehension. However, the content analysis of student essays showed that causal/consequence connectives were used more often in the argumentations than in the summaries. Students assigned the argument writing task also wrote essays with more transformed and added information (see Figure 14.2). In line with Wiley and Voss (1999), the authors suggested that argument writing promotes readers' deep comprehension and integration of the texts.

These findings indicate that there is "something special" (Wiley & Voss, 1999, p. 6) about writing an argument from multiple texts, something that prompts students to construct their own representation of the texts. Wiley and Voss (1999) suggested

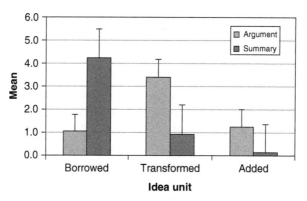

Figure 14.2 *Mean number of idea units in students' essays as a function writing task and type of idea unit category in the study by Le Bigot and Rouet (2007)*

that the argument instruction may prompt readers to bridge together different pieces of evidence in support of their own conclusion, and thus to construct a more integrated causal model than other types of instructions. They also conjectured that students might interpret argument writing as more personally engaging, raising their level of involvement in the task.

However, mixed – and even contradictory – findings have also been reported in the literature regarding the effects of tasks assignments on multiple-text comprehension. For instance, Bråten and Strømsø (2009) found that undergraduate students writing arguments or summaries from multiple texts had a better understanding than those who read in order to produce a general overview, but they did not find any difference between the argument and summary conditions. In another study, Gil and colleagues (2010b) even found an opposite effect of task instructions with better understanding and integration in a summary writing task compared with a task requiring readers to "express and justify your personal opinion." Several reasons may explain the discrepancy, including differences in the prompt ("write an argument" vs. "express and justify your personal opinion"), the type of materials (answer has to be constructed vs. answer can be selected from the documents; Britt & Rouet, 2012), and readers' characteristics. Indeed, Gil and colleagues (2010b) found that argument writing was only beneficial to readers holding more sophisticated epistemological beliefs. However, personal epistemology affected just one of several dependent measures, providing only partial support in favor of this assumption. In yet another study, however, Bråten and Strømsø (2009) found that students with more sophisticated beliefs benefitted more from the argument task than students with more naïve beliefs. The impact of readers' characteristics on their comprehension of multiple texts is further discussed in the next section.

In sum, while some studies demonstrated beneficial effects of argument task instructions on readers' comprehension of multiple texts (Le Bigot & Rouet, 2007; Wiley et al., 2009; Wiley & Voss, 1999), others found no difference between argument and summary instructions (Bråten & Strømsø, 2009), and some even found benefits of the summary tasks (Gil et al., 2010b). Consequently, it is still unclear whether and in what ways argument and summary tasks affect processing during multiple-text reading. Hagen, Braasch, and Bråten (2014) tried to disentangle this question by looking at "online" measures of multiple-text comprehension instead of postreading measures as in the studies cited above. To do so, Hagen and colleagues (2014) analyzed the different kinds of notes undergraduate students spontaneously took while reading multiple texts and related them to postreading comprehension scores in argument versus summary writing task conditions. They found no differences in the sheer amount of different types of notes produced as a function of reading to construct an argument versus a summary. However, readers in the argument and summary conditions displayed different relationships between the kinds of notes they took during reading and their comprehension. For the argument condition, there were several positive correlations between the notes taken and the intratextual and intertextual comprehension scores. For the summary condition, there were no significant relationships between note-taking and comprehension scores. These analyses suggest a difference in the quality of strategic processing of multiple texts between the conditions in favor of the argumentation task.

Finally, even if the results are still not clear-cut as regards the effects of the specific tasks assigned to students while reading multiple texts, one conclusion that can be drawn from these studies is that instruction promoting a "deeper" processing of the relationships among concepts and ideas in each text, and between concepts and ideas across texts (as it is somewhat the case for argumentation), would be beneficial for multiple-text comprehension.

Other types of instruction have also shown to prompt better multiple-text comprehension. For example, Linderholm, Therriault, and Kwon (2014, Study 2) examined the influence of self-explaining while reading science texts on undergraduate students' comprehension, memory, and integration of multiple-text ideas. They randomly assigned the participants to a control condition (i.e., read silently for comprehension) or to a self-explain condition. Participants who self-explained during reading obtained better scores on a postreading comprehension questionnaire compared with controls. The authors concluded that instructions to self-explain *during* reading promote multiple-text comprehension, perhaps because they enhance readers' ability to monitor their comprehension (i.e., how well they are meeting the goal of the task). The aforementioned study by de Pereyra and colleagues (2014, Experiment 2) provides additional support by showing that instructions to evaluate the source of a statement during reading increases readers' memory for source–content links to a large extent compared with instructions to evaluate the plausibility of the story. Likewise, Stadtler and colleagues (2015) found that providing fourteen-year-old gymnasium (upper-track middle school) students with a short text informing them about author competence, bias, and other issues regarding information quality was enough to improve students' attention to source information while performing a Web-based inquiry task about the risks associated with aspartame. They also found an increase in students' citation of sources in support of their own position and their memory for source-content links. Finally, Kammerer, Amann, and Gerjets (2015) found positive effects with short, self-administered instructional intervention about the issue of Web-based information quality on low-education adults' attention to and selection of reliable web pages as part of an Internet search scenario dealing with a health-related controversy. Interestingly, the intervention also affected participants' epistemic beliefs related to the Internet as evidenced in a questionnaire that participants completed both one week before and one week after the instructions. After the intervention, participants agreed more with statements reflecting a belief in justification through multiple sources (compared with other types of justifications such as personal belief or authority).

Our brief review of the literature demonstrates that some specific task instructions are effective at enhancing students' multiple-text comprehension. However, it is worth noting that several of these studies also showed that not all readers respond in the same way to the same task instructions (e.g., Bråten, & Strømsø, 2009; Gil et al., 2010). Indeed, some characteristics of the readers themselves are likely to influence multiple-text processing and to mediate the effects of task instructions.

Reader Factors

The ability to spontaneously notice and evaluate sources as well as skill in learning from and using multiple documents varies considerably across readers (Anmarkrud, Bråten, & Strømsø, 2014; Goldman et al., 2012; Strømsø, Bråten, & Britt; 2010; Strømsø et al., 2013; Wineburg, 1991). While some of this variability can be due to task factors and to text factors, as discussed in the previous sections, research has begun to identify important individual differences that contribute to this variability.

As with comprehending a single text, prior knowledge on the topic itself has been shown to affect multiple-document comprehension (Braasch et al., 2013; Bråten, Strømsø, & Britt, 2009; Gil et al., 2010a; Rouet et al., 1997; Strømsø, Bråten, & Samuelstuen, 2008; Strømsø & Bråten, 2009). Knowledge of the genre (such as an argument schema) can also affect learning from multiple documents (e.g., Kopp, 2013). Knowledge is important both to make inferences across documents and to create a task model with appropriate goals and actions to control reading behavior (Britt, Rouet, & Durik, 2018; Rouet, Britt, & Durik, 2017). Knowledge of the genre, topic, domain, or discipline has been useful as a covariate or as a means of understanding to whom the target factor generalizes.

There is also evidence that noticing and evaluating sources is a skill in itself (Rouet et al., 1996; Stahl et al., 1996; Wineburg, 1991). In general, within one's discipline, experts typically comprehend and evaluate sources when reading (Bazerman, 1985; Shanahan, Shanahan, & Misischia, 2011; Wineburg, 1991). In contrast, developing readers from elementary school through college and discipline novices often fail to attend to sources and do not evaluate them in the way experts do (Barzilai, Tzadok, & Eshet-Alkalai, 2015; Brem, Russels, & Weems, 2001; Britt & Aglinskas, 2002; Gerjets, Kammerer, & Werner, 2011; Maggioni & Fox, 2009; Macedo-Rouet et al., 2013; Nokes, Dole, & Hacker, 2007; Stadtler & Bromme, 2007; Stahl et al., 1996; VanSledright & Kelly, 1998; Wineburg, 1991). Skill in noticing and evaluating sources will of course directly affect one's memory for source information, enabling the use of this information in their postreading activities (such as essay writing). But source evaluations have also been shown to predict learning from multiple documents (Barzilai & Eshet-Alkalai, 2015; Bråten et al., 2009; Goldman et al., 2012; Strømsø et al., 2010; Wiley et al., 2009).

The role of readers' epistemic beliefs in learning from multiple documents has received considerable support (Barzilai & Eshet-Alkalai, 2015; Bråten et al., 2013; Bråten et al., 2011; Griffin et al., 2012; Kammerer, et al., 2015; Mason, Ariasi, & Boldrin, 2011; Pieschl, Stahl, & Bromme, 2008). One approach to understanding epistemic beliefs is to ask readers to endorse statements about their beliefs about what knowledge really is (certain vs. tentative and simple vs. complex) and how we gain knowledge (internal self vs. external authority and justification through observation authority vs. reason–rules–evaluation sources) (Hofer & Pintrich, 1997; Bråten et al., 2011). For example, readers who view knowledge as tentative and changeable respond better to argument tasks than those who believe knowledge is certain and unchanging (e.g., Bråten & Strømsø, 2010; Gil et al., 2010). Again, these effects can be viewed as important factors that will influence readers' goals and actions while reading (Britt et al., 2018). In a recent study, Bråten and colleagues (2014) found that both topic knowledge and epistemic beliefs were related to increased strategic behavior to make cross-text connections (Figure 14.3).

In contrast, the role of topic beliefs is only just beginning to be examined (for a review of beliefs and discourse processing, see Wolfe & Griffin, 2017). For

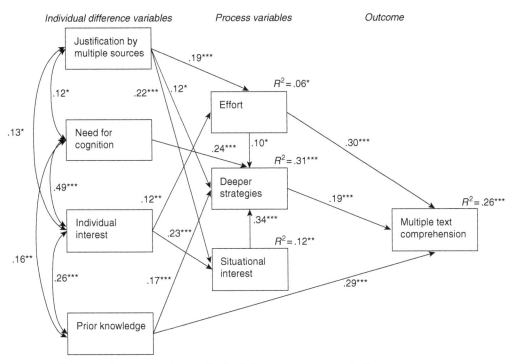

Figure 14.3 *Model linking individual characteristics to multiple-text comprehension (Bråten et al., 2014)*

example, Maier and Richter (2013) found that readers learned more information that was consistent with their prior beliefs than information that was belief-inconsistent when reading multiple documents on a topic. However, this effect was only found when the two sides were presented as a block rather than alternating perspectives ("texts"). To date, the effects of beliefs on learning, evaluating, and using information from multiple documents require much more research.

Surprisingly, very few studies on multiple-text comprehension have investigated the role of other predictors widely studied in the context of single-text reading, such as fluent reading, vocabulary, or working memory. Bråten and colleagues (2012) found that word recognition skills predicted learning from and comprehending multiple texts in 10th graders after controlling for their prereading topic knowledge (but see Bråten & Strømsø, 2010, and Strømsø et al., 2008). Even fewer studies have investigated the impact of readers' working memory capacities on their comprehension of multiple texts. Banas and Sanchez (2012) have nonetheless demonstrated that students with higher working memory were more able to connect information across multiple texts compared with lower-memory students. A study by Burton and Daneman (2007) has also found a relation between working memory and epistemic knowledge. More precisely, epistemic knowledge enabled low-span readers to compensate for their limited resources in processing texts. Future research should therefore take into account those dimensions of individual differences when examining readers' comprehension of multiple texts.

Teaching Students to Comprehend Multiple Texts

Early studies suggested that young students do not always benefit from reading multiple texts. For instance, after asking 10th grade Advance Placement students to read eleven documents related to the Tonkin Gulf Incident, Stahl and colleagues (1996) observed that the largest increase in knowledge occurred after reading the first text, and that students' mental model of the situation did not change much after the second text. Students' notes reflected very little in terms of evaluation of the information read. Stahl and his colleagues concluded that "For most of these students . . ., simply presenting them with multiple texts did not encourage them to think like historians" (p. 448).

The text and task effects reviewed in the sections above suggest that it takes specific conditions to enhance students' comprehension of multiple texts and that targeted interventions may improve their ability to do so in the absence of specific support. In single-text reading, several studies have demonstrated that readers' processing and comprehension of text are influenced by task instructions such as "reading for entertainment" or "reading to prepare for an exam" (e.g., Narvaez, van den Broek, & Ruiz, 1999). Students' reading comprehension can also be improved through the teaching of strategies (e.g., McNamara et al., 2006; Paris, Cross, & Lipson, 1984; Spörer, Brunstein, & Kieschke, 2009).

Over recent decades, research has also investigated the instructional tools and conditions that may foster students' multiple-text comprehension. Britt and

Aglinskas (2002) designed and tested the Sourcer's Apprentice, a tutoring system aimed at teaching multiple-text comprehension heuristics (i.e., sourcing, corroboration, contextualization). The Sourcer's Apprentice implemented naturalistic multiple-text reading scenarios, whereby students were invited to study texts related to a specific question or issue. As they were studying the texts, the students had to identify and select relevant details from each text and drag and drop them onto icons representing the category of information, e.g., author identity, motives, and so forth. In three small-scale experiments, the authors tested the effects of the tutorial compared with regular classroom instruction in groups of high school students. During a posttest, students trained with the Sourcer's Apprentice outperformed control students on measures of source use in postreading essays (see also Pérez et al., 2018).

Nokes and colleagues (2007) asked 11th grade students to use historian heuristics (i.e., sourcing, corroboration, and contextualization) before they read multiple texts as part of a series of ten history lessons. They found that these instructions combined with the reading of diversified texts were very beneficial for students and increased students' understanding of the texts' contents, compared with more traditional approaches involving textbook-like expository texts and/or content-oriented instruction. More recently, Walraven, Brand-Gruwel, and Boshuizen (2013) implemented a classroom intervention program targeting 9th grade students' Internet search and evaluation skills. The students worked over a cycle of eleven sessions during which they confronted the issue of searching and evaluating information online and performed a series of inquiry tasks involving the search of information about various topics in twentieth-century history with the use of a worksheet. During the sessions, the students had the opportunity to discuss their activity with their peers and the teacher. The authors found a significant condition × time interaction whereby trained students outperformed control students on a posttest. However, the effects of the intervention failed to transfer to a similar task involving biology materials instead of history.

Wiley and colleagues (2009) designed an instructional intervention program called SEEK (Source, Evidence, Explanation, Knowledge). The program comprised prompting students with questions they should bear in mind while reading documents from the Web (e.g., Who is the author? How reliable is the information?); providing students with heuristics on how to answer these questions (e.g., "You can figure this out from ... what training the person has, what their current occupation is"); allowing the students to apply these heuristics to a set of documents with the help of a scoring template; and, finally, comparing their ratings with an "expert" rank ordering of the documents. A control group simply read and ranked the same documents without the support of any declarative information or feedback through the "expert" rankings. Students instructed using SEEK gave more contrasted rankings to reliable versus less reliable texts compared with those in the control condition. They checked the information more often and wrote better essays in a transfer task involving multiple-text inquiry learning. Mason, Junyent, and Tornatora (2014) reported similar positive outcomes using a version of the SEEK methodology with 9th graders.

Braasch and colleagues (2013) trained high school students to reflect on multiple-text reading strategies using a "contrasting-cases" instructional method. The method consisted of presenting a short text passage along with two fictitious student "scripts" reporting the strategies of the students as they were studying the passage. One script reported efficient strategies (e.g., looking at the author, the type of document, the date of publication) whereas the other reported less efficient strategies (e.g., ignoring source features, basing trustworthiness evaluations solely on the presence/absence of keywords), based on the literature on expertise in multiple-text comprehension. The participants were invited to identify the strategies reported in each script, to assess each strategy as effective versus less effective, and to explain their assessment. In an application session, the participants were asked to study a set of six texts dealing with the geophysical phenomenon of El Niño. Compared with a control group who received traditional classroom instruction, the students who had taken the strategy instruction session included more scientific concepts from more useful documents in their essays and offered more justifications based on source features to evaluate documents' trustworthiness.

Stadtler and colleagues (2016) trained twenty-year-old students in a vocational school to reflect on source information when reading multiple texts. The training was implemented as a single 90-minute in-class session. In the pre- and posttests, the students were given pairs of texts dealing with social-scientific topics. Within each pair, the texts were attributed to either two experts, or to one expert and one nonexpert. In addition, the texts provided either consistent or discrepant information. The students were asked to decide which texts they agreed with (as a forced choice between text A and B) and to justify their response. The training session was made up of four modules, during which the experimenters introduced the social division of cognitive labor (module 1), discussed the construct of expertise (module 2), asked students to discuss authors' competence in a set of texts (module 3), and had students practice the criterion task with three examples (module 4). At the posttest, trained students were more likely to side up with texts issued by more competent sources and to justify their preference based on source features. Regardless of condition, students also remembered source details better when the texts they had read disagreed on the issue than when they agreed, thus replicating the DISC effect (see the section on "Text Factors").

In total, there is accumulated evidence that students from middle school to postsecondary education can be trained to skillfully read multiple texts and, in particular, to interpret and evaluate the description of information sources, a key process toward the construction of integrated documents models from multiple texts. It remains to be seen, however, how the procedures that have been found efficient can be transferred in regular educational settings.

Conclusions and Perspectives

In this chapter, we have presented an introduction to the comprehension of multiple texts, considered from both a theoretical and an instructional perspective.

At a theoretical level, research on multiple-text comprehension was able to capitalize on thirty years of research on single-text comprehension to elicit some of the additional processes and resources required when comprehending multiple texts.

At a practical level, the past decades have seen a growing emphasis on students' ability to learn independently from various sources of information. This emphasis reflects in part a shift in favor of constructivist instructional approaches (to the detriment of so-called transmissive approaches whereby a single source communicates knowledge to the student). It also reflects an even deeper and more pervasive transformation in postindustrial societies, whereby the digital revolution has brought ever-growing amounts of information within the reach of students at all levels of the curriculum. Whether teachers and other content-experts like it or not, students, but also patients and consumers, are a lot more likely than before to retrieve information from the Internet on virtually any topic of interest. Therefore, educating readers on the selection, evaluation, and careful integration of information from multiple sources has become of critical interest.

Research has mostly approached multiple-text comprehension using information processing frameworks. However, as repeatedly noted in this chapter, it is difficult to characterize readers' behaviors without taking account of their reasons for engaging in reading and their interest in doing to. A critical challenge for future research will be to integrate constructs of student motivation and engagement, together with theoretical accounts of cognitive processes and representations.

References

Albrecht, J. E. & O'brien, E. J. (1993). Updating a mental model: Maintaining both local and global coherence. *Journal of Experimental Psychology: Learning, Memory, and Cognition*, *19*(5), 1061.

Anmarkrud, Ø., Bråten, I., & Strømsø, H. I. (2014). Multiple-documents literacy: Strategic processing, source awareness, and argumentation when reading multiple conflicting documents. *Learning and Individual Differences*, *30*, 64–76. http://dx.doi.org/10.1016/j.lindif.2013.01.007

Banas, S. & Sanchez, C. A. (2012). Working memory capacity and learning underlying conceptual relationships across multiple documents. *Applied Cognitive Psychology*, *26*(4), 594–600.

Barzilai, S. & Eshet-Alkalai, Y. (2015). The role of epistemic perspectives in comprehension of multiple author viewpoints. *Learning and Instruction*, *36*, 86–103.

Barzilai, S., Tzadok, E., & Eshet-Alkalai, Y. (2015). Sourcing while reading divergent expert accounts: Pathways from views of knowing to written argumentation. *Instructional Science*, *43*(6), 737.

Bazerman, C. (1985). Physicists reading physics: Schema-laden purposes and purpose-laden schema. *Written Communication*, *2*, 3–23.

Braasch, J. L. G., Bråten, I., Strømsø, H. I., Anmarkrud, Ø., & Ferguson, L. E. (2013). Promoting secondary school students' evaluation of source features of multiple documents. *Contemporary Educational Psychology*, *38*, 180–195. http://dx.doi.org/10.1016/j.cedpsych.2013.03.003

Braasch, J. L., McCabe, R. M., & Daniel, F. (2016). Content integration across multiple documents reduces memory for sources. *Reading and Writing*, *29*(8), 1571–1598.

Braasch, J. L. G., Rouet, J.-F., Vibert, N., & Britt, M. A. (2012). Readers' use of source information in text comprehension. *Memory and Cognition*, *40*, 450–465. https://doi.org/10.3758/s13421-011-0160-6.

Bråten, I., Anmarkrud, Ø., Brandmo, C., & Strømsø, H. I. (2014). Developing and testing a model of direct and indirect relationships between individual differences, processing, and multiple-text comprehension. *Learning and Instruction*, *30*, 9–24.

Bråten, I., Ferguson, L., Anmarkrud, Ø., & Strømsø, H. (2013). Prediction of learning and comprehension when adolescents read multiple texts: The roles of word-level processing, strategic approach, and reading motivation. *Reading and Writing*, *26*, 321–348.

Bråten, I. & Strømsø, H. I. (2009). Effects of task instruction and personal epistemology on the understanding of multiple texts about climate change. *Discourse Processes*, *47*(1), 1–31.

(2010). When law students read multiple documents about global warming: Examining the role of topic-specific beliefs about the nature of knowledge and knowing. *Instructional Science*, *38*, 635–657.

Bråten, I., Strømsø, H. I., & Britt, M. A. (2009). Trust matters: Examining the role of source evaluation in students' construction of meaning within and across multiple texts. *Reading Research Quarterly*, *44*, 6–28.

Bråten, I., Strømsø, H., Britt, M. A., & Rouet, J.-F. (2011). The role of epistemic beliefs in the comprehension of multiple expository texts: Towards an integrated model. *Educational Psychologist*, *46*, 48–70.

Bråten, I., Strømsø, H., & Salmerón, L. (2010). Trust and mistrust when students read multiple information sources about climate change. *Learning and Instruction*, *21*, 180–192.

Brem, S. K., Russell, J., & Weems, L. (2001). Science on the Web: Students' evaluation of scientific arguments. *Discourse Processes*, *32*, 191–213.

Britt, M. A. & Aglinskas, C. (2002). Improving students' ability to identify and use source information. *Cognition and Instruction*, *20*, 485–522.

Britt, M. A., Perfetti, C. A., Sandak, R., & Rouet, J. F. (1999). Content integration and source separation in learning from multiple texts. In S. R. Goldman, A. C. Graesser, & P. van den Broek (eds.), *Narrative comprehension, causality, and coherence: Essays in honor of Tom Trabasso* (pp. 209–233). Mahwah, NJ: Lawrence Erlbaum.

Britt, M. A., & Rouet, J. -F. (2012). Learning with multiple documents: Component skills and their acquisition. In M.J. Lawson and J.R. Kirby (Eds.), *Enhancing the Quality of Learning: Dispositions, Instruction, and Learning Processes*, (pp. 276–314). Cambridge University Press.

Britt, M. A., Rouet, J.-F., & Durik, A. M. (2018). *Literacy beyond text comprehension: A theory of purposeful reading*. New York: Routledge.

Burton, C. & Daneman, M. (2007). Compensating for a limited working memory capacity during reading: Evidence from eye movements. *Reading Psychology*, *28*(2), 163–186.

De Pereyra, G., Britt, M. A., Braasch, J. L. G, & Rouet, J. F. (2014). Reader's memory for information sources in simple news stories: Effects of text and task features. *Journal of Cognitive Psychology*, *24*(2), 187–204.

Gerjets, P., Kammerer, Y., & Werner, B. (2011). Measuring spontaneous and instructed evaluation processes during Web search: Integrating concurrent thinking-aloud protocols and eye-tracking data. *Learning and Instruction*, *21*(2), 220–231.

Gil, L., Bråten, I., Vidal-Abarca, E., & Strømsø, H. I. (2010). Summary versus argument tasks when working with multiple documents: Which is better for whom? *Contemporary Educational Psychology, 35,* 157–173.

(2010b). Understanding and integrating multiple science texts: Summary tasks are sometimes better than argument tasks. *Reading Psychology,* 31, 30–68.

Glenberg, A. M., Meyer, M., & Lindem, K. (1987). Mental models contribute to foregrounding during text comprehension. *Journal of Memory and Language, 26,* 69–83.

Goldman, S. R., Braasch, J. L. G., Wiley, J., Graesser, A. C., & Brodowinska, K. (2012). Comprehending and learning from Internet sources: Processing patterns of better and poorer learners. *Reading Research Quarterly, 47,* 356–381. https://doi.org/10.1002/RRQ.027

Griffin, T. D., Wiley, J., Britt, M. A., & Salas, C. R. (2012). The role of CLEAR thinking in learning science from multiple-document inquiry tasks. *International Electronic Journal of Elementary Education, 5,* 63–78.

Hagen, Å. M., Braasch, J. L., & Bråten, I. (2014). Relationships between spontaneous note-taking, self-reported strategies and comprehension when reading multiple texts in different task conditions. *Journal of Research in Reading, 37,* 141–157.

Hofer, B. K. & Pintrich, P. R. (1997). The development of epistemological theories: Beliefs about knowledge and knowing and their relation to learning. *Review of Educational Research, 67*(1), 88–140.

Jurica, P. J. & Shimamura, A. P. (1999). Monitoring item and source information: Evidence for a negative generation effect in source memory. *Memory and Cognition, 27*(4), 648–656.

Kammerer, Y., Amann, D., & Gerjets, P. (2015). When adults without university education search the Internet for health information: The roles of Internet-specific epistemic beliefs and a source evaluation intervention. *Computers in Human Behavior, 48,* 297–309. https://doi.org/10.1016/j.chb.2015.01.045

Kintsch, W. (1988). The role of knowledge in discourse comprehension: A construction-integration model. *Psychological review, 95*(2), 163.

Kintsch, W. & van Dijk, T. A. (1978). Toward a model of text comprehension and production. *Psychological Review, 85,* 363–394.

Kintsch, W., & Young, S. R. (1984). Selective recall of decision-relevant information from texts. *Memory and Cognition, 12*(2), 112–117.

Kopp, K. (2013). Selecting and using information from multiple documents for argumentation. Unpublished dissertation, Northern Illinois University, DeKalb, IL. http://search.proquest.com/docview/1459216967.

Le Bigot, L. & Rouet, J.-F. (2007). The impact of presentation format, task assignment, and prior knowledge on students' comprehension of multiple online documents. *Journal of Literacy Research, 39,* 445–470.

Lelivrescolaire (2017). Habiter une métroploe d'un pays emergent: Mumbai (2/2) [to live in the capital of an emerging country: Mumbai (2/2)]. https://fr.calameo.com/read/000596729dc5e7968d39c

Linderholm, T., Therriault, D. J., & Kwon, H. (2014). Multiple science text processing: Building comprehension skills for college student readers. *Reading Psychology, 35*(4), 332–356.

Macedo-Rouet, M., Braasch, J.G.L., Britt, M.A., & Rouet, J.-F. (2013). Teaching fourth and fifth graders to evaluate information sources during text comprehension. *Cognition and Instruction, 31,* 204–226.

Maggioni, L. & Fox, E. (2009). Adolescents' reading of multiple history texts: An interdisciplinary investigation of historical thinking, intertextual reading, and domain-specific epistemic beliefs. Paper presented at the Annual Meeting of the American Educational Research Association, San Diego, CA.

Maier, J. & Richter, T. (2013). Text belief consistency effects in the comprehension of multiple texts with conflicting information. *Cognition and Instruction*, *31*(2), 151–175.

Mason, L., Ariasi, N., & Boldrin, A. (2011). Epistemic beliefs in action: Spontaneous reflections about knowledge and knowing during online information searching and their influence on learning. *Learning and Instruction*, *21*, 137–151. doi:10.1016/j.learninstruc.2010.01.001

Mason, L., Junyent, A. A., & Tornatora, M. C. (2014). Epistemic evaluation and comprehension of web-source information on controversial science-related topics: Effects of a short-term instructional intervention. *Computers and Education*, *76*, 143–157.

McNamara, D. S., Kintsch, E., Songer, N. S., & Kintsch, W. (1996). Are good texts always better? Interactions of text coherence, background knowledge, and levels of understanding in learning from text. *Cognition and Instruction*, *14*(1), 1–43.

McNamara, D.S., O'Reilly, T., Best, R., & Ozuru, Y. (2006). Improving adolescent students' reading comprehension with iSTART. *Journal of Educational Computing Research*, *34*, 147–171.

Narvaez, D., van den Broek, P., & Ruiz, A. (1999). The influence of reading purpose on inference generation and comprehension in reading. *Journal of Educational Psychology*, *3*, 488–496.

Nokes, J. D., Dole, J. A., & Hacker, D. J. (2007). Teaching high school students to use heuristics while reading historical texts. *Journal of Educational Psychology*, *99*(3), 492.

Paris, S. G., Cross, D. R. & Lipson, M. Y. (1984). Informed strategies for learning: A program to improve children's reading awareness and comprehension. *Journal of Educational Psychology*, *76*, 1239–1252.

Pieschl, S., Stahl, E., & Bromme, R. (2008). Epistemological beliefs and self-regulated learning with hypertext. *Metacognition and Learning*, *3*, 17–37.

Pérez, A., Potocki, A., Stadtler, M., Macedo-Rouet, M., Paul, J., Salmerón, L., & Rouet, J-F. (2018). Fostering Teenagers' Assessment of Information Reliability: Effects of a Classroom Intervention focused on Critical Source Dimensions. *Learning and Instruction*, *58*, 53–64.

Perfetti, C. A., Rouet, J.-F., & Britt, M. A. (1999). Towards a theory of documents representation. In H. van Oostendorp & S. Goldman (eds.) *The construction of mental representations during reading* (pp. 99–122). Mahwah, NJ: Lawrence Erlbaum.

Rouet, J.-F. & Britt, M. A. (2011). Relevance processes in multiple document comprehension. In M. T. McCrudden, J. P. Magliano, & G. Schraw (eds.), *Text relevance and learning from text* (pp. 19–52). Greenwich, CT: Information Age Publishing.

(2014). Learning from multiple documents. In R.E. Mayer (ed.) *Cambridge handbook of multimedia learning*, 2nd edn (pp. 813–841). Cambridge: Cambridge University Press. https://doi.org/10.1017/cbo9781139547369.039

Rouet, J.-F., Britt, M. A., & Durik, A. (2017). RESOLV: Readers' representation of reading: Contexts and tasks. *Educational Psychologist*, *52*(3), 200–215. https://doi.org/10.1080/00461520.2017.1329015

Rouet, J.-F., Britt, M. A., Mason, R. A., & Perfetti, C. A. (1996). Using multiple sources of evidence to reason about history. *Journal of Educational Psychology*, *88*(3), 478–493.

Rouet, J.-F., Favart, M., Britt, M. A., & Perfetti, C. A. (1997). Studying and using multiple documents in history: Effects of discipline expertise. *Cognition and Instruction, 15*, 85–106.

Rouet, J.-F., Le Bigot, L., de Pereyra, G., & Britt, M. A. (2016). Whose story is this? Discrepancy triggers readers' attention to source information in short narratives. *Reading and Writing, 29*, 1549–1570. https://doi.org/10.1007/s11145-016-9625-0

Rouet, J.-F., Levonen, J., Dillon, A. P. and Spiro, R. J. (eds.) (1996). *Hypertext and cognition.* Mahwah, NJ: Lawrence Erlbaum.

Salmerón, L., Macedo-Rouet, M., & Rouet, J.-F. (2016). Multiple viewpoints increase students' attention to source features in social question and answer forum messages. *Journal of the Association for Information Science and Technology. 67*, 2404–2419. https://doi.org/10.1002/asi.23585

Shanahan, C., Shanahan, T., & Misischia, C. (2011). Analysis of expert readers in three disciplines: History, mathematics, and chemistry. *Journal of Literacy Research, 43* (4), 393–429.

Spörer, N., Brunstein, J. C., & Kieschke, U. (2009). Improving students' reading comprehension skills: Effects of strategy instruction and reciprocal teaching. *Learning and Instruction, 19*, 272–286.

Stadtler, M. & Bromme, R. (2007). Dealing with multiple documents on the WWW: The role of metacognition in the formation of documents models. *International Journal of Computer Supported Collaborative Learning, 2*, 191–210.

Stadtler, M., Paul, J., Globoschütz, S., & Bromme, R. (2015). Watch out! – An instruction raising students' epistemic vigilance augments their sourcing activities. In: D. C. Noelle, R. Dale, A. S. Warlaumont, J. Yoshimi, T. Matlock, C. D. Jennings, & P. P. Maglio (eds.), *Proceedings of the 37th annual conference of the Cognitive Science Society* (pp. 2278–2283). Austin, TX: Cognitive Science Society.

Stadtler, M., Scharrer, L., Brummernhenrich, B., & Bromme, R. (2013). Dealing with uncertainty: Readers' memory for and use of conflicting information from science texts as function of presentation format and source expertise. *Cognition and Instruction, 31*, 130–150.

Stadtler, M., Scharrer, L., Macedo-Rouet, M., Rouet, J. F., & Bromme, R. (2016). Improving vocational students' consideration of source information when deciding about science controversies. *Reading and Writing, 29*(4), 705.

Stahl, S. A., Hynd, C. R., Britton, B. K., McNish, M. M. & Bosquet, D. (1996). What happens when students read multiple source documents in history? *Reading Research Quarterly, 31*, 4, 430–456.

Strømsø, H. I. & Bråten, I. (2009). Beliefs about knowledge and knowing and multiple-text comprehension among upper secondary students. *Educational Psychology, 29*, 425–445.

Strømsø, H. I., Bråten, I., & Britt, M.A. (2010). Reading multiple texts about climate change: The relationship between memory for sources and text comprehension. *Learning and Instruction, 20*, 192–204.

Strømsø, H. I., Bråten, I., Britt, M. A., & Ferguson, L. E. (2013). Spontaneous sourcing among students reading multiple documents. *Cognition and Instruction, 31*, 176–203. doi:10.1080/07370008.2013.769994

Strømsø, H. I., Bråten, I., & Samuelstuen, M. S. (2008). Dimensions of topic-specific epistemological beliefs as predictors of multiple-text understanding. *Learning and Instruction, 18*, 513–527. doi:10.1016/j.learninstruc.2007.11.001.

Trabasso, T. & van den Broek, P. (1985). Causal thinking and the representation of narrative events. *Journal of Memory and Language, 24*, 612–630.

Turner, K. & Greene, E. (1977). *The construction and use of a propositional text base.* Technical report No. 63, University of Colorado.

van Dijk, T. A. & Kintsch, W. (1983). *Strategies of discourse comprehension.* Hillsdale, NJ: Lawrence Erlbaum.

VanSledright, B. A. & Kelly, C. (1998). Reading American history: The influence of multiple sources on six fifth graders. *The Elementary School Journal, 98*(3), 239–265.

Voss, J.-F. & Wiley, J. (1997). Developing understanding while writing essays in history. *International Journal of Educational Research, 27*, 255–265.

Walczyk, J. J., Kelly, K. E., Meche, S. D., & Braud, H. (1999). Time limitations enhance reading comprehension. *Contemporary Educational Psychology, 24*, 156–165.

Walraven, A., Brand-Gruwel, S., & Boshuizen, H. P. A. (2013). Fostering students' evaluation behavior while searching the Internet. *Instructional Science, 41*, 125–146.

Wiley, J., Goldman, S., Graesser, A., Sanchez. C., Ash, I. & Hemmerich, J. (2009) Source evaluation, comprehension, and learning in internet science inquiry tasks. *American Educational Research Journal, 46*, 1060–1106. http://dx.doi.org/10.3102/0002831209333183

Wiley, J. & Voss, J. F. (1996). The effects of "playing historian" on learning in history. *Applied Cognitive Psychology, 10*(7), 63–72.

    (1999). Constructing arguments from multiple sources: Tasks that promote understanding not just memory for text. *Journal of Educational Psychology, 91*, 301–311.

Wilson, E. J. & Sherrell, D. L. (1993). Source effects in communication and persuasion research: A meta-analysis of effect size. *Journal of the Academy of Marketing Science, 21*, 101–112. 10.1007/BF02894421

Wineburg, S. S. (1991). Historical problem solving: A study of the cognitive processes used in the evaluation of documentary and pictorial evidence. *Journal of Educational Psychology, 83*, 73–87.

    (1994). The cognitive representation of historical texts. In G. Leinhardt, I. Beck & C. Stainton (eds.) *Teaching and learning in history* (pp. 85–135). Hillsdale, NJ: Lawrence Erlbaum.

Wolfe, M. B. & Griffin, T. D. (2017). Beliefs and discourse processing. In M. F. Schober, D. N. Rapp, & M. A. Britt (eds.), *Handbook of discourse processes*, 2nd edn (pp. 295–314). New York: Routledge.

15 Interventions to Promote Reading for Understanding

Current Evidence and Future Directions

Elizabeth A. Stevens and Sharon Vaughn

Introduction

The Significance of Reading for Understanding

Beginning reading instruction emphasizes the foundation skills of reading such as learning the alphabetic principle and acquiring word reading proficiency. Students learn how to decode words, sentences, and connected text developing phonemic awareness, or an awareness of words within sentences, syllables within words, and finally sounds within words. Simultaneously, students work on fluent, automatic word recognition developing a sight word vocabulary (e.g., was, have, some, the) or words that can be recognized immediately without sounding out individual phonemes. Once students acquire proficient word reading, the focus of reading instruction shifts from "learning to read" to "reading to learn" (Chall, 1983).

While most students acquire proficiency in the foundation skills of reading within the first couple of years of reading instruction, reading comprehension is an increasingly complex task with text difficulty, background knowledge, and vocabulary knowledge providing demands on student performance. In contrast to the early elementary grades, as students move through the grades, content learning in social studies, science, and math brings expectations for reading for understanding. Students are expected to be proficient readers of grade-level texts and beyond in order to learn academic content (Brozo, 2009; Hagaman, Casey, & Reid, 2016; Toste, Fuchs, & Fuchs, 2013). The stakes are higher; reading comprehension difficulty may impact not only reading performance but also general content area

This research was supported in part by grant P50 HD052117-07 from the Eunice Kennedy Shriver National Institute of Child Health and Human Development.

The research reported here was also supported by the Institute of Education Sciences, U.S. Department of Education, through Grant R305A150407, Examining the Efficacy of Differential Levels of Professional Development for Teaching Content Area Reading Strategies, to The University of Texas at Austin. The content is solely the responsibility of the authors and does not necessarily represent the official views of the Eunice Kennedy Shriver National Institute of Child Health and Human Development, the National Institutes of Health, the Institute of Education Sciences, or the U.S. Department of Education.

knowledge. Contributing to the demands on text difficulty is federal legislation (e.g., Every Student Succeeds Act, 2016) with accountability requirements resulting in complex texts to meet rigorous state and national standards (e.g., Common Core State Standards or other progressive state standards).

In addition to keeping up with an accelerated curriculum, students need advanced literacy skills in order to understand text (Goldman, Snow, & Vaughn, 2016). For example, students must be able to infer the meaning of unknown words, understand and analyze various text structures, integrate information across texts, synthesize textual information with existing knowledge, and critique arguments presented in text (Goldman et al., 2016). These demands cannot be underestimated; even students who have mastered word reading accuracy and fluency may experience difficulties understanding text (Goldman et al., 2016). Students who master the application of literacy skills in various contents (e.g., reading via technology) are more competitive within the global economy (Biancarosa & Snow, 2006). Current employment opportunities require employees to communicate effectively, analyze information, and solve complex problems (National Education Summit on High Schools, 2005). Adequate reading comprehension is a critical life skill; students with proficient reading comprehension skills are more successful in society, the workforce, and social settings (Biancarosa & Snow, 2006).

Students with Reading Comprehension Problems

The National Center for Education Statistics conducts a National Assessment of Educational Progress (NAEP) in reading every other year (NCES, 2015). The results of the NAEP provide an indication of student progress over time. The 2015 data indicate more than half of 4th, 8th, and 12th grade students are struggling readers. Only 36 percent of 4th graders, 34 percent of 8th graders, and 37 percent of 12th graders read at a proficient level. Disturbingly, results from the 2013 NAEP assessment were similar for 4th and 12th graders; the percentage of 8th graders meeting a proficient level in reading declined from 2013 to 2015. This suggests many students do not demonstrate the necessary skills to read and understand grade-level texts.

Reading performance is particularly low for students with identified disabilities, including students identified as learning disabled, those with behavior disorders, and students with cognitive impairments. In 2015, 12 percent of 4th graders, 8 percent of 8th graders, and 12 percent of 12th graders with disabilities performed at a proficient level in reading (NCES, 2015). The National Longitudinal Transition Study-2, which examined ten years of high school transcript data for secondary students with disabilities, confirmed students with disabilities lag behind general education peers in academic performance (Newman et al., 2011). In general, students with disabilities earn fewer credits, take fewer academic courses, maintain a lower grade point average, and have a higher course failure rate compared with the general student population.

In sum, many high school graduates lack the literacy skills needed to be successful in employment (National Education Summit on High Schools, 2005). There is a pressing need for evidence-based reading interventions in schools. Unfortunately, most teachers view themselves as content area teachers, emphasizing content learning rather than reading to understand content (Edmonds et al., 2009). Other teachers assume students who can accurately decode text can also read for understanding (Edmonds et al., 2009). As a result of the emphasis on content understanding and the misconception that fluent word reading suggests adequate comprehension, there is a lack of formal reading instruction beyond the elementary grades (Kamil et al., 2008).

A Historical Perspective of Reading Comprehension Instruction

Assessing Rather Than Teaching

We learned most of what we know about reading comprehension instruction over the past forty years. In 1978, Dolores Durkin conducted an observation study of 3rd through 6th grade reading and social studies classrooms to examine the state of reading comprehension instruction. Findings revealed a dearth (i.e., less than 1 percent of the instructional time observed) of explicit comprehension instruction (Durkin, 1978). Teachers allocated most instructional time to assessing students' understanding through literal comprehension questions. Furthermore, content area instruction (e.g., social studies) was not utilized as an opportunity to teach reading comprehension. Teachers made little to no modifications for struggling readers, instruction continued even if students demonstrated misunderstanding, and students spent little time actually reading texts. This seminal work provided the impetus for a lasting line of intervention research targeting reading comprehension instruction (e.g., Brown & Day, 1983; Jitendra, Hoppes, & Xin, 2000).

1970s and 1980s: Theories of Meaning and Cognitive Strategy Instruction

During the decades following Durkin's observation study, reading research consisted of a movement toward cognitive strategy instruction. Researchers tried to identify how readers construct meaning as they read. Various theories emerged, which influenced the nature and type of comprehension strategy instruction investigated. A strategy generally refers to a set of actions taken to accomplish a specific goal; a cognitive strategy, however, refers to specific mental steps a reader uses to arrive at a specific goal (i.e., understanding text; van Dijk & Kintsch, 1983). Cognitive strategy instruction verbalizes the mental processing used to understand text; if the mental steps can be explained and modeled, then struggling readers can emulate such processing and thus improve their reading comprehension.

For example, Kintsch and van Dijk (1978) proposed a summarization model theorizing the way in which readers develop a global understanding of text. Identifying main ideas and summarizing text facilitates comprehension because it helps the reader remember the important information (e.g., Jitendra et al., 2001). According to the theory, the reader applies specific subskills using the text's micro-structure (i.e., meaning units that comprise the text's base) in order to develop an overall essence of the text. The reader is taught to apply five steps to summarize text: (1) delete trivial information; (2) delete redundant information; (3) generalize information using a superordinate, categorical name (e.g., *farm animals* for cows, pigs, horses, and chickens); (4) select the main idea topic sentence from the text; and (5) develop the main idea sentence if one is not explicitly stated. Subsequent research investigated teaching students these steps to develop a macrostructure of texts (e.g., Brown & Day, 1983; Gajria & Salvia, 1992; Gallini et al., 1993; Weisberg & Balajthy, 1990).

Anderson and Pearson (1984) suggested another theoretical framework – schema theory – that influenced reading research. A student's knowledge is organized into units, or schema. Schema can be thought of as the knowledge or understanding related to the key idea or concept. The reader develops understanding of text when new information can be integrated into an existing schema. Therefore, a familiar schema will facilitate swift processing of text (Anderson, 1984). Reading compre-hension instruction should employ techniques that activate a reader's prior knowl-edge. This supports reading comprehension because textual information can be situated within an existing knowledge representation. Instructional strategies include building background knowledge, activating prior knowledge (i.e. discuss students' existing knowledge about a topic or concept related to the upcoming text), making predictions based on the reader's existing schema, and making connections between the text and the reader's prior knowledge (Anderson, 1984).

Allan Paivia (1971, 1986) propelled the dual coding theory, which suggests that mental images, or visual representations of text content, increase the reader's memory of text. The theory is rooted in the notion that mental processing consists of two distinct representations: verbal and visual imagery. Memory consists of these two systems that can operate independently, simultaneously, or in an interconnected way. Dual coding theorists believe that linking text and images improves recall. In other words, if text reading is supported by visual imagery, the reader is more likely to recall the text because both verbal and visual representations are stored and linked in memory. Thus, reading instruction should emphasize visualization of text elements while reading. Research in dual coding theory examined the effects of training students to construct mental images while reading (e.g., Levin, 1973; Pressley, 1976).

Toward the end of the 1980s, Gough and Tumner (1986) introduced the Simple View of Reading. They posit that reading comprehension is the product of listening comprehension (i.e., linguistic comprehension or the process of interpreting sen-tences and discourse) and decoding (i.e., accurate and fluent word recognition). In order to adequately comprehend text, students need strong decoding *and* language comprehension skills. Based on this formula, Gough and Tumner (1986) suggested three types of specific reading disability: (1) adequate language comprehension but limited decoding skill (i.e., dyslexia); (2) adequate decoding skill but limited lan-guage comprehension (i.e., hyperlexia); (3) weaknesses in both areas (i.e., garden-variety poor reader). Based on this framework, teaching reading must incorporate a bottom-up, analytic approach to reading words but also background knowledge and vocabulary instruction in order to develop adequate language comprehension.

Late 1980s and 1990s: Explicit Instruction in Comprehension Strategies

Reading research efforts changed moving into the 1990s; the effects of comprehension strategy instruction shifted from simply teaching strategies to teaching students *how* and *when* to use the strategies. This transition to a more active approach to strategy use was influenced heavily by the reader-response theory. Rosenblatt (1978) suggests that meaning does not reside solely in the text but occurs as a result of the interaction between the reader and the text. Consequently, interpretation changes from reader to reader, depending on the reader's perspective and background knowledge. Reading instruction, therefore, should encourage students to engage in an active, meaning-making process as they read.

A hallmark of reader-response theory is reciprocal teaching. Palincsar and Brown (1984) identified the following as the most important activities for enhancing reading comprehension skills: (1) set a clear purpose for reading, (2) activate background knowledge, (3) focus on the most important content, (4) make connections between new content and prior knowledge, (5) monitor understanding, and (6) make and revise inferences. Reciprocal teaching is a collaborative learning approach in which students work in small groups to summarize, question, clarify, and make predictions while reading. Collaborative learning allows for text-based discussion in which the teacher and students model mental processing of text. Palincsar and Brown (1984) selected these practices (i.e., summarizing, questioning, clarifying, and predicting) because they improve comprehension while simultaneously encouraging readers to monitor their understanding. In other words, identifying the main idea of a passage supports retention of the most important information; however, if the reader cannot identify the main idea, a breakdown in comprehension has occurred and fix-up strategies (e.g., rereading, asking questions) are needed to repair the misunderstanding.

The importance of explicit mental modeling, often referred to as a think-aloud, was further investigated in an experiment conducted by Duffy and colleagues (1987). Treatment teachers provided direct explanation of the mental acts used when applying reading comprehension strategies. In contrast to previous instruction (i.e., teaching and memorizing skills in isolation), students learned how to monitor understanding while reading, stop reading when they encountered difficulty, select an appropriate strategy from their toolbox, and apply the strategy to repair understanding. This study is important, however, for another reason. Mental modeling was embedded in an instructional routine that allowed for gradual release of responsibility to students. Teachers (1) explained the strategy; (2) modeled the strategy while reading, including explaining the mental acts involved in using the strategy; and (3) allowed students to practice with support. In other words, Duffy and colleagues introduced the explicit, systematic instructional routine that is frequently used in reading comprehension practices.

Twenty years following the release of Durkin's observation study, Pressley and colleagues (1998) conducted an observation study of 4th grade classrooms in New York. Unfortunately, the authors observed a similar pattern of assessing rather than teaching reading comprehension skills. Teachers asked more questions related to comprehension processes (e.g., summarizing, predictions, confusing aspects of text) but students were not taught how to engage in comprehension processing and monitoring while reading. Pressley indicated "students were prompted to generate the types of ideas that might occur to strategic readers as they read, but they were not actually taught the strategies themselves, how to use them, or the utility of the strategies" (p. 299). Furthermore, observations revealed a lack of self-regulation strategy instruction; students were simply expected to develop self-regulation skills naturally. Although researchers investigated explicit modeling of text processing for more than a decade, it didn't appear these practices were being implemented in classrooms.

The Turn of the Century: The Influence of Legislation and Policy on Reading Research

The new millennium brought about federal legislation that impacted the course of reading instruction. The Every Student Succeeds Act (ESSA, 2016), formerly known as the No Child Left Behind Act (NCLB, 2001), emphasizes equal opportunity for all students in public education, regardless of race, socioeconomic status, disability, or home language. The law aims to improve achievement by ensuring that all students are college- and career-ready. NCLB introduced a heightened level of accountability in the public education system; schools were expected to monitor individual student growth via high-stakes assessment. Consequently, NCLB exposed achievement gaps for minority and low-income students. Under NCLB, federal funding allocated to Title I schools required teachers to identify and use evidence-based reading practices for kindergarten through 3rd grade reading instruction. In addition to the push for increased accountability and use of evidence-based practices in public education, Congress called for increased rigor in educational research by passing the Education Sciences Reform Act of 2002. This law established the Institute of Education Sciences (IES), the research branch of the US Department of Education. IES put forth new standards (e.g., randomized control trials and evaluation of student growth using standardized measures) to evaluate the quality of evidence for specific instructional practices.

Finally, the Individuals with Disabilities Education Improvement Act (IDEIA, 2004) redefined the way in which schools identified students with learning disabilities – most of whom demonstrate significant reading difficulties. Prior to this law, schools used a discrepancy between IQ and achievement as one of the criteria for identification of learning disability and access to special education services. In contrast, IDEIA (2004) suggests a multitiered system of support for identifying students with learning disabilities. Students move through increasingly intensive levels of intervention based on inadequate response to previous, less-intensive tiers (Vaughn & Fuchs, 2003). The intention is that students who demonstrate persistent low response to research-based interventions would be considered for referral for special education.

Response to intervention (RTI) is conceptualized as a process that prevents school failure by providing universal research-based instruction for all students. Furthermore, it is designed to meet the academic and behavioral needs of all students by providing increasingly more intensive tiers of intervention to align with the instructional needs of students (Vaughn & Fletcher, 2012). Initially, all students are screened for reading difficulty at the beginning of the year. Classroom teachers provide high-quality instruction to all students (Tier 1), using the screening results to identify particular student needs and match instruction accordingly. Students who score below the screening benchmark receive supplemental instruction in addition to Tier 1 instruction. This supplemental instruction is typically referred to as Tier 2-type intervention. These increasingly intensive tiers of intervention are also thought of within a multitiered system of support (MTSS). Tier 2 intervention targets students' reading needs (i.e., phonemic awareness, phonics, vocabulary, reading fluency, and comprehension) and typically provides additional instruction for 20–30 minutes a day for three to five days per week. Progress monitoring occurs at least once per month, and students who respond minimally to Tier 2 intervention move to even more intensive intervention (i.e., Tier 3). School-based teams design and implement Tier 3 intervention in which students receive daily instruction targeting specific needs; progress monitoring occurs on a weekly basis. Data collected via progress monitoring may be used for special education referrals and possible identification of a learning disability. While the number of tiers of intervention provided by a particular school or district may be more than three, intensifying implementation focuses on increasing the dosage of instruction (number of times per week, the length of time of instruction), the personnel providing the instruction (e.g., moving from general education teacher to special education teacher), and adjusting the type of instruction to meet the individual needs of the students.

These legislative changes also shifted the landscape of educational research addressing reading comprehension. Federal funding targeted high-quality research designs that prioritized studies that implemented randomized control trials and used rigorous analysis procedures and well-developed measures.

What Have We Learned from Nearly Four Decades of Research on Reading Comprehension?

1980–2004: Struggling Readers Benefit from Reading Interventions

In this section, we will present the findings from several key meta-analytic reviews within the field of reading intervention research. Meta-analyses summarize the effect of a treatment on a particular outcome by reporting an average treatment effect across a set of studies; each study-wise effect is weighted based on its precision.

Scammacca and colleagues (2007) conducted a meta-analysis of nearly 25 years of reading intervention research for struggling readers (e.g., readers with significant reading problems or students with reading disabilities). They aimed to answer the following questions: (1) How effective are reading interventions for struggling readers? (2) How effective are reading interventions on measure of reading comprehension? The authors systematically searched the literature to locate studies that met the following criteria: (1) published between 1980 and 2006, (2) participants were struggling readers in Grades 4–12, (3) the intervention targeted reading instruction (i.e., word study, fluency, vocabulary, and/or reading comprehension strategies), and (4) employed an experimental, quasi-experimental, or multiple-treatment design.

The search resulted in thirty-one studies, with twenty-three reporting reading comprehension outcomes. The results indicated that struggling readers benefit from reading interventions, particularly reading comprehension strategy instruction. The authors reported a statistically significant pooled estimate of 0.97 for the effect of reading interventions ($k = 23$) on reading comprehension outcomes. A separate meta-analysis reported on findings from studies that used standardized measures of reading ($k = 8$) resulting in a smaller estimate (ES = 0.42) that was not statistically significant. The authors also reported on analyses that examined the effects of treatments on reading comprehension measures only (not all reading measures). The effect size estimate for reading comprehension measures was large and statistically significant (ES = 1.35) for reading comprehension strategy interventions. However, when including only standardized reading comprehension measures, the estimate was 0.54.

These results suggest that reading interventions, particularly comprehension strategy interventions, improved struggling readers' comprehension by more than one standard deviation. The difference in the magnitude of the effect represented by all measures versus standardized measures is an important finding. The estimates resulting from standardized measures provide a less optimistic picture of the effectiveness of reading interventions. One reason for this may be that standardized measures are less aligned to an intervention than proximal, researcher-developed measures. It is also possible that the researcher developed measures yield a less reliable index of reading comprehension. Edmonds and colleagues (2009) found a similar pattern in their meta-analysis of reading interventions for students in Grades 6 through 12; the mean effect of interventions on unstandardized measures was almost double that of standardized measures. It's important to consider the type of measures contributing to the pooled estimate when interpreting meta-analytic results; while standardized measures present lower effects, they are also considered more representative of generalized reading skill.

The authors (Edmonds et al., 2009) examined interventions (i.e., comprehension strategies, word study, fluency, multicomponent, and vocabulary) as a potential moderator of intervention effectiveness. The results indicated that students benefit from word-level and text-level interventions. Word study interventions, targeting automatic word recognition and fluent reading of multisyllabic words, produced significant gains (ES = 0.60) on all reading measures but differences were not significant when examining the effect on reading comprehension measures only (ES = 0.40). The largest effects were found with interventions targeting vocabulary instruction (ES = 1.62); however, these studies did not include standardized vocabulary measures. As such, the estimate may inflate the effect of vocabulary interventions without knowing their impact when measured by more generalized assessments. Previous research identified fluency interventions as a promising practice for improving reading comprehension for elementary students with learning disabilities (Chard, Vaughn, & Tyler, 2002; Stevens, Walker, & Vaughn, 2017). Scammacca and colleagues (2007) found no significant differences for the effect of fluency interventions on struggling readers' reading comprehension (ES = – 0.07 standardized measures; ES = 0.26 all measures). Similar findings in other meta-analyses (e.g., Edmonds et al., 2009) suggest that fluency interventions improve reading comprehension for younger students but fluency interventions may not be associated with improved outcomes in reading comprehension in older struggling readers. Finally, multicomponent reading interventions (i.e., targeting word study, fluency, vocabulary, and/or reading comprehension) resulted in moderate to large effects on reading comprehension measures (ES = 0.59 standardized measures; ES = 0.80 all measures) but these differences were not significant.

Additional moderator analyses examined the impact of grade level on overall intervention effectiveness across outcome measures. Students in upper elementary and middle school students showed the greater gains in reading comprehension (ES = 0.47 standardized measures; ES = 1.11 all measures) than students in high school (ES = 0.14 standardized measures; ES = 0.59 all measures). For both grade groupings, the effects on standardized reading comprehension measures were not significant. This finding suggests that it may be more difficult to remediate students' reading difficulties as they progress through the grades, providing an impetus for early reading intervention. In spite of this finding, older readers have demonstrated beneficial effects from reading intervention, so practitioners and researchers should avoid an "it's too late to remediate" mentality.

2005–2011: A Trend Toward Smaller Effects

Scammacca and colleagues (2015) updated the prior meta-analysis to include reading intervention studies published between 2005 and 2011. In contrast to the results from studies published between 1980 and 2004 (i.e., pooled ES = 0.97), the mean estimate for the effect of reading interventions on all reading comprehension outcomes (standardized and researcher developed) yielded a statistically significant yet much smaller effect (ES = 0.24). The analysis using only standardized comprehension measures resulted in a significant mean effect of 0.19. A similar pattern yielding smaller effects resulted for the effect of reading comprehension interventions on reading comprehension outcomes. A moderator analysis found publication year to be a statistically significant predictor of effect size when standardized and unstandardized measures were included in the model.

It appears that reading intervention research conducted more recently is associated with lower effect sizes than early research. There are several interpretations for the decreasing trend in effect size over time. At the turn of the century, the passage of NCLB (i.e., currently known as ESSA, 2016) changed the instructional practices in schools. Within an environment of increased accountability, schools began monitoring individual student growth at a heightened level. In response to high-stakes testing results, the implementation of school-based interventions targeting all students' needs (i.e., students receiving Tier 1 instruction and Tier 2 or Tier 3 intervention) became increasingly important. Prior to legislation at the turn of the century, experimental studies often compare the treatment group to a control condition in which the students did not receive any instruction. This is a true no-treatment condition, representing the effect of a reading intervention compared with no additional intervention. However, this was no longer the case in the counterfactual. Due to NCLB and RTI, the comparison group often received some type of school-provided intervention. Consequently, the effects of more recent studies may be smaller because they represent the impact of the treatment relative to another school-provided intervention.

The Education Sciences Report Act (2002) also impacted effect size estimates as IES called for more rigorous research designs, including the use of standardized measures. Prior to 2000, reading intervention experiments rarely used standardized measures, which are associated with lower effect size estimates due to assessing more generalized reading skill that is less aligned with the intervention itself. Standardized measures may more accurately reflect students' improvement in reading skill, particularly when asked to apply those skills in new or different ways. Scammacca and colleagues (2015) suggested another reason for the change in effect size over time: recent research includes much larger samples. Almost 70 percent of the 1980–2004 studies included 40 or fewer participants compared with only 17.5 percent in 2005–2011 studies. A quarter of the studies conducted between 2005 and 2011 included 100 or more participants compared with only 6.3 percent in the previous set of studies.

Intervention Features That Impact Effectiveness

When interventions are associated with improved outcomes, it is helpful to better understand the features of instruction that are associated with these outcomes. One feature of instruction to consider is the amount of time the intervention is provided. In 1980–2004, less than 20 percent of the studies provided more than 16 hours of intervention, whereas most of the studies in the 2005–2011 corpus provided more than 16 hours of intervention. Moderator analyses of all of the studies (i.e., 1980–2011) resulted in a significantly larger mean effect for shorter interventions. Interventions providing 5 hours or less or 6–15 hours resulted in significantly larger effects than interventions providing 26 hours or more (Scammacca et al., 2015). It seems somewhat contradictory that interventions that are provided for briefer periods are associated with greater effects. One explanation may be that students respond initially to additional instruction as part of a novelty effect but that this novelty effect wears off over time. Future studies are needed to help understand the duration of interventions and their outcomes.

In the 1980–2004 set of studies, researcher-implemented interventions resulted in significantly higher effect size estimate than those implemented by teachers; however, there were no significant differences in the 2005–2011 studies (Scammacca

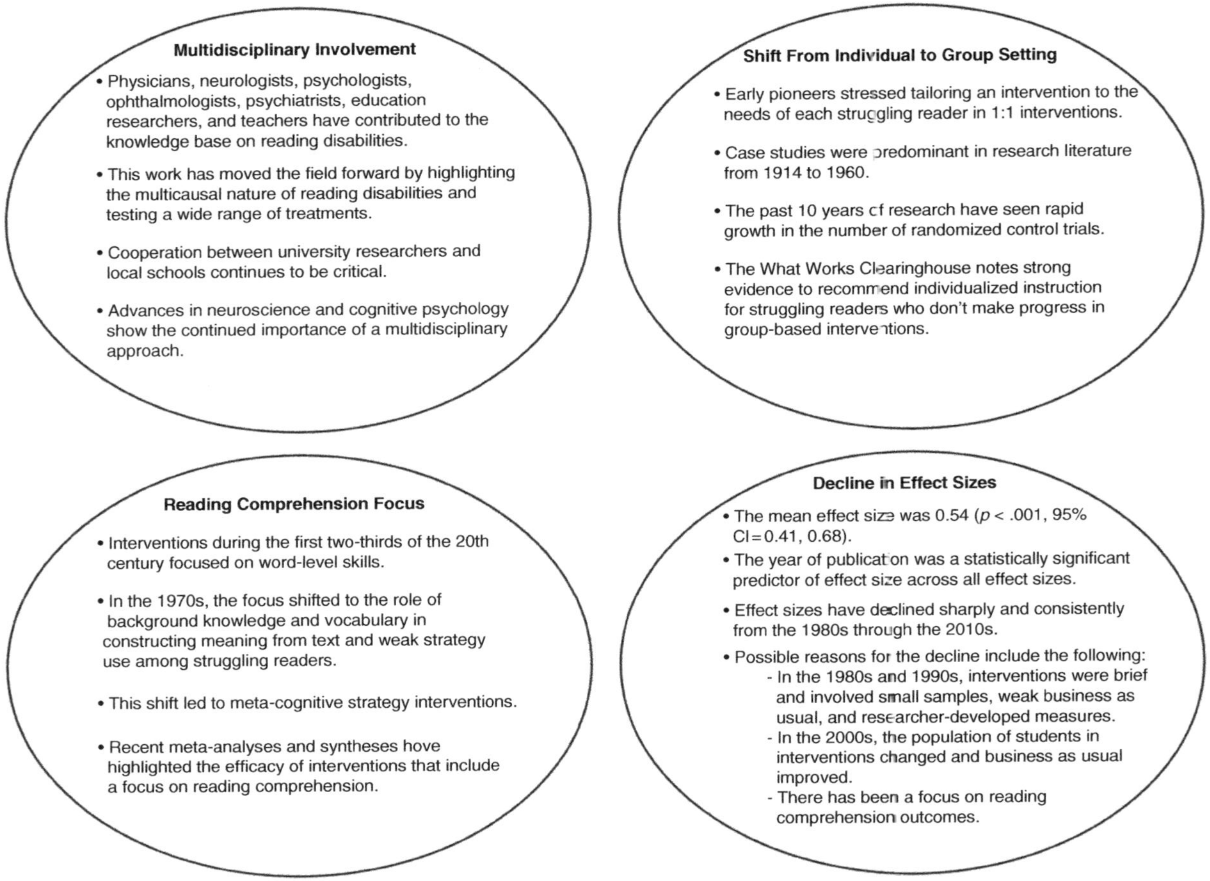

Multidisciplinary Involvement

- Physicians, neurologists, psychologists, ophthalmologists, psychiatrists, education researchers, and teachers have contributed to the knowledge base on reading disabilities.

- This work has moved the field forward by highlighting the multicausal nature of reading disabilities and testing a wide range of treatments.

- Cooperation between university researchers and local schools continues to be critical.

- Advances in neuroscience and cognitive psychology show the continued importance of a multidisciplinary approach.

Reading Comprehension Focus

- Interventions during the first two-thirds of the 20th century focused on word-level skills.

- In the 1970s, the focus shifted to the role of background knowledge and vocabulary in constructing meaning from text and weak strategy use among struggling readers.

- This shift led to meta-cognitive strategy interventions.

- Recent meta-analyses and syntheses have highlighted the efficacy of interventions that include a focus on reading comprehension.

Shift From Individual to Group Setting

- Early pioneers stressed tailoring an intervention to the needs of each struggling reader in 1:1 interventions.

- Case studies were predominant in research literature from 1914 to 1960.

- The past 10 years of research have seen rapid growth in the number of randomized control trials.

- The What Works Clearinghouse notes strong evidence to recommend individualized instruction for struggling readers who don't make progress in group-based interventions.

Decline in Effect Sizes

- The mean effect size was 0.54 ($p < .001$, 95% CI = 0.41, 0.68).

- The year of publication was a statistically significant predictor of effect size across all effect sizes.

- Effect sizes have declined sharply and consistently from the 1980s through the 2010s.

- Possible reasons for the decline include the following:
  - In the 1980s and 1990s, interventions were brief and involved small samples, weak business as usual, and researcher-developed measures.
  - In the 2000s, the population of students in interventions changed and business as usual improved.
  - There has been a focus on reading comprehension outcomes.

Figure 15.1 *Themes identified from Scammacca et al. (2016)*

et al., 2015). Researcher-provided and teacher-provided interventions yielded similar mean estimates on all measures of reading comprehension (ES = 0.20, 0.25) as well as standardized measures of reading comprehension (ES = 0.16, 0.19). This finding indicates that teachers have provided effective interventions to struggling readers, which is less costly and builds the capacity to provide interventions in schools. Finally, there were no significant differences in intervention effectiveness by grade level (i.e., 4th–5th graders, 6th–8th graders, and 9th–12th graders), suggesting that struggling readers between grades 4 through 12 benefit equivalently from targeted reading intervention. This synthesis does not examine effects on reading comprehension outcomes for students with reading problems in younger grades (1st through 3rd grade) where impacts have typically been higher than 4th grade and above.

Struggling Readers' Response to Increasingly Intensive Levels of Support

A key component of RTI is that schools address all students' reading needs via increasingly intensive levels of support. It is likely that 3 to 5 percent of students will not respond to Tier 1 instruction and Tier 2 reading intervention, requiring intensive intervention provided more frequently over an extended period of time. The evidence suggests that reading interventions result in improved reading comprehension for struggling readers, but what about those students with intractable reading difficulties requiring the most intensive level of support?

Vaughn and colleagues (2010) conducted a longitudinal study with a cohort of middle school students to examine their response to increasingly intensive levels of intervention. The results of this study shed light on the challenges involved when intervening with students with intractable reading difficulties. In the first year of the study, 6th graders with reading difficulties (i.e., identified by failing scores on the state's standardized reading comprehension test at the end of 5th grade) were randomly assigned to receive a Tier 2 intervention or a business-as-usual comparison condition. Treatment and comparison content area teachers received professional development on the integration of vocabulary and reading comprehension practices in content area instruction; as such, all students benefited from enhanced Tier 1 instruction. Students in the treatment condition received a yearlong, daily Tier 2 intervention in groups of ten to fifteen students. The intervention targeted reading comprehension, word recognition, vocabulary, and fluency. Students made minimal gains on measures of decoding, comprehension, and fluency, revealing older students may have more significant needs than that which can be remediated in one year (e.g., limited vocabulary and background knowledge; Solis et al., 2014).

Students deemed limited responders at the end of the Tier 2 intervention (i.e., identified using standardized reading test at the end of 6th grade) were randomly assigned in Grade 7 to a standardized intervention, an individualized intervention, or a comparison condition (Vaughn, Wexler et al., 2011). The standardized intervention provided a standard treatment protocol to all students, whereas students in the individualized conditions received targeted instruction based on their specific needs. For example, in the standardized condition all students received the same amount of time allocated to each of the components of reading (i.e., phonics, word reading, fluency, vocabulary, and comprehension), whereas in the individualized intervention the treatment was customized to respond to students' particular needs (e.g., some students received more time on comprehension and less on word reading). The Tier 3 intervention was provided daily for the entire school year in small groups of five students. After a second year of treatment, there were no significant differences between the standardized and the individualized treatments; however, both conditions significantly outperformed the comparison group with moderate effects in reading comprehension. There were no significant differences between the groups on word reading, decoding, or fluency measures.

Finally, after two years of intervention, limited responders were again identified and provided a third year of increasingly intensive intervention in Grade 8 (Vaughn, Wexler et al., 2012). Students received an individualized, intensive daily reading intervention in even smaller groups of two to four students. Interventionists used the posttest data from the previous year and frequent progress-monitoring data to tailor the instruction to students' needs in phonics, word reading, fluency, vocabulary, and reading comprehension. Treatment students significantly outperformed the comparison condition on standardized measures of reading comprehension (ES = 1.20) and word identification (ES = 0.49). These effect sizes, however, are somewhat misleading. Although they suggest the treatment group made substantial gains in reading comprehension and word identification relative to the comparison group, the treatment group's pretest and posttest scores on these measures were actually quite similar. The large effects in reading comprehension occurred due to the comparison group's decreasing performance from pretest to posttest (e.g., Gates-MacGinitie Passage Comprehension pretest $M = 85.98$, posttest $M = 74.48$).

These studies demonstrate that students requiring Tier 3 intervention may need long-term intensive instruction (i.e., over several years) simply to maintain performance levels. It may be unrealistic, however, to expect these students to make substantial improvement in reading such that they close the achievement gap with typically achieving peers. The declining performance of the comparison group in the third year of this longitudinal study provides a compelling reason to implement sustained intensive interventions for students who are limited responders.

Wanzek and colleagues (2013) synthesized studies published between 1995 and 2011 that examined intensive interventions (i.e., provided for at least seventy-five sessions) for students in Grades 4–12. The authors aimed to answer two questions: (1) How effective are intensive interventions in improving reading outcomes for students with reading difficulties or disabilities? and (2) What features of intensive interventions are associated with improved outcomes for students? The systematic search resulted in nineteen studies, ten of which met criteria for a meta-analysis. These studies contained features of rigorous educational research recommended by the IES (e.g., random assignment to condition, use of standardized measures), thus enhancing our confidence in the validity of the findings. The intensive interventions differ from the studies reported in the previous meta-analyses in that they were provided with increased frequency (i.e., number of sessions per week), duration (i.e., total length of the intervention), and intensified instructional delivery in response to more frequent progress monitoring. Most studies implemented multicomponent interventions targeting phonics or word recognition, spelling, fluency, vocabulary, and comprehension. Results of the meta-analysis yielded statistically significant, small effects ranging from 0.10 to 0.16 on measures of reading comprehension, reading fluency, word reading, word reading fluency, and spelling. Moderator analyses showed no difference in intervention effectiveness based on hours of intervention, group size, or grade level. Students with intractable reading difficulties may need long-term interventions to make minimal gains in reading outcomes.

Reading for Understanding: Practices That Work

Across the evidence base, certain practices are recommended to improve readers' comprehension before, during, and after reading. These practices are recommended because there is research documenting their efficacy. This section explains and provides examples of these research-based practices.

Before Reading

Building background knowledge. Since reading comprehension is affected by students' accessing relevant background knowledge to connect to the text, providing students with critical background knowledge prior to reading is an essential feature of effective reading comprehension instruction. For some students, building background knowledge involves encouraging them to access the background knowledge that they have. For example, students might be prompted to "think about what you know about whales, where they live, and how they communicate and consider that as you read the next passage." However, this approach is unlikely to be successful for many students with reading difficulties because they do not have adequate background knowledge to access. Thus, teachers need to do more than encourage them to access their background knowledge; they need to assist students in acquiring the necessary background knowledge to understand the new text. For example, prior to reading text, students with reading comprehension difficulties benefit from practices that build their existing knowledge of the text's content. Students who approach text with some familiarity of the content (i.e., schema theory; Anderson & Pearson, 1984) have better understanding than those who read text without any prior knowledge of the topic. Building background knowledge prepares students to understand text by preteaching important information (i.e., critical to understanding the text) prior to reading. This may include providing students with historical context or discussing an important concept. The purpose is to build students' existing schema so they can integrate new information from the text. The intention is that this building of background knowledge occurs relatively quickly with specific purposes and may involve mechanisms such as 3-minute videos, instruction on key words, or reviewing previous knowledge. Building background knowledge is *not* asking students what they already know about the topic (see activating prior knowledge); it is not possible to activate students' background knowledge if they do not have any prior knowledge of the topic. It is important for practitioners to distinguish between activating and building prior knowledge and to identify when to use each practice before reading.

One way to build background knowledge is by providing an overarching big idea, often related to the entire unit of instruction (Vaughn et al., 2013). In a brief summary (i.e., three sentences or less), teachers remind students of the unit big idea (e.g., "Remember that we are learning about the early civilizations in Texas"), situate new learning with previous learning (e.g., "Yesterday you learned about Paleoamericans' way of life, but today you're going to learn about a Native American tribe, the Comanche"), and provide students with a comprehension purpose question or issue related to the text (e.g., "As you read today, think about how the Comanche Indians were skilled warriors"). Teachers might consider posting the comprehension purpose question or issue so that students can reference it while reading. Questions or key issues should direct students to the main idea, encouraging them to focus on the most important aspects of the text while reading. It's important to circle back to the comprehension purpose question after reading; students can discuss the question in pairs or small groups.

Another way to build students' background knowledge is by previewing and providing brief explanations of important concepts or ideas (Vaughn et al., 2013). For example, teachers may preteach important proper nouns (e.g., Stephen Austin established the first colony in Texas). Teachers can also build students' background knowledge by using a short video, photograph, or map related to the text content. Asking questions about the visual or video prompts discussion, connects new learning with prior learning, and contextualizes the text content for students. Visuals may be particularly helpful when reading social studies texts as they provide students with mental images of the time period. Finally, teachers may ask students to preview the text, highlighting important text features (e.g., headings, bold words, maps, figures) prior to reading (Simmons et al., 2010). This provides students with a sense of how the information will be organized.

Activating prior knowledge. Practitioners often confuse building background knowledge with activating background knowledge but they are distinct practices and serve different purposes. Activating prior knowledge is a practice that should be used when students already have existing knowledge about the text content. For example, if students have already read and learned about renewable resources, then building their background knowledge is not needed. It is important, however, to bring students' existing knowledge about renewable resources to the forefront of their minds. In this case, students benefit from previewing the text, thinking about what they already know about the topic, and making predictions about what they will learn (Klingner et al., 2004; Vaughn, Klingner et al., 2011).

Explicit vocabulary instruction. In addition to building background knowledge, students benefit from explicit vocabulary instruction across content area. In other words, vocabulary instruction that includes social studies, science, and mathematics as well as language arts. A high level of vocabulary knowledge is associated with high levels of reading comprehension (Elleman et al., 2009). One of the ways that students improve their vocabulary knowledge is through wide reading of a range of text types. Students who read more acquire greater vocabulary through access to a range of words in text that they are unlikely to encounter in oral language alone (Stanovich & Cunningham, 1993). Unfortunately, students with reading difficulties often spend less time reading, which negatively impacts their vocabulary development. Elleman and colleagues (2009) found that struggling readers benefit three times as much as students without reading problems from vocabulary intervention (i.e., in improving reading comprehension outcomes). As such, it is critical that interventionists provide explicit vocabulary instruction to students with reading comprehension difficulties.

Knowing which words to teach is an ongoing question that many educators ask. While there is no one right way to select words, the following procedures may be useful to practitioners when selecting which words to teach: (1) less is more, so select two to three words per text; and (2) choose words with high content value and high utility (Beck, McKeown, & Kucan, 2002; Hairrell et al., 2010; Vaughn et al., 2013). Of course, words that students are not familiar with are a high priority. Teachers should consider which words are critical to students' understanding of the text and words that can be utilized across multiple content areas (e.g., the women's suffrage *movement* versus the *movement* of water in phases of the water cycle).

Students benefit from explicit vocabulary instruction that incorporates multiple strategies to learn and to apply terms (Beck et al., 2002). In other words, simply providing students with definitions will not be sufficient. Research-based practices include providing a student-friendly definition, illustration of the word's meaning, word associations (i.e., other words that are related in some way to the new term), student-generated examples (e.g., use the word in a sentence), and examples and nonexamples of the word (Beck et al., 2002; Simmons et al., 2010; Vaughn et al., 2013). Additionally, teachers may consider using a turn-and-talk question, which prompts students to engage in a discussion using the new term. Students need multiple exposures to a new word, providing many opportunities to connect the word to the content learned (Vaughn et al., 2013). Graphic organizers can be used to support word learning using these strategies (see Figure 15.2).

Explicit vocabulary instruction includes practices that facilitate independent word learning. One way for students to acquire words independently is through the use of context clues (Simmons et al., 2010). With repeated practice, students can learn to infer the meaning of unfamiliar words using the clues or information provided in the text. For example, context clues may provide the definition (e.g., *Plateaus*, high stretches of flat land, are common in Africa) or a synonym (e.g., The government held a *convention* to write a new constitution. At the three-day meeting, they wrote Texas's new constitution) for the target word. General context clues do not explicitly state the meaning of the word (i.e., as with definition and synonym clues); in this case, students use their background knowledge and the context to infer the meaning of the target term (e.g., Sam was *lethargic* and didn't have energy to get out of bed).

Another way to acquire words is through explicit instruction in morphology. Morphology is the study of morphemes, the smallest unit of meaning in a word. This includes knowledge of prefixes, suffixes, roots, and word transformations (i.e., spelling and sound changes when morphemes are added or removed from a word; e.g., politics, politician, political; Kieffer & Lesaux, 2007). When students have an

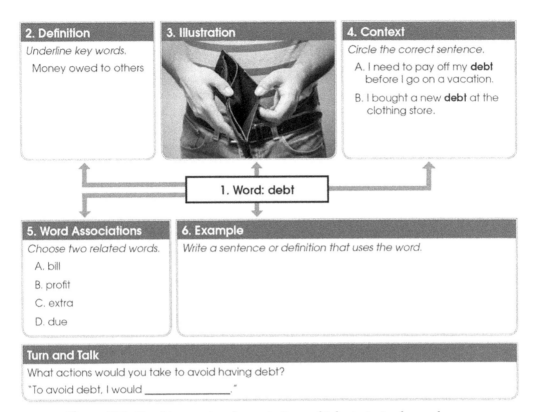

Figure 15.2 *Graphic organizer demonstrating multiple strategies for word learning*

understanding of word structures, they are able to break down an unfamiliar word into its subparts (i.e., morphemes) in order to better understand text. Students' morphological understanding is related to their reading comprehension, and this becomes increasingly important as they move through the grades (Kieffer & Lesaux, 2007). Kieffer and Lesaux (2007) recommend teaching morphology as an explicit cognitive strategy: (1) identify an unfamiliar term, (2) analyze the word for known morphemes, (3) use the word parts to infer the meaning of the word, and (4) check the inferred meaning against the word's context. For example, knowing that the prefixes *in-, im-, ir-, and il-* mean not, students can infer the meaning of the words *inaccurate, impolite, irresponsible*, and *illogical*. As students practice this skill, they break words apart into prefixes, bases or roots, and suffixes to determine meaning (e.g., *inactivity* contains the prefix *in-* meaning not, the base *active*, and the suffix *–ity* meaning quality of). It is important that students practice the application of these cognitive strategies while reading text.

During Reading

Good readers recognize when their understanding breaks down and they employ practices to repair their understanding. Struggling readers, however, need to be taught how to monitor their understanding while reading. This section describes evidence-based practices for improving students' reading for understanding; these practices help students to recognize when they have an incomplete understanding of text and to repair misunderstandings to improve comprehension.

Asking and answering questions. Asking and answering questions prompts discussion and provides the opportunity to clarify any misunderstandings in content knowledge (Vaughn et al., 2013). Questioning while reading can be teacher-generated or student-generated. Initially, it is important for teachers to model how to ask different question types and to vary their question types in order to elicit a range of levels of thinking about text. For example, questions that start with "Where" and "When" often require students to recall or consider what was in the text. Questions that start with "How" or "Why" require students to integrate, reflect, and or consider inferences about the text and previous knowledge or reading. In addition to having teachers ask a range of question types, there is value in having students generate questions that they ask themselves or others. For example, with upper elementary students, teachers might ask students to ask "What," "When," or "Where" questions initially. These questions are typically easier for students to generate. Teachers can ask students to work in small groups and generate questions about text and then call on others in the group to answer them. As students acquire greater proficiency with these question types, they can practice more challenging questions such as those that ask about "How" or "Why." Of course, these are not the only question types available to teachers and students. Questions that ask students to compare texts, contrast ideas in one text with those in another text, and other ways that encourage students to use multiple texts to integrate, synthesize, and compare texts can be exceedingly helpful in improving reading comprehension. Questioning can also facilitate connections between new information in the text and previously taught vocabulary terms or the overarching big idea or question guiding a unit or set of texts (see the section on "building background knowledge").

Monitoring comprehension. Many students with reading comprehension problems do not adequately monitor their text understanding while they read. They perceive reading as a task in which they "plow through words" with little consideration of whether the words make sense and how the various elements of the story or information in the text go together. A significant part of reading comprehension is connecting the information within text and connecting what you are reading with what you already know. One practice for improving students' understanding of text while reading is "click and clunk." The click and clunk strategy teaches students to monitor understanding of the text by identifying clicks, parts of the text that make sense, and clunks, any misunderstanding that the student encounters, including vocabulary words or ideas (Klingner et al., 2004; Vaughn, Klingner et al., 2011). Through teacher modeling of when text "clicks," teachers demonstrate reading proficiency and asking themselves questions to make sure they understand what they are reading. After students observe the teacher's model, they are provided structured opportunities to practices with shorter texts (e.g., paragraphs) and then increasing to longer texts. Learning to identify "clunks" is taught in a similar way with the teacher initially modeling reading and identifying words or ideas that don't make sense. Students learn to identify "clunks" and then to apply fix-up strategies to repair misunderstandings or words they don't know. A fix-up practice is a set of actions, or tools, that students can use when encountering difficulty with the task. Fix-up practices may include rereading the sentence to look for key ideas, rereading the sentences before and after the clunk, or looking for known word parts (e.g., prefixes, suffixes, roots).

Main ideas and summarization. Summarization is another research-based practice for improving reading comprehension (Brown & Palincsar, 1987; Duke & Pearson, 2008; Watson et al., 2012). Explicit main idea instruction is often included in multicomponent reading interventions (e.g., Wanzek et al., 2016). Summarizing text is a complex process that requires readers to monitor their understanding, identify important information, and eliminate irrelevant details (Jitendra et al., 2001). A critical component of the summarization process is students' skill in identifying main ideas; this process improves comprehension because it helps the reader remember the important information (e.g., Hagaman et al., 2016).

Paraphrasing is one way to support students' identification of main ideas while reading. Schumaker, Denton, and Deshler (1994) introduced the RAP strategy (i.e., read a paragraph, ask yourself what was the main idea and two details, put the main idea and details into your own words). Another paraphrasing strategy is Get the Gist, which is a key comprehension activity in the multicomponent interventions Collaborative Strategic Reading and Peer Assisted Learning Strategies (Saenz, Fuchs, & Fuchs, 2005; Vaughn, Klingner et al., 2011). Get the Gist (see Figure 15.3) is a three-step paraphrasing process (1) identify the most important "who" or "what" in the text, (2) identify the most important thing about the "who" or "what"; and (3) write the gist in ten words or less. Requiring students to master the first step in the process and using graphic organizers are ways to scaffold instruction.

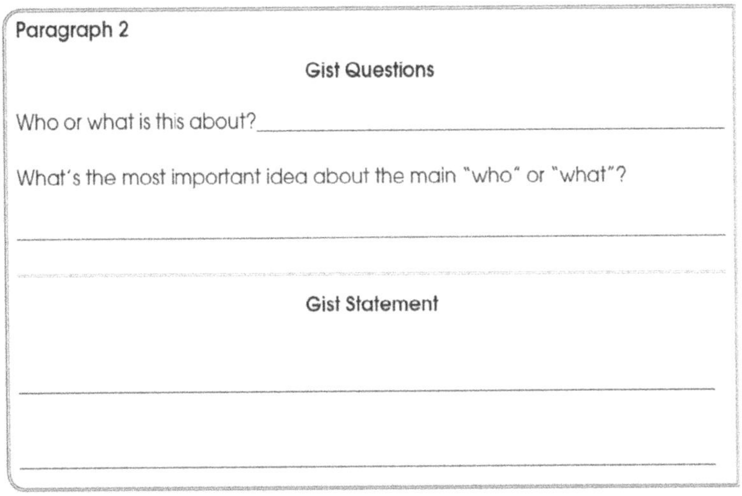

> Paragraph 2
>
> Gist Questions
>
> Who or what is this about?_____
>
> What's the most important idea about the main "who" or "what"?
>
> _____
>
> Gist Statement
>
> _____

Figure 15.3 *Get the Gist graphic organizer*

Identifying the most important part of the section may be difficult for students; process-specific feedback may guide students in applying fix-up practices during the paraphrasing process. Fix-up practices may include checking the headings or topic sentence to provide a clue regarding that section's main idea, rereading the text, or verifying one's main idea statement with self-questioning: (1) Is this the most important event that happened in this paragraph (i.e., narrative)? (2) Does the whole paragraph tell about this idea (i.e., expository)? Once students develop main idea statements across several sections, the gists can be combined to develop a summary of the entire text.

After Reading

During reading practices support comprehension monitoring and identifying the key ideas while students read. After reading activities provide students the opportunity to reflect on the content of the entire passage. Two evidence-based practices, question generation and wrap-up statements, support students in reflecting on the meaning of the passage as a whole.

Question generation. In addition to asking and answering questions while reading, opportunities to ask and discuss questions after reading is associated with improved outcomes (Raphael & Pearson, 1985). Many of the productive questions that teachers ask can lead students to think more about text and connect through discourse with others in the class. Additionally, students can ask questions of themselves or others to improve understanding. Students ask questions that can be answered in the text, which improves memory, content knowledge, and highlights the most important information (Klingner et al., 2004; Vaughn, Klingner et al., 2011). Teachers can help students learn to generate and organize questions based on a hierarchy of lower- to higher-level thinking (e.g., the answer is explicitly stated in one part of the text, the answer requires the reader to synthesize information in various parts of the text, and the answer requires the reader to use his or her prior knowledge and information in the passage). Question generation allows teachers to evaluate students' reading comprehension based on (1) the quality of the question asked and (2) whether or not the question can be answered using the text.

Summarize. Learning to summarize increasingly lengthy text by providing the key ideas is an important way to demonstrate text understanding and improve learning. A summary may also be considered a final wrap-up statement. When students learn to generate main ideas during text reading, summarizing is less difficult because they can access main ideas as a resource for integrating a summary of the entire passage (Klingner et al., 2004; Vaughn, Klingner et al., 2011). After examining the section-level main ideas for all parts of the text, students can integrate these main ideas to produce a text-level summary. This task supports students in organizing information from the reading and focusing on the most important information. These statements also serve as a discussion springboard as the class can discuss which statements best represent the key ideas presented in the text.

Discussion-Based Comprehension

Discussion-based practices provide opportunities for students to describe their understanding of text, use text to support their views, integrate and respond to comments of other students, and remember what they read. Many of these discourse-based practices are embedded within collaborative grouping opportunities (Klingner et al., 2004; Simmons et al., 2010; Vaughn, Klingner et al., 2011; Vaughn et al., 2013). This is an important aspect of instruction for students with reading comprehension difficulties because it allows for text-based discussion, opportunities to hear the views of others and to adjust their own views, and ways to synthesize learning and comprehension (Goldman et al., 2016). Struggling readers benefit from listening to others' thought processes about text. Participating in text-based conversation may support students' motivation, engagement, and understanding of text (Vaughn et al., 2013).

Intensifying Intervention for Students with Persistent Reading Comprehension Difficulties

The practices previously discussed are associated with improved outcomes for many readers with reading comprehension difficulties; however, it is often necessary to provide more intensive instruction for some students with reading difficulties who continue to display significant challenges. This section reviews four approaches to intensify interventions: intensify the instructional delivery, integrate self-regulation and executive functioning strategies, increase dosage, and reduce group size (Vaughn et al., 2012).

Intensify Instructional Delivery

Intensive intervention (i.e., Tier 3) differs from previous instruction in content and delivery. The content targets each student's needs as determined by frequent progress monitoring. Curriculum-based measures (e.g., letter-sound fluency, oral reading fluency) can be used frequently and are relatively easy to administer. Graphing the results provides teachers with immediate feedback on student performance. If progress-monitoring data reveal limited response, then the intervention must be adapted and intensified to meet the student's needs. A specific reading program, approach, or practice will not be sufficient to meet students' needs.

Intensive intervention provides explicit, systematic instruction. Explicit instruction refers to a sequence in which teachers (1) tell students what it is they need to know, (2) model the task step-by-step, (3) provide guided practice in which the task is repeated with students' help, and (4) provide independent practice in which students conduct the task without guidance or support. Instruction is also systematic, meaning complex skills are broken into smaller, more manageable parts. Teachers instruct students in the easier subskills first and then proceed to the more difficult components; scaffolding is provided as needed throughout the process. Teachers may cycle back through the process in order to provide more modeling, extended opportunities for practice with feedback, and temporary support that is reduced as students become more proficient with the task. Feedback plays a critical role in students' acquisition of new skills. Struggling students often require many practice opportunities to master a new skill; as such, task-specific and process-specific feedback allows students to hone their skills (Hattie & Timperley, 2007).

Self-Regulation and Executive Functioning Strategies

Students with reading comprehension difficulties also may have challenges with executive function (e.g., memory and attention) and self-regulation (e.g., monitoring one's own behavior or thinking). Combining reading instruction with strategies that support self-regulation and executive functioning improves outcomes for struggling readers. Using "during reading" strategies and goal setting facilitate students' regulation of their understanding while reading text. Students benefit from evaluating their learning goals, charting progress, and reflecting on what's working well and what needs improvement in order to meet the goal.

Increase Dosage

Increasing the quantity of instruction is an important characteristic of intensifying intervention because it allows for increased learning time and practice opportunities. This can be accomplished by increasing the length of each session, number of sessions per week, or total sessions. This is particularly important for older struggling readers, as they often need extended time (i.e., more than one year) in intervention. Other factors to consider when determining dosage are the difficulty of academic tasks and students' stamina. For example, first graders struggling with reading comprehension may benefit from shorter sessions (i.e., 30 minutes) twice per day rather than 60 minutes once a day.

Reduce Group Size

Reducing group size intensifies intervention by promoting attention and engagement in academic tasks. Research shows that the smaller group sizes (i.e., one to four students) yield the highest effects for students in Grades K through 3 (Wanzek & Vaughn, 2007). Practitioners should consider using other resources (e.g., computer programs, volunteers, paraeducators) to assist with practice opportunities while reserving time with the teacher for systematic and explicit instruction in new tasks. Reducing group size may not be as important for older struggling readers. Vaughn, Wanzek, and colleagues (2010) found that group size was not associated with increased reading performance for middle school students. It may be that adolescent readers make gains regardless of receiving instruction in small (i.e., four to five) or large (i.e., ten to twelve students) groups. Although more research is needed to determine the optimal group size for adolescent struggling readers, providing intensive intervention in larger groups is less costly and may be more feasible for schools.

Future Research Directions

Current evidence supports the effectiveness of reading interventions for students with reading comprehension difficulties; however, improving reading comprehension for students with significant reading problems is unlikely to occur quickly. In spite of the increasing knowledge base about reading comprehension instruction, many questions remain regarding the effects of comprehension interventions, particularly for secondary struggling readers. Other than Vaughn and colleagues' longitudinal work described previously (Vaughn, Cirino et al., 2010; Vaughn, Wexler et al., 2011; Vaughn, Wexler et al., 2012), no other studies have examined the effects of continued, increasingly intensive tiers of support for older students with limited RTI.

Future research might further examine the best ways to provide long-term, intensive interventions for middle and high school students with intractable reading difficulties. Current evidence suggests large groups may be as effective as small groups for older struggling readers but further research is needed to identify the most optimal instructional grouping. School systems might consider individualized versus standardized approaches to providing intensive intervention. Given the training required to prepare teachers to provide effective reading intervention, using a standardized approach with larger groups of students may be more feasible and manageable for middle and high schools. Providing additional instructional time may be easier in the elementary grades due to more flexible scheduling; schools may need to consider options for alleviating scheduling barriers so that multiyear, sustained interventions can be provided.

Researchers might also consider examining the most effective components to include in multicomponent interventions. How can each component (e.g., summarization instruction) be strengthened? Are there ways to adjust multicomponent interventions to meet individual students' needs? For example, how might students respond when provided more of one component (i.e., based on needs identified through progress monitoring) versus another? Finally, students apply learned strategies within the context of the intervention but often have difficulty generalizing skill use during independently reading. Researchers might examine ways to support skill generalization as well as the application of strategies in new and various contexts.

In addition to the many questions related to instruction that research might address, there are other theoretical questions that might improve our understanding of reading comprehension instruction (Compton et al., 2014). For example, it may be that the "next generation" of reading interventions would more fully consider the role of word reading and word meaning as well as how language, knowledge, and learning contribute to our understanding of texts. Particularly for developing readers after Grade 4, understanding text deeply requires significant knowledge about the topic but also knowledge of language structures that allow accessing text. How we devise instructional supports to enhance these mechanisms will likely determine our success in designing even more robust interventions for students with significant reading difficulties.

References

Anderson, R. C. (1984). Role of the reader's schema in comprehension, learning, and memory. In R. Anderson, J. Osborn, & R. Tierney (eds.), *Learning to read in American schools: Basal readers and content texts* (pp. 243–257). Hillsdale, NJ: Lawrence Erlbaum.

Anderson, R. C. & Pearson, P. D. (1984). A schema-theoretic view of basic processes in reading. In P. D. Pearson (ed.), *Handbook of reading research* (pp. 255–291). Mahwah, NJ: Lawrence Erlbaum.

Beck, I.L., McKeown, M.G., & Kucan, L. (2002). *Bringing words to life: Robust vocabulary instruction.* New York: Guilford.

Biancarosa, C. & Snow, C. E. (2006). *Reading next – A vision for action and research in middle and high school literacy: A report to Carnegie Corporation of New York,* 2nd edn. Washington, DC: Alliance for Excellent Education.

Brown, A. L. & Day, J. D. (1983). Macrorules for summarizing texts: The development of expertise. *Journal of Verbal Learning and Verbal Behavior, 22*(1), 1–14. https://doi .org/10.1016/S0022-5371(83)80002-4

Brown, A. L. & Palincsar, A. S. (1987). Reciprocal teaching of comprehension strategies: A natural history of one program for enhancing learning. In J. Day & J. Borkowski (eds.), *Intelligence and exceptionality: New directions for theory, assessment, and instructional practices* (pp. 81–132). Westport, CT: Ablex Publishing.

Brozo, W. G. (2009). Response to intervention or responsive instruction? Challenges and possibilities of response to intervention for adolescent literacy. *Journal of Adolescent and Adult Literacy, 53,* 277–281. https://doi.org/10.1598/JAAL.53.4.1

Chall, J. S. (1983). *Learning to read: The great debate.* New York: McGraw-Hill.

Chard, D. J., Vaughn, S., & Tyler, B. (2002). A synthesis of research on effective interventions for building reading fluency with elementary students with learning disabilities. *Journal of Learning Disabilities, 35,* 386–406. https://doi.org/10.1177/ 00222194020350050101

Compton, D. L., Miller, A. C., Elleman, A. M., & Steacy, L. M. (2014). Have we forsaken reading theory in the name of "quick fix" interventions for children with reading disability? *Scientific Studies of Reading, 18*(1), 55–73. https://doi.org/10.1080/ 10888438.2013.836200

Duffy, G. G., Roehler, L. R., Sivan, E., Rackliffe, G., Book, C., Meloth, M. S., . . . & Bassiri, D. (1987). Effects of explaining the reasoning associated with using reading strategies. *Reading Research Quarterly, 22*(3), 347–368. https://doi.org/10.2307/747973

Duke, N. K. & Pearson, P. D. (2008). Effective practices for developing reading comprehension. *The Journal of Education, 189*(1/2), 107–122

Durkin, D. (1978). What classroom observations reveal about reading comprehension instruction. *Reading Research Quarterly, 14,* 481–533.

Edmonds, M. S., Vaughn, S., Wexler, J., Reutebuch, C., Cable, A., Tackett, K. K., & Schnakenberg, J. W. (2009). A synthesis of reading interventions and effects on reading comprehension outcomes for older struggling readers. *Review of Educational Research, 79,* 262–300. https://doi.org/10.3102/0034654308325998

Elleman, A., Lindo, E. J., Murphy, P., & Compton, D. (2009). The impact of vocabulary instruction on passage-level comprehension of school-age children: A meta-analysis. *Journal of Research on Educational Effectiveness, 2*(1),1–44. https://doi.org/10.1080/ 19345740802539200

Every Student Succeeds Act (2015). Pub. L. No. 114–95 § 114 Stat. 1177 (2015–2016).

Gajria, M. & Salvia, J. (1992). The effects of summarization instruction on text comprehension of students with learning disabilities. *Exceptional Children, 58*(6), 508–516. https://doi.org/10.1177/001440299205800605

Gallini, J. K., Spires, H. A., Terry, S., & Gleaton, J. (1993). The influence of macro and micro-level cognitive strategies training on text learning. *Journal of Research and Development in Education, 26*(3), 164–178.

Goldman, S. R., Snow, C., & Vaughn, S. (2016). Common themes in teaching reading for understanding: Lessons from three projects. *Journal of Adolescent and Adult Literacy, 60*(3), 255–264. https://doi.org/10.1002/jaal.586

Gough, P. B. & Tunmer, W. E. (1986). Decoding, reading, and reading disability. *Remedial and Special Education, 7*(1), 6–10.

Hagaman, J. L., Casey, K. J., & Reid, R. (2016). Paraphrasing strategy instruction for struggling readers. *Preventing School Failure: Alternative Education for Children and Youth, 60*(1), 43–52. https://doi.org/10.1080/1045988X.2014.966802

Hairrell, A., Simmons, D., Swanson, E., Edmonds, M., Vaughn, S., & Rupley, W. H. (2010). Translating vocabulary research to social studies instruction: Before, during, and after text-reading strategies. *Intervention in School and Clinic, 46*(4), 204–210. https://doi.org/10.1177/1053451210389606

Hattie, J. & Timperley, H. (2007). The power of feedback. *Review of Educational Research, 77*(1), 81–112. https://doi.org/10.3102/003465430298487

IDEIA (Individuals With Disabilities Education Improvement Act), 20 U.S.C. § 1400 (2004) *Biennial report to Congress: Institute of Education Sciences*. http://ies.ed.gov/pdf/biennialrpt05.Pdf

Jitendra, A. K., Chard, D., Hoppes, M. K., Renouf, K., & Gardill, M. C. (2001). An evaluation of main idea strategy instruction in four commercial reading programs: Implications for students with learning problems. *Reading and Writing Quarterly, 17*(1), 53–73. https://doi.org/10.1080/105735601455738

Jitendra, A. K., Hoppes, M. K., & Xin, Y. P. (2000). Enhancing main idea comprehension for students with learning problems: The role of a summarization strategy and self-monitoring instruction. *The Journal of Special Education, 34*(3), 127–139. https://doi.org/10.1177/002246690003400302

Kamil, M. L., Borman, G. D., Dole, J., Kral, C. C., Salinger, T., & Torgesen, J. (2008). *Improving adolescent literacy: Effective classroom and intervention practices: A Practice Guide (NCEE #2008–4027)*. Washington, DC: National Center for Education Evaluation and Regional Assistance, Institute of Education Sciences, and US Department of Education. http://ies.ed.gov/ncee/wwc.

Kieffer, M. J. & Lesaux, N. K. (2007). Breaking down words to build meaning: Morphology, vocabulary, and reading comprehension in the urban classroom. *The Reading Teacher, 61*(2), 134–144. https://doi.org/10.1598/RT.61.2.3

Klingner, J. K., Vaughn, S., Arguelles, M. E., Hughes, M. T., & Leftwich, S. A. (2004). Collaborative strategic reading "real-world" lessons from classroom teachers. *Remedial and Special Education, 25*(5), 291–302.

Levin, J. R. (1973). Inducing comprehension in poor readers: A test of a recent model. *Journal of Educational Psychology, 65*(1), 19–24. https://doi.org/10.1037/h0034818

National Education Summit on High Schools. (2005). *An action agenda for improving America's high schools*. www.achieve.org/SummitActionAgenda

NCES (National Center for Education Statistics). (2015). *The nation's report card: Trends in academic progress 2015 (NCES 2015–136).* Washington, DC: National Center for Education Statistics, Institute of Education Sciences, and US Department of Education.

NCLB (No Child Left Behind Act). (2001). Pub. L. No. 107–110, § 115, Stat. 1425 (2002).

Newman, L., Wagner, M., Huang, T., Shaver, D., Knokey, A.-M., Yu, J., . . . Cameto, R. (2011). *Secondary school programs and performance of students with disabilities. A special topic report of findings from the national longitudinal transition Study-2 (NLTS2) (NCSER 2012–3000).* Washington, DC: National Center for Special Education Research and US Department of Education.

Paivia, A. (1971). *Imagery and verbal processes.* New York: Holt, Rinehart & Winston.

  (1986). *Mental representations: A dual-coding approach.* New York: Oxford University Press.

Palincsar, A. S. & Brown, A. L. (1984). Reciprocal teaching of comprehension-fostering and comprehension-monitoring activities. *Cognition and Instruction, 1,* 117–175. https://doi.org/10.1207/s1532690xci0102_1

Pressley, G. M. (1976). Mental imagery helps eight-year-olds remember what they read. *Journal of Educational Psychology, 68*(3), 355–359. https://doi.org/10.1037/0022–0663.68.3.355

Pressley, M., Wharton-McDonald, R., Mistretta-Hampston, J., & Echevarria, M. (1998). Literacy instruction in 10 fourth-grade classrooms in upstate New York. *Scientific Studies of Reading, 2*(2), 159–194. https://doi.org/10.1207/s1532799xssr0202_4

Raphael, T. E. & Pearson, P. D. (1985). Increasing students' awareness of sources of information for answering questions. *American Educational Research Journal, 22* (2), 217–235.

Rosenblatt (1978). *The reader, the text, the poem: The transactional theory of the literary work.* Carbondale: Southern Illinois University Press.

Saenz, L., Fuchs, L., & Fuchs, D. (2005). Peer-assisted learning strategies for English language learners with learning disabilities. *Exceptional Children, 71*(3), 231–247. https://doi.org/10.1177/001440290507100302

Scammacca, N., Roberts, G., Vaughn, S., Edmonds, M., Wexler, J., Reutebuch, C. K., & Torgesen, J. K. (2007). *Interventions for adolescent struggling readers: A meta-analysis with implications for practice.* Portsmouth, NH: RMC Research Corporation, Center on Instruction.

Scammacca, N. K., Roberts, G., Vaughn, S., & Stuebing, K. K. (2015). A meta-analysis of interventions for struggling readers in grades 4–12: 1980–2011. *Journal of Learning Disabilities, 48*(4), 369–390. https://doi.org/10.1177/0022219413504995

Schumaker, J. B., Denton, P. H., & Deshler, D. D. (1994). *The paraphrasing strategy: Instructor's manual.* Lawrence: University of Kansas Institute for Research in Learning Disabilities.

Simmons, D., Hairrell, A., Edmonds, M., Vaughn, S., Larsen, R., Willson, V., . . . & Byrns, G. (2010). A comparison of multiple-strategy methods: Effects on fourth-grade students' general and content-specific reading comprehension and vocabulary development. *Journal of Research on Educational Effectiveness, 3*(2), 121–156. https://doi.org/10.1080/19345741003596890

Solis, M., Miciak, J., Vaughn, S., & Fletcher, J. M. (2014). Why intensive interventions matter: Longitudinal studies of adolescents with reading disabilities and poor

reading comprehension. *Learning Disability Quarterly, 37*(4), 218–229. https://doi
.org/10.1177/0731948714528806

Stanovich, K. E. & Cunningham, A. E. (1993). Where does knowledge come from? Specific
associations between print exposure and information acquisition. *Journal of
Educational Psychology, 85*(2), 211–229. https://doi.org/10.1037/
0022–0663.85.2.211

Stevens, E. A., Walker, M. A., & Vaughn, S. (2017). The effects of reading fluency interventions on the reading fluency and reading comprehension performance of elementary
students with learning disabilities: A synthesis of the research from 2001 to 2014.
Journal of Learning Disabilities, 50(5), 576–590. https://doi.org/10.1177/
0022219416638028

Toste, J. R., Fuchs, D., & Fuchs, L. S. (2013). Supporting struggling readers in high school.
In R. T. Boon & V. G. Spencer (eds.), *Adolescent literacy* (pp. 79–91). Baltimore,
MD: Brookes.

van Dijk, T. A. & Kintsch, W. (1983). *Strategies for discourse comprehension*. New York:
Academic Press.

Vaughn, S. & Fletcher, J. M. (2012). Response to intervention with secondary school students
with reading difficulties. *Journal of Learning Disabilities, 45*(3), 244–256. https://
doi.org/10.1177/0022219412442157

Vaughn, S. & Fuchs, L. S. (2003). Redefining learning disabilities as inadequate response to
instruction: The promise and potential problems. *Learning Disabilities Research
and Practice, 18*(3), 137–146. https://doi.org/10.1111/1540–5826.00070

Vaughn, S., Cirino, P. T., Wanzek, J., Wexler, J., Fletcher, J. M., Denton, C. D.,… Francis, D. J.
(2010). Response to intervention for middle school students with reading difficulties:
Effects of a primary and secondary intervention. *School Psychology Review, 39*(1), 3–21.

Vaughn, S., Klingner, J. K., Swanson, E. A., Boardman, A. G., Roberts, G., Mohammed, S. S.,
& Stillman-Spisak, S. J. (2011). Efficacy of collaborative strategic reading with
middle school students. *American Educational Research Journal, 48*(4), 938–964.
https://doi.org/10.3102/0002831211410305

Vaughn, S., Swanson, E. A., Roberts, G., Wanzek, J., Stillman-Spisak, S. J., Solis, M., &
Simmons, D. (2013). Improving reading comprehension and social studies knowledge in middle school. *Reading Research Quarterly, 48*(1), 77–93. https://doi.org/
10.1002/rrq.039

Vaughn, S. Wanzek, J., Murray, C. S., & Roberts, G. (2012). *Intensive interventions for
students struggling in reading and mathematics: A practice guide*. Portsmouth, NH:
RMC Research Corporation, Center on Instruction.

Vaughn, S., Wanzek, J., Wexler, J., Barth, A., Cirino, P. T., Fletcher, J. M.,… Francis, D. J.
(2010). The relative effects of group size on reading progress of older students with
reading difficulties. *Reading and Writing, 23*, 931–956. https://doi.org/10.1007/
s11145-009-9183-9

Vaughn, S., Wexler, J., Leroux, A., Roberts, G., Denton, C., Barth, A., & Fletcher, J. M.
(2012). Effects of intensive reading intervention for eighth-grade students with
persistently inadequate response to intervention. *Journal of Learning Disabilities,
45*(6), 515–525. https://doi.org/10.1177/0022219411402692

Vaughn, S., Wexler, J., Roberts, G., Barth, A. A., Cirino, P. T., Romain, M. A., … &
Denton, C. A. (2011). Effects of individualized and standardized interventions on
middle school students with reading disabilities. *Exceptional Children, 77*(4),
391–407. https://doi.org/10.1177/001440291107700401

Wanzek, J. & Vaughn, S. (2007). Research-based implications from extensive early reading interventions. *School Psychology Review, 36*(4), 541–561.

Wanzek, J., Vaughn, S., Scammacca, N., Gatlin, B., Walker, M. A., & Capin, P. (2016). Meta-analyses of the effects of tier 2 type reading interventions in Grades K-3. *Educational Psychology Review, 28*(3), 551–576. https://doi.org/10.1007/s10648-015-9321-7

Wanzek, J., Vaughn, S., Scammacca, N. K., Metz, K., Murray, C. S., Roberts, G., & Danielson, L. (2013). Extensive reading interventions for students with reading difficulties after grade 3. *Review of Educational Research, 83*(2), 163–195. https://doi.org/10.3102/0034654313477212

Watson, S. M. R., Gable, R. A., Gear, S. B., & Hughes, K. C. (2012). Evidence-based strategies for improving the reading comprehension of secondary students: Implications for students with learning disabilities. *Learning Disabilities Research and Practice, 27*(2), 79–89. https://doi.org/10.1111/j.1540–5826.2012.00353.x

Weisberg, R. K. & Balajthy, E. (1990). Development of disabled readers' metacomprehension ability through summarization training using expository text: Results of three studies. *Journal of Reading, Writing, & Learning Disabilities International, 6*(2), 117–136. https://doi.org/10.1080/0748763900060204

PART IV

General Learning Strategies

16 When Does Interleaving Practice Improve Learning?

Paulo F. Carvalho and Robert L. Goldstone

Introduction

As you flip through the pages of this handbook you will notice that the content does not seem to be randomly organized. The content of the handbook is *sequenced* in a particular way: foundations before general strategies, background before applications, and so on. The editors envisaged a sequence of topics, the authors of each topic envisaged a sequence of information in each chapter, and so forth. We selected a particular sequence because we considered it to be effective. Deciding how to sequence information takes place all the time in educational contexts, from educators deciding how to organize their syllabus to educational technology designers deciding how to organize a piece of educational software, from handbook editors and writers deciding how to organize their materials, to students making decisions as to how to organize their study. One might imagine that as long as all students study the same materials, regardless of the sequence in which they study it, they will all learn the same information. This could not be further from the truth. In this chapter, we review evidence of how and why the sequence of study changes what is learned. In doing so, we uncover the powerful ways in which sequence can improve or deter learning.

How Does the Sequence of Study Affect Learning and Why Does It Matter?

Cognitive psychologists have long identified the powerful effect that the sequence in which information is presented has on cognition and, specifically, on learning and memory. The main research question is, given the same amount and nature of training, how is learning affected by changing the sequence in which the information is presented? This question has a long history in cognitive science because it has the potential to inform theories of learning. If learning is the process of connecting and integrating new information into existing structures, then which information is learned first should have an impact on how later information is integrated and ultimately what is learned. Thus, studying sequencing effects can help us understand the learning *process*. Of course, these findings can also directly inform practice by helping educational designers, teachers, and students know which factors to consider when deciding how to sequence learning materials.

For example, Elio and Anderson (1984) proposed that learning should start with low-variability items (e.g., items that do not differ much from one another or from the central tendency of the category) and items with greater variability should be introduced later (for similar evidence with young learners, see Sandhofer & Doumas, 2008). When learning about mammals, one should probably start by studying deer, gazelles, moose, and impalas, and only after having covered these more similar types of mammals move to bats and whales. However, not all learners benefit from this approach. Elio and Anderson (1984) also showed that if the learners' approach to the task is to consciously generate hypotheses of category membership, the pattern of results is reversed. One possibility is that how the learner approaches the task changes what type of information gets encoded and, consequently, what information is more relevant (Elio & Anderson, 1984); when learners are asked to generate explicit hypotheses, starting with low-variability items could lead them to be biased toward incorrect or partial classification rules (in the example above, that all mammals have four legs, for example). In these conditions, starting with high-variability items helps learners to not settle on incorrect hypotheses, whereas when learners are not trying to create explicit rules, the initially reduced variability leads learners to abstract common properties that are likely to characterize most, if not all, items of the category (Elio & Anderson, 1984).

Consistent with these results, it has also been suggested that for optimal transfer of category learning, the study situation should emphasize items that promote a coherent generalization based on the properties that occur more frequently (Elio & Anderson, 1981). Moreover, in situations where one needs to learn several items that promote different types of generalizations, best learning is achieved by studying items close in time that promote similar generalizations (Elio & Anderson, 1981; Mathy & Feldman, 2009).

Students often struggle to decide whether to get difficult material out of the way by studying it early or studying it last. In general, research seems to indicate that learning benefits from study with examples organized in increasing order of complexity or difficulty, i.e., from the easiest and simplest to the hardest and more complex (Hull, 1920; Terrace, 1964). But the reverse pattern has also been shown. For example, Lee and colleagues (1988) showed that learners who start by studying examples other learners classified incorrectly made fewer errors during later classification tests than learners who studied the examples in the opposite order. One possibility is that starting with difficult items might be beneficial only for concepts organized around a clear rule, whereas the reverse is true for concepts requiring the integration across different dimensions (Spiering & Ashby, 2008). Why? When learners study easy items, for which identifying the classification rule is easy, closer in time, they will identify the rule faster and with ease. This is good for learning. But when there is no such rule, studying together items that are easy to categorize together might lead learners to assume a rule that is not correct or only partially correct (Spiering & Ashby, 2008).

Three important aspects are salient from the above brief review of sequencing effects in learning: (1) learning takes place by integrating previous experience with current experience and is sensitive to which sequence is used; (2) no one way of sequencing is optimal for everyone, every time, and with every material; and (3) the optimal sequence depends on a match between the learning process and the properties of the sequence. These conclusions will set the stage for our overview of one particular sequencing effect: the learning impact of interleaved practice.

The Case of Blocked and Interleaved Practice

School involves learning different topics across and within several disciplines. For example, a math course might involve learning about area, perimeter, volume, and so on. The above discussion implicitly envisions sequences of study materials where one topic is introduced and finished before the next one, but it does not have to be that way. When different topics are studied separately, we have *blocked practice* – a textbook might start with a section on calculating area, practice problems on area, and only then move on to perimeter, and so on. This sequence can perhaps consider difficulty and prerequisites, as discussed above, in how to decide how to order these blocks, that is, whether area or perimeter should happen first.[1] By most accounts, albeit a general and quantifiable metric of content similarity has not yet been devised, most learning and practice tools (classes, textbooks, tutoring systems, etc.), are organized this way (Bjork, Dunlosky, & Kornell, 2013).

However, another possibility is to alternate practice of different topics, i.e., *interleaved practice*. This could mean, for example, introducing area, perimeter and volume in the same session and practicing them in alternating or random order. Although arguably not as common in educational practice, interleaved practice has received recent support from educational researchers, suggesting that it might yield substantial benefits over the traditional blocked practice.

Our focus in the remainder of this chapter will be in understanding when and how interleaved practice can improve learning but also when it does not and when blocked practice should be used instead. We will start with a brief overview of empirical evidence in favor of interleaved practice. We will then cover evidence of negative or neutral effects of interleaved practice and conclude with a theoretical framework to help understand – and predict – when interleaved practice should be used.

Using Interleaved Practice to Boost Learning

Interleaved practice has been demonstrated to improve learning compared with blocked practice in many different situations, from motor behavior to learning psychology concepts in the classroom. When learners interleave practice of different topics, concepts, or actions, learners continuously need to monitor and change their

---

[1] Though Lee and colleagues' (1988) proposal of starting with harder materials before easy materials can yield learning benefits, in practice, learning must be sequenced in such a way so that all prerequisites to current learning have been previously introduced and mastered. For example, although calculus is harder than addition, one must start with addition because calculus would be impossible without knowing addition.

response with different contexts, and simultaneously maintaining several responses in working memory results in better retention at delayed tests. This process creates beneficial contextual interference (Lee & Magill, 1985; Paas, 1992; Shea & Kohl, 1991). Early evidence for this proposal comes from studies in motor learning. For example, Ste-Marie and colleagues (2004) trained elementary school children's handwriting skills for three letters (*h*, *a*, and *y*) either in a blocked or random (interleaved) sequence. Children who practice the letters interleaved (randomly presented) retained more of their training in a delayed test of letter writing skills than those who practice the letters blocked. Follow-up studies showed that children who practiced the letters interleaved were also faster at writing a new word (hay) in delayed tests. Similar results have been demonstrated with other motor skills (Shea & Morgan, 1979).

However, the increase in contextual interference associated with interleaved practice has an important consequence: students' performance during learning is markedly worse in interleaved than in blocked practice (Shea & Morgan, 1979; Ste-Marie et al., 2004). Because of this mismatch between study and test performance, interleaved practice has been classified as a "desirable difficulty" – a study practice that, counterintuitively, reduces performance during learning but improves long-term learning (Bjork, 1994).

Rohrer and colleagues have proposed a similar framework (Rohrer, Dedrick, & Burgess, 2014) for the demonstrated benefits of interleaved practice in the domain of mathematics learning (Rohrer, 2012, 2015; Rohrer & Taylor, 2007). The authors propose that when practice of different types of mathematics problems are interleaved, students attend more to which procedure needs to be applied for each type of problem; they not only learn the procedure better but also when to apply it (see also Li, Cohen, & Koedinger, 2013). Consistent with this proposal, research has demonstrated that students not only learn better (as measured in delayed test) following interleaved practice but also make fewer confusion errors, i.e., they are less likely to apply the wrong procedure to a problem (Rohrer & Taylor, 2007). In addition, Wahlheim, Dunlosky, and Jacoby (2011) showed that blocked study results in decreased encoding of immediate repetitions of the same category. The authors analyzed memory performance at test for items that had been studied as a function of which position in the study sequence the item had been studied (i.e., was it the first, second, third, and so on to be studied?). The results showed a decreasing function for blocked practice, with learners more accurately classifying earlier items into the correct category than later ones. For interleaved practice, however, there was no difference in categorization performance across study positions. One interpretation of the results is that, in later presentations in the blocked sequence, learners did not attend to the items to the same extent as the earlier ones and therefore do not recall them as well.

Interleaved practice has also been shown to benefit concept learning and generalization. Kornell and colleagues (Kornell & Bjork, 2008; Kornell et al., 2010) have demonstrated in laboratory studies that learners remember the style of new artists better following interleaved practice (for examples of the artists, see Figure 16.1).

Pessani Paintings

Stratulat Paintings

Braque Paintings

Cross Paintings

Figure 16.1 *Examples of paintings and artists used by Kornell and colleagues (Kornell & Bjork, 2008; Kornell et al., 2010)*

More than that, they are better at identifying new paintings from those artists and telling apart studied from not studied artists.

Expanding on this work, Kang and Pashler (2012) replicated Kornell and colleagues' results and directly tested the possibility that the benefits of interleaved practice might, at least in part, be due to the increased spacing between repetitions of the same category. The authors contrasted learners' test performance following a spaced practice sequence (in which repetitions of each category were spaced in time but not interleaved – like blocked study with added temporal spacing between repetitions) with a blocked practice condition and an interleaved condition. Learners' classification of new paintings at test was best following interleaved practice. Moreover, blocked and spaced practice resulted in equivalent test performances. These results suggest that the benefits of interleaved practice are tied not to the increased temporal lag between practices of the same type of material or response but to the temporal contiguity among items of different concepts or that require different responses.

Birnbaum and colleagues (2013) used pictures of butterflies from different species to test people's acquisition of natural animal categories (species) following interleaved and blocked practice. They found that interleaved practice results in best learning of butterfly species and improved generalization to new exemplars of each species. This study also replicated Kang and Pashler's (2012) finding that temporal spacing between presentation of different concepts during interleaved practice reduces its benefits. Interestingly, the opposite was seen for blocked practice: increasing the temporal spacing between repetitions of the same category improved learning (albeit not above the levels seen following interleaved practice; for similar results using a discrimination task with artificial stimuli, see Mitchell, Nash, & Hall, 2008).

Interleaved practice has also been shown to improve learning of verbal concepts, specifically in educational contexts. For example, Introductory Psychology students were better at identifying new situations exemplifying psychology concepts such as "foot-in-the-door technique" and "hindsight bias" when they had practiced by studying examples of these concepts interleaved (Rawson, Thomas, & Jacoby, 2015). Similarly, college students were better at identifying psychological disorders when they practiced each disorder by studying representative cases interleaved, regardless of whether these were presented visually or aurally (Zulkiply et al., 2012), and medical students were better at interpreting exams following interleaved practice with x-ray images (Rozenshtein et al., 2016) and EEG results (Hatala, Brooks, & Norman, 2003). Studies have also found benefits of interleaved practice for neuroanatomy students learning to classify new structures (Pani, Chariker, & Naaz, 2012) and college students learning to classify mathematical functions (McDaniel, Fadler, & Pashler, 2013), to mention a few.

Generally, there is an assumption that interleaved practice will result in greater longer-term benefits than what would be possible with blocked practice. For instance, Rohrer, Dedrick, and Stershic (2015) created an intervention for middle school math class that included blocked or interleaved study of four types of problems followed by a review session of all the problems studied. Either one or thirty days after the end of the review session students completed a test. The results showed an overall benefit for interleaved study. Interestingly, the numerical benefit of interleaved practice over blocked practice increased with increasing retention intervals. Similar results have been found using an online tutor system to deliver practice math activities (Ostrow et al., 2015).

It is possible, however, that the benefit of retention interval seen here is orthogonal to the relative benefits of different sequences. It is possible, for example, that greater delays between the end of study and test promote better performance for all sequences of study, the difference being that one characteristic of interleaved study is that it includes a more even distribution of the problems across the entire learning sequence. Rohrer and colleagues (2014) report partial evidence for this possibility in an experiment comparing interleaved and blocked practice of mathematical problems in a naturalistic setting that did not include a review session before test.

The results show that the benefit of interleaved over blocked practice is smaller for materials studied in earlier blocks, that is, for materials for which the period between last study and test was the longest for blocked practice and increases monotonically with decreasing retention intervals between the end of blocked practice and test. These results indicate that although retention interval may play a role, it is not limited to interleaved practice.

Overall, the evidence of the benefits of interleaved practice is encouraging and has led to the development of several intervention studies and learning systems that incorporate interleaved practice as one of their key aspects. These interventions have shown improved learning and instructional outcomes in domains as diverse as geology (Andrews & Frey, 2015), biochemistry (Horn & Hernick, 2015), physiology (Linderholm, Dobson, & Yarbrough, 2016), neuroanatomy (Chariker, Naaz, & Pani, 2011; Pani et al., 2012), and plant biology (Kirchoff et al., 2014). However, we should note, there has, to date, not been a large-scale classroom randomized controlled trial of the benefits of interleaved practice as a learning and teaching tool, and the existence of null results in applied studies (e.g., Dobson, 2011) still warrants some caution.

To summarize this section, interleaved practice shows great promise as an easy-to-implement way to improve learning. It has been shown to positively change learning in a wide range of domains and populations, including in classroom studies. However, it is important to keep in mind that, as we noted before, at least in what concerns sequencing effects in learning, no single sequence seems to benefit all types of situations. Moreover, students seem to prefer blocked study when given the chance (Carvalho et al., 2016; Kornell & Bjork, 2008; Tauber et al., 2013; Yan et al., 2017) and this preference seems particularly resistant to change (Yan, Bjork, & Bjork, 2016). Thus, it is important to look not only at the uses of interleaved practice but also at the positive uses of blocked practice.

Using Blocked Practice to Boost Learning

Despite what the previous section might make one think, blocked practice is not always a poor choice. There is considerable evidence that blocked practice can result in improved or equally effective learning as interleaved practice, and also across a varied set of domains, from abstract stimuli and motor behavior to psychology concepts. For example, Kurtz and Hovland (1956) demonstrated, using abstract stimuli, that people remembered the properties of studied items better and were better at describing the main characteristics of each of four categories, when study had been blocked by category. Similarly, Whitman and Garner (1963) had adult participants learn two categories organized by the relational structure of geometrical objects in a figure. The results showed that participants achieved criterion more quickly when stimuli from the same category (i.e., that shared the same relational structure) were studied blocked. More recently, benefits of blocked practice have been demonstrated with several different types of artificial stimuli (Carvalho & Goldstone, 2014b, 2017b; Zulkiply & Burt, 2013). One important idea put forward by this research is that concept learning does not have to always take place by contrasting a to-be-learned concept with other concepts. It is possible – perhaps sometimes preferable – to learn concepts in isolation as with blocked practice. Learning the concepts in isolation allows one to focus on their positive characterizations and not on how positive examples contrast with negative examples (Goldstone, 1996).

Evidence of positive effects of blocked practice also seems to question the proposal that contextual interference benefits learning, as discussed in the previous section. In fact, research in motor behavior has also shown that blocked practice can sometimes improve learning compared with interleaved practice. Hebert, Landin, and Solmon (1996) taught undergraduate students enrolled in tennis classes different ground strokes, either blocked or interleaved. They found that low-skilled students (as measured before starting training) learned the ground strokes better with blocked practice and performed better in a delayed posttest compared with interleaved practice. No significant difference between the two practice schedules was found for high-skilled students at posttest. Similar results have been found when comparing young and older learners' acquisition of motor skills in blocked or interleaved practice (Al-Mustafa, 1989; Farrow & Maschette, 1997; Pigott & Shapiro, 1984; Pinto-Zipp & Gentile, 1995). This pattern of results, in addition to other evidence of lack of difference between the two sequences of study (see Wulf & Shea, 2002), seems to indicate that perhaps the benefits of interleaved practice are connected exactly with situations that the contextual interference theory proposes that it should benefit the least from: those in which memory and attentional demands are relatively low, such as with experts, adults, or longer study times. When attentional and memory demands are increased, as might be expected for novices, younger learners, and shorter study times, the pattern is reversed and blocked practice is frequently more beneficial (Wulf & Shea, 2002). However, Sana, Yan, and Kim (2016) recently demonstrated that when learning three different statistics concepts (Kruskal–Wallis, Wilcoxon signed-rank, and Chi-squared tests), learners with high working memory capacity benefited from blocked practice to the same extent as interleaved practice, whereas learners with lower working memory capacity benefited more from interleaved practice.

Still in the math domain, Rau, Aleven, and Rummel (2013) conducted a classroom study with 5th and 6th grade math students learning fractions using different representations (e.g., pie charts, number lines, and sets) with a math tutor. Their results demonstrate a benefit in immediate and delayed tests of blocked practice by representation compared with interleaving the representations. Additionally, these benefits were particularly pronounced for low-skill students. Thus, blocked practice may not only be more beneficial overall but also especially help those students who are more likely to struggle with the materials being presented. Interleaved study might be too challenging for low-skill students.

Although one could argue that the benefits of blocked practice are tied to specific material or individual differences, that does not seem to be the case. For example, Kost, Carvalho, and Goldstone (2015) used Kornell and Bjork's (2008) artists' styles to show that blocked practice can also improve learning of natural categories that have been shown before to benefit from interleaved practice. Kost and colleagues

(2015) demonstrated that, in a condition where learners had the opportunity to study each painting more than once and were asked to "guess" the category assignment and provided with feedback, learners were better at classifying old and new paintings from artists studied using blocked practice. When study did not include repetition or active guessing from the learners, interleaved practice was again more beneficial, as previous research had indicated.

Blocked practice can also improve verbal learning. For example, Carpenter and Mueller (2013) showed that non-French speakers learned orthographic-to-phonological mappings in French (i.e., "-eau" and the corresponding sound /o/ in the words "bateau," "carreau," and "corbeau," and "-er" and the sound /e/ in the words "adosser," "attraper," and "baver") better when they studied different words with the same mapping blocked (bateau, carreau, corbeau, adosser, attraper, baver, etc.) rather than when words with different mappings were studied interleaved (bateau, adosser, carreau, attraper, corbeau, baver, etc.). Similarly, Sorensen and Woltz (2016) conducted a study investigating the effect of blocked and interleaved practice in learning the association between novel words and groups of English words. For example, the new association between "things found underground" (such as cave, roots, potato, and tunnel) and the novel word "brask." They found that blocked practice resulted in better performance in implicit (categorization of novel words, e.g., worm, gopher, well, and aquifer, into one of the new verbal categories) and explicit tests (definition of the grouping rule for the new categories). Moreover, Rawson and colleagues (2015) demonstrated that when undergraduate Introductory Psychology students were presented a definition before studying several examples of different psychological concepts such as "foot-in-the-door," blocked practice resulted in better subsequent classification of novel examples compared with interleaved practice.

It is important to note that the benefits of blocked practice are not limited to immediate testing as one might initially predict based on results from the contextual interference literature and temporal spacing theories. For example, Carvalho and Goldstone showed benefits of blocked practice at different intervals, including from 3 minutes to up to three days, for both memory (Carvalho & Goldstone, 2017b) and categorization (Carvalho & Goldstone, 2014a).

Finally, despite the widely held belief that students might not study using the best sequence, benefits of blocked study have been found in self-regulated learning. If left to organize their study, students prefer to block practice by studying items from the same category close in time (Tauber et al., 2013) and, because blocked practice is often thought to result in worse learning (Bjork et al., 2013), one might assume that students' choices are not optimal and result in worse learning. Carvalho and colleagues (2016) tested this possibility in a classroom study with Introductory Psychology students learning the concepts of mean, median, and mode – three measures of central tendency in statistics. After completing a short pretest, students were provided with practice materials of these three concepts in an online platform. Students were free to study the materials in any order they wished. The posttest was a set of questions regarding these concepts introduced in the students' midterm exam. As predicted, students showed a high preference to block their study. More importantly, higher rates of blocked practice were associated with higher posttest scores, controlling for pretest differences (see Figure 16.2). This relationship was not present in a control group of students who did not choose how to organize their study but were instead yoked to a sequence chosen by another student.

To summarize this section, blocked practice shows great promise as a simple way to improve learning. It has been shown to positively affect learning in a wide range of domains and populations, including in classroom studies (Monteiro et al., 2017). However, as reviewed in the previous section, interleaved practice also has demonstrable benefits. Thus, whether interleaved or blocked practice is more beneficial cannot be answered in terms of main effects but rather in how sequencing interacts with other factors. In the next section, we discuss a theoretical framework that can help make this decision.

How to Decide Whether to Use Interleaved or Blocked Practice?

Two important conclusions can be taken from the previous discussion. On the one hand, there might not be a single sequence that improves all learning, all the time, for

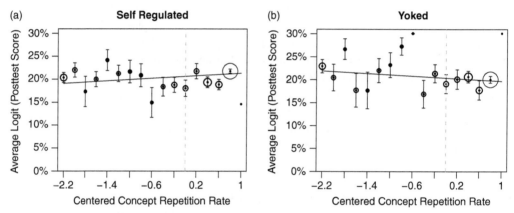

Figure 16.2 *Average posttest score by concept repetition rate for the (a) self-regulated and (b) yoked groups in Carvalho and colleagues (2016; reprinted with permission)*

Students were divided into bins by their adjusted rate of repetition and average posttest scores (Logit transformed) within each bin were plotted. Concept repetition rate was adjusted by subtracting the average rate of repetition for the entire group from the rate of repetition for the bin – a value of 0 in the x-axis indicates mean concept repetition rate (represented by the vertical dashed line) and increasing values indicate increasing difference from average. The values in the y-axis represent Logit transformed posttest scores. Each point in the graph lies at the center of a 20%-wide interval of concept repetition rates, and represents the average posttest score among students whose concept repetition rates fell in that interval. The number of students in each bin is represented by the area of the circles surrounding the data points. The regression lines represent best-fitting lines of the regression analyses assuming average values for all predictors other than concept repetition rate.

all the students. On the other hand, sequence does have the potential to improve learning and it is a relatively easy-to-implement intervention in most educational settings and beyond. Where does this leave us? We believe that the development of a theory that can account for the pattern of results observed, and predict when and why interleaved or blocked practice will be beneficial, will allow for the comprehensive use of sequence of study to make learning better.

We (Carvalho & Goldstone, 2015b, 2017b) have proposed that the effect of different sequences on learning efficacy might not be due to the sequence per se but the effect that sequencing has on a general-purpose learning process. Our account of why the sequence of study changes learning can predict most of the results described above and help guide educators, students, and learning scientists on deciding which sequence to use.

The Sequential Attention Theory (SAT; Carvalho & Goldstone, 2015b, 2017b) posits that interleaved and blocked practice emphasize different aspects of the learning materials or situation and, therefore, the best sequence of study is the one that emphasizes the most challenging aspect(s) of the learning situation. As an example, if learning is hard because it is difficult to distinguish two concepts, then one would want to use a sequence that emphasizes exactly that: interleaved study. Conversely, if learning is hard because it is difficult to identify common aspects among examples of the same concept, then one would want to use a sequence that emphasizes exactly that: blocked study. Overall, this description is consistent with previous proposals (Birnbaum et al., 2013; Carpenter & Mueller, 2013; Carvalho & Goldstone, 2014b, 2015a; Goldstone, 1996; Higgins & Ross, 2011; Higgins, 2017; Mathy et al., 2013; Noh et al., 2016; Rawson et al., 2015; Sandhofer & Doumas, 2008; Zulkiply & Burt, 2013) and seems to match the main findings in the literature we described thus far (see the sections that follow for details). However, this description by itself *does not explain why this is the case*. SAT goes one step further by describing the learning mechanism which gives rise to these differences – a mechanism that can be tested and implemented in educational tools.

SAT (Carvalho & Goldstone, 2015b, 2017b) proposes that learning is a sequential process of item-by-item comparisons to emphasize important stimulus characteristics. During learning, learners compare the current item with the previously studied one and, depending on the assignment of the previous and current items, attend to similarities or differences between the two items. This assumption is consistent with behavioral and modeling results in the category learning literature, showing that recent categorization events play a stronger role in a novel categorization decision than do older events and that categorization decisions are not based on a veridical analysis of the distribution of exemplars across time (e.g., more recent examples are more emphasized; Jones & Sieck, 2003; Stewart & Brown, 2004; Stewart, Brown, & Chater, 2002) but are context- and task-specific (Mack & Palmeri, 2015; Markman & Ross, 2003; Palmeri & Mack, 2015; Ross, 2000). Moreover, this proposal is also congruent with recent neurophysiological evidence suggesting the important role of pattern completion for learning and the role of the hippocampus in providing details not only about past events but also about the relationship between events to create learning (Mack & Preston, 2016; Schlichting & Preston, 2015; Zeithamova, Schlichting, & Preston, 2012).

During each learning moment (e.g., a trial in a laboratory task), the learner evaluates similarities and differences between the current stimulus and the recollection they have of the previous item(s), as well as the category assignment of the previous exemplar and the current one. If the previous and current items belong to the same category, attention will be directed toward their similarities. However, if they belong to different categories, attention will be directed toward their differences. Across time, attention will be increasingly shifted toward relevant within-category similarities and between-category differences. This will, in turn, affect category representations, which will affect categorization decisions and recollection. With each new learning moment, the relevant properties will be progressively better encoded whereas irrelevant ones will be poorly encoded or not encoded at all.

When categories are studied interleaved, the number of transitions between objects of different categories is frequent, which will result in attending to differences between categories on most trials by the process just described. In the same way, when categories are studied blocked, the likelihood of a within-category transition is high, which will increase attention toward within-category similarities by the same process. Furthermore, this process can also lead to encoding information that might not be central for learning the categories. For example, blocked practice would lead learners to encode similarities among items of the same category that will end up also being present in the other category and, therefore, cannot discriminate between the two categories (see Figure 16.3 for a schematic representation of this proposal).

The process of sequential shifts of attention toward similarities or differences among studied items will give rise to overall different attention patterns and this, according to SAT, is the reason why interleaved study leads to better encoding of differences between categories and blocked practice leads to better encoding of similarities among items of the same category. Carvalho and Goldstone (2017b) showed

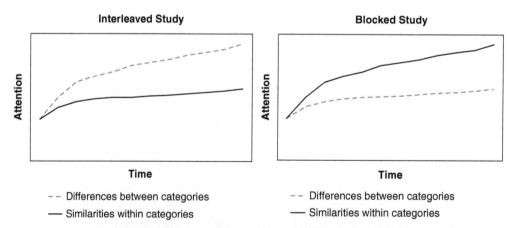

Figure 16.3 *Schematic representation of the mechanism proposed in Sequential Attention Theory (SAT) for how each sequence leads to attending to different properties of the studied materials (from Carvalho & Goldstone, 2017b. Reprinted with permission from the American Psychological Association)*

evidence for this mechanism in a series of laboratory studies. The researchers probed what learners attend to, encoded, and remembered from materials studied interleaved or blocked. If the differences seen between the two practice sequences are due to different attentional patterns during learning, using an eye tracker, we should see that learners look at different aspects of the study materials depending on the sequence of study. That is exactly what Carvalho and Goldstone found. Whereas during interleaved practice learners attended to sequential differences between study items, during blocked practice learners showed no such bias. Moreover, Carvalho and Goldstone probed learners' memory and categorization of new items and found that, following blocked practice, learners were more sensitive to changes in characteristic properties of the concepts that did not discriminate between the categories but were frequent in each category. Conversely, following interleaved practice, learners ignored those properties and were more sensitive to infrequent but discriminative properties (those that helped tell the categories apart).

Finally, SAT makes a series of predictions about factors that should modulate the benefit of interleaved and blocked practice. Next, we will briefly review some of these factors. In the final section, we will propose future directions and other modulating factors that have not yet been tested in the literature.

Different Types of Concepts

The type of concepts being studied will change which aspects are harder to learn and should be attended to. Telling alligators and crocodiles apart requires fine discrimination among similar concepts whereas identifying whether a physics problem requires classical or quantum theoretical constructs requires the identification of common characteristics across a highly varied set of classical and quantum physics problems. Situations such as the former would benefit from interleaved practice, whereas the latter would benefit from blocked practice. Consistent with this proposal, interleaved practice improves learning of, for example, highly similar abstract categories (Carvalho & Goldstone, 2014b, 2014a; Zulkiply & Burt, 2013), rule-based categories (Noh et al., 2016), the style of similar artists (Kang & Pashler, 2012; Kornell & Bjork, 2008; Kornell et al., 2010), confusable natural bird categories (Wahlheim et al. 2011), related mathematical and verbal concepts (Rawson et al., 2015; Rohrer et al., 2015; Rohrer & Taylor, 2007; Taylor & Rohrer, 2010), and motor behaviors (Tse & Altarriba, 2010). Conversely, blocked practice improves learning of, for example, highly dissimilar abstract categories (Carvalho & Goldstone, 2014b, 2014a; Kurtz & Hovland, 1956; Zulkiply & Burt, 2013), information integration categories that require noticing several similarities among items of the same category (Noh et al., 2016), and identifying a phoneme as present in orthographically diverse words (Carpenter & Mueller, 2013).

Different Types of Study Activities

Different study tasks might lead students to focus on different aspects of the same concept (Markman & Ross, 2003; Yamauchi & Markman, 2000). For example, teachers often use inference activities that present a series of different scenarios or sentences with a common underlying principle to stimulate students to make inferences during reading. Inference-making is an important skill for reading proficiency (McNamara & Kintsch, 1996) that is part of the common core standards (National Governors Association Center for Best Practices, Council of Chief State School Officers, 2010). This activity will tend to benefit from blocked study, as learners will more easily be able to identify and infer the common aspects across multiple scenarios if these are presented close in time, instead of interleaved with other scenarios with different inferences. Conversely, when asked to complete classification activities such as sorting different animals into classes – an important skill in biology education (National Research Council, 2012) – students focus on the properties that distinguish the animals and that can help in dividing into different classes. This type of learning activity will benefit from interleaved practice (e.g., practice classifying animals of different classes together, instead of only one class at a time), as students will more easily be able to identify the differences between the classes than if they study only one item at a time.

Consistent with this prediction, Carvalho and Goldstone (2015a) demonstrated that, when using the same learning materials, interleaved practice promoted learning in a classification task whereas blocked practice promoted learning in an inference task. Similar results with different materials were found by Kost and colleagues (2015). Rawson and colleagues (2015) found a similar interaction by manipulating whether the concept definition was presented along with examples (which arguably makes it more of an inference task) or not (which arguably makes it more of a classification task).

Different Types of Testing Activities

Different testing activities also recruit different knowledge. If the test activity requires knowing the discriminating properties among different options – such as the commonly used multiple-choice test – not having encoded these properties would result in low performance. Conversely, if the test task requires the student to recruit the details about how different examples fit together (i.e., the characteristics properties of a concept, as would arguably be the case with providing definitions for studied concepts), perhaps knowing only the discriminating properties would impair performance. Consistent with this proposal, Carvalho and Goldstone (2017a) demonstrated that learners provided more correct definitions for psychology concepts studied blocked than interleaved, but there were no differences between the two practice sequences for other types of tests (multiple-choice, writing new examples, matching definitions with the correct concept). Similar results were found by Carvalho and Albuquerque (2012) using a memory test. In that study, learners learned to discriminate two images along one dimension using either interleaved or blocked practice. When during a test learners had to tell apart studied items from novel items that differed along the discriminating dimension, interleaved practice improved learning. Conversely, if the memory test included distractors that varied from studied items along a different dimension, there was no difference between the two practice sequences (see also de Zilva, Mitchell, & Newell, 2013).

Different Types of Learners

SAT describes the attentional process for an average adult. However, different developmental stages, levels of expertise, and working memory capacity change how the attentional process operates, with consequences for which practice sequence is better.

There are documented developmental differences in how children and adults deploy attention. For example, younger children are more likely to distribute attention inconsistently among dimensions whereas older children are able to consistently focus on a single dimension during learning (Cook & Odom, 1992; Smith & Kemler, 1978; Strutt, Anderson, & Well, 1975; Thompson & Markson, 1998). Similarly, in categorization tasks, it has been shown that infants and children do not optimize attention toward task-relevant properties of the materials being studied whereas adults show such optimization (Best, Robinson, & Sloutsky, 2011; Best, Yim, & Sloutsky, 2013), with consequences for what is remembered from learning (Deng & Sloutsky, 2016). Thus, for the young attentional system, interleaved practice might pose special challenges because it is particularly hard to focus on specific dimensions of change among many, and attend only to that. This means that even though interleaved practice directs attention toward relevant differences among successive items, if the attentional system cannot focus on a reduced number of dimensions and is instead attracted by overall variation, then the high amount of variation during interleaved practice (varying stimuli and varying responses) can delay learning. During blocked practice, on the other hand, learners do not need to focus their attention on particular differences but rather attend to all properties of the material being studied. Successive similarities among items of the same category will be more frequent and potentially better encoded, resulting in successful learning.

This interpretation is consistent with the results already discussed, showing that young children benefit more from blocked practice whereas adults benefit more from interleaved practice for the same types of materials (Al-Mustafa, 1989; Farrow & Maschette, 1997; Pigott & Shapiro, 1984; Pinto-Zipp & Gentile, 1995). Moreover, it is consistent with results showing that, for young children, the benefits of interleaved practice increase with decreased perceptual complexity of the materials studied – less complex materials will have fewer features competing for attention, which will help children focus on the relevant feature. That is, when fewer dimensions change from one study moment to the next, children can benefit from interleaved practice, but there is no difference between the two sequences for more perceptually complex materials (Albaret & Thon, 1998).

Similarly, experts are able to focus their attention on specific components of the task and ignore others whereas novices tend to show less organized attention

(Beilock et al., 2002; Kioumourtzoglou et al., 1998; Werner & Thies, 2000). Experts are also able to select and manage which information is relevant from an array whereas novices tend to attend to all information presented (Carter et al., 1988). Thus, novices, those who do not have relevant prior knowledge that might help identify which dimensions might be relevant for learning, might not be able to benefit from interleaved practice because they are not able to organize their attention to focus on only the relevant changes from one learning moment to the next. Conversely, experts, who more easily organize their attention based on previous knowledge, can successfully benefit from interleaved practice and identify relevant differences between successive items (Hebert et al., 1996). Consistent with this proposal, Shea, Kohl, and Indermill (1990) demonstrated that increasing amounts of practice with a new complex task (from 50 to 400 practice opportunities) increased the benefits of interleaved practice. At low levels of practice (50 practice opportunities), blocked practice resulted in better learning.

Finally, for simplicity, in our description of the sequential attention process during learning – which we argued gives rise to differences between interleaved and blocked practice – we assumed that learners consider only the previous item to establish sequential comparisons and decide what to attend to in each learning moment. What would happen if learners could maintain more information in memory? Individuals with higher working memory capacity are able to maintain in memory and simultaneously operate with a large set of information (Engle & Kane, 2003; Kane et al., 2004; Unsworth & Engle, 2007). Moreover, these individuals also are better at controlled search from long-term memory and focused attention (Unsworth & Engle, 2007; Unsworth & Spillers, 2010). One prediction, then, would be that higher working memory capacity would be related with reduced differences between interleaving and blocked practice because learners can use more information in the sequential attentional learning process. The results from the work by Sana and colleagues (2016) as described are consistent with this proposal; for individuals with higher working memory spans (a measure of working memory capacity), the benefits of interleaved practice were less pronounced than for individuals with lower working memory spans (for whom, interleaved practice was more beneficial). The less information one can maintain and operate in working memory simultaneously, the more beneficial temporal contiguity of contrasting cases is, because it will result in heightened attention toward the relevant properties which would otherwise not be possible.

Conclusion: What Now?

We started this chapter by arguing that sequencing decisions happen all the time in educational settings and might seem inconsequential. The evidence presented here paints a picture of an important influence of how study practice is organized, be it interleaved, blocked, hard-to-easy, easy-to-hard, and so on. It is also important to emphasize that it is quite apparent from the available evidence that there is no one-size-fits-all solution in terms of best sequence of study. Thus, future research should focus on understanding the underlying learning process as an online process that takes place over time. As such, learning is influenced by the sequence of study in, hopefully, predictable ways. We believe real progress in this area will come from mechanistic theories and models grounded on solid laboratory and in vivo research. It will most likely not be enough to demonstrate that interleaved practice works or not – we should strive to explain in detail the learning process that is changed by interleaved practice. Only the existence of strong theories and models will allow successful and systematic use of different sequences of practice as a tool to improve learning. We believe SAT is a good initial model to understanding the learning process and how it is changed by sequence, but it can certainly be improved, expanded, or challenged.

Additionally, there are several areas where research is still lacking. For example, most research either does not include or ignores the fact that students often study the same materials several times, perhaps always in the same sequence. What consequences does repeating the same sequence of items have? Initial evidence from Kost and colleagues (2015) shows that repetition of the sequence of learning improves learning during blocked practice. One possibility is that the repetition allows learners to contrast the category similarities acquired during the first pass-through with other categories during subsequent repetitions. However, these more complex learning sequences are still very much an open question, even though they are common in students' practice.

Moreover, in our effort to find the best sequence between interleaved and blocked practice, we might also have missed the opportunity to find the best sequence that includes both interleaved and blocked practice. If one sequence directs attention toward similarities among successive items and the other differences between successive items, a carefully crafted version mixing the two might be the best of both worlds.

Similarly, not every blocked sequence is equal. For example, it is possible that the way blocked practice is implemented will have an impact in its effectiveness. One way blocked practice is often implemented is by studying all materials of one concept before starting the next (e.g., Kornell & Bjork, 2008; Rawson et al., 2015; Ste-Marie et al., 2004; Zulkiply & Burt, 2013). This implementation might, in effect, reduce the potential benefits of blocked practice by reducing students' opportunity to test hypotheses during study and reducing attention to the task – both factors that have been shown to matter for improved learning (Abel & Roediger, 2017; Karpicke & Blunt, 2011; Wahlheim et al., 2011). However, it is possible to equate the informativity, attention, and the ability to generate hypotheses between interleaved and blocked practice. For example, Carvalho and Goldstone (2014a, 2014b, 2015a) have implemented blocked practice by including reduced alternation between categories (25 percent of transitions are changes between concepts). Conversely, interleaved practice includes a high level of alternation between categories (75 percent transitions are changes between concepts). This approach allows students to generate hypotheses and test them in both sequences, and makes both sequences unpredictable and therefore equates for attentional demands. This approach also matches how students often decide to block their study (Carvalho et al., 2016; Tauber et al., 2013). It is currently unclear whether, when the two sequences are implemented in such a way, it is possible to increase the range of situations that benefit from blocked practice.

There is also a lack of research that investigates differences in learning between concepts studied in different positions during blocked practice. As we mentioned earlier in this chapter, early research on sequential effects on learning focused on finding which concepts should be studied first and which should be studied afterword. However, most research on interleaved versus blocked practice compares interleaved practice with a randomized version of blocked practice, where this factor is "controlled for" by careful experimental practice. Perhaps a carefully crafted blocked practice that considers difficulty level to determine the order of the concepts is a more appropriate sequence to compare with interleaved practice. Consistent with this prediction, Patel, Liu, and Koedinger (2015) recently demonstrated that middle school students practicing fraction addition and fraction multiplication showed equivalent learning with interleaved and blocked practice if blocked practice started with fraction multiplication followed by fraction addition. When blocked practice started with fraction addition, however, students performed worse than in interleaved practice. This research is initial evidence that bringing to bear early research on concept sequencing to the study of interleaved and blocked practice can prove fruitful.

Learning is also complex in terms of multidimensionality of the learning materials, a factor often ignored in current research. For example, when sequencing practice of different concepts (addition, subtraction, multiplication) with different types of problems, should one interleave the concepts and block the types of problems, interleave both, or any other combination? To date, only one study by Rau and colleagues (2013) probed this question. The authors found that in the context of fraction learning with different types of problems and representations, best learning was achieved by interleaving type of problem and blocking type of representation. Further study is needed to identify common properties across multi-dimensional materials, where one dimension benefits from interleaved practice and the other from blocked practice, to extrapolate general principles to support implementation and theoretical understanding.

Another important area is investigating to what extent students' decisions influence and shape the effect of different sequences. Although it is possible that blocked practice might not be optimal for certain situations, when students decide to block their study (and they often do), it might result in best learning. This is because the attentional and memory demands of self-regulated tasks differ from tasks where information is not controlled by the learner (Gureckis & Markant, 2012; Markant & Gureckis, 2014; Markant, Settles, & Gureckis, 2016). Most current studies have not compared students' performance between self-regulated and yoked study to identify the impact of self-regulation on the effectiveness of different sequences of study to promote learning (however, see Carvalho et al., 2016). We see the study of sequencing in self-regulated practice as a major next step in this line of research – not only because it can provide novel insights not currently available but also as an entry way into understanding how to change and improve metacognitive awareness to the benefits of choosing the right sequence of study for the right situation.

References

Abel, M. & Roediger, H. L. (2017). Comparing the testing effect under blocked and mixed practice: The mnemonic benefits of retrieval practice are not affected by practice format. *Memory and Cognition, 45*(1),81–92. https://doi.org/10.3758/s13421-016-0641-8

Albaret, J. M. & Thon, B. (1998). Differential effects of task complexity on contextual interference in a drawing task. *Acta Psychologica, 100*(1–2), 9–24.

Al-Mustafa, A. A. (1989). Contextual interference: Laboratory artifact or sport skill learning related? (Doctoral dissertation).

Andrews, S. E. & Frey, S. D. (2015). Studio structure improves student performance in an undergraduate introductory soil science course. *Natural Sciences Education, 44*(1), 60. https://doi.org/10.4195/nse2014.12.0026

Beilock, S. L., Carr, T. H., MacMahon, C., & Starkes, J. L. (2002). When paying attention becomes counterproductive: Impact of divided versus skill-focused attention on novice and experienced performance of sensorimotor skills. *Journal of Experimental Psychology: Applied, 8*(1), 6–16. https://doi.org/10.1037//1076-898X.8.1.6

Best, C. A., Robinson, C. W., & Sloutsky, V. M. (2011). The effect of labels on children's category learning. In *Proceedings of the 33rd Annual Conference of the Cognitive Science Society* (pp. 3332–3336). Austin, TX.

Best, C. A., Yim, H., & Sloutsky, V. M. (2013). The cost of selective attention in category learning: Developmental differences between adults and infants. *Journal of Experimental Child Psychology, 116*(2), 105–119. https://doi.org/10.1016/j.jecp.2013.05.002

Birnbaum, M. S., Kornell, N., Bjork, E. L., & Bjork, R. A. (2013). Why interleaving enhances inductive learning: The roles of discrimination and retrieval. *Memory and Cognition, 41*(3), 392–402. https://doi.org/10.3758/s13421-012-0272-7

Bjork, R. A. (1994). Memory and metamemory considerations in the training of human beings. In J. Metcalfe & A. P. Shimamura (eds.), *Metacognition: Knowing about knowing* (pp. 185–205). Cambridge, MA: MIT Press.

Bjork, R. A., Dunlosky, J., & Kornell, N. (2013). Self-regulated learning: Beliefs, techniques, and illusions. *Annual Review of Psychology, 64*, 417–444. https://doi.org/10.1146/annurev-psych-113011-143823

Carpenter, S. K. & Mueller, F. E. (2013). The effects of interleaving versus blocking on foreign language pronunciation learning. *Memory and Cognition, 41*(5),671–682. https://doi.org/10.3758/s13421-012-0291-4

Carter, K., Cushing, K., Sabers, D., Stein, P., & Berliner, D. (1988). Expert-novice differences in perceiving and processing visual classroom information. *Journal of Teacher Education, 39*(3), 25–31. https://doi.org/10.1177/002248718803900306

Carvalho, P. F. & Albuquerque, P. B. (2012). Memory encoding of stimulus features in human perceptual learning. *Journal of Cognitive Psychology, 24*(6), 654–664. https://doi.org/10.1080/20445911.2012.675322

Carvalho, P. F., Braithwaite, D. W., de Leeuw, J. R., Motz, B. A., & Goldstone, R. L. (2016). An in vivo study of self-regulated study sequencing in introductory psychology courses. *Plos One*, *11*(3), e0152115. https://doi.org/10.1371/journal.pone.0152115

Carvalho, P. F. & Goldstone, R. L. (2014a). Effects of interleaved and blocked study on delayed test of category learning generalization. *Frontiers in Psychology*, 5, 936. https://doi.org/10.3389/fpsyg.2014.00936

(2014b). Putting category learning in order: Category structure and temporal arrangement affect the benefit of interleaved over blocked study. *Memory and Cognition*, *42*(3), 481–495. https://doi.org/10.3758/s13421-013-0371-0

(2015a). The benefits of interleaved and blocked study: Different tasks benefit from different schedules of study. *Psychonomic Bulletin and Review*, *22*(1), 281–288. https://doi.org/10.3758/s13423-014-0676-4

(2015b). What you learn is more than what you see: What can sequencing effects tell us about inductive category learning? *Frontiers in Psychology*, *6*, 505. https://doi.org/10.3389/fpsyg.2015.00505

(2017a). The most efficient sequence of study depends on the type of test. Manuscript under review.

(2017b). The sequence of study changes what information is attended to, encoded, and remembered during category learning. *Journal of Experimental Psychology: Learning, Memory, and Cognition*.

Chariker, J. H., Naaz, F., & Pani, J. R. (2011). Computer-based learning of neuroanatomy: A longitudinal study of learning, transfer, and retention. *Journal of Educational Psychology*, *103*(1),19–31. https://doi.org/10.1037/a0021680

Cook, G. L. & Odom, R. D. (1992). Perception of multidimensional stimuli: A differential-sensitivity account of cognitive processing and development. *Journal of Experimental Child Psychology*, *54*(2), 213–249.

Deng, W. S. & Sloutsky, V. M. (2016). Selective attention, diffused attention, and the development of categorization. *Cognitive Psychology*, *91*, 24–62. https://doi.org/10.1016/j.cogpsych.2016.09.002

de Zilva, D., Mitchell, C. J., & Newell, B. R. (2013). Eliminating the mere exposure effect through changes in context between exposure and test. *Cognition and Emotion*, *27*(8), 1345–1358. https://doi.org/10.1080/02699931.2013.775110

Dobson, J. L. (2011). Effect of selected "desirable difficulty" learning strategies on the retention of physiology information. *Advances in Physiology Education*, 35(4),378–383.

Elio, R. & Anderson, J. R. (1981). The effects of category generalizations and instance similarity on schema abstraction. *Journal of Experimental Psychology: Human Learning and Memory*, *7*(6), 397–417.

(1984). The effects of information order and learning mode on schema abstraction. *Memory and Cognition*, *12*(1), 20–30.

Engle, R. W. & Kane, M. J. (2003). Executive attention, working memory capacity, and a two-factor theory of cognitive control, *44*, 145–199. https://doi.org/10.1016/S0079-7421(03)44005-X

Farrow, D. & Maschette, W. (1997). The effects of contextual interference on children learning forehand tennis groundstrokes. *Journal of Human Movement Studies*, *33*, 47–67.

Goldstone, R. L. (1996). Isolated and interrelated concepts. *Memory and Cognition*, *24*(5), 608–628.

Gureckis, T. M. & Markant, D. B. (2012). Self-directed learning: A cognitive and computational perspective. *Perspectives on Psychological Science: A Journal of the Association for Psychological Science, 7*(5), 464–481. https://doi.org/10.1177/1745691612454304

Hatala, R. M., Brooks, L. R., & Norman, G. R. (2003). Practice makes perfect: The critical role of mixed practice in the acquisition of ECG interpretation skills. *Advances in Health Sciences Education: Theory and Practice, 8*(1), 17–26.

Hebert, E. P., Landin, D., & Solmon, M. A. (1996). Practice schedule effects on the performance and learning of low- and high-skilled students: An applied study. *Research Quarterly for Exercise and Sport, 67*(1),52–58. https://doi.org/10.1080/02701367.1996.10607925

Higgins, E. J. (2017). The complexities of learning categories through comparisons. Psychology of Learning and Motivation, 66, 43–77. https://doi.org/10.1016/bs.plm.2016.11.002

Higgins, E. J. & Ross, B. H. (2011). Comparisons in category learning: How best to compare for what? In L. Carlson, C. Holscher, & T. Shipley (eds.), *Proceedings of the 33rd annual conference of the Cognitive Science Society* (pp. 1388–1393). Austin, TX: Cognitive Science Society.

Horn, S. & Hernick, M. (2015). Improving student understanding of lipids concepts in a biochemistry course using test-enhanced learning. *Chemical Education Research and Practice, 16*(4), 918–928. https://doi.org/10.1039/C5RP00133A

Hull, L. (1920). Quantitative aspects of evolution and concepts: An experimental study. *The Psychological Monographs, 28*(1), 1–86.

Jones, M. & Sieck, W. R. (2003). Learning myopia: An adaptive recency effect in category learning. *Journal of Experimental Psychology. Learning, Memory, and Cognition, 29*(4), 626–640.

Kane, M. J., Hambrick, D. Z., Tuholski, S. W., Wilhelm, O., Payne, T. W., & Engle, R. W. (2004). The generality of working memory capacity: A latent-variable approach to verbal and visuospatial memory span and reasoning. *Journal of Experimental Psychology. General, 133*(2), 189–217. https://doi.org/10.1037/0096–3445.133.2.189

Kang, S. H. K. & Pashler, H. (2012). Learning painting styles: Spacing is advantageous when it promotes discriminative contrast. *Applied Cognitive Psychology, 26*(1), 97–103. https://doi.org/10.1002/acp.1801

Karpicke, J. D. & Blunt, J. R. (2011). Retrieval practice produces more learning than elaborative studying with concept mapping. *Science, 331*(6018), 772–775. https://doi.org/10.1126/science.1199327

Kioumourtzoglou, E., Kourtessis, T., Michalopoulou, M., & Derri, V. (1998). Differences in several perceptual abilities between experts and novices in basketball, volleyball and water-polo. *Perceptual and Motor Skills, 86*(3), 899–912. https://doi.org/10.2466/pms.1998.86.3.899

Kirchoff, B. K., Delaney, P. F., Horton, M., & Dellinger-Johnston, R. (2014). Optimizing learning of scientific category knowledge in the classroom: The case of plant identification. *CBE Life Sciences Education, 13*(3), 425–436. https://doi.org/10.1187/cbe.13–11-0224

Kornell, N. & Bjork, R. A. (2008). Learning concepts and categories: Is spacing the "enemy of induction"? *Psychological Science, 19*(6), 585–592. https://doi.org/10.1111/j.1467–9280.2008.02127.x

Kornell, N., Castel, A. D., Eich, T. S., & Bjork, R. A. (2010). Spacing as the friend of both memory and induction in young and older adults. *Psychology and Aging*, *25*(2), 498–503.

Kost, A. S., Carvalho, P. F., & Goldstone, R. L. (2015). Can you repeat that? The effect of item repetition on interleaved and blocked study. In D. C. Noelle, R. Dale, A. S. Warlaumont, J. Yoshimi, T. Matlock, C. D. Jennings, & P. P. Maglio (eds.), *Proceedings of the 37th annual meeting of the Cognitive Science Society* (pp. 1189–1194). Austin, TX: Cognitive Science Society.

Kurtz, K. H. & Hovland, C. I. (1956). Concept learning with differing sequences of instances. *Journal of Experimental Psychology*, *51*(4),239–243. https://doi.org/10.1037/h0040295

Lee, E. S., MacGregor, J. N., Bavelas, A., Mirlin, L., & et al. (1988). The effects of error transformations on classification performance. *Journal of Experimental Psychology: Learning, Memory, and Cognition*, *14*(1), 66–74. https://doi.org/10.1037/0278-7393.14.1.66

Lee, T. D. & Magill, R. A. (1985). Can forgetting facilitate skill acquisition? In D. Goodman, R. B. Wilberg, & I. M. Franks (eds.), *Differing perspectives in motor learning, memory, and control* (pp. 3–22). Amsterdam: North-Holland.

Li, N., Cohen, W. W., & Koedinger, K. R. (2013). Problem order implications for learning. *International Journal of Artificial Intelligence in Education*, *23*(1–4), 71–93. https://doi.org/10.1007/s40593-013–0005-5

Linderholm, T., Dobson, J., & Yarbrough, M. B. (2016). The benefit of self-testing and interleaving for synthesizing concepts across multiple physiology texts. *Advances in Physiology Education*, *40*(3), 329–334. https://doi.org/10.1152/advan.00157.2015

Mack, M. L. & Palmeri, T. J. (2015). The dynamics of categorization: Unraveling rapid categorization. *Journal of Experimental Psychology. General*, *144*(3), 551–569. https://doi.org/10.1037/a0039184

Mack, M. L. & Preston, A. R. (2016). Decisions about the past are guided by reinstatement of specific memories in the hippocampus and perirhinal cortex. *Neuroimage*, *127*, 144–157. https://doi.org/10.1016/j.neuroimage.2015.12.015

Markant, D. B. & Gureckis, T. M. (2014). Is it better to select or to receive? Learning via active and passive hypothesis testing. *Journal of Experimental Psychology. General*, *143*(1), 94–122. https://doi.org/10.1037/a0032108

Markant, D. B., Settles, B., & Gureckis, T. M. (2016). Self-Directed learning favors local, Rather than global, Uncertainty. *Cognitive Science*, *40*(1), 100–120. https://doi.org/10.1111/cogs.12220

Markman, A. B. & Ross, B. H. (2003). Category use and category learning. *Psychological Bulletin*, *129*(4), 592–613. https://doi.org/10.1037/0033-2909.129.4.592

Mathy, F. & Feldman, J. (2009). A rule-based presentation order facilitates category learning. *Psychonomic Bulletin and Review*, *16*(6), 1050–1057. https://doi.org/10.3758/PBR.16.6.1050

Mathy, F., Haladjian, H. H., Laurent, E., & Goldstone, R. L. (2013). Similarity-dissimilarity competition in disjunctive classification tasks. *Frontiers in Psychology*, *4*, 26. https://doi.org/10.3389/fpsyg.2013.00026

McDaniel, M. A., Fadler, C. L., & Pashler, H. (2013). Effects of spaced versus massed training in function learning. *Journal of Experimental Psychology. Learning, Memory, and Cognition*, *39*(5), 1417–1432. https://doi.org/10.1037/a0032184

McNamara, D. S. & Kintsch, W. (1996). Learning from texts: Effects of prior knowledge and text coherence. *Discourse Processes*, *22*(3), 247–288. https://doi.org/10.1080/01638539609544975

Mitchell, C. J., Nash, S., & Hall, G. (2008). The intermixed-blocked effect in human perceptual learning is not the consequence of trial spacing. *Journal of Experimental Psychology: Learning, Memory, and Cognition*, *34*(1),237–242.

Monteiro, S., Melvin, L., Manolakos, J., Patel, A., & Norman, G. (2017). Evaluating the effect of instruction and practice schedule on the acquisition of ECG interpretation skills. *Perspectives on Medical Education*, *6*(4), 237–245.

National Governors Association Center for Best Practices, Council of Chief State School Officers. (2010). *Common Core State Standards: English Language, Arts & Literacy in History/Social Studies, Science, and Technical Subject*. www.corestandards.org/wp-content/uploads/ELA_Standards1.pdf

National Research Council. (2012). *A framework for K-12 science education: Practices, Crosscutting concepts, and Core ideas*. Washington, DC: National Academies Press. https://doi.org/10.17226/13165

Noh, S. M., Yan, V. X., Bjork, R. A., & Maddox, W. T. (2016). Optimal sequencing during category learning: Testing a dual-learning systems perspective. *Cognition*, *155*, 23–29. https://doi.org/10.1016/j.cognition.2016.06.007

Ostrow, K., Heffernan, N., Heffernan, C., & Peterson, Z. (2015). Blocking vs. interleaving: Examining single-session effects within middle school math homework. In C. Conati, N. Heffernan, A. Mitrovic, & M. F. Verdejo (eds.), *Artificial intelligence in education*, Vol. 9112 (pp. 338–347). Cham: Springer. https://doi.org/10.1007/978-3-319–19773-9_34

Paas, F. G. (1992). Training strategies for attaining transfer of problem-solving skill in statistics: A cognitive-load approach. *Journal of Educational Psychology*, *84*(4), 429–434. https://doi.org/10.1037/0022–0663.84.4.429

Palmeri, T. J. & Mack, M. L. (2015). How experimental trial context affects perceptual categorization. *Frontiers in Psychology*, *6*, 180. https://doi.org/10.3389/fpsyg.2015.00180

Pani, J. R., Chariker, J. H., & Naaz, F. (2012). Computer-based learning: Interleaving whole and sectional representation of neuroanatomy. *Anatomical Sciences Education*, *6*(1), 11–18.

Patel, R., Liu, R., & Koedinger, K. (2015). When to block versus interleave practice? Evidence against teaching fraction addition before fraction multiplication. In A. Papafragou, D. Grodner, D. Mirman, & J. C. Trueswell (eds.), *Proceedings of the 38th annual conference of the Cognitive Science Society* (pp. 2069–2074). Austin, TX: Cognitive Science Society.

Pigott, R. E. & Shapiro, D. C. (1984). Motor schema: The structure of the variability session. *Research Quarterly for Exercise and Sport*, *55*, 41–45.

Pinto-Zipp, G. & Gentile, A. M. (1995). Practice schedules in motor learning: Children vs. adults. *Society of Neuroscience: Abstracts*, *21*, 1620.

Rau, M. A., Aleven, V., & Rummel, N. (2013). Interleaved practice in multi-dimensional learning tasks: Which dimension should we interleave? *Learning and Instruction*, *23*, 98–114. https://doi.org/10.1016/j.learninstruc.2012.07.003

Rawson, K. A., Thomas, R. C., & Jacoby, L. L. (2015). The power of examples: Illustrative examples enhance conceptual learning of declarative concepts. *Educational Psychology Review*, *27*(3), 483–504. https://doi.org/10.1007/s10648-014–9273-3

Rohrer, D. (2012). Interleaving helps students distinguish among similar concepts. *Educational Psychology Review, 24*(3), 355–367.

(2015). Student instruction should be distributed over long time periods. *Educational Psychology Review, 27*(4), 635–643. https://doi.org/10.1007/s10648-015-9332-4

Rohrer, D., Dedrick, R. F., & Burgess, K. (2014). The benefit of interleaved mathematics practice is not limited to superficially similar kinds of problems. *Psychonomic Bulletin and Review, 21*(5), 1323–1330. https://doi.org/10.3758/s13423-014-0588-3

Rohrer, D., Dedrick, R. F., & Stershic, S. (2015). Interleaved practice improves mathematics learning, *107*(3), 900–908.

Rohrer, D. & Taylor, K. (2007). The shuffling of mathematics problems improves learning. *Instructional Science, 35*(6), 481–498.

Ross, B. H. (2000). The effects of category use on learned categories. *Memory and Cognition, 28*(1), 51–63.

Rozenshtein, A., Pearson, G. D. N., Yan, S. X., Liu, A. Z., & Toy, D. (2016). Effect of massed versus interleaved teaching method on performance of students in radiology. *Journal of the American College of Radiology, 13*(8), 979–984. https://doi.org/10.1016/j.jacr.2016.03.031

Sana, F., Yan, V. X., & Kim, J. A. (2016). Study sequence matters for the inductive learning of cognitive concepts. *Journal of Educational Psychology.*

Sandhofer, C. M. & Doumas, L. A. A. (2008). Order of presentation effects in learning color categories. *Journal of Cognition and Development, 9*(2), 194–221.

Schlichting, M. L. & Preston, A. R. (2015). Memory integration: Neural mechanisms and implications for behavior. *Current Opinion in Behavioral Sciences, 1*, 1–8. https://doi.org/10.1016/j.cobeha.2014.07.005

Shea, C H & Kohl, R. M. (1991). Composition of practice: Influence on the retention of motor skills. *Research Quarterly for Exercise and Sport, 62*(2), 187–195. https://doi.org/10.1080/02701367.1991.10608709

Shea, C. H., Kohl, R., & Indermill, C. (1990). Contextual interference: Contributions of practice. *Acta Psychologica, 73*(2), 145–157. https://doi.org/10.1016/0001-6918(90)90076-R

Shea, J. B. & Morgan, R. L. (1979). Contextual interference effects on the acquisition, retention, and transfer of a motor skill. *Journal of Experimental Psychology: Human Learning and Memory, 5*(2), 179–187.

Smith, L. B. & Kemler, D. G. (1978). Levels of experienced dimensionality in children and adults. *Cognitive Psychology, 10*, 502–532.

Sorensen, L. J. & Woltz, D. J. (2016). Blocking as a friend of induction in verbal category learning. *Memory and Cognition, 44*(7), 1000–1013. https://doi.org/10.3758/s13421-016-0615-x

Spiering, B. J. & Ashby, F. G. (2008). Initial training with difficult items facilitates information integration, but not rule-based category learning. *Psychological Science, 19*(11), 1169–1177. https://doi.org/10.1111/j.1467-9280.2008.02219.x

Ste-Marie, D. M., Clark, S. E., Findlay, L. C., & Latimer, A. E. (2004). High levels of contextual interference enhance handwriting skill acquisition. *Journal of Motor Behavior, 36*(1), 115–126.

Stewart, N. & Brown, G. D. A. (2004). Sequence effects in the categorization of tones varying in frequency. *Journal of Experimental Psychology: Learning, Memory, and Cognition, 30*(2), 416–430.

Stewart, N., Brown, G. D. A., & Chater, N. (2002). Sequence effects in categorization of simple perceptual stimuli. *Journal of Experimental Psychology: Learning, Memory, and Cognition*, *28*(1), 3–11.

Strutt, G. F., Anderson, D. R., & Well, A. D. (1975). A developmental study of the effects of irrelevant information on speeded classification. *Journal of Experimental Child Psychology*, *20*(1), 127–135. https://doi.org/10.1016/0022–0965(75)90032–6

Tauber, S. K., Dunlosky, J., Rawson, K. A., Wahlheim, C. N., & Jacoby, L. L. (2013). Self-regulated learning of a natural category: Do people interleave or block exemplars during study? *Psychonomic Bulletin and Review*, *20*(2), 3560363.

Taylor, K. & Rohrer, D. (2010). The effects of interleaved practice. *Applied Cognitive Psychology*, *24*(6), 837–848.

Terrace, H. S. (1964). Wavelength generalization after discrimination learning with and without errors. *Science*, *144*(361), 78–80.

Thompson, L. A. & Markson, L. (1998). Developmental changes in the effect of dimensional salience on the discriminability of object relations. *Journal of Experimental Child Psychology*, *70*(1), 1–25. https://doi.org/10.1006/jecp.1998.2445

Tse, C.-S. & Altarriba, J. (2010). Does survival processing enhance implicit memory? *Memory and Cognition*, *38*(8), 1110–1121.

Unsworth, N. & Engle, R. W. (2007). The nature of individual differences in working memory capacity: active maintenance in primary memory and controlled search from secondary memory. *Psychological Review*, *114*(1), 104–132. https://doi.org/10.1037/0033-295X.114.1.104

Unsworth, N. & Spillers, G. J. (2010). Variation in working memory capacity and episodic recall: the contributions of strategic encoding and contextual retrieval. *Psychonomic Bulletin and Review*, *17*(2), 200–205. https://doi.org/10.3758/PBR.17.2.200

Wahlheim, C. N., Dunlosky, J., & Jacoby, L. L. (2011). Spacing enhances the learning of natural concepts: an investigation of mechanisms, metacognition, and aging. *Memory and Cognition*, *39*(5), 750–763. https://doi.org/10.3758/s13421-010–0063-y

Werner, S. & Thies, B. (2000). Is "change blindness" attenuated by domain-specific expertise? An expert-novices comparison of change detection in football images. *Visual Cognition*, *7*(1–3), 163–173. https://doi.org/10.1080/135062800394748

Whitman, J. R. & Garner, W. R. (1963). Concept learning as a function of form of internal structure. *Journal of Verbal Learning and Verbal Behavior*, *2*(2), 195–202.

Wulf, G. & Shea, C. H. (2002). Principles derived from the study of simple skills do not generalize to complex skill learning. *Psychonomic Bulletin and Review*, *9*(2), 185–211.

Yamauchi, T. & Markman, A. B. (2000). Inference using categories. *Journal of Experimental Psychology. Learning, Memory, and Cognition*, *26*(3), 776–795.

Yan, V. X., Bjork, E. L., & Bjork, R. A. (2016). On the difficulty of mending metacognitive illusions: A priori theories, fluency effects, and misattributions of the interleaving benefit. *Journal of Experimental Psychology: General*, *145*(7), 918–933.

Yan, V. X., Soderstrom, N. C., Seneviratna, G. S., Bjork, E. L., & Bjork, R. A. (2017). How should exemplars be sequenced in inductive learning? Empirical evidence versus learners' opinions. *Journal of Experimental Psychology: Applied*

Zeithamova, D., Schlichting, M. L., & Preston, A. R. (2012). The hippocampus and inferential reasoning: Building memories to navigate future decisions. *Frontiers in Human Neuroscience*, *6*, 70. https://doi.org/10.3389/fnhum.2012.00070

Zulkiply, N. & Burt, J. S. (2013). The exemplar interleaving effect in inductive learning: moderation by the difficulty of category discriminations. *Memory and Cognition, 41* (1), 16–27. https://doi.org/10.3758/s13421-012–0238-9

Zulkiply, N., McLean, J., Burt, J. S., & Bath, D. (2012). Spacing and induction: Application to exemplars presented as auditory and visual text. *Learning and Instruction, 22*(3), 215–221. https://doi.org/10.1016/j.learninstruc.2011.11.002

17 Correcting Student Errors and Misconceptions

Elizabeth J. Marsh and Emmaline Drew Eliseev

Introduction

Overview and History

Mistakes are common in education and sometimes are even encouraged as part of the learning process. Young children, for example, are often instructed to "invent" spellings while writing, as this approach leads them to write longer texts (albeit with more spelling errors; Clarke, 1988). Many textbook chapters prompt students to answer "prequestions" about material that has not yet been covered, with the goal of guiding their reading (Pressley et al., 1990). Learning to debug errors in computer code is considered integral to learning to program (e.g., Klahr & Carver, 1988). In general, the prevailing zeitgeist is for educational practice to encourage learners to have a growth mindset and to accept mistakes as part of the learning process (Yeager & Dweck, 2012).

Such practices differ greatly from what was considered ideal practice prior to the 1970s. Perhaps most notably, the behaviorist B. F. Skinner argued strongly against a "trial-and-error" view of learning in favor of avoiding errors when possible (Skinner, 1953). The emphasis was on *errorless learning* (Terrace, 1963), meaning that learning conditions should allow students to learn without ever making a mistake (under the logic that errors had the potential to interfere with learning the correct responses). This perspective is an "early selection" model of errors, in that it aims for errors to never occur in the first place. Such an approach is insufficient for two reasons: First, in at least some instances, making a mistake may help learning (e.g., Kornell, Hays, & Bjork, 2009). Second, and more practically, it is virtually impossible to prevent a learner from ever making mistakes, necessitating a mechanism for error correction (a "late correction" model).

The Importance of Error Correction

Understanding how to correct errors is crucial, as uncorrected errors have the potential to be problematic. For example, students who do not receive feedback on their answers on a multiple-choice test are at risk for later reproducing some of the multiple-choice lures they selected (for a review, see Marsh et al., 2007). A student who incorrectly selects "mice" as the answer to the multiple-choice question "With the increase in nutrias in the U.S., which animal's population decreased?: (a) beavers, (b) mice, (c) moles, (d) muskrats" will be more likely to answer "mice" to a later short-answer version of the question ("With the increase in nutrias in the U.S., which animal's population decreased?") than if they had never answered the multiple-choice question at all. This problem occurs with college students, high school students (Fazio, Agarwal et al., 2010), and even elementary school children (Marsh, Fazio, & Goswick, 2012). The problem is not question-specific, in that incorrectly selecting "gravitation" in response to the question "What biological term describes fish slowly adjusting to water temperature in a new tank?: (a) acclimation, (b) gravitation, (c) maturation, (d) migration" affects responses to conceptually similar questions, such as "Animals that thicken their fur during winter are exhibiting what biological phenomenon?" (Marsh et al., 2007). Fortunately, there is a relatively simple solution: Tell students the correct answer (Butler & Roediger, 2008) – previewing one of the main messages of this chapter.

Uncorrected errors have consequences beyond believing a single falsehood is true; conceptual misunderstandings can interfere with new learning of other related information. Students enter the classroom with naïve theories about how things work, based on their own experiences as well as portrayals in film and television, and such beliefs are thought to impede acquisition of fundamental concepts in fields such as chemistry (e.g., Nakhleh, 1992), physics (e.g., Carey, 1986), and computer programming (e.g., Clancy, 2004). It is for this reason that teachers often try to anchor new concepts on familiar objects and systems (e.g., using the solar system to teach about the atom), to make sure they are using the correct mental model for the problem.

Defining Feedback

Broadly, we consider feedback to be any information that has the potential to affirm or update a student's knowledge (as opposed to feedback regarding student behavior or motivation, for example). Our definition of feedback is not tied to a particular type of error and it can take many forms, including but not limited to marks indicating whether an answer is right or wrong, the correct answer to a problem or question, an explanation of why an answer is the correct one, or a new way of thinking about a complex system. It can occur at different grain sizes, providing only the needed correction or contextualizing the correction within a larger unit (e.g., an entire textbook chapter or lesson). Feedback could come from another person (such as a teacher), from places such as the Internet or a book, or even from oneself (such as when one looks up the answer to check their work). In short, we endorse a broad definition of feedback in this chapter, with the different instantiations tied together by the *need to correct something* – meaning that even entire lessons may serve as feedback if the student enters with a misconception.

Methods for Studying Error Correction

Overview

There are hundreds of demonstrations of the power of feedback. Feedback is typically considered to be one of the most powerful tools in the teacher's toolbox, yielding a large effect size (average Cohen's d greater than 0.7; Hattie, 2012, 2015). The benefits of providing feedback are larger than those of other common recommendations to teachers, such as having students spread out learning over time (spacing; $d = 0.60$), create concept maps ($d = 0.64$), review worked examples ($d = 0.37$), and engage in peer tutoring ($d = 0.55$) (Hattie, 2015).

One of our favorite experimental examples comes from Pashler and colleagues (2005) because they separated the effects of feedback on maintaining correct answers versus correcting errors. That is, they argued that some of the inconsistent effects in the literature likely occurred because these two types of responses were treated as the same, when feedback should have less of an impact on correct answers (given that, by definition, there is nothing to correct). Their participants received two chances to study a list of twenty Luganda–English word pairs (e.g., *leero–today*), before taking a translation test (*leero–?*). On this initial test, the groups performed similarly (as expected), translating about 40 percent of words correctly – meaning that there were plenty of errors to be corrected. Critically, some subjects received no feedback about their answers, others were told whether each translation was correct or not, and a third group was told the correct translation of each Luganda word (additional controls were run to rule out possible confounds but we will not discuss those further). Of interest was the learner's ability to maintain their correct responses, as well as to correct their errors, both relatively immediately and after a delay.

While participants did forget some of their correct translations over the course of one week, this effect was similar across feedback conditions. Error correction, in contrast, depended on the feedback condition: Errors were only corrected after receiving answer feedback, not correct/incorrect feedback, and this pattern held both immediately and on a test one week later (although the expected forgetting happened over the course of a week). These effects were very large – receiving correct answer feedback following a mistake improved final performance by 494 percent. Such powerful effects are consistent with past reviews of the literature showing large benefits of feedback.

Pashler and colleagues' results highlight our first piece of advice: When students make an error, it is better to provide the correct answer than to simply mark it as incorrect. We reached a similar conclusion when we tested students on what they learned from reading short passages describing history, geography, and science (Fazio, Huelser et al., 2010). Answer feedback is even the better choice when correcting errors made on a multiple-choice test (Marsh et al., 2012). This finding with multiple-choice tests is particularly discouraging about the usefulness of right/ wrong feedback, as such feedback does provide information in this case – it allows the learner to winnow down the remaining choices. But of course this benefit is contingent on learners' ability to correctly eliminate lures, leading to the finding shown in Figure 17.1: Following errors on a multiple-choice test, receiving right/wrong feedback led to intermediate performance on a final test, between the levels observed following no feedback versus answer feedback. The benefit of right/wrong feedback dropped as narrowing down the choices became harder (with three remaining choices, for example, as opposed to one) – after being told one made an error on a four-alternative multiple-choice question, performance was not much higher than if one had received no feedback at all.

In another study, we examined whether receiving right/wrong feedback (and the knowledge of what one does vs. does not know) indirectly benefits learning, by guiding learners' future study efforts – but, unfortunately, our data did not support this idea. After reading texts and receiving feedback, readers received a second chance to read the passages, at their own pace. However, all readers benefited from rereading, even if they had not received any feedback at all. One possibility is that right/wrong feedback often does not provide any additional information to the learner – there are many cases where learners have a good sense of what they do versus do not know without feedback, such as translations of foreign vocabulary or simple facts (e.g., Hart, 1967). However, there are also cases where people do not realize they are making mistakes, something we turn to in the next section of this chapter.

Errors Made with Confidence

We know intuitively that not all errors are the same – it is one thing to correct an incorrect translation and another to correct a misunderstanding of why seasons occur. These two example errors differ in many ways, including but not limited to the

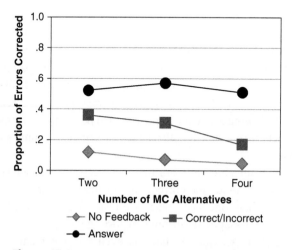

Figure 17.1 *Proportion of errors corrected on the final test based on feedback condition (no feedback, correct/incorrect, answer feedback) and the number of multiple-choice alternative answer choices (two, three, four) on an initial multiple-choice test (after Marsh et al., 2012)*

complexity of the error (a simple factual error vs. a conceptual misunderstanding of a system), confidence in one's response (which likely will be lower for the failed translation than one's faulty explanation of the seasons), content domain (language vs. science), and so on.

As a starting point, we can examine other errors that are similar to the incorrect translations in most ways but differ in one key aspect. For example, many people believe that George Washington had wooden teeth or that Marie Antoinette said "let them eat cake," even though neither is true. Structurally, these errors are like the incorrect translations, in that they are relatively simple paired associates, with the "George Washington–wooden teeth" association needing to be updated to "George Washington–dentures made of bone and other nonwood materials." The difference is that these misconceptions are likely believed with much higher confidence than errors made when translating recently learned foreign words. In other words, we can examine either materials that elicit a range of confidence or a set designed to elicit high-confidence errors, to examine whether one's confidence in an error affects one's ability to correct it.

Intuitively, one might expect that beliefs held with high confidence would be harder to correct, as they likely reflect stronger representations in memory. However, numerous studies demonstrate that people are more likely to correct high-confidence errors than low-confidence ones (*the hypercorrection effect*; Butterfield & Metcalfe, 2001). Given feedback, most people, for example, are more likely to correct their misconception that Sydney is the capital of Australia than an error about the capital of Botswana. This pattern is observed across ages; for example, adolescents are more likely to correct high-confidence misconceptions about science, such as "The largest part of the Sahara consists of sand" and "When in a heavy thunderstorm, it is safest to lie down flat on the ground," than misconceptions that were held with lower confidence (Van Loon et al., 2015). Even young children show a higher correction rate for high-confidence errors than erroneous guesses (Marsh et al., 2012; Metcalfe & Finn, 2012).

One explanation is that people likely have greater confidence when answering questions about topics they already know something about (i.e., most Americans know more about Australia than Botswana) and that knowledge supports encoding of the feedback (for related ideas about how knowledge may support hypercorrection, see Metcalfe & Finn, 2011). A second explanation involves people's subjective feelings when faced with a large discrepancy between their confidence and accuracy – a surprising error increases attention to the feedback, with consequent benefits for memory. This claim is supported by experiments showing that people take longer to respond to a secondary tone detection task when feedback mismatches their expectations (suggesting they were distracted by the feedback; Butterfield & Metcalfe, 2006). Similarly, people are more likely to remember the color of the feedback when receiving feedback in response to correct guesses and high-confidence errors (Fazio & Marsh, 2009), supporting the hypothesis that surprising feedback directs attention toward the feedback.

The classroom implications of these results are less clear; we do not wish educators to resort to "gimmicky" feedback in order to "surprise" their students.

Rather, such results should provide reassurance that answer feedback will be sufficient even in cases where students are confident in their answers.

Misunderstandings

Misunderstanding how echolocation works is a different problem from not being able to produce the term echolocation in response to a description of how bats navigate. The first involves misunderstanding a process whereas the second is a fairly straightforward memory problem, involving forgetting of a specific term. This difference has implications for what information the feedback should convey; simply telling someone the answer works in the case of simple errors (as described in the previous two sections) but may be insufficient with more complex errors.

Many educators and researchers assume that more feedback is better. For example, educational software programs (especially Intelligent Tutoring systems) often respond to wrong answers with an explanation of *why* the answer is wrong (e.g., Graesser et al., 2005). Educators provide in-line comments on student essays, summary statements on student work, and comments on exams (e.g., Tomas, 2014). However, the experimental evidence is mixed as to whether there are added benefits from providing information beyond the correct answer (for a review, see Kulhavy & Stock, 1989; for a meta-analysis, see Bangert-Drowns et al., 1991). For example, students whose multiple-choice selections revealed misconceptions about science (such as the belief that an individual insect can become immune to pesticides) benefited as much from correct answer feedback as explanations of why their choices were wrong (i.e., that natural selection operates at the species level, not the individual level; Gilman, 1969). Similarly, it was just as effective to tell middle school children the correct answers to factual questions as to have them find the answers in their text (with line numbers to ensure they could find them; Peeck, 1979).

One issue that makes it hard to draw conclusions across studies is that the "extra information" added to the feedback takes many forms or, other times, is not specified in enough detail to evaluate. Students might receive explanations of why answers are incorrect (e.g., Kulhavy et al., 1985), reread exact texts to discover why their errors were wrong (Andre & Thieman, 1988), or be directed to look at a particular place in a text to find the correct information (Peeck, 1979), among other variations. This issue is highlighted in a study where introductory psychology students were assigned to one of four conditions, so that after each multiple-choice exam they either received no feedback, compared their answers with the correct answers written on the board, listened to the instructor discuss each question, or were directed to reread textbook passages relevant to the questions they missed (Sassenrath & Garverick, 1965). Feedback helped performance on later exam questions that tapped retention (questions that were repeated from the midterm) but it did not matter whether students received answer feedback or listened to the instructor's discussion. It is hard to draw strong conclusions about feedback content from this study, however, because it is not clear whether or not students interacted during the instructor's discussion of the feedback, nor what content was discussed. (Did the teacher focus on elaborating the correct answer by explaining why some answers were wrong? etc.) Furthermore, even the answer feedback condition was unusual, in that it involved self-grading (comparing one's answers with those on the blackboard) and as such involved the students more than simply viewing answer feedback.

Logically, it is not clear why students would need more information than the answer to improve on a final test containing exactly the same questions as before – in such a situation, retention is required, not explanation or elaboration of knowledge. The advantage of elaborated feedback should be greatest on final tests that require going beyond retention to demonstrate a deeper understanding of the key concepts and applications of one's knowledge to novel situations. Returning to the study of introductory psychology students just discussed, the data hint at this possibility. In addition to repeating questions from the midterm, the final test included new questions that were conceptually related to some of the midterm questions, to test transfer of learning. On these transfer questions, performance was best in the discussion condition, with checking one's answers a close second. Again, it is not clear exactly what the teacher discussed but it seems reasonable to assume that a word "discussion" would involve more than just providing the answer.

We tested these ideas more directly in our own work, where students learned about complex scientific processes such as understanding how bread rises or how tornadoes form (Butler, Godbole, & Marsh, 2013). After reading the scientific texts, students took an open-ended test probing definitions of the concepts; critically, after each response, students received no feedback, were told the correct answer to the question, or received the answer in combination with an explanation that had been presented in the earlier text (Butler et al., 2013). Two days later, students took a final test that included some of the same definitional questions as on the first test, as well as novel inference questions. For example, the final test required students to name the process that facilitates gas exchange in the alveoli (definitional question) and to explain why breathing pure oxygen helps people who have trouble breathing (inference question). When faced with the same definitional questions as on the initial test, students benefited from having received feedback – but it did not matter if the feedback contained the right answer or an explanation (see Figure 17.2). In contrast, when faced with novel inference questions, students who had received explanation feedback outperformed those who had only received answer feedback. The extra information in the explanation feedback was unnecessary when the test tapped retention of answers; the explanation feedback was needed when the test required transfer of knowledge to a new context.

Conceptual Change

Even if a student understands a concept, he or she may struggle to understand how that concept interacts with other concepts or how to generalize that knowledge to a new problem. Students may sometimes have an incorrect mental model of a situation; in this case, what needs to be changed is the larger mental representation not just a specific fact or concept. We discussed earlier how feedback can be useful in correcting simple errors and here we will focus on how feedback can be used to correct a student's flawed mental representation of broad conceptual information.

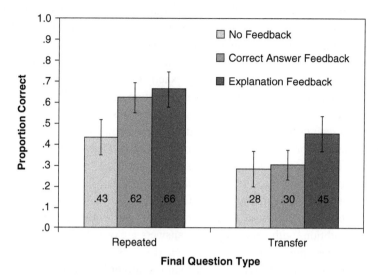

Figure 17.2 *The effect of feedback type (no feedback, correct answer feedback, explanation feedback) on repeated questions compared with transfer questions (from Butler, Godbole, & Marsh, 2013, p. 292. Adapted with permission from the American Psychological Association)*

Of course, correcting a misconception of an entire system is unlikely to occur with the kind of simple feedback described thus far – one cannot encapsulate the entirety of evolution into a single sentence, for example. Here is where the line begins to blur between learning and correction; the first time students learn about motion and friction, for example, should it be called "learning" (as it is the first school lesson on the topic) or a correction (given that the student enters the classroom with naïve incorrect beliefs about the concepts)?

For example, consider students' misunderstanding of emergent properties in science (Chi, 2005). This example requires an understanding of the differences between direct and emergent processes, so we review these first. Direct processes involve a series of sequential stages – examples include the cycles of the moon, the circulation of blood in the body, and the stages of mitosis (Chi et al., 2012). One stage is the *direct* result of an agent, prior process, or stage. In contrast, emergent processes are nonsequential and based on unconstrained, continuous action (Chi et al., 2012). The end result *emerges* from the set of actions but is not caused by any one agent or action. Examples include osmosis, heat flow, and natural selection. Consider how a student's response to a question about diffusion (an emergent process) suggests that he or she is incorrectly applying a direct process model. When describing the exchange of CO_2 and O_2 in the lungs, the student stated: "the capillaries that are in your lungs would ... let the oxygen come in through the space in its walls and then the carbon dioxide would go out ... because ... it wants to get out into a lower concentration, so all the carbon dioxide would want to go through so it would be in a lower concentration" (Chi, 2005, p. 185). The student uses sequential language, stating that oxygen *first* comes in *and then* carbon dioxide goes out. This student also treats diffusion as an intentional process where oxygen *wants* to get in and carbon dioxide *wants* to get out. In reality, CO_2 and O_2 (and all molecules) are in constant motion (Brownian motion), moving from areas of high to low concentration – and it is these collective movements that yield diffusion, not one molecule causing another to move.

To teach emergent processing, Chi and colleagues created a module that (1) defined and differentiated the two types of processes, (2) gave everyday examples of each, and (3) prompted the student to examine how the processes played out in the everyday examples. For direct processes, students learned about wolf pack hunting and skyscraper construction; for emergent processes, students learned about schools of fish and movement in crowds. The examples were chosen to have familiar structures that students could easily understand. In the third part of the module, students identified whether the examples fit the criteria of direct versus emergent properties, as they had learned about in the beginning of the module. For example, students identified whether all agents had an equal role (indicative of an emergent process) or not (suggesting a direct process) – for example, noting that the architect's role is different from the welder (skyscraper example) but that no single fish drives the school of fish. To test the effectiveness of this module, Chi and colleagues assigned 8th and 9th grade students to complete the emergent processing module or a control science module; all students later completed a module on diffusion and took a test that tapped standard misconceptions about diffusion. Students who completed the emergent processing module (the "feedback" targeting the misconception) endorsed fewer of the misconceptions than did the students who completed the control module, although questions about the generality of this work remain.

Conceptual change is required to fix misconceptions of many complex processes, such as understanding how evolution works or why we experience seasons. Many examples can also be drawn from physics, where many students (and adults!) possess naïve beliefs about force and motion that are incorrect. For example, many people struggle to understand the concept of curvilinear motion. When people are shown the image in (the incomplete version of) Figure 17.3 of a ball on a string spun in a circle and asked to predict the path of the ball if the string were to break, they often incorrectly assume the untethered ball would continue moving in a circular pattern.

Although many people struggle with abstract physics problems, people are more likely to correctly solve such problems if they are framed within a familiar context. For example, most people have at one point in their lives engaged in a water fight, spraying others with a garden hose. If Figure 17.3 is interpreted as a person holding a garden hose (black line), people do not predict that the water will follow the curve of the hose but, instead, correctly predict that the water will shoot directly out of the hose (in a straight line, independent of the curvature of the hose). In this and other examples, the feedback involves drawing students' attention to familiar past experiences, to help them understand their mistakes in more abstract situations.

This section emphasizes the many different forms feedback can take, from simply indicating whether an answer is correct or incorrect to an entire learning module. The challenge is for educators to know what is needed, and when – points we cover in the next section.

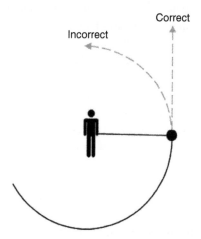

Figure 17.3 *The ball and string problem, which tests a person's understanding of curvilinear motion (after Kaiser, Jonides, & Alexander, 1986)*

This schematic shows correct and incorrect responses (dashed lines) to the ball and string problem, which tests a person's understanding of curvilinear motion.

Advice for Educators

Overview

The laboratory is obviously very different from the classroom – and even with that expectation, we were shocked at the differences we experienced when we started working in undergraduate engineering classrooms. Our experiments did not translate in the ways we expected them to – students worked together on assignments, teachers unknowingly ruined manipulations, and people cheated (Butler et al., 2014). We can only imagine the challenges involved in working in classrooms with younger students. We are not surprised that some laboratory findings do not translate to the classroom; a once-significant effect may be swamped in the classroom when the experimenter can no longer control for other factors that carry more weight.

Fortunately, it is clear that receiving feedback benefits students learning authentic educational materials, although sometimes learning is measured outside of assignments contributing to course grades. The benefits occur with such varied educational topics as soil ecology (Farragher & Szabo, 1986), army ants (Surber & Anderson, 1975), glaciers (More, 1969), the human eye (Kulhavy, Yekovich, & Dyer, 1976), and introductory psychology (e.g., Kulhavy & Anderson, 1972). Increased exposure to feedback matters; for example, the number of optional homework feedback sessions attended is correlated with final course grades (Núñez-Peña, Bono, & Suárez-Pellicioni, 2015). Quality of feedback also matters; 6th grade students' math achievement improved after teachers received training on what to include in their written feedback to homework (Elawar & Corno, 1985).

Given that feedback helps, what do educators need to know? What might surprise them? In the following section, we try to be more specific than simply advising teachers to "give feedback."

Know the Few Situations Where Feedback May Be Unnecessary

The title of this section may appear to directly contradict everything we have written thus far – so it is worth reiterating that most of the time feedback is important to provide. However, in schools, time is a precious and limited resource – critically, time spent doing one activity is at the cost of another. It remains an open question how educators should decide to spend valuable class time, given that the time used to distribute feedback could be used for other learning activities known to benefit learning, such as retrieving information from memory (i.e., flashcards, quizzes; McDaniel et al., 2011) or writing to learn activities (for a meta-analysis, see Bangert-Drowns, Hurley, & Wilkinson, 2004; see also Klein and Van Dijk, Chapter 8, this volume).

One situation was alluded to earlier in this chapter: Feedback has relatively little effect on the maintenance of correct answers, *unless* they were guesses (Butler & Roediger, 2008). In contrast, feedback is absolutely crucial for error correction and should not be skipped. The logical extension of these findings is that feedback may not be necessary if student performance is uniformly high. This point was captured in a laboratory study where undergraduates received a fixed amount of time to learn two lists of Swahili–English translations (Hays, Kornell, & Bjork, 2010). After an initial study phase, students completed a series of test-feedback trials (akin to going through a pack of flashcards repeatedly). Feedback viewing was required for one list (every flashcard had to be turned over), whereas it could be skipped for the other list, as determined by either the computer or the learner. In this case, skipping feedback (whether determined by the computer or the student) meant that students spent more time practicing retrieval (as opposed to reading feedback), which led to more correct translations a day later (reflecting the known memorial benefits of retrieving information from memory; e.g., Roediger & Butler, 2011). It should be noted, however, that participants' judgments about whether or not to skip feedback viewing were excellent, with 85 percent of their feedback choices lining up with their actual performance. As covered in the next section, students are not always so calibrated at judging their need for feedback, meaning it is likely safer for the teacher to make the decision that feedback is unnecessary.

Ensure That Students Look at the Feedback

In the section "Errors Made With Confidence", we argued that surprising feedback was better attended to, with consequent benefits for later correction (Fazio & Marsh, 2009). Yet it is difficult to directly generalize these results to educational practice – not all feedback surprises the learner and, in many cases, the teacher has no idea if students even looked at the feedback, let alone understood it. In the laboratory, we can address these problems, requiring feedback to stay on the computer screen for a set period of time, instructing students to respond after reading it, or asking students to make a judgment that shows they processed it for meaning (e.g., Lhyle & Kulhavy, 1987). However, educators normally do not have the option of forcing students to spend a set amount of time reading feedback, given that time spent on review means less time for new learning activities.

Furthermore, attention is not guaranteed, even in a relatively captive classroom given that laptops distract (Fried, 2008) and minds wander (see review by Szpunar, Moulton, & Schacter, 2013). The laboratory likely underestimates the challenges of directing a learner's attention to processing feedback in authentic educational settings, where feedback processing is often left to the discretion of students. We have all seen students recycle their commented papers as they walk out the classroom door, or experienced empty office hours when no students stop by to view their exams (which were not returned in order to protect a bank of test questions). Existing data confirm these anecdotal impressions. For example, one set of researchers took advantage of the practice of allowing third-year medical students to submit a self-addressed stamped envelope (SASE) so feedback on their essay could be mailed to them. This essay was a five-page review piece and a passing grade was required to advance to the next grade. Unfortunately, less than half of the students provided the SASE, meaning most of the students did not receive any feedback on their written work (Sinclair & Cleland, 2007). Perhaps most discouraging, students who likely needed the feedback the most (the ones with lower course grades) were the least likely to provide an envelope so that the feedback could be mailed.

In our study in an engineering classroom, we used an online homework system that allowed us to automatically collect records of whether or not individual students clicked on problem-by-problem feedback (Mullet et al., 2014). This system also made it possible to require feedback viewing, if desired. In one section of the course, feedback viewing was required and counted toward the class grade. In the other section, feedback viewing was optional, as is the norm in most college courses. The results were striking: When feedback viewing was required, 94 percent of students clicked on the links. In contrast, students in the feedback-optional section only clicked on the feedback links for 47 percent of the problems. For a given problem, students viewed the feedback sooner and more frequently in the feedback-required section than in the optional section. These different behaviors were associated with differences in performance on the course exams – students who had been required to view the feedback answered 10 percent more exam questions correctly than did the students for whom feedback viewing was optional.

Why did students sometimes fail to access the feedback provided to them? One possibility is that students simply punt on tasks that do not contribute directly to their grades. A second possibility is that students may not always be calibrated enough to know when to look at the feedback. It is entirely possible that the students in the engineering classroom study believed they looked at the feedback when they really needed it – which would suggest a metacognitive problem, not a laziness problem. Both are likely involved, but here we focus on the metacognitive issue.

Correctly skipping feedback depends critically on people's awareness of when they made mistakes. In the Hays and colleagues (2010) study discussed in the previous section, students benefited from the ability to skip feedback – but those students were very good at knowing which Swahili words they could not translate, with 85 percent of their feedback choices lining up with their actual performance. We cannot assume similar calibration of learning with more complex materials. It may be obvious when one does not know the translation of a foreign word but much harder to judge the quality of one's essay or whether a math problem was solved correctly. Second, students in that study likely benefited from skipping feedback because they replaced that time with another learning activity – skipping feedback on some trials allowed them to spend more time retrieving other information. We do not have any data on this point but we doubt that the students in our feedback-optional section used the time they saved on some other additional activity for the class.

Ensure That Students Process the Feedback Correctly

Our engineering students benefited from clicking on the feedback links – but it should be noted that we do not know if they actually read the content, whether they thought about it, and so on. In some instances, additional steps may be necessary to ensure that students actually process the feedback. For example, in one study, experimenters attempted to leverage the known benefits of active processing (e.g., Slamecka & Katsaiti, 1987) by requiring students to unscramble the words in the feedback message (that is, the correct multiple-choice alternative was presented in scrambled format). This strategy only helped when the experimenters added a task to make sure that students actually processed the feedback for meaning, in this case, by requiring them to write out the correct unscrambled version of the feedback (Lhyle & Kulhavy, 1987).

More generally, feedback will fail if students do not understand it or fail to understand how it contradicts their own answer. This may be particularly important in situations where people are self-grading or peer-grading – if they do not apply a rubric correctly, they will not realize an error has been made. In one study, students were asked to define terms such as "the fundamental attribution error" and then compare their answers to correct definitions (Rawson & Dunlosky, 2007). The critical finding is that sometimes students could not understand how their incorrect answer differed from the correct one. A similar finding has been reported with example generation, with students asked to generate examples of concepts failing to understand how their answers fell short when provided with feedback (Zamary, Rawson, & Dunlosky, 2016).

Don't Assume That Corrections Are Permanent

There is no "mastery" level that guarantees information will always be known – for example, we have all experienced tip-of-the-tongue states whereby something we know is currently "out of reach." More generally, forgetting increases as the cues in the environment change and as time passes since learning and using a piece of information. The most well-known educational example of this problem is the so-called summer learning loss whereby students appear to lose large amounts of information over summer vacation (Cooper et al., 1996). One issue involves how to reactivate that previously learned information; another problem involves the potential resurgence of an earlier error.

First, consider the problem whereby a student has forgotten the meanings of core concepts from a class. In at least some cases, the simple solution involves simple reexposure to the material – the same way a tip-of-the-tongue state is often resolved when someone takes pity on the speaker and fills in the missing word. In our own work, we have shown that a multiple-choice test can serve the same function; after knowledge about the Treaty of Versailles is forgotten, solving the multiple-choice question "What peace treaty ended World War I?" is sufficient to reactivate it (while also providing formative assessment to the teacher). One problem involves identifying which information should be revisited; when we investigated these issues in a pharmacology classroom, we relied on the instructor to identify foundational material that students were supposed to know from prerequisite coursework (Butler et al., under review). For three of the course's six units, students answered multiple-choice questions on related foundational material (which units were assigned to the intervention versus control were counterbalanced across subjects). Pretesting indicated that students were unable to produce 75 percent of the foundational material at the start of the course (even though it all had been covered in prerequisites for the course); multiple-choice testing (without feedback) led to significant improvement on a later test of that foundational material. To our knowledge, this is the first demonstration of stabilizing access to foundational knowledge in a classroom setting but there is still much to be learned about how to identify which knowledge needs to be reactivated and how often – a point we return to at the end of this chapter.

The second problem involves the resurgence of errors. Spontaneous recovery of undesirable behaviors is common – the drinker who abstained from alcohol can "fall off the wagon," a frequent flyer may become anxious after numerous smooth flights, and long-debunked beliefs (i.e., that the world is flat) become popular again. In education, this problem is particularly problematic when dealing with confidently held misconceptions. Earlier in this chapter, we discussed how people are more likely to correct high-confidence errors such as "Sydney is the capital of Australia" than erroneous guesses, given feedback. This result is surprising because confidently held errors would be expected to be harder to correct – and yet increased attention to the feedback leads to a higher correction rate. But what happens after time has passed? Forgetting of the recent event (the feedback) will occur at a faster rate than forgetting of the misconception (this is Jost's Law; Jost, 1897) – meaning that, at some point in time, the misconception will be stronger in memory than the feedback. A week later, it was errors such as "Sydney is the capital of Australia" that were most likely to reappear (Butler, Fazio, & Marsh, 2011).

Finally, vestiges of misconceptions may remain even though students show knowledge of the correct information. For example, young children often believe that the ability to move is a prerequisite for life, a belief that is at odds with plants being alive. The remnant of this belief shows up when undergraduates are asked to quickly classify a series of items as living versus nonliving; they are slower and less accurate to classify plants than animals, even after controlling for word frequency (Goldberg & Thompson-Schill, 2009). Even PhDs in biology show a similar effect when told to make their decisions quickly, despite having spent an average of twenty years as biology faculty. Under the right circumstances, an ingrained false belief may coexist with its correction. Similarly, even though most people know that density determines whether an object floats or sinks in water, they are slower to make decisions when mass and density are not positively correlated, reflecting the child-hood tendency to relate buoyancy and size (Potvin et al., 2015).

Student Preferences Do Not Always Align with the Best Learning Strategies

Student beliefs about learning are notoriously incorrect. For example, many students prefer to use inefficient study strategies such as rereading their textbooks and rewriting their notes instead of engaging in self-testing (Karpicke, Butler, & Roediger, 2009). Cramming is another popular, yet ineffective, study technique often used by students. In fact, students believe they learn more when their study sessions are massed together even though this is not true – they actually learn more when they spread out their study sessions (Kornell, 2009). These metacognitive illusions likely occur because easy practice feels good, even if it does not promote long-term learning. That is, rereading a text is easier than reading it for the first time, and a translation is easily retrieved if I just tested myself with the same flashcard two trials ago – tricking the learner into believing they are good study strategies (see Bjork & Schmidt, 1992). It matters what students like, as their preferences are correlated with their teacher ratings (Beleche, Fairris, & Marks, 2012) which in turn often play a role in how teachers are evaluated in their jobs.

Students tend to like feedback that includes written comments, although the need for them likely varies depending on the nature of the comment and the type of to-be-learned information. While students value written feedback, not all written feedback is viewed as helpful (Weaver, 2006). A common complaint of students is that the written feedback they received on their assignments was unclear, confusing, and needed to include more details in order for students to understand how to improve (Ferguson, 2011; Walker, 2009). Earlier we discussed how feedback need not always contain an explanation of why a particular answer is right or wrong – but students like to receive feedback that explains their grade. For instance, one student com-plained that there were "not enough comments to justify the grade given" (Ferguson, 2011, p. 57). Specifically, students prefer feedback that contains comments on the quality of their main ideas rather than specific details. Unsurprisingly, students like to see positive comments to build their confidence included with more critical feedback indicating how to improve their work (Ferguson, 2011).

A second misconception of students is that feedback should be provided as soon as possible (of course, this preference likely also reflects their desire to know their grades). This belief is not limited to students; it occurs in contemporary educational programs and is often considered a positive feature of an assessment if feedback can be immediate – Coursera touts immediate feedback to student responses in massive open online courses (MOOCs) and teachers can purchase the Immediate Feedback Assessment Technique (IF-AT) testing system (where students uncover a star if they scratch off the correct answer to a multiple-choice question; Epstein, Epstein, & Brosvic, 2001; Epstein & Brosvic, 2002). This belief traces back to B. F. Skinner, who showed that animals required immediate reinforcement to learn an association between a lever press and a food reward (see review by Renner, 1964). However, the results with humans are actually quite mixed, with some studies (mostly classroom studies) showing a benefit of immediate feedback whereas others (mostly laboratory studies) show a benefit of delaying feedback (for meta-analysis, see Kulik & Kulik, 1988). Despite the ambiguous success of immediate feedback, students show a strong preference of using the IF-AT where they receive immediate corrective feedback over traditional multiple-choice testing (Dibattista, Mitterer, & Gosse, 2004). On written assignments, university students preferred feedback to be returned in two to three weeks, as long as it was before the start of the next assignment (Ferguson, 2011).

In our own work on this issue, we used an online homework system that allowed us to carefully control the timing of feedback (Mullet et al., 2014). Students in upper-level undergraduate engineering classes received identical feedback on their homework assignments; the only difference was whether the feedback was delivered immediately after the homework deadline or delayed by one week. Grades on course exams were higher following delayed feedback, even after controlling statistically for the shorter retention interval. However, students failed to recognize the benefits of delayed feedback. When asked which feedback schedule they preferred and which one was more effective, the overwhelming majority of students reported a strong preference for immediate feedback. This was true regardless of whether they experienced both schedules of feedback within their course (a within-subjects design) or only experienced one of the two schedules (a between-subjects design). Thus, there was a metacognitive disconnect between the feedback timing schedule that students preferred and what actually helped them to learn.

Given the general importance of student ratings in teacher evaluations, we understand why teachers might be loath to implement a strategy that promotes learning but is almost universally disliked. One possibility is to explain upfront to students the reasons for one's choices (which is possible in practice, albeit not in a controlled experiment) – in teaching, we have found that students interpret delayed feedback as evidence that the teacher does not care or is procrastinating; it may not be possible to completely manage this impression but explaining the reasoning will not hurt and has the potential to help.

Consider Students' Preexisting Beliefs and Motivations to Change

From the instructor's perspective, feedback consists of relatively neutral information (other than the negative affect associated with making a mistake). However, learners enter the classroom with preexisting beliefs and differ in their motivation to change them. No one is surprised by a lack of change when one simply tells a climate change doubter to believe science on global warming – a different approach is needed. Even in a study with relatively neutral statements (e.g., telling students that they were wrong for believing that bulls become enraged by the color red), students indicated that they did not believe all of the feedback. That is, the more confident students were in their initial responses, the less likely they were to believe the feedback, as rated on a 0 (do not believe the feedback at all) to 100 (absolutely believe the feedback) scale (Rich et al., 2017). Belief in the feedback, in turn, was related to later corrections of the errors.

This type of situation is also one where explanation feedback can help. It makes sense that when someone is motivated to believe something, he or she will need more evidence to reject it. Accordingly, participants who received both the right answer and the explanation behind it were more successful at correcting their misconceptions than participants who only received feedback with the correct answer (Rich et al., 2017). That is, receiving the following feedback, "The color red does not enrage bulls (the correct answer) because bulls do not see the color red, and, instead, attack because they perceive the matador as a threat (the explanation)" (Rich et al., 2017, p. 492), is more likely to increase your belief in the feedback and help you correct your misconception than only receiving "The color red does not enrage bulls (the correct answer)" (Rich et al., 2017, p. 492). When tackling students' mistaken beliefs, feedback is only helpful in correcting misconceptions if it is believed. Providing explanations in addition to the correct answer is a good way to refute the misconception and help students accept the feedback as true.

Conclusions

Open Questions

One open question involves the value of personalized feedback. Personalized learning is, in general, a hot topic in education – it is very appealing to think about adjusting the curriculum and feedback to a particular learner. While there are many commercial products touting personalized learning, in most cases we know little about the nature of the underlying algorithms. From the academic perspective, the best evidence for personalized learning comes from work looking at the effects of different practice schedules on the retention of Spanish vocabulary words (Lindsey et al., 2014). Grade 8 students practiced Spanish vocabulary via an online flashcard (retrieval followed by feedback) tutoring system called the Colorado Optimized Language Tutor (COLT). In a standard practice condition, practice was massed – one-third of the words were assigned to be translated chapter-by-chapter, so that older chapters were never revisited as the class progressed through the book. In a spaced condition, the scheduler had one-third of the words revisited later in the course – practice was spread out over time. In a third condition, analytics were used to individually determine the practice schedule for one-third of the words; the analytics drew on both the learner's data and a large amount of data about past learners to make predictions about which items needed the most practice. Briefly, the results showed that children learned the words in the personalized spacing condition best, followed by those in the spaced condition, with the worst retention of words in the standard practice condition (especially those that had occurred early in the course).

Feedback was provided in all three COLT learning conditions, so the current data do not tell us anything about how feedback should be scheduled. However, some evidence suggests that the temporal spacing of feedback is similar to that of retrieval (Smith & Kimball, 2010). That is, a fair amount of evidence suggests that the interval between learning opportunities should be between 5 percent and 20 percent of the desired retention interval (Cepeda et al., 2008) – and this same formula works for the timing of feedback.

Final Thoughts

Vague advice to educators can be harmful rather than helpful if principles are implemented in a way that changes the processing involved. One concern is that we are simply asking too much of teachers, who are already often following mandated curricula – especially since we suspect many of the chapters in this volume are providing other pieces of advice. However, we encourage teachers to keep in mind (1) the benefits of delaying feedback and (2) the resurgence of errors over time. To the extent that new topics build on old ones, there may be a natural spacing of feedback over time. The teacher can also watch for any indicators that students are regressing, which could trigger a need for review. More generally, we encourage teachers to think more flexibly about the definition of feedback. Feedback could take the form of a multiple-choice quiz (Cantor et al., 2015), a student presentation, or an in-class review game – it does not have to take the form of responses to a test or other graded assignment.

References

Andre, T. & Thieman, A. (1988). Level of adjunct question, type of feedback, and learning concepts by reading. *Contemporary Educational Psychology, 13*(3), 296–307.

Bangert-Drowns, R. L., Hurley, M. M., & Wilkinson, B. (2004). The effects of school-based writing-to-learn interventions on academic achievement: A meta-analysis. *Review of Educational Research, 74*(1), 29–58.

Bangert-Drowns, R. L., Kulik, C. L. C., Kulik, J. A., & Morgan, M. (1991). The instructional effect of feedback in test-like events. *Review of Educational Research, 61*(2), 213–238.

Beleche, T., Fairris, D., & Marks, M. (2012). Do course evaluations truly reflect student learning? Evidence from an objectively graded post-test. *Economics of Education Review, 31*(5), 709–719.

Bjork, R. A., Dunlosky, J., & Kornell, N. (2013). Self-regulated learning: Beliefs, techniques, and illusions. *Annual Review of Psychology, 64*(1), 417–444.

Butler, A. C., Black-Maier, A. C., Campbell, K., Marsh, E. J., & Persky, A. M. (under review). Stabilizing access to marginal knowledge in a classroom setting.

Butler, A. C., Fazio, L. K., & Marsh, E. J. (2011). The hypercorrection effect persists over a week, but high-confidence errors return. *Psychonomic Bulletin and Review, 18*(6), 1238–1244.

Butler, A. C., Godbole, N., & Marsh, E. J. (2013). Explanation feedback is better than correct answer feedback for promoting transfer of learning. *Journal of Educational Psychology, 105*(2), 290–298.

Butler, A. C., Karpicke, J. D., & Roediger, H. L. III (2007). The effect of type and timing of feedback on learning from multiple-choice tests. *Journal of Experimental Psychology: Applied, 13*(4), 273–281.

Butler, A. C., Marsh, E. J., Slavinsky, J. P., & Baraniuk, R. G. (2014). Integrating cognitive science and technology improves learning in a STEM classroom. *Educational Psychology Review, 26*(2), 331–340.

Butler, A. C. & Roediger, H. L. (2008). Feedback enhances the positive effects and reduces the negative effects of multiple-choice testing. *Memory and Cognition, 36*(3), 604–616.

Butterfield, B. & Metcalfe, J. (2001). Errors committed with high confidence are hypercorrected. *Journal of Experimental Psychology: Learning, Memory, and Cognition, 27*(6), 1491–1494.

   (2006). The correction of errors committed with high confidence. *Metacognition and Learning, 1*(1), 69–84.

Cantor, A. D., Eslick, A. N., Marsh, E. J., Bjork, R. A., & Bjork, E. L. (2015). Multiple-choice tests stabilize access to marginal knowledge. *Memory and Cognition, 43*(2), 193–205. http://dx.doi.org/10.3758/s13421-014-0462-6

Carey, S. (1986). Cognitive science and science education. *American Psychologist, 41*(10), 1123–1130.

Cepeda, N. J., Vul, E., Rohrer, D., Wixted, J. T., & Pashler, H. (2008). Spacing effects in learning a temporal ridgeline of optimal retention. *Psychological Science, 19*(11), 1095–1102.

Chi, M. T. (2005). Commonsense conceptions of emergent processes: Why some misconceptions are robust. *The Journal of the Learning Sciences, 14*(2), 161–199.

Chi, M. T., Roscoe, R. D., Slotta, J. D., Roy, M., & Chase, C. C. (2012). Misconceived causal explanations for emergent processes. *Cognitive science, 36*(1), 1–61.

Clancy, M. (2004). Misconceptions and attitudes that interfere with learning to program. In S. Fincher & M. Petre (eds.), *Computer science education research* (pp. 85–100). CRC Press.

Clarke, L. K. (1988). Invented versus traditional spelling in first graders' writings: Effects on learning to spell and read. *Research in the Teaching of English, 22*(3), 281–309.

Cooper, H., Nye, B., Charlton, K., Lindsay, J., & Greathouse, S. (1996). The effects of summer vacation on achievement test scores: A narrative and meta-analytic review. *Review of Educational Research, 66*(3), 227–268.

Dibattista, D., Mitterer, J. O., & Gosse, L. (2004). Acceptance by undergraduates of the immediate feedback assessment technique for multiple-choice testing. *Teaching in Higher Education, 9*(1), 17–28.

Elawar, M. C. & Corno, L. (1985). A factorial experiment in teachers' written feedback on student homework: Changing teacher behavior a little rather than a lot. *Journal of Educational Psychology, 77*(2), 162–173. https://doi.org/10.1037/0022–0663.77.2.162

Epstein, M. L. & Brosvic, G. M. (2002). Students prefer the immediate feedback assessment technique. *Psychological Reports*, *90*(3, suppl.), 1136–1138.

Epstein, M. L., Epstein, B. B., & Brosvic, G. M. (2001). Immediate feedback during academic testing. *Psychological Reports*, *88*(3), 889–894.

Farragher, P. & Szabo, M. (1986). Learning environmental science from text aided by a diagnostic and prescriptive instructional strategy. *Journal of Research in Science Teaching*, *23*(6), 557–569.

Fazio, L. K., Agarwal, P. K., Marsh, E. J., & Roediger, H. L., III (2010). Memorial consequences of multiple-choice testing on immediate and delayed tests. *Memory and Cognition*, *38*(4), 407–418. http://dx.doi.org/10.3758/MC.38.4.407

Fazio, L. K., Huelser, B. J., Johnson, A., & Marsh, E. J. (2010). Receiving right/wrong feedback: Consequences for learning. *Memory*, *18*(3), 335–350.

Fazio, L. K. & Marsh, E. J. (2009). Surprising feedback improves later memory. *Psychonomic Bulletin & Review*, *16*(1), 88–92.

Ferguson, P. (2011). Student perceptions of quality feedback in teacher education. *Assessment and Evaluation in Higher Education*, *36*(1), 51–62. https://doi.org/10.1080/02602930903197883

Fried, C. B. (2008). In-class laptop use and its effects on student learning. *Computers and Education*, *50*(3), 906–914.

Gilman, D. A. (1969). Comparison of several feedback methods for correcting errors by computer-assisted instruction. *Journal of Educational Psychology*, *60*(6, Pt. 1), 503–508.

Goldberg, R. F. & Thompson-Schill, S. L. (2009). Developmental "roots" in mature biological knowledge. *Psychological Science*, *20*(4), 480–487.

Graesser, A. C., Chipman, P., Haynes, B. C., & Olney, A. (2005). AutoTutor: An intelligent tutoring system with mixed-initiative dialogue. *IEEE Transactions on Education*, *48*(4), 612–618.

Hart, J. T. (1967). Second-try recall, recognition, and the memory-monitoring process. *Journal of Educational Psychology*, *58*(4), 193–197.

Hattie, J. (2012). *Visible learning for teachers: Maximizing impact on learning*. New York: Routledge.

  (2015). The applicability of visible learning to higher education. *Scholarship of Teaching and Learning in Psychology*, *1*(1), 79–91. https://doi.org/10.1037/stl0000021

Hays, M. J., Kornell, N., & Bjork, R. A. (2010). The costs and benefits of providing feedback during learning. *Psychonomic Bulletin and Review*, *17*(6),797–801.

Jost, A. (1897). Die Assoziationsfestigkeit in ihrer Abha¨ngigkeit von der Verteilung der Wiederholungen [The strength of associations in their dependence on the distribution of repetitions]. *Zeitschrift fur Psychologie und Physiologie der Sinnesorgane*, *16*, 436–472.

Kaiser, M. K., Jonides, J., & Alexander, J. (1986). Intuitive reasoning about abstract and familiar physics problems. *Memory and Cognition*, *14*(4), 308–312.

Karpicke, J. D., Butler, A. C., & Roediger III, H. L. (2009). Metacognitive strategies in student learning: Do students practise retrieval when they study on their own?. *Memory*, *17*(4), 471–479.

Klahr, D. & Carver, S. M. (1988). Cognitive objectives in a LOGO debugging curriculum: Instruction, learning, and transfer. *Cognitive Psychology*, *20*(3), 362–404.

Kornell, N. (2009). Optimising learning using flashcards: Spacing is more effective than cramming. *Applied Cognitive Psychology*, *23*(9), 1297–1317. https://doi.org/10.1002/acp.1537

Kornell, N., Hays, M. J., & Bjork, R. A. (2009). Unsuccessful retrieval attempts enhance subsequent learning. *Journal of Experimental Psychology: Learning, Memory, and Cognition*, *35*(4), 989–998. https://doi.org/10.1037/a0015729

Kulhavy, R. W. & Anderson, R. C. (1972). Delay-retention effect with multiple-choice tests. *Journal of Educational Psychology*, *63*(5), 505–512. https://doi.org/10.1037/h0033243

Kulhavy, R. W. & Stock, W. A. (1989). Feedback in written instruction: The place of response certitude. *Educational Psychology Review*, *1*(4), 279–308.

Kulhavy, R. W., White, M. T., Topp, B. W., Chan, A. L., & Adams, J. (1985). Feedback complexity and corrective efficiency. *Contemporary Educational Psychology*, *10* (3), 285–291.

Kulhavy, R. W., Yekovich, F. R., & Dyer, J. W. (1976). Feedback and response confidence. *Journal of Educational Psychology*, *68*(5), 522–528.

Kulik, J. & Kulik, C. (1988). Timing of feedback and verbal learning. *Review of Educational Research*, *58*(1), 79–97. www.jstor.org/stable/1170349

Lhyle, K. G. & Kulhavy, R. W. (1987). Feedback processing and error correction. *Journal of Educational Psychology*, *79*(3), 320.

Lindsey, R. V., Shroyer, J. D., Pashler, H., & Mozer, M. C. (2014). Improving students' long-term knowledge retention through personalized review. *Psychological Science*, *25* (3), 639–647.

Maier, U., Wolf, N., & Randler, C. (2016). Effects of a computer-assisted formative assessment intervention based on multiple-tier diagnostic items and different feedback types. *Computers and Education*, *95*, 85–98.

Marsh, E. J., Fazio, L. K., & Goswick, A. E. (2012). Memorial consequences of testing school-aged children. *Memory*, *20*(8), 899–906.

Marsh, E. J., Lozito, J. P., Umanath, S., Bjork, E. L., & Bjork, R. A. (2012). Using verification feedback to correct errors made on a multiple-choice test. *Memory*, *20*(6), 645–653.

Marsh, E. J., Roediger, H. L., Bjork, R. A., & Bjork, E. L. (2007). The memorial consequences of multiple-choice testing. *Psychonomic Bulletin and Review*, *14*(2), 194–199.

McDaniel, M. A., Agarwal, P. K., Huelser, B. J., McDermott, K. B., & Roediger, H. L., III, (2011). Test-enhanced learning in a middle school science classroom: The effects of quiz frequency and placement. *Journal of Educational Psychology*, *103*(2), 399–414.

Metcalfe, J. & Finn, B. (2011). People's hypercorrection of high-confidence errors: Did they know it all along? *Journal of Experimental Psychology: Learning, Memory, and Cognition*, *37*(2), 437–448.

(2012). Hypercorrection of high confidence errors in children. *Learning and Instruction*, *22* (4), 253–261.

More, A. J. (1969). Delay of feedback and the acquisition and retention of verbal materials in the classroom. *Journal of Educational Psychology*, *60*(5), 339–342. https://doi.org/10.1037/h0028318

Mullet, H. G., Butler, A. C., Verdin, B., von Borries, R., & Marsh, E. J. (2014). Delaying feedback promotes transfer of knowledge despite student preferences to receive feedback immediately. *Journal of Applied Research in Memory and Cognition*, *3*(3), 222–229.

Nakhleh, M. B. (1992). Why some students don't learn chemistry: Chemical misconceptions. *Journal of Chemical Education, 69*(3), 191–196.

Núñez-Peña, M. I., Bono, R., & Suárez-Pellicioni, M. (2015). Feedback on students' performance: A possible way of reducing the negative effect of math anxiety in higher education. *International Journal of Educational Research, 70,* 80–87.

Pashler, H., Cepeda, N. J., Wixted, J. T., & Rohrer, D. (2005). When does feedback facilitate learning of words? *Journal of Experimental Psychology: Learning, Memory, and Cognition, 31*(1), 3–8.

Peeck, J. (1979). Effects of differential feedback on the answering of two types of questions by fifth-and sixth-graders. *British Journal of Educational Psychology, 49*(1), 87–92.

Potvin, P., Masson, S., Lafortune, S., & Cyr, G. (2015). Persistence of the intuitive conception that heavier objects sink more: A reaction time study with different levels of interference. *International Journal of Science and Mathematics Education, 13*(1), 21–43.

Pressley, M., Tanenbaum, R., McDaniel, M. A., & Wood, E. (1990). What happens when university students try to answer prequestions that accompany textbook material? *Contemporary Educational Psychology, 15*(1), 27–35.

Rawson, K. A. & Dunlosky, J. (2007). Improving students' self-evaluation of learning for key concepts in textbook materials. *European Journal of Cognitive Psychology, 19*(4–5), 559–579.

Renner, K. E. (1964). Delay of reinforcement: A historical review. *Psychological Bulletin, 61*(5), 341–361. https://doi.org/10.1037/h0048335

Rich, P. R., Van Loon, M. H., Dunlosky, J., & Zaragoza, M. S. (2017). Belief in corrective feedback for common misconceptions: Implications for knowledge revision. *Journal of Experimental Psychology: Learning, Memory, And Cognition, 43*(3), 492–501. https://doi.org/10.1037/xlm0000322

Roediger, H. L. & Butler, A. C. (2011). The critical role of retrieval practice in long-term retention. *Trends in Cognitive Sciences, 15*(1), 20–27. https://doi.org/10.1016/j.tics.2010.09.003

Sassenrath, J. M. & Garverick, C. M. (1965). Effects of differential feedback from examinations on retention and transfer. *Journal of Educational Psychology, 56*(5), 259–263.

Schmidt, R. & Bjork, R. (1992). New conceptualizations of practice: Common principles in three paradigms suggest new concepts for training. *Psychological Science, 3*(4), 207–217.

Sinclair, H. K. & Cleland, J. A. (2007). Undergraduate medical students: Who seeks formative feedback? *Medical Education, 41*(6), 580–582.

Skinner, B. F. (1953). *Science and human behavior.* New York: Simon and Schuster.

Slamecka, N. J. & Katsaiti, L. T. (1987). The generation effect as an artifact of selective displaced rehearsal. *Journal of Memory and Language, 26*(6), 589–607.

Smith, T. A. & Kimball, D. R. (2010). Learning from feedback: Spacing and the delay–retention effect. *Journal of Experimental Psychology: Learning, Memory, and Cognition, 36*(1), 80–95. https://doi.org/10.1037/a0017407

Surber, J. R. & Anderson, R. C. (1975). Delay-retention effect in natural classroom settings. *Journal of Educational Psychology, 67*(2), 170–173. https://doi.org/10.1037/h0077003

Szpunar, K. K., Moulton, S. T., & Schacter, D. L. (2013). Mind wandering and education: From the classroom to online learning. *Frontiers in Psychology, 4,* 495.

Terrace, H. S. (1963). Errorless transfer of a discrimination across two continua. *Journal of the Experimental Analysis of Behavior*, *6*(2), 223–232.

Tomas, C. (2014). Marking and feedback provision on essay-based coursework: A process perspective. *Assessment and Evaluation in Higher Education*, *39*(5), 611–624. https://doi.org/10.1080/02602938.2013.860078

Van Loon, M. H., Dunlosky, J., Van Gog, T., Van Merriënboer, J. J., & De Bruin, A. B. (2015). Refutations in science texts lead to hypercorrection of misconceptions held with high confidence. *Contemporary Educational Psychology*, *42*, 39–48.

Walker, M. (2009). An investigation into written comments on assignments: Do students find them usable? *Assessment and Evaluation in Higher Education*, *34*(1), 67–78. https://doi.org/10.1080/02602930801895752

Weaver, M. (2006). Do students value feedback? Student perceptions of tutors' written responses. *Assessment and Evaluation in Higher Education*, *31*(3), 379–394. https://doi.org/10.1080/02602930500353061

Yeager, D. S. & Dweck, C. S. (2012). Mindsets that promote resilience: When students believe that personal characteristics can be developed. *Educational Psychologist*, *47*(4), 302–314.

Zamary, A., Rawson, K. A., & Dunlosky, J. (2016). How accurately can students evaluate the quality of self-generated examples of declarative concepts? Not well, and feedback does not help. *Learning and Instruction*, *46*, 12–20.

18 How Multimedia Can Improve Learning and Instruction

Richard E. Mayer

The Multimedia Principle

Over the course of human history, the primary mode of communication in education has been with words, including spoken words (e.g., in lectures) and printed words (e.g., in books). This chapter explores the straightforward idea that human communication can be improved when pictures are added to words. In short, the idea motivating this chapter is that people learn better from words and pictures than from words alone. This statement summarizes what has been called the *multimedia principle*, which has become a fundamental principle of instructional design based on a growing body of research evidence (Butcher, 2014; Clark & Mayer, 2016; Mayer, 2009, 2014a).

Multimedia instruction (or a multimedia instructional message) refers to a lesson containing both words and pictures, where the words can be in spoken form or printed form and the pictures can be in static form (such as illustrations, charts, graphs, or photos) or dynamic form (such as animation or video). Multimedia instruction – educational communications that use words and graphics – can be presented in books, in live slideshow presentations, in e-learning on computers, or even in video games or virtual reality.

The rationale for multimedia instruction is both practical and theoretical. On the practical side, the multimedia principle – i.e., adding pictures to words – has potential to contribute to the science of instruction by improving how well students understand academic material; and, on the theoretical side, the multimedia principle has the potential to contribute to the science of learning by yielding the basis for theories of how people learn authentic academic content rather than contrived laboratory materials.

The goal of this chapter is to explore the potential of the multimedia principle for improving how people understand communications about academic content, as measured by their ability to take what they have learned and apply it to new situations (i.e., to be able to solve transfer problems). After a brief introduction, this chapter explores the historical foundations of multimedia learning, the evidence for the multimedia principle, the theoretical basis for how the multimedia principle works, the instructional implications of the multimedia principle, and future directions for the multimedia principle.

Preparation of this chapter was supported by Grant N000141262046 from the Office of Naval Research.

Historical Overview of the Multimedia Principle

The multimedia principle is at once both an old idea, dating back hundreds of years to the work of Comenius on the first multimedia textbook in the seventeenth century, and a new idea, inspired by ever-expanding advances in computer technology that allow dazzling graphics in the digital age.

The first children's multimedia textbook was published in Nuremberg in 1657 by John Amos Comenius. His book, *Orbis Pictus* (translated as "the world in pictures" or simply "visible world"), contained nearly 200 pages, with each page containing a black line drawing ranging from the parts of a house to a barbershop to creatures that live on land and water. Each element in the drawing was numbered, and below was a legend that gave the name in Latin and in the language of the reader for each numbered object, along with some description. The goal was to provide to children "a picture and nomenclature of all the chief things in the world ... so they may see nothing which they know not how to name and that they may name nothing which they cannot show." Comenius' guiding theory was that "there is nothing in the understanding, which was not before in the sense," which is consistent with the premise of the cognitive theory of multimedia learning that understanding is enhanced when learners can mentally connect words and graphics. On the practical side, *Orbis Pictus* became the bestselling textbook in Europe for a century, insuring its place as the world's first educational classic. In the subsequent centuries, picture books became the staple of children's textbooks, but modern analyses of the use of illustrations in textbooks show that most serve little or no pedagogical value and in some cases can even be distracting (Levin & Mayer, 1993).

Advances in computing technology in today's digital age have reignited educators' interest in multimedia forms of communication because of the ease with which it is now possible to render illustrations, photos, animation, and video and incorporate them with audio and text. Access to the Internet, mobile computing, and interactive virtual reality have made multimedia learning available when and where the learner wants it. Such advances have prompted calls for expanding the concept of literacy to new media in which students learn to create and comprehend multimedia messages (Mayer, 2008). Today's forms of multimedia instruction have expanded beyond paper-based formats to live slideshow formats to computer-based formats, including e-learning, video games, and virtual reality.

However, just because an educational technology exists does not mean that it will be used productively. For example, Cuban (1986) provides a history of educational technology in the twentieth century, including motion pictures in the 1920s, radio in the 1930s, educational TV in the 1950s, and machine-based programmed instruction in the 1960s. In each case, strong claims were made for the educational potential of the cutting-edge technology of the day, but, within a decade, it became clear that the technology had failed to revolutionize education. Today's cutting-edge technologies have prompted some visionaries to call for revolutionizing education – putting multimedia learning experiences online and making better use of game-like activities to accelerate learning (Gee, 2003; McGonical, 2011; Prensky, 2006; Schank, 2002).

The lessons concerning the educational technologies of the twentieth century should caution us to replace a *technology-centered approach* – designing instruction based on what cutting-edge technology can do without regard to how people learn – with a *learner-centered approach* – designing instruction, often multimedia instruction, based on an understanding of how people learn regardless of the medium used to deliver the instruction (Mayer, 2009). This chapter takes a learner-centered approach to designing multimedia instruction in the digital age based on the idea that instructional media do not cause learning but rather instructional methods cause learning (Clark, 2001). The next sections examine what the research has to say about how to design effective multimedia learning experiences for learners.

Evidence Concerning the Multimedia Principle

I stumbled into the field of multimedia learning about thirty years ago as part of my search for techniques that help people learn in ways that allow them to subsequently apply what they have learned to new situations. I was trying to figure out how to help people understand scientific explanations of how cause-and-effect systems work. For example, consider a verbal description of how a bicycle tire works: "When the handle is pulled up, the piston moves up, the inlet valve opens, the outlet valve closes, and air enters the lower part of the cylinder. When the handle is pushed down, the piston moves down, the outlet valve opens, and air moves out through the hose." This is a somewhat accurate – if brief – explanation of how the pump works, but you may wonder how well people understand this communication.

Our research shows that after students listen to this explanation, they are not able to generate many useful answers to transfer questions such as the troubleshooting question, "Suppose you push down and pull up several times but no air comes out. What could have gone wrong?," or the redesign question, "What could be done to make a pump more effective, that is, to move more air more rapidly?" (Mayer & Anderson, 1991).

However, consider what happens if we add a simple animation depicting the movement of the handle, piston, and valves in a pump in sync with the narration, as summarized in Figure 18.1. Our research (Mayer & Anderson, 1991) shows that students who received multimedia instruction generated more than twice as many useful answers to transfer questions than students who received only the narration without any animation. The effect size was greater than $d = 1$, which means that adding the animation to the narration pushed transfer performance up by more than one standard deviation, which is considered a large effect for an instructional intervention.

Overall, in each of the eight experimental comparisons conducted in our lab involving brief explanations of how pumps work, how car braking systems work, how electrical generators work, how lightning storms develop, and how to add and subtract with signed numbers, students who learned with words and graphics performed better than students who learned with words alone, yielding a median effect size of $d = 1.39$ (Mayer, 2009). Being able to improve transfer

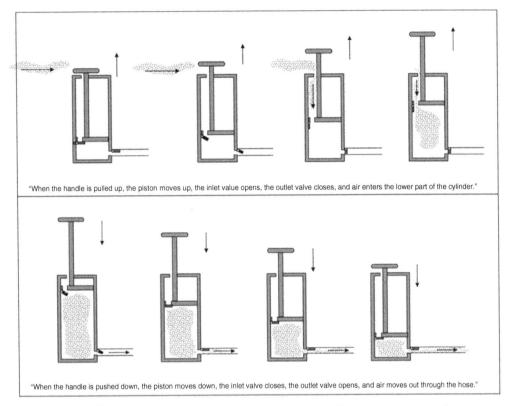

"When the handle is pulled up, the piston moves up, the inlet value opens, the outlet valve closes, and air enters the lower part of the cylinder."

"When the handle is pushed down, the piston moves down, the inlet valve closes, the outlet valve opens, and air moves out through the hose."

Figure 18.1 *Frames from narrated animation on how a bicycle tire pump works*

performance by more than a standard deviation is an exciting prospect because most instructional interventions do not generate that level of effect (Hattie, 2009). The next step in this research program was to determine how best to design multimedia instruction.

How the Multimedia Principle Works

In order to explain the multimedia principle and to determine how best to design multimedia instruction, classic theories of learning based mainly on rote learning of word lists need to be modified and expanded. For example, an explanation for the multimedia principle is provided by the cognitive theory of multimedia learning, as summarized in Figure 18.2 (Mayer, 2009, 2014a). The cognitive theory of multimedia learning is based on three key ideas from cognitive science:

Dual-channel principle: The human information processing system contains separate channels for verbal and pictorial information (Paivio, 1986; Baddeley, 1992). This is reflected in a verbal channel across the top row of Figure 18.2 and a pictorial channel across the bottom of Figure 18.2.

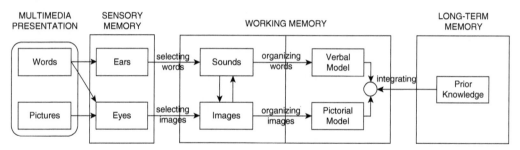

Figure 18.2 *Cognitive theory of multimedia learning*

Limited capacity principle: Only a few items can be processed in a channel at any one time (Baddeley, 1992; Sweller, Ayres, & Kalyuga, 2011). This is reflected in the working memory box in the middle column of Figure 18.2.

Active processing principle: Meaningful learning requires appropriate cognitive processing during learning, including attending to relevant information, mentally organizing it into a coherent structure, and integrating it with relevant prior knowledge (Mayer, 2009; Wittrock, 1989). This is reflected in the arrows for selecting, organizing, and integrating in Figure 18.2.

The boxes in Figure 18.2 represent memory stores and the arrows represent cognitive processes during learning. The first box in Figure 18.2 consists of the multimedia instructional message, which consists of words and pictures. The second box represents *sensory memory* – spoken words are held briefly in auditory sensory memory whereas pictures and printed words are held briefly in visual sensory memory. If the learner pays attention, as indicated by the *selecting* arrows, some of the words and images are transferred to *working memory* for further processing within a system that has limited processing capacity in each channel. In working memory, the learner can arrange words (including printed words transformed from the visual channel) into a verbal model and images into a pictorial model, as indicated by the *organizing* arrows. The final box is *long-term memory*, which contains a permanent storehouse of knowledge. The learner activates relevant prior knowledge and brings it into working memory, where it is connected with the incoming information and where the verbal and pictorial models are connected, as indicated by the *integrating* arrows.

Overall, meaningful learning occurs when the learner engages in appropriate cognitive processing during learning, including selecting relevant words and images from the multimedia message for further processing in working memory, mentally organizing the words into a coherent structure (or verbal model) and the images into a coherent structure (or pictorial model), and integrating the verbal and pictorial representations with each other and with relevant prior knowledge activated from long-term memory. The main challenge in instructional design is to guide learners to engage in these process, while not overloading their limited processing capacity in each channel of working memory. This challenge can be addressed by designing multimedia instruction in ways that minimize extraneous processing (i.e., cognitive processing that does not support the instructional objective, which can be caused by poor instructional design), manage essential processing (i.e., cognitive processing aimed at representing the presented material in working memory, which depends on the complexity of the material for the learner), and foster generative processing (i.e., cognitive processing aimed at making sense of the material, which depends on the learner's motivation to exert effort). In short, designing effective multimedia instruction requires not only presenting the relevant material but also guiding the learner's cognitive processing of the material.

Implications of the Multimedia Principle for Instructional Design

In attempting to apply the multimedia principle to practical educational venues such as classroom instruction, textbooks, and online instruction, it becomes clear that some ways of incorporating graphics are more effective than others. This section explores principles for how to design multimedia instruction that are based on replicated research findings (as reported in primary source publications) and grounded in cognitive theories of how people learn.

Table 18.1 lists eleven evidence-based principles for the design of multimedia instruction – including slideshow presentations, textbooks, online instruction, and educational games. The first column gives the name of the principle, the second column gives a brief description of the principle, the third column lists the median effect size based on published experiments comparing the transfer test performance of students who learned with the standard version of the lesson versus those who learned with an enhanced version that added the target feature, and the fourth column shows the number of experiments showing a positive effect out of the total number of experiments. We focus on principles that yield median effect sizes greater that $d = 0.40$, which is considered substantial enough to be practically important for education (Hattie, 2009).

The first five principles address the instructional goal of reducing extraneous processing – cognitive processing during learning that does not support the instructional goal. The theoretical rationale for reducing extraneous processing is that working memory capacity is limited, so if a learner allocates too much cognitive processing capacity to extraneous processing during learning there will not be enough cognitive capacity left to fully engage in essential processing (i.e., cognitive processing aimed at mentally representing the essential information in working memory) and generative processing (i.e., cognitive processing aimed at reorganizing the material and integrating it with relevant knowledge activated from long-term memory).

The *coherence principle* is that people learn better when extraneous material is excluded rather than included (Mayer, 2009; Mayer & Fiorella, 2014). Extraneous material includes unneeded detail in graphics, background music, or interesting but irrelevant facts in the text. For example, consider a slideshow lesson on how a virus causes a cold, such as exemplified in Figure 18.3 (Mayer et al., 2008). In the slide, we

Table 18.1 *Evidence-based principles for the design of multimedia instruction*

Principle	Description	ES	No.
Principles for reducing extraneous processing in multimedia learning			
Coherence principle	Eliminate extraneous material.	0.86	23/23
Signaling principle	Highlight essential material.	0.41	24/28
Spatial contiguity principle	Place printed words near corresponding graphics.	1.10	22/22
Temporal contiguity principle	Present corresponding narration and graphics simultaneously.	1.22	9/9
Redundancy principle	Do not add printed onscreen text that duplicates narrated graphics.	0.86	16/16
Principles for managing essential processing in multimedia learning			
Segmenting principle	Break lesson into manageable parts.	0.77	10/10
Pretraining principle	Provide pretraining in names and characteristics of key elements.	0.75	13/16
Modality principle	Present words in spoken form.	0.76	53/61
Principles for fostering generative processing in multimedia learning			
Personalization principle	Use conversational language.	0.79	14/17
Voice principle	Present spoken text with an appealing human voice.	0.74	5/6
Embodiment principle	Use humanlike gestures.	0.40	13/13

Note. ES = median effect size based on Cohen's d; No. = number of positive effects out of total number of comparisons.

have added two sentences at the end of the paragraph that present an interesting but irrelevant fact (which can be called a *seductive detail*). Students learned better when seductive details were excluded from the virus lesson (d = 0.80). Overall, across twenty-three of twenty-three experimental comparisons, students performed better on transfer tests when extraneous material was excluded, yielding a median effect size of d = 0.86, which is considered a large effect. Thus, more learning occurs when less is presented, that is, when the instructional message is kept as simple as possible. Some possible boundary conditions are that the coherence principle applies most strongly for learners with low working memory capacity, when the lesson is presented at a fast pace not under the learner's control, and when the extraneous material is highly distracting (Rey, 2012).

The *signaling principle* (also called the *cueing principle*) is that people learn better when essential material is highlighted (Mayer, 2009; Mayer & Fiorella, 2014; van Gog, 2014). Highlighting of printed text can involve the use of color, underlining, bold, italics, font size, font style, or repetition. Highlighting of spoken text can involve speaking louder or with more emphasis. Highlighting of graphics includes the use of arrows, color, flashing, and spotlights. For example, in a narrated

Step5: Breaking Free from the Host Cell
The new parts are packaged into new virus within the host cell. The new viruses break free from the host cell. In some cases, they break the host cell open, destroying the host cell in the process, which is called lysis. In other cases, they punch out of he cell membrane surrounding them, which is called budding. A study conducted by researchers at Wilkes University in Wilkes-Barre, Pennsylvania, reveals that people who make love once or twice a week are more immune to colds than folks who abstain from sex. Researchers believe that the bedroom activity somehow stimulates an immune-boosting antibody called IgA.

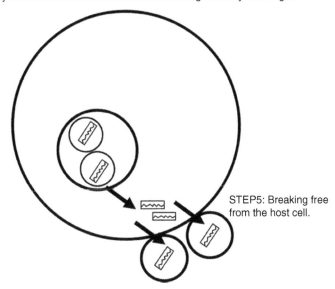

STEP5: Breaking free from the host cell.

Figure 18.3 *Do people learn better when we add interesting but extraneous text?*

slideshow lesson on how airplanes achieve lift, signaling involved adding headings such as "Wing Shape: Curved Upper Surface Is Longer," and emphasizing key words, such as the emboldened words in the following phrase: "surface on **top** of the wing is **longer** than on the **bottom**." Mautone and Mayer (2001) reported better transfer test performance for students who learned from a signaled multimedia lesson than from a nonsignaled lesson ($d = 0.65$). Overall, there was a positive signaling effect in twenty-four of twenty-eight published experimental comparisons, yielding a median effect size of d = 0.41, which is considered in the small to medium range. Some possible boundary conditions are that the signaling effect can be stronger for low-knowledge learners (Naumann, et al., 2007), when the graphics are complex (Jeung, Chandler, & Sweller, 1997), and when signaling is used sparingly (Stull & Mayer, 2007).

The *spatial contiguity principle* is that people learn better when printed words are placed near to rather than far from corresponding graphics (Ayers & Sweller, 2014; Ginns, 2006; Mayer & Fiorella, 2014). For example, Figure 18.4a shows a version of a lesson on car braking systems with the words presented as a caption at the bottom of the page or screen (i.e., separated presentation) whereas Figure 18.4b shows the words placed near the part of the graphic they describe (i.e., integrated presentation). Johnson and Mayer (2012) reported that students performed substantially better on transfer tests when they received integrated presentations rather than separated

(a) Separated Presentation

When the driver steps on the car's brake pedal, a piston moves forward inside the master cylinder. The piston forces brake fluid out of the master cylinder and through the tubes to the wheel cylinders. In the wheel cylinders, the increase in fluid pressure makes a smaller set of pistons move outward. These smaller pistons activate the brake shoes. When the brake shoes press against the drum, the wheel stops or slows down.

(b) Integrated Presentation

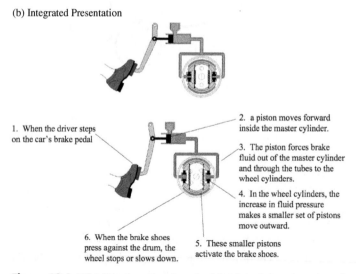

Figure 18.4 *Which instructional method leads to better learning about braking systems?*

presentations, even though the words and graphics were identical in both treatments ($d = 0.73$). Overall, there was a positive effect for spatial contiguity in twenty two out of twenty two published experiments, yielding a median effect size of $d = 1.22$, which is a large effect. Some possible boundary conditions are that the spatial contiguity effect can be stronger when learners are low in prior knowledge (Mayer et al., 1995) and when the material is complex (Ayres & Sweller, 2014).

The *temporal contiguity principle* is that people learn better from a narrated lesson, when the spoken words are presented simultaneously with the corresponding graphics such as drawings, animation, or video (Ginns, 2006; Mayer & Fiorella, 2014). In successive presentation, the spoken words are presented before (or after) the graphics are presented. In nine out of nine published experimental comparisons, students performed better on transfer tests with simultaneous rather than successive presentations, yielding a median effect size of $d = 1.22$, which is a large effect. Some possible boundary conditions are that the temporal contiguity principle is diminished when the material is very simple (Ginns, 2006), when the material is presented in very short chunks (Mayer, et al., 1999; Moreno & Mayer, 1999; Schuler et al., 2012), and when the lesson is slow-paced or under learner control (Michas & Berry, 2000).

The *redundancy principle* is that people learn better from narration and graphics than from narration, graphics, and redundant printed text (Adesope & Nesbit, 2012; Kalyuga & Sweller, 2014; Mayer & Fiorella, 2014). For example, Figure 18.5a shows a slide from a lesson on lightning that includes animation and narration, whereas Figure 18.5b shows a slide that includes animation, narration, and onscreen text that duplicates the narration. Mayer, Heiser, and Lonn (2001) reported that students performed better on transfer tests when they received a narrated animation rather than a narrated animation with redundant onscreen text ($d = 0.77$). Overall, in sixteen of sixteen published experiments, people performed better on transfer tests when redundant onscreen text was excluded rather than included, with a median effect size of $d = 0.86$, which is a large effect. Some important boundary conditions are that the redundancy principle may not apply when no graphics are presented (Moreno & Mayer, 2002), only a few key words are printed on the screen (Mayer & Johnson, 2008), or the onscreen text is worded differently than the spoken text (Yue, Bjork, & Bjork, 2013).

The next three principles in Table 18.1 are aimed at managing essential processing (i.e., cognitive processing for mentally representing the essential material in working

(a) Animation and Narration   **(b) Animation, Narration, and On-Screen Text**

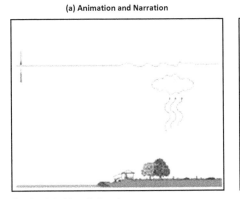

As the air in this updraft cools, water vapor condenses into water droplets and forms a cloud.

"As the air in this updraft cools, water vapor condenses into water droplets and forms a cloud".   "As the air in this updraft cools, water vapor condenses into water droplets and forms a cloud".

Figure 18.5 *Which instructional method leads to better learning from an online slideshow?*

memory). When the material is complex for the learner, the amount of essential processing required to mentally represent the material may overload working memory capacity. In this case, the learner needs to be able to manage his or her processing capacity in a way that allows for representing the essential material. Three techniques for accomplishing this goal are breaking the essential material into manageable parts (i.e., segmenting), learning about the names and characteristics of key elements before the lesson is presented (i.e., pretraining), and presenting words in spoken form rather than printed form (i.e., modality).

The *segmenting principle* calls for breaking a multimedia lesson into manageable parts (Mayer & Pilegard, 2014). For example, rather than presenting a 2.5 minute narrated animation on lighting formation as a continuous presentation, suppose we break it into sixteen segments, each about 10 seconds long with about one sentence, and allow the learner to click on a CONTINUE key to go to the next segment. A sample slide is shown in Figure 18.6. This design allows the learner to digest one step in the process of lightning formation before going on to the next one. Mayer and Chandler (2001) found that students performed better on transfer tests when they received segmented rather than continuous lessons on lightning formation, with an effect size of $d = 1.13$. The segmenting principle was supported in ten of ten published experiments, yielding a median effect size of $d = 0.79$, which is nearly a large effect. Concerning boundary conditions, the segmenting principle may apply more strongly for students with low working memory capacity (Lusk et al., 2009) and for students who are low-achieving (Ayres, 2006).

The *pretraining principle* calls for teaching students about the names and characteristics of key elements before presenting the multimedia lesson (Mayer & Pilegard, 2014). For example, before presenting a narrated animation depicting how a car's braking system works, students can be presented with a diagram of the braking system showing the key parts – e.g., brake petal, piston, wheel cylinders, and brake shoes – as

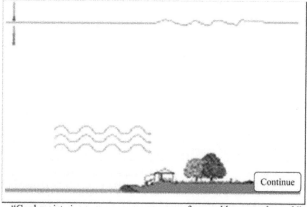

"Cool moist air moves over a warmer surface and becomes heated."

Figure 18.6 *Do people learn better when a CONTINUE button is added after each segment?*

shown in Figure 18.7. When the learner clicks on a part, such as the piston, the computer shows that the part is called a piston and tells the learner that the piston can move forward and back. Mayer, Mathias, and Wetzell (2002) found that students who received this pretraining before the multimedia lesson performed better on transfer

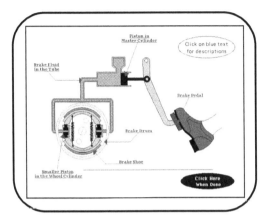

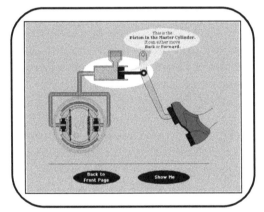

Figure 18.7 *Do people learn better when they receive pretraining in the names and characteristics of the key elements?*

tests than those who received no pretraining ($d = 0.86$). In thirteen of sixteen published experiments, pretrained learners performed better on transfer tests than non–pretrained learners, with a median effect size of $d = 0.75$, which is in the medium range. An important boundary condition is that the pretraining principle may apply to low-knowledge but not high-knowledge learners (Pollock, Chandler, & Sweller, 2002).

The *modality principle* is that people learn better from multimedia presentations when the words are spoken rather than printed (Low & Sweller, 2014; Mayer & Pilegard, 2014). The rationale is that the visual channel may become overloaded by having to process both graphics and printed words, but processing capacity in the visual channel can be freed up when the words are spoken and therefore processed in the verbal channel. For example, Figure 18.8(a) shows a frame from a narrated animation on lightning whereas Figure 18.8(b) shows a frame from the same lesson with words printed on the screen as a caption. Mayer and Moreno (1998) found strong evidence that students performed better on transfer tests when the words were spoken rather than printed for this fast-paced animation that was presented under system control ($d = 1.49$). The modality principle is the most studied of all the multimedia design principles, with positive effects found in fifty-three of sixty-one published experiments, yielding a median effect size of $d = 0.76$, which is in the medium range. Some of the boundary conditions identified in the literature are that the effect can be eliminated when the lesson is self-paced (Tabbers, Martens, & van Merrienboer, 2004) or when the verbal segments are long and complex for learners (Schuler et al., 2012).

The final three principles in Table 18.1 are intended to foster generative processing, that is, cognitive processing aimed at making sense of the presented material. Even if cognitive capacity is available, learners may not be motivated to use it to process the material deeply. Social cues can help motivate learners to engage in deeper processing because people tend to want to understand what a communication partner is telling them. Thus, principles based on social cues are intended to make learners feel as if they are in a conversation with the instructor, that is, they feel that

(a) Animation and Narration

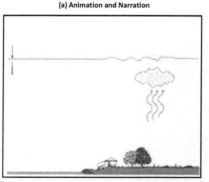

"As the air in this updraft cools, water vapor condenses into water droplets and forms a cloud".

(b) Animation, Narration, and On-Screen Text

As the air in this updraft cools, water vapor condenses into water droplets and forms a cloud.

"As the air in this updraft cools, water vapor condenses into water droplets and forms a cloud".

Figure 18.8 *Which instructional method leads to better learning from an online slideshow?*

Table 18.2 *Portions of nonpersonalized and personalized text from a narrated animation on how the human respiratory system works*

Nonpersonalized Version

"During inhaling, the diaphragm moves down creating more space for the lungs, air enters through the nose or mouth, moves down through the throat and bronchial tubes to tiny air sacs in the lungs ... "

Personalized Version

"During inhaling, your diaphragm moves down creating more space for your lungs, air enters through your nose or mouth, moves down through your throat and bronchial tubes to tiny air sacs in your lungs ... "

the instructor is a social partner. This approach yields the newest of the multimedia design principles, including using conversational language (personalization principle), using an appealing human voice (voice principle), and using humanlike gestures (embodiment principle).

The *personalization principle* is that people learn better from a multimedia lesson when the words are in conversation style rather than formal style (Ginns, Martin, & Marsh, 2013; Mayer, 2014b). For example, Table 18.2 shows a portion of the words from a lesson on how the human respiratory system works presented in third-person form (e.g., "the lungs") or in first- and second-person form (e.g., "your lungs"). Students performed better on a transfer test when the words were in conversational style (i.e., in first- and second-person form), with an effect size of $d = 0.79$ (Mayer et al., 2004). Overall, there were positive effects in fourteen of seventeen published experiments on personalization (including polite vs. direct wording), yielding a median effect size of $d = 0.79$ which is nearly a large effect. Concerning boundary conditions, the personalization principle works best for less knowledgeable learners (McLaren, DeLeeuw, & Mayer, 2011a, 2011b; Wang et al., 2008) and lower achieving learners (Yeung et al., 2009) as well as with shorter lessons (Ginns et al., 2013).

The *voice principle* is that people learn better from multimedia lessons involving spoken words when the narrator has an appealing human voice rather than a machine voice or an unappealing voice (Mayer, 2014b). In five out of six experimental comparisons, people learned better from narrated animations – such as a 2.5 minute animated presentation on lightning formation (Mayer, Sobko, & Mautone, 2003) – when the words were spoken in an appealing human voice rather than in a machine voice or in an unappealing human voice, yielding a median effect size of $d = 0.74$. An important boundary condition is that the positive impact of a human voice can be overturned by the use of negative social cues such as presenting an onscreen agent that does not engage in humanlike gesturing (Mayer & DaPra, 2012).

The *embodiment principle* is that people learn better from multimedia lessons in which an onscreen agent or instructor uses humanlike gesture (Mayer, 2014b). For example, Mayer and DaPra (2012) presented students with a narrated slideshow lesson on how solar cells work in which an onscreen animated pedagogical agent stood next to the slide (as shown in Figure 18.9) and either displayed humanlike gestures or did not move during the lesson. Students learned better when the

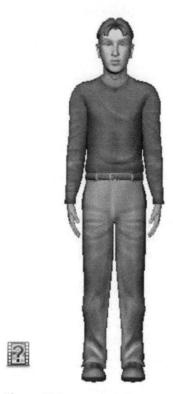

Figure 18.9 *Do people learn better when an onscreen agent uses humanlike gestures or stands still?*

onscreen agent used humanlike gestures ($d = 0.92$). Overall, in thirteen of thirteen published experiments, students performed better on transfer tests when they learned from onscreen agents or instructors that exhibited humanlike gestures, yielding a median effect size of $d = 0.40$. Concerning boundary conditions, the embodiment effect is reduced or eliminated when the lesson contains negative social cues such as a machine voice (Mayer & DaPra, 2012).

What happens when we combine these principles within the context of an actual classroom? Issa and colleagues (2013) compared how beginning medical students learned from a standard slideshow lesson or from a lesson in which the slides were modified based on multimedia design principles such as in Table 18.1. On a transfer test administered four weeks later, students in the modified group outperformed those in the standard group with an effect size of $d = 1.17$, even though the content was the same. This study – and similar ones (Harskamp, Mayer, & Suhre, 2007; Issa et al., 2011) – suggest that applying multimedia principles to the design of classroom instruction can greatly increase student learning.

What happens when we apply multimedia design principles to the design of educational games? In a more recent review, Mayer (2014c) found that students learned more from educational games when they were based on the personalization, pretraining, modality, and redundancy principles. Thus, principles of multimedia design appear to apply in game-based venues as well as in paper-based and computer-based lessons.

In summary, Table 18.1 lists eleven evidence-based principles of multimedia design that are intended to maximize the effectiveness of multimedia instruction. Each has important boundary conditions, largely consistent with the cognitive theory of multimedia learning.

Future Directions for the Multimedia Principle

Some potential future directions for principles of multimedia learning are listed below.

1. Studies examining design principles for multimedia instruction have been forged mainly in short-term laboratory studies, so future research is needed to examine how the principles apply in more authentic educational environments such as with real students in real classrooms and over longer time periods including the use of delayed tests.
2. Studies examining design principles for multimedia instruction have been conducted mainly looking at one feature at a time, so future research is needed to determine what happens when multiple features are used in conjunction with each other.
3. Studies on design principles for multimedia instruction have focused mainly on helping students learn conceptual knowledge (such as explanations of how a scientific system works), so future research is needed to determine whether the principles also apply for other kinds of learning objectives in the revised Bloom's taxonomy including learning facts, procedures, and strategies (Anderson, et al., 2001).
4. As the field progresses, it is useful to develop converging evidence on the boundary conditions for each multimedia design principle. In particular, most of the research supporting this chapter was conducted with low-knowledge learners (or beginners), and there is emerging evidence that the principles may not apply to high-knowledge learners (or experts). Kalyuga (2014) uses the term *expertise reversal effect* to refer to the finding that instructional manipulations that benefit learning for beginners do not work for experts or may even be detrimental to experts. Research is needed to determine if the expertise reversal principle applies to each multimedia design principle.
5. In light of technological advances, it is useful to determine the extent to which multimedia design principles apply to new media such as learning in virtual reality, video games, massive open online courses (MOOCs), and interactive e-books.
6. Finally, as the field progresses, the theories underlying the principles need to be sharpened and expanded to include motivational, metacognitive, affective, and social factors.

What should not change in the future is a focus on rigorous scientific methods grounded in research-based theories of how people learn. Over the past thirty years, educational and cognitive psychology have amassed encouraging evidence that human understanding can be improved substantially when we add appropriate graphics to text. The power of multimedia learning has useful practical implications for the design of instruction and useful theoretical implications for the science of learning. In multimedia learning, pictures do not replace words but rather work together with words to form an instructional message that results in deeper understanding.

References

Adesope, O. O. & Nesbit, J. C. (2012). Verbal redundancy in multimedia learning environments: A meta-analysis. *Journal of Educational Psychology*, *104*, 250–263.

Anderson, L. W., Karthwohl, D. R., & Airasian, P. W. et al. (2001). *A taxonomy for learning, teaching, and assessing: A revision of Bloom's taxonomy of educational objectives*. New York: Longman.

Ayres, P. (2006). Impact of reducing intrinsic cognitive load on learning in a mathematical domain. *Applied Cognitive Psychology*, *20*(3), 287–298.

Ayres, P. & Sweller, J. (2014). The split attention principle in multimedia learning. In R. E. Mayer (ed.), *The Cambridge handbook of multimedia learning*, 2nd edn (pp. 206–226). New York: Cambridge University Press.

Baddeley, A. D. (1992). Working memory. *Science*, *255*, 556–559.

Butcher, K. R. (2014). The multimedia principle. In R. E. Mayer (ed.), *The Cambridge handbook of multimedia learning*, 2nd edn (pp. 174–205). New York: Cambridge University Press.

Clark, R. C. & Mayer, R. E. (2016). *e-Learning and the science of instruction*, 4th edn. Hoboken, NJ: Wiley.

Clark, R. E. (2001). *Learning from media*. Greenwich, CT: Information Age Publishing.

Comenius, J. A. (1887). *Orbis pictus*. Syracuse, NY: Bardeen.

Cuban, L. (1986). *Teachers and machines: The classroom use of technology since 1920*. New York: Teachers College Press.

Gee, J. P. (2003). *What video games have to teach us about learning and literacy*. New York: Palgrave Macmillan.

Ginns, P. (2006). Integrating information: A meta-analysis of spatial contiguity and temporal contiguity effects. *Learning and Instruction*, *16*, 511–525.

Ginns, P., Marin, A. J., & Marsh, H. M. (2013). Designing instructional text for conversational style: A meta-analysis. *Educational Psychology Review*, *25*, 445–472.

Harskamp, E. G., Mayer, R. E., & Suhre, C. (2007). Does the modality principle for multimedia learning apply to science classrooms? *Learning and Instruction*, *17*, 465–477.

Hattie, J. (2009). *Visible learning*. New York: Routledge.

Issa, N., Mayer, R. E., Schuller, S., Wang. E., Shapiro, M. B., & DaRosa, D. A. (2013). Teaching for understanding in medical classrooms using multimedia design principles. *Medical Education*, *47*, 388–396.

Issa, N., Schuller, M., Santacaterina, S., Shapiro, M., Wang, M., Mayer, R. E., & DaRosa, D. A. (2011). Applying multimedia design principles enhances learning in medical education. *Medical Education*, *45*, 818–826.

Jeung, H., Chandler, P., & Sweller, J. (1997). The role of visual indicators in dual sensory mode instruction. *Educational Psychology*, *17*, 329–433.

Johnson, C. & Mayer, R. E. (2012). An eye movement analysis of the spatial contiguity effect in multimedia learning. *Journal of Experimental Psychology: Applied*, *18*, 178–191.

Kalyuga, S. (2014). The expertise reversal principle in multimedia learning. In R. E. Mayer (ed.), *The Cambridge handbook of multimedia learning*, 2nd edn (pp. 576–597). New York: Cambridge University Press.

Kalyuga, S. & Sweller, J. (2014). The redundancy principle in multimedia learning. In R. E. Mayer (ed.), *The Cambridge handbook of multimedia learning*, 2nd edn (pp. 247–262). New York: Cambridge University Press.

Levin, J. R. & Mayer, R. E. (1993). Understanding illustrations in text. In B. K. Britton, A. Woodworth, & M. Binkley (eds.), *Learning from textbooks* (pp. 95–113). Hillsdale, NJ: Lawrence Erlbaum.

Low, R. & Sweller, J. (2014). The modality principle in multimedia learning. In R. E. Mayer (ed.), *The Cambridge handbook of multimedia learning*, 2nd edn (pp. 227–246). New York: Cambridge University Press.

Lusk, D. L., Evans, A. D., Jeffrey, T. R., Palmer, K. R., Wikstrom, C. S., & Doolittle, P. E. (2009). Multimedia learning and individual differences: Mediating the effects of working memory capacity with segmentation. *British Journal of Educational Technology*, *40*(4), 636–651.

Mautone, P. D. & Mayer, R. E. (2001). Signaling as a cognitive guide in multimedia learning. *Journal of Educational Psychology*, *93*, 377–389.

Mayer, R. E. (2008). Multimedia literacy. In D. J. Leu, J. Coiro, M. Knobel, & C. Lankshear (eds.), *Handbook of research on new literacies* (pp. 359–377). Mahwah, NJ: Lawrence Erlbaum.

(2009). *Multimedia learning*, 2nd edn. New York: Cambridge University Press.

(ed.) (2014a). *The Cambridge handbook of multimedia learning*, 2nd edn. New York: Cambridge University Press.

(2014b). Principles based on social cues in multimedia learning: Personalization, voice, image, and embodiment principles. In R. E. Mayer (ed.), *The Cambridge handbook of multimedia learning*, 2nd edn (pp. 345–368). New York: Cambridge University Press.

(2014c). *Computer games for learning: An evidence-based approach*. Cambridge, MA: MIT Press.

Mayer, R. E. & Anderson, R. B. (1991). Animations need narrations: An experimental test of a dual-coding hypothesis. *Journal of Educational Psychology*, *83*, 484–490.

Mayer, R. E. & Chandler, P. (2001). When learning is just a click away: Does simple user interaction foster deeper understanding of multimedia messages? *Journal of Educational Psychology*, *93*, 390–397.

Mayer, R. E. & DaPra, C. S. (2012). An embodiment effect in computer-based learning with animated pedagogical agent. *Journal of Experimental Psychology: Applied*, *18*, 239–252.

Mayer, R. E., Fennell, S., Farmer, L., & Campbell, J. (2004). A personalization effect in multimedia learning: Students learn better when words are in conversational style rather than formal style. *Journal of Educational Psychology*, *96*, 389–395.

Mayer, R. E. & Fiorella, L. (2014). Principles for reducing extraneous processing in multimedia learning: Coherence, signaling, redundancy, spatial contiguity, and temporal contiguity. In R. E. Mayer (ed.), *The Cambridge handbook of multimedia learning*, 2nd edn (pp. 345–368). New York: Cambridge University Press.

Mayer, R. E., Griffith, E., Jurkowitz, I. T. N., & Rothman, D. (2008). Increased interestingness of extraneous details in multimedia science presentation leads to decreased learning. *Journal of Experimental Psychology: Applied*, *14*, 329–339.

Mayer, R. E., Heiser, H., & Lonn, S. (2001). Cognitive constraints on multimedia learning: When presenting more material results in less understanding. *Journal of Educational Psychology*, *93*, 187–198.

Mayer, R. E. & Johnson, C. I. (2008). Revising the redundancy principle in multimedia learning. *Journal of Educational Psychology*, *100*, 380–386.

Mayer, R. E., Mathias, A., & Wetzell, K. (2002). Fostering understanding of multimedia messages through pre-training: Evidence for a two-stage theory of mental model construction. *Journal of Experimental Psychology: Applied*, *8*, 147–154.

Mayer, R. E. & Moreno, R. (1998). A split-attention effect in multimedia learning: Evidence for dual processing systems in working memory. *Journal of Educational Psychology*, *90*, 312–320.

Mayer, R. E., Moreno, R., Boire, M., & Vagge, S. (1999). Maximizing constructivist learning from multimedia communications by minimizing cognitive load. *Journal of Educational Psychology*, *91*, 638–643.

Mayer, R. E. & Pilegard, C. (2014). Principles for managing essential processing in multimedia learning: Segmenting, pretraining, and modality principles. In R. E. Mayer (ed.), *The Cambridge handbook of multimedia learning*, 2nd edn (pp. 379–315). New York: Cambridge University Press.

Mayer, R. E., Sobko, K., & Mautone, P. D. (2003). Social cues in multimedia learning: Role of speaker's voice. *Journal of Educational Psychology*, *95*, 419–425.

Mayer, R. E., Steinhoff, K., Bower, G., & Mars, R. (1995). A generative theory of textbook design: Using annotated illustrations to foster meaningful learning of science text. *Educational Technology Research and Development*, *43*, 31–43.

McGonical, J. (2011). *Reality is broken: Why games make us better and how they can change the world*. New York: Penguin.

McLaren, B. M., DeLeeuw, K. E., & Mayer, R. E. (2011a). Polite web-based intelligent tutors: Can they improve learning in classrooms? *Computers and Education*, *56*, 574–584.

(2011b). A politeness effect in learning with web-based intelligent tutors. *International Journal of Human-Computer Studies*, *69*, 70–79.

Michas, I. C. & Berry, D. (2000). Learning a procedural task: Effectiveness of multimedia presentations. *Applied Cognitive Psychology*, *14*, 555–575.

Moreno, R. & Mayer, R. E. (1999). Cognitive principles of multimedia learning: The role of modality and contiguity. *Journal of Educational Psychology*, *91*, 358–368.

(2002). Verbal redundancy in multimedia learning: When reading helps listening. *Journal of Educational Psychology*, *94*, 156–163.

Naumann, J., Richter, T., Flender, J., Cristmann, U., & Groeben, N. (2007). Signaling in expository hypertexts compensates for deficits in reading skill. *Journal of Educational Psychology*, *99*, 791–807.

Paivio, A, (1986). *Mental representations: A dual-coding approach*. Oxford: Oxford University Press.

Pollock, E., Chandler, P., & Sweller, J. (2002). Assimilating complex information. *Learning and Instruction*, *12*, 61–86.

Prensky, M. (2006). *Don't bother me mom – I'm learning!* St. Paul, MN: Paragon House.

Rey, G. D. (2012). A review and meta-analysis of the seductive detail effect. *Educational Psychology Review*, *7*, 216–237.

Schank, R. C. (2002). *Designing world-class e-learning*. New York: McGraw-Hill.

Schuler, A., Scheiter, K., Rummer, R., & Gerjets, P. (2012). Explaining the modality effect in multimedia learning: Is it due to a lack of temporal contiguity with written text and pictures? *Learning and Instruction*, *22*, 92–102.

Stull, A. & Mayer, R. E. (2007). Learning by doing versus learning by viewing: Three experimental comparisons of learner-generated versus author-provided graphic organizers. *Journal of Educational Psychology*, *99*, 808–820.

Sweller, J., Ayres, P., & Kalyuga, S. (2011). *Cognitive load theory*. New York: Springer.

Tabbers, H. K., Martens, R. L., & van Merrienboer, J. J. G. (2004). Multimedia instructions and cognitive load theory: Effects of modality and cueing. *British Journal of Educational Psychology*, *74*, 71–81.

van Gog, T. (2014). The signaling (or cueing) principle in multimedia learning. In R. E. Mayer (ed.), *The Cambridge handbook of multimedia learning*, 2nd edn (pp. 263–278). New York: Cambridge University Press.

Wang, N., Johnson, W. L., Mayer, R. E., Rizzo, P., Shaw, E., & Collins, H. (2008). The politeness effect: Pedagogical agents and learning outcomes. *International Journal of Human-Computer Studies*, *66*, 98–112.

Wittrock, M. C. (1989). Generative processes of comprehension. *Educational Psychologist*, *24*, 345–376.

Yeung, A., Schmid, S., George, A. V., & King, M. M. (2009). Using the personalization hypothesis to design e-learning environments. In M. Gupta-Bhowon, S. Jhaumer-Laulloo, H. K. L. Wah, & P. Ramasami (eds.), *Chemistry education is the ICT age* (pp. 287–300). Berlin: Springer.

Yue, C. L., Bjork, E. L., & Bjork, R. A. (2013). Reducing verbal redundancy in multimedia learning: An undesired desirable difficulty? *Journal of Educational Psychology*, *105*, 266–277.

19 Multiple-Choice and Short-Answer Quizzing on Equal Footing in the Classroom

Potential Indirect Effects of Testing

Mark A. McDaniel and Jeri L. Little

Laboratory findings show that taking a test on to-be-learned material produces better final test performance on that material than does simply restudying the material, especially when the final test is administered after a delay (for recent reviews, see Roediger & Butler, 2011; Roediger & Karpicke, 2006; for a recent meta-analysis, see Rowland, 2014). This effect – termed the *testing effect* – has become a compelling example of how basic findings in cognitive psychology can be fruitfully applied to education (e.g., Belluck, 2011; Carey, 2010). One reason that the testing effect has received so much attention is that the benefits of testing can be directly and easily implemented in the classroom. That is, rather than used simply as summative assessments, quizzes (or tests) can be used to promote learning and retention, and students can be advised to use self-testing methods, such as flashcards (Kornell & Bjork, 2008) and recitation (McDaniel, Howard, & Einstein, 2009), to study rather than reread their textbooks and notes. Further, it is straightforward for instructors and students to apply testing as a learning method to a wide range of subjects; indeed, it is difficult to imagine a substantive high school or college course for which using testing as a learning tool is not possible.

Additionally, current technology makes it easy to quiz students during lectures (e.g., with clickers), which promotes learning in addition to increasing engagement (e.g., Buhay, Best, & McGuire, 2010; Lantz & Stawiski, 2014; Mayer et al., 2009; Smith et al., 2009). As well, research demonstrating the applied value of the testing effect is now relatively extensive, having been conducted in authentic educational settings in middle school (e.g., McDaniel et al., 2011), high school (e.g., Agarwal et al., 2014; McDermott et al., 2014), college (e.g., Glass, Brill, & Ingate, 2008; Lyle & Crawford, 2011; Trumbo et al., 2016), and medical school (e.g., Larsen, Butler, & Roediger, 2008). (For an early review of the testing effect in the classroom, see Bangert-Drowns, Kulik, & Kulik, 1991; and for a recent review, see Fiorella & Mayer, 2015.)

Yet closer examination reveals that there is an intriguing dissociation between the standard laboratory findings and theory of the testing effect on the one hand and recent results from classroom experiments on the other hand. We first highlight this dissociation, which centers on the issue of how the format of the test influences subsequent test performance, offer possible explanations for the dissociation, and then discuss an explanation based on indirect effects of testing that likely play a role

480

in testing effects observed in educational contexts. For purposes of clarity and consistency, we will use the term "quiz" to refer to an initial test and "exam" to refer to a subsequent final test, even when describing laboratory results.

Recall Versus Recognition

Taking a test requires the learner to retrieve information from memory. The cognitive processes exerted to achieve retrieval are viewed as promoting retention. Various theoretical viewpoints emphasize that the more activated or engaged these processes are, the better retention of the tested information will be as indicated by a final test (e.g., the retrieval difficulty hypothesis, Bjork & Bjork, 1992; the bifurcation framework, Halamish & Bjork, 2011; Kornell, Bjork, & Garcia, 2011; the encoding elaboration or variability view of retrieval, Carpenter, 2009; McDaniel & Masson, 1985; Pyc & Rawson, 2010; and distinctive processing of tested information, Kuo & Hirshman, 1997; Peterson & Mulligan, 2013). Generally, theories of memory assume that recall requires more extensive retrieval processes than does recognition (e.g., SAM, Raaijmakers & Shiffrin, 1981; two-process generation-recognition models, Kintsch, 1978; Jacoby & Hollingshead, 1990; Guynn et al., 2014). Accordingly, the notion is that an initial quiz that requires recall will generally produce better subsequent test performance than will an initial quiz that is based on recognition.

Results from laboratory studies are in accord with this expectation: Initial quizzes requiring free-recall or cued-recall have been shown to produce better exam performance than initial recognition quizzes (e.g., yes/no recognition or forced alternative recognition tests; see Butler & Roediger, 2007; Glover, 1989; Kintsch, 1978). As shown in Figure 19.1, this pattern tends to hold even when the final test is a recognition test, a test that aligns with an initial recognition test but not an initial recall test (Glover, 1989). Multiple-choice tests are often argued to rely on recognition rather than recall (e.g., Newble, Baxter, & Elmslie, 1979), and, in line with this presumption, laboratory research has generally shown initial quizzes with short-answer questions to be more effective for learning than those with multiple-choice questions (e.g., Anderson & Biddle, 1975; Hamaker, 1986; Kang, McDermott, & Roediger, 2007; Rowland, 2014; for an exception, see Little et al., 2012).

Note that if initial recognition tests produce substantially higher correct responding than initial recall tests and feedback is not provided, then final test performance can be higher after a recognition (e.g., multiple-choice) test (Kang et al., 2007, Experiment 1; Little et al., 2012; McDaniel & Masson, 1985). However, it remains the case that the "strengthening" effect of successful recall is more potent than that of successful recognition. This strengthening effect is best revealed by going beyond conditionalizing final test performance on initial correct quiz performance; conditionalization can artifactually favor recall relative to recognition because of potential item-selection artifacts (e.g., successful recall may disproportionately favor easier items relative to successful recognition). Figure 19.2 shows that "S" (strengthening) scores, which adjust for item selection artifacts, confirm that recall of an item produces a higher likelihood of later retention than does recognition of the item

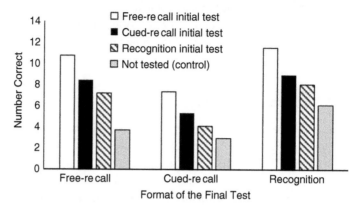

Figure 19.1 *Correct performance on a final free-recall test (Experiment 4a), a final cued-recall test (Experiment 4b), and a final recognition test (Experiment 4c) as a function of initial test type (from Glover, 1989. Adapted with permission from the American Psychological Association)*

The final free-recall test assessed idea units recalled (24 possible); the cued-recall and recognition tests also had 24 items possible.

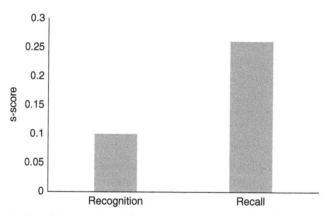

Figure 19.2 *Enhancement of subsequent retrieval (recall) following initial recall vs. initial recognition of an item*

The values are s-scores, a final memory score that factors out possible item-selection components that can differ when final performance is conditionalized on initial recall vs. recognition (results from McDaniel & Masson, 1985; SDs not reported).

(McDaniel & Masson, 1985). This pattern supports the theoretical assumption that more extensive (effortful) retrieval required by recall is more beneficial than the less extensive retrieval required for recognition. The upshot is that the results from the laboratory strongly suggest that to gain the most benefit from quizzing in classroom practice (in which feedback would almost always be provided), quizzes that require production (recall) are preferred over quizzes in which the answer must be recognized but not produced (multiple-choice questions, for example). Indeed, this has been the received conclusion from the laboratory literature: "the benefits of testing are greater when the initial test is a recall (production) test rather than a recognition test" (McDaniel, Roediger, & McDermott, 2007, p. 200).

Classroom Testing Effects

Several classroom experiments have implemented quizzing conditions that directly evaluate the above suggestion. In a web-based college course, McDaniel, Wildman, and Anderson (2012) investigated the effects of either multiple-choice or short-answer quiz questions on performance on course exams. Both the multiple-choice and short-answer questions used the same question stem (but different students saw either the multiple-choice or short-answer version of the question). For instance, the question stem, "Tissue covering the brain and spinal cord can become infected, a condition known as _____" could appear either in multiple-choice or short-answer format. For multiple-choice, the stem was followed by four possible alternatives (i.e., *encephalitis, caudal, efferent, meningitis*, for the example above); for short-answer, the student had to generate (recall) the answer. Correct answer feedback was given following each quiz. As shown in Figure 19.3, both types of quiz questions produced better performance on exams (all multiple-choice) relative to a no-quiz condition and relative to a condition in which students restudied the target fact or concept. Importantly for present purposes, the magnitude of the testing effect was surprisingly as large for multiple-choice quiz questions as for short-answer (recall) quiz questions.

This finding was unanticipated given the laboratory testing-effect findings (e.g., Glover, 1989; Kang et al., 2007), some classroom research (e.g., McDaniel et al., 2007), and the theoretical accounts of the laboratory testing effects. Perhaps this

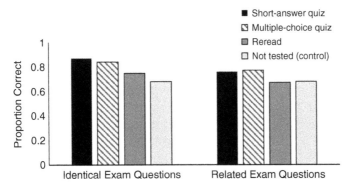

Figure 19.3 *Exam performance for identical and related questions as a function of initial quiz format (from Experiment 1 of McDaniel et al., 2012. Adapted with permission)*

pattern was obtained because the multiple-choice format of the exams aligned with multiple-choice quizzes, providing some advantage to the multiple-choice quiz questions. Yet there was a critical aspect of the McDaniel and colleagues' (2012) quizzing paradigm not typically found in the laboratory paradigms (and even some classroom paradigms). In laboratory paradigms, the quiz is typically presented once prior to the final test, whereas, in the McDaniel and colleagues' study students were strongly encouraged (through points given for quiz completion) to take the quizzes four times prior to an exam. Students generally did so, as the average number of times students took the quizzes in Experiment 1 was 3.87 for short-answer questions and 3.22 for multiple-choice questions (students read the statements an average of 3.38 times). And by the fourth quiz, performance on both the multiple-choice and short-answer items was nearly identical and quite high (97 and 96 percent for short-answer and multiple-choice conditions, respectively).

Accordingly, another tentative interpretation is that in taking four repeated quizzes, students were able to overlearn the content, thereby offsetting the presumed mnemonic benefits of initial short-answer relative to initial multiple-choice quizzing (although it is interesting that repeated exposure to statements did not result in such overlearning; McDaniel et al., 2012). In line with this interpretation, in a classroom study (i.e., web-based Brain and Behavior course) in which short-answer quiz questions were shown to be better for learning than were multiple-choice questions, questions were only answered for practice once (McDaniel et al., 2007).

Both of these just-mentioned interpretations were informed by subsequent classroom experiments with middle school and high school students (McDermott et al., 2014). In these experiments, the quizzes were taken either two or three times and the exams consisted of both multiple-choice and short-answer questions. As shown in Figure 19.4, both multiple-choice and short-answer quiz questions produced significantly higher performance on the exams than did a restudy condition and a no-quiz control; and the magnitude of this testing effect generally did not significantly differ as a function of quiz question format (multiple-choice, short-answer). The critical new finding was that the statistically equivalent testing effect across the multiple-choice and short-answer quiz formats was observed for both multiple-choice exam items (see the right side of the upper and lower panels of Figure 19.4 for middle school and high school students, respectively) and for short-answer exam items (left side of upper and lower panels of Figure 19.4). (In Experiment 3, with middle school students, the short-answer quiz items advantaged short-answer exam items significantly more than did multiple-choice quiz items; 81 percent vs. 78 percent for each quiz format, respectively.) In an additional instance, the multiple-choice quiz format produced better exam performance on short-answer items than did the short-answer quiz format (Experiment 1a), and this held for end-of-semester final exams.

Practical Implications. These initial findings indicate that, in a classroom context, multiple-choice quizzes are associated with testing effects that are of similar magnitude, and sometimes of greater magnitude, than the testing effects associated with short-answer quizzes. Further, this pattern holds regardless of whether summative

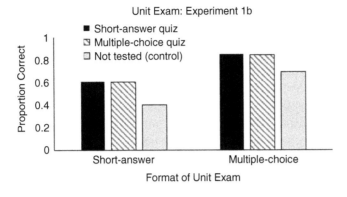

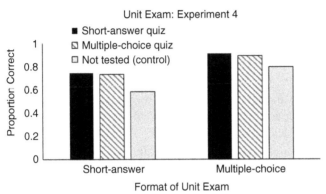

Figure 19.4 *Exam performances from Experiments 1b and 4 of McDermott et al. (2014) as a function of quiz format and exam format (adapted with permission from the American Psychological Association)*

Experiment 1b was conducted in a middle school science class, and Experiment 4 was conducted in a high school history class. Both multiple-choice and short-answer quizzes enhance later exam performance in middle and high school classes.

exams are multiple-choice or short-answer. Before considering how this pattern might be reconciled with laboratory testing effects, let's first consider the practical implications.

In McDermott and colleagues (2014), students spent more time answering the short-answer quizzes than they did answering the multiple-choice quizzes. Indeed, the short-answer quizzes took teachers 2.5 times as long to administer as did the multiple-choice quizzes. Short-answer quizzing is not as efficient as multiple-choice quizzing. Accordingly, classroom time spent on quizzing would be minimized and classroom efficiency maximized by administering multiple-choice quizzes instead of short-answer quizzes, *without sacrificing the benefits to learning*. A second advantage is that multiple-choice quizzes require less of the teacher's time for grading. In fact, grading can be easily automated for multiple-choice quizzes.

Additionally, the finding that multiple-choice questions can serve in such a useful way in the classroom is especially exciting given the increasing inclusion of audience-response systems (e.g., "clickers," handheld devices that allow students to respond to questions) in the classroom, particularly in large university lecture halls where instructor–student interaction is often limited (e.g., Buhay et al., 2010; Lantz & Stawiski, 2014; Mayer et al., 2009; Smith et al., 2009). One advantage of clickers is that they provide instructors and their students with real-time feedback about student learning. Although there are software alternatives to the traditional clicker that allow for short-answer responses, most audience-response system technology tends to rely on students providing a predetermined choice among a set of alternatives; that is, clickers are ideal for multiple-choice quizzing and, indeed, clickers have been shown to be fruitful for learning. For example, Mayer and colleagues (2009) showed that students scored higher on course exams (i.e., in an education psychology class) when they used clickers during lecture (i.e., 2–4 questions per lecture) than when they did not.

Furthermore, Smith and colleagues (2009) found that answering clicker questions in the classroom can serve as a springboard for fruitful peer discussion that increases learning. In a physics course, students answered a question, then engaged in discussion with peers before answering the same question and then a new conceptually related (isomorphic) question. Their results suggested that answering multiple-choice questions followed by peer discussion led to robust gains in learning. For example, in the physics course, when asked for the first time, only 52 percent of questions were answered correctly; however, of the 48 percent of questions answered incorrectly initially, 42 percent were then answered correctly the second time around. Although a commonsense explanation is that less knowledgeable students simply used the answers from their more knowledgeable peers, this did not seem to explain the effect because following incorrect and then correct responding to the initial question, 77 percent of isomorphic questions were answered correctly without any consultation between students.

Reconciling the Apparent Paradox of Laboratory and Classroom Testing Effects

We suggest that the disparate findings described in the previous sections across the laboratory and the classroom reflect a major difference between how the testing effect is investigated in the laboratory and the classroom. In the laboratory, participants study the material (usually presented in written form), take the quiz, and then are given the final test. There is typically no opportunity for restudy of the material before or after the quiz. By sharp contrast, in a classroom study, students are not restricted from engaging in additional study of target material after completing reading assignments and attending class lectures. For instance, in McDaniel and colleagues (2012) and McDermott and colleagues (2014), students could elect to study before taking the quizzes (e.g., a review quiz) and in between taking the quizzes and the exams.

In short, whereas the laboratory studies are designed to investigate and isolate the direct effects of retrieval practice on subsequent test performance, the classroom studies open the door for potential "indirect" effects of quizzing (Roediger, Putnam, & Smith, 2011). In fact, the absence of an advantage of short-answer quizzes over multiple-choice quizzes in the classroom experiments may signal that the effects of quizzing in the classroom are likely a consequence of various indirect factors in addition to potential direct benefits of quizzing. The reasoning is that direct effects of quizzing are usually reflected by more robust effects of quizzing involving relatively more retrieval (short-answer quizzes) relative to quizzing involving less retrieval and more recognition (multiple-choice tests). This is a critical point to appreciate: Classroom experiments that demonstrate the testing effect cannot be definitively interpreted in terms of the direct effects of retrieval practice.

In the remainder of this chapter, we consider several indirect effects of quizzing that are likely candidates for mediating the benefits of quizzing on learning when quizzing is used to stimulate learning in classroom contexts. We then close the chapter by revisiting the effects of multiple-choice quizzing. This penultimate section reveals that strategically designed multiple-choice quizzes may advantage learning in ways that recall (short-answer) quizzes do not.

Indirect Effects of Testing: A Potent Effect

The potency of the testing effect in some classroom studies may be attributed, at least in part, to indirect benefits that frequent testing provides. That is, in addition to the benefits that retrieval directly provides for learning, frequent quizzing may provide additional benefits indirectly. In this section, we discuss how quizzing induces students to study more, reduces their anxiety about test-taking, and provides students with increased metacognitive awareness of what they know and do not know, which in turn helps them to allocate their future study effectively. Table 19.1 shows five indirect benefits that we discuss in the present chapter, as well as four additional benefits discussed by Roediger and colleagues (2011).

Frequent testing leads to frequent studying. One of the most obvious indirect effects of frequent quizzing is that students may study more frequently. Many students procrastinate in their studies, but quizzes provide students with a concrete incentive to study. For example, Mawhinney and colleagues (1971) showed that students tended to study most frequently right before tests, with more studying occurring with more frequent testing. Following from that work, in two different courses (Learning and Memory, Introductory Psychology), Leeming (2002) showed that having a short exam (quiz) at the start of every class led to improved grades as compared with previous classes in which fewer exams had been given. Although students self-reported that they were initially skeptical of the procedure of frequent quizzing, they agreed that such quizzing led them to study more than they did for other classes (70 percent in Learning and Memory; 65 percent in Introductory Psychology). Additionally, the majority of students reported that they kept up with course content better than they did in other courses (91 percent in Learning and Memory; 85 percent in Introductory Psychology) and that they learned more than

Table 19.1 *Indirect benefits of testing*

Benefit 1	Testing encourages frequent study
Benefit 2	Testing reduces anxiety*
Benefit 3	Testing improves metacognitive monitoring
Benefit 4	Testing improves subsequent studying
Benefit 5	Testing facilitates the retrieval of information that was not tested
Additional indirect benefits enumerated by Roediger et al. (2011)	
Benefit 6	Testing prevents interference from prior material when learning new material
Benefit 7	Testing produces better organization of knowledge
Benefit 8	Testing improves transfer of knowledge to new contexts
Benefit 9	Testing provides feedback to instructors

Note. Indirect benefits 6–9 were addressed by Roediger, Putnam, and Smith (2011). * = not mentioned by Roediger et al.

they would have with fewer exams (79 percent in Learning and Memory; 85 percent in Introductory Psychology). Lyle and Crawford (2011) provided additional evidence for this finding by comparing two introductory statistics courses that were taught during the same semester. In one section, students were given a low-stakes quiz at the end of every lecture; in the other, students were only given the main exams. In addition to performing better on the final exam, the quiz-a-day section reported positive feelings about the frequent quizzing.

Frequent quizzing lowers test anxiety. Some in the popular media have objected to the recommendations that educators should increase testing (i.e., give a steady dose of low- or no-stakes quizzes) on the grounds that students are already too "stressed out" with the increased demands of standardized testing (and the usual classroom examinations). The premise is that implementing quizzing as a standard classroom practice will increase test-anxiety, an unwelcome outcome based on the assumption that students already suffer from excessive test anxiety (as parodied in a cartoon in which a distraught child awakens her parents, saying "I dreamed I was being chased by a giant standardized test"). Agarwal and colleagues (2014) investigated this premise in a public middle school and high school in which the students had participated in year-long quizzing programs as part of a large-scale classroom study. Quizzing was implemented in the classrooms with clickers and was frequent, occurring at least once a week. The study spanned a variety of content areas, including English, history, mathematics, science, and Spanish.

More than 1,300 middle school students and 100 high school students who had participated in the quizzing study were given a survey at the end of the academic year to assess their reactions to the extensive quizzing. Of interest for present purposes are the responses to the question: "Did clicker quizzes make you more or less nervous for unit tests?" In answering the question, students were told to consider their experience in the particular class in which they were given quizzes relative to their classes in which the quizzing program was not implemented. Overall, a clear majority of students (72 percent) indicated that frequent quizzing made them less nervous about their unit tests. Only 6 percent responded that the quizzing made them more nervous. This general pattern held for middle and high school and across the different types of courses. Thus, the only published study investigating the relation between frequent no- or low-stakes quizzing (quiz scores had little or no impact on course grade) and anxiety suggests that no- or low-stakes quizzing attenuates anxiety about course exams.

Quizzing improves metacognitive accuracy. Another indirect benefit of quizzing in the classroom (or at home) is that quizzing helps students assess their knowledge. In fact, students tend to use flashcards or practice tests for this benefit, being unaware of the direct benefits of quizzing (Hartwig & Dunlosky, 2012; Kornell & Bjork, 2007); and teachers often give frequent quizzes so that they can accurately assess their students' knowledge, not necessarily for the direct benefits of quizzing.

How do we know whether testing leads to more accurate metacognitive assessment on the part of learners? Assessment of one's learning has often been examined in the laboratory by having participants study word pairs and then make judgments about their likelihood of future recall (e.g., Dunlosky & Nelson, 1991; Karpicke, 2009; King, Sechmeister, & Shaughnessy, 1980; Koriat & Bjork, 2006; Kornell & Rhodes, 2013; Kornell & Son, 2009; Lovelace, 1984; Soderstrom & Bjork, 2014; Tullis, Finley, & Benjamin, 2013). Confidence ratings and judgments of learning (JOLs) are common measures for assessing metacognitive monitoring. For example, participants may rate the likelihood (on a scale) that they will be able to recall the target when later given the cue. When comparing JOLs following testing to those following restudy, laboratory research has shown that JOLs are more accurate following testing, as evidenced by their higher correlation with actual performance in the former rather than latter case (e.g., Kornell & Son, 2009; Little & McDaniel, 2015). Participants often inaccurately predict that they will remember more following a restudy session than following a testing session.

The accuracy of metacognitive monitoring is important because it is commonsensical that monitoring judgments would influence restudy allocation. Several ideas about how learners allocate their restudy time have been put forward, but two prominent views are the discrepancy-reduction view (e.g., Dunlosky & Hertzog, 1998; Dunlosky & Thiede, 1998) and the region of proximal learning view (e.g., Metcalfe & Kornell, 2005). The discrepancy-reduction view suggests that learners will allocate the most time to information that is least well learned – that is, presumably information given the lowest JOLs in a procedure assessing metacognitive monitoring. The region of proximal learning view suggests that individuals will allocate the most time to difficult but learnable items, perhaps giving up on the items given the lowest JOLs in favor of those given moderately low JOLs. A discrepancy-reduction allocation strategy has been suggested in some studies focusing on text materials, in that negative correlations between JOLs and study time are reported (Thomas & McDaniel, 2007; the strategy may be especially evident for more skilled readers, Martin, Nguyen, & McDaniel, 2016).

The critical issue turns now to the extent to which the effectiveness of the discrepancy-reduction restudy strategy depends on accurate metacognitive monitoring. As noted above, common sense tells us that if monitoring is relatively inaccurate (which is not uncommon for educationally authentic materials; e.g., Glenberg & Epstein, 1985; Maki et al., 1990), then students' sensible reliance on a discrepancy-reduction strategy should be unfruitful. Thomas and McDaniel (2007) directly informed this issue in a laboratory experiment that implemented encoding activities that either attenuated or augmented monitoring accuracy. An encoding task that focused learners on details (reinserting missing letters in the text) enhanced monitoring accuracy for a detail-oriented test (gamma correlation between predicted and actual performance = 0.62) but undermined monitoring accuracy for a conceptual-oriented test (correlation = −0.13); and an encoding task that focused learners on relationships among concepts (reordering randomly ordered sentences) enhanced monitoring accuracy for the conceptual test (correlation = 0.55) but undermined monitoring for the detail test (correlation = 0.06). Nevertheless, regardless of monitoring accuracy (and encoding condition), learners' restudy policies followed a discrepancy-reduction pattern: When allowed to restudy the texts, study time increased for content that learners judged to be not well learned (i.e., a negative correlation).

Did the discrepancy-reduction strategy produce effective restudying? It depended on the monitoring accuracy supported by the particular learning condition. For the conditions in which monitoring accuracy hovered around 0, restudy did not improve learning (as assessed by a cued-recall test) relative to participants who were not given a restudy opportunity (restudy = 0.31; no restudy = 0.36). A dramatically different pattern emerged for the conditions in which monitoring accuracy was high: Restudy ($M = 0.84$) produced a notable improvement over no restudy ($M = 0.62$). Accordingly, we would strongly expect that if testing improved monitoring accuracy in classroom learning, then students' study effectiveness would improve.

Relatively little work has examined the influence of quizzing on metacognitive monitoring and subsequent restudy time allocation with materials like those used in the classroom. An exception is a laboratory experiment that examined metacognitive monitoring and restudy time allocation following the reading of text passages (Little & McDaniel, 2015; Experiment 2). In this experiment, participants were provided with passages about the geography, climate, and people of six different regions of the world. Participants thus read eighteen sections of information with eight sentences (or facts) each. After their initial reading of these materials, participants either reread the information or took a quiz for which they were supposed to recall as much information as possible. Following the quiz or rereading, participants provided estimates of how many facts (out of eight possible) they thought that they would be able to recall for each of the eighteen sections on a final test two days later. After making these estimates, they were given the chance to restudy information from half of the geographic regions, and the time spent on each sentence was recorded. Forty-eight hours later, they took a final test for which they had to recall as much as they could remember about each of the regions. This procedure allowed the researchers to examine metacognitive monitoring, how individuals controlled their restudy, and the consequent performance following restudy as compared with not.

Several interesting results emerged. First, consistent with what we have discussed thus far, recalling information (quizzing) was better for learning than was rereading, both for the information that students had a chance to restudy and for information that they did not. Secondly, as can be seen in Figure 19.5, participants' estimations about their future recall were more accurate (as evidence by higher gamma correlations) following testing than following rereading; and those estimations predicted, to some extent, how they allocated future study (see region of proximal learning, Metcalfe & Kornell, 2005). Finally, the benefit of testing compared to rereading was larger following restudy than not following restudy, with one possible reason being that allocation of restudy time following testing was more effectively deployed than that following rereading, owing to the more accurate metacognitive monitoring. We focus on this potential restudy-allocation (indirect) effect of quizzing next.

Quizzing and metacognitive control. In classroom studies of the testing effect, researchers have not assessed students' restudy behaviors (in terms of what is studied) after administration of quizzes. Indeed, this would be a Herculean challenge. Consequently, McDaniel and colleagues (2015, Experiment 2) attempted to closely approximate key features of classroom learning in a laboratory experiment that investigated how quizzing influences restudy activity. In an initial session, college participants studied a thirty-eight-page packet on experimental methods in psychology that was excerpted from a standard textbook. Two days later, one group of participants took a multiple-choice quiz on key concepts from the text (e.g., "reliability," "validity," "independent variable"). As in a classroom, participants were given feedback on what items they answered correctly and what items they missed (but the correct answers were not provided). With this feedback in hand, the participants were then allowed to restudy the material for 15 minutes. These participants were instructed to highlight what they were restudying so that the

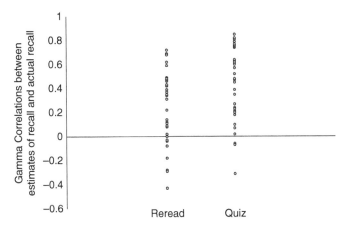

Figure 19.5 *Gamma correlations representing, for each participant in the reread and quiz conditions, respectively, the relationship between estimates of fact recall and actual recall for each section (after Little & McDaniel, 2015. Adapted with permission)*

experimenters could identify what was studied followed the quiz. Another group of participants was not given a quiz but instead was given time to again study the material (comparable to the time the quiz group was taking the quiz). Then this "study-only" group was instructed to restudy the material and highlight what they were restudying (paralleling the restudy instructions for the quiz group). Five days later, participants returned to the lab and were given a short-answer test on the research methods concepts.

Of interest were the particular concepts highlighted by the quiz group versus the study-only group. Two categories of concepts were identified: concepts that had been quizzed (and were subsequently tested on the short-answer test) and untested concepts. In general, the study-only group highlighted more concepts than did the quiz group. Interestingly, both groups highlighted more quizzed than unquizzed concepts, suggesting that the quizzed concepts were identified by learners in both groups as the main concepts. However, the proportion of tested concepts highlighted (relative to the total number of concepts highlighted by a participant) was significantly higher in the quiz than the study-only group. Quizzing thus promoted somewhat more focus in restudy than did study alone.

A critical question is whether the participants in the quiz group focused their restudy on concepts related to quiz items not correctly answered – i.e., a discrepancy-reduction restudy policy. The results were decisive on this point: Incorrect concepts were highlighted 78 percent of the time, whereas concepts related to correctly answered quiz items were highlighted less than 45 percent of the time. This pattern directly supports the premise that testing – in this case multiple-choice quizzing – elicits restudy focused on content that the learner has not learned well.

Importantly, this indirect effect of multiple-choice quizzing translated into better final test performance. The quiz group performed significantly better than the study-alone group for short-answer questions targeting definitions and applications. In addition, the quiz group performed significantly better on the final test than a third group that received several quizzes (with feedback) but was not allowed to restudy. Thus, restudy following quizzing was more beneficial for learning than repeated quizzing alone (direct effects of testing). These patterns align with the hypothesis proposed at the outset. Classroom testing effects may well reflect both direct and indirect effects of testing, with indirect effects of testing likely stimulated by multiple-choice tests (as well as by short-answer tests).

When Multiple-Choice Quizzes Might Be Better Than Short-Answer Quizzes

Throughout this chapter, we have discussed the nature of quiz format, focusing especially on multiple-choice versus short-answer formats because of their common use in educational contexts. In this final section, we highlight the idea that the type of processing that a quiz question induces or requires is more important than the format of a quiz question itself. The implication is that the general assumption that cued-recall or short-answer quizzes induce retrieval, whereas multiple-choice quizzes induce recognition, is incomplete. To the extent that a short-answer question requires deeper processing than a multiple-choice question, we should expect that such questions (without regard to the indirect benefits that they might engender) should lead to better retention of that information. However, multiple-choice questions need not rely on recognition or otherwise shallow processing. Such questions can be constructed to necessitate deep processing of the question and its answer – as well as consideration of related information. As any student knows, questions that have multiple answers that seem plausible require a lot of thought to choose the correct answer: Students often consider why certain choices are incorrect in order to reject them and choose the correct answer (Little, Frickey, & Fung, 2018).

Consistent with this theme, recent laboratory experiments showed that multiple-choice questions with competitive (plausible) alternatives were not worse than short-answer questions for the later retention of tested information (Little et al., 2012; this effect persisted even at 48 hours; Little & Bjork, 2012). Importantly, multiple-choice questions (relative to short-answer questions) improved participants' ability to retain related but not initially tested information pertaining to the incorrect alternatives. For example, if a participant read a passage about Yellowstone National Park and were then asked which geyser is the *oldest* geyser in the park (Answer: Castle Geyser), they were better able to recall on a later cued-recall test that Steamboat Geyser is the *largest* geyser in Yellowstone, provided that Steamboat Geyser had been an incorrect alternative for a multiple-choice question on an earlier quiz. A simple explanation regarding why this benefit might occur is that instead of leading participants to deeply process the question and alternatives, exposure to Steamboat Geyser as a choice in the initial test simply made it easier for participants to recall it as the answer. However, inconsistent with this simple explanation, alternatives had to be plausible answers for a given question in order for such benefits in performance to arise (Little & Bjork, 2015).

These laboratory findings were then put to the "test" in a college research methods course (Bjork, Little, & Storm, 2014). Both previously tested and related information was retained better (higher exam performance) following initial multiple-choice quizzing, compared with information for which no related information had been previously quizzed.

So are multiple-choice tests better than short-answer tests for the retention of related information? Although several findings suggest that cued-recall testing often fails to improve recall of related information or even impairs it (Carroll et al., 2007; Chan, 2009; Little, Storm, & Bjork, 2011), in a notable exception, Chan, McDermott, and Roediger (2006) showed that following the reading of a passage about toucans, participants who answered cued-recall questions were more likely to correctly recall the answers to related questions on a final test 24 hours later than were participants who read comparable statements or who did not do anything after reading. Chan and colleagues, like Little and colleagues (2012), argued that the questions asked on the initial quiz sometimes led to the spontaneous recall of related information that would be tested later; and such spontaneous recall of this related information during the initial quiz is what supported enhanced retention later. That is, it is not the format that is critical – it is how much and what the quiz questions make the student think about that is important.

A related issue regarding quizzing in the classroom is what effect quizzing might have when students are unlikely to answer correctly on that quiz. This question is relevant to the present chapter because sometimes instructors give pretests or use clicker questions in the classroom to assess students' knowledge before instruction (Glass et al., 2008). Multiple-choice quizzes may serve as valuable learning tools even if they are provided prior to the study event (Little & Bjork, 2011; 2016). For example, Little and Bjork (2016) showed that multiple-choice quizzes helped learners retain information pertaining to the question directly quizzed as well as to information pertaining to the incorrect alternatives, improving performance for that related information as compared to cued-recall quizzes additionally, the benefit persisted over a 48-hour interval. Although the majority of this work on the benefits of multiple-choice pretesting has been completed in the laboratory, Bjork, Soderstrom, and Little (2015) report an unpublished study completed by Bjork and Soderstrom in which students in a research methods course were given multiple-choice pretests prior to instruction in some lectures (no pretests were given in other lectures). Questions were displayed on a large screen prior to lecture and no feedback was given. Performance on the final exam showed improved performance for the pretested questions compared with control questions from lectures not preceded by questions. Additionally, performance for initial non–pretested related questions were better than performance for control questions. It should be noted that, at present, the effect of pretesting on learning in the classroom is less well documented than is the benefit of posttesting in the classroom, and at least one published study failed to find a benefit in a middle school classroom (McDaniel et al., 2007)

In short, although laboratory research has often implemented multiple-choice quizzes that rely on recognition, with these quizzes producing worse later retention than recall-based quizzes it is not necessarily the case that multiple-choice quizzes need only rely on recognition. When multiple-choice questions are constructed with plausible alternatives, they can lead to deep processing. In classroom settings, such multiple-choice questions could be constructed (and maybe already are), and accordingly, in classroom applications of the testing effect, it is likely that multiple-choice quizzing would produce benefits comparable with or superior to that of short-answer quizzes.

Conclusions

We began this chapter by emphasizing that laboratory experiments generally converge on the conclusion that the testing effect is more robust following initial recall than initial recognition quizzes. Moreover, this pattern aligns well with theoretical ideas that recall is a more demanding and deeper retrieval process than is recognition. In light of this empirical and theoretical literature, extension of the testing effect to classroom applications has assumed that quizzes requiring recall (short-answer quizzes) will be more beneficial to outcomes on summative exams than quizzes requiring recognition (multiple-choice quizzes). Indeed, this assumption is found in practical manuals for teachers on how to use testing to enhance learning (e.g., Agarwal et al., 2013). Thus, one of the most puzzling findings of the initial research examining the testing effect in the classroom is that the benefit of testing is as robust with multiple-choice quizzes as it is with short-answer quizzes. A major theme in this chapter is that rather than view this finding from classroom experiments as anomalous, we suggest that the finding signals the presence of potent indirect effects of quizzing that have been relatively unexplored in the literature.

We identified five indirect benefits of testing that, based on available research, likely augment the direct effects of testing in authentic educational settings. With frequent quizzing, students may study more regularly. Frequent quizzing might lower test anxiety, thereby improving students' performances on summative tests. Quizzing can improve the accuracy of students' self-assessments of what they know and do not know (metacognitive monitoring); as a consequence, students' study policies can be more effectively implemented. Quizzing, for example with strategically constructed multiple-choice quizzes, can stimulate consideration of information not directly tested and thereby improve learning of that nontested material. There may be other indirect effects (see Table 19.1), and these also merit investigation. In light of the findings that multiple-choice and short-answer quizzes have led to similar improvements on classroom exams, we suggest that indirect effects of testing in the classroom, effects that theoretically could be stimulated by both multiple-choice and short-answer quizzes, are likely as important as the direct effects of testing that have been isolated and emphasized in laboratory experiments.

References

Agarwal, P. K., D'Antonio, L., Roediger, H. L., McDermott, K. B., & McDaniel, M. A. (2014). Classroom-based programs of retrieval practice reduce middle school and high school students' test anxiety. *Journal of Applied Research in Memory and Cognition*, *3*, 131–139.

Agarwal, P. K., Roediger, H. L., McDaniel, M. A., & McDermott, K. B. (2013). *How to use retrieval practice to improve learning*. Washington: University in St. Louis.

Anderson, R. C. & Biddle, W. B. (1975). On asking people questions about what they are reading. In G. H. Bower (ed.), *The psychology of learning and motivation*, Vol. 9 (pp. 89–132). New York: Academic Press.

Bangert-Drowns, R. L., Kulik, J. A., & Kulik, C. L. C. (1991). Effects of frequent classroom testing. *The Journal of Educational Research*, *85*(2), 89–99.

Belluck, P. (2011). To really learn, quit studying and take a test. *New York Times*. January 20, 2011.

Bjork, R. A. & Bjork, E. L. (1992). A new theory of disuse and an old theory of stimulus fluctuation. In A. Healy, S. Kosslyn, & R. Shiffrin (eds.), *From learning processes to cognitive processes: Essays in honor of William K. Estes*, Vol. 2 (pp. 35–67). Hillsdale, NJ: Lawrence Erlbaum.

Bjork, E. L., Little, J. L., & Storm, B. C. (2014). Multiple-choice testing as a desirable difficulty in the classroom. *Journal of Applied Research in Memory and Cognition, 3*, 165–170.

Bjork, E. L., Soderstrom, N. C., & Little, J. L. (2015). Can multiple-choice testing induce desirable difficulties? Evidence from the laboratory and the classroom. *The American Journal of Psychology, 128*, 229–239.

Buhay, D. Best, L. A., & McGuire, K. (2010). The effectiveness of library instruction: Do students response systems (clickers) enhance learning? *The Canadian Journal for the Scholarship of Teaching and Learning, 1*, 5.

Butler, A. C. & Roediger, H. L. (2007). Testing improves long-term retention in a simulated classroom setting. *European Journal of Cognitive Psychology, 19*, 514–527.

(2008). Feedback enhances the positive effects and reduces the negative effects of multiple-choice testing. *Memory and Cognition, 36*, 604–616.

Carey, B. (2010). Forget what you know about good study habits. *New York Times.* September 6, 2010.

Carpenter, S. K. (2009). Cue strength as a moderator of the testing effect: The benefits of elaborative retrieval. *Journal of Experimental Psychology: Learning, Memory, and Cognition*, 35, 1563–1569.

Carroll, M., Campbell-Ratcliffe, J., Murnane, H., & Perfect, T. (2007). Retrieval-induced forgetting in educational contexts: Monitoring, expertise, text integration, and test format. *European Journal of Cognitive Psychology, 19*, 580–606.

Chan, J. C. K. (2009). When does retrieval induce forgetting and when does it induce facilitation? Implications for retrieval inhibition, testing effect, and text processing. *Journal of Memory and Language, 61*, 153–170.

Chan, J. C. K., McDermott, K. B., & Roediger, H. L. (2006). Retrieval-induced facilitation: Initially nontested material can benefit from prior testing of related material. *Journal of Experimental Psychology: General, 135*, 553–571.

Dunlosky, J. & Hertzog, C. (1998). Training programs to improve learning in later adulthood: Helping older adults educate themselves. In D. J. Hacker, J. Dunlosky, & A. C. Graesser (eds.), *Metacognition in educational theory and practice* (pp. 249–275). Mahwah, NJ: Lawrence Erlbaum .

Dunlosky, J. & Thiede, K. W. (1998). What makes people study more? An evaluation of factors that affect self-paced study. *Acta Psychologica, 98*, 37–56.

Fiorella, L. & Mayer, R. E. (2015). *Learning as a generative activity: Eight learning strategies that promote understanding.* New York: Cambridge University Press.

Glass, A. L., Brill, G., & Ingate, M. (2008). Combined online and in-class pretesting improves exam performance in general psychology. *Educational Psychology, 28*, 483–503.

Glenberg, A. M. & Epstein, W. (1985). Calibration of comprehension. *Journal of Experimental Psychology: Learning, Memory, & Cognition, 11*, 702–718.

Glover, J. A. (1989). The" testing" phenomenon: Not gone but nearly forgotten. *Journal of Educational Psychology, 81*, 392–399.

Guynn, M. J. & McDaniel, M. A. (1999). Generate – sometimes recognize, sometimes not. *Journal of Memory and Language, 41*, 398–415.

Guynn, M. J., McDaniel, M. A., Strosser, G. L., Ramirez, J. M., Castleberry, E. H., & Arnett, K. H. (2014). Relational and item-specific influences on generate-recognize processes in recall. *Memory and Cognition, 42*, 198–211.

Halamish, V. & Bjork, R. A. (2011). When does testing enhance retention? A distribution-based interpretation of retrieval as a memory modifier. *Journal of Experimental Psychology: Learning, Memory, and Cognition, 37*(4), 801–812.

Hamaker, C. (1986). The effects of adjunct question on prose learning. *Review of Educational Research, 56*, 212–242.

Hartwig, M. K., & Dunlosky, J. (2012). Study strategies of college students: Are self-testing and scheduling related to achievement?. *Psychonomic Bulletin and Review, 19*, 126–134.

Jacoby, L. L. & Hollingshead, A. (1990). Toward a generate/recognize model of performance on direct and indirect tests of memory. *Journal of Memory and Language, 29*, 433–454.

Kang, S. H., McDermott, K. B., & Roediger, H. L., III (2007). Test format and corrective feedback modify the effect of testing on long-term retention. *European Journal of Cognitive Psychology, 19*, 528–558.

Karpicke, J. D. (2009). Metacognitive control and strategy selection: Deciding to practice retrieval during learning. *Journal of Experimental Psychology: General, 138*, 469–486. https://doi.org/10.1037/a0017341

King, J. F., Zechmeister, E. B., & Shaughnessy, J. J. (1980). Judgments of knowing: The influence of retrieval-practice. *American Journal of Psychology, 93*, 329–343.

Kintsch, W. (1978). More on recognition failure of recallable words: Implications for generation-recognition models. *Psychological Review, 85*, 470–473.

Koriat, A. & Bjork, R. A. (2006). Illusions of competence during study can be remedied by manipulations that enhance learners' sensitivity to retrieval conditions at test. *Memory and Cognition, 34*, 959–972. https://doi.org/10.3758/BF03193244

Kornell, N. & Bjork, R. A. (2007). The promise and perils of self-regulated study. *Psychonomic Bulletin and Review, 14*, 219–224. https://doi.org/10.3758/BF03194055
(2008). Optimising self-regulated study: The benefits – and costs – of dropping flashcards. *Memory, 16*(2), 125–136.

Kornell, N., Bjork, R. A., & Garcia, M. A. (2011). Why tests appear to prevent forgetting: A distribution-based bifurcation model. *Journal of Memory and Language, 65*, 85–97.

Kornell, N. & Rhodes, M. G. (2013). Feedback reduces the metacognitive benefit of tests. *Journal of Experimental Psychology: Applied, 19*, 1–13.

Kornell, N. & Son, L. K. (2009). Learners' choices and beliefs about self-testing. *Memory, 17*, 493–501.

Kuo, T. & Hirshman, E. (1997). The role of distinctive perceptual information in memory: Studies of the testing effect. *Journal of Memory and Language, 36*, 188–201.

Lantz, M. E. & Stawiski, A. (2014). Effectiveness of clickers: Effect of feedback and the timing of questions on learning. *Computers in Human Behavior, 31*, 280–286.

Larsen, D. P., Butler, A. C., & Roediger, H. L., III (2008). Test-enhanced learning in medical education. *Medical Education, 42*(10), 959–966.

Leeming, F. C. (2002). The exam-a-day procedure improves performance in psychology classes. *Teaching of Psychology, 29*, 210–212.

Little, J. L. & Bjork, E. L. (2011). Pretesting with multiple-choice questions facilitates learning. In L. Carlson, C. Hölscher, & T. Shipley (eds.), *Proceedings of the 33rd annual conference of the Cognitive Science Society* (pp. 294–299). Austin, TX: Cognitive Science Society.
(2015). Optimizing multiple-choice tests as tools for learning. *Memory and Cognition, 43*, 14–26.

(2016). Multiple-choice pretesting potentiates learning of related information. *Memory and Cognition*, *44*, 1085–1101.

Little, J. L., Bjork, E. L., Bjork, R. A., & Angello, G. (2012). Multiple-choice tests exonerated, at least of some charges fostering test-induced learning and avoiding test-induced forgetting. *Psychological Science*, *23*, 1337–1344.

Little, J. L., Frickey, E. A., & Fung, A. K. (2018). The role of retrieval in answering multiple-choice questions. *Journal of Experimental Psychology: Learning, Memory, and Cognition*. https://doi.org/10.1037/xlm0000638

Little, J. L. & McDaniel, M. A. (2015). Metamemory monitoring and control following retrieval practice for text. *Memory and Cognition*, *43*, 85–98.

Little, J. L., Storm, B. C., & Bjork, E. L. (2011). The costs and benefits of testing text materials. *Memory*, *19*, 346–359.

Lovelace, E. A. (1984). Metamemory: Monitoring future recallability during study. *Journal of Experimental Psychology: Learning, Memory, and Cognition*, *10*, 756–766.

Lyle, K. B. & Crawford, N. A. (2011). Retrieving essential material at the end of lectures improves performance on statistics exams. *Teaching of Psychology*, *38*, 94–97.

Maki, R. H., Foley, J. M., Kajer, W. K., Thompson, R. C., & Willert, M. G. (1990). Increased processing enhances calibration of comprehension. *Journal of Experimental Psychology: Learning, Memory, & Cognition*, *16*, 609–616.

Martin, N. D., Nguyen, K., & McDaniel, M. A. (2016). Structure building differences influence learning from educational text: Effects on encoding, retention, and metacognitive control. *Contemporary Educational Psychology*, *46*, 52–60.

Mawhinney, V. T., Bostow, D. E., Laws, D. R., Blumenfeld, G. J., & Hopkins, B. L. (1971). A comparison of students studying-behavior produced by daily, weekly, and three-week testing schedules. *Journal of Applied Behavior Analysis*, *4*, 257–264.

Mayer, R. E., Stull, A., DeLeeuw, K., Almeroth, K., Bimber, B., Chun, D., Bulger, M., Campbell, J., Knight, A., & Zhang, H. (2009). Clickers in college classrooms: Fostering learning with questioning methods in large lecture classes. *Contemporary Educational Psychology*, *34*, 51–57.

McDaniel, M. A., Agarwal, P. K., Huelser, B. J., McDermott, K. B., & Roediger III, H. L. (2011). Test-enhanced learning in a middle school science classroom: The effects of quiz frequency and placement. *Journal of Educational Psychology*, *103*, 399–414.

McDaniel, M. A., Anderson, J. L., Derbish, M. H., & Morrisette, N. (2007). Testing the testing effect in the classroom. *European Journal of Cognitive Psychology*, *19*(4–5), 494–513.

McDaniel, M. A., Bugg, J. M., Liu, Y., & Brick, J. (2015). When does the test-study-test sequence optimize learning and retention? *Journal of Experimental Psychology: Applied*, *21*, 370–382.

McDaniel, M. A., Howard, D. C., & Einstein, G. O. (2009). The read-recite-review study strategy effective and portable. *Psychological Science*, *20*(4), 516–522.

McDaniel, M. A. & Masson, M. E. (1985). Altering memory representations through retrieval. *Journal of Experimental Psychology: Learning, Memory, and Cognition*, *11*(2), 371–385.

McDaniel, M. A., Roediger, H. L., & McDermott, K. B. (2007). Generalizing test-enhanced learning from the laboratory to the classroom. *Psychonomic Bulletin and Review*, *14*(2), 200–206.

McDaniel, M. A., Wildman, K. M., & Anderson, J. L. (2012). Using quizzes to enhance summative-assessment performance in a web-based class: An experimental study. *Journal of Applied Research in Memory and Cognition*, *1*(1), 18–26.

McDermott, K. B., Agarwal, P. K., D'Antonio, L., Roediger, H. L., III & McDaniel, M. A. (2014). Both multiple-choice and short-answer quizzes enhance later exam performance in middle and high school classes. *Journal of Experimental Psychology: Applied*, *20*, 3–21

Metcalfe, J. & Kornell, N. (2005). A region of proximal learning model of study time allocation. *Journal of Memory and Language*, *52*, 463–477.

Nelson, T. O. & Dunlosky, J. (1991). When people's judgments of learning (JOLs) are extremely accurate at predicting subsequent recall: The "delayed-JOL effect." *Psychological Science*, *2*, 267–270.

Newble, D. I., Baxter, A., & Elmslie, R. G. (1979). A comparison of multiple-choice tests and free-response tests in examinations of clinical competence. *Medical Education*, *13*, 263–268.

Peterson, D. J. & Mulligan, N. W. (2013). The negative testing effect and the multifactor account. *Journal of Experimental Psychology: Learning, Memory, and Cognition*, *39*, 1287–1293.

Pyc, M. A. & Rawson, K. A. (2010). Why testing improves memory: Mediator effectiveness hypothesis. *Science*, *330*, 335.

Raaijmakers, J. G. & Shiffrin, R. M. (1981). Search of associative memory. *Psychological Review*, *88*(2), 93–134.

Rawson, K. A., Dunlosky, J., & Thiede, K. W. (2000). The rereading effect: Metacomprehension accuracy improves across reading trials. *Memory and Cognition*, *28*, 1004–1010.

Roediger, H. L. & Butler, A. C. (2011). The critical role of retrieval practice in long-term retention. *Trends in Cognitive Sciences*, *15*, 20–27.

Roediger, H. L. & Karpicke, J. D. (2006). The power of testing memory: Basic research and implications for educational practice. *Perspectives on Psychological Science*, *1*, 181–210.

Roediger, H. L., III, Putnam, A. L., & Smith, M. A. (2011). Ten benefits of testing and their applications to educational practice. In J. P. Mestre & B. H. Ross (eds.), *Psychology of learning and motivation: Cognition in education*, Vol. 55 (pp. 1–36). Oxford: Elsevier.

Rowland, C. A. (2014). The effect of testing versus restudy on retention: A meta-analytic review of the testing effect. *Psychological Bulletin*, *140*, 1432–1463.

Smith, M. K., Wood, W. B., Adams, W. K., Wieman, C., Knight, J. K., Guild, N., & Su, T. T. (2009). Why peer discussion improves student performance on in-class concept questions. *Science*, *323*(5910), 122–124.

Soderstrom, N. C. & Bjork, R. A. (2014). Testing facilitates the regulation of subsequent study time. *Journal of Memory and Language*, *73*, 99–115.

Thomas, A. K. & Mcdaniel, M. A. (2007). Metacomprehension for educationally relevant materials: Dramatic effects of encoding-retrieval interactions. *Psychonomic Bulletin and Review*, *14*, 212–218.

Trumbo, M. C., Leiting, K. A., McDaniel, M. A., & Hodge, G. K. (2016). Effects of reinforcement on test-enhanced learning in a large, diverse introductory college psychology course. *Journal of Experimental Psychology. Applied*.

Tullis, J. G., Finley, J. R., & Benjamin, A. S. (2013). Metacognition of the testing effect: Guiding learners to predict the benefits of retrieval. *Memory and Cognition*, *41*, 429–442.

20 Collaborative Learning

The Benefits and Costs

Timothy J. Nokes-Malach, Cristina D. Zepeda, J. Elizabeth Richey, and Soniya Gadgil

A ubiquitous feature of human activity is working and learning with others. Whether we are at home, school, or work we are likely to be interacting and engaging with others to accomplish our goals. Those others often include family, friends, teachers, students, and coworkers. Each of us has likely encountered situations in which these collaborative activities have gone well and we accomplished our goals or even surpassed them. Many of us have also experienced scenarios in which the collaborative activity failed or was not as efficient, effective, or productive as it could have been. What accounts for success in one scenario and failure in another? What are the key factors that support or inhibit productive collaboration? The study of collaborative learning has a long history of research in psychology to answer questions such as these. This research covers a wide array of perspectives and approaches, including cognitive, social, educational, and socio-cultural. A common aim across these different perspectives is to understand how collaborative learning works, that is, to identify the mechanisms and factors that underlie its success and failure.

Our goal for this chapter is to draw from these different perspectives and approaches to understand the potential benefits and costs of collaborative learning. We begin by providing a brief overview of the history of research on collaborative learning. Next, we define collaborative learning for the purposes of this chapter and describe three common approaches used to study it. We then review results from these approaches in which we separate the benefits from the costs and discuss the cognitive and social mechanisms proposed to account for those outcomes. Afterwards, we describe four theoretical frameworks that incorporate some of these mechanisms to account for the findings. Finally, we discuss the implications of these findings for education and future research.

A Brief History of Collaborative Learning

Collaborative learning has been a topic of interest for several thousand years. Many educational practices of the past included elements of collaborative learning. For example, the Roman rhetorician Quintilian's view of teaching focused

This work was supported by grant DUE-1534829 from the National Science Foundation and grant No. 220024083 from the James S. McDonnell Foundation. We thank the editors for very helpful comments on earlier drafts of the manuscript.

on teachers and students writing together and peers giving feedback and constructive criticism to one another (Bloodgood, 2002). Another historical precursor is the centuries-old practice of apprenticeship in learning new trades and skills. Apprenticeship is a source of inspiration to some of the ideas present in current theories of cognitive apprenticeship (Brown, Collins, & Duguid, 1989), situative learning (Greeno, 1998), and communities of practice (Lave & Wegner, 1991) developed in the 1980s and early 1990s.

We do not unpack these more distal histories of collaborative learning (though it would be fascinating to do so) but begin closer to our modern-day context and describe some major contributions of psychological research on collaborative learning in the twentieth century. The scientific study of collaboration is almost as old as the discipline of psychology itself. Classic studies such as the rope-pulling task by Ringelmann (1913; Kravitz & Martin, 1986), which showed that the individual effort exerted by each member of a group decreases linearly as the group size increases, paved the way for a rigorous study of group work.

Foundational thinkers in social psychology such as Kurt Lewin (1890–1947) set the stage for a program of research on group dynamics and the importance of interdependence of individuals in groups. Lewin examined how perceptions of interdependence affect an individual's sense of responsibility and contribution. A major focus of this work was how task interdependence, i.e., the degree to which individuals shared a joint goal, mattered to the success of the group (Lewin, 1935, 1948). Another one of his major influences was the establishment of the Research Center for Group Dynamics at the Massachusetts Institute for Technology in 1945. In 1948, the center moved to the University of Michigan where it is still active today. The center has had a major impact on many faculty and students interested in understanding group dynamics.

One of Lewin's students, Morton Deustch (1920–2017), continued this work and helped to develop a theory of cooperation and competition (Deutsch, 1949, 1973). Deutsch proposed that the interdependence of goals among group members greatly impacts their interactions and, thereby, group success. Cooperative goals were hypothesized to promote positive interdependence based on communication and exchange and lead to successful collaborative outcomes. In contrast, competitive goals were hypothesized to promote negative interdependence and hinder group success. These core ideas were then further developed and extended in many contexts, including student learning in the classroom. For example, David and Roger Johnson at the University of Minnesota have developed an impressive program of research over the past 50 years dedicated to understanding and facilitating cooperation in classroom settings (Johnson & Johnson, 1989, 2009; Johnson, Johnson, & Smith, 1998).

Jean Piaget (1896–1980) also had a large impact on collaborative learning research through his theory of learning, which focused on mechanisms of change including equilibration, assimilation, and accommodation (Piaget, 1932, 1950, 1975/ 1985). He defined equilibration as a driving force of cognitive change (e.g., seeking consistency and coherence in thought and understanding). Although Piaget was primarily focused on change processes *within the individual*, cognitive conflict and working with others could provide one pathway to create such change. This work had a significant impact on cognitive approaches aimed at understanding individual learning mechanisms in the context of learning and problem-solving with others (e.g., Goldbeck & El-Moslimany, 2013; O'Donnell & Hmelo-Silver, 2013; Tudge & Winterhoff, 1993). It also has had a direct impact on social approaches to understanding collaborative learning in relation to conflict regulation (e.g., Buchs et al., 2004; Butera & Darnon, 2017).

Vygotsky (1896–1934) was another pioneer of work in collaborative learning. He proposed the zone of proximal development in which interaction between a novice and a more expert adult or peer facilitates learning (Vygotsky, 1978). We see reverberations of this idea throughout modern research investigating the interaction between the individual, others, and the environment (e.g., Hakkarainen et al., 2013; Tudge & Winterhoff, 1993). A second critical feature of his work was a focus on historical-cultural aspects of learning. Vygotsky argued that learning and development do not proceed in universal stages but rather that they are directly influenced by the environment and culture of the learner. His work had a profound impact on multiple perspectives on collaborative learning, especially sociocultural views.

In this chapter, we focus on three approaches that have been firmly anchored in this historical context: social/cognitive, educational, and sociocultural. We focus on these perspectives because they provide complementary questions, methods, and results that are rarely brought together in a single paper or chapter (see Dillenbourg et al., 1996). Together they capture a wide variety of collaborative outcomes and theory to account for these results. Examining just one would likely focus on just some of the costs and/or benefits.

Approaches to Collaborative Learning

We define *collaboration* as an interaction among individuals in a dyad or group that aims to accomplish or achieve a common goal (Dillenbourg et al., 1996; Kirschner, Paas, & Kirschner, 2009a). Similar to a recent literature review we conducted on this topic, we focus on dyads of two people and groups between three and six people (Nokes-Malach, Richey, & Gadgil, 2015). We do not review work on larger groups ($N > 6$) or from the team performance literature in which different members have specialized complementary skills that need to be utilized to accomplish the group goal (for reviews, see De Dreu & Weingart, 2003; Stewart, 2006).

We define *learning* broadly to include situations in which there is some measure of what was learned from an earlier task or activity (see Figure 20.1 for an illustration of three common collaborative learning and performance scenarios). Each of these scenarios has been associated with a particular theoretical approach including social/cognitive, educational, and sociocultural, and each answers different questions about collaborative learning and performance.

We will describe each approach and its associated methodologies, as well as identify mechanisms that could result in benefits and/or costs of collaboration. These approaches are overlapping and without firm boundaries. They do not have

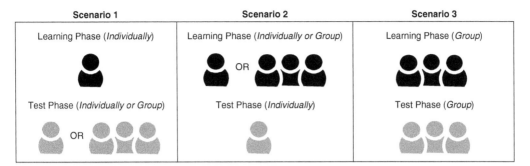

Figure 20.1 *Illustration of the three common collaborative scenarios*

distinguishing features but rather a set of features that tend to co-occur to define the approach, including the types of research questions asked, learning content (puzzle tasks, word lists, or academic content), context (lab or classroom), elements of study design (Figure 20.1), and so on. We acknowledge that some researchers use multiple approaches or combine approaches. For example, our own work is informed by all three approaches.

Cognitive and Social Approaches

Research adopting cognitive and social psychological perspectives has focused on comparing the similarities and differences in learning and performance when people work together versus alone to perform a task. Paper titles such as "When two is too many: Collaborative encoding impairs memory" (Barber, Rajaram, & Aron, 2010) and "Many hands make light the work" (Latané, Williams, & Harkins, 1979) have captured these types of questions. This work has primarily focused on tasks such as memorizing (e.g., Harris, Barnier, & Sutton, 2013; Meade, Nokes, & Morrow, 2009; Rajaram & Pereira-Pasarin, 2010), problem-solving, (e.g., Laughlin et al., 2006; Nokes-Malach, Meade, & Morrow, 2012), brainstorming (e.g., Paulus & Yang, 2000), and physical tasks like clapping or shouting (Latané, et al., 1979). Researchers from this perspective have typically conducted laboratory experiments in which they randomly assigned participants to either a group or individual condition at learning or test (see Figure 20.1, scenarios 1 and 2).

In scenario 1, all participants learn individually and then are tested either individually or in groups. This is a common design to examine the effects of collaboration on the recall of prior knowledge, and has been used extensively in the collaborative memory literature (e.g., Basden et al., 1997; Blumen & Stern, 2011; Harris, Paterson, & Kemp, 2008). In scenario 2, participants learn either individually or as a group and then are tested individually (e.g., Gadgil & Nokes-Malach, 2012; Paulus & Yang, 2000). For example, in a study in which students were learning how to write scientific summaries (Gadgil & Nokes-Malach, 2012), students were first assigned to work either with a partner or individually on an error-detection writing task during the learning phase. All students were then later assessed individually on a summary writing task.

Of course, there are several variations of these two basic scenarios including designs that manipulate collaboration at learning *and* test. For example, in some studies of collaborative memory, participants study the materials collaboratively or alone, and then later recall that knowledge either with a partner or alone (e.g., Barber et al., 2010; Finlay, Hitch, & Meudell, 2000). Similar research designs have been used in problem-solving (e.g., Laughlin, Carey, & Kerr, 2008). This general approach focuses on manipulating the independent variable of collaboration (i.e., working together or not) as well as various other variables (e.g., group size, type of collaborative scaffold, prior knowledge of collaborators) to test hypotheses about the mechanisms and factors that affect successful collaboration.

A major issue in research on collaborative learning is determining how to measure the cost or benefit of group learning and performance outcomes. Research in cognitive and social psychology has focused on the type of contrast condition or standard to which the collaborative group is compared (Hill, 1982; Lorge et al., 1958; Steiner, 1966). In this work, two levels of analysis have been identified. One level of analysis is defined by comparing the collaborative group with the average individual. Called the "average individual" comparison, this approach treats the group as the unit of analysis and assesses whether the average group performs the task more accurately or efficiently than the average individual. For example, imagine a memory task comparing group recall and individual recall after an initial study session. Participants would study a list of ten items (A–J) individually and at test they would recall that list either with their partner (dyad) or alone. The average individual comparison would be to compare the average number of items recalled by the dyads to the average number of items recalled by the individuals (see Figure 20.2). As a simplistic illustration, let's compare one dyad to two individuals. Imagine the dyad recalled seven items on the list (e.g., A, B, C, D, E, F, and J), while individual participant 1 recalled six items (A, B, C, G, H, I) and individual participant 2 recalled four items (A, D, E, J). The two individuals would have recalled on average 50 percent of the items and, thus, the dyad would have recalled more than the average individual (70% > 50%). Research has shown that there are often advantages when comparing the group to the average individual (for reviews, see Hill, 1982; Kerr & Tindale, 2004).

The second type of analysis helps answer the question of how working in a group affects learning and performance compared to the pooled outcome of working alone. In order to make this comparison, the collaborative dyad or group condition must be compared with what has been called a *nominal group*, in which performance is pooled or summed across the same number of individuals as are in the collaborative group (Rajaram & Pereira-Pasarin, 2010). There are a number of ways to create nominal groups, including summing scores to create post hoc groups or algorithms that make estimates of the nominal group based on individual performance scores (Kelley & Wright, 2010; Schwartz, 1995; Wright, 2007). For example, in our simplistic illustration of the memory recall paradigm above, we can see that if we pool together the two individuals' unique (non-redundant) responses, they would

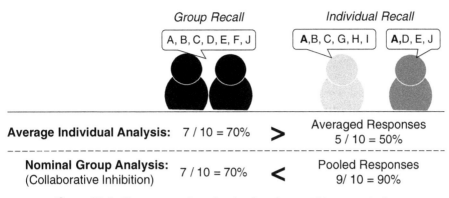

Group Recall   *Individual Recall*

A, B, C, D, E, F, J   **A**,B, C, G, H, I   **A**,D, E, J

Average Individual Analysis: 7 / 10 = 70%   **>**   Averaged Responses
5 / 10 = 50%

Nominal Group Analysis: 7 / 10 = 70%   **<**   Pooled Responses
(Collaborative Inhibition)   9/ 10 = 90%

Figure 20.2 *Illustration of two levels of analysis within scenario 1*

have recalled nine items (A, B, C, D, E, G, H, I, J) out of ten, or 90 percent of the list. This example illustrates that although they recalled fewer responses when averaged (50%), the individuals actually recalled more unique responses than the dyad when summed across individuals (Figure 20.2).

When the collaborative dyad or group performs less well than the nominal dyad or group, it is called *collaborative inhibition* (Weldon & Bellinger, 1997) and has been interpreted as individuals in the group not performing up to their predicted potential. In contrast, when the collaborative group performs better than the nominal group this is called *collaborative facilitation* or *synergy* (Meade et al., 2009; Nokes-Malach et al., 2012) and is interpreted as individuals in the group performing better than their predicted potential based on individual performance. For example, imagine in our memory recall paradigm that the collaborative dyad recalls all ten items and has 100 percent recall and the individuals in the nominal group recall the same number as described above. This would be an example of collaborative facilitation because the collaborative group's recall (100%) would be better than that of the nominal group (90%). Next, we describe a second major approach to research on collaborative learning that comes from educational psychology.

Educational Psychology Approaches

Educational psychologists have used a myriad of methods to study collaborative learning. Research questions from this perspective often focus on understanding how different types of instruction can facilitate productive collaboration and learning outcomes. Much of this research has been conducted in classroom contexts, often comparing different types of instructional activities to one another. This work has covered a wide variety of content domains and tasks, including mathematics (Kolloffel, Eysink, & de Jong, 2011; Schwarz, Neuman, & Biezuner, 2000; Slavin, Leavey, & Madden, 1984), science (Kirschner, Paas, & Kirschner, 2009b; Springer, Stanne, & Donovan, 1999; Sampson & Clark, 2009), and language arts (Kim, 2008; Stevens & Slavin, 1995; Stevens, Slavin, & Farnish, 1991), among others, as well as varied age groups ranging from preschoolers to adults (for reviews, see Johnson & Johnson, 1989; Slavin, 1995).

The most commonly used study design within the educational approach assigns students to work in collaboration with others (group) or to work alone (individual), and then tests all students individually (Figure 20.1, scenario 2). This design answers the question about what was learned at an individual level of analysis. If there is a difference between the two conditions at test, then it is attributed to the manipulation of being in a dyad or group versus in an individual condition during the learning phase. Some studies also compare two or more collaborative conditions to one another to see which leads to better learning, instead of comparing an individual and collaborative condition. In such studies, students learn collaboratively and then are tested individually to understand what kinds of collaborative instructional strategies are most effective (e.g., Souvignier & Kronenberger, 2007) or what types of group compositions (e.g., same or mixed ability) lead to successful collaborative learning.

These research designs capture several features of common educational practices and curricula that encourage students to collaborate during learning and then give individual assessments. For example, in K-12 science classes, students frequently learn together in small groups (e.g., with their lab partners) but are then tested individually. When researchers investigate collaboration in the classroom, these condition assignments typically happen at the classroom level, i.e., some classrooms do group work whereas other classrooms do individual assignments (e.g., Mevarech, 1985). Occasionally, the group versus individual comparison happens within the classroom using a counterbalanced design, such that the conditions are switched for the next session and each student has the opportunity to participate in both conditions. Other types of methods include pull-out studies, interviews, and laboratory contexts (for an overview of methods and context, see Hmelo-Silver et al., 2013).

Many variables have been examined using this approach. Five key variables that Johnson and Johnson (2009) have investigated include positive interdependence (mutual goals), individual accountability within the group, promotive interaction (i.e., encouraging each other's efforts), the appropriate use of social skills, and group processing (i.e., reflecting on performance). The role of each of these variables in relation to collaborative benefits and costs has been studied extensively. Next, we describe the sociocultural approach to studying collaborative learning.

Sociocultural Approaches

A primary focus of the sociocultural approach is to understand how interactions between group members and the environment support or inhibit collaborative outcomes. This approach treats the dyad or group as the unit of analysis as opposed to the individual within the group and does not often compare groups or dyads to individuals (e.g., Barron, 2000; Engle & Conant, 2002; Greeno & MMAP, 1997; Harris, Yuill, & Luckin, 2008; Roschelle, 1992; Roschelle & Teasley, 1995). Instead, much of the work involves examining collaborative interactions for insights on the affordances and constraints that lead to more versus less successful collaborative outcomes. Success or failure is determined by whether and how the group has accomplished its goal(s). This approach has typically focused on academic content in classroom settings. For example, in Engle and Conant (2002) the researchers examined how groups of four or five students collaborated on biology projects in their middle school science classes. The project spanned many weeks of class and consisted of a variety of group activities, including determining which endangered animal to study, researching that animal, writing individual chapters of the report, collaborative writing of the introduction and conclusion of the report, and presenting the report to the other student groups.

A typical design is to compare different groups with one another or the same group with itself at different points in time and then analyze process data to assess which factors and mechanisms are associated with the benefits and costs of collaboration (e.g., Figure 20.1, scenario 3). Researchers typically video record student talk and behaviors during the learning phase (Jeong, 2013; Sawyer, 2013). This serves as the primary data source and the researchers code and analyze the discourse and behaviors for different types of interactions. In many studies, there is some later assessment taken as a group, individually, or both. However, in contrast to the previous scenarios, the test phase is not always well differentiated from the learning phase. For example, in the Engle and Conant (2002) study, the test phase can be conceptualized as the final biology report given. In other cases, researchers have looked for evidence of change whether it be in solving new problems later in the activity (e.g., Roschelle, 1992) or new thinking or reasoning about an old problem (e.g., Engle & Conant, 2002). In the next section, we review findings from these three approaches on the benefits and costs of collaborative learning.

Table 20.1 *Summary of three common approaches to examining collaborative learning*

| Approach | Focus | Methodologies | | |
		Research Design(s)	Level of Analysis	Setting
Social and Cognitive	Comparing the similarities and differences of learning and performance when people work together versus when they work alone to perform a task	Scenarios 1 & 2, Combination of 1 & 2	Individual & Group	Mostly Laboratory
Educational	Understanding how different types of instruction can facilitate productive collaboration and learning outcomes	Scenario 2	Individual	Mostly Classroom
Sociocultural	Understanding how interactions between group members and the environment support or inhibit collaborative outcomes	Scenario 3	Group	Mostly Classroom

Reviewing the Costs and Benefits of Collaborative Learning

Collaborative Benefits

Research from these three approaches has shown a multitude of benefits from collaboration. Many of these findings come from work using the cognitive and social psychological approaches with a group level of analysis, in which groups performed better than the average individual (Figure 20.1, scenario 1). Research on collaborative memory has routinely shown this effect (for a review, see Rajaram & Pereira-Pasarin, 2010). This benefit has been observed for memory of a wide array of materials, including word lists (Andersson & Rönnberg, 1995; Experiment 1; Basden et al., 1997), stories (Weldon & Bellinger, 1997; Experiment 2), problem-solving scenarios (Meade et al., 2009), pictures (Finlay et al., 2000; Experiment 1), and videos (Andersson & Rönnberg, 1995; Experiment 2). Similar benefits for groups performing better than the average individual have been found for a variety of other tasks, including category learning (Voiklis & Corter, 2012), video game learning (Arthur et al., 1997), and problem-solving tasks (Laughlin et al., 2006).

There is also extensive evidence from the educational psychology approach for the benefits of learning in a group versus learning individually, especially outside of the laboratory in classroom contexts (Figure 20.1, scenario 2). These tasks include model-building tasks (Azimitia, 1988), hypothesis generation (Teasley, 1995), and problem-solving tasks (Kischner et al., 2009b, 2011). For example, a meta-analysis reported in Johnson, Johnson, and Smith (2007) compared cooperative groups, which they defined by positive interdependence (e.g., shared goals or rewards), with individualistic groups, which they defined by their lack of social interdependence. They found an overall positive effect ($d = 0.53$) of cooperative instruction over individualistic instruction (for similar results, see Springer et al., 1999).

In addition to finding benefits at the group level, a few studies have examined whether there is collaborative facilitation or synergy at the individual level of analysis by comparing whether the group outcomes exceed the performance of nominal groups (Figure 20.2). A few studies have shown benefits of collaborative facilitation, including Meade and colleagues (2009) and Paulus and Yang (2000). In sum, the benefits of group learning and performance at the group level of analysis are extensive. This research has mainly investigated what cognitive and social mechanisms support collaborative gains. We review these mechanisms next.

Mechanisms Underlying Benefits

Cognitive Factors

One important cognitive factor is the role of prior knowledge in promoting successful learning and performance. When individuals in a group have *complementary knowledge*, they can combine their knowledge to either improve recall or solve problems that they could not solve alone. For example, a study by Canham, Wiley, and Mayer (2012) compared two types of dyads. In one type of dyad, each learner received different background knowledge on a statistics concept and, in the other type of dyad, both learners received the same background knowledge. Those who received different background information spent more time understanding and developing a solution with their partner and performed better on transfer questions about the material than those who were given the same background information.

Similar results have been found in a study comparing older couples who reported that they were typically responsible for remembering different kinds of everyday information and couples who reported having the same responsibilities (Harris et al., 2011). Those who reported remembering different kinds of information performed better in recalling information from episodic stories and autobiographical recall tasks. Another study showed that when individuals in a group are given instructions for remembering different portions of the to-be-learned information, they remember more compared with when they are given the same material (Basden et al., 1997).

Another way prior knowledge can support collaboration is through *cross-cuing*. This is when one person in the group recalls information that then cues other group members' recall. Cross-cuing rests on the assumption that group members have *shared knowledge* that can serve as a source of cues and related target responses. For example, in the study on older couples' recall, cuing was associated with better recall performance (Harris et al., 2011). A similar result was found in the Meade and colleagues (2009) study examining expert and novice pilots' recall of prior flight scenarios. Expert dyads were more likely to elaborate on each other's contributions when recalling elements of the problem, which was related to overall better recall.

Both complementary and shared prior knowledge structures are theorized to contribute to a reduction in cognitive load (the amount of mental effort being expended in working memory). Dividing the information among collaborative partners is one way to potentially reduce any one person's cognitive load. Similarly, shared prior knowledge might reduce the cognitive load because that shared knowledge does not need to be discussed or stored in working memory as it has already been encoded into long-term memory (Ericsson & Kintsch, 1995).

Two other cognitive factors thought to support collaborative benefits are reexposure and retrieval practice. *Reexposure* is the idea that when recalling information in a group, a given individual will be reexposed to information they may have forgotten from the encoding phase (Rajaram & Pereira-Pasarin, 2010). When a partner recalls prior information, they effectively have an additional opportunity to learn that piece of information. A second beneficial memory process is *retrieval practice*, the act of attempting to retrieve information, which can promote learning and later recall (Roediger & Karpicke, 2006). Although retrieval practice is not a uniquely collaborative activity, some prior work suggests that retrieval practice is particularly beneficial when the learner is given immediate feedback on performance (Roediger & Butler, 2011). One advantage of working in a dyad or a group is that participants can provide immediate feedback to one another on the accuracy of their answers (or at least whether they agree or disagree).

Providing feedback is related to the process of *error-correction* by which individuals ask each other questions and critique each other's thinking as they recall or solve problems. Individuals may put a particular idea or hypothesis to multiple tests before settling on a solution. For example, Weigold, Russell, and Natera (2014) showed participants ten different word lists, each of which was semantically related to one word that was not presented (the non-presented critical word). Collaborative groups were least likely to recall the non-presented critical words, compared to both nominal groups and individuals. Collaborators engaged in successful error-correction by rejecting other group members' false recall, which led to higher accuracy in recall.

A powerful mechanism of individual and collaborative learning is *explanation*. Individuals who generate explanations are more likely to identify what they do not understand, and the process of generating explanations provides them an opportunity to address that lack of understanding or fill in knowledge gaps (Chi et al., 1989; Chi et al., 1994). In collaborative learning scenarios, other members in the group may benefit from hearing the proposed explanation (Webb, Troper, & Fall, 1995). For example, Okada and Simon (1997) found that dyads were more successful at discovering scientific principles than individuals and attributed their success to their greater use of explanation-guided experimentation.

Social Factors

There are also several social factors that have been hypothesized to support collaborative benefits. One is through the *joint management of attention*. Group members are more likely to succeed if they share attention than if each member focuses on different aspects of the problem. If they focus on different aspects, then they also have to take more time and effort to integrate those ideas. Teasley and Roschelle (1993) proposed the idea of a joint-problem space as the coordination of goals, knowledge about the problem or task, and awareness of possible solution steps. Barron (2003) conducted a qualitative analysis of twelve triads of 6th graders working on a problem-solving task and found that triads who were successful in establishing a joint problem-solving space had better problem-solving outcomes. Members of successful groups showed better coordination and considered proposals from all group members. Less successful groups had at least one self-focused group member who was reluctant to accept others' proposals and such groups were rarely able to establish a joint problem-solving space.

Relatedly, research on the construction of *common ground* shows that building a shared understanding facilitates collaborative success. For example, Meade and colleagues (2009) had expert, novice, and nonpilots read flight problem scenarios and then later recall those scenarios either alone or in collaboration with another participant of the same level of expertise. Expert dyads showed collaborative gains on recall compared with nominal groups where novices and nonpilots did not (see Table 20.2). Experts were also more successful than novices in establishing common ground. To understand the development of common ground, the researchers analyzed dyads' discourse patterns and found that experts were more likely than novices to acknowledge, restate, and elaborate on each other's contributions. One possible source contributing to the experts' abilities to develop common ground may be from their formal training to work with team members such as establishing common ground with the copilot and air traffic control. Another potential contribution could have been the group's high levels of shared prior knowledge, which may have reduced cognitive load.

A third social factor that impacts the success of collaborative learning concerns the *negotiating of multiple perspectives*. Understanding a partner's perspective means coming to terms with new information that one would not have been exposed to otherwise. For instance, Schwartz (1995) compared problem-solving representations of individuals and dyads across several complex science topics and found that learners who worked together produced more abstract representations. Schwartz argued that these representations likely helped learners with different perspectives to coordinate their understanding to solve the problems. In other words, creating a representation that two different individuals could both understand in a meaningful way seemed to push them toward creating a more abstract representation of the problem.

A closely related factor that can also contribute to collaborative benefits involves how an individual relates to and engages with the potential conflict that can be created when working in a collaborative group. There is a long history of work on *conflict regulation* in social psychology that has differentiated between two types of conflict regulation: epistemic and relational (Doise & Mugny, 1984; Mugny, De Paolis, & Carugati, 1984). Epistemic regulation is hypothesized to be productive whereas relational regulation is hypothesized to be detrimental to group learning and performance. We refer to epistemic regulation here and relational regulation in the "Collaborative Costs" section. Epistemic regulation involves focusing on the task and the answers and is related to improved learning (Doise & Mugny, 1979, 1984). Relational regulation focuses on relative levels of competence and demonstrating one's own superiority.

Table 20.2 *Mean proportion of segments recalled by experts, novices, and nonpilots as a function of individual or collaborative recall (after Meade, Nokes, & Morrow, 2009, p. 43. Copyright 2009 Psychology Press, an imprint of the Taylor and Francis Group. Reprinted by permission of the publisher)*

	Experts	Novices	Nonpilots
Nominal group	0.52 (0.18)	0.51 (0.13)	0.41 (0.10)
Collaborative	0.68 (0.15)	0.46 (0.08)	0.33 (0.14)
Average individual	0.33 (0.16)	0.28 (0.14)	0.23 (0.11)
Effect Size	0.97	−0.48	−0.67

Note. Standard deviations are in parentheses. Effect sizes are based on a comparison between nominal group and collaborative conditions ($N = 96$).

Collaborative Costs

Given the two levels of analysis (individual versus nominal) and the variety of study designs described in the "Approaches to Collaborative Learning" section, the results for collaborative costs can be operationalized in a variety of ways. Here, we briefly review three. The first is from the research on collaborative inhibition (Figure 20.2). As described in the previous section, collaborative inhibition is when the group performs worse than the nominal group, showing that the individuals in the group are not performing up to their predicted potential. There are many studies showing such deficits on a variety of memory recall tasks. In these experiments, participants first memorize the materials individually and then attempt to recall them either with another person or alone (Figure 20.1, scenario 1). The typical result shows that the collaborative group recalls fewer items than the nominal group, suggesting that the individuals within the group are not performing at their predicted potential. These results have been found for different age groups, including children, adults, and older adults, and across types of relationships ranging from strangers to couples and friends (for a review, see Rajaram & Pereira-Pasarin, 2010).

In addition to these memory tasks, there are a few other tasks that have shown collaborative inhibition effects. One is from the Nokes-Malach and colleagues (2012) study in which nonpilots working in dyads performed worse than those solving the problems alone. Collaborative inhibition has also been found in a classroom writing task in which students worked either with a partner or alone to find writing errors in a text (Gadgil & Nokes-Malach, 2012). Students who worked with another student were less likely to find grammatical errors in the writing than those working alone.

A second type of collaborative cost comes from collaborative memory research that has examined the acquisition of false memories. In this research, investigators have examined what they call contagion memory effects, in which one partner in a group falsely recalls a piece of information and another participant mistakenly encodes that information as being from the original study material. The majority of research exploring this phenomenon has used laboratory experiments in which a confederate in the group falsely recalls information during group recall and then later all participants are tested individually on what they remember from the original list. This work shows that false memories can spread during collaboration, and several studies have demonstrated that the contagion effect is robust even when participants are warned that false recall can be a problem in group settings (Meade & Roediger, 2002; Roediger, Meade, & Bergman, 2001). We know of no work that has examined this phenomenon in educational settings, but it would be informative to understand whether this result happens in group school work and whether there is any relation to the large literature on student misconceptions.

A third type of cost is when the group performs *equal to or worse than* the average individual. This result appears to occur less often than collaborative inhibition, but there are a few examples in the literature (Crooks et al., 1998; Kirschner et al., 2011; Leidner & Fuller, 1997; Tudge, 1989). For instance, Tudge (1989) showed that elementary students working alone performed better than students working in dyads in solving conservation balance beam problems. In another example, Leidner and Fuller (1997) found that students working alone performed better than students working in pairs in an information management course. To explain collaborative inhibition, contagion effects, and poor group performance, several different cognitive and social mechanisms have been proposed. We describe these mechanisms below.

Mechanisms Underlying the Costs

Cognitive Factors

One mechanism that negatively affects collaborative learning and performance is the *coordination costs* of working with other individuals (Clark & Brennan, 1991; Steiner, 1972). When working in a group, members typically need to figure out each individual's role. For example, in a problem-solving task, the group has to decide who will work on which aspects of the problem (e.g., who will read the problem aloud), how they will resolve differences of perspective or strategy, and how they will evaluate potential solutions and reach consensus. Figuring out the logistics of who is contributing to which component of the task and integrating those contributions creates additional cognitive demands. Ivan Steiner (1972) in his classic work on collaboration referred to this additional coordination cost as "process loss."

Similar to this view, Kirschner and colleagues (2009a) have described a cognitive load approach to understanding collaborative learning. When comparing the group with individual learning and performance, they propose that there will be collaborative costs when the task is simple and benefits when the task is complex. The idea is that when the task is simple and the individual could learn the information or solve the problem without assistance, working with others simply increases the coordination costs and cognitive load without improving outcomes. In contrast, when the task is complex it is thought to require more cognitive resources than an individual can provide and therefore they are benefited by assistance from others. Kirshner and colleagues (2009b) tested this hypothesis by comparing participants' ratings of mental effort (a measure of cognitive load) after various learning and test tasks. Participants learned in groups of three or individually on either simple or complex learning materials in biology. All students were then tested individually on a transfer test. For the simple materials, they found that participants working in groups did not differ from those working individually in their mental effort ratings at learning. However, the participants who learned individually reported lower mental effort than participants in the group condition at test. This result suggests there might be a cost for group learning when materials are simple. For the complex materials, the authors found a different pattern of results. The participants in the group reported lower levels of mental effort at learning and at test than the participants who learned individually. These results were consistent with the hypothesis that the complexity of the materials interacts with cognitive load during group work.

Another type of cognitive cost is *production blocking* (Diehl & Stroebe, 1987). This cost is based on the idea that typically only one person in a group talks at a time so that others may hear what that person is saying. When one person is speaking, it effectively blocks or prevents others from talking, causing a delay in making one's contribution. This delay may cause others to forget their ideas, decide that their contributions are no longer relevant, or be less motivated to come up with new ideas during the delay. Further, processing what another person is saying may interfere with one's thinking. For example, Diehl and Stroebe (1987) showed that when group members were only allowed to say their thoughts when given permission (i.e., blocked from stating their thoughts as they occurred), they produced fewer solutions than a group and nominal group that could say their thoughts freely. This finding suggests that if a group member dominates a collaboration, then they might be reducing the productivity of the group by limiting the others' abilities to contribute.

A closely related concept to production blocking is the *retrieval strategy disruption hypothesis* (Basden et al., 1997). This hypothesis states that as one person in a group starts recalling information aloud, this information disrupts other group members' memory retrieval processes because individuals typically vary in their recall strategies and have idiosyncratic output orders. For example, if the task is to recall a list of items and one individual attempts to recall the list in alphabetical order (apple, aardvark, bassoon, baker ...) whereas another person attempts to recall the list by category (apple, grapes, orange, kiwi ...), one strategy interferes with the other as the item order does not align across the two. Evidence for this hypothesis comes from a series of experiments showing that groups performed worse than nominal groups when the number of categories to be recalled was large rather than small (Basden et al., 1997; Experiment 1). In contrast, when the participants had nonoverlapping parts of the list to be recalled or people were forced to adopt the same recall strategy (e.g., recall a single category at a time), there were no differences between groups and nominal groups (Basden et al., 1997; Experiments 3 and 4), that is, collaborative inhibition was eliminated. Another factor that has been shown to attenuate or eliminate this cost is the type of test employed. For example, using cued recall or recognition tests as opposed to a free recall test will attenuate inhibition effects (Finlay et al., 2000). These factors aim to minimize idiosyncratic recall based on specific retrieval strategies. Two other factors that reduce inhibition are to include repeated study or test trials (Congleton & Rajaram, 2011; Pereira-Pasarin & Rajaram, 2011) or to involve a delay of two or more hours between study and test (Congleton & Rajaram, 2011).

Social Factors

Several social factors have also been proposed to account for the costs of collaborating. One factor that is often examined in group performance is *social loafing* (Latané et al., 1979). As the number of people in a group increases, each individual contributes less effort because of the belief that someone else will pick up the slack (i.e., diffusion of responsibility). Research on this topic initially focused on physical tasks such as clapping or shouting (Latané et al., 1979) but has since been replicated on other tasks, including brainstorming (Harkins & Petty, 1982), perceptual counting (Matsui, Kakuyama, & Onglatco, 1987), and evaluating poems and editorials (Petty et al., 1977). The majority of these tasks have been examined from a performance perspective and few have been examined using learning paradigms that test what has been learned. A meta-analysis by Karau and Williams (1993) found that a number of variables moderate social loafing effects, with loafing decreasing when there is potential for performance evaluation, higher task value, higher group value, when the expectations of the coparticipants were low, when group size decreased, when tasks were more complex versus simple, and when individuals perceived their contributions as unique, among others.

Another social factor that can produce detriments in group performance is *fear of evaluation*. In this case, the individual is afraid to put forward risky solutions to other group members for fear of being incorrect or not consistent with group strategies. For example, Collaros and Anderson (1969) showed that when individuals were told that one or all other members of their group were experts, they were more reluctant to offer ideas because they feared criticism, felt inhibited, or feared disapproval from others in the group. They also withheld more ideas than a control condition that was not told about the expert status of their group members. Although there is evidence for fear of evaluation on group performance in some contexts, research on the role of evaluation apprehension in brainstorming productivity failed to account for the collaborative inhibition effect (Diehl & Stroebe, 1987). A closely related idea is research on *self-attention* (Mullen 1983, 1987). This work has examined the negative outcomes of focusing on one's competence when working in groups as compared to when working alone. The idea is that working with others in particular contexts increases attention to one's performance or competence and that this increased attention to oneself leads to decreased performance.

The complement of epistemic regulation in the benefits section is relational regulation. When individuals in a group are focused on *relational regulation* they are engaged with thinking about issues of status and competence, which takes attention away from the task at hand. This type of regulation is associated with poor performance and learning outcomes (Doise & Mugny, 1984).

Theoretical Frameworks of Collaborative Learning

In this section, we point to four theoretical frameworks of collaborative learning that bring together several of the aforementioned processes to explain collaborative benefits and costs. The first is Rajaram and Pereira-Pasarin's (2010) collaborative memory framework. This framework brings together several of the cognitive mechanisms described in the benefits and costs sections (see Figure 20.3). The goal of the framework is to describe how cognitive processes that occur during collaboration create positive and negative effects on later individual learning measures. The positive influences include reexposure, relearning via retrieval (retrieval practice), and error pruning (error correction). The negative influences include social contagion errors (contagion memory effects), blocking that leads to forgetting

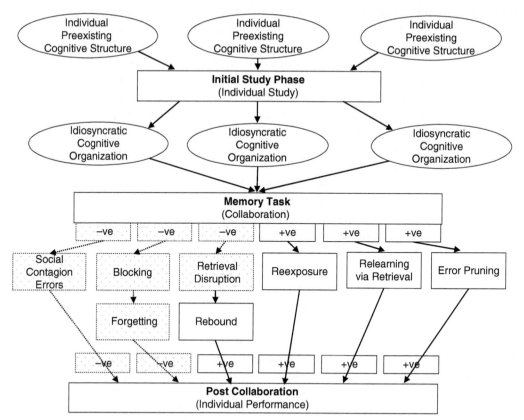

Figure 20.3 *Illustration of Rajaram and Pereira-Pasarin's (2010) theoretical framework of the cognitive mechanisms underlying effects of collaboration on memory (after Rajaram & Pereira-Pasarin, 2010, p. 651. Copyright 2010. Reprinted with permission from SAGE Publications)*

The ovals at the top and center represent three different individuals. Negative influences of collaboration are identified with a "–ve" and positive influences of collaboration are identified with a "+ve."

(production blocking), and retrieval disruption. Rebound is a mitigating process that can follow retrieval disruption once the disruptive cues of collaborators' recall are removed; when rebound occurs, items that had disappeared during collaborative recall reappear when the individual recalls the items alone. Although this framework includes several cognitive mechanisms, it does not include most of the social mechanisms.

The second is M. T. H. Chi's Interactive-Constructive-Active-Passive (ICAP) framework that relates learning activities, cognitive engagement, and learning outcomes to one another (Chi, 2009; Chi & Wylie, 2014). In this framework, Chi and colleagues hypothesize that as cognitive engagement increases so do learning outcomes. At the top of the engagement activities hierarchy are interactive behaviors defined as "dialogues that meet two criteria: (a) both partners' utterances must be primarily constructive, and (b) a sufficient degree of turn taking must occur" (Chi &

Wiley, 2014, p. 223). Chi defines constructive behaviors as learners generating outputs that go beyond the information given in the learning activity (e.g., asking questions, generating inferences). This framework captures many of the proposed mechanisms for collaborative benefits reviewed in this chapter and has related those mechanisms to student behaviors when engaging in learning activities in small group contexts.

The third and fourth frameworks are closely related in that they both examine the relation between group knowledge and task affordances. Nokes-Malach and colleagues (2012) propose the *zone of proximal facilitation*, hypothesizing that collaborative facilitation will occur when the prior expertise of the group's knowledge and the complexity of the task afford constructive and interactive processes between group members. A fourth and related proposal by Kirschner and colleagues (2009a) uses a cognitive-load analysis of the learning or problem-solving activity to develop their framework. They predicted that complex tasks will result in collaborative success because of the pooling of memory resources. In contrast, simple tasks will result in poorer performance or no gains because individuals could perform those tasks well alone and, therefore, the cost of group coordination outweighs the cognitive benefits of collaboration. These two frameworks provide explanations for why in some circumstances the cognitive/memory resources of the group lead to process loss (simple tasks) whereas in others they can lead to process gains (complex tasks).

These frameworks integrate different pieces of literature to provide a guide to understanding how, when, and why different mechanisms of collaborative learning produce beneficial processes and outcomes. However, each framework carves out only part of the underlying mechanisms. Combining these frameworks and integrating more of the social mechanisms can provide a more holistic yet fine-grained approach to understanding how all these mechanisms work together to produce efficient, effective, and productive collaborative learning outcomes. One difficulty in developing such a framework is that there are several different approaches to examining collaborative learning. In this chapter, we reviewed work from the three different perspectives, but there is also work from a self-regulated learning perspective (for an overview, see Hadwin, Järvelä, & Miller, 2011) and computer-supported collaborative learning (CSCL) perspective (see Hmelo-Silver et al., 2013, chaps. 22–28) that goes beyond the scope of this chapter. Although we have made much progress in understanding collaborative learning, there is much more work to be done to integrate these different perspectives and approaches into a larger framework or taxonomy.

Educational and Instructional Implications

As discussed in our review, research from cognitive, social, and educational psychology as well as the learning sciences has made important contributions to understanding how collaboration works. Unfortunately, findings from basic research do not often get incorporated in instructional practice (Vanderlinde & van Braak, 2010). In this section, we provide six specific strategies that teachers and instructional designers can implement to mitigate the cognitive and social costs and maximize the benefits of collaboration.

Strategy 1: Keep Coordination Costs Low to Reduce Process Loss

Reducing process loss by keeping coordination costs low leads to better learning from collaboration. There are multiple ways to keep coordination costs low, including providing a script, repeated practice, and grouping collaborators with shared expertise. Providing a script for collaboration has been shown to improve collaborative learning over nonscripted conditions (O' Donnell, 1999; Rummel & Spada, 2005). A collaboration script describes the roles of participants, their actions, and the sequence of events that they engage in during collaboration. The collaboration script eliminates the extraneous cognitive load of figuring out task logistics, thus combating process loss.

When collaborators share expertise, they may be able to establish common ground more quickly and spend less time coordinating their different areas of knowledge and assumptions (Canham et al., 2012; Nokes-Malach et al., 2012). However, combining collaborators with different areas of expertise or prior knowledge may promote deeper discussions and greater conceptual learning, highlighting the importance of considering goals of the task when deciding how to structure a collaboration.

Strategy 2: Carefully Consider Task Complexity

Collaborative success hinges upon whether the task is complex enough to warrant working in a group. Tasks that involve simple recall or rote memorization often suffer from collaborative inhibition, as the costs of collaboration may outweigh the benefits. Studies that compared individual and collaborative learning across simple and complex tasks found that while complex tasks benefited from collaboration, learning on simple tasks was actually hindered (Kirschner et al., 2011). We recommend designing collaborative activities for tasks that are complex and that require higher-order thinking or problem-solving rather than for those that involve only rote memorization. When thinking about the difficulty of the task, it is important to consider the prior knowledge of the group members, as a task that is complex for a novice may be simple for someone with greater expertise. If the group members have the opportunity to combine their different pieces of prior knowledge, then they will benefit more from the task as new knowledge will be shared and there will be more opportunities for elaboration.

Strategy 3: Minimize Fear of Evaluation

Social factors such as fear of evaluation often hinder collaborative success. Some prior research has shown that fear of evaluation or evaluation apprehension is reduced when participants are told that observers will be a source of future help (e.g., Geen, 1983). Studies have also shown that cooperation rather than competition leads to better learning in groups (e.g., Johnson & Johnson, 1994). Thus, underscoring the message that group members are not competitors, but should support each other in successfully completing the task will lead to better learning.

Another technique to minimize fear of evaluation is to include self-affirmation writing activities. For example, studies have shown asking students to write about a value that is important to them improves performance and learning and significantly reduces the racial achievement gap between African-American and white students (Cohen et al., 2006) and Latinx-American and white students (Sherman et al., 2013).

Strategy 4: Promote Use of Productive Conflict Regulation Strategies

Conflict is a natural consequence of working in a group. To the extent that such conflicts focus on the content of the material to be learned, or in other words are of an *epistemic* nature, they lead to greater motivation and successful collaborative learning outcomes. Conversely, conflicts that question a group member's competence or are *relational* in nature lead to decreased motivation and worse learning from collaboration (Darnon, Buchs, & Butera, 2002). Collaborative groups should be reminded that criticizing their peers' ideas is okay but personal attacks are not. Giving students guidelines for thinking about how the things they say affect other people might be particularly useful in these situations. Relatedly, helping students process negative feedback may be another way to alleviate this barrier. For example, instructors can make clear that making errors and receiving negative feedback are an important part of learning.

Strategy 5: Promote Motivation – Mastery Goals, Growth Mindsets, and Task Value

Students' goals for engaging in a learning activity have a profound influence on how and how much they learn. Mastery goals, wherein students are focused on learning and extending their own mastery, have been shown to be more adaptive, compared with performance goals that are focused on comparing one's performance to a normative standard. In collaborative learning, past research has shown that individuals who reported having performance goals shared less information with partners compared with those who reported having mastery goals (e.g., Poortvliet et al., 2007). Darnon and colleagues (2006) found that mastery goals are related to epistemic regulation whereas performance goals are related to relational regulation, suggesting that the induction of mastery goals during group activities may attenuate the cost of social comparison. To promote mastery goals, instructors should continually emphasize the importance of learning and growth over grades.

Additionally, feedback from teachers and peers should focus on students' growth in relation to their past competence, and normative comparisons should be avoided. One strategy to help students view their group work from a growth mindset perspective is to provide them with constructive strategies such as those described in strategy 4 (e.g., criticizing ideas but not people). The focus is not on the person's ability but on the understanding of the task.

Another way to increase student learning in collaborative contexts and attenuate the potential cost of social loafing is to help them see the value in the task and in working in a group. Prior work has shown that when students have a higher task and group value, they are more likely to engage in the task (Karau & Williams, 1993). Telling students how to approach or engage in the task is one part of the puzzle but the other parts involve telling students why they are engaging in the task and the benefits that they gain from working together.

Strategy 6: Build Social and Cognitive Factors That Support Collaboration into the Task Design

Cognitive processes such as reexposure, retrieval practice, error-correction, and explanation-generation are some of the key mechanisms underlying successful collaboration. Instructional tasks should be designed such that the cognitive processes that underlie good collaboration are key features. For example, programming is a task that often involves a significant amount of debugging and can benefit from learning collaboratively. Likewise, science concepts that involve learning about cause and effect often require generating explanations and inferences and could benefit from collaboration. Tasks that require rote learning or memorization should be avoided because they are likely to cause inhibition rather than facilitation. Key social processes such as sharing joint attention, building common ground, and negotiating multiple perspectives can also be incorporated into task design. For example, one could have students first complete an assignment individually that provides background knowledge for the collaborative task, thereby creating a shared knowledge source that students can draw from when building common ground during problem-solving (e.g., Gadgil & Nokes-Malach, 2012).

These strategies could be used alone or in combination to facilitate collaborative benefits and minimize the costs. We advocate that instructors adopt an active measurement perspective when implementing such strategies to see whether the instructional strategies are working as intended. That is, it would be helpful for the instructor to get feedback on whether the strategy is in fact improving learning by giving pre- and posttests. Also, surveys may be administered to see how students are relating to one another to resolve conflicts.

Conclusion

Much work remains in further integrating the social/cognitive, educational, and sociocultural approaches and the variety of methods, results, and mechanisms reviewed in this chapter. Bringing together these approaches is a first step toward future theoretical innovation and empirical tests to better understand how the cognitive and social mechanisms are interrelated. Research on collaborative learning presents a unique opportunity to construct a more general theory of learning that incorporates multiple psychological mechanisms working at different levels of analysis, including both the individual and the group.

References

Andersson, J. & Rönnberg, J. (1995). Recall suffers from collaboration: Joint recall effects of friendship and task complexity. *Applied Cognitive Psychology*, *9*(3), 199–211.

Arthur, W., Jr., Day, E. A., Bennett W., Jr., McNelly, T. L., & Jordan, J. A. (1997). Dyadic versus individual training protocols: Loss and reacquisition of a complex skill. *Journal of Applied Psychology*, *82*(5), 783–791.

Barber, S. J., Rajaram, S., & Aron, A. (2010). When two is too many: Collaborative encoding impairs memory. *Memory and Cognition*, *38*(3), 255–264.

Barron, B. (2000). Achieving coordination in collaborative problem-solving groups. *The Journal of the Learning Sciences*, *9*(4), 403–436.

(2003). When smart groups fail. *The Journal of the Learning Sciences*, *12*(3), 307–359.

Basden, B. H., Basden, D. R., Bryner, S., & Thomas III, R. L. (1997). A comparison of group and individual remembering: Does collaboration disrupt retrieval strategies? *Journal of Experimental Psychology: Learning, Memory, and Cognition*, *23*(5), 1176–1189.

Basden, D. R., Basden, B. H., & Galloway, B. C. (1977). Inhibition with part-list cuing: Some tests of the item strength hypothesis. *Journal of Experimental Psychology: Human Learning and Memory*, *3*, 100–108.

Bloodgood, J. W. (2002). Quintilian: A classic educator speaks to the writing process. *Reading, Research, and Instruction*, *42*(1), 30–43.

Blumen, H. M. & Stern, Y. (2011). Short-term and long-term collaboration benefits on individual recall in younger and older adults. *Memory and Cognition*, *39*(1), 147–154.

Brown, J. S., Collins, A., & Duguid, P. (1989). Situated cognition and the culture of learning. *Educational Researcher*, *18*, 32–42.

Buchs, C., Butera, F., Mugny, G., & Darnon, C. (2004). Conflict elaboration and cognitive outcomes. *Theory into Practice*, *43*, 23–30.

Butera, F. & Darnon, C. (2017). Competence assessment, social comparison, and conflict regulation. In A. J. Elliot & C. S. Dweck (eds.), *Handbook of competence and motivation: Theory and application* (pp. 192–213). New York: Guilford Press.

Canham, M. S., Wiley, J., & Mayer, R. E. (2012). When diversity in training improves dyadic problem solving. *Applied Cognitive Psychology*, *26*, 421–430.

Chi, M. T. H. (2009). Active-constructive-interactive: A conceptual framework for differentiating learning activities. *Topics in Cognitive Science*, *1*(1), 73–105.

Chi, M. T. H., Bassok, M., Lewis, M. W., Reimann, P., & Glaser, R. (1989). Self-explanations: How students study and use examples in learning to solve problems. *Cognitive Science*, *13*, 145–182.

Chi, M. T. H., de Leeuw, N., Chiu, M. H., & LaVancher, C. (1994). Eliciting self-explanations improves understanding. *Cognitive Science*, *18*, 439–477.

Chi, M. T. H. & Wiley, R. (2014). The ICAP framework: Linking cognitive engagement to active learning outcomes. *Educational Psychologist*, *49*(4), 219–243

Clark, H. H. & Brennan, S. E. (1991). Grounding in communication. In L. B. Resnick, J. M. Levine, & S. D. Teasley (eds.), *Perspectives on socially shared cognition* (pp. 127–149). Washington, DC: American Psychological Association.

Cohen, G. L., Garcia, J., Apfel, N., & Master, A. (2006). Reducing the racial achievement gap: A social-psychological intervention. *Science*, *313*, 1307–1310.

Collaros, P. A. & Anderson, L. R. (1969). Effect of perceived expertness upon creativity of members of brainstorming groups. *Journal of Applied Psychology, 53*(2), 159–163.

Congleton, A. R. & Rajaram, S. (2011). The influence of learning methods on collaboration: Prior repeated retrieval enhances retrieval organization, abolishes collaborative inhibition, and promotes post-collaborative memory. *Journal of Experimental Psychology: General, 140*(4), 535–551.

Crooks, S. M., Klein, J. D., Savenye, W., & Leader, L. (1998). Effects of cooperative and individual learning during learner-controlled computer-based instruction. *The Journal of Experimental Education, 66*(3), 223–244.

Darnon, C., Buchs, C., Butera, F. (2002). Epistemic and relational conflicts in sharing identical vs. complementary information during cooperative learning. *Swiss Journal of Psychology, 61*(3), 139–151.

Darnon, C., Muller, D., Schrager, S. M., Pannuzzo, N., & Butera, F. (2006). Mastery and performance goals predict epistemic and relational conflict regulation. *Journal of Educational Psychology, 98*(4), 766–776.

De Dreu, C. K. & Weingart, L. R. (2003). Task versus relationship conflict, team performance, and team member satisfaction: A meta-analysis. *Journal of Applied Psychology, 88*(4), 741–749.

Deutsch, M. (1949). A theory of cooperation and competition. *Human relations, 2*, 129–152. (1973). *The resolution of conflict.* New Haven, CT: Yale University Press.

Diehl, M. & Stroebe, W. (1987). Productivity loss in brainstorming groups: Toward the solution of a riddle. *Journal of Personality and Social Psychology, 53*, 497–509.

Dillenbourg, P., Baker, M., Blaye, A., & O'Malley, C. (1996). The evolution of research on collaborative learning. In E. Spada & P. Reiman (eds.), *Learning in humans and machine: Towards an interdisciplinary learning science* (pp. 189–211). Oxford: Elsevier.

Doise, W. & Mugny, G. (1984). *The social development of the intellect.* International Series in Experimental Social Psychology, vol. 10. London: Pergamon Press.

Engle, R. A. & Conant, F. R. (2002). Guiding principles for fostering productive disciplinary engagement: Explaining an emergent argument in a community of learners classroom. *Cognition and Instruction, 20*(4), 399–483.

Ericsson, K. A. & Kintsch, W. (1995). Long term working memory. *Psychological Review, 102*, 211–245.

Finlay, F., Hitch, G. J., & Meudell, P. R. (2000). Mutual inhibition in collaborative recall: Evidence for a retrieval-based account. *Journal of Experimental Psychology: Learning, Memory, and Cognition, 26*(6), 1556–1567.

Gadgil, S. & Nokes-Malach, T. J. (2012). Overcoming collaborative inhibition through error correction: A classroom experiment. *Applied Cognitive Psychology, 26*(3), 410–420.

Geen, R. G. (1983). Evaluation apprehension and the social facilitation/inhibition of learning. *Motivation and Emotion, 7*(2), 203–212.

Goldbeck, S. L. & El-Moslimany, H. (2013). Developmental approaches to collaborative learning. In C. E. Hmelo-Silver, A. Chinn, C. K. K. Chan, & A. M. O'Donnel (eds.), *The international handbook of collaborative learning* (pp. 41–56). New York and London: Routledge.

Greeno, J. G. (1998). The situativity of knowing, learning, and research. *American Psychologist, 53*, 5–26.

Greeno, J. & The Middle-School Mathematics through Applications Project Group (MMAP). (1997). Theories and practices of thinking and learning to think. *American Journal of Education*, *106*(1), 85–126.

Hadwin, A. F., Järvelä, S., & Miller, M. (2011). Self-regulated, co-regulated, and socially shared regulation of learning. *Handbook of self-regulation of learning and performance*, *30*, 65–84.

Hakkarainen, K., Paavola, S., Kangas, K., & Seitama-Hakkarainen, P. (2013). Sociocultural perspectives on collaborative learning: Toward collaborative knowledge creation. In C. E. Hmelo-Silver, C., Chinn, C. K. K. Chan, & A. M. O'Donnell (eds.), *International handbook of collaborative learning* (pp. 57–73). New York: Routledge.

Harkins, S. G. & Petty, R. E. (1982). Effects of task difficulty and task uniqueness on social loafing. *Journal of Personality and Social Psychology*, *43*(6), 1214–1229.

Harris, C. B., Barnier, A. J., & Sutton, J. (2013). Shared encoding and the costs and benefits of collaborative recall. *Journal of Experimental Psychology: Learning, Memory, and Cognition*, *39*(1), 183.

Harris, C. B., Paterson, H. M., & Kemp, R. I. (2008). Collaborative recall and collective memory: What happens when we remember together? *Memory*, *16*(3), 213–230.

Harris, A., Yuill, N., & Luckin, R. (2008). The influence of context-specific and dispositional achievement goals on children's paired collaborative interaction. *British Journal of Educational Psychology*, *78*(3), 355–374.

Harris, C. B., Keil, P. G., Sutton, J., Barnier, A. J., & McIlwain, D. J. F. (2011). We remember, we forget: Collaborative remembering in older couples. *Discourse Processes*, *48*, 267–303.

Hill, G. W. (1982). Group versus individual performance: Are n + 1 heads better than one. *Psychological Bulletin*, *91*(3), 517–539.

Hmelo-Silver, C. E., Chinn, C. A., Chan, C. K. K., & O'Donnell, A. (eds.). (2013). *The international handbook of collaborative learning*. New York: Routledge.

Jeong, H. (2013). Verbal data analysis for understanding interactions. In C. E. Hmelo-Silver, C., Chinn, C. K. K. Chan, & A. M. O'Donnell (eds.), *International handbook of collaborative learning* (pp. 57–73). New York: Routledge.

Johnson, D. W. & Johnson, R. T. (1989). *Cooperation and competition: Theory and research*. Edina, MN: Interaction Book Company.

(1994). *Learning together and alone: Cooperative, competitive, and individualistic learning*, 4th edn. Needham Heights, MA: Allyn and Bacon.

(2009). An educational psychology success story: Social interdependence theory and cooperative learning. *Educational Researcher*, *39*(5), 365–379.

Johnson, D. W., Johnson, R. T., & Smith, K. A. (1998). *Active learning: Cooperation in the college classroom*. Edina, MN: Interaction Book Company.

Johnson, D. W., Johnson, R. T., & Smith, K. (2007). The state of cooperative learning in postsecondary and professional settings. *Educational Psychology Review*, *19*(1), 15–29.

Karau, S. J. & Williams, K. D. (1993). Social loafing: A meta-analytic review and theoretical integration. *Journal of Personality and Social Psychology*, *65*(4), 681–706.

Kelley, M. R. & Wright, D. B. (2010). Obtaining representative nominal groups. *Behavior Research Methods*, *42*(1), 36–41.

Kerr, N. L. & Tindale, R. S. (2004). Group performance and decision making. *Annual Review of Psychology*, *55*, 623–655.

Kim, Y. (2008). The contribution of collaborative and individual tasks to the acquisition of L2 vocabulary. *The Modern Language Journal, 92*(1), 114–130.

Kirschner, F., Paas, F., & Kirschner, P. A. (2009a). A cognitive load approach to collaborative learning: United brains for complex tasks. *Educational Psychology Review, 21*(1), 31–42.

(2009b). Individual and group based learning from complex cognitive tasks: Effects on retention and transfer efficiency. *Computers in Human Behavior, 25*(2), 306–314.

(2011). Task complexity as a driver for collaborative learning efficiency: the collective working-memory effect. *Applied Cognitive Psychology, 25*(4), 615–624.

Kolloffel, B., Eysink, T. H., & de Jong, T. (2011). Comparing the effects of representational tools in collaborative and individual inquiry learning. *International Journal of Computer-Supported Collaborative Learning, 6*(2), 223–251.

Kravitz, D. A. & Martin, B. (1986). Ringelmann rediscovered: The original article. *Journal of Personality and Social Psychology, 50*(5), 936–941.

Latané, B., Williams, K., & Harkins, S. (1979). Many hands make light the work: The causes and consequences of social loafing. *Journal of Personality and Social Psychology, 37*(6), 822–832.

Laughlin, P. R., Carey, H. R., & Kerr, N. L. (2008). Group-to-individual problem-solving transfer. *Group Processes and Intergroup Relations, 11*(3), 319–330.

Laughlin, P. R., Hatch, E. C., Silver, J. S., & Boh, L. (2006). Groups perform better than the best individuals on letters-to-numbers problems: Effects of group size. *Journal of Personality and Social Psychology, 90*(4), 644–651.

Lave, J. & Wenger, E. (1991). *Situated learning: Legitimate peripheral participation.* New York: Cambridge University Press.

Leidner, D. E. & Fuller, M. (1997). Improving student learning of conceptual information: GSS supported collaborative learning vs. individual constructive learning. *Decision Support Systems, 20*(2), 149–163.

Lewin, K. (1935). *A dynamic theory of personality.* New York: McGraw-Hill.

(1948). *Resolving social conflict.* New York: Harper.

Lorge, I., Fox, D., Davitz, J., & Brenner, M. (1958). A survey of studies contrasting the quality of group performance and individual performance. *Psychological Bulletin, 55,* 337–372.

Matsui, T., Kakuyama, T., & Onglatco, M. U. (1987). Effects of goals and feedback on performance in groups. *Journal of Applied Psychology, 72,* 407–415.

Meade, M. L., Nokes, T. J., & Morrow, D. G. (2009). Expertise promotes facilitation on a collaborative memory task. *Memory, 17*(1), 39–48.

Meade., M. L. & Roediger, H. L. (2002). Explorations in the social contagion of memory. *Memory and Cognition, 30(7),* 995–1009.

Mevarech, Z. R. (1985). The effects of cooperative mastery learning strategies on mathematics achievement. *The Journal of Educational Research, 78*(6), 372–377.

Mugny, G., De Paolis, P., & Carugati, F. (1984). Social regulations in cognitive development. In W. Doise & A. Palmonari (eds.), *Social interaction in individual development* (pp. 127–146). Cambridge: Cambridge University Press.

Mullen, B. (1983). Operationalizing the effect of the group on the individual: A self-attention perspective. *Journal of Experimental Social Psychology, 19*(4), 295–322.

(1987). Self-attention theory. In B. Mullen & G. R. Goethals (eds.), *Theories of group behaviour* (pp. 125–146). New York: Springer-Verlag.

Nokes-Malach, T. J., Meade, M. L., & Morrow, D. G. (2012). The effect of expertise on collaborative problem solving. *Thinking and Reasoning*, *18*(1), 32–58.

Nokes-Malach, T. J., Richey, J. E., & Gadgil, S. (2015). When is it better to learn together? Insights from research on collaborative learning. *Educational Psychology Review*, *27*(4), 645–656.

O'Donnell, A. M. (1999). Structuring dyadic interaction through scripted cooperation. In A. M. O'Donnell & A. King (eds.), *Cognitive perspectives on peer learning* (pp. 179–196). Mahwah, NJ: Lawrence Erlbaum.

O'Donnell, A. M. & Hmelo-Silver, H. E. (2013). What is collaborative learning: An overview. In C. E. Hmelo-Silver, C. A. Chinn, C. K. K. Chan, & A. O'Donnell (eds.), *The international handbook of collaborative learning* (pp. 1–15). New York: Routledge.

Okada, T. & Simon, H. A. (1997). Collaborative discovery in a scientific domain. *Cognitive Science*, *21*(2), 109–146.

Pereira-Pasarin, L. & Rajaram, S. (2011). Study repetition and divided attention: Effects of encoding manipulations on collaborative inhibition in group recall. *Memory and Cognition*, *39*, 968–976.

Petty, R. E., Harkins, S. G., Williams, K. D., & Latane, B. (1977). The effects of group size on cognitive effort and evaluation. *Personality and Social Psychology Bulletin*, *3*(4), 579–582.

Piaget, J. (1932). *The language and thought of the child*, 2nd edn. London: Routledge and Kegan Paul.

(1950). *The psychology of intelligence*. London: Routledge and Kegan Paul.

(1975/1985). *The equilibration of cognitive structures: The central problem of intellectual development*. Chicago, IL: University of Chicago Press.

Paulus, P. B. & Yang, H. C. (2000). Idea generation in groups: A basis for creativity in organizations. *Organizational Behavior and Human Decision Processes*, *82*, 76–87.

Poortvliet, P. M., Janssen, O., Van Yperen, N. W., & Van de Vliert, E. (2007). Achievement goals and interpersonal behavior: How mastery and performance goals shape information exchange. *Personality and Social Psychology Bulletin*, *33*(10), 1435–1447.

Rajaram, S. & Pereira-Pasarin, L. P. (2010). Collaborative memory: Cognitive research and theory. *Perspectives on Psychological Science*, *5*(6), 649–663.

Ringelmann, M. (1913). Recherches sur les moteurs animes: Travail de rhomme [Research on animate sources of power: The work of man]. *Annales de I'Institut National Agronomique*, *12*, 1–40.

Roediger, H. L. & Butler, A. C. (2011). The critical role of retrieval practice in long-term retention. *Trends in Cognitive Sciences*, *15*(1), 20–27.

Roediger, H. L. & Karpicke, J. D. (2006). The power of testing memory: Basic research and implications for educational practice. *Perspectives on Psychological Science*, *1*, 181–210.

Roediger, H. L., Meade, M. L., & Bergman, E. T. (2001). Social contagion of memory. *Psychonomic Bulletin and Review*, *8*(2), 365–371.

Roschelle, J. (1992). Learning by collaborating: Convergent conceptual change. *Journal of the Learning Sciences*, *2*(3), 235–276.

Roschelle, J. & Teasley, S. D. (1995). The construction of shared knowledge in collaborative problem solving. In C. O'Malley (ed.), *Computer-Supported Collaborative Learning* (pp. 69–197). Berlin: Springer-Verlag.

Rummel, N. & Spada, H. (2005). Learning to collaborate: An instructional approach to promoting collaborative problem solving in computer-mediated settings. *Journal of the Learning Sciences, 14*, 201–241.

Sampson, V. & Clark, D. (2009). The impact of collaboration on the outcomes of scientific argumentation. *Science Education, 93*(3), 448–484.

Sawyer, R. D. (2013). Learning to walk the talk: Designing a teacher leadership EdD program as a laboratory of practice. *Planning and Changing, 44*(3/4), 208–220.

Schwartz, D. L. (1995). The emergence of abstract representations in dyad problem solving. *The Journal of the Learning Sciences, 4*, 321–354.

Schwarz, B. B., Neuman, Y., & Biezuner, S. (2000). Two wrongs may make a right . . . if they argue together! *Cognition and Instruction, 18*(4), 461–494.

Sherman, D. K., Hartson, K. A., Binning, K. R., Purdie-Vaughns, V., Garcia, J., Taborsky-Barba, S., . . . Cohen, G. L. (2013). Deflecting the trajectory and changing the narrative: How self-affirmation affects academic performance and motivation under identity threat. *Journal of Personality and Social Psychology, 104*(4), 591–618.

Slavin, R. E. (1995). *Cooperative learning: Theory, research, and practice*, 2nd edn. Boston, MA: Allyn & Bacon.

Slavin, R., Leavey, M., & Madden, N. (1984). Combining cooperative learning and individualized instruction: Effects on student mathematics achievement, attitudes, and behaviors. *Elementary School Journal, 84*, 409–422.

Springer, L., Stanne, M. E., & Donovan, S. S. (1999). Effects of small-group learning on undergraduates in science, mathematics, engineering, and technology: A meta-analysis. *Review of Educational Research, 69*(1), 21–51.

Souvignier, E. & Kronenberger, J. (2007). Cooperative learning in third graders' jigsaw groups for mathematics and science with and without questioning training. *British Journal of Educational Psychology, 77*(4), 755–771.

Steiner, I. D. (1966). Models for inferring the relationships between group size and potential group productivity. *Behavioral Science, 11*, 273–283.

(1972). *Group processes and productivity*. New York: Academic Press.

Stevens, R. J. & Slavin, R. E. (1995). Effects of a cooperative learning approach in reading and writing on academically handicapped students. *The Elementary School Journal, 95*(3), 241–262.

Stevens, R. J., Slavin, R. E., & Farnish, A. M. (1991). The effects of cooperative learning and direct instruction in reading comprehension strategies on main idea identification. *Journal of Educational Psychology, 83*(1), 8–16.

Stewart, G. L. (2006). A meta-analytic review of relationships between team design features and team performance. *Journal of management, 32*(1), 29–55.

Teasley, S. D. (1995). The role of talk in children's peer collaborations. *Developmental Psychology, 31* (2), 207–220.

Teasley, S. D. & Roschelle, J. (1993). Constructing a joint problem space: The computer as a tool for sharing knowledge. In S. P. Lajoie & S. J. Derry (eds.), *Computers as cognitive tools* (pp. 229–258). Hillsdale, NJ: Lawrence Erlbaum.

Tudge, J. (1989). When collaboration leads to regression: Some negative consequences of socio-cognitive conflict. *European Journal of Social Psychology, 19*(2), 123–138.

Tudge, J. R. H. & Winterhoff, P. A. (1993). Vygotsky, Piaget, and Bandura: Perspectives on the relations between the social world and cognitive development. *Human Development, 36*, 61–81.

Vanderlinde, R. & van Braak, J. (2010). The gap between educational research and practice: Views of teachers, school leaders, intermediaries and researchers, *British Educational Research Journal, 36*(2), 299–316.

Voiklis, J. & Corter, J. E. (2012). Conventional wisdom: Negotiating conventions of reference enhances category learning. *Cognitive Science, 36*(4), 607–634.

Vygotsky, L. S. (1978). *Mind in society: The development of higher psychological processes.* Cambridge, MA: Harvard University Press.

Webb, N. M., Troper, J. D., & Fall, R. (1995). Constructive activity and learning in collaborative small groups. *Journal of Educational Psychology, 87,* 406–423.

Weigold, A., Russell, E. J., & Natera, S. N. (2014). Correction of false memory for associated word lists by collaborating groups. *The American Journal of Psychology, 127*(2), 183–190.

Weldon, M.S. & Bellinger, K.D. (1997). Collective memory: Collaborative and individual processes in remembering. *Journal of Experimental Psychology: Learning, Memory, and Cognition, 23,* 1160–1175.

Wright, D. B. (2007). Calculating nominal group statistics in collaboration studies. *Behavior Research Methods, 39,* 460–470.

21 Self-Explaining

Learning About Principles and Their Application

Alexander Renkl and Alexander Eitel

Introduction

Imagine a graduate student who has conducted experiments on how to exploit cognitive science effects for meaningful learning. She has obtained nice results and wants to write a first manuscript. She has already read much of the APA manual, and she had a look at Internet sites providing tips on scientific writing. Hence, she has already "heard" about principles of scientific writing such as "preparing hypotheses in the introduction," "concise style," and "parallel construction." However, she is unsure how to apply such principles to her own paper. Her advisor gave her two recently submitted, well-written papers on a similar topic that were first-authored by fellow graduate students.

Such "model submissions" will certainly prove useful for our graduate student. However, when trying to write concisely or to use parallel construction, she cannot merely copy passages from the model papers and just replace some concepts. In fact, she must clarify to herself which passages were written concisely, where parallel constructions were used, and how the hypotheses were prepared in the introduction. Ideally, she will even notice and explain to herself which passages could have been made even more concise, where an opportunity for parallel construction has been overlooked, and which hypothesis has been suboptimally prepared. In short, our student has to self-explain several model papers in order to understand how abstract principles of scientific writing can be instantiated in a problem case (here: a manuscript).

This introductory example illustrates several important issues: (1) The "self" in self-explanation has a double meaning; first, the explanations are provided by the learners themselves (in contrast to instructional explanation) and, second, these explanations are provided for themselves (in contrast to explanations for teaching something to somebody). (2) Self-explaining should help learners acquire cognitive skills that are based on an understanding of domain principles and their application. (3) Self-explanations can in particular help interrelating principles and concrete cases. A self-explaining student learns how to "interpret" (here: evaluate) cases (here: sample manuscripts) in terms of the relevant principles and how abstract principles can be applied in concrete cases. (4) Our introductory example also shows that providing good self-explanations is a challenging task. Hence, many students might need support to provide self-explanations that really help them learn (e.g., Renkl et al., 1998; Rittle-Johnson, Loehr, & Durkin, 2017).

One frequently employed support procedure is the use of self-explanation prompts. Figure 21.1 provides such a prompt. This screenshot is taken from an example-based learning environment for (mathematics) teachers in which they can learn how to effectively design worked examples for high school instruction (Hilbert et al., 2008). The teachers learn about design principles by comparing worked examples for high school students that conform or do not conform to these principles. In Figure 21.1, they learn about the "(meaningful) building-blocks principle" (Renkl, 2014b), which states that, in the beginning of skill acquisition, the students should be confronted with examples in which single solution steps are clearly marked so that the student can understand the rationale for these single steps (see right side of Figure 21.1); other formulae (see left side of Figure 21.1) might be computationally more efficient but they are very hard to understand for students just beginning to learn about a mathematical topic. Note also that the teachers are guided in processing these two examples by a prompt that requires them to explain which example better fosters students' understanding and why (see lower left side of Figure 21.1).

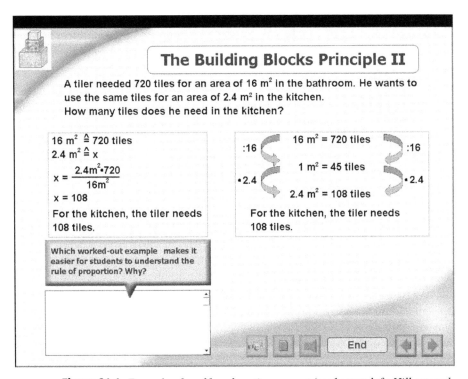

Figure 21.1 *Example of a self-explanation prompt (see bottom left; Hilbert et al., 2008. Reprinted with permission)*

In particular, the "why" part of this question should lead the teachers to interrelate the "(meaningful) building-blocks principle" and the example cases at hand.

In the following, we present the historical roots of the self-explanation effect and explain why we focus on principles-based self-explanations. We discuss the learning domains for which such self-explanations might be a beneficial learning activity and we present a theory about why this is the case. A major part of this chapter discusses research that informs how to effectively implement learning by self-explaining. We also outline promising lines for further research on self-explanations. Finally, we summarize what practice recommendations can be provided on the basis of the present state-of-the-art.

The Self-Explanation Effect: Its Historical Roots

Chi and colleagues (e.g., Chi et al., 1989) analyzed students' processing of worked examples (domain: Newton's laws) and they related interindividual differences in this processing to later problem-solving performance on transfer problems. These authors found that the successful problem-solvers had provided more self-explanations while studying the worked examples' solution procedures. This finding was called the self-explanation effect. VanLehn, Jones, and Chi (1992) summarized this effect in the following four findings: "1. Good solvers uttered more self-explanations during example studying. 2. Their self-monitoring statements during example studying were more accurate. 3. They made fewer references to examples during problem solving. 4. Their references to examples during problem solving were more accurate" (p. 8). The self-explanations mentioned in the first finding included inferences about operations and their preconditions, their consequences, and their goals; they also referred to the meaning of mathematical expressions. Many of these explanations included references to the laws, concepts, and definitions described in an introductory text on Newton's laws. Early studies on self-explanations saw their primary function as filling in the details that the usual worked examples from textbooks omit and relating general knowledge about the domain (i.e., about domain concepts and principles) to the specific examples at hand (e.g., Chi & Bassok, 1989; Chi et al., 1989, VanLehn et al., 1992).

The self-explanation effect was initially established just by correlational findings (e.g., Chi et al., 1989; Renkl, 1997). Subsequent studies also provided experimental evidence for this effect by showing, for example, that students prompted to self-explain worked examples had better final learning outcomes than nonprompted students (e.g., Hilbert & Renkl, 2009; Atkinson, Renkl, & Merrill, 2003). Such effects were typically found in conjunction with learning outcomes assessed via conceptual knowledge (i.e., understanding domain concepts and principles) and/or problem-solving performance on transfer problems (e.g., Aleven & Koedinger, 2002; De Caro & Rittle-Johnson, 2012; Hilbert & Renkl, 2009; McEldoon, Durkin, & Rittle-Johnson, 2012).

The construct of self-explanations has attracted considerable attention since the seminal studies by Chi and colleagues (e.g., Chi et al., 1989). It was used in studies on additional learning methods such as learning from text (Chi et al., 1994), learning from visual displays (e.g., Ainsworth & Loizou, 2003; De Koning et al., 2011), learning from (science) simulations (Morrison et al., 2015), or game-based learning (Johnson & Mayer, 2010). Having students self-explain is now recommended in educational practice guides (e.g., Dunlosky et al., 2013; Pashler et al., 2007).

As use of this construct has become so widespread, its meaning has changed. For example, Chi (2000) now sees (at least some) self-explanations as the process by which learners revise and improve their yet imperfect mental models. Presumably due to the widely varying use of this construct, its recent characterizations are rather general such as "inferences by the learner that go beyond the given information" (Rittle-Johnson et al., 2017) or explaining "the content of a lesson to themselves by elaborating upon the instructional material presented" (Fiorella & Mayer, 2015, p. 125). If one relies on such definitions, it is hard to draw the boundaries between other established constructs in research on learning such as "elaborative inferences" (in text learning; Singer, 1994) or "elaboration strategies" (Weinstein & Mayer, 1986). It is also questionable whether all the phenomena labeled self-*explanations* in previous research can be justifiably called *explanation* (for discussions about the concept of explanation, see, e.g., Keil, 2006; Kiel, 1999; Lombrozo, 2012).

Given that even the initial characterization of self-explanation already included relatively heterogeneous phenomena (see the four findings reported by VanLehn et al., 1992) and given that the subsequent extensions led to very general characterizations, there would appear to be little justification for discussing the learning effects of self-explanations and their use in (classroom) instruction on a general level. It is highly probable that different types of self-explanations have different functions, lead to better learning via different mechanisms, and should not be regarded as a unitary construct when providing practice recommendations. In the next section, we will outline which type of self-explanations we focus on in this chapter and what important function such self-explanations fulfill.

Principle-Based Self-Explanations

We focus on principle-based self-explanations (Renkl, 1997): Learners "self-explain" a step in a problem solution (e.g., physics problem) or a feature of an object (e.g., the appearance of an animal) in reference to an underlying principle (e.g., one of Newton's laws or mimicry). Such self-explanations were part of the initial self-explanation concept (e.g., VanLehn et al., 1992). They can also reasonably be called *explanations*. Although the concept of explanation can have different meanings (e.g., Keil, 2006; Lombrozo, 2012), explaining a case in terms of underlying principles is a quite prototypical case of explanation. This type of explanation fits the subsumption and unification accounts of explanation (e.g., Lombrozo, 2012). These accounts regard a case as explained when it is subsumed under a more general pattern (e.g., Newton's laws or the general strategy of mimicry).

Domains of Application

Principle-based self-explanations are important because they help solve the educational problem of how to enable learners to apply general, learned principles to new problem cases (Schalk, Saalbach, & Stern, 2016). In most subjects taught in school, there are important principles to be learned as a mental tool for analysis and problem-solving. For example, students should learn about theorems in mathematics, about laws in physics and chemistry, about general biological phenomena (e.g., mimicry), about the principle of separation of powers in social studies, or about different types of ethical views or arguments in religious and ethics classes (e.g., deontological and consequentialist views or arguments). Hence, the concept of principle-based self-explanation (in the following mostly just called self-explanation) is relevant to learning in diverse school subjects.

Of course, fostering principle-based self-explanations only makes sense in learning domains in which general principles apply. In their recent review on prompted self-explanations, Rittle-Johnson and Loehr (2017) came to the conclusion that self-explanations work in only those domains in which general principles predominate and where there are not too many exceptions to those principles. For example, self-explanations are of rather less use in second-language learning when there are numerous exceptions to general grammar rules (Wylie, Koedinger, & Mitamura 2010; Wylie et al., 2011).

To prevent any misunderstanding of this restriction to principle-based domains, it should be noted that learning via principle-based self-explanations has been successfully employed in areas that initially would not appear to be principled. For example, prompting principle-based self-explanations helps with acquiring the technique of concept mapping as a learning strategy (e.g., Hilbert & Renkl, 2009), learning to collaborate (Rummel, Spada, & Hauser, 2009), or learning to argue in a scientifically sound way (Hefter et al., 2014). In such cases, it is important to identify powerful heuristics ("rules of thumb") as principles whose implementation genuinely support learning by concept mapping, collaborating productively, or arguing in a differentiated way.

Principle-Based Self-Explanations: Theoretical Assumptions

The following theory is based on work by Renkl (e.g., 2014a, b, 2015) that mainly focused on self-explanations while learning from worked examples. However, the theoretical assumptions on the effects of principle-based self-explanations for worked examples can be generalized to other learning methods such as learning by problem-solving.

As already mentioned, principle-based self-explanations serve the function of interconnecting knowledge about principles and problem cases in which these principles apply. Multiple example cases are usually considered when learning via self-explanations. These cases can be mathematical problems to be solved (e.g., Aleven & Koedinger, 2002; McEldoon et al., 2012), video clips of effective classroom instruction (e.g., Seidel, Blomberg, & Renkl, 2013; Moreno & Valdez, 2007), or worked examples of effectively designed instructional materials for high school instruction (see Figure 21.1; Cho & Lee, 2013; Hilbert et al., 2008; Schworm & Renkl, 2006). By self-explaining multiple cases, the learners finally acquire a knowledge structure where a principle and multiple cases are represented in an interconnected manner (Renkl 2014b, 2015). Figure 21.2 illustrates such a knowledge structure for the case of a principle from probability theory (i.e., the multiplication law). A goal during the initial stages of knowledge acquisition is that learners have represented principles, multiple problem cases, and the interrelations between the principles and the problem cases as shown in Figure 21.2 (e.g., Nokes-Malach et al., 2013; Renkl, 2015). The learners should know not only that a problem "somehow" relates to a principle but also how it corresponds exactly to a principle (in Figure 21.2 the multiple arrows connecting the principle and the problem cases represent such mapping in detail). Such interconnected knowledge enables the learners to interpret problem cases in terms of the underlying principles, and they know how principles can be applied or instantiated to solve problem cases.

Note that, in the beginning, a principle might first be represented just as a (relatively isolated) fact (e.g., multiplication rule in probability: p (A and B) = p(A) × p(B)). Only after self-explaining multiple example cases and mapping different entities from, let us say, the mathematical examples' different cover stories (e.g., red marbles or a certain defect in a product), have the students learned that different entities can correspond to a formula element (e.g., "p(A)" can correspond to red marbles or a certain defect). Now, the representation of the principle has become schematic. A schematic representation means that there are abstract slots that can be filled in with the specifics of (new) example cases. In other words, different concrete cases can be interpreted and solved by a principle's schema-like representation.

Given that a learner has acquired a knowledge structure, as depicted in Figure 21.2, there are two main routes by which principles can be applied to transfer problems (e.g., Didierjean & Cauzinille-Marmèche, 1998; Ross, 1989; see Figure 21.3).

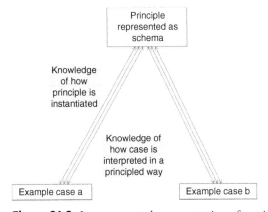

Figure 21.2 *Interconnected representation of a principle and multiple example cases (after Renkl, 2017b, reprinted with permission from Springer Nature)*

Note that multiple example cases typically means more than two cases; for the sake of clarity, just two example cases are depicted here.

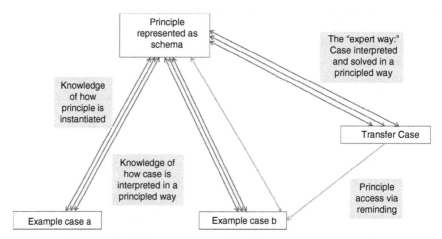

Figure 21.3 *Two routes of transfer based on an interconnected representation of a principle and multiple cases (after Renkl, 2017b. Reprinted with permission from Springer Nature)*

The direct route means that learners can interpret transfer cases directly in terms of the underlying principles. In other words, they can "see through" the surface features (e.g., numbers and objects in a mathematical word problem) and select the correct principles (e.g., mathematical theorems) to interpret and solve transfer problems (Chi & VanLehn 2012). This route usually requires relatively high learner expertise.

Analogical reasoning research has shown that there is also an indirect route (e.g., Ross, 1989). Many learners cannot directly activate the appropriate principle when they encounter a problem but they are reminded of a similar problem. If this similar problem is represented in relation to the underlying principle, the learners can obtain indirect access to the relevant principle, that is, by the "detour" via a similar problem. When relating these assumptions to the type of typical learning goals assessed in studies on self-explanations, self-explanations should lead to better transfer performance and better conceptual knowledge as the representation of the principles becomes more elaborate.

In summary, principle-based self-explanations increase the likelihood that principles and example cases will be represented in an interconnected manner. Thereby, the representation of the principle becomes schematic. New cases can be mapped to this schematic representation directly or via the detour of similar example cases (remindings).

Implementing Effective Learning by Self-Explaining

Although learning by (principle-based) self-explaining can be viewed as a generally effective method (Fiorella & Mayer, 2015; Rittle-Johnson et al., 2017), the details on how it is implemented determine its actual effects in a specific learning setting (see also Rittle-Johnson & Loehr, 2017). In the following five sections, we discuss exemplary research on important factors that moderate the effectiveness of learning by self-explaining and that should be taken into account when implementing this learning method.

Self-Explanation Prompts Providing Varying Degrees of Structure

As most learners do not spontaneously engage in principle-based self-explanations (e.g., Renkl, 1997), they need support. One support procedure is prompting self-explanations (see Figure 21.1 for such a prompt). Researchers have investigated a wide variety of different prompt types that differ in the amount of structure they provide for the learners (see Wylie & Chi, 2014). On the one end of the dimension (i.e., lowly structured), "generic" prompts are used that do not specify the specific information a learner should provide (i.e., prompts for a great variety of learning contents). For example, Wong, Lawson, and Keeves (2002) had their 9th grade students learn about the angle-in-a-semi-circle theorem (geometry) and its application. These authors compared a self-explanation condition to a control condition in which the students engaged in their usual study strategies. In the self-explanation condition, rather general prompts were used (e.g., "How does the new piece of information help me solve the sample problem?"). The self-explanation group outperformed the control group in a final posttest. This effect was primarily due to superior (far) transfer performance (problems where additional theorems had to be used).

On the other end of the dimension (i.e., highly structured), prompts constrain and, therefore, help the learners to provide principle-based self-explanations. For example, Atkinson and colleagues (2003) had their learners study worked examples from probability. After each solution step, the learners in the prompted self-explanation condition had to select from a list one of four probability principles that was applied in that specific solution step. In two experiments, such menu-based prompting (Wylie & Chi, 2014) fostered final performance on both near transfer problems (isomorphic to the examples presented during learning) and far transfer problems (with changes in the mathematical structure).

Many studies have successfully employed self-explanation prompts that are between the extremes just described. See, for example, the type of prompt displayed in Figure 21.1: "Which worked-out example makes it easier for students to understand the rule of proportion? Why?" This prompt is open (in the sense that there is no prestructured answer) but the prompt is tailored to the specific learning materials and the type of information expected is specified (Schworm & Renkl, 2006). Even more structured – but not yet fully structured, as in Atkinson and colleagues (2003) – is the type of assisting prompt used by Berthold and colleagues (Berthold, Eysink, & Renkl, 2009; Berthold & Renkl, 2009); answers to self-explanation prompts were initially supported by fill-in-the-blank self-explanations (see Figure 21.4). This type of prompting also fostered learning outcomes (Berthold et al., 2009).

The recent reviews on (prompting) self-explanations by Fiorella and Mayer (2015), Rittle-Johnson et al. (2017), and Wylie and Chi (2014) suggest that the more structured options are the "safer bets" to foster students' learning outcomes (see also van der Meij & de Jong, 2011). More open prompts may be too difficult to

5. Example Task: Mountainbike III

You and your friend take part in a two-day mountain bike course. Each day of the course the instructor brings along 5 helmets, each one of a different color (orange, silver, brown, red, and green). The helmets are handed out randomly and given back to the instructor at the end of the day.
What is the probability that you and your friend get the red and the green helmet on the first day of the course (it does not matter who gets which color)?

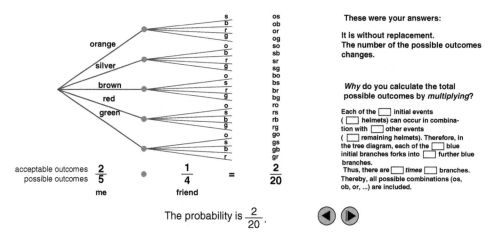

Figure 21.4 *Example of assisted prompting by using fill-in-the-blanks self-explanations (see bottom right; from Berthold & Renkl, 2009. Reprinted with permission from the American Psychological Association)*

answer correctly, meaning they may sometimes even have detrimental effects, at least on certain aspects of the learning outcomes (e.g., Berthold & Renkl, 2009: positive effect on conceptual knowledge but negative effect on procedural knowledge). Furthermore, an advantage of prompts with a highly prestructured answer format is that feedback on their correctness can be easily provided (Rittle-Johnson et al., 2017), as was, for example, done in Atkinson and colleagues (2003). A possible reason why Wong and colleagues (2002) detected positive effects from their open prompts may be that they provided a short training intervention to enable an adequate response to the prompts.

In summary, highly structured prompting procedures are usually preferable to prompt principle-based self-explanations. This is at least true when the students are not trained (or experienced) self-explainers, as was the case in most studies.

Self-Explanation Training Interventions

A variety of training approaches have been developed and tested (e.g., Bielaczyc, Pirolli, & Brown, 1995; McNamara, 2004). We discuss some training interventions that targeted, at least among others, principle-based self-explanations.

Hodds, Alcock, and Inglis (2014) as well as Renkl and colleagues (1998; Stark et al., 2002) have developed short-training interventions that can be applied within 20 minutes. During these training sessions, students are first informed about the importance of self-explanations. Second, a model shows them how to self-explain with one worked example from mathematics (Hodds et al.: proof; Renkl et al.: interest calculation). Third, the students practice self-explaining with another example. The students in the training conditions then continue to work without further guidance. The training approach adopted by Hodds and colleagues (2014) and by Renkl and colleagues (1998) fostered self-explanations (including principle-based self-explanations) in a later unguided example or proof study (see also Stark et al., 2002). The training interventions also fostered learning outcomes (Hodds et al.: proof interpretation; Renkl et al.: transfer problems in the area of interest calculation). In addition, Renkl and colleagues (1998) found that the overall benefits of the training intervention were greater for low-prior knowledge learners; Hodds and colleagues detected no such differential effectiveness with their training intervention.

Although these training interventions were successful, they are limited by the fact that the training is carried out working with the same type of problems presented later for learning by self-explaining. Hence, mere "intra-topic" transfer was required from the learners. It is an open question whether such training interventions can exert more general effects (e.g., when learning from examples from a different topic or even a different domain).

There is some evidence that transfer effects to different topics are achievable. Chi and VanLehn (2010) had their learners work in an intelligent tutoring system called "Pyrenees" that demanded, among other things, a focus on domain principles. The learners were prompted to reason about *probability* principles in order to determine sought values and they had to apply the principles to the problems at hand. The authors found that at least the weaker students demonstrated an enhanced principle-emphasis when learning *physics* later in another intelligent tutoring system (i.e., "Andes").

Busch, Renkl, and Schworm (2008) developed a short-term training intervention on self-explanation strategies. One trained strategy was principle-based self-explanations (i.e., relating problem elements to underlying principles). More specifically, Busch and colleagues used the topic of fables to show the learners (undergraduate students) that it is necessary to refer to underlying principles (e.g., animals as actors; moral in the end) in order to identify whether a story is a fable or not and to construct a fable. Remarkably, this short-term intervention (about 30 minutes) revealed transfer effects to an example-based learning environment on scientific argumentation. Trained learners provided more self-explanations on argumentation examples (i.e., referring to argumentative structures) and produced more sophisticated written arguments in a posttest later on.

Whereas the training intervention by Busch and colleagues (2008) stressed different types of self-explanations, Renkl, Solymosi, and Erdmann (2013) focused their training intervention for high school students (about 30 minutes) on principle-based self-explanations. They used the topic of fables as a "verbal" training domain (as Busch et al., 2008) and mathematics as an "algorithmic" training domain.

The transfer domain referred to the basics of Kelley's (1971) attribution theory and its application to educational contexts (this transfer domain fitted nicely into the curriculum of the psychology course the trained high school students were taking). The training was, however, only partially successful, as compared to a control group who received instruction about mnemonic strategies. About two-thirds of the trained students applied the trained self-explanation strategy to learning about attribution theory and profited accordingly with respect to their learning outcomes. However, the remaining third of the trained students, that is, those who were "unconvinced," did not exhibit superior learning outcomes.

In summary, principle-based self-explanations can be successfully fostered by short-term training interventions. However, interventions aiming to transfer self-explanation skills to different domains still need to be optimized.

Working Memory Load Induced by the Basic Learning Arrangement

Note that learning by self-explaining cannot be regarded as a stand-alone learning method. Students learn by self-explaining while engaging in a basic learning arrangement requiring, for example problem solving, studying worked examples, or watching videos or animations. In this context, it is again important to note that learners find self-explaining a demanding task (see the previous two sections on prompting and training). Hence, a learning arrangement that asks learners to self-explain should not impose high load on working memory from the basic learning arrangement or method (e.g., learning by problem solving or by animations); otherwise the learners' capacities might be overtaxed (e.g., Fiorella & Mayer, 2015; Sweller, 2006). For example, de Koning and colleagues (2011) found that self-explaining an animation fostered learning only when the demands of processing the provided animation, and thereby the cognitive load, were reduced by attention-guiding cues added to the animation.

Johnson and Mayer (2010) found that prompted self-explanation fostered learning from a game-based environment compared with a condition without prompts, but only if the explanation could be selected from a menu; self-explanations prompts that required the student to generate the explanation and type it into a box were not helpful. The authors argued that typing the text might interrupt the learner's game flow and pose extraneous demands that do not foster understanding (see also Große & Renkl, 2006; Hoogerheide et al., 2016; Sweller, 2006). In other words, if the means by which self-explanations have to be generated impose an extraneous load, no positive effects on learning outcomes are likely.

A classical method of reducing extraneous (i.e., unnecessary) cognitive load in initial cognitive skill acquisition (Cooper & Sweller, 1987; Sweller & Cooper, 1985) is to present the students worked examples for study instead of problems to be solved (see also Renkl, 2014b). Aleven, Renkl, and colleagues (e.g., Schwonke et al., 2009; Salden et al., 2009) investigated in a series of studies two conditions: (1) studying worked examples that gradually fade away so that more and more problem-solving is demanded later on (Renkl & Atkinson, 2003; Renkl, 2014b) and (2) solving problems right from the beginning. These two conditions were implemented in an intelligent tutoring system (Cognitive Tutor; Koedinger & Corbett, 2006) and the learners were prompted to provide principle-based self-explanations for all solution steps (irrespective of whether they were worked-out or had to be solved). In several experiments, combining self-explaining with (faded) worked examples was superior to problem-solving (see Salden et al., 2010). Similarly, Rummel and colleagues (2009) found that it was effective to add an elaboration-support procedure (consisting of instructional hints focusing on underlying principles and self-explanation prompts) to worked examples of productive collaboration (here: in form of video models); adding this elaboration support to a condition of learning by (scripted) doing had hardly any positive effects. Note that also in research on worked examples there is emphasis on the particular efficacy of combining examples and self-explanation support (e.g., Renkl, 2014b; Renkl, 2017a).

In summary, prompting self-explanations is most promising when the basic learning arrangement or the way the self-explanations are required does not impose high (extraneous) load. A particularly promising combination is prompting self-explanations while studying worked examples – that can also take on the form of (video) models (see van Gog & Rummel, 2010; Renkl, 2014b).

Self-Explaining Correct and Incorrect Solutions

Several studies have shown that it can help learning to self-explain not only correct solutions but a set of correct and incorrect solutions (e.g., Adams et al., 2014; Booth et al., 2013; Curry, 2004; Siegler, 2002; Siegler & Chen, 2008). For example, Durkin and Rittle-Johnson (2012) had 4th and 5th graders study worked-out number line tasks (placing a decimal on the number line). Each task was solved by two fictitious students who had placed a decimal on a number line and justified their choice. Half of the participating students compared two correct solutions with different justifications (explanation prompts: "1. How is Matt's way different from Laura's way? 2. Explain why both ways of thinking are correct" [p. 208]); the other half of the participating students compared a correct and an incorrect solution (explanation prompts: "1. How is Matt's way different from Justin's way? 2. Why can't you solve the problem Justin's way?" [p. 208]). The participating students who self-explained correct and incorrect solutions exhibited superior procedural knowledge at the immediate posttest and superior conceptual knowledge at a (two weeks) delayed posttest.

These findings might be qualified by Große and Renkl (2007) who found that studying and self-explaining correct and incorrect examples might benefit stronger students but overwhelm those with low prior knowledge, in particular when the errors are not explicitly labeled as such. However, Durkin and Rittle-Johnson (2012) found that students with low prior knowledge also profited from self-explaining correct and incorrect solutions. This difference might be due to the fact that Durkin and Rittle-Johnson (2012) – in contrast to Renkl and Große (2007) – presented their correct and incorrect solution side by side, making them easily comparable.

The interpretation that a side-by-side presentation might be an important factor helping all students learn is backed up by Oser and Spychiger's theory of "negative knowledge" (Oser & Spychiger, 2005). They postulate that the representation of wrong procedures or concepts (i.e., negative knowledge) might be useful. However, the incorrect knowledge should be represented in connection with the corresponding correct knowledge and ideally with strategies on how to prevent errors (i.e., application of the incorrect knowledge). In this case, negative knowledge's function is to remind learners of potential error sources and therefore help avoid errors (Gartmeier et al., 2010).

In summary, the effects of self-explaining can be optimized by having students study correct and incorrect solutions. The correct and incorrect solutions are best presented side by side.

Phase of Cognitive Skill Acquisition

There are several models of cognitive skill acquisition postulating stages in which learning fulfills different functions (e.g., Anderson, Fincham, & Douglass, 1997; Renkl, 2014b; Schunk & Zimmermann, 2007; VanLehn, 1996). Without going into the details of these models and their not-too-profound differences, what can be said is that learners should first understand the domain principles (or rules) and their applications. Later on, one major goal of learning is to form action rules and automate them (Renkl, 2014b). As principle-based self-explanations foster the understanding of principles and their application but not automation, it is obvious that learners should self-explain at the beginning of cognitive skill acquisition. Later, self-explaining can be considered a redundant activity that unnecessarily restricts learners' cognitive capacities (see also Kalyuga & Renkl, 2010; Kalyuga & Singh, 2016).

Beyond these theoretical considerations, there are empirical studies that back up these arguments. For example, Pirolli and Recker (1994) detected a diminishing return effect from self-explanations, that is, when learners keep on self-explaining, this learning activity gradually loses its effectiveness. In other words, after the self-explanations have (more or less) fulfilled the function of interconnecting principles with multiple examples, they have little added value. Note also that some studies found that fostering self-explanation is especially helpful for less advanced learners (i.e., those in earlier stages of skill acquisition) (e.g., Conati & VanLehn, 2000; Renkl et al., 1998). Finally, Rittle-Johnson and colleagues (De Caro & Rittle-Johnson, 2012; Matthews & Rittle-Johnson, 2009) found that self-explaining (instead of practicing more problems) does not reveal significant added value if there are prior learning periods that tap on (conceptual) contents similar to those addressed by the self-explanation prompts. Hence, if the students have already understood the principles and their application, additional self-explanations are no longer very helpful, at least, they are no more helpful than using the same learning time to solve additional practice problems.

In summary, it makes sense to prompt self-explanations at the beginning of cognitive skill acquisition. When students have already gained understanding of the principles and their application, self-explaining becomes a redundant learning activity that does not help reach important goals in later stages of skill acquisition such as automation.

Promising Avenues of Further Research

Three promising avenues of further research are outlined below. Firstly, self-explanation has developed into a "shimmering" and very prominent construct used in a wide variety of contexts. Even right from the beginning of the respective research, rather heterogeneous learning activities have been subsumed under this construct, as already outlined (see VanLehn et al., 1992). We doubt that all the heterogeneous learning activities subsumed under the umbrella of self-explanations foster learning via the same mechanism, and that the same practice recommendations apply to different types of self-explanation. In addition, we question whether some types of self-explanations actually count as "explanations." Against this background, we plead for further theoretical and empirical work (1) to systematize different types of self-explanations more profoundly and (2) to determine which mechanisms contribute to the effects of different types of self-explanations. Future studies should also confirm that it makes sense to separate principle-based self-explanation from other types of self-explanations, as we did in this chapter.

Secondly, providing productive self-explanations is a demanding task (see also Fiorella & Mayer, 2015). In some cases, prompting arrangements foster learning only when they support correct and focused self-explanations (see Rittle-Johnson et al., 2017; Wylie & Chi, 2014). In other cases, open prompts that leave learners with a lot of freedom regarding how to react to a prompt also support learning (e.g., Schworm & Renkl, 2006). Given the general instructional principle to provide as little support as possible but as much as necessary (see the assistance dilemma in Koedinger & Aleven, 2007, and the expertise-reversal effect (Kalyuga & Renkl, 2010), it would be worthwhile to develop procedures of self-explanation support that can adapt to the groups of learners at hand or, even better, to the individual learner. Inexperienced students should receive structure-providing prompts; more advanced students should be given more open prompt types. Further studies should analyze whether this type of adaptational self-explanation support is actually most effective, and most efficient, for cognitive skill acquisition (see also Wylie & Chi, 2014).

Thirdly, there are a number of studies showing that self-explanations can be successfully trained (e.g., Bielaczyc et al., 1995; Hodds et al., 2014). However, these interventions usually comprise just short-term training sessions. They might work when the training domain is the same as the application domain (e.g., Renkl et al., 1998) or when a specific new transfer domain is targeted (Busch et al., 2008). However, there is a lack of evidence as to whether trained students can become good self-explainers in the sense that they can apply this learning strategy to a variety of learning contents. Longer interventions are required to train such generalizable self-explanation skills and it takes long-term studies to test the effectiveness of such interventions (see also Rittle-Johnson et al., 2017).

"All Things Considered": What Are the Practice Recommendations?

We provide three recommendations that apply if the instructional goal is that the students should acquire cognitive skills based on underlying domain principles and if the students are in initial stages of skill acquisition. These recommendations should be regarded as a package. Disregarding any one of these recommendations may lead to restricted learning outcomes.

Have the students self-explain example cases in a principle-based manner. As detailed in the section on theoretical assumptions, this learning method directly addresses the goal of fostering cognitive skills based on an understanding of underlying principles. Empirical studies confirm this assumption (e.g., Atkinson et al., 2003; Schworm & Renkl, 2007; Hefter et al., 2014). In the section on implementing effective learning by self-explaining, we have, however, shown that the details regarding how learners have to self-explain make a difference.

Make informed decisions about the details of how students learn by self-explaining. As we have shown, it is usually advisable to use types of prompts that provide some structure (e.g., menu-based prompts), at least if your students are not trained or experienced self-explainers (see assistance dilemma or expertise-reversal effects). You may also consider using a training intervention to enable your students to provide good self-explanations to prompts without much structure (see Wong et al., 2002).

The positive effects of principle-based self-explaining may also be compromised if the basic learning arrangement already imposes a high cognitive load. In this case, additionally inducing substantial load by requiring learners to provide principle-based self-explanations might overwhelm them. One tried-and-tested option to reduce (unnecessary) cognitive load is to use worked examples instead of problems to be solved at the beginning of cognitive skill acquisition. There are many more options to reduce (unnecessary) cognitive load that cannot be discussed within the scope of this section (for details, see, e.g., Clark, Nguyen, & Sweller, 2006; Clark & Mayer, 2016).

In particular, if you teach a domain in which learners commit typical errors, it makes sense to have them self-explain correct and incorrect solutions. These correct and incorrect solutions are best presented side by side. Such an arrangement helps learners to represent in their memory correct and incorrect knowledge in an integrated manner, which helps them to avoid errors in the future (Oser & Spychiger, 2005).

Finally, fade out the self-explaining requirements if your students proceed in cognitive skill acquisition and have already understood the application of the principle(s). Now may be the time to automate parts of the skill; self-explaining does not help in this respect.

Assess self-explanation quality. Learning by self-explaining – as with any other learning method – is not the "silver bullet" for fostering learning in each and every context. This is even true when following the guidelines in the previous section. Unfortunately, research has not (yet) provided enough evidence to determine a priori with great certainty whether a specific learning-by-self-explaining arrangement will work well in a given context. Hence, teachers should design their instruction in such a way that students leave "tracks" that reveal something about the quality of their self-explanations. It is not enough for teachers "just" to monitor self-explanation answers from individual students in a question–answer classroom period. Methods are preferable that provide a more complete and accurate picture of how individual students in a classroom are reacting to self-explanation demands. For example, selections from menus or written entries into boxes on worksheets (see Figures 21.1 and 21.4) provide more diagnostic information about a classroom. If your students are unable to provide correct principle-based explanations, an (additional) short training intervention or prompting procedure that provides more structure might be necessary. On the other hand, if a large majority of your students can quickly provide correct self-explanations, this learning activity may become redundant.

In summary, having students self-explain in a principle-based manner has the potential to substantially foster the initial acquisition of cognitive skills. However, a number of guidelines must be taken into account to enhance the probability that this learning method's potential is fully exploited. Presently, these guideline are imperfect. However, as research on self-explanation is such a busy and productive field, we can anticipate "more perfect" instructional guidelines in the (near) future.

Stop, Before You Go!

We nearly forgot about our poor graduate student struggling with her first manuscript. What can we finally say about her situation? It is in fact a good idea to give her two (or more) model submissions, in particular when her advisor encourages her to analyze the model submissions in terms of the writing principles that were realized or ignored (see the recommendation *Have the students self-explain example cases in a principle-based way*).

To optimize the use of the model submissions, her advisor should *make informed decisions about the details of how students learn by self-explaining.* If the graduate student is a genuinely inexperienced writer, the advisor might first take an article they had both already read while setting up the experiments. They may jointly analyze parts of this article with respect to the realization of writing principles. Such a *short training intervention* might help the graduate student when she later analyzes the model submissions on her own.

The advisor would ideally select model submissions on a topic closely resembling the to-be-written manuscript's topic. Moreover, the model submissions should not be overly complex in their theoretical arguments and methodology (*reducing unnecessary cognitive load*). If the topic is unfamiliar and the contents too complex, too much of the graduate student's cognitive capacities will be "absorbed" by trying to understand what the paper is about (see Renkl, Hilbert, & Schworm, 2009). As a consequence, self-explanations referring to writing principles would be hindered.

Another potential factor that might overtax the graduate student is that there are many writing principles that could or should be considered. Actually, it is not possible to refer to all of them while self-explaining when reading a model submission. Hence, the advisor might propose a handful of writing principles to focus on in the first step (*reducing cognitive load*).

It is highly improbable that the advisor can provide model submissions in which all sections are superbly written. However, suboptimal model submissions might not be a real problem. The advisor might say, for example, that the graduate student should compare the beginning of both discussions:

> In submission A, there is a precise and concise summary of the findings, including clear statements revealing support or nonsupport of the main hypotheses.
> In contrast, in submission B, there is a summary of findings that more or less repeats what was written in the prior section. Have a close look at the differences between the papers in order to see how a good discussion should start.

In other words, the advisor can encourage *self-explaining correct and incorrect* (here better: *very good and suboptimal*) solutions to the problem of starting a discussion.

With respect to the recommendation "*assess self-explanation quality*," the advisor may invite the graduate student to a short get-together for the coming week. In this meeting, the graduate student should say whether she had been able to "see" the extent to which the principles were realized in the model submissions. To validate the student's self-assessment, the advisor might ask the student to provide examples of well-written and not so well-written paragraphs and to justify her evaluations. On this basis, our graduate student and her advisor can decide together as to whether studying the model papers really helped or whether more support should be provided.

References

Adams, D. M., McLaren, B. M., Durkin, K., Mayer, R. E., Rittle-Johnson, B., Isotani, S., & van Velsen, M. (2014). Using erroneous examples to improve mathematics learning with a web-based tutoring system. *Computers in Human Behavior, 36*, 401–411.

Ainsworth, S. & Loizou, A. T. (2003). The effects of self-explaining when learning with text or diagrams. *Cognitive Science, 27*, 669–681.

Aleven, V. A. & Koedinger, K. R. (2002). An effective metacognitive strategy: Learning by doing and explaining with a computer-based cognitive tutor. *Cognitive Science, 26*, 147–179.

Anderson, J. R., Fincham, J. M., & Douglass, S. (1997). The role of examples and rules in the acquisition of a cognitive skill. *Journal of Experimental Psychology: Learning, Memory, and Cognition, 23*, 932–945.

Atkinson, R. K., Renkl, A., & Merrill, M. M. (2003). Transitioning from studying examples to solving problems: Combining fading with prompting fosters learning. *Journal of Educational Psychology, 95*, 774–783.

Berthold, K., Eysink, T. H., & Renkl, A. (2009). Assisting self-explanation prompts are more effective than open prompts when learning with multiple representations. *Instructional Science, 37*, 345–363.

Berthold, K. & Renkl, A. (2009). Instructional aids to support a conceptual understanding of multiple representations. *Journal of Educational Psychology, 101*, 70–87.

Bielaczyc, K., Pirolli, P. L., & Brown, A. L. (1995). Training in self-explanation and self-regulation strategies: Investigating the effects of knowledge acquisition activities on problem solving. *Cognition and Instruction, 13*, 221–252.

Booth, J. L., Lange, K. E., Koedinger, K. R., & Newton, K. J. (2013). Using example problems to improve student learning in algebra: Differentiating between correct and incorrect examples. *Learning and Instruction, 25*, 24–34.

Busch, C., Renkl, A., & Schworm, S. (2008). Towards a generic self-explanation training intervention for example-based learning. In P. A. Kirschner, F. Prins, V. Jonker, & G. Kanselaar (eds.), *Proceedings of the 8th International Conference of the Learning Sciences 2008* (CD-ROM version only). Utrecht: International Conference of the Learning Science.

Chi, M. & VanLehn, K. (2010). Meta-cognitive strategy instruction in intelligent tutoring systems: How, when, and why. *Educational Technology and Society, 13*, 25–39.

Chi, M. T. H. (2000). Self-explaining expository texts: The dual processes of generating inferences and repairing mental models. In R. Glaser (ed.), *Advances in instructional psychology* (pp. 161–238). Hillsdale, NJ: Lawrence Erlbaum.

Chi, M. T. H. & Bassok, M. (1989). Learning from examples via self-explanations. In L. B. Resnick (ed.), *Knowing, learning, and instruction: Essays in honor of Robert Glaser* (pp. 251–282). Hillsdale, NJ: Lawrence Erlbaum.

Chi, M. T. H., Bassok, M., Lewis, M. W., Reimann, P., & Glaser, R. (1989). Self-explanations: How students study and use examples in learning to solve problems. *Cognitive Science, 13*, 145–182.

Chi, M. T., deLeeuw, N., Chiu, M. H., & LaVancher, C. (1994). Eliciting self-explanations improves understanding. *Cognitive Science, 18*, 439–477.

Chi, M. T. H. & VanLehn, K. A. (2012). Seeing deep structure from the interactions of surface features. *Educational Psychologist, 47*, 177–188.

Cho, Y. H. & Lee, S. E. (2013). The role of co-explanation and self-explanation in learning from design examples of PowerPoint presentation slides. *Computers and Education, 69*, 400–407.

Clark, R. C. & Mayer, R. E. (2016). *e-Learning and the science of instruction: Proven guidelines for consumers and designers of multimedia learning*, 4th edn. San Francisco, CA: Wiley.

Clark, R. C., Nguyen, F., & Sweller (2006). *Efficiency in learning: Evidence-based guidelines to manage cognitive load*. San Francisco, CA: Wiley.

Conati, C. & VanLehn, K. (2000). Further results from the evaluation of an intelligent computer tutor to coach self-explanation. In G. Gauthier, C. Frasson, & K. VanLehn (eds.), *Proceedings of the 5th International Conference on Intelligent Tutoring Systems* (pp. 304–313). Berlin: Springer.

Cooper, G. & Sweller, J. (1987). Effects of schema acquisition and rule automation on mathematical problem-solving transfer. *Journal of Educational Psychology, 79*, 347–362.

Curry, L. A. (2004). The effects of self-explanations of correct and incorrect solutions on algebra problem-solving performance. In K. Forbus, D. Gentner, & T. Regier (eds.),

Proceedings of the 26th conference of the Cognitive Science Society (p. 1548). Mahwah, NJ: Lawrence Erlbaum.

De Caro, M. S. & Rittle-Johnson, B. (2012). Exploring mathematics problems prepares children to learn from instruction. *Journal of Experimental Child Psychology*, *113*, 552–568.

De Koning, B. B, Tabbers, H. K, Rikers, R. M. J. P, & Paas, G. W. C. (2011). Improved effectiveness of cueing by self-explanations when learning from a complex animation. *Applied Cognitive Psychology*, *25*, 183–194.

Didierjean, A. & Cauzinille-Marmèche, E. (1998). Reasoning by analogy: Is it schema-mediated or case-based?. *European Journal of Psychology of Education*, *13*, 385–398.

Dunlosky, J., Rawson, K. A., Marsh, E. J., Nathan, M. J., & Willingham, D. T. (2013). Improving students' learning with effective learning techniques: Promising directions from cognitive and educational psychology. *Psychological Science in the Public Interest*, *14*, 4–58.

Durkin, K. & Rittle-Johnson, B. (2012). The effectiveness of using incorrect examples to support learning about decimal magnitude. *Learning and Instruction*, *22*, 206–214.

Fiorella, L. & Mayer, R. E. (2015). *Learning as a generative activity: Eight learning strategies that promote understanding*. New York: Cambridge University Press.

Gartmeier, M., Bauer, J., Gruber, H., & Heid, H. (2010). Workplace errors and negative knowledge in elder care nursing. *Human Resource Development International*, *13*, 5–25.

Große, C. S. & Renkl, A. (2006). Effects of multiple solution methods in mathematics learning. *Learning and Instruction*, *16*, 122–138.

(2007). Finding and fixing errors in worked examples: Can this foster learning outcomes? *Learning and Instruction*, *17*, 612–634.

Hefter, M. H., Berthold, K., Renkl, A., Riess, W., Schmid, S., & Fries, S. (2014). Effects of a training intervention to foster argumentation skills while processing conflicting scientific positions. *Instructional Science*, *42*, 929–947.

Hilbert, T. S. & Renkl, A. (2009). Learning how to use a computer-based concept-mapping tool: Self-explaining examples helps. *Computers in Human Behavior*, *25*, 267–274.

Hilbert, T. S., Renkl, A., Schworm, S., Kessler, S., & Reiss, K. (2008). Learning to teach with worked-out examples: A computer-based learning environment for teachers. *Journal of Computer-Assisted Learning*, *24*, 316–332.

Hodds, M., Alcock, L., & Inglis, M. (2014). Self-explanation training improves proof comprehension. *Journal for Research in Mathematics Education*, *45*, 62–101.

Hoogerheide, V., Deijkers, L., Loyens, S. M., Heijltjes, A., & van Gog, T. (2016). Gaining from explaining: Learning improves from explaining to fictitious others on video, not from writing to them. *Contemporary Educational Psychology*, *44*, 95–106.

Johnson, C. I. & Mayer, R. E. (2010). Applying the self-explanation principle to multimedia learning in a computer-based game-like environment. *Computers in Human Behavior*, *26*, 1246–1252.

Kalyuga, S. & Renkl, A. (2010). Expertise reversal effect and its instructional implications: Introduction to the special issue. *Instructional Science*, *38*, 209–215.

Kalyuga, S. & Singh, A. M. (2016). Rethinking the boundaries of cognitive load theory in complex learning. *Educational Psychology Review*, *28*, 831–852.

Keil, F. C. (2006). Explanation and understanding. *Annual Review of Psychology*, *57*, 227–254.

Kelley, H. H. (1971). *Attribution in social interaction*. New York: General Learning Press.

Kiel, E. (1999). *Erklären als didaktisches Handeln [Explaining as instructional action]*. Würzburg: Ergon.

Koedinger, K. R. & Aleven, V. (2007). Exploring the assistance dilemma in experiments with cognitive tutors. *Educational Psychology Review, 19*, 239–264.

Koedinger, K. R. & Corbett, A. T. (2006). Cognitive tutors: Technology bringing learning sciences to the classroom. In R. K. Sawyer (ed.), *The Cambridge handbook of the learning sciences* (pp. 61–78). New York: Cambridge University Press.

Lombrozo, T. (2012). Explanation and abductive inference. In K. J. Holyoak & R. G. Morrison (eds.), *The Oxford handbook of thinking and reasoning* (pp. 260–276). Oxford: Oxford University Press.

Matthews, P. & Rittle-Johnson, B. (2009). In pursuit of knowledge: Comparing self-explanations, concepts, and procedures as pedagogical tools. *Journal of Experimental Child Psychology, 104*, 1–21.

McEldoon, K. L., Durkin, K. L., & Rittle-Johnson, B. (2013). Is self-explanation worth the time? A comparison to additional practice. *British Journal of Educational Psychology, 83*, 615–632.

McNamara, D. S. (2004). SERT: Self-explanation reading training. *Discourse Processes, 38*, 1–30.

Moreno, R. & Valdez, A. (2007). Immediate and delayed effects of using a classroom case exemplar in teacher education: The role of presentation format. *Journal of Educational Psychology, 99*, 194–206.

Morrison, J. R., Bol, L., Ross, S. M., & Watson, G. S. (2015). Paraphrasing and prediction with self-explanation as generative strategies for learning science principles in a simulation. *Educational Technology Research and Development, 63*, 861–882.

Nokes-Malach, T. J., VanLehn, K., Belenky, D. M., Lichtenstein, M., & Cox, G. (2013). Coordinating principles and examples through analogy and self-explanation. *European Journal of Psychology of Education, 28*, 1237–1263.

Oser, F. & Spychiger, M. (2005). *Lernen ist schmerzhaft: Zur Theorie des Negativen Wissens und zur Praxis der Fehlerkultur [Learning is painful: On a theory of negative knowledge and on the practice of error management]*. Weinheim: Beltz.

Pashler, H., Bain, P. M., Bottge, B. A., Graesser, A., Koedinger, K., McDaniel, M., & Metcalfe, J. (2007). Organizing instruction and study to improve student learning. *IES Practice Guide. NCER 2007–2004*. Washington, DC: National Center for Education Research.

Pirolli, P. & Recker, M. (1994). Learning strategies and transfer in the domain of programming. *Cognition & Instruction, 12*, 235–275.

Renkl, A. (1997). Learning from worked-out examples: A study on individual differences. *Cognitive Science, 21*, 1–29.

(2014a). *Theoretische Konzepte und Prinzipien auf den Schulalltag beziehen: Ein wenig Theorie und darauf begründete Vorschläge für die Referendariatsausbildung [Relating theoretical concepts and principles to classroom practice: A bit of theory and delineated recommendations for teacher education]*. Seminar, 2(2014), 9–16.

(2014b). Towards an instructionally-oriented theory of example-based learning. *Cognitive Science, 38*, 1–37.

(2015). Different roads lead to Rome: The case of principle-based cognitive skills. *Learning: Research & Practice, 1*, 79–90.

(2017a). Instruction based on examples. In R. E. Mayer & P. A. Alexander (eds.), *Handbook of research on learning and instruction*, 2nd edn (pp. 325–348). New York: Routledge.

(2017b). Learning from worked-examples in mathematics: Students relate procedures to principles. *ZDM Mathematics Education, 49*, 571–584.

Renkl, A. & Atkinson, R. K. (2003). Structuring the transition from example study to problem solving in cognitive skills acquisition: A cognitive load perspective. *Educational Psychologist, 38*, 15–22.

Renkl, A., Hilbert, T., & Schworm, S. (2009). Example-based learning in heuristic domains: A cognitive load theory account. *Educational Psychology Review, 21*, 67–78.

Renkl, A., Solymosi, J., Erdmann, M., & Aleven, V. (2013). Training principle-based self-explanations: Transfer to new learning contents. In M. Knauff, M. Pauen, N. Sebanz, & I. Wachsmuth (eds.), *Proceedings of the 35th Annual Conference of the Cognitive Science Society* (pp. 1205–1210). Austin, TX: Cognitive Science Society.

Renkl, A., Stark, R., Gruber, H., & Mandl, H. (1998). Learning from worked-out examples: The effects of example variability and elicited self-explanations. *Contemporary Educational Psychology, 23*, 90–108.

Rittle-Johnson, B. & Loehr, A. M. (2017). Eliciting explanations: Constraints on when self-explanation aids learning. *Psychonomic Bulletin and Review, 24*, 1501–1510.

Rittle-Johnson, B., Loehr, A. M., & Durkin, K. (2017). Promoting self-explanation to improve mathematics learning: A meta-analysis and instructional design principles. *ZDM Mathematics Education, 49*, 599–611.

Ross, B. H. (1989). Remindings in learning and instruction. In S. Vosniadou & A. Ortony (eds.), *Similarity and analogical reasoning* (pp. 438–469). Cambridge: Cambridge University Press.

Rummel, N., Spada, H., & Hauser, S. (2009). Learning to collaborate while being scripted or by observing a model. *International Journal of Computer-Supported Collaborative Learning, 4*, 69–92.

Salden, R., Aleven, V., Renkl, A., & Schwonke, R. (2009). Worked examples and tutored problem solving: Redundant or synergistic forms of support? *Topics in Cognitive Science, 1*, 203–213.

Salden, R., Koedinger, K. R., Renkl, A., Aleven, V., & McLaren, B. M. (2010). Accounting for beneficial effects of worked examples in tutored problem solving. *Educational Psychology Review, 22*, 379–392.

Schalk, L., Saalbach, H., & Stern, E. (2016). Approaches to foster transfer of formal principles: Which route to take? *PloS One, 11*, e0148787.

Schunk, D. H. & Zimmerman, B. J. (2007). Influencing children's self-efficacy and self-regulation of reading and writing through modeling. *Reading and Writing Quarterly, 23*, 7–25.

Schwonke, R., Renkl, A., Krieg, K., Wittwer, J., Aleven, V., & Salden, R. (2009). The worked-example effect: Not an artefact of lousy control conditions. *Computers in Human Behavior, 25*, 258–266.

Schworm, S. & Renkl, A. (2006). Computer-supported example-based learning: When instructional explanations reduce self-explanations. *Computers and Education, 46*, 426–445.

(2007). Learning argumentation skills through the use of prompts for self-explaining examples. *Journal of Educational Psychology, 99*, 285–296.

Seidel, T., Blomberg, G., & Renkl, A. (2013). Instructional strategies for using video in teacher education. *Teaching and Teacher Education, 34*, 56–65.

Siegler, R. S. (2002). Microgenetic studies of self-explanation. In N. Granott & J. Parziale (eds.), *Microdevelopment: Transition Processes in Development and Learning* (pp. 31–58). New York: Cambridge University Press.

Siegler, R. S. & Chen, Z. (2008). Differentiation and integration: Guiding principles for analyzing cognitive change. *Developmental Science, 11*, 433–448.

Singer, M. (1994). Discourse inference processes. In M. A. Gernsbacher (ed.), *Handbook of psycholinguistics* (pp. 479–515). San Diego: Academic Press.

Stark, R., Mandl, H., Gruber, H., & Renkl, A. (2002). Conditions and effects of example elaboration. *Learning and Instruction, 12*, 39–60.

Sweller, J. (2006). The worked example effect and human cognition. *Learning and Instruction, 16*, 165–169.

Sweller, J. & Cooper, G. A. (1985). The use of worked examples as a substitute for problem solving in learning algebra. *Cognition and Instruction, 2*, 59–89.

Van der Meij, J. & de Jong, T. (2011). The effects of directive self-explanation prompts to support active processing of multiple representations in a simulation-based learning environment. *Journal of Computer-Assisted Learning, 27*, 411–423.

Van Gog, T. & Rummel, N. (2010). Example-based learning: Integrating cognitive and social-cognitive research perspectives. *Educational Psychology Review, 22*, 155–174.

VanLehn, K. (1996). Cognitive skill acquisition. *Annual Review of Psychology, 47*, 513–539.

VanLehn, K., Jones, R. M., & Chi, M. T. (1992). A model of the self-explanation effect. *The Journal of the Learning Sciences, 2*, 1–59.

Weinstein, C. E. & Mayer, R. E. (1986). The teaching of learning strategies. In M. Wittrock (ed.), *Handbook of research on teaching* (pp. 315–327). New York: Macmillan.

Wong, R. M. F., Lawson, M. J., & Keeves, J. (2002). The effects of self-explanation training on student's problem solving in high-school mathematics. *Learning and Instruction, 12*, 233–262.

Wylie, R. & Chi, M. T. H. (2014). The self-explanation principle in multimedia learning. In R. E. Mayer (ed.), *The Cambridge handbook of multimedia learning*, 2nd edn (pp. 413–432). New York: Cambridge University Press.

Wylie, R., Koedinger, K., & Mitamura, T. (2010). Analogies, explanations, and practice: Examining how task types affect second language grammar learning. In V. Aleven, J. Kay, & J. Mostow (eds.), *Proceedings of the 10th International Conference on Intelligent Tutoring Systems* (pp. 214–223). Berlin: Springer.

Wylie, R., Sheng, M., Mitamura, T., & Koedinger, K. R. (2011). Effects of adaptive prompted self-explanation on robust learning of second language grammar. In G. Biswas, S. Bull, J. Kay, & A. Mitrovic (eds.), *Proceedings of the 15th International Conference on Artificial Intelligence in Education* (pp. 588–590). Berlin: Springer.

22 Enhancing the Quality of Student Learning Using Distributed Practice

Melody Wiseheart, Carolina E. Küpper-Tetzel, Tina Weston, Alice S. N. Kim, Irina V. Kapler, and Vanessa Foot-Seymour

Whether you are an educator or a student, effective time management is critical to achieving success in the formal education system. For educators, the expectation is that a significant amount of curriculum can be covered in a condensed period of time. The goal is to maximize the amount of learning that takes place in the classroom so that students are prepared for the grade level or course that will follow. For students, the expectation is that a range of subject materials will be studied and tested in a short amount of time. This system of learning prioritizes the quantity of knowledge conveyed to students over the quality of students' learning – that is, long-lasting comprehension and retention of the material. In preparation for an upcoming test or exam, teachers and students must decide what material to review and when and how to review it. To maximize the use of limited learning time, it is important to identify learning strategies that will be not only effective but also *efficient* tools for promoting long-term retention of classroom materials.

The field of cognitive psychology offers a wealth of insight on how to enhance knowledge retention. Particularly, researchers have consistently shown the benefit of repetition or reviewing of newly learned information on long-term memory. As explained in the writings of memory researcher Ebbinghaus (1885/1964), "with any considerable number of repetitions a suitable distribution of them over a space of time is decidedly more advantageous than the massing of them at a single time" (p. 89). This phenomenon is called the *distributed practice effect* or *spacing effect*, and it refers to the finding that when reviewing previously learned material, distributing or "spacing" a set amount of study time across sessions leads to better memory performance in the long run than "massing" or cramming the same amount of study time into a single session. A typical research design for investigating the spacing effect consists of two study events and one test event. During the first study event, new material is introduced and learned (sometimes to a criterion); during the second study event, the same material is reviewed; and during the test event, the material is tested (Figure 22.1). The time interval between the first and second study events is referred to as the *interstudy interval*; it can be short/massed (e.g., immediate or a few seconds later) or long/spaced (e.g., minutes, hours, or days later). The time interval between the last study event and the test event is referred to as the *retention interval*; it can also be short (e.g., an immediate test or a test in 5 minutes) or long (e.g., a test a month or year away). Therefore, the distributed practice effect can be studied in both single-session experiments as well as multiday experiments.

Basic research design

Example: (a) Massed interstudy interval; (b) Spaced interstudy interval

Example: (c) Short retention interval; (d) Long retention interval

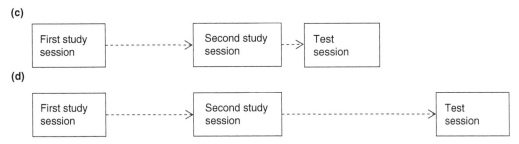

Figure 22.1 *A basic distributed practice research design*

During the first study event, new material is introduced and learned. During the second study event, the material is reviewed. During the test event, individuals are tested on their memory for the material. The time interval that passes between the first and second study events is referred to as the interstudy interval. It is either (a) short/massed or (b) long/spaced. The time interval that passes between the second study event and the test event is referred to as the retention interval. It is either (c) short or (d) long. Note: Some researchers refer to interstudy interval as gap or lag.

In this chapter, we provide a brief historical overview of the distributed practice effect and its theoretical underpinnings. We highlight important studies across a range of different subject matters that demonstrate the versatility of this phenomenon, particularly as it relates to education. We close with a discussion on how teachers and students can incorporate distributed practice into everyday instruction and study, as well as how researchers can address limitations of the current literature.

Historical Studies and Key Findings of the Distributed Practice Effect

Ebbinghaus (1885/1964) conducted the earliest known research documenting distributed practice benefits. He ran a series of experiments on himself to determine how to minimize the amount of time it took for him to relearn a set of material. He found that spacing the study of simple verbal material across several days instead of massing all study into a single day resulted in fewer relearning trials to achieve perfect acquisition. Around the same time, Jost (1897; described in Hovland, 1939) administered a paired-associate task with a fixed number of learning trials, similar to many modern-day distributed practice studies. He also found a distributed practice benefit for simple verbal material. Lashley (1915) subsequently examined skill learning in archery and found that when fewer arrow shots were made per day (40 vs. 20 vs. 5, to a grand total of 320), subjects' final shooting accuracy increased.

Since the work of Ebbinghaus, hundreds of studies have investigated the distributed practice effect, most of which are in the verbal learning domain (e.g., studies that employed words, paired-associates, sentences, or text passages as the study material). Meta-analyses estimate that about 75 percent of 400 plus verbal learning studies in the distributed practice literature show a spacing advantage, about 15 percent show a massing advantage, and the remaining 10 percent of studies show no difference between spacing and massing conditions (Cepeda et al., 2006; Moss, 1995). Generally, reported effect sizes are large; however, as we will discuss in the section "Generalizability of the Distributed Practice Effect," the magnitude of the distributed practice benefit may depend on a variety of factors, such as type of content or skill being reviewed.

Early researchers wondered whether final test performance always benefited from spacing, regardless of the retention interval. Robinson (1921), for example, compared a single massed learning session to two shorter sessions spaced out by 24 hours. He found that spacing only improved performance on the final test when the retention interval was 24 hours. Massed and spaced conditions resulted in identical test performance when the retention interval was only 5 minutes or 20 minutes (average of Tables III and IV in Robinson, 1921, p. 332). This is perhaps the first study showing that a spaced interstudy interval (in this example, 1 day) does not always optimize final test performance. Years later, Glenberg (1976) formally reported that the interstudy interval and retention interval interact, such that the optimal amount of spacing (or time) between the two learning events is different depending on when the final test takes place (see also Cepeda et al., 2008).

Data from Glenberg's (1976) experiments convincingly demonstrate that the effect of interstudy interval is nonmonotonic; that is, increasing the interstudy interval (i.e., amount of time) between study sessions will benefit retention to a point, after which additional increases in interstudy interval will lead to poorer retention (Peterson et al., 1963). The point at which the shift takes place is the optimal interstudy interval for the given retention interval (Glenberg, 1976). Generally speaking, for a test that occurs immediately after learning (i.e., short retention interval), the optimal interstudy interval is massed. Conversely, for a test that occurs further into the future (i.e., a longer retention interval), the optimal interstudy interval is spaced. Glenberg's findings helped to clarify earlier reviews of the distributed practice effect that had not considered retention interval as a factor of interest and therefore had reported incomparable results across some experiments (e.g., Ruch, 1928). Additionally, Glenberg's work paved the way for contemporary mathematical models of the spacing effect that seek to determine the optimal interstudy interval for a host of time scales ranging from seconds to years (Lindsey et al., 2009; Küpper-Tetzel & Erdfelder, 2012).

Thus, memory researchers of the 1960s and 1970s formally defined variables such as interstudy interval and retention interval and demonstrated how these variables (and their interaction) influence the magnitude of the distributed practice benefit (Glenberg, 1979; Hintzman, 1974; Melton, 1970). This work was groundbreaking as it began to clarify the question, "What is the best way to distribute my studying?" (Answer: "Depends on when your test is.")

Explanations of the Distributed Practice Effect

As interest around distributed practice grew in the 1960s, researchers focused their efforts on understanding why the effect occurred and how it could be so remarkably consistent across people and across learning tasks. Two of the major historical theories put forth as explanations of the distributed practice effect – study-phase retrieval and contextual variability – still remain popular today (for a comprehensive review, see Küpper-Tetzel, 2014). Study-phase retrieval theory suggests that greater difficulty retrieving an earlier learning instance of an item leads to greater strengthening of the memory trace for this item during a subsequent learning event (Delaney, Verkoeijen, & Spirgel, 2010; Hintzman & Block, 1973; Murray, 1983; Thios & D'Agostino, 1976). In other words, when retrieval is effortful at the second study event, the difficulty in reaccessing the information improves the likelihood of remembering that item on a final test. However, if too much time has passed between the first and second study events, and the item has been forgotten by the second study events, study-phase retrieval will not take place. The initial memory trace of the item will not be reinforced and final memory for the item will inevitably suffer. This theory suggests that a learner should choose interstudy intervals that are long enough to make retrieval during a subsequent study session effortful, but still successful, meaning that the interstudy interval will vary depending on the to-be-learned material and the characteristics of the learner. Study-phase retrieval theory does not make strong predictions due to its lack of specificity about the retrieval process (e.g., what are the specific factors that affect the likelihood of successful study-phase retrieval?), and therefore may not be a sufficient explanation for the spacing effect. It also conflicts with research suggesting that the ideal interstudy interval should be determined by the desired length of retention (e.g., Cepeda et al., 2008).

Contextual variability theory suggests that cues such as mood, environmental context, and mental images are encoded alongside items as they are learned

(Estes, 1955; Glenberg, 1979). These cues fluctuate over time and spacing helps to increase cue variability. It is assumed that the probability of successful recall will depend on whether contextual cues at the final test can be used to retrieve previously learned information from memory. The greater the overlap between cues at test and cues stored in memory from each study event, the higher the chances that the target information will be retrieved. When the retention interval is long, greater cue variability during learning increases the probability of retrieval at test; it is assumed that greater cue variability is more likely to occur if practice is spaced out in time. In contrast, when the retention interval is short, relatively less cue variability increases the probability of retrieval at test; it is assumed that less cue variability is more likely to occur if practice is massed. Similarly to study-phase retrieval theory, contextual variability theory lacks specificity (e.g., how can fluctuations in context and cue/trace overlap be measured?) and does not account for the full range of distributed practice effects reported in the literature.

Study-phase retrieval theory and contextual variability theory are not mutually exclusive. Recently, researchers have evaluated the probability of a hybrid account as an explanation of the distributed practice effect – for example, a combination of contextual variability mechanisms with some other mechanism(s), such as study-phase retrieval (Benjamin & Tullis, 2010; Delaney et al., 2010; Lindsey et al., 2009; Mozer et al, 2009; Raaijmakers, 2003). Hybrid accounts acknowledge that no single-mechanism account has been able to account for the wide range of distributed practice findings.

Metacognition and the Distributed Practice Effect

Ironically, although the distributed practice effect is clear across a range of different topics and activities, related research studies in the field of metacognition (i. e., awareness of one's own thinking or behavior) show that the strategy is not used by most learners. On the contrary, most students believe that cramming will improve their memory prior to a test (Kornell, 2009; Kornell & Bjork, 2008; McCabe, 2011; Son & Simon, 2012; Zechmeister & Schaughnessy, 1980). Technically, this belief is correct. Since semesters are the norm in traditional education systems, and tests are often given within weeks of learning a set of material, it is often the case that shorter-term retention is evaluated (days or weeks) rather than longer-term retention (months or years). As we have discussed, when the retention interval is short, a short interstudy intervals will be optimal.

Unfortunately, massing gives the illusion that memory storage is strong and will last for a long time. This belief is incorrect; massing creates more salient memory traces that are prone to forgetting, while spacing produces memory traces that are less salient at the time of initial learning but are more robust to forgetting. (Rohrer & Taylor, 2007, fig. 1B shows that massed memory traces leave memory more quickly; Cepeda et al., 2008, fig. 3a shows that short interstudy interval memory traces are stronger for short retention intervals, whereas long interstudy interval traces are weaker for short retention intervals and are stronger at long retention intervals.) We return to these points in the following sections.

Distributed Practice Schedules

In a more complex distributed practice research design, to-be-learned material is reviewed more than once. Material is introduced during the first study event, reviewed once (second study event), and then reviewed a second time (third study event), before eventually being tested. In this design, the interstudy interval between the first study event and the second study event may be varied, *and* the interstudy interval between the second study event and the third study event may be varied. This research design naturally presents more options for the timing of when material is reviewed; researchers have defined these options as equal, expanding, or contracting learning schedules (Figure 22.2). Studies that have investigated the optimal learning schedule for verbal material across three study events have reported mixed results (e.g., Balota, Duchek, & Logan, 2007; Cull, 2000; Kang et al., 2014). Not surprisingly, the optimal learning schedule is also likely to depend on retention interval. For example, Küpper-Tetzel, Kapler, and Wiseheart (2014) found that contracting learning schedules benefited participants' cued recall memory at shorter retention intervals, and expanding and equal learning schedules benefited participants' cued recall memory at a longer retention interval.

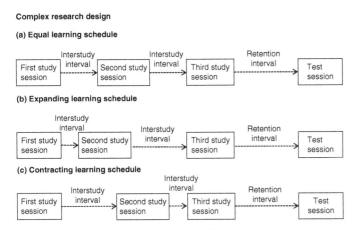

Figure 22.2 *A complex distributed practice research design where three different learning schedules are compared against each other*

In the equal learning schedule (a), the interstudy interval between the first and second study events is the same length as between the second and third study events. In the expanding learning schedule (b), the interstudy interval between the first and second study events is shorter than the interstudy interval between the second and third study events. In the contracting learning schedule (c), the interstudy interval between the first and second study events is longer than the interstudy interval between the second and third study events. Across all three learning schedules, retention interval is fixed, as is total time from first to last study event.

Studies on the distributed practice effect have expanded further to include the concept of "interleaving." Interleaving is the practice of mixing different types of learning activities within a single block of time rather than distributing blocks of the same activity across time. For the sake of conciseness, we do not review any interleaving studies in this chapter. Instead, we refer readers to Chapter 16 in this volume.

Generalizability of the Distributed Practice Effect

The distributed practice effect has been found across different age groups, in addition to different skills and domains. The benefits of distributed practice on knowledge retention have been reported in infants (e.g., Rovee-Collier, Evancio, & Earley, 1995), preschool children (e.g., Toppino, Kasserman, & Mracek, 1991), elementary school children (e.g., Rea & Modigliani, 1987), middle school children (e.g., Carpenter, Pashler, & Cepeda, 2009; Küpper-Tetzel, Erdfelder, & Dickhäuser, 2014), and healthy young and old adults (e.g., Cepeda et al., 2008; Simone, Bell, & Cepeda, 2013). It has been demonstrated in memory-impaired populations, which speaks to its robustness (Balota et al., 2006; Cermak et al., 1996; Green et al., 2014). This large collection of research, which taps into various populations across the life span, suggests that distributed practice can improve how people of all ages learn and retain new information.

To determine the extent to which distributed practice improvements can be generalized, researchers have searched for ways to categorize learning outcomes. Gagné (1977, 1984) outlined five major types of learning outcomes: intellectual skills, verbal information (i.e., verbal learning), cognitive strategies, motor skills, and attitudes. He posited that these categories of learning outcomes have the following characteristics: they are clear in terms of final performance made possible by the learning; they apply to a diverse set of human activities; they require that learning tasks be specific to the category; and, most pertinently, they "differ in the nature of information-processing demands for its learning. Specifically, each kind of outcome requires different (a) substantive type of relevant prior learning, (b) manner of encoding for long-term storage, and (c) requirements for retrieval and transfer of new situations" (Gagné, 1984, p. 378). Research on distributed practice effects has explored three of the five learning categories: verbal information, motor skills, and intellectual skills. Verbal learning happens orally or through writing and consists of facts, conceptual ideas, and other information. Motor skills, on the other hand, are organized sets of actions, such as playing an instrument or throwing a ball. Both simple motor actions and skills executed as part of a complex activity are included in this category. Intellectual skills include higher-order acts of thinking, such as solving mathematical problems or correcting grammar. Outside Gagné's framework, several investigations on distributed practice have been conducted in the context of a fourth learning outcome – social and emotional skills. Social and emotional skills include sensitivity to others' needs and fear responses such as phobias.

Meta-analytic data suggest that the effect size of the distributed practice effect varies across domains, with a large effect size for verbal learning ($d = 0.85$; Cepeda et al., 2006; Moss, 1995) and a medium effect size for motor skills learning ($d = 0.5$; Donovan & Radosevich, 1999; Lee & Genovese, 1988). We estimate a medium effect size for intellectual skills learning ($d = 0.5$; based on Foot, 2016; Kapler, Weston, & Wiseheart, 2015; Vlach & Sandhofer, 2012) and a small effect size for social and emotional skills ($d = 0.2$; based on Korben, 1976; Rowe & Craske, 1998).

Tables 22.1, 22.2, 22.3, and 22.4 provide a list of distributed practice studies across a range of different subjects, organized by three of Gagné's (1977, 1984) five learning outcomes, as well as the social and emotional skills domain. Studies with potential confounds (e.g., different number of relearning trials during session 2 for each experimental condition; different retention intervals for each experimental condition) are included to demonstrate the range of topics that have been investigated, but are marked as confounded. The verbal learning literature is so large that we have chosen to highlight only a small subset of studies in Table 22.1. The other three learning outcomes have much smaller literatures; thus, we have included many (although not all) of these studies in Tables 22.2, 22.3, and 22.4. Because the distributed practice literature is, on the whole, very large, it is not surprising that there is a range of reported effect sizes (weak to strong) and, in some cases, reports of mixed findings.

In the sections that follow, we highlight details for a subset of studies listed in Tables 22.1, 22.2, and 22.3 that had the primary goal of translating the distributed practice effect to educational materials and/or educationally relevant time schedules. Contrary to classic distributed practice studies, many of the studies we review are not formal laboratory studies. The emergence of field and simulated-field studies demonstrates a paradigm shift by the research community toward understanding the distributed practice effect in real-world learning environments. We have emphasized disciplines that, in our opinion, offer empirically sound studies, and these disciplines should provide an understanding of the types of learning that will and will not demonstrate distributed practice benefits.

Verbal Learning

Simple word recall and phonics learning. In a traditional distributed practice study, Seabrook, Brown, and Solity (2005: Experiment 3) taught sounds associated with phonemes (i.e., phonics) to five-year-olds in a classroom setting. Massed practice was compared with a 2 minute interstudy interval and the retention interval was two weeks. Distributed study led to greater phonics improvement than massed study in this sample.

Word and fact learning. Sobel, Cepeda, and Kapler (2011) examined vocabulary learning among 5th grade students, using a typical teaching method employed by elementary school teachers. Students studied and practiced recalling definitions of Graduate Record Examinations (GRE) words and practiced using them in sentences. They compared massed practice to one-week spaced practice and the retention

Table 22.1 *Distributed practice studies of verbal learning*

Subject / Skill	Brief Study Description	Time Scale of Interstudy Interval / Retention Interval	Effect Size~	Number of Study Sessions	Notes	References
Medical Treatment	Dementia patients used spaced retrieval to learn names of friends.	Days / Days and Weeks	Weak	9	* %	Hawley (2002)
	Multiple sclerosis patients learned a paragraph of text and a route on a map.	Mins / Secs and Mins	Weak	3		Goverover et al. (2009)
	A developmental amnesia patient (case study) learned words and paired associates.	1 Day / Days	Strong	2		Green et al. (2014)
	Children diagnosed with speech apraxia completed a speech therapy intervention.	Days / n/a	Mixed	4 or 16	* ^	Webb (2011)
	Children born with a cleft palate practiced speech intelligibility.	Days / n/a	Weak	15 or 104	* ^	Pamplona et al. (2005)
Medical Training	Undergraduate students learned to recognize faces.	Secs / Secs	Mixed	3		Wogalter, Jarrard, & Cayard (1991)
	Medical students studied for a medical licensing exam.	Weeks / Weeks	Strong	Multiple	*	Kerfoot et al. (2011)
History	8th grade students learned US history facts.	Weeks / Months	Strong	2		Carpenter, Pashler, & Cepeda (2009)
Language	5th grade students memorized the definitions of Graduate Record Examinations (GRE) words.	Weeks / Months	Strong	2		Sobel, Cepeda, & Kapler (2011)
	Elementary school children learned basic vocabulary in a classroom field study.	Weeks / Days and Weeks	Weak	Multiple		Goossens et al. (2016)
	6th grade students memorized German–English word pairs.	Days / Months	Strong	2		Küpper-Tetzel, Erdfelder, & Dickhäuser (2014)

Description	Interval	Strength	N		Citation
5th grade students completed computerized spelling drills.	Days / Weeks	Strong	3		Fishman, Keller, & Atkinson (1968)
Elementary school children practiced reading fluency.	Days / n/a	Weak	12	<	LaRocco (2008)
Kindergarten students practiced reading fluency.	Days / n/a	Weak	15	<	Griffin (2009)
Elementary school children (with and without language impairments) learned verbs.	Days / Secs and 1 Week	Mixed	4		Riches, Tomasello, & Conti-Ramsden (2005)
At-risk kindergarten students learned phonemic awareness.	Days and Weeks / Secs and Weeks	Mixed	24		Ukrainetz, Ross, & Harm (2009)
High school students memorized English–French word pairs.	Days / Secs and Days	Strong	3		Bloom & Shuell (1981)
Elementary school students learned phonics.	Mins / Weeks	Strong	3		Seabrook, Brown, & Solity (2005), Exp. 3
Undergraduates memorized GRE words using flashcards.	Hours and Days / 1 Day	Strong	4		Kornell (2009), Exp. 2
Undergraduates read and comprehended expository narratives.	1 Week / Secs and Days	Strong	2		Rawson & Kintsch (2005)
Undergraduates read and comprehended expository narratives.	Secs and Days and Weeks / Days	Mixed	2		Verkoeijen, Rikers, & Ozsoy (2008)
Undergraduates learned face-name pairs.	Secs / Mins	Strong	3		Carpenter & DeLosh (2005)

% See Creighton, van der Ploeg, and O'Connor (2013) and Oren, Willerton, and Small (2014) for extensive reviews; all but one reviewed study contained a confound.

* Study contains a potential confound.

< Study did not have a retention interval.

~ Weak indicates not significant or small effect size; strong indicates medium or large effect size and significant or likely to be significant; mixed indicates both weak and strong results.

This table demonstrates the scope of existing research. It is not a complete review.

Table 22.2 *Distributed practice studies of motor skills*

Subject / Skill	Brief Study Description	Time Scale of Interstudy Interval / Retention Interval	Effect Size~	Number of Study Sessions	Notes	References
Aviation	Undergraduates practiced controlling the altitude of a model airplane using a pulley.	Secs / n/a	Strong	Dozens	* ^	Farr, Dey, & Bloch (1956)
Fine Motor	Undergraduates learned to maintain a ratio of keypresses with each of four keys.	Mins and 1 Day / 1 Day	Strong	3		Shea, Lai, Black, & Park (2000), Exp. 2
Gross Motor	Experienced weightlifters practiced lifts.	Mins / n/a	Strong	1	^	Joy et al. (2013)
	Experienced weightlifters practiced lifts.	Secs / n/a	Strong	1	^	Kreutzer (2014)
	Experienced weightlifters practiced lifts.	Secs / n/a	Weak	1	^	Lawton, Cronin, & Lindsell (2006
	Experienced weightlifters practiced lifts.	Days / Days	Strong	12	^	Oliver (2012)
	Experienced weightlifters practiced lifts.	Secs / n/a	Strong	1	^	Willardson & Burkett (2006a, 2006b)
	Undergraduates adapted to biceps strength training.	Mins and Days / Weeks and months	Weak	1 or 3		Calder & Gabriel (2007)
	Undergraduates learned how to balance on a stabilometer.	Mins or 1 Day / 1 Day	Strong	2		Shea et al. (2000), Exp. 1
Medical Training	Medical students practiced bronchoscopy skills.	Mins and Weeks / 1 Month	Weak	3		Bjerrum et al. (2016)
	Medical students practiced endoscopy skills.	Mins and Days / 1 Week	Mixed	3		Verdaasdonk et al. (2007)
	Adult novices practiced laparoscopy skills.	Mins / 5 Mins 1 Week / 2 Weeks	Mixed	3	*	Gallagher, Jordan-Black, & O'Sullivan (2012)
	Medical students practiced laparoscopy skills.	Mins / Mins	Strong	1 or 4		Mackay et al. (2002)

Domain	Description	Acquisition / Retention	Evidence	Number	Symbol	Citation
	Medical students practiced laparoscopy skills.	Mins and 1 Week / 2 Weeks and 1 Year	Mixed	1 or 3		Spruit, Band, & Hamming (2015)
	Medical students practiced vascular anastomosis skills.	Weeks and Months / Mins and Months	Weak	4		Mitchell et al. (2011)
	Medical students practiced vascular anastomosis skills.	Mins and 1 Week / Mins and 1 Month	Mixed	4		Moulton et al. (2006)
Military Training	Undergraduates learned command-and-control skills in a simulated naval warfare environment.	Days / Months	Weak	5 or 9	*	Arthur et al. (2007)
	Adults learned a radar position task (similar to radar intercept missions during flight combat).	Mins and Days / 1 Week	Weak	4		Fleishman & Parker (1962)
	Army reserves practiced machine gun assembly and disassembly.	Weeks / Weeks	Weak	1 or 2	*	Schendel & Hagman (1980)
	Army reserves practiced rifle firing skills.	Days / 1 Day	Mixed	10	*	McGuigan & MacCaslin (1955)
Music	Experienced pianists learned a series of short piano compositions.	Mins and Hours and Days / 2 Weeks	Mixed	1 or 2		Rubin-Rabson (1940)
	Novice pianists learning a melodic sequence.	Mins and Hours and 1 Day / n/a	Mixed	3	<	Simmons (2012)
	Novice undergraduates learning familiar and unfamiliar melodic sequences on a piano.	Mins / Mins	Weak	2		Wiseheart, D'Souza, & Chae (2017)
Sports	Adults learning archery skills.	Days / n/a	Strong	6 to 72	<	Lashley (1915)
	Undergraduates learning to bounce a basketball into the basket from the foul line.	Mins and 1 Day / Mins and Days and Weeks	Mixed	4		Singer (1965)
	Elementary school children learning to dribble a basketball.	Mins / Mins	Strong	2		Christina (1974)
	High school students practicing volleyball serves.	Days / n/a	Weak	6 or 18	<	Fitzgerald (1952)

Table 22.2 (*cont.*)

Subject / Skill	Brief Study Description	Time Scale of Interstudy Interval / Retention Interval	Effect Size~	Number of Study Sessions	Notes	References
	High school students practicing javelin throws.	Days / Months	Weak	34	*	Murphy (1916)
	Undergraduate physical education students learning archery and badminton.	Days / n/a	Mixed	16 or 19	<	Young (1954)
	Undergraduates learning to swim.	Days / n/a	Weak	Variable (5+)	*^	Scott (1954)
	Undergraduate physical education students learning to juggle.	Days / n/a	Strong	Variable (6+)	<	Knapp & Dixon (1950)
	Novice undergraduates practicing putting skills.	Mins and Days / Days and Weeks	Strong	4		Dail & R. Christina (2004)
	Novice high school students practicing putting skills.	Mins / Days	Weak	12		Lynch (1971)
	Novice undergraduates practicing billiards set shots.	Days / 1 Year	Strong	9		Lawrence (1949); Miller (1948)
	Undergraduates learning how to dribble a soccer ball.	Days and Weeks / Days and 1 Month	Strong	3		Murphree (1971)
	Undergraduates learning gymnastics skills.	Mins / n/a	Mixed	10	<	Kleinman (1976)
Vocation	High school students learning typing skills.	Days / n/a	Weak	9	<	Dritsas (1950)
	High school students learning welding skills.	Days / 1 Day	Strong	7 to 20		Drake (1981; 1987)
	Postal workers learning keyboard skills on mail sorting machines.	Hours / Months	Weak	60		Baddeley & Longman (1978)
	Utility employees memorizing computer shortcut keys.	Mins and 1 Day / 1 Week	Strong	4		Rogers (2004)

* Study contains a potential confound.

< Study did not have a retention interval.

~ Weak indicates not significant or small effect size; strong indicates medium or large effect size and significant or likely to be significant; mixed indicates both weak and strong results.

Table 22.3 *Distributed practice studies of intellectual skills*

Subject / Skill	Brief Study Description	Time Scale of Interstudy Interval / Retention Interval	Effect Size~	Number of Study Sessions	Notes	References
Aviation	Aviation students interpreted noisy or distorted air traffic communications between pilots and controllers.	Days / 2 Weeks	Weak	2 to 16		Tobias (1976), Exp. 2
Language	Undergraduates corrected verb errors in text passages.	Days / Weeks and Months	Strong	5		Bird (2010)
Mathematics	Middle school students studied math units.	Weeks / Days	Strong	Multiple	*	Wineland & Stephens (1995)
	8th grade students studied mathematics.	Days / Weeks	Weak	Multiple	*	Liang (1970)
	8th grade students studied mathematics.	Days / Months	Mixed	Multiple	*	Weaver (1976)
	High school students solved plane geometry problems.	Days / Secs and Weeks	Strong	7	*	Yazdani & Zebrowski (2006)
	High school students learned algebra rules.	Days / Months	Weak	Multiple	*	Urwiller (1971)
	Undergraduates solved precalculus problems.	Days / Days	Weak	Multiple	*	Revak (1997)
	Undergraduates learned statistics.	Day / Days	Strong	4	*	Smith & Rothkopf (1984)
	Undergraduates learned statistics.	Secs and Weeks / Months	Strong	Multiple	*	Budé et al. (2011)
	Undergraduates used mathematical reasoning to solve a water displacement problem.	Mins / Mins and 1 Day	Weak	8		Hunt (1969)
	Undergraduates used mathematical reasoning to solve a water displacement problem.	Mins / Mins	Weak	9		Scheel (2007)
	Undergraduates learned algebra rules.	Days / Weeks	Mixed	4	*	Mayfield & Chase (2002); Kim (2003)

Table 22.3 (cont.)

Subject / Skill	Brief Study Description	Time Scale of Interstudy Interval / Retention Interval	Effect Size~	Number of Study Sessions	Notes	References
	Undergraduates solved permutation problems.	1 Week / Weeks	Strong	2		Rohrer & Taylor (2006), Exp. 1
	Undergraduates solved permutation problems.	1 Week / 1 Week	Strong	2		Rohrer & Taylor (2007), Exp. 1
Media Literacy	Elementary school children learned to judge the credibility of a series of websites.	1 Day and 1 Week / Weeks	Strong	3		Foot (2016)
Science	Elementary school children learned biology facts about food chains and reasoning about food chain consequences.	Days / 1 Week	Strong	4		Gluckman, Vlach, & Sandhofer (2014); Vlach & Sandhofer (2012)
	Middle school students learned biology concepts.	Days / Days and Weeks	Strong	Multiple		Reynolds & Glaser (1964), Exp. 1
	High school students learned physics concepts.	Days / Weeks	Strong	Multiple	*	Grote (1995)
	Undergraduates learned astronomy concepts.	Mins / Secs	Strong	3		Lu (1978)
	Undergraduates learned meteorology facts and applied concepts.	Days / Months	Strong	2		Kapler, Weston, & Wiseheart (2015)
Vocational Training	Adults enrolled in labor education classes practiced computer skills, issues in collective bargaining and handling grievances, union leadership, and commonsense economics.	Days and Weeks / Months	Mixed	6	*	Hertenstein (2000)
	Bank employees learned effective sales techniques.	Days / Weeks	Strong	6	*	Kauffeld & Lehmann-Willenbrock (2010)

* Study contains a potential confound.

~ Weak indicates not significant or small effect size; strong indicates medium or large effect size and significant or likely to be significant; mixed indicates both weak and strong results.

Table 22.4 *Distributed practice studies of social and emotional skills*

Subject / Skill	Brief Study Description	Time Scale of Interstudy Interval / Retention Interval	Effect Size~	Number of Study Sessions	Notes	References
Social & Emotional Training	Elementary school children learned emotional coping skills.	Days / n/a	Weak	12	^	Tran (2007)
	Undergraduates learned assertiveness skills.	Weeks / Weeks and Months	Weak	1 or 6		El-Shamy (1976); Korben (1976)
	Undergraduates with arachnophobia completing therapy for extinction of a fear response to spiders.	Mins / Weeks	Strong	1		Rowe & Craske (1998)
	Adult participants enrolled in sensitivity training.	Mins or Days / Months	Weak	1 or dozens		Bare & Mitchell (1972)

^ Study did not have a retention interval.

~ Weak indicates not significant or small effect size; strong indicates medium or large effect size and significant or likely to be significant; mixed indicates both weak and strong results.

interval was five weeks. Students in the spaced condition recalled almost triple the number of definitions on the final test. Using similar stimuli, Kornell (2009) asked undergraduate students to learn GRE words using digital flashcards in an online study. In the spaced condition, participants studied words in a single large stack of twenty cards and the entire stack was presented in the same order four consecutive times. In the massed condition, participants studied the same twenty words in four small stacks of five cards each. Stack #1 was presented four consecutive times, stack #2 was presented four consecutive times, and so forth for all four stacks. Participants were tested for their memory of the words after a median retention interval of 24 hours (range: 17–41 hours). Recall of the word meanings on the final test was, on average, 13 percent higher for words learned in the spaced condition.

In a classroom study, Carpenter, Pashler, and Cepeda (2009) tested 8th grade students on their knowledge of US history facts. After their regularly scheduled exam for the class, students completed delayed relearning of material at interstudy intervals of either one week or sixteen weeks. When tested nine months later, students who had relearned at the sixteen-week interval demonstrated better performance.

Goossens and colleagues (2016) ran field experiments in schools comparing long (two-week) versus short (one-week) interstudy intervals for 2nd, 3rd, 4th, and 6th grade students learning vocabulary words with retention intervals from one to eleven weeks (retention interval varied by age group). Contrary to the evidence presented thus far, the researchers found no systematic differences between the interstudy interval conditions and final memory performance using two different types of tests (cued recall and multiple choice). When they found a difference, it was in the opposite direction, with shorter interstudy intervals outperforming longer ones. However, in the light of previous studies that have revealed a systematic relationship between interstudy interval and retention interval, it is possible that the shorter interstudy interval was better suited for the given retention interval. In addition, field studies like this one introduce higher levels of environmental noise, which can increase error variance in the data and decrease chances of finding an experimental effect.

Second-language learning. Bloom and Shuell (1981) studied vocabulary learning in high school students memorizing English–French vocabulary as part of their regular classwork. Learning took place using multiple-choice, fill in the blank, and cued recall tests. Massed practice and a one-day interstudy interval were compared, and retention intervals of 0 minutes and four days were included. Groups performed equally at the immediate test, and the spaced group showed better performance four days later.

Küpper-Tetzel, Erdfelder, and Dickhäuser (2014) asked 6th grade students in a German school to restudy German–English vocabulary either immediately (massed condition), one day later, or ten days later (two spaced conditions with different interstudy intervals). Final memory tests were given after one week or thirty-five days. In line with previous findings (e.g., Cepeda et al., 2008; Glenberg, 1976), results showed that the optimal interstudy interval for a test one week later was one day, whereas students tested one month later benefited from an interstudy interval of up to ten days.

Text comprehension. Rawson and Kintsch (2005) investigated whether distributed practice aids comprehension of text narratives. Participants read a 2,000-word *Scientific American* excerpt once, twice in a massed fashion, or twice with one week between sessions. They were tested for their comprehension of the passage immediately after the second study session or after a retention interval of two days. Again, the optimal rereading interval depended on the retention interval; massed rereading was best for the immediate test group whereas spaced rereading was best for the delayed test group. Verkoeijen, Rikers, and Ozsoy (2008) replicated the results of this study using three interstudy intervals (massed, four days, and three and a half weeks) and a single two-day retention interval. In the context of their study design, the optimal interstudy interval was four days.

Motor Skills Learning

Sports. Distributed practice has been applied to training protocols in a number of different sports, including golf, basketball, and soccer. For example, Dail and Christina (2004) examined novice golfers (young adults) practicing their putting skills. Massed practice was compared to a one-day interstudy interval, and the golfers' putting performance was assessed following one-, seven-, and twenty-eight-day retention intervals. Distributed practice resulted in better acquisition of golf putting skills as well as improved retention of these skills.

Christina (1974) investigated basketball dribbling in 4th grade students, with dribbling speed as a dependent variable. Massed practice was compared to a 12 minute interstudy interval in which other skills were practiced. The design of this study had additional complexities; overlapping the distributed practice intervention, both massed and spaced groups received distributed practice at several-day interstudy intervals (i.e., several practice sessions occurred during Tuesday and Thursday physical education class sessions). Still, after a formal five-day retention interval, the distributed practice group dribbled faster than the massed group.

Murphree (1971) examined ability to dribble a soccer ball in undergraduates without soccer experience. One group received three consecutive days of practice, a second group received six sessions over three weeks, plus a 20 second rest between trials, and a third group received six sessions over three weeks, plus a 5 minute rest between trials. There was a no practice control group. Retention intervals of several days (exact number not specified) and one month were used. Increasingly spaced groups showed larger gains during skill acquisition. The 5 minute interstudy interval produced the highest scores after each retention interval. There was no evidence of forgetting during the one-month retention interval.

Vocation. Two studies have been conducted examining the effects of distributed practice on welding skills (Drake, 1981, 1987). In both studies, a large number of practice sessions were given, with 5 hours' total training time at welding skills in all conditions. Giving a larger number of shorter training sessions, a form of distributed practice, resulted in higher-quality welding.

Surgical skills. Several researchers have investigated whether distributed practice helps future doctors improve their surgical skills. Bjerrum and colleagues (2016) examined bronchoscopy training using massed practice or a one-week interstudy interval, and a one-month retention interval. Using five different measures of quality of bronchoscope usage, no differences were found between massed and spaced groups.

Verdaasdonk and colleagues (2007) examined endoscopic skills using 15 minute and one-day interstudy intervals, and a one-week retention interval. The spaced group completed tasks faster but no spacing benefit in accuracy was observed. Surgical skills studies show that there are limitations to motor skills benefits from distributed practice. It might be that complex motor skills are less likely to show a distributed practice benefit, while basic motor skills (e.g., repetitive hand movements) are more likely show a benefit.

Intellectual Skills

Mathematics. Rohrer and Taylor (2006) examined permutation problem-solving (sometimes known as transformations in the education domain) in a group of undergraduates, using massed practice and a one-week interstudy interval, and one- and four-week retention intervals. Massed and spaced groups performed equally well at the one-week retention interval, however, the spaced group performed twice as well as the massed group at the four-week retention interval. Rohrer and Taylor (2007) performed a similar study, with less practice per learning session, and found a spacing benefit at the one-week retention interval.

Science. In two studies, 1st and 2nd grade children learned basic biology information using massed versus spaced learning schedules (Gluckman, Vlach, & Sandhofer, 2014; Vlach & Sandhofer, 2012). Children memorized facts about food chains as well how to generalize consequences of disruptions to the food chain. The researchers used interstudy intervals of zero days and one day, and a retention interval of one week. Both massed and spaced lessons benefited memory for facts, with a larger increase in recall for spaced learning. However, only spaced learning resulted in generalization skill improvements. A review of category learning by Vlach (2014) suggests that distributed practice helps infants and preschool aged children to generalize to novel exemplars of a category.

Reynolds and Glaser (1964) examined learning of biology concepts (via computer instruction and testing) in middle school classrooms. In their second experiment, massed and one-day interstudy intervals were compared (intervals estimated, as not explicitly stated by the authors), and retention intervals of ten days and thirty-one days were used. Distributed practice benefited final test performance at both retention intervals.

Lu (1978) taught undergraduates astronomy facts using audio lectures, using either massed learning one concept at a time, or distributed learning in which concepts were repeated throughout the lecture. In the spaced group, a specific interstudy interval was not used. Rather, concepts were repeated and related to new content that was presented in later parts of the lecture. Spaced learning resulted in higher test scores immediately following the lecture.

Kapler and colleagues (2015) presented a lecture on meteorology to a group of undergraduates in a simulated classroom study. Students completed a comprehension test immediately after the lecture to ensure learning had taken place. After interstudy intervals of either one day or eight days, students reviewed the content of the lecture in an online quiz containing both short answer questions and equivalent multiple-choice questions (to ensure relearning had taken place). After a retention interval of thirty-five days, students were tested for their fact knowledge as well as their ability to apply learned information to solve a series of novel problems. Students in the spaced group outperformed students in the massed group on both factual knowledge and application skills, though the effect size was smaller for the latter.

Literacy. Foot (2016) taught 4th through 6th grade students a set of criteria for evaluating the credibility of a website (i.e., media literacy). Credibility lessons were presented on three consecutive days or one lesson per week. After a thirty-five-day retention interval, students in the spaced group recalled more of the criteria and were better able to explain their credibility rating of a novel website compared to students in the massed group.

Bird (2010) taught undergraduate students with intermediate English language proficiency to correctly use verb tenses, with interstudy intervals of three days and fourteen days, and retention intervals of seven days and sixty days. After the seven-day retention interval, both interstudy interval conditions performed equally well (both groups improved in comparison to pretest). After the sixty-day retention interval, students in the fourteen-day condition demonstrated better language reasoning skills than students in three-day interstudy interval condition, indicating a distributed practice benefit for long-term retention.

Summary of Findings

The distributed practice effect appears to be most beneficial for mastering fact learning (e.g., word recall, vocabulary, second-language learning, text comprehension). Although rote memory of words and facts may sound like a shallow type of learning, many disciplines require good foundational knowledge before higher-order thinking skills enter the learning process (e.g., medicine, engineering, law).

Motor skills also benefit from distributed practice, such as in sports training and basic motor training. Unlike verbal learning studies, motor skills studies typically employ several practice sessions, not just the two sessions (basic research design) or even three sessions (complex research design) that characterize the majority of the literature. Motor skills learning is not simply defined by a single correct or incorrect answer; rather outcome measures such as timing, balance, and coordination are uniquely measured and reported. It appears that less forgetting takes place between study sessions during motor practice (e.g., Murphree, 1971; Wiseheart et al., 2017), which may have important implications for theory development of the distributed practice effect.

Evidence for the distributed practice effect in the domain of intellectual skills suggests that this strategy may be applied to higher-level thinking abilities, although the effect might not be as strong. The broad nature of this domain makes generalizations from the data more difficult. It is a challenge for researchers to define what exactly is meant by terms such as conceptual learning, intellectual skills, and critical thinking skills. Moreover, assessing this type of learning is difficult when, like motor learning, there is typically no "correct" answer. Despite these complications, research in this area may contribute to theory development. For example, in the study by Kapler and colleagues (2015), distributed practice improved participants' application skills not only for items that were reviewed at the second study session but also for items that were *not reviewed* at the second study session. This outcome suggests that when learning is not single-fact–based but rather unit- or concept-based (i.e., holistic), distributed practice may have effects on the entire learning experience. Reviewing one concept may implicitly prompt the learner to think of other (nonreviewed) concepts, thereby strengthening memory for all of the information.

Recommendations for Integrating Distributed Practice into Classroom Instruction

As our review of the literature demonstrates, researchers have put great effort into translating distributed practice from the lab into real (or simulated) classrooms and/or using real curricula (e.g., Foot, 2016; Kapler et al., 2015). Generally, the results are positive, which is impressive considering the added variability and complexities of real-world learning (e.g., students missing classes, student distraction, preknowledge of curriculum material; but see Goossens et al., 2016). The field is at a point where preliminary recommendations can be made to educators and students about how and when to integrate distributed practice into classroom learning. These recommendations may challenge traditional curriculum structure, requiring educators to put more emphasis on integration or restructuring of material rather than simply covering a quantity of information.

Distributed practice is appealing for integration into classroom instruction due to its beneficial effects on learning, reliability across participants and time scales, as well as its versatile potential for implementation. Table 22.5 lists a number of suggestions for implementing a distributed practice strategy into real-world classroom instruction. From the educator's point of view, teachers may choose to space out homework practice (Laing & Peterson, 1973; Peterson, 1971), to administer weekly review quizzes and/or cumulative tests, or choose textbooks that include opportunities for distributed practice (e.g., for a review, see Hood & Ivie, 2003; see also Baldree, 2003; Harden & Stamper, 1999; cf. Johnson & Smith, 1987; Klingele & Reed, 1983; Saxon, 1982). From the student's point of view, learners may choose to

Table 22.5 *Suggestions for implementing distributed practice into classroom instruction*

Teaching Tool	Implementation Techniques
Homework	Students complete at least one practice item from the previous class/week in the homework assigned for the current class/week.
Weekly quizzes	In-class (or online) quizzes that cover material from the previous class/week. Quizzes can be graded for accuracy or simply for completion.
Cumulative exams	Final assessments that cover entire contents of a course. This approach works well in combination with weekly quizzes so that the amount of to-be-learned material is not overwhelming.
Textbooks	Books, articles, and other reference materials that use a distributed practice or interleaving approach.
Technology	Apps, games, and study reminders that integrate distributed practice in entertaining (and portable) ways.

allocate their study time in more efficient ways. They may download games and apps or set study reminders on their electronic devices that maximize learning, even while they are on the go from home to school. We are aware of a number of smartphone apps (e.g., Eidetic, Memrise) that use distributed practice (and also adjust number of learning trials throughout the learning process) to help the learner maximize their performance (e.g., flashcards for the verbal GRE; flashcards for second-language learning). By applying a distributed learning approach, students will be forced to rethink conventional study habits. Study habits that are fluid and that involve little mental effort generally do not support long-term maintenance of knowledge. Rather, when acquisition is made slower or more difficult, as it is with distributed practice, long-term retention is supported. Researchers have termed this type of learning "desirably difficult" (Bjork & Bjork, 2011).

Optimal interstudy intervals for classroom learning depend mostly on how long information needs to be retained, and there is no definitive answer to this question. As study-phase retrieval theory suggests, difficult-to-learn information should be reviewed at shorter time intervals to ensure it is not completely forgotten at review. Yet assuming a desire for long-term retention, contextual variability theory suggests that information should be reviewed at an interval spaced far enough in time that contextual cues in the learning environment have a chance to vary. This review schedule will increase the likelihood that contextual cues at study and test will match, thereby aiding final retrieval. We recommend that study sessions be spaced widely (e.g., across days or weeks) so that the chances of long-term retention are maximized.

A Paradigm Shift in Pedagogical Practices

Although we can make predictions about what information will benefit from distributed practice and at what learning schedules, and we can make recommendations for how to implement spacing into everyday practice, the strategy can only fully be integrated into real educational contexts if educators and policy advisors seriously rethink traditional pedagogical practices. As Vash (1989) writes, "education policy setters know perfectly well [distributed practice] works better; they don't care. It isn't tidy. It doesn't let teachers teach a unit and dust off their hands quickly with a nice sense of 'Well, *that's* done'" (p. 1547). Vash alludes to the fact that many teachers are accustomed to covering topics in chunks, only once per semester, and giving noncomprehensive tests. Teachers are constrained by time and have a lot of curriculum to cover within a narrow time frame. Given these pressures, a unit-by-unit teaching approach might appear to be the best (and perhaps only) option. As discussed at the outset of the chapter, this type of teaching prioritizes the quantity of the content covered over integration of students' knowledge throughout their educational experience. Distributed practice is a strategy that, if used effectively, can vastly improve the quality of student learning and at no (or very little) additional time cost.

Limitations and Directions for Future Research

The distributed practice effect has been studied exhaustively in the laboratory. Although many of these lab studies have involved rigorous experimental methods, others contain confounds in experimental design or analysis problems that preclude interpretation of findings. For example, it is critical that retention interval is controlled across all interstudy interval conditions, which can be particularly problematic in list learning paradigms of the distributed practice effect (although applicable to multiday paradigms, too). Furthermore, equating the number of learning trials across conditions and including a discrete retention interval(s) are also critical design decisions.

A great number of studies evaluating the distributed practice effect in classrooms have appeared in the last decade. This is a promising shift in the published literature and we look forward to more of this work. Well-conducted classroom studies require collaborations between psychologists (who have expertise in research design) and field-specific experts and affiliates, such as school boards, principals, and teachers (who have expertise in curriculum and implementation). These collaborations between distributed practice experts and experts outside psychology are needed so that students in a wide range of fields, including outside traditional academia, can benefit from use of distributed practice. Tables 22.1, 22.2, 22.3, and 22.4 provide a good representation of fields that are ripe for future collaborations. Future hallmark studies will be those that employ a large number of classrooms, teachers, and disciplines and that, ideally, use a randomized controlled trial approach to compare the distributed practice strategy to whatever is the current status quo for classroom learning. We encourage improved dialogue among all collaborators.

Whether in the laboratory or in the classroom, more studies are needed that investigate the distributed practice effect outside of the verbal learning domain. While difficult to design and conduct, and requiring dedication to strong and respectful collaborations, these types of studies are needed to bridge the gap between laboratory and classroom.

Overall, we believe that educators and students alike need to take a hard look at why we teach and why we are motivated to learn. Using detrimental learning strategies like cramming might be a viable option for an immediate assessment, but research shows that in the long run it is often ineffective. Students will need to invest more time in relearning the material if it is needed again in the future. In comparison to other educational interventions, distributed practice has been ranked quite high (#27 out of 195 in a review by Hattie, 2015), and it can and should be used to improve classroom outcomes (e.g., American Association for the Advancement of Science, 1962; Carpenter et al., 2012; Dempster, 1987, 1988; Kiepert, 2009; Pashler et al., 2007). Based on the available empirical evidence and the potential ease with which distributed practice can be implemented, we endorse the use of distributed practice as a means for enhancing the quality of student learning.

References

American Association for the Advancement of Science (1962). Strengthening the behavioral sciences. *Science*, *136*(3512), 233–241. https://doi.org/10.1126/science.136.3512.233

Arthur, W.Jr., Day, E. A., Villado, A. J., Boatman, P. R., Kowollik, V., Bennett Jr., W., & Bhupatkar, A. (2007). *Decay, transfer, and the reacquisition of a complex skill: An investigation of practice schedules, observational rehearsal, and individual differences*. Woburn, MA: Aptima.

Baddeley, A. D. & Longman, D. J. A. (1978). The influence of length and frequency of training session on the rate of learning to type. *Ergonomics*, *21*(8), 627–635. https://doi.org/10.1080/00140137808931764

Baldree, C. L. (2003). The effectiveness of two mathematical instructional programs on the mathematics growth of eighth grade students. (Unpublished doctoral dissertation). University of Georgia, Athens, GA.

Balota, D. A., Duchek, J. M., & Logan, J. M. (2007). Is expanded retrieval practice a superior form of spaced retrieval? A critical review of the extant literature. In J. S. Nairne (ed.), *The foundations of remembering* (pp. 83–105). New York: Psychology Press.

Balota, D. A., Duchek, J. M., Sergent-Marshall, S. D., & Roediger III, H. L. (2006). Does expanded retrieval produce benefits over equal-interval spacing? Explorations of spacing effects in healthy aging and early stage Alzheimer's disease. *Psychology and Aging*, *21*(1), 19–31. https://doi.org/10.1037/0882–7974.21.1.19

Bare, C. E. & Mitchell, R. R. (1972). Experimental evaluation of sensitivity training. *The Journal of Applied Behavioral Science*, *8*(3), 263–276. https://doi.org/10.1177/002188637200800301

Benjamin, A. S. & Tullis, J. (2010). What makes distributed practice effective? *Cognitive Psychology*, *61*(3), 228–247. https://doi.org/10.1016/j.cogpsych.2010.05.004

Bird, S. (2010). Effects of distributed practice on the acquisition of second language English syntax. *Applied Psycholinguistics*, *31*(4), 635–650. https://doi.org/10.1017/S0142716410000172

Bjerrum, A. S., Eika, B., Charles, P., & Hilberg, O. (2016). Distributed practice. The more the merrier? A randomised bronchoscopy simulation study. *Medical Education Online*, *21*(1), 30517. https://doi.org/10.3402/meo.v21.30517

Bjork, E. L. & Bjork, R. A. (2011). Making things hard on yourself, but in a good way: Creating desirable difficulties to enhance learning. In M. A. Gernsbacher, R. W. Pew, L. M. Hough, & J. R. Pomerantz (eds.), *Psychology and the real world: Essays illustrating fundamental contributions to society* (pp. 56–64). New York: Worth Publishers.

Bloom, K. C. & Shuell, T. J. (1981). Effects of massed and distributed practice on the learning and retention of second-language vocabulary. *Journal of Educational Research*, *74*(4), 245–248. https://doi.org/10.1080/00220671.1981.10885317

Budé, L., Imbos, T., van de Wiel, M. W., & Berger, M. P. (2011). The effect of distributed practice on students' conceptual understanding of statistics. *Higher Education*, *62*(1), 69–79. https://doi.org/10.1007/s10734-010-9366-y

Calder, K. M. & Gabriel, D. A. (2007). Adaptations during familiarization to resistive exercise. *Journal of Electromyography and Kinesiology*, *17*(3), 328–335. https://doi.org/10.1016/j.jelekin.2006.02.006

Carpenter, S. K., Cepeda, N. J., Rohrer, D., Kang, S. K., & Pashler, H. (2012). Using spacing to enhance diverse forms of learning: Review of recent research and implications for instruction. *Educational Psychology Review*, *24*(3), 369–378. https://doi.org/10.1007/s10648-012-9205-z

Carpenter, S. K. & DeLosh, E. L. (2005). Application of the testing and spacing effects to name-learning. *Applied Cognitive Psychology*, *19*(5), 619–636. https://doi.org/10.1002/acp.1101

Carpenter, S. K., Pashler, H., & Cepeda, N. J. (2009). Using tests to enhance 8th grade students' retention of U.S. history facts. *Applied Cognitive Psychology*, *23*(6), 760–771. https://doi.org/10.1002/acp.1507

Cepeda, N. J., Pashler, H., Vul, E., Wixted, J. T., & Rohrer, D. (2006). Distributed practice in verbal recall tasks: A review and quantitative synthesis. *Psychological Bulletin*, *132*(3), 354–380. https://doi.org/10.1037/0033-2909.132.3.354

Cepeda, N. J., Vul, E., Rohrer, D., Wixted, J. T., & Pashler, H. (2008). Spacing effects in learning: A temporal ridgeline of optimal retention. *Psychological Science*, *19*(11), 1095–1102. https://doi.org/10.1111/j.1467-9280.2008.02209.x

Cermak, L. S., Verfaellie, M., Lanzoni, S., Mather, M., & Chase, K. A. (1996). Effect of spaced repetitions on amnesia patients' recall and recognition performance. *Neuropsychology*, *10*(2), 219. https://doi.org/10.1037/0894-4105.10.2.219

Christina, W. B. (1974). The effects of massed and distributed practice on the performance of a gross motor skill. (Master's thesis). The College at Brockport, New York.

Cull, W. L. (2000). Untangling the benefits of multiple study opportunities and repeated testing for cued recall. *Applied Cognitive Psychology*, *14*(3), 215–235. https://doi.org/10.1002/(SICI)1099-0720(200005/06)14:3<215::AID-ACP640>3.0.CO;2-1

Dail, T. K. & Christina, R. W. (2004). Distribution of practice and metacognition in learning and long-term retention of a discrete motor task. *Research Quarterly for Exercise and Sport*, *75*(2), 148–155. https://doi.org/10.1080/02701367.2004.10609146

Delaney, P. F., Verkoeijen, P. P., & Spirgel, A. (2010). Spacing and testing effects: A deeply critical, lengthy, and at times discursive review of the literature. *Psychology of Learning and Motivation*, *53*, 63–147. https://doi.org/10.1016/S0079-7421(10)53003-2

Dempster, F. N. (1987). Time and the production of classroom learning: Discerning implications from basic research. *Educational Psychologist*, *22*(1), 1–21. https://doi.org/10.1207/s15326985ep2201_1

(1988). The spacing effect: A case study in the failure to apply the results of psychological research. *American Psychologist*, *43*(8), 627–634. https://doi.org/10.1037/0003-066X.43.8.627

Descours, K. (2013). Teachers' perceptions of critical thinking. (Unpublished master's thesis). York University, Toronto, ON.

Diekelmann, S., Wilhelm, I., & Born, J. (2009). The whats and whens of sleep-dependent memory consolidation. *Sleep Medicine Reviews*, *13*, 309–321. https://doi.org/10.1016/j.smrv.2008.08.002

Donovan, J. J. & Radosevich, D. J. (1999). A meta-analytic review of the distribution of practice effect. *Journal of Applied Psychology*, *84*(5), 795–805. https://doi.org/10.1037/0021–9010.84.5.795

Drake, J. B. (1981). The theory of distributed practice as related to acquisition of psychomotor skills by adolescents in a selected curricular field. *The High School Journal*, *65*(1), 26–32.

(1987). Effects of distributed practice theory on arc welding skill development of agriculture students. *Journal of the American Association of Teacher Educators in Agriculture*, *28*(3), 16–21. https://doi.org/10.5032/jaatea.1987.03016

Dritsas, A. (1950). A study to determine the effectiveness of a relative massing time pattern as compared with an additive time pattern on skill development in typewriting. (Unpublished doctoral dissertation). Boston University, Boston, MA.

Ebbinghaus, H. (1885/1964). *Memory: A contribution to experimental psychology* (trans. H. A. Ruger, C. E. Bussenius, & E. R. Hilgar). New York: Dover Publications.

El-Shamy, S. E. (1976). The effects of time-spacing on outcomes in assertion training for women: The effectiveness of a workshop model (Unpublished doctoral dissertation). Indiana University, Bloomington, IN.

Estes, W. K. (1955). Statistical theory of distributional phenomena in learning. *Psychological Review*, *62*(5), 369–377. https://doi.org/10.1037/h0046888

Farr, R. G., Dey, M. K., & Bloch, E. (1956). The airplane control test: A compensatory pursuit task. *Perceptual and Motor Skills*, *6*(3), 77–80. https://doi.org/10.2466/pms.1956.6.3.77

Fishman, E. J., Keller, L., & Atkinson, R. C. (1968). Massed versus distributed practice in computerized spelling drills. *Journal of Educational Psychology*, *59*(4), 290–296. https://doi.org/10.1037/h0020055

Fitzgerald, M. A. (1952). The effect of two time patterns on developing a secondary motor skill. (Unpublished doctoral dissertation). Boston University, Boston, MA.

Fleishman, E. A. & Parker Jr, J. F. (1962). Factors in the retention and relearning of perceptual-motor skill. *Journal of Experimental Psychology*, *64*(3), 215–226. https://doi.org/10.1037/h0041220

Foot, V. (2016). *Judging Credibility: Can spaced lessons help students think more critically online?* (Unpublished master's thesis). York University, Toronto, ON.

Gagné, R. M. (1977). *The conditions of learning*, 3rd edn. New York: Holt, Rinehart, and Winston.

(1984). Learning outcomes and their effects. *American Psychologist*, *39*(4), 377–385. https://doi.org/10.1037/0003-066X.39.4.377

Gallagher, A. G., Jordan-Black, J. A., & O'Sullivan, G. C. (2012). Prospective, randomized assessment of the acquisition, maintenance, and loss of laparoscopic skills. *Annals of Surgery, 256*(2), 387–393. https://doi.org/10.1097/SLA.0b013e318251f3d2

Glenberg, A. M. (1976). Monotonic and nonmonotonic lag effects in paired-associate and recognition memory paradigms. *Journal of Verbal Learning and Verbal Behavior, 15*(1), 1–16. https://doi.org/10.1016/S0022-5371(76)90002-5

(1979). Component-levels theory of the effects of spacing of repetitions on recall and recognition. *Memory and Cognition, 7*(2), 95–112. https://doi.org/10.3758/BF03197590

Gluckman, M., Vlach, H. A., & Sandhofer, C. M. (2014). Spacing simultaneously promotes multiple forms of learning in children's science curriculum. *Applied Cognitive Psychology, 28*(2), 266–273. https://doi.org/10.1002/acp.2997

Goossens, N. A. M. C., Camp, G., Verkoeijen, P. P. J. L. et al. (2016). Distributed practice and retrieval practice in primary school vocabulary learning: A multi-classroom study. *Applied Cognitive Psychology, 30*(5), 700–712. https://doi.org/10.1002/acp.3245

Goverover, Y., Hillary, F. G., Chiaravalloti, N., Arango-Lasprilla, J. C., & DeLuca, J. (2009). A functional application of the spacing effect to improve learning and memory in persons with multiple sclerosis. *Journal of Clinical and Experimental Neuropsychology, 31*(5), 513–522. https://doi.org/10.1080/13803390802287042

Green, J. L., Weston, T., Wiseheart, M., & Rosenbaum, R. S. (2014). Long-term spacing effect benefits in developmental amnesia: Case experiments in rehabilitation. *Neuropsychology, 28*(5), 685. https://doi.org/10.1037/neu0000070

Griffin, C. S. (2009). A comparison of the effectiveness and efficiency of traditional phonics-distributed practice, traditional phonics-massed practice, and incremental rehearsal on kindergarten students' letter-sound correspondence performance. (Unpublished doctoral dissertation). The Ohio State University, Columbus, OH.

Grote, M. G. (1995). Distributed versus massed practice in high school physics. *School Science and Mathematics, 95*(2), 97–101. https://doi.org/10.1111/j.1949-8594.1995.tb15736.x

Harden, R. M. & Stamper, N. (1999). What is a spiral curriculum? *Medical Teacher, 21*(2), 141–143. https://doi.org/10.1080/01421599979752

Hattie, J. (2015). The applicability of visible learning to higher education. *Scholarship of Teaching and Learning in Psychology, 1*(1), 79. https://doi.org/10.1037/stl0000021

Hawley, K. S. (2002). Spaced-retrieval effects on name-face recognition in older adults with probable Alzheimer's disease. (Unpublished master's thesis). Louisiana State University, Baton Rouge, LA.

Hertenstein, E. J. (2000). The interaction between learning goal orientation and differentially distributed-practice training designs in labor education. (Unpublished doctoral dissertation). University of Illinois at Urbana-Champaign, Urbana, IL.

Hintzman, D. L. (1974). Theoretical implications of the spacing effect. In R. L. Solso (ed.), *Theories in cognitive psychology: The Loyola Symposium* (pp. 77–99). Potomac, MD: Erlbaum.

Hintzman, D. L., Block, R. A., & Summers, J. J. (1973). Modality tags and memory for repetitions: Locus of the spacing effect. *Journal of Verbal Learning and Verbal Behavior, 12*(2), 229–238. https://doi.org/10.1016/S0022-5371(73)80013-1

Hood, T. & Ivie, S. D. (2003). Is Saxon Math the answer? *Journal of Philosophy and History of Education, 53*, 64–82.

Hovland, C. I. (1939). Experimental studies in rote-learning theory. V. Comparison of distribution of practice in serial and paired-associate learning. *Journal of Experimental Psychology*, *25*(6), 622–633. https://doi.org/10.1037/h0062807

Hunt, B. J. (1969). The effects of massed and distributed practice on problem solving (Unpublished doctoral dissertation). University of Nebraska, Lincoln, NE.

Johnson, D. M. & Smith, B. (1987). An evaluation of Saxon's algebra text. *The Journal of Educational Research*, *81*(2), 97–102. https://doi.org/10.1080/00220671.1987.10885804

Jost, A. (1897). Die Assoziationsfestigkeit in ihrer Abhängigkeit von der Verteilung der Wiederholungen [The strength of associations in their dependence on the distribution of repetitions]. *Zeitschrift für Psychologie und Physiologie der Sinnesorgane*, *14*, 436–472.

Joy, J. M., Oliver, J. M., McCleary, S. A., Lowery, R. P., & Wilson, J. M. (2013). Power output and electromyography activity of the back squat exercise with cluster sets. *Journal of Sports Sciences*, *1*, 37–45.

Kang, S. H., Lindsey, R. V., Mozer, M. C., & Pashler, H. (2014). Retrieval practice over the long term: Should spacing be expanding or equal-interval? *Psychonomic Bulletin and Review*, *21*(6), 1544–1550. https://doi.org/10.3758/s13423-014-0636-z

Kapler, I. V., Weston, T., & Wiseheart, M. (2015). Long-term retention benefits from the spacing effect in a simulated undergraduate classroom using simple and complex curriculum material. *Learning and Instruction*, *36*, 38–45. https://doi.org/10.1016/j.learninstruc.2014.11.001

Kauffeld, S. & Lehmann-Willenbrock, N. (2010). Sales training: effects of spaced practice on training transfer. *Journal of European Industrial Training*, *34*(1), 23–37. https://doi.org/10.1108/03090591011010299

Kerfoot, B. P., Shaffer, K., McMahon, G. T., Baker, H., Kirdar, J., Kanter, S., Corbett Jr., E. C., Berkow, R., Krupat, E., & Armstrong, E. G. (2011). Online "spaced education progress-testing" of students to confront two upcoming challenges to medical schools. *Academic Medicine*, *86*(3), 300–306. https://doi.org/10.1097/ACM.0b013e3182087bef

Kiepert, M. H. (2009). An examination of repetition and the spacing effect in the classroom: A self-report survey of teachers. (Unpublished doctoral dissertation). Temple University, Philadelphia, PA.

Kim, C. (2003). Cumulative review: Effects of random alternation of review items on mathematics problem solving. (Unpublished doctoral dissertation). West Virginia University, Morgantown, WV.

Kleinman, M. (1976). The effects of practice distribution on the acquisition of three discrete motor skills. *Research Quarterly. American Alliance for Health, Physical Education and Recreation*, *47*(4), 672–677.

Klingele, W. E. & Reed, B. W. (1984). An Examination of an incremental approach to mathematics. *Phi Delta Kappan*, *65*(10), 712–13.

Knapp, C. G. & Dixon, W. R. (1950). Learning to juggle: I. A study to determine the effect of two different distributions of practice on learning efficiency. *Research Quarterly. American Association for Health, Physical Education and Recreation*, *21*(3), 331–340.

Korben, D. L. (1976). The effects of distributed practice versus massed practice, and behavioral modeling versus script modeling, on assertive training with females. (Unpublished doctoral dissertation). Indiana University, Bloomington, IN.

Kornell, N. (2009). Optimizing learning using flashcards: spacing is more effective than cramming. *Applied Cognitive Psychology*, *23*(9), 1297–1317. https://doi.org/10.1002/acp.1537

Kornell, N. & Bjork, R. A. (2008). Optimising self-regulated study: The benefits – and costs – of dropping flashcards. *Memory*, *16*(2), 125–136. https://doi.org/10.1080/09658210701763899

Kornell, N. & Bjork, R. A. (2008). Learning concepts and categories is spacing the "enemy of induction"? *Psychological science*, *19*(6), 585–592. https://doi.org/10.1111/j.1467-9280.2008.02127.x

Kreutzer, A. (2014). Acute kinematic, kinetic, and hormonal responses to cluster sets in parallel back squat exercise in trained and untrained young men utilizing hypertrophic intensities. (Unpublished master's thesis). Texas Christian University, Fort Worth, TX.

Küpper-Tetzel, C. E. (2014). Strong effects on weak theoretical grounds: Understanding the distributed practice effect. Zeitschrift für Psychologie *[Journal of Psychology]*, *222*, 71–81. https://doi.org/10.1027/2151-2604/a000168

Küpper-Tetzel, C. E. & Erdfelder, E. (2012). Encoding, maintenance, and retrieval processes in the lag effect: A multinomial processing tree analysis. *Memory*, *20*(1), 37–47. https://doi.org/10.1080/09658211.2011.631550

Küpper-Tetzel, C. E., Erdfelder, E., & Dickhauser, O. (2014). The lag effect in secondary school classrooms: Enhancing students' memory for vocabulary. *Instructional Science*, *42*(3), 373–388. https://doi.org/10.1007/s11251-013-9285-2

Küpper-Tetzel, C. E., Kapler, I. V., & Wiseheart, M. (2014). Contracting, equal, and expanding learning schedules: The optimal distribution of learning sessions depends on retention interval. *Memory and Cognition. 42*(5), 729–741. https://doi.org/10.3758/s13421-014-0394-1

Laing, R. A. & Peterson, J. C. (1973). Assignments: Yesterday, Today, and Tomorrow – Today. *The Mathematics Teacher*, *66*(6), 508–518.

LaRocco, A. J. (2008). An investigation of the repeated reading intervention for improving reading fluency: A doctoral dissertation. (Unpublished doctoral dissertation). University of Iowa, Iowa City, IA.

Lashley, K. S. (1915). The acquisition of skill in archery. *Papers from the Department of Marine Biology of the Carnegie Institution of Washington*, *7*, 105–128.

Lawrence, D. H. (1949). Acquired distinctiveness of cues: I. Transfer between discriminations on the basis of familiarity with the stimulus. *Journal of Experimental Psychology*, *39*(6), 770–784. https://doi.org/10.1037/h0058097

Lawton, T. W., Cronin, J. B., & Lindsell, R. P. (2006). Effect of interrepetition rest intervals on weight training repetition power output. *The Journal of Strength and Conditioning Research*, *20*(1), 172–176.

Lee, T. D. & Genovese, E. D. (1988). Distribution of practice in motor skill acquisition: Learning and performance effects reconsidered. *Research Quarterly for Exercise and Sport*, *59*(4), 277–287. https://doi.org/10.1080/02701367.1988.10609373

Liang, R. A. (1970). Relative effects of massed and distributed scheduling of topics on homework assignments of eighth grade mathematics students. (Unpublished doctoral dissertation). Ohio State University, Columbus, OH.

Lindsey, R., Mozer, M. C., Cepeda, N. J., & Pashler, H. (2009). Optimizing memory retention with cognitive models. In A. Howes, D. Peebles, & R. Cooper (eds.), *Proceedings of the ninth international conference on cognitive modeling (ICCM)*. Manchester: University of Manchester.

Lu, P. K. (1978). Three integrative models of kinetic structure in teaching astronomy. *Journal of Research in Science Teaching*, *15*(4), 249–255. https://doi.org/10.1002/tea.3660150403

Lynch, G. I. S. (1971). Effects of three practice conditions on the acquisition of golf skill. (Unpublished doctoral dissertation). Texas Tech University, Lubbock, TX.

Mackay, S., Morgan, P., Datta, V., Chang, A., & Darzi, A. (2002). Practice distribution in procedural skills training. *Surgical Endoscopy*, *16*(6), 957–961. https://doi.org/10.1007/s00464-001–9132-4

Mayfield, K. H. & Chase, P. N. (2002). The effects of cumulative practice on mathematics problem solving. *Journal of Applied Behavior Analysis*, *35*(2), 105–123. https://doi.org/10.1901/jaba.2002.35–105

McCabe, J. (2011). Metacognitive awareness of learning strategies in undergraduates. *Memory and Cognition*, *39*(3), 462–476. https://doi.org/10.3758/s13421-010–0035-2

McGuigan, F. J. & MacCaslin, E. F. (1955). Whole and part methods in learning a perceptual motor skill. *The American Journal of Psychology*, *68*(4), 658–661. https://doi.org/10.2307/1418796

Miller, A. G. (1948). The effect of various interpolated time patterns on motor learning. (Unpublished doctoral dissertation). Boston University, Boston, MA.

Melton, A. W. (1970). The situation with respect to the spacing of repetitions and memory. *Journal of Verbal Learning and Verbal Behavior*, *9*(5), 596–606. https://doi.org/10.1016/S0022-5371(70)80107–4

Mitchell, E. L., Lee, D. Y., Sevdalis, N., Partsafas, A. W., Landry, G. J., Liem, T. K., & Moneta, G. L. (2011). Evaluation of distributed practice schedules on retention of a newly acquired surgical skill: a randomized trial. *The American Journal of Surgery*, *201*(1), 31–39. https://doi.org/10.1016/j.amjsurg.2010.07.040

Moss, V. D. (1995). The efficacy of massed versus distributed practice as a function of desired learning outcomes and grade level of the student. (Unpublished doctoral dissertation). Utah State University, Logan, UT.

Moulton, C. E., Dubrowski, A., Macrae, H., Graham, B., Grober, E., & Reznick, R. (2006). Teaching surgical skills: What kind of practice makes perfect? *Annals of Surgery*, *244*(3), 400–409. https://doi.org/10.1097/01.sla.0000234808.85789.6a

Mozer, M. C., Pashler, H., Cepeda, N. J., Lindsey, R., & Vul, E. (2009). Predicting the optimal spacing of study: A multiscale context model of memory. In Y. Bengio, D. Schuurmans, J. Lafferty, C. K. I. Williams, & A. Culotta (eds.), *Advances in Neural Information Systems 22*. San Diego, CA: Neural Information Processing Systems Foundation.

Murray, J. T. (1983). Spacing phenomena in human memory: A study phase retrieval interpretation. (Unpublished doctoral dissertation). University of California, Los Angeles, Los Angeles, CA.

Murphree, T. R. (1971). Effects of massed and distributed practice upon motor learning and retention of a novel gross motor task. (Unpublished doctoral dissertation). North Texas State University, Denton, TX.

Murphy, H. H. (1916). Distribution of practice periods in learning. *Journal of Educational Psychology*, *7*(3), 150–162. https://doi.org/10.1037/h0074113

Oliver, J. M. (2012). *Intra-set rest intervals in hypertrophic training: Effects on hypertrophy, strength, power, and myosin heavy chain composition* (Unpublished doctoral dissertation). Texas A&M University, College Station, TX.

Pamplona, C., Ysunza, A., Patiño, C., Ramírez, E., Drucker, M., & Mazón, J. J. (2005). Speech summer camp for treating articulation disorders in cleft palate patients. *International Journal of Pediatric Otorhinolaryngology, 69*(3), 351–359. https://doi.org/10.1016/j.ijporl.2004.10.012

Pashler, H., Bain, P. M., Bottge, B. A., Graesser, A., Koedinger, K., McDaniel, M., & Metcalfe, J. (2007). *Organizing instruction and study to improve student learning* (NCER 2007–2004). Washington, DC: National Center for Education Research, Institute of Education Sciences, and US Department of Education. http://ncer.ed.gov.

Peterson, J. C. (1971). Four organizational patterns for assigning mathematics homework. *School Science and Mathematics, 71*(7), 592–596. https://doi.org/10.1111/j.1949-8594.1971.tb13760.x

Peterson, L. R., Wampler, R., Kirkpatrick, M., & Saltzman, D. (1963). Effect of spacing presentations on retention of a paired associate over short intervals. *Journal of Experimental Psychology, 66*(2), 206–209. https://doi.org/10.1037/h0046694

Raaijmakers, J. G. (2003). Spacing and repetition effects in human memory: Application of the SAM model. *Cognitive Science, 27*(3), 431–452. https://doi.org/10.1207/s15516709cog2703_5

Rasch, B. & Born, J. (2013). About sleep's role in memory. *Physiological Reviews, 93*(2), 681–766. https://doi.org/10.1152/physrev.00032.2012

Rawson, K. A. & Kintsch, W. (2005). Rereading effects depend on time of test. *Journal of Educational Psychology, 97*(1), 70–80. https://doi.org/10.1037/0022-0663.97.1.70

Rea, C. P. & Modigliani, V. (1987). The spacing effect in 4- to 9-year-old children. *Memory and Cognition, 15*(5), 436–443. https://doi.org/10.3758/BF03197733

Revak, M. (1997). Distributed practice: More bang for your homework buck. *Florida Journal of Educational Research, 37*(1), 36–48.

Reynolds, J. H. & Glaser, R. (1964). Effects of repetition and spaced review upon retention of a complex learning task. *Journal of Educational Psychology, 55*(5), 297–308. https://doi.org/10.1037/h0040734

Riches, N. G., Tomasello, M., & Conti-Ramsden, G. (2005). Verb learning in children with SLI: Frequency and spacing effects. *Journal of Speech, Language, and Hearing Research, 48*(6), 1397–1411. https://doi.org/10.1044/1092-4388(2005/097)

Robinson, E. S. (1921). The relative efficiencies of distributed and concentrated study in memorizing. *Journal of Experimental Psychology, 4*(5), 327–343. https://doi.org/10.1037/h0073490

Rogers, D. (2004). Evaluating spacing of practice effects on the learning of shortcut keys (Unpublished master's thesis). San Jose State University, San Jose, CA.

Rohrer, D. & Taylor, K. (2006). The effects of overlearning and distributed practise on the retention of mathematics knowledge. *Applied Cognitive Psychology, 20*, 1209–1224. https://doi.org/10.1002/acp.1266

(2007). The shuffling of mathematics problems improves learning. *Instructional Science, 35*(6), 481–498. https://doi.org/10.1007/s11251-007-9015-8

Rovee-Collier, C., Evancio, S., & Earley, L. A. (1995). The time window hypothesis: Spacing effects. *Infant Behavior and Development, 18*(1), 69–78. https://doi.org/10.1016/0163-6383(95)90008-X

Rowe, M. K. & Craske, M. G. (1998). Effects of an expanding-spaced vs massed exposure schedule on fear reduction and return of fear. *Behaviour Research and Therapy*, *36* (7–8), 701–717. https://doi.org/10.1016/S0005-7967(97)10016-X

Rubin-Rabson, G. (1940). Studies in the psychology of memorizing piano music: II. A comparison of massed and distributed practice. *Journal of Educational Psychology*, *31*(4), 270–284. https://doi.org/10.1037/h0061174

Ruch, T. C. (1928). Factors influencing the relative economy of massed and distributed practice in learning. *Psychological Review*, *35*(1), 19–45. https://doi.org/10.1037/h0074423

Saxon, J. (1982). Incremental development: A breakthrough in mathematics. *The Phi Delta Kappan*, *63*(7), 482–484.

Seabrook, R., Brown, G. D. A., & Solity, J. E. (2005). Distributed and massed practice: From laboratory to classroom. *Applied Cognitive Psychology*, *19*(1), 107–122. https://doi.org/10.1002/acp.1066

Scheel, M. H. (2007). Massing practice increases rate and errors on a virtual water jar task. (Unpublished doctoral dissertation). University of Nevada, Reno, Reno, NV.

Schendel, J. D. & Hagman, J. D. (1980). *On sustaining procedural skills over prolonged retention intervals* (Research Report No. 1298). Alexandria, VA: Army Research Institution for the Behavioral and Social Sciences. (Accession No. AD-A120 758)

Scott, M. G. (1954). Learning rate of beginning swimmers. *Research Quarterly. American Association for Health, Physical Education and Recreation*, *25*(1), 91–99.

Shea, C. H., Lai, Q., Black, C., & Park, J. H. (2000). Spacing practice sessions across days benefits the learning of motor skills. *Human Movement Science*, *19*(5), 737–760. https://doi.org/10.1016/S0167-9457(00)00021-X

Simmons, A. (2012). Distributed practice and procedural memory consolidation in musicians' skill learning. *Journal of Research in Music Education*, *59*(4), 357–368. https://doi.org/10.1177/0022429411424798

Simone, P. M., Bell, M. C., & Cepeda, N. J. (2013). Diminished but not forgotten: Effects of aging on magnitude of spacing effect benefits. *The Journals of Gerontology Series B: Psychological Sciences and Social Sciences*, *68*(5), 674–680. https://doi.org/10.1093/geronb/gbs096

Singer, R. N. (1965). Massed and distributed practice effects on the acquisition and retention of a novel basketball skill. *Research Quarterly. American Association for Health, Physical Education and Recreation*, *36*(1), 68–77.

Smith, S. M. & Rothkopf, E. Z. (1984). Contextual enrichment and distribution of practice in the classroom. *Cognition and Instruction*, *1*(3), 341–358. https://doi.org/10.1207/s1532690xci0103_4

Sobel, H. S., Cepeda, N. J., & Kapler, I. V. (2011). Spacing effects in real-world classroom vocabulary learning. *Applied Cognitive Psychology*, *25*(5), 763–767. https://doi.org/10.1002/acp.1747

Son, L. K. & Simon, D. A. (2012). Distributed learning: Data, metacognition, and educational implications. *Educational Psychology Review*, *24*(3), 379–399. https://doi.org/10.1007/s10648-012-9206-y

Spruit, E. N., Band, G. P., & Hamming, J. F. (2015). Increasing efficiency of surgical training: effects of spacing practice on skill acquisition and retention in laparoscopy training. *Surgical Endoscopy*, *29*(8), 2235–2243. https://doi.org/10.1007/s00464-014-3931-x

Thios, S. J., & D'Agostino, P. R. (1976). Effects of repetition as a function of study-phase retrieval. *Journal of Verbal Learning and Verbal Behavior, 15*(5), 529–536. https://doi.org/10.1016/0022–5371(76)90047–5

Tobias, J. V. (1976). *Massed versus distributed practice in learned improvement of speech intelligibility* (Report No. FAA-AM-76–3). Oklahoma City, OK: FAA Civil Aeromedical Institute, Office of Aviation Medicine, Federal Aviation Administration.

Toppino, T. C., Kasserman, J. E., & Mracek, W. A. (1991). The effect of spacing repetitions on the recognition memory of young children and adults. *Journal of Experimental Child Psychology, 51*(1), 123–138. https://doi.org/10.1016/0022–0965(91)90079–8

Tran, O. T. K. (2007). Promoting social and emotional learning in schools: An investigation of massed versus distributed practice schedules and social validity of the Strong Kids curriculum in late elementary aged students. (Unpublished doctoral dissertation). University of Oregon, Eugene, OR.

Ukrainetz, T. A., Ross, C. L., & Harm, H. M. (2009). An investigation of treatment scheduling for phonemic awareness with kindergartners who are at risk for reading difficulties. *Language, Speech, and Hearing Services in Schools, 40*(1), 86–100. https://doi.org/10.1044/0161–1461(2008/07–0077)

Urwiller, S. L. (1971). A comparative study of achievement, retention, and attitude toward mathematics between students using spiral homework assignments and students using traditional homework assignments in second year algebra. (Unpublished doctoral dissertation). University of Nebraska-Lincoln, Lincoln, NE.

Vash, C. L. (1989). Comment on Dempster. *American Psychologist, 44*(12), 1547. https://doi.org/10.1037/0003-066X.44.12.1547.a

Verdaasdonk, E. G. G., Stassen, L. P. S., Van Wijk, R. P. J., & Dankelman, J. (2007). The influence of different training schedules on the learning of psychomotor skills for endoscopic surgery. *Surgical Endoscopy, 21*(2), 214–219. https://doi.org/10.1007/s00464-005-0852-8

Verkoeijen, P. P. J. L., Rikers, R. M. J. P., & Ozsoy, B. (2008). Distributed rereading can hurt the spacing effect in text memory. *Applied Cognitive Psychology, 22*(5), 685–695. https://doi.org/10.1002/acp.1388

Vlach, H. A. (2014). The spacing effect in children's generalization of knowledge: allowing children time to forget promotes their ability to learn. *Child Development Perspectives, 8*(3), 163–168. https://doi.org/10.1111/cdep.12079

Vlach, H. A. & Sandhofer, C. M. (2012). Distributing learning over time: The spacing effect in children's acquisition and generalization of science concepts. *Child Development, 83*(4), 1137–1144. https://doi.org/10.1111/j.1467–8624.2012.01781.x

Weaver, J. R. (1976). The relative effects of massed versus distributed practice upon the learning and retention of eighth grade mathematics. (Unpublished doctoral dissertation). University of Oklahoma, Norman, OK.

Webb, C. L. (2011). Schedule distribution and motor learning guided treatment with childhood apraxia of speech. (Unpublished master's thesis). East Carolina University, Greenville, NC.

Willardson, J. M. & Burkett, L. N. (2006). The effect of rest interval length on the sustainability of squat and bench press repetitions. *Journal of Strength and Conditioning Research, 20*(2), 400–403.

Wineland, J. N. & Stephens, L. (1995). Effects of spiral testing and review on retention and mathematical achievement for below-average eighth-and ninth-grade students.

International Journal of Mathematical Education in Science and Technology, 26(2), 227–232. https://doi.org/10.1080/0020739950260207

Wiseheart, M., D'Souza, A. A., & Chae, J. (2017). Lack of spacing effects during piano learning. *PLoS ONE, 12*, e0182986. https://doi.org/10.1371/journal.pone.0182986

Wogalter, M. S., Jarrard, S. W., & Cayard, J. A. (1991). Massed versus distributed exposure and imaging of faces: Changing the test view. *Current Psychology, 10*(4), 281–288. https://doi.org/10.1007/BF02686900

Yazdani, M. A. & Zebrowski, E. (2006). Spaced reinforcement: An effective approach to enhance the achievement in plane geometry. *Journal of Mathematical Sciences and Mathematics Education, 1*(1), 37–43.

Young, O. G. (1954). Rate of learning in relation to spacing of practice periods in archery and badminton. *Research Quarterly. American Association for Health, Physical Education and Recreation, 25*(2), 231–243.

Zechmeister, E. B. & Shaughnessy, J. J. (1980). When you know that you know and when you think that you know but you don't. *Bulletin of the Psychonomic Society, 15*(1), 41–44. https://doi.org/10.3758/BF03329756

PART V

Metacognition

23 Self-Regulation in Computer-Assisted Learning Systems

Roger Azevedo, Nicholas V. Mudrick, Michelle Taub, and Amanda E. Bradbury

Computer-assisted learning systems (CALSs) such as intelligent tutoring systems (ITSs), game-based learning environments (GBLEs), and virtual reality (VR) have the potential to transform educational outcomes by supporting and augmenting learners' ability to accurately monitor and regulate key cognitive, affective, metacognitive, motivational, and social processes. CALSs can now be outfitted with natural language processing, machine vision, haptic devices, and physiological sensors that can potentially improve learners' self-regulation while significantly challenging current frameworks, models, and theories of self-regulation. These advances can significantly augment existing CALSs both as research tools and as instructional tools. For example, including natural language processing in CALSs will allow for the collection of concurrent verbalizations that can be coded in real time to *measure* the deployment of metacognitive judgments (e.g., determine the relevance of instructional material) as well as be used by the system to determine whether the learner needs *scaffolding* to address particular metacognitive challenges (e.g., inability to determine the relevance of instructional material). Despite the temptation to design and instrument CALSs with the most recent technological advances, researchers need to make theoretically driven and empirically based decisions based on current models, frameworks, and theories of self-regulated learning (SRL).

The goal of this chapter is to present research on self-regulation in CALSs by providing examples from contemporary CALSs and also how we use multimodal multichannel data to examine cognitive, affective, and metacognitive (CAM) self-regulatory processes in these systems. Specifically, our chapter focuses on the role, measurement, and support of CAM processes during learning and problem-solving with

This chapter was supported by funding from the National Science Foundation (DRL#1431552; DRL#1660878, DRL#1661202) and the Social Sciences and Humanities Research Council of Canada (SSHRC 895-2011-1006). Any opinions, findings, conclusions, or recommendations expressed in this material are those of the author(s) and do not necessarily reflect the views of the National Science Foundation or Social Sciences and Humanities Research Council of Canada.

The authors would also like to thank members of the SMART Lab at NCSU for their assistance and contributions.

We acknowledge that motivational and social self-regulatory processes are key to understanding self-regulated learning; however, in this chapter we only focus on cognitive, affective, and metacognitive processes due to space limitations.

CALSs. The structure of our chapter is as follows. First, we will provide a brief history of research on SRL with CALSs and discuss how different CALSs have been used to study and foster SRL. We will then present and discuss conceptual and theoretical issues derived from several models, frameworks, and theories of SRL that focus on CAM processes. Following this, we discuss several dichotomies related to CAM and the challenges they pose for the measurement and support of SRL with CALSs. Lastly, we present challenges and future directions that need to be addressed by researchers.

History of Research on SRL and CALS

The last several decades have seen major shifts in conceptual, theoretical, methodological, and analytical advances that have challenged research on the effectiveness and design of CALSs, as evidenced by certain movements such as cognitivism, constructivism, radical constructivism, constructionism, situated cognition, embodied cognition, and so on (see Dunlosky & Rawson, Mayer & Alexander, 2017; Sawyer, 2014; introductory chapter, this volume). Additionally, research methodologies have become more intricate, as researchers have sought to explore the underlying learning processes students use with CALSs. For instance, studies have shifted from experimental designs using pretest/posttest designs (i.e., product data) to including self-reports (e.g., learners' self-perceptions of strategy use, metacognition, motivation, emotions) and, more recently, process data (see Azevedo, Taub, & Mudrick, 2018). Process data (e.g., eye tracking, log files, facial expressions of emotions, physiological sensors, screen recordings, gestures, learner–artificial agent interactions) allow researchers to capture the CAM SRL processes students deploy when learning with CALSs in real time (Taub & Azevedo, 2016a). CALSs were originally designed purely as an instructional tool, but with the ability of process data to detect complex CAM processes in real time, CALSs are now being used to better understand the complex learning processes students engage in during learning, problem-solving, conceptual understanding, scientific reasoning, and so on (see Azevedo & Aleven, 2013; Schunk & Greene, 2017). Additionally, research has expanded from focusing solely on cognitive processes during learning to including other areas such as the metacognitive and affective processes involved in learning. Further, a plethora of studies have provided clear evidence that there is no one-size-fits-all CALS; therefore, the ultimate goal is to develop adaptive CALSs that can accurately detect students' CAM SRL processes and then act on this information by providing timely, intelligent, and adaptive scaffolding specific to each student's needs. In the next section, we describe several types of CALSs and how they measure and foster CAM SRL.

Computer-Assisted Learning Systems: An Overview

There are several different types of CALSs, including multimedia, hypermedia, ITSs, GBLEs, teachable agents, computer-supported collaborative learning (CSCL) environments, robots, and more recently intelligent virtual humans (IVHs), virtual reality (VR), augmented reality (AR), and tangible computing. Mayer (2014a) defines multimedia learning as knowledge construction and building mental representations from text (e.g., spoken, written) and pictures (e.g., illustrations, videos, animations, photos) while hypermedia is defined as knowledge construction from computer-based media (text, images, videos, etc.) navigable via hyperlinks (e.g., the internet; Azevedo & Cromley, 2004). Several studies have demonstrated the educational effectiveness as well as the promotion of self-regulation in both multimedia and hypermedia learning environments (Azevedo, 2014; Azevedo et al., 2012; Mayer, 2014a). For instance, hypermedia can provide learners with a wealth of nonlinear information including text, diagrams, animations, and videos; however, many students lack the CAM SRL skills necessary to effectively navigate these systems (Azevedo et al., 2017; Bannert & Reimann, 2012). Early work with the hypermedia environment Encarta found that training SRL skills prior to using the hypermedia environment led to more sophisticated mental models of the circulatory system compared to a control (Azevedo & Cromley, 2004). Additionally, Bannert and Reimann (2012) found that SRL prompts embedded within a hypermedia environment improved overall learning compared to a control; however, the best effects were observed when students received a short training on SRL in addition to the SRL prompts.

ITSs are computerized learning environments designed to mimic expert human tutors' pedagogical moves (e.g., feedback, scaffolding) by using computational models from the fields of cognitive psychology and artificial intelligence (Aleven & Koedinger, 2016; Kulik & Fletcher, 2016) to provide learners with individualized, adaptive, and intelligent scaffolding in real time. A recent meta-analysis found that students who used an ITS outperformed students who received traditional classroom instruction 92 percent of the time (Kulik & Fletcher, 2016). ITSs have a long tradition in cognitive and educational psychology and learning sciences and have been built to address learning and problem-solving issues in several well-structured as well as ill-structured domains for learners of all ages (e.g., Cognitive Tutors for algebra problem-solving, AutoTutor for physics misconceptions, MetaTutor for teaching biology and self-regulated learning; for an extensive review, see Wolff, 2009). The majority of research on ITSs has focused on learners' cognitive and metacognitive SRL processes while some recent systems are now addressing learners' affective processes such as Graesser and D'Mello's (2012) extensive work on AutoTutor and other affect-sensitive CALSs.

There is a tremendous emphasis on designing and using GBLEs to promote learning across domains and for learners of all ages (Mayer, 2014b). Some GBLEs are designed to train SRL skills along with educational content embedded within a narrative (e.g., Crystal Island; Rowe et al., 2011) while others can be level-based with new problems being presented at each level (e.g., Physics Playground; Shute et al., 2016). Past research on GBLEs has demonstrated mixed results in terms of their educational effectiveness (Mayer, 2014b); however, a recent meta-analysis found that GBLEs were more educationally effective compared to traditional instructional methods (Clark et al., 2016). Other types of CALSs, such as open-ended systems like Teachable Agents (e.g., Betty's Brain, SimStudent) were explicitly designed using the learning-by-teaching paradigm in which students learn material by teaching a peer agent (Biswas, Segedy, & Bunchongchit, 2016; Matsuda, 2013). Several studies have demonstrated their educational effectiveness (Biswas et al., 2010, 2016; Matsuda, 2013). Additionally, teachable agents, such as Betty in Betty's Brain, can provide SRL support by having students monitor the learning of the teachable agent via questions and quizzes, therefore monitoring their own understanding. In contrast, CSCL environments are designed to facilitate knowledge and expertise sharing via collaborative activities (e.g., Lin et al., 2016). Past research with CSCL environments including Bioworld and Quest Atlantis demonstrated increased learning gains for Quest Atlantis and improved diagnostic reasoning after using Bioworld (Barab et al., 2007; Lajoie et al., 2015). CSCL systems are currently being used as testbeds to evaluate assumptions of co-regulated, socially shared regulated learning (Järvelä et al., 2016).

As technology advances so do opportunities to design more sophisticated CALSs that were not possible decades ago. For example, VR, AR, and tangible computing are the newest CALSs, and, as the technology becomes more readily available, new games, virtual environments, and simulations are being developed. For example, VR has been around since the 1960s (Heiling, 1962); however, widespread dissemination was limited due to practical and technological constraints (Merchant et al., 2014). VR is an artificial immersive environment in which students experience a virtual world via a head-mounted display. AR layers computer-generated images across real-world stimuli via a head-mounted display or handheld computer (e.g., tablet, cellphone). Where VR diverts attention away from the real world, AR enhances it. A recent meta-analysis gauging the effectiveness of VR-based instruction on learning outcomes in K-12 and higher education found that VR is an effective educational tool with an effect size of 0.36 (Merchant et al., 2014) while a meta-analysis of AR-based instruction found a moderate positive effect on student performance with an effect size of 0.56 (Santos et al., 2014). We argue that both VR and AR likely require a high degree of SRL skills (e.g., monitoring effective strategy use, coordinating relevance of multiple information sources) due to the unmatched affordances provided by these environments (e.g., realism that may reduce misconceptions in science; immersion and presence may sustain motivation and positive emotions while allowing prolonged persistence during complex problem-solving); however, despite its importance, there is a dearth of research studying the SRL processes students employ or fail to employ during learning with these environments.

CALSs and Self-Regulated Learning: Examples

In this section, we describe how SRL has been used to both design and measure SRL processes in several CALSs. For example, MetaTutor is an adaptive hypermedia-based ITS designed to detect, model, and foster students' SRL while learning about the human circulatory system (Azevedo & Witherspoon, 2009). The design of MetaTutor is based on Winne and Hadwin's model of SRL (2008; Winne, 2018) and Mayer's (2014a, 2014b) Cognitive Theory of Multimedia Learning and has undergone several redesigns based on extensive SRL research with the system for over a decade (Azevedo et al., 2010; Duffy & Azevedo, 2015; Harley et al., 2018; Taub & Azevedo, 2016a, 2016b). MetaTutor provides feedback and scaffolding via four pedagogical agents – Gavin the Guide, Pam the Planner, Sam the Strategizer, and Mary the Monitor – each embodying theoretical assumptions underlying monitoring and regulation of cognitive and metacognitive SRL processes (see Figure 23.1 for a screenshot of the MetaTutor interface). In addition to collecting pretest, posttest, and other self-report measures of metacognition, motivation, and emotions, MetaTutor has been used as a research tool that collects multichannel multimodal process SRL data during learning via the use of log files, eye tracking, videos of facial expressions of emotions, screen recordings, physiological activity, and learner–agent dialogue.

CRYSTAL ISLAND is a narrative-centered GBLE designed to foster students' SRL, scientific reasoning, literacy, and problem-solving skills (Rowe et al., 2011). The game is experienced in first-person perspective and is set on a tropical island where students learn of a mysterious illness infecting the community. Taking a protagonist role, participants explore the island, collecting clues as they speak with residents and patients, read and answer content on microbiology, and use lab equipment to scan food items, all to discover the source, identity, and best treatment option for the infectious disease. CRYSTAL ISLAND has been used in several lab experiments involving undergraduates, and has also been used in thousands of middle school classrooms to engage students in microbiology content-learning and problem-solving (e.g., Taub, Mudrick et al., 2017; Taub, Azevedo et al., 2018). Additionally, the system was first developed over a decade ago and has since served

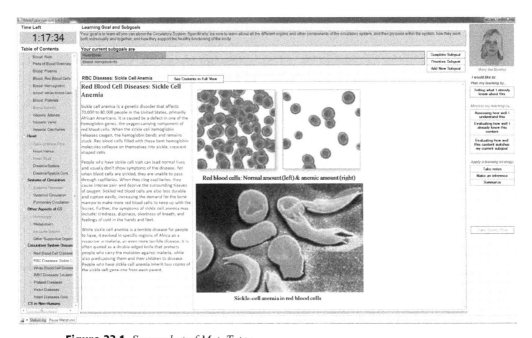

Figure 23.1 *Screenshot of MetaTutor*

as a research and educational tool for investigating game-based learning behaviors related to SRL including emotions, motivation, engagement, presence, and agency (e.g., Bradbury, Taub, & Azevedo, 2017; Sawyer et al., 2017).

The design of Betty's Brain is based on the learning-by-teaching paradigm (Bargh & Schul, 1980) to improve SRL and STEM learning (Biswas et al., 2016) for adolescents. To teach Betty, students first learn science content (ecology) and then construct causal concept maps illustrating ecological processes. Next, they ask Betty questions by getting her to take quizzes on the content, which she answers based on what she was taught (i.e., what information and links students include in their concept map). Her performance on these quizzes provides students with feedback on what information needs to be added to the concept map and what information in the concept map may be incorrect, prompting students to identify strategies for adding relevant information and identifying errors (Biswas et al., 2016). The quizzes are administered by a mentor agent named Mr. Davis who students can seek help from at any time by clicking the "*Ask Mr. Davis*" button. Mr. Davis can answer questions such as "How do I build a concept map?," "How do I search for specific information in the resources?," and so on. Additionally, when the student is not performing well, Mr. Davis can suggest a certain learning strategy to get them back on track. Later versions of the system also include a motivational component by having Betty express happiness when her quiz scores improve and disappointment when her quiz scores fail to improve (Biswas et al., 2016).

In this section, we described how several contemporary CALSs have been designed to measure and foster SRL by embodying assumptions of various models. In addition, we have also described how they have been instrumented as research tools to collect learning outcomes, self-reports, and rich, temporally unfolding SRL process data to detect, measure, and understand the role of CAM processes during learning, problem-solving, and so on across domains and learners while addressing contextual constraints related to the collection of process data (e.g., the scaling up of CALSs as educational and research tools, from the research laboratory to schools and informal settings, limits the ability to collect precise eye-tracking data from learners due to a variety of economic, privacy, and pragmatic issues).

Conceptual and Theoretical Issues Derived from Models on Cognitive, Affective, and Metacognitive Self-Regulated Learning Processes

In this section, we focus on describing and critiquing how three leading models of CAM SRL processes have been used with multimodal multichannel process data to explain, measure, and understand these processes in CALSs. Specifically, we present the assumptions and mechanisms, and discuss the levels of explanation (i.e., grain size) and empirical support for Winne & Hadwin's (2008) information processing theory (IPT) of SRL; Greene & Azevedo's (2009) extension of the IPT model of SRL, which details macro- and micro-level SRL processes; and D'Mello & Graesser's (2012) model of Affective Dynamics, which describes the underlying affective processes that may occur during learning with CALSs. We also focus our critique on the limitations of these models and question how we can use them to understand multimodal multichannel CAM SRL process data during learning with CALSs. We end this section by listing questions arising from the conceptual dichotomies presented in the use of these models to understand CAM SRL processes during learning with CALSs.

Winne & Hadwin's Information Processing Theory of Self-Regulated Learning

Winne & Hadwin's (2008) IPT of SRL is one of the leading theories used to detect, measure, and interpret SRL process data to examine the temporal unfolding of SRL during learning with CALSs. The model assumes that SRL is an event and is dependent on the relationship between the learner's accurate metacognitive monitoring and control (i.e., regulation) of different cognitive operations (i.e., SMART processes) over four loosely sequenced, recursive learning phases (i.e., task definition, goal setting and planning, engaging in cognitive operations, and adaption). Winne (2018) suggests that during each of these four phases, self-regulated learners engage in one or many cognitive operations as they concurrently monitor the quality of the outcomes from these processes. For example, learners engage in *searching* for specific information within the learning content, *assembling* that learned information with previously learned information, *rehearsing* the information by preserving it in working memory, and *translating* information by changing its representation (e.g., creating a diagram from reading a text), while concurrently *monitoring* the quality of the outcomes from these SMART processes, based on internal standards.

   In addition to the enactment of these five cognitive operations, the model specifies that SRL unfolds over four phases. In phase one, self-regulated learners define the learning task based on their perceptions, as well as the constraints of the task. During phase two, the learners generate goals and plans for future learning strategies. In phase three, self-regulated learners engage in the previously discussed cognitive operations based on their plans and goals of phase two. Lastly, in phase four, learners adapt their strategies based on their performance and output of their enacted learning strategies. As a loosely sequenced and recursive model, the IPT model of SRL specifies that learners do not always progress through these phases in a sequential manner and instead are constantly moving between these phases as they self-regulate their learning.

   As Winne & Hadwin's (2008) model assumes SRL is an event, it is an optimal model to use when examining how cognitive and metacognitive SRL processes unfold during learning with CALSs (Winne & Azevedo, 2014). There is extensive empirical evidence in support of using Winne & Hadwin's (2008) model to examine these processes during learning with CALSs (see Azevedo et al., 2013, 2017; Taub et al., 2014; Taub et al., 2017). However, there are also several issues regarding its ability to explain, describe, and predict SRL processes with multimodal multichannel process data during learning with CALSs. Specifically, the model argues for mechanisms that span across micro and macro levels and, as such, does not expand on some processes that are necessary to explain SRL during learning with CALSs. For example, how are learners' internal conditions (e.g., prior knowledge) enacted during learning? Can they be accessed in real time during learning with CALSs? What process data are required to assess how a learner evaluates their products based on their internal standards? Can CALSs be designed to make these real-time processes visible to facilitate learners' metacognitive monitoring and control during learning?

Furthermore, as the model is loosely sequenced and recursive, it does not specify the optimal sequence, temporality, or dynamics of cognitive and metacognitive processes that learners need to engage in during learning, making it difficult for CALSs to respond to the learner effectively by tailoring individualized, adaptive scaffolding and support. For example, is there an optimal period of time during which learners define the task and, if so, how do we assess if a learner does not accurately perceive and define the learning task? Although the model has recently begun to address learners' affective and motivational processes during learning (e.g., as internal conditions; see Winne, 2018), the model does not account for the specific influence of these processes and instead implies that SRL is dependent on cognitive and metacognitive processes. Lastly, the model is based on the assumption that learners can inherently engage in these learning phases and self-regulate their learning. However, it is possible that some learners may not be able to effectively enact some of these processes. If so, how can CALSs provide support and adapt their scaffolding and feedback to learners who cannot appropriately define their task or set appropriate learning goals and so on?

Greene & Azevedo's Macro- and Micro-Level Framework of Self-Regulated Learning

The seminal work on metacognition (e.g., Dunlosky & Metcalfe, 2009; Nelson & Narens, 1990) and SRL (e.g., Bjork, Dunlosky, & Kornell, 2013; Hacker, Dunlosky, & Graesser, 2009) has been influential in developing Greene and Azevedo's (2009) macro- and micro-level framework of SRL, which expands on Winne & Hadwin's (2008) model of SRL by detailing specific macro- and micro-level, valenced, cognitive, and metacognitive processes that students enact during SRL. As it is an extension of Winne and Hadwin's (2008) model, it is based on the same assumptions that SRL is an event that is dependent on the interplay between accurate metacognitive monitoring and regulation (of cognitive learning strategy use). The Greene & Azevedo (2009) framework argues that SRL is comprised of five macro-level processes of planning, monitoring, strategy use, perceptions of task difficulty and demands, and interest, and within these macro-level processes are thirty-five specific micro-level processes. In addition to defining these processes, the framework indicates that micro-level cognitive and metacognitive judgments are valenced. In general, valence indicates the accuracy (i.e., positive or negative) of a learner's own evaluations, familiarity with, or understanding of their judgments (Azevedo et al., 2013). For example, when a learner performs (e.g., via a mouse click on an interface element or a concurrent utterance during learning with a CALS) a content evaluation (CE; an evaluation of the relevancy of the content to the learner's current goal, within the macro-level category of monitoring), the evaluation could be positively valenced (i.e., the content is relevant to their goal), or negatively valenced (i.e., the content is irrelevant to their goal). Alternatively, when learners engage in prior knowledge activation (PKA; searching for relevant prior knowledge before beginning the learning task, within the macro-level category of planning), a positively valenced PKA would indicate the learner recalled relevant learning material, while a negatively valenced PKA would indicate that the learner could not recall relevant information. The inclusion of valence within the framework contextualizes these cognitive and metacognitive processes within the specific learning context that may change depending on the learning task, CALS, and so on. For example, a learner may make a negatively valenced PKA (i.e., activate irrelevant prior knowledge) when learning about the different vessels of the human heart with a hypermedia system but may make a positively valenced PKA (i.e., activate relevant prior knowledge) when learning about the circulatory system of invertebrates in a VR system.

Like Winne and Hadwin's (2008) model, there exists substantial empirical support for Greene and Azevedo's (2009) framework of SRL to detect and explain what SRL processes occur and influence learning outcomes during learning with a CALS (see Azevedo et al., 2013, 2017; Taub et al., 2014). However, there are also similar issues for using this framework to identify, explain, and predict cognitive and metacognitive SRL processes with multimodal multichannel process data during learning with CALSs. Despite defining specific cognitive and metacognitive SRL processes, the model does not specify the optimal sequence, temporality, or dynamics of how these processes should unfold. For example, what is the optimal length of a specific sequence of micro-level SRL processes? Is there a difference between the quality and quantity of these micro-level processes during learning? Does engaging in more processes contribute to higher learning outcomes? And does the quality of these processes improve over time? Additionally, as this framework was derived from analyzing think-aloud data during experiments involving a hypermedia learning system (e.g., Greene & Azevedo, 2009), it may not be representative of how these processes may unfold during learning with different types of CALSs. For example, rereading (RR; under the macro-level category of strategy use) may not be an appropriate process to examine in a VR-based learning environment with different representations of information. Lastly, similar to Winne & Hadwin's (2008) model, Greene & Azevedo's (2009) framework focuses primarily on cognitive and metacognitive processes at the expense of the affective. As such, it offers no specific information regarding when, why, or how learners' emotions can influence the accuracy of their metacognitive monitoring or the deployment of effective cognitive learning strategies.

D'Mello & Graesser's Dynamics of Affective States Model

Unlike the previously discussed models that focused exclusively on cognitive and metacognitive processes, D'Mello & Graesser's (2012) Dynamics of Affective States model focuses on the learner-centered emotions that can occur during learning with CALSs. Derived from research on emotions during learning with AutoTutor the model assumes that: (1) learners' cognitive and affective processes during learning are linked during learning; (2) learners typically experience a specific subset of discrete, learner-centered emotions; and (3) the interplay between these emotions can differentially influence their learning outcomes.

The model predicts that learners in a state of deep learning (i.e., complex learning where they demonstrate high levels of conceptual understanding) are in a base state of flow/engagement. Once the learner encounters an impasse (i.e., discrepancy in the presented information) they experience a state of cognitive disequilibrium (i.e., state of uncertainty arising from the discrepancy) and subsequently experience confusion. If the learner does not effectively resolve this confusion by engaging in effortful problem-solving to identify the source of the discrepancy (e.g., discrepancy between representations of information), they can transition into a state of frustration. However, if the learner is successful in their problem-solving, they can transition back to a state of engagement/flow. Once the learner experiences frustration, the model predicts that persistent failure and blockage to the learner's goals as they experience their frustration can subsequently lead to boredom and task disengagement.

The Dynamics of Affective States model is one of the leading models used to describe emotions during learning with CALSs and is based on empirical evidence detailing the presence of these discrete emotions, as well as their dynamics over time (see D'Mello & Graesser, 2012; D'Mello et al., 2014). The model can be easily extended to explain affective processes with multimodal multichannel process data during learning with other CALSs as it assumes that emotions are temporally dependent and unfold over time. However, there are several theoretical and conceptual issues regarding its descriptive and explanatory adequacy for examining emotions during learning with CALSs. First, the model does not provide a concrete operational definition of the engagement/flow state learners experience when they engage in deep learning. As such, there remains an open question regarding how researchers can empirically assess engagement/flow with multimodal multichannel process data during learning with CALSs. Additionally, this model is limited in the number and types of the discrete emotions that it examines and predicts and cannot offer explanations or predictions regarding the presence of other emotions that can occur in academic settings (e.g., pride, anxiety; Pekrun et al., 2011). Furthermore, while the grain size of this model is primarily micro-level discrete emotions (e.g., confusion, frustration), it does not include all possible learning-centered emotions nor does it emphasize the potential expression of basic emotions (e.g., anger) in cases where CALSs are used in nontraditional educational purposes (e.g., recently diagnosed breast cancer patient learning about basic biomedical knowledge with a MetaTutor-like CALS).

Lastly, the model is also based on the assumption that learners can effectively engage in emotion regulation processes (e.g., Gross, 2015) and can transition between emotions. However, if learners are not effective emotion regulators do they perpetually disengage from the task because of their inability to transition from confusion back to a state of engagement/flow? Additionally, can learners engage in other emotion-regulation strategies (e.g. attentional deployment) other than the effortful problem-solving specified in the model? Although the model assumes that cognition and affective processes during learning cannot be separated, it does not account for the presence of metacognitive monitoring processes that may influence the emotions experienced. For example, can learners experience confusion because of their inaccurate metacognitive judgments? Lastly, it also lacks assumptions regarding the temporality of affective states. For instance, how long does a person need to be in a state of confusion before transitioning to frustration?

Conceptual and Theoretical Dichotomies Related to CAM SRL Processes Related to CALSs

The previously described models and theories have been the leading frameworks researchers have used to examine CAM SRL processes with multimodal multi-channel process data during learning with CALSs. However, there are several remaining questions when using these models to explain CAM SRL processes with multimodal multichannel process data that can be organized by four conceptual dichotomies. In this section, we describe each dichotomy and raise several issues based on the models presented and discussed in the previous section by focusing on detection and measurement of CAM SRL processes during learning with CALSs. We end this section by presenting a table (see Table 23.1) with process-specific (i.e., cognitive, affective, and metacognitive) research questions based on the subcategories of these dichotomies.

The first conceptual dichotomy that arises from these models deals with the **quality vs. quantity** of the CAM SRL processes. Within this conceptual dichotomy we argue that there are three specific subcategories related to the (1) frequency and (2) duration of as well as the (3) latency between the CAM SRL processes described in each model. For example, are higher frequencies of CAM SRL processes indicative of more effective SRL? What are the key components that distinguish low- vs. high-quality SRL (e.g., copying information vs. paraphrasing when given the opportunity to take notes during learning with a CALS) and are these dependent on the specific learning context, individual differences, task demands, and so on? Many of these models are primarily descriptive of the CAM SRL processes they discuss but do not address the qualitative features of these processes (e.g., quality of inferences). Instead, these models imply that a higher frequency and longer duration, as well as a shorter latency between these processes, are indicative of effective SRL during learning. For example, both Winne & Hadwin (2008) and Greene & Azevedo (2009) imply that engaging in more cognitive processes can contribute to higher learning outcomes. Alternatively, the model of Affective Dynamics implies that shorter latencies between emotional state transitions (e.g., confusion to engagement/flow)

Table 23.1 *Sample questions and data sources based on conceptual dichotomies about cognitive, affective, and metacognitive (CAM) self-regulated learning processes*

Dichotomies	Cognitive		Affective		Metacognitive	
	Sample question	Data	Sample question	Data	Sample question	Data
Quality vs. Quantity						
Frequency	Does taking more notes contribute to better learning outcomes?	LF	Does a higher frequency of confusion negatively impact learning?	LF, FE, EDA	Do more inaccurate judgments of learning (JOLs) contribute to more frequent episodes of confusion?	LF, FE, EDA
Duration	Do longer periods of summarizing lead to higher quality summaries?	LF	Do extended periods (i.e., states) of emotion contribute to higher arousal?	FE, EDA	Do shorter time periods in making judgments of learning (JOLs) contribute to lower absolute accuracy?	LF, ET
Latency	What contributes to the period of time between a learner selecting a new page of content and deciding to take notes?	LF, FE, ET, EDA	What is the average amount of time between a learner encountering an impasse or discrepancy and experiencing confusion?	LF, FE, ET, EDA	How long is the optimal amount of time for detecting (metacognitive evaluation) relevant information and making an accurate (metacognitive judgment) content evaluation?	LF, ET
Macro vs. Micro						
Granularity	How does the complexity of the text influence the learner's ability to make an accurate summary?	LF, ET	Do facial expressions of confusion that last for only 1 second impact learning outcomes?	LF, FE, EDA	How long does a learner engage in monitoring judgments vs. how long do learners engage in judgments of learning, feelings of knowing, content evaluations, vs. how long do learners engage in positive or negative judgments of learning, in positive or negative feelings of knowing, in positive or negative content evaluations, etc.?	LF
Valence	What causes a learner to	LF, ET	Can experiencing more positive	FE, EDA	To what extent do accurate judgments of	LF

Table 23.1 (*cont.*)

Dichotomies	Cognitive		Affective		Metacognitive	
	Sample question	Data	Sample question	Data	Sample question	Data
	accurately summarize relevant instructional materials?		emotions (e.g., joy) influence the experience of negative emotions (e.g., confusion, frustration, boredom)?		learning predict increased learning outcomes?	
Interplay	At what point does individual variation in the deployment of valence-level process use lead us to examine micro-level processes?	LF, ET, FE, EDA	How does a learner's negatively valenced mood influence their ability to regulate their confusion?	FE, EDA	How can we distinguish macro-level monitoring from micro-level planning processes and does this evidence represent the development of SRL skills?	LF, ET

Time vs. Event

Dichotomies	Cognitive		Affective		Metacognitive	
Thresholding	How long should a learner attempt to activate their prior knowledge?	LF	How long does an emotion need to last for it to be considered an episode?	FE, EDA	At what point does a macro-level planning phase transition into a micro-level monitoring judgment?	LF, ET

Discrete vs. Co-occurrence

Dichotomies	Cognitive		Affective		Metacognitive	
Parallel	Can cognitive strategy use (e.g., note-taking and summarizing) co-occur or is co-occurrence only possible across cognitive, affective, and metacognitive processes (e.g., note-taking while metacognitively monitoring and facially expressing joy)?	LF	Can learners experience co-occurring confusion and frustration (and are these detection techniques such as video of facial expressions)?	FE, EDA	Can learners make judgments of learning when they are summarizing the learning content?	LF, ET

Table 23.1 (*cont.*)

Dichotomies	Cognitive		Affective		Metacognitive	
	Sample question	Data	Sample question	Data	Sample question	Data
Serial	Should learners engage in note taking on every page?	LF	At what point does confusion transition into frustration?	FE, EDA	Should previewing learning content always be followed by a content evaluation?	LF, ET
Causation	When reading text, what causes the learner to inspect the corresponding diagram?	LF, FE, ET, EDA	To experience frustration, do learners need to first experience confusion?	FE, EDA	Which specific cues cause learners to engage in judgments of learning?	LT, FE, ET, EDA
Correlation	Are individual differences correlated with increased note taking?	LF, FE, ET, EDA	Do higher levels of confusion lead to higher levels of frustration?	FE, EDA	Are more accurate judgments of learning associated with more accurate content evaluations?	LF

Note. LF = log file, FE = facial expressions of emotion, ET = eye tracking, EDA = electrodermal activity. We acknowledge that this table does not include all possible multimodal multichannel SRL process data (e.g., concurrent think-aloud data). Please note that this table does not include a comprehensive list of all possible questions, issues, and multimodal multichannel SRL processes data.

contribute to increased learning outcomes. As such, these conceptual issues must be addressed in future work to interpret learners' CAM SRL processes with multimodal multichannel process data during learning with CALSs.

A second dichotomy presented in these models relates to their descriptions of **macro- vs. micro-level** CAM SRL processes. Within this conceptual dichotomy, we argue there are three specific subcategories related to the (1) granularity (i.e., levels of description), (2) valence (i.e., specific features related to each process), and (3) interplay between these levels (i.e., micro-level processes influencing macro-level processes and vice versa). The grain size of CAM SRL processes described in these models range from the micro to the macro level. As such, these differing levels of description make the theoretical interpretation of the interplay between CAM SRL processes difficult and pose questions regarding the interpretation of the multimodal multichannel process data. For example, does a micro-level emotional state (e.g., a 1 second state of confusion) influence a learner's macro-level monitoring (e.g., judgment of learning) during a 2-hour learning session? Should grain size be standardized when examining these processes with multimodal multichannel process data? Or does the predictive ability between macro- and micro- SRL processes differ based on the specific CAM process, temporal dynamics, evidence of adaptivity during learning, development of SRL competencies during learning with CALSs, and so on? As such, issues related to grain size, valence, and the interplay between micro and macro levels are important issues to consider when interpreting CAM SRL processes.

The third dichotomy deals with the **time vs. event-based** thresholds needed to theoretically interpret CAM SRL processes during learning with CALSs. Specifically, these models do not address how long CAM SRL processes last or how many CAM SRL processes *should* occur during SRL. Furthermore, these theories are limited in descriptions on how to identify the occurrence of CAM SRL processes and, as such, researchers are left with several open questions related to the identification of time- or event-based SRL processes. For example, does time thresholding (i.e., the amount of time a process needs to occur before being considered present) influence our theoretical understanding of how a process occurs during learning with CALSs? How long do CAM SRL processes need to occur for to be psychologically meaningful and detectable by multimodal multichannel process measures (and requiring intelligent intervention by a CALS)? More research is needed to identify the behavioral signatures of CAM SRL processes in order to identify how and when certain processes can be considered psychologically meaningful and influential for understanding their contributions to learning (e.g., longer periods of confusion, an optimal number of summaries) and where CALSs can potentially intervene to facilitate SRL (e.g., repeated evidence of a lack of ability to control metacognitive discrepancies).

The last conceptual dichotomy arising from these models deals with issues related to interpreting CAM SRL processes as **discrete events vs. co-occurring processes**. Within this dichotomy, we argue there are four subcategories related to interpreting CAM SRL as (1) parallel or (2) serial processes, as well as how these processes (3) correlate with and/or (4) cause each other. Although these models interpret CAM SRL processes as events that unfold over time (e.g., Winne, 2018), they do not specify if these processes occur in a serial or parallel fashion. For example, does a learner monitoring themselves by using a judgment of learning (JOL) that leads to the use of a cognitive strategy to reread stop the cognitive learning strategy of rereading or does the learner use that cognitive strategy that leads to metacognitive monitoring or does the learner concurrently judge their learning as they continue reading? Alternatively, can a learner experience confusion and frustration simultaneously or does confusion need to serve as the precursor? This issue becomes more complicated as researchers and designers consider measuring CAM processes using multimodal multichannel data – e.g., is confusion expressed before, during, or after the onset of a metacognitive judgment such as a JOL? If there is a transition from confusion to frustration, does that affective transition happen serially or in parallel as a result of repeated cognitive strategy use? One can see how using multimodal multichannel SRL process data can begin to address these questions (e.g., Azevedo et al., 2018) to both extend models of SRL as well as design SRL-sensitive CALSs. Lastly, although some models identify specific causal relationships (e.g., experiencing cognitive disequilibrium after encountering an impasse in the learning content), there are still questions regarding the correlations between CAM SRL processes. For example, are there certain affective states that are more likely to be present when making an inaccurate JOL? Can we profile learners based on these correlations to identify optimal scaffolding and feedback during learning with CALSs?

We end this section by presenting an initial list of process-specific (i.e., cognitive, affective, and metacognitive) research questions based on the subcategories of the conceptual dichotomies (see Table 23.1). We also provide examples of the types of multimodal multichannel process data that can be used to detect, interpret, and analyze these processes during learning with CALSs.

Assessing Self-Regulation Using Multimodal Multichannel Process Data

There are many ways to assess SRL during learning with CALSs using different types of data, such as self-report questionnaires or multimodal multichannel data of real-time temporally unfolding processes. Using multimodal multichannel data to measure SRL can be particularly useful because it allows us to use both obtrusive (e.g., prompted to make a metacognitive judgment) and unobtrusive (e.g., log files) methods to measure learners' overt (e.g., making a summary after inspecting diagrams and reading text) and covert (e.g., gaze behaviors of reading behavior and diagram inspection) SRL behaviors, as opposed to relying on self-perceptions of how they engaged, activated, used, reflected, and so on. There are various different types of data channels we can use to assess SRL, and selecting the most appropriate data will depend on the research questions being posed, experimental design of the study, design of the CALSs themselves, and other critical issues (e.g., scaling up from lab to outside the lab, securing the privacy and anonymity of learners, pragmatic issues related to conducting data in real-world contexts such as classrooms). In the following section, we will provide examples of how different types of data channels can be used to assess CAM SRL processes, as well as the challenges we face when using these data.

CALSs as a Research and Learning Tool

One advantage of developing CALSs is that they can be used as both research tools and learning tools. For learning, they can be used to ensure that students of all ages and ability levels are learning and engaging in effective self-regulation. This is clearly beneficial as we are aiming to improve educational opportunities for students. CALSs can also be used as a research tool, such that not only do we allow students to learn with these systems but we collect large amounts of data that inform us *how* students are learning, including what types of self-regulation (i.e., metacognitive monitoring and cognitive learning strategies) they are (or are not) engaging in, when they use them, and whether or not they are used effectively.

When using CALSs to conduct research, the researchers themselves have many design considerations they have to make based on the research questions and hypotheses they want to answer – what is the research design and what are the logistical considerations they have to make – which will then inform the types of data they want to collect (for examples, see Hacker et al., 2009; Schunk & Greene, 2017). First, the specific research questions that researchers want answered by developing these systems will impact how they design the CALS and the data they want to collect. For example, if researchers are interested in how a pedagogical agent's facial expressions impact a student's facial expressions during learning with a multimedia environment, the system has to include agents that are capable of emoting facial expressions that are commonly found across teachers, tutors, and previous research on students (e.g., confusion and its benefits for learning; D'Mello et al., 2014). Additionally, since the question also aims to investigate students' emotions, the study protocol must also include collecting emotion data from students during learning. In contrast, if the research is to assess how students self-initiate the use of cognitive and metacognitive processes during learning with MetaTutor, and how this impacts their overall performance on the posttest, the system itself must support engaging in these processes (e.g., the SRL palette), and the study protocol must include a posttest (e.g., Taub et al., 2014). Thus, these questions, and the specificity of these questions, will guide researchers toward using CALSs as a research tool.

Moreover, the research design itself will also impact how research is conducted assessing these systems. Specifically, using a within-subjects vs. between-subjects design will impact how the researcher can assess the effectiveness of these systems for fostering SRL and learning. When comparing a within- vs. between-subjects design, there can be benefits and drawbacks to each design. A within-subjects design will expose the students to all conditions the system entails, such as progressing through a series of trials that expose students to all combinations of different discrepancy types (e.g., Burkett & Azevedo, 2012). This is a beneficial design because it allows us to examine how students change over time and specifically across different contexts. If a student was interacting with a pedagogical agent that emoted different facial expressions, we could determine how these different emotions impact performance across different trials. However, these designs can be time-consuming, and although trials are randomly ordered, there is still the chance of an order effect, such that a student becomes more familiar with each trial as they complete more of them. In contrast, a between-subjects design is not subject to the effects of trial; however, it can pose an unfair advantage or disadvantage to students in each condition, such that a student who receives prompts and feedback has the advantage of knowing their progress and getting assistance when they perform poorly, but a student who does not receive this assistance has a disadvantage because they are not taught which processes to engage in or told how they performed. Therefore, based on these design decisions, assessing how the system fosters the use of CAM processes will differ based on the design choice, such that there will be more time-varying data and data for all conditions for all students from a within-subjects design.

Finally, when designing these experimental procedures, a researcher must consider the logistics of the study, including how much time there is and how many experimenters there are that have the expertise in setting up and calibrating the participant. Specifically, calibrating the experimental equipment can add up to 30–60 minutes during data collection and so, in addition to the learning session, which can last upwards of 1–3 hours, the entire procedure can last a relatively long time and potentially induce undue fatigue, stress, and so forth on participants. In addition, the setup itself can be complicated and so the experimenter must have adequate expertise in calibrating the equipment, which includes troubleshooting errors. Thus, to set up a study, the more advanced the technology being used, the more difficult it can be to run the study itself, which is a consideration all researchers must be prepared to make when testing CALSs.

For this chapter, we focus on CALSs as a research tool, such that we discuss how we can use multimodal multichannel data to examine students' CAM processes during learning with CALSs. In the next section, we review some of the different types of data we can use to assess these processes.

Types of Multimodal Multichannel SRL Process Data

There are many different data channels we can use to assess self-regulation during learning with CALSs. We can use eye-tracking data to examine where students are fixating (i.e., focusing on for at least 250 milliseconds; Rayner, 2009) during learning, which can be indicative of focused attention on particular areas of the screen (Scheiter & Eitel, 2016) thus demonstrating students are probably monitoring based on where they are paying attention in the CALS. Eye-tracking data can also be used to investigate students' saccades, which are rapid movements between fixations (Rayner, 2009), and can indicate students are reading content or are assessing whether or not the content is relevant to their overall learning goals. We can also investigate regressions, which involves a student returning back to a previously fixated-on area of interest (Rayner, 2009), indicating a student is rereading because they do not understand the content. Eye-tracking data are increasingly being used to assess self-regulation during learning with CALSs (Conati, Jaques, & Muir, 2013; Scheiter & Eitel, 2016; Taub & Azevedo, 2016a), revealing how it can be useful to assess where students are focusing on the system during learning.

Another type of data includes videos of facial expressions of emotions that reveal which emotions students are expressing during learning with CALSs. Students can experience a range of basic (joy, anger, surprise, fear, disgust, sadness) or learning-centered (confusion, frustration, boredom) emotions during learning, which research has shown can impact how they engage in self-regulation and overall performance (D'Mello et al., 2014; Mudrick et al., 2017). When investigating facial expressions of emotions, software (such as FACET; iMotions, 2017) can measure the evidence of these emotions (e.g., onset, triggering event, frequency, duration, latency between states, context, alignment with other cognitive and metacognitive processes), defined as the likelihood of human coders coding for that emotion, using a logarithmic (base 10) scale. Therefore, evidence scores of 1, 2, or 3 indicates the likelihood of 10, 100, or 1,000 human expert coders coding for that emotion, respectively. Furthermore, a positive value would indicate the likelihood of an emotion being coded as present, while a negative value indicates the likelihood of an emotion being coded as absent. Thus, in addition to identifying which emotions students are experiencing during learning with CALSs, we can also identify which emotions students are not expressing. For example, if the software detects the student is confused during learning but not frustrated, this can indicate the student is trying to reestablish cognitive equilibrium (D'Mello & Graesser, 2012) by engaging in effective self-regulation strategies. In contrast, if a student is expressing frustration, perhaps they need further assistance to help them regulate this frustration so as to not lead them to a state of boredom (D'Mello & Graesser, 2012). As such, examining students' facial expressions of emotions can also inform us about how students are learning with CALSs.

A third data type is log-file data, which include time-stamped, behavioral indicators of students' interactions with a system – i.e., the entire sequence of learner-initiated and system-initiated actions with the CALS at the millisecond level listing what, when, and for how long the learner and system initiated all behavioral actions (e.g., what page they click on, when, and for how long). When extracting log-file data, there are many activities or behaviors that can be extracted, which can usually provide contextual information about what the student is doing. For example, if a student has just completed a subgoal, the log file will indicate the time at which they completed the previous subgoal and began the new subgoal; and since completing a subgoal requires students to complete a ten-item quiz, the log file will also indicate the start and end time of taking the quiz, indicating the duration of that quiz as well as specific responses to each quiz question, allowing the researcher to know how the student performed on the quiz. As another example, log files can be used to assess gameplay activity, such that we can determine which location the student is in (Bradbury et al., 2017), which activities they engage in at each location (e.g., read four books, talked to one nonplayer character), and the outcome of these activities (e.g., number of concept matrix attempts, food item testing positive or negative for pathogenic substances). As such, log files allow us to calculate frequencies, durations, specific responses to, and all other behavioral variables that researchers might want in order to determine what students were doing during learning (Taub, Azevedo et al., 2018). These data are typically indicative of cognitive strategy use (e.g., taking notes, summarizing) and can be used to infer metacognitive processes (unless they are embedded self-report measures of metacognitive judgments) during learning with CALSs, as affective data are typically measured using sensing devices.

Finally, another measure of affective data includes electrodermal activity (EDA), which is a measure of students' physiological arousal, (e.g., heart rate variability, skin conductance, galvanic skin response) measured with wearable biosensors (e.g., Shimmer GSR+, Empatica E4). EDA is an umbrella term used to describe any type of electrical phenomena present in the skin (Boucsein, 2012) and can be processed to measure skin conductance response (SCR) events derived from phasic EDA. Specifically, EDA is comprised of two components: tonic and phasic. Tonic EDA, commonly referred to as skin conductance level, is activity that varies over time in the absence of environmental effects or external stimuli (Hardy et al., 2013). In contrast, phasic activity consists of fast increases in skin conductance forming a peak with a slower decline back to baseline and has been shown to respond to the presence of specific environmental stimuli (e.g., images, smells, cognitive processes, affective states; Benedek & Kaernbach, 2010; Boucsein, 2012). Research examining students' emotions using physiological measures has primarily examined the size, duration, and frequency of students' SCR events as they engage in different learning tasks (Arguel et al., 2016; Brawner, & Gonzalez, 2016; Harley et al., 2015). Furthermore, research has also identified that SCR events can predict students' perceptions of the relevance of information in retrieval tasks (Barral et al., 2015) or affective responses to specific learning events (e.g., negative feedback; Hardy et al., 2013). Thus, we can use these data to examine the number of SCR events as students read content, take quizzes, make metacognitive judgments, and engage in hypothesis testing during learning. We can also examine how the number of SCR events impact students' abilities to deem pages as relevant to their subgoals, or how students' emotions impact how they respond to reading pages vs. completing quizzes vs. talking to nonplayer characters vs. testing items during learning with different CALSs. Overall, these different types of data can be used to assess different types of cognitive, affective, and metacognitive processes during learning with CALSs. In the next section, we demonstrate specific examples of how we have assessed CAM processes using different data types.

Using Multimodal Multichannel Data to Measure CAM Processes

The abovementioned data can be useful for assessing self-regulation during learning with CALSs. Specifically, we can take different approaches to analyzing data for CAM processes. In the following section, we provide specific examples of using different data channels to investigate different CAM processes during learning with different types of CALSs.

Figure 23.2 illustrates how a student can engage in several cognitive, affective, and metacognitive processes during learning with two different CALSs (MetaTutor, CRYSTAL ISLAND) and how we can use different data channels to measure these different CAM processes. For cognitive processes (under the "Cognitive" header in Figure 23.2), we can use MetaTutor to examine how students are taking notes. To do so, we can use log-file data to examine the frequency of taking notes (Taub et al., 2014), the duration of how long they spent taking notes (overall, and for each separate instance), and the content of those notes (e.g., Trevors et al., 2014). In addition, we can use eye-tracking data to examine how long students spent fixating on the notes (e.g., Taub & Azevedo, 2016a). With CRYSTAL ISLAND, we can investigate students' cognitive learning strategy use based on how they solved the concept matrix after reading a book; examine their log-file behavior, how long they spent reading a book and completing its concept matrix; and how many attempts they made to complete the matrix correctly. Additionally, we can examine their eye-tracking behavior to reveal the proportion of time they spent fixating on the text and the concept matrices, and how this impacted their performance (Taub et al., 2017). As such, we can use both log files and eye-tracking data to examine how students engage in cognitive self-regulation processes during learning with different CALSs.

Figure 23.2 *Examples of specific uses of multimodal multichannel data to investigate CAM processes with different CALSs*

To assess affective processes (under the "Affective" header in Figure 23.2), we can use both facial expressions of emotions and EDA data. During learning with MetaTutor, we can measure how students' facial expressions of emotions impacted their proportional learning gain and we can assess how students' emotions varied in different locations in CRYSTAL ISLAND (Bradbury et al., 2017). We can also investigate heart rate variability and skin conductance response in terms of how they changed over different content pages about the circulatory system in MetaTutor and across different activities (e.g., reading books vs. talking to nonplayer characters vs. testing food items) during gameplay with CRYSTAL ISLAND. Finally, we can use all these data to create emotion heat maps, which indicate the prevalence of emotions over time, where more prevalent emotions are in red and the least prevalent emotions are in blue. As such, we can use these emotion heat maps to indicate emotions while interacting with all of these CALSs, where we can indicate if, for example, a student had high levels of confusion at the beginning of the learning session, followed by high levels of frustration as time progressed, indicating the student might have been on a path toward disengagement (D'Mello & Graesser, 2012). Therefore, using both video and EDA data can be used to assess students' emotions during learning with different types of CALSs.

For assessing metacognitive processes during learning with CALSs ("Metacognitive" header in Figure 23.2), we can use multimodal multichannel data. First, while a student is reading text content and inspecting diagrams during learning with MetaTutor, we can use eye-tracking data to indicate gaze patterns between the text and diagram, representing metacognitive monitoring to coordinate informational sources. We can also investigate hypothesis-testing behavior and how students monitored the food items they were testing during gameplay with CRYSTAL ISLAND. The log files can indicate when students used the scanning device as well as how long students spent testing food items with the scanner and which food items students were testing for (Taub et al., 2018). As another example, we can use log-file data from MetaTutor, such that we can examine students' metacognitive judgments, including which judgment (e.g., content evaluation) they were making and what their responses were (e.g., concurrent verbalizations). We can also examine students engaging in metacognitive processes by using the SRL palette in MetaTutor, such that students can choose to engage in a judgment of learning, feeling of knowing, and content evaluation. We can use eye-tracking data to examine the time spent fixating on the SRL palette (Taub & Azevedo, 2016a, 2016b) as well as use the log files to examine when in the learning session students selected to use these processes, which process they selected, how long they spent engaging in the process, and their response (e.g., this page is relevant to my subgoal). Thus, using log-file and eye-tracking data can provide many details on how students are using metacognitive processes during learning with CALSs.

Given these examples, it is evident that multimodal multichannel data can provide great insight into how learners are using cognitive, affective, and metacognitive processes as they learn with different types of CALSs. However, when selecting which data to use, researchers should always use theoretically driven and empirically based justification when selecting data channels. In the next section, we will provide a list of questions that researchers should ask themselves prior to choosing their use of data types.

Selecting the Appropriate Multimodal Multichannel Data

A common misconception about using multimodal multichannel data is that the more data types you have, the more information you will obtain; however, this is not the case. There are many considerations a researcher has to make regarding their research questions, hypotheses, and learning context that will inform them of which data channels are the most appropriate, instead of using data channels that cannot address their research goals. In addition, there are theoretical dichotomies (see details in Table 23.1) that can also impact the selection of different data channels. In this section, we will discuss these considerations in more detail to help researchers select which type of data they should collect to conduct appropriate analyses to investigate CAM processes during learning with CALSs.

Contextual Considerations. A researcher's research questions and hypotheses will impact the data they should use because only certain data channels will be able to address the questions and provide evidence supporting or not supporting the hypotheses. For example, if a research question were to investigate how students' quiz scores differ based on the condition they were assigned to in MetaTutor, it would be appropriate to use log files to determine their quiz scores, while it would not be appropriate to use eye-tracking data or affect data because those data would not provide information on students' quiz scores. Alternatively, if the research question were to examine how students' emotions differ between the two conditions, it would be appropriate to use emotion data, but not eye-tracking or log-file data because they would not allow the researcher to test the hypotheses they formed regarding this research question. Thus, in these cases, we demonstrate how using all data types will not always be useful.

The specific learning context will also play an important role in determining which data channels to collect. Depending on where students are learning (e.g., lab, classroom, home) and what type of CALS they are using, some types of data will be more appropriate than others. For example, if students are learning with a CALS in a classroom and researchers are conducting a classroom study, collecting log-file data and EDA data are feasible to collect because they do not have additional limitations in terms of data collection, such that when collecting video and eye-tracking data, this requires a controlled setting where students must sit still and avoid movement and touching their face. These limitations make it difficult to collect these data channels in the classroom, which is therefore another factor that influences choosing data types. In contrast, a controlled laboratory study does not pose any limitations in terms of moving around the lab; however, when using the eye tracker, it is important to remember that the lighting has to be at an appropriate brightness so as not to interfere with pupil size measurement. As such, based on the design setting, there are different types of limitations and actions to be taken to avoid data collection issues and, depending on the research setting, this can impact which data to collect, and how.

Theoretical Dichotomies. In addition to the contextual considerations, selecting an accurate data type will also depend on factors mentioned in the theoretical dichotomies table from the previous section (see Table 23.1), where the appropriate data type(s) will depend on the type of variable and the specific CAM process being analyzed. From Table 23.1, it is evident that for cognitive and metacognitive processes, log-file data can always be used to answer research questions related to the use of these processes, whether it examines quality vs. quantity, macro vs. micro level, time vs. event, or discrete vs. co-occurring variables. However, with more specific and detailed questions examining variables considering different dichotomies, using more data channels will be necessary. For example, a simple question for cognitive processes (based on the frequency level in Table 23.1) can ask if taking more notes leads to better learning outcomes, while a simple question for metacognitive processes (based on the correlation subcategory in Table 23.1) can ask if more accurate judgments of learning are associated with more accurate content evaluations. Both of these questions would require the use of log-file data only, thus making them simpler to address. In contrast, a more complex question for cognitive processes (based on the interplay subcategory in Table 23.1) might ask at what point does individual variation in micro-level (e.g., take notes, summarize) processes lead us to examine macro-level (e.g., learning strategies) processes, while a metacognitive question (based on the causation subcategory in Table 23.1) might ask which specific cues cause students to engage in judgments of learning. Both of these research questions are far more complex and, as such, to answer them would require the use of many data channels, such as eye tracking, facial expressions, and EDA, in addition to log files.

For affective processes, a simpler question will also require fewer data channels; however, these are facial expressions and/or EDA data. For example, based on a valence subcategory as described in Table 23.1, this type of question would ask if experiencing a positive emotion (e.g., joy) influences expressing negative emotions (e.g., confusion), which would require using facial expression and/or EDA data only. In contrast, a more complex question (based on the latency subcategory in Table 23.1) might ask about the average amount of time occurring between encountering an impasse and expressing confusion, which would require the use of log files and eye tracking with facial expression and/or EDA data. Thus, as with cognitive and metacognitive processes, the appropriate data channels to answer questions related to affect at different complexity levels will differ, where more complex questions require the use of more data channels.

Overall, based on all CAM processes, it appears that to include more contextual information in a research question (e.g., what is a student's level of frustration while making inaccurate metacognitive judgments, or what contributes to the period of time between opening a new content page and deciding to take notes), the researcher needs to include more than only facial expression or log-file data, respectively, but to include multiple data channels that inform the researcher of the data they need to answer their research questions. Based on these examples, if the researcher wants to investigate a student's level of frustration during learning they would only need to include facial expression and/or EDA data; or to investigate taking notes alone this would only need log-file data. However, once the researcher wants to know *when, where,* or *how* (when making a metacognitive judgment or selecting a new page, on page 6 of the CASL or when in the infirmary of CRYSTAL ISLAND, or the level of accuracy of this judgment), the researcher needs to include other data channels as well. Thus, to investigate CAM processes during learning with CALSs, there are many different types of research questions to pose and, depending on the level of specificity of the research questions, using more than one data channel will be necessary and will also depend on the specific details of the research question.

Implications of Using Multimodal Multichannel Data

Based on all these examples, it is evident that there are many different ways we can analyze data using the same data channel (e.g., frequency vs. duration), and how we can use multiple different data channels to investigate one research question. In addition to selecting which data channel to use to answer these research questions, one more distinction must be made between using data to assess the *quality* vs. the *quantity* of an SRL process, which may require the use of the same data channel, however in different ways. For example, assessing the use of cognitive strategies, such as taking notes, can be measured by the frequency of use of the note-taking feature, which assesses the quantity of taking notes. However, this does not guarantee that all of these notes contain correct information and so, in order to assess the quality of these notes, further processing of the notes, such as using Latent Semantic Analysis, should be applied. This still involves using the log-file data; it just requires further processing. In contrast, some research questions can involve using more than one data channel to assess the quantity of a CAM process. This can include using both log-file and eye-tracking data to assess if a longer duration engaging in a metacognitive judgment increases its accuracy. However, to assess the quality of the metacognitive judgment, we will not be able to use eye-tracking data and will only assess the accuracy based on the log files, which indicate the student's response to the judgment. Thus, we infer from the eye tracking that the student is fixating on the text and diagram to make the judgment, but to assess the actual quality of that judgment, we would not be able to infer this from the eye-tracking data. As such, not only is it important to differentiate between investigating the quantity and quality of the CAM process but it is also necessary to make this distinction of which data channels will generate these different types of data.

In addition to discussing how these dichotomies impact selecting the appropriate data channel to help us respond to our research questions, selecting the appropriate data channel will also inform us of which specific type of data analysis to conduct. It is beyond the scope of this chapter to address the different types of statistical tests and analysis techniques (e.g., machine learning); however, we do note that the selection of a data analysis technique will also depend on the research questions as well as data channel and variable type (e.g., frequency vs. duration; one time point vs. multiple time points). For example, if a researcher wants to address the total time students were confused during learning, they can use a total duration variable, or proportion of time spent confused compared with the total time spent expressing all emotions (i.e., total session time), and can compare the difference in expressing confusion between conditions using traditional inferential statistics, such as a *t*-test or ANOVA. However, if the researcher wants to narrow down when specific instances of durations of confusion occurred during learning, and how each instance impacted overall learning, a multilevel modeling approach would be more appropriate. As such, not only is it important to make choices about your research questions for selecting the appropriate data channel but doing so will also be important toward conducting data analysis, demonstrating the close relationship between all the steps toward conducting a research study.

Overall, using multimodal multichannel data is a beneficial approach to measuring self-regulation because it allows us to pose more sophisticated research questions, allowing us to get a more in-depth depiction of how students are engaging in different types of cognitive, affective, and metacognitive processes during learning with CALSs, which can ultimately lead the way for designing CALSs that can foster self-regulation and adapt to how students self-regulate during learning.

Future Directions and Conclusions

The area of SRL and CALSs has reached an unprecedented moment in history of human learning where we can strategically use our models, frameworks, and theories of SRL to intelligently design CALSs with recent technological advances to measure CAM processes as well as support and foster SRL. Below are a few examples of work that could advance our measurement and understanding of CAM SRL processes with CALSs.

One area of research focuses on the measurement and analysis of learners' CAM processes in real time while solving complex STEM and non-STEM problems that require the use of computational thinking (CT) skills (e.g., abstractions and pattern generalization) using VR as both a research and a learning tool. For example, measuring metacognition by converging online trace multimodal multichannel process data (e.g., eye tracking, facial expressions, EDA, log files, concurrent verbal utterances, gestures, body movements), self-reports, and learning outcomes. The results of this type of study can be used to develop a VR metacognition training module (also delivered by VR) that can reify metacognitive monitoring and control processes (e.g., replaying a teacher's gaze behavior and associated verbal explanations of her metacognitive monitoring and control processes while solving a complex STEM problem). This example naturally leads to dealing with issues of domain specificity, training and transfer of CAM SRL skills, and the development of SRL competencies.

Another area stems from the growing interdisciplinary research documenting adolescents' inability to accurately monitor and regulate their CAM processes during learning about complex STEM material, which negatively impacts their academic achievement, persistence, engagement, and interest in STEM and in pursuing STEM careers. One promising approach has been to use VR or other immersive systems (e.g., AR, tangible computing) that can intrinsically foster and sustain motivational (e.g., situational interest, persistence, task value, intrinsic motivation, self-efficacy) and affective (e.g., joy, curiosity, pride) processes while allowing learners to focus on cognitive and metacognitive processes necessary to perform accurately when solving complex STEM problems. More specifically, we assume that fostering and sustaining motivational processes and affective states will allow learners to (1) practice a myriad of cognitive learning strategies (e.g., hypothesizing, summarizing, making inferences) and (2) practice making accurate metacognitive monitoring judgments (e.g., judgments of learning, feeling of knowing, monitoring progress toward goals, content evaluation).

A much-needed area of research involves the embodiment of theoretical assumptions of models, theories, and frameworks described earlier as affordances of CALSs. While many systems reviewed in this chapter have accomplished this challenge, there are still constructs, mechanisms, and assumptions that have yet to be embodied in CALSs. For example, most models of metacognition and SRL make assumptions about internal standards used to monitor and control. However, none of the existing CALSs model learners' internal standards nor do they make them visible to learners and teachers so they can potentially use them as feedback to monitor the accuracy of their metacognitive processes. Internal standards can be illustrated as part of the CALSs interface and be augmented with other data visualizations (Azevedo et al., 2018) that provide the learner with information regarding the accuracy of their self-regulatory skills.

Lastly, there are other constructs and mechanisms of SRL (e.g., calibration, adaptivity, self-modification, dysregulation, efficacy) that can be measured through the use of multimodal multichannel data during learning and problem-solving with CALS. Such endeavors, as illustrated in this chapter, along with the key questions presented in Table 23.1, will significantly advance the science of learning with CALSs. This effort will involve interdisciplinary researchers, including psychologists, educational researchers, and instructional designers working alongside statisticians, engineers, computer scientists, and AI researchers to detect, model, track, and foster CAM SRL processes with CALSs. An interdisciplinary approach will advance (1) our models and theories (e.g., test and extend current assumptions by including micro-level and valence in Greene and Azevedo [2009] processes in Winne's [2018] model) and (2) provide intelligent, adaptive scaffolding that addresses learners' real-time self-regulatory needs during learning with CALSs.

In conclusion, the future of self-regulation and CALS is very bright as recent technological advances allow for unsurpassed approaches to design sophisticated systems that can measure and foster SRL. In this chapter, we presented a brief historical review of research on SRL and CALSs; discussed the role, measurement, and support of CAM processes during learning and problem-solving with CALSs; presented ways of measuring and fostering SRL with CALSs; discussed conceptual and theoretical issues derived from several models, frameworks, and theories of SRL; discussed several dichotomies related to CAM and the challenges they pose for the measurement and support of SRL with CALSs; and presented challenges and future directions that need to be addressed by researchers.

References

Aleven, V. & Koedinger, K. (2016). An interview reflection on "Intelligent tutoring goes to school in the big city." *International Journal of Artificial Intelligence in Education*, *26*, 13–24.

Arguel, A., Lockyer, L., Lipp, O. V., Lordge, J. M., & Kennedy, G. (2016). Inside out: Detecting learners' confusion to improve interactive digital learning environments. *Journal of Educational Computing Research*, *55*, 526–551.

Azevedo, R. (2014). Issues in dealing with sequential and temporal characteristics of self- and socially-regulated learning. *Metacognition and Learning*, 9, 217–228.

Azevedo, R. & Aleven, V. (eds.). (2013). *International handbook of metacognition and learning technologies*. Amsterdam: Springer.

Azevedo, R. & Cromley, J. G. (2004). Does training on self-regulated learning facilitate students' learning with hypermedia? *Journal of Educational Psychology*, 96, 523–535.

Azevedo, R., Feyzi-Behnagh, R., Duffy, M., Harley, J., & Trevors, G. (2012). Metacognition and self-regulated learning in student-centered learning environments. In D. Jonassen & S. Land (eds.), *Theoretical foundations of student-center learning environments*, 2nd edn (pp. 171–197). New York: Routledge.

Azevedo, R., Harley, J., Trevors, G., Duffy, M., Feyzi-Behnagh, R., Bouchet, F., & Landis, R. S. (2013). Using trace data to examine the complex roles of cognitive, metacognitive, and emotional self-regulatory processes during learning with multi-agent systems. In R. Azevedo & V. Aleven (eds.), *International handbook of metacognition and learning technologies* (pp. 427–449). Amsterdam: Springer.

Azevedo, R., Johnson, A., Chauncey, A., & Burkett, C. (2010). Self-regulated learning with MetaTutor: Advancing the science of learning with metacognitive tools. In M. Khine & I. Saleh (eds.), *New science of learning* (pp. 225–247). New York: Springer.

Azevedo, R., Mudrick, N. V., Taub, M., & Wortha, F. (2017). Coupling between metacognition and emotions during STEM learning with advanced learning technologies: A critical analysis, implications for future research, and design of learning systems. In T. Michalsky & C. Schechter (eds.), *Self-regulated learning: Conceptualization, contribution, and empirically based models for teaching and learning* (pp. 1–18). New York: Teachers College Press.

Azevedo, R., Taub, M., & Mudrick, N. V. (2018). Using multi-channel trace data to infer and foster self-regulated learning between humans and advanced learning technologies. In D. Schunk & J. A. Greene (eds.), *Handbook of self-regulation of learning and performance*, 2nd edn (pp. 254–270). New York: Routledge.

Azevedo, R. & Witherspoon, A. M. (2009). Self-regulated learning with hypermedia. In D. J. Hacker, J. Dunlosky, & A. C. Graesser (eds.), *Handbook of metacognition in education* (pp. 319–339). Mahwah, NJ: Routledge.

Bannert, M. & Reimann, P. (2012). Supporting self-regulated hypermedia learning through prompts. *Instructional Science*, 40, 193–211.

Barab, S., Dodge, T., Tuzun, H., Job-Sluder, K., Jr., R. C., Gilbertson, J., et al. (2007). The Quest Atlantis project: A socially-responsive play space for learning. In B. E. Shelton & D. Wiley (eds.), *The design and use of simulation computer games in education* (pp. 159–186). Rotterdam: Sense Publishers.

Bargh, J. A. & Y. Schul. (1980). On the cognitive benefits of teaching. *Journal of Educational Psychology*, 72, 593–604.

Barral, O., Eugster, M. J. A., Ruotsalo, T., Spapé, M. M., Kosunen, I., Ravaja, N., Kaski, S., & Jacucci, G. (2015). Exploring peripheral physiology as a predictor of perceived relevance in information retrieval. In O. Brdiczka, P. Chau, G. Crenini, S. Pan, & P. O. Kristensson (eds.), *Proceedings of the 20th international conference on intelligent user interfaces*, (pp. 389–399). New York: ACM.

Benedek, M. & Kaernbach, C. (2010), Decomposition of skin conductance data by means of nonnegative deconvolution. *Psychophysiology*, 47, 647–658.

Biswas, G., Jeong, H., Kinnebrew, J. S., Sulcer, B., & Roscoe, R. (2010). Measuring self-regulated learning skills through social interactions in a teachable agent environment. *Research and Practice in Technology Enhanced Learning*, *5*, 123–152.

Biswas, G., Segedy, J. R., & Bunchongchit, K. (2016). From design to implementation to practice a learning by teaching system: Betty's Brain. *International Journal of Artificial intelligence in Education*, *26*, 350–364.

Bjork, R. A., Dunlosky, J., & Kornell, N. (2013). Self-regulated learning: Beliefs, techniques, and illusions. *Annual Review of Psychology*, *64*, 417–444.

Boucsein, W. (2012). *Electrodermal activity*. New York: Springer.

Bradbury, A.E., Taub, M., & Azevedo, R. 2017. The effects of autonomy on emotions and learning in game-based learning environments. In G. Gunzelmann, A. Howes, T. Tenbrink, & E. J. Davelaar (eds.), *Proceedings of the 39th annual meeting of the Cognitive Science Society* (pp. 1666–1671). Austin, TX: Cognitive Science Society.

Brawner, K. W. & Gonzalez, A. J. (2016). Modeling a learner's affective state in real time to improve intelligent tutoring effectiveness. *Theoretical Issues in Ergonomics*, *17*, 183–210.

Burkett, C. & Azevedo, R. (2012). The effect of multimedia discrepancies on metacognitive judgments. *Computers and Human Behavior*, *28*, 1276–1285.

Clark, D. B., Tanner-Smith, E. E., & Killingsworth, S. S. (2016). Digital games, design, and learning: A systematic review and meta-analysis. *Review of Educational Research*, *86*, 79–122.

Conati, C., Jaques, N., & Muir, M. (2013). Understanding attention to adaptive hints in educational games: An eye-tracking study. *International Journal of Artificial Intelligence in Education*, *23*, 136–161.

D'Mello, S. K. & Graesser, A. C. (2012). Dynamics of affective states during complex learning. *Learning and Instruction*, *22*, 145–157.

D'Mello, S. K., Lehman, B. Pekrun, R., & Graesser, A. C. (2014). Confusion can be beneficial for learning. *Learning and Instruction*, *29*, 153–170.

Duffy, M. & Azevedo, R. (2015). Motivation matters: Interactions between achievement goals and agent scaffolding for self-regulated learning within an intelligent tutoring system. *Computers in Human Behavior*, *52*, 338–348.

Dunlosky, J. & Metcalfe, J. (2009). *Metacognition: A textbook for cognitive, educational, life span and applied psychology*. Newbury Park, CA: SAGE.

Greene, J. A. & Azevedo, R. (2009). A macro-level analysis of SRL processes and their relations to the acquisition of a sophisticated mental model of a complex system. *Contemporary Education Psychology*, *34*, 18–29.

Gross, J. (2015). Emotion regulation: Current status and future prospects. *Psychological Inquiry*, *26*, 1–26.

Hacker, D. J., Dunlosky, J., & Graesser, A. C. (2009). *Handbook of metacognition in education*. New York: Routledge.

Hardy, M., Wiebe, E. N, Grafsgaard, J. F., Boyer, K. E., & Lester, J. C. (2013). Physiological responses to events during training: Use of skin conductance to inform future adaptive learning systems. In Proceedings of the human factors and ergonomic society 57th annual meeting (pp. 2101–2105).

Harley, J. M., Bouchet, F., Hussain, M. S., Azevedo, R., & Calvo, R. (2015). A multi-componential analysis of emotions during complex learning with an intelligent multi-agent system. *Computers in Human Behavior*, *48*, 615–625.

Harley, J. M., Taub, M., Azevedo, R., & Bouchet, F. (2018). "Let's set up some subgoals": Understanding human-pedagogical agent collaborations and their implications for learning and prompt and feedback compliance. *IEEE Transactions on Learning Technologies*, *11*, 54–66.

Heilig, M. (1962). *United States Patent No. #3,050,870*. Alexandria, VA: United States Patent Office.

iMotions. (2017). *Attention tool (Version 6.3)* [Computer software]. Boston, MA: iMotions Inc.

Järvelä, S., Malmberg, J., & Koivuniemi, M. (2016). Recognizing socially shared regulation by using the temporal sequences of online chat and logs in CSCL. *Learning and Instruction*, *42*, 1–11.

Kulik, J. A. & Fletcher, J. D. (2016). Effectiveness of intelligent tutoring systems: A meta-analytic review. *Review of Educational Research*, *86*, 42–78.

Lajoie, S. P., Poitras, E. G., Doleck, T., & Jarrell, A. (2015). Modeling metacognitive activities in medical problem-solving with BioWorld. In A. Peña-Ayala (ed.), *Metacognition: Fundamentals, applications, and trends. A profile of the current state-of-the-art* (pp. 323–343). New York: Springer.

Lin, M., Preston, A., Kharrufa, A., & Kong, Z. (2016). Making L2 learners' reasoning skills visible: The potential of computer supported collaborative learning environments. *Thinking Skills and Creativity*, *22*, 303–322.

Matsuda, N., Yarzebinski, E., Keiser, V., Raizada, R., Cohen, W. W., Stylianides, G. J., & Koedinger, K. R. (2013). Cognitive anatomy of tutor learning: Lessons learned with SimStudent. *Journal of Educational Psychology*, *105*, 1152–1163.

Mayer, R. E. (2014a). *Computer games for learning: An evidence-based approach*. Cambridge, MA: MIT Press.

 (ed.). (2014b). *The Cambridge handbook of multimedia learning*, 2nd edn. Cambridge, MA: Cambridge University Press.

Mayer, R. E. & Alexander, P. A. (eds.). (2017). *Handbook of research on learning and instruction*, 2nd edn. New York: Routledge.

Merchant, Z., Goetz, E. T., Cifuentes, L., Keeney-Kennicutt, W., & Davis, T. J. (2014). Effectiveness of virtual reality-based instruction on students' learning outcomes in K-12 and higher education: A meta-analysis. *Computers and Education*, *70*, 29–40.

Mudrick, N. V., Rowe, J., Taub, M., Lester, J., & Azevedo, R. (2017). Toward affect-sensitive virtual human tutors: The influence of facial expressions on learning and emotion. In C. Busso & J. Epps (eds.) *Proceedings of the 2017 seventh international conference on affective computing and intelligent interaction (ACII)* (pp. 184–189). Washington, DC: IEEE Computer Society.

Nelson, T. O. & Narens, L. (1990). Metamemory: A theoretical framework and new findings. *The Psychology of Learning and Motivation*, *26*, 125–173.

Pekrun, R., Goetz, T., Frenzel, A. C., Barchfeld, P., & Perry, R. P. (2011). Measuring emotions in students' learning and performance: The achievement emotions questionnaire (AEQ). *Contemporary Educational Psychology*, *36*, 36–48.

Rayner, K. (2009). Eye movements and attention in reading, scene perception, and visual search. *The Quarterly Journal of Experimental Psychology*, *62*, 1457–1506.

Rowe, J. P., Shores, L. R., Mott, B. W., & Lester, J. C. (2011). Integrating learning, problem solving, and engagement in narrative-centered learning environments. *International Journal of Artificial Intelligence in Education*, *21*, 115–133.

Santos, M. E. C., Chen, A., Taketomi, T., Yamamoto, G., Miyazaki, J., & Kato, H. (2014). Augmented reality learning experiences: Survey of prototype design and evaluation. *IEEE Transactions on Learning Technologies*, *7*, 38–56.

Sawyer, R. K. (2014). *The Cambridge handbook of the learning sciences* New York: Cambridge University Press.

Sawyer, R., Smith, A., Rowe, J., Azevedo, R., Lester, J., & Carolina, N. (2017). Is more agency better? The impact of student agency on game-based learning. In André E., Baker R., Hu X., Rodrigo M., & B. du Bouley (eds.) *Proceedings of the 18th international conference on artificial intelligence in education* (pp. 335–346). Amsterdam: Springer.

Scheiter, K. & Eitel, A. (2016). The use of eye tracking as a research and instructional tool in multimedia learning. In C. A. Was, F. J. Sansosti, & B. Morris (eds.), *Eye-tracking technology applications in educational research* (pp. 143–164). Hershey, PA: IGI Global.

Schunk, D. & Greene, J. (2017). *Handbook of self-regulation of learning and performance*, 2nd edn. New York: Routledge.

Taub, M. & Azevedo, R. (2016a). Using multi-channel data to assess, understand, and support affect and metacognition with Intelligent Tutoring Systems. In A. Micarelli, J. Stamper, & K. Panourgia (eds.), *Proceedings of the 13th international conference on intelligent tutoring systems* (pp. 543–544). Amsterdam: Springer.

(2016b). *Using eye-tracking to determine the impact of prior knowledge on self-regulated learning with an adaptive hypermedia- learning environment?* In A. Micarelli, J. Stamper, & K. Panourgia (eds.), *Proceedings of the 13th international conference on intelligent tutoring systems* (pp. 34–47). Amsterdam: Springer.

Taub, M., Azevedo, R., Bouchet, F., & Khosravifar, B. (2014). Can the use of cognitive and metacognitive self-regulated learning strategies be predicted by learners' levels of prior knowledge in hypermedia-learning environments? *Computers in Human Behavior*, *39*, 356–36.

Taub, M., Azevedo, R., Bradbury, A. E., Millar, G. C., & Lester, J. (2018). Using sequence mining to reveal the efficiency in scientific reasoning during STEM learning with a game-based learning environment. *Learning and Instruction*, *54*, 93–103.

Taub, M., Mudrick, N. V., Azevedo, R., Millar, G. C., Rowe, J., & Lester, J. (2017). Using multi-channel data with multi-level modeling to assess in-game performance during gameplay with Crystal Island. *Computers in Human Behavior*, *76*, 641–655.

Taub, M., Mudrick., N., Bradbury, A. E., & Azevedo, R. (in press). Self-regulation, self-explanation, and reflection in game-based learning. In J. Plass, B. Horner, & R. Mayer (eds.), *Handbook of game-based learning*. Boston, MA: MIT Press.

Trevors, G., Duffy, M., & Azevedo, R. (2014). Note-taking within MetaTutor: Interactions between an intelligent tutoring system and prior knowledge on note-taking and learning. *Educational Technology Research and Development*, *62*, 507–528.

Winne, P. H. (2018). Cognition and metacognition in self-regulated learning. In D. Schunk & J. Greene (eds.), *Handbook of self-regulation of learning and performance* (2nd edn) (pp. 36–48). New York: Routledge.

Winne, P. H. & Azevedo, R. (2014). Metacognition. In K. Sawyer (ed.), *Cambridge handbook of the learning sciences*, 2nd edn. (pp. 63–87). Cambridge, MA: Cambridge University Press.

Winne, P., & Hadwin, A. (2008). The weave of motivation and self-regulated learning. In D. Schunk & B. Zimmerman (eds.), *Motivation and self-regulated learning: Theory, research, and applications* (pp. 297–314). New York: Taylor & Francis.

Wolff, B. (2009). *Building intelligent interactive tutors: Student-centered strategies for adaptive e-learning*. Burlington, MA: Morgan Kaufmann.

24 Improving Students' Metacomprehension Accuracy

Thomas D. Griffin, Marta K. Mielicki, and Jennifer Wiley

Improving Students' Metacomprehension Accuracy

Reading assignments are still a primary means by which students learn in their courses. Often, students will have to complete readings for multiple topics within a limited amount of time. And, as course exams approach, they must regulate their time and efforts in what and how they study in order to optimize learning and test performance across topics and courses. Theoretically, optimal study regulation will depend on how accurately students can monitor and self-assess their comprehension of various pieces of text, in order to avoid wasting time by restudying mastered material or by continuing to employ ineffective strategies that are not leading to comprehension (Thiede & Dunlosky, 1999; Winne & Hadwin, 1998). This monitoring of ongoing learning processes has been referred to as *metacognitive monitoring* or, in the context of text comprehension, *metacomprehension* (Maki & Berry, 1984). How accurate learners are in monitoring and judging their progress is *metacomprehension accuracy*.

The earliest research to approach the issue of monitoring during text comprehension employed error-detection paradigms (e.g., Markman, 1977). Readers' failure to notice or mention errors in texts has been claimed to indicate their failure to monitor the coherence of their mental representations of the text. However, there are many alternative explanations for readers' failure to mention errors, such as a lack of comprehension itself or a presumption that the texts are error-free and that any confusion is their own fault (see Markman, 1979). Other research has attempted to use online measures of reading behaviors (e.g., reading slow-downs when encountering contradictions) to show error detection and thus implicate comprehension monitoring (Otero, 1998; Wiley & Myers, 2003), but many alternative explanations exist for slow-downs in reading times as well.

The earliest studies that attempted to directly assess the accuracy of monitoring during text comprehension using a judgment paradigm were initiated by Maki and Berry (1984), and Glenberg and Epstein (1985). The basic paradigm is outlined in

The authors were supported by grants from the National Science Foundation (DUE 1535299) and the Institute of Education Sciences (R305A160008) during the preparation of this chapter. All opinions expressed herein are those of the authors and do not necessarily reflect those of the funding agencies. The authors thank Keith W. Thiede and Tricia A. Guerrero for their comments on this chapter.

Figure 24.1 (minus the effective manipulations shown in the shaded box). It involves participants reading multiple texts, providing predictive judgments of comprehension for each text, and answering test questions for each text. These researchers borrowed the paradigm from two decades of research on metamemory, where learners were asked to predict their future ability to recall/recognize general facts, presented pictures, or studied word pairs (e.g., Flavell, Freidrichs, & Hoyt, 1970; Hart, 1965; Nelson & Narens,1980). These simpler learning materials were replaced with texts typically ranging from 200 to 1,000 words, and the monitoring judgments about memory were replaced with judgments of "comprehension," "understanding," or predictions of performance on a "test of comprehension." The majority of research on metacomprehension of text has followed Nelson's (1984) advice regarding measures of metamemory accuracy, by focusing primarily on relative accuracy computed via intra-individual correlations between an array of judgments and an array of test performances rather than difference scores between judgments and tests, whether signed or absolute.

Since these initial studies, there have now been over eighty experiments that have measured the relative accuracy of judgments of comprehension for texts. Across studies, methodological approaches have varied greatly, from the length of text that corresponds to each monitoring judgment to whether the tests focus on memory for the isolated ideas explicitly stated in the text versus comprehension of the implied logical and causal relations among various concepts. In this chapter, the former type of test is considered to reflect metamemory for text, whereas the latter is considered to reflect metacomprehension. As suggested by both theory and empirical findings, accurate metamemory and metacomprehension for text are distinct constructs, rely on different types of judgment cues, and can be impacted in opposite ways by a given

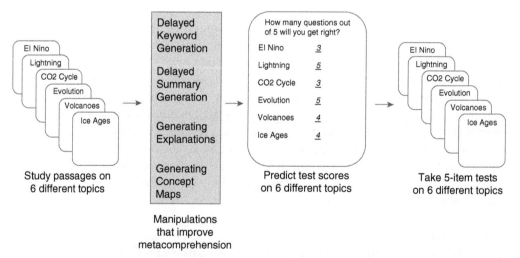

Figure 24.1 *Overview of the standard metacomprehension paradigm (minus the shaded box)*

The shaded box shows manipulations that increase access to situation-model–based cues and improve metacomprehension accuracy.

manipulation. The main focus of this chapter is providing an overview of effective manipulations specifically for improving metacomprehension. In general, students' ability to accurately monitor their own comprehension of text is quite poor. Several reviews have reported average levels of metacomprehension accuracy around 0.27 in baseline conditions without special instructions or activities (Dunlosky & Lipko, 2007; Maki, 1998a, 1998b; Thiede et al., 2009). However, a substantial body of evidence has begun to accumulate suggesting that there are several instructional conditions that can lead to significant improvements, such as those shown in the shaded box in Figure 24.1. Before turning to the research on these effective manipulations, it is important to situate that literature within a theoretical context and discuss relevant methodological concerns.

Monitoring and Other Components of Metacognition

Hacker (1998) identified two different concepts in the literature commonly referred to as "monitoring." An approach used primarily by educational researchers uses "comprehension monitoring" in a broad sense to refer to any deliberate attention that learners pay to their learning goals, use of strategies, and learning progress. This approach generally utilizes assessments such as self-report scales of strategy knowledge and strategy use, rather than focusing on accurate monitoring of ongoing learning (for a review, see Dinsmore, Alexander, & Loughlin, 2008). The second approach, used primarily by cognitive psychologists, focuses on learners' monitoring of ongoing learning. Monitoring is measured by having students make explicit judgments of their current level of learning or understanding. Using this approach, comprehension monitoring *accuracy* can be computed by comparing judgments to performance on objective tests of comprehension. Identifying the conditions that improve performance on these metacomprehension accuracy measures is the focus of this chapter.

Monitoring progress of ongoing learning was central to Flavell's (1979) original conception of metacognition and he distinguished it from the types of more general meta-knowledge that are assessed by self-reported study strategies. Metacognition entails two levels of processing that are reflected in the predominant models of metacognition and self-regulated learning (SRL; Griffin, Wiley, & Salas, 2013; Metcalfe, 2002; Nelson & Narens, 1990; Pintrich, Wolters, & Baxter, 2000; Thiede & Dunlosky, 1999; Winne & Hadwin, 1998; Zimmerman, 2002). As shown in the shaded portion at the bottom of Figure 24.2, object-level processing entails the application of a priori knowledge and assumptions about particular tasks, strategies, or a learner's abilities that can be used to implement cognitive actions to increase learning. The upper unshaded area is meta-level processing that entails metacognitive reactions to subjective *experiences* of internal states that occur as a result of the cognitive actions and reflect how learning is progressing. Only by monitoring these experiences during a learning episode can one be aware of actual variations in learning that arise from interactions among the specific texts or learning material, contextual factors, and how well the reader actually executes any learning

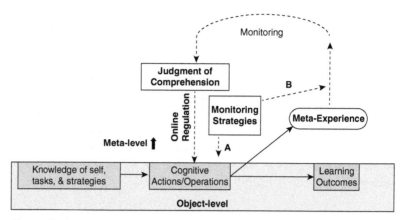

Figure 24.2 *A process model of metacognition during learning*

strategies. Such monitoring allows the learner to make adjustments and regulate learning beyond what is afforded by limited, and often inaccurate, a priori assumptions and expectations about learning. This feedback loop of actively monitoring subjective experiences during learning is what Flavell meant by "monitoring" and makes metacognition qualitatively distinct from the cognitive processes or operations that learners engage in at the "object" level (Fischer & Mandl, 1984; Griffin et al., 2013; Nelson & Narens, 1990).

The focus of research on monitoring accuracy has been to identify effective metacognitive strategies, which, as Flavell (1979) argued, are strategies specifically for aiding the accurate *monitoring* of learning rather than more general cognitive/ study strategies that directly aid learning itself. The distinction lies in the learner's purpose for using a strategy. The same activity (e.g., practice tests or self-explaining what was just read) could be employed as a cognitive strategy to improve retention or comprehension or, alternatively, it could be used as a metacognitive strategy to generate meta-experiences to serve as cues of how well one already comprehends the material. Learners know and can apply cognitive strategies that impact object-level processing and directly affect learning outcomes without involving meta-level processes. Nearly all models of SRL have at least an implicit recognition that the mere application of study strategies does not inherently entail meta-level processing or monitoring of ongoing learning (e.g., Hacker, Keener, & Kircher, 2009; Nelson & Narens, 1990; Pintrich et al., 2000; Winne & Hadwin, 1998). Instead, what is critical is that students are using a strategy specifically to actively reflect on their learning progress.

How Are Metacognitive Judgments Made?

The prevailing theoretical framework that guides research on monitoring accuracy is Koriat's (1997) cue-utilization theory, which presumes that learners cannot directly observe their own level of understanding and must make use of indirect cues to infer it. Koriat discussed two classes of cues from which learners draw inferences that form the basis of their judgments and performance predictions. One class is comprised of cues that are tied to learners' internal online subjective experiences that result from their cognitive processing in the specific situation. Koriat labeled these *mnemonic cues* because his focus was on monitoring during memorization tasks. These cues include the subjective sense of ease or fluency during learning (Benjamin & Bjork, 1996; Dunlosky & Nelson, 1992). The other kinds of cues are tied to objective features of the learning situation. These cues can be either *intrinsic* to the materials and task demands (e.g., relatedness of word pairs, memory of details versus conceptual application) or *extrinsic* to the task or stimuli but instead related to the context (e.g., how many times items were studied or what strategy was used). Griffin, Jee, and Wiley (2009) pointed out that these intrinsic and extrinsic cues depend on the application of a priori knowledge or assumptions, whereas the mnemonic cues are meta-experiences tied to actually constructing a particular mental representation during a learning episode. Thus, the explicit judgments of learning (JOLs) that people are asked to make can either be inferred based in actual monitoring of meta-experiences or be inferred based on general heuristic knowledge or assumptions about learning.

General heuristic knowledge may sometimes be useful in predicting aggregate levels of learning because such knowledge is informed by the information one has acquired about oneself and various factors related to learning from prior experience. If one has generally done better on tests than one's peers, then knowledge of this could accurately predict doing better than one's peers on average on any future test. In fact, such heuristic knowledge could be used to predict other people's understanding as well as one's own. However, such knowledge will not aid in the prediction of within-person variability in learning because it fails to incorporate the countless and often highly context-dependent factors that impact comprehension of a particular text at a particular moment. Predicting context-dependent learning that varies within-person across topics requires attention to those subjective, online meta-experiences at the center of the metacognitive monitoring construct. This general point leads to two more specific arguments. The first is that it is preferable to have a measure of monitoring accuracy that is sensitive to these online experiences. The second is that it is preferable if that measure also is sensitive to diagnostic cues that predict actual comprehension. These two points are discussed further in the following sections.

Differences Between Measures of Monitoring Accuracy: Relative Versus Absolute Measures

Research on monitoring accuracy relies on having learners make explicit judgments about their level of learning, understanding, or comprehension (JOLs, JOUs, JOCs), or predictions of performance (POPs) on upcoming tests. The accuracy of these judgments is determined by comparing them with actual performance on subsequent tests assumed to be objective measures of actual comprehension. Various measures of metacomprehension compare predictions with actual performance but they do so in different ways. Three independent measures of judgment–performance relations have been employed by metacomprehension researchers: *absolute accuracy, confidence bias*, and *relative accuracy* (Griffin et al., 2009; Maki 1998a). *Absolute accuracy* is the mean of the absolute (or mean squared) deviations between judged and actual performance. For absolute accuracy measures, lower values indicate better accuracy. A related outcome measure, *confidence bias*, concerns the directionality of these deviations, computed as the mean of the signed difference between each judgment and corresponding test score. This measure, sometimes referred to as overconfidence (for positive values) or underconfidence (for negative values), does not reflect the level of accuracy in terms of the number or magnitude of judgment errors but rather in terms of whether those judgment errors are systematically biased in one direction (Yates, 1990). Both absolute accuracy and confidence bias are statistically dependent on marginal mean performance levels and this allows for nonmetacognitive influences on these accuracy measures (for a longer discussion, see Nelson, 1984).

Therefore, a third measure, relative accuracy, has become the main measure of interest for most metacomprehension research. Relative accuracy quantifies an individual's accuracy in predicting performance on one text relative to other texts in terms of an intra-individual correlation between the individual's performance predictions and the individual's test scores (e.g., Gamma or Pearson). Nelson (1984) strongly recommended computing relative accuracy using intra-individual correlations over measures of absolute accuracy because the latter are so directly dependent on aggregate levels of test performance. Two people who engage in identical metacognitive processes will wind up with drastically different absolute accuracy scores simply because one did worse on the tests. Similarly, the overall difficulty of the tests can increase or decrease absolute accuracy.

To appreciate the differences between these measures, consider Figure 24.3 that illustrates two sets of hypothetical predictive judgments and two sets of performance on comprehension tests for texts on six different topics. For the purposes of this illustration, the topics have been arranged in order from the text that was understood the best to the text that was understood the least, for a set of easy tests and a set of hard tests. Relative accuracy is the intra-individual correlation between the array that results from an individual learner's judgments and the array that results from that individual's actual performance on the corresponding tests. If the reader makes Judgment A on each topic, then it would result in perfect relative accuracy (both with the easy and hard tests) because the judgments vary in parallel with variations in test performance. In contrast, if the reader makes Judgment B on each topic, it would result in weak relative accuracy (at the typically observed 0.28) because these judgments sometimes vary in the opposite direction relative to test performance. Importantly, the general difficulty level of the tests does not impact the relative accuracy scores. However, the general difficulty level of the tests makes a large difference in absolute accuracy. When absolute accuracy is computed as the mean of the absolute differences between each judgment–performance pair, lower scores mean less error and greater accuracy. When the tests are generally easy, Judgment

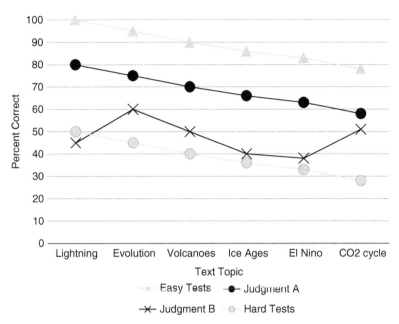

Figure 24.3 *An illustration of how test difficulty impacts absolute but not relative accuracy*

A would lead to much better absolute accuracy than Judgment B (20 versus 40.17). In contrast for difficult tests, Judgment A would have far worse accuracy than Judgment B (30 versus 10.33).

Although it is pragmatically useful for learners to know whether they have mastered material in an absolute sense (Dunlosky & Rawson, 2012), measures of absolute accuracy have less utility for advancing theories of monitoring because they confound effects due to object-level processes with meta-level processes. In some cases, this problem can be reduced by using comprehension performance measures as statistical controls when analyzing effects on absolute metacomprehension accuracy (Griffin et al., 2009). In contrast, relative accuracy provides a measure that is orthogonal to test performance and average judgment magnitude. This means it is also orthogonal to absolute accuracy so they are not measures of the same psychological construct. The differences between the constructs of absolute and relative accuracy are important theoretically as relative accuracy is the more direct reflection of how well a learner is engaging in effective monitoring of meta-experiences during learning. Maki and colleagues (2005) pointed out that "participants have to use their *experience* with the *specific* task in order to produce accurate relative judgments across parts of that task" (p. 729, emphasis added). The low levels of relative accuracy that are generally obtained in studies of metacomprehension (Dunlosky & Lipko, 2007; Maki, 1998a, 1998b; Thiede et al., 2009) may result from individuals' inability to distinguish their level of learning from specific texts from their assumed ability to learn from text in general. In contrast, heuristic knowledge about one's general ability can produce judgments that are accurate in an absolute sense. As a byproduct of how they are computed, absolute accuracy measures are sensitive to anything that impacts average judgment magnitude, such as a priori heuristic assumptions. In contrast, high relative accuracy can only be achieved by relying on cues that reflect the context-dependent variations in how well one is actually comprehending information from text to text and from moment to moment. In other words, differences in relative accuracy will be more reflective of how well learners are actually monitoring meta-experiences created while processing the material.

Several studies have indirectly illustrated this point by showing the greater sensitivity of absolute accuracy measures to differences in learners' heuristic assumptions. Griffin and colleagues (2009) showed that having more general domain knowledge and self-reported prior domain familiarity predicted higher judgments and greater absolute accuracy but not relative accuracy. This held after controlling for knowledge effects on test performance itself and even when participants only saw text titles and did not even read the texts before making their judgments and taking the tests. In addition, an index of how much each participant based their judgments on prior familiarity was correlated with absolute accuracy scores. In contrast, prior general knowledge and familiarity had no relation with relative accuracy. Thus, when readers used a priori heuristic knowledge unrelated to meta-experiences during text processing to make judgments, this led to better absolute accuracy but not better relative accuracy.

Other studies have suggested that absolute accuracy is more sensitive to heuristic cues, although this point was not made explicitly by the authors of those studies. Generalized a priori expectations about how hard the tests will be are a form of general heuristic knowledge independent of monitored meta-experiences. Maki (1998a) manipulated learners' prior heuristic knowledge about test difficulty by telling them that the "typical" score was either high or low. This heuristic knowledge had a large impact on learners' judgment magnitudes and the group that was told that the tests were easy had much higher absolute accuracy in both experiments ($ds = 0.74$ and 0.99), whereas this knowledge had only a small effect on relative accuracy in one experiment ($d = 0.29$) and no effect in the second experiment. Zhao and Linderholm (2011) found the same effect, except in the reverse direction, such that the group given the expectancy of difficult tests had the best absolute accuracy. In Maki (1998a) the tests happened to be easy (75 percent correct), whereas the tests were more difficult (50 percent correct) in Zhao and Linderholm (2011). This is an empirical example of the problem illustrated in Figure 24.3 in which the same manipulation is used in two studies, and may have the same impact on metacognitive processes, and yet produces opposite results in terms of absolute accuracy depending on how difficult or easy the researchers chose to make the tests (for a conceptually similar argument, see Connor, Dunlosky, & Hertzog, 1997).

Besides heuristics about tests, there are also heuristics that learners hold about themselves, the learning materials, and different media that help them learn. Kwon and Linderholm (2014) found that students' a priori heuristic beliefs about their general reading skill predicted their overall judgment magnitude for specific texts ($r = 0.44$) even better than their actual reading skill ($r = 0.29$), and predicted absolute accuracy and confidence bias. Ackerman and Goldsmith (2011) found that when learners were given a set amount of study time for each text, there was a bias for making higher judgments when the texts were read on computer screens versus on paper, despite no effect of text presentation on actual test performance. On-screen reading produced higher overconfidence and worse absolute accuracy but there was no impact on relative accuracy.

Ackerman and Goldsmith's (2011) findings suggest that readers apply a general heuristic about learning with technology, which is related to the heuristic about multimedia learning suggested by Serra and Dunlosky (2010). In their experiments, Serra and Dunlosky collected an initial set of predictive judgments prior to reading, when learners only knew they would read "a short science text about how lightning storms develop" in the text-only condition or "a short science text with diagram" in the multimedia conditions. Serra and Dunlosky found higher prereading judgments in the multimedia conditions than the text-only condition. Because readers had not yet seen the texts, these higher judgments could only be due to learners applying a general heuristic that multimedia helps learning. Further, reliance on this heuristic persisted into a second set of postreading judgments, even after learners read the texts and saw that the "diagrams" were merely decorative photos without conceptual relevance to how lightning storms develop. As shown in Table 3 of their paper (p. 705), the test items were generally very difficult, with participants on average getting only 33 percent correct, whereas average postreading judgments of test performance were nearly twice as high (62 percent), indicating overconfidence in all but a few participants. Serra and Dunlosky did not report absolute accuracy but, given that almost all participants were overconfident in all conditions, absolute accuracy can be estimated from the mean performance and mean per-paragraph judgment scores reported in table 3 of their paper. The inflated judgments in the photos condition led to worse estimated absolute accuracy in the multimedia conditions compared to the text-only condition (37.3 vs. 29.7). However, the same heuristic also led to better absolute accuracy in a multimedia condition that had conceptually useful images. This multimedia condition produced inflated judgments similar to those seen in the nonuseful photo condition but also markedly increased test performance up to 43 percent correct. This resulted in an estimated absolute accuracy that was actually better (23.6) than that of the text-only condition. In contrast, the per-paragraph relative accuracy was unaffected by the multimedia heuristic.

In sum, absolute accuracy appears highly sensitive to variability in heuristic cues that are not tied to monitoring of meta-experiences during learning and varies depending on test difficulty. While better absolute accuracy may sometimes reflect more accurate heuristic assumptions held by readers, it can also reflect whether these assumptions happen to match the average difficulty level of the tests created by researchers or instructors.

The previously mentioned measure of confidence bias, the simple signed average of judgment–performance difference scores, shares many of the interpretation issues as absolute accuracy because it is also orthogonal to relative accuracy and dependent on mean test performance and mean judgments. However, when construed as a measure of monitoring accuracy, confidence bias is particularly problematic.

In contrast to the standard absolute accuracy measure, and as its name implies, this bias score does not reflect accuracy in terms of how *much* error was in a person's judgments, but rather it reflects the extent to which a person's errors were either random (thus cancelling each other out to produce a bias score close to zero) or systematically biased in one direction (to overestimate or underestimate performance). When comparing conditions in a study, mean bias scores do not reflect the magnitude of the difference between judgments and performance, but rather whether the people in a condition shared the same directional bias. Since the least amount of bias (a difference score of zero) falls in the middle of all possible bias scores, a difference between means may not even reflect more or less bias but merely that one subgroup was overconfident while another was equally underconfident. Bias and absolute accuracy can be unrelated or negatively related but will be positively related if the majority of a sample happens to share the same directional bias (such as when the tests are generally difficult, so performance is consistently below judgments). If researchers create especially hard tests to ensure variability on their measure, this is likely to produce general overconfidence. In sum, absolute accuracy, relative accuracy, and confidence bias are the three most common outcome measures reported in metacomprehension research and are sometimes treated as interchangeable despite being largely unrelated. These measures generally are not suited to test the same theories or hypotheses.

A final measure that is reported from time to time is an inter-person correlation, where a mean judgment and mean performance score is calculated for each person, then the two measures are correlated at the level of study condition. Readers of this literature need to be aware that there are instances where such "inter-individual" correlations are incorrectly reported as "intra-individual" correlations. Some signals that the correlations are inter-individual are when they are reported as correlation coefficients tested against zero. With relative accuracy intra-individual correlations, the actual Gamma or Pearson scores are only for an individual person so they would not be reported as correlations with confidence intervals. Instead, mean scores and variation indices (like standard deviations) would be reported for each study condition and tested against each other.

Pilegard and Mayer (2015) argue that an inter-person correlation reflects whether learners can predict their own performance relative to the performance of others. However, it is unclear what this construct could mean or how it could inform regulation of study behaviors. There is no statistical or conceptual overlap between these inter-individual correlations and relative accuracy as computed by intra-individual correlations. This inter-individual measure also does not have a straightforward connection to absolute accuracy. The inter-person correlation reflects whether the people within a given condition share the same direction and magnitude of confidence bias. Two conditions could be identical in absolute error but, if the errors in one condition are more systematically biased in the same direction, then the mean confidence bias will be greater and the inter-individual correlation will be stronger in that condition. This makes it unclear whether such a measure has any theoretical or pragmatic utility.

Gamma versus Pearson as relative accuracy measures. Although Nelson (1984) suggested using intra-individual Goodman–Kruskal Gamma correlations as the basis for computing relative accuracy for studies on metamemory, other arguments can be made in favor of using Pearson to compute relative accuracy for studies on metacomprehension. The original recommendation for using Gamma was based in metamemory work where performance measures (memory tests) were dichotomous (recall or no recall). In such instances, it makes sense to compute a tally of hits and misses as an accuracy measure, which is what is involved in computing Gamma. Computing Gamma entails making a set of pairwise comparisons, tabulating the number of times that two judgments differ in the same direction (concordance/hit) versus opposite direction (discordance/miss) as the difference between the corresponding pair of test performances. Gamma attends only to the frequency of hits and misses, completely ignoring the large variance in how close those hits and misses actually are. The Pearson–Gamma tradeoff is one of making an assumption of linearity in the variance of the judgment scale versus completely discarding most of the variance information that nondichotomous scales yield.

In contrast to metamemory studies, most studies in the metacomprehension literature use comprehension tests with multiple items and are therefore collecting more continuous measures of performance. When comparing Pearson and Gamma even for dichotomous performance measures, Schwartz and Metcalfe (1994) noted "a subject might be revealing something real and interesting ... by giving values of .49, .50, and .51 for the three items in one list [rather than] .01, .50, and .99," yet "gamma discards this information" (p. 105). Griffin, Wiley, and Thiede (2008) further noted that when judgments are predicting *continuous* comprehension scores derived from multi-item tests, then the case for Pearson is stronger due to the extreme amount of information that Gamma discards. Also, the linearity assumption is more sound when readers are judging the number of test items they will correctly answer rather than endorsing subjective abstractions like being "somewhat confident" in one's answer. It is easy to find fault with any correlational method based on only six judgment–test pairs per participant, as is common in studies on text metacomprehension. However, there is no easy solution to this problem given the goal of exploring the monitoring of deeper comprehension processes, which requires using texts of sufficient length and complexity to support the construction of explanatory models and a single judgment for each text that reflects the reader's monitoring of the quality and completeness of their representation of each explanation as a whole. This generally makes collecting a much larger number of judgment–performance pairs untenable in metacomprehension experiments.

Benjamin and Diaz (2008, p. 78) provide evidence that a variant of signal-detection measures (D_a) is preferable to Gamma, in part, because it does not "discard vast amounts of information" that the pairwise approach of Gamma does. According to their approach, D_a gives consideration to the number of judgment levels between any two judgments (however, for a D_a measure based on the same dichotomous hits and misses categorizations as Gamma, see Masson & Rotello, 2009). Although Benjamin and Diaz (2008) also critique Pearson for its linearity assumption, the simulations and conclusions resulting from their approach apply to metamemory paradigms with dichotomous test performance (e.g., recall or no recall) and may have limited validity for typical metacomprehension paradigms. The computation of D_a is a function of X and Y coordinates, where X is the probability of one outcome (e.g., successful recall) for a given judgment level and Y is the probability of the other outcome (e.g., failed recall) at that judgment level. Each item used to compute those probabilities has its own independently rated judgment, unlike metacomprehension paradigms where a judgment applies only to the continuous aggregate score on multi-item tests. It is unclear how this D_a approach could be validly applied to continuous performance scales. Recoding continuous scores into dichotomous categories (e.g., by computing a median split) would discard much of the magnitude information just as Gamma does. In addition, Benjamin and Diaz (2008) show failed linearity tests for Gamma and Pearson at their minimum and maximum boundaries of +1.0 and −1.0 when using dichotomous performance measures. However, when performance is measured on a continuous interval scale with a range of values, extreme Pearson values are uncommon, because they require predicting the precise direction and magnitude of each relative difference. Finally, the recommended design for computing D_a entails twenty observations per judgment level per participant. As noted above, this is untenable within the prevailing metacomprehension paradigm where readers are being asked to reflect on their comprehension of the complex relations among ideas from each text as a whole.

The magnitude information ignored by Gamma (and by D_a measures used with nondichotomous performance measures) will tend to reduce the number of observed unique accuracy scores, increase standard deviations, and lead to ceiling/floor effects due to more observations being pushed to the maximum and minimum values of ±1.0. For example, consider the results of one metacomprehension study (Wiley et al., 2017: Experiment 1) for which both judgments and performance were assessed on 6-point scales. In a sample of eighty-three participants, there were only twenty unique values for relative metacomprehension accuracy as computed with Gamma, including sixteen scores of 0, twenty-two scores of +1.0 and thirteen scores of −1.0. In contrast, there were sixty-eight unique values for relative metacomprehension accuracy as computed with Pearson, with only eight scores of 0, one score of +1.0 and zero scores of −1.0. Thus, Pearson provided a more continuous, normally distributed, and sensitive metric of covariance between predictions and test scores. The mean Gamma and Pearson were similar at 0.16 and 0.14 but the medians (0.00 vs. 0.13) and modes (1.00 vs. 0.00) reflect abnormal distribution for Gamma scores that are problematic for use as an outcome measure in tests of means. Gamma also resulted in larger standard deviations (0.15), as did D_a (0.41) than did Pearson (0.11), producing smaller effect sizes and less theoretically coherent results across the three experiments for both Gamma and D_a than for Pearson.

The prior observation that Gamma ignores potentially meaningful differences in judgment magnitude (Schwartz & Metcalfe, 1994) becomes doubly problematic when meaningful differences in test performance magnitude are also ignored. Imagine two different people both score a 0 percent, 1 percent, 99 percent, and 100 percent on four different tests. Thus, they had two tests they did almost as poorly as possible on and two they did almost as well as possible on. Of the six possible pairs of tests, four pairs have huge differences that likely reflect reliable and meaningful differences in level of understanding, while Test 1 versus Test 2, and Test 3 versus Test 4 show the smallest possible 1 percent difference that is probably not meaningful or reliable. Now imagine that Person 1 gave the judgment predictions of 1 percent, 0 percent, 100 percent, and 99 percent. They were almost perfectly correct in predicting the four biggest pairwise differences that reflect real differences in understanding, and only failed to predict the relative order in the two pairs with the tiny 1 percent difference in understanding. In contrast, imagine Person 2 gave predictions of 0 percent, 99 percent, 1 percent, and 100 percent. Although Person 2 predicted the two tiny differences in performance, they were only at random chance (two of four) in predicting which of the two they would almost ace and which they would get near the lowest score possible. Arguably, any valid measure of relative accuracy should give Person 1 a much higher accuracy score than Person 2, which Pearson does (0.99 versus 0.02), but Gamma treats them as identically accurate (both 0.33) because both people had four concordances and two discordances. This makes Gamma more influenced than Pearson by the smallest least reliable differences in test performance. Once again, this problem for Gamma is particular to the complexities of text metacomprehension research because dichotomous memory tests have only one possible magnitude of difference in performance.

A conservative approach followed by increasing numbers of metacomprehension researchers is to compute and report multiple measures of relative accuracy including Pearson and Gamma (and D_a when possible and appropriate). Often these alternative measures show similar patterns and reporting each allows the reader to make connections to the existing literature. However, when they diverge, it should not be presumed that the results are unreliable, but rather it could be that the methodological paradigm makes some measures more reliable and valid than others. With continuous performance measures and judgments made about that aggregate performance, Pearson may be the more psychologically valid and statistically powerful approach. Our own work in metacomprehension generally finds that Pearson scores provide more observations, more unique values, fewer extreme scores, lower standard deviations, and more normal distributions that are appropriate for testing differences in accuracy between conditions in general linear models.

Cues That Predict Comprehension of Text

In addition to using a measure of monitoring accuracy that is sensitive to readers' online experiences, monitoring will theoretically be more effective when the cues that readers use as a basis for their judgments are more diagnostic for predicting comprehension (Dunlosky, Mueller, & Thiede, 2016). As already noted, cues based in heuristics are unlikely to reflect differences in comprehension across a set of texts. In addition, the use of different types of cues that are tied to meta-experiences may not all be equal. A central premise of the *situation-model approach to metacomprehension* (Wiley, Griffin, & Thiede, 2016) is that some meta-experiences (i.e., cues) may be more indicative of one's ability to recall or recognize explicitly stated text information, and other meta-experiences may be more reflective of one's ability to recognize valid inferences and connections merely implied by the text, to connect new information to prior knowledge, or to apply it to new situations (Rawson, Dunlosky, & Thiede, 2000; Wiley, Griffin, & Thiede, 2005). This notion is rooted in the prevailing theory about different levels of representation that are constructed during text comprehension (Kintsch, 1998). Kintsch's framework distinguishes several levels at which text information is represented: the surface level where exact word-forms and syntax are represented; the text-base level where explicitly stated individual idea units are represented; and the situation-model level where the meaning of concepts and their relations with each other and with existing knowledge are represented as an integrated and coherent whole. The quality of one level of representation does not necessarily correspond to the others. Complete surface-level memory for words can be achieved without any comprehension of the relations among concepts, and surface-level information can quickly fade from memory, while a more conceptual understanding based in the situation-model level remains (Kintsch et al., 1990). Further, it is the situation-model level representation that is most important for comprehension (Kintsch, 1994; Wiley et al., 2005).

Based on these premises, the *situation-model approach* suggests that the most predictive cues for judging comprehension will be those that reflect the quality of the situation model that the reader has constructed. Such cues could include fluency and ease of processing when trying to build bridging inferences or to engage in end-of-paragraph wrap-up, or the experience of success or difficulty when trying to summarize or explain ideas from the text. Thiede and colleagues (2010) asked readers to report what cues they had used to guide their judgments of comprehension. Reported cues were classified into three broad types: superficial, memory-based, and comprehension-based. Superficial cues could include some of the general heuristic cues described above, such as familiarity with or interest in the topic of the text. These cues are not necessarily tied to any representation of the actual text being read. Memory-based cues entail being able to recall or restate parts of the text whereas comprehension-based cues entail being able to explain the meaning of a text. Some examples of the types of cues readers reported were being able to remember ideas in a text (memory-based), whether they thought they could explain the meaning of the text to someone else (comprehension-based), and whether they felt that the topic was boring (superficial). Thiede and colleagues (2010) found that comprehension-based cues, though rarely reported, were associated with the highest levels of metacomprehension accuracy. However, even memory-based cues led to accurate predictions of test performance in a delayed generation condition. Jaeger and Wiley (2014) also examined readers' self-reported use of either comprehension-based or noncomprehension-based cues and found that use of comprehension-based cues led to higher metacomprehension accuracy. Further, Wiley, Jaeger and colleagues (2017) found that prompting readers to use comprehension-based cues (e.g., "Do you think you could explain the causal process of digestion to a friend?") led to higher relative accuracy than prompting them to use more superficial and memory-based cues (e.g., "How much of the text do you feel like you would be able to recall?"). Getting readers to generate and attend to diagnostic cues is the crux of several instructional contexts that have showed improvements over typical levels of relative metacomprehension accuracy.

Effective Interventions for Improving Metacomprehension

There is now a substantial body of work that has demonstrated the effectiveness of several types of activities in improving relative metacomprehension accuracy. Four main approaches are discussed below. Most of the approaches, such as those shown in the shaded box in Figure 24.1, impose alternative or additional processing tasks designed to help students generate more diagnostic cues, whereas other approaches guide students toward selecting the most diagnostic cues from those that are available (Griffin et al., 2013; Wiley, Griffin et al., 2016; Wiley et al., 2016). Each of these approaches can be thought of as supporting the use of diagnostic cues during monitoring in slightly different ways and their two paths (A and B) are illustrated in Figure 24.2. However, they are all generally consistent with the theoretical assumptions proposed by the *situation-model approach*. Although the majority of these studies have been done in laboratory contexts with undergraduate participants, several have now been done in classroom contexts and with younger students.

Delayed generation tasks. Activities using delayed generation tasks, including delayed keyword and delayed summarization tasks, have been shown to improve metacomprehension accuracy, presumably because they help readers to generate cues related to the situation model. In the original study using a delayed-generation paradigm, Thiede and Anderson (2003) found that relative metacomprehension accuracy was higher for students who wrote summaries after a delay and then judged their performance than for groups who either wrote a summary immediately after reading or who wrote no summaries. Similarly, Thiede, Anderson, and Therriault (2003) showed that a delayed keyword generation task, where students were asked to list keywords that captured the gist of a text, produced the same boost in relative metacomprehension accuracy relative to generating keywords immediately after reading or not generating keywords. In addition to observing benefits for relative metacomprehension accuracy, Thiede and colleagues (2003) also found that delayed keyword generation led to more effective self-regulation of study. Participants in the delayed keyword generation condition were more likely to select texts for restudy based on perceptions of how well the texts had been learned during initial reading than participants in the immediate and no generation conditions. Although the three groups did not differ in performance on the initial comprehension test, the delayed keyword generation group outperformed both other groups on the final comprehension test, which occurred after restudy, and made the greatest gains in performance between the first and final comprehension tests. These findings suggest that delayed keyword generation may not only improve relative metacomprehension accuracy but also lead to more effective restudy behavior and, ultimately, gains in learning.

Why do delayed generation tasks improve relative metacomprehension accuracy? Both components, the generation activity and the delay, play a role. First, generating a summary or keywords may allow a reader to reflect on how successfully he or she is able to retrieve information during generation (see the modified feedback hypothesis described by Glenberg et al., 1987). Accordingly, a text may receive a high rating of comprehension if the person is able to retrieve a great deal of information about the text during generation; whereas, a text may receive a low rating of comprehension if the person struggles to retrieve information about the text. Second, the timing of the generation task is critical. Kintsch and colleagues (1990) showed that surface memory for text decays over time, whereas the situation model is robust to such decay. When writing a summary immediately after reading, a person may have easy access to their surface model (or episodic memory for the text) and can use this information to generate a summary. However, relying on the surface model as a basis for a judgment of comprehension fails to improve accuracy because performance on the immediate summary task and the later comprehension test are determined by different levels of representation. In contrast, when writing a summary after a delay, the findings by Kintsch and colleagues (1990) suggest that a person will likely have relatively greater access to the situation model of a text. Thus, using the experience of writing a summary after a delay as a basis of a judgment of comprehension improves accuracy because performance in both the delayed summary task and on the comprehension test are both based in the situation model.

Thiede, Dunlosky, and colleagues (2005) tested this explanation for delayed generation effects by independently varying several different features of generation tasks, including the types of delay and the nature of the generation task. Consistent with the *situation-model approach*, the critical feature for improving metacomprehension accuracy was a delay between reading and generation, because only this delay forces readers to rely on their situation model to generate the keywords and thus to generate cues related to the quality of that situation model. Other delays (between generation and judgment or between the generation task for one text and the next) did not improve accuracy. Performing nongenerative tasks at a delay, such as reading a list of provided keyword or prompting readers to "think about the text," also did not improve accuracy. The key to producing better monitoring was making readers perform a specific type of generative self-test.

Improvements in relative monitoring accuracy due to engaging in delayed generation tasks have now been replicated by several labs in a variety of contexts. Anderson and Thiede (2008) found benefits of delayed summary generation in a sample of US college students. Shiu and Chen (2013) replicated delayed keyword effects with a sample of Chinese college students. Thiede and colleagues (2010) showed benefits of delayed summary generation for both typical and at-risk college readers, and found that the delay changed the nature of the cues produced during keyword generation such that they became far more predictive of performance on inference tests. In addition, benefits of delayed keyword tasks have now been shown with younger students reading expository texts in the context of science lessons. Several studies have shown that even middle school students can benefit from delayed keyword generation tasks when making judgments of comprehension (de Bruin et al., 2011; Thiede et al., 2012, 2017). However, de Bruin et al. (2011) found that 4th graders were not able to benefit from a delayed keyword activity, which suggests that delayed generation benefits may not extend to younger readers.

The fact that a delay by itself is insufficient to improve judgment accuracy underscores a critical difference between metacomprehension of text and metamemory for simpler materials, like paired associates. In metamemory paradigms, a delay before judgment does notably improve accuracy (Nelson & Dunlosky, 1991; Rhodes & Tauber, 2011). The judgment prompt for paired associates is essentially the same as the testing prompt. Thus, the learner can attempt to self-test and generate a test answer as part of the judgment process, which produces diagnostic cues for predicting that performance. However, in metacomprehension paradigms the judgment is about comprehension of complex, interrelated concepts. Unlike in metamemory paradigms, there is no one-to-one mapping between the judgment and testing prompts because the judgment prompts are far broader and more abstract than the actual test items. Thus, a delay between reading and judgment is not sufficient to improve relative metacomprehension accuracy. Rather, the delay merely moderates whether the generation task produces cues that reflect the situation model rather than surface memory.

Rereading. Another activity that can help students to improve their metacomprehension accuracy is rereading a text before making judgments of comprehension. Sizable increases in monitoring accuracy have been observed as a result of prompting college students to read each text in a set twice in succession before making their judgments (Dunlosky & Rawson, 2005; Rawson et al. 2000). However, rereading was not found to be an effective activity for improving metacomprehension accuracy among 7th graders presented with a set of expository texts as part of their science lessons (Redford et al., 2012). Why might rereading be an effective strategy? Dunlosky and Rawson (2005) have noted that "rereading may afford more resources for comprehension monitoring" (p. 51). During an immediate second reading, many of the subprocesses involved in reading do not need to be reexecuted (e.g., Millis, Simon, & tenBroeck, 1998; Perfetti, 1985). Importantly, Dunlosky and Rawson (2005) found greater benefits from immediate rereading than from delayed rereading.

This reduction in the need for low-level text processing during immediate rereading allows readers to focus more attention at the meta-level during a second pass and may have implications for readers who struggle to monitor during reading. To test this hypothesis, Griffin and colleagues (2008) examined effects of rereading as a function of individual differences in both comprehension skill and working memory capacity (WMC). When readers were low in comprehension skill or WMC, their metacomprehension accuracy after a single reading was limited. However, following immediate rereading their metacomprehension improved such that they were just as accurate as readers with more comprehension skill or WMC. Griffin and colleagues (2008) argued that rereading helps metacomprehension by allowing readers a second chance to attend to monitoring cues, which can be especially beneficial for readers whose limited comprehension skill or attentional resources prevent them from attending to anything but low-level text processing during the first reading. Unlike the benefits of delayed generation discussed above, the benefits of rereading are not rooted in drawing the reader's attention to situation model-based cues per se. Instead, by decreasing reading-related processing demands, rereading may be beneficial because it helps readers (particularly struggling ones) to be able to attend to any meta-level experiences at all rather than rely on heuristic cues that are just as available before and after reading.

Explanation and concept map generation tasks. While delayed generation activities may prompt attention to an already constructed situation-model, self-explanation may encourage efforts to construct a situation model during reading and thereby help readers to generate relevant cues about that level of comprehension. Self-explanation is the activity of explaining to oneself during reading in an effort to understand and integrate new information (Chi, 2000). Griffin and colleagues (2008) tested the hypothesis that self-explanation during rereading might improve relative accuracy by generating meta-experiences such as a subjective sense of difficulty in generating an explanation or a sense of explanatory coherence. Participants were randomly assigned to one of three groups. One group read each text once, a second group read each text twice, and a third group read each text twice and engaged in self-explanation of connections between parts of the text during rereading. Metacomprehension accuracy was higher in the rereading condition relative to the single reading condition, but the group that self-explained during rereading had significantly better metacomprehension accuracy than the other two groups. Fukaya (2013) has also replicated the benefits of having participants generate explanations using a set of illustrated texts about "How Things Work." Across two studies, engaging in generation of explanations following reading led to higher accuracy than being told to "expect" to have to generate explanations or generating keywords immediately.

Griffin and colleagues (2008) found that even readers with limited resources, due to low WMC or low comprehension skill, benefited from self-explanation above mere rereading. They suggested that the benefits from self-explanation on monitoring accuracy may be due to specific types of meta-experiences and cues generated by the task. However, in this study, participants always engaged in self-explanation during a second reading. Further, the rereading condition suggested that a second reading was critical for these struggling readers. So, it is plausible that struggling readers will only benefit from the types of cues generated by tasks like self-explanation if they are able to attend to meta-experiences in general, which is made possible by a second reading.

More recent work has begun to explore the use of concept-mapping tasks as learning activities and artifacts that might help to improve the metacomprehension accuracy of readers with resource limitations. Concept-mapping was considered to be a promising candidate for a learning activity to the extent that it may help readers deal with the competing demands of reading and monitoring. Since the text is available during the mapping activity, and the activity creates a visual representation of the situation model, concept-mapping tasks may be especially appropriate for students who have limited processing resources (Stensvold & Wilson, 1990). Indeed, in a review of the literature, Nesbit and Adesope (2006) concluded that concept-mapping tasks were the most effective activities for improving learning from text for younger, less-skilled, or at-risk readers.

In addition, constructing concept maps should help readers generate diagnostic comprehension cues. Weinstein and Mayer (1986) suggested that instructing students to create concept maps of texts during reading helps them to identify the connections among concepts, which improves comprehension. From this perspective, concept-mapping is similar to self-explanation, as both tasks should help readers construct and attend to the underlying causal models of the subject matter, thereby generating meta-experiences that reflect the quality of their mental representation of those causal models. Consistent with this reasoning, Thiede and colleagues (2010: Experiment 2) tested the effectiveness of a set of concept-mapping activities on improving metacomprehension accuracy in a sample of college students enrolled in a remedial reading course. In a within-subjects design, initial relative metacomprehension accuracy was obtained using the standard paradigm. That is, students read a series of texts, judged their comprehension of each text, and then completed a comprehension test for each text. Participants then received lessons on how to construct causal concept maps from short scientific texts and completed the standard metacomprehension paradigm again, but this time they constructed concept maps while reading. Constructing concept maps while reading improved both comprehension and relative metacomprehension accuracy.

Similar studies with middle school students have shown that simply prompting students to generate concept maps, or to fill in concept maps immediately after reading, does not lead to higher levels of metacomprehension accuracy among younger readers (Redford et al., 2012; van Loon et al., 2014). However greater improvements were found when younger readers were shown a good example and given instruction in how to create and use concept maps for understanding (Redford et al., 2012) and when readers were given a template to fill in after a delay (van Loon et al., 2014). Under these conditions, concept-map generation activities seemed to help young readers use cues based in their situation model when making judgments of comprehension.

The benefits of concept-map generation are consistent with benefits found with other tasks that may also direct the reader's attention to the situation model. Thomas and McDaniel (2007) found that sentence sorting (a task which relies on the reader's situation model) improves accuracy for predicting performance on thematic questions, while letter insertion (filling in missing letters in words, which does not rely on the reader's situation model) improves accuracy for predicting performance on detail questions. These different effects for comprehension and detail questions harken back to the difference between metacomprehension and metamemory for text paradigms discussed above. Tasks that generate meta-experiences tied to the situation model should lead to benefits specifically when readers are asked to predict performance on comprehension questions rather than detail (memory) questions because only the former are likely to depend directly on the quality of the situation model. In contrast, answering detail questions is more likely to depend on surface memory and text-base representations. When tests consist of detailed memory questions, then monitoring should benefit from tasks that generate meta-experiences related to those levels of representation.

Learning goals and cue selection. A common feature of the manipulations discussed so far is that they directly prompt the reader to engage in additional processing tasks in order to generate the meta-experiences that readers can draw on as diagnostic cues for the judgments of comprehension. More recently, studies have been exploring instructional conditions that may help readers select the most diagnostic cues for comprehension monitoring. One example is giving students the expectancy that their comprehension will be assessed with inference tests rather than memory tests. This work takes as its starting point the premise that students need to have a valid reference for what it means to "comprehend" an expository text in order to make judgments that predict comprehension (Wiley et al., 2005). Without specific instructions about what comprehension entails, what goals for reading should be, and what comprehension tests will be like, students may select memory-based cues instead of comprehension-based cues as the basis for their judgments.

Encoding the exact ideas from a text into memory may be a student's default setting for reading. Many studies have demonstrated that people tend to be better at predicting their ability to answer detail questions, or questions that rely on their memory for specific terms, as opposed to comprehension questions that rely on the ability to integrate, connect, or apply information from the text (Dunlosky, Rawson, & Middleton, 2005; Ozuru, Kurby, & McNamara, 2012; Rawson & Dunlosky, 2007; Thiede et al., 2012; Thomas & McDaniel, 2007; Weaver & Bryant, 1995; Wiley, Griffin, & Thiede, 2008).

Using memory-based cues as a basis for JOLs from a text will generally be an effective strategy if future tests ask for specific terms, details, or ideas directly stated by a text. Further, this behavior is certainly important for some subject matters and learning contexts. However, if tests require students to gain conceptual understanding, for example of scientific processes and phenomena from expository text, then it is important to prompt students to override the "reading for memory" setting. In order to engage in accurate monitoring, readers need to appreciate that their goal for reading is understanding how or why a phenomenon or process occurs, and that they will need to make connections and causal inferences across sentences. Instilling appropriate reading goals may be particularly important when readers are tasked with understanding science texts.

Thiede, Wiley, and Griffin (2011) tested the hypothesis that test expectancy impacts metacomprehension accuracy by manipulating whether students were provided with an explicit statement about the nature of comprehension, an explicit statement about the nature of the final test items they should expect, and example test items for a practice text (on a different topic than the target texts). This test-expectancy manipulation was highly effective for a sample of graduate students in educational psychology. Griffin, Wiley, and Thiede (2018) found similar improvements among a sample of undergraduates. Participants in the comprehension expectancy condition were better able to predict performance on comprehension items for target texts over no-expectancy and memory-expectancy conditions. Further, when a self-explanation prompt was combined with comprehension test expectancy, the benefits were additive and led to the highest levels of comprehension monitoring accuracy. This combined benefit could reflect the two distinct paths of monitoring strategies shown in Figure 24.2. An added cognitive activity like self-explanation allows learners to generate useful meta-experiences (Path A), while the comprehension test-expectancy allows learners to select the more diagnostic experiences available to them when making their judgments (Path B).

It is encouraging that similar benefits have also been found for this combined manipulation in a real classroom context (Wiley et al., 2016). Students in a research methods course were randomly assigned to receive the same combined test expectancy and self-explanation intervention used in Wiley and colleagues (2008). Both the combined-manipulation group and a control group read six texts on research methods topics and made monitoring judgments. A week later, the groups were reminded of their judgments and given time to restudy before taking quizzes on all the texts. Not only did students who received the combined test expectancy and self-explanation instruction have higher monitoring accuracy but they were also more likely to restudy the texts in a strategic manner (rather than just reread in order) and their restudy was more effective in producing learning gains evidenced by their quiz scores.

Comprehension-based curricular experience. The test-expectancy studies have attempted to give students a better understanding of appropriate goals for comprehending expository science texts as part of experimental manipulations. However, if prior literacy instruction already provides students with this knowledge, then they should be in a better position to engage in accurate comprehension monitoring. Indeed, Thiede and colleagues (2012) found that 7th and 8th grade students whose early literacy education focused on deep understanding and experience with inference tests demonstrated better metacomprehension accuracy than students with more typical schooling experience. Moreover, superior monitoring accuracy led to better decisions about which texts to restudy and produced significantly better overall comprehension. A potential explanation for this result is that prior experiences with inference tests created an expectancy that led students to select more diagnostic cues when judging their comprehension. Commander and colleagues (2014) reported a similar advantage in metacomprehension accuracy for Chinese college students over American college students. They suggested this advantage could be due to the emphasis that Chinese reading instruction puts on "meaning making."

Taken together, the above studies suggest that when readers rely on appropriate cues for judging their comprehension, either by engaging in activities that help them to generate more diagnostic cues or by having reading goals or curricular experience that direct them toward the selection of more diagnostic cues, they are able to engage in more accurate comprehension monitoring.

Conclusions and Future Directions

Without special instructions or activities, most students tend to have very poor metacomprehension accuracy, and several reviews have reported average levels of metacomprehension accuracy around .27 in baseline conditions

(Dunlosky & Lipko, 2007; Maki, 1998a, 1998b; Thiede et al., 2009). However, a substantial body of evidence emerging from studies inspired by the *situation-model approach* to metacomprehension indicates that there are a number of conditions that can lead to significant improvements in metacomprehension accuracy. The *situation-model approach* suggests that the most predictive cues for judging metacomprehension will be those that reflect the quality of the situation model that the reader has constructed. Such cues could include a sense of fluency and ease of processing when trying to build bridging inferences or engage in end-of-paragraph wrap-up, or the experience of success or difficulty when trying to summarize or explain ideas from the text. A growing number of studies have demonstrated that conditions that prompt readers to rely on appropriate cues for judging their comprehension, either by engaging in activities that help them to generate meta-experiences that can serve as diagnostic cues or by having reading goals or curricular experience that direct them toward the selection of more diagnostic cues, can successfully improve students' comprehension monitoring.

The results of several studies using instructional and test-expectancy manipulations suggest that it is important for teachers to give students clear goals for reading and clear expectations about the nature of test items. There seems to be sufficient support to recommend instruction aimed at teaching students about the difference between what it means to remember a text versus what it means to comprehend the ideas and arguments a text is making. In addition, students could be encouraged to keep this distinction in mind while reading, using it to help them make better judgments of whether they have actually comprehended a text. This ability to judge comprehension should then positively impact learners' decisions about what to restudy. The results of several studies also suggest that students could be prompted to engage in tasks like concept-mapping and self-explanation, not merely to directly improve comprehension but also to improve metacomprehension. Of the various effective activity manipulations, delayed keywords and summaries appear to be the simplest to implement in the classroom. However, such simple tasks may lack the direct benefits to comprehension itself that more involved tasks, such as self-explanation and concept mapping, have been shown to produce.

Although a substantial number of studies have been able to show improvements in metacomprehension accuracy, there are still several important directions for future research. First, it is important to note that most of this work has examined comprehension monitoring from plain expository texts. However, in many contexts expository texts are accompanied by instructional adjuncts such as images, animations, and analogies. These adjuncts are often included with the goal of supporting better student understanding. While these adjuncts could potentially improve both comprehension and metacomprehension outcomes, they have also been suggested to lead to illusions of understanding (Jaeger & Wiley, 2014, 2015; Wiley, Jaeger, et al., 2017: Wiley, Sarmento, et al., 2017). More work is needed to understand how teachers can help students gain only the benefits of including instructional features such as visualizations and analogical examples.

Further attention to the fact that almost none of the metacomprehension accuracy studies have explicitly informed readers about the potential metacognitive purpose of the various additional tasks or instructions is also needed. It is likely that readers would assume the focus of additional tasks is on comprehension itself and readers may not treat the tasks as part of a metacognitive strategy. There is no obvious reason that overt awareness of this metacognitive utility should undermine the observed benefits. It may even boost the effects, but this is an untested empirical question. In addition, although several studies have now been done in classroom contexts and with younger students, much more work is needed to test to what extent findings obtained with undergraduate samples and in laboratory contexts will generalize to other samples and contexts.

The focus of this chapter has been on relative metacomprehension accuracy, but more work is needed that measures both absolute and relative accuracy because they are likely to have distinct implications. However, it is crucial that the findings be evaluated independently for each measure. Researchers should avoid lumping the two sets of results together as though they are alternative convergent measures of the same phenomena. Divergent results from the two measures are to be expected, and when different measures fail to show the same result, this should not be seen as a failure to replicate. Instead, more careful attention is needed to how each might contribute to effective SRL, and what conditions are likely to cause improvements in each of the measures.

Finally, there is a great need for more research on how and when improvements in metacomprehension accuracy lead to improvements in self-regulated study and learning outcomes. More work is needed to understand the relation between improving metacomprehension accuracy and causing positive changes in study behaviors that improve learning outcomes. A major obstacle to achieving these goals is that it appears impossible for the same study to assess the full causal chain from predictive monitoring accuracy, to restudy, and to final level of comprehension. If readers make judgments prior to restudy, then the final test performance cannot serve as a valid measure of metacomprehension. Effective restudy should mean that learners are selectively restudying each text relative to how much their learning would benefit. Thus, effective restudy is likely to alter the relative comprehension levels among the texts and thus reduce how well they correlate with the pre-restudy judgments. Readers who most effectively use their metacomprehension judgments to guide restudy will appear to have lower metacomprehension accuracy if computed using post-restudy tests. A seeming solution to this problem is to test for comprehension prior to restudy regulation and use this performance to assess metacomprehension accuracy. However, that testing gives learners test experience and implicit feedback about performance on objective tests that they can use to guide their restudy. That undermines the ability to draw any inferences about whether actual metacognitive monitoring during initial learning is playing a critical role in later study regulation. Thus, researchers will need (and hopefully reviewers will appreciate this need) to piece together the chain of causality from initial experiments that show the impact of a manipulation on monitoring accuracy and follow-up experiments that show the same manipulation impacting restudy regulation and ultimately learning. Similarly, much more work is needed to understand how to achieve long-term benefits from interventions. These kinds of projects are important for providing empirical support in order to make the strongest recommendations for education.

References

Ackerman, R. & Goldsmith, M. (2011). Metacognitive regulation of text learning: On screen versus on paper. *Journal of Experimental Psychology: Applied*, *17*, 18–32.

Anderson, M. & Thiede, K. W. (2008). Why do delayed summaries improve metacomprehension accuracy? *Acta Psychologica*, *128*, 110–118.

Benjamin, A. S. & Bjork, R. A. (1996). Retrieval fluency as a metacognitive index. In L. M. Reder (ed.), *Implicit memory and metacognition* (pp. 309–338). Hillsdale, NJ: Erlbaum.

Benjamin, A. S. & Diaz, M. (2008). Measurement of relative metamnemonic accuracy. In J. Dunlosky & R. A. Bjork (eds.), *Handbook of memory and metamemory* (pp. 73–94). New York: Psychology Press.

Chi, M. T. H. (2000). Self-explaining: the dual processes of generating inferences and repairing mental models. In R. Glaser (ed.), *Advances in instructional psychology* (pp. 161–238). Mahwah, NJ: Lawrence Erlbaum.

Commander, N. E., Zhao, Y., Li, H., Zabrucky, K. M., & Agler, L. M. L. (2014). American and Chinese students' calibration of comprehension and performance. *Current Psychology*, *33*, 655–671.

Connor, L. T., Dunlosky, J., & Hertzog, C. (1997). Age-related differences in absolute but not relative metamemory accuracy. *Psychology and Aging*, *12*, 50–71.

de Bruin, A. B. H., Thiede, K. W., Camp, G., & Redford, J. (2011). Generating keywords improves metacomprehension and self-regulation in elementary and middle school children. *Journal of Experimental Child Psychology*, *109*, 294–310.

Dinsmore, D. L., Alexander, P. A., & Loughlin, S. M. (2008). Focusing the conceptual lens on metacognition, self-regulation, and self-regulated learning. *Educational Psychology Review*, *20*, 391–409.

Dunlosky, J. & Lipko, A.R. (2007). Metacomprehension: A brief history and how to improve its accuracy. *Current Directions in Psychological Science*, *16*, 228–232.

Dunlosky, J., Mueller, M. L., & Thiede, K. W. (2016). Methodology for investigating human metamemory. In J. Dunlosky, & S. K. Tauber (eds.), *The Oxford handbook of metamemory* (pp. 23–38). Oxford: Oxford University Press

Dunlosky, J. & Nelson, T. O. (1992). Importance of the kind of cue for judgments of learning (JOL) and the delayed-JOL effect. *Memory and Cognition*, *20*, 374–380.

Dunlosky, J. & Rawson, K. A. (2005). Why does rereading improve metacomprehension accuracy? Evaluating the levels-of-disruption hypothesis for the rereading effect. *Discourse Processes*, *40*, 37–55.

    (2012). Overconfidence produced underachievement: Inaccurate self evaluations undermine students' learning and retention. *Learning and Instruction*, *22*, 271–280.

Dunlosky, J., Rawson, K. A., & Middleton, E. L. (2005). What constrains the accuracy of metacomprehension judgments? Testing the transfer-appropriate-monitoring and accessibility hypotheses. *Journal of Memory and Language, 52,* 551–565.

Fischer, P. M. & Mandl, H. (1984). Learner, text variables, and the control of text comprehension and recall. In H. Mandl, N. L. Stein, & T. Trabasco (eds.), *Learning and comprehension of text* (pp. 213–254). Hillsdale, NJ: Lawrence Erlbaum.

Flavell, J. H. (1979). Metacognition and cognitive monitoring: A new area of cognitive-developmental inquiry. *American Psychologist, 34,* 906–911.

Flavell, J. H., Friedrichs, A. G., & Hoyt, J. D. (1970). Developmental changes in memorization processes. *Cognitive Psychology, 1,* 324–340.

Fukaya, T. (2013) Explanation generation, not explanation expectancy, improves metacomprehension accuracy. *Metacognition Learning, 8,* 1–18.

Glenberg, A. M. & Epstein, W. (1985). Calibration of comprehension. *Journal of Experimental Psychology: Learning, Memory, and Cognition, 11,* 702–718.

Glenberg, A. M., Sanocki, T., Epstein, W., & Morris, C. (1987). Enhancing calibration of comprehension. *Journal of Experimental Psychology: General, 116,* 119–136.

Griffin, T. D., Jee, B. D., & Wiley, J. (2009). The effects of domain knowledge on metacomprehension accuracy. *Memory and Cognition, 37,* 1001–1013.

Griffin, T. D., Wiley, J., & Salas, C. (2013). Supporting effective self-regulated learning: The critical role of monitoring. In R. Azevedo & V. Aleven (eds.) *International handbook of metacognition and learning technologies* (pp. 19–34). New York: Springer Science.

Griffin, T. D., Wiley, J., & Thiede, K. W. (2008). Individual differences, rereading, and self-explanation: Concurrent processing and cue validity as constraints on metacomprehension accuracy. *Memory and Cognition, 36,* 93–103.

Griffin, T. D., Wiley, J., & Thiede, K. W. (2018). The effects of comprehension-test expectancies on metacomprehension accuracy. *Journal of Experimental Psychology: Learning, Memory, and Cognition.* Advance online publication: http://dx.doi.org/10.1037/xlm0000634

Hacker, D. J. (1998). Self-regulated comprehension during normal reading. In D. J. Hacker, J. Dunlosky, & A. C. Graesser (eds.), *Metacognition in educational theory and practice* (pp. 165–191). Mahwah, NJ: Lawrence Erlbaum.

Hacker, D. J., Keener, M. C., & Kircher, J. C. (2009). Writing is applied metacognition. In D. J. Hacker, J. Dunlosky, & A. C. Graesser (eds.), *Handbook of metacognition in education* (pp. 154–172). New York: Routledge.

Hart, J. T. (1965). Memory and the feeling-of-knowing experience. *Journal of Educational Psychology, 56,* 208–216.

Jaeger, A. J. & Wiley, J. (2014). Do illustrations help or harm metacomprehension accuracy?. *Learning and Instruction, 34,* 58–73.

    (2015). Reading an analogy can cause the illusion of comprehension. *Discourse Processes, 52,* 376–405.

Kintsch, W. (1998). *Comprehension: A paradigm for cognition.* New York: Cambridge University Press.

Kintsch, W., Welsch, D., Schmalhofer, F., & Zimny, S. (1990). Sentence memory: A theoretical analysis. *Journal of Memory and Language, 29,* 133–159.

Koriat, A. (1997). Monitoring one's own knowledge during study: A cue-utilization approach to judgments of learning. *Journal of Experimental Psychology: General, 126,* 349–370.

Kwon, H. & Linderholm, T. (2014). Effects of self-perception of reading skill on absolute accuracy of metacomprehension judgments. *Current Psychology, 33,* 73–88.

Maki, R. H. (1998a) Metacomprehension of text: Influence of absolute confidence level on bias and accuracy. In D. L. Medin (ed.) *The psychology of learning and motivation: Advances in research and theory* (pp. 223–248). San Diego, CA: Academic Press.

(1998b). Test predictions over text material. In D.J. Hacker, J. Dunlosky, & A.C. Graesser (eds), *Metacognition in educational theory and practice* (pp. 117–144). Mahwah, NJ: Lawrence Erlbaum.

Maki, R. H. & Berry, S. L. (1984). Metacomprehension of text material. *Journal of Experimental Psychology: Learning, Memory, and Cognition, 10,* 663–679.

Maki, R. H., Shields, M., Wheeler, A. E., & Zacchilli, T. L. (2005). Individual differences in absolute and relative metacomprehension accuracy. *Journal of Educational Psychology, 97,* 723–731.

Markman, E. M. (1977). Realizing that you don't understand: A preliminary investigation. *Child Development, 48,* 986–992.

(1979). Realizing that you don't understand: Elementary school children's awareness of inconsistencies. *Child Development, 50,* 643–655.

Masson, M. E. & Rotello, C. M. (2009). Sources of bias in the Goodman–Kruskal gamma coefficient measure of association: Implications for studies of metacognitive processes. *Journal of Experimental Psychology: Learning, Memory, and Cognition, 35,* 509–527.

Metcalfe, J. (2002). Is study time allocated selectively to a region of proximal learning? *Journal of Experimental Psychology: General, 131,* 349–363.

Millis, K. K., Simon, S., & tenBroek, N. S. (1998). Resource allocation during the rereading of scientific texts. *Memory and Cognition, 26,* 232–246.

Nelson, T. O. (1984). A comparison of current measures of feeling-of-knowing accuracy. *Psychological Bulletin, 95,* 109–133.

Nelson, T. O. & Dunlosky, J. (1991). When people's judgments of learning (JOLs) are extremely accurate at predicting subsequent recall: The "delayed-JOL effect." *Psychological Science, 2,* 267–270.

Nelson, T. O. & Narens, L. (1980). A new technique for investigating the feeling of knowing. *Acta Psychologica, 46,* 69–80.

(1990). Metamemory: A theoretical framework and new findings. In G. H. Bower (ed.), *The psychology of learning and motivation, 26,* pp. 125–141. New York: Academic Press.

Nesbit, J. C. & Adesope, O. O. (2006). Learning with concept and knowledge maps: A meta-analysis. *Review of Educational Research, 76,* 413–448.

Otero, J. (1998). Influence of knowledge activation and context on comprehension monitoring of science texts. In D. J. Hacker, J. Dunlosky, & A. C. Graesser (eds.), *Metacognition in educational theory and practice* (pp. 145–164). Mahwah, NJ: Lawrence Erlbaum.

Ozuru, Y., Kurby, C. A., & McNamara, D. S. (2012). The effect of metacomprehension judgment task on comprehension monitoring and metacognitive accuracy. *Metacognition and Learning, 7,* 113–131.

Perfetti, C. A. (1985). *Reading ability.* New York: Oxford University Press.

Pilegard, C. & Mayer, R. E. (2015). Within-subject and between-subject conceptions of metacomprehension accuracy. *Learning and Individual Differences, 41,* 54–61.

Pintrich, P. R., Wolters, C. A., & Baxter, G. P. (2000). Assessing metacognition and self-regulated learning. In G. Schraw & J.C. Impara (eds.), *Issues in the measurement of metacognition* (pp. 43–97). Lincoln, NE: Buros Institute of Mental Measurements.

Rawson, K. A. & Dunlosky, J. (2007). Improving students' self-evaluation of learning for key concepts in textbook materials. *European Journal of Cognitive Psychology, 19,* 559–579.

Rawson, K. A., Dunlosky, J., & Thiede, K. W. (2000). The rereading effect: Metacomprehension accuracy improves across reading trials. *Memory and Cognition, 28,* 1004–1010.

Redford, J. S., Thiede, K. W., Wiley, J., & Griffin, T. D. (2012). Concept mapping improves metacomprehension accuracy among 7th graders. *Learning and Instruction, 22,* 262–270.

Rhodes, M. G. & Tauber, S. K. (2011). The influence of delaying judgments of learning on metacognitive accuracy: A meta-analytic review. *Psychological Bulletin, 137,* 131–148.

Schwartz, B.L. & Metcalfe, J. (1994). Methodological problems and pitfalls in the study of human metacognition. In J. Metcalfe & A. P. Shimamura (eds.), *Metacognition: Knowing about knowing* (pp. 93–113). Cambridge, MA: MIT Press.

Scrra, M. J. & Dunlosky, J. (2010). Metacomprehension judgments reflect the belief that diagrams improve learning from text. *Memory, 18,* 698–711.

Shiu, L. & Chen, Q. (2013). Self and external monitoring of reading comprehension. *Journal of Educational Psychology, 105,* 78–88.

Stensvold, M. S. & Wilson, J. T. (1990). The interaction of verbal ability with concept mapping in learning from a chemistry laboratory activity. *Science Education, 74,* 473–480.

Thiede, K. W. & Anderson, M. C. M. (2003). Summarizing can improve metacomprehension accuracy. *Contemporary Educational Psychology, 28,* 129–160.

Thiede, K. W., Anderson, M. C. M., & Therriault, D. (2003). Accuracy of metacognitive monitoring affects learning of texts. *Journal of Educational Psychology, 95,* 66–73.

Thiede, K. W. & Dunlosky, J. (1999). Toward a general model of self-regulated study: An analysis of selection of items for study and self-paced study time. *Journal of Experimental Psychology: Learning, Memory, and Cognition, 25,* 1024–1037.

Thiede, K. W., Dunlosky, J., Griffin, T. D., & Wiley, J. (2005). Understanding the delayed-keyword effect on metacomprehension accuracy. *Journal of Experimental Psychology: Learning, Memory, and Cognition, 31,* 1267–1280.

Thiede, K. W., Griffin, T. D., Wiley, J., & Anderson, M. C. M. (2010). Poor metacomprehension accuracy as a result of inappropriate cue use. *Discourse Processes, 47,* 331–362.

Thiede, K. W., Griffin, T. D., Wiley, J., & Redford, J. (2009). Metacognitive monitoring during and after reading. In D. J. Hacker, J. Dunlosky, & A. C. Graesser (eds). *Handbook of metacognition in education* (pp. 85–106). New York: Routledge.

Thiede, K. W., Redford, J. S., Wiley, J., & Griffin, T. D. (2012). Elementary school experience with comprehension testing may influence metacomprehension accuracy among seventh and eighth graders. *Journal of Educational Psychology, 104,* 554–564.

(2017). How restudy decisions affect overall comprehension for 7th grade students. *British Journal of Educational Psychology, 84,* 590–605.

Thiede, K. W., Wiley, J., & Griffin, T. D. (2011). Test expectancy affects metacomprehension accuracy. *British Journal of Educational Psychology, 81,* 264–273.

Thomas, A. K. & McDaniel, M. A. (2007). The negative cascade of incongruent task-test processing in memory and metamemory. *Memory and Cognition, 35,* 668–678.

van Loon, M. H., de Bruin, A. B. H., van Gog, T., van Merrienboer, J. J. G., & Dunlosky, J. (2014). Can students evaluate their understanding of cause-and-effect relations? The effects of diagram completion on monitoring accuracy. *Acta Psychologica, 151,* 143–154.

Weaver, C. A. & Bryant, D. S. (1995). Monitoring of comprehension: The role of text difficulty in metamemory for narrative and expository text. *Memory and Cognition, 23,* 12–22.

Weinstein, C. E. & Mayer, R. E. (1986). The teaching of learning strategies. In M. C. Wittrock (ed.), *Handbook on research in teaching,* 3rd edn. (pp. 315–327). New York: Macmillan.

Wiley, J., Griffin, T. D., Jaeger, A. J., Jarosz, A. F., Cushen, P. J., & Thiede, K. W. (2016). Improving metacomprehension accuracy in an undergraduate course context. *Journal of Experimental Psychology: Applied, 22,* 393–405.

Wiley, J., Griffin, T. D., & Thiede, K. W. (2005). Putting the comprehension in metacomprehension. *Journal of General Psychology, 132,* 408–428.

  (2008). To understand your understanding, you must understand what understanding means. In B. C. Love, K. McRae, & V. M. Sloutsky (eds.), *Proceedings of the 30th annual conference of the Cognitive Science Society* (pp. 817–822). Austin, TX: Cognitive Science Society.

  (2016). Improving metacomprehension with the situation-model approach. In K. Mokhtari, *Improving reading comprehension through metacognitive reading instruction for first and second language readers* (pp. 93–110). Lanham, MD: Rowman & Littlefield.

Wiley, J., Jaeger, A. J., Taylor, A. R., & Griffin, T. D. (2017). When analogies harm: The effects of analogies and valid cues on the metacomprehension of science text. *Learning and Instruction,* 55, 113–123. https://doi.org/10.1016/j.learninstruc.2017.10.001

Wiley, J. & Myers, J. L. (2003). Availability and accessibility of information and causal inferences from scientific text. *Discourse Processes, 36,* 109–129.

Wiley, J. Sarmento, D., Griffin, T. D., & Hinze, S. R. (2017). Biology textbook graphics and their impact on expectations of understanding, *Discourse Processes, 54,* 463–478.

Winne, P. H. & Hadwin, A. F. (1998). Studying as self-regulated learning. In D. J. Hacker, J. Dunlosky, & A. C. Graesser (eds.), *Metacognition in educational theory and practice* (pp. 277–304). Mahwah, NJ: Lawrence Erlbaum.

Yates, J. E (1990). *Judgment and decision-making.* Englewood Cliffs, NJ: Prentice-Hall.

Zhao, Q. & Linderholm, T. (2011). Anchoring effects on prospective and retrospective metacomprehension judgments as a function of peer performance information. *Metacognition and Learning, 6,* 25–43.

Zimmerman, B. J. (2002). Becoming a self-regulated learner: An overview. *Theory into Practice, 41,* 64–72.

25 Calibration and Self-Regulated Learning

Making the Connections

Douglas J. Hacker and Linda Bol

Introduction

As educators, we all can rest assured that our students fully understand our teaching and transfer their learning beyond the classroom to achieve college success and career fulfillment. After all, a major goal of formal education is to equip students with the capabilities to educate themselves throughout their lifetime (Bandura, 1993; Zimmerman, 2008). Why would we settle for anything less?

Regrettably, although this may be the case for some of our students, it certainly is not the case for all. An often missing yet critical component of formal education is helping students become self-regulatory agents of their own thinking. To become self-regulated learners would entail at a minimum that students learn to establish their own goals for learning, develop plans to achieve those goals, monitor the deployment and progress of those plans, exert control and change plans when necessary, and judge when these have been achieved. Moreover, the self-regulated learner must be motivated to ensure the accuracy of each of these processes throughout learning. When students are inaccurate in their self-monitoring, the goals selected may be inappropriate to the task, progress toward them misestimated, changes to them never made or made at inappropriate times, and judgments of achieving them misaligned with actual learning. Thus, above all else, productive self-regulation requires that students accurately monitor their cognitive and affective states and processes. That is, they must be well calibrated and equipped with strategies to maintain or reestablish accuracy so that effective control over their learning can be maintained.

Model of Self-Regulated Learning

As researchers of self-regulated learning, many of us have based our notions of self-regulation on Zimmerman and colleagues' social cognitive model of self-regulation (Schunk & Zimmerman, 1997; Zimmerman, 2008; Zimmerman & Kitsantas, 2002; Zimmerman & Moylan, 2009). The model of self-regulation is illustrated in Figure 25.1. Central to this model of self-regulation is a personal feedback loop in which social, environmental, or personal information about one's performance is used to guide and direct future cognitive, affective, or behavioral states or actions regarding learning. The personal feedback loop consists of three cyclical phases: forethought, performance, and self-reflection.

The forethought phase consists of a task analysis process in which tasks are broken down into constituent elements so that the learner can form learning goals and initiate strategic planning to learn. Close and accurate monitoring and control of the development of this task analysis will do much to ensure a more successful learning outcome. Driving this phase are self-motivation beliefs, which are derived from several sources, including the learner's sense of self-efficacy, expectations for success, interest in learning, and a learning goal orientation or a belief that, through effort, mental ability can be increased.

The performance phase consists of self-control and self-observation. Self-control includes strategies that can be applied to specific aspects of a learning task or strategies that can be applied to learning tasks in general. The ultimate goal of these strategies is to exert control over oneself or one's environment so that optimal conditions for learning are established. To ensure that self-control strategies are having their desired

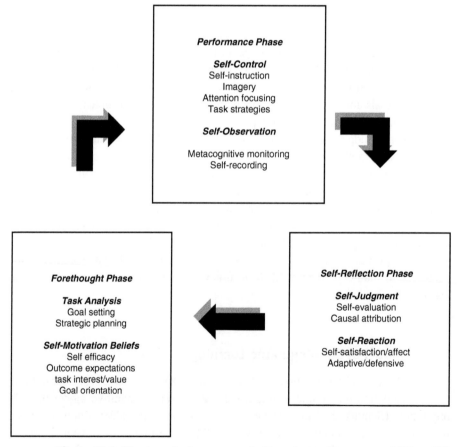

Figure 25.1 *Phases and subprocesses of self-regulation (Zimmerman, 2008, p. 178. Reprinted with permission from SAGE Publications)*

outcomes on learning, the learner must engage in self-observation. Self-observation, or metacognitive monitoring, allows a learner to take stock of one's knowledge, thoughts, and actions before and during learning, and is essential for making progress toward one's learning goals.

Finally, the self-reflection phase consists of self-judgments and self-reactions. Self-judgments involve establishing a standard for performance, monitoring one's performance in relation to that standard, and judging whether the standard is being met or has been met. If the standard has been met and the learning goals developed in the forethought phase have been achieved, the specific learning task has been accomplished. If, however, the learner judges that the standard has not been met, and the learner is sufficiently motivated, he or she must decide to return to the forethought phase to modify existing goals and planning strategies or develop new ones, engage in self-control and self-observation in the performance phase, and again monitor one's performance and judge whether the new or modified standards have been met in the self-reflection phase. The learner's self-reactions to his or her self-judgments play a critical role in the decision to continue the cycle of self-regulation. Negative reactions caused perhaps by attributing failure to external causes can lead to learned helplessness and will likely end the learning cycle of self-regulation. Positive reactions coming from a strong sense of self-efficacy will likely keep the learner engaged in the cycle.

In sum, self-regulated learning depends on the orchestration of many components embedded in each of the three cyclical phases and, in each of the phases, metacognitive monitoring and control play a role. Critical to successful learning is accurate monitoring and control of the development of learning goals in the forethought phase, the progress of one's learning in the performance phase, and the evaluation of one's standards for learning in the self-reflection phase. The study of calibration, defined as a measure of the degree to which people's subjective judgments of performance correspond to their actual performance (Keren, 1991; Lichtenstein, Fischhoff, & Phillips, 1982; Lin & Zabrucky, 1998; Nietfeld, Cao, & Osborne, 2006; Winne, 2004; Yates, 1990), helps us understand the accuracy of the learner's monitoring. In addition, research on calibration has provided us with insights into whether the learner exerts control of learning in response to monitoring and ultimately increases performance.

Prior Review of Calibration Studies

The review by Hacker, Bol, and Keener (2008) of classroom studies of calibration presented a complex picture of monitoring, control, and performance. In general, people tend to be overconfident when monitoring their abilities or knowledge. However, the association between monitoring and performance presents a more nuanced picture. In general, lower-achieving students show low accuracy and overconfidence, and higher-achieving students show higher accuracy and slight underconfidence. The results of interventions designed specifically to improve monitoring accuracy have been mixed. Providing feedback and practice alone appears to be insufficient for improving accuracy, but when explicitly provided in a more concentrated intervention, they can increase accuracy. Reflection and instruction on self-assessment and monitoring can be effective, but effective for only higher-achieving students. External rewards and incentives also can be effective, but effective for only lower-achieving students. Familiarizing students with the type of test and test content improved monitoring accuracy in two studies but was not replicated in a third. And, given the strong stability of monitoring judgments across tasks and in spite of performance, the possibility must be entertained that such judgments are based on stable and persistent personality traits, such as explanatory or attributional style.

To date, the majority of the calibration research has been focused on whether students can accurately monitor their knowledge and skills and what strategies can be applied to improve accuracy. In addition, much research has shown an association between monitoring accuracy and performance. However, researchers have not yet adequately investigated causal connections between monitoring and control: Do students actually utilize the output of monitoring to control cognitive activities? Even more important, researchers have rarely investigated causal connections between monitoring and control with the quality of performance: Is performance enhanced under conditions of effective monitoring and control? The end goal of our research cannot be simply to examine the extent and accuracy of metacognitive monitoring. As educators and researchers, we need to focus on what students do with their monitoring to control learning and whether learning is enhanced as a consequence.

Current Review of Calibration Studies

In this chapter, we have reviewed the calibration research since our last review (Hacker et al., 2008). Our review is organized in three sections: (1) research that has examined factors that may contribute to calibration; (2) research that has investigated whether calibration accuracy can be improved; and (3) research that has sought to establish a link between calibration accuracy and academic performance. We have provided greater detail of the studies than what is typically given in a literature review so that the reader can obtain a more complete understanding of the methods that have been used to investigate calibration and whether those methods have led to increased accuracy or performance. After our reviews, we then interpret the overall findings in terms of the three phases of self-regulated learning that we described earlier and their implications for learning.

In our selection of research to be reviewed, we have attempted to be as inclusive as possible but, considering the large number of studies that have been published since 2008, we have narrowed our review of the calibration literature mainly to studies that have been conducted in actual classroom contexts. However, we also have included some laboratory studies of calibration based on the potential contributions of their findings to classroom practices. Though these studies were conducted in laboratory settings, the tasks were more authentic and directly applicable to classrooms. Our early argument (Hacker et al., 2000) remains that the context of the classroom matters in investigations of self-regulation. Although the threats to the internal validity of studies conducted in classrooms are many in comparison to laboratory studies, the need to understand self-regulation and learning of students immersed in more authentic contexts over time and under more motivating circumstances outweigh these threats. Because self-regulated learning occurs in specific academic domains, it seems imperative that we study how students monitor and regulate their learning within those domains (Alexander et al., 2011). Finally, we focus exclusively on calibration, or absolute accuracy, and do not include studies of relative accuracy. Although there have been many important studies conducted since 2008 that have used relative accuracy, the construct is theoretically and empirically distinct from absolute accuracy.

Factors That May Contribute to Calibration

Since the earliest studies of calibration, there have been at least three consistent findings: (1) people tend to be overconfident in their judgments of performance, with lower performance associated with greater overconfidence; (2) people show considerable stability in their judgments, with stability in judgments oftentimes exceeding stability in performance; and (3) postdicted judgments of performance tend to be more accurate than predicted judgments. Although these findings have been commonplace in the calibration research, there is still considerable question as to the factors that may be contributing to them. The following nine studies attempt to bring some resolve to that question (see Table 25.1). The first four studies focus on postdictions of performance, the next one focuses on predictions of performance, and the last four focus on both.

Working with 72 sophomore, junior, and senior college students in a research methods course, Dinsmore and Parkinson (2013) investigated, among other things, the factors that potentially influence students' postdictive confidence judgments. Although the researchers did not actively integrate the use of calibration into the course, they did use student performance on recall items from two passages they were asked to read on topics specific to research methods. Recall performance on these items was used as a measure of knowledge and confidence judgments were used to calculate calibration. Students also responded to the open-ended item, "Please explain how you arrived at or what you considered when making your confidence judgment." Responses were coded using categories based on Bandura's (1986) model of reciprocal determinism, which included prior knowledge, characteristics of the text, characteristics of the item, guessing, other considerations, and combinations of these five.

The results indicated that students mostly used text and item characteristics (i.e., task elements) to explain their confidence ratings, but they also used prior knowledge (i.e., person elements) of the texts' content to a lesser extent, and many students used a combination of both. The researchers concluded that interventions designed to

Table 25.1 *Studies on factors that may contribute to calibration*

Source	Participants	Context	Task	SRL Phase	Factors
Dinsmore & Parkinson (2013)	72 undergrads	Lab	Research methods exams	Self-Reflection	Postdictions are based on knowledge of text and items, and prior knowledge secondarily
García et al. (2016)	524 5th and 6th graders	Lab	Math problems	Forethought, Performance, & Self-Reflection	Greater planning leads to better postdiction accuracy
Schneider et al. (2014)	107 undergrads	Classroom	High-stakes pharmacy exam	Self-Reflection	Higher performance contributed to more accurate postdictions; involvement with a high-stakes test may engage students in greater questioning of their responses
List & Alexander (2015)	205 undergrads	Lab	Passages on developmental psychology & astrophysics	Self-Reflection	Greater accuracy of postdictions result when judgments of performance focus on directness of questions or familiarity with domain
Foster et al. (2017)	87 undergrads	Classroom	Calibration practice and reflection for educational psychology exams	Forethought & Self-Reflection	Wishful thinking may contribute to predictions; practice, reflection, and prior exam score did not increase accuracy; judgments remained stable
Bol et al., 2010	77 6th grade students	Classroom	High-stakes math test	Forethought, Performance, & Self-Reflection	Accurate predictions reflected effort and studying, ability, and prior performance; postdictions reflected students knowing the answer, expectations of test difficulty, studying, and effort
Serra & DeMarree (2016) Study 1	485 undergrads	Classroom	General psychology course	Forethought	Students' desired grade was a stronger predictor of exam and course predictions than actual grades
Serra & DeMarree (2016) Study 2	59 undergrads	Classroom	Research methods course	Self-Reflection	Students' desired grade was a stronger predictor of exam postdictions than actual grades
Serra & DeMarree (2016) Study 3	60 undergrads	Classroom	Research methods course	Self-Reflection	Students' desired grade was a stronger predictor of exam postdictions than actual grades; the effects from desired grade decreased across the semester, suggesting that students adjusted their desires across the semester to more realistically reflect actual performance

increase calibration accuracy and performance need to focus on task and person factors.

García and colleagues (2016) focused on factors influencing calibration using younger students. They investigated factors involved in the metacognitive processing of 524 Grade 5 and 6 students as they solved mathematics problems. Metacognition was measured using the Triple Task Procedure in Mathematics (TTPM). The TTPM requires participants to perform three tasks simultaneously: a primary task (solving two mathematics problems), a secondary probe task (time to respond to a tone presented periodically), and a task to identify their current thoughts or actions by selecting from a theoretically driven categorization of processes. During a regularly scheduled mathematics class, students were administered the TTPM for each of the two mathematics problems and, after each problem, were asked to provide a postdiction on their performance in terms of success or failure.

The researchers found that only about 30–35 percent of the students could solve the problems, and the students were poorly calibrated, showing strong overconfidence with greater overconfidence for low achievers. There were some differences noted in the processes that accurate and inaccurate students used during problem-solving. Accurate students spent more time planning but less time writing and reviewing than inaccurate students. The researchers concluded that 5th and 6th grade students lack effective metacognitive skills that would be necessary for them to monitor their own solution processes or use different strategies.

Schneider and colleagues (2014) investigated the link between achievement level and calibration accuracy in preparation for a high-stakes exam in a college-level pharmacy program. They explored students' judgments of performance on the exam and whether they could identify their incorrect answers. One hundred and seven students completed the high-stakes exam intended to assess whether they were prepared to advance in their pharmacy program. During the administration of the test, the pharmacy students were asked to identify up to ten questions they felt certain they had answered incorrectly. They were also asked to express in a percentage how well they had done on the exam.

All analyses were conducted by first dividing students into quartiles based on their exam scores. Results concerning the selection of ten incorrect answers showed that higher-performing students were better at selecting incorrect answers than lower-performing students. Calibration, assessed by correlating postdictions with actual performance, showed a moderate correlation (0.41), with 86 percent of the students underestimating their actual performance. Contrary to most calibration studies, students in the lowest quartile were the best estimators of their performance.

The purpose of List and Alexander's (2015) lab study was to identify the criteria students use when justifying their judgments of confidence and to examine whether judgments of confidence differ depending on the type of question posed (discrete vs. open-ended) and the domains (developmental psychology vs. astrophysics) in which the judgments occur. Two hundred and five undergraduate students were given either a discrete question requiring a single answer or an open-ended question requiring a more elaborate answer regarding information provided in seven texts. The questions and texts were about either developmental psychology or astrophysics. After answering the question, they were asked to rate their confidence in their answer and to justify their rating. They were then presented with a second question (counterbalanced between discrete or open-ended) and additional texts (counterbalanced between psychology and astrophysics) followed by the confidence rating and justification.

Results showed that the majority of participants' justifications for their postdictions were text-directed. For example, the response "I believe the source that gave me the information was very reliable" (p. 417) was coded as a text-directed justification, indicating that their confidence judgments were based more on features of the texts or information conveyed rather than on factors extrinsic to the text. Of the text-directed justifications, more were focused on the quality, accuracy, or trustworthiness of the source type rather than on surface or superficial features of the content. Also, there were more text-directed justifications generated for discrete questions than open-ended questions in developmental psychology than astrophysics. The researchers attributed this to the directness of the discrete questions and the greater familiarity with developmental psychology. Justifications for confidence judgments were frequently based on the ease of finding the answer, and with greater ease came greater confidence in their judgments. Participants who were more accurate in responding to the discrete questions were more likely to cite text-directed justifications; that is, they were finding the answers in the texts. Participants who were inaccurate more often justified their confidence in personally directed ways; that is, they believed they knew the answer from prior knowledge but were incorrect in their beliefs.

Other researchers have shown that practice alone does not seem to improve calibration accuracy. Foster and colleagues' (2017) study investigated whether providing students with multiple opportunities to make calibration judgments on exams throughout a semester-length college course would contribute to increased calibration accuracy. Eighty-seven undergraduate students enrolled in an introductory educational psychology course predicted performance on thirteen 35-item multiple-choice exams, each administered once a week and covering course material for only that week. On completion of each exam, students received their score and were asked to reflect on how their predictions compared with their actual performance. Students then predicted how well they would do on the next exam administered one week later.

Not too surprisingly, students were overconfident in their predictions but, contrary to hypotheses, students showed worsening accuracy across the semester. In an analysis to show whether students relied on past exam performance to make their predictions, results showed that students were remarkably stable in their overconfidence across the exams regardless of prior exam performance. Thus, it appears that memory for past exam performance played a minor role in students' predictions of performance. An additional analysis showed that past performance would have in fact served as a good basis for future predictions and yet students did not rely on it. The researchers speculated that this disregard for actual performance when predicting performance may reflect "wishful thinking" on students' part, or how they want to perform rather than how they actually will perform.

In a descriptive, comparative design, Bol and colleagues (2010) explored the accuracy of middle school students' predictions and postdictions on a high-stakes mathematics exam. A total of seventy-seven 6th grade students from two regular and two honors sections of basic math courses participated. Students were asked to predict and postdict their scores and to judge whether they would fail, pass, or pass advanced. They were also asked to respond to open-ended questions prior to and after taking the exam about the bases of their predictions and postdictions.

A median split was used to divide students into high- and low-achievement groups. Although all students were overconfident in their judgments, the higher-achieving students were significantly more accurate on both predictions and post-dictions than lower-achieving students. Overconfidence was also apparent in their judgments about whether they would fail, pass, or pass advanced on the exam. Only four students (6 percent) predicted that they would fail the exam when in fact 40 percent failed. Over half predicted that they would receive pass advanced scores when only 24 percent actually scored in this highest category. The same pattern of findings was observed for postdictions.

The open-ended responses were coded into categories. When asked "Why do you predict you will get this score?," most responses reflected effort or study as the reason for students' predictions. They also made reference to basing judgments on their math ability and prior performance in their math classes. After taking the test, students were asked to explain why their predictions and postdictions were accurate or inaccurate. Frequent categories included that they knew how many they answered correctly, that they expected the test to be easier or harder, and they believed that their studying or effort preparing for the exam influenced their judgments.

In three studies, Serra and DeMarree (2016) tested the hypothesis that students are consistently overconfident in their judgments of exam performance because their judgments are potentially biased by their desired level of performance. Study 1 was conducted with 485 college students enrolled in a general psychology course. Students were asked two questions about their performance on the final exam for the course: "What grade do you realistically want to earn on your final exam in this course?" and "What grade do you think you will actually earn on your final exam in this course?" Students responded using a whole number in the range 0–100 percent. The same two questions were asked about their final grade for the entire course. Both predictions of exam and course grades showed the typical pattern found in most calibration research: high overconfidence of lower-performing students and slight underconfidence of higher-performing students. In regression analyses, desired grade was shown to be a stronger predictor of exam predictions and course predictions than actual grades. Thus, students' desired grade could be a significant source of bias in their predictions of performance contributing to overconfidence.

In study 2, Serra and DeMarree followed essentially the same procedures with 59 students in a college research methods course. They first asked students to indicate what grade that wanted to earn on their final exam but, in this case, they asked students to postdict their performance once they had finished the exam. Results of the regression analysis showed that both desired and actual grades were significant contributors to postdictions but desired grades were a slightly stronger contributor than actual grades.

Once again, the results supported the researchers' hypothesis that student's desired grade could be a source of bias in their judgments of performance, resulting in overconfidence.

Finally, in the third study, 60 students enrolled in another research methods course provided their desired grades and postdicted grades on four exams administered across the semester. Using multilevel modeling, the researchers found results similar to the first two studies: Both desired grades and actual grades significantly contributed to postdicted grades, with desired grades showing a stronger contribution than actual grades. The researchers also examined whether the effect of desired grades on postdictions diminished after being shown repeatedly throughout the semester that they were being overly optimistic. The effects from desired grades did decrease across the semester, suggesting that students adjusted their desires across the semester to more realistically reflect actual performance.

Summary. These nine studies have identified a variety of factors that may contribute to calibration judgments and these factors appear to vary depending on whether the judgment of performance is a prediction or postdiction. As mentioned previously, postdictions are generally more accurate than predictions. This finding can be plausibly attributed to greater knowledge of the task once it has been completed and, consequently, a person can make more informed judgments concerning whether the task and its demands have been mastered.

Support for this "greater knowledge of the task" hypothesis can be found in multiple sources: Dinsmore and Parkinson (2013) showed that postdictions were influenced by reactions to the task and questions; List and Alexander (2015) showed that greater accuracy was associated with features of the task, such as directness of the question, ease in finding an answer, and greater familiarity with the domain of the task; and Bol and colleagues (2010) showed that participants' postdictions were influenced by factors such as knowing they answered questions correctly or incorrectly or that they had expected the task to be either easier or more difficult. Moreover, as shown by García and colleagues (2016), if the tasks are too difficult for students to master, their ability to make accurate postdictions was compromised. The students who had devoted more time to planning for the task did show greater postdictive accuracy, which may indicate that planning helps to form a more complete mental representation of the task, resulting in better assessments that the task had or had not been completed. Also, when the task makes greater demands on the students, such as the high-stakes exam that Schneider and colleagues (2014) used in their study, the typical high overconfidence of lower-performing students changed dramatically so that they exhibited greater accuracy than the higher-performing students.

In contrast, predictions of performance carry with them greater uncertainty than postdictions. Students may have developed their knowledge in the domain that is the focus of their judgments but their representation of the task is still imperfect, even in cases such as Foster and colleagues (2017) when students were provided with thirteen opportunities to predict their exam performance. Each exam may bear some resemblance to previous exams, but exactly what knowledge is to be probed each time remains uncertain. In response to this "uncertainty hypothesis," students provide highly stable and safe predictions of average or slightly above-average performance, thereby minimizing the potential discrepancies between judgments and performance. What is surprising is that students had at their disposal a stronger factor as the basis for making predictions, that is, their prior exam score, but they appeared to have ignored it and continued with a stable average or slightly above-average prediction of performance.

When faced with the uncertainty of making predictions, students also may turn to other factors on which to base their judgments. Serra and DeMarree (2016) showed that "desired" grade was a significant contributor to students' predictions and post-dictions over and above actual performance and across multiple exams. Although the biasing effect of "desired" grade did decrease with repeated testing, it still remained a significant contributor. This appraisal was also voiced by Foster and colleagues (2017), who speculated that students' predictions of performance may reflect "wishful thinking." Finally, Bol and colleagues (2010) showed that, in the absence of knowing the task and its demands, students could rely on only what they knew for certain; that is, their judgments relied on how much effort and studying they had put forth, the extent of their knowledge in the domain, and their prior experiences of taking exams.

Thus, students' postdictions appear to be influenced by factors of certainty gained from knowledge of the task, the task demands, and their knowledge of what questions they believed were correct or incorrect. When making predictions, students do not have those cognitive and metacognitive advantages and must use factors peripheral to the task and their actual performance. In this case, the best factors on which to rely seemed a good safe prediction of average or slightly above average or their desired or wished for grade.

Improving Calibration Accuracy

As described earlier, productive self-regulated learning requires that students accurately monitor their cognitive and affective states and performance. Without accurate monitoring, effective self-regulation of learning will be compromised. Therefore, improving the accuracy of students' judgments of performance remains an important focus of research. Although we found numerous studies dealing with calibration accuracy, we identified three that were focused on conditions that potentially improve accuracy, which are described in Table 25.2. The other studies examined the relations between calibration accuracy and academic performance. This latter group of studies is described in the following section.

In an experiment by Hawthorne, Bol, and Pribesh (2017), 596 undergraduate students were administered a high-stakes writing exam required for graduation. Students were randomly assigned to one of three conditions that were designed to test the effects of rubrics on calibration accuracy: (1) a global condition, wherein students made global predictions and postdictions; (2) a global and general writing criteria condition, wherein students made global predictions and postdictions and were provided with a rubric consisting of general writing criteria (i.e., organization, development and analysis, sentence structure, and grammar, diction, and mechanics) and made criteria-based predictions and postdictions; and (3) a global and detailed

Table 25.2 *Studies on improving calibration accuracy*

Source	Participants	Context	Treatment	SRL Phase	Calibration
Hawthorne et al. (2017)	596 undergrads	Classroom	Rubric details/ high-stakes writing exam	Forethought & Self-Reflection	No improvement in calibration accuracy due to writing rubrics; using detailed criteria to make judgments improved calibration accuracy for the criterion of organization
Krebs & Roebers (2010)	107 children (8–9 vs. 11–12)	Lab	Liberal vs. strict scoring scheme/ test after watching film on sugar production	Forethought, Performance, & Self-Reflection	No improvement in calibration accuracy or regulation of performance due to scoring schemes
Hadwin & Webster (2013)	170 undergrads	Classroom	SRL course/ setting current and past study goals	Forethought & Self-Reflection	No improvement in accuracy in judgments of goal attainment; higher-achieving students were more accurate at assessing past goal attainment than lower-achieving students

writing criteria condition, wherein students made global predictions and postdictions and were provided with an analytic rubric with detailed performance criteria and made criteria-based predictions and postdictions.

Results showed no main effect of rubrics on calibration accuracy. However, when students were grouped into the highest- and lowest-achieving quartiles based on total SAT scores, predictions and postdictions were more accurate for the highest-achieving students on criterion and global measures of calibration. Students in the detailed rubric conditions had higher postdictive accuracy for the organization criteria than did students in the general rubric condition regardless of achievement level. However, contrary to expectations, there was not a significant interaction between achievement level and rubric condition.

Krebs and Roebers (2010) conducted an experiment to investigate children's ability to metacognitively monitor and regulate their test-taking behavior. The researchers used a factorial design ($2 \times 3 \times 3$) with 107 children aged 8–9 and 11–12. The first factor was age group, the second factor was experimental condition, and the third was item difficulty (easy, difficult, or unanswerable). Children were assigned to either a liberal scoring condition in which they received 5 bonus points for a correct answer, 1 bonus point for an incorrect answer, and 0 bonus points for answers they crossed out. Other children were assigned to a strict scoring condition in which they received 1 bonus point for a correct answer, lost 3 points for an incorrect answer, and got 0 bonus points for answers crossed out. The children in the two conditions were told that they could cross out any answers they thought to be incorrect. Children in the control condition were told only that they could cross out answers they believed were incorrect. The children watched a 7 minute film on sugar production two times with a one-week delay. After the second showing, the children completed a twenty-six-item cloze test and told to answer all questions (forced report). Of the twenty-six items, eighteen were answerable based on details in the film and eight were unanswerable because no details on them had been provided. The children then made postdictive confidence judgments on a seven-point Likert scale, indicating how confident they were that their answers were correct. Finally, they were told that they had the option to cross out answers they thought were incorrect (free report). Strategic regulation was operationalized as the option to withdraw answers during free report. Confidence judgments for each item were averaged for correct and incorrect answers on easy and difficult items and for crossed-out and maintained answers.

Results showed that the manipulation to impose different scoring schemes appeared to have little impact on the monitoring accuracy or regulation of test performance. Regardless of condition and age, analyses of children's monitoring indicated that they gave lower confidence judgments to incorrect than correct answers on easy questions, but only older students gave lower confidence judgments for incorrect versus correct answers on difficult items. Thus, older children were better than younger children at monitoring the uncertainty in their answers. As to the regulation of test-taking behavior, regardless of age or scoring scheme, children crossed out more incorrect answers to difficult questions than easy questions; however, only older students were better able to regulate their answers by appropriately crossing out incorrect answers to unanswerable than answerable questions. In sum, although children from both age groups exhibited abilities to monitor and regulate their test performance, developmental differences were shown by the older children exhibiting significant improvements in both monitoring and regulation over younger children.

Hadwin and Webster's (2013) study was conducted with 170 undergraduate students enrolled in a semester-length course to instruct students on how to self-regulate their learning. In contrast to other studies of calibration, which have used academic performance as the object of calibration, this study investigated the accuracy of confidence judgments and attainment of personal studying goals. During a nine-week period of the course, students received extensive training on self-regulated learning and were then expected to use what they had learned to set studying goals and evaluate progress toward those goals in another course in which they were enrolled. Students provided confidence judgments concerning whether they would attain the current goal in the upcoming week and how well they had attained the preceding week's goal. The researchers found that students' accuracy did not increase over time but they were more accurately calibrated with self-evaluations of current goal attainment than past goal attainment. Also, students with higher grade point averages had confidence judgments that more closely corresponded with their perceptions of past success than students with lower grade point averages. The findings suggest that there is stability in students' judgments of goal attainment, and those judgments may be more heavily influenced by the current goal context than by perceptions of past successes in attaining goals. However, higher-achieving students seemed to have benefited in their assessments of goal attainment based on past goals for studying, indicating that some reflection on past goals may help when planning for future goals.

Summary. Although there are only three studies reviewed in this section, the findings provide additional insights into conditions that can potentially improve calibration accuracy. More will be said about ways to improve calibration accuracy in the next section, but those studies also can be tied to performance.

The three studies reviewed here differed greatly in the object of participants' judgments: Students in Hawthorne and colleagues (2017) judged whether their writing performance was affected as a function of level of detail in rubrics; the children in Krebs and Roebers (2010) judged whether they were able to discriminate between easy versus difficult questions and answerable versus unanswerable questions; and the students in Hadwin and Webster (2013) judged whether their studying goals had been attained. In two cases, calibration accuracy was not increased, regardless of experimental manipulations or prolonged instruction. In Hawthorne and colleagues (2017), only postdictive accuracy was sensitive to the level of rubric detail and for only one writing criterion. These studies speak to the difficulties encountered when attempting to assist students in making more accurate judgments of their cognitions or behaviors, and they focus greater attention on the circumstances when accuracy is actually increased.

The three studies also point to the important role that greater ability or knowledge plays in calibration accuracy. In two of the studies, higher-achieving students were more accurate than lower-achieving students and, in the third study, older students with assumed greater knowledge were more accurate than younger students. However, it is important to point out that lower-achieving or less knowledgeable students are not incapable of accurate monitoring. They were able to make accurate judgments and, in some circumstances, were on a par with higher-achieving or more knowledgeable students. In the Krebs and Roebers (2010) study, less knowledgeable students were as capable as more knowledgeable students in regulating their test taking behaviors, and Hawthorne and colleagues (2017) showed that lowest achieving students seemed to anticipate low writing scores as reflected in their calibration judgments. This should be encouraging news for any advocate of self-regulated learning. The reasons for greater accuracy may be due in part to greater knowledge or ability but, as indicated from studies reviewed earlier, there are many other contributing factors.

Improving Calibration and Performance

Attempts to improve calibration accuracy *and* performance have met with mixed results (Hacker et al., 2008). We have ample correlational evidence that calibration accuracy is linked to performance, yet experimental studies designed to show causal connections between prediction or postdiction accuracy and performance are rare. Making causal connections between improvements in calibration that lead to improvements in performance are critical for informing classroom practice. We reviewed eleven studies conducted in either classrooms or laboratories aimed at improving both calibration accuracy and performance. Six of these studies showed increases in calibration accuracy and performance (see Table 25.3) and five of them showed some increases in calibration accuracy but not performance (see Table 25.4). Although the research outcomes continue to be mixed, these eleven studies have helped to isolate the conditions that can lead to increased accuracy and performance.

Studies showing positive effects on both accuracy and performance. Bol and colleagues (2012) showed positive effects on both calibration accuracy and performance in high school biology classrooms. Employing a (2 × 2) quasi-experimental factorial design with eighty-two students from four classrooms, the researchers investigated whether guidelines or no guidelines in either group or individual settings impacted accuracy and performance. The guidelines asked students to assess: (1) how well they were learning specific concepts, (2) their confidence in learning, and (3) their areas of strengths and weaknesses in understanding the concepts. Students from the four classrooms then predicted and postdicted their performance on a unit exam on biology.

The analyses indicated a significant interaction between guidelines and setting for both prediction and postdiction accuracy. Those students who received guidelines in group settings versus individually were more accurately calibrated. The results also showed main effects for guidelines and setting on exam scores. Those with guidelines had significantly higher scores than those who did not; and those that reviewed in group settings also outscored students who reviewed individually. It seems logical that the guidelines helped students better judge whether they knew the content, and having social comparisons and interactions may have further promoted accurate metacognitive judgments. This greater accuracy then contributed to enhanced achievement on the unit exam.

In two studies, Callender, Franco-Watkins, and Roberts (2016) investigated whether incentives, feedback, and instruction on metacognition and making confidence judgments influence test performance and calibration accuracy. Moreover, the researchers argued that because calibration accuracy is measured by examining the correspondence between judged performance and actual performance, changes in calibration accuracy over time can occur because performance has changed, judgments have changed, or both have changed. In study 1, the researchers used archival data from a college course on decision-making with 127 undergraduate students. In the course, students received: (1) instruction on the concepts related to calibration; (2) instruction on how to make confidence judgments; (3) immediate feedback, explanations, and information on their answers and their calibration accuracy; (4) instruction to review

Table 25.3 *Studies showing positive effects on accuracy and performance*

Source	Participants	Context	Treatment	SRL Phase	Calibration and performance
Bol et al. (2012)	82 high school students	Classroom	Guidelines in groups or individually to self-monitor and regulate predictions and postdictions/ biology exam	Forethought, Performance & Self- Reflection	Guidelines in groups increased prediction and postdiction accuracy and performance increased
Callender et al. (2016)	217 undergrads	Classroom	Extensive feedback instruction on calibration, practice, and incentives/ decision-making exam	Forethought, Performance& Self-Reflection	Feedback on performance and judgments of performance increased postdiction accuracy and performance increased
DiGiacomo & Chen (2016)	30 7th grade students	Classroom	Item-level judgments, learning SRL model, feedback, explaining calibration accuracy, and using reflective worksheet/ math problems	Forethought, Performance & Self-Reflection	Comprehension treatment increased prediction and postdiction accuracy and performance increased
Gutierrez & Schraw (2015)	107 undergrads	Lab	Strategy training and incentives/comprehension of a psychology text	Forethought, Performance & Self-Reflection	Strategy training and incentives increased postdiction accuracy and performance increased
Dunlosky & Rawson (2012) Experiment 1	48 undergrads	Lab	Idea-unit judgments or no standards used in learning key terms in psychology/retention of learning key terms	Performance& Self-Reflection	Idea-unit judgments increased postdiction accuracy and retention increased
Dunlosky & Rawson (2012) Experiment 2	158 undergrads	Lab	Idea-unit judgments used in learning key terms in psychology/retention of learning key terms	Performance & Self-Reflection	Idea-unit judgments increased postdiction accuracy and retention increased; greater accuracy associated with further studying

Table 25.4 *Studies showing positive effects on accuracy but not performance*

Source	Participants	Context	Treatment	SRL Phase	Calibration	Performance
Miller & Geraci (2011) Study 1	130 undergrads	Classroom	Incentives and feedback/ exams in cognitive psychology	Forethought & Performance	Prediction accuracy did not increase	No effects
Miller & Geraci (2011) Study 2	81 undergrads	Classroom	Incentives and feedback/ exams in cognitive psychology	Forethought & Performance	Prediction accuracy increased for only lower- achieving students	No effects
Labuhn et al. (2010)	90 5th grade students	Lab	Mastery or social standards and individual or social feedback/math problems	Forethought, Performance & Self-Reflection	Standards did not increase prediction or postdiction accuracy/feedback increased postdiction accuracy/feedback increased prediction and postdiction accuracy of at-risk participants	No effects
Huff & Nietfeld (2009)	118 5th grade students	Lab	Fix-up strategies vs. monitoring training/ reading comprehension	Performance & Self-Reflection	Fix-up strategies and monitoring training increased postdiction accuracy	No effects
Reid et al., (2016)	80 undergrads	Lab	Cognitive, metacognitive strategies, or both/ reading comprehension	Performance	Mixed-strategy use increased prediction accuracy	No effects

how their judgments matched their performance; and (5) incentives in the form of extra points on their exam scores if they were within a specified range of postdiction accuracy. Students were given two exams during the semester. On completing an exam, they were asked to rate their performance. Study 2, conducted with ninety undergraduates from the same course, was the same as study 1 except that students participated in either a Feedback or No Feedback condition. In the No Feedback condition, there was no feedback given on the exams and no instructions to review how students' judgments matched their performance.

Findings from the two studies showed that the extensive instruction, practice, incentives, and feedback were associated with improved accuracy and performance from the first to the second exam. The results of the second study point more directly at the importance of receiving feedback; that is, students who received feedback decreased their overconfident judgments and improved their performance, whereas students who did not receive feedback did not have significant change to either. For the lowest achieving group, performance changes occurred more frequently than judgment changes and, for the highest performing groups, changes in one or both measures occurred. Thus, improvement in accuracy may not be due solely to improvements in judgments but also to changes in performance. The researchers suggested that feedback on both performance and judgments may help students to better self-regulate their study behaviors.

In their attempts to increase accuracy and performance, DiGiacomo and Chen (2016) focused their study on a comprehensive treatment that incorporated specific strategies to increase self-regulated learning. These researchers conducted an experiment with thirty 6th and 7th grade students who were learning a unit on probability over five class sessions. Students were assigned to either a self-regulated learning treatment or control group, both of which worked in small groups. The self-regulated learning treatment components included (1) judging math questions by making predictive and postdictive confidence judgments by item; (2) teaching a model of self-regulated learning; (3) providing feedback on review questions; (4) providing a graph of calibration accuracy as well as explanation; and (5) using a reflective worksheet that guided students' understanding. Students in the control group received math instruction that did not contain any of the active elements of the treatment.

The results revealed more accurate predictions and postdictions as well as higher scores on math problems for treatment compared with control students. Additional qualitative findings inform the question of what factors contribute to calibration accuracy. Students in the treatment condition were more likely to base their predictions on metacognitive processes and self-concept, whereas control students were more likely to base their judgments on item characteristics, prior knowledge, and guessing. Furthermore, greater calibration accuracy was associated with greater use of prior knowledge to make postdictions, whereas less accuracy was associated with reported guessing.

In a (2 × 2 × 2) factorial design study intended to increase accuracy and performance, Gutierrez and Schraw (2015) manipulated strategy instruction and incentives. Participants took a pretest that consisted of reading a text on behaviorism and related theories; answering twenty multiple-choice questions and judging their performance on each; and a posttest that consisted of rereading the text, answering forty multiple-choice questions, and rating their confidence on each. Participants were 107 undergraduate students recruited from psychology or educational psychology courses. The strategy training was a one-hour session that focused on seven general strategies designed to improve monitoring and regulation, including (1) reviewing main objectives, (2) summarizing, (3) rereading, (4) using contextual cues, (5) highlighting text, (6) relating similar questions, and (7) using diagrams and tables. Incentives were a monetary reward ($10) if participants scored eighty or better on the posttest.

The results showed that strategy training improved calibration accuracy and performance from pretest to posttest. Also, the use of incentives showed a main effect on performance and calibration. Moreover, the combination of strategies and incentives positively impacted performance, confidence, and calibration. The researchers concluded that strategy instruction improved both performance and self-regulation by "providing participants with explicit techniques to process and monitor new information" (p. 398). They also speculated that the incentives may have improved calibration and performance by motivating participants to use the intervention strategies.

In two lab studies, Dunlosky and Rawson (2012) evaluated the extent to which accuracy of monitoring is associated with increased retention. In the first study, forty-eight undergraduate students were randomly assigned to either a no-standard group or an idea-unit group. The task was learning key term definitions from a short passage on social attribution theory. Each key term and its definition were presented one at a time for an initial self-paced study trial, after which, practice sessions began that asked participants to type out as much of the definition of each key term as they could remember. For the no-standard group, participants were prompted to rate their confidence in their responses on a 3-point scale (no credit, partial credit, or full credit). For the idea-unit group, a yes/no check box was presented with each idea unit contained in the definition of each key term, and the participants were asked to indicate which of the idea units were in their response. They were then asked to self-score in the same manner as the no-standard group. Participants were repeatedly presented the key terms for test–judge–study trials until each participant had indicated three times that a key term would be correctly recalled. Two days after the practice sessions, participants returned for a retention test in which they were asked to type as much of the correct definition of each key term as they could remember. Results showed that, although both groups were overconfident, participants in the idea-unit condition were better calibrated and their retention was better than participants in the no-standard group.

In their second study, 158 undergraduates followed the same procedures that were used for the idea-unit group in study 1. Results showed that the participants who showed the greatest overconfidence had judged nearly 65 percent of their responses as correct when they were actually incorrect and the least overconfident participants had judged only about 10 percent of their responses as correct when they were actually incorrect. Further analyses showed that the relation between overconfidence and performance on the retention test was mediated by the practice trials. That is, high overconfidence was associated with less practice and less practice was associated with poorer performance. The results from both studies suggest that highly overconfident participants had prematurely ended further study and consequently performed poorly on the retention test. Participants who were more accurately calibrated monitored their knowledge of the key terms, engaged in further study, and performed better on the retention test.

In an experiment, Morrison and colleagues (2015) examined the effects of generative strategies on calibration accuracy and learning physics principles. They assigned eighty-five undergraduate students to one of three conditions: (1) paraphrase strategy, (2) prediction and self-explanation strategy, and (3) control (no generative strategy use). Participants in the paraphrase group were prompted to paraphrase their observations on an assignment and a principle embedded in the assignment. Participants in the prediction and self-explanation group first predicted the relationship between variables in the assignment and then self-explained differences between their prediction and actual results. Participants in the control group used no generative strategy with the assignment. The assignment involved a computer simulation with five sequential assignments to learn physics principles. The sessions were up to two hours in duration. The dependent variables were test scores (twenty-two multiple-choice and twelve short-answer items), prediction, and postdiction accuracy. Results revealed the effectiveness of using generative learning strategies. Participants in the two generative learning groups had higher scores on recall, evaluation, and transfer type items, and greater prediction accuracy but not postdiction accuracy than participants in the control group.

Studies showing positive effects on accuracy but not performance. Miller and Geraci (2011) sought to improve calibration and performance by administering interventions that focused strongly on incentives and feedback. In two studies, college students, 130 in study 1 and 81 in study 2, enrolled in a cognitive psychology course were asked to predict their grade before taking each of four exams across a semester. Students were incentivized to give accurate predictions by earning extra credit when their predictions were correct. After each exam, the course instructor also displayed feedback for students consisting of the average grade and prediction for the class and encouraged students to reflect on their accuracy. In the second study, the instructor further encouraged students to either improve their predictions by lowering them, because most students were overconfident, or attempt to raise their grades. Results from the first study showed that both high- and low-performing students did not improve their accuracy or their grades across the four exams. In the second study, accuracy increased only for low performing students and once again there was no improvement in exam score for either low- or high-performing students across the four exams.

Types of standards and feedback were compared to determine their influence on metacognitive judgments and performance. Labuhn, Zimmerman, and Hasselhorn (2010) conducted a (3 × 3) factorial experiment using ninety 5th grade students assigned to one of nine conditions (ten per group) to investigate the effects of individual versus social comparison feedback on calibration accuracy and mathematics performance. The three standards conditions were (1) mastery standards, (2) social standards, and (3) no standards. In the mastery standards conditions, participants were told "Everyone can succeed. One can learn to perform well at this task. It is great if you do the best you can and try to improve your own skills step by step." Participants in the social standards group were told "Students perform differently at this task. Some do very well at it, others don't do so well. We will see how well you do." Students in the control group received no information about standards. The three feedback conditions were (1) individual feedback, (2) social comparison feedback, and (3) no feedback. Participants who received individual feedback graphed their scores on mathematics problems. Those who received social comparison feedback graphed their scores and were told how other students had performed. Last, participants in the no feedback group received no feedback on their performance. Another independent variable was whether participants were overconfident (i.e., at-risk students). The experimental task consisted of eight mathematics problems. Participants engaged in the experimental task individually during a 40 minute session. The dependent variables were math scores, prediction and postdiction of performance, and bias scores.

Results showed no significant differences due to standards on participants' calibration accuracy or performance; however, there were effects of feedback. Participants who received either type of feedback produced more accurate postdictions than participants who did not, but there no differences in performance. For the at-risk participants, feedback led to both better predictive and postdictive accuracy and marginally increased performance with social comparison feedback tending to be more supportive than individual feedback.

In an attempt to improve calibration accuracy and reading comprehension, Huff and Nietfeld (2009) conducted a quasi-experimental study in which strategies to increase comprehension monitoring were taught to 118 5th grade students over a fourteen-day period. Four classrooms of students were assigned to one of four conditions. As pre- and postintervention assessments, students in all four conditions read two selections from the Gates–MacGinitie Reading Comprehension Tests, answered comprehension questions, and provided a confidence judgment on each question. Students in one classroom read twelve practice passages and answered comprehension questions about them but did not receive any calibration instruction. Students in a second classroom did not receive the twelve practice passages nor did they receive any calibration instruction. Students in a third classroom received direct instruction using think-aloud methods on how to apply "Fix-Up" strategies during reading. In addition, they read the twelve practice passages with comprehension questions, and each passage was marked at two locations with an asterisk that served to remind them to stop and self-monitor their reading. After each passage, students answered the comprehension questions and gave a confidence rating on each answer. Students in the remaining classroom followed the same procedures and they were provided with monitoring accuracy training that consisted of being given the correct answers after answering and asked to reflect on the accuracy of their judgments.

Results indicated that students who received the Fix-Up strategies and Fix-Up strategies with accuracy training showed greater confidence and calibration accuracy but increases in comprehension did not differ across classrooms. One explanation offered by the researchers for a lack of differences in comprehension was that students who received the Fix-Up strategies with or without accuracy training may have improved their monitoring abilities but they did not improve their control of reading. Successful self-regulated learning requires not only accurate monitoring of learning but strategic control of learning.

Reid, Morrison, and Bol (2016) used an experimental design in a laboratory study to examine whether strategy prompts embedded in a text would improve calibration accuracy and comprehension. Eighty college undergraduates were randomly assigned to one of four conditions and asked to read a text on photography. In the cognitive strategy condition, participants used a generative strategy that prompted them to summarize the content of the preceding page before moving on to the next page. In the metacognitive strategy condition, participants responded to metacognitive prompts that were embedded throughout the text, such as "Am I distracted during learning the materials?" In the mixed strategy use condition, participants were asked to summarize and respond to metacognitive prompts on separate pages of the text. Finally, participants in the control condition simply read the text. A pretest on knowledge of photography and a posttest on comprehension of the text were administered. Immediately after reading, participants were asked to predict their score on the comprehension test. Finally, participants rated themselves on the levels of cognitive effort needed to complete the task, and they rated themselves seven times during reading on how hard they had to work to understand the text.

Results showed that participants in the mixed strategy condition showed the most accurate predictions; however, there were no differences among the four conditions on comprehension. Participants in the mixed and cognitive conditions reported the highest levels of cognitive load and the highest levels of mental effort during reading, and participants in the metacognitive and control groups reported low levels of cognitive load and mental effort. Putting forth more cognitive effort to monitor oneself and generate a summary appears to have had positive effects on the accuracy of one's self-judgments. Surprisingly, this greater effort exerted over reading did not contribute to greater comprehension.

Summary. Attempts to improve calibration accuracy and performance continue to meet with mixed results. On the one hand, there are studies that were conducted in classrooms and laboratories with high school, college, or younger students, using a variety of treatments and tasks, and the end results have been increases in both calibration accuracy and performance. On the other hand, there are studies that have been conducted under similar circumstances and the end results have been occasional increases in calibration accuracy and no increases in performance. Bringing some coherence to these contradictory results presents no small challenge to researchers and educators.

As a result of our analyses of these studies, we would like to suggest that successful interventions to increase accurate monitoring, regulation, and performance appear to have three factors in common: (1) they clearly target specific content that is to be learned; (2) they provide explicit instruction in processes that aid in both monitoring and regulating learning of that content; and (3) they consist of multiple procedures for monitoring and regulating learning.

In each of the studies reported in Table 25.3, there is evidence of these three factors. Bol and colleagues (2012) provided explicit guidelines in a group context that asked students to (1) assess how well they were learning specific concepts, (2) assess their confidence in learning, and (3) assess their areas of strengths and weaknesses in understanding specific biology concepts. Callender and colleagues (2016) (1) taught students about calibration, (2) instructed them on how to make confidence judgments, (3) explained how to review the relation between judgments and performance, (4) provided immediate feedback on their answers and calibration accuracy, and (5) administered incentives for accurate calibration to increase motivation on a decision-making test. DiGiacomo and Chen (2016) (1) asked students to practice making predictions and postdictions, (2) taught them a model of self-regulated learning, (3) gave feedback on review questions, (4) provided explanations on how well calibrated students were, and (5) asked students to reflect on their understanding of concepts on probability. Gutierrez and Schraw (2015) provided strategy training that consisted of seven general strategies to improve monitoring and regulation, including (1) reviewing main objectives, (2) summarizing, (3) rereading, (4) using contextual cues, (5) highlighting text, (6) relating similar questions, and (7) using diagrams and tables, and they administered incentives for accurate calibration to increase motivation to comprehend a text on psychology. Dunlosky and Rawson (2012) asked participants to (1) provide yes/no judgments of learning on each idea unit contained in each key term within a text on social attribution theory and (2) had students test, judge, and study until they indicated three times that a key term would be correctly recalled. Finally, Morrison and colleagues (2015) asked their participants in two-hour sessions (1) either to paraphrase their observations on an assignment on physics and a principle embedded in the assignment or to predict the relation between variables in an assignment; and (2) to self-explain the differences between predictions and actual results.

In contrast, although some of the studies that showed no effects on increasing performance did have clearly targeted content as part of their interventions, they appeared to lack the strong focus on the explicit processes that aid in both monitoring and regulation of that content and had fewer procedures in place to monitor and regulate learning. Some of these studies were able to increase calibration accuracy but none of them led to increases in performance. Miller and Geraci (2011) provided incentives for accurate predictions on four exams across a semester-length course on cognitive psychology, displayed group feedback on performance and accuracy, and encouraged students to reflect on and improve their predictions. Although there were multiple procedures in place, the procedures focused mainly on monitoring and not regulation. Labuhn and colleagues (2010) gave simple mastery or socially oriented statements to do well on mathematics problems, which had no effect on prediction or postdiction accuracy or performance, although their feedback after the problems were completed helped with more accurate postdictions. Huff and Nietfeld (2009) instructed two of their treatment groups to engage in strategies that asked them to use

Fix-Up strategies to increase reading comprehension and prompted them to self-monitor their reading, which increased postdiction accuracy but not performance. The authors suggested that their intervention may have focused only on monitoring but not control of reading, resulting in increased calibration accuracy but not comprehension. Finally, Reid and colleagues (2016) had participants in a treatment group summarize the content of each page of a text and prompted them to monitor their comprehension. This group did improve their monitoring of comprehension as shown by increased prediction accuracy but there was no focus on regulation and no increases in comprehension.

In sum, we propose that the degree of success for an intervention to self-regulate learning will be directly related to the degree to which the intervention focuses learners on specific content to learn, engages them in explicit instruction on how to monitor and regulate their learning of that content, and contains multiple procedures that include a focus on both the monitoring and the regulating of learning. In the final section of this chapter, we provide theoretical support for this proposal.

Theoretical Interpretations and Learning Implications

At the outset of this chapter, we described Zimmerman and colleagues' theory of self-regulated learning (Schunk & Zimmerman, 1997; Zimmerman, 2008; Zimmerman & Kitsantas, 2002; Zimmerman & Moylan, 2009). The research on calibration reviewed here provides insights into each of the three cyclical phases of that theory: forethought, performance, and self-evaluation. Based on the empirical evidence discussed in this review, we have proposed that for successful self-regulated learning, specific content must be clearly targeted for learning, explicit instruction in processes that aid in both monitoring and regulating must be taught, and that instruction must consist of multiple procedures for monitoring and regulating of learning. In this section, we will discuss how the empirical evidence supports the theoretical claims and learning implications associated with each major phase in Zimmerman's model as well as the cyclical interactions among components of these phases.

Forethought

According to Zimmerman's model, the forethought phase encompasses task analysis, learning goals, strategic planning, and self-motivation beliefs. Calibration can be conceptualized as a type of task analysis in that learners are asked to make predictions about how well they will perform on a task or how confident they are in their upcoming performance. Many of the calibration studies reviewed here have targeted this initial phase. However, just having students make predictions is not sufficient for increasing accuracy or performance. Predictions made in concert with other factors or interventions are more effective. For example, Bol and colleagues (2012) demonstrated that calibration practice structured by guidelines led to increased calibration accuracy and performance. Also, Callender and colleagues (2016) and DiGiacomo and Chen (2016) showed that explanations and practice of calibration combined with feedback or reflection improved calibration and performance outcomes. Effective interventions at the forethought phase meet earlier described criteria of focusing on specific content.

Another intervention targeting the forethought phase is the provision of incentives for calibration accuracy or performance. Incentives align with the forethought phase in that they motivate students and add task value. Gutierrez and Schraw (2016) found that incentives coupled with cognitive strategies promoted calibration accuracy, confidence, and performance. Callender and colleagues (2016) further provided evidence of the effectiveness of incentives combined with feedback and instruction on calibration. Incentives were also shown to improve calibration accuracy among lower-achieving students in one of the studies conducted by Miller and Geraci (2011). Though not reviewed in this literature review due to the earlier date of publication, we observed a similar pattern of results in Hacker, Bol, and Bahbahani (2008) in which incentives were effective for lower- but not higher-achieving students. A plausible argument is that higher-achieving students are already motivated to perform well and make accurate judgments; therefore, there is no value added by providing extra incentives. In contrast, lower-achieving students profit from incentives because they are less intrinsically motivated to perform well.

Surprisingly, the two studies that specifically targeted goal setting and strategic planning did not demonstrate strong positive effects on calibration. Hadwin and Webster (2013) reported that students overall did not improve their accuracy in judging goal attainment during a course on self-regulated learning even though higher-achieving students were somewhat better at assessing past goal attainments. In the García and colleagues (2016) study, students' ability to make accurate self-judgments was compromised by the difficulty of the task. Participants who spent more time engaged in strategic planning for the problem did see improvements in their self-observations of performance, which increased the accuracy of their judgments; however, the self-observations may have simply served as a reflection that the children knew the task demands were too great for them. When task demands are moderately difficult, planning and goal setting may lead to better metacognitive accuracy.

The studies also shed some light about what does not seem to work with respect to the forethought phase. Outcome expectations are one part of self-motivational beliefs in this phase. Some results (e.g., DiGiacomo and Chen, 2016; Foster et al., 2017) tell us that guessing and wishful thinking about performance outcomes may contribute to stable predictions and yet accuracy may be left unaffected. Similarly, Serra and DeMarree (2016) showed that students' desired grade outcomes contributed more to predictive and postdictive accuracy than did actual grades, though these effects did decrease somewhat over the semester. Unrealistic outcome expectations are also reflected in the ubiquitous overconfidence among lower-achieving students (Bol et al., 2010; Foster et al, 2017). Uncertainty and wishful thinking likely work in tandem to influence these metacognitive judgments. Factors and operations at the performance phase may diminish these detrimental effects.

To summarize, interventions that focus primarily at the forethought phase may focus students on specific targeted content, but they appear to lack sufficient emphasis on explicit instructions on how to monitor and regulate study or do not contain multiple procedures for monitoring and regulating. Adding these components in the other two phases may be essential for successful self-regulated learning. We turn to these phases next.

Performance

One subarea of the performance phase is self-observation. Self-observation entails metacognitive monitoring and self-control. Calibration is often associated with metacognitive monitoring, which we argue can occur during any of the three phases but, during the performance phase, it reflects monitoring of the task itself. One example of calibration in the context of monitoring of the task comes from Huff and Nietfeld (2009) who used "Fix-Up" strategies and training to accurately monitor. Grade 5 students made item-by-item confidence judgments. Although calibration improved, performance did not, and, as noted previously, this may have been due to the absence of explicit instruction of self-control strategies applied in the performance phase. Krebs and Roebers' study (2010) provides another good example of metacognitive monitoring and self-control during the performance phase. During the task, students had to discriminate between easy, difficult, and unanswerable items as well as correct and incorrect items. The intervention to increase accuracy was not successful; however, both the younger and the older children who participated exhibited abilities to monitor and self-control their test performance, with the older children showing greater monitoring accuracy and self-control than younger children. Similarly, Dunlosky and Rawson (2012) found that making idea-unit judgments during the task, a kind of monitoring judgment, led to better self-control over self-study and both postdiction accuracy and retention were increased.

Other studies have focused more squarely on self-control within the performance phase. The idea here is that effective learning strategies, general or specific, applied during the performance phase should promote more accurate calibration and performance. Morrison and colleagues (2015) taught students generative learning strategies in the form of paraphrasing and self-explanation with predictions. Their hypotheses were confirmed in that the generative strategies led to better accuracy and higher achievement. Similarly, Reid and colleagues' (2016) use of a generative cognitive strategy involving summarization and metacognitive monitoring prompts during reading led to improved calibration accuracy but not comprehension.

Interventions that focus on all three phases also apply clearly to the performance phase. These interventions will be discussed in a subsequent section in which we contend that the most successful approaches for improving metacognitive judgments and performance are those that are multifaceted and span the three phases of self-regulated learning.

Self-Reflection

The self-reflection phase of the theoretical model includes self-judgment and self-reaction. With reference to calibration, postdictions are a salient example of self-judgment and more specifically self-evaluation. Postdictions elicit self-evaluations about how well one performed after completing a task. However, postdictions are also influenced by self-reactions, which are affective responses to one's performance. For instance, the phenomenon of overconfidence among lower-achieving students may be due to defensive postures adopted in order to preserve a sense of self-worth (Hacker et al., 2008). These types of self-reactions may also help explain the stability of calibration judgments and the tendency to base postdictions on desired performance rather than actual performance (Serra & DeMarree, 2016).

Results from several studies illuminate how various factors within the self-reflection phase contribute to calibration accuracy. Perhaps the most robust finding in the calibration literature is the strong association between achievement level and accuracy. As repeatedly noted, achievement level is a strong predictor of postdiction accuracy; however, factors other than achievement may be contributing to postdictions. Factors such as attribution style, knowledge or focus of items and task, feedback, and domain familiarity have been shown to contribute to postdictions. Dinsmore and Parkinson (2013) found that making postdictions required participants to make self-judgments based on the outcomes of their performance, and the accuracy of their judgments was associated with learners' focus on elements of the task and their prior knowledge. Labuhn and colleagues (2010) found that participants responded to feedback on their performance, which led to increased postdiction accuracy. List and Alexander (2015) suggested that a participant's focus on task performance can be more salient than personal beliefs about performance when self-judgments of the task are focused on the directness of the task questions, which resulted in greater accuracy. Task direction or specificity was manipulated in the Hawthorne and colleagues (2017) study by varying the level of detail in writing rubrics. Having more detailed rubrics was associated with better postdictions. Bol and colleagues (2010) related their findings to attributions for calibration accuracy. Students attributed their postdiction accuracy to their feelings of knowing, expectations about test difficulty, and how much effort or study they put into preparing for the exam, the task, and their prior experiences with similar tasks.

Other factors within the self-reflection phase that contribute to calibration accuracy are related to self-reactions or affective constructs. As with the study of predictions (Foster et al., 2017), findings reported by Serra and DeMarree (2016) suggest that postdictions may be based on desired grades, factors that are not likely to lead to increased metacognitive accuracy. Postdiction accuracy may depend on the importance of the task or exam, cycling back to self-motivation and task value represented in the forethought phase. Schneider (2014) concluded that a high-stakes exam may engage students in greater questioning of their responses. However, this does not always result in good postdiction accuracy. When presented with high-stakes exams, students in the Bol and colleagues (2010) study and the Hawthorne and colleagues (2017) study did not make accurate postdictions, but the populations of students were low-achieving and the type of exam was not directly compared. Nevertheless, it stands to reason that postdictions would be affected by the stakes of the task.

Across Self-Regulated Learning Phases

Earlier we argued that the success of an intervention designed to self-regulate learning will depend on whether the intervention focuses learners on specific content, engages them in explicit instruction on how to monitor and regulate their learning of that content, and features multiple procedures that include a focus on both the monitoring and the regulating of learning. Here, we extend this argument by saying that an intervention to self-regulate learning will be more successful for improving metacognitive accuracy and performance if it contains strategies that target all three phases of Zimmerman's model. Furthermore, calibration can occur at all three phases and could be explicitly targeted to increase metacognitive accuracy. The dynamic and cyclical nature of the model should be recognized and the lines between phases may be blurred as learners move back and forth among phases to meet task demands.

Three studies are particularly good exemplars of interventions meeting all criteria and resulting in improved calibration and performance. They also illustrate how interventions may strongly focus on one phase that likely makes the operations at other phases more successful. DiGiacomo and Chen's (2016) intervention began with an overview of Zimmerman's model. For the forethought and performance phases, they used structured and guided questions to review the material and made predictive and postdictive confidence judgments across trials. Strategies at the self-reflection phase were particularly strong. Calibration judgments were graphed, students received feedback on their review questions, and they completed self-reflective worksheets. Gutierrez and Schraw (2015) focused strongly on the performance phase of the intervention by training students how to use cognitive strategies and how they related to calibration accuracy. Incentives were used to motivate students reflecting forethought. Self-reflection was elicited by making confidence judgments after completing items and responding to questions about the self-perceptions of training effectiveness and items on metacognitive awareness. Though the intervention was brief, it used multiple strategies across phases. Finally, Bol and colleagues (2012) used guiding questions in the forethought phase to help students not only more accurately predict their exam performance but strategically plan their test review activities. Group settings led to discussion among students in the performance phase, and students self-reflected on how well they had performed when making postdictions after having taken the exam.

Conclusion

We have argued that a critical component of formal education is helping students become self-regulatory agents of their own thinking and that successful self-regulation requires that students accurately monitor their cognitive and affective states and processes. That is, they must be well calibrated and equipped with strategies to maintain or reestablish monitoring accuracy so that effective control over their learning can be maintained. The studies we have reviewed here were conducted in the contexts of classrooms and laboratories, and although there is less methodological rigor in classroom studies in comparison to laboratory studies, which restricts generalizability, the fact that the contexts of the classroom studies have expanded to many different content areas with students of a wide variety of ages certainly helps to overcome this restriction.

As was shown in our review, calibration is a complex psychological construct, and efforts to increase accuracy do not always end successfully. However, there are conditions under which calibration accuracy is increased and there are conditions under which accuracy and learning are increased. Improving both is no small task, but we believe – based on the empirical findings reviewed here and in prior reviews – that interventions to increase accuracy will be more successful if (1) they clearly target specific content that is to be learned, (2) they provide explicit instruction in processes that aid in both monitoring and regulating learning of that content, and (3) they consist of multiple procedures for monitoring and regulating learning. Including these three components in classroom instruction will initially add much to the already large demands placed on educators. But, if the end result of these efforts is reflected in the sentiments attributed to Maria Montessori, they are efforts well spent: "The greatest sign of success for a teacher . . . is to be able to say, The children are now working as if I did not exist."

References

Alexander, P. A., Dinsmore, D. L., Parkinson, M. M., & Winters, F. I. (2011). Self-regulated learning in academic domains. In B. J. Zimmerman & D. H. Schunk (eds.), *Handbook of self-regulation of learning and performance* (pp. 393–407). New York: Routledge.

Bandura, A. (1986). *Social foundations of thought and action: A social cognitive theory.* Englewood Cliffs, NJ: Prentice Hall.

(1993). Perceived self-efficacy in cognitive development and functioning. *Educational Psychologist, 28*, 117–131.

Bol, L., Hacker, D., Walck, C., & Nunnery, J. (2012). The effects of individual or group guidelines on the calibration accuracy and achievement of high school biology students. *Contemporary Educational Psychology, 37*, 280–287.

Bol, L., Riggs, R., Hacker, D., Dickerson, D., & Nunnery, J. (2010). The calibration accuracy of middle school students in match classes. *Journal of Research in Education, 21*, 81–96.

Callender, A. A., Franco-Watkins, A. M., & Roberts, A. S. (2016). Improving metacognition in the classroom through instruction, training, and feedback. *Metacognition and Learning, 11*, 215–235.

DiGiacomo, G. & Chen, P. P. (2016). Enhancing self-regulatory skills through an intervention embedded in middle school mathematics curriculum. *Psychology in the Schools*, *53*, 601–616.

Dinsmore, D. L. & Parkinson, M. M. (2013). What are confidence judgments made of? Students' explanations for their confidence ratings and what that means for calibration. *Learning and Instruction*, *24*, 4–14.

Dunlosky, J. & Rawson, K. A. (2012). Overconfidence produces underachievement: Inaccurate self evaluations undermine students' learning and retention. *Learning and Instruction*, *22*, 271–280.

Foster, N. L., Was, C. A., Dunlosky, J., & Isaacson, R. M. (2017). Even after thirteen class exams, students are still overconfident: the role of memory for past exam performance in student predictions. *Metacognition and Learning*, *12*(1), 1–19. https://doi.org/10.1007/s11409-016–9158-6.

García, T., Rodríguez, C., González-Castro, P., González-Pienda, J. A., & Torrance, M. (2016). Elementary students' metacognitive processes and post-performance calibration on mathematical problem-solving tasks. *Metacognition and Learning*, *11*(2), 139–170. https://doi.org/10.1007/s11409-015–9139-1.

Gutierrez, A. & Schraw, G. (2015). Effects of strategy training and incentives on students' performance, confidence, and calibration. *The Journal of Experimental Education*, *83*, 386–404.

Hacker, D. J., Bol, L., Bahbahani, K. (2008). Explaining calibration in classroom contexts: The effects of incentives, reflection, and attributional style. *Metacognition and Learning*, *3*, 101–121.

Hacker, D. J., Bol, L., Horgan, D., & Rakow, E. A. (2000). Test prediction and performance in a classroom context. *Journal of Educational Psychology*, *92*, 160–170.

Hacker, D. J., Bol, L., & Keener, M. C. (2008). Metacognition in education: A focus on calibration. In J. Dunlosky, & R. Bjork (eds.), *Handbook of memory and metacognition* (pp. 429–455). Mahwah, NJ: Lawrence Erlbaum.

Hadwin, A. F. & Webster, E. A. (2013). Calibration in goal setting: Examining the nature of judgments of confidence. *Learning and Instruction*, *24*, 37–47.

Hawthorne, K., Bol, L., & Pribesh, S. (2017). Can providing rubrics for writing tasks improve developing writers' calibration accuracy? *Journal of Experimental Education*, *85*, 689–708. https://doi.org/10.1080/00220973.2017.1299081.

Huff, J. D. & Nietfeld, J. L. (2009). Using strategy instruction and confidence judgments to improve metacognitive monitoring. *Metacognition and Learning*, *4*, 161–176.

Keren, G. (1991). Calibration and probability judgments: Conceptual and methodological issues. *Acta Psychologica*, *77*, 217–273.

Krebs, S.S. & Roebers, C.M. (2010). Children's strategic regulation, metacognitive monitoring, and control processes during test-taking. *British Journal of Educational Psychology*, *80*, 325–340.

Labuhn, A. S., Zimmerman, B. J., & Hasselhorn, M. (2010). Enhancing students' self-regulation: The influence of feedback and self-evaluative standards. *Metacognition and Learning*, *5*, 173–194.

Lichtenstein, S., Fischhoff, B., & Phillips, L. D. (1982). Calibration of probabilities: The state of the art to 1980. In D. Kahneman, P. Slovic, & A. Tversky (eds.) *Judgment under uncertainty: Heuristics and biases*. Hillsdale, NJ: Lawrence Erlbaum.

Lin, L. & Zabrucky, K. M. (1998). Calibration of comprehension: Research and implications for education and instruction. *Contemporary Educational Psychology*, *23*, 345–391.

List, A. & Alexander, P. A. (2015). Examining response confidence in multiple text tasks. *Metacognition and Learning*, *10*, 407–436.

Miller, T. M. & Geraci, L. (2011b). Training metacognition in the classroom: The influence of incentives and feedback on exam predictions. *Metacognition and Learning*, *6*, 303–314.

Morrison, J., Bol, L., Ross, S., & Watson, G. (2015). Paraphrasing and prediction with self-explanation as generative strategies for learning science principles. *Education Technology: Research and Development*, *63*, 861–882.

Nietfeld, J. L., Cao, L., & Osborne, J. W. (2006). Metacognitive monitoring accuracy and student performance in the postsecondary classroom. *The Journal of Experimental Education*, *74*, 7–28.

Schneider, E. F., Castleberry, A. N., Vuk, J., & Stowe, C. D. (2014). Pharmacy students' ability to think about thinking. *American Journal of Pharmaceutical Education*, *78*, 1–5.

Schunk, D. H. & Zimmerman, B. J. (1997). Social origins of self-regulatory competence. *Educational Psychologist*, *32*, 195–208.

Serra, M. J. & DeMarree, K. G. (2016). Unskilled and unaware in the classroom: College students' desired grades predict their biased grade predictions. *Memory and Cognition*, *44*, 1127–1137.

Reid, A. J., Morrison, G. R., & Bol, L. (2016). Knowing what you know: Improving metacomprehension and calibration accuracy in digital text. *Educational Technology Research and Development*, https://doi.org/10.10007/s11423-016-9454-5.

Winne, P. H. (2004). Students' calibration of knowledge and learning processes: Implications for designing powerful software learning environments. *International Journal of Educational Research*, *41*, 466–488.

Yates, J. F. (1990). *Judgment and decision making*. Englewood Cliffs, NJ: Prentice-Hall.

Zimmerman, B. J. (2008). Investigating self-regulation and motivation: Historical background, methodological developments, and future prospects. *American Educational Research Journal*, *45*, 166–183.

Zimmerman, B. J. & Kitsantas, A. (2002). Acquiring writing revision and self-regulatory skill through observation and emulation. *Journal of Educational Psychology*, *94*, 660–668.

Zimmerman, B. J. & Moylan, A. R. (2009). Self-regulation: Where metacognitive and motivation intersect. In D. J. Hacker, J. Dunlosky, & A. C. Graesser (eds.), *Handbook of metacognition in education* (pp. 299–315). New York: Routledge.

26 Teachers' Judgments of Student Learning of Mathematics

Keith W. Thiede, Steven Oswalt, Jonathan L. Brendefur, Michele B. Carney, and Richard D. Osguthorpe

A Brief History of Teacher Judgments

More than three decades ago, Richard Shavelson published an article in which he discussed the importance of teachers accurately monitoring their students' states of mind (Shavelson, 1978). He noted, "Teachers' estimates of student 'state of mind' – cognitive, emotional, motivational – provide primary information in deciding how to teach" (p. 37). He noted at the time there was no direct empirical evidence that teachers accurately monitor their students' states of mind and called for more research into this critical issue. Since then a great deal of research has focused on teachers' diagnostic competence (Artelt & Rausch, 2014) and has shown that teachers are not particularly adept at monitoring students' emotional states (e.g., Spinath, 2005) or their motivational states (e.g., Givvin et al., 2001). Moreover, the accuracy of teachers' judgments of students' cognitive states (e.g., current level of learning) varies widely from teacher to teacher and from one study to the next (for a recent review of this literature, see Südkamp, Kaiser, & Möller, 2012).

The importance of accurately judging student learning is highlighted in models of instruction, which describe teaching as the interplay between teachers' judgments of student learning and their decisions about subsequent instruction (e.g., Box, Skoog, & Dabbs, 2015; Donovan, Bransford, & Pellegrino, 2000; Ready & Wright, 2011; Ruiz-Primo & Furtak, 2007). According to these models, in order to judge the quality of their instruction and to make informed adjustments as they unfold in their classrooms, teachers need to be able to accurately assess their students' learning. Although the importance of accurately judging student learning holds across all domains, it may be particularly important in teaching mathematics, where teachers are often inadequately prepared, especially at the elementary level (e.g., Ball, Hill, & Bass, 2005; Lampert, 2001; Loucks-Horsley et al., 2003). As stated by the National Council of Teachers of Mathematics (NCTM, 2000), "Effective mathematics teaching requires understanding what students know and need to learn and then challenging and supporting them to learn it well" (p. 16).

Despite the importance of judgment accuracy in instruction, few studies have (1) investigated how teachers judge their students' learning or (2) developed interventions to improve judgment accuracy. Instead, teacher judgment research has examined how accuracy is affected by the characteristics of the judgment, test, students, and teachers (Südkamp et al., 2012). This body of research has shown that judgment accuracy is better when teachers are informed about the nature of the test prior to judging student performance than when they are uninformed (e.g., Feinberg & Shapiro, 2009; Hoge & Coladarci, 1989) and when tests are more closely related to classroom curricula than when they are more general standardized tests (e.g., Feinberg & Shapiro, 2003; Jenkins & DeMaray, 2016). Judgment accuracy has been affected by subject area being judged in some studies (language arts vs. mathematics: Demaray & Elliot, 1998) but not others (Hinnant, O'Brien, & Ghazarian, 2009). Judgment accuracy is better when teachers judge performance of higher achieving students than lower achieving students (e.g., Hurwitz, Elliot, & Braden, 2007), and although the organization of content in mathematics lessons differs for expert and novice teachers (Leinhardt & Smith, 1985), judgment accuracy is not influenced by teaching experience (Leinhardt, 1983).

To move the field forward and develop programs to improve teachers' judgment accuracy, a theory of what drives judgment accuracy is needed. The present chapter offers a start in this direction by first distinguishing two types of judgment accuracy that can potentially influence instructional practice. Given this potential, the second section considers teacher judgments from a self-regulated learning perspective, which highlights the connection between accurate teacher judgments, effective instruction, and change in student achievement. After establishing this important connection, the third section introduces the cue-utilization framework of metacognitive monitoring (Koriat, 1997) as a guide for improving judgment accuracy. Building on this framework, the fourth section presents some data as evidence of the link between cue utilization and judgment accuracy. The final section then provides future directions for research that aims to improve judgment accuracy and further establish its interdependence with good instructional practice and gains in student learning.

Different Measures of Judgment Accuracy and Why Accuracy Matters

Researchers operationalize judgment accuracy in different ways. One way to operationalize judgment accuracy is the degree to which the predicted level of performance (i.e., the judgment) is related to the actual level of a student's performance on a test. For instance, imagine a teacher having just finished a lesson on two-digit addition judges that a student could correctly solve nine of ten items on a test, but in fact discovers that the student was only able to correctly solve five of ten items. The match between predicted and actual level of performance is called *absolute accuracy* (in the metacognition literature) and is often reported as confidence bias (i.e., average predicted performance minus average actual performance computed across students). A teacher may decide the pacing of a lesson based on whether he or she judges the class understands the material. Much like the teacher in the example above who overestimated the student's performance by four points, overconfidence in judgments is typically found in the literature (e.g., Bates & Nettelbeck, 2001; Rausch et al. 2016; Sudkamp & Möller, 2009). This overconfidence may lead a teacher to move on before students truly understand the material, and under-confidence may lead a teacher to move through a lesson more slowly than necessary.

Judgment accuracy has also been operationalized as the degree to which judgments discriminate between different levels of performance across students. This kind of accuracy has been called *relative accuracy* (in the metacognition literature) and has been reported as the intra-individual correlation between predicted and actual performance computed across students (e.g., Coladarci, 1986; Helmke & Schrader, 1987; Thiede et al., 2015). Again, imagine the teacher above, who just completed the lesson, surveyed the class, and judged students' level of understanding. Although she was overconfident, if she has strong relative accuracy, then she will be able to correctly identify those students who need additional instruction and those who have already mastered two-digit addition. The teacher may use her judgments to decide how to work individually with students (providing additional attention to struggling students or challenging more advanced students). A teacher who accurately assesses individual learning, discriminating whether or not students are proceeding toward the learning goal, can tailor instruction to the individual needs of students; whereas, a teacher who cannot accurately discriminate levels of student learning may allocate attention to individual students less effectively.

It is important to note that absolute accuracy and relative accuracy are statistically independent of one another (Dunlosky & Thiede, 2013). To illustrate the possible relations between absolute and relative accuracy, we have created data for four teachers, each of whom is predicting the performance of five students on a test with eight questions. As seen in Table 26.1, Teacher 1 is neither overconfident nor underconfident because the confidence bias (average predicted performance minus average actual performance computed across students) is zero; this represents perfect absolute accuracy. Teacher 1 also has perfect relative accuracy – as the correlation

Table 26.1 *Illustrations of the relation between absolute and relative accuracy*

Performance	Teacher 1		Teacher 2		Teacher 3		Teacher 4	
	Predicted	Actual	Predicted	Actual	Predicted	Actual	Predicted	Actual
Student 1	8	8	8	5	8	4	8	1
Student 2	7	7	7	4	7	5	7	2
Student 3	6	6	6	3	6	6	6	3
Student 4	5	5	5	2	5	7	5	4
Student 5	4	4	4	1	4	8	4	5
Average	6	6	6	3	6	6	6	3
Accuracy								
Absolute	0		+3		0		+3	
Relative	+1.0		+1.0		−1.0		−1.0	

between predicted and actual performance computed across the five students is $+1.0$. Teacher 2 is overconfident by an average of three points but the correlation between predicted and actual performance is still perfect $(+1.0)$; thus, Teacher 2 has poor absolute accuracy but perfect relative accuracy. Teacher 3 has perfect absolute accuracy but has relative accuracy of -1.0, which is perfectly inaccurate (the student the teacher predicted would do worst on the test actually did best and vice versa). Teacher 4 has poor absolute accuracy and poor relative accuracy.

Judgment accuracy could influence instructional decisions. For instance, Teachers 2 and 4 are quite overconfident. They think their students will get on average six points on the test, which may be well enough for the teacher to proceed to the next topic (as it may be for Teachers 1 and 3, given their perfect absolute accuracy). Unfortunately, these teachers may have moved on too soon because their students did not understand the materials as well as predicted. Regarding relative accuracy, Teachers 1 and 2 were able to accurately discriminate the students who would do better on the test from those who would do worse. These teachers might allocate more time to work individually with Students 4 and 5 (who actually did worse on the test). By contrast, Teachers 3 and 4 had perfectly inaccurate relative accuracy. The students they predicted would do worse on the test actually did best and the students they predicted would do best actually did worse. These inaccurate judgments might cause these teachers to allocate more time to work with Students 4 and 5 when in fact these students understood the materials better than the other students. Moreover, these teachers might choose not to work with Students 1 and 2, who could have used additional help understanding the materials.

In the teacher judgment literature, teachers are most often asked to predict individual student performance for the whole test (called global judgments: Artelt & Rausch, 2014). However, in some studies, teachers have been asked to predict individual student performance on each item of the test. Coladarci (1986) recommended making item-by-item predictions because the item-level predictions could provide information about which items the teacher thought the student could answer correctly; therefore, these predictions provided more diagnostic information. Moreover, these item-level predictions could be aggregated to provide test-level predictions and used to compute absolute and/or relative accuracy.

When judgments are made for each individual item of a test, the degree to which item-level predictions of student performance match actual performance has been called *hit rate* (e.g., Gabriele, Joram, & Park, 2016). In some studies, hit rate has been reported as a percent agreement among a teacher's predictions and his or her individual students' correct responses on individual test items computed across the students in a class (see Coladarci, 1986; Gabriele et al., 2016). Other researchers have provided different approaches to calculating hit rate. For example, Carpenter and colleagues (1989) and Peterson, Carpenter, and Fennema (1989) computed hit rate as the raw number of matches (correct and incorrect performance) across all items and across students rather than as a percent agreement. In these studies, the hit rate has described the match between levels of predicted and actual performance; thus, this type of hit rate is more like absolute accuracy than relative accuracy. That said, item-by-item predictions could have been used to compute either of these kinds of accuracy.

To summarize, *absolute accuracy* describes the match between predicted and actual levels of performance – and could inform the pace at which a teacher proceeds through a lesson. *Relative accuracy* describes how well a teacher discriminates between students with higher levels of understanding and those with lower levels of understanding – and could inform how a teacher tailors instruction to individual students. These terms for judgment accuracy are commonly used in the metacognition literature; we purposely imported them for use in the teacher judgment literature to draw other parallels between these areas of research. First, we will extend the framework of metacognition developed by Nelson and Narens (1990) to help clarify the importance of *accurate* judgments in teacher judgment research. Second, we will apply the cue-utilization framework of metacognitive monitoring (Koriat, 1997) to guide research to improve the accuracy of teacher judgments.

A Self-Regulated Learning Prospective of Teacher Judgments

In their seminal chapter, Nelson and Narens (1990) provided a framework for thinking about how various metacognitive judgments were related to different control processes and the acquisition, retention, and retrieval of knowledge, which helped conceptualize the role of metacognitive judgments in learning. In particular, the framework highlighted the interplay between monitoring and control in learning. For instance, as a student prepares for an upcoming test, the student monitors his or her progress toward a learning goal (e.g., by making a judgment of learning) and then uses the information from monitoring to make decisions about which materials to restudy (see the leftmost part of Figure 26.1). Nelson and Narens (1990) suggested that more accurate metacognitive monitoring should lead to more effective study decisions, which in turn should lead to better learning outcomes.

The Nelson and Narens framework helped clarify the theoretical link between metacognitive monitoring, control, and learning – and motivated research to establish empirical links between the components of the model. That is, it motivated research exploring and identifying factors that influence the accuracy of metacognitive judgments (for overviews of this research, see Dunlosky &

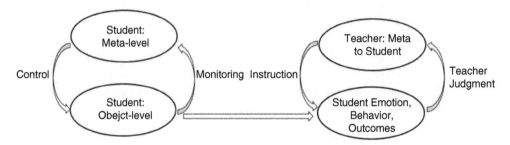

Figure 26.1 *Monitoring and control for students and teachers*

Metcalfe, 2009; Dunlosky & Bjork, 2008). It also motivated research examining the link between metacognitive judgments and subsequent behavior (e.g., Dunlosky & Thiede, 2004; Son & Metcalfe, 2000) and ultimately research examining the role of metacognitive judgments and regulation of study on learning. The Nelson and Narens framework elevated the importance of research seeking to improve the accuracy of monitoring, which was the beginning component in the causal chain. The framework also provided the impetus for research that produced empirical evidence that learning is related to both absolute accuracy (Dunlosky & Rawson, 2012) and relative accuracy (e.g., Rawson, O'Neil, & Dunlosky, 2011; Thiede, Anderson, & Therriault, 2003; Thiede et al., 2012), with higher levels of accuracy supporting greater achievement.

This framework of self-regulated learning associated with the robust body of literature on metacognitive judgments has strong application to teacher judgments. Much as more accurate monitor of learning should lead to more effective regulation of study, which should support greater achievement for students, more accurate monitoring of student learning should help a teacher make better decisions to tailor instruction to the needs of students (see Figure 27.1), which should support greater student learning. This bird's-eye perspective guides research but it is important to acknowledge that teachers' diagnostic competence includes a wide range of judgments (Artelt & Rausch, 2014). Much as different metacognitive judgments are expected to guide different control processes, different teacher judgments are expected to guide different instructional practices. For example, judging a student is not interested in a certain mathematical concept may lead a teacher to discuss the practical importance of the concept. By contrast, judging the strategy a student may use to solve a particular kind of problem may lead a teacher to provide additional instruction to scaffold use of more effective problem-solving strategies. Thus, it is important to specify the judgments being studied and how these judgments are hypothesized to guide instruction and contribute to learning. In the case of teachers' judgments of student learning, the accuracy of judgments influence certain instructional decisions – and the accuracy (whether absolute or relative) is crucial because it influences the effectiveness of instruction and how these variables affect student learning across time (see Figure 26.2).

Although we know of no studies providing empirical evidence of the link between judgment accuracy and subsequent instruction – which may be due to difficulties related to reliably measuring different aspects of instruction (Ball & Rowan, 2004) – research has examined the accuracy of teachers' judgments of student learning and its relation to student achievement as part of professional development around mathematics instruction.

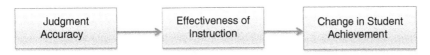

Figure 26.2 *Link between teacher judgment accuracy and student achievement*

One example of research that has examined the relation between teachers' judgment accuracy and student achievement is Cognitively Guided Instruction (CGI). CGI is a professional development program designed to improve mathematics instruction by focusing on students' mathematical thinking. CGI promotes dialog among students and the teacher to increase teachers' knowledge of how students solve problems and think about mathematics. The program presumably should improve the accuracy of teacher judgments about their students' learning and thereby improve instruction, which should increase student learning. However, the findings of CGI are inconsistent.

For example, Carpenter and colleagues (1989) had teachers predict what strategies six students (randomly selected from the class) would use to solve each problem and whether they would correctly solve each problem in a set of problems. They then examined the relation between teachers' judgment accuracy (absolute) and students' performance on the standardized test of mathematics. Teachers' judgment accuracy regarding strategy use was not related to student achievement; however, judgment accuracy regarding correctly solving problems was related to student achievement. In another study of CGI, Gabriele and colleagues (2016) found judgment accuracy regarding correctly solving problems was not related to student achievement. Several factors differed across these studies, so it is difficult to explain the inconsistent findings.

Regardless of the inconsistent findings across these studies, the correlation across teachers' judgment accuracy and student achievement is difficult to interpret. That is, between-class differences in student performance, which would commonly exist in studies conducted in a naturalistic setting, would influence the strength and direction of the correlation. For instance, consider a teacher who has perfect judgment accuracy. If the teacher was working in a class with high-achieving students, she is contributing to a positive correlation. By contrast, if the teacher is working in a class with low-achieving students, she is contributing to a negative correlation. This does not mean the correlation does not have meaning but it does suggest the correlation needs to be interpreted with caution – as a positive correlation (Carpenter et al., 1989) or the lack of a significant correlation (Gabriele et al., 2016) could be an artifact of between-class differences in student achievement.

One way to control for between-class differences in test performance is to examine the relation between judgment accuracy and *change* in student achievement. This eliminates the effect of between-class differences on the correlation. If testing occurs annually or at the beginning and the end of a school year, this score could capture the change over a single academic year, which corresponds to the time the student has worked with a particular teacher.

Thiede and colleagues (2015) examined the relation between the accuracy of teachers' judgments of student learning on change in student achievement. They worked with a school district to create sets of elementary schools matched on prior math achievement, proportion of students on free or reduced lunch (socioeconomic status), and proportion of English-language learners. They then randomly assigned schools to a professional development or a control group. The key outcome variables were teachers' judgment accuracy and change in student achievement (measured by performance on a standardized test administered by the district).

The treatment group received the Developing Mathematical Thinking (DMT) professional development that hinges on five key dimensions of classroom practice: (1) focusing on students' initial ideas through problem-solving; (2) encouraging multiple solution strategies and models; (3) pressing students conceptually; (4) maintaining a focus on the structure of the mathematics; and (5) addressing misconceptions (Brendefur et al., 2015; Brendefur et al., 2016). DMT was chosen because its multidimensional framework for teaching encourages teachers to monitor their students' mathematical ideas and to then modify their instruction based on what they observed from several perspectives. The model supports ongoing formative assessments but does not include specific, focused professional development in the vocabulary and mechanics of formative assessment itself.

Thiede and colleagues (2015) found accuracy of teachers' judgments was greater for teachers who participated in the DMT professional development than for those who did not. They then examined the relation between judgment accuracy and change in student achievement – both teacher-level variables. The correlation was +0.32. Thus, as in self-regulated learning by individual students, where greater learning was associated with more accurate monitoring of learning, greater gains in student achievement were associated with teachers who had greater judgment accuracy. Given this link between judgment accuracy and gains in student achievement, Thiede and colleagues suggest it is important to find ways to improve the accuracy of teachers' judgments of students' learning.

Improving Teachers' Judgment Accuracy

The cue-utilization framework of metacognitive monitoring (Koriat, 1997) provides a model for understanding how to improve monitoring accuracy. This framework states that monitoring accuracy is largely determined by the cues people use to make judgments. Monitoring accuracy will be better when people base their judgments on cues that are predictive of subsequent test performance and worse when they use cues that are not predictive of subsequent performance. Thus, poor monitoring accuracy occurs when people use cues that are not diagnostic of subsequent test performance (Benjamin, Bjork, & Schwartz, 1998; Hertzog et al. 2003; Robinson, Hertzog, & Dunlosky, 2006; Thiede et al., 2010) or when they do not use cues that are diagnostic of subsequent test performance (Koriat & Bjork, 2005; van Loon et al., 2014). In other words, monitoring accuracy is related to whether or not people use the right cues.

In similar fashion, the accuracy of teacher judgments is related to whether or not teachers use diagnostic cues that are predictive of student performance. So, what cues are used to judge student learning and which cues are most diagnostic of test performance? Research into student characteristics that influence judgment accuracy has identified potential cues used by teachers to judge student learning. Some cues that influence teachers' judgment may not be particularly diagnostic of test performance. For instance, demographic variables (gender and ethnicity) are only diagnostic when these variables explain a substantial proportion of variance in test performance. Yet we know that teachers' judgments are influenced by gender (Helwig, Anderson & Tindal, 2001; Mizala, Martínez, & Martínez, 2015) and ethnicity (Martínez, Stecher, & Borko, 2009) – although perhaps only to a small degree. Hecht and Greenfield (2002) showed that gender explained unique variance in teacher judgments beyond that explained by past performance and classroom behavior, but gender accounted for only 1 percent to 2 percent of the variance in teacher judgments. Thus, demographic variables do not likely contribute a great deal to the accuracy of teacher judgments (Kaiser, Südkamp, & Möller, 2017).

Teachers' judgments are also influenced by students' behavior. That is, judgments are influenced by students' engagement in class (Kaiser et al., 2013; Jenkins & Demaray, 2016), interest in domain being studied (Kikas, Silinskas, & Soodla, 2015), effort and conduct (Bennett et al., 1993), and verbal assertiveness, compliance, and self-control (Hecht & Greenfield, 2002; Jenkins & Demaray, 2016). To the degree these behaviors are predictive of student performance, these might be diagnostic cues. However, there are likely situations in which student behavior is not related to learning or a teacher inaccurately interprets the behavior; in these situations, the use of these behaviors to judge student learning will negatively affect judgment accuracy.

Teachers' judgments are also influenced by factors beyond the students themselves. For example, judgments are influenced by the match between teachers' and students' personality characteristics (measured by a personality inventory: Rausch et al., 2016). Judgments are also influenced by teachers' perceptions of parents' educational values (Hauser-Cram, Sirin, & Stipek, 2003). Again, these factors may well be related to student achievement, that is, they may be diagnostic cues. However, to the degree that these factors are not predictive of student learning or to the degree to which teachers inaccurately judge these factors, these factors will decrease the accuracy of teachers' judgments of student learning.

One of the best predictors of future performance is past performance, that is, past performance is a highly diagnostic cue. Teacher judgments are influenced by students' past performance (Hecht & Greenfield, 2002; Martínez et al., 2009). When teachers base their judgments on past performance on tests highly related to the upcoming test, this cue will be diagnostic. However, judgments are also influenced by past performance in domains related to the upcoming test (e.g., performance in science may be used as a cue to predict performance on a test of mathematics; Dompnier, Pansu, & Bressoux, 2006) and scholastic history in general (Dusek & Joseph, 1983). Again, the diagnosticity of past performance as a cue for predicting future performance is a function of the alignment of cues and subsequent performance – accuracy will increase as the alignment increases.

One way to increase the diagnosticity of cues is to more frequently assess student learning (Martínez et al., 2009) and use student-centered instructional techniques that promote conversations about learning among students and between students and the teacher (Connor et al., 2014; Curby, Rimm-Kaufman, & Cameron Ponitz, 2009).

Instructional practices that provide information to guide subsequent instruction are often referred to as *formative assessments*.

During lesson planning, educational objectives, instruction, and assessments are all aligned as a lesson is designed (e.g., Airasian & Russell, 2007; Shavelson et al., 2008). Assessments include both summative assessments – those used to assign grades – and formative assessments, which typically occur during instruction. Formative assessments serve multiple purposes, such as providing teachers information about students' progress toward educational objectives or the effectiveness of a particular approach to teaching (Stiggins & Chappuis, 2006). Formative assessments also provide timely feedback to students and guide their subsequent study (e.g., Stiggins, 2008). When objectives, instruction, and assessments are well aligned, formative assessments provide diagnostic cues for predicting performance on summative assessments (student achievement).

In summary, there are a variety of cues that might inform teachers' judgments of student performance. Some of these cues include demographic variables (such as gender and ethnicity), student behavior (such as level of student engagement), personality match between teacher and student, the value that parents place on education, and past performance of students. Of these possible cues, past performance is one of the most diagnostic cues for predicting future performance of students; therefore, increased use of formative assessment should improve the accuracy of teacher judgments.

Relating Teacher Judgments to Use of Formative Assessment

We hypothesized that the accuracy of teacher's judgments of student learning would be related to use of formative assessment. To evaluate this hypothesis, we used an observation checklist (Oswalt, 2013) to gather data on the use of formative assessment by sixteen teachers. These teachers averaged fifteen years of experience and were evenly distributed across grade levels 2 through 5. The checklist was developed to assess five key components of formative assessment defined by Wiliam (2010): (1) Learning Targets: Clarifying and sharing learning intentions and criteria for success; (2) Monitoring Student Learning: Engineering effective classroom discussions, questions, and learning tasks; (3) Feedback: Providing feedback that moves learners forward; (4) Self-Assessment: Activating students as the owners of their own learning; and (5) Peer-Assessment: Activating students as instructional resources for one another. Oswalt (2013) conducted a validation study and showed the five scales of the instrument had substantial test–retest reliability (weighted Cohen's kappas from 0.71 to 0.82), moderate levels of inter-rater reliability (weighted Cohen's kappas from 0.44 to 0.57), and good to acceptable levels of internal consistency reliability (Cronbach's alphas from 0.68 to 0.91 – the Self-Assessment scale had poor internal consistency reliability, Cronbach's alpha = 0.40). Each teacher was observed multiple times over a two-week period (on average 3.0 times) as they taught mathematics. For each teacher, an average score was computed across the classroom observations on each of the five scales. As seen in

Table 26.2 *Descriptive statistics of formative assessment scales and correlations with measures of judgment accuracy (N = 16)*

Assessment	Mean (SE)	Relative Accuracy	Absolute Accuracy
Learning Target	1.74 (0.13)	0.14	0.06
Monitoring	2.80 (0.13)	0.72**	0.02
Feedback	2.53 (0.15)	0.58*	0.00
Self-Assessment	1.43 (0.07)	−0.05	−0.16
Peer Assessment	1.44 (0.15)	0.02	−0.13

Note. Items were scored on a scale from 1 = "No evidence of use" to 5 = "Pervasive effect use."

* Indicates significance at the 0.05 level.

** Indicates significance at the 0.01 level.

the leftmost column of Table 26.2, teachers were observed effectively using practices to monitor student learning (e.g., teachers used effective questioning strategies, teacher elicited evidence of both factual/procedural knowledge and deeper conceptual knowledge) and provide feedback (e.g., teacher provided accurate feedback to assist learning, teacher provided feedback that describes specific strengths and suggests strategies for learning) more than other practices. Teachers did little by way of effectively creating situations to help students self-assess and self-regulate their learning or providing opportunities to evaluate their peers. Teachers also did not frequently provide clear expectations of learning and well-defined standards for high-quality work; thus, although it is fairly common to present learning targets, the teachers in this study did not clarify learning targets during instruction.

To obtain measures of judgment accuracy, each teacher previewed the test of mathematical skill, which had good reliability (Cronbach's alphas greater than 0.80). Teachers predicted the number of items each student would correctly answer on the test and then administered the test to students (the experimenters scored the test). We computed relative accuracy and absolute accuracy (confidence bias) for the test.

We operationalized relative accuracy as the intra-individual correlation between each teacher's predicted performance and actual student performance. We operationalized absolute accuracy as the average predicted performance minus average actual performance computed across students (confidence bias). For these sixteen teachers, the mean relative accuracy was 0.58 ($SE = 0.06$), which was above chance accuracy, $t(15) = 9.78, p < 0.001$. The mean absolute accuracy was 0.43 ($SE = 0.29$) – twelve of the sixteen teachers were overconfident about their students' performance and four were underconfident. We took the absolute value of the bias scores and computed the mean absolute bias ($M = 0.89, SE = 0.20$). Teachers' predicted scores were on average off by 0.89 items on the five-item test, which was different from zero, $t(15) = 4.39$, $p = 0.001$. The correlation between relative accuracy and absolute accuracy did not differ from zero ($r = -0.05$, $p > 0.10$).

To test the hypothesis that formative assessment is related to judgment accuracy, we computed the correlations between the five formative assessment scale scores and the two measures of judgment accuracy. As seen in Table 26.2, scores on the *Monitoring* scale were significantly related to judgment accuracy. Higher relative accuracy for the mathematics skill test was associated with higher scores on the monitoring scale (e.g., more frequent use of effective questioning strategies, ongoing monitoring, variable questioning methods). The high correlation between judgment accuracy and effective questioning may be intuitively obvious. Nonetheless, this is empirical evidence showing a connection between judgment accuracy and instructional practice.

Higher relative accuracy was also significantly associated with higher scores on the feedback scale (e.g., teacher provided accurate feedback to assist learning, teacher provided feedback that describes specific strengths and suggests strategies for learning). Monitoring and feedback likely go hand in hand conceptually and in practice – that is, teachers who can effectively monitor students' learning are better able to use the information to provide evaluative feedback. In fact, scores on these scales were highly correlated ($r = 0.80$, $p < 0.001$).

It is notable that the other components of formative assessment were not related to relative accuracy, nor were any components related to absolute accuracy. It could be that these other components were not related to teachers' judgment accuracy because these were less frequently used/observed classroom practices, or it could also be a function of the small sample size.

Most important, these findings are consistent with the hypothesis that the accuracy of teacher's judgments of student learning will be related to use of formative assessment. In particular, relative judgment accuracy was related to two components of formative assessment: use of effective monitoring and providing feedback that moves learners forward. However, absolute judgment accuracy was not related to the measures of formative assessment. Relative accuracy and absolute accuracy are different measures and are not necessarily related to one another (Dunlosky & Thiede, 2013); thus, they may be influenced by different factors/processes – that seems to be the case with the teachers who participated in this study.

Summary and Future Directions

Models of instruction describe the importance of teachers' judgments in guiding instructional practice (e.g., Ready & Wright, 2011; Ruiz-Primo & Furtak, 2007; Stein et al., 2008). Regardless of judgment accuracy, judgments influence instruction. For instance, even though teachers may not be able to accurately assess student motivation (e.g., Givvin et al., 2001), student motivation (engagement, interest in learning) affects instruction (Nurmi, 2012). Teachers find more enjoyment and are more involved with students who are more engaged and interested in classroom activities than for those less engaged and disinterested (Hughes et al., 2008;

Skinner & Belmont, 1993). Thus, it is important to study teacher judgments because the judgments themselves affect instruction and student learning. That said, it is especially important to study the accuracy of teacher judgments and the factors that influence judgment accuracy.

Considering teacher judgments from a self-regulated learning perspective provides a context to appreciate the importance of judgment accuracy. In models of self-regulated learning (e.g., Thiede & Dunlosky, 1999), accurate monitoring is crucial to making good decisions related to regulating study (Winne & Perry, 2000). Less accurate monitoring leads to less effective regulation of study and less than optimal learning, whereas more accurate monitoring leads to more effective regulation of study and better learning outcomes (e.g., Thiede et al., 2003). Likewise, less accurate teacher judgments lead to less effective instruction and less than optimal student achievement, whereas more accurate teacher judgments lead to more effective instruction and improved student achievement (Thiede et al., 2015). Thus, it is important to find ways to improve the accuracy of teachers' judgments.

The cue-utilization framework (Koriat, 1997) suggests that judgment accuracy is determined by the cues used to make a judgment. The teacher judgment literature has identified several cues used by teachers to judge student learning. Some are likely less diagnostic of student test performance (e.g., classroom behavior: Bennett et al., 1993) than others (e.g., past performance: Hecht & Greenfield, 2002). Martínez and colleagues (2009) suggested one way to focus teachers on more diagnostic cues is to increase the frequency of assessment in the classroom. That is, increasing the use of formative assessment should focus teachers on more valid cues and increase the accuracy of their judgments of student learning. The results of our investigation provide empirical evidence to support this claim. We showed that relative judgment accuracy was positively correlated with more frequent use of effective questioning strategies, ongoing monitoring, and variable questioning methods.

Despite the evidence showing that accuracy of teachers' judgments is related to gains in student achievement (Thiede et al., 2015), there have been few interventions designed explicitly to improve the accuracy of teachers' judgments. For example, CGI (Carpenter et al., 1989) is a professional development program primarily developed with a goal of changing classroom mathematics instructional practices, and certainly accuracy of teachers' judgments is a key outcome variable for the evaluation of CGI. However, the primary outcome variables for evaluating the CGI program were teachers' instructional practice and student achievement. Given that effective use of CGI presumably leads to a better understanding of students' thinking about mathematics, and judgment accuracy would serve as a good proxy for teachers' knowledge of student learning, it seems that judgment accuracy could have served as a check of the fidelity of implementing CGI. That is, researchers could use judgment accuracy to identify teachers needing additional professional development.

Related to the idea of a check on implementation, we recommend gathering data on teachers' judgment accuracy to examine the fidelity of professional development on formative assessment. Some professional development programs in formative assessment have been shown to improve formative assessment practices and improve student achievement (Robinson et al., 2014), while others have increased teachers' knowledge of assessment but have not changed classroom practice or student achievement (Randel et al., 2016). Judgment accuracy data could help identify teachers in need of additional professional development. Although judgment accuracy only provides information on the monitoring component of formative assessment and fails to provide information related to whether teachers use this information to adjust instruction, accurate monitoring of student learning is necessary for effective adjustment of instruction; therefore, this seems like useful information that is much easier to reliably interpret than classroom observations.

References

Airasian, P. W. & Russell, M. K. (2007). *Classroom assessment*, 6th edn. New York: McGraw-Hill.

Artelt, C. & Rausch, T. (2014). Accuracy of teacher judgments. In S. Krolak-Schwerdt, S. Glock, & M. Böhmer (eds.). *Teachers' professional development: Assessment, training, and learning* (pp. 27–43). Rotterdam: Sense Publishers.

Ball, D. L., Hill, II. C., & Bass, H. (2005). Knowing mathematics for teaching: Who knows mathematics well enough to teach third grade, and how can we decide?. *American Educator, 29*(3), 14–46.

Ball, D. L. & Rowan, B. (2004). Introduction: Measuring instruction. *The Elementary School Journal, 105*(1), 3–10.

Bates, C. & Nettelbeck, T. (2001). Primary school teachers' judgments of reading achievement. *Educational Psychology, 21*(2), 177–187.

Benjamin, A. S., Bjork, R. A., & Schwartz, B. L. (1998). The mismeasure of memory: When retrieval fluency is misleading as a metamnemonic index. *Journal of Experimental Psychology: General, 127*(1), 55–68.

Bennett, R. E., Gottesman, R. L., Rock, D. A., & Cerullo, F. (1993). Influence of behavior perceptions and gender on teachers' judgments of students' academic skill. *Journal of Educational Psychology, 85*(2), 347–356.

Box, C., Skoog, G., & Dabbs, J. M. (2015). A case study of teacher personal practice assessment theory and complexities of implementing formative assessment. *American Educational Research Journal, 52*(5), 956–983.

Brendefur, J. L., Carney, M. B., Hughes, G., & Strother, S. (2015). Framing professional development that promotes mathematical thinking. In E. Ostler (ed.), *Emerging trends and perspectives in STEM learning*.

Brendefur, J. L., Thiede, K. T., Strother, S., Jesse, D., & Sutton, J. (2016). The effects of professional development on elementary students' mathematics achievement. *Journal of Curriculum and Teaching, 5*(1), 1–15.

Carpenter, T. P., Fennema, E., Peterson, P. L., Chiang, C., & Loef, M. (1989). Using knowledge of children's mathematical thinking in classroom teaching: An experimental study. *American Educational Research Journal, 26*(4), 499–531.

Clark, C. M. & Peterson, P. L. (1986). Teachers' thought processes. In M. C. Wittrock (ed.), *Third handbook of research on teaching* (pp. 255–296). New York: Macmillan.

Coladarci, T. (1986). Accuracy of teacher judgments of student responses to standardized test items. *Journal of Educational Psychology, 78*(2), 141–146.

Connor, C. M., Spencer, M., Day, S. L., Giuliani, S., Ingebrand, S. W., McLean, L., & Morrison, F. J. (2014). Capturing the complexity: Content, type, and amount of instruction and quality of the classroom learning environment synergistically predict third graders' vocabulary and reading comprehension outcomes. *Journal of Educational Psychology, 106*(3), 762–778.

Curby, T W., Rimm-Kaufman, S. E., & Cameron Ponitz, C. (2009). Teacher-child interactions and children's achievement trajectories across kindergarten and first grade. *Journal of Educational Psychology, 101*(4), 912–925.

Demaray, M. K. & Elliot, S. N. (1998). Teachers' judgments of students' academic functioning: A comparison of actual and predicted performance. *School Psychology Quarterly, 13*(1), 8–14.

Dompnier, B., Pansu, P., & Bressoux, P. (2006). An integrative model of scholastic judgments: Pupils' characteristics, class context, halo effect and internal attributions. *European Journal of Psychology in Education, 21*(2), 119–133.

Donovan, M. S., Bransford, J. D., & Pellegrino, J. W. (eds.). (2000). *How people learn: Bridging research and practice.* Washington, DC: National Research Council and National Academy Press.

Dunlosky, J. & Bjork, R. A. (2008). *Handbook of metamemory and memory.* New York: Psychology Press.

Dunlosky, J. & Metcalfe, J. (2009). *Metacognition.* Thousand Oaks: CA: SAGE Publications.

Dunlosky, J. & Rawson, K. A. (2012). Overconfidence produced underachievement: Inaccurate self evaluations undermine students' learning and retention. *Learning and Instruction, 22*(4), 271–280.

Dunlosky, J. & Thiede, K. W. (2004). Causes and constraints of the shift-to-easier-materials effect in the control of study. *Memory and Cognition, 32*(5), 779–788.

(2013). Four cornerstones of calibration research: Why understanding students' judgments can improve their achievement. *Learning and Instruction, 24*(1), 58–61.

Dusek, J. D. & Joseph, G. (1983). The bases of teacher expectancies: A meta-analysis. *Journal of Educational Psychology, 75*(3), 327–346.

Feinberg, A. B. & Shapiro, E. S. (2003). Accuracy of teacher judgment of oral reading fluency. *School Psychology Quarterly, 18*(1), 52–65.

(2009). Teacher accuracy: An examination of teacher-based judgments of students' reading with differing achievement levels. *The Journal of Educational Research, 102*(6), 453–462.

Gabriele, A. J., Joram, E., & Park, K. H. (2016). Elementary mathematics teachers' judgment accuracy and calibration accuracy: Do they predict students' mathematics achievement outcomes? *Learning and Instruction, 45*(1), 49–60.

Givvin, K. B., Stipek, D. J., Salmon, J. M., & MacGyvers, V. L. (2001). In the eyes of the beholder: Students' and teachers' judgments of students motivation. *Teaching and Teacher Education, 17*(3), 321–331.

Hauser-Cram, P., Selcuk, R. S., & Stipek, D. (2003). When teachers' and parents' values differ: Teachers' ratings of academic competence in children from low-income families. *Journal of Educational Psychology, 95*(4), 813–820.

Hecht, S. A. & Greenfield, D. B. (2002). Explaining the predictive accuracy of teacher judgments of their students' reading achievement: The role of gender, classroom behavior, and emergent literacy skills in longitudinal sample of children exposed to poverty. *Reading and Writing, 15*(7–8), 789–809.

Helmke, A., & Schrader, F. W. (1987). Interactional effects of instructional quality and teacher judgement accuracy on achievement. *Teaching and Teacher Education, 3*(2), 91–98.

Helwig, R., Anderson, L., & Tindal, G. (2001). Influence of elementary student gender on teachers perceptions of mathematics achievement. *Journal of Educational Research, 95*(1), 93–102.

Hertzog, C., Dunlosky, J., Robinson, A. E., & Kidder, D. P. (2003). Encoding fluency is a cue utilized for judgments about learning. *Journal of Experimental Psychology: Learning, Memory, and Cognition, 29*(1), 22–34.

Hinnant, J. B., O'Brien, M., & Ghazarian, S. R. (2009). The longitudinal relations of teacher expectations to achievement in the early school year. *Journal of Educational Psychology, 101*(3), 662–670.

Hoge, R. D. & Coladarci, T. (1989). Teacher-based judgments of academic achievement: A review of literature. *Review of Educational Research, 59*(3), 297–313.

Hughes, J. N., Luo, W., Kwok, O. M., & Loyd, L. K. (2008). Teacher-student support, effortful engagement, and achievement: A 3-year longitudinal study. *Journal of Educational Psychology, 100*(1), 1–14.

Hurwitz, J. T., Elliot, S. N., & Braden, J. P. (2007). The influence of test familiarity and student disability status upon teachers' judgments of students' test performance. *School Psychology Quarterly, 22*, 115–144.

Jenkins, L. N. & Demaray, M. K. (2016). Teachers' judgments of academic achievement of children with and without characteristics of inattention, impulsivity, and hyperactivity. *Contemporary School Psychology, 20*(2), 183–191.

Kaiser, J., Retelsdorf, J., Südkamp, A., & Möller, J. (2013). Achievement and engagement: How student characteristics influence teacher judgments. *Learning and Instruction, 28*(1), 73–84.

Kaiser, J., Südkamp, A., & Möller, J. (2017). The effects of student characteristics on teachers' judgment accuracy: Disentangling ethnicity, minority status, and achievement. *Journal of Educational Psychology, 109*(6), 871–888.

Kikas, E., Silinskas, G., & Soodla, P. (2015). The effect of children's reading skill and interest on teacher perceptions of children's skill and individualized support. *International Journal of Behavioral Development, 39*(5), 402–412.

Koriat, A. (1997). Monitoring one's own knowledge during study: A cue-utilization approach to judgments of learning. *Journal of Experimental Psychology: General, 126*(4), 349–370.

Koriat, A. & Bjork, R. A. (2005). Illusions of competence in monitoring one's knowledge during study. *Journal of Experimental Psychology: Learning, Memory, and Cognition, 31*(2), 187–194.

Lampert, M. (2001). *Teaching problems and problems of teaching.* New Haven, CT: Yale University Press.

Leinhardt, G. (1983). Novice and expert knowledge of individual student's achievement. *Educational Psychologist, 18*(2), 165–179.

Leinhardt, G. & Smith, D. A. (1985). Expertise in mathematics instruction: Subject matter knowledge. *Journal of Educational Psychology, 77*(3), 247–271.

Loucks-Horsley, S., Love, N., Stiles, K.E., Mundry, S., & Hewson, P.W. (2003). *Designing professional development for teachers of science and mathematics.* Thousand Oaks, CA: Corwin Press.

Martínez, J. F., Stecher, B., & Borko, H. (2009). Classroom assessment practices, teacher judgments, and student achievement in mathematics: Evidence from the ECLS. *Educational Assessment, 14*(1), 78–102.

Mizala, A., Martínez, F., Martínez, S. (2015). Pre-service elementary school teachers' expectations about student performance: How their beliefs are affected by their mathematics anxiety and student's gender. *Teaching and Teacher Education, 50*(1), 70–78.

NCTM (National Council of Teachers of Mathematics). (2000). *Principles and standards for school mathematics*. Reston, VA: NCTM.

Nelson, T. O. & Narens, L. (1990). Metamemory: A theoretical framework and new findings. In G. H. Bower (ed.), *The psychology of learning and motivation*, vol. 26, pp. 125–141. New York: Academic Press.

Nurmi, J. E. (2012). Students' characteristics and teacher-child relationships in instruction: A meta-analysis. *Educational Research Review, 7*(3), 177–197.

Oswalt, S. G. (2013). Identifying formative assessment in classroom instruction: Creating an instrument to observe use of formative assessment in practice (Doctoral dissertation). http://scholarworks.boisestate.edu/cgi/viewcontent.cgi?article=1772&context=td.

Peterson, P. L., Carpenter, T., & Fennema, E. (1989). Teachers' knowledge of students' knowledge in mathematics problem solving: Correlational and case analyses. *Journal of Educational Psychology, 81*(4), 558–569.

Randel, B., Apthorp, H., Beesley, A. D., Clark, T. F., & Wang, X. (2016). Impacts of professional development in classroom assessment on teacher and student outcomes. *The Journal of Educational Research, 109*(5), 491–502.

Rausch, T., Karing, C., Dörfler, T., & Artelt, C. (2016). Personality similarity between teachers and their students influences teacher judgment of student achievement. *Educational Psychology, 36*(5), 863–878.

Rawson, K. A., O'Neil, R., & Dunlosky, J. (2011). Accurate monitoring leads to effective control and greater learning of patient education materials. *Journal of Experimental Psychology: Applied, 17*(3), 288–302.

Ready, D. D. & Wright, D. L. (2011). Accuracy and inaccuracy in teachers' perceptions of young children's cognitive abilities the role of child background and classroom context. *American Educational Research Journal, 48*(2), 335–360.

Robinson, E. A., Hertzog, C, & Dunlosky, J. (2006). Aging, encoding fluency, and metacognitive monitoring. *Aging, Neuropsychology, and Cognition, 13*(3–4), 458–478.

Robinson, J., Myran, S., Strauss, R., & Reed, W. (2014). The impact of an alternative professional development model on teacher practices in formative assessment and student learning. *Teacher Development, 18*(2), 141–162.

Ruiz-Primo, M. A. & Furtak, E. M. (2007). Exploring teachers' informal formative assessment practices and students' understanding in the context of scientific inquiry. *Journal of Research in Science Teaching, 44*(1), 57–84.

Shavelson, R. J. (1978). Teachers' estimates of student "states of mind" and behavior. *Journal of Teacher Education, 29*(5), 37–40.

Shavelson, R. J., Young, D. B., Ayala, C. C., Brandon, P. R., Furtak, E., Ruiz-Primo, M. A., Tomita, M. K., Yin,Y. (2008). On the impact of curriculum-embedded formative assessment on learning: A collaboration between curriculum and assessment developers. *Applied Measurement in Education, 21*(4), 295–314.

Skinner, E. & Belmont, M. (1993). Motivation in the classroom: Reciprocal effects of teacher behavior and student engagement across the school year. *Journal of Educational Psychology*, *85*(4), 571–581.

Son, L. K. & Metcalfe, J. (2000). Metacognitive control strategies in study-time allocation. *Journal of Experimental Psychology: Learning, Memory, and Cognition*, *26*(1), 204–221.

Spinath, B. (2005). Accuracy of teacher judgments on student characteristics and the construct of diagnostic competence. *Zeitschrift Fur Padagogische Psychologie*, *19*(1), 85–95.

Stein, M. K., Engle, R. A., Smith, M. S., & Hughes, E. K. (2008). Orchestrating productive mathematical discussions: Five practices for helping teachers move beyond show and tell. *Mathematical Thinking & Learning*, *10*(4), 313–340.

Stiggins, R. (2008). *Student-involved assessment for learning.* Upper Saddle River: NJ: Pearson.

Stiggins, R. J. & Chappuis, J. (2006). What a difference a word makes: Assessment "for" learning rather than assessment "of" learning helps students succeed. *Journal of Staff Development*, *27*(1), 10–14.

Südkamp, A., Kaiser, J., & Möller, J. (2012). Accuracy of teachers' judgments of students' academic achievement: A meta-analysis. *Journal of Educational Psychology*, *104* (3), 743 762.

Südkamp, A. & Möller, J. (2009). Reference-group-effects in a simulated classroom: Direct and indirect judgments. *Zeitschrift Fur Padagogische Psychologie*, *23*(1), 161–174.

Thiede, K. W., Anderson, M. C. M., & Therriault, D. (2003). Accuracy of metacognitive monitoring affects learning of texts. *Journal of Educational Psychology*, *95*(1), 66–73.

Thiede, K. W., Brendefur, J. L., Osguthorpe, R. D., Carney, M.B., Bremner, A., Strother, S., Oswalt, S., Snow, J. L. Sutton, J., & Jesse, D. (2015). Can teachers accurately predict student performance? *Teaching and Teacher Education*, *49*(1), 36–44.

Thiede, K.W. & Dunlosky, J. (1999). Toward a general model of self-regulated study: An analysis of selection of items for study and self-paced study time. *Journal of Experimental Psychology: Learning, Memory, & Cognition*, *25*(4), 1024–1037.

Thiede, K. W., Griffin, T. D., Wiley, J., & Anderson, M.C.M. (2010). Poor metacomprehension accuracy as a result of inappropriate cue use. *Discourse Processes*, *47*(4), 331–362.

Thiede, K.W., Redford, J.S., Wiley, J., & Griffin, T.D. (2012). Elementary school experience with comprehension testing may influence metacomprehension accuracy among 7th and 8th graders. *Journal of Educational Psychology*, *104*(3), 554–564.

Van Loon, M. H., de Bruin, A. B. H., van Gog, T., van Merriënboer, J. J. G., & Dunlosky, J. (2014). Can students evaluate their understanding of cause-and-effect relations? The effect of diagram completion on monitoring accuracy. *Acta Psychologica*, *151* (1), 143–154.

Wiliam, D. (2010). An integrative summary of the research literature and implications for a new theory of formative assessment. In H. L. Andrade & G. J. Cizek (eds.), *Handbook of formative assessment* (pp. 18–40). New York: Routledge.

Winne, P. H. & Perry, N. E. (2000). Measuring self-regulated learning. In M. Boekaerts and P. Pintrich (eds.), *Handbook of self-regulation* (pp. 531–566). New York: Academic Press.

27 Learning Strategies and Self-Regulated Learning

Philip H. Winne and Zahia Marzouk

A Select History of Learning Strategies

While they are not the earliest North American writings about learning strategies, B. A. Hinsdale's (1910)*The art of study*, G. V. N. Dearborn's (1916) text *How to learn easily* and G. M. Whipple's (1916) first edition of *How to learn easily* mark launching points for early scholarly attention to learning strategies. Allowing for differences in terminology then versus now, these authors' accounts about how to study foreshadowed modern conceptions of learning strategies, metacognition, self-regulated learning (SRL), and volition.

Hinsdale (1910) viewed learning as a self-driven, life-long activity: "Every one must make his own knowledge, for man is a knowledge-maker by nature ... The child is engaged in making knowledge from his earliest days" (pp. 11–12). Casting studying as a practical art, Hinsdale foreshadowed a key role for metacognition and challenges of productive self-regulated learning:

> It is practice and study, then, and not simply study that makes one perfect in an art. But everything depends upon the kind of practice. Mere mechanical grinding ... will never bring perfection. Practice must be intelligent, or it must be conducted according to a right method. Now some happy pupils may, without great loss of time, find out this method for themselves, but the majority of pupils will not be able to do so.

Alas, he saw little remedy in schooling: "In the schools, the art of study is taught, for the most part, indirectly, wholly at random, and very imperfectly" (p. 25).

Dearborn (1916) seems the least optimistic and most socioeconomically rigid of the aforementioned trio. He opined: "For it is possible, if not probable, that a certain percentage of a class ... can never be a success at any learned pursuit" (p. 1). For him, the key to successful study was, first, interest – "Whatever be the means, we must have interest" (p. 3) – supplemented by a dogged pursuit of maximizing the "joy-efficiency ratio" (p. 12) in the learning process. He distinguished deliberate study (i.e., deliberate practice; Campitelli & Gobet, 2011) as dependent on inhibitory control (e.g., Baker, 2016) spiced with volition (Corno, 1994): "All sorts of sensory stimuli have to be kept out of the effective mind. The desire to change must be inhibited ... Study, then ... is the forcing of the mental processes along new pathways" (p. 14). "We should beware of false study . . . If we cannot force an interest or attention on what we are studying, we should rest . . . or . . . we should give it up" (p. 15). Dearborn judged learners are intrinsically challenged to study strategically: "The mind, then, is in general a capable instrument but not so as an instrument of precision"(p. 38). In a delightfully titled chapter, "Is your 'thinker' in order," Dearborn echoed Hinsdale: "A truly educated man knows how to think, and, more-over, he has the process habituated ... [but] the present school system does not educate as yet in this" (p. 148). He forcefully characterized learning as a skill: *"Learning and all mentation are related to that form of personal ability which we have denoted as skill"* (p. 163, emphasis in original).

Whipple's (1916) view foreshadowed today's attention to growth mindset (e.g., Dweck, 2008): "most studying is real work, and that most boys and girls have to acquire the art of studying as they have to acquire many other habits and skills necessary to success in life" (p. 4). He predicted great need for learners to master productive learning strategies: "Students in both high school and college have been studying, it is true, for years, but too often ... have not formed right habits of mental work, and indeed, do not even know how to go about the development of an adequate method or plan for such work" (p. 4). He proposed thirty-eight rules, many of which were prescient. Rule 18 presaged learners should be learning scientists engaged in self-regulated learning (Winne, 1997, 2017b): "Find out by trial whether you suc-ceed better by beginning with the hardest or with the easiest task when you are confronted with several tasks of unequal difficulty" (p. 20). He anticipated transfer appropriate processing (McDaniel & Kearney, 1984) in rule 19: "In general, use in your studying the form of activity that will later be demanded when the material is used" (p. 21). In rule 20, he took a side in the modern discussion of restudying according to the model of maximum discrepancy and the model of proximal learning (Metcalfe, 2009): "Give most time and attention to the weak points in your knowl-edge or technique" (p. 21). Rule 25 anticipated the spacing effect (Son, 2010): "When or drill or repetition is necessary, distribute over more than one period the time given to a specified learning" (p. 27). Elaboration and mnemonics were fore-seen in rule 35: "When the material to be learned by heart presents no obvious rational associations, it is perfectly legitimate to invent some artificial scheme learning and recalling it" (p. 34).

Leaping forward approximately a half-century, theoretical and empirical research on learning blossomed under the umbrella of cognitive skills. A launching point was Flavell, Friedrichs, and Hoyt's (1970) study that examined strategies kindergarten, Grade 2, and Grade 4 children used to memorize information and how these children described their strategies. The early age at which learning strategies appeared au naturel was a mild surprise. What mattered far more was their assertion that a child's "knowledge and awareness of his own memory system is a particularly important and timely research problem" (p. 324). This is metacognition, "mentally inspecting cognition and its attributes – how one thinks and with what information one thinks; and of mentally charting then following a path of action toward achieving a goal" (Winne, 2017a, p. 10; Winne & Azevedo, 2014). Features of metacognition in learning strategies, as we describe later, are key today, nearly a half-century onward.

Edited volumes soon appeared entitled *Thinking and learning skills* (vol. 1: Segal, Chipman, & Glaser, 1985; vol. 2: Chipman, Segal, & Glaser, 1985) and *Learning and study strategies* (Weinstein, Goetz, & Alexander, 1988), among others (Jones & Idol, 1990; Idol & Jones, 1991). The scope of learning strategies was immense. Learners' ages spanned preschool through adulthood. Subject matters ranged over reading, mathematics, writing, and science. Forms of thinking, including problem-solving, critical thinking, and creativity were investigated. Motivation was acknowledged. The message was cheery: Learners can be taught about and will use learning strategies with very well-planned instructional designs and some attention to motivating them. Mild benefits to achievement could be achieved. Disappointingly, effects typically were short-lived and transfer was feeble, if it occurred at all. Weak points in learners' applications of learning strategies were cataloged – for example, the production deficiency, when learners fail to recognize a strategy they could use; the utilization deficiency, when learners have not fully automated a strategy so using it actually depresses performance (see Winne, 1997, 2010); and waning motivation.

Information about learning strategies is more than abundant. A Google search for the exact phrase "learning strategies" (May 10, 2017 at 11:45) identified about 3.08 million items on the internet. There is a staggering diversity of lists, typologies, hierarchies, tables, charts, acronyms, maxims, diagrams, cartoons, surveys, self-help sites, and even corporations. Clearly, learning strategies are deemed important. Restricting this set to intersect with "learning science" reduces this set dramatically to a "mere" 119,000.

Do learning strategies matter to students? Canada's Amazon bookstore returned 1,018 results when we searched for "learning strategies" (May 10, 2017 at 11:50). There appears to be a healthy market for books about what learning strategies there are and how they might be applied. Every postsecondary institution we know of offers some mix of in-person coaching services, workshops, and online materials to help students develop more effective study techniques. Karpicke, Butler, and Roediger (2009) surveyed undergraduates about study strategies they used when studying. Slightly more than 68 percent reported using three or more strategies. We conclude, "Yes, students value learning strategies."

Basic Concepts: Learning Tactics, Learning Strategies, and Self-Regulated Learning

A learning tactic is a single or a very short sequence of operations a learner applies to information. For example, if a learner wants to remember definitions of terms, a potential tactic might be to mentally rehearse a paired associate, e.g., "verisimilitude – the appearance of being true or real." After several repetitions, test by reviewing each term in the list and trying to recite the definition of each, and then checking the match between recall and the definition provided by the text or glossary.

Learners activate tactics in the context of specific conditions they perceive. Thus, a succinct model for a learning tactic is IF-THEN. IFS identify the set of conditions under which the learner is reminded about and entertains carrying out a particular (set of) operation(s). In the just given example, there are at least two conditions: the nature of information to be learned (paired associate) and value attached to knowing the definition of a new word. THEN represents one or more operations the learner applies to information and, in some tactics, manipulation of physical objects. In the previous example, the learner might have written each term on one side of an index card, the definition on the other side, and flip a card after trying to recall a term's definition to check completeness and accuracy. Another example: IF reading a text and encountering a baffling term, THEN put your finger on the term and read on to expand context as a basis for inferring the meaning of the new term.

A more complete model of tactic adds three further elements: (1) features of the product generated by the tactic's operation(s) and (2) an evaluation of the product relative to (3) standards the learner adopts for evaluating products in the present context. To integrate this set of features with the IF-THEN components of a learning tactic, we apply a common learning tactic: IF a list of items or a multipart name needs to be remembered, assemble an acronym to represent each item in a list defined by the items' first letters. The result is COPES (Winne, 1997, 2017b) based on the first letter of conditions (or context, IFS), operations (THEN), products, evaluations, and standards. Standards for evaluating a product generated by applying this tactic, the acronym COPES, are each binary: Is each component represented in the acronym? Can each component be recalled given its first letter? Does the acronym meaningfully associate to what it represents, for example: "A learner COPES with tasks using learning tactics." The COPES comprising a task is summarized in Table 27.1.

Beyond the IF-THEN architecture of a learning tactic, tactics have two key characteristics. First, a tactic inherently expresses orientation toward a goal. Goals are operationally defined by the standards a learner uses to evaluate products. That is, learners consider applying a learning tactic in relation to how the tactic fits a purpose. Even a tactic of trial-and-error responses to a situation reflects a goal to produce a product with particular attributes, e.g., an answer to the teacher's question or a solution to a problem. If goals were not constitutive of a learning tactic, any

Table 27.1 *COPES features of a task*

Conditions	Features in the external environment plus elements of a learner's mental state that the leaner perceives can influence performance.
Operations	Primitive, tactical (IF-THEN) and strategic (conditionally linked tactics) manipulations of information.
Product(s)	New or transformed information created by operations. Information can describe any feature of a task, its COPES.
Evaluation	A comparison judging attributes of a product relative standards the learner adopts for the product.
Standards	Optimal or sufficient qualities of a product.

product would be acceptable. Because tactics are oriented toward goals, tactics inherently relate to motivation, an account for why learners approach particular goals. We elaborate more about motivation in the section "Conceptualizing Learning Strategies as Decision-Making, Hot and Cold." As well, tactics – specifically, the operation(s) that animate a tactic – are means for solving problems about how goals can be achieved. This foreshows our later examination of learning strategies.

Second, tactics are skills. Thus, learners are deliberate when they apply a tactic. First attempts to apply a tactic are neither fluid nor quick. As a result, the learner perceives greater effort is required to do it. With practice, the pace of execution quickens, the tactic becomes more fluid (vs. punctuated), and the learner's perception of effort required declines. Commonly, there is also an improvement in the alignment of products to standards (goals). After extensive practice, a tactic becomes automated. In this state, a learner barely needs to attend to specifics of the tactic's COPES to apply it to good effect. An example is the undergraduate student who rapidly and with barely perceptible reflection reliably identifies (IF) disciplinary terms while reading new content and highlights (THEN) corresponding text that defines or describes significant features of those terms, e.g., the name of a person who coined the label for a significant psychological effect or basic tenets of a major theory.

Learning tactics serve as building blocks for multitactic learning strategies (Derry, 1990; McKeachie, 1988). Learning strategies have three important qualities beyond those of their component tactics. First, learning strategies unfold in "steps" when prior events produce updates to conditions, the IFs of tactics. That is, strategies involve sequentially context-sensitive decisions about which tactic should be applied under evolving conditions.

Second, because learning strategies are comprised of at least two tactics – one just applied and a choice to reapply that same tactic or switch to a new one – learning strategies have a temporal pattern. If an immediately prior tactic was productive, it may be repeated depending on the learner's judgment of whether doing so moves closer to the overall goal of a task. If the prior tactic was not productive, the learner has three options: (1) Repeat the prior tactic. This reflects an interpretation that the context requires "stronger" or repeated expression of that just-used tactic. One of us often observes our spouse clicking the same button on a web page when a website doesn't respond as expected. (2) Replace the prior tactic with another judged to have a greater probability of success. If the button doesn't "seem" to work, search for a menu option. (3) Abandon the task. As we discuss in the next section, these choices create opportunities for researchers to explore how learners value each option.

The third key feature of a learning strategy arises from the first two. Strategies unfold as branching and sometimes cyclically recursive patterns. Across the timeline of work on a task, as each successive tactic is applied, products and evaluations of them update conditions the learner may consider in deciding what to do next. A learner who inspects this history of strategic learning activities and forecasts whether and how it might be improved is a self-regulating learner (Winne, 2010, 2017b). Later, we sketch how learning strategies can be quantitatively described using graph theory (Winne, Gupta, & Nesbit, 1994).

Conceptualizing Learning Strategies as Decision-Making, Hot and Cold

We adopt the axiom that learners are inherently self-regulating learners (Winne, 1995a, 1995b). We note choices learners make in regulating their learning may well differ from those considered ideal by learning scientists or teachers. How does a learner decide which strategy to select and whether to adapt a standard strategy when working on everyday academic tasks? We propose learners choose strategies and tactics based on two importantly different categories of information.

One category of information is relatively objective, a set of factual features of a task (Hadwin & Winne, 2012; McKeachie, 1988). Examples are the availability of information resources ("Can I Google it?") and tools (a notepad where information can be offloaded to address challenges caused by the limited capacity of working memory) and time available. It is important to point out learners may not recognize some elements of a task's conditions that empirical research indicates affect learning. Also, learners' subjective interpretations about features of a task may mistake objective features of context. Judging the match of objective conditions to a tactic or strategy is fundamentally a mechanical, a "cold" process. The question is straightforward: Does the array of conditions of a task "fit" conditions that set a stage for applying a particular tactic?

The second major category of conditions learners consider when deciding to apply a particular tactic or strategy sets a stage for a quite different decision-making process. This category of information is a mixture of internal factors, particularly motivational factors and emotions associated to motivational factors (Winne & Hadwin, 2008). Motivation and associated emotions account for "why individuals or organisms behave as they do: What gets their behavior started, and what directs, energizes, sustains, and eventually terminates action" (Graham & Weiner, 2012, p. 367). Translating to the case of choosing learning tactics and strategies, we pose as a key question: How does motivation affect learners' choices about tactics and strategies when several are judged a good fit to the current conditions of a task? This is the key question learners face when enacting learning strategies.

To answer this question, we turn to theories of and research on motivation. We aggressively condense this huge and complex literature by introducing another first-letter mnemonic, AEIOU (Winne & Marx, 1987). The letter A represents an attribution, the explanation a learner constructs for the evaluation made of a product (Weiner, 2010). Fundamentally, "Why was the product a success or a failure?" Attribution theorists classify causes that form explanations used in answering this question according to three factors: (1) locus, internal to the person or external in the environment; (2) the learner's ability to control causes of success/failure; and (3) the stability or predictability of a cause. Causes articulate to emotions. For example, explaining failure as due to an internal, uncontrollable, invariant factor such as intelligence gives rise to the emotion of shame. Attributing success to an internal, controllable and adaptable factor, such as effort, prompts a feeling of pride. The letter E in the AEIOU complex represents an efficacy expectation. This is a learner's interpretation about having sufficient skill to carry out an operation, a tactic, or strategy under the conditions of a task (Bandura, 1997). The letter I marks the incentive or value the learner associates with the product of a task. What is the worth of the product? Letter O is the learner's outcome expectation (Bandura, 1997). What will or could be the product generated when a particular tactic or strategy is applied under particular conditions? In passing, we point out learners' judgments of efficacy, predictions about incentive(s) linked to products, and outcome(s) are theoretically probabilities although learners may treat them as binaries.

The final letter in the AEIOU model marks utility. Utility represents a learner's aggregate appraisal about whether to apply a tactic or strategy formed on the basis of the profile of A, E, I, and O components. We theorize learners choose the tactic that has sufficient utility, i.e., is satisficing (Simon, 1956). Because learners have memories of past experience, previously used tactics that fit current "cold" (cognitive) conditions of a task have an initial utility value. This index may be adjusted to accommodate updates to a task's conditions. After applying a selected tactic, learners may adjust the tactic's entire profile of A, E, I, and O that aggregate to form utility. For example, learners may increase their efficacy expectation if an immediately prior perceived effort in applying a tactic was less than forecast before the tactic was enacted. Our approach parallels Koriat's (2007) conceptualization of metacognition and consciousness.

Analysis of Hypothetical Studying Illustrating COPES and AEIOU

Son and Metcalfe (2000: Experiment 1) invited undergraduates to study the biographies of eight famous people published in *Encyclopedia Britannica*. First, learners read a one-paragraph introduction to each biography and judged how easy each would be to learn and how interesting each was. Then, the learners were allowed 30 minutes to study the set of biographies under instructions to either "study ... there will be

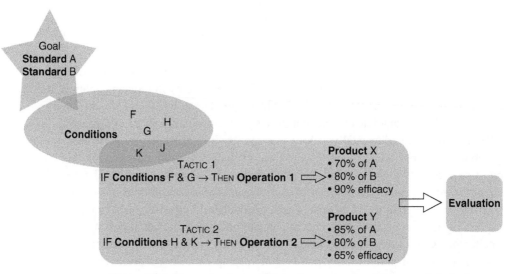

Figure 27.1 *Example of standards and a motivational factor weighed when judging utility*

a memory test ... testing material from all 8 biographies" or "free-read" with no mention of a test. Both groups were told, "You may read the biographies as you wish, choosing each of them for as long as you like. You can always go back to one that you've already read, and don't worry if you don't get through all of them" (p. 209).

With random assignment to groups and rigorous experimental controls, the single difference in objective conditions between groups was the instruction to study for a memory test versus read freely. It did not have a statistically identifiable effect on the groups' average memory for information. In both groups, learners learned more and studied longer the biographies they predicted would be easier to learn. Biographies predicted to be more interesting were better recalled but difference in instructions affected studying. Learners reading freely spent more time reading material they perceived as interesting than learners who expected a test.

COPES. Learners expecting a test did not know the kind of test they would receive. Undergraduates report they adjust tactics they use in relation to item formats (Scouller, 1998), so we infer learners reading freely used different tactics than learners expecting a test. Because achievement didn't differ between groups and traces of learners' tactics and strategies weren't gathered, we interpret (1) learners didn't use different tactics to study despite what peers describe about studying (Winne & Jamieson-Noel, 2002) or (2) whatever various tactics learners used in this study generated approximately equivalent products. We believe the latter is the case. The free-reading learners decided to read more of the interesting material than learners who expected a test. Different standards free-readers used to evaluate products of operations led them to choose different materials.

AEIOU. We omit here speculation about attributions as we find no grounds in the data or design of Son and Metcalfe's study to support more than pure guesswork.

We assume learners in the free-reading group were very clear about the outcome to be generated when they read freely because they previewed each of the biographies. Since they have a lifetime of experience with tactics for free-reading, we predict they also would be very clear in predicting efficacy in applying those well-worn tactics. Assuming undergraduates in a psychology lab experiment assigned reading materials actually believe there won't be a test, and were explicitly granted opportunity to choose what they prefer to read and to study each "for as long as you like," incentive should be rather positive. The utility of satisfying interest was unfettered by an incentive to learn.

In comparison, learners expecting a test of an unknown kind would necessarily be less certain about the outcome to achieve. Therefore, if different tactics generate different outcomes and assuming they have multiple tactics in their toolkits and have differential outcome expectations for those tactics, these learners also likely have greater variance in efficacy expectations. We believe quite probably that efficacy expectations are less positive given they were told the test would span all eight biographies but were told "don't worry if you don't get through all of them." That these learners spent more time studying less interesting materials might well reflect their utility calculations. Coverage of content using "build knowledge" tactics trumped a "follow your interests" approach that called on tactics for relating new information to personalized memories.

Are Learning Strategies Effective? Empirical Findings

In the period 1975–1995, learning strategies and component study tactics received increased attention in the postsecondary arena. One account for this was that, because institutions needed to bolster enrollments in the face of declining budgets, they sought to support students with less well-developed study skills whom they admitted (McKeachie, 1988). A popular form of research was correlating achievement with learners' self-reported use of learning strategies, such as Robinson's well-known SQ3 R method (survey question, read, recite, review) or various methods that represented "deep processing" (e.g., see Winne & Perry, 2000; Winne, Zhou, & Egan, 2011). Johns and McNamara's (1980) review of studies about SQ3 R in particular led them to conclude "support for SQ3 R is based more on opinion than on empirical fact" (p. 1).

In this context, Hadwin and Winne (1996) undertook a review of studies relating learning strategies to achievement. They filtered the literature to focus on studies in which students were supported to some degree in applying strategies but were not "controlled" to do so, as was common in laboratory studies. In other words, students could self-regulate learning. Their conclusions were not cheerful. There were few studies to review. Of 566 candidate articles, only sixteen met best-evidence criteria that included empirical evidence of students actually applying strategies they were taught. "There [was] a very scant research base upon which to ground recommendations for study tactics that populate the many handbooks available (e.g., Pauk, 1991) or to justify mounting costly programs that promise to improve students' study skills" (p. 711). Concept mapping, self-questioning, and monitoring time spent studying showed modest benefits, as did underlining (or highlighting). Other oft-recommended strategies – creating graphic organizers, outlines, or annotations of text – were not productive.

A dozen years later, one of us (Winne, 2013) conducted a similar review, including an outline of methodological issues bearing on research about learning strategies and their potential effects on achievement. Major meta-analyses of specific study tactics and learning strategies in the intervening period were summarized: Caverly, Orlando, and Mullen (2000), Hattie, Biggs, and Purdie (1996), Mulcavy-Ernt and Caverly (2009), Robbins et al. (2004), Credé and Kuncel (2008), Sitzmann and Ely (2011), and Richardson, Abraham, and Bond (2012). Acknowledging limits to interpretation arising from various methodological issues, I concluded the

> research has not yet generated consistent or strong evidence that applying tactics for studying generates significantly more or more robust knowledge. On the other hand, there is practically no evidence that study tactics are detrimental except for the potential issue of whether time taken to learn and use them costs learners time that might be better spent studying in whatever ways learners do. (Winne, 2013, p. 395)

At approximately the same time, two other important reviews were published. Dunlosky and colleagues (2013) surveyed research about ten study tactics learners could use with little training and across a wide array of contexts. To each, they assigned a utility value representing the tactic's benefit to learning across diverse learners, varied materials, different criterion tasks, challenges to implementing the tactic, and breadth of contexts in which the tactic could apply. Summarizing, high-lighting, generating a keyword mnemonic, using imagery to learn from text, and rereading were judged to have low utility. Elaborative interrogation (answering "Why is that so?"), self-explaining, and interleaving different kinds of tasks in practice were assigned moderate utility. Practice testing and distributing practice gained ratings of high utility. Overall, Dunlosky and colleagues noted these

> learning techniques … will not be a panacea for improving achievement for all students, and perhaps obviously, they will benefit only students who are motivated and capable of using them. Nevertheless, when used properly, we suspect that they will produce meaningful gains in performance in the classroom, on achievement tests, and on many tasks encountered across the life span. (p. 47)

The most recent meta-analysis of research investigating effects of teaching learners about learning strategies was produced by Donker and colleagues (2014). They distinguished three categories of strategies. Cognitive strategies develop understanding when learners rehearse, elaborate, and/or organize information in a particular domain. Metacognitive strategies activate cognitive strategies and adjust them when learners plan, monitor, and evaluate work on tasks. Management strate-gies are used to orchestrate the learner's effort, support from peers and instructors, and affordances within the learning environment. Across 58 separate studies exam-ining 95 interventions that generated 180 effect sizes, Donker and colleagues calculated a mean Hedges' $g = 0.66$ ($SE = 0.05$). They concluded "students' academic performance can indeed be improved by the instruction of learning strategies [and] performance was almost always improved by a combination of strategies" (p. 14).

Closely aligned to learning strategies in general are strategies readers use to understand expository text. A meta-analysis by Hebert and colleagues (2016) inves-tigated effects on comprehension, recall, and retention of teaching learners to identify and analyze information based on structural components in texts, e.g., description, sequence, cause–effect, compare–contrast, and problem–solution (Meyer, 1975). Across 45 reports producing a total of 323 effect sizes, Hebert and colleagues reported robust variance estimates of effect sizes of 0.57 for researcher created measures of reading comprehension, 0.62 when comprehension was mea-sured for information in text structures not taught after learners had been taught about another text structure, and 0.15 when comprehension was measured using norm-referenced measures. They concluded while the

> consistency and magnitude of the effects of TSI [text structure instruction] on researcher created expository reading outcomes and transfer measures were notable … more research is needed focusing on the instructional aspects of text structure interventions and whether certain aspects of instruction in text structures are differentially effective for specific subgroups of students or age ranges. (pp. 622–623)

Based on these various reviews and meta-analyses, we recommend adopting a cautious yet modestly optimistic position: learning strategies have potential to positively affect achievement. All these reports note the presence of moderator variables, e.g., student characteristics (socioeconomic status, cognitive classifications), subject matter, and the nature of measures of achievement, particularly whether outcome measures were developed by researchers to align with the purpose of a study. As well, important methodological features curtail a robust conclusion. Key among these is whether a study gathered documentation about whether, under what conditions, and how frequently learners actually used a learning strategy.

Foci in Contemporary Research

Viewed through a lens of self-regulated learning, learners face many decisions in the course of studying. Topics of their decisions have at least three foci: selecting content to study, choosing tactics and strategies to use, and deciding whether to persist or terminate study (see Nelson & Naren, 1994). In other words, learners metacognitively regulate the *what* and the *how* of studying (Kornell & Bjork, 2007). In the next sections, space allows reviewing a small sample of studies with findings that accord with the AEIOU model as a lens for viewing decisions learners make when exercising metacognitive control in selecting content for study and tactics/strategies for studying content.

Decisions About What to Study

A prominent early model of decision-making about what to study was Dunlosky and Hertzog's (1998) discrepancy reduction (DR) model. This model identifies several features of a studying task. First, for each "bit" of content, learners evaluate the discrepancy between how well they know a "bit" and their learning goal. Content perceived to have the greatest discrepancy on this dimension is labeled most difficult, and that is what learners select to study, thus allocating more study time to difficult content. Learners terminate studying when they decide the state of their knowledge matches metacognitive standards that define their goal for learning.

We theorize elements of the AEIOU model play important roles in learners' decisions about what to study. Consider first learners' outcome expectation (O), the clarity and accuracy of their prediction about the product to be created, and their efficacy expectation (E), their prediction about having capability to apply a tactic successfully. Theide and Dunlosky (1999: Experiment 1) assigned undergraduates a relatively challenging learning goal to recall twenty-four of thirty paired associate items or a relatively easy goal to recall six of thirty paired associate items. We interpret outcome expectations were equally clear for both groups. Learners assigned the challenging goal selected more items to restudy. Learners assigned the easier goal selected easier items for restudy, contrary to the prediction of the DR model. Making a bold assumption that learners had equal efficacy expectations about the tactic for learning each paired associate item, we interpret learners' choices about what to study reflected a difference in incentive.

Son and Metcalfe (2000) elaborated studies of the DR model. They reviewed nineteen research papers that showed learners in thirty-five out of forty-six experimental groups allocated more time to items judged more difficult. This finding supports the DR model. However, findings in studies where participants studied longer texts or sonnets showed the DR model oversimplifies decisions about selecting content. We propose AEIOU factors influenced learners' decisions about which content to study. First, when learners expected a test, they selected more difficult items to study (Experiments 1 & 2) except when they were under time pressure, in which case they choose easier items to study (Experiment 3). Assuming outcome expectations for whatever tactic(s) each learners used were clear and incentive was equivalent across these experiments, we interpret differences in efficacy expectations led to differences in deciding which content to study. Specifically, time pressure changed efficacy expectations. Also, results from Experiments 1, 2, and 3 showed learners allocated more studying time to content they judged interesting. We conjecture differential incentive accounts for this effect.

Instability of the DR model's prediction, that learners prefer to study the most difficult content, prompted Metcalfe (2002) to propose learners choose to study content within a region of proximal learning (RPL), where content is judged close to rather than distant from the threshold of being learned. Positioning and span of the RPL were hypothesized to vary according to learners' expertise, an objective indicator of efficacy expectation, and in relation to two factors that plausibly modulate efficacy expectations, the number of study trials available and time available to study. A further hypothesis reflects our conception of utility as a composite of motivational factors. Metcalfe (2002) showed learners shift content choices to study more difficult English–Spanish paired associates if they have more expertise, are allowed more time, and are granted more study trials. Novices, presumably holding lower efficacy expectations, selected easier items for study. When learners studied over multiple trials, we interpret their efficacy expectation elevated as traced by a shift in their choosing to study more difficult items in later trials after mastering items at lower or medium levels of difficulty.

A similar pattern relating to efficacy expectations can be ascribed to participants in the study by Metcalfe and Kornell (2003). Learners studied easier Spanish–English pairs first, which took less time; then, they chose medium difficulty pairs for study. Starting with easier items first is consistent with lack of certainty about efficacy. As participants learned, efficacy was bolstered and they subsequently decided to study more difficult items. It is tempting to add to this interpretation that learners made attributions to effort that supported a shift to selecting more difficult items to study. But this study offers no independent indication about effort.

Thiede, Anderson, and Therriault's (2003) study, in which learners generated keywords and their decisions about what to restudy, shines some light on the attribution and incentive facets of the AEIOU model. Learners in this experiment studied seven texts of modest length (1,118–1,595 words). When they generated keywords at a delay, after reading all texts, compared with generating keywords for a text immediately after reading it or not generating keywords at all, two effects were observed for the group that delayed generating keywords: Judgments of learning were more accurate. Decisions to restudy texts favored those judged less well learned. The latter effect aligns with an interpretation that learners generating keywords at delay held a belief, a "self-explanation," that additional effort spent to learn the more challenging content would pay off. These learners made an accurate prediction. The additional effort they chose to invest to restudy texts judged more difficult (less well learned) boosted their achievement relative to their peers who generated keywords immediately after studying a text the first time or didn't generate keywords.

Dunlosky and Thiede (2004) presented learners with paired associates to learn, one pair at a time, then invited them to restudy the associate to each stimulus by making selections from stimuli presented one at a time or from a display that showed all stimuli at once. The latter presentation format permits learners to develop a plan for selecting items for restudy whereas the one-at-a-time format does not. Items selected for restudy varied according to an interaction of judgments of learning about each paired associate and presentation format. This accords with an interpretation that incentives and efficacy expectation, operationalized as a judgment of learning, modulate a learner's strategy for restudying.

Efficacy expectations originate not only based on judgments of whether content is learned. Changes in the rate of learning (jROL) also can provide input to a learner's efficacy expectation and interact with incentive to add knowledge to memory. This was demonstrated in Metcalfe and Kornell's (2005) studies. The observed learners stopped restudying content when they decided extra effort (time) would not pay off.

Decisions About How to Study

Journals in and cognate to learning science abound with laboratory-based studies in which learners are taught or encouraged to apply a learning tactic and strategy as they study content ranging from paired associates to relatively short but authentic texts. Hundreds of studies and multiple meta-analyses report small to moderate benefits to comprehension, recall, problem-solving, and transfer for various tactics and strategies. But, as noted, studies of tactics and strategies in more realistic settings are less sanguine, particularly for tactics that learners can learn mostly on their own (Dunlosky et al., 2013).

Why do positive findings in hosts of lab-based studies dissolve in authentic contexts? We offer three propositions. First, materials studied and the time frame available for studying in lab studies are quite different than is the case on campus and in classrooms. While research probably is needed to validate this reason, noteworthy questions for research are what specifically differs in these respects and how those factors affect exercise of metacognitive control over tactics and strategies. Second, learners may not be very aware of effective tactics and strategies; or, if they are aware, they may reject them or not have skill in applying them. Surveys of undergraduates (e.g., Hartwig & Dunlosky, 2012; Kornell & Bjork, 2007; Karpicke et al., 2009) lend support to this proposition. More potent evidence is the plethora of studies in lab settings that demonstrate that under controlled conditions learners who are known to be skilled and documented to use particular learning tactics and strategies outperform comparison groups who study with tactics and strategies they bring to the research setting. Third, learners well equipped with potentially effective learning tactics and strategies may poorly manage metacognitive control; in other words, they may engage in unproductive decision-making about how to study. The literature is rather vacant about this third proposition.

Differential incentives associated with alternative tactics may be a major factor influencing learners' choices to deploy learning tactics. Bjork's (1994) concept of desirable difficulty acknowledges learners can judge the effort in applying a particular tactic to be unwarranted. It has broad support as an account for learners' rejection of tactics such as spaced practice and interleaved practice. We view this finding as strong representation of the utility facet of the AEIOU model.

Topics for Further Research on Learning Strategies

Scholars ranging from Hinsdale (1910) to Bandura (1977) recognize learning can proceed by observation. To our knowledge, there are no published studies describing how learners develop learning strategies by observing others. Given students of all ages across diverse settings rarely receive direct instruction in learning strategies – e.g., only 20 percent of undergraduates in Kornell and Bjork's (2007) survey reported they studied as they did because they were taught to study that way – we recommend research that investigates how students observe peers as a means to develop personal learning tactics and strategies.

Do learners apply tactics and strategies differently in everyday studying than in laboratory studies? We don't know. While some laboratory studies used "approximately authentic" materials (e.g., recall of information about biographies, sonnets; Son & Metcalfe 2000), studying in the lab differs in potentially significant ways from everyday studying. For example, Kornell and Bjork (2007) noted "students ... often find themselves making study decisions by triage instead of by trying to maximize long-term learning. Applying research on cognition to education requires focusing on the system level – on the relationship between courses, on instructional activities and requirements, and so forth" (p. 223). Software such as the nStudy system we are developing (Winne, 2017c) might help close this gap. nStudy can record fine-grained, time-stamped traces that reflect tactics and strategies students use as they study online websites, pdf documents, and video. Because some of nStudy's features are configurable and it is designed to use trace data in generating learning analytics for students, self-regulating learners can carry out their own programs of research in partnership with learning scientists (see Winne, 2006, 2017c).

So far, research on learning strategies has been fairly hyperopic, focusing on the strategy as a whole but not often tracing components and their arrangements. Quantitative tools such as conditional probabilities, graph theory (Winne et al., 1994), and process mining (see Winne, 2014) hold promise for representing and quantifying attributes of IF-THEN models of learning tactics and the more complex arrangements of tactics that form learning strategies. Here's a hypothetical example.

Consider a simple strategy for building understanding about technical terms, e.g., in psychology: concept, schema, interference. Suppose a learner studies an online text using nStudy and is told each term is printed with italic style when it is introduced and defined. We assume this perceptual cue allows the learner to identify terms without error. When nStudy is provided the list of terms, traces can be logged about how the learner operates on terms while studying. Suppose the first time "concept" appears the learner does not highlight it but the first time "schema" appears the learner highlights it and its definition. When these terms appear later in the text, nStudy records how the learner operates on information, specifically, whether the learner (1) does nothing observable, (2) highlights the term again, (3) retreats into the text to review the term's definition at the point it was first introduced, or (3) creates at this later point in the text a note elaborating information about the term in relation to new context. For sake of this example, suppose nStudy's log shows the learner retreated to the term "concept," then returned to the spot where the term was used in a new context and created a note elaborating information relating to "concept." In contrast, for "schema," nStudy's log shows a different pattern. The learner did not retreat or make an elaborative note about this term is its new context. Instead, information at this later point in the text was highlighted.

These patterns of engagements with information trace simple learning strategies under a plausible (and testable) assumption about the learner metacognitively monitoring knowledge and highlighting what is judged important but not yet learned well enough. In the case of the term "concept," the learner did not highlight it when it was introduced; the learner later judged knowledge was not sufficient to understand and hence retreated. Reviewing then elaborating as a means to better understand the term per se and weave its meaning with information presented in the new context, if repeated across terms, appears to be a tactic the learner has confidence to carry out (efficacy expectation) and perceives "to work" (incentive associated with the outcome, an elaborative note). Attributing growth in knowledge to this self-regulated, effortful approach to studying supports a feeling of satisfaction. A parallel analysis can be developed for the case of terms such as "schema."

Each learner will not apply these two strategies uniformly. Translating the time-stamped trace data to a transition matrix allows the use of graph theoretic indexes to characterize a learner's strategy. Each learning event – encounter italicized (new) term, highlight italicized term, retreat to italicized term, highlight information where term is used in a new context, and create elaborative note – defines a row of the transition matrix. Columns of the transition matrix are the same traces in the same sequence. Suppose the first event observed is when an italicized term is encountered. Identify the row for this event and, after the second event is observed, identify the column of the matrix describing that event and place a tally in the cell at the intersection of the row (first event) and column (second event). The second event used to identify a row of the transition matrix – it is now a preceding event – and the event following it identifies a column of the matrix. A tally is recorded in the cell at this intersection, and so on.

From a transition matrix populated with tallies, a graph can be developed showing how events "flow" in relation to one another. An index reflecting the probability a learner highlights italicized terms can be formed: Divide (1) the number of tallies in the cell defined by the intersection of the row for encountering an italicized term and the column of highlights of italicized terms by (2) the number of italicized terms. Under our assumption, this index reflects the learner's judgment about prior knowledge of terms presented in the text. Larger patterns of transitions characterize strategic features of studying. For example, a learning analytic could describe how regularly the learner retreats to review a term's definition for terms first judged already understood (not highlighted) versus judged not known (highlighted). Another might describe whether elaborative notes are a preferred product for expanding understanding about terms judged known when they are first encountered versus not known when introduced. Research on creating learning analytics to guide self-regulated learning is just beginning (see Roll & Winne, 2015). Given learners' aversions to desirable difficulties, theorizing then testing how to convey learning analytics so AEIOU profiles favor self-regulating learning (Marzouk et al., 2016; Winne et al., 2017) will be important features of that research if it is to influence how learners study beyond the laboratory.

References

Baker, L. (2016). The development of metacognitive knowledge and control of comprehension. *Improving Reading Comprehension through Metacognitive Reading Strategies Instruction*, 1.

Bandura, A. (1977). *Social learning theory*. Englewood Cliffs, NJ: Prentice-Hall.

(1997). *Self-efficacy: The exercise of control*. New York: W. H. Freeman.

Bjork, R. A. (1994). Memory and metamemory considerations in the training of human beings. In J. Metcalfe & A. P. Shimamura (eds.), *Metacognition: Knowing about knowing* (pp. 185–206). Cambridge, MA: MIT Press.

Campitelli, G. & Gobet, F. (2011). Deliberate practice: Necessary but not sufficient. *Current Directions in Psychological Science*, *20*(5), 280–285.

Caverly, D. C., Orlando, V. P., & Mullen, J. L. (2000). Textbook study reading. In R. F. Flippo & D. C. Caverly (eds.), *Teaching reaching and study strategies at the college level* (pp. 86–165). Newark, DE: International Reading Association.

Chipman, S. F., Segal, J. W., & Glaser, R. (1985). *Thinking and learning skills. Vol. 2: Research and open questions*. Hillsdale, NJ: Lawrence Erlbaum.

Corno, L. (1994). Student volition and education: Outcomes, influences and practices. In B. J. Zimmerman & D. H. Schunk (eds.). *Self-regulation of learning and performance* (pp. 229–254). Hillsdale, NJ: Lawrence Erlbaum.

Credé, M. & Kuncel, N. R. (2008). Study habits, skills, and attitudes: The third pillar supporting collegiate academic performance. *Perspectives on Psychological Science*, *3*, 425–453.

Dearborn, G. V. N. (1916). *How to learn easily: Practical hints on economical study*. Boston, MA: Little, Brown and Company.

Derry, S. J. (1990). Learning strategies for acquiring useful knowledge. B. F. Jones & L. Idol (eds.) *Dimensions of thinking and cognitive instruction* (pp. 347–379). Hillsdale, NJ: Lawrence Erlbaum.

Donker, A. S., de Boer, H., Kostons, D., Dignath van Ewijk, C. C., & van der Werf, M. P. C. (2014). Effectiveness of learning strategy instruction on academic performance: A meta-analysis. *Educational Research Review, 11*,1–26.

Dunlosky, J. & Hertzog, C. (1998). Training programs to improve learning in later adulthood: Helping older adults educate themselves. *Metacognition in educational theory and practice, 249,* 276.

Dunlosky, J. & Thiede, K. W. (2004). Causes and constraints of the shift-to-easier-materials effect in the control of study. *Memory and Cognition, 32(5),* 779–788.

Dunlosky, J., Rawson, K. A., Marsh, E. J., Nathan, M. J., & Willingham, D. T. (2013). Improving students' learning with effective learning techniques: Promising directions from cognitive and educational psychology. *Psychological Science in the Public Interest, 14*(1), 4–58.

Dweck, C. S. (2008). *Mindset: The new psychology of success.* Random House Digital.

Flavell, J. H., Friedrichs, A. G., & Hoyt, J. D. (1970). Developmental changes in memorization processes. *Cognitive Psychology, 1*(4), 324–340.

Graham, S. & Weiner, B. (2012). Motivation: Past, present and future. In K. R. Harris, S. Graham, & T. Urdan (eds.), *APA Educational psychology handbook. Vol. 1: Theories, constructs, and critical issues.* Washington, DC: American Psychological Association.

Hadwin, A. F. & Winne, P. H. (1996). Study strategies have meager support: A review with recommendations for implementation. *Journal of Higher Education, 67,* 692–715.

(2012). Promoting learning skills in undergraduate students. In M. J. Lawson & J. R. Kirby (eds.), *Enhancing the quality of learning: Dispositions, instruction, and mental structures* (pp. 201–227). New York: Cambridge University Press.

Hartwig, M. K. & Dunlosky, J. (2012). Study strategies of college students: Are self-testing and scheduling related to achievement?. *Psychonomic Bulletin and Review, 19(1),* 126–134.

Hattie, J., Biggs, J., & Purdie, N. (1996). Effects of learning skills interventions on student learning: A meta-analysis. *Review of Educational Research, 66,* 99–136.

Hebert, M., Bohaty, J. J., Nelson, J. R., & Brown, J. (2016). The effects of text structure instruction on expository reading comprehension: A meta-analysis. *Journal of Educational Psychology, 108*(5), 609–629.

Hinsdale, B. A. (1910). *The art of study.* New York: American Book Company.

Idol, L. & Jones, B. F. (1991). *Educational values and cognitive instruction: Implications for reform.* Hillsdale, NJ: Lawrence Erlbaum.

Johns, J. L. & McNamara, L. P. (1980). The SQ3 R study technique: A forgotten research target. *Journal of Reading, 23,* 705–708.

Jones, B. F. & Idol, L. (eds.) (1990). *Dimensions of thinking and cognitive instruction.* Hillsdale, NJ: Lawrence Erlbaum.

Karpicke, J. D., Butler, A. C., & Roediger III, H. L. (2009). Metacognitive strategies in student learning: Do students practise retrieval when they study on their own? *Memory, 17*(4), 471–479.

Koriat, A. (2007). Metacognition and consciousness. In P. D. Zelazo, M. Moscovitch, & E. Thompson (eds.), *Cambridge handbook of consciousness* (pp. 289–325). New York: Cambridge University Press.

Kornell, N. & Bjork, R. A. (2007). The promise and perils of self-regulated study. *Psychonomic Bulletin & Review, 14*(2), 219–224.

Marzouk, Z., Rakovic, M., Liaqat, A., Vytasek, J. Samadi, D., Stewart-Alonso, J., Ram, I., Woloshen, S., Winne, P. H., & Nesbit, J. C. (2016). What if learning analytics were based on learning science? *Australasian Journal of Educational Technology, 32*(6). https://ajet.org.au/index.php/AJET/article/view/3058/1433

McDaniel, M. A. & Kearney, E. M. (1984). Optimal learning strategies and their spontaneous use: The importance of task-appropriate processing. *Memory & Cognition, 12*(4), 361–373.

McKeachie, W. J. (1988). The need for study strategy training. In C. E. Weinstein, E. T. Goetz, & P. A. Alexander (eds.), *Learning and study strategies: Issues in assessment, instruction, and evaluation* (pp. 3–9). San Diego, CA: Academic Press.

Metcalfe, J. (2002). Is study time allocated selectively to a region of proximal learning? *Journal of Experimental Psychology-General, 131(3),* 349–363.

Metcalfe, J. & Kornell, N. (2003). The dynamics of learning and allocation of study time to a region of proximal learning. *Journal of Experimental Psychology: General, 132 (4),* 530–542

(2005). A region of proximal learning model of study time allocation. *Journal of Memory and Language, 52(4),* 463–477.

Metcalfe, J. (2009). Metacognitive judgments and control of study. *Current Directions in Psychological Science, 18,* 159–163.

Meyer, B. J. F. (1975). *The organization of prose and its effects on memory.* Amsterdam: North-Holland Publishing.

Mulcavy-Ernt, P. I. & Caverly, D. C. (2009). Strategic study-reading. In R. F. Flippo & D. C. Caverly (eds.), *Handbook of college reading and study strategy research* (pp. 177–198). New York: Routledge.

Nelson, T. O. & Narens, L. (1994). Why investigate metacognition? In J. Metcalfe & A. P. Shimamura (eds.), *Metacognition: Knowing about knowing* (pp. 1–25). Cambridge, MA: MIT Press

Pauk, W. (1991). *How to study in college.* Boston, MA: Houghton Mifflin Company.

Richardson, M., Abraham, C., & Bond, R. (2012). Psychological correlates of university students' academic performance: A systematic review and meta-analysis. *Psychological Bulletin, 138,* 353–387.

Robbins, S. B., Lauver, K., Le, H., Davis, D., Langley, R., & Carlstrom, A. (2004). Do psychosocial and study skill factors predict college outcomes? A meta-analysis. *Psychological Bulletin, 130,* 261–288.

Roll, I. & Winne, P. H. (2015). Understanding, evaluating, and supporting self-regulated learning using learning analytics. *Journal of Learning Analytics, 2*(1), 7–12.

Scouller, K. (1998). The influence of assessment method on students' learning approaches: Multiple choice question examination versus assignment essay. *Higher Education, 35,* 453–472

Segal, J. W., Chipman, S. F., & Glaser, R. (1985). *Thinking and learning skills. Vol. 1: Relating instruction to research.* Hillsdale, NJ: Lawrence Erlbaum.

Simon, H. A. (1956). Rational choice and the structure of the environment. *Psychological Review, 63*(2), 129–138.

Sitzmann, T. & Ely, K. (2011). A meta-analysis of self-regulated learning in work-related training and educational attainment: what we know and where we need to go. *Psychological Bulletin, 137,* 421–42.

Son, L. K. (2010). Metacognitive control and the spacing effect. *Journal of Experimental Psychology: Learning, Memory, and Cognition, 36*(1), 255–262.

Son, L. K. & Metcalfe, J. (2000). Metacognitive and control strategies in study-time allocation. *Journal of Experimental Psychology: Learning, Memory, and Cognition*, *26*(1), 20 r-221.

Thiede, K. W., Anderson, M., & Therriault, D. (2003). Accuracy of metacognitive monitoring affects learning of texts. *Journal of Educational Psychology*, *95(1)*, 66–73.

Thiede, K. W. & Dunlosky, J. (1999). Toward a general model of self-regulated study: An analysis of selection of items for study and self-paced study time. *Journal of Experimental Psychology: Learning, Memory, and Cognition*, *25* (4), 1024.

Weiner, B. (2010). The development of an attribution-based theory of motivation: A history of ideas. *Educational Psychologist*, *45*(1), 28–36.

Weinstein, C. E., Goetz, E. T., & Alexander, P. A. (1988). *Learning and study strategies. Issues in assessment, instruction and evaluation*. San Diego, CA: Academic Press.

Whipple, G. M. (1916). *How to study effectively*. Bloomington, IL: Public School Publishing.

Winne, P. H. (1995a). Inherent details in self-regulated learning. *Educational Psychologist*, *30*, 173–187.

(1995b). Self regulation is ubiquitous but its forms vary with knowledge. *Educational Psychologist*, *30*, 223–228.

(1997). Experimenting to bootstrap self-regulated learning. *Journal of Educational Psychology*, *89*, 397–410.

(2006). How software technologies can improve research on learning and bolster school reform. *Educational Psychologist*, *41*, 5–17.

(2010). Bootstrapping learner's self-regulated learning. *Psychological Test and Assessment Modeling*, *52*, 472–490.

(2013). Learning strategies, study skills and self-regulated learning in postsecondary education. In M. B. Paulsen (ed.), *Higher education: Handbook of theory and research*. Vol. 28 (pp. 377–403). Dordrecht: Springer.

(2014). Issues in researching self-regulated learning as patterns of events. *Metacognition and Learning*, *9(2)*, 229–237.

(2017a). The trajectory of research on self-regulated learning. In T. Michalsky (ed.), *Yearbook of the National Society for the Study of Education. Vol. 116: Self-regulated learning: Conceptualizations, contributions, and empirically based models for teaching and learning*. Chicago, IL: National Society for the Study of Education

(2017b). Cognition and metacognition in self-regulated learning. In D. Schunk & J Greene (eds.), *Handbook of self-regulation of learning and performance*. (2nd ed. New York, NY: Routledge.

(2017c). Leveraging big data to help each learner upgrade learning and accelerate learning science. *Teachers College Record*, *119*(3), 1–24.

Winne, P. H. & Azevedo, R. (2014). Metacognition. In R. K. Sawyer (ed.), *The Cambridge handbook of the learning sciences*, 2nd edn (pp. 63–87). Cambridge: Cambridge University Press.

Winne, P. H., Gupta, L., & Nesbit, J. C. (1994). Exploring individual differences in studying strategies using graph theoretic statistics. *Alberta Journal of Educational Research*, *40*, 177–193.

Winne, P. H. & Hadwin, A. F. (2008). The weave of motivation and self-regulated learning. In D. H. Schunk & B. J. Zimmerman (eds.), *Motivation and self-regulated learning: Theory, research, and applications* (pp. 297–314). Mahwah, NJ: Lawrence Erlbaum.

Winne, P. H. & Jamieson-Noel, D. L. (2002). Exploring students' calibration of self-reports about study tactics and achievement. *Contemporary Educational Psychology, 27,* 551–572.

Winne, P. H. & Marx, R. W. (1987). The best tool teachers have: Their students' thinking. In D. Berliner & B. Rosenshine (eds.), *Talks to teachers: A festschrift for N. L. Gage* (pp. 267–304). New York: Random House. *Note: This article was misprinted identifying Marx as first author.*

Winne, P. H. & Perry, N. E. (2000). Measuring self-regulated learning. In M. Boekaerts, P. Pintrich, & M. Zeidner (eds.), *Handbook of self-regulation* (pp. 531–566). Orlando, FL: Academic Press.

Winne, P. H., Vytasek, J. M., Patzak, A., Rakovic, M., Marzouk, Z., Pakdaman-Savoji, Ram, I., Samadi, D., Lin, M. P. C., Liu, A., Liaqat, A., Nashaat, N., Mozaffari, Z., Stewart-Alonso, J., & Nesbit, J. C. (2017). Designs for learning analytics to support information problem solving. In J. Buder & F. W. Hesse (eds.) *Informational environments: Effects of use, effective designs* (pp. 249–272). New York: Springer.

Winne, P. H., Zhou, M., & Egan, R. (2011). Designing assessments of self-regulated learning. In G. Schraw & D. H. Robinson (eds.), *Assessment of higher-order thinking skills* (pp. 89–118). Charlotte, NC: Information Age Publishing.

Index

CPSIA information can be obtained
at www.ICGtesting.com
Printed in the USA
LVHW110237221221
706918LV00005B/163